Encyclopedia of
American Architecture

Encyclopedia of American Architecture

WILLIAM DUDLEY HUNT, Jr., FAIA

McGRAW-HILL BOOK COMPANY

New York St. Louis San Francisco Auckland Bogotá
Hamburg Johannesburg London Madrid Mexico
Montreal New Delhi Panama Paris São Paulo
Singapore Sydney Tokyo Toronto

Library of Congress Cataloging in Publication Data

Hunt, William Dudley.
  Encyclopedia of American architecture.

  Includes index.
  1.   Architecture—United States—Dictionaries.
I. Title.
NA705.H86   720′.973   80-11589
ISBN   0-07-031299-0

1234567890   HDHD   89876543210

*The editors for this book were Thomas H. Quinn and Margaret Lamb,
the designer was Naomi Auerbach, and the production supervisor
was Paul A. Malchow. It was set in Optima Medium
by The Clarinda Company.*

Printed and bound by Halliday Lithograph.

CONSULTING EDITORS

Mary E. Osman
Senior Editor, *The AIA Journal*

Caleb Hornbostel
Architect and Adjunct Associate Professor, Temple University

Joseph W. Molitor
Architect and Architectural Photographer

Contents

CONTENTS

Preface

This book presents, in words and pictures, the vast breadth of American architecture. It is intended to be of interest and use to people who want to know about the culture and the environment in which they live and how it came to be that way. Students of all ages, people who own or will some day own buildings, those who occupy and use buildings, those interested in history or the contemporary scene all should find information of interest and value. The book is also intended for those who must know about architecture: architects, landscape architects, engineers, interior designers, city planners, building owners and developers, real estate people, artists, contractors, construction financiers, conservationists, furniture designers, product manufacturers, government officials, and building managers. For such people, the articles on their own specialties may seem elementary, but those on the many other subjects should be useful.

In any work of this sort, there are obvious limitations. A whole library would be required to contain relatively complete information on all the elements involved in American architecture. In a single book, choices and compromises must be made, and this is certainly true of the present volume. The professional language of architecture also presents problems. The semantics are dealt with by using the proper specialized terms, but always defining them at the same time in everyday language.

In this book, an attempt has been made to discuss all the major elements of American architecture in enough depth to explain the general facts and principles of each, but not to become so complete or technical that only experts would require or understand so much information. The purpose is to inform the reader, not to be obscure.

Another important decision about the organization of this book involved methods for handling the participation in architecture of women, as well as minority and other special groups of people. Serious consideration was given to some special groups of people. Serious consideration was given to some special emphasis in the book, for example, a separate article on women in architecture. The final decision was based on the simple conviction that accomplishment in architecture today is not limited by sex, skin color, place of birth or aspects of that sort. The real limits are those of talent, training, knowledge, skills, and the will to work, and are therefore applicable to all people, regardless of sex, color, or other such attributes.

Therefore women and members of minority and special groups have been included in articles of this book wherever they have been found to have made notable accomplishments in architecture. That their numbers included here are relatively small reflects social conditions of the past. In the future, their numbers can confidently be expected to increase radically.

Although an attempt has been made to make the book as complete, interesting, and useful as possible, it is a foregone conclusion that such a broad, large, general work will have imperfections. For example, while the work of a very large number of architects and other environmental designers is discussed or illustrated, major articles are included on the lives and work of only about 50 architects, considered the most important in American history. Only a few living architects are the subjects of individual articles, most of them retired or nearing the end of their careers. The major deterrent to the selection of other living architects was the extreme difficulty of understanding and evaluating current work. To have the proper perspective of current architecture, while standing so close to it, seems to be almost impossible for most people, the author included. Another author might have handled this problem differently and might have selected some architects not included here.

Other articles in this book discuss various major aspects of architecture, including building types, systems, materials, structures, and the like; periods or movements in American architecture; the environment design professions and the building industry; and architectural practice. Another author might have chosen to eliminate some of the articles included here, substitute others, shorten or lengthen still others. The articles that are included were selected and their lengths and depths of coverage determined, only after many hours of thought, discussion, and study of their appropriateness to understanding American architecture and their value to those who want or need to know about it. The articles are as factual, straightforward, and objective as it was possible to make them.

The overall organization of the book was chosen to make it as useful as possible to readers. There are 202 articles, arranged alphabetically. The articles are as broad in scope as seemed feasible and their titles are as generic as possible. Articles may be classified into seven major categories: individual architects and firms; the building industry; building types; components and systems of buildings; history of architecture; materials of construction; and practice of architecture. A large number of miscellaneous articles are also included that do not fit neatly in such categories.

Generally, each article begins with a definition of its title, discusses principles of the subject and other important aspects, and then proceeds to the history or biography of the subject. Technical or professional terms are defined at the places at which they are first used. The articles also include cross-references to others that are closely related.

At the end of articles, guidelines to further related information are included: other articles in this book; other books containing information on the subjects; magazines and other publications; and associations, organizations, or other sources. A large number of photographs, drawings, tables, and charts contribute to the understanding of the text of the articles. The very complete and detailed index is an important and useful guide to information contained in the book on thousands of architectural and related subjects.

This book took six years to research and write. In the course of the work, some 8,000 architectural and related terms were collected and analyzed and over 1,000 books were consulted, along with a great many magazine articles and other data. Perhaps the most important source of information and inspiration was the great number of friends, acquaintances, and other people who gave their time, talents, and knowledge in order to help the book become a reality. While a list of all of them is not possible, some must be mentioned, including Allen Freeman, managing editor of the *AIA Journal*; Harold Hauf, FAIA, architect and educator; Blake Hughes, publisher of *Architectural Record*; Douglas Haskell, FAIA, former editor of *Architectural Forum*; Robert Packard, AIA, architect and editor of the seventh edition of the AIA/Ramsey and Sleeper *Architectural Graphic Standards*; and architects Hugh Stubbins, FAIA, Merle Westlake, AIA, and Stephen Jacobs, AIA. All helped a great deal.

Then there are a number of people without whom the book could not have been written, even in six years. They include Susan Cosgrove Holton and Stephanie C. Byrnes of the AIA Library; Mary E. Fenelon, who did a masterful job of reading and typing the final manuscript; and my wife, Gwen Munson Hunt, who not only was able to live with the typing of an intermediate draft from an incredibly marked-up earlier draft, but also has managed to stay on speaking terms with the author.

The photographers' credits in the book comprise a blue-ribbon list of a great many of the best architectural photographers in the United States. Their help is appreciated and special mention must be made for that of Jack Hedrich of Hedrich-Blessing.

Credit must also be given to editor Thomas H. Quinn, editing supervisor Margaret Lamb, production supervisor Paul Malchow, and designer Naomi Auerbach for talented and efficient editing, design, and production of the book.

Finally, there is a small group of people whose help was absolutely essential in the preparation of this book, the consulting editors, who did research, gave counsel, read manuscripts, and did other invaluable services. They are Mary E. Osman, senior editor, the *AIA Journal*; Caleb Hornbostel, architect and educator; and Joseph W. Molitor, architectural photographer and architect.

The writing involved a long and arduous struggle to achieve a book that, though inevitably imperfect, will be of interest and value to its readers and bring with it some degree of understanding the culture and architecture of America. If so, the book will have served its intended purpose.

The writing of the book has been an interesting and gratifying experience, accomplished in spite of the need for carrying on other editorial work at the same time and in spite of the fact that the window in front of the author, when seated at his typewriter, overlooks the North River leading to the Chesapeake Bay, in Tidewater Virginia, and then to all the seas and oceans of the world.

William Dudley Hunt, Jr.

Encyclopedia of
American Architecture

AIRPORT An architectural complex consisting of runways, buildings, and related facilities for the takeoff, landing, and handling of airplanes and other aircraft and their crews, passengers, and cargoes.

Types There are three major types of airports: air carrier, general aviation, and military. Air carrier airports are designed for use by scheduled airlines. General aviation airports are for all types of civilian aircraft, except those of the airlines. Business, pleasure, and charter aircraft use general aviation airports, as do air taxis that fly to air carrier airports and between small towns. Facilities for general aviation are also provided at air carrier airports, often in buildings separated from the passenger terminals. Military airports are for the armed services, including the U.S. Air Force, Army, Navy, and Marines. They are also used by Reserve and National Guard units of the services. The major military airports are operated by the armed services, but facilities at commercial airports are sometimes used.

Air carrier airports serve various kinds of airlines, classified according to the areas served. Regional airlines serve regions such as the Southeastern or Northeastern United States. Trunk airlines serve larger areas, such as all the Eastern states. International airlines fly between countries.

General aviation airports are classified into basic utility for small airplanes, general utility for larger propeller airplanes, basic transport for small jets, and general transport for larger jets. Special types of general aviation airports are heliports for helicopters, which can land in small areas, including the tops of buildings; and the seaplane bases for seaplanes and amphibians, which can land on both land and water. In later years, short takeoff and landing (STOL) aircraft and vertical takeoff and landing (VTOL) aircraft have been developed. If they should come into widespread use, special airports may be provided for them.

In the United States, there are over 12,000 airports, most of which are relatively small. Only about 1,000 can be used by aircraft that carry 20 or more passengers. And only slightly over 500 are used by scheduled airlines. While very few new airports are being built, continuing changes in aircraft and increases in their size, range, speed, and numbers cause existing airports to become obsolescent much faster than most other building types. Their modernization and replacement, therefore, and the design of a few new ones make airports not only an important building

type but one that is interesting and challenging to architects.

Elements The major elements of an air carrier airport are air-traffic control and navigational facilities, runway and taxiway system, ground handling systems, passenger handling systems, and ground transportation systems. Although the design of airports is involved with all these systems, the major portions handled by architects are those having to do with passenger handling and ground transportation. The other elements are primarily handled by engineers who specialize in their design.

Sometimes the term *airside,* or *fieldside,* is used to indicate runways for takeoffs and landings, and for other facilities required by the aircraft themselves. The term *landside* is often used for facilities required by passengers and their luggage, freight, and mail. Often engineers design the airside and architects the landside. However, they must work closely together if the design of an airport is to be a success. They must also work with the airlines, often called the carriers, and with those who will operate the airport.

Design In the design of an air carrier airport, primary consideration must be given to the relationships between the apron, the terminal, and ground transportation. The apron is the area between the airside, or runway-taxiway, part of the airport and the terminal, the building in which the requirements of passengers and other functions are handled. On the apron, aircraft arrive and depart, load and unload, at connections with the terminal called gates, and here the aircraft are serviced with fuel, passenger meals, and so on. In the terminal, passengers check baggage, purchase tickets, and so on. In the ground transportation area, provisions are made for arriving and departing passengers, sometimes called *deplaning* and *enplaning* passengers, to reach the terminal by automobile, limousine, bus, taxicab, or on foot. Parking lots and sometimes garages are provided for short-term and long-term parking by passengers, visitors, and employees.

At the junction of the apron with the terminal, the gates allow passengers to *enplane* or *deplane,* or to board or depart from the aircraft. There are four major methods of providing gates. The simplest, used at small terminals, is the linear method in which the gates are placed on the side of the terminal facing the apron. For larger terminals, piers, sometimes called fingers, project from the terminal proper and aircraft

AIRPORT Separate Terminal Buildings, John F. Kennedy International (1942–62, with some buildings later), New York, N.Y. [Consulting architect: Wallace K. Harrison. Architects of terminals: International Arrivals Building (1957), Skidmore, Owings and Merrill; Pan American (1961), Tibbetts, Abbett, McCarthy and Stratton; Trans World (1960), Eero Saarinen; Domestic Arrivals (1969), I. M. Pei; Northwest (1962), White and Mariani; Eastern (1959), Chester L. Churchill; American (1960), Kahn and Jacobs; United (1961), Skidmore, Owings, and Merrill.]

AIRPORT Centralized Terminal Buildings, O'Hare International (1963), Chicago, Ill. [Architects: C. F. Murphy Assoc. (Hedrich-Blessing)]

are parked alongside; the third method uses satellite buildings which are smaller elements located away from the main terminal and connected to it with corridors or concourses. The fourth type, not used to any great extent so far, is the transporter method, which utilizes mobile lounges. In this case, aircraft are parked at some distance from the terminal and passengers transported to and from them in vehicles that resemble buses, which can be driven in either direction and have special provisions for connecting with both the aircraft and the terminal building.

The Terminal In some air carrier airports, a single terminal building is used by all the airlines. In other airports, there may be a group of terminal buildings, each used by one or more airlines. In any terminal, there are several kinds of space: passenger and public areas; management offices; areas used by the airlines; special facilities such as the control tower, from which aircraft air and ground traffic are directed, a weather station, and, for international airports, customs, health, and immigration services.

In any terminal, an important design problem is the flow of passengers from ground transportation to baggage check-in to ticket counters to the departure lounge at the gate. In recent years, this flow has become even more complicated by the need for security checks to prevent hijacking and other threats. For *de-planing* passengers, the flow is from the lounge at the gate to baggage claim and to ground transportation. In addition, most airports make provisions for many other needs and wishes of passengers and visitors, including rest rooms, newsstands, restaurants, bars and lounges, banks, shops, and in some cases even hotels and motion picture houses. Freight, or air cargo, including mail, is often handled along with passenger luggage at small airports. In larger ones, special provisions must be made, including separate terminals designed specifically for freight. At almost all airports, except the very smallest, hangars are provided for the maintenance of aircraft.

General aviation, whether located at an air carrier airport or at a general aviation airport, utilizes many of the same elements as the air carriers, runways, taxiways, and so on. However, runways are usually shorter and terminal provisions much simpler. For these purposes, an individual or organization called a "fixed base operator" provides flight and weather information, fuel, hangars and tie-down space for aircraft, and maintenance.

Airports, particularly air carrier airports, confront architects and engineers with very complex design problems. Because of the interrelationships between the complicated requirements of the airlines, management, passengers, and visitors; and the extremely

AIRPORT Interior, O'Hare International Airport (1963), Chicago, Ill. [*Architects: C. F. Murphy Assoc. (Hedrich-Blessing)*]

AIRPORT Centralized Terminal Building, Lambert–St. Louis (1956), with later additions), St. Louis, Mo. [*Architects: Hellmuth, Yamasaki and Leinweber; additions: Hellmuth, Obata and Kassabaum. (Hedrich-Blessing)*]

high degree of technological requirements of the aircraft, including servicing, maintenance, and control; the need for safety and security; and the great and growing number of people using airlines; the design of airports has become highly specialized. Most airport design is therefore handled by architects and engineers with the experience, knowledge, and foresight to design facilities that will function properly for the aircraft and the people who will use them some 10 years later, when their construction has been completed.

History The history of airports is relatively short, beginning with the work of the Wright brothers, Orville (1871–1948) and Wilbur (1867–1912), that resulted in the first flight on December 17, 1903, at Kitty Hawk, N.C. For many years, airports were pastures or fields level enough for the early airplanes to take off and land. Barns were used as hangars and any gas pump served for refueling. As time went on, improvements were made in the form of dirt (later asphalt and concrete) airstrips and mats. In 1925 the first scheduled airline was started. By that time, there were about 1,000 airports in the United States, most of them quite primitive. By the beginning of World War II, their number had more than doubled. Today there are more than 12,000 U.S. airports and their number is still growing.

Related Articles GARAGE; ROAD AND TRAFFIC DESIGN.

Further Reading Blankenship, Edward G.: *The Aiport*, Praeger, New York, 1974, Horonjeff, Robert: *Planning and Design of Aiports*, McGraw-Hill, New York, 1975.

Sources of Additional Information Air Transport Association of America, 1709 New York Ave., N.W., Washington, D.C. 20006; Aircraft Owners and Pilots Assoc., 7315 Wisconsin Ave., Bethesda, Md. 20014

ALUMINUM A lightweight, silvery-colored, non-magnetic metal used extensively in buildings, in extruded, forged, stamped, rolled, and cast form, for windows, doors, roofing, wall covering, wiring, hardware, and a host of other purposes. Called aluminium in England, Canada, and some other countries, aluminum is one of the most versatile of metals.

Extraction Aluminum is a very abundant element, occurring in almost all soils and rocks, but only in compounds, not as a native metal. Bauxite ore, composed primarily of alumina, or aluminum oxide, and other oxides, is the source of the metal. The separation of aluminum from the other materials in bauxite ore is a two-stage process. In the first stage, bauxite is crushed, mixed with lime, soda ash, and hot water and pumped into digester tanks. There the action of the chemicals and the introduction of steam dissolves the alumina, leaving the other materials as solids, which are filtered out. In a precipitator, the dissolved alumina cools and precipitates into crystals, from which the water is removed in a rotary kiln, leaving pure alumina. During the process the alumina changes into sodium aluminate, aluminum hydrate, and back into alumina.

In the second stage, the alumina is dissolved in cryolite, a compound of sodium, fluorine, and aluminum, in an electrolytic cell, through which current is passed to break down the alumina into carbon dioxide and molten aluminum, which is approximately 99 percent pure. Once started, the second stage is continuous, aluminum being removed periodically and alumina, cryolite, and other materials added. The molten aluminum is siphoned off into large ladles and either poured directly into molds to form pigs weighing 50 pounds each or fluxed, skimmed, and cast into ingots. For most architectural uses, pig or ingot aluminum is remelted and alloyed before further processing into various products.

Properties Among the properties of aluminum that make it so important in architecture are its lightness, about one-third that of other common metals, and its easy workability by most methods, including, most importantly, extrusion, a process involving drawing the metal through dies to produce shapes. Other properties include resistance to corrosion through the formation of aluminum oxide on the surface which then resists further deterioration, relatively high conduction of both heat and electricity, and reflection qualities. Aluminum is nonpoisonous and nonflammable, though it does have a relatively low melting point. While pure aluminum is soft and has relatively low strength, both properties may be improved considerably by proper alloying and various metalworking techniques.

Aluminum for use in architecture may be obtained in bars, rods, wire, cable, plate, sheet, foil, pipe, and structural shapes, and in complete products such as nails, rivets, hardware, windows, doors, and many others. Such products may be made by all the major production methods: forging, casting, extrusion, pressing, molding, stamping, cold or hot rolling, and so on. Aluminum may be fastened in many ways such as nailing, riveting, welding, brazing, and soldering, and adhesion with glues or other adhesives.

Alloys Aluminum alloys are available in great variety. Among the major metals with which aluminum is alloyed are copper, manganese, silicon, magnesium, and zinc. Among the large number of alloys are types suitable for a host of architectural purposes. Special alloys are available for producing plate, sheet, and other shapes by rolling—forcing hot metal between rollers; others are for extrusion—forcing hot metal through dies; others are made for casting—pouring the molten metal into molds made of sand, cast iron, or steel; and still others for forging—utilizing forging presses or hammers to form the metal. The choice of an alloy for a specific architectural purpose is heavily dependent on the forming method to be used.

The choice of an alloy for a specific architectural purpose is also dependent on the function to be served. For example, the alloys used most often for structural members are usually quite different from those used for other purposes. Aluminum structural members are often alloys with copper or with a combination of magnesium and silicon, while hardware is often made of alloys with magnesium alone. Aluminum manufacturers and suppliers furnish information on the various alloys and their uses.

Aluminum is widely used without the addition of finishes, other than various surface textures. Many people find the natural color pleasing and, under most conditions other than near bodies of salt water, the metal is resistant to corrosion. However, aluminum may also be finished with a number of materials, including wax, plastic coating, paint, plating of other metals, and porcelain enamel. By making a selection from the types of finishes available, it is possible to obtain aluminum in plain, textured, highly polished, or matte finishes, exposing the color of the natural metal or in a variety of colors. A most important aluminum finishing method is called anodizing. This is an electrolytic process which builds up a clear protective coating of aluminum oxide on the surface of the metal. The color of anodized aluminum depends on the alloy used and includes a range of grays. Color anodizing produces a range of colors in the aluminum oxide coating by means of dyes or by adding various metals in small quantities.

Architectural Products Any list of architectural products made of aluminum would be a very long one. Among the major products are structural members, including beams, tees, angles, channels, zees, and square, rectangular, and round pipe; roofing and siding, including flat, corrugated, and other shapes; roofing, including crimped, shingles, and others; flashing, copings, gravel stops, gutters, and downspouts, or leaders; windows and doors; curtain walls and storefronts; railings, grilles, stair treads, and fences; insect screens; ceiling products; movable partitions; heating and air-conditioning ducts; hardware; and others. Such products come in a great variety of sizes, alloys, finishes, and colors. Aluminum is also used for wiring and, in the form of foil, for insulation and vapor barriers and under plastic laminated materials for countertops to make them resistant to heat, including damage from cigarettes. Powdered aluminum, actually miniscule flakes, is sometimes used in paints.

Aluminum appeals to architects as a material because of its inherent characteristics and properties and for its versatility. Particularly appealing is the ease of extrusion of the metal, using low-cost dies that make special applications economically feasible that might not be if other metals were used. Also of appeal is the variety of surface textures, as well as the great number of colors, available through color anodizing at relatively low costs.

When selecting products of aluminum, architects and other environmental designers should make sure the proper alloys, forming methods, and finishes are used for the specific purposes intended. Designing special products or usages of aluminum requires considerable knowledge of its properties and characteristics, and those of its alloys, and its fabrication and finishing. When designing structures of aluminum, careful attention must be paid to the properties and characteristics of aluminum that are quite different from those of other structural materials.

History Although natural compounds containing aluminum were used for various purposes in ancient times, the metal itself was not separated from the compounds until the 19th century. And aluminum did not make its appearance in architecture until the late 19th century, making it one of the very few really

ALUMINUM Alcoa Building (1952), Pittsburgh, Pa. [*Architects: Harrison and Abramovitz, in association with Mitchell and Ritchey and Altenhof and Brown. (Richard Wurts)*]

modern building materials. The discovery of aluminum and its later extraction and development was an international effort.

In 1809 the English chemist Sir Humphry Davy (1778–1829) first demonstrated that alum contained an unknown metal, which he named aluminum. The Danish physicist Hans Christian Oersted (1777–1851) produced the first aluminum powder in 1825. A German chemist, Friedrich Wöhler (1800–82), made the first aluminum particles in 1845 and discovered the properties of the metal, including its light weight. In 1854 a French chemist, Henri Étienne Sainte-Claire Deville (1818–81), developed a method for melting the particles to produce bars of the metal. In the same year a German chemist, Robert Wilhelm Bunsen (1811–99), accomplished the same feat. The new metal was then more costly than gold. Emperor Napoleon III (1808–73) of France had a set of aluminum tableware made for his most honored guests; his less important guests dined with gold and silver tableware.

In 1884 the first aluminum to be used in architecture was the 6-pound cap of the Washington Monument, Washington, D.C., designed by Robert Mills (1781–1855). The price of aluminum had come down from that of the time of Napoleon III, when it was about $550 per pound, to about $12, which was still too expensive for most uses. In 1886 the American chemist Charles Martin Hall (1863–1914) and the French metallurgist Paul Louis Toussaint Héroult (1863–1914) independently developed methods for the electrolytic production of aluminum, the basis of the methods still used today. Within six years, the price per pound had dropped to about 60 cents and the future of aluminum as a material for architectural and other purposes was ensured.

The major uses of aluminum in the early 20th century were for such purposes as cooking pots and pans and other small utensils and devices. The first structural uses were in dirigibles and these were followed by widespread uses in the aircraft industry. By the beginning of the second quarter of the 20th century, aluminum began to be used in buildings, on a somewhat tentative basis at first. As time went by, its use spread rapidly, not only to a great number of architectural elements, including curtain walls, but also to many other industries, including aircraft, automobiles, bridges, and others. Today aluminum is used in many ways in architecture and has become one of the most important materials.

Related Articles Various articles on structures, components, and systems in architecture.

Further Reading Peter, John: *Aluminum in Modern Architecture*, vol. 1, Reynolds Metals Company (distributed by Reinhold), Louisville, Ky., 1956; Weidlinger, Paul: *Aluminum in Modern Architecture—Engineering Design and Details*, vol. 2, Reynolds Metal Company (distributed by Reinhold), Louisville, Ky., 1956.

Sources of Additional Information Aluminum Assoc., 750 Third Ave., New York, N.Y. 10017; Architectural Aluminum Manufacturers Assoc., 35 E. Wacker Dr., Chicago, Ill. 60601.

APARTMENT

APARTMENT Originally a dwelling room, now usually a group of rooms used as a dwelling, or an apartment building or apartment house which contains a number of such groups of rooms. Apartment buildings assumed importance in the United States as cities became more crowded, causing land values to increase and available land to decrease. Apartment buildings are enjoying increasing acceptance by those who choose to live in close proximity to other people, shops and stores, and often jobs and recreational facilities, with relative safety and ease of maintenance. An apartment often provides increased living space and more amenities than a single-family house that costs the same amount of money. Because of their popularity and increasing numbers in suburbs as well as in urban areas, apartment buildings have become one of the major building types in architecture today.

Types There are several different kinds of apartment buildings. A garden apartment, usually found in the suburbs and one to three stories in height, is an apartment building in which some or all of the individual units have private gardens of limited size or share an outdoor garden area. In some cases, each garden apartment unit occupies only a single floor, but in others the units have two stories. When similar apartment buildings are located in more highly populated areas, as in cities, they are frequently called townhouses.

Often the terms *high-rise* and *low-rise,* and sometimes *medium-rise,* are applied to apartment buildings. There is little agreement about the exact definitions of these terms. However, it is generally accepted that any apartment over three, or possibly four, stories in height must be served by elevators, while the lower buildings may be walk-up apartments. If low-rise apartments are defined as walk-ups, perhaps medium-rise might mean those from about five to nine stories; and high-rise, those more than nine. If an apartment building requires elevators, its design and construction will differ markedly from those that only require stairs.

An apartment hotel combines some of the qualities of both hotels and apartments. For example, it might have more or less permanent residents as in an apartment, but might provide public spaces for dining and other purposes and maid and maintenance service as in a hotel.

Formerly, all apartments were rented or leased by the occupants. Such apartment units are available furnished, with all major pieces of furniture and furnishings provided and sometimes with such things as dishes and linen. Unfurnished apartments usually have only the major kitchen equipment, the remainder of the furniture and furnishings to be supplied by the occupants. In later years, there has been a growing tendency toward ownership of some apartments by their occupants. Occupant-owned apartments may be condominiums or cooperatives.

Ownership A condominium is an apartment building, in which the occupants own their own indi-

APARTMENT High-Rise, Lake Point Tower (1968), Chicago, Ill. [*Architects: Schipporeit and Heinrich. (Hedrich-Blessing)*]

APARTMENT Low-Rise, Greenfield Housing (1949), Greenfield, Mass. [Architects: Sargent, Webster, Crenshaw and Folley. (Joseph W. Molitor)]

vidual apartment units and share ownership with all other occupants of common areas, such as halls, elevators, swimming pool, outside areas, and so on. In a condominium, the maintenance and upkeep of these common areas and of the overall building are usually performed by people who handle the work for the benefit of all occupants, who pay a fee for these services. In some cases, the occupants also pay an additional fee for which they receive janitorial, maintenance, and other services within their apartments.

In a cooperative, the occupants share ownership in the entire apartment building, but do not own their individual apartment units, leasing their units from the cooperative in which they are stockholders. As in a condominium, cooperative apartment occupants usually pay a fee for upkeep, maintenance, and so on. Also property taxes are paid on the entire building and prorated among the owners.

The most obvious advantage of both condominiums and cooperatives is that of ownership as opposed to renting. With this comes the advantages that other homeowners have of acquiring equity and various tax advantages. Since cooperatives and condominiums are generally nonprofit, their occupant-owners can ordinarily afford nicer apartments than they might in a rental apartment building.

Unit Variations Apartment units vary considerably in size, number of rooms, and degree of luxury. The smallest, an efficiency apartment, has a single major room for living, dining, and sleeping; a kitchen; and a bathroom. Larger apartments, like single-family

houses, may have any number of rooms, large or small. Apartments of all sizes may range from somewhat simple, utilitarian types to the utmost in luxury, with costs and rentals reflecting the various degrees between. Apartment units may occupy one floor, two floors, or sometimes more. If a unit occupies two floors, it is called a duplex apartment, not to be confused with a duplex house, which means a double house for two families. If the apartment unit occupies three floors, it is called a triplex.

Building Complexes At one time, the most usual apartment development consisted of a single building placed on a single site. Such a building might contain a few individual units or hundreds. Of increasing importance are complexes consisting of two or more apartment buildings on one site, with landscaped areas, automobile parking spaces, and sometimes recreational facilities, such as swimming pools and tennis courts, shared between them. In some cases, the development goes much further, providing on a single site a shopping center, a motion picture house, and other amenities. A further development is the multiuse center which not only contains elements of this kind but also may provide hotel or motel facilities, a convention center, and offices. In most cases, this multiplicity of usage is provided in a group of buildings, designed and constructed in such a way as to complement each other. In some cases, though, many of these uses may be combined into a single high-rise building.

In the last few years, another method for providing housing has been the planned unit development. Such developments provide open spaces, recreation facilities, churches, schools, and shops, as well as dwellings, for a relatively large number of families. A typical planned unit development might include multifamily residences, such as high-rise apartments and townhouses as well as single-family and two-family homes.

Elements The planning of apartment buildings involves three major elements: private areas, public areas, and administration-service areas. The private areas are the apartment units. These ordinarily contain rooms or spaces, as in a single-family house, for sleeping, dining, food preparation, and so on. The public area includes the lobby or vestibule, stairs and elevators, corridors, parking facilities, and sometimes a mailroom. Also often included are other shared facilities, such as laundry rooms, bulk storage for tenants, recreational facilities, and community rooms for games and dining. There may be shops and service establishments in the building. The administration-service area includes office space for the management, storage rooms, and space for mechanical equipment and sometimes maintenance shops.

American Development In colonial America, land was plentiful and inexpensive and most people lived in single-family houses. As land became less available and more expensive, construction of apartments began, first in New York City in the mid-19th century and

APARTMENT Low-Rise, Lake Shore Housing (1971), Buffalo, N.Y. [*Architect: Paul Rudolph. (Joseph W. Molitor)*]

later in other large cities. Prior to about 1870, these buildings were tenements, which originally simply meant apartments but which came to mean buildings for housing great numbers of poor families in large cities. Often shabbily built, overcrowded, unsafe, and unsanitary, the tenements were not desirable places to live. The conditions of the tenements and their eventual deterioration into slums slowed the development of more suitable forms of multiple housing for many years.

In spite of the bad reputation of tenements, the continuing growth of city populations gradually led to construction of better apartment buildings, beginning about 1875 in New York City and few years later in Chicago. The evolution of the modern apartment had begun. Technological developments, including steel-framed structural systems, electric lighting, and greatly improved elevators, helped speed the evolution. Better planning of apartment buildings and individual apartment units soon followed. Early in the 20th century, passage of laws protecting the safety and health of apartment dwellers gave a tremendous boost to the development of apartments. This led to a great boom in apartment construction in larger cities after 1921, a boom that spread to the smaller cities and towns and then to the suburbs. In most urban areas today, single-family houses have largely been supplanted by apartments. And apartment living has come to be very acceptable, even desirable, for a large number of people. With the continuing scarcity and high cost of land, the trend can be expected to continue.

Related Articles HOUSE; HOUSING.

Further Reading Alpern, A.: *Apartments for the Affluent*, McGraw-Hill, New York, 1975; *Architectural Record: Apartments, Townhouses and Condominiums*, McGraw-Hill, New York, 1975; Macsai, John, E. P. Holland, H. E. Nachman, and J. Y. Yacker: *Housing*, John Wiley, New York, 1976.

Periodical *Apartment Business*, 5 S. Wabash Ave., Chicago, Ill. 60603.

ARCH A structural element that usually supports the weight of a building or other structure above a door, window, or other opening in a wall. Originally, arches were constructed from a number of small wedge-shaped masonry units, of brick, stone, or tile called *voussoirs*, set in such a way as to form an opening that curved upward from the sides. Curved arches may take many forms, including semicircle, horseshoe, and lancet (pointed). Arches may also be flat.

Masonry arches derive their strength by transferring weight, or thrust, laterally from unit to unit starting at the crown in the top unit, the keystone, down the sides or haunches to the bottom of the arch to what is called the spring line. At the spring line, the weight, or thrust, is transferred from the arch to a wall or other structural element. This may be a pier, which is a heavy type of column designed to take the thrust. The pier may be assisted in this by a buttress, another structural element placed to help take the thrust. An arcade is a line of arches resting on columns, arranged so that the thrust at the bottom of each arch is resisted by the thrust from the arches on either side.

Elements of an Arch The rise of an arch is the height from the springer to the keystone and the span

ARCH Contemporary brick, Dutch Lane School (1974), Freehold, N.Y. [*Architect: Warren Ashley. (Joseph W. Molitor)*]

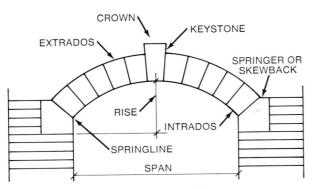

ARCH Components of masonry segmental type.

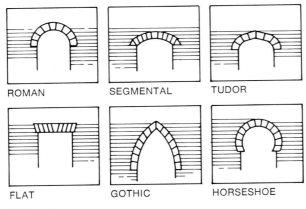

ARCH Masonry types.

is the width between springers. An archivolt is an ornamental molding on the face of an arch, and an extrados is the line or surface of the exterior of an arch at the outside edge of the units or voussoirs. This is the line which the archivolt follows. An intrados is the line or surface at the interior of an arch at the inside edge of the voussoirs. A springer, or skewback, is the unit at the bottom of the side of an arch.

Today arches are also made of wood, steel, and reinforced concrete, utilizing many of the same principles but with the lateral thrust at the spring line reduced to a minimum so that heavy piers or buttresses are not required.

History The principles of the arch were discovered in Mesopotamia at least 6,000 years ago. The ancient Babylonians and Egyptians used arches, as did the Greeks. The Romans developed arch design to a high level, especially in the semicircular form. In the Gothic architecture of the Middle Ages, the pointed arch was widely used and highly developed. In Renaissance buildings, there was a return to the round form.

American Development The Spanish began using masonry, including arches, in St. Augustine in 1565. Early in the 17th century, perhaps as early as 1610 at Jamestown, the manufacture of brick in the English colonies in America began, and stone quarrying soon followed. The masonry arch then followed and has been an important structural element of American architecture ever since. At first, masonry buildings and arches were relatively uncommon in the colonies. Later the use of stone and brick became widespread not only for large, important buildings but also for houses. Today arches of masonry are still used in buildings but arches of the newer materials of laminated wood, steel, and reinforced concrete are more prevalent.

Related Articles BRICK; CONCRETE: DOME; MASONRY STRUCTURE; STONE; TILE; VAULT; WOOD.

ARCHITECTURE The art and science of buildings, groups of buildings, and other structures that are functional, soundly constructed, economical, and esthetic. The term *architecture* can also be applied to buildings, groups of buildings, and other structures that fulfill these requirements. Although the word *architect* is sometimes used in a general sense, such as in speaking of God as the Architect of the Universe, the more specific meaning today denotes a person who has been educated and has gained experience in architecture and, having passed comprehensive examinations, is registered or licensed to practice architecture. In ancient Greece an architect was called *architekton*, arch technician or builder; in Rome this became *architectus*.

Attributes Marcus Vitruvius Pollio, usually called simply Vitruvius, a Roman architect and writer, who lived in the first century A.D., defined architecture in his famous book, *De architectura*. Vitruvius said architecture consisted of order, arrangement, proportion, symmetry, decor, and distribution. These dicta are still widely followed today and mean, in modern terms, that architecture must have its details adjusted properly, the details must be assembled together properly, the parts of a building must be of proper sizes and proportion in relation to other parts and to the building as a whole, the parts of the building must be in harmony with each other and balanced, all parts of a building must be assembled into an ensemble, and materials and other parts of the building must be economically sound.

The most famous quotation from *De architectura* is "strength, utility, grace," which Vitruvius required of buildings if they were to be called architecture. The English poet and diplomat Sir Henry Wotton (1568–1639) paraphrased Vitruvius some 1,500 years later with his, "firmness, commodity and delight." In any case, what they both meant was that architecture should be functional or useful, strongly and economically built, and esthetic or beautiful.

Later architects have maintained that the principles of architecture can be conceived in two words: function and form. To be functional, a building must provide shelter in a manner that is comfortable and efficient. Form refers to all the elements involved in the appearance of the building, both inside and outside. Architects of various eras have had different attitudes about these principles. For example, in the 20th century some architects maintained that "form follows function," a dictum of the great pioneer of the modern movement Louis Henri Sullivan (1856–1924). Although Sullivan did not adhere strictly to this principle, other architects interpreted it to mean that if a building is made to be functional, its proper form will be directly derived from its functions. Other 20th-century architects maintain that the form of a building is the primary concern; the function, secondary. Since architecture is the only major art that is truly functional, this is like arguing that the science of architecture can somehow be separated from that of the art. Most architects would not agree with this premise.

Another method for describing the attributes of architecture entails dividing it into what are thought to be the basic determinants—natural, cultural, and technical—that affect it. Natural characteristics are those of climate, geology, and geography. Cultural characteristics are those having to do with sociological and related aspects, such as religion, ideals, governments, and the like. Technological characteristics are those that have to do with materials, structures, and systems used in architecture and the methods used for their construction. For his famous book, *A History of Architecture on the Comparative Method*, first published in 1896 and still in print in its eighteenth edition, Sir Banister Fletcher (1866–1953) analyzed world architecture on the basis of what he considered the six influences on it: geographical, geological, climatic, religious, social, and historical.

Because of the great scope of architecture, none of the analytical methods is perfect. Yet all are valid in their own ways. A person who would attempt to understand architecture can certainly start with them as guides which can lead to further study, knowledge, and appreciation.

Functions of Architects. The functions of architects are varied and numerous. The primary ones are programming, the study and analysis of architectural problems and preparation of programs describing the problems; preparation of preliminary drawings, often called schematic designs, followed by further study resulting in more detailed drawings, called design development drawings; preparation of construction documents, working drawings and specifications, from which the building may be constructed; and construction administration, including inspection of the construction, previously called supervision, to ensure that the work is properly performed.

In the performance of these functions, architects are usually assisted by technicians, draftsmen, specification writers, and others; and architects oversee and coordinate the work of other professionals, including engineers, landscape architects, interior designers, and other consultants. Architects occasionally perform some of these services themselves or with the aid of employees, partners, or other associates. In addition, architects often perform a myriad of other services, including feasibility studies, market and merchandising analyses, project development, research, testing, and product design. Architects are sometimes active in such fields as city planning.

Related Articles Various articles in this book are concerned with the major aspects of architecture and of the profession and practice of architecture. Several historical articles trace the history of architecture in America and many articles on other subjects contain historical information. Articles are also included on the lives of notable American architects. The functions of architects are discussed in articles on various phases; see, for example, articles entitled design, architectural; programming; specification; working drawing. A number of articles are included on other aspects of architecture; for example, see computer; drafting; model making; rendering. See also articles entitled career; education; engineering; landscape architecture; planning, city. A series of articles covers the important materials, equipment, and systems used in architecture.

Further Reading Burchard, John, and Albert Bush-Brown: *The Architecture of America*, Little, Brown, Boston, 1961; Cowan, Henry J.: *Master Builders—A History of Structural and Environmental Design from Ancient Egypt to the Nineteenth Century*, John Wiley, New York, 1977; Cowan, Henry J.: *Science and Building—Structural and Environmental Design in the Nineteenth and Twentieth Centuries*, John Wiley, New York, 1978; Fletcher, Sir Banister: *A History of Architecture on the Comparative Method*, 18th ed., Charles Scribner's, New York, 1975; Giedion, Sigfried: *Space, Time and Architecture*, 5th ed., Harvard University Press, Cambridge, Mass., 1967; Hamlin, Talbot: *Architecture—An Art for All Men*, Columbia University Press, New York, 1947; Hamlin, Talbot: *Architecture Through the Ages*, rev. ed., Putnam, New York, 1953; Harris, Cyril M., ed.: *Dictionary of Architecture and Construction*, McGraw-Hill, New York, 1975; Rasmussen, Steen Eiler; *Experiencing Architecture*, rev. ed., MIT Press, Cambridge, Mass., 1962.

Source of Additional Information. The American Institute of Architects, 1735 New York Avenue, N.W., Washington, D.C. 20006.

Periodicals *AIA Journal*, 1735 New York Avenue, N.W., Washington, D.C. 20006; *Architectural Record*, 1221 Avenue of the Americas, New York, N.Y. 10020; *Progressive Architecture*, 600 Summer St., Stamford, Conn. 06904.

ART IN ARCHITECTURE Paintings, sculpture, and other art forms, which enhance the esthetic effect of architecture. From the time prehistoric humans first decorated the walls of caves, art has been an integral and important aspect of architecture.

The fine arts are often defined as painting, drawing, sculpture, and architecture and sometimes include poetry, music, dance, and drama. While the latter four arts are often enjoyed in or near buildings, art in architecture usually means the visual arts, mainly painting and sculpture, but often includes such useful arts as furniture, furnishing, and industrial design.

Types Art in architecture, fine arts and others, can be classified into four major types: those that are attached to and are, to an extent, integral with buildings, for example, walls with murals or carvings; independent artworks placed in buildings, for example, paintings on canvas or freestanding sculpture; architectural ornament, which is integral with buildings; and architecture itself as sculptural or other art forms.

Art in architecture may be attached to, located in or on, or integrated with every conceivable architectural element, including walls, floors, ceilings, fireplaces, chimneys, grilles or screens, doors, windows, towers, and exteriors of buildings and their sites. Other elements of architecture, such as landscaping, furniture and furnishings, lighting, fabrics, and graphic arts, may be used in conjunction with art in architecture and, in some cases, may be works of art in themselves. Works of art today may be created in almost every conceivable material and combination of materials: aluminum, brass, brick, bronze, ceramics, concrete, copper, glass, iron, plastics, stainless and other types of steel, stone, terra-cotta, terrazzo, tile, and wood. Some artists have gone even further, working with light or with sand or soil.

Among the major types of art intended to enhance architecture are sculpture—freestanding, integrated into walls and other elements, relief carving and engraving, constructions, and mobiles; painting, both independent paintings and those on walls—murals and frescoes; stained glass; mosaics of tile, glass, and other materials; and various structures, including the building themselves or such elements as bell towers, fountains, and reflecting pools. In many cases, artists work with mixed media, for example, a combination of painting and sculpture; and in others they combine major elements to produce a complete work of art, such as sculpture in conjunction with a fountain.

Acquisition Artworks for placement or integration into architecture may be acquired in two ways: direct purchase of existing works or commission of new works made especially for specific buildings. In either case, the art to be acquired must meet certain standards of taste, economics, and function. Taste in art varies as much as it does in architecture. Therefore, art forms that please an owner may not please the architect. Decisions on such matters are not always easy and must be handled with tact and diplomacy. Sometimes the architect and owner defer such decisions to museum directors or art professors, or they may be asked to aid in decisions.

In any case, artworks should be compatible with the buildings in which they will be located; architectural settings must be appropriate; the medium or media must be correct. In addition, a work of art should serve a purpose as an important, strong focal point in a building, a somewhat incidental ornament, or any other. Although not all would agree, many would consider the most important attribute to be that the art should exist in harmony with the architecture, enhancing it rather than competing with it.

The economics of art in architecture are also important. Works of art, especially those by established dead or living artists, can be very expensive. Complete understanding on this subject between owners and architects is essential. While works of art may be profitable financial investments, the first consideration should be the pleasure and fulfillment that can come from art. However, from an owner's point of view, the financial investment may be of considerable importance. Works of lesser known, often younger, artists may well fulfill the purposes of art in architecture at relatively low costs. It should also be remembered that works of art may be imported from foreign countries, under the proper circumstances, without payment of import duties.

Should the decision be made to acquire the art by direct purchase, additional factors should be taken into consideration. Existing works are ordinarily for sale in any of the media mentioned above, with the exception of those that are integrated directly into the architecture of the building, such as wall carvings or murals. In addition, one may purchase drawings or original prints, such as etchings, lithographs, wood engravings, woodcuts, engravings, or silk-screen prints (serigraphs). Original prints, as distinguished from reproductions, are conceived and executed by artists in limited quantities, after which the etching plates, lithograph stones, silk screens, and so on are defaced or destroyed.

In purchasing works of art, consideration should also be given to the intended locations in buildings and to whether the locations will be permanent or temporary. Some architects and owners prefer to rotate works of art, displaying them for a time and then replacing them with others. Some art museums and other institutions lend or rent works of art, thus making it possible to show and rotate examples in buildings, without making an actual purchase. Some also offer lease-purchase plans, in which rental fees may later be applied to purchases. In the purchase of artworks, the integrity of art dealers or other sources is of utmost importance. Thus not only the works of art but the reputation of the dealer should be acceptable. Certificates of authenticity should be required, signed by experts who guarantee the works.

When works of art are specifically commissioned for buildings, additional considerations must be made. First, there should be complete understanding

ART IN ARCHITECTURE Sculptured clock, Grand Central Station (1913), New York, N.Y. [*Architects: Reed and Stem; Warren and Wetmore. Sculptor: Jules Coutan. (Joseph W. Molitor)*]

ART IN ARCHITECTURE Sculpture, Federal Center (1964), Chicago, Ill. [*Architects: Ludwig Mies van der Rohe; Schmidt, Garden and Erikson; C. F. Murphy Associates; A. Epstein and Sons. Sculptor: Alexander Calder. (Hedrich-Blessing)*]

between owners and architects on the works to be commissioned, artists to be selected, and costs of the artworks. Artists may be selected directly by the architect or owner; by the two together; by an art committee that might include the owner, architect, and experts from museums, universities, or other institutions; or by competitions, in which a few artists are asked to submit conceptual drawings or models. In competitions, it is customary to pay fees to the artists for their submissions. The winners may be required to apply the fees toward the total cost of the works.

In addition to the quality of work, an artist should be selected for compatibility, competence, and dependability. The artist must be expected to perform properly and, most importantly, must work smoothly and creatively with the architect. However, it would be self-defeating if an adequate degree of creative freedom were not granted the artist.

Firm agreements should be reached at the beginning, regarding location, size, materials, scale, cost, and schedule for completion of the artwork. In addition, agreements should be reached on detailed specifications for the work; submissions by the artist of preliminary models or sketches; their approval by the owner and architect; and periodic visits to the artist's studio by the architect to determine progress and problems and to aid the artist in the work and arrangements for installation of the art in the building. Guarantees should be required, often for two years, of the permanence of the materials and other factors. All the factors listed and any others that apply in individual cases should be made part of written agreements between owners and artists.

Architects sometimes design works of art that are to be executed by others or, in a few cases, by the architects themselves. In all cases, architects must provide the proper physical environment for works of art, which are often affected, sometimes extremely, by humidity, ventilation, temperature, light, and other conditions. In some cases, as in weathering steel or bronze sculptures, the gradual change in the surface or the acquiring of patina are normal and expected. In other cases, the conditions in which a work of art exists can cause it to deteriorate or eventually to be destroyed. The requirements for each work of art in architecture must be individually determined and provided for.

History The earliest known art forms are from the Paleolithic or Old Stone Age, about 20,000 B.C. These are common stone tools into which ornament was chipped by hand. The earliest known art in architecture, dating from about five centuries later, is found in various European caves. Both the tools and the cave art show a sophistication indicating that they evolved from earlier and more primitive efforts.

In the caves, art of about 15,000–10,000 B.C. includes the marvelous cave paintings at Altamira, Spain, and Lascaux, France; the rock carvings at La Magdeleine Cave, Penne, France; and the rock engravings in the Cave of Addaura, Monte Pellegrino,

Palermo, Italy. Not very much is known about art in architecture in the New Stone, or Neolithic, Age, which began about 8000 B.C., because by that time humans had begun to build tents and huts, none of which has survived. However, some of their other art forms, such as tools, have survived.

In ancient Egypt, Mesopotamia, and other parts of the Middle East and Mediterranean area, beginning sometime between 5000 and 4000 B.C., more permanent buildings were constructed and ornamented with various art forms. These included wall paintings, now known as mural paintings or murals; freestanding sculpture; sculpture on walls, either with raised figures or in intaglio, incised into the wall surfaces; and engaged sculpture, in which figures are almost freestanding but are partly attached to walls or other architectural elements. The sculpture of these cultures was mostly in stone and many examples have survived.

Wall paintings were usually on stone and some of these also still exist. Another form of art in architecture of the era was the use of sculptural ornament on columns, both freestanding and attached to buildings or engaged, and on their tops or capitals, and for other architectural elements of buildings, thus beginning a tradition that has persisted almost until the present time. In addition, other types of art were integrated into the buildings, including sculptured walls of glazed brick, copper sculptures, and mosaics, ornamental areas made by arranging small pieces of stones or tile or other material to form decorative patterns.

Early Art Forms The names of the artists who created the great variety of art forms in architecture of these early times are unknown. So many great examples of their work have survived that only a few can be mentioned here: in Egypt—the temples of Karnak (c. 1500–300 B.C.) and Luxor (c. 1400–1300 B.C.) at Thebes, Queen Hatshepsut (c. 1500 B.C.) at Deir el-Bahari, Abu Simbel (c. 1300 B.C.) and Edfu (c. 300 B.C.); in Assyria—the city of Khorsabad (705 B.C.), Iraq, including the Temple of King Sargon II (722–705 B.C.); in Crete—the Palace of King Minos (c. 1600 B.C.), Knossos. Many art objects that were originally parts of ancient buildings and also others have been removed from their original sites and are now in museums around the world. For example, the great sculptured brick walls of the Ishtar Gate (c. 575 B.C.), originally in Babylon of King Nebuchadnezzar II (605–563 B.C.), were removed to the State Museum of Berlin, Germany, where they were restored and reconstructed.

The ancient Greeks performed prodigious feats in the incorporation of art, particularly sculpture, into their buildings. Some of the sculptures were free standing; others are integral parts of the buildings they adorn. The Greeks were particularly fond of ornamenting certain parts of their buildings with sculpture, believed to have been originally painted in bright colors. They ornamented the tops, or capitals,

ART IN ARCHITECTURE   Bell tower, St. John's Abbey Church (1967), Collegeville, Minn. [*Architect: Marcel Lajos Breuer. (Hedrich-Blessing)*]

ART IN ARCHITECTURE Sculpture, Pan American Building (1963), New York, N.Y. [*Architects: Emery Roth and Sons. Architectural design consultants: Walter Adolf Gropius and Pietro Belluschi. Sculptor: Richard Lippold. (Joseph W. Molitor)*]

of columns with stylized sculpture; the triangular gable ends, or pediments, with sculptured groups; the portions of buildings between the tops of columns and the undersides of roofs, or friezes; and other parts of their buildings. An interesting Greek form employed sculptured female figures, called caryatids, as columns to support the roofs in certain buildings. It is known that the Greeks employed wall paintings in buildings, but none has survived.

The great surviving examples of Greek art in architecture would make a very long list. Some of the most important are the buildings on the Acropolis, Athens, including the Parthenon (c. 432 B.C.), by the architects Ictinus and Callicrates (both 5th century B.C.); the Propylaea (c. 432 B.C.) by Mnesicles (5th century B.C.), who also designed the Erechtheion (c. 405 B.C.), together with the caryatids of its Porch of Maidens; and the little Temple of Athena Nike (c. 427 B.C.), probably by Callicrates.

It is thought that the incomparable sculptor Phidias (c. 500–c. 432) created a great sculpture of Athena that was placed in the center of the Parthenon and another Athena nearby and that he may have contributed to the sculptures of the friezes and pediments of the Parthenon. The *Athena* sculptures disappeared long ago and no other works by Phidias are known to exist. This was almost the fate of a later great sculptor, Praxiteles (c. 370–c. 330 B.C.); only a few of his works still exist, including *Hermes,* at Olympia, where it was found.

It is a wonder that anything remains of the buildings on the Acropolis, when it is remembered that the Persians tried to destroy it in 480 B.C., that the Parthenon was converted first into a Byzantine and then into a Roman Catholic church and finally into a mosque by the Turks, who came close to destroying it when gunpowder stored in it exploded in 1687. And then in 1803, Englishman Thomas Bruce, Lord Elgin (1766–1841), removed much of the remaining sculpture from the Parthenon and shipped it to the British Museum, London, where today it remains as a spectacular exhibit called the Elgin marbles.

The Etruscans (forerunners of the Romans) used art in architecture, including wall painting, wood carving, and sculptured terra-cotta. The best-preserved examples are at Tarquinia, Italy, where the *Tomb of Hunting and Fishing* (c. 520 B.C.) wall paintings are thought by some authorities to be similar to the lost ones of the Greeks.

The Romans continued the use of art in architecture, though much of it was derived from the Greeks who are better known for artistic ability than are the Romans. The Romans ornamented the capitals of columns and other elements of buildings, placing on them sculptures of various sorts, including friezes, mosaics, and wall paintings or murals. They also further developed sculptured plaster, which had been used to some extent by earlier cultures. The Romans are believed to have developed true fresco painting, a method in which the paints are applied to wet, lime-plastered walls. Other types of fresco painting, utilizing dry plaster with binders to make paint adhere to it, had been used in more ancient cultures. Many of the Roman works of art were by Greek artists, but their work is not the equal of that of earlier times. The Romans erected many monuments and memorials, which appeared everywhere in honor of almost every historical event and included columns, obelisks, and triumphal arches. Most of these were highly decorated with sculpture and other ornamental forms.

Many examples of Roman art in architecture have survived, including some triumphal arches and other monuments. Among the most notable examples in Rome are the Arch of Titus (A.D. 82), the Column of Trajan (A.D. 113), the Column of Marcus Aurelius (A.D. 174), and the Arch of Constantine (A.D. 312), all erected to memorialize Roman emperors. The most striking examples of Roman wall paintings are in the ancient cities of Pompeii and Herculaneum, buried by an eruption of Mount Vesuvius in A.D. 79, and preserved under the cinders and ashes until their rediscovery in the 18th century. Many examples of Roman sculpture have also been preserved there.

Art in architecture continued to be used in Early Christian and Byzantine churches, and included wall and ceiling paintings, mosaics, ornamented architectural elements, sculpture, frescoes, and encaustic, a painting method utilizing a binder of wax or wax and resin to make the paint adhere. Although used earlier in the Orient, bits of colored glass were used, in Early Christian and Byzantine churches, for the first time in Europe, becoming the forerunner of the great stained-glass windows. Among the important buildings containing art of the times are the Byzantine churches of Santa Sophia (536), also called Hagia Sophia, in Istanbul, and San Marco (1085, with later additions), Venice.

Middle Ages At the beginning of the Middle Ages, Romanesque architecture laid the groundwork for the great development of art in architecture that came to fruition in the Gothic style, particularly in monumental sculpture, mostly in stone. Other types of art in both eras were bronzes in sculptures, sculptured doors, other architectural elements, and stained glass, which was developed to a very high point. Much of the great Romanesque and Gothic art in architecture was of a religious nature, and appeared mostly in and on the great churches and cathedrals of the time.

While a list of the best examples would be very long indeed, some must be mentioned. Among the most notable churches and cathedrals are: in France—Abbaye-aux-Hommes (1086), Caen; Notre Dame de Paris (1163–1250); Saint Madeleine (1206), Vezelay; Chartres (1194–1260), with north tower later; Rheims (1211–90), towers later; and Amiens (1220–88); in England—Durham (1093–1133) and Salisbury (1220–70); in Germany—Cologne (1248–1880); in Italy—Pisa (1092); Monreale (1182); Palermo (1170–85); and Florence (1296–1462), designed by Arnolfo di Cambio (1232–c. 1300), with great dome added later by Filippo Brunelleschi (c. 1377–1446).

Many nonreligious buildings of the Middle Ages also contain notable examples of art in architecture. These buildings and the churches and cathedrals, with some exceptions, were designed by master builders and their art created by unknown artists. This is very unfortunate since they created not only some of the greatest buildings of all times but some of the greatest art in architecture.

During the Middle Ages, and even earlier, some notable artists created a number of important works of art in architecture. Among the many works are the religious frescoes (1306) of the painter, sculptor, and architect Giotto di Bondone (c. 1276–c. 1337), usually called Giotto, in the Arena Chapel (1305), Padua, Italy. In a secular vein, Ambrogio Lorenzetti (c. 1300–c. 1348) painted *Good and Bad Government* (1340) in the Palazzo Pubblico (1309) in Siena, Italy. Among the many great sculptures of the time are the pulpit (1260) by Nicola Pisano (1220–84), in the Baptistery (1278) at Pisa, Italy. In 1310, his son, Giovanni Pisano (1245–1314), architect, sculptor, and painter, created another sculptured pulpit for the nearby Cathedral of Pisa (1092). Aslo in this building group is the campanile (1174), the famous leaning tower of Pisa. Sculptured bronze doors, called the *Gates of Paradise*, were completed in 1447 by Lorenzo Ghiberti (1378–1455) for the Baptistery of the Cathedral of Florence, Italy. Another famous masterpiece is the Ghent Altarpiece (1432), by the brothers van Eyck, Hubert (c. 1366–1426) and Jan (c. 1370–1440), in Saint Bavon Church (14th century) at Ghent, Belgium.

Renaissance During the Renaissance, the tradition of art in architecture was continued and developed to a high point, not only because of the interest in art among the nobility and the wealthy but many of the greatest architects of the time were also among the greatest artists in other media, particularly in painting and sculpture.

The magnificent works of art in architecture during the Renaissance form a very long list. Only a few can be mentioned here. First among them must be the sculptures of Donatello (c. 1386–1466), particularly those for the Cathedral and other churches in Florence. Among the greatest frescoes are those of Giovanni da Fiesole (1387–1455), known as Fra Angelico, in the Monastery of San Marco (1450), Florence; the *Last Supper* (1498) of Leonardo da Vinci (1452–1519) in Santa Maria della Grazie (15th century), Milan; the frescoes (1511 and 1513) of Raphael Santi (1483–1520), known as Raphael, in the Vatican and the Villa Farnesina (1511), both in Rome; those of Tiziano Vescelli (1477–1576), known as Titian, in San Nicolò dei Frari (1526) in Venice; and the wall and ceiling frescoes (1512) and *The Last Judgment* (1541) by Michelangelo Buonarroti (1475–1564) in the Sistine Chapel (begun 1508) at the Vatican, Rome.

Among many later important works are the frescoes (1525) of Antonio Allegri da Correggio (1494–1534), known as Correggio, in the Parma Cathedral and in other buildings in Parma; the frescoes of Jacopo Robusti (1518–94), known as Tintoretto, in several churches in Venice; and the great sculptured throne of Saint Peter (1666) by Gian Lorenzo Bernini (1598–1680) in the Cathedral of Saint Peter (1506–1667), Rome. Architecture of the Renaissance not only formed a background for works of art but was itself richly ornamented.

Toward the end of the Renaissance, the ornamentation of buildings increased to a point that, beginning with the Baroque style and especially the Rococo that followed it, the art in architecture cannot really be separated from the architecture itself. By the 18th century, in buildings such as the Kaisersaal (1744), in the Palace, Wurzburg, Germany, by Balthasar Neumann (1687–1753), the murals by Giovanni Battista Tiepolo (1696–1770) and other ornament almost succeed in hiding the building itself.

During the 18th and 19th centuries, the use of ornament in buildings continued but became more subdued and more architectural. The great era of integration of art into architecture that developed during the Renaissance was superseded by times in which many architects sought to integrate art into their work but not always with the great success of the past. Murals and sculpture were often used, but now in many cases, the works of art were accomplished independently of buildings in which they were then placed. Freestanding works of art, such as memorials and monuments, were prevalent, and architects and sculptors often worked together on these.

Modern Movement During the late 19th century, with the beginning of the modern movement in architecture, deliberate efforts were made by many architects to eliminate ornament in an attempt to make their buildings look more functional. Some architects, including Louis Henri Sullivan (1856–1924), attempted to integrate ornament with modern buildings. But these were not the highly ornamented exteriors and interiors of what is probably the last great ornamented building of its kind, the Paris Opéra (1874), by Jean Louis Charles Garnier (1825–98).

A few other attempts were made in the late 19th and early 20th centuries to bring art back into an integral relationship with architecture. One involved the undulating and sinuous lines of the Art Nouveau style, exemplified by the Tassel House (1893) in Brussels, Belgium, by Victor Horta (1861–1947). Art Nouveau, however, never really became well-established in architecture. Another attempt was in the sculptural building designs of the great Spanish architect, Antoni Gaudí (1852–1926), whose most notable buildings are the Casa Milá (1910) and the Church of Sagrada Familia (1926), both in Barcelona. For the most part, architects of the modern movement avoided everything that resembled ornament and turned away from other forms of art in architecture.

U.S. Art Programs Some attempts were made in the

ART IN ARCHITECTURE Sculpture, Cranbrook Academy (1941), Bloomfield Hills, Mich. [*Architect: Eliel Saarinen. Sculptor: Carl Milles. (Hedrich-Blessing)*]

ART IN ARCHITECTURE Sculpture, Daley Center (1965), Chicago, Ill. [*Architects: C. F. Murphy Associates; Loebl, Schlossman and Bennett; Skidmore, Owings and Merrill. Sculptor: Pablo Picasso. (Hedrich-Blessing)*]

United States beginning in the 1930s to restore art to a place in architecture. A few architects designed buildings in which works of art were placed. At the time, the U.S. government gave art in architecture considerable impetus with its Public Works of Art Project, part of the Work Projects Administration. Almost 4,000 artists were paid by the government to produce paintings and sculpture, some 16,000 pieces in public buildings, mostly post offices, and others that were donated to public institutions.

In 1962 President John F. Kennedy (1917–63) instituted another program to bring art into the architecture of the federal government, authorizing the payment of up to 1 percent of the cost of government buildings for works of art. The actual percentage allowed is 0.5 percent. A number of cities, including New York and Philadelphia, instituted similar allowances for artwork. Another federal government boost to art, including art in architecture, was the establishment in 1965 of the National Foundation of Arts and Humanities. One of its branches, the National Endowment for the Arts, provides grants to artists for the furtherance of their creative work. The other branch, the National Endowment for Humanities, provides similar grants in its field.

Private, corporate, and institutional clients of architects have become increasingly interested in art in their buildings in recent years. Today many companies make allowances for art in building budgets, as do many individuals. Because of this growing interest, the number of buildings with integrated art is growing rapidly. Some buildings, and groups of buildings, now look almost like art galleries.

For example, Lincoln Center for the Performing Arts (1968), New York City, has an array of art by leading artists of the time, including sculptures by Englishman Henry Moore (1898–   ) and by Americans Alexander Calder (1898–1977) and Richard Lippold (1915–   ); murals by Frenchman Raoul Dufy (1877–1953) and Russian Marc Chagall (1887–   ); and a bronze fountain by American architect Philip Cortelyou Johnson (1906–   ).

The United Nations Headquarters (1953), New York City, also contains a sizable collection of art in architecture, including murals by Frenchman Fernand Léger (1881–1955), American Fritz Glarner (1899–1972), and Brazilian Candido Portinari (1903–62); and stained glass by Chagall. The Graduate Center, Harvard University, Cambridge, has sculpture by Lippold, a mural by the Spaniard Joan Miró (1893–   ), wood relief sculptures by Frenchman Jean Arp (1887–1966), and a sculptured brick chimney by German-American Josef Albers (1888–1976).

Many other works of art are to be found in recent buildings all over the United States: public buildings, schools and universities, churches, shopping centers, airports, office buildings, and almost every other building type. Although a great deal of progress has been made, many people think there has not been enough. One who has actively attempted to improve the situation for many years is Polish-American architect, watercolorist, and writer Louis Gordon Redstone (1903–   ).

Related Articles DESIGN, ARCHITECTURAL; ESTHETICS; GARDEN; HISTORY OF ARCHITECTURE; MUSEUM.

Further Reading Bitterman, Eleanor: *Art in Modern Architecture*, Reinhold, New York, 1952; Damaz, Paul F.: *Art in European Architecture*, Reinhold, New York, 1956; Janson, H. W.: *History of Art—A Survey of the Major Visual Arts from the Dawn of History to the Present Day*, Harry N. Abrams, New York, 1962; Myers, Bernard S., and Shirley D. Myers: *McGraw-Hill Dictionary of Art*, 5 vols., McGraw-Hill, New York, 1974; *McGraw-Hill Encyclopedia of World Art*, 15 vols., McGraw-Hill, New York, 1967; Redstone, Louis G.: *Art in Architecture*, McGraw-Hill, New York, 1968.

Sources of Further Information American Federation of Arts, 41 E. 65th St., New York, N.Y. 10021; National Endowment for the Arts, 2401 E St., N.W., Washington, D.C. 20506; National Institute of Arts and Letters and American Academy of Arts and Letters, 633 W. 155th St., New York, N.Y. 10032.

ASSOCIATION, BUILDING INDUSTRY

An organization of people with some common interest. Sometimes called business, professional, or trade associations, organizations of this type are nonprofit; their major purpose is the accomplishment of important goals for members that they cannot accomplish as individuals. Such goals often include promotion of the services or goals of the members to the public; cooperation with other organizations; influencing legislation; maintaining good relations with governments; education, ethics, and public relations; and ensuring the competence of members and others.

It is estimated that there are over 6,000 organizations of this type in the United States, ranging in size from very small to very large and representing almost every conceivable interest. Some organizations are composed of individual members; others of corporations, companies, or groups.

In the building industry, there is a large number of such organizations. In addition, there is an even larger number whose goals and work affect the building industry in some way. Some of these are listed in individual articles in this book. The most important ones may be divided into major groups in much the same manner that the building industry may be divided, for example, design, construction, ownership, finance, real estate, and regulation. The other group deeply involved in building, the users, have no associations to represent them, unless some of the consumer groups might be considered as performing this task.

Building industry designers are those who design and perform professional services for buildings and other structures: architects, engineers, landscape architects, planners, interior designers, and technicians.

The AIA The most important association in architecture is the American Institute of Architects (AIA). Founded in New York City in 1857 by 13 architects led by Richard Upjohn (1802–78), who served 18 years as

ASSOCIATION, BUILDING INDUSTRY Headquarters of the American Institute of Architects (1972), Washington, D.C. [*Architects: The Architects Collaborative. (Ezra Stoller)*]

its first president, the AIA was the second national organization of architects in the United States. The first was the American Institution of Architects, founded in 1836 in New York City, which lasted only a few years. Since architecture was in the beginning stages of becoming a profession in the United States, the AIA grew very slowly until 1867, when the first local chapter was organized in New York City. Other chapters soon followed and membership grew, but it still numbered only a few hundred in 1887, thirty years after its founding.

In 1884 a rival organization, the Western Association of Architects, was founded, and in 1889 it merged into the AIA. Membership continued to grow slowly until 1920, when it had reached about 1,500. Growth was somewhat more rapid from that year until the end of World War II, when the membership was slightly more than 5,000. Then membership growth accelerated until it reached about 12,000 in 1957, a hundred years after the founding of the AIA. Today the membership is about 26,000.

The organization of the AIA includes the national body which is governed by national officers who are elected at large by delegates to national conventions, and by members of the board of directors who are elected from the next lower level of organization, the

18 regions, each composed of one or more states. In addition, there is another level composed of states, some of which have state associations with their own officers and directors. The lowest echelon consists of chapters, which operate on local levels and have their own officers.

Membership in the AIA consists of individuals who, with a few exceptions, are all registered or licensed architects and who were formerly called corporate members but now simply members. The AIA associate members are not registered or licensed architects, but they work for architects or in fields related to architecture. Members of both classifications are not only national members but also members of state associations, where they exist, and local chapters. There are also local memberships, of chapters only, for newly registered architects and those in related fields. There is also a category of student members, intended for students in architectural schools, which has a local and national organization of its own, called the Associated Student Chapters of AIA (ASC/AIA). Every prospective member is expected to declare intention of complying with the bylaws and ethical standards of the AIA.

Management of the AIA is conducted by a national organization staff, headed by an executive vice president, located in Washington, D.C. Major divisions, with titles that reflect their services, are program development, component affairs, education and professional development, government affairs, practice and design, conventions, and public relations. In addition, the AIA has four operative wholly owned subsidiaries, the AIA Research Corporation, Production Systems for Architects and Engineers, Inc., the AIA Corporation, and the AIA Foundation.

On the state association and chapter levels, management is provided by small staffs headed by component executives who are often called executive directors. The work of the AIA goes on at all levels: national, state, and chapter. In addition to the functions performed by staff members, a large number of committees work on various types of architectural and related problems. Committees are organized, according to their functions, into commissions, such as education and research, institute and component affairs, community services, professional practice, government relations, building design, and environment.

The AIA performs many services for its members: maintenance of liaison with other organizations in the building industry and with governments; publications, including a magazine, AIA Journal, newsletters, studies, books, and contracts and other legal forms; provision of insurance programs; continuing education, and others.

The AIA on the local, state, and national levels presents a number of awards to architects and those in related fields each year. A fellowship is the highest award that can be given to a member for accomplishments, except for the Gold Medal, which may be given to only one architect a year. Members ordinarily use the letters AIA after their names, unlike doctors and other professionals who use the initials of their professional degrees. Fellows of the AIA use the initials FAIA.

Other Associations Associations that represent the interests of other professionals who perform portions of the design services for buildings offer services to their members that are similar to those of the AIA, though they may differ in some details. The most important of these in the order of their founding are American Society of Civil Engineers (ASCE) in 1852, divided into divisions, of which the most important to architecture are structural, sanitary, soil mechanics and foundations, and surveying; American Society of Mechanical Engineers (ASME), 1880; Institute of Electrical and Electronics Engineers (IEEE), organized in 1884 and merged with radio engineers in 1963; American Society of Landscape Architects (ASLA), 1899; Illuminating Engineering Society (IES), 1906; American

Institute of Planners (AIP), 1917; Acoustical Society of America (ASA), 1929; National Society of Professional Engineers (NSPE), 1934; American Society of Planning Officials (ASPO), 1934; Construction Specifications Institute (CSI), 1956; and American Society of Heating, Refrigerating and Air Conditioning Engineers (ASHRAE); 1959.

Important associations for constructors, those who produce materials for builders and those who actually construct buildings, exist for every type of system, product, and material and for all the functions in construction. The three most closely connected with building construction are: Associated General Contractors of America (AGC), founded in 1918; the Producers' Council (PC), 1921, and National Association of Home Builders (NAHB) of U.S.A., 1942.

Owners of buildings are represented by the National Association of Building Owners and Managers, founded in 1908 (now the Building Owners and Managers Association International), and by other groups.

Financiers have a number of associations, of which the most important to the building industry are American Bankers Association, founded in 1875; U.S. Savings and Loan League, 1892; and the Mortgage Bankers Association of America, 1914.

Real estate interests are represented by a number of associations. The most important to the building industry are American Society of Real Estate Counselors, founded in 1953; National Association of Real Estate Boards, 1908 (which became the National Association of Realtors in 1973); and the Society of Industrial Realtors, 1941.

The regulators formulate and enforce codes and standards for the building industry and are government employees. Many of them, along with others interested in this work, belong to associations. Among the most important of these associations are National Fire Protection Association (NFPA), founded in 1896; American Society for Testing and Materials (ASTM), 1898; Building Officials and Code Administrators International (BOCA), 1915; International Conference of Building Officials (ICBO), 1922; and the Southern Building Code Congress (SBCC), 1944.

The names and addresses of the associations discussed above, as well as many others, are listed at the end of articles on specific subjects.

Related Articles Many of the articles in this book discuss specific subjects.

Further Reading Banister, Turpin: *The Architect at Mid-Century—Evolution and Achievement*, 2 vols., Reinhold, New York, 1954; Saylor, Henry H.: *The AIA's First Hundred Years*, the American Institute of Architects, Washington, 1957.

Periodicals See articles on specific subjects.

BACON, HENRY American architect (1866–1924). If he had not designed another building, Henry Bacon would be remembered for the Lincoln Memorial (1922), Washington, D.C. This monumental building brought him world fame when it was finished shortly before he died and has come to be one of the most respected and loved structures in the United States.

Equally respected and loved is the great sculpture in the building of the seated Abraham Lincoln (1809–65) by the noted sculptor Daniel Chester French (1850–1931). This collaboration between architect and sculptor culminated an association between the two men that had lasted a great number of years and produced more than 50 monuments located in many parts of the United States.

Bacon designed a great number of other monuments, including some for which the sculptor was the noted Augustus Saint-Gaudens (1848–1907). All his monumental works were in the Eclectic Beaux Arts style so popular at the time. His buildings were in the same mode. Many of them were considered very distinguished at the time they were constructed, but later generations have tended to regard them as merely representative of the Beaux Arts tradition of the time, not the finest buildings of that time.

Lincoln Memorial Henry Bacon's masterpiece, the Lincoln Memorial, was a hit from the first and has become even more so with the passing years. So impressed were his fellow architects that they staged its dedication like a latter-day grand opera which might have been composed by Richard Wagner (1813–83). It began on May 18, 1923, during the convention of the American Institute of Architects (AIA), with the annual banquet at tables along the reflecting pool in front of the Memorial.

At the end of the banquet as the architects and their guests stood alongside the reflecting pool, a decorated barge with a great yellow sail, drawn by ropes by architecture students, slowly made its way toward the Memorial which was illuminated from within with violet-colored lights. At the foot of the Memorial waited officers and former officers of the AIA, bearing colorful banners. Waiting with them were the President of the United States, Warren Gamaliel Harding

BACON, HENRY Lincoln Memorial (1922), Washington, D.C. (M. E. Warren)

(1865–1923), and former President William Howard Taft (1857–1930), then Chief Justice of the Supreme Court, standing between incense-burning braziers.

On the barge were the architect Henry Bacon and the sculptor Daniel Chester French and members of the U.S. Marine Corps Band, all dressed in colorful medieval cloaks, illuminated by what was called the "fire of inspiration." From muted trumpets came "Walther's Prize Song" from Wagner's opera *Die Meistersinger*. After disembarking from the barge, Henry Bacon received from President Harding the Gold Medal of the American Institute of Architects, its greatest honor for an architect. The Memorial was then dedicated as a national shrine. The ceremonies ended with the playing of the national anthem by the Marine Band and the bursting high overhead of a single star shell.

Life   Henry Bacon was born at Watseka, Ill., on November 26, 1866, the son of an engineer. In 1881 he entered the Chauncey Hall School in Boston and, after graduation, entered the architectural school of the University of Illinois, Urbana, in 1884. After staying only a year, Bacon went to work in an architectural office in Boston and then went to New York City to work for McKim, Mead and White, where he came under the influence of their eclectic architecture, which was based on the principles of design of the École des Beaux Arts in Paris. In 1889 Bacon won the important Rotch Traveling Scholarship and went to Europe for two years to study and travel. After returning to New York City, he again entered the office of McKim, Mead and White in 1891, and stayed there until 1897, when he opened his own office. During his professional career, he designed buildings of many types, including churches, hospitals, libraries, banks, railroad stations, schools, and office buildings. He was best known for his designs for monuments and memorials.

Toward the end of his life, Bacon received many honors, including membership in the National Academy of Arts and Sciences and the National Institute of Arts and Letters. As mentioned previously, he also won the Gold Medal of the American Institute of Architects in 1923 for his design for the Lincoln Memorial. Less than a year later, on February 14, 1924, Henry Bacon died. It was a tragic year for architecture. On April 14 Louis Henri Sullivan died, and 10 days later Bertram Grosvenor Goodhue died.

Related Articles   ART IN ARCHITECTURE; BEAUX ARTS, ÉCOLE DES; CAPITAL, UNITED STATES; CRAM, GOODHUE AND FERGUSON; ECLECTIC ARCHITECTURE; MCKIM, MEAD AND WHITE; MONUMENT.

BANK   A type of building, or portion of a building, in which financial transactions are performed, including receiving, protecting, and lending money. Several other types of financial institutions whose functions resemble those of banks are sometimes called banks. A credit union is a cooperative that receives funds for deposit and makes loans to its members. Land banks lend money on real estate, as do mortgage companies; investment banks distribute corporate securities.

Types   Banks provide a number of services, including savings accounts, checking accounts, loans, safety deposit boxes and vault storage, and trust management. A commercial bank usually performs all these and other functions. Commercial banks may be either national or state banks, according to which governmental body charters and supervises them. Savings banks, chartered and supervised by the states, perform more limited services, mostly confined to savings accounts and loans. Trust companies, most of which are banks, manage trusts, receive deposits of money or other valuables, and make loans. Central banks are owned and operated by the government, such as the 12 Federal Reserve Banks of the United States. These banks perform services for other banks, such as issuing bank notes, clearing and collecting checks, making loans to the banks, and acting as depositories for government funds.

Elements   The major elements of banks are public spaces, operations departments, and the executive suite. Other elements are the legal department, the mailroom, and data-processing (computer) facilities. The public spaces include the lobby where tellers are located for easy accessibility to the customers; the officers' area where bank officials are available for consultation, making loans, and other functions; and the safety deposit vault located conveniently nearby. The public spaces also include the drive-in and sidewalk, or walk-up, tellers' windows and the automated banking system where customers may activate computers to make transactions.

The operations departments are behind the scene to customers. They include bookkeeping, data-processing, clerical, mail, records, and employees' areas. The trust department and often an auditorium for meetings are included. The executive suite contains offices for the officers of the bank and their assistants, and conference rooms. Many banks also have building departments used by the people who maintain the building and handle the renting of office space to other businesses.

History   Banking has existed since ancient times, first practiced by money changers and money lenders who later received deposits of money from their customers to hold for safekeeping. The first bank, in the modern sense of the word, was the Banco di Rialto in Venice, Italy, established in 1587. In 1694 the Bank of England was established and the business of banking has continued to grow ever since. With the growth of banking came the establishment of bank buildings as an important building type.

American Development   In colonial times, attempts were made to establish banks, but none succeeded. There were loan offices but no real banks.

BANK   Southeast National (1975), Orlando, Fla. [*Architects: Langdon and Wilson. (Hedrich-Blessing)*]

BANK Federal Reserve (1972), Minneapolis, Minn. [*Architect: Gunnar Birkerts. (Hedrich-Blessing)*]

The first commercial bank in the United States, the Bank of North America, was established in Philadelphia in 1781 by Robert Morris, who was superintendent of finance for the colonies. The first state-chartered bank, the Bank of Massachusetts, was established in Boston in 1784. The First Bank of the United States (1798), in Philadelphia, was the first bank in which the U.S. government had a financial in-

terest. Its architect was Samuel Blodget. The Second Bank of the United States (1818), also in Philadelphia, was designed by William Strickland (1787–1854). The original buildings of the last two banks are still in existence.

Over the years, banks have continued to add new services and new buildings have been built to accommodate them. In 1816, the first savings bank was es-

BANK Southern Ohio (1972), Cincinnati, Ohio. [*Architects: RTKL Assoc. (Joseph W. Molitor)*]

tablished; in 1822, the first trust company; and in 1910, the first postal savings bank. In 1946 the first drive-in bank was built in Chicago, a trend that has continued in complete drive-in banks and as one of the services of regular banks. A recent development has been the automated teller system, by means of which check cashing, deposits, and other transactions may be handled by a computer activated by the customer's identification and instructions.

Over the years, the design of banks has greatly changed. Now banks tend to be as open, spacious, and well furnished as any other commercial establishment that hopes to attract customers. Just a few years ago, most banks were austere, the tellers hiding in forbidding cages instead of working at open counters as they now do. Another somewhat recent development is the construction of banks in large office buildings, portions of which are used for banking operations, with other spaces occupied by other businesses.

BAUHAUS, STAATLICHES (STATE BUILDING SCHOOL) Famous German school of architecture

and other design arts. From 1919, when it was founded by architect Walter Adolf Gropius, the Bauhaus has had an important influence on design of buildings, furniture, manufactured products, and other arts. The original Bauhaus was formed by Gropius, who became its director, by combining two other schools in Weimar, Germany: the Grand Ducal Saxon School of Applied Arts and the Grand Ducal Academy of Arts.

Principles The Bauhaus was founded in a time of eclecticism in architectural and other design. The modern movement, then in its infancy, was deeply affected by this new school that revolutionized the principles of design and their teaching. The most important principles were: the machine and industrial production are the new media of design and designers must understand and exploit the media; to accomplish this, designers and others involved must collaborate rather than working only as individuals; all elements of design are completely interdependent on one another; education of designers must integrate practical training in workshops actually engaged in production with sound training in the theoretical

BAUHAUS, STAATLICHES   School Building (1925), Dessau, Germany.
[*Architect: Walter Adolf Gropius. (The Architects Collaborative)*]

aspects of design. As Gropius said, "The object of the Bauhaus was not to propagate any 'style,' system or dogma, but simply to exert a revitalizing influence on design."

Curriculum   For the new school, Gropius devised a new curriculum that required all students to take a preliminary course in the fundamentals of design that are common to all of the arts. Their interrelationships were studied in a broad way that would prepare students, as whole designers, to further pursue specialized studies within an overall system. Each student then entered a workshop of his own choosing, where the studies were taught by two masters: one in handcrafts and one in design. The workshops served as laboratories in which students could develop their own ideas, with help from the staff masters and from visiting experts. After the first three years, students were required to pass a difficult examination before being allowed to proceed to building training. For those who went on, the training included practical work in building sites and materials, drafting, engineering, and design. Those who finished the course were awarded the Master Certificate of the Bauhaus, and went on to become architects or designers in other fields.

Masters   To ensure that the instruction and other work at the Bauhaus would be of the highest order, Gropius attracted top-quality teachers, or masters, to the faculty. The list sounds like a who's who of mod-

ern design and the arts. Among those who became the most famous are Josef Albers (1888–1976), German painter, graphic artist, and educator; Herbert Bayer (1900–   ), Austrian graphic artist; Marcel Lajos Breuer (1902–   ), Hungarian architect; Lyonel Feininger (1871–1956), American painter; Wassily Kandinsky (1866–1944), Russian painter; Paul Klee (1879–1940), Swiss-German painter; Ludwig Mies van der Rohe (1886–1969), German architect; and Lazlo Moholy-Nagy (1895–1946), Hungarian designer and artist. All these masters except Kandinsky and Klee later came to America to live and work.

With a superior faculty and a strong curriculum, the Bauhaus had great success with its students. Starting in 1919, all went well for several years, but Weimar, the capital of Germany after World War I, became one of the first cities to feel the growing reaction in Germany to the continuing inflation and political problems that later would bring the Nazis into power. The reaction was felt in attitudes toward the arts and architecture as well.

Later History   In 1925 Gropius moved the school to Dessau where the political atmosphere was better, and there designed new buildings (1925) which were among his best ever. The growing unrest in the country forced Gropius to resign as director in 1928 and go back into private practice. A faculty member, Hannes Meyer (1889–1954) became director and served until 1930, when Ludwig Mies van der Rohe took over.

Mies was the director until 1932 when the Dessau school was closed and in temporary quarters in Berlin until the school was permanently closed by the Nazis in 1933.

A total of only about 1,250 students had attended the Bauhaus, but its influence went much further than the numbers would indicate. One of the former faculty members, Moholy-Nagy, continued the programs in the United States through the establishment of a school in Chicago, the Institute of Design, which was called the New Bauhaus. Gropius went to Harvard University in 1937 and became chairman of the department of architecture, and in 1938 Marcel Breuer joined him as a design professor. That same year, Mies went to the Armour Institute in Chicago, later renamed Illinois Institute of Technology, to become director of architecture.

Through the efforts of such people as these, the principles of the Bauhaus were preserved, further developed, and disseminated to thousands of future architects and other designers.

Related Articles BREUER, MARCEL LAJOS; EDUCATION; GROPIUS, WALTER ADOLF; MIES VAN DER ROHE, LUDWIG.

Further Reading Wingler, Hans M.: *The Bauhaus—Weimar, Dessau, Berlin, Chicago*, MIT Press, Cambridge, Mass., 1968.

BEAUX ARTS, ÉCOLE DES Famous French school of the fine arts—architecture, painting, and sculpture—located in Paris. Although the Paris school is the one usually referred to in architectural circles, there were schools of the same name located in eight other French cities.

The École des Beaux Arts and its predecessors dominated the teaching of architecture in France for almost 300 years, from 1671 until 1968. They also dominated the teaching of painting and sculpture and, later, of related arts during the same period. In addition, this influence was international. Students from countries other than France were freely admitted and, beginning in the middle of the 19th century, a large number of American architects were educated there. These architects came back to the United States, trained young people in the principles of the Beaux Arts, and founded American architectural schools. Gradually, the influence of the Beaux Arts philosophy spread and deepened until it dominated American architectural education well into the 20th century. Architectural schools taught Beaux Arts principles; and design problems, to be solved by students, were prepared and judged by Beaux Arts architects. This became the accepted tradition in American architectural

BEAUX ARTS, ÉCOLE DES Exterior, Grand Central Station (1913), New York, N.Y. [*Architects: Reed and Stem; Warren and Wetmore. (Irving Underhill, Library of Congress) See color section for additional illustration.*]

BEAUX ARTS, ÉCOLE DES Interior, Grand Central Station (1913),
New York, N.Y. [*Architects: Reed and Stem; Warren and Wetmore.
(Library of Congress)*]

education until the 1930s, when Walter Adolf Gropius (1883–1969) began to divert the architectural school at Harvard University, Cambridge, Mass., away from Beaux Arts philosophies toward those of the Bauhaus, the school he had founded in Germany. Other American schools later followed the lead of Harvard toward teaching modern principles, but the Beaux Arts system did not die out in the United States until after World War II.

Thus it may be seen that the philosophy of the Beaux Arts was a dominant factor in American architecture for approximately 100 years. Although the philosophy of the École changed somewhat over the years of its existence, it was in the main academic and conservative. In its later years, some of its professors and graduates turned toward the modern movement in architecture, but education in the École was primarily based on scholarly study of the architecture of the past. For some years, the style most emulated was that of Classical Greece. Later, all styles of the past were embraced and students began to design buildings in eclectic styles, but always based on proper scholarship.

Composition The central and all-important theme in Beaux Arts architecture was composition, which was the essential act of architectural design or making a whole, as in a building, of its parts. Composition in this sense has several elements, including proportion, scale, contrast, balance, rhythm, unity, and character.

Proportion means the relationship of one part of a building to the whole building and to the other parts. Scale is the factor that permits comparisons of proportions in relation to one another and to some abstract unit of measurement, such as the human figure. Contrast means differences in parts of buildings, as in form, mass and shape, line size, tone, and so on. Balance means a state of equalization or equilibrium in the form of a building and its parts and may be symmetrical, having identical forms on both sides of an axis, or asymmetrical, in which balance is obtained with forms that are not identical on the sides of an axis. Rhythm means the organized repetition of elements so that they flow from one to the other with regularity and accents; in music, rhythm is produced by sounds; in architecture, mostly by forms. Unity involves bringing together all the elements of architecture into a harmonious whole. Character is the aggregate of the elements of a building that makes it individual or unique.

Education Although changes were made in education at the École des Beaux Arts over the years, in the important things it remained much the same as when it was founded. In general, the requirements for admission were simple: attainment of age fifteen and no more than thirty, and the successful completion of oral and written entrance examinations in mathematics, descriptive geometry, history, drawing, and architectural design. Entrance was open to all male students, regardless of nationality; in 1900 the first women were admitted. Although there was no

tuition, students were charged rent for the studios in which they studied, fuel for heating, and oil for lighting; some students paid fees to the design professors.

Upon passing the examinations, an applicant, called an *aspirant,* was admitted to the second, or *seconde,* class. Attendance at lectures was optional and no examinations were given except in scientific subjects. Each new student, or *nouveau,* was also admitted to a studio, or *atelier,* of a practicing architect called a *patron,* in which to learn architectural design, or composition as it was usually called. In an *atelier* the *nouveau* learned by designing series of projects, or *projets,* in competitions, or *concours.* These projects were generally of two types: sketches, or *esquisses,* which usually lasted 12 hours and required one drawing, and rendered projects, or *projets rendus,* which lasted about two months and usually required three large drawings or renderings. Students could participate in as many *concours* as they wished, with a minimum of two a year, and after receiving an adequate number of points, called *valeurs,* in the competitions and in mathematics, construction, and perspective, a *nouveau* could enter the first, or *première,* class and become an old student, or *ancien élève.* Completion of the *seconde* class usually took from two to four years.

Work in the first class could also be done at a student's own pace. There were six *esquisses* and six *projets rendus* each year and a student could participate in any or all of these. At first, there was no official graduation. Students simply stayed as long as they wished and left the school when they wanted to. However, they were not eligible to remain in the École after age thirty. After 1867, students could participate in an annual special competition for diplomas.

In all the competitions, awards were made to students who did the best work. In some, these were medals, or *médailles;* in others, *mentions.* Money prizes were also awarded. The highest prize of all was the *Grand Prix de Rome,* a special competition held each year for French students only. This was the ultimate honor at the École. The winner received all expenses for study at the French Academy in Rome for four or more years at first, and later for two years of study and two of travel.

Work in the *ateliers* was the most important part of education at the École. *Ateliers* varied in size from only 1 student to 100 or more, with the average size about 20 in the middle of the 19th century. Some of these were *ateliers officiels,* in which the fees of the *patrons* were paid by the government. Others were *ateliers libres,* in which *patrons* were paid by the students. The *ateliers* were governed by the students, each group electing one of its members, called a *massier,* to take charge of its common fund. The *patron* regularly gave instructions and the students helped each other, the *anciens élèves* by criticizing the work of the *nouveaux,* who in turn helped the older students make their drawings and renderings.

In general, a student participated in competitions, or *concours*, by choice. If the student decided to participate, a separate enrollment was required for each *concours*. After the student had signed in, a copy of the program for the *concours* was furnished. The student then went into a small cubicle, or went *en loge*. Twelve hours were allocated for study of the problem and preparation of a sketch, called a *parti*, showing ideas for solution of the problem. At the end of the allotted time, the student signed out and turned in the sketch, retaining a copy.

Returning to the *atelier*, the student developed the idea, with critical help from the *patron*, and prepared drawings and submitted them to the school on the scheduled completion day for judgment. If the student's drawings did not reflect the original ideas of the *parti*, the submission was declared out of competition, or *hors-concours*, and no credit was given. As time for submissions approached, students usually worked day and night to complete their drawings. On the last day, their drawings were transported to the school on hand-drawn carts, called *charrettes*. Thus the last struggle to complete the work came to be called a *charrette* and a student so engaged was said to be *en charrette*.

Although the École des Beaux Arts no longer exists and architecture and architectural education have changed radically, many of the old French terms are still in use in the United States and elsewhere today.

American Students Before the closing of the École, a great many Americans were educated there. The first was Richard Morris Hunt (1827–95), who went to the École in 1846. Some of the most notable of the later students were Henry Hobson Richardson (1838–86), Charles Follen McKim (1847–1909), Louis Henri Sullivan (1856–1924), Ernest Flagg (1857–1947), John Merven Carrère (1858–1911), Thomas Hastings (1860–1929), Bernard Maybeck (1862–1957), Whitney Warren (1864–1943), Chester Holmes Aldrich (1871–1940), John Russell Pope (1874–1937), William Adams Delano (1874–1960), Paul Philippe Cret (1876–1947), Raymond Mathewson Hood (1881–1934), and George Howe (1886–1955). Julia Morgan (1872–1957) was the first American woman to graduate from the Beaux Arts.

History The Ecole des Beaux Arts, together with its predecessors, had a long and often turbulent history that lasted almost 300 years. In 1648, the Royal Academy of Painting and Sculpture in Paris was founded. The Royal Academy of Architecture, founded in 1671, had as its first professor and director François Blondel (1617–86). It had a curriculum consisting of theory of architecture, mathematics, mechanics, military architecture, perspective, and stonecutting. Some years later, building construction was added. Early in the 18th century, competitions were instituted, in which students vied for prizes. The first regular annual competition was held in 1720 and this started a tradition that was to be followed, with some breaks in continuity, for almost 250 years. The annual competition

came to be called the *Grand Prix* and later the *Grand Prix de Rome*, since its award brought with it a scholarship to the French Academy in Rome. The annual competition, and others, became the most important factor in architectural education in France for almost as long.

Other than the institution of competitions, the curriculum in the academy, including lectures and student design problems, changed very little until the advent of the French Revolution. Beginning in 1789, the famous French painter Jacques-Louis David (1748–1825) led a fight to abolish the academies along with other royal institutions. The fight was successful and the royal academies were abolished in 1793, only to be reconstituted a short time later without the royal designation. Architect Julien-David Leroy (1724–1803), who had taught at the architectural academy since 1762 and was well thought of by the painter David, was appointed head of the new academy and served in that capacity until his death. In 1795 the academy was renamed the Special School of Architecture and joined to the also newly renamed Special School of Painting and Sculpture.

During the years since its beginning, the École des Beaux Arts did not have many students, for example, only 28 in 1717, and 47 in 1746. During the period Leroy was its head, 1793–1803, a total of only 37 students were admitted. The curriculum remained very much like it had been before the Revolution, consisting of lectures, monthly student design problems, and the annual competition for the *Grand Prix de Rome*. The design philosophy of the school was based on the architecture of ancient Greece.

In another school in Paris, the École Polytechnique, some architectural courses were taught but never a full program as in the special school. The professor of architecture at the École Polytechnique was Jean-Nicolas-Louis Durand (1760–1834), who espoused free use of all architectural styles. After the death of Leroy, Léon Dufornoy (1754–1818) became the head of the Special School and continued the Greek classical tradition started by Leroy. Annual enrollments began to increase, from 6 in 1803 to 38 in 1818.

In 1814 the monarchy was reestablished in France under Louis XVIII (1755–1824). In 1816 the King ordered the special schools to be combined under the name of the École Royale et Spéciale des Beaux Arts. The decree became official in 1819 and the school's name was modified to École Royale des Beaux Arts. Nothing much, other than the name, was changed until 1863. By 1851 the student body in architecture had grown to 281. In 1846 the first American Student, Richard Morris Hunt, enrolled in the École, and was subsequently followed by other American students. In 1848 the second French Republic was established with Charles Louis Napoléon Bonaparte (1808–73), a nephew of the first Emperor Napoléon (1769–1821), as president. In 1852 Louis Napoléon was declared Emperor Napoléon III.

For some time previously, controversy had raged

concerning the orthodox teaching of architecture at the École. The opposition to the teaching was led by Henri Labrouste (1801–75) and later by Eugène Emmanuel Viollet-le-Duc (1814–79). Finally, mostly because of the campaign of Viollet-le-Duc against the orthodoxy of the school, Napoléon III ordered a reform of the policies in 1863. The school was then reorganized. Some professors were dismissed and others appointed to take their places. The admission age for students was changed. The judgment of the competition for the *Grand Prix de Rome* was changed and the prize itself became two years in Rome and two years for travel. Lecture courses were made mandatory rather than optional. The most far-reaching change was that the school was placed under the direction of the government of France rather than under the appointed academy members. The academy members protested vehemently and brought suit. The students rioted and the professors were embroiled in controversy. As a result of the uproar, most of the reforms were gradually rescinded.

It was another development in 1867 that changed the nature of architectural education at the École more than all the reforms of 1863. This was the institution of a diploma to be given to graduates who successfully completed a special competition. Few students attempted the competition and the diploma was largely ignored until 1887, when the government awarded a diploma to each living winner of the *Grand Prix de Rome*. Students now remained at the École from five to seven years, though theoretically the diploma was available after two years, seeking the award of an *Architecte D.P.L.G. (diplôme par le gouvernement)*. Thus a certain consistency and continuity, which had not existed before, was established in the educational process of the École.

By 1890, there were 606 students enrolled in architecture at the École; by 1906, 950 students; and by 1920, 1,100 students. By that time, architecture that seemed to have been designed on the basis of the principles of the École was called Beaux Arts architecture. After World War I, the school's philosophies were vigorously opposed by architects of other countries, particularly Walter Adolf Gropius and the others of the Bauhaus in Germany and the great Swiss architect practicing in France, Charles Édouard Jeanneret, called Le Corbusier (1887–1965). These and other men were engaged in developing what came to be called modern architecture and in pioneering educational principles for architectural schools. The academic classicism of the Beaux Arts was anathema to them.

World War II, when France was mostly occupied by the Germans, brought further problems. The postwar years were not much better. The French economy was depressed and money was scarce. In the 1950s, when the economy began to recover, inflation set in. In spite of these problems, the architectural enrollment of the École rose to 2,780 in 1967. In 1968 student rioting broke out at the University of Paris and spread to the Sorbonne and then to the École. In June 1968, students were evicted and locked out of the École; during that summer the students prevented the competition for the *Grand Prix de Rome* from being held and in the fall prevented the school from reopening.

In December 1968 President Charles de Gaulle (1890–1970) reorganized architectural education in France. The *Grand Prix de Rome* was abolished. The École was replaced by a number of schools called pedagogical units in various parts of France, including eight in Paris. Each unit now teaches architecture in its own manner. The grand and controversial history of the École des Beaux Arts and its predecessors, which had lasted almost 300 years, had come to an end.

Related Articles BAUHAUS, STAATLICHES; CRET, PAUL PHILIPPE; DESIGN, ARCHITECTURAL; ECLECTIC ARCHITECTURE; EDUCATION; HOOD, RAYMOND MATHEWSON; HUNT, RICHARD MORRIS; MAYBECK, BERNARD; MCKIM, MEAD AND WHITE; POPE, JOHN RUSSELL; RICHARDSON, HENRY HOBSON; SULLIVAN, LOUIS HENRI.

Further Reading Curtis, Nathaniel Cortlandt: *Architectural Composition*, J. H. Jansen, Cleveland, 1928; Drexler, Arthur, ed.: *The Architecture of the École des Beaux Arts*, the Museum of Modern Art (distributed by MIT Press), New York, 1977; Pickering, Ernest: *Architectural Design*, 2d ed., John Wiley, New York, 1941.

Source of Further Information National Institute for Architectural Education, 20 W. 40th St., New York, N.Y. 10018.

BELLUSCHI, PIETRO

Italian-American architect (1899–   ). Particularly noted for his religious buildings and for his masterful use of wood, Belluschi spent much of his career in and around Portland, Ore. And a full and influential career it has been.

After receiving engineering degrees, never having had any formal architectural education, and immigrating to the United States, speaking little English, Belluschi spent 18 years in a Portland architectural office that produced eclectic work in many styles. He instituted a modern design philosophy. The changes he made had a quiet drama about them, just as much of his later work would have that quality.

Regional Characteristics Beginning in the late 1930s and early 1940s, Belluschi developed an architecture that nestled into its Pacific Northwest setting as if it had grown there. Using wood, often combined with stone which he remembered with pleasure from his boyhood in Italy, he designed buildings, in particular houses and churches, that were closely related to the climate, landscape, materials, needs, and qualities of the region in which they were built. Along with a few other Northwest architects of the time, he created a truly regional architecture in a part of the world that was quite different from that in which he grew up. Yet he never allowed himself to become stereotyped. At the time when he was designing wood houses and churches with regional character, he also designed office buildings and other types that were quite different—modern skeleton structures with plain geometric surfaces of thin stone, glass, and aluminum. His ability to design buildings to fit their purpose and

BELLUSCHI, PIETRO Platt House (1941), Portland, Ore. *(Pietro Belluschi)*

to integrate them into their setting continued in his later work.

Belluschi's houses have been highly praised for their functional plans and human qualities as well as their regional characteristics. Partaking of the same qualities, his many churches are even more admired. As he stated on many occasions, Belluschi tried all of his life to achieve an architecture of attainment and restraint. Most who have experienced his buildings would agree that he succeeded admirably. And his architecture and philosophy have had considerable influence on the work of other architects.

Academic Career Belluschi also deeply influenced architects and architecture through his academic career. For 15 years, he was dean of the School of Architecture and Planning of the Massachusetts Institute of Technology, Cambridge, and lectured at many other schools. His philosophy of a quiet architecture, that is, original and of high quality, yet attainable and harmonizing with its setting, was imparted to a great number of students at MIT and to many young architects who worked for or were associated with him. And other people who have become familiar with his

work and philosophy have learned a great deal about what constitutes the finest architecture.

Buildings The first important building by Belluschi was the Portland Art Museum (1932), designed when he was working in the firm of Albert E. Doyle. He added a wing in 1939 and another in 1970. When the first two wings had been completed, the museum brought Belluschi considerable recognition, as did the Finley Mortuary (1937), also in Portland. During the depression years few buildings were completed, but beginning about 1940, Belluschi began designing a great number. Over the years, he designed houses, churches, office buildings, banks, stores, shopping centers, schools, hospitals, fountains, and many other types, including a drive-in restaurant.

Among the best of his buildings were houses, the most notable of which are: Sutor (1938), Portland; Meyes (1940), Seattle; Joss (1940), Portland; Kerr (1941), Gearhart, Ore.; Coats (1941), Tillamook, Ore.; and Menefee (1948), Yamhill, Ore.

Churches There is widespread agreement that Belluschi's finest designs were for religious buildings. Starting with his first church, the St. Thomas More

BELLUSCHI, PIETRO Kerr House (1941), Gearhart, Ore. *(Pietro Belluschi)*

Chapel (1941), Portland, still considered one of his best, he gained an international reputation for buildings of this type. Some of his finest churches are: Zion Lutheran and Central Lutheran, both completed in Portland in 1951; First Presbyterian (1941), Cottage Grove, Ore.; Central Lutheran (1952), Eugene, Ore.; Episcopal Church of the Redeemer (1959; see illustrations in article religious building), Baltimore, in association with Rogers and Taliaferro; Trinity Episcopal Church (1963), Concord, Mass.; and St. Mary's Cathedral (1971), San Francisco, in association with Mc-Sweeney, Ryan and Lee and the great Italian engineer Pier Luigi Nervi (1891–1979).

Office Buildings In the design of office buildings, Belluschi has been a leader in a way that is different from his work with houses and churches. In his first important office building for the Oregonian Publishing Co. (1948) in Portland, he made a design for a simple rectangular mass, faced with marble and granite, and with large expanses of windows. The design of this building was completely overshadowed by that of another finished in the same year, the Equitable Building (see illustration in article modern architecture), now the Commonwealth Building, also in Portland. Here, in a 12-story office building, Belluschi produced what many think is a masterpiece of modern architecture. This office building, with a curtain wall of tinted glass and aluminum and with the structure expressed on the exterior, has been called the logical conclusion of the trends in tall building design started by Major William Le Baron Jenney (1832–1907) and the other talented members of the Chicago school of architecture in the late 1800s.

BELLUSCHI, PIETRO Exterior, St. Thomas More Chapel (1941), Portland, Ore. *(Pietro Belluschi)*

BELLUSCHI, PIETRO Interior, St. Thomas More Chapel (1941), Portland, Ore. *(Pietro Belluschi)*

BELLUSCHI, PIETRO Exterior, Trinity Episcopal Church (1963), Concord, Mass. *(Joseph W. Molitor)*

BELLUSCHI, PIETRO Exterior, St. Mary's Cathedral (1971), San Francisco, Calif. [*Belluschi, in association with McSweeney, Ryan and Lee and Pier Luigi Nervi. (Morley Baer)*]

BELLUSCHI, PIETRO Interior, Trinity Episcopal Church (1963), Concord, Mass. *(Joseph W. Molitor)*

BELLUSCHI, PIETRO Interior, St. Mary's Cathedral (1971), San Francisco, Calif. [*Belluschi, in association with McSweeney, Ryan and Lee and Pier Luigi Nervi. (Morley Baer)*]

Belluschi never did another office building that excelled in the way the Equitable did. Later, with Walter Adolf Gropius (1883–1969), he acted as design consultant on the Pan American Building (1963; see illustration in article art in architecture), New York City, by architects Emery Roth and Sons, but it was not considered up to the standards of either consultant. He also was associated as design consultant, with the firms of Wurster, Bernardi and Emmons, and Skidmore, Owings and Merrill, for the design of the Bank of America headquarters (1971; see illustration in article Wurster, William Wilson) in San Francisco, a much better designed building.

Life Pietro Belluschi was born in Ancona, Italy, on August 18, 1899. When he was six years old, his family moved to Rome, where he spent most of his early years. As a boy, he was interested in drawing and in high school he became interested in architecture. At seventeen, he enlisted in the Italian Army in World War I, and served three years. Belluschi entered the school of engineering of the University of Rome and graduated in 1922, with a doctor of engineering degree. In 1923, as an exchange student, he came to the United States and entered Cornell University, Ithaca, N.Y., and received a civil engineering degree in 1924.

After leaving Cornell, Belluschi worked for a while in Idaho as an electrician's helper and then went to Portland, Ore., where he was employed in 1925 by the well-established and successful office of the eclectic architect Albert E. Doyle (1877–1928). When Doyle died two years after Belluschi began work in the office, several other members of the firm left. In 1928 Belluschi became chief designer of the firm and in 1932, a partner. During this period of his life, Belluschi was deeply affected by the philosophy of Harry Wentz, a Portland artist and art teacher who was inspired by the regional qualities of the Northwest and by Japanese architecture. In 1929 Belluschi became a naturalized U.S. citizen.

In 1931 Belluschi designed his first important building, the Portland Art Museum, and gained a measure of national recognition for his effort.

In 1934 Belluschi married Helen Hemmila and they had two children. That same year, he went to Europe where he studied the modern architecture being built and the old medieval churches and villages. On his return, he decided to design buildings that would be expressions of their own time, but founded in the great cultural traditions of the past.

After becoming chief designer, Belluschi produced a steady flow of well-designed buildings. In 1943 he had become so successful that he acquired the Doyle firm and changed its name to his own. The good designs continued and brought him an international reputation as a designer and as one of the foremost proponents of regional architecture.

In 1951 Belluschi decided to devote much of his time and energies to education and became dean of the School of Architecture and Planning of Massachusetts Institute of Technology. Leaving Portland, he formed an association with Skidmore, Owings and Merrill, one of the greatest and most successful of American architectural firms. In spite of Belluschi's deep involvement in architectural and planning education, he still managed to design many buildings, often in association with other architects. During his very prolific career, the total reached well over 1,000 buildings.

In 1962 Belluschi's wife died. He continued at MIT until 1965, when he retired. In that same year, he married Marjorie Bruckner. After retirement from the deanship, he became more active in architectural practice and later moved back to Oregon. Pietro Belluschi has received many honors, including a number of honorary doctor's degrees, election to fellowship in the American Academy of Arts and Sciences and to membership in the National Institute of Arts and Letters. In 1972 the architects of his adopted country awarded him their highest honor, the Gold Medal of the American Institute of Architects.

Related Articles CONTEMPORARY ARCHITECTURE; COPPER ALLOY [for illustration of Student Center, Goucher College (1963), Towson, Md.]; EDUCATION; JENNEY, WILLIAM LE BARON; MODERN ARCHITECTURE; RELIGIOUS BUILDING [for illustration of the Priory of St. Gregory the Great (1961), Portsmouth, R.I.]; SKIDMORE, OWINGS AND MERRILL.

Further Reading Stubblebine, Jo, ed.: The Northwest Architecture of Pietro Belluschi, F. W. Dodge, New York, 1953.

BOGARDUS, JAMES

American inventor (1800–74). As an inventor, James Bogardus originated a great number and variety of devices, including clocks, cotton spinning machinery, engraving machines, gas meters, and mechanical pencils. Some of these were important contributions and were quite successful.

Cast-Iron Buildings In architecture, Bogardus is remembered for other reasons. He was the first American to develop practical methods for the construction of skeleton frames of cast iron for buildings. And he was the first to prefabricate almost every part of a building, transport the parts to the site, and erect the building in record time, sometimes in a few weeks. Whereas cast iron had been used previously, starting in England, for the construction of portions of the frames of buildings and bridges, Bogardus was the first to develop a system for an entire building: a five-story factory he built for himself in New York City in 1849. This building had prefabricated cast-iron columns, piers, beams, and wall panels and was constructed in a few weeks. Some 10 years later, it was disassembled.

Thus Bogardus accomplished the early pioneering work that led eventually to wrought-iron and later steel skeleton-framed buildings and to the tall buildings, or skyscrapers, of today. His earlier buildings were not completely framed with cast iron. Eventually, Bogardus developed methods for making cast-iron fronts for buildings, another element of architecture that soon spread from New York City, where he first used it, to other parts of the country. These fronts might be considered the forerunners of the curtain walls of metals and other materials in use today.

After his first cast-iron building, Bogardus built others in many places, including Baltimore, Washington, Chicago, and Cuba. But he did more of them in New York City than anywhere else. Most of his buildings were demolished long ago. In New York City the only examples that remain are two warehouses in very poor condition on Leonard Street, one of which Bogardus built for himself. Another interesting structure thought to be by Bogardus that still exists is a cast-iron watchtower (1857), or fire tower, in Mount Morris Park, New York City. Another of his New York City works, the Laing Warehouses (1949), later known as the Bogardus Building, was torn down in the 1960s, after the cast-iron wall panels had been carefully removed. The panels were stolen; how and by whom has never been established.

Life James Bogardus was born in Catskill, N.Y., on

BOGARDUS, JAMES 85 Leonard St. Building (1860), New York, N.Y. Only authenticated Bogardus building remaining in New York City. (Joseph W. Molitor)

March 14, 1800. He did not do well in school, attending only at irregular intervals until he was fourteen years of age. Then he was apprenticed to a watchmaker. He never went back to school. After completing his apprenticeship in his early 20s, he went to New York City where he embarked on a life of invention.

When Bogardus was twenty-eight years old, he received a considerable amount of publicity by winning a gold medal for his invention of an eight-day clock. He continued to invent devices of many kinds for the rest of his life. In 1831 he married Margaret Maclay, the daughter of a minister. They had children, but none survived to adulthood.

Starting in the 1840s, Bogardus developed systems for the use of cast iron in buildings, some of which were inventions that he patented. Much of the remainder of his life was spent designing and constructing cast-iron buildings and other structures and further developing inventions of this sort. He became a successful manufacturer of cast-iron systems and parts for buildings, which were used by others in their buildings, and a very successful designer and constructor of buildings.

In his lifetime, Bogardus did not receive much credit for pioneering skeleton-frame construction for buildings and prefabrication. After his death, on April 13, 1874, he gradually slipped into relative obscurity, his name but an occasional footnote in books and other references on architecture.

Related Articles IRON; JENNEY, WILLIAM LE BARON; MODERN ARCHITECTURE; STRUCTURE.

BOOK, ARCHITECTURAL Although other meanings have been used in past eras, the word *book* today commonly means a work of considerable length, about 96 pages or more, printed on paper which has been assembled and bound into a cover. From very early times, a great number of architectural books have been written and published for use by both professionals in architecture and laymen. Many of these books, some by architects, have greatly and even profoundly influenced architecture.

Composition Books are classified as softbound, with flexible covers usually of heavy paper; or hardbound, with stiff covers usually of cardboard covered with cloth, paper, leather, or other materials. Each leaf of paper in a book has two sides or pages. The top of a book, of its pages, is the head; the bound edge is the back; the opposite edge is the front; and the bottom is the foot. The area in which type and illustrations occur on a page is called the type page and the space around it, the margins. The inside edge at the binding is the gutter. Often included on the pages are the titles of chapters or other information; if at the top of pages, these are called running heads; if at the bottom, running feet. Also on the pages are page numbers or folios.

Upon opening a book, the first double sheet is ordinarily attached to the inside of the front cover, and the last, to the back cover. These are the endpapers and may contain illustrations or other decorative matter. The first printed page, other than the endpapers, is the half-title page which contains only the title of the book. This is the first page of a series called the front matter. The second printed page is the title page which contains not only the title but the author's name, the publisher's name, the place of publication, and sometimes other matter. On the back of the title page is the copyright page which usually includes other information, such as a Library of Congress number and an International Standard Book Number (ISBN). The next page, sometimes several pages, in the front matter is usually the table of contents. There may then be a list of illustrations, an enumeration and background of contributors, a dedication page, a foreword written by someone other than the author, and a preface written by the author to explain the reasons for the book and to acknowledge those who helped in its preparation. If many people have to be acknowledged, an acknowledgment page follows the preface. There may be other pages in the front matter.

After the front matter comes the text, or main body, of the book. This is usually divided into chapters but may be divided into parts which are subdivided into chapters. Notes may be placed at the end of each chapter or footnotes at the bottom of text pages, particularly in scholarly books.

After the main body of a book comes the back matter. This may consist of appendixes to furnish supplementary information to the main text, often a bibliography, and, most importantly, an index. In some architectural books, more than one index is used for clarity and usefulness to readers. For example, there might be a general index plus indexes of architects, buildings, places, and so on.

The covers of books are ordinarily stamped with the titles, author's names and publishers on the back, sometimes called the shelf-back or spine, and sometimes also stamped on the front. Most stamping is with colored ink; however, in blind stamping, only an impression is made without using ink. Most books have jackets, sometimes called dust jackets, which are printed separately and folded around the book.

Classifications Books are usually classified into four major kinds: trade, including novels and others intended for the general public; textbooks, intended for instruction in schools, colleges, and universities; reference books, including dictionaries, encyclopedias, and the like; and professional books, for specialized use by those who need them in their vocations. Most architectural books fall in the professional category and in the reference group. There is also a fifth category, reprint books, usually less expensive versions of published books. Reprints may be made from all kinds of books.

As in many other categories of professional books, architectural books are often written by people whose main occupation is other than writing, including the teaching and practice of architecture professions. Thus it might be said that writers of architectural books are often members of their own audience.

Launching a Book An architect, or a person in a field related to architecture, who wants to write a book usually starts by preparing an outline of the book, together with a prospectus telling the purpose or objective of the book, what is to be included, the audience for whom it is intended, how the writing will be accomplished, the intended length of the manuscript, the number and character of the illustrations, and the schedule for completion of the work.

With this information in hand and perhaps with the addition of sample chapters, a publisher can decide about the feasibility of publishing the book. During the writing of the book, an editor works with the author to assist with problems that may arise. Architect-authors often make their own drawings or have them prepared under their supervision. When the manuscript and illustrations are ready and accepted by the publisher, the book is put into production. The book is styled by a designer; a copy editor corrects the manuscript; the materials are typeset; the author and copy editor read the galleys, long sets of typeset matter, not yet divided into pages, for errors; the corrected galleys are returned to the compositor to effect necessary changes and to be divided into pages; page proofs are sent to the author and editors who read them for errors.

After some time, usually a matter of months after the start of production, everything is ready for printing. The printed sheets are folded and then gathered into signatures which are groups of 16, 32, or 64 consecutive pages and the signatures are arranged in the proper order, or collated; the book is then bound. The book is inserted into a jacket and is now ready to be marketed. For most architectural books, marketing is effected by advertising in architectural and related magazines, by direct mail promotion, and, in the case of textbooks, by salespeople, called college travelers, who call on educators and bookstores.

Purposes of Architectural Books Books have exerted a powerful influence on architects and their architecture from the time of the Romans. Books have deeply affected architectural design. They have been used for the espousal of architectural philosophies and for education, not only in schools, colleges, and universities but for self-education. In the early days of American colonial architecture, books were the training source of many gentlemen-architects, who had no other way to learn about architecture. Since that time, a major purpose of architectural books has been the continuing education of architects after they have entered practice. This list of purposes of architectural books might be expanded considerably.

Hundreds of thousands of architectural and related books have been published and new ones appear every year. Although many architectural books are mentioned or listed in other articles in this book, it is impossible to do justice to their scope, breadth, and impact. However, some books have had such a powerful effect on architecture that they must be mentioned here.

Influential Architectural Books The first great architectural book, still of considerable influence today, was *De architectura,* written by Marcus Vitruvius Pollio, usually called Vitruvius, a Roman architect of the first century B.C., about whom very little is known. In this book, not published until 1486, Vitruvius attempted to analyze the elements of good architecture. His principles are still quoted. Another book of importance to architecture was the *Historia Naturalis,* written by scholar Gaius Plinius Secundus (A.D. 23–79), usually called Pliny the Elder. This monumental work, the only one of Pliny's many books that is still in existence, discussed architecture, along with all the known sciences of the time.

During the Renaissance a number of Italian architects wrote important books. The first architectural book printed from movable type was *Architecture in Ten Books* by Leon Battista Alberti (1404–72), published in 1485. Giacomo Barozzi da Vignola (1507–73) wrote *The Five Orders of Architecture,* published in 1563. These books greatly influenced later architects who designed in the Classic Revival and Eclectic styles.

Another important book was *Lives of the Most Eminent Painters, Sculptors, and Architects,* published in 1550, by Giorgio Vasari (1511–74), who was a painter as well as an architect. Although not gathered into a book, the engravings of Giovanni Battista Piranesi

(1720–78) presented the most complete view of Roman architecture of his time and of the past. Perhaps the most important book of all was *The Architecture of A. Palladio*, by Andrea Palladio (1518–80), first published in 1570 and translated into English in 1716. This book became the most used guide to classical architecture for the architects who later designed Classic Revival buildings.

Many other architects wrote books about classical architecture. Among the most important were those by the English architects—James Gibbs (1682–1754), who wrote *Book of Architecture*, 1728, and *Rules for Drawing the Several Parts of Architecture*, 1732; and Inigo Jones (1573–1652), who wrote *Designs*, a two-volume book published in 1770. Also of importance were books by Scottish architects, in particular, those of the brothers Adam, the first of which was *Ruins of the Palace of Diocletian in Dalmatia*, by Robert Adam (1728–92), published in 1764; equally important is *Works in Architecture of Robert and James Adam*, in three volumes published in 1773, 1779, and 1822, and written by Robert Adam and his brother, James Adam (1730–94). Another ambitious publishing project was the *Vitruvius Brittanicus*, published in five volumes, 1715–71, the first volume by Colen Campbell (c. 1676–1729), the next four by other authors. One of the many important books by French architects is *L'Architecture Français* by Jacques François Blondel (1705–44), published in four volumes, 1752–56.

Many architects and others wrote books of importance in the era of Gothic Revival architecture and later. Among the most influential are those of the Pugins, father and son. The father, Augustus Charles Pugin (1762–1832), wrote *Architectural Antiquities of Normandy*, 1828, *Examples of Gothic Architecture*, vol. 1, 1828, and in collaboration with his son, Augustus Welby Northmore Pugin (1812–52), *Examples of Gothic Architecture*, vol. 2, 1838. The younger Pugin wrote other books, including *The True Principles of Pointed or Christian Architecture*, 1841. The books of the French architect Eugène Emmanuel Viollet-le-Duc (1814–79) were also noteworthy; his most important was the 10-volume *Dictionary of French Architecture*, published in 1854–69. Also important were those of the Englishman Batty Langley (1696–1751), including his *Gothic Architecture Improved by Rules and Proportion*, published in 1742.

English critics produced evaluative works. John Ruskin (1819–1900) wrote *Seven Lamps of Architecture*, 1849, and *Stones of Venice*, published in three volumes, 1853. The English critic and painter Sir Charles Lock Eastlake (1793–1865) wrote *A History of the Gothic Revival in England*, published in 1872.

A great number of books on architecture and related subjects were published in the late 19th and in the 20th centuries and many new ones are constantly being published. Some of the most influential have been written by architects, including Louis Henri Sullivan (1856–1924), Ralph Adams Cram (1863–1942), Walter Adolf Gropius (1883–1969), Eliel Saarinen (1873–1950), and Frank Lloyd Wright (1869–1959). Some have been written by architecture critics and historians, including important works by Montgomery Schuyler (1843–1914) and Lewis Mumford (1895–   ). Far too numerous to mention here, many relevant works are discussed or listed in other articles in this book.

History The forerunners of books, clay tablets with symbols, existed in Mesopotamia from about 50 centuries before the birth of Christ. Beginning about the 25th century B.C., the Egyptians used a paperlike substance, papyrus, made from the bark of a plant, instead of clay. Papyrus was usually made into long sheets or rolls, called scrolls. Although papyrus was a better writing material than clay, it decayed quickly. The ancient Greeks also used papyrus scrolls. The Romans invented a new kind of writing material, parchment, made from untanned skins of animals. For the finest work, they used a top grade of parchment called vellum. At first, parchment or vellum was made into scrolls, but beginning about the second century A.D., sheets of vellum were folded, gathered, and sewn together very much like the pages of a modern book. Such a gathering was called a codex. During the Middle Ages, vellum was used extensively by monks who copied books by hand.

Inventions In China two important inventions eventually revolutionized the making of books. In the second century A.D. the Chinese invented paper and about the 9th century they printed the first book from type made of baked clay. It is thought that paper was introduced into Europe in the 12th century by merchants who had traveled to China. However, printing with movable type was developed independently in Europe, probably by Johann Gutenberg (c. 1397–1468). One of the world's most famous books is Gutenberg's *Latin Bible*, printed about 1456 with movable cast-lead type. Originally known as the *Mazarin Bible*, it is now generally called the *Gutenberg Bible*. More than 40 copies are still in existence.

After the invention of movable type, the growth of printing and the publication of books was very rapid. Early books, printed before the 16th century, are called *incunabula*, from the Latin word for cradle. By the 16th century, many books were published, some of them among the most beautiful examples of book design, printing, and binding of all time. Woodcuts, carved designs on blocks of wood, usually by hand, came into use for printing illustrations. Woodcuts were cut into the side grain of woodblocks. This process was followed by wood engraving, cut into the end grain of wood blocks, first by hand and then by machine, allowing more detail than in woodcuts. Later in the 15th century, engravings were made on copper, allowing still more detail and a longer useful life. In the 19th century, engravings were often made on steel, further extending the number of printing impressions that could be made from a single plate. All these and other methods are still in use by artists today, but in book printing they have been supplanted by new methods.

For more than 300 years after the invention of movable type, books were printed in much the same manner, with hand-cast type, set by hand, printed on handmade paper on hand-operated wooden presses. This is how the books of the first American printer, Stephen Daye (c. 1594–1668), were produced in Cambridge, Mass., starting in 1640. In the early 18th century machines were invented for making paper, and in the early 19th century an all-metal press was developed. Soon afterward, a machine-driven press was developed and in 1845, a revolving cylinder press. In 1865 a web press, using paper in rolls rather than in single sheets, was invented. These were the last great improvements in printing machinery until the 20th century.

Other inventions improved the type used for printing. First, in 1725 came the stereotype, a device for casting type in large plates, in molds usually made of paper pulp, and still in use today mostly by newspapers. Then in 1839 stereotypes were mostly superseded by the invention of the electrotype, a method of casting type in metal-coated wax molds made by electroplating.

In 1852 a new process was developed for printing illustrations and other content. The photoengraving process involves exposing a photographic negative against a metal plate, coated with a substance that may be hardened by light. Then the metal plate is exposed to acid that eats away the parts of the plate not covered by the coating. A line engraving, or line cut, is an engraving of line drawings or similar matter and shows only the lines without shading. A halftone engraving is photographed through a screen that produces small dots, which show tones or shading when printed. Halftones are used for photographs and similar matter.

All these developments helped in the growth of printing and book publishing. Another development in 1884 speeded up the growth considerably; this was the invention of the Linotype, a machine for setting type and still in use today, by Ottmar Mergenthaler (1854–99). This was closely followed in 1887 by another machine for this purpose, the Monotype, also still in use.

Other Improvements The 20th century has seen a number of improvements in printing methods, including in 1902 methods for controlling the cleanliness, humidity, and temperature of the air in printshops, problems that had always made consistent printing difficult. Then in 1904 the offset press was invented, utilizing the techniques of photolithography. Heretofore, printing was done by letterpress. In the new method, called offset printing, printing plates are made by sensitizing metal, to which the matter to be printed is then transferred by a photographic process. On the press, this printing plate transfers the inked image to a rubber cylinder which in turn transfers the image to the paper or other material.

The offset method of printing is based on the principles of lithography, or stone printing, invented in 1796. The original form of lithography, still used by artists, involves drawing on a porous stone (found chiefly in Germany) with greasy crayon, ink, or pencil, wetting the stone with water and inking the stone with greasy ink which adheres only to the drawing, not to the other parts of the stone. Paper is then printed by pressing it on the inked stone. At first, offset printing could not achieve the quality of the letterpress, but in recent years it has been greatly improved and has become the most important method for printing books and many other materials.

Color printing can be accomplished on either letterpress or offset press. For such work, separations must be made dividing the material to be printed into its component colors, usually four—black, magenta (red), yellow, and cyan (blue)—for most work. For special printing such as reproduction of great paintings, more than four colors are often used. From each color separation, a separate plate is made and each is printed in succession.

Other 20th-century developments of importance in printing include the invention of xerography, or photocopying, in 1937, a form that requires no ink; and the invention of cold setting of type, starting with the first commercial phototypesetting machines in 1947. Another development is setting type by computer, which began in 1962.

All these developments have contributed to the great flow of books of all kinds, including many on architecture, in the 20th century.

Related Articles CRITICISM, ARCHITECTURE; GRAPHIC DESIGN; LIBRARY; MAGAZINE, ARCHITECTURAL.

Further Information American Institute of Architects Library, 1735 New York Avenue, N.W., Washington, D.C. 20006; Avery Library, Columbia University, New York, N.Y. 10027; Library of Congress, 10 First St., S.E., Washington, D.C. 20540.

BOTANICAL BUILDING A structure for shelter and display of plants for scientific, educational, and artistic purposes. The botanical building is often located in a botanical garden, an outdoor area in which plants are grown for the same purposes, or in an arboretum, an outdoor area in which trees, shrubbery, and other woody plants are grown. Sometimes botanical and zoological gardens, or zoos, are combined.

Functions Botanical gardens and buildings are often located in universities or other institutions where plants are studied. Various functions are performed, including collection and cultivation, classification, breeding and hybridization, and research and experimentation of plants. Botanical institutions often maintain libraries of books and other information on plants and present educational programs for adults and children. Permanent displays are usually available, in which plants are labeled with their common and scientific names. In many botanical gardens and buildings, plants are displayed in areas that approximate their natural habitats, such as temperate, tropical, or

BOTANICAL BUILDING Exterior, Climatron (1960), Missouri Botanical Garden, St. Louis. [*Architects: Murphy and Mackey; Dome, R. Buckminster Fuller. (Hedrich-Blessing)*]

BOTANICAL BUILDING Interior, Climatron (1960), Missouri Botanical Garden, St. Louis. [*Architects: Murphy and Mackey; Dome, R. Buckminster Fuller. (Hedrich-Blessing)*]

desert zones. In others, plants are arranged according to cultural requirements as indoor, rock, or aquatic gardens.

Although botanical buildings are not an important building type in terms of the number built, they do represent an interesting architectural challenge. They must be designed in such a way that climatological conditions found in nature may be duplicated artificially. The sun must be controlled, along with the humidity, temperature, soil conditions, insects, and plant diseases. These conditions are provided by such architectural means as the conformation, orientation, and placement of the buildings, and by mechanical and electrical systems designed to produce requisite environmental states.

Greenhouse A special kind of botanical building in increasingly widespread use is the greenhouse, a glass or plastic enclosed building in which plants may be grown under controlled conditions the year round. Greenhouses are used in botanical gardens, by commercial growers, and by individuals who like to grow things as a hobby or for the table. Greenhouses usually have shading devices to control the sun and range from simple types to those with built-in heating and ventilating equipment and piped-in water supplies. They range in size from small units that attach to a window to commercial units covering acres of ground. Greenhouses may be framed with wood, steel, or aluminum; many prefabricated types are available.

Development One of the earliest botanical, and zoological, gardens in Europe, the *Jardin des Plantes*, Paris, was established in 1626 and is still one of the best and most extensive institutions of its kind in the world. Another famous one that still survives is the Royal Botanic Garden, known as Kew Gardens, established in 1760 in Surrey, just west of London. In 1728 American botanist John Bartram (1699–1777) established the first botanical garden in Philadelphia, and built his house there in 1731. Both garden and house still exist and, now known as Bartram's Gardens, are open to the public. There are a number of botanical gardens all over the United States, including the Brooklyn Botanic Garden; the New York Botanical Garden, New York City; the Missouri Botanical Garden, St. Louis; and the U.S. National Arboretum, Washington, D.C.

Related Articles GARDEN; ZOOLOGICAL BUILDING.

BREUER, MARCEL LAJOS Hungarian-American architect (1902–   ). After having been a student and a faculty member at the Bauhaus in Germany, Marcel Lajos Breuer came to the United States in 1937 to join Walter Adolf Gropius (1883–1969) on the faculty of Harvard University and as a partner in architectural practice.

Assessment Breuer has had a brilliant career in education and in furniture design, but he is first and foremost an architect. And his architecture is thought by many to embody all the elements that the best ar-

BREUER, MARCEL Robinson House (1947), Williamstown, Mass.
(Marcel Breuer)

chitecture must contain. His buildings solve the problems contained in their programs. The materials used are a combination of the traditional such as wood and brick with newer types such as concrete and metal. The designs are inventive, without gimmicks, and strictly of their time rather than some past historic era. There is a naturalness about his buildings, a neatness in their form and appearance. Somehow, they always seem to combine a sort of quiet excitement with serene contentment, an accomplishment not often achieved in the architecture of today.

Works Starting with his early work in Germany and other parts of Europe, Breuer has produced a steady stream of notable buildings, almost all of the highest quality. His first building was a house in Germany in 1932. This was followed by an apartment building (1933) in Zurich, Switzerland, for Dr. Sigfried Giedion (1888–1968), the eminent art and architecture historian and critic, who wrote one of the most influential books on architecture of all time, *Space, Time and Architecture*, first published in 1941 and still in print, in a fifth revised edition (Harvard University Press, 1967).

After coming to the United States, Breuer continued to design houses and other residential buildings exclusively until he was almost fifty. His first American buildings were designed in partnership with Gropius in and around Cambridge. Among these were the house for Gropius (1937; illustrated in Gropius article) and that for Breuer himself (1939), both in Lincoln, Mass.; the University House (1938), Cohasset, Mass.; and the Aluminum City Terrace Housing (1941; illus-

trated in Gropius article), New Kensington, Pa., near Pittsburgh.

After leaving Gropius to start his own firm, Breuer continued to design houses, including the Geller House (1945), Lawrence, N.Y., and the Robinson House (1947), Williamsburg, Mass., and has continued to design houses ever since. Breuer also designed a house which was constructed in the garden of the Museum of Modern Art, New York City, in 1949. This house brought him to the attention of architects and the general public as nothing had before. He soon received commissions for other houses and for larger buildings.

Notable buildings by Breuer include the Ferry Cooperative Dormitory (1951), Vassar College, Poughkeepsie, N.Y.; the UNESCO Headquarters (1958), Paris, designed in association with Pier Luigi Nervi (1891–1979) and Bernard Zehrfuss (1912–   ); the IBM Building (1962), La Gaude, France; Whitney Museum of American Art (1966), New York City; St. John's Abbey Church and College buildings (1967), Collegeville, Minn.; the U.S. Department of Housing and Urban Development Building (1967), Washington, D.C.; New York University Technology buildings (1969); and the Murray Lincoln Center (1973), University of Massachusetts, Amherst, Mass.

Life Marcel Lajos Breuer was born in Pecs, Hungary, on May 22, 1902. After graduating from school in Pecs, he enrolled in 1920 in the Bauhaus founded by Walter Adolf Gropius in Weimar, Germany. In 1924 he received his degree and joined the faculty as a master of carpentry, remaining there until 1928. In 1926 he

BREUER, MARCEL UNESCO Headquarters (1958), Paris, France. [*Breuer, in association with Bernard Zehrfuss and Pier Luigi Nervi. (Dominique Lajoux)*]

BREUER, MARCEL St. John's Abbey Church (1967), Collegeville, Minn. *(Hedrich-Blessing)*

BREUER, MARCEL St. John's College (1967), Collegeville, Minn. *(Hedrich-Blessing)*

married Martha Erps; the marriage ended in divorce. While at the Bauhaus, he designed several modern chairs and other furniture, using bent, tubular steel frames for the first time.

In 1928 both he and Gropius left the Bauhaus faculty, and Breuer established an architectural practice in Berlin. In 1931, when the worldwide Depression and the Nazi influence had almost brought architectural commissions to a halt, he managed both to practice and to travel in other parts of Germany and Europe and in North Africa. While in Berlin, he designed interiors, a few houses, and an apartment building. He also designed more chairs, of plywood and metals, which are still considered among the best examples of modern furniture. In 1935 he went to England, where Gropius had set up a practice, and formed a partnership with F. R. S. Yorke (1906–   ) which lasted until 1937.

Soon after Gropius arrived at Harvard University in 1937 to assume the chairmanship of the department of architecture, Breuer joined him on the faculty as a de-

sign professor and stayed until 1941. Also in 1937 the two architects started an architectural practice in Cambridge that lasted until 1942. In 1940 Breuer married Constance Leighton.

In 1942 Breuer organized his own practice in Cambridge, and in 1946 moved his office to New York City, where it remains today, carried on by his associates since his retirement in 1977. Breuer has received many honors for his contributions to architecture and for his significant building designs. These include several honorary doctors' degrees, including one from Harvard. He was elected a member of both the American Academy of Arts and Sciences and the National Institute of Arts and Letters. In 1968 he received the highest award of the architects of his adopted country, the Gold Medal of the American Institute of Architects. In 1975 he had the honor of having his tubular chair of 1929 again put into production by a leading furniture manufacturer, certainly an indication of the lasting freshness and originality of his designs.

BREUER, MARCEL Murray Lincoln Center (1973), University of Massachusetts, Amherst, Mass. [*Breuer, in association with Herbert Beckhard. (Ben Schnall)*]

Related Articles BAUHAUS, STAATLICHES; CONTEMPORARY ARCHITECTURE; EDUCATION; FURNITURE; GROPIUS, WALTER ADOLF; MODERN ARCHITECTURE. For illustrations of IBM Laboratory (1974), Boca Raton, Fla., see CONCRETE; LABORATORY; STAIR.

Further Reading Blake, Peter: *Marcel Breuer—Architect and Designer,* Museum of Modern Art, New York, 1949, Breuer, Marcel: *Sun and Shadow—The Philosophy of an Architect,* Dodd, Mead, New York, 1955; Jones, Cranston, ed.: *Marcel Breuer, Buildings and Projects, 1921–1961,* Praeger, New York, 1962.

BRICK A masonry unit usually made of kiln-burned clay, but sometimes of other materials, used in architecture for construction of walls and other purposes. From the earliest times to today, brick has been one of the most important building materials. The major type of brick used today and the one most frequently referred to when using the word *brick* is made of clay fired in kilns to impart hardness, strength, and resistance to moisture. Other types include cement, sand-lime, and adobe brick types. Cement brick, some-

times called concrete brick, is made of portland cement and aggregates, very much like other types of concrete. Adobe brick is very much like that used by ancient people, and is made of sun-dried clay.

Kiln-Burned Brick This brick is usually made by the stiff-mud process, in which just enough water is added to the ground clay to allow it to be extruded through a die into a ribbon. The ribbon is then sliced with wires to form bricks. Sometimes a vacuum pump is used to remove air from the clay to make the bricks stronger. The shaped bricks are dried at 100 to 300°F (38 to 149°C) and then burned in kilns at 1600°F (871°C) or higher. Other methods for making brick include the soft-mud process, in which a greater quantity of water is used with the clay, and the dry-press process, in which almost no water is used.

The two most important types of kiln-burned brick are building brick, sometimes called common brick; and facing or face brick. The main differences between the two types are appearance and use; face brick has a better appearance and is used for exposed

BRICK IBM Building (1974), Harrisburg, Pa. [*Architect: Donald Coupard. (Joseph W. Molitor)*]

brickwork left in its natural state; building brick is used mostly for hidden work or for exposed work where appearance is unimportant or the brickwork will be painted. Building brick comes in three grades: SW, MW, and NW; SW for conditions of heavy rainfall and freezing, MW for moderate conditions, and NW for minimal conditions. Face brick also comes in three grades—FBX, FBS, and FBA—generally denoting the degree of perfection of the bricks, from the most perfect to the least. All grades of both types of brick generally have high strength against crushing (compression) and bending, but less strength against stretching (tension). All are relatively impervious to water pene-

tration and are incombustible. However, bricks with various degrees of strength and other characteristics may be obtained. Both building and face brick may be obtained either solid or cored, with vertical holes through the centers.

Other important types of kiln-burned bricks include glazed, flooring, and paving. Glazed brick, solid or cored, is face brick which has a surface glaze produced by gases or with ceramic materials. It comes in two grades, S (select) and SS (select sized), in which face dimension variations are minimal. These bricks may be obtained with either one of two faces glazed. Flooring brick is hard and dense and is used in build-

BRICK Drake Center (1975), Drake University, Des Moines, Iowa.
[*Architect: Harry Weese. (Hedrich-Blessing)*]

ings, such as factories, in which floors must resist heavy wear and hard treatment. Flooring brick comes in several grades for various uses. Paving brick is also hard and dense, and may be used in buildings of all types.

Special types include fire, refractory, and acid. Firebricks are made of special clays that are resistant to heat for such purposes as lining the interiors of fireplaces. Refractory bricks are similar but will withstand even higher temperatures, such as those in industrial furnaces. Acid bricks are produced for use in chemical plants, laboratories, and the like. Also available are thin-brick veneers used to simulate real walls.

Bricks may be preassembled into panels with cement plastic mortar which has high tensile strength, but the more general method involves laying them in mortar, one by one. Bricks may also be obtained in special shapes for making arches, trim around windows and doors, and other purposes. Such shapes are usually made in molds. Various surface textures are available, including smooth; grooved, or scored; scratched, or combed; roughened; water-struck, in which molds have been wetted; and sand-struck, in which sand was used on the sides of molds. Bricks may also be obtained in a variety of earth colors, and glazed bricks in additional colors.

Sizes Regular brick comes in a variety of sizes in addition to the usual nominal size of about 4 by 8 by slightly more than 2 inches. In general, there are two

systems for brick sizes: the modular and the nonmodular. The modular sizes differ from the others in that they produce even multiples of 4-inch increments, or modules, including the mortar joints that separate the bricks. Thus a brick that is nominally 4 inches deep and 8 inches long will actually be slightly less than those dimensions, to allow for the width of the mortar joints. A regular modular brick has a nominal size of 4 by 8 by 2⅔ inches, if it is to be laid with ⅜-inch mortar joints. The actual dimensions of the brick will be smaller so that a brick, with its mortar joint, will be an even 8 inches in length; and three brick courses in height, including mortar joints, will be an even 8 inches high. Nonmodular brick come in sizes that do not produce even dimensions when laid in walls or other structures.

In addition to the regular-sized bricks, there are a variety of other sizes, all nominal, including Norman brick, 12 inches long; Roman brick, 12 inches long but only 2 inches high; and jumbo brick, 12 inches long, 4 inches high, and 6 or 8 inches thick. Flooring and paving bricks come in various sizes, from about ½ to 2½ inches thick, and from 4 to 16 inches in the other dimensions. Paving brick may be obtained in rectangular, square, and hexagonal shapes.

Brick Laying Bricks are usually laid in a manner that allows their joints to be staggered to produce stronger walls or other building elements. This is ordinarily accomplished by placing individual bricks in

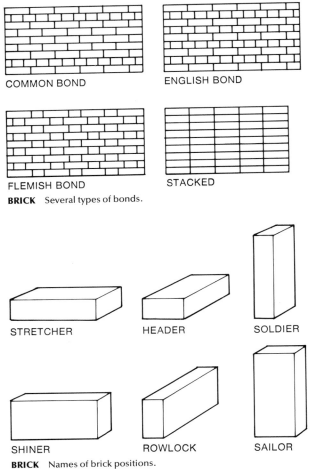

COMMON BOND

ENGLISH BOND

FLEMISH BOND

STACKED

BRICK Several types of bonds.

STRETCHER

HEADER

SOLDIER

SHINER

ROWLOCK

SAILOR

BRICK Names of brick positions.

different positions, to produce a bond. The two most common ways of placing bricks in walls are with the long side showing, in which a brick is called a stretcher, and with the end showing, in which it is called a header. By alternating headers and stretchers in various ways, good bonds are produced, along with ornamental patterns. The most commonly used bonds in the United States are the English, in which courses are alternately composed of stretchers and headers; the Flemish, in which stretchers and headers alternate in courses; and the common, or American, in which every fifth or sixth course is composed of headers, while others are stretchers. A number of other bonds are also used and sometimes bonding is accomplished by means of metal ties. Where only stretchers are used with both horizontal and vertical mortar joints continuous, the brick is said to be stacked. This method is not usually employed for structural building elements unless bonded with ties.

Brick floors may be laid flat or on edge. A number of patterns may be used, including running, in which bricks, flat or on edge, are laid like stretchers in a wall, for example, along a walk; and cross, in which the bricks are laid with their long dimensions at right angles to a walk. Brick floors may also be laid in other

patterns, such as herringbone, basket weave, and diagonal.

Other Types of Bricks Cement, or concrete, and sand-lime bricks are generally available in sizes similar to those for kiln-burned brick. Both types are naturally gray, but other colors may be introduced by adding various mineral pigments. These colored types are not recommended for use in sunlight because of fading. Adobe bricks, used mostly in arid climates such as the Southwest, are generally the colors of the clays from which they are made. Adobe bricks are usually larger than regular brick and may only be used for buildings of one to a few stories in height. They must be laid on top of waterproof foundations, must be protected from precipitation by overhangs and finishes of plaster or adobe, and must be laid with mortar made of adobe.

While regular bricks are relatively impervious to water infiltration, some types are often treated with silicone or other materials to increase resistance. Joints are also important in preventing water from entering. Another problem that sometimes occurs is discoloration, called efflorescence, caused by salts within the brick or mortar that are brought to the surface by water action. Efflorescence can also cause deterioration of brick and the mortar joints. To avoid this problem, brick should be carefully selected and mortars carefully formulated and applied. If efflorescence occurs, it can be removed by scrubbing with dilute hydrochloric acid followed by rinsing with clear water. However, no method to completely stop efflorescence is known.

Bricks of so many varied sizes, colors, shapes, and types are available that architects and other environmental designers have a wide selection at their disposal. Types should be selected according to the function, textures, and colors desired; the bonds to be used; and other technical and design considerations. Brick is widely used in many ways in both exteriors and interiors of buildings today. Many people think it one of the finest materials for imparting warmth, texture, and other desirable qualities into architecture.

History Other than wood and mud, brick is the oldest material used in architecture. When bricks were first made has not been established, but brick fragments made about 4000 B.C. have been found in Mesopotamia. It is believed that brick making began many centuries before that time. In this area, the principle of the corbel for spanning an opening is thought to have been developed. A corbel, thought to be the forerunner of the arch, vault, and dome, was constructed by projecting each higher course of brick, or stone, slightly farther out from the sides until the highest courses met in the middle.

The earliest bricks were made by fashioning clay into shapes and drying them in the sun. Fire-burned brick making developed somewhat later, first utilizing open fires into which the formed bricks were placed and later using kilns. Fire-burned bricks were mostly used for special purposes such as facings for walls. The process of applying impervious coatings, often in color, fired on bricks in kilns, calling glazing, was also discovered very early. Plain and glazed bricks were often laid in bitumen.

Brick was widely used in Mesopotamia because of the shortage of lumber and stone. In ancient Egypt and Greece, brick was also used, usually without mortar, but only to a limited extent since other materials were available. The Romans used both sun-dried and kiln-dried bricks, leaving them exposed in modest buildings and covering them with stone or plaster in more important ones. The Romans sometimes laid brick without mortar, but also often used mud, lime mortar, or lime, with crushed tiles or sand, for that purpose. Roman bricks were usually wider and longer than those of today, but thinner to resist warping and cracking. Brick walls were bonded, much as they are today.

Brick was widely used in Early Christian and Byzantine architecture, often left exposed in the former and frequently highly ornamented with marble or other stone or with glass mosaics in the latter. Romanesque architecture utilized brick in many buildings. During the Middle Ages brick was no longer used extensively. However, brick was an important element of architecture, especially in France and Germany where it was often molded or carved into ornamental shapes and laid in widely varied patterns. Brick was also used in Italy and to some extent in England. By the 16th century, English brick sizes had been standardized, generally at 4½ inches thick, by 9 inches long, by 2 inches high. Before standardization, sizes had varied from 8 to 11 inches long and of various thicknesses. English brickwork generally utilized English bond, with alternate courses of headers and stretchers, but sometimes used Flemish bond, with stretchers and headers alternated in each course. Since bricks were often misshaped or distorted, they were usually laid with thick mortar joints.

By the time of the Renaissance, good brick in standard sizes had become widely available and was used in buildings of all types. Some of the finest buildings were of brick or brick combined with stone. While brick is often thought of as a less costly material than stone, this was not always the case in this period, except in areas where no local stone existed. By the 16th and 17th centuries in Europe, brick had become less expensive and was used more extensively. By the 18th century, brick was plastered or stuccoed, painted, and scored to resemble stone.

American Development Although wood was the prevalent material for buildings in early colonial America, brick was also widely used. Bricklayers and brick makers were among the first colonists at Jamestown, and it is believed that they constructed kilns and made brick early in the 17th century, possibly about 1610, three years after the colony was founded. The Spanish had made brick in St. Augustine, Fla., and other colonies much earlier.

Brick has always been produced locally, partly because of difficulties in shipping the relatively heavy and bulky materials and partly because the raw materials are found almost everywhere. In spite of this, bricks for a few buildings in the colonies were imported from England and other places. Both sun-dried and kiln-dried bricks were used in the colonies, the former mainly in the Southwest and the latter elsewhere.

Bricks were molded by hand usually in wooden molds and then dried. For the most part, except in the Southwest, they were then burned in kilns of various types, usually fueled with wood. Colonial bricks varied in size from place to place. However, most were of excellent quality, comparable to bricks made in Europe. American bricklayers were, for the most part, also as capable as those in the countries from which they had emigrated. Bricks were usually laid in English bond, but later Flemish bond became quite popular and other bonds were also used. Bricks were generally laid in mortar composed of sand and lime, often obtained from oyster shells in the coastal colonies.

By the middle of the 18th century, bricks for sale were made in many locations in the colonies. And bricks were also made on or near the sites of many individual buildings and were widely used for buildings of all types. All this brick was molded by hand. About the end of the 18th century, attempts were made to produce brick-making machines and by the second quarter of the 19th century, a few bricks were produced in machines that mixed the ingredients, extruded the mixture through dies into ribbons of clay, and then cut the ribbons into individual bricks. By the end of that century, almost all bricks were made by machine. Essentially, this established the method used for the manufacture of brick today.

From the beginning of brick making in America to the present, brick has been an important building material in every era. Some of the finest houses and buildings of other types were constructed of brick. Brick continues to be an important building material today, particularly in houses and other buildings of relatively small size. Brick is also sometimes used very effectively in larger buildings, but the last use for bearing walls in a tall building was in the Monadnock Building (1891), Chicago, designed by Burnham and Root. This 16-story building has 6-foot brick walls in the first story.

Related Articles ARCH; DOME; FIREPLACE; MASONRY STRUCTURE; TILE; VAULT; WALL.

Further Reading Brick Development Assoc.: *Bricks — Their Properties and Use*, the Construction Press, London, 1974; McKee, Harley J.: *Introduction to Early American Masonry — Stone, Brick, Mortar and Plaster*, National Trust for Historic Preservation and Columbia University, Washington, 1973.

Sources of Additional Information Brick Institute of America, 1750 Old Meadow Rd., McLean, Va. 22101; International Masonry Inst., 823 15th St., N.W., Washington, D.C. 20005.

BRIDGE A structure that spans a river, a depression, or some other space, usually providing a passageway for people, automobiles, or other vehicles. Although many bridges would not be considered architecture by most people, and engineers now usually design them, there are numerous notable bridges which many observers consider architecture of high excellence.

Types Bridges may be fixed or movable. Fixed bridges are built permanently in place; movable bridges, sometimes called drawbridges, are designed so that portions may be raised or moved aside to allow ships to pass unobstructed. The major types of movable bridges are swing, lift, and bascule. A portion of a swing bridge may be turned to a position approximately at a right angle to the bridge proper, allowing ships to pass through. A lift bridge can be raised with counterweights, between two towers, allowing ships to pass underneath. A bascule bridge has counterweights on one end that allow the other end to be raised as if the bridge were on a pivot. A special kind of bridge is a viaduct, used for carrying automobiles or trains over low-lying ground, valleys, or other obstructions.

Bridges may be constructed of most structural materials, including wood, stone, cast or wrought iron, aluminum, steel, and reinforced concrete. The earliest bridges were wood, a material now little used except for small footbridges. Stone and wrought and cast iron, in their time the most important bridge materials, have been largely supplanted by steel and reinforced concrete.

Structural Systems Three major structural systems are used in bridges: beam, arch, and suspension. A beam structure can range from the smallest and simplest, for example, a log spanning a stream, to a large reinforced concrete bridge system with many spans resting on vertical supports, called piers, set on foundations in a river or lake bottom. An advanced use of the beam for relatively long spans utilizes trusses, made up of steel components joined together to form strong rigid frames. Arched bridges, originally of masonry but today of steel or reinforced concrete, are curved to allow the higher portions to be supported by the lower, transferring the weight down to piers or the ground. Suspension bridges are hung on towers, originally with vines, then with ropes, and later with chains. Today such bridges are suspended with great cables made of steel wire.

A more unusual structural type is the pontoon bridge, supported on floats and used for temporary purposes, such as military operations. A special type of beam, the cantilever, is sometimes used in bridges. A cantilever is a beam so constructed as to project beyond the pier that supports it. Cantilever bridges usually have two cantilever spans with their ends anchored on the banks of the water body. Their cantilevered ends ordinarily do not meet but instead support a third span suspended between them. Another special type of beam bridge utilizes a fixed frame, sometimes called a portal frame. In this type of frame, the beam and its supports are of one piece or monolithic, and the entire structure acts together to support the weight.

History The earliest bridges, in prehistoric times, were probably trees that fell across streams or depressions. These were followed by bridges constructed of logs and by ropes made of twisted vines in pairs, one to walk on and one to hold on to. Masonry bridges of brick and stone are known to have been constructed in the Middle East at least as early as 4000 B.C. Many of these used arched construction, a method later highly developed by the Romans. Stone has continued to be used to some extent well into the 20th century. In medieval Europe, stone bridges were often picturesquely lined with small shops. Metal bridges, of wrought or cast iron, both arch and suspension types, were first built in Europe in the late 18th century.

American Development The first bridges in colonial America were built of wood. This tradition continued for some time. Some of the most pleasant examples were covered bridges, a type that had its origins in other countries. Later stone was used for bridges, but the most significant developments were in metals. Architect Henry Hobson Richardson (1838–86) designed a fine, small stone bridge (1811) in the Fenway, Boston. Architect Paul Philippe Cret (1876–1947) designed a number in and around Philadelphia.

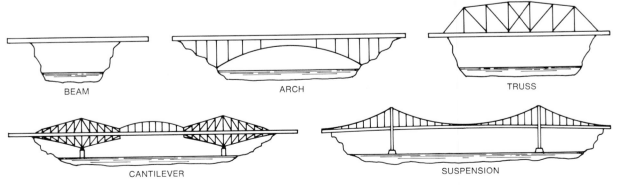

BEAM   ARCH   TRUSS

CANTILEVER   SUSPENSION

BRIDGE Types.

BRIDGE Brooklyn (1883), New York, N.Y. [*Engineer: John Augustus Roebling. (Detroit Photographic Co., Library of Congress)*]

BRIDGE Brooklyn (1883), New York, N.Y. [*Engineer: John Augustus Roebling. (Wayne Andrews)*]

BRIDGE Verrazzano-Narrows (1964), New York, N.Y. [*Engineer:
Othmar Hermann Ammann. (Wurts Brothers)*]

PRE-COLUMBIAN ARCHITECTURE Pueblo Bonito (c. 1100), Chaco Canyon National Park, N. Mex. [*Architect: unknown. (David Muench)*]

SPANISH COLONIAL ARCHITECTURE San Xavier del Bac (c. 1797), Tucson, Ariz. [*Architect: unknown. (David Muench)*]

ENGLISH COLONIAL ARCHITECTURE   Old Ship Meeting House
(*c.* 1681), Hingham, Mass. [*Architect: unknown. (Steve Rosenthal)*]

MODERN ARCHITECTURE Taliesin West (1938–59), Maricopa County, near Phoenix, Ariz. [*Architect: Frank Lloyd Wright. (Hedrich-Blessing)*]

MODERN ARCHITECTURE Johnson Wax Co. Research Tower (1949), Racine, Wis. [*Architect: Frank Lloyd Wright. (Ezra Stoller)*]

MODERN ARCHITECTURE   Johnson House (1949), New Canaan,
Conn. [*Architect: Philip Johnson. (Ezra Stoller)*]

MODERN ARCHITECTURE   Illinois Institute of Technology (1952),
Chicago, Ill. [*Architect: Ludwig Mies van der Rohe. (Hedrich-Blessing)*]

MODERN ARCHITECTURE Lever House (1952), New York, N.Y.
[*Architects: Skidmore, Owings and Merrill. (Joseph W. Molitor)*]

MODERN ARCHITECTURE Seagram Building (1958), New York, N.Y.
[*Architects: Ludwig Mies van der Rohe and Philip Johnson, in
association with Kahn and Jacobs. (Joseph W. Molitor)*]

CONTEMPORARY ARCHITECTURE Richards Laboratory (1961),
University of Pennsylvania, Philadelphia, Pa. [*Architect: Louis Isadore
Kahn. (Joseph W. Molitor)*]

CONTEMPORARY ARCHITECTURE Dulles International Airport
(1963), Chantilly, Va., near Washington, D.C. [*Architects: Eero
Saarinen, in association with Ellery Husted. (Joseph W. Molitor)*]

CONTEMPORARY ARCHITECTURE Boston City Hall (1968), Boston,
Mass. [*Architects: Kallmann, McKinnell and Knowles; Campbell,
Aldrich and Nulty. (Ezra Stoller)*]

CONTEMPORARY ARCHITECTURE   World Trade Center (1973), New
York, N.Y. [*Architects: Minoru Yamasaki, in association with Emery
Roth and Sons. (Joseph W. Molitor)*]

An early pioneering steel-arched bridge is the Eads (1874) in St. Louis, designed by and named for engineer James Buchanan Eads (1820–87). But it is in steel suspension bridges that American bridge design talent has been at its best. First developed in Europe, steel suspension bridges, each seemingly more daring than the last, have been built in the United States since the late 19th century. One of the earliest and best is the Brooklyn Bridge (1883), New York City, designed by John Augustus Roebling (1806–69), a German-American engineer, with its construction directed by his son, Washington Augustus (1837–1926), also an engineer. This bridge was followed by the George Washington Bridge (1931), New York City, designed by Swiss-American engineer Othmar Hermann Ammann (1879–1965), with Cass Gilbert (1858–1934) as consulting architect; the Golden Gate Bridge (1937), San Francisco, by engineer Joseph B. Strauss (d. 1938), with Ammann as a consulting engineer and Irving F. Morrow as consulting architect; and the Verrazano-Narrows Bridge (1964), with the longest span in the world, 4,260 feet, also designed by Ammann. Americans have not done so well with the design of reinforced concrete bridges. Although pioneering designs were made in the early 20th century by European engineers and architects, the Swiss engineer Robert Maillart (1872–1940) was the acknowledged master of their design. During the 1940s Frank Lloyd Wright (1869–1959) proposed daring designs for reinforced concrete bridges, including one between San Francisco and Alameda. It would have had a garden in the center between the roadways; but like others he proposed, it was never built.

Related Articles ARCH; CRET, PAUL PHILIPPE; ENGINEERING; GILBERT, CASS; RICHARDSON, HENRY HOBSON; STRUCTURE; WRIGHT, FRANK LLOYD.

Further Reading Mock, Elizabeth B.: *The Architecture of Bridges*, Museum of Modern Art, New York, 1949; Plowden, David: *Bridges—The Spans of North America*, Viking Press, New York, 1974.

BUCKLAND, WILLIAM English-American architect (1734–74). Many colonial architects prepared designs for buildings as an avocation while supporting themselves by some other unrelated trade or profession. Others, including William Buckland, were builders by trade who prepared designs for buildings and erected them. Buckland, trained in London as a carpenter and joiner, worked as designer and builder, interior designer, and wood-carver on his buildings. The interiors for Gunston Hall, Fairfax Co., Va., was his first job in the colonies, starting in 1755. After working on other buildings nearby, of which little is known, he moved to Annapolis, where he designed

BUCKLAND, WILLIAM Hammond-Harwood House (1774), Annapolis, Md. *(M. E. Warren)*

a number of notable houses. The best-known and most noted is the Hammond-Harwood House (1774). Georgian in style, this house has been called the finest colonial town house in America. The fine details, inside and out, show it to be the work of a talented architect and builder, who was totally involved in all the parts of the house, in the manner in which the parts relate to each other and to the whole building. While the design shows indications of adaptation from influential architectural books of the time, it also shows the architect to have been a creative, trained craftsman who made adaptations with an originality and freedom not often found in the work of the more academic architects of the period.

Works William Buckland's career as an architect and builder lasted less than 20 years, from 1755 to the year of his death, 1774. It is assumed that he designed a number of buildings, but only about 10 have been attributed to him with any accuracy. Among these are Strawberry Hill (about 1766) near Annapolis; Raspberry Plain (1771), Loudoun Co., Va.; and the Chase-Lloyd House (1774), Annapolis; only the Chase-Lloyd House still exists. Three other great Annapolis houses, on which Buckland is known to have worked and is believed to have been the architect, are the Paca House (1763), the Ridout House (1763), and the Brice House (about 1770).

Life William Buckland was born on August 14, 1734, in England. At about fourteen, he was apprenticed to his uncle in London to learn the joiner's and carpenter's trade. Six years later, he came to America as an indentured servant to George Mason, owner of Gunston Hall. Buckland designed some exterior details for this house, and the interiors which have become known as among the most beautiful in any colonial house. While indentured, and for a while after being released, he worked on buildings by other architects and, later, on buildings for which he was the architect and builder. About 1770 he moved to Annapolis and established his own workshop, which he operated until his death in December 1774, at age forty.

Related Articles COLONIAL ARCHITECTURE; GEORGIAN ARCHITECTURE.

Further Reading Beirne, Rosamond Randall, and John Henry Scarff: *William Buckland, 1734–1774: Architect of Virginia and Maryland,* Maryland Historical Society, Baltimore, 1958.

BUILDING CODES AND STANDARDS
In law, a code may refer to any law or statute, but more properly means a collection of statutes on a subject. A standard is a rule, usually part of a set of rules, established by an authority, but having no legal standing except when referenced or cited in a code or other statute.

Range of Regulations Architecture today is subject to a vast set of codes and statutes which govern many aspects of the methods, materials, systems, types, and sizes of buildings, and almost every other facet of design and construction. In general, these codes and statutes are part of the laws of states, counties, and municipalities, but some are federal laws effective throughout the country. Most of them include certain standards by reference. Other standards also affect architecture, though they are not regulatory in a legal sense. These are standards developed by insurance companies and lending institutions to control certain aspects of the buildings that they insure or finance. Another example is the kind of standards of design and construction required by such organizations as hotel, food, or automobile service station chains.

Governmental Regulations In general, architects and others participating in building design and construction must abide by the provisions of the codes, statutes, and regulations of the municipalities, counties, and states in which their buildings will be constructed. First, they must comply with zoning codes that determine which buildings may be built where, including land uses, sizes and bulks of buildings, densities or how many families or people will be permitted per acre, provisions for light and air, and parking. Next there is the subdivision ordinance or code which governs how land may be subdivided. The third major type, the building code, determines how buildings may be constructed, including many details of construction, materials, fire-resistant qualities, exits, stairs, floor and roof load capacities, and many others. In addition, there may be separate housing codes for single-family and multifamily dwellings. There are also other types of codes, including those for plumbing, electrical work, and fire safety. In addition, building construction must be in conformance with a number of federal statutes: the Occupational Safety and Health Act (OSHA); the Architectural Barriers Act, governing design for the handicapped in federal buildings and those financed by the federal government; and the National Environmental Policy Act, governing the effects of construction on the environment.

In addition, construction with loans insured by the Federal Housing Administration (FHA) of the U.S. Department of Housing and Urban Development (HUD) must conform to the property standards of the FHA; and those guaranteed by the Veterans Administration, to its construction standards. Hospitals must be constructed in conformance with regional, state, and federal statutes; schools, colleges, and universities, with state educational statutes; and so on.

Taken together, the codes, statutes, and regulations affecting architecture contain a bewildering array of legal requirements that sometimes seem to threaten to drown architecture in a sea of red tape and bureaucracy. No reasonable person would argue with their intent: the preservation of the health, safety, and welfare of those who occupy or use the buildings, and the protection of their surroundings and the environment. However, many think that much of their content could be considerably simplified or even eliminated. And some believe that a part of the content may even be detrimental.

Authoritative Organizations Although some local codes have been prepared individually to answer specifically local needs, many are based on one or more national model codes and standards. These are codes and standards prepared by national authoritative organizations and kept up to date at intervals. Other than the federal government and its publications, the most important of these organizations and their most important publications include: American Insurance Association, formerly the National Bureau of Fire Underwriters—National Building Code and Fire Prevention Code; American National Standards Institute (ANSI)—ANSI Standards; American Society for Testing and Materials (ASTM)—ASTM Standards; Building Officials and Code Administrators International (BOCA)—Basic Building Code, Basic Mechanical Code, Basic Plumbing Code, Basic Fire Prevention Code; International Conference of Building Officials (ICBO)—Uniform Building Code, Uniform Mechanical Code, Uniform Plumbing Code, Uniform Sign Code, Uniform Fire Code; National Fire Protection Association (NFPA)—Life Safety Code, National Electric Code, National Fire Prevention Code, National Fire Codes; and the Southern Building Code Congress (SBCC)—Standard Building Code, Standard Mechanical Code, Standard Plumbing Code, Standard Fire Prevention Code.

All these organizations publish codes and standards other than those mentioned, including ones on housing, gas uses, types of construction, and other subjects. Some codes and standards of these organizations, such as those of ANSI and NFPA, are incorporated into statutes of localities all over the United States; others such as those of BOCA, ICBO, and SBCC are used only in certain regions of the country, for example, the SBCC codes in the Southern states.

Architecture and building construction are certainly made more difficult by the mass of regulations contained in codes, statutes, and other laws. Just how difficult can be gathered from a typical situation, in which an architect might design 10 single-family houses for a builder who has a small firm. For this project, the architect and builder will have to deal with at least 15 major codes, ordinances, and standards if the houses are to be VA and FHA approved. And in some building projects, additional statutes would apply in certain cases, including those concerned with environmental impact, water pollution, air pollution, and wetlands conservation and protection.

To the extent that these codes and ordinances and standards contribute to health, wealth, and safety and to the protection of the environment, both the architect and the builder, whoever they may be, would probably agree that the time, money, and effort spent to meet the requirements were well spent.

History In very early times, humans made laws governing conduct even before they developed writing. The earliest laws appear to have included architecture and building construction. One of the most important discoveries of all time was the finding in 1901 of the stone slab upon which was carved the Code of Hammurabi, who was king of Babylon for 43 years during the 18th century B.C. This code contains some 300 legal provisions concerning the rights of people under the authority of the law. The code is thought to have been based on still older laws of the Sumerians and Akkadians. Among the subjects covered are tariffs, wages, trade, military service, and business.

One important part of the Code of Hammurabi contains laws concerning land and building construction. Hammurabi expected good building construction, for one of his provisions was: "If a builder has built a house for a man and his work is not strong, and if the house he has built falls in and kills the householder, that builder shall be slain." Evidently Hammurabi took the responsibilities of builders and, by implication, of architects quite seriously.

Other ancient civilizations developed laws, including those for building construction, most of which were concerned with safety. The Romans devised many types of building regulations, and some of these have survived, in particular those having to do with fire safety. The first real legal profession began in Rome and in the fifth century B.C. an important set of laws was developed, called the Law of the Twelve Tables. Another important development was the codification of Roman law in the *Corpus Juris Civilis,* under Emperor Justinian I (A.D. 483–565). This code laid the foundation for the laws of most European countries.

During the Middle Ages canon law, the legal system of the Roman Catholic Church, took the place to some extent of Roman law, and the Germanic codes also were important. During the Renaissance, Roman law was revived and, along with canon and Germanic law, it influenced the development of new codes of law. The most important was the Code Napoléon, a system developed and codified by a group of experts appointed by Emperor Napoléon (1769–1821). The Code Napoléon had great influence on the laws of European countries.

The laws of the United States generally follow the English system of common law, which is based on judicial decisions rather than on statutes. An exception is Louisiana, in which much of the law is still based on the Code Napoléon. In states that were originally settled by the Spanish, such as Texas and California, some vestiges of Spanish law still remain.

In all the above systems of law, there have been provisions for regulating architecture and building construction. For example, the Code Napoléon contains an article that says in effect that if a building should fall, either in whole or in part, within 10 years after its construction, because of bad workmanship or bad soil, its architect and workmen shall pay for the loss. Many other regulations of architecture and building construction had been made into law earlier. For example, the London Building Act of 1667, passed after the great fire a year earlier which had almost destroyed London, prohibited timber-framed houses in the city and contained a number of other safety provisions, such as minimum wall thicknesses and requirements for noninflammable roofs.

American Development In the English colonies in America, common law was in effect. This situation still exists today, though, starting in the early 19th century, various statutes have been adopted and collected into codes to supplement the common law. In the Spanish and French colonies in America, codes were also established. Some of these early codes regulated buildings, though they were not so highly developed and complete as the building codes of today. New York City passed the first housing code in 1867 and the first zoning code in 1913.

Great numbers of statutes affecting architecture and building construction have since been passed all over the nation by municipal, county, state, and federal governments. Building codes are in existence in almost every town and city in the United States, and some also exist for counties and states. Zoning codes are in existence in most jurisdictions, the only major U.S. city without one being Houston, Tex.

Related Articles EARTHQUAKE PROTECTION; ECOLOGY; FIRE PROTECTION; GOVERNMENT; HANDICAPPED, FACILITIES FOR THE; LIGHTNING PROTECTION; PRACTICE OF ARCHITECTURE.

Further Reading Bockrath, Joseph T.: *Environmental Law for Engineers, Scientists and Managers*, McGraw-Hill, New York, 1977; Various codes and standards listed in this article, published by organizations listed below.

Sources of Additional Information American Institute of Architects, 1735 New York Ave., N.W., Washington, D.C. 20006; American Insurance Assoc., 85 John St., New York, N.Y. 10038; American National Standards Inst., 1430 Broadway, New York, N.Y. 10018; American Society for Testing and Materials, 1916 Race St., Philadelphia, Pa. 19013; Building Officials and Code Administrators International, 1313 E. 60th St., Chicago, Ill. 60637; Environmental Protection Agency, 401 M St., S.W., Washington, D.C. 20460; International Conference of Building Officials, 5360 S. Workman Mill Rd., Whittier, Calif. 90601; National Fire Protection Assoc., 470 Atlantic Ave., Boston, Mass. 02210; Southern Building Code Congress, 3617 Eight Ave., S., Birmingham, Ala. 35222; U.S. Department of Commerce, National Bureau of Standards, Washington, D.C. 20234; U.S. Department of Health and Human Services, Deputy Commissioner for Handicapped, 330 Independence Ave., S.W., Washington, D.C. 20201; U.S. Department of Housing and Urban Development, 451 Seventh St., S.W., Washington, D.C. 20410; U.S. Department of Labor, Occupational Safety and Health Administration, 200 Constitution Ave., N.W., Washington, D.C. 20210.

BUILDING INDUSTRY

BUILDING INDUSTRY The loosely knit, diverse group of individuals and organizations that performs the many functions necessary to bring buildings into being. Often thought of as only consisting of those who design buildings and those who construct them, the building industry is actually much more complex. The major elements include designers, constructors, owners, users, financiers, real estate agents, and regulators. All are essential in transforming a need for a building from an idea to a completed structure.

The Designers Buildings and their surroundings are designed by a group of professionals: architects, engineers, planners, landscape architects, interior designers, and others. Technicians, draftsmen, specification writers, and others assist them, working together with the professionals to create building designs and to prepare working drawings and specifications that indicate what is to be constructed, and coordinating the work so that the actual construction will conform to the intent of the working drawings and specifications. Ordinarily, an architect has the overall responsibility for these activities. And the architect has the specialized responsibility for the concept of the building or its design. The engineers, usually working in architects' offices or as consultants to them, are responsible for their own specialized activities: the structural engineer for the structure, the electrical engineer for electrical systems, and the mechanical engineer for mechanical systems such as plumbing and heating. The planners, usually called city planners, are responsible for the design of the city or part of the city in which buildings are to be located. Sometimes they work on an area in which only a relatively small number of buildings are to be placed in a group. Landscape architects are responsible for the design and coordination of the exterior areas around buildings, interior designers for the interiors, road and traffic designers for provisions for automotive requirements. At times, the services of other professional are required, for example, in a theater, an acoustical or lighting expert, or both. An industrial designer may be called upon if specialized equipment is to be designed into a building. Various combinations of these professionals may be required on buildings of varying sizes, purposes, and complexity. For a small single-family house, for example, the architect and his technicians might perform all or most of the functions named.

The Constructors The people who actually construct buildings are contractors, manufacturers, and the building trades. Contractors, sometimes called builders for houses, manage the actual construction work: general contractors or builders having responsibility for the entire building, subcontractors for specialized portions such as plumbing, electrical, or roofing work. The most usual method for accomplishing this work is the general contract method, in which a general contractor signs a contract with an owner, for an agreed-upon price, to construct a building in a manner required by the working drawings and specifications prepared by the architect and other design professionals. The general contractor makes contracts with the subcontractors needed to perform specialized phases of the work. The contractors then proceed to construct the building utilizing the abilities of those in the building trades, the carpenters, electricians, plumbers, roofers, and so on who actually perform the labor.

In a more recent variation of this process, the owner employs a project, or construction, manager who performs duties similar to those of the general contractor, but for an agreed-upon fee or salary instead of a price for the entire construction work. Advantages claimed for this method are faster completion of the building at a lower cost to the owner.

Other important constructors are the manufacturers, sometimes called producers, who produce and distribute building materials and equipment. In a way, they function in a role similar to that of the other constructors, except that their work is accomplished in factories rather than on building sites. With the growth of prefabrication, the assembly of smaller parts into large assemblies or systems, such as a whole wall, in factories, the role of producers and production trades has grown while that of contractors and building trades has diminished.

The Owners Of great importance are the owners, without whose needs and requirements for buildings and furnishing of capital for their design and construction there would be no building industry. In general, an owner may be an individual, as the owner of a private house, a private group, as a corporation or partnership that owns an office building, or a government representing its constituents, as a post office. The owner, called the client by the architect and other design professionals, is the individual or group who makes contracts with them and with the constructors for the design and the construction.

The Users The needs and desires of people who actually use buildings, whether they be workers in offices, salespeople and customers in stores, tenants in public housing, or others, have not always been given serious consideration by the other groups in the building industry. Recently, users have come to be considered of prime importance and in some cases have been given a role in the design and construction decisions that affect their lives and welfare. In fact, a movement called advocacy architecture or planning has come into being, in which architects and other professionals devote their professional practice or a portion of it to the representation of the rights of those who use buildings.

The Financiers This group furnishes the capital in the form of money and credit, and is an important element of the building industry. While such needs are often supplied in part by owners, it is common practice for a large percentage of the money for buildings to come from investors, banks, insurance companies, savings and loan organizations, and other investors. They finance the purchase of land, furnish money on a short-term basis or interim financing, during the construction process, and make long-term loans to owners, usually taking a mortgage on the building and the land on which it is located. As a result of their investment policies, such financiers exert a strong influence on building construction. The government strongly influences financing of buildings through its Federal Housing Administration and Veterans Administration guarantees of private loans and through the activities of various regulating agencies.

The Real Estate Agents Through their active participation in the buying, selling, leasing, and development of land and buildings, the real estate agents perform important functions in the building industry.

Real estate brokers find buyers for those who wish to sell property and manage the transactions. Developers, sometimes called entrepreneurs or promoters, assemble land on which buildings can be constructed to meet needs and procure financing for the projects, often taking a financial interest themselves. Real estate appraisers estimate the value of land and buildings; counselors advise owners and investors; managers administer leasing, maintenance, and other business matters for buildings.

The Regulators On every governmental level, from that of the smallest township to the federal, an important element of the building industry is the regulator, who formulates and enforces the rules for building design and construction. The federal government affects building construction by such means as the Occupational Safety and Health Act (OSHA) which governs the safety and health of those who work on and in buildings. The National Environmental Policy Act regulates construction that may affect the quality of the environment. The regulations of the Federal Housing Administration (FHA) govern the construction of houses for which it guarantees loans. On state, county, and local levels the use of land is governed by regulations of land-use agencies. The size and other factors of buildings allowed to be constructed on individual sites are regulated by zoning laws and their construction, by building codes.

American History In the earliest times in America, there was no building industry as such. If a person decided to build a house, he simply cleared a site, cutting trees that were then worked into lumber with hand tools, and started the construction of the building. Such a house was not really designed but rather grew out of the needs of the family that would occupy it and the available materials and labor, usually members of the family and neighbors; its plan and appearance reflected houses in the builder's native country.

Soon after the founding of the first English colonies in the early 17th century, artisans and craftsmen arrived from Europe. These carpenters, joiners, bricklayers, painters, and plasterers performed much of the construction work. Designs for houses and other buildings were made by amateur gentlemen-architects who learned from books and by craftsmen-architects who learned from practicing their trades as well as from books. Most of these early architects acted as their own engineers, and in the case of the craftsmen-architects, as the constructors of the buildings as well. Many of the craftsmen-architects were master carpenters. And master carpenters usually directed the work of construction for buildings designed by the gentlemen-architects.

The manufacturing of building products began

early, brick making as early as 1610 in Jamestown, Va., and 1629 in Salem, Mass. Water-powered sawmills for processing lumber were established about the same time in Maine as well as near Jamestown. Other industries, including the quarrying of stone and the making of window glass, followed soon after.

By the middle of the 18th century the functions of designers and constructors were beginning to become established. This trend continued into the 19th century with an accelerated pace brought on by industrialization, invention, and education. By the beginning of the 20th century most of the present-day elements of the building industry were established and recognized. The architects had organized a national association, the American Institute of Architects, in 1857; the civil engineers had founded the American Society of Civil Engineers in 1852, in spite of the fact that the functions of architects and engineers were not really separated until the late 19th century and have continued to overlap to this day.

Labor Groups Labor movements had existed in one form or another from colonial days; by the beginning of the 20th century they had achieved a solid place in the building industry mainly through the efforts of the American Federation of Labor, founded in 1886, which represented the interests of the craftsmen who worked on buildings. Although the Associated General Contractors of America was not founded until 1918, there had been an organization of master craftsmen who directed the work of building construction as far back as 1724. This was the year of the founding of the Carpenters' Company of the City and County of Philadelphia, an organization still in existence. This group, with a membership of master carpenters who directed the construction of buildings, and many of whom acted as architects, might be called a link between the guilds of the Middle Ages and the labor unions and contractors of today.

Paralleling the development of the designers and constructors has been that of the other important elements of the building industry, the owners, financiers, realtors, and regulators. And the users are finally coming into their own position of importance.

Related Articles ARCHITECTURE; ASSOCIATION, BUILDING INDUSTRY; BUILDING CODES AND STANDARDS; BUILDING TRADE; CARPENTERS' COMPANY; CONSTRUCTION, BUILDING; ELECTRICAL ENGINEERING; FINANCE; GOVERNMENT; INTERIOR DESIGN; LANDSCAPE ARCHITECTURE; MECHANICAL ENGINEERING; PLANNING, CITY; ROAD AND TRAFFIC DESIGN; STRUCTURAL ENGINEERING; SURVEYING.

BUILDING TRADE
One of the specialized types of work performed by workers who construct buildings and other structures. The major building trades today are bricklayers, carpenters, electricians, ironworkers, painters, plasterers, plumbers, steam fitters, and roofers.

Bricklayers lay brick and other types of masonry products. Carpenters are divided among rough carpenters, who build wood frameworks for buildings and wood forms for concrete work; and finish carpenters, who handle such work as hanging doors, installing windows, putting hardware in place, and installing wood baseboards and other trim. Electricians install wiring, switches, outlets, switchboards, and other electrical equipment. Ironworkers erect beams, trusses, columns, and other parts of the structural frames of steel buildings. Painters apply paints and other finishes to the interiors and exteriors of buildings. Plasterers apply and finish plaster and related products in the interiors of buildings. Plumbers install water, gas, and sewer piping; and bathroom, kitchen, laundry, and other equipment. Steam fitters install heating, ventilating, and air-conditioning equipment and ductwork and related items. Roofers install roofing and related items.

Members of the building trades usually work for general contractors, or builders, who are responsible for the complete construction of building projects; or for subcontractors, who are responsible for portions of it, such as mechanical, electrical, or painting work. Workers in the building trades often become general contractors or subcontractors after having gained knowledge and experience.

Trade Unions Today most building trade work in the United States is handled by members of trade unions. Labor unions are divided generally into craft unions and industrial unions. A craft union includes all workers employed in a single craft. Most of the building construction unions are craft unions, such as the electricians, carpenters, plumbers, and so on. An industrial union includes all workers employed in a single industry, such as automobile manufacturing or mining. Industrial union members participate in the building industry because ordinarily they fabricate parts and components, such as structural steel, windows, hardware, and so on in factories. They also become involved in a larger way when building components or whole buildings are prefabricated or preassembled in factories.

Labor unions control most of the training of young people who wish to become master or journeyman workers in the crafts and industries. This is often accomplished through apprenticeship programs, which specify schedules of study and experience. To qualify for apprenticeship, a young person must ordinarily be between age sixteen and twenty-four, a high school graduate, and often must pass tests or have other qualifications. The young person must also join the union which administers the apprenticeship program. Apprentices then follow prescribed training schedules that include working in a single craft, study, and often courses in a technical school. The period of apprenticeship varies but the normal time is approximately four years before an apprentice can complete the training. To prepare for careers in given crafts, many young people take vocational courses in secondary schools or attend trade or vocational schools after graduation from high school. For people who like to work with their hands, constructing portions of buildings and other structures, careers in the building trades can be very satisfying.

History In ancient times, the concept of labor was based on the use of slaves to do the work. In ancient cultures, including Greece and Rome, this was most often the case. During the Middle Ages, with the decline of slavery and the spread of Christianity, laborers gained status and became respected community members. Skilled craftsmen and artisans formed guilds which fixed prices, set standards and wages, and determined who could practice the crafts, much as do the labor unions of today. Workers were classified according to their knowledge and abilities as apprentices, those learning a craft; journeymen, those who were proficient in it; and masters, those who were highly skilled. Some labor unions still follow this practice today. The guild system began to die out with the end of the Middle Ages and the advent of capitalism, which required free markets in goods and labor.

In Europe as well as in colonial America the status of workers declined after the Middle Ages. Workers were expected to work long hours in unhealthy environments for low wages. And child labor was accepted as a normal state of affairs.

American Development In colonial America, there were attempts to induce Indians to act as laborers but to no avail. The colonists then turned to other involuntary laborers: slaves, convicts, and debtors. Another source of labor was indentured servants, people brought from Europe who had agreed to work for a period of time, often seven years or more, in return for their passage to America and freedom at the end of the indentured period. Another method was cooperative effort, such as people joining forces in raising a barn. In time, skilled artisans and craftsmen were brought to America from Europe and they trained others. Some of the early American architects were craftsmen, who had been trained in their crafts rather than in architecture.

Apprenticeship was also widespread in early American colonies. Young boys were apprenticed to masters of various trades, by whom they were instructed. Unlike apprentices of today, those of colonial times often lived with their masters and worked for them for periods of seven years or more, for no wages, in return for the training and upkeep received. After that, the apprentice could become a journeyman and later a master.

The first real labor union in the United States was that of the shoemakers, founded in 1792 in Philadelphia. The Carpenters' Company had been founded in that city in 1724, but it functioned more like a medieval guild than like a modern union. In the 1800s many local unions were founded, and in 1852 the first national union, the International Typographical Union, was started; it exists to this day. The American Federation of Labor (AFL) was founded in 1886 and the Congress of Industrial Organizations (CIO), in 1938. The two organizations merged into the AFL-CIO in 1955. This union includes in its membership those who work in the building trades. Working conditions and pay scales in the building trades have been vastly improved during the 20th century, primarily due to the efforts of the unions.

Related Articles BUILDING INDUSTRY; CARPENTERS' COMPANY; CONSTRUCTION, BUILDING.

Source of Additional Information American Federation of Labor and Congress of Industrial Organizations (AFL-CIO), 815 16th St., N.W., Washington, D.C. 20006.

BULFINCH, CHARLES

BULFINCH, CHARLES American architect (1763–1844). Born into a prominent and wealthy Boston family, and educated at Harvard, though not in architecture, Charles Bulfinch occupied city and later national government positions most of his life. This did not prevent him from becoming an architect; many think him one of the greatest. That he considered himself an architect and that others accepted him as one is certain. Other American architects of Bulfinch's time and before were either architect-builders who primarily constructed buildings, with the design secondary, or amateur gentlemen-architects who designed buildings as an avocation while pursuing some other career. Bulfinch, though he certainly started out as the latter kind, soon found himself almost totally involved with architecture.

Architectural Plans Bulfinch was one of the first American architects known to have used drawings extensively for the construction of buildings. Before him such drawings were few and sketchy. Perhaps even more importantly, Bulfinch also used drawings to study the design of the building. Thus he took a giant step toward becoming what would now be called a professional architect. He seems professional in other ways too. Bulfinch was deeply concerned in the everyday operations in constructing buildings. His involvement was not that of the architect-builder who actually worked on buildings but much more like that of later professional architects who supervised the construction to ensure that designs were carried out properly and that the workmanship was acceptable.

Although self-taught from books, as were the other colonial architects, Bulfinch was not satisfied with the design of buildings by adaptation of elements of architecture selected from books. As have architects who came after him, Bulfinch attempted to understand the buildings, their materials, the methods by which they were constructed, and their functions. And also like later architects, he became aware of the importance of the surroundings of the buildings, that is, their relationship to streets and walkways, parks and city, and other buildings in their vicinity.

Boston It has been said that Bulfinch changed Boston from a provincial town with meager buildings and meandering streets into a city of taste, of handsome buildings placed in a setting of parks and trees and plantings. In the 30-odd years he practiced in Boston, Bulfinch accomplished much that merits such an accolade. Part of the reason was the excellence of his buildings, but of almost equal importance was his in-

BULFINCH, CHARLES Massachusetts State House (1798), Boston.
(Wayne Andrews)

volvement in every aspect and activity of the city through civic work, as a member, and chairman, of the board of selectmen. In this capacity, he came to understand Boston and its needs thoroughly.

The early work of Bulfinch was Georgian in character, though late Georgian as influenced by the brothers Adam. His later buildings demonstrate a maturing process that led him more toward the Classic Revival style that had come to be the preferred style of such architects as Thomas Jefferson and Benjamin Henry Latrobe. In his first major buildings, the Federal Street Theater and Franklin Crescent houses (1794), Bulfinch demonstrated his concern with the totality of architecture and its surroundings. This was ambitious architecture indeed for its time, the late 18th century, and place, provincial Boston. As might a present-day architect, Bulfinch conceived the design as a master plan for two curved buildings each of which would contain 16 connected houses, placed at opposite sides of a landscaped oval park. At one end was the

theater, forming a focal point for the whole composition. All three buildings were to be brick and were designed to complement each other in style and scale. Only one of the crescent buildings and the theater were actually built. Where the other crescent would have been, detached houses by Bulfinch were substituted. Neither the theater nor the crescent building has survived.

The architect's next major building, the Massachusetts State House (1798), has survived in good condition, though it is now only a part of a much larger complex, having been added on to several times. The State House is a simple rectangular building in plan and exterior, two stories high with a basement, and a porch or portico in front, the whole crowned by a dome. The walls are of brick, the portico and columns of wood, and the dome of wood boards, matched and worked to fit tightly against each other. The elegant proportions of the building, the use of arches with slender columns above, the relationship of the dome

BULFINCH, CHARLES Lancaster Meeting House or First Church of Christ (1817), Lancaster, Mass. *(Wayne Andrews)*

to the other elements, and the spacious and richly ornamented interiors caused the building to be called a masterpiece immediately upon its completion. It is still considered one of the greatest American buildings and a very high point in Bulfinch's architectural career.

Other Works After this triumph, Bulfinch went on to design some 40 other public buildings and churches. Among the most important public buildings still in existence are the Old Connecticut State House (1796), Hartford; the Old Maine State House (1829), in Augusta, and now much altered; University Hall, Harvard University (1815), Cambridge; and the Massachusetts General Hospital (1820), Boston, a building now called the Bulfinch Pavilion and a relatively small part of a large hospital complex. This was the architect's last building in Boston, the city upon which his buildings had so great and lasting an effect. Of the five Bulfinch churches in Boston, only New North Church (St. Stephen's Catholic), completed in

1804, remains. It is not considered one of Bulfinch's best designs and has been much modified and was even moved back for a street widening. Fortunately preserved is the church which is considered the architect's best, some think his best building of any kind, the Lancaster Meeting House (First Church of Christ) built in Lancaster, Mass., in 1817.

Charles Bulfinch designed a number of houses, many of them on or around Beacon Hill in Boston. Their impact on Boston was probably stronger than that of his public buildings or even his churches since the houses and their settings established an atmosphere of charm and beauty which has been preserved in the Beacon Hill area to this day. Bulfinch designed both single detached houses and row or attached houses. Most of the latter are now gone but a notable exception is the Chestnut Street block containing numbers 13 to 17. Several of his detached houses still exist in Boston as well as in other Massachusetts towns. Among the finest are the three

BULFINCH, CHARLES Exterior, First Otis House (1796), Boston, Mass. *(Wayne Andrews)*

BULFINCH, CHARLES Interior, First Otis House (1796), Boston, Mass. *(Wayne Andrews)*

houses he designed for Harrison Gray Otis, a prominent and powerful Boston politician. These houses are the First Otis House (1796), the only one with the original interiors; the Second Otis House (1800), usually considered the finest of the three; and the Third Otis House (1806), the architect's last great house in Boston.

Life Charles Bulfinch was one of the first great American-born architects. Born in Boston, on August 8, 1763, into a well-to-do and prominent family, he was graduated from Harvard in 1781, one of the first American architects to complete a college education. His interest in architecture seems to have been awakened when he spent two years (1785–87) touring France and Italy, at the suggestion of Thomas Jefferson, and England. Upon his return from Europe, he entered the accounting room of a Boston merchant, a position which left him time to study architectural books and to dabble in design and construction much as did other amateur gentlemen-architects.

As early as 1787, soon after his return from Europe, Bulfinch gave an indication of his future dedication to architecture by submitting the first plans for a new Massachusetts State House, a project that was to elude him until he was selected to design the building in 1795. During these early years, he also designed other important buildings, but continued to have only a casual involvement in architecture until he went bankrupt in 1796.

In 1791 he was elected to the board of selectmen of Boston, a position in which he served, except for four years, until he left for Washington in 1817. For the last 18 of these years, he was the board's chairman, a position not unlike that of a mayor. At about the time of his bankruptcy, he resigned from the board to devote himself fully to architecture. Returning to the board in

1799, he soon found himself deeply involved in all of the governmental, commercial, and financial affairs of Boston. From that time, his civic work and his architecture went hand in hand and complemented each other. As an architect, he designed government buildings, churches, wharves, warehouses, schools, markets, prisons, banks, hospitals, theaters, multifamily houses, and numerous single-family houses. In addition, he planned portions of Boston.

His city honored him for his civic work and for his architecture early in life and this appreciation was to continue. His civic work primarily belonged to Boston, but his architecture came to belong to the country. In 1817 James Monroe, (1758–1831), newly inaugurated president of the United States, appointed him to replace Benjamin Henry Latrobe (1764–1820) as architect in charge of rebuilding the U.S. Capitol (see color section and illustration in article capital, United States), burned by the British in 1814. Bulfinch continued in this position until 1829. During this time he joined the two wings with a central dome and designed the west portico with steps and terrace forming the approach to it, completing the building for the first time since its construction had begun. Bulfinch's dome was later replaced by a larger and grander one, but the west front remains. After 1830 Bulfinch returned to Boston where he lived in retirement until his death on April 4, 1844.

Related Articles Capital, United States; Classic Revival Architecture; Colonial Architecture; Georgian Architecture.

Further Reading Bulfinch, Ellen Susan, ed.: *The Life and Letters of Charles Bulfinch*, Houghton-Mifflin, Boston, 1896; Kirker, Harold: *The Architecture of Charles Bulfinch*, Harvard University Press, Cambridge, 1969; Place, Charles A.: *Charles Bulfinch: Architect and Citizen*, DaCapo, New York, 1968.

BURNHAM AND ROOT American architectural firm. This partnership, formed in 1893 by Daniel Hudson Burnham (1846–1912), architect and city planner, and John Wellborn Root (1850–91), architect, became one of the most prominent and successful in America in its time. It was the ideal partnership. The two architects shared a mutual respect and affection. And the talents of one complemented those of the other perfectly. Burnham was good-natured, energetic, practical, and a good executive. He brought commissions into the office and was master of the technical, utilitarian, and financial aspects of architecture. On the other hand, Root was a dreamer and artist, creative and deeply interested in culture. It has been said

BURNHAM AND ROOT Exterior, The Rookery (1886), Chicago, Ill. *(Hedrich-Blessing)*

BURNHAM AND ROOT Closeup, The Rookery (1886), Chicago, Ill.
(Hedrich-Blessing)

that Burnham saved Root from becoming a dilettante-architect and in turn was saved from being only a businessman-architect. In any case, they were a good team and went on to design a great number of distinguished buildings.

Firm's Works During the first years of the firm's existence, Burnham and Root did mostly houses. The first big commission was for the Montauk Block (1882), now demolished, followed by the Calumet Building (1884), both in Chicago, composed of masonry with cast-iron columns. These were followed by other masonry buildings in Chicago, the most notable being the Rookery (1886), named for its site where flocks of pigeons had formerly roosted, and the Monadnock Building (1891; see illustrations in article modern architecture and in color section), the last tall building, 16 stories, with brick bearing walls. Then came the first all-steel skeleton-framed building, the Rand-McNally Building (1890), since demolished. In Chicago the firm did several metal skeleton-framed buildings that were designed before Root's death and constructed afterward. Among these were the Great Northern Hotel (1892) with a wrought-iron and steel frame and the Masonic Temple (1892) with a steel

skeleton and at the time the tallest, 20 stories, building in the world. Both were later demolished.

Considered the finest by the firm is the Reliance Building (1895; see illustrations in article modern architecture and in color section), the design for which had begun before Root's death and was completed by Charles B. Atwood (1848–95), who was in charge of the design department. In this building came the logical conclusion in the design of Chicago skyscrapers. The structural skeleton is steel and the walls are terra-cotta and glass, expressing the structure underneath. The proportions and details are skillfully handled and balanced.

After the untimely death of Root in 1891, Burnham changed the firm's name to D. H. Burnham and Company and continued in practice. The practice grew but the design was never quite the same. Burnham produced a great number of buildings, many of them very good ones. But now they were in eclectic styles, particularly the Renaissance, which were popular in the Eastern United States. None approached the invention and daring of those of Burnham and Root. Among the most notable are Field Museum of Natural History (1900), the Fisher Building (1896), and the Railway Exchange Building (1904), all in Chicago; and the Flatiron, formerly Fuller, Building (1902) in New York City.

In his later years Burnham became seriously interested in city planning. With Root, he had designed the master plan for the World's Columbian Exposition (1893; see illustration in article exposition) in Chicago. As early as 1897, he had begun thinking about a great plan for the development of the Chicago lakefront in collaboration with Edward H. Bennett and Jens Jensen (1860–1951). Later, with Jensen as the landscape architect, Burnham was to see this work re-sult in the construction of Grant Park and the other great Chicago parks beginning in 1904 and, ultimately, in his widely admired Chicago Plan of 1909. He made other plans for a number of other cities, including Baltimore, Duluth, and San Francisco, and for Manila and Baguio, the Philippines.

Burnham had said, "Make no little plans; they have no magic to stir men's minds." In everything he did, in architecture, planning, and practice, he followed his own dictum.

Burnham's Life Daniel Hudson Burnham was born near Henderson, N.Y., on September 4, 1846, and

BURNHAM AND ROOT Interior, The Rookery (1886), Chicago, Ill.
(Hedrich-Blessing)

BURNHAM AND ROOT Field Museum of Natural History (1900), Chicago, Ill. [Architects: D. H. Burnham and Co. (Hedrich-Blessing)]

BURNHAM AND ROOT Flatiron, formerly Fuller, Building (1902), New York, N.Y. [Architects: D. H. Burnham and Co. (Wurts Brothers)]

moved to Chicago with his family when he was nine years old. An indifferent student, he graduated from Central High School with a poor record, except for freehand drawing in which he excelled. After failing the entrance examinations of both Harvard and Yale, he tried one thing after another, all for short periods, working as a clerk in a retail store, mining in Nevada, running for the Illinois senate, a race in which he was defeated, working in the architectural office of Wil-

liam Le Baron Jenney (1832–1907), and attempting to start his own office.

In 1872 he went to work in the Chicago architectural office of Carter, Drake and Wight. He admired Peter B. Wight (1838–1925), who taught him a great deal about buildings. Having had no academic training in architecture and a short apprenticeship, Burnham formed a partnership in 1873 with a man who had both the training and experience, John Wellborn Root. Both were working in the office of Carter, Drake and Wight at the time. The partnership, after a slow start, flourished and grew. One of its first draftsmen was William Holabird (1854–1923), who later made a reputation in his own right. The partnership lasted until Root's death, and produced a number of notable buildings.

In 1876, Burnham married Margaret Sherman, the daughter of his first important client, wealthy Chicago stockyard executive John B. Sherman. Two years earlier, Burnham and Root had completed a large and fashionable house for Sherman. Within ten years after the marriage, Daniel and Margaret Burnham had two daughters and three sons born to them. Two of the sons, Hubert and Daniel, Jr., eventually became architects and joined their father's firm.

After Root's death, Burnham carried on alone, renaming the firm D. H. Burnham and Company. Burnham began to broaden his interests. He was named chief of construction and then chief consulting architect for the World's Columbian Exposition. During this period another architect destined for success, Dwight Perkins (1867–1941), ran the office, and Charles B. Atwood was in charge of design. His office grew to be the largest in Chicago and he established branch offices in New York and San Francisco. He became quite active in the work of his profession, serving in a number of capacities, including that of president of the American Institute of Architects, 1894–95. He worked diligently, along with Charles Follen McKim (1847–1929) and others, for the establishment of the American Academy in Rome.

After 1900 the administration of the firm was under Ernest Robert Graham (1868–1936), who had joined it in 1888. Burnham died on June 1, 1912, in Heidelberg, Germany, and Graham continued the firm in partnership with Burnham's sons, Hubert and Daniel, Jr. This was a productive firm and was later continued as Graham, Anderson, Probst and White.

Root's Life John Wellborn Root was born on January 10, 1850, in Lumpkin, Ga., of a well-to-do family. As a child, he showed great interest in nature and talent in the arts, beginning serious study of drawings when he was seven and the piano at twelve. General William Tecumseh Sherman's troops drove Root's family out of their home when he was fourteen. He was then sent to school in Liverpool, England, where he studied architecture and music and further developed his interest in the other arts.

In 1866 Root entered New York University from which he was graduated in 1869 with a B.S. in civil engineering and a brilliant record. He had also distinguished himself in drawing and music, composing and playing both the piano and organ. After graduation, he entered the office of James Renwick (1818–95), the noted Gothic Revival architect in New York City, staying there in 1869 and 1870. He was strongly influenced by Renwick, and Gothic details were to appear in all his buildings. In 1871 he went to Chicago to work in the office of Carter, Drake and Wight, where he met Daniel Hudson Burnham, the man who would most influence the rest of his career. In 1873 the two formed a partnership that produced many fine buildings and lasted until Root's death.

Root's interest in the arts continued throughout his life. In Chicago he produced amateur plays, concerts, and recitals and even achieved something of a professional status as a critic, reviewing concerts and operas for the *Chicago Tribune*.

In 1880 Root married Mary Louise Walker, who died of tuberculosis six weeks after the wedding. In 1882 he married Dora Louise Monroe. Their son, John Wellborn Root (1887–1963), became a successful architect. Root's sister-in-law, Harriet Monroe (c. 1860–1936), became well known both as the founder of *Poetry* magazine, which published most of the great American poets of the day, and as the biographer of her brother-in-law.

Root practiced architecture less than 20 years. He died on January 15, 1891; though only forty-one, he had accomplished a great deal. He had pursued the ideas of the Chicago school to a high peak of excellence.

Related Articles HOLABIRD AND ROCHE; JENNEY, WILLIAM LE BARON; MODERN ARCHITECTURE.

Further Reading Hines, Thomas S.: *Burnham of Chicago: Architect and Planner*, Oxford University Press, New York, 1974; Hoffmann, Donald: *The Architecture of John Wellborn Root*, Johns Hopkins University Press, Baltimore, 1973; Monroe, Harriet: *John Wellborn Root: A Study of His Life and Work*, Prairie School Press, Park Forest, Ill., 1966 (Facsimile reprint of 1896 edition).

CAPITAL, UNITED STATES The seat of the federal government in Washington, District of Columbia. Washington and the District of Columbia are unique in many ways, not the least of which is in the architecture.

Residence Act In 1790 the U.S. Congress passed the Residence Act authorizing President George Washington (1732–99) to select a site of not more than 100 square miles on the Potomac River for the location of a federal district to be used as the nation's capital. In 1791 Washington chose the present site of exactly 100 square miles, 10 miles on each side, incorporating the existing Maryland towns of Georgetown, Carrollsburg, and Hamburg, and a portion of Virginia. Later that year he received approval from Congress to add the town of Alexandria, Va., to the district, but Alexandria was ceded back to Virginia in 1846.

Early in 1791 Washington appointed Major Pierre Charles L'Enfant (1754–1825), French engineer who had served in the Continental Army during the American Revolution, to survey, map, and make plans for the city to be built in the federal district. After he had prepared excellent plans for the city, still much admired today, L'Enfant was dismissed in 1792, but not before he had indelibly stamped the city with the pattern that has lasted ever since. Work began on the laying out of the city, its streets and buildings. And this work has been going on ever since.

Design Competitions In 1792 competitions were held for the design of the two most important buildings, the Capitol and the President's House, as the White House was known then, and construction began on the White House the same year and on the Capitol, the following year. Of all the important government buildings in Washington, these two have had the longest and most interesting histories.

When the competition for the Capitol was held in 1792, there were 17 entries and the winner, who submitted his entry three months late, was a doctor of medicine and amateur architect, William Thornton (1759–1828). When it became apparent that Thornton was unqualified to construct the building, a French architect, Stephen Hallet (1755–1825), the runner-up in the competition, was employed, but after disagreements with Thornton and the Commissioners of the Federal Buildings, he was dismissed in 1794. An Irish architect, James Hoban (c. 1762–1831), who had won the competition for the President's House, was given the title of surveyor of public buildings and replaced

Hallet, who remained as his assistant. By 1800 they had finished the north wing and Congress moved in for the first time. (See color section for additional illustration.)

In 1803 Benjamin Henry Latrobe (1764–1820), who had come to America from England five years before, was given the appointment by President Thomas Jefferson (1743–1826) that had been Hoban's and the south wing was started. This wing was finished by 1807 and the north wing altered. Latrobe also had his problems with Thornton and later on with Jefferson. In 1812, after funds for the work had run out, Latrobe left his position.

During the War of 1812, on August 24, 1814, the British burned the Capitol, along with the White House and other Washington buildings. In 1815 Latrobe was again appointed to his old position and

CAPITAL, UNITED STATES. Rapid Rail Transit System (1976–90) Washington Metropolitan Area Transit Authority (METRO), Washington, D.C. [*Architect: Harry Weese & Associates; Engineers; LeLeuw, Cather & Co., Inc. (Paul Myatt)*]

CAPITAL, UNITED STATES U.S. Capitol Building (begun 1793), Washington, D.C. [*Architects: William Thornton, Benjamin Henry Latrobe, Charles Bulfinch, Robert Mills, Thomas Ustick Walter, and others. (Joseph W. Molitor)*]

CAPITAL, UNITED STATES White House (begun 1792). [*Architects: James Hoban, Benjamin Henry Latrobe, and others. (White House)*]

took on the job of rebuilding the Capitol. He restored the building and designed many of the interiors, and then, under pressure, resigned his position in 1817. Charles Bulfinch (1763–1844) was then appointed and during his tenure, which lasted until 1829, the central link between the wings was completed along with a dome, designed by him generally following the Thornton scheme. In 1836 Robert Mills (1781–1855) was appointed architect of public buildings, which included work on the Capitol, and served until 1851.

In 1850 a competition was held for the design of a new dome. It was won by Thomas Ustick Walter (1804–87), who then became architect of the Capitol, replacing Mills. During Walter's tenure, not only was the present dome completed but the wings were extended for both the House of Representatives and the Senate. After the completion of Walter's work on the Capitol in 1865, little was done other than remodeling, plumbing, and electrical work and construction of related buildings until the middle of the 20th century. In 1962 the east front was extended outward some 30 feet after a bitter struggle involving the government and preservationists. In 1970 George Malcolm White (1920–   ) became architect of the Capitol and has since recommended extending the west front, again a very controversial issue.

The White House, designed by James Hoban, went into construction in 1792 shortly after the architect won the competition. The runner-up was Secretary of State Thomas Jefferson, who had submitted an anon-

ymous design. In 1800, with the building still incomplete, President John Adams (1735–1826) moved in with his family. In 1807, after Jefferson had become president, Latrobe added terrace pavilions on both sides, worked on the interiors, and designed porticoes. In 1814 the White House was burned by the British, but was saved from total destruction by a thunderstorm. The president at the time, James Madison (1751–1836), and his family moved into the Octagon House (1800), designed by Dr. William Thornton for Col. John Tayloe III (1771–1828) and now owned by the American Institute of Architects. By 1815 the White House had been rebuilt. In 1824 Hoban added the south portico that Latrobe had designed and in 1829, the north portico.

In 1849 landscape architect Andrew Jackson Downing (1815–52) redesigned the grounds and also worked on those of the Capitol and the Smithsonian Institution. Subsequently, few changes were made except the installation of plumbing and electricity. In 1902 the White House was extensively remodeled by McKim, Mead and White and the East Gallery and Executive Office Wing were added. While Harry S Truman (1884–1972) was president, the White House was badly in need of repairs and much of the structure of the building was removed and replaced with steel framing. The exterior walls were not changed and the interiors were reinstalled.

Government Buildings In Washington there are significant buildings of many kinds and eras, some of

CAPITAL, UNITED STATES Old State, War and Navy Building (1888), now the Executive Office Annex, Washington, D.C. [*Architect: Arthur B. Mullett. (Joseph W. Molitor)*]

which are discussed elsewhere in this book. The buildings of the U.S. government alone make the city a virtual museum of the history of architecture in this country after colonial times. The Capitol and the White House are the oldest government buildings. Many of the other early buildings are now gone. Those still in existence include the Navy Yard buildings (1804) by Latrobe and the Marine Barracks (1805) by George Hadfield (c. 1764–1826). In the old Congressional Cemetery, established in 1807, architects Thornton, Hadfield, and Mills are buried, surrounded by the tombs of senators and congressmen and by a number of monuments designed by Latrobe.

Among the later government buildings are the Old City Hall (1850) by Hadfield, now the D.C. Courthouse; the Old Patent Office (1867), restored (1969) as the National Portrait Gallery; the Old Post Office (1869), later restored as offices and shops; and the Treasury Building (1869), the last three by Mills. Still later are the Old Pension Building (1883), now scheduled to become a museum, by General Montgomery Meigs (1816–92); the Old State, War and Navy Building (1888), now the Executive Office Annex, by Arthur B. Mullet (1834–90); and another Old Post Office (1899) by Willoughby J. Edbrooke (1843–96), one of the few Romanesque Revival buildings in Classic Revival Washington.

Early in the 20th century congressional office buildings were built, designed by Carrère and Hastings, who divided the work between them, John Merven Carrère (1858–1911) assuming responsibility for the Old Senate Office Building (1909) and Thomas Hastings (1860–1929), for the Old House Office Building (1908).

In the 1920s and 1930s a large group of buildings for various departments of the government were built in an area that was cleared and is now called the Federal Triangle. All of the buildings are Eclectic Classic Revival and seem like throwbacks to an earlier era. During the same period the Supreme Court Building (1935) was designed by Cass Gilbert (1859–1934). In 1937 the Federal Reserve Building, designed by Paul Philippe Cret (1876–1945), was built. These buildings were the last great examples of the academic phase of Classic Revival architecture in Washington.

Although it took a long time coming, modern architecture finally arrived in official Washington. Modern buildings, constructed in the past few years, include the New Executive Office and Court of Claims buildings (1968), designed in conjunction with the restoration of the buildings around Lafayette Square, across from the White House, by John Carl Warnecke (1919–   ). Others are the Office of the Department of Housing and Urban Development (1968), designed by Marcel Lajos Breuer (1902–   ) in association with James A. Nolen (1913–   ) and Herbert H. Swinburne (1912–   ), and the International Monetary Fund Building (1973), designed by Vincent Kling (1916–   ).

Smithsonian Institution One of the most interest-

CAPITAL, UNITED STATES U.S. Supreme Court Building (1935), Washington, D.C. [*Architect: Cass Gilbert. (Joseph W. Molitor)*]

CAPITAL, UNITED STATES Air and Space Museum (1975), Washington, D.C. [*Architects: Hellmuth, Obata and Kassabaum. (Joseph W. Molitor)*]

ing groups of buildings in Washington, really not a group since they are scattered, are the buildings of the Smithsonian Institution. It was founded in 1846 with a bequest, in 1829, of some $550,000 from an Englishman, James Smithson (1765–1829), who had never seen the country to which he left his money. The Smithsonian has since grown to include a number of activities and buildings in Washington and in other locations. The first building was designed by James Renwick, Jr. (1818–95) in Gothic Revival style and was completed in 1849. Another Renwick building, the Old Corcoran Gallery (1859), later used by the Court of Claims, was restored in 1972 and renamed for its architect as the Renwick Gallery. The first Smithsonian building was followed by another Gothic Revival design for the Arts and Industries Building (1880) by Cluss and Schulze.

In later years other buildings were constructed, including the Museum of Natural History (1910) by Hornblower and Marshal, the Freer Gallery (1923) by Charles A. Platt (1861–1933), and the National Gallery of Art (1941) by John Russell Pope (1874–1937). After some years of building inactivity, the Smithsonian constructed the Museum of History and Technology (1964) by McKim, Mead and White, and Steinmann, Cain and White. The newest buildings are the Hirshhorn Museum (1975) by Skidmore, Owings and Merrill and the Air and Space Museum (1975) by George F. Hellmuth (1907–   ), Gyo Obata (1923–   ), and George E. Kassabaum (1920–   ). In 1969 the Old Patent Office (1867), designed by Mills, was restored and converted into the National Portrait Gallery. In 1978 an extension of the National Gallery, designed by Ieoh Ming Pei (1917–   ), was completed.

In addition to the museums and galleries, the Smithsonian directs the activities of the National Zoological Park, founded in 1890, and the John F. Kennedy Center for the Performing Arts (1969), designed by Edward Durell Stone (1902–78).

Other interesting public buildings, owned by governments other than the United States, are the embassies. Many of these are located in what were once fine old homes lining Massachusetts Avenue.

Related Articles PUBLIC BUILDING; Individual architects and firms; Various building type articles.

Further Reading Cox, Warren, J., Hugh Newell Jacobsen, Francis D. Lethbridge, and David R. Rosenthal: *A Guide to the Architecture of Washington, D.C.*, 2d ed., McGraw-Hill, New York, 1972.

CAREER
The lifework of a person who becomes a professional architect or an architectural technician. Simply defined, architecture is the art and science of buildings. And good buildings should be functional, soundly constructed, economical, and esthetic.

Judging by this, careers in architecture might seem quite limited in scope and diversity. Actually, the opposite is the case; those trained in architecture often achieve a level of knowledge, understanding, and proficiency that prepares them for many kinds of careers in architecture and related fields.

Some people, after fulfilling the educational, experience, and examination requirements to become registered or licensed professional architects, start a one-person office. In such an office, the architect must perform all the functions of the profession, many of which, in larger offices, would be performed by specialists, technicians, and professionals in fields related to architecture.

Functions of an Office Thus a young architect starting out, and probably handling only small buildings such as modest one-family houses at first, would have to perform a host of functions. These functions would include management of the office; sales, obtaining commissions for buildings; programming, study or research and preparation of the goals and problems to be solved in buildings; design of buildings; preparation of drawings and renderings or models, indicating how the buildings have been designed; design of the structural, mechanical, and electrical systems; drafting of working drawings from which buildings may be constructed; preparation of specifications, describing the materials, equipment, and workmanship required in the construction; preparation of estimates of the costs of construction; and administration of the construction process, including inspection of the work, to ensure that it is performed properly. And an individual practicing architecture completely alone would have to perform many other related functions.

In architectural schools, students are educated to perform all these functions. However, in the practical world of today, most individuals do not perform all the functions, though they must be conversant with the entire spectrum.

In practice, an individual architect usually employs architectural technicians, trained to perform certain phases of the work, such as drafting, specification writing, and inspection of the work. Professional consulting engineers perform most or all of the structural, mechanical, and electrical design, drafting, specification writing, and construction administration. And specialist professionals are engaged when needed in such fields as acoustics, lighting, and so on. In such an office the individual architect would still perform a large number of functions.

The next step might be a partnership of two architects, who divide the architectural functions. For example, one architect might manage the office, obtain commissions, work with clients, and perform related functions, while the other might handle the programming, design, and direction of the production of construction documents, the working drawings and specifications from which buildings will be constructed. In larger offices, specialization may be greater, with certain people functioning only in management, others in sales, others as designers, others in production, and so on.

As a result of the fact that architectural offices tend to grow into larger ones in which specialization is practiced to some degree, there are career opportunities of many kinds in architectural offices today. There is a place for the talented manager, the talented salesperson, the talented production director, and the talented designer.

Related Fields In addition, many who are educated as architects make their careers, entirely or partly, in related fields, such as city or regional planning, landscape architecture, interior design, furniture design, industrial design, or in teaching, writing, or editorial work.

Some architects eventually start their own offices or become partners or stockholders in architectural firms. Others work for architectural firms, for government agencies on all levels, for associations, for product manufacturers, for magazine or book publishers, in research organizations, in colleges and universities, in construction management firms, and for many other types of organizations.

Thus an architect may work in a small or large firm; practice alone or work for any of a variety of types of enterprises; remain a generalist or become a specialist; work on small buildings, large ones, or all sizes; specialize in one building type or a few types or do all kinds; work on quiet, introspective projects such as in research or gregarious, outgoing ones such as sales, in a professional office, a business, a nonprofit institution, or for a government agency. The possibilities are almost endless and varied.

Many details of other aspects of architectural practice functions and other matters related to careers in the profession of architecture are to be found in other articles in this book, as are those for the related professions of engineering, interior design, landscape architecture, and city planning, or in other occupations, such as building construction. Also included in these articles is information on the educational and other requirements for those who would like to consider careers as technicians in drafting, specification writing, and other functions of architecture and related fields.

Aptitudes and Skills In the past, it was said that a young person considering architecture as a career should have an interest in mathematics, sciences, and art. And the young person should have demonstrated talents in creative pursuits, along with aptitudes and abilities in drawing. All of these are still important today, but taken alone are an oversimplification of the case. Architects today practice in such a variety of ways and in such a large number of specialties that the attempt in past times to educate every student to become a first-rate architectural designer has been outmoded.

In the creation of fine architecture, designers are still very important, but people with other talents are also needed. The aptitudes needed in a designer include creative ability, drawing skill, and the ability to analyze complicated problems that are part engineering, part function, and part esthetics, all to be properly combined in buildings to serve the needs of people. Although such aptitudes are of help to an architect who will manage a large firm, the essential ones are those required in a manager of any business: executive ability; financial acumen; the ability to manage and work with other people; initiative; and a deep sense of responsibility to architecture, the firm, clients, those who work for and with the firm, and the public. Other types of careers in architecture require different aptitudes.

Some maintain that the most important aspect of the decision to go into architecture is a deep interest in the environment and the people in it. A person motivated toward architecture should be an observer of the environment and the buildings in it. Such a person sees things that make deep impressions, positively and negatively. A fine building or a beautiful park evoke a positive reaction. On the other hand, such a person will see things that are very much in need of improvement and will believe that they can be improved. This is the sort of person who is motivated toward architecture.

Another person, such as one who is so motivated by people that the environment in which they exist seems unimportant, might well choose to seek a career in another field than architecture. Although the most successful architects often achieve comfortable incomes, some even relatively high ones, general income levels in architecture are lower than in many other professional occupations. Therefore the prime motivation toward a career in architecture should be the opportunity for achievement, not for wealth.

Education A young person who has decided to go into architecture should take a broad, college preparatory course in secondary school, including sciences, mathematics, social sciences, and humanities. Few secondary schools offer courses in architecture or architectural drawing. Some architecture educators maintain that art and mechanical drawing courses in secondary schools are helpful. Others believe that unless the art courses can be made highly creative, they may do more harm than good. And mechanical drawing courses often teach methods and types of drawing that may be equally harmful.

Architectural curricula in colleges and universities vary somewhat in length and form. The most prevalent today is a five-year program that leads to a bachelor of architecture (B. Arch.) professional degree, but there is a trend toward six-year programs. In other universities only graduate work is offered in architecture, or combined undergraduate-graduate programs. In some of these institutions, a student is expected to take four years of architecture leading to a bachelor of arts (A.B.) or bachelor of science (B.S.) degree in architecture, not professional degrees, then go on to two years of graduate work leading to a B.Arch. or a master's degree (M.Arch.), both professional degrees. In a few universities the first nonprofessional degree may be taken in any discipline and is then followed by three or more years in graduate architectural work. Other schools have been experimenting with variations of these systems. Some students, having obtained B.Arch. degrees, go on to earn M.Arch. degrees, and a few go on to the advanced degree of doctor of philosophy (Ph.D.). A small number engage in post-doctoral studies.

In a five-year architectural school students take courses in mathematics, sciences, social sciences, and humanities, and professional courses in such subjects as art and architectural history, architectural design, structures, mechanical and electrical equipment, and city planning. In graduate architectural school programs offering first professional degrees, only professional courses are taught. Architectural technicians often obtain their education in technical or vocational schools or in two-year prearchitectural schools. For further information on education for architecture, see the article entitled education.

License After obtaining a professional degree in architecture, a graduate must become registered or licensed in one of the states or territories before being called an architect or practicing architecture. To accomplish this, a person with a degree from an accredited school must complete three years of practical experience, called an internship, in an architectural office or in other approved work. Summer work may be counted. The candidate for registration or licensing must be at least twenty-one and must pass a comprehensive professional examination. These professional examinations are given by state and territory registration or licensing boards and consist of five parts: the first four are from 3½ to 5 hours long each, and each contains 100 to 150 multiple-choice questions on environmental analysis, architectural programming, design and technology, and construction; and a fifth part which consists of multiple-choice questions on design and a 10-hour design problem.

For people who have not received professional architectural degrees from accredited architectural schools, graduation from high school or its equivalent, a combination of 12 years of practical experience and architectural education, and the successful completion of an equivalency examination and the professional examination are required. The equivalency examination has three parts: history of architecture, 2 hours; design, including both building design and site planning, 10 hours; and construction theory and practice, 8 hours, covering structures, building construction, mechanical equipment, and professional administration.

A person who successfully passes the professional examination is then registered or licensed to practice architecture and use the title architect in the state which administered the examination. And a person who has applied and qualified for registration or license may obtain certification by the National Council of Architectural Registration Boards (NCARB) attesting to qualification for registration or licensing in other states and territories. Some progress has also been made in a movement to extend reciprocal licensing or registration to foreign countries.

An architectural license or registration must be re-newed each year, or in some states, every two years. This is a personal license or registration issued only to individuals, who may then practice architecture in the states of issuance. These architects may sign working drawings and other construction documents and place their seals on them, certifying that they were prepared by them or under their direction, but they may not sign or place their seals on construction or other documents prepared in any other manner. A movement is under way to require continuing education of registered or licensed architects as a prerequisite for renewal of registration or license and some states have adopted rules to this effect.

Related Articles ARCHITECTURE; BUILDING INDUSTRY; CONSTRUCTION, BUILDING; EDUCATION; ENGINEERING; INTERIOR DESIGN; LANDSCAPE ARCHITECTURE; PLANNING, CITY; Also articles on architectural practice, such as design and drafting.

Further Reading McLaughlin, Robert: *Architect—Creating Man's Environment*, Macmillan, New York, 1962; *NCARB Architectural Registration Handbook—A Test Guide for Professional Examination Candidates*, current edition, McGraw-Hill, New York; Piper, Robert: *Opportunities in Architecture Today*, rev. ed., Vocational Guidance Manuals, Louisville, Ky., 1975.

Sources of Additional Information The American Institute of Architects, Association of Collegiate Schools of Architecture, National Architectural Accrediting Boards, Inc., National Council of Architectural Registration Boards, all at 1735 New York Ave., N.W., Washington, D.C. 20006; American Personnel and Guidance Assoc. 1605 New Hampshire Ave., N.W., Washington, D.C. 20036; National Institute for Architectural Education, 20 W. 40th St., New York, N.Y. 10018.

Periodicals *Journal of Architectural Education*, 1735 New York Ave., N.W., Washington, D.C. 20006; *Vocational Guidance Quarterly*, 1605 New Hampshire Ave., N.W., Washington, D.C. 20036.

CARPENTERS' COMPANY An organization of builders and architects, founded about 1724 by master carpenters and still in existence. The full name of the organization is the Carpenters' Company of the City and County of Philadelphia. The Company is a sort of combination of a medieval guild with a modern labor union and a professional association. It was modeled after the Worshipful Company of Carpenters, London, under whose rules many of the Philadelphia carpenters had served their apprenticeships.

Company Controls For a long time after its founding, the Company dominated building, construction, and architecture too, for its members were master builders, or builder-architects, who both designed and constructed structures. Controls over construction were exercised in various ways. The Company strictly limited the number of its members and the members controlled the selection of those allowed to join. Starting with 10 to 15 members, the Company had grown to a membership of about 60 by the middle of the 18th century. It was the custom at this time for sons of deceased members to join without paying entrance fees. Thus membership became something of a family affair.

Members of the Company were close to govern-

CARPENTERS' COMPANY Carpenters' Hall (1773), Philadelphia, Pa. [*Architect: Robert Smith. (Detroit Photographic Co., Library of Congress)*]

CARPENTERS' COMPANY Independence Hall (1755), Philadelphia, Pa. [*Architect: Edmund Woolley. (Library of Congress)*]

ment officials in the city and, through their influence, obtained preferential treatment when construction projects were contemplated. Company members were the chief employers of other construction craftsmen and laborers. In addition, the Company obtained a considerable amount of control of the pricing of construction and maintained secret price books. One of these books, first published in 1786, was republished in 1971. However, the Company never did gain real control of the building industry.

A rival organization, the Friendship Carpenters' Company of Philadelphia, was founded in 1769. For some years the two companies competed, while making some halfhearted attempts to cooperate with each other. In 1785 the newer organization was merged into the older. The Carpenters' Company provided education for and assistance to its members. Although it never had an organized apprenticeship system, its individual members trained new craftsmen. And when the Library Company was formed in 1732, some of its new members who were also Carpenters' Company members saw to it that the first books purchased were concerned with architecture.

Accomplishments The greatest accomplishments of the Carpenters' Company are to be found in the buildings its members designed and constructed in late-18th-century Philadelphia. The earliest builder-architect was James Portues, sometimes spelled Porteus (c. 1660–1737). He designed and built a number of houses in and around the city, most of which were later demolished. A masterpiece, believed to have been built from his design, is Christ Church (1774) which still stands. Two other Company members, John Harrison, Jr. (d. 1760) and Robert Smith (1722–77), added a steeple in 1754. Smith, a most successful member of the Carpenters' Company, designed and built a number of notable buildings in Philadelphia, among them several houses and a dormitory (1763) at Philadelphia College, now the University of Pennsylvania, and the Walnut Street Prison (1776), both demolished. He also designed Nassau Hall (1756) at Princeton University and University Hall (1771) at Brown University, then called Rhode Island College, in Providence, both still standing, and the Mad House (1769) at Williamsburg, Va., since demolished. One of Smith's most distinguished buildings is Carpenters' Hall (1773), which he designed for the Company. This building was used for the meetings of the First Continental Congress in 1774.

The crowning achievement of the great era of the Carpenters' Company is Independence Hall (1775), formerly the State House of the Province of Pennsylvania. Here were held the Second Continental Congress, starting in 1775, and the Constitutional Convention, starting in 1787. And in this building, the Declaration of Independence was debated and signed and the Constitution drafted, debated, and signed. The designer of Independence Hall was a Carpenters' Company member, Edmund Woolley (1696–1771), about whom almost nothing else is known.

By the end of the 18th century, the grand era of the Carpenters' Company was drawing to a close. Architects not members of the Company, and even from places other than Philadelphia, were now called upon to design many Philadelphia buildings. Nevertheless, the Carpenters' Company has carried on to this day.

Related Articles BUILDING INDUSTRY; COLONIAL ARCHITECTURE; GEORGIAN ARCHITECTURE.

Further Reading Peterson, Charles E., ed.: *Building Early America—Contributions Toward the History of a Great Industry*, Chilton, Radnor, Pa., 1976; Peterson, Charles E., ed.: *The Carpenters' Company of the City and County of Philadelphia 1786 Rule Book*, Bell, a division of Crown, New York, 1971.

CEILING The overhead interior surface of a building or room. In times past, ceilings were often highly ornamented, important determinants of architectural design. Today, except for those ceilings in which the roof structure is exposed or expressed, ceilings are usually designed to be as plain, simple, and unobtrusive as possible.

Types Other than those with exposed roof structures, ceilings are usually one of two types: ceilings fastened to the undersides of roof structures; or suspended or hung from the structures. In buildings today, though ceilings are not as important design elements as in the past, they are of more importance functionally since they are often acoustically treated; have thermal insulation above them, particularly in flat-roofed buildings; and often house air-conditioning and heating diffusers, ductwork, electrical wiring, and light fixtures. In a suspended ceiling system, all such devices and systems may be easily installed below the structure and then may be concealed above the ceiling, if required. Suspended ceilings are often made so that there is easy access to the space over them for repairs, maintenance, and modifications. In ceilings attached directly to the underside of structures, ducts must be run alongside beams or joists or through them.

Finishes Today finishes for ceilings, suspended or not, are usually plaster, gypsum board, acoustical tiles, or other materials, and sometimes wood. Ceilings are generally painted; wallpapered; stained, in the case of wood; or furnished with factory-applied coatings or primers, as in the case of acoustical tile.

Suspended ceilings can be obtained in a number of types of integrated systems, utilizing metal channels, hangers and runners to support acoustical tiles, lighting fixtures, and heating and air-conditioning diffusers. These are complete systems in which acoustical tiles of various kinds may be clipped or otherwise attached. Insulation and vapor barriers may be supported above them if required. Acoustical tiles of various materials are available, either made with quite porous textures or with holes in them. They include tiles made from wood; mineral or glass fibers, either plain or perforated; and perforated metal or asbestos-cement tile, above which is placed the acoustical material. Acoustical ceilings made of mineral fibers and

binders or other materials may also be sprayed on or applied with trowels like plaster.

Many ceilings are finished with plaster, often called the wet system, troweled onto metal or gypsum lath. Plaster may be applied in two coats: the scratch coat and the brown coat. Three-coated plaster is recommended, and required over metal lath. In addition to the other coats, it has a third or finish coat. Scratch and brown coats are usually composed of portland cement, lime, and sand mixed with water. Finish-coat plaster is often composed of a special cement (Keene's), lime, and water. Acoustical materials may be substituted for the sand in plaster.

In dry systems, boards of gypsum with surfaces of paper are often used. They are ordinarily nailed in place and are available with depressed edges that allow for taping and filling with special cements to conceal joints. Other dry systems include paneling of plywood or sometimes solid wood, asbestos-cement board, and boards made from various wood and other vegetable fibers.

Lighting Fixtures are available in sizes to fit properly into suspended ceiling systems. Some ceilings, often called luminous ceilings, are designed to appear as single lighting sources covering large portions of or entire ceilings of rooms. Of metal or plastic, luminous ceilings may have small louvers, sometimes called egg crates, through which light enters rooms, or plastic sheets, often corrugated, for this purpose. Both types are hung in suspended ceiling systems and the actual light fixtures placed above them. In some cases the spaces above ceilings are divided in such a way that they act as ducts for warm-air heating, with the ceilings acting as radiant panels. In other types, copper tubing, through which hot water flows, or electrical cables are embedded in the ceilings for the same purpose. Ceilings have been developed in which all of the aspects of heating and cooling, lighting, acoustics, and so on are integrated. Ceiling materials and construction are governed by applicable building and other codes, particularly where they are used for fire protection of structures.

History The first ceilings in buildings constructed in ancient times were the undersides of animal skins, brush, or thatch used to cover primitive huts or tents. Such ceilings, if so they can be called, exposed both structures, the limbs of trees or poles and the undersides of roofs. Thus began a tradition that lasted thousands of years until about the beginning of the Renaissance.

By about 3000 B.C. in the civilizations around the Mediterranean Sea, ceilings were often treated as major architectural elements and highly ornamented. Coffered ceilings, with deeply recessed panels and often highly ornamented, were introduced at this time. Both exposed ceilings and coffering became traditions that have lasted until today. The early Persians used exposed roof structures with beams and brackets and with planks, all highly ornamented, while the Mesopotamians often used vaults. The ancient

Greeks also utilized coffered ceilings of wood, with the roof structures exposed. They often painted the ceilings in several colors. They also constructed roofs and ceilings of stone, often coffering them to resemble wood construction; sometimes they used no ceiling at all, only the undersides of sloping roofs.

For the most important buildings, the Egyptians used stone in roof structures, often coffered below and painted in various colors. The Romans also used coffered ceilings, sometimes of stone, carved with patterns, and at others of stucco, modeled with patterns of foliage and other forms and sometimes also ornamented with paint. In Byzantine architecture, the undersides of domes were often entirely covered with mosaics.

In Gothic architecture, ceilings were usually the undersides of vaults, often unornamented except for the forms of the ribs where vaults intersected, or exposed wood structures, especially in England, that often were highly ornamented with carvings. During the Renaissance, ceilings were generally constructed under roof structures, completely concealing the structures from view. Ceilings were generally flat or vaulted and almost always highly ornamented in the more important buildings. During this period, coved ceilings, those that have decorative elements at the line of junction of ceilings with walls, were also used. Often curved or angular, the coves were usually highly ornamented. Coffered ceilings were also used. Many ceilings of the era were elaborately ornamented with wood carvings, plaster forms, gilding, or murals. After the Renaissance, in the Baroque period of architecture, ceilings were given a profusion of paintings and carved and molded forms in plaster and other materials, completely hiding the structural and functional aspects. This was the ultimate stage of a philosophy of design that had started during the Renaissance.

By the 18th century, the design of ceilings had begun to move away from the elaborate and sometimes unrestrained ornament of Renaissance and Baroque architecture. Instead, refined, often delicate forms, derived from Classical architecture, came into use in the United States as well as in Europe.

American Development In the earliest colonial times, ceilings in America had been quite plain and utilitarian for the most part. By the beginning of the 18th century, they followed the models in use in Europe. During the Classic and Gothic Revival periods of architecture, ceilings in America were usually derived from those of these past periods. In the Eclectic period, ceilings were derived from those of any of the past periods upon which the styles of individual buildings were based. There was also a return to highly ornamented ceilings.

With the beginning of the modern movement in architecture in the 19th century, ceiling design went in two widely varied directions: one toward completely plain, unornamented flat ceilings, and the other toward the exploitation of structure by exposing it in the interiors of buildings. Both trends continue today, simple flat ceilings being used in most of the usual types of skeleton-framed buildings and in houses, and exposed structural systems in the ceilings of buildings with advanced structural systems, such as space frames and folded plates.

Related Articles ART IN ARCHITECTURE; CONCRETE STRUCTURE; FIRE PROTECTION; HEATING, VENTILATING, AND AIR CONDITIONING; LIGHTING; MASONRY STRUCTURE; ORNAMENT; ROOF; SOUND CONTROL; STEEL STRUCTURE; WOOD-FRAME STRUCTURE.

CLASSIC REVIVAL ARCHITECTURE

A movement, or style, in architecture that used forms derived from the architecture of the classic periods in Greece and Rome. Sometimes called the neoclassic style, the movement began in the United States toward the end of the American Revolution, when architects turned away from the Georgian style architecture of England. In its place, they espoused an architecture they considered more appropriate for a new republic and turned to the Greeks and Romans for inspiration. Although not all architectural scholars would agree, Classic Revival architecture may be divided into three main trends: the Federal style, the Roman Revival style, and the Greek Revival style.

The Federal Style This style, which began about the time of the Revolution and lasted into the 19th century, was not radically different from Georgian architecture (see the article entitled Georgian architecture). Some maintain that the Federal style was actually a continuation of the Georgian, varying only in relatively small details and in the scale of buildings. The Federal style, conservative as it was, produced some notable architecture, in particular that of Charles Bulfinch (1763–1844) and Samuel McIntire (1757–1811).

The Roman Revival Style On the other hand, the Roman Revival style, though it retained some vestiges of the Georgian, was an attempt to create a monumental American architecture that would reflect the grandeur of the concept of the new republic. While the Federal style was conservative and traditional, the new Roman Revival style was individualistic. Sometimes called the idealistic phase of the Classic Revival movement, the Roman phase is considered to have begun with the Virginia State Capitol (1791), Richmond, designed by Thomas Jefferson (1743–1826), and derived from the Roman Maison Carrée (c. 16 B.C.), Nîmes, France. Roman Revival architecture is thought to have reached its peak about 1820, but continued to be an important style until the beginning of the Civil War.

Typical of Roman Revival architecture were such forms as columns, or orders; large imposing porticoes; gable roofs, with great pediments; and domes. All of Jefferson's greatest buildings are in the Roman style, notably the Rotunda, derived from the Pantheon (A.D. 124), Rome, Italy, and the other buildings at the University of Virginia, Charlottesville. In his

CLASSIC REVIVAL ARCHITECTURE Gore Place (1804), Waltham, Mass. [*Architect: unknown. (Wayne Andrews)*]

CLASSIC REVIVAL ARCHITECTURE City Hall (1811), New York, N.Y. [*Architects: Mangin and McComb. (Wayne Andrews)*]

own great house, Monticello, in Charlottesville, Jefferson provided a masterful example of the change from the Georgian to the Roman Revival style. Construction, tearing down, and rebuilding of this house continued from about 1770 to almost the end of his life. By 1775 the house was virtually completed in the Georgian style, but Jefferson soon started to remodel and rebuild it in the Roman Revival style, essentially completing this work in 1808. The Monticello of today, in Roman style, is quite different from the first version. (See color section for illustrations of the Rotunda and Monticello.)

The Roman Revival style was used for a great number of important buildings. Considered by many the greatest of these is the U.S. Capitol Building, upon which construction began in 1793. Other notable buildings in this style include the White House, begun in 1792 and designed by James Hoban (c. 1762–1821), and the Cathedral of the Assumption (1818), Baltimore, designed by Benjamin Henry Latrobe (1764–1820). The style was also used for many great houses in various parts of America, sometimes in various combinations with the Greek Revival style. (See color section for illustration of U.S. Capitol Building.)

The Greek Revival Style This style, occasionally called the national phase of Classic Revival architecture, is thought to have begun in the United States with the Bank of Pennsylvania (1801), Philadelphia, designed by Latrobe. Although the architect used the Greek Ionic order and other Greek details, the essential character of this building, with vaults and a dome, was Roman. Other later Greek Revival buildings, and there were many of them, including houses and commercial, public, and other types all over the United States, were more purely Greek in derivation. Greek Revival became more firmly established in American architecture than did the Roman, and persisted until the Civil War and afterward to an extent, even into the present century.

Two of the earliest proponents of the style were

both former employees of Latrobe, Robert Mills (1781–1855) and William Strickland (1787–1854). Strickland designed what many believe to be the first purely Greek Revival building in America, the Second Bank of the United States (1824), Philadelphia, and went on to design many others. Mills also became firmly committed to the style and designed numerous Greek Revival buildings, including the Treasury Building (1842), Washington.

As time went by, the Greek Revival style became predominant, though Roman forms and details were sometimes combined with it. Most of the greatest architects of the first half of the 19th century designed buildings in this style, including John Haviland (1792–1852), Thomas Ustick Walter (1804–87), Isaiah Rogers (1800–69), Ammi B. Young (1798–1874), Gideon Shryock (1802–80), and James Gallier, Sr. (1798–1868). Some of these and other architects of the time were dedicated to the Greek Revival style, while others sometimes worked in other styles.

Greek Revival architecture soon became familiar to most educated people in the United States and was as greatly admired as were the principles of Greek democracy. This was the first style to become almost completely acceptable in all parts of the country for buildings of every kind. Buildings designed like Greek temples, with classic orders, porticoes, and pediments, were constructed everywhere. Books of details were published showing the orders and other parts of the style, and these became familiar to the carpenters as well as the architects of the time.

By the beginning of the Civil War, the style had been completely accepted by most architects and their clients. Not only were standard details available but standard columns and other elements were being manufactured. About 1840, some architects turned away from the Classic Revival toward other styles; see, for example, articles entitled eclectic architecture; Gothic revival. After the Civil War, Classic Revival buildings continued to be designed, even into the 20th century, but the style never again had the

CLASSIC REVIVAL ARCHITECTURE Capitol (1833), Raleigh, N.C. [*Architects: Town, Davis and Paton. (Wayne Andrews)*]

CLASSIC REVIVAL ARCHITECTURE Oak Alley Plantation (1836), Vacherie, La. [*Architect: unknown. (Wayne Andrews)*]

CLASSIC REVIVAL ARCHITECTURE Elias Brown House (1835), Old Mystic, Conn. [*Architect: unknown. (Wayne Andrews)*]

CLASSIC REVIVAL ARCHITECTURE Federal Hall National Memorial (1842), formerly Subtreasury Building and Customs House, New York, N.Y. [*Architects: Town and Davis. (Joseph W. Molitor)*]

force and vitality it had once had, particularly from about 1820 to 1860.

A very large number of Classic Revival buildings are still in existence all over the United States. A complete listing would be a very long one indeed. In addition to those mentioned above, others are discussed in articles on various architects of the period and in other articles in this book.

Principles of Classicism The Classic Revival period in architecture was one of deep beliefs in the principles of classicism: in reason, ideals, and analysis; in what were considered to be universal truths; and in the good and the beautiful, meaning that which was clear, symmetrical, reposeful, and derived from traditional classical forms. With the beginning of Gothic Revival architecture, architects and others turned away from classical principles to those of romanticism, in many ways the antithesis of the classical ideals. This led first to the Gothic Revival style and then to the many others that are spoken of collectively as the Eclectic architecture of the second half of the 19th

and the early part of the 20th centuries.

Related Articles COLUMN; ECLECTIC ARCHITECTURE; GEORGIAN ARCHITECTURE; HISTORY OF ARCHITECTURE; JEFFERSON, THOMAS; LATROBE, BENJAMIN HENRY; PRESERVATION; Various articles on other classic revival architects.

Further Reading Hamlin, Talbot: *Greek Revival Architecture in America,* Oxford University Press, London, 1944; See also listings in articles entitled colonial architecture, Georgian architecture, and history of architecture.

Sources of Additional Information See listing in the article entitled history of architecture.

CLIMATE Over a period of many years, the weather conditions that exist in an area, such as a continent, a country, a city, a building site, or even a portion of a site. The climate in which a building will be placed is one of the major considerations in architecture. Climatology is the science of climate and its relation to animal and plant life. Climate is concerned with long-term conditions; and weather, with short-term conditions. Both climate and weather are concerned with five major conditions: temperature, wind, sun, humidity, and precipitation in the form of rain, sleet, snow, and hail.

Determinants and Zones The major determinant of climate is the distance of an area from the equator, or its latitude. Other important determinants include an area's altitude, terrain or topography, prevailing winds, and proximity of water bodies, particularly oceans. Climates are often classified into five major zones, based on the relation of the climate to the vegetation in the area. The zones are rainy tropical, dry or desert, warm-temperate, cool-snow-forest, and polar. Climates may also be classified into nine zones: rainy tropical; alternately wet and dry tropical; semi-arid; desert; warm rainy; dry summer, rainy winter; cold moist; polar; and ice cap. Often zones are spoken of in other terms, such as the equatorial zones or doldrums, which have high temperatures and heavy rainfall; subtropical; or the horse latitudes, usually taken to be in the neighborhood of 30° latitude, north or south. Another zone which has a dry, mild climate is sometimes said to have a Mediterranean type of climate and is found on the west coasts of continents, north of the subtropical zone. It is characterized by mild temperatures, with moderate rain in winter and dry summers.

U.S. Zones In architecture, all climate zones are important. The United States has almost all zones, the major ones being warm, rainy in the Southeastern states; cold moist in the Northern states and much of Alaska; semiarid in the Western states; warm with dry summers and rainy winters on much of the West Coast; and desert in the Southwestern states. In addition, the Pacific Northwest and the coastal lands of Alaska have warm, rainy climates; northern Alaska's climate is polar in nature; and Hawaii has a mild, rainy climate, with little seasonal change in temperature. American architects design buildings to be constructed in all these areas. And many of them design buildings to be constructed in foreign countries where other zones, such as rainy tropical, are to be found.

Effects on Architecture The determinants of climate, latitude, altitude, terrain, prevailing winds, and water bodies deeply affect architecture. The latitude of a building site affects the path of the sun from sunrise to sunset, the height to which it will rise at noon, and the length of days. These factors in turn determine the heating effect of the sun and the hours of daylight. For example, in the north middle latitudes between the tropical and polar zones, the sun usually rises toward the southeast, reaches its highest point in the southern sky at noon, and sets toward the southwest. On the day of the summer solstice, about June 21, the sun rises at the point farthest north of east that it will have all year, progresses to its highest point of the year in the southern sky, and sets at the point farthest north of west of the year. This is also the longest day of the year, the daylight hours exceeding those of the night. After the summer solstice, the sun

rises farther to the south, reaches a lower point in the sky at noon, and sets farther to the south with each succeeding day until the winter solstice, about December 21, is reached. On that day, the sun rises at its most southeasterly position, progresses to its lowest point in the southern sky at noon, and sets in its most southwesterly position of the year. This is the shortest day of the year, with the nighttime hours exceeding those of the day. After the winter solstice, the process repeats itself, in reverse, the sun rising more toward the northeast each day, climbing higher in the sky, and setting more toward the northwest until the summer solstice is again reached. On two days of the year, the vernal equinox, about March 21, and the autumnal equinox, about September 21, the sun rises in the due east and sets in the due west, providing days and nights of equal length.

While the latitude of an area is the most important determinant of climate, altitude, or elevation above sea level, is also important, since temperatures are usually colder at higher than at lower altitudes. Also lower barometric pressures at higher elevations have some effect, and rainfall tends to increase with increases in altitude up to about 6,000 feet above sea level and then to decrease above that level.

Terrain has considerable effect on climate. Some surfaces, such as sand, rock, and pavement, absorb more heat than do water, forests, and meadows. Thus sand, rock, and pavement give off more heat to the lower atmosphere than do water, forests, or meadows. Mountains or hills generally receive more rainfall than flat areas, since moist air carried past the highest terrain feature is forced to rise, becomes cooler, and cannot hold as much moisture as warm air.

Mountains block winds and valleys channel them, thus affecting the flow of cool or warm air toward various areas. These and other conditions determine prevailing winds, the normal direction of wind flow, in various areas. Water bodies also have a considerable effect on climate. The larger the body of water, the greater will be its effect. Water bodies do not become as cold in winter as the land adjacent to them, or as warm in summer. Water bodies therefore have a moderating effect on the land areas near them, producing milder climates in coastal areas than in those farther inland. On the west coasts of continents, where prevailing winds are usually from the west, climates are usually mild. They are often rainy because the winds bring moisture from the ocean. West coastal mountain areas are often very rainy since the winds bring considerable moisture which is forced to fall when the winds rise to pass over the mountains.

Most of the foregoing discussion is particularly directed to the climates of relatively large areas, which are often called macroclimates. But the same conditions also affect smaller climates, often called microclimates, as might exist on a specific building site, or even in one area of the site, such as a sunny patio or a shaded backyard. Architecture is affected by both macroclimates and microclimates. In addition to the conditions already discussed, microclimates are affected by such conditions as relatively small terrain features: rocks, banks, surrounding buildings or other structures, and trees and other vegetation.

Building Types Climate affects architecture in a number of ways. Since it affects animal and vegetable life, it affects the lives of human beings and the living things with which they surround themselves. One of the most important social questions related to architecture is concerned with differences in the way people live and act in different climates and methods by which architecture can serve their varied needs. Meeting such needs requires considerable variation in the types of buildings constructed in various regions. Thus at the risk of oversimplification, building forms throughout history have tended to vary in design according to the climates in which they were built, becoming closed-in insulated structures, with few small openings and pitched roofs in cold areas; structures with heavy walls, small openings, and flat roofs in hot, arid zones; open structures with pitched roofs in hot, humid areas; and so on. Climate continues to affect the form of buildings today as it did in the past. Architects must study climatic effects on their designs to produce solutions that properly meet the requirements of various climates. Climate also affects other architectural considerations in buildings, such as plans, which, for example, can be more open in temperate than in colder climates.

Weather Controls Climate also deeply affects architecture in another way: the control of its effects on buildings. Such controls fall into three major categories: provision of more desirable climates within buildings, portions of them, and on their sites; protection of buildings and their occupants from extreme climatic or weather conditions, such as hurricanes and floods; and production of energy for use in buildings from climatic phenomena, such as solar radiation and the force of winds. For further discussion on protection from climatic conditions, see the article entitled weather protection; and on production of energy, the article entitled energy.

Control of climates within buildings may be classified into two major types: those of an engineering nature and those of an architectural nature. Engineering controls include mechanical and electrical systems employed to create artificial climatic conditions within buildings. This subject is discussed in the article entitled heating, ventilating, and air conditioning.

Perhaps the most important architectural control is building orientation, the placement on a site to take advantage of desirable climatic conditions, such as the heat of the sun in winter and prevailing winds in summer, and to minimize undesirable effects of the sun in summer and cold winds in winter. Proper orientation also may reduce the amount of heating and air conditioning required and have other desirable effects, such as improvement of the quality of lighting in buildings. Some architects maintain that the walls of buildings should be considered as filters. In this view, walls, together with their openings and other devices, act to allow wind, heat, light, and so on to enter buildings when needed or to be excluded when they are not. Such a filter may also modify entry, such as in heat-absorbing glass which allows light to enter or louvers which permit wind to enter but direct its flow.

Other important architectural controls include materials and systems. Horizontal and vertical sunshades can aid in controlling the entry of sun into buildings, allowing it to come in during winter and excluding it during summer. Trees and other vegetation may also be used for the same purpose, and in addition may serve to channel winds in desirable directions or act as windbreaks. Garden walls or other structures may serve the same functions. Insulation retains heat inside in winter and blocks it from entry in summer. Double glazing of windows, or storm windows and doors, serves a similar purpose while also minimizing entry of drafts.

In addition, the major building materials used have a considerable impact on the control of climate in buildings. Heavy masonry walls tend to block the entry of heat more than thin metal or wood-framed walls. On the other hand, masonry walls also retain the heat they absorb longer than the other types, radiating it back after the air cools.

From the foregoing discussion, it may be seen that the proper handling of climatic considerations in architecture involves a number of factors and complications. Proper handling must begin with the programming phase, in which accurate information, both macroclimatic and microclimatic, is gathered and analyzed, and continue during the design phases. If the right decisions are made in these first phases, it will be easier to make decisions during the preparation of working drawings and specifications.

Data-gathering Techniques A number of techniques have been derived for study of the effects of climate on buildings and their occupants, and a considerable amount of data is available. After obtaining accurate data on a specific site for a building, architects and other design professionals use a number of tools for their analysis and for proper climatic design of buildings and other structures. Charts and tables of climatic data are available, including sun charts and tables that contain information on the timing and paths of the sun relative to the earth for various latitudes and times of the year.

Calculators and other devices may be used for this and other purposes. Formulas also have been derived for calculations of such information. Thus a choice of methods is available to an individual user. Some experts believe that calculations of this sort should be worked out with formulas, while charts, tables, and other devices serve only for quick approximations and for checking the results derived from the calculations. Some experts recommend the use of models for checking the effects of the sun and wind.

History Although weather changes take place on a regular basis, sometimes very rapidly, changes in climate occur very slowly. It is thought that climate has changed very little during the period of recorded history. Before that, great changes took place during what is called the Pleistocene Epoch, sometimes called the Ice Age, when sheets of ice, or glaciers, moved down from the polar regions into the areas south of them.

Beginning about 2 million years ago, there have been four major periods of the Ice Age. Each lasted many thousands of years and was separated from the next by a warmer period in which the ice melted. In North America the Ice Ages, or glaciation periods, from the oldest to the latest, are the Nebraskan, Kansan, Illinoisan, and Wisconsin. The warmer periods between, the interglacial periods, from first to latest, are Aftonian, Yarmouth, and Sangamon. The first Ice Age in North America, the Nebraskan, started about 600,000 years ago and lasted about 64,000 years. The Aftonian interglacial period started about 536,000 years ago and lasted 60,000 years. The latest North American period of glaciation, the Wisconsin, began about 115,000 years ago and ended more than 10,000 years ago.

Since the end of the Wisconsin glaciation period, no great climatic changes have occurred. However, there have been periods, lasting from 35 to 100 years, when general warming or cooling trends have been recorded. Some scientists believe that these climatic cycles occur on a regular basis. In any case, from about the middle of the 19th to the middle of the 20th centuries, somewhat higher temperatures have been observed, particularly in the middle and higher latitudes of the Northern Hemisphere. Since the middle of the 20th century, the trend has been toward lower temperatures. However, some scientists see a trend toward warmer, more humid weather for the remainder of the century.

Related Articles DESIGN, ARCHITECTURAL; ELECTRICAL ENGINEERING; ENERGY; HEATING, VENTILATING, AND AIR CONDITIONING; INSULATION, THERMAL; LIGHTNING PROTECTION; MECHANICAL ENGINEERING; PROGRAMMING; WATERPROOFING; WEATHER PROTECTION.

Further Reading Aronin, Jeffrey E.: *Climate and Architecture*, Reinhold, New York, 1953; Fry, Edwin Maxwell, and Jane Drew: *Tropical Architecture in the Dry and Humid Zones*, Batsford, London, 1964; Olgyay, Aladar, and Victor Olgyay: *Solar Control and Shading Devices*, Princeton University Press, Princeton, N.J., 1957; Olgyay, Victor: *Design with Climate —Bioclimatic Approach to Architectural Regionalism*, Princeton University Press, Princeton, N.J., 1963; Oliver, John E.: *Climate and Man's Environment —An Introduction to Applied Climatology*, John Wiley, New York, 1973.

Source of Additional Information U.S. Department of Commerce, National Weather Service, National Oceanic and Atmospheric Administration, 6010 Executive Blvd., Rockville, Md. 20852.

COLLEGE AND UNIVERSITY BUILDING A building in an institution for higher learning and research,

located on a campus. A college is an institution dedicated to only one branch of knowledge, such as a liberal arts or medical college. A university is an institution dedicated to many branches of knowledge. These individual branches within a university are also referred to as colleges. Special types are junior colleges which ordinarily offer only freshman and sophomore courses, and community colleges which offer courses to students who usually live at home and commute to the colleges. There are also undergraduate, graduate, and professional colleges.

Campus Size Many colleges in the past were small and had all their facilities in one or a few buildings. Today some universities have student bodies numbering in the tens of thousands and have campuses that provide all the facilities of a small city, in addition to classroom and other educational buildings. Some universities have branches located in various parts of their states, thereby bringing higher education to students in the various localities, allowing for some specialization among the branches, and avoiding the problems of one campus becoming too large for proper education. In spite of this, some campuses have more than 50,000 students. In comparison, many of the smallest colleges have less than 100 students. In the past, there were colleges for men and women, but the current trend is toward coeducational colleges.

Operation Colleges and universities are operated by private or governmental groups. Private colleges and universities are sometimes sponsored by religious groups, sometimes by other groups, often with the help of endowments, money given by philanthropists. Government-sponsored colleges and universities include state universities; community colleges, sponsored by state or local governments; and those sponsored by the federal government, such as the armed services academies. Governing the affairs of most colleges and universities are boards of trustees or regents, elected or appointed by the sponsors.

Organization A college or university is organized with an administration, a faculty, a student body, and a maintenance group. The administration ordinarily consists of a president or chancellor, along with other executives who have duties as deans, controllers, and so on. The faculty consists of the professors of various ranks and instructors, organized into a department, such as biology or mathematics, with a chairman of each department. In a university, each college usually has a dean, who is its administrative head. Members of the student body enroll and take courses in the individual colleges. Maintenance includes grounds keeping, janitorial services, repair shops, and the like.

Campus Buildings Although all the buildings on a college or university campus are involved in the education of students in some way, the elements may be divided into those that are primarily educational, such as classroom buildings; residential, such as dormitories; administrative, such as offices; athletic, such as gymnasiums; and miscellaneous, such as cafeterias. In addition to regular classroom buildings, many

COLLEGE AND UNIVERSITY Foothill College (1962), Los Altos Hills, Calif. [*Architect: Ernest J. Kump, in association with Masten and Hurd. Landscape architects: Sasaki and Walker. (Morley Baer)*]

other types of educational facilities may be provided, including laboratory and research buildings, theaters, auditoriums, and computer centers. Some of these buildings may also be used for administrative, recreational, or other purposes.

Residential facilities include dormitories, which usually have been restricted to men or women but today also include coed buildings, in which each sex occupies a separate wing or an alternate floor. Although some dormitories have single rooms, most have double rooms for two students. Three-student rooms have been used, but were not successful. In some cases, two or more rooms are organized into suites, often with shared baths. In other cases, baths for a relatively large number of people, or gang baths, are provided. This is not considered to be the best planning solution but may be dictated by economy. Dormitories often have communal areas used by some or all of the occupants, including lounges, libraries, mailroom, dining or vending facilities, laundry rooms, and date rooms. On some campuses, apartments are provided for married students, and facilities are available for mobile homes and trailers. Fraternity and sorority houses often have dormitory rooms in addition to other facilities for members.

Administrative facilities in colleges and universities often include separate buildings for the office of the president and other officials as well as offices in the educational buildings for the college deans and others. Also provided are shops for repair and maintenance work, and often a communications center.

Athletic buildings provide for several types of ac-

tivity: physical education, intramural sports and games, intercollegiate sports, and recreation. Outdoor areas are also required, including such facilities as stadiums, practice fields, tennis courts, golf courses, swimming pools, and playing fields. Some of the buildings are gymnasiums for physical education and sports; field houses for dances, assemblies, and other events as well as athletics; and specialized buildings for indoor swimming, handball, and so on.

Important miscellaneous buildings are the cafeterias and other dining facilities for students, faculty, and administrators. Also of great importance is the library, without which a college or university cannot operate properly. Other buildings often provided are chapels, observatories, and student unions. In fact, buildings of almost every type may be found on campuses, for example, hospitals in medical schools, farm buildings in agricultural schools, churches in theological schools, and so on.

There are more than 2,200 colleges and universities in the United States with student bodies of 200 or larger. Of these, about 100 have colleges of architecture. The construction of new colleges and universities accelerated after World War II, but has now declined. However, the remodeling and replacement of older buildings and the construction of new buildings on existing campuses make this an important building type. And design of a college or university campus, or a building on a campus, is one of the most interesting and gratifying commissions to an architect.

History Early colleges came into existence first in Italy, including one founded at Salerno in the ninth

COLLEGE AND UNIVERSITY Exterior, Southeastern Missouri State College (1975), Cape Girardeau, Mo. [*Architects: Pearce Corp. (Hedrich-Blessing)*]

COLLEGE AND UNIVERSITY Interior, Southeastern Missouri State College (1975), Cape Girardeau, Mo. [*Architects: Pearce Corp. (Hedrich-Blessing)*]

century that specialized in medicine and one founded at Bologna in the twelfth that specialized in law. The first universities included these two, a few hundred years later, and also the University of Paris and the Universities of Oxford and Cambridge in England, all founded in the 12th or early 13th century. The first in America was the University of Santo Domingo, founded in 1538, in what is now the Dominican Republic; and it was followed by the universities of Mexico, Mexico City, and San Marcos, Lima, Peru, both founded in 1551.

American Colonial Universities The first university in the English colonies in America was planned to be built near Richmond, Va., in 1619, but the project was abandoned. The first actually built was Harvard College, now University, in Cambridge, Mass., in 1636, followed by the College of William and Mary, Williamsburg, Va., in 1693. Other early American universities were Saint John's (1696), Annapolis, Md.; Yale (1701), New Haven, Conn.; Princeton (1746), Princeton, N.J.; Columbia (1754), New York City; and Pennsylvania (founded as a charity school, in 1740), Philadelphia.

Since the founding of Harvard, a very large number of architects, including some of the greatest, have designed campuses and their buildings. The earliest American college building still in existence is the so-called Wren building (1695) at William and Mary, its design traditionally attributed to the great English architect, Sir Christopher Wren (1632–1723).

Further Reading *Architectural Record: Campus Planning and Design,* McGraw-Hill, New York, 1972.

Source of Additional Information American Association for Higher Education; Association of State Colleges and Universities; Association of American Universities; American Association of Community and Junior Colleges, all at 1 Dupont Circle, N.W., Washington, D.C. 20036.

COLONIAL ARCHITECTURE
The architecture of the colonists in America, beginning with the rude structures of the earliest settlers and continuing to the time of the American Revolution. Although architecture of this period is sometimes spoken of as the Colonial style, the phrase is a misnomer. There was no such single style, but a number of different styles, varying considerably between the English, Dutch, Spanish, French, and other colonists, at various periods of time and between the various geographical regions.

Early Colonization The time of the founding of the earliest colonies that eventually became the United States is often taken to mark the beginning of the colonization of America. Actually, of course, the process began much earlier, with the colonization of Greenland by the Norseman Eric the Red, about 985. The mainland is believed to have been discovered by Leif Ericson, son of Eric, about the year 1000, and colonized a short time later. Leif Ericson named the land he found Vinland, variously held to have been Newfoundland, Labrador, or New England. The Greenland colony lasted several hundred years and then died out

and that in Vinland only a few years. Theories have been advanced, but remain unproven, that Irish adventurers, and possibly others, reached North America about the same time or earlier.

The first colony in America after the time of the Norse efforts was established by Columbus, during his voyage in 1492, on the island of Española, now the Dominican Republic. The colony had disappeared when he returned the following year. He established another colony in 1493, near where the first one had been. In 1486 this colony was moved to Santo Domingo, and became the first permanent colony in America. Other colonies, in various locations in the Carribean and in Central and South America, soon followed. The earliest colony directly related in any way to the future United States, San Juan, Puerto Rico, was founded in 1521.

U.S. Settlements The first permanent settlement in what became mainland United States was founded by the Spanish in St. Augustine, Fla., in 1565, six years after an earlier attempt had failed at Pensacola, Fla. The first permanent English settlement was made at Jamestown, Va., in 1607, following an earlier colonization effort at Roanoke Island, N.C., in 1584, which disappeared with scarcely a trace. After several earlier attempts had failed in other locations, the French finally established permanent colonies at Mobile, Ala., in 1710 and at New Orleans, La., in 1718. Earlier, in 1626, the Dutch had founded New Amsterdam, now New York City, and the Swedish had founded, in 1638, Fort Christian, which later became Wilmington, Del. Following these early colonies, others were established in many parts of what are now the United States.

Early Structures The first settlers in America generally constructed buildings much like those they had known in the countries from which they had come, with materials most easily obtained. Thus half-timbered houses were built in Jamestown soon after it was founded. In Spanish Florida wood was used along with brick; and in the Spanish Southwest, mostly adobe. In New England and the other English colonies, wood was used at first and later brick. While many of the earliest colonial houses resembled those in the home countries of the settlers, numerous houses were much more primitive, a fact that has been somewhat overlooked in histories of the period.

Many of the early settlers lived in caves, either natural or dug into the sides of hills. Others lived in huts, the lower halves of which were pits dug into banks or cliffs, the upper halves of limbs and brush, sometimes covered with mud or sod, and with roofs of limbs covered with tree bark, sod, or brush. In other cases, the settlers constructed houses copied from the wigwams of the Indians. Chimneys were often constructed of fieldstone or of a combination of sticks, grass or brush, and clay. Contrary to popular belief, the use of log cabins did not originate in America but in the northern countries of Europe. The first log cabins in America were constructed by the Swedish settlers in

COLONIAL ARCHITECTURE Parson Capen House (1683), Topsfield, Mass. [*Architect: unknown. (Wayne Andrews)*]

Delaware, beginning about 1638. Later, German immigrants to Pennsylvania and other places also built log cabins. Still later, pioneers built log cabins in the West. Another type of early building was the sod house, constructed of dirt and used mostly in the Midwest. Although it is not widely known, many Americans still lived in such primitive dwellings at the time of the Revolutionary War and even later.

For the most part, the settlers soon moved out of their first primitive dwellings into more permanent types, modeled after those in Europe. Most of the more permanent houses were quite modest in size, had few rooms, and were constructed of materials easily obtainable locally. In time, mainly because of differences in climate, materials available, national origins and preferences of the colonists, regional styles of architecture became established.

Regional Styles The major early styles in the English colonies were Northern, or New England, Colonial; the Southern Colonial. Another major style from the early 1600s to well into the 1800s was Dutch Colonial, mostly in what is now New York City and its environs and northern New Jersey. In the areas that became the State of Florida and the Southwestern

states, Spanish Colonial was the prevailing style from the time of the earliest settlements until almost the middle of the 19th century. The French Colonial style, originally established in the area that became Canada, prevailed in the areas that became southern Mississippi, Alabama, and Louisiana and up the Mississippi River to St. Louis, during the 18th century. Much of the colonial architecture before the end of the 17th century, and even afterward in some instances, was designed by architects whose names are unknown.

New England Colonial Style Early New England Colonial structures were built almost entirely of wood, except for fireplaces and chimneys which were usually of stone. Most had heavy, half-timber frames which were filled in with wattle and daub, a mixture of clay or lime with straw. In other cases, the frames were covered with clapboard. Chimneys, were usually built inside houses for additional warmth. Most of these early houses were derived from English rural architecture of the time. At first, only one room was provided on the ground floor with a sleeping loft above, but later houses had several rooms on each of two floors. Roofs over the main portions were gable types, and often one-story kitchens were built on the

COLONIAL ARCHITECTURE Rocky Hill Meeting House (1785), Amesbury, Mass. [*Architect: unknown. (Wayne Andrews)*]

back sides and covered with lean-to roofs. Windows were small because of the severity of the winter and houses were usually compact, without porches, for the same reason. Sometimes the second story projected out beyond the first-story wall. In time, buildings other than houses were also built in New England. Notable among them were religious buildings, meeting houses, which were also built of wood until late in the 17th century, when brick and stone came into use.

Unlike the South, where brick was used much earlier and nearly all the early 17th-century wooden buildings have long since disappeared, a number of early wooden buildings still exist in New England. Unlike those in the South, they were protected from deterioration by the colder, drier climate. Among the existing 17th-century Colonial buildings, some of the most notable houses are Fairbanks House (1636), Dedham, Mass.; Whipple House (c. 1639), Ipswich, Mass.; Scotch-Boardman House (c. 1651), Saugus, Mass.; Richard Jackson House (1664), Portsmouth, R.I.; The House of the Seven Gables (c. 1669), Salem, Mass., made famous in the book of that title by Nathaniel Hawthorne (1804–64); the Paul Revere House

(c. 1676), Boston, equally famous as the home of the great silversmith and patriot, Paul Revere (1735–1818); and the Parson Capen House (1683), Topsfield, Mass. The only 17th-century meeting house still in existence, considered by many as one of the finest buildings in the United States, is the Old Ship Meeting House (1681; see color section), Hingham, Mass. Another interesting early building is the Jail (1652) in York, Maine.

Southern Colonial Style In the English colonies that later became the Southern states, Southern Colonial architecture was, like that of New England, derived from English rural architecture. At first of wood, later often of brick, the earliest buildings were quite similar to those of New England: small with one or a few rooms and sleeping loft, with small windows, but with chimneys usually attached to exterior walls. Later, houses became much more open in plan because of the milder climate, and much larger and imposing than most of those in New England. In the South, the early great houses were mostly located on plantations of many acres, owned and operated by gentlemen-planters, while New England houses were more typically located in towns and owned by merchants. In the South, other types of buildings were also constructed, the most important of which were churches. Though almost all of the early Southern Colonial buildings were destroyed long ago, several remarkable examples still exist relatively small distances from each other in tidewater Virginia.

The oldest, and possibly the oldest English colonial building in America, is St. Luke's Church (1632) in Isle of Wight County, near Smithfield, Va. Almost as old and possibly the oldest existing English colonial house is the Adam Thoroughgood House (c. 1636), near Norfolk, Va. Both of these buildings are quite Gothic in character. Perhaps the last surviving house in America in the Jacobean style, named for King James I (1566–1625) of England, is in Surry, Va. It is now called Bacon's Castle (c. 1655), after Nathaniel Bacon (1647–76), who led an ill-fated rebellion against the English in 1676. At one point during the rebellion, Bacon's followers seized the house and it has been called by his name since that time. Bacon's Castle gives early and considerable indication of the grandeur of future Southern plantation houses that followed it. Not far away, another building, the Thomas Rolfe House (1652), is more typical of the residential architecture of its time. It is much smaller, having only four rooms, and unpretentious.

Dutch Colonial Style Dutch Colonial buildings were derived from those in the Netherlands, from which the settlers had come. Dutch Colonial houses were of two major types: one had steep, double-pitched, modified gambrel roofs with overhangs, or eaves, only on the front and back and with chimneys on both ends; the other type was similar, but had gable roofs with flared eaves. Gambrel roofs were sometimes used in early New England in the South, but these are thought to have been borrowed from the styles of the Dutch. Dutch Colonial buildings were generally of wood at first, but later stone was often used. Although the Dutch colonists often used solid doors, they became noted for the so-called Dutch door, divided horizontally in the middle so that either the top or bottom half could be opened independently of the other.

Only a moderate number of Dutch Colonial houses exist today. Some of the most notable are Pieter Claessen Wyckoff House (c. 1641), Brooklyn, New York City, probably the oldest building in the state; Ackerman House (1704), Hackensack, N.J.; Bries House (1723), Greenbush, N.Y.; Dyckman House (c. 1783), New York City; and Vreeland House (1818), Englewood, N.J. Settlers from many other countries eventually affected Colonial architecture, particularly in the middle colonies of Maryland, Pennsylvania, Delaware, and New Jersey. In addition to the English and Dutch who settled in some of these places, Swedish, German, Scottish, and Welsh immigrants also settled there. None of them established strong styles as did the English and Dutch, but they nevertheless stamped their architecture with their own traditions.

Spanish Colonial Style Spanish Colonial architecture began in Central and South America, earlier than in

COLONIAL ARCHITECTURE Exterior, Bacon's Castle (c. 1655), Surrey, Va. [Architect: unknown. (Thomas L. Williams, Association for the Preservation of Virginia Antiquities)]

COLONIAL ARCHITECTURE Interior, Bacon's Castle (c. 1655), Surry, Va. [Architect: unknown. (Thomas L. Williams, Association for the Preservation of Virginia Antiquities)]

COLONIAL ARCHITECTURE St. Luke's Church (1632), Isle of Wight Co., Va. [Architect: unknown. (Ken Cassell)]

COLONIAL ARCHITECTURE Philipsburg Manor (c. 1680), N. Tarrytown, N.Y. [*Architect: unknown. (Joseph W. Molitor)*]

COLONIAL ARCHITECTURE San Estevan (c. 1642), Acoma, N. Mex.
[*Architect: unknown. (Wayne Andrews)*]

the areas that later became the United States. However, it soon spread to what became the State of Florida and along the Gulf Coast to the Southwest to California, and eventually to New Orleans. Spanish
architecture in the colonies was mainly of brick, or
adobe, after the time of the earliest wood buildings.
It was unlike other architecture in America at that
time. The English and Dutch settlers based their
buildings on rural types in their homelands, and produced buildings that were mostly medieval, or
Gothic, in character. The Spanish, on the other hand,
produced a more exuberant architecture more akin to
the Baroque style then in favor on the European con-

tinent. However, Spanish Colonial architecture was
never as dramatic and ornamented in what became
the United States as it was in Mexico and other places
farther south.

Many Spanish Colonial buildings are still in existence, primarily forts (see the article entitled military
buildings), churches, and government buildings. In
St. Augustine, in addition to the fort and a few other
old buildings, is located the oldest Spanish Colonial
house, now called the Spanish Treasurer's House (c.
1695). Its first story is built of coquina, limestone from
fossil seashells; and the second, of wood. In New Orleans are located some important Spanish Colonial

buildings, including the old Spanish Town Hall, the Cabildo (1795), and the nearby Presbytere (1794–1813), both now used as museums, and the Cathedral of St. Louis (1794, and later remodeled).

The greatest collections of existing Spanish Colonial buildings in the United States exist in the Southwest and in California. In the Southwest, some of the most notable churches include San. Estévan (c. 1642), Acoma, N.Mex.; Nuestra Señora de la Asunción (1692), Zia Pueblo, N.Mex.; San José (1706), Old Laguna Pueblo, N.Mex.; San José y San Miguel de Aguayo (1731), San Antonio, Tex.; The Alamo (1757), San Antonio, the scene, in 1836, of the great battle for Texas independence from Mexico; San Francisco (c. 1772), Ranchos de Taos, N.Mex.; and San Xavier del Bac (1797; see color section), Tucson, Ariz. Among the most notable California Spanish mission churches are San Carlos Borremeo (1797), Carmel; San Juan Capistrano (1806); and Santa Barbara (1820). A number of other Spanish Colonial buildings still exist in California and in the Southwest. Among the most interesting are the Governor's Palace (1614), Santa Fe, N.Mex., and the Governor's Palace (1749), San Antonio, Tex.

French Colonial Style Early French Colonial architecture in what eventually became the United States, like that in the other colonies, reflected the buildings the settlers had known in Europe. At first very primitive and impermanent, French Colonial architecture soon progressed to better designed and constructed and more permanent types. Several things made French Colonial architecture quite different from that in the other colonies. One was a system called *briquette entre poteaux,* which employed structures of wood, with the spaces between filled in with brick and the walls stuccoed.

Other differences came from the hot, humid climate and the heavy rainfall of Louisiana and the Mississippi River Valley. One answer to this problem was the provision of considerable numbers of large windows, surrounded by great verandas that not only shaded the windows and walls from the sun but provided protected outdoor living space. Another answer was the construction of raised cottages, which have the main living areas on the second floor and other floors above, while only service and storage areas are located on the ground floor. Thus the early permanent French Colonial buildings, while derived from those in France, soon developed into a regional style, well adapted to the habits of their occupants and the climate of the area in which they were built.

While French Colonial buildings still exist in a number of places, the greatest number are in Louisiana, including New Orleans and the bayou country. The great era of French Colonial architecture in New Orleans began with the founding of the city in 1718 and continued until 1769, when Louisiana was ceded to Spain. Louisiana came back to France in 1799, but only for four years until the Louisiana Purchase in 1803. The French Colonial style continued to influence the architecture of New Orleans and other places in Louisiana for many years after that date.

In New Orleans, there are a number of French Colonial buildings, including examples of many types, such as small houses and plantation houses. Some of the most important are Ursuline Convent (c. 1727); Madame John's Legacy, a house thought to be the oldest in the Mississippi Valley and to have been built in the early 18th century; Lafitte's Blacksmith Shop, thought to be almost as old and to have been occupied by the pirate, Jean Lafitte (c. 1780–c. 1826); and the Spanish Customs House (c. 1784), actually a relatively small plantation house built during the Spanish regime but French Colonial in character.

Outside New Orleans, several great plantation houses of the era still exist. Among the most notable are Ormond Plantation (c. 1790), St. Charles Parish; Parlange Plantation (c. 1750), Pointe Coupee Parish; Voisin Plantation (c. 1785), St. John the Baptist Parish; and Rienzi (c. 1800), Lafourche Parish.

Beginning in the early part of the 18th century, architecture in the English colonies and in the former Dutch colonies, by then also English, gradually changed from the colonial styles of the past to the style then most important in England, the Georgian (see the article entitled Georgian architecture). Other styles continued in these colonies for quite a long time, but the Georgian eventually prevailed. In the French and Spanish colonies, which became states later, the early colonial styles continued until well into the 19th century. And Dutch Colonial also continued to an extent, alongside the Georgian, in parts of New York, New Jersey, and other places settled by the Dutch.

The 13 original states, which had all started out as proprietary colonies, those controlled by individuals under grants from European rulers, or as corporate colonies, controlled by groups chartered by the rulers. By the beginning of the Revolutionary War, eight of the colonies had become what were called Royal Colonies, under the direct control of the king of England. They were Georgia, Massachusetts, New Hampshire, New Jersey, New York, North Carolina, South Carolina, and Virginia. Maryland, Pennsylvania, and Delaware remained proprietary. Connecticut and Rhode Island were still corporate colonies.

Very little architectural construction took place during the Revolution. Afterward, the new states turned away from the Georgian of the English toward other styles thought to be more appropriate to the newly formed republic. For a discussion on the new kind of architecture, eventually called Classic Revival, see the article entitled classic revival architecture.

Related Articles CLASSIC REVIVAL ARCHITECTURE; GEORGIAN ARCHITECTURE; HISTORY OF ARCHITECTURE; PRE-COLUMBIAN ARCHITECTURE; PRESERVATION; Various articles on colonial architects.

Further Reading Farrar, Emmie Ferguson: *Old Virginia Houses —The Mobjack Bay Country and Along the James,* combined edition, Bonanza Books, New York, reprint of separate editions of 1955 and 1957, Hastings House, New York; Forman, H. Chandlee: *The Virginia Eastern Shore and Its British Origins —History, Gardens and Antiquities,* Eastern Shore Publishers' Assoc., Easton, Md., 1975; John, Fitshugh: *The Architects of the American Colonies, or Vitruvius Americanus,* Barre Publishers, Barre, Mass., 1968; Overdyke, W. Darrell: *Louisiana Plantation Homes—Colonial and Ante Bellum,* Architectural Book Publishing Co., New York, 1965; Pierson, William H., Jr.: *American Architects and Their Buildings—The Colonial and Neoclassical Styles,* Doubleday, New York, 1970.

Sources of Additional Information See listing in the article entitled history of architecture.

COLUMN In the trabeated, or post and lintel, structural system, a structural member that is usually relatively long and slender, vertical, and supports weights and other loads above it. Columns are sometimes called posts or pillars. A pier is like a thick column, relatively short usually, which supports very heavy loads such as those of arches, vaults, or domes. Columns and piers may be either freestanding or attached to walls, the latter often called engaged. A rectangular column or pillar attached to a wall is often called a pilaster.

Functions Columns have been one of the most important elements in architecture since ancient times. They have functioned as vertical structural members carrying loads from the structures above them throughout history from the time of the earliest civilizations. Columns continue to perform this important function today. In the past, the major materials for columns were wood, stone, and later cast and wrought iron. Today wood is still important but steel and reinforced concrete have virtually replaced the other materials.

Until the end of the 19th and the beginning of the 20th century, columns performed another immensely important function, as one of the primary determinants of architectural design. In every era, from the beginning of architecture to the 20th century, the esthetic design of columns and their uses as ornament have deeply affected the overall appearance, architectural effects, and other qualities of buildings. Today the ornamental functions of columns have virtually disappeared, leaving as their only function that of structural members.

History Little is known about the first uses of columns in buildings. However, by the beginning (about 3000 B.C.) of the ancient civilizations around the Mediterranean Sea, in the Middle East, Egypt, Crete and other islands of the Aegean Sea, and on the mainland of Greece, columns had come to be used extensively, and in some cases as very important elements of architecture.

The Mesopotamians did not use columns to any extent, but the Persians developed highly ornamental columns of wood and stone, with tops, or capitals, and scrolls and brackets above depicting bulls, sometimes with human heads, and dragons. In Crete and in the early years on the mainland of Greece, square stone columns were used, but the most common type

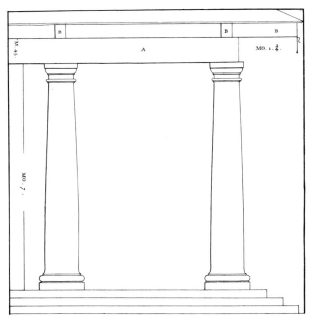

COLUMN Roman Order, Tuscan. *(Andrea Palladio:* The Four Books of Architecture, *Dover Publications)*

was round, made of wood and usually tapered, with a capital similar to that of later Greek Doric columns. In Egypt, square pillars of stone and round columns were used. Ordinarily, the columns were built up in sections, or drums, each placed on top of the one below. Column shafts were often ornamented, as were capitals, the major types of which had stylized versions of papyrus bundles in bell or bud shapes, lotus flowers, or palm leaves. Sometimes the heads of gods were used on capitals and sometimes their figures were used for entire columns. Some column shafts were simple cylinders and others were fluted.

Most of the styles of columns of these ancient civilizations have had little effect on the architecture in America. An exception is the Egyptian style, which was used sometimes on certain buildings of the Eclectic era and a few earlier and later ones.

Greek Columns The design of columns was a great accomplishment of the ancient Greeks. Eventually, they refined their designs to a very high degree of excellence, which have been models for architects ever since. Also they produced a system with three types, called orders, for the design of columns and related elements. The later Greek columns were of marble, constructed by placing a series of drums in layers.

Orders The three Greek orders, from the simplest to the most ornamental and from the earliest to the latest developed, are the Doric, Ionic, and Corinthian. An order is considered to consist of the shaft of the column, with its top, or capital, and its base, if it has one, together with the horizontal structural member, or entablature, it supports. The entablature is divided into three parts, the lowest being the architrave, the middle part the frieze, and the highest the

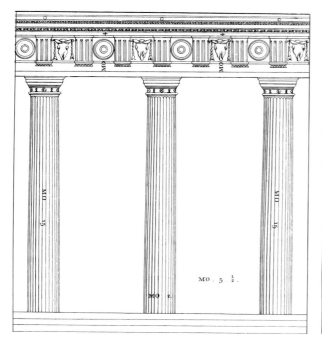

COLUMN Roman Order, Doric. *(Andrea Palladio:* The Four Books of Architecture, *Dover Publications)*

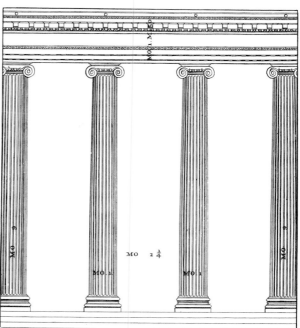

COLUMN Roman Order, Ionic. *(Andrea Palladio:* The Four Books of Architecture, *Dover Publications)*

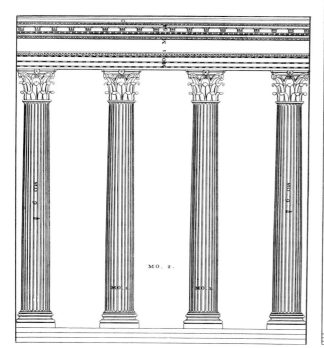

COLUMN Roman Order, Corinthian. *(Andrea Palladio:* The Four Books of Architecture, *Dover Publications)*

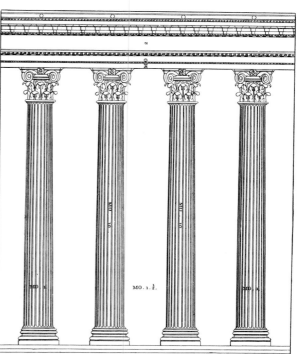

COLUMN Roman Order, Composite. *(Andrea Palladio:* The Four Books of Architecture, *Dover Publications)*

cornice. Very definite proportions and forms for all of these elements and for the relationships between the elements were established. The orders played a very important role in Greek architecture, becoming the single most important element that determined the appearance of buildings. Although the Greek orders are often thought of as comprising a rigid standardized system, they never were that to the Greeks, who varied them considerably in every building they designed and constructed.

The Doric order was relatively plain and dignified. Without a base, the columns were generally fluted, but not always, tapered toward the simple capital and entablature above. The Ionic order, more slender and somewhat more ornamental than the Doric, was also fluted and tapered to a capital with volutes similar to those of the spiral structure of some seashells. Almost always, the volutes were placed on the insides and outsides of the capitals, except at corners of buildings. The Corinthian order was the most ornamental of the three, mainly because of the capital, which was like an inverted bell with acanthus leaves, and more delicately detailed than those of the other orders. Otherwise, the Ionic and Corinthian orders were similar, except that in the Corinthian, columns were even more slender than those of the Ionic.

The Greeks were masters of architectural design. To make sure that buildings and their elements had the proper appearance, they introduced methods of design which corrected for optical errors inherent in the human eye. The major methods involved the subtle curving of horizontal and vertical lines to make them appear straight to viewers and the inclination of vertical elements to make them appear to be absolutely vertical rather than as if they were leaning. In columns, optical corrections were made by subtly curving the shafts, giving them what is called *entasis*.

Roman Columns The Romans used columns which they adapted from those of the Greeks, changing them to meet their own purposes. While Greek columns of fine marble were generally fluted, the Romans usually eliminated the flutes, finding them unsuitable for the granite and other stones at their disposal. Their columns were made in one piece, that is, monolithic. The Romans also placed lines of columns, or colonnades, over other colonnades, or superimposed them, something the Greeks never did. The Roman taste for grandeur and ornament is reflected in their columns. The original Greek Doric order was modified, making the column shafts taller and more slender, and bases were added. The Ionic order was made less refined and more ornamented, eventually having capitals with volutes on all four sides. Neither order gained the acceptance with the Romans of the Corinthian, which was their favorite, and which they developed to a highly ornate state. The Romans occasionally used an order called the Tuscan, similar to the Doric, which they adapted from the architecture of the Etruscans, who were the early inhabitants of west-central Italy. More to their liking, and highly ornamented, was a new order, the Composite, which they developed by combining some of the characteristics of the Ionic with those of the Corinthian.

The columns, and the complete orders, of both Greece and Rome have had great influence on subsequent architecture, including that of the Renaissance and the Classic Revival and Eclectic periods that followed, in America as well as in Europe.

Early Christian and Byzantine Columns In the architecture of the years immediately following the Roman era, columns in both Early Christian and Byzantine buildings generally utilized the Roman orders. In fact, many of the columns in Early Christian churches were actually removed from older Roman buildings. Byzantine architecture soon discarded the old orders, to develop newer types better suited for the support of arches and domes. Capitals became very ornate; some prevalent types were the bird and basket, and the cushion. During the Romanesque period, columns in Italy were often monolithic as they had been in Roman times, but were usually made up from smaller pieces of stone in other countries. Romanesque columns or piers were generally heavy and large, somewhat crudely made, often relatively short, with capitals adapted from those of Rome. Sometimes several columns were grouped together in a sort of cluster. The columns of none of these eras has deeply affected those in America.

Gothic Columns The opposite is true of the Gothic era, which followed the Romanesque. Architecture in Europe as well as in America has been deeply affected by the Gothic, particularly in the design of churches in the Gothic Revival and Eclectic periods. Gothic columns or piers came in a great variety. Some were simple, cylindrical shafts, with or without capitals, while others utilized various kinds of clusters with highly ornamented capitals.

Designs of columns varied so much from country to country during the Gothic era and between buildings and at different times, it is impossible to generalize about them. In England, for example, columns varied from short cylinders with unornamented square capitals to tall, slender types in the shape of octagons and other polygons, with designs on the shafts and highly ornamented capitals with foliage forms.

Renaissance Columns During the Renaissance, architects turned away from the column forms used in Gothic times, back to those of the classical era, in particular to the classic Roman orders. Columns were used structurally or purely for decorative effects, either freestanding or engaged. Two widely divergent philosophies of column design seem to have existed during the Renaissance: one that produced a variety of types with various kinds of ornament not only on the capitals but also on the shafts, and another that attempted to codify and standardize designs, based on the five Roman orders.

Standardization The move toward standardization was probably started by the first publication in Latin, in 1486, and subsequent publication in Italian, in 1521, of a book written in the first century B.C. by a Roman architect of that era, Marcus Pollio Vitruvius. The thoughts of Vitruvius, including those on the orders, had a considerable effect on Renaissance architects. The move toward standard design of columns was accelerated by the publication of two books by two Italian architects who were contemporaries, Giacomo Barozzi da Vignola (1507–73) and Andrea Palladio (1508–80). Palladio's book, published in 1570, greatly influenced architects of the Classic Revival era, including Americans, even more. Vignola's book, published in 1562, also influenced architects of the time,

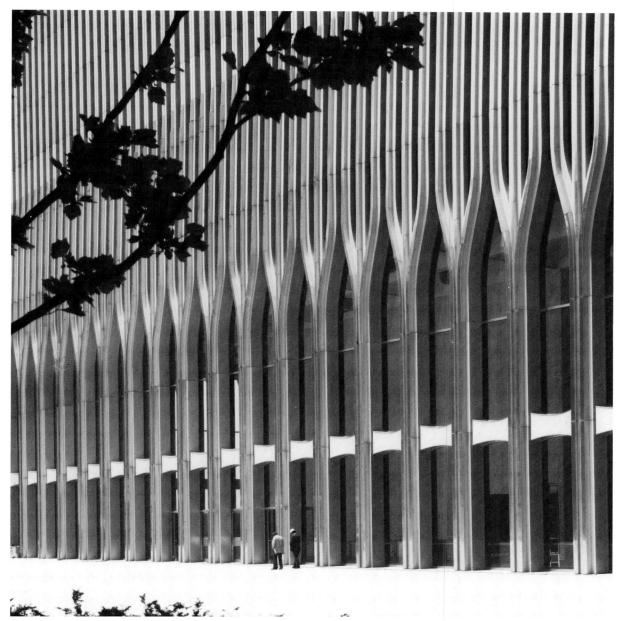

COLUMN Contemporary, World Trade Center (1973), New York, N.Y. [*Architects: Minoru Yamasaki and Emery Roth and Sons. (Hedrich-Blessing)*]

and later in the Classic Revival era. Particularly influential were his standardized designs and proportions for the classical Roman orders.

American Development From the time of the early colonies, the design of columns generally followed the prevailing styles in Europe, in wood at first and later in wood or stone. The books of Palladio and Vignola were used for inspiration and information as were others on similar subjects published mostly in England, including those of James Gibbs (1682–1754), Inigo Jones (1573–1652), and Colen Campbell (c. 1676–1729). Many early American architects learned architecture from studying such books and went on to

design buildings, using the orders much as they were presented in the books.

As was the practice elsewhere, many American architects did not slavishly copy the orders as standardized by the authors of such books. Although an American, upon occasion, would copy a column design and an order for a given building straight from a book or from some specific classic or Renaissance building, many of the buildings they designed employed columns that were inspired or derived from books or older buildings. In this way, a vast vocabulary of column types, roughly identifiable as having been derived from the orders, appeared in American buildings, particularly up to the end of the Classic Revival period. The columns for Gothic Revival buildings in America were designed in a similar manner. After that, during the Eclectic period, column designs were derived or reproduced from a variety of sources and styles, including Egyptian, Muslim, and other styles. Some column types were so popular that they became widely available as stock items in wood.

In the latter half of the 19th century, with the beginning of what became the modern movement in architecture, the use of ornamental columns declined and was replaced by types that were frankly only structural in function. An exception was the attempt by some architects to reproduce, in cast-iron and wrought-iron columns, the designs of the classic orders. Thus iron columns on buildings looked superficially like Greek, Roman, and Renaissance forms. Because of their extremely slender shafts and other factors inherent in the nature of iron as a material, these columns actually appeared quite different. Iron columns were also often offered as stock items. However, an era of structural design of columns, without regard to their ornamental effect, had begun and it eventually brought the use of ornamental columns, except for an occasional resurgence, virtually to an end in the 20th century.

Related Articles ART IN ARCHITECTURE; BOOK, ARCHITECTURAL; DESIGN, ARCHITECTURAL; HISTORY OF ARCHITECTURE; MOLDING; ORNAMENT; Various articles on phases of American architectural history.

COMMUNICATION SYSTEM In buildings, the provisions for delivering information from person to person or place to place. Important types include intercommunication systems, commonly called intercoms; telephones; alarm systems; sound systems; and security systems. (See articles entitled fire protection; security systems.)

Many people would agree that the highest form of communication between persons takes place in conversation, face to face. In the complex world of today, face-to-face conversation is not always possible. Therefore a vast array of types of communication devices and systems have been developed. All are important in architecture. Although some people may believe it possible to communicate directly from person to person through extrasensory perception (ESP), most communication systems used in architecture today rely on the senses, in particular those of sight and hearing. Architects and other environmental designers must be familiar with these systems and provide for their proper design and installation when and where they are needed in buildings.

Sound Systems The simplest communication systems used in buildings are those that rely on sounds from bells, buzzers, horns, or chimes to relay certain simple messages. Perhaps the simplest of all is a door

knocker that tells people that a visitor or some other person has arrived at a house, apartment, or other building. A door-bell system serves the same purpose and requires only the provision of a simple button, a transformer, low-voltage wiring and a bell, buzzer, or chime to announce the visitor. Equally as simple are such devices as horns to communicate simple facts, such as the end and start of work shifts in factories. Such communication systems may be manually operated or automatic.

In schools, colleges, and universities similar systems are used to signal the end and beginning of class periods, lunch hours, and other activities. These systems are usually automated by tying them in with clock systems that not only give the time in various areas but automatically trip the bells or other sound devices at the proper time. Often called clock and program systems, a communication system of this type may be controlled by a master clock. Another type operates in a similar manner, but does not have a master clock. In either case, the system may have only a single scheduled program or several. If more than one is required, a program instrument is used. A variation of such systems is a complete sound system, which allows for paging, music, and other transmissions, in addition to signaling the ending and beginning of class periods.

Other sound systems, similar to those already discussed, include paging, nurses' call, and similar types. Some of these systems require wiring, microphones, loudspeakers, and other equipment. In others, such as doctors' call systems, radio transmissions are used to activate devices, some of which are portable and may be carried in a pocket or on a belt, which signal to a person that a telephone call should be placed to a paging center. Another relatively simple system, sometimes installed in large homes or other buildings, uses annunciators, devices that register numbers indicating the location of a person who wishes assistance or service.

Telephone The most important sound communication system is the telephone, essential in buildings of every type. Modern telephone service requires good design and planning in all buildings. In offices, hospitals, and many other complex types telephone systems may also be very complex, requiring special satellite closets in which cable connections may be made, equipment rooms, apparatus closets and spaces, and conduits for vertical and horizontal placement of cables. Telephones today serve many communication needs, including local and long-distance calls and intercommunication within buildings. Private intercom systems, utilizing speaker-receivers wired together or transmitting radio signals, may also be used for intercommunication in buildings. Call directors are used for controlling up to 30 different telephone lines. A relatively large organization may require a private branch exchange (PBX), with an operator's console and equipment room.

Special kinds of telephone equipment may be required in a building, including speakerphones that allow conversations to be heard by several people in a room; automatic dialers that use plastic cards, magnetic tape, or other devices; or answering devices. Private lines, sometimes called tie lines, may be required, for example, between the headquarters of a company and its branches. Wide-area-transmission-service (WATS) lines, allowing unlimited long-distance calls to designated places for a set fee, may be required, as may mobile telephones in automobiles or other vehicles. Private lines are also used for such purposes as the transmission of written information by teletype, graphic material by facsimile or telephoto, or radio and television programs from networks to local stations. Telephone lines may also be used for transmission of information between computers.

The design and installation of telephone systems is quite complicated today. Telephone companies have staffs of consultants, specialists in telephone communications, whose function it is to advise architects and other environmental designers regarding the proper design and installation of such systems. Because of the importance of good telephone systems in buildings today, their increasing complexity and need for space, such consultants should be called in early in the design of buildings. In addition, installation costs are rising rapidly for telephone systems that are flexible, complete, designed for later developments and improvements, and often located in hidden conduits, shafts, and other places in buildings.

Specialized Sound Systems Another kind of communication system often used in buildings is a sound system, over which public address announcements, music, and sometimes other types of communication may be broadcast in buildings. Systems of this type may be quite simple or very complex, ranging from a public address system in a school auditorium, consisting of a microphone, or more than one, an amplifier, and loudspeakers, to a complete system in a multiuse recreational building, with the equipment named and in addition, record players, radio receivers, tape players, and other equipment. In some of the most completely equipped buildings, motion picture and television facilities are also provided. In some buildings, music is piped to various rooms. In others, such as schools or colleges, special provisions are often made for listening or viewing by individuals or small groups. Closed-circuit television is also sometimes provided. Central antenna systems may be required in buildings such as hotels and others.

In specialized buildings, such as theaters, opera houses, concert halls, and the like, very complete sound systems with very high-quality components such as those named are usually required, along with complex instrument panels, or consoles, from which the various components may be controlled. Motion picture houses have their own special requirements and most other types of theater and music buildings require facilities for showing motion picture film.

The design and installation of such audio, video, and audiovisual systems are quite complex and grow more complex with time. Provision for such systems must be made in many building types; for example, in theaters or concert halls such provision is a major consideration. Today numerous community auditoriums and similar buildings are being constructed. In many of these, hockey, basketball, tennis, and other athletic events are staged, along with dance recitals, plays, rock groups, symphony orchestras, and other types of entertainment. Not only are effective sound systems required for such buildings but they must have extreme flexibility. In all but the simplest of sound systems, specialists are required for proper design and installation.

Monitoring and Control Another major type of communications system used in buildings involves the monitoring and control of various functions. For example, in hospitals, remote systems are required for monitoring the vital signs of patients in intensive care wards. Closed-circuit television is often used in hospitals for observation of such patients and is used in many other ways in other types of buildings. Processes in chemical plants or within furnaces in factories may be monitored by television, when no other visual method would be possible. Children in nursery schools may be similarly monitored during free play periods. Many other uses may also be made of such systems.

Another important type of monitoring and control system in buildings consists of control centers in which various processes may be monitored on instruments, controlled when necessary, and recorded on tape, charts, or in other ways when required. In a large office building, for example, a control panel may be used to monitor and control temperatures in the building, airflow, electrical devices, and water, mechanical, and other systems. In a factory, such a control center may be used to monitor and control industrial processes. In smaller buildings with relatively simple functions, such systems may not be required or may be of minimal complexity. In larger, more complex types, the systems are often very sophisticated.

Resident Systems While houses and other residential buildings are often thought of as relatively simple building types, in actuality they are not, since they combine facilities under one roof for so many varied kinds of human activities. Communication systems in houses and other residences may also be quite complex and complete. In addition to the usual door-bell and telephone requirements, houses and other residences often have smoke detectors; burglar alarms; intercom systems, including instruments outside for identification of callers; closed-circuit television for monitoring nurseries, for example; rooftop antennas, some of which are electrically operated; maid call annunciators; telephone systems utilizing master stations and jacks for portable instruments; radio and television sets; and often very complete sound and music systems with amplifiers, tape decks, radio receivers or tuners, record changers and players, microphones, and elaborate speaker systems.

Written Communications In this time of electronics, it is easy to forget that written communications have existed for a much longer time than the electronic. The major written communications used in architecture involve both outside and internal services. In single-family houses, a mailbox usually suffices for the former and perhaps a bulletin board for the latter. In apartment houses and some other building types, such as small office buildings, banks of mailboxes may be provided. In other larger buildings, mailrooms are ordinarily required for the receipt and sending of mail. Mail chutes for letters and bundle drops for packages are used for mailing articles. Sometimes, in very large buildings, conveyors are installed to transport mail from floor to floor.

Internal, sometimes called interoffice, written communications within buildings are often handled, routed, and carried to their destinations by the same people who handle the incoming and outgoing regular mail, using the same mailrooms. For a small business or other organization, a mailroom may be quite simple in design and small in size; but for larger ones, mailrooms may require a considerable amount of equipment for receiving, sorting, temporary storage, and delivery of mail. In some cases, such mailrooms may also be quite large in size. In any case, architects and other environmental designers must provide proper facilities and equipment for mail. Before proceeding with such designs, it is necessary to check the relevant regulations and other requirements of the U.S. Postal Service as well as the requirements of the users of buildings.

A method for handling written communications in buildings, used widely in the past but less so today, is a pneumatic tube system. Used in such building types as department stores, transportation buildings, factories, and hospitals, pneumatic tube systems consist of tubing connecting various areas of a building, through which small carriers travel propelled by air pressure or vacuum. In addition to written communications, some pneumatic tube systems have the advantage of being able to transport small articles that can fit into carriers of up to about 3 by 11 by 16 inches in size.

In practice, most electronic communication systems are designed by electrical engineers, particularly those who specialize in such work. Complete sound and music systems are often designed by other specialists. Both mechanical and electrical engineers are involved in the design of control systems. In the design of all such systems, the engineers must work closely with each other and with architects.

History In the earliest primitive times, communications between people in buildings could only be accomplished by speaking to each other face to face or, later, by written communications that were hand delivered from one person to another. Still later, communications were printed and the first practical typewriter, invented in 1867, made private business communications fast and efficient. Other communication devices included mechanical bells and speaking tubes that carried the voice through piping or tubing. The real history of intercommunications in buildings begins with the invention of the telephone in 1876, by Alexander Graham Bell (1847–1922). A few years later, there were more than 1,000 telephones in the United States.

In 1878 the first telephone exchange, serving 21 customers, was installed in New Haven, Conn. Long-distance calling began in 1881 between Boston and Providence, R.I., and in 1884 a line was opened between New York City and Boston. Transcontinental calls between New York City and San Francisco began in 1913, transatlantic calls via radiotelephone between New York City and London in 1927, and long-distance calls by coaxial cable between New York City and Philadelphia in 1936. Many improvements have since been made in telephone instruments, lines, and equipment until today the telephone is the most important communication system used in architecture, for both internal and external messages.

Other communication systems used in architecture include radio, first used in 1895 by Italian engineer Marchese Guglielmo Marconi (1874–1937) and considerably improved during the 20th century, and television, first developed in the 19th century but not used commercially until the 1930s and not widely accepted until after World War II. Television now includes closed-circuit broadcasting and international broadcasting via satellite. Computers have had wide applications in communications in the second half of the 20th century (see the article entitled computer). Computer and other electronic communication systems are being rapidly improved and expanded today and new developments of importance in architecture can be expected to continue.

Related Articles COMPUTER; ELECTRICAL ENGINEERING; ELECTRIC POWER AND WIRING; FIRE PROTECTION; SECURITY SYSTEMS; SOUND CONTROL; THEATER.

Source of Additional Information Institute of Electrical and Electronics Engineers (IEEE), 345 E. 47th St., New York, N.Y. 10017.

COMPLEX, ARCHITECTURAL

A group of buildings, for single or multiple purposes, on one site. Architectural complexes have been designed by architects for a very long time in such projects as colleges and universities, schools, apartments, and shopping centers. See articles entitled apartment; college and university building; school; shopping center.

Categories Architectural complexes fall into two major categories: the type for which master plans are made by an architect or other design professionals for long-term development, often with buildings by other architects; and the type for which both the master plan and the buildings are made by one architect. For example, many colleges and universities have had master plans and buildings designed by one architect, while in others the master plan was made and buildings added later by the same architect, by another architect, or by several architects. In the case of a university that has been in existence a long time, one architect may have made the original master plans, to be followed by buildings by various architects, designed over a period of time ranging up to 300 years or more in the United States. In such a case, it is not uncommon for the original master plan to have been revised or redesigned one or more times by other architects.

In any case, the design of architectural complexes, of whatever type, involves more than just the design of a single building. The relationships between the buildings and the open spaces around them, the landscaping, and other elements they share, must all be designed properly if success is to be achieved.

Single-Purpose Complexes Most of the earlier architectural complexes in the United States were designed for a single purpose. Industrial buildings were gathered into industrial parks, shops and stores into shopping centers, college buildings onto campuses, buildings for music and drama into cultural centers, and so on.

Mixed-Use Centers A later development has been what is called mixed-use, or multiuse, sometimes called MXD, centers. In these centers, many kinds of functions can be served, including hotel and motel lodging, convention facilities, apartments and other housing, offices, shopping, and cultural activities.

The pioneering mixed-use center is Rockefeller Center, New York City, completed in 1940, and designed by an association of three architectural firms: Reinhard and Hofmeister; Corbett, Harrison and MacMurray; and Hood and Fouilhoux. In Rockefeller Center are to be found such uses as offices, restaurants, theaters, recreational facilities, stores, exhibition rooms, broadcasting stations, and museums.

Some years later, architects and others began to think about providing mixed-use centers in other cities. It was felt that the segregation of complexes by a single type of function was not always the best solution. The downtown areas of cities had traditionally been places where many functions were served in close juxtaposition to each other. Why not try to bring this idea back into new projects in urban locations? In the middle 1950s some attempts were made to accomplish this, the most notable being the Back Bay Center proposal made for Boston in 1954. Architects Pietro Belluschi (1899–), Walter Bogner (1899–), Carl Koch (1912–), Hugh Stubbins (1912–), and The Architects Collaborative set up a separate office to design the center. The proposal met with great critical acclaim, but was never built.

Other mixed-use centers, with office, shopping, and transportation functions, were proposed about the same time, including Penn Center, Philadelphia, designed by Vincent Kling (1916–), and Place Ville Marie, Montreal, Canada, by Ieoh Ming Pei (1917–),

COMPLEX, ARCHITECTURAL Rockefeller Center (1940), New York, N.Y. [*Architects: Reinhard and Hofmeister; Corbett, Harrison and MacMurray; Hood and Fouilhoux. (Thomas Airviews)*]

COMPLEX, ARCHITECTURAL Rockefeller Center (1940), New York, N.Y. [*Architects: Reinhard and Hofmeister; Corbett, Harrison and MacMurray; Hood and Fouilhoux. (Bo Parker)*]

COMPLEX, ARCHITECTURAL Constitution Plaza (1964), Hartford, Conn. [*Architect: Charles DuBose. Landscape architects: Sasaki, Dawson and DeMay. (Joseph W. Molitor)*]

COMPLEX, ARCHITECTURAL Constitution Plaza (1964), Hartford, Conn. [*Architect: Charles DuBose. Landscape architects: Sasaki, Dawson and DeMay. (Joseph W. Molitor)*]

both finished in the 1960s. Many others have been proposed in recent years and a number of them have been built in cities all over the United States. In all there are more than 100 already constructed and being planned, including 6 in Atlanta. Many predict that the trend will continue.

Today most mixed-use centers being designed encompass a large number of functions that reflect the life of the central city. Their designs are based on the principle of fully integrating the various functions into the buildings and other spaces, rather than simply placing each function in a separate building within the group. Many centers utilize central malls, often multilevel, in which many uses are provided and which also serve to connect and give access to the other buildings of the group. Thus the mall and the buildings surrounding it take on a life very much like the busy lives of downtown areas of cities long ago before the great exodus of people to the suburbs. With so many functions to be provided and integrated with each other, the design of multiuse centers presents tremendous problems to architects. If the problems can be solved properly, the results can be very significant contemporary architecture.

Related Articles APARTMENT; HARRISON, WALLACE KIRKMAN; PRACTICE OF ARCHITECTURE; Articles on other individual building types.

Further Reading Witherspoon, Robert E., Jon P. Abbett, and Robert M. Gladstone: *Mixed Use Developments—New Ways of Land Use,* Urban Land Institute, Washington, 1976.

COMPUTER A machine or device that handles information through calculation and measurement. Computers have many uses in architecture and related fields. Sometimes their functions are called automatic data processing (ADP) or electronic data processing (EDP).

Types There are two major types of computers: analog and digital. Analog computers, which measure quantities in terms of other quantities, have been used in architecture for many years and are still widely used today. A slide rule, for years used for making numerical calculations by distance measurements, is an analog computer. So is an alcohol, or mercury, thermometer which measures temperature in terms of the length of a fine line of one of the fluids.

A more recent development is the digital computer, which makes calculations by counting numbers, or digits. Digital computers in the past, such as adding machines and cash registers, did the counting by movements of wheels, drums, or other mechanical means. Electronic analog and digital computers were developed in the 20th century, starting about 1930, and have been vastly improved over the years. Electronic analog computers operate by the measurement of electrical currents and are mostly used for special purposes. They are not as accurate as electronic digital computers, which may be used for special purposes, but are mostly general-purpose types that can be used for numerous applications. A very common type is the hand-held, or pocket, calculator which has largely supplanted the slide rule. Other electronic digital computers are much larger, more complex, and capable of many types of activities. In some ways, they have revolutionized architecture, as they have other fields of endeavor. And as improvements continue to be made, they can be expected to contribute to further changes.

Function Digital computers function by counting binary numbers, those which have only two digits. Examples of binary situations are those which can be expressed by yes or no, on or off, up or down, right or left, and so on. Decimal numbers have 10 digits, from 0 to 9, but binary numbers have only two, 0 and 1. A typical binary number is 10011 which equals 19 in the decimal system. In the binary number 10011, the first digit on the right stands for 1×2^0, or 1 in the decimal system; the next digit stands for 1×2^1, or 2; the next for 0×2^2, or 0; the next for 0×2^3, or 0; and the digit on the extreme left stands for 1×2^4, or 16. By adding, the decimal number is found to be $1 + 2 + 0 + 0 + 16 = 19$. Digital computers operate by binary means that involve electrical currents that are on or off, magnetization that is north or south, switches that are open or closed, or other processes of this sort that represent the two digits of the binary numbers. In this way, great quantities of binary numbers may be counted very accurately and rapidly by computers.

Computer technology has brought with it a new set of terms. One of these is bit which stands for 1 binary digit; another is byte which stands for 8 bits. Digital computers handle calculations by counting large numbers of bits and bytes.

Digital computers come in various sizes and capacities. The smallest can perform arithmetic calculations with reasonable speed and have limited logical or reasoning capabilities. Larger machines calculate faster than small ones, have greater logical capabilities, and have storage and printing capabilities. The largest machines calculate still faster, have larger storage capacities and may have capabilities for performing several calculations at once, for graphical displays, and for communicating with other computers.

Basic Components In all computers, of whatever size, there are five basic components: input unit, which sends data and instructions; memory unit, which receives and stores data and instructions; control unit, which takes instructions from the memory and transmits them to the arithmetic unit; the arithmetic unit, which performs the mathematical functions; and output unit, which records or delivers the results or information to the user.

Operation A computer operator operates and controls a computer from a unit called a console. Data and instructions, or input, are given to the computer in various ways. The operator may set switches or push buttons, a method that is very slow, only about 2 characters per minute; or a typewriter may be used, raising the speed to about 300 characters per minute. One of the most common input methods is by means of punched cards, in which holes have been made on keypunch machines, very much like typewriters, operated by keypunch operators. The cards are read into the computer by a card reader that can handle 1,000 or more cards a minute. Input from magnetic tape, which is very similar to that used in tape recorders, can reach speeds up to 100,000 characters per minute.

Other types of input methods include punched paper tape, magnetic ink as used on bank checks, and optical scanners that work somewhat like the human

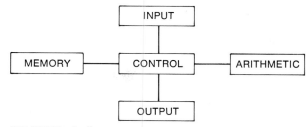

COMPUTER Basic components.

eye. For computer graphical work and drafting, two input methods are in use: a light pen with which the operator may draw on the face of a cathode-ray tube, and a digitizing table which contains a grid of wires activated by drawing on it with a stylus.

Memory Storage Memory units utilize storage of four types. The basic type is a core which contains thousands of little rings that may be magnetized in a clockwise or counterclockwise direction. A core is usually used for the working memory storage, but it is expensive, has a small capacity, and is slow. For larger amounts of information, drums, disks, or magnetic tapes are used. Transfer of information between the different types is efficient and easy.

Output from computers may take a number of forms such as punched cards or tape, magnetic tape, automatic typewriting, automatic typesetting, high-speed printing, drawings, images on screens similar to those of television sets, and so on. The output of a computer may also be transmitted by radio or telephone to other computer equipment in distant places.

Computer Language In order for people to give data and instructions to computers, it is necessary to translate ordinary human language into computer language. Computer languages must be based on the binary system. To do this, a program is written for the computer using certain words or symbols. The first type used was called machine language and involved programs using the binary digits, 0 and 1; this was slow and cumbersome. Other computer languages have been developed, including assembly or symbolic, and compiler, using only simple words which the computer translates into binary machine language. A later language is called problem-oriented and uses ordinary English phrases. Typical compiler languages include common business-oriented language (COBOL), used for business transactions, and formula transaction (FORTRAN), used in problem solving. Others are also available for specific purposes.

To prepare a program or a set of instructions for a computer, a computer programmer starts with the selection of the proper computer language for the task that the computer will perform and with a description of the task, including the input information required, processing to be performed, and the required output.

Sometimes such information is prepared by system analysts. From this information, a systems flowchart may be prepared, indicating how the various activities involved will pass through the computer operations. From the flowchart, the programmer then prepares coding sheets of the program in computer language. From these coding sheets, cards may be punched and if required, the cards may be read by a machine that transmits the information to units that record it on magnetic tape.

Architectural Uses In architecture, a great many important functions may be vastly improved and speeded up by the use of digital computers. Among them are engineering design and calculations, including structural, mechanical, electrical, and others; cost estimating and control; specification writing and printing; accounting and bookkeeping; management of offices and projects; systems analysis; programming; design; analysis of specific building types; drafting; preparation of working drawings; and project scheduling. Another important use of computers in architecture, not fully developed so far, is in storage and retrieval of information on building systems, materials, products, design factors, and the like.

The growth of computer technology and usage has created many career opportunities. Most require college education, with emphasis on mathematics and computer courses. Some of the jobs are systems analyst, who studies uses, programming, and operation of computers; design engineer, who performs research, development, and design work on computers; computer programmer, who prepares programs; computer operator, who operates the machines; and service engineer, who maintains and repairs the machines.

Architectural, engineering, and other professional schools now offer courses in computer programming and operation as part of their regular curricula, thus providing their graduates with some knowledge and experience in computer capabilities and uses. There are also opportunities in architectural, engineering, and other related offices for career programmers and operators.

History A device using beads for solving arithmetic problems, called an abacus, is probably the earliest form of computer. In various forms, it was used by the ancient Chinese, Egyptians, Greeks, and Romans. Other devices were developed later, including the slide rule which makes calculations by the positioning of sliding or revolving scales. The modern slide rule was invented in the middle of the 19th century and was based on a logarithmic scale made by English mathematician Edmund Gunter (1581–1626), who pioneered many surveying instruments.

The first mechanical digital computer was developed in the early 1800s by the Englishman Charles Babbage (1792–1871). He called it an analytical engine, but never completed building it after the English government turned it down. Not much happened in the field for almost 100 years, until 1928, when American electrical engineer Vannevar Bush (1890–1974) developed the first electronic analog computer; he called it a differential analyzer. In 1944 a mechanical-electrical digital computer was developed at Harvard University, and in 1946 the first one using vacuum tubes was built at the University of Pennsylvania. During the same period, the principles of computer memories were introduced.

People in the computer industry call the computers of various eras generations of computers. The first generation appeared on the market during the 1950s, using electronic circuits controlled by vacuum tubes. The second generation came on the market in the early 1960s. They were more dependable and faster, as much as 10 times faster, than those they superseded, mainly because they used transistors instead of vacuum tubes. The third generation, using miniature electronic circuits, were introduced in the late 1960s and are sometimes 100 times faster than those of the second generation.

Computers have caused many great changes in the ways people do business and live their daily lives, and in architecture. One of the most spectacular results of their use has been the space program. With the aid of computers, Alan B. Shepard, Jr. (1923–   ), was the first American in space on May 5, 1961; John Glenn (1921–   ) was the first to orbit the earth on February 20, 1962; and Neil Armstrong (1930–   ) was the first man on the moon on July 20, 1969. Possibly more spectacular achievements may be made in the future, with the aid of computers. Certainly computers will continue to deeply affect people's lives and architecture.

Related Articles CONSTRUCTION CONTRACT ADMINISTRATION; COST CONTROL; DESIGN, ARCHITECTURAL; DRAFTING; ELECTRICAL ENGINEERING; MECHANICAL ENGINEERING; PRACTICE OF ARCHITECTURE; PROGRAMMING; SPECIFICATION; STRUCTURAL ENGINEERING; WORKING DRAWING.

Further Reading Eastman, Charles M., ed.: *Spatial Synthesis in Computer-Aided Building Design*, John Wiley, New York, 1975; Guttridge, Byron, and Jonathan R. Wainwright: *Computers in Architectural Practice*, Halsted Press of John Wiley, New York, 1973; Harper, Neil G., ed.: *Computer Applications in Architecture and Engineering*, McGraw-Hill, New York, 1968; Paterson, John: *Information Methods—For Design and Construction*, John Wiley, New York, 1977.

CONCRETE An important building material, usually consisting of portland cement, aggregates, and water which, when mixed together and poured into forms, set into a hard strong material that resembles stone. Earlier, concrete, mostly made with natural cements, was generally used without reinforcement. Today the material most widely used is reinforced concrete, which has steel bars or mesh embedded in the other materials for added strength.

Uses Concrete, usually reinforced, has wide uses in architecture, including foundations, floor slabs, structures, piping, sidewalks, roads, parking lots, and driveways. Portland cement also has many other uses for example, for making mortar for brick and stone masonry; in plaster; for finishing interior walls and ceilings; in stucco for finishing exterior walls; in the production of asbestos-cement boards, shingles, and other products; in terrazzo flooring; for making concrete, or cement, brick and concrete block; and in paints.

Composition   Concrete is composed of four major ingredients: cement, most often portland cement today; fine aggregates, mostly sand; coarse aggregates, such as gravel; and water. The types of materials used, their proportions, or mixes, and the ratio between the cement and water, called the water-cement ratio, are the major determinants of the strength and other properties of concrete. In addition, in reinforced concrete, the steel bars or mesh determine certain strength and other properties.

Portland Cement   This cement is manufactured, under highly controlled conditions, from about 60 percent lime, 25 percent silica, 10 percent alumina, and smaller quantities of iron oxide and gypsum, the latter to control the hardening or setting time of the cement. The manufacture of portland cement involves mixing, crushing, and grinding the raw materials and burning them in a kiln, in which they are placed dry or mixed with water. The burning produces marble-sized clinkers, which are ground, often with added gypsum, to a fine powder ready to be used.

Eight types of portland cement are used in architecture. Type I is for general use; II for slower setting and less generated heat, in massive structures such as large retaining walls or dams; III, high early strength; IV, low heat slow setting; and V, called sulfate-resisting, for uses in which the concrete must resist damage from alkaline water or soils. The other three types, IA, IIA, and IIIA, are similar in composition to I, II, and III, but are air-entrained cements and have a great number of entrapped air bubbles. The air-entrained types have increased resistance to freezing and thawing.

Special types of portland cement include white, waterproof white, pozzolanic, and blast-furnace slag cements. Other cements that are employed in architecture include aluminous, for use where extremely high temperatures are to be encountered; plastic, with plasticizers added to types I and II portland cement, for use in mortars, plaster, and stucco; Keene's cement, for hard-finish coats of plaster; and oxychloric, for floors.

Aggregates   Fine aggregates for concrete, mortar, and plaster are usually sands of various kinds, with granules ranging from $1/16$ to $1/4$ inch in diameter. They must be free of organic or other harmful materials, and are usually washed, graded for size, and may be otherwise treated before being used in concrete. Coarse aggregates used in concrete, but not in mortar or plaster, are over $1/4$ inch in diameter and include natural materials, such as gravel or crushed stone, and manufactured materials, such as expanded blast-furnace slag or expanded burned clay or shale. The manufactured kinds are considered lightweight aggregates, and are used in applications in which that characteristic is important, together with insulating qualities. Other lightweight aggregates include minerals, such as vermiculite, perlite, and diatomite. Lightweight concretes made with such aggregates vary considerably in shrinkage, strength, and insulating qualities. Those made with expanded shale or clay are relatively the strongest and shrink the least. Next in strength are concretes made with expanded clay or shale, and the weakest are those made with diatomite, vermiculite, or perlite, which have the highest insulating qualities.

Water-Cement Ratio   In addition to the selection of the proper types of portland cement and aggregates, the correct water-cement ratio for various purposes must be selected. The water-cement ratio determines the strength of the concrete, other than that derived from reinforcement, its durability, and other qualities. In concrete, the compressive strength or ability to resist forces that push upon it, developed in 7 and 28 days after placement, are usually specified, based on building and other codes and accepted practices. The water-cement ratio largely determines such strengths. Such ratios vary widely, from about 1.0, with equal parts, by weight, of water and cement, developing a compressive strength of 1,750 lb/sq in, in 28 days, to 0.40, 40 percent as much water as cement, by weight, which produces 6,000 lb/sq in, in the same time. Data of this sort may be accurately obtained by testing actual specimens. On building sites, the usual method is a slump test, which involves filling a standard metal cone on a flat surface with concrete mix. The mix is rodded with a standard-sized rod and the cone raised to release the concrete. The empty cone is then placed adjacent to the concrete and the distance from the top of the cone to the top of the concrete measured. The distance indicates the water-cement ratio.

Placement   Concrete in architecture is usually poured in place on building sites or precast, either in manufacturing plants or on the sites. In either case, it is generally poured into molds or forms made of wood, metal, or plastic, and sometimes reinforced paper for columns. Concrete can also be set into place in other ways, by using special machinery. Forms for precast concrete and other standard applications are often made of metal and are reusable. In other cases, special forms must be designed. Since they must carry the load of the concrete until it has cured, such forms are usually designed by structural engineers.

The placing of concrete must be strictly controlled. Either very hot or very cold temperatures will affect curing and ultimate strength. Regular testing of sample cylinders are made during the pouring of concrete, in a manner specified by building and other codes. Most concrete poured on building sites comes ready-mixed in trucks. They must not be allowed to transport the mix too far. The concrete must be placed carefully in layers and each succeeding layer must be placed before the previous one starts to set. The concrete must not be allowed to drop very far, no more than about 5 feet for hidden work and 3 feet for exposed. Sometimes vibrators must be used to ensure proper placement in the forms. In cold weather, calcium chloride is sometimes used to hasten setting and the concrete is covered with insulating materials. Another method, more often used today, involves heating the materials and the space around the poured concrete. Many other approved methods and precautions must be taken to ensure proper placement and curing of concrete.

Many types of finishes may be given to concrete. Textures may be obtained by lining forms with materials, such as sandblasted plywood, plastics, rubber mats, and hardboard. Aggregates of various kinds, such as marble and granite, may be exposed on the surface of concrete. The surfaces of concrete may also be finished by various processes, such as grinding, bushhammering, sandblasting, or polishing. In addition, various pigments may be added to concrete mixes to produce a range of colors.

Versatility Concrete is a very versatile material and as such is widely used in architecture for many purposes. Many architects and other environmental designers prefer concrete as a material, because it is plastic and may be formed in the manner they wish, to materials such as steel that come in stock sizes. The plasticity and workability of concrete can also cause difficulties in design if it is used in ways not appropriate to its nature, for example, in certain extreme forms or as fake stone. Concrete must be designed, mixed, placed, and otherwise cared for properly if it is to perform properly. Thus, for all but the simplest applications, concrete structures and many other types of uses require the attention of highly qualified structural engineers to perform design, detailing, and other professional services.

History Cements, materials such as mud and clay, which when placed wet, dry to form hard adhesives, were used in architecture from early primitive times. The use of gypsum followed. All of the early uses were as mortar for use in masonry buildings. The time of the first use of concrete for structural purposes has not been determined, possibly as early as 1000 B.C.

The first recorded uses of concrete as a structural material were made by the Romans, beginning about 200 B.C. It soon became their favorite structural material for buildings, aqueducts, bridges, and other purposes. Roman concrete was made with a natural cement, called pozzolana, a volcanic ash found at Pozzuoli, Italy, near Mount Vesuvius. Mixed with slaked lime, or water and lime, pozzolana formed a quite strong cement mortar with which concrete could be made. This was called hydraulic mortar because it was virtually waterproof and could be used for buildings and other structures, including those placed under water.

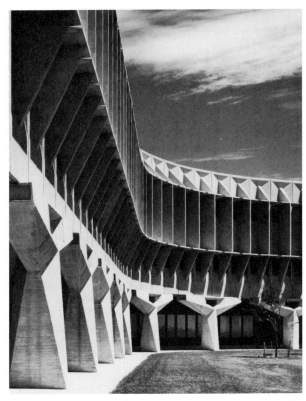

CONCRETE STRUCTURE IBM Building (1974), Boca Raton, Fla. [*Architects: Marcel Lajos Breuer and Robert Gatje. (Joseph W. Molitor)*]

CONCRETE STRUCTURE IBM Building (1971), Hamden, Conn. [*Architect: Eliot Noyes. (Joseph W. Molitor)*]

As aggregates in concrete, the Romans used a variety of materials, including broken stone, brick, or other clay objects. Instead of mixing the aggregate with the other materials and water, as is the practice today, the Romans usually placed the aggregate where they wanted it and then covered it with mortar, repeating the process as required by the structure being built. Large-sized, heavy aggregates were usually placed in the lower part of a structure, such as a wall, covered with mortar, and then followed by alternating layers of aggregate and mortar, with the smaller and lighter aggregates toward the top.

Roman concrete was used as a compressive material, one that can withstand weights that push on it. Centuries passed before reinforcing allowed concrete to be used in other types of structures. Roman concrete structures were often very large and massive, as required by the compressive forces, and well engineered. In addition to walls, the Romans built arches, vaults, and domes of the material. They knew how to use formwork to hold the concrete in place while it was curing. They often made the framework out of durable materials, such as brick, and left it in place instead of removing it as is the practice today. Although Roman concrete was often left exposed, the more usual procedure, especially in important buildings, was to cover it with a veneer of brick, stone, or stucco. Before the end of their era, the Romans exploited mass concrete to the ultimate, producing large, daring, and well-engineered structures of many kinds.

In addition to pozzolana cement, the Romans sometimes used other natural types. And lime mortar, used as a cementing material long before, was sometimes employed. However, lime mortar is relatively weak and, not being waterproof, must be protected. The Romans therefore preferred the other material. After the era of the Romans, the use of concrete in architecture virtually came to a halt.

During the Middle Ages, concrete was used only on rare occasions. Instead, lime mortar was often used for such purposes as the construction of rubble-stone cores of structural members that were then covered with finished stone. It is believed that the rubble was laid as stone is today, by placing a layer of mortar upon which the stones were then placed, instead of in the opposite manner used by the Romans. During the Renaissance, lime mortars were used but cement mortars, only very rarely. Such was the situation until the 18th century.

In 1752 an English engineer, John Smeaton (1724–92), rediscovered the making of hydraulic cement and used it first as mortar for a stone lighthouse in 1759, which he designed for Eddystone, England. After that, several other people developed cements. The first portland cement, named for Isle of Portland stone and for which it was at first considered a substitute, was patented by an English bricklayer, Joseph Aspdin (1779–1855), in 1824. For some years, it was used only in mortar for masonry work and mass concrete. But the beginning of the modern use of concrete had been assured.

American architects and engineers excelled in innovation and invention using structural steel, beginning in the 19th century. Innovation and invention in concrete, beginning in the same century, was almost exclusively the province of European architects and engineers for many years. Precast concrete was made in England about 1832. Reinforced concrete was patented by a Frenchman, Joseph Monier (1823–1906), in 1857. Prestressed concrete was used in Germany as early as 1886, but its uses in architecture were pioneered by the French engineer, Eugéne Freyssinet (1879–1962), in the 1920s and 1930s.

Many other great contributions of the development of concrete in architecture were made during the first half of the 20th century by such people as the French architect Auguste Perret (1874–1954), the Swiss-French architect Le Corbusier (1887–1965), the Swiss engineer Robert Maillart (1872–1940), the Italian engineer Pier Luigi Nervi (1891–1979) and the Spanish architect Felix Candela (1910–   ).

In later years, American architects and engineers have also been quite inventive and innovative in the use of concrete. Among them are architect Frank Lloyd Wright (1867–1959) and engineer Othmar Hermann Ammann (1879–1965). Others have also been involved in the development of structural concrete and their work is discussed in various articles in this book.

Related Articles BRIDGE; CONCRETE STRUCTURE; DAM; FIRE PROTECTION; FOUNDATION; MASONRY STRUCTURE; STRUCTURAL ENGINEERING; STRUCTURE; Various articles on architects and building components and systems.

Sources of Additional Information American Concrete Inst., P.O. Box 19150, Detroit, Mich. 48219; Portland Cement Assoc., Old Orchard Rd., Skokie, Ill. 60076.

CONCRETE STRUCTURE A building or other structure in which the structural frame, columns, joists, beams, girders, floors, and roof, and sometimes walls, elevator shafts, and vent shafts, are of concrete, which is usually reinforced with steel bars or mesh. Although used to some extent before, concrete first became a popular structural material during the time of the Romans, when it was used in mass without reinforcement. After the time of the Romans, concrete was used very little in architecture until the 18th century. Beginning in the late 19th century, with the development of reinforced concrete, its use in architecture has grown until the present time, when it is one of the most important materials for structures and other purposes.

Concrete is used today in mass, without reinforcement, in dams and other heavy construction. For the most part, reinforced concrete is used in buildings for such purposes as structures, walls, foundations, floors, walkways, driveways, roads, parking lots, and roofs. For the general subject of concrete, including portland cement and fine and coarse aggregates from which it is made, see the article entitled concrete.

Uses other than for structural frames of buildings, such as walls, foundations, paving, concrete or cement, brick, and concrete block masonry are discussed in articles in this book on various building components and systems.

Reinforced Concrete In addition to foundations (see the article entitled foundation), major structural uses of reinforced concrete are made in architecture. Reinforced concrete may be poured in place on building sites or precast, either on the sites or in manufacturing plants. Poured-in-place concrete is placed in forms in buildings in the exact locations where it will remain. Precast concrete is also placed in forms but after curing, it is moved into the final locations in buildings. The major advantage of precast concrete is that it can be poured under controlled conditions on the ground or on tables in standard, often reusable forms, that do not need structural supports while the concrete is curing. Poured-in-place concrete, on the other hand, except for floor slabs on grade or other similar applications, must be supported until it cures, with often elaborate, strong, engineered formwork and shoring. Thus precast concrete may often be considerably less expensive than poured-in-place concrete.

Poured-in-place concrete can be used for any structural purpose for which concrete is suitable. Precast concrete is often used for relatively small components, such as stair treads, curbs and gutters for roadways, and curtain-wall panels. A great number of structural components are precast today, including columns, joists, beams, girders, and decking units for floors and roofs. Such components are available in most localities in a limited range of sizes and strengths. For relatively large buildings, special sizes may be produced.

Precast concrete may also be used for very large structural components, such as entire walls or floors. For entire walls or portions of them, a system called tilt-up is often employed. Tilt-up construction consists of precasting a wall, or portion of one, on the ground in special forms, allowing the concrete to cure, and then tilting the entire assembly into place in a building, usually with the aid of cranes. Tilt-up walls may be structural, or loadbearing, or nonloadbearing. With this system, it is possible to cast walls with windows, doors, and other components in place. In tilt-up work, it is necessary to coat the forms with a bond-breaking agent, such as wax, paraffin, oil, paper, or others, to allow the precast walls to be detached easily from the forms.

Another technique for precasting entire floors and roofs, or large portions of them, is the lift-slab method. In general, the lift-slab method involves the erection of columns for a building, pouring a slab on grade around the columns, and then pouring additional slabs on top of the first, with bond-breaking materials between them. Each slab is then lifted into place with powerful jacks attached to columns, the columns being extended as required. The lift-slab system has the advantages of simple formwork, no need for shoring, work performed on the ground level, and speedy erection.

Steel-Reinforcing Types Reinforced concrete may be either poured in place or precast. The major structural principle of reinforced concrete is the combination of the high compressive strengths, resisting forces that push on it, of concrete with the high tensile strength, resisting forces that pull, of steel reinforcing. Steel reinforcing for use with concrete is of three general types: bars, often called rebars; welded wire mesh; and wire rope or cable. Rebars are available in a number of sizes, plain or deformed. The deformed bars have raised projections for better bonding with the concrete, and are designated by numbers, from the smallest number, 3 (about ⅜ inch in diameter) to the largest number, 18 (about 2¼ inches in diameter). Rebars are used for reinforcing beams, girders, columns, and other structural members. Welded wire mesh, sometimes called welded wire fabric, consists of wires welded to each other, at right angles, or sometimes welded to form triangles. Welded wire fabrics, made from wire of various gauges ranging from about 0.06 inch in diameter to about 0.5 inch, is used for reinforcing floors, roofs, walls, and similar structural components. Wire rope or cable is used for reinforcing prestressed concrete components.

The most widely used method for placing reinforcement in concrete structures involves locating carefully designed rebars or mesh, or both, in forms, supporting and tying them together properly, and then pouring concrete around them to make the proper bond and develop the required strength. Another method, often used today, is prestressing, which involves stretching the reinforcing steel to place it in tension, thereby placing the concrete in compression, before the building loads are placed on it. Prestressing has several advantages, including reduced sizes of structural members, use of lesser quantities of reinforcing steel and concrete, and resistance to cracking. Prestressing is accomplished by two methods: pretensioning and posttensioning. In pretensioning, the reinforcing is prestressed and then the concrete is poured around it. When the concrete has cured, the steel is released and the bond between steel and concrete maintains the tension in the one and the compression in the other. In posttensioning, tubes or other devices are placed in the form and the concrete poured around them. After the concrete has cured, reinforcing is inserted in the tubes, tensioned and anchored at the ends of the members. Both prestressing methods are widely used, sometimes in combination.

In reinforced concrete work, there are strict requirements of building and other codes and good practice for overlapping of bars or other reinforcing for the bending of bars, tying of reinforcing, amount of coverage of reinforcing by concrete, and many other factors. There are also strict requirements for joints between concrete pours, called construction joints, and for expansion joints. Construction joints must be designed and located properly and the concrete pours keyed to each other properly. Expansion joints are usually located at points where cracks are likely to occur, such as the intersections of wings of a building, and are also provided in long walls or other building elements. Expansion joints must also be designed and located properly.

In addition to the usual ingredients in concrete (portland cement, fine and coarse aggregates, and water); other materials, called admixtures, are often used for special purposes. Many types of admixtures are available, including those that retard the time of hardening, those that accelerate it, those that make concrete more waterproof, and those that make concrete mixes more workable.

Shapes Concrete is a plastic material and as such may be used to produce a great many shapes. The most common shapes are square or round columns, rectangular beams and girders, and flat slab floors and roofs. However, columns and other structural members may be formed in many other shapes. They may also be reinforced in only one direction, called a one-way system, as is usual in beams and girders and sometimes used in slabs; or in two directions, two-way systems, as most often used in slabs.

A form of slab often used is ribbed and consists of tee-shaped beams placed in a series, and either poured in place or precast. A variation of this, often referred to as a waffle, flat-plate slab, has ribs in two directions at right angles to each other. These slabs are poured over series of square forms.

Many other shapes are possible with reinforced concrete, including arches, vaults, and domes. Often used in buildings today are various shapes usually classified as thin shells. These shells may be designed in a number of shapes and can be very thin as compared to other structures, since reinforced concrete in the shells transmits direct compressive stresses throughout their entire areas. Often only enough concrete is required for the minimum allowable covering of the reinforcing, sometimes as little as a few inches in a very large shell, with some thickening near columns or other supports.

One of the simplest, thin-shell structures is called a folded-plate roof. It consists of thin-shell concrete plates connected together to form a series of triangles or other shapes when viewed from the end. Other types of thin-shell concrete structures include domes, barrel and other vaults, and hyperbolic paraboloids. While most thin-shell structures of these types are usually poured in place, precast units are sometimes available.

Tables of properties and characteristics of commonly used concrete structural members can be easily obtained. However, the use of such members and the design of more complex ones and of buildings with reinforced concrete structures require the services of skilled and talented structural engineers. As a plastic material which can be controlled and formed

almost at the will of architects and engineers, reinforced concrete is very versatile. Since it can be controlled and formed so readily, many architects and other environmental designers prefer it for many uses in buildings and other structures to any other structural material. The previous discussion of the properties and uses of concrete is general and can only be considered as a guideline. In practice, the design of reinforced concrete structures must follow the applicable building and other codes and the principles of good engineering, architecture, and construction.

History During the Roman period, and even earlier, concrete was used as a structural building material. The early uses were all in mass as a structural material dependent on its strength in compression. After the time of the Romans, concrete was no longer used to any extent as a structural material until the 18th century, when it again began to be used in mass as a compressive material. During the 19th century, reinforced concrete was developed.

Today mass concrete is sometimes used for such purposes as the structures of dams. In architecture, concrete has come into its own only in the reinforced and prestressed types.

Many of the early innovations in concrete were made in Europe; for further discussion see the article entitled concrete. In the United States, architects and engineers of the era were primarily concerned with steel structures. They still are to some extent, but interest in concrete as a structural material has grown rapidly in the United States in recent years. Reinforced concrete has been used in the United States as a structural material since about the beginning of the 20th century. None of the early American reinforced concrete buildings were as daring and innovative as those being built in Europe at the same time.

Later, American architects and engineers began to design innovative reinforced concrete structures. Some of the notable examples are the State Fair and Exposition Building (1955), Raleigh, N.C., designed by architect Matthew Nowicki (1910–49) in association with William Henry Dietrick (1905–   ) and with Frederick Severud (1899–   ) as the engineer; the Administration Building (1939) and Research Building (1950) for S. C. Johnson and Sons Company, Racine, Wis., by Frank Lloyd Wright (1867–1959); the Hayden Planetarium (1935), Chicago, by Trowbridge and Livingston; Lambert Airport (1955), St. Louis, by Hellmuth, Yamasaki and Leinweber; the Guggenheim Museum (1959), New York City, by Wright; and several buildings by Eero Saarinen (1910–61).

Today American architects and engineers continue to be interested in reinforced concrete and to use it in relatively high-rise buildings and others and in such systems as folded plates and domes.

Related Articles BRIDGE; CONCRETE; DAM; STRUCTURAL ENGINEERING; STRUCTURE; Various articles on building components and systems.
Further Reading Parker, Harry, and Harold D. Hauf: *Simplified Design of Reinforced Concrete*, 4th ed., John Wiley,

New York, 1976; Waddell, J.: *Concrete Construction Handbook,* 2d ed., McGraw-Hill, New York, 1974; Wilby, C. B., and I. Khwaja: *Concrete Shell Roofs,* John Wiley, New York, 1977.

Sources of Additional Information American Concrete Inst., P.O. Box 19150, Detroit, Mich. 48219; Concrete Reinforcing Steel Inst., 228 N. LaSalle St., Chicago, Ill. 60601; Portland Cement Assoc., Old Orchard Rd., Skokie, Ill. 60076.

CONSTRUCTION, BUILDING

The activities required to put all the parts together, make all the assemblies, install all the systems, and perform other functions necessary for constructing buildings, from preliminary site work to final finishes. In general, builders or home builders construct buildings, in particular they direct, and have overall responsibility for the construction. People who handle such work for larger and more complex buildings are usually called contractors, because they often contract with owners for the construction of buildings. However, architects sometimes perform the functions of contractors. Contractors fall into two major categories: general contractors who usually contract with owners for and have responsibility for entire buildings, and subcontractors who contract either with general contractors or owners for specialized portions of buildings, such as electrical, heating, or plumbing work.

Contracting Firms General contracting or building firms are organized in two major ways. One type of organization is large and complete, and usually constructs the basic parts of buildings, foundations, structure, carpentry work, and so on, with its own crews, using its own machinery and equipment, and subcontracting only the specialties, such as electrical, heating and air-conditioning, and plumbing work. This type of organization has been somewhat replaced by general contracting or building firms that own little or no machinery or equipment; have a relatively small number of regular employees, mostly management and supervisory people; and subcontract almost all of the phases of the work.

General Contracts General contracts for building construction are of two major types: the competitive bidding type and the negotiated type. For a competitive contract, the architect ordinarily receives bids from several general contractors, often ones who have been prequalified for competence, financial status, and other requisites. The contract is ordinarily awarded to the low bidder, though it need not always be, except in most government work. In a negotiated contract, the owner, with the counsel of the architect and often other consultants, awards the contract to the contractor thought to be the best choice for the job, without requiring bids. In either case, the contract is between the owner and the contractor. Subcontracts for various portions of the work may be included in the total price of the general contractor or they may be separate contracts between the owner and the subcontractors. For most public work, laws require that bids must be solicited by advertising. For private work, bids may be solicited through advertising or by invitations to contractors.

Construction Contracts Contracts for construction work are generally of two types: for a stipulated dollar amount, sometimes called a lump-sum contract; or for the actual cost of the construction work plus a stipulated fee, sometimes called a cost-plus contract. There are numerous advantages and disadvantages in each type of contract for construction work. The exact form to be used depends on the individual situation, and the alternatives must be thoroughly studied by the owner and architect.

Construction contracts, of whatever type, are based on construction documents prepared by the architect, engineers and other consultants, and their technicians. Construction documents primarily consist of a set of drawings, furnished as prints, now usually black-line or blue-line rather than blueprints, and a set of specifications, a book of instructions. The drawings show what is to be constructed and the specifications complement the drawings with verbal information on the construction. Drawings are made up into sets that include sheets on the purely architectural work and others on the various engineering aspects, such as structural, electrical, and mechanical work. Specifications have two main sections: the general conditions and the technical sections. The general conditions contain information on definitions: roles of the owner, architect, contractor, and subcontractors; insurance; changes in the work; and so on. The technical sections are organized in a manner that divides the actual construction work into 16 divisions, such as general requirements, site work, concrete work, masonry work, and so on. Sometimes supplementary construction documents may be required in specific situations.

After a general contractor has been selected, a contract is signed between the owner and the general contractor, or contracts between the owner and the general contractor and subcontractors. Often contractors are required to post bonds. Performance bonds provide for the award of payments, damages, to the owner if the contractors fail to perform their work properly, and labor and materials bonds guarantee payment of material and services bills from suppliers and the wages of workers if the contractors do not pay them.

Building Construction After the contract has been signed and the necessary building permits have been obtained, the actual construction of the building can begin. The general contractor oversees and manages the work, often by employing superintendents who perform these functions. Subcontractors manage their own work under the overall direction of the superintendent. And the construction work of the project goes forward, usually starting with site work that may include grading and excavation, proceeding to foundation work and then to framing the building. During these phases, some subcontractors start their work, at this stage called roughing-in, by putting in the first portions of piping, ductwork, electrical conduits, and so on. Gradually, the structure proceeds and the exterior covering of the walls begins. The last structural member at the top of the building is raised into place and the building is said to have been topped-out. It is a tradition in some places for the last structural member to carry a tree, and sometimes a flag, up with it. The covering of the exterior is then completed and the roofing is installed. At this point, the building has been completely enclosed, or weathered-in. Interior work begins; the subcontractors proceed with their work; windows, doors, and other items are installed. Finally, after some months for a small building or years for a large one, the building is completed.

During the construction the architect, engineers, and other consultants, or technicians representing them, will have made regular inspections of the work to ensure that it has been properly constructed and that the work is accomplished on schedule. Periodically, usually at the end of each month, the contractor will have made applications for progress payments, which the architect, after having made sure that they are correct, will have certified for payment by the owner and the owner will have paid.

Many other functions will probably have been performed by the architect, engineers, and other consultants, such as approval of material samples; tests and reports; checking of large-scale drawings, called shop drawings, made by subcontractors or suppliers to indicate exactly how they will fabricate or construct parts of the building; and checking and approval of change orders.

At the end of construction, the contractor delivers warranties, guarantees, maintenance schedules and instructions, and other pertinent information to the architect for the owner, and the architect certifies to the owner that the job has been completed. The contractor receives the final payment and the owner receives the keys to the building.

Sometimes, particularly for projects in which there have been substantial changes during construction, the architect, engineers, and other consultants may prepare as-built drawings, showing the actual construction. These are based on a set of construction documents, maintained at the site by the contractor, on which all changes are noted. If defects appear during the guarantee or warranty periods for the whole building or any of its parts, the contractors are required under their contracts to correct them.

For a single-family house, only a few workers may have been involved in the construction; for a high-rise office building or skyscraper, there may have been thousands. But each building will have been constructed of thousands of items of materials and products, each studied, designed, and painstakingly put into place.

Construction Management Another method for handling the actual construction of buildings that has increasingly been utilized during recent years is construction management. Although this phrase may be applied to the functions a general contractor, builder, or subcontractor perform in building construction, the new meaning is management of construction projects by people who work directly for owners in a manner similar to the way architects work. A construction manager, or more frequently a construction management firm, is engaged by an owner as an agent to oversee and direct the construction, and is paid a fee for these services in a manner similar to the fees paid other professionals: the architect, engineers, and consultants. The construction manager then contracts with others, in the name of the owner, for construction of the building. This may be by means of a general contract with subcontracts, but the more usual form is a series of subcontracts between the owner and the various contractors, including, in some cases, a subcontract for the work usually performed by a general contractor.

Several major advantages are claimed for the construction management system. A construction manager may be engaged early, at the beginning of the architectural process as a consultant on construction materials and processes to the owner and architect; the owner may be able to maintain more control over the project; the time required to design and build a project may be shortened, thereby saving considerable money; and the profits of the usual general contractor, if any, accrue to the owner. Many construction managers learned their business as general contractors; but others, including architects and engineers, have entered the field, either by specializing in construction management or by creating subsidiaries or departments that specialize in it.

Construction work, as contractors or construction managers, appeals to many people, who like work on the construction of buildings and other structures that is part sedentary office work and partly active on-the-job work and that combines business priniciples with the chance to create something. And many are drawn to construction because it offers a chance for a degree of independence, to work for oneself and to become an owner of a business.

In the past, many contractors came from a background of work in the building trades, and others from engineering or sometimes architecture. Today many of the people who eventually become contractors or construction managers are graduates of building construction programs in colleges. Often four years in duration and attached to architectural schools, building construction curricula usually offer B.S. degrees to students who complete the prescribed general courses and the specialized courses in such fields as building materials, structures, systems and equipment, architectural drafting, economics, business law, construction administration, estimating, scheduling, and procedures.

History Humans have constructed structures from the earliest primitive times. From the time of the most ancient cultures, the design and construction of buildings were considered to be related parts of a single function. As the concept of architects, those who devoted their careers to buildings and other structures, came to be accepted, it was also accepted that they would be responsible for both the design and the construction. This principle was followed for many centuries and in its most developed form produced the master builders of the ancient cultures in Mesopotamia, Egypt, Greece, and Rome. During the Middle Ages, the concept of the master builder persisted in the construction of the great Gothic cathedrals and other buildings. During the Renaissance, a division developed between those who designed buildings, the architects, and those who constructed them, the contractors. During the 17th century, the separation widened.

American Development   In colonial America, many of the early builders designed their own buildings and some of them became accomplished architects as well as craftsmen. As was happening in Europe, architects in America were either gentlemen-architects, who had learned their architecture from books and from whose designs others did the actual construction, or builder-architects or craftsmen-architects, who had learned their architecture from actual construction experience and generally designed and built their own projects. In a sense, the latter were still master builders. By the 18th century the time of the builder-architects was almost past, and by the 19th century it was gone. Since then, design has been the province of professional designers, architects, engineers, and others; and construction, the province of constructors, builders, and contractors. With the advent of construction management, some architects believe that some of the advantages of the master-builder system can again be achieved. And some architects today contract for the construction of buildings.

Related Articles   BUILDING INDUSTRY; Various articles on building materials and systems.

Further Reading   Clough, Richard H.: *Construction Contracting*, 3d ed., John Wiley, New York, 1974; Douglas, Clarence J., and Elmer L. Munger: *Construction Management*, Prentice-Hall, Englewood Cliffs, N.J., 1969; Foxhall, William B.: *Professional Construction Management and Project Administration*, 2d ed., the American Institute of Architects and *Architectural Record*, Washington, 1976; Merritt, Frederick S., ed.: *Building Construction Handbook*, 3d ed., McGraw-Hill, New York, 1975; Volpe, S. Peter: *Construction Management Practices*, John Wiley, New York, 1972.

Sources of Additional Information   American Subcontractors Assoc., 815 15th St., N.W., Washington, D.C. 20005; Associated General Contractors of America, 1957 E St., N.W., Washington, D.C. 20006; National Association of Home Builders of U.S., 15th and M Sts., N.W., Washington, D.C. 20005.

Periodicals   *Constructor*, 1957 E St., N.W., Washington, D.C. 20006; *NAHB Journal of Homebuilding*, 15th and M Sts., N.W., Washington, D.C. 20005; *Professional Builder*, 5 S. Wabash Ave., Chicago, Ill. 60603.

CONSTRUCTION CONTRACT ADMINISTRATION

The management of the construction of a building by an architect, together with engineers and other design professionals and technicians, as the representative of the building owner. Construction contract administration is ordinarily the last phase of what are called the basic services of architects, the preceding ones being the schematic design, design development, construction contract documents, and bidding or negotiation phases.

Formerly called supervision, the name of the administration phase was changed in the 1950s to avoid confusion with the supervision or superintendence of construction by contractors and because the earlier term did not reflect the full extent of an architect's duties and responsibilities during construction.

Administration Phase   The construction contract administration phase begins after a contractor has been selected to do the construction work. The services of an architect and other design professionals from that time on are mainly concerned with ensuring that the construction work conforms to the working drawings, specifications, and other contract documents and that the work is carried out efficiently, safely, economically, and on schedule.

The position of an architect in this phase is somewhat different from that in the preceding phases. In those phases, an architect acts primarily as a professional engaged by an owner to produce specific results, such as a design, contract documents, and so on, that will be in the owner's best interests. During the construction contract administration phase, an architect performs different functions: impartial interpretation of the contract documents and the performance of both owner and contractor as required by those documents. In the first phases, the architect is in the position of a professional actually performing services for a client, but in the administration phase, the architect assumes a position more like that of an arbiter or judge, even though still working for the client.

Basic Services   In the actual administration of construction contracts, an architect performs a number of specific services. In the performance of these services, assistance may come from technicians or other architectural staff members. Also, assistance in the administration of the engineering portions of the work and that of other design professionals is provided by the engineers and the others involved. In addition to the general administration of the work, an architect performs such services as the following: advising and consulting the owner and transmitting the owner's instructions to the contractor; periodic visits to the job to observe and inspect the work for progress and quality; receiving the contractor's applications for progress payments, usually on a monthly basis; verification of the work completed and certification to the owner; review and approval of samples, large-scale fabrication drawings (called shop drawings); and so on; preparation of change orders, for changes in the work approved by the owner; and final inspection, receipt of guarantees and warranties, and certification of the final payment to the contractor.

This brief description does not do justice to the great number of small and large questions that come up in the course of the construction of even smaller buildings. Some of these are solved without involving the architect and other design professionals, but others may require conferences, discussions, tests, and other procedures and may involve a number of people and many hours of time.

Other Services Architects and other design professionals also may perform other services during the construction phase, such as extra design, analysis, survey or cost estimating work, and preparation of as-built drawings, showing how a building was actually constructed. All of these are considered additional services and are not included in the fees paid by owners to architects for basic services. Also not included in the basic services is the cost of a full-time project representative, formerly called a clerk of the works. Sometimes, particularly on a large and complex building, it is considered desirable to have a full-time person on the construction job to represent the interests of the owner. When this is necessary, a project representative performs this function. Ordinarily selected, employed, and directed by the architect, a project representative's salary is paid by the owner.

While an architect and other design professionals or their representatives make only periodic visits to a construction site as required, a full-time project representative remains on the site during working hours each day when construction work is being performed. A project representative performs functions similar to those of an architect, but on a full-time rather than a part-time basis. The project representative also maintains files at the site, attends conferences there and reports on them to the architect, and performs other functions required for the orderly, timely, and economic progress of the work. Ordinarily, a project representative may not authorize deviations from the contract documents, perform any part of the work that is the responsibility of the contractor, or issue certificates of payment.

Construction contract administration occupies a very important place in architectural services. Without good construction, a building cannot become what it is intended to be even if its design is excellent and its contract documents properly prepared. Thus the administration phase should effectively complete the execution of architecture that began with a problem, a program, and a design. The functions of the architect and other construction contract administrators can ensure that this happy result actually occurs.

Others engaged in the construction having major functions are craft specialists, the manufacturers, the subcontractors, and the contractors. The work of the contractor is of primary importance, for it includes the responsibility for all the parts, components, and systems that make up the building and for all of the labor and other work that erects them there. The contractor must keep schedules, including those for deliveries of materials as well as of construction; must understand the contract documents and construct the building in accordance with them; must direct the construction with skill; and must meet payrolls and pay material invoices, keep accounts, and perform a myriad of other functions. And legally, the contractor, not the architect, is responsible to the owner for proper construction.

Construction contract administration services of architects are usually performed by three types of people: architects themselves, employees of architects who are themselves architects, and technicians, many of whom learned their craft in actual construction work. In order to do administration work of this kind properly, a person must have knowledge and experience in materials, systems, construction methods, contracts, and other practical matters of building construction, as well as in the principles of architecture.

History In the earliest days, administration of building construction was performed by those who did the work, that is, the workers, then for many hundreds of years by architects, or master builders, who not only designed the buildings but directed and worked on the construction. Not until the Renaissance did architects leave the construction of buildings to the builders. Thus it might be said that construction contract administration resembling the practice today came into being at that time.

American Development In colonial America, architects were either self-taught from books or had learned architecture by participating as craftsmen in its construction. The self-taught gentlemen-architects sometimes performed services very much like the construction contract administration of today and the craftsmen-architects performed the functions of contractors as well as those of architects. Most of these early architects practiced architecture only part-time as one of their pursuits. When architecture became a profession in America as first practiced by such architects as Charles Bulfinch (1763–1844) and Benjamin Henry Latrobe (1764–1820), supervision, or construction contract administration, became one of the important services they performed for their clients.

Related Articles CONSTRUCTION, BUILDING; COST CONTROL; DESIGN, ARCHITECTURAL; ENGINEERING; PRACTICE OF ARCHITECTURE; SPECIFICATION; WORKING DRAWING.

Further Reading Dubin, Martin D.: *Architectural Supervision of Modern Buildings*, Reinhold, New York, 1963; MacFarlan, A. A.: *Architectural Supervision on Site*, Applied Science Publishers, London, 1973; McKaig, Thomas: *Field Inspection of Building Construction*, McGraw-Hill, New York, 1958.

CONSTRUCTION MATERIALS The physical substances of which buildings are constructed. Because of the broad and almost all-encompassing nature of architecture, it is hard to conceive of a material that serves no useful purpose in architecture. However, some of these uses are relatively minor. The major materials of architecture can be classified into the natural, those that may be used in buildings without significant changes, and those that come from nature but must be considerably modified before being used. The major natural materials used today are stone and wood. The major modified or man-made materials include metals, such as aluminum, copper alloys, iron, and steel; ceramic materials, such as brick, glass, and tile; concrete; and plastics. A host of other materials are also of importance in architecture.

Construction materials then are the stuff from which buildings are made. They are used in structures, without which buildings would not stand. They are used in enclosures, such as walls and roofs, without which buildings would offer little shelter to humans. They are used for the manufacture of the myriad pieces that go to make up complete buildings, together with their systems. They are used for making ornamental features. Thus it may be seen that knowledge of the properties, applications, and economics of materials is absolutely necessary in architecture. And every person who contributes to the creation of architecture must have such knowledge.

Many architects maintain that materials, in addition to their important technical functions, are one of the primary determinants of architectural design. They believe that building designs, in order to produce excellent architecture, must utilize materials in a manner that fully exploits their unique characteristics and that fully expresses those characteristics. Although an oversimplification, it might be said that in this view, stone, a material that efficiently resists compressive forces (those that push on it) but is relatively inefficient in resisting tensile forces (those that pull), should be used in a manner that exploits and expresses the compression forces. And in addition, stone should be used in a manner that exploits and expresses its nature as a material that can be sawed or carved but cannot be extruded into long, thin pieces as can a material like aluminum.

Other characteristics of stone should also be expressed and exploited. Most of all, the stone must look like what it is, not like some other material with different properties and characteristics. In this view of materials as a major determinant of architecture, plastic wall or floor coverings should exploit and express their own nature and not, for example, be given a stone finish, texture, or pattern. The proper expression and exploitation of materials goes much further, into what some have called honesty of use, into good craftsmanship, and even into advanced philosophical theories of the nature of materials and their uses.

The view of materials as one of the primary determinants of architectural design was essentially developed in the late 19th and 20th centuries. In earlier periods, architects do not seem to have been too concerned with this principle. The architects of ancient Greece used stone in a trabeated, or post and lintel, structural system, one with vertical members, posts, or columns supporting horizontal members, lintels, or beams. The result is considered to be excellent architecture. On the other hand, the master builders of the Middle Ages used stone to produce great cathedrals, also considered to be of great excel-

lence, with an arcuated structural system, based on the principles of the arch. It is difficult to determine which method properly expressed and exploited the nature of stone. From the earliest times, buildings with structures of one material have been covered, or veneered, with another. For example, the Romans habitually constructed buildings of brick or concrete and covered them with stone or plaster. Many other examples could be cited in later periods.

Today many architects believe that the proper use of materials in architecture involves truthfulness to their innate natures, insofar as possible. Thus reinforced concrete, with which, unlike stone, great spans may be achieved, is used in a manner that expresses that fact. And concrete, as is fitting to a man-made material, is finished to look like concrete not like imitation marble or granite. Some architects do not agree with this position.

In any case, the selection of materials for use in architecture involves a number of considerations, including quantitative factors such as size, weight, and shape; chemical and physical properties such as strength, workability, durability, hardness and rigidity, compatibility with other materials, quality, and appearance; and a much more elusive factor, the character imparted by materials to buildings or portions of them.

For further discussion on all major materials used in architecture, see articles entitled aluminum; brick; concrete; copper alloy; glass; iron; plastics; steel; stone; tile; wood. Some discussion is also included in the articles on building components and systems, in which various materials are used.

Minor Materials However, a number of others, though not considered major materials, do have important functions in architecture. These include asbestos, asphalt, coal tar, gypsum, lead, Monel metal, terneplate, porcelain enamel, rubber, sand, gravel, slag, paper, and textiles. Many other metals and materials are also used in conjunction with architecture, in alloys of other metals; as ingredients of paints, coatings, and adhesives for plating or other coatings of materials; and many other uses.

Asbestos is a fibrous mineral used for many purposes in architecture. One of the major uses is in asbestos-cement which is made of portland cement and asbestos, in shingles, boards and sheet (flat or corrugated), in a number of sizes and thicknesses. These products are nonflammable, fire resistant, and long lasting and are used mainly for exterior and interior siding and for roofing. Asbestos-cement pipe, available in a range of sizes, is used for such purposes as sewers, drainage, and electrical conduits. Asbestos papers and textiles are used for retarding fire in various architectural components.

Asphalt and coal tar are bituminous products, natural or manufactured, mostly derived from coal or petroleum. Both are used for waterproofing, for paving streets and highways, in the construction of built-up roofs, as ingredients in certain paints and coatings, and in the manufacture of such products as resilient flooring, paving blocks, and building papers or felts.

Gypsum is a mineral that when heated, or calcined, loses most of the water it contains, and then cements together in any shape desired when water is added to it. Most gypsum is used in architecture for important functions, such as a major ingredient of plaster, plaster lath, and gypsum board, sometimes called sheet rock; in roof decking, both precast and poured; in tile, boards, and blocks for partitions; and for fire protection of columns and other structural elements.

Lead is used in architecture, mainly because of its heavy weight and softness, for such purposes as special flashing; rough hardware items, such as expansion shields for anchoring bolts or screws in masonry; equipment in laboratories; and as a shield against the radiation of atomic reactors and x-rays. It is also used in coatings for other materials, in paints, and in alloys with other metals.

Monel metal is an alloy composed of 66 percent nickel, 31.5 percent copper, and 2.5 percent iron, manganese, silicon, and other ingredients. It is very resistant to corrosion and does not stain most other materials. Relatively expensive, Monel metal is used mostly for laboratory sinks and other equipment and for high-quality roofing and flashing. Terne is an alloy of 80 percent tin with 20 percent lead, used to provide a protective coating for steel, in a product called terneplate. Terne-coated stainless or copper-bearing steel is called short terne and is used for roofing, flashing, gutters, and downspouts, or leaders. Terne-coated steel of other types, called long terne, is used for doors, door frames, and roofing. The stainless steel type need not be painted, but painting is recommended for the others.

Porcelain enamel, which is neither a procelain nor an enamel, is composed of metal, usually steel or aluminum, on which vitreous surfaces have been fused by high heat. The vitreous, glasslike finishes make the metals highly impervious to moisture, chemicals, pollution, and other hazards, except direct impact or bending. The base metals impart considerable strength to the material. Porcelain enamel may be obtained in a great variety of colors and in various sizes of sheets, panels, and other forms. The material is used mostly for exterior and interior wall panels and for kitchen and other equipment.

Rubber is made from a milky secretion, or latex, about 99 percent of which is obtained from rubber trees (Hevea brasiliensis), though other trees and plants also produce latex. Some 90 percent of the world's supply of rubber comes from Malaysia, Indonesia, and other countries in the Far East. Rubber has many uses in architecture: for resilient flooring, gaskets, and glazing strips; in paints and other coatings, and toppings for concrete floors; and as adhesives. Today many synthetic rubbers are used for similar purposes; one of the best known and most widely used is neoprene.

Sand, gravel, and slag (a by-product of blast-furnace production of iron) have a number of uses in architecture. Sand is a major ingredient of concrete, mortar, plaster, stucco, and terrazzo and is used for other purposes, such as fill. Gravel is used as an aggregate in concrete; for setting beds under concrete slabs; for finishing built-up roofs; for fill around buildings, particularly where good drainage is required; and for walkways and roadways. Slag is used for similar purposes and also in the manufacture of portland cement, mineral wool, and concrete block.

Paper is used quite often in building construction, in such products as building and roofing papers and felts; flashing; coverings for other materials, such as gypsum board; and wall coverings. Paper forms are often used for pouring concrete. In combination with other materials, such as asphalt, coal tar, plastics, and the like, papers are often used for waterproofing and similar purposes. Textiles are also used extensively in architecture, not only in interiors for carpeting, curtains, furniture upholstery, and the like but outside as outdoor carpeting and for awnings. Textiles are also used for roofing structures that are supported by air.

Historical Development In prehistoric times, humans lived in natural caves or those they dug. When humans began to construct rudimentary shelters, they turned to the materials that were close at hand and easy to work with. Thus the first man-made shelters are believed to have been rude huts made of poles covered with brush, leaves, or thatch; or tents made with poles covered with animal skins. Since these early buildings were made of organic materials that disintegrated very quickly, almost no remains of them have been found. However, it is known that the first building materials were mostly wood, which has continued to be an important building material ever since. Another early building material was mud.

Later, when more elaborate structures were constructed, wood was most likely to be used in areas where trees were plentiful. Elsewhere, early builders turned to other materials that were plentiful, including turf, mud, and adobe. Thus the concept of using materials that were available locally was established very early and became a regional tradition in architecture, which has lasted, though it has not always been honored, to the present time.

In the Neolithic period, European buildings continued to be constructed mostly of wood which was plentiful and well adapted to the climate. Early buildings in the Middle East and in Egypt utilized wood as a material, but the limited supplies were soon exhausted, and some wood was imported. Since the supply of clay in those areas was almost inexhaustible, most buildings were constructed of sun-dried brick, though wood continued to be used in a limited way. In time, bricks were burned in kilns improving their strength, making them more uniform in size and shape, and improving their resistance to water penetration. Brick, like wood, thus was established as an important building material in early times and has continued to be important to the present day.

In the Middle East, with little wood and almost no stone, brick has continued to be the major building material to this day. In Egypt, on the other hand, ample supplies of stone allowed the more important buildings to be constructed of that material. Terracotta was used after methods of glazing this material and brick were developed. Other materials also came into use, including bitumen for waterproofing and plaster made of clay or mud.

Although the ancient Greeks first constructed buildings of wood and then of brick, they had an abundance of fine stone, primarily limestone and marble. During the classical period in Greece, all the important buildings were of stone. At first, limestone with a rough surface was used with a covering of plaster made of burned limestone. Later buildings were of marble cut with precision, smoothly finished, and erected with accurate joints. Iron had been available as a building material for a long time, but was not much used until the time of the Greeks and then for only minor purposes, such as attachment of sculpture to buildings. Roofs were generally of marble or terracotta tiles. By the time of the construction of the Parthenon (432 B.C.), the Greeks had begun using some wrought-iron beams in their structures.

The Romans continued the use of stone as a building material, quarrying it not only in Italy but in Greece and other places. They also used brick extensively in their buildings and other structures. The most striking development by the Romans was the widespread use of concrete for buildings and other purposes. Roman concrete was composed of a natural volcanic earth, called pozzolana, found near Naples and in other places in Italy. Pozzolana was mixed with burned, slaked lime to form a good, strong cement. Cement mortar was then made into concrete by combining it with broken bricks or stones. Most of the concrete used in buildings was then plastered or covered with thin sheets, or veneers, of marble.

After the first century A.D., the Romans used concrete more often than any other building material. They continued to use stone, especially for covering concrete walls and other structures. They also used wood for framing walls and roofs and for floors. Wood-framed Roman buildings are not so well known as those of other materials since none of them has survived. The most used roofing materials were terracotta tiles, but stone slates were also used for this purpose. Glass was used in windows by the Romans beginning about the middle of the first century B.C. The first glass was colored, but later the Romans discovered a method of making relatively clear glass. Their method was later lost and was not rediscovered until the 15th century.

For various parts of buildings, the Romans used other materials, including wood for doors and bronze for both windows and doors, and, in a few cases, for columns and other structural purposes. Iron was sometimes used for structural members.

After the era of the Romans, few innovations were made in building materials for quite a long time. By the 7th century, both tin and lead were sometimes used for roofs, and iron was used for hardware and grilles. Other than these, the most prevalent building materials were those that had been used in the past. During the Middle Ages, the use of stone increased, particularly in important buildings such as cathedrals. These usually were of stone, with wood-framed roof structures. In England, brick making resumed in the 13th century, after a lapse of more than 800 years. Glass also began to be more widely used in windows, not only of churches and cathedrals but in larger houses. The glass was thick, uneven, and greenish, and came only in small pieces that were held together with strips of lead. Wood was also extensively used in the Middle Ages, a time when methods for framing heavy timbers were developed. Also half-timber structures were constructed. These employed heavy timbers in their structural systems with plaster filling the spaces between the timbers. Concrete fell into disuse during the Middle Ages.

During the Renaissance, few innovations were made in building materials. Architects of the period seemed content to stay with materials that had been used before, but with increasing refinement in their treatment. Stone continued to be the most important building material for all but the simplest buildings, but wood and brick were used extensively. Concrete was used sparingly, but iron came to be used more often than before, especially for structural members. Window glass was improved considerably and was used in buildings of all types. Renaissance architects made great progress in the use of traditional materials in innovative structural ways, but developed no important new materials.

After the Renaissance, building materials were mostly brick, stone, and wood, varying between localities mainly because of availability. In cities, because of fire hazards, stone was the favored material and brick was also used. Beginning in the early 19th century, a number of people developed artificial cements, whose manufacture was not dependent on natural materials, such as pozzolana. The most successful came to be called portland cement, because it was supposed to produce a concrete that could be substituted for Isle of Portland stone. Invented by an English mason and builder, Joseph Aspdin (1779–1855), this cement in time revolutionized building construction and remains a very important material today. With the advent of artificial cement, concrete began to be used more extensively in buildings and other structures.

Although it had been used to some extent much earlier, iron started to become an important building material during the 18th century and came into its own during the 19th. Both wrought and cast iron were utilized, first for the structures of bridges, then for those of buildings. Later, both materials were used for other architectural purposes, such as in decorative ironwork and even for entire fronts, or facades, of some buildings. Although steel had been manufactured in relatively small quantities for several centuries, it was only used for minor parts of buildings until the late 19th century, when the architects of the so-called Chicago school began to design steel-framed tall buildings. The use of steel in structures has since become standard practice everywhere.

Concrete had been extensively used by the Romans, fell into disuse for an extended period, then once again became an important building material in the 19th century. Until that time, it was always used as mass concrete, which had great strength in compression but much less in tension. In the 19th century, various experiments were made involving the embedding of iron rods in concrete to improve its tensile strength. This marked the beginning of the development of reinforced concrete.

Beginning in the 19th century and continuing to the present time, many other materials have been developed and are now used in buildings. Almost every material known has some usefulness in building construction. Most types of metals are used to some extent. Composite materials, in which two or more materials are combined, are used extensively. Plastics have assumed an important position in building construction. Research and development continues at the present time, and it can be expected that new materials will be forthcoming as well as new uses for older types and new uses of materials in combinations.

American Development The history of materials in building construction in America generally parallels that elsewhere. In early colonial days, the materials used were those available locally, wood generally in the Eastern and Southern states, brick and other clay products in the Southwest. Stone also began to be used early in American history. It was plentiful in some areas and quarrying was started early. For many years, stone was the preferred material for the most important buildings.

As cast and wrought iron became available, American architects turned to those materials, with which they pioneered in the design of tall buildings. They also pioneered in the use of steel in tall buildings. Reinforced concrete became an important American building material. And American architects have been enthusiastic users of most other new materials that have been developed. Today the most important materials used in American architecture are aluminum, brick, concrete, copper, glass, iron, miscellaneous metals, plastics, steel, stone, tile, and wood.

Related Articles DESIGN, ARCHITECTURAL; STRUCTURE; Various articles on specific materials, structural methods, and building systems and components.

Further Reading Brady, G.: *Materials Handbook*, 10th ed., McGraw-Hill, New York, 1971; Hornbostel, Caleb: *Construction Materials—Types, Uses and Applications*, John Wiley, New York, 1978; Hornbostel, Caleb, and William J. Hornung: *Materials and Methods for Contemporary Construction*, Prentice-Hall, Englewood Cliffs, N.J., 1974; Smith, R.: *Materials of Construction*, 2d ed., McGraw-Hill, New York, 1973.

CONTEMPORARY ARCHITECTURE Although the word *contemporary*, strictly speaking, means living, occurring, or existing at the same time and therefore might be applied to any era, the meaning here is taken to be architecture of the present era. Sometimes the phrase *modern architecture* is used to denote such current work. That phrase is equally inaccurate, but because of its widespread acceptance in this sense it has been used in this book to denote the architecture of the late 19th and early 20th centuries, from the beginning of the revolt against eclecticism and the development of a new type of architecture that would be of its own time. For purposes of convenience in this book, the end of modern architecture has been taken to have occurred with the deaths of the great modern masters: Frank Lloyd Wright (1867–1959), Le Corbusier (1887–1965), Ludwig Mies van der Rohe (1886–1969), and Walter Adolf Gropius (1883–1969), in the 1950s and 1960s. Thus in this book both phrases are somewhat arbitrary. Also the eras overlap, since many of the architects practicing today or who practiced recently were already in practice before the death of the last master.

Contemporary Architects Some notable architects, born early in the 20th century, are still in practice, including Philip Cortelyou Johnson (1906–   ); and Minoru Yamasaki (1912–   ); see articles entitled Johnson, Philip Cortelyou; Yamasaki, Minoru. Marcel Lajos Breuer (1902–   ) and Wallace Kirkman Harrison (1895–   ) practiced until recently; see the articles entitled Breuer, Marcel Lajos; Harrison, Wallace Kirkman. Other important contemporary architects, still in practice or who practiced until recently, include Paul Albert Thiry (1904–   ), Harry Weese (1915–   ), Edward Larrabee Barnes (1915–   ), Bertrand Goldberg (1913–   ), Hugh Stubbins (1912–   ), John Johansen (1916–   ), Cloethiel Woodard Smith (1910–   ), John Lyon Reid (1906–   ), Paul Schweicker (1903–   ), Ralph Rapson (1914–   ), and Paul Rudolph (1918–   ).

Important contemporary architects who emigrated to the United States include Gunnar Birkerts (1925–   ), from Latvia; Ieoh Ming Pei (1917–   ), from China; Kevin Roche (1922–   ), from Ireland; Cesar Pelli (1926–   ), from Argentina; and Ulrich Franzen (1922–   ), from Germany. Other contemporary architects of importance include Victor Lundy (1923–   ), Robert Venturi (1925–   ), and his wife, Denise Scott-Brown (1931–   ); Charles Willard Moore (1925–   ); and Richard A. Meier (1934–   ). Among the firms of importance today are Davis and Brody; Gwathmey and Siegel; MLTW/Turnbull; Hartman and Cox; McCue, Boone and Tomsick (MBT); Geddes, Brecher, Quarles and Cunningham; Hardy, Holzman, Pfeiffer; and Mitchell and Giurgola.

Firms Today a number of relatively large firms offer not only basic architectural services but engineering and various combinations of landscape architecture, interior design, graphic design, construction

CONTEMPORARY ARCHITECTURE Marina City (1967), Chicago, Ill. [*Architect: Bertrand Goldberg. (Hedrich-Blessing)*]

CONTEMPORARY ARCHITECTURE Blue Cross Building (1968), Chicago, Ill. [*Architects: C. F. Murphy Assoc. (Hedrich-Blessing)*]

CONTEMPORARY ARCHITECTURE Bronx Development Center (1977), Bronx, N.Y. [*Architect: Richard Meier. (Ezra Stoller)*]

management, and other services. Some of these firms have been in existence for a long time. One of the oldest is Shepley, Bulfinch, Richardson and Abbott, which grew out of the practice of Henry Hobson Richardson (1838–86), established in 1865. The firm, in spite of a number of name changes, still practices in Boston. Perhaps the oldest firm still in practice, which also has had a number of name changes, established in 1853, is Smith, Hinchman and Grylls, of Detroit, whose president, for a number of years, was Robert Frank Hastings (1914–73), and whose current president is Philip J. Meathe (1926–   ). Perkins and Will, in Chicago, was founded in 1935 by Lawrence Bradford Perkins (1907–   ) and Philip Will (1906–   ); Skidmore, Owings and Merrill in 1936, New York and other offices, by Louis Skidmore (1897–1962), Nathaniel Alexander Owings (1903–   ), and John Ogden Merrill (1896–1975). Welton Becket and Associates, Los Angeles, Calif., and other offices, was founded in 1933 by Welton David Becket (1902–69) and Walter Wurdeman (1902–48); Caudill, Rowlett and Scott, Houston, Tex., founded in 1946 by William Wayne Caudill (1914–   ), John Miles Rowlett (1923–78), and Wallie Eugene Scott, Jr. (1921–   ); The Architects Collaborative (TAC), Cambridge, Mass., founded in 1946 by Walter Adolf Gropius and a group of young architects; and Hellmuth, Obata and Kassabaum, founded in 1955 by George Francis Hellmuth (1907–   ), George Edward Kassabaum (1920–   ), and Gyo Obata (1923–   ). Of course, there is not sufficient space to list the many other excellent American architects and firms practicing today. However, the work of quite a few is shown in the many illustrations in this book.

Complex Problems   The problems faced by these architects today are very complex and their attempts to solve them are varied and inventive. Many people have tried to analyze this situation and have mostly failed to shed much light on either the problems or their solutions. This is understandable for many reasons. First, there is the complexity of life in today's world. Second, very few philosophers, architects, or critics have ever been able to analyze properly and draw meaningful conclusions about contemporary periods. And perhaps most important of all, those who try are often poorly equipped in breadth of knowledge, depth of thought, objectivity, and purity of purpose for such Herculean tasks as the analysis and drawing of conclusions about people, life, and architecture in the present era. However, it seems to be a necessity that humans attempt to understand themselves and the world in which they live. And no harm will be done if the pronouncements and manifestos of those who believe they have found the answers are received with patience, skepticism, and, above all, a sense of humor. No attempt at any real analysis, much less drawing conclusions, will be made here. Rather, the discussion will attempt to develop some degree of understanding of the state of contemporary architecture as it reflects the state of life and thought in the world today.

On the one hand, life is full of stresses, rapidly changing, and impermanent. Today is an era of violence, small wars, threats of wars, hijacking of airplanes, terrorists, bombings, kidnappings, increase in violent crimes of all kinds. It is a time of political unrest; demonstrations, peaceful and otherwise; and widespread and frequent strikes, even among public protectors, such as fire fighters. There is increasing permissiveness in ethics, morals, sex, and most of the

CONTEMPORARY ARCHITECTURE   Crown Center (1972), Kansas City, Mo. [Architect: Edward L. Barnes. (Hedrich-Blessing)]

CONTEMPORARY ARCHITECTURE Ford Foundation Building (1967), New York, N.Y. [*Architects: Kevin Roche and John Dinkeloo. (Ezra Stoller)*]

CONTEMPORARY ARCHITECTURE Hallowell Social Center (1975), Mount Holyoke College, South Hadley, Mass. [*Architect: Hugh Stubbins. (Joseph W. Molitor)*]

other principles of civilized human life. There are accompanying decreases in esthetics and other standards, and in manners, and increases in the use of alcohol, drugs, and other mind-modifying substances and practices. It is a time of extreme social stresses, caused by minority groups, special-interest groups of other kinds, and people with high-speed, high-pollution-producing, high-noise-level machines of various kinds. There is worldwide, seemingly uncontrollable and unending inflation.

On the other hand, today's world is one of rising expectations among people for better, more comfortable, and more meaningful lives. It is a time of increasing freedom for nations and liberties and human rights for individuals. There is increasing concern for the needs of ordinary citizens, often referred to as consumers, even though almost always also producers. There is increasing concern for the sociological and humanistic aspects of human life. There is increasing concern for other living things sharing planet earth, with conservation and elimination of pollution in the atmosphere, water bodies, and the earth. This is a time of scientific and technological exploits of many kinds. It is a time of interest in history and of preservation or restoration of the historic past, including its architecture.

All this adds up to a confused world in which to create architecture. In other arts, it has led, in recent years, to such movments as Op art, using forms, color, and other means for producing abstract sensations in the human eye; Pop art, using comic strips, soup cans, and other everyday objects as the basis for paintings; Happenings, events intended to be works of art through the presentation of certain experiences; Earthworks, sculptures, usually large scale, created in the earth itself; and others.

Many people have found these movements baffling but also often inventive and satisfying in newly discovered kinds of ways. In any case, of the so-called fine arts, only architecture is expected to be useful. Such experimentation in the other fine arts may be accepted or rejected by each individual. In architecture, most users or consumers do not have that choice. And many users find themselves baffled by the architecture of today. This confusion also extends itself to many of the owners of buildings, to the clients of architects, and to not a few architects.

Building Designs Many architects are producing very competent, often excellent, building designs. They have learned how to exploit the great technology of the time in daring structures, masterful use of materials, and sophisticated and efficient systems, such as heating and air conditioning, lighting, and so on. They know how to produce comfortable interiors. And above all, many have learned to provide for the sociological, humanistic, esthetic, and other needs of the people who occupy or use the buildings. Nevertheless, there is unrest among architects today. And the critics and others who attempt to analyze and draw conclusions about the architecture of today often add to the unrest. No wonder that owners and users are perplexed.

Current Labels To gain some appreciation of the problems, it may help to look at some of the phrases or labels being attached to the architecture of today. One such label is postmodernism, a word meaning simply after, or later than, modernism. This implies that the modern movement has ended. Other phrases include neorationalism, postfunctionalism, contextualism, allusionism, ornamentalism, and historicism. Now rationalism is the philosophy that holds that knowledge comes from reason, independently of the senses. Thus neorationalism must mean rationalism that is new.

CONTEMPORARY ARCHITECTURE Coogan House (1972), Long Island, N.Y. [*Architects: Gwathmey and Siegel. (Ezra Stoller)*]

CONTEMPORARY ARCHITECTURE Venturi House (1964), Philadelphia, Pa. [*Architects: Venturi and Rauch. (Ezra Stoller)*]

Function has long been one of the determinants of good architecture; thus postfunctionalism can only mean that architecture has gone beyond that to a stage in which being functional is no longer required. Context means the part of anything, particularly in writing or literature, in which the meaning is to be found. Thus, contextualism, in architecture, may denote its meaning, but in a literary sense. An allusion is an indirect reference to something. In architecture, does allusionism refer to the same thing? And does ornamentalism in architecture mean the addition of something intended only to embellish, decorate, or adorn? And does historicism in architecture mean the attempt to add to modern building designs forms from the historic past, a sort of latter-day eclecticism?

Historicism   In any case, there appears to be a sort of historicism in these times that seems to cause many present-day architectural designs to be derived from historic eras, including the present one. An example may clarify the situation. One architect may design an award-winning building, using the latest technology, techniques, and forms and, for his next building, select forms from past periods, while using present-day technology and techniques, perhaps in a less than forthright manner. Another architect, who has excelled in forms reminiscent of those of the past but not really derivative from them, designs his next building in a form similar to that which the first architect has only recently discarded.

One architect lauds the glories claimed to be observed in the shoddy, often subhuman environment of the Times Square area of New York City or the garish environment of the gambling casino area of Las Vegas, Nev. Another builds only underground. Still another designs buildings with ornament, seemingly derived from the past, but actually more of a caricature of historic forms, embellished with some of the effects of the latest *avant garde* movements in painting, sculpture, or the other arts. Some architects design buildings with exposed, and exploited, examples of technology, such as heating and air-conditioning ductwork, plumbing stacks, and others. Some paint these and other portions of their buildings in very bright colors to form abstractions, such as may be found in certain types of painting. Some decorate their buildings with what they call supergraphics, large, often brightly colored, ornamental forms derived from typography and other graphic design elements.

In 1974 a book by Walter C. Kidney, entitled *The Architecture of Choice—Eclecticism in America 1880—1930,* was published by George Braziller, New York City. Some think the author stopped his work too soon, that the architecture of choice, or eclecticism, has been reborn today in the designs of many contemporary architects. Traditionally, eclectic architecture has denoted a style, or movement, in which forms and details are selected from any of the styles of the past, either from one building or style, or from several recombined into a single building. If the con-

temporary movement in architecture is indeed eclectic, the definition will require expansion to include such selection and recombination not only of forms and details of the past but of the present.

In addition, there seems to be historicism of another sort extant today. This seems to involve a return to something resembling the ideas of the movement in architecture called Mannerism, which occurred in the 16th century as a revolt against the rules and principles of the Renaissance. In Mannerism, the accepted forms, proportions, and other elements of architecture and other arts were discarded in favor of confused and often arbitrary juxtapositions of forms and deliberate distortions of scale and proportion, often resulting in bizarre examples of sculpture, painting, and architecture. Some architects today seem to believe that, above all things, they must be original at any cost; some seem to be always seeking new thrills. And the result is often similar to that of mannerist architecture.

In spite of all the confusion, many individual architects and firms continue to design excellent buildings that serve their purposes, function well, serve the needs and desires of the people who use them, and fulfill the requirements of their owners. Many of these building projects are large and complex; many are composed of several buildings and related areas; some are for multiple uses, requiring unusual skills in handling relationships between elements. Undoubtedly, such architects will continue to design excellent buildings and young architects will come along in time to perform just as well and even better. In time also, an analysis of and conclusions about the present era will be possible, and the era will take its proper place in history. At that time, it may well be that the confusion of the present will be found to have been mostly a matter of thrill seeking or even of semantics. (For additional illustrations, see color section.)

Related Articles   ECLECTIC ARCHITECTURE; HISTORY OF ARCHITECTURE; MODERN ARCHITECTURE; Various articles on modern and contemporary architects.

Further Reading   See listings in articles entitled history of architecture; modern architecture.

Periodicals   *AIA Journal,* 1735 New York Ave., N.W., Washington, D.C. 20006; *Architectural Record,* 1221 Avenue of the Americas, New York, N.Y. 10020; *Progressive Architecture,* 600 Summer St., Stamford, Conn. 06904; Various foreign architectural magazines.

COPPER ALLOY   An alloy made from copper with tin, zinc, or other metals. Used in architecture for a great many purposes, the major copper alloys include true bronze, containing tin; bronzelike alloys, containing one or more other metals, such as zinc, lead, or nickel, and nonmetallic elements, such as silicon; brass, containing zinc, and sometimes lead, tin, manganese, or silicon. Other alloys include copper-nickels; nickel silvers, with copper and the other two metals; and leaded coppers. Pure copper has a minimum of 99.3 percent copper.

Properties of Copper   Copper has high electrical

and thermal conductivity. It is extremely ductile, capable of being stretched without breaking, and malleable, capable of being shaped or otherwise worked without breaking. It is nonmagnetic, highly resistant to corrosion by air or salt water, but not resistant to acids and alkalies. When exposed to air, copper and its alloys acquire a coating, called a patina, that protects them from further corrosion. Admired by many as an admirable property of copper and its alloys, patinas gradually change the surface colors to grayish green in about six years of exposure. Copper and its alloys can be efficiently worked by all the current metalworking methods, including casting, extrusion, bending, drawing, forging, welding, brazing, and soldering.

Properties of Copper Alloys Copper alloys generally have properties and characteristics similar to those of copper. However, some alloys are strong enough to be used for certain structural purposes and have other properties and characteristics that vary somewhat from those of copper. A great number of copper alloys are available today. Some of those most used include commerical bronze, with 90 percent copper, 10 percent zinc; red brass, 85 percent copper, 15 percent zinc; cartridge brass, 70 percent copper, 30 percent zinc; Muntz metal, 60 percent copper,

40 percent zinc; architectural bronze, 57 percent copper, 40 percent zinc, 3 percent lead; silicon bronze, 97 percent copper, 3 percent silicon; nickel silver, 65 percent copper, 25 percent zinc, 10 percent nickel; and leaded nickel silver, 45 percent copper, 42 percent zinc, 10 percent nickel, 2 percent manganese, 1 percent lead. As may be seen, the so-called commercial and architectural bronzes of today are actually brasses, since they contain zinc rather than tin. Silicon bronze is not a true bronze either, since it contains no tin. The only true bronze used in architecture today is statuary bronze, composed of copper, tin, and various combinations of other metals, including zinc, lead, and nickel. Different alloys, all containing tin, yield varying characteristics and colors. Statuary bronze is used in architecture for such purposes as sculpture, ornament, and hardware.

Uses Pure copper is used for many purposes in architecture, including roofing, flashing, insect screening, hardware, piping, and electric wiring. Copper alloys are used for an even greater variety of purposes, including curtain walls, storefronts, doors and frames, plumbing fixtures, windows, furniture, flag poles, railings, and many other kinds of equipment for buildings. Copper is also used in other ways, for example, as an alloying metal in steel to improve its

COPPER ALLOY Student Center, Goucher College (1963), Towson, Md. [Architect: Pietro Belluschi. (Joseph W. Molitor)]

corrosion resistance, as a pigment in coatings, for the plating of other metals, and as a wood preservative.

Production Copper is produced by several processes, including a type that involves crushing and grinding the ore in a mill, with water, into slurry; mixing the slurry with oil and chemicals in a floating tank, which causes the copper-bearing particles to rise to the surface, forming a froth of copper concentrate which is about one-third or less pure copper; after the froth has been scraped off, the concentrates are again ground, passed through flotation tanks, and filtered. From the mill, the copper concentrate goes to a smelter where it is heated in a reverberatory furnace, forming copper matte, still quite impure. It is then put into a converter, where silica is added and air is forced through the molten copper matte, producing blister copper which has a purity of 97 percent or more. The blister copper is then placed in a firecoating or electrolytic furnace for further refining. About half the copper used in the United States comes from recycled products. Copper in products to be recycled has a value of as much as 90 percent of that of the primary metal.

Finishes Copper alloys may be obtained with a number of different kinds of finishes, including asfabricated; buffed, the result of grinding, polishing, and buffing; directional textured; and nondirectional textured. Directional-textured finishes are available in five grades, from the finest to the coarsest, called fine satin, medium satin, coarse satin, uniform, and brushed. A relatively expensive finish is the handrubbed. Nondirectional textured finishes come in fine, medium, and coarse matte. Copper alloys may also be colored with chemicals, laminated with protective plastics, or coated with plastic coatings.

In using copper alloys in architecture, care must be taken not to connect them directly to other metals and not to place copper alloys where water can run off them onto other metals. Because of galvanic action or electroysis, copper alloys, low in the galvanic scale, will cause deterioration, or even destruction, of most other commonly used metals. Copper alloys should never be used where sulfur is present and should be used with care where acids and alkalies are present. Moisture runoff from copper alloys may stain some kinds of stone and other materials.

Copper and its alloys are very important in architecture, particularly those cases which call for high-quality materials. In many instances, and for many functions, copper and its alloys are considered the best choices possible.

History Some doubt exists about which metal, gold or copper, was first used by humans and when. Both occur naturally, gold almost always in veins, lodes, or placer deposits; and copper in particles, nuggets, and sometimes masses. Since many other metals are found only in ores or in combination with other minerals, it is understandable that gold and copper, followed by silver and lead, were the first usable metals.

It is believed that the first copper was used by humans during the Neolithic, or New Stone, Age, beginning about 5000 B.C. Some believe the metal may have been used 3,000 years earlier. However, no objects made of the metal at that time have been found.

There is little evidence that any considerable progress was made in the use of copper until about 3000 B.C., which is assumed to be the beginning of the Bronze Age. About that time, various methods of extracting copper from ore were developed, along with the process of annealing by heating the metal. As time went on, methods for melting, casting, and other techniques were developed, along with methods of extracting already alloyed bronze. By about 1400 B.C., methods for alloying copper with tin to produce bronze had been discovered.

Most of the early uses of copper and bronze were for relatively small, functional articles, such as tools and containers for food and drink, and later for weapons, armor, and works of art. The first use of copper or bronze in architecture has not been established. However, the use of these metals for ornamental sculpture, furniture, and small hardware and fittings certainly began about 1000 B.C., for doors shortly afterward, and was well established by about 600 B.C. in the Middle East as well as in Egypt. Between those dates, alloying copper with zinc to form brass was discovered. From that time, copper alloys have been important architectural materials. And bronze has been considered, in almost every era, to be one of the finest architectural and sculptural materials. In the earliest days, the main source of copper was on the island of Cyprus, Cyprium in Latin, from which came the Latin word *cuprum* or, in English, copper. Today the United States leads the world in mining copper, over half of it coming from Arizona.

The ancient Greeks used bronze for sculpture, for fittings to hold sections of columns together, and for attaching various architectural elements to buildings. The Etruscans also used bronze for sculpture and other purposes. The Romans used copper and bronze extensively in architecture and for sculpture, ornament, roofing, doors, furniture, candelabra, fittings for stone and brick elements, and many other purposes. In the Pantheon (A.D. 124), the Romans used bronze girders, since removed, for the structure of the roof of the portico and gold-plated copper or bronze tiles, later replaced with lead, for the roofing of the dome. After the Romans, copper production came almost to a halt and the small amount produced went mostly into utensils and ornaments for religious purposes.

During the Renaissance, copper alloys were used extensively. Bronze was a preferred material for sculpture, including sculptured doors, other ornamental purposes, and parts of furniture. Other copper alloys were widely used for many purposes similar to those of today. Since the Renaissance period, in America as well as in other places copper alloys have continued to be of great importance in architecture.

Related Articles ART IN ARCHITECTURE; DOOR; ELECTRIC POWER AND WIRING; HARDWARE; ORNAMENT; PLUMBING; ROOFING; WATERPROOFING.
Source of Additional Information Copper Development Assoc., 405 Lexington Ave., New York, N.Y. 10017.

COST CONTROL The process undertaken to ensure that the amount of money spent for a building or other structure will be kept within its budget or other proper limits. Control of costs of architectural and related services and actual construction has always been an important consideration in architecture. Since costs of construction have been rising rapidly for many years, it is even more important to keep costs under strict control. And it can be expected that continued inflation will cause construction costs to rise further in the future, making controls increasingly important.

Proper cost controls start at the beginning of an architectural project, when a need for a building or other structure has been identified. They should continue through all the phases of architectural and related services, through the construction, and, according to some experts, through the whole life of a building or structure. Good cost control requires that reliable data be available and that the data be interpreted properly by trained, intelligent cost experts, using up-to-date methods for analysis and projections. While architects and other design professionals may not be legally responsible for the construction costs of projects, they have responsibilities for keeping their clients informed of probable costs and for having clients approve their estimates.

Estimates An estimate is an approximate calculation of the costs of construction of a building. Architects, other design professionals, and others in the building industry utilize estimates of two major types: unit estimates and quantity estimates. Unit estimates are based on the principle of establishing a price for each unit of a certain kind that will go into a building or other structure, such as square feet of floor area. The unit price multiplied by the total number of units establishes the total cost. Quantity estimates are based on the principle of actually determining the exact number of items to go into a building or other structure, such as doors, windows, cubic yards of concrete, and so on, and then determining the complete cost of these items as constructed into the building or structure, including purchase price, delivery to the site, labor, overhead, and profit of contractors. These prices are then added to establish an estimated total cost. In an inflationary era, this total estimated cost must then be projected to the time of actual construction to determine what the total estimated cost will be when the effects of inflation have been considered.

Unit estimating is not as accurate or reliable as quantity estimating. Some unit-price estimating systems, beginning with the least reliable and proceeding to the most reliable, are the area, or square-foot, method; volume, or cubic-foot method; and the unit-of-use method, which uses, for example, the estimated cost per hospital bed or school pupil. While all these methods are frequently employed, they are, at best, only useful for early, very rough estimates of construction costs. Another method, more refined than the others, is the unit-of-enclosure system, which requires determination of the total quantity of construction: walls, floors, roofs, and so on enclosing a building. This quantity is then multiplied by a unit rate, derived from reliable data. The quantity estimating method, called quantity surveying in England and sometimes in this country, is the most reliable and accurate current method.

For estimating by means of the area and volume unit methods, systems have been established for the relative values given to areas and volumes of various types. While practices vary, a typical square-foot system might assign full value to ordinary floor areas in buildings measured from exterior wall to exterior wall; and for special areas, decreased values such as ⅔ of regular floor areas to heated garages, enclosed walkways, and porches; ½ value to unheated garages and penthouses; ⅓ value to carports, nonenclosed porches, and walkways; and ¼ value to roof overhangs.

After the determination of the number of square feet of area for each of the elements of the structure listed above, each total is multiplied by its proper fractional value, and the gross area determined. The gross total, in square feet, is then multiplied by an estimated cost per square foot to determine the total estimated cost of the building. The cost per square foot to be used is usually derived from published cost indexes for specific building types, modified by as much applicable information as can be gathered. Some of the modifiers might include the area of the country in which the building site is located, inflation and other cost-increasing factors during the time between the estimate and that of construction, seasonal cost factors such as the possibility of slowdowns because of bad weather, the effect of unusual design factors, and so on.

In a similar way, the other unit estimate methods entail totaling the units and multiplying them by unit prices to determine the gross total estimated costs of buildings. Quantity estimating also makes use of unit prices, but in this case they are prices for relatively small elements of buildings and therefore may be more accurate.

Quantity estimating is more accurate in another important way since it involves actually counting the materials, equipment, and so on that will go into a building and then establishing a unit price for each that may then be multiplied by the total quantities. While the other methods might be called rule-of-thumb methods, a quantity estimate, if done properly, will result in an accurate list of everything that will go into the construction of a building.

Quantity estimating begins with a takeoff: a list of all the materials, equipment, and other items in a building. An estimator usually develops a takeoff from working drawings and specifications either in their completed form or in some intermediate stage before completion. It is also possible to take off quantities, approximately, before the working drawings and specifications have been prepared. However, the more complete the information available, the more accurate the takeoff and therefore the estimate that can be made.

Experienced estimators stress the necessity of an orderly, methodical approach to takeoffs. Although procedures may vary, one method is to prepare takeoffs for general construction work in an order similar to the following: concrete work, masonry work, carpentry work; finishing work; excavation; and site work. To these must be added the takeoffs of specialized work, including such items and systems as plumbing, heating and air conditioning, electrical work, structural steelwork, and others. After the takeoff has been completed, an estimate of the cost of each group of items may be made. Then the overall estimate may be prepared, including labor and materials for each of the categories in the takeoff, to which are added the prices of subbids, if any, and the contractor's overhead and profit.

Estimators Making of reliable estimates depends on many things. First, of course, it depends on good estimators, who not only know construction and architecture but have inquisitive attitudes that lead them to investigate every possible source of pricing information. And they must approach estimating jobs as controllers as well as evaluators of costs. A good estimator is always on the lookout for information on such factors as wage scales; labor problems; local material prices; special work rules; special building code requirements; shortages of labor or materials; degree of competition among contractors, suppliers, and others; and any other information that may be of help in the estimating process.

In addition to information of this sort, estimators use data from other sources, including national and other cost indexes, unit price manuals of various types, and valuation and appraisal manuals. A large number of these are available today. Price indexes showing relative changes in costs of construction over the years can be obtained from several sources. One of the leading ones is published by *Engineering News-Record* magazine. Some architects prepare their own indexes.

Estimating is the most important tool of cost control. Estimates may be of several kinds. General contractors make estimates, using quantity takeoffs to price their bids on construction projects; as do subcontractors for their bids on specialized portions of the construction, such as electrical work, plumbing, heating and air conditioning.

Architects and other design professionals use estimating as a tool with which to control the costs of construction so that the buildings they design can be built within the budgets or other limits established by owners. This entails beginning the cost control program at the beginning of the performance of architectural services, or even before. Most contracts or agreements between owners and architects require that architects perform certain cost control activities as part of their basic services. Usually, these activities include preparing for the owner statements of probable cost during the schematic design phase, updated versions during the design development phase, and further refined versions during the construction documents phase. All these statements should be based on the best information and estimates possible at each phase. Some believe that proper cost control should begin even before the schematic phase, at the time of program preparation, and that cost control does not end until the construction has been completed within the budget or other amount to which an owner has agreed.

Unit estimating methods are widely used in the early phases of architectural services, while quantity estimating is generally used in the construction document phase. Some architects believe that unit pricing methods should not be the basis of the early estimates, but should only be used as rules of thumb. In their place, they suggest that quantity takeoffs can be made even in the earliest stages if they are approached with knowledge, imagination, and creative ability. It is obviously more difficult, and less accurate, to make a takeoff of a building when only preliminary design drawings have been made. However, some architectural offices do just that.

Budget Estimates Cost control begins with the preparation of a budget estimate, which must be made at a time when only the building program, and perhaps some early sketchy ideas of the building concept, are available for estimating. Thus budget estimates must be based on data that are ordinarily much less reliable than that of quantity takeoffs. In order for a budget estimate to be as realistic and reliable as possible, it must be made by expert cost control people who use every device at their disposal, including their knowledge of the type of buildings the firm produces as well as cost data. As in other types of estimates, those for budgets require orderly, methodical processes.

Although the process may vary somewhat, budget estimates ordinarily include separate items for the costs of site work, structure, exterior and interior finishes, electrical work, plumbing, heating, air conditioning, fire protection, elevators, and the like. They also include estimated costs of special work required by unusual site or soil conditions, special equipment, provisions for future alterations or expansion, construction schedules, type of construction contracts, landscaping, signs, art allowances, and so on. In addition, in order to furnish owners with budgets for entire project costs and not just those of the construction, budget estimates include the cost of architectural and other professional fees, surveys, insurance, legal fees, financing costs, and any other costs directly related to projects. From a budget estimate, a project budget can be prepared for the approval of the owner. Ensuring that the project costs stay within a budget then becomes the goal of all further cost control efforts.

During the schematic design phase, budget estimates can be considerably refined. Although unit estimating may be the basis, a quantity takeoff may be started to help in the refinement of the earlier estimated costs. Cost controls practiced by designers and others involved in the work may be directed toward ensuring that the project can be constructed within the budget. The estimate made at this time indicates budgetary problems, if they exist, and often indicates the building elements in which the problems occur.

During the design development phase, further efforts to keep the costs under control are made by designers, project architects, and others working on projects. A more refined estimate can now be prepared, based on more complete information than was previously available. Additional quantity takeoffs may be made of certain elements of the proposed building. While the working drawings and specifications are being prepared, further refinements may be made in the estimate and after these documents have been finished, the takeoffs may be completed and a further refined estimate made. During this phase, controls of costs may be more difficult because of the great number of specific decisions that must be made and because a number of people may be working on the job.

Cost control during the construction contract administration phase is mainly devoted to keeping changes from being made in a building. Such changes may result from various causes. The worst, from a cost control standpoint and for other reasons, are changes made necessary by errors or omissions in the working drawings or specifications, or changes made necessary by misunderstandings between the architect and owner. Obviously, the need for such changes must be eliminated in the preceding phases of the work, before construction begins. Other changes during construction may be initiated by the owner, contractors, or architect. Regardless of the source of the ideas for such changes, they must be dealt with firmly. If they will result in sufficient benefits in the building, are economically feasible, and are approved by the owner, such changes may be justified. Otherwise there is a risk of exceeding a budget that has been carefully guarded by all the cost control activities in the phases that preceded construction.

Construction Variables   It has often been said that the three variables in building construction work are quantity, quality, and cost. For example, if a building of a certain size, or quantity, is required at a certain specific cost, the quality of the building will be determined by the other two factors. Of course, this can work in several ways: any of the variables can become fixed, while the other two vary; any two can be fixed, and so on. But it is not possible to fix all three.

Recently, a fourth variable, the time of construction, has become of extreme importance because of rising costs of construction due to inflation and other factors. This has resulted in a situation that causes a building designed at a certain time to cost considerably more if it is built some years later. This situation makes estimating and cost control more difficult since factors have to be applied to today's costs to determine those of tomorrow. In addition, the actual time required to design a building, prepare construction documents, take bids, and construct it will greatly affect the cost. In general, the faster these phases can be accomplished, the lower will be the cost of the building. This situation has produced some new ways of handling the phases of architectural services and construction.

Architectural Service Methods   Today the most used method of architectural services is still the traditional one, beginning with schematic design and ending with construction contract administration. However, two other methods, the phased system, sometimes called fast-track, and the design-build system, have come into use. In the phased system, after schematic designs have been approved, the project work is separated into what are sometimes called bid packages. Design development and construction contract documents are prepared for each package, and each is then contracted for, without waiting for completion of the documents for the other packages. Thus construction can begin on site work, foundations, and so on, long before construction documents have been completed for work that comes later. Considerable time may be saved on certain architectural projects, with requirements that fit into this system, by allowing the design and construction-document phases to overlap to some extent with the construction phases.

The design-build system is essentially a method of placing complete responsibility for architectural and related services and construction on one organization, that of an architect, contractor, or construction manager. Often used for technically complex projects, such as petrochemical plants, the design-build system also allows projects to be separated into packages as in phased construction and also makes time-savings possible in the overall process. Variations of these systems are sometimes used; one is the turnkey system, which is quite similar to the design-build system.

Work Schedule Systems   The new systems all have as their major purpose the saving of building costs through acceleration of the processes required to produce a building. Another aspect of cost control and saving money are systems for scheduling the work. In the past, such systems were primitive, mostly dependent on bar charts upon which the various activities could be shown. Bar charts are still used to some extent, but they have been joined by much more sophisticated methods and techniques for scheduling the work.

One of the most widely used techniques is known as the critical path method (CPM). The critical path method utilizes diagrams upon which lines are placed, each representing a task or activity that must take place in the construction of buildings. CPM diagrams are also used for scheduling activities involved in architectural services and for many other purposes. Each line on a CPM diagram represents one activity and each is connected in order to the activity that follows it. Arrowheads are placed at the ends of all lines, indicating the order in which the activities take place and the end of each activity. Each arrow is labeled with the title of the activity it represents and the arrowheads are numbered with event numbers. At the midpoint of each arrow, the normal time, in days, to complete the event is placed. A complete CPM diagram is called a network. The critical path consists of the sequence of activities representing the minimum length of time in which the project may be completed.

The CPM system allows projects to be properly scheduled, gives indications of possible problems, and allows actual problems to be identified early, thus helping to keep projects on schedule and to control their costs. The use of CPM is more complicated than is indicated by the short description given here, but the system is not overly complicated and can be used either manually or with the aid of a computer. Another system, with some similarities to CPM, called program evaluation and review techniques (PERT), was developed by the U.S. Navy in connection with its Polaris missile project. PERT can be used as a cost control system without networks, and some think it superior to CPM for continuous project cost control. Other methods are also available, and it may be expected that new ones will be developed in the not too distant future.

Other Techniques A number of other systems and techniques have been developed to aid in cost control. One of these is value engineering, developed about the end of World War II. Value engineering is a technique for determination of the lowest costs for the proper accomplishment of the function of anything, such as a building project. This technique attempts to eliminate unnecessary costs by examining each item on the basis of what the item is, what it will do, what it will cost, what other item or items will do what the first does, and at what cost.

Another comparatively recent technique is life-cycle cost analysis. This system involves not only the cost of construction or even the cost of completely producing a project but the total cost of a building throughout its useful life from start to finish. Life-cycle costing takes into consideration the costs of architectural and related services and construction, together with costs for capital, financing, and interim and long term; costs of use, operations, heating, cooling, alterations, repairs, improvements, replacement, and delays in use caused by weather or strikes; and lost revenues if a project is not constructed. From this list, it may be seen that life-cycle analysis is complex and demanding. However, in no other way can owners or investors completely understand the total costs involved in building projects.

All the cost control techniques described may be handled, at least partly, on computers. Some architects have established computer operations in their offices or through the use of terminals that connect with computers, which the architects time-share with other users. A number of private companies offer computer estimating and cost controls, and other organizations, such as the American Insititute of Architects, have such systems under study or development.

Formerly, the people most directly involved in cost control in architectural and other design offices were estimators. For a very long time, much of the public and many clients of these professionals believed that the estimators and the architects they worked for did not really do a very good job. One of the harshest, and most frequently heard, criticisms of architects was their often seeming disinterest in cost control and their inability to perform architectural services which would ensure that buildings could be constructed within their budgets.

Today the situation has changed. Estimators still perform important functions in cost control, but architects generally cannot be satisfied with anything less than the best cost controls. Therefore it has become necessary for all the people who perform any of the functions in architectural and related services to become cost conscious and to participate in cost control. The estimator of the past has had to change into the cost manager of today. Often in the past, estimators were trained on the job in construction under experienced estimators. Some of the cost managers of today have been trained in the same manner, but they have also had to learn many new techniques and to develop attitudes that enable them to perform positive, creative functions in the production of building designs and buildings.

Related Articles COMPUTER; PRACTICE OF ARCHITECTURE; Articles on various phases of architectural services.

Further Reading Deatherage, G.: *Construction Scheduling and Control*, McGraw-Hill, New York, 1965; Dell'Isola, Alphonse J.: *Value Engineering in the Construction Industry*, Construction Publishing Company, New York, 1974; Foster, Newman: *Construction Estimates from Take-Off to Bid*, 2d ed., McGraw-Hill, New York, 1972; Hunt, William Dudley, Jr., ed.: *Creative Control of Building Costs*, McGraw Hill, New York, 1967; Peurifoy, Robert L.: *Estimating Construction Costs*, 2d ed., McGraw-Hill, New York, 1976.

CRAM, GOODHUE AND FERGUSON

CRAM, GOODHUE AND FERGUSON American architectural firm. Founded in 1899 as a successor to Cram and Wentworth, Cram, Goodhue and Ferguson established themselves as the leading church architects in the United States and as the foremost proponents of the Eclectic Gothic style. The partners were Ralph Adams Cram (1863–1943), Bertram Grosvenor

Goodhue (1869–1924), and Frank Ferguson (1861–1926).

With two talented designers, Cram and Goodhue, and Ferguson to run the office, the new firm made rapid progress. Soon numerous commissions for important buildings came in. Some of these were from clients who were impressed with the firm; others came as a result of the publicity gained from Cram's books and, in particular, his lectures. Others were won in competitions. Soon the firm had become a great success that lasted for more than a decade.

At the beginning, the working relationships between the two major partners, Cram and Goodhue, were excellent. Cram usually initiated the design, plans, and overall appearance of buildings. Then Goodhue took over, developing details and ornament. The two partners complemented each other very well. As time went on, each began to design his own buildings and, in some cases, each developed a design for a single building, presenting both to a client or in a competition. Athough their predominant style was Gothic, they did buildings in Colonial, Georgian, and other styles.

Goodhue eventually became disenchanted with the dedication of his partner to Gothic architecture. Competition between the two men grew. After Goodhue moved to New York in 1903 to start a branch office, the rift widened. Finally, in 1914 Goodhue left to start his own practice in New York City. And Cram went on practicing in Boston with Ferguson, under the name of Cram and Ferguson.

Works The first commissions of the firm were for small, insignificant work, remodeling and the like. This did not last long and soon they were being chosen for, or winning in competitions, a large number of important buildings. Beginning with All Souls Church (1894), Ashmont, Mass., the first in Gothic style, produced when the firm name was Cram and Wentworth, the architects designed many other churches. Among the best were All Saints (1895), Brookline, Mass.; St. Stephen's (1900), Cohasset, Mass.; First Baptist (1909), Pittsburgh, the U.S. Military Academy Chapel (1910), West Point, N.Y.; Park Avenue Christian Church (1911), New York City; Euclid Avenue Presbyterian (1911), Cleveland; Fourth Presbyterian (1912), Chicago; and Hope Presbyterian (1912), St. Paul, Minn.

The firm's most significant buildings, other than churches, were at West Point, where Cram, Goodhue and Ferguson designed a number of buildings beginning in 1903. Appropriately, their last building together was a church, St. Thomas's, New York City, completed about 1914, the year Goodhue left.

Cram's Life Ralph Adams Cram was born in 1863, in Hampton Falls, N.H., the son of a Unitarian minister. After graduating from high school, he toured Europe. Interested in many cultural subjects, including art and architecture, he went to Boston where he wrote articles on art for the *Boston Transcript,* and in 1881 he joined the firm of Rotch and Tilden as an apprentice, staying there until 1885.

After participating in competitions in which he did well but did not win, he again went to Europe, this time specifically to study buildings. Coming back greatly impressed with Gothic architecture and the medieval spirit, he started his own architectural prac-

CRAM, GOODHUE AND FERGUSON Exterior, Park Avenue Christian Church (1911), New York, N.Y. *(Wurts Brothers)*

CRAM, GOODHUE AND FERGUSON Interior, Park Avenue Christian Church (1911), New York, N.Y. *(Wurts Brothers)*

CRAM, GOODHUE AND FERGUSON Exterior, St. Thomas' Episcopal Church (1914), New York City. *(Wurts Brothers, Library of Congress)*

CRAM, GOODHUE AND FERGUSON Interior, St. Thomas' Episcopal Church (1914), New York City. *(Wurts Brothers)*

tice in Boston in partnership with Charles Wentworth (1861–97). Their first commissions were for modest houses and remodeling. In 1891 Bertram Grosvenor Goodhue joined the firm and in 1897, became a partner. In 1899 Frank Ferguson joined, to take care of the business end of things, and the firm was renamed Cram, Goodhue and Ferguson.

Cram was a prolific writer and speaker. In his lifetime, he wrote 24 books on a variety of subjects, including art, architecture, philosophy, and religion. The books and speeches brought the firm to the attention of potential clients all over the country and soon commissions started to come into the office in increasing numbers. Cram, and the firm, became the foremost proponents of Gothic architecture of the time. Their architectural work was mostly Gothic, and Cram's books and speeches espoused the cause of that style.

In 1903 Goodhue went to New York City to open a branch office for the firm. After that, the two partners drifted apart, not only because of the physical separation of the offices but because of competition between the two and Goodhue's increasing unhappiness with the Gothic style.

In 1889 Cram and Goodhue had submitted separate designs in the competition for the Cathedral Church of St. John the Divine (begun in 1892 and still incomplete) in New York City. Neither won, the commission going to Heins and La Farge. In 1911 Cram was appointed architect for the building and remained in

that position until 1942, when he died. He managed to complete a major portion of the cathedral during his lifetime, and succeeded in changing its design from the Romanesque-Byzantine style of his predecessor to Gothic. Although Cram and Ferguson designed other buildings after 1911, the cathedral occupied most of Cram's time for the remainder of his life. At various times, Cram acted as supervising architect at Princeton University, and Bryn Mawr, Mount Holyoke, and Wellesley colleges. On September 22, 1942, Ralph Adams Cram died, having been one of the most successful architects of his era and certainly the most dedicated to medievalism.

Goodhue's Life Bertram Grosvenor Goodhue was born in Pomfret, Conn., on April 28, 1869. He was educated at the Collegiate and Commercial Institute, New Haven, Conn., but left in 1884, when he was only fifteen to go to work in New York City for James Renwick, Jr. (1818–95), a famous architect who designed buildings in the Gothic Revival style. Within two years, Goodhue had become the chief draftsman for the firm. Thoroughly indoctrinated in the design of Gothic Revival buildings and an accomplished draftsman, in 1891 Goodhue left Renwick to join the firm of Ralph Cram in Boston, and in 1897 he became a partner. In 1914 Goodhue left to start his own office in New York City.

Goodhue practiced as an individual architect for another 10 years. He was one of the finest draftsmen of his time and designed a number of distinguished buildings in many eclectic styles, including Spanish Colonial Revival, sometimes called Spanish Baroque; Gothic Revival; and a style that was almost modern but still derivative from the past.

After leaving Cram, Goodhue was appointed chief architect for the Panama-California Exposition (1915) in San Diego, Calif. He was successful in making the architectural theme of the fair the Spanish Colonial, or Spanish Baroque, Revival style. In addition, he designed buildings for the fair, some of which, including the California Building, still exist.

During his remaining years, Goodhue produced a number of other important buildings, all of them eclectic, including the Church of St. Vincent Ferrer (1918) and St. Bartholomew's Church (1923), both in New York City; the Los Angeles Public Library (1924); and the Rockefeller Memorial Chapel, University of Chicago, finished in 1928 after the architect's death. Also completed in 1928 was the building generally considered his best, the Nebraska State Capitol, Lincoln. Toward the end of his life, Goodhue seemed to be progressing toward an architecture that would be more specifically modern. But this was cut short by his death at fifty-five, on April 21, 1924.

Related Articles Book, Architectural; Eclectic Architecture; Exposition; Gothic Revival Architecture; Renwick, James, Jr.

Further Reading Cram, Ralph Adams: *My Life in Architecture,* Little Brown, Boston, 1936; Maginnis, Charles D.: *The Work of Cram and Ferguson, Including Work by Cram, Goodhue and Ferguson,* Pencil Points Press, New York, 1929; Whitaker, Charles H., ed.: *Bertram Grosvenor Goodhue—Architect and Master of Many Arts,* DaCapo Press, New York, 1976.

CRET, PAUL PHILLIPPE French-American architect (1876–1945). As a practicing architect for more than 40 years and as a teacher of architecture for more than 30, Paul Phillipe Cret strongly influenced the design of buildings, not only those of his many students and associates but those of other architects of the time. A talented designer and teacher, Cret was a man of high principles and deep knowledge. He was respected and revered by all who knew him.

Cret was an eclectic architect, a very talented one, who designed excellent buildings in styles derived from the great buildings of the past. Trained at the École des Beaux Arts in Paris, his whole philosophy was imbued with Beaux Arts traditions. He taught Beaux Arts design by Beaux Arts methods and he designed buildings in the same manner. He was not an

CRAM, GOODHUE AND FERGUSON State Capitol (1928), Lincoln, Neb. [*Architect: Bertram Grosvenor Goodhue. (Macdonald photo, Library of Congress)*]

CRET, PAUL PHILIPPE Pan American Union Building (1907), Washington, D.C. [*Architects: Cret, in association with Albert Kelsey. (Library of Congress)*]

innovator, and his whole career was spent outside the mainstream of what became modern architecture. Nevertheless, he designed a number of fine buildings in various styles that are still well thought of today and transmitted to his students a knowledge of good architecture and a sensitivity to its design.

Works His first commission in America was the Pan American Union Building (1907), formerly called the International Bureau of American Republics, in Washington, designed in association with Albert Kelsey. Many consider this his best building, a Classic eclectic design with fine detailing and a beautiful garden with a reflecting pool. In any case, it was the forerunner of the kind of designs that would flow from his office afterward. His next important work was the

Public Library (1915), Indianapolis, Ind., for which he won a competition in association with the firm of Zantzinger, Borie and Medary, and this was followed by the Detroit Institute of Fine Arts (1922), designed in association with the same firm. Both buildings are notable examples of his eclectic architecture.

Over the years, Cret designed several houses, though they were a small part of his work. On the other hand, he designed a great number of monuments and memorials, several of them in Europe in commemoration of World War I. Others of importance are the Washington Memorial Arch (1912), Valley Forge, Pa.; Providence War Memorial (1927), Providence R.I.; and the Gettysburg Peace Memorial (1938), Gettysburg, Pa. He also designed a number of bridges. In fact, it is hard to cross any body of water in Philadelphia without using a Cret bridge. Among the most notable are the Delaware River Bridge (1922), the University Avenue Bridge (1925), and Henry Avenue Bridge (1927). Two bridges in Washington are also of note: Klingle Valley (1931) and Calvert Street (1933).

Paul Cret designed many other kinds of buildings, including museums, libraries, government buildings, apartments, university buildings, and courthouses. He even designed interiors for many of the great railroad trains of his era, including the Zephyrs, the Santa Fe Super-Chief and the Silver Meteor, and the Empire State.

Cret continued to practice architecture until he died, producing designs of good taste and refinement. Some of the most important buildings are the Rodin Museum (1928), Philadelphia; Folger Shakespeare Library (1929), Washington; and the Federal Reserve Building (1935), Washington.

Life   Paul Phillippe Cret was born in Lyons, France, on October 21, 1876. At an early age, while working in the architectural office of his uncle, Johannes Bernard, he seems to have decided to become an architect. Entering the École des Beaux Arts in Lyons, he won an important prize for his work and a scholarship to the École des Beaux Arts in Paris. A good student, he won many prizes there. American students at the École, who had previously attended the University of

CRET, PAUL PHILIPPE   Folger Shakespeare Library (1929), Washington, D.C. *(Theodore Horydczak, Library of Congress)*

CRET, PAUL PHILIPPE   Institute of Fine Arts (1922), Detroit, Mich. *(Detroit Publishing Co., Library of Congress)*

Pennsylvania, recommended Cret for a position teaching design at the latter school. He accepted and came to Philadelphia in 1903 to join the faculty, a position he held, with the exception of the World War I years, until 1937.

Soon after arriving in America, Cret went back to France to marry Marguerite Lahalle in 1904. The next few years were devoted to teaching until he won (with Albert Kelsey) a major competition for the design of the Pan American Union Building (1907) in Washington. During his career, he won six additional major competitions. The Pan American Union Building started his architectural practice, but he designed only a few other buildings before World War I. Still a French citizen, he was called into the French army in 1914 and after the war, came back to the University of Pennsylvania in 1919. He had been decorated for his service and had partly lost his hearing.

Soon after the war, General John J. Pershing appointed him first consulting architect to the American Battle Monuments Commission, a post in which he served the rest of his life. This began an important part of Cret's architectural practice, the design of memorials, three of them for the commission and a number of others. Other important building commissions came his way and the small office Cret had started grew to 25 people, almost all of them his former students. Four students became partners in the firm, though it was always called simply by his name until his death. The partners were John Harbeson, William Hough, William Livingston, and Roy Larson.

The work of the firm was varied, from the usual architectural types—residences, libraries, office and commercial buildings—to monuments and bridges, and from 1933 on, interiors of railroad trains. Cret continued to teach, in his office, as well as classes at the university. He was known by students, clients, and employees as a kind and gentle man, devoted to those with whom he was associated. He was witty and well read. Dedicated to architecture, he spent most of his time in the drafting rooms where the work was going on rather than in his private office. His deafness did not slow his interests and activities. Later in life, after he lost the use of his voice from cancer of the throat, he carried a pad and pencil with which he communicated.

The architecture of Paul Cret was widely admired and brought him many honors, including the Gold Medal of the American Institute of Architects in 1938. After his death on September 8, 1945, his partners continued his firm under the name of Harbeson, Hough, Livingston and Larson.

Related Articles ECLECTIC ARCHITECTURE; EDUCATION.
Further Reading White, Theo B. ed.: *Paul Philippe Cret— Architect and Teacher*, the Art Alliance Press, Philadelphia 1973.

CRITICISM, ARCHITECTURE The act or skill of analyzing and judging architecture. Although perhaps not as highly developed or as widely practiced as crit-

icism of art, music, drama, or literature, architecture criticism today may often make valuable contributions to architecture.

In architecture, the word *criticism* has several meanings. In architectural schools, students receive criticisms which are analyses and judgments, positive and negative, of their design work by their professors, who in this case are called design critics. In a similar sense, the word can be used to denote other actions, such as the criticism of a designer's work in an architectural office by an architect-principal or chief designer, or criticism of an architect's work by clients or by users of buildings. Although all these interpretations are extremely important, the type of criticism under discussion here is that performed by architecture critics, amateur and professional.

Purposes of Criticism Critical writings on architecture can come in many forms, from short articles or essays that appear in magazines and other places to books. While open to considerable interpretation, the avowed purposes of most critics are the analysis and understanding of architecture, identification and judgment of what is good and bad in it, interpretation of its effects on society and the environment, and provision of guidelines by which architecture might be made better. By providing insight and information of these kinds, a critic expects to influence architects and other designers; clients and other consumers of architecture; and governmental, real estate, and financial forces toward the goal of better architecture and ultimately a better environment. Furthermore, critics believe they may discover something of the nature of future issues and solutions of problems caused by them.

Types Criticism may be divided into two major types: objective, sometimes called normative, in which a work of architecture or another art object is judged on the basis of criteria or doctrines that are as free of personal bias as possible; and impressionistic, sometimes called interpretative, in which judgments are made on the basis of the effect of the work of art on the critic. A review is a form of criticism usually written soon after a book has been published, a play has opened, or a building has been completed. Some reviews are impressionistic, while others are descriptive, mentioning only the facts without making judgments about the subject of the review.

Some believe that architecture criticism should be concerned with the totality of buildings, that is, with their functions or purposes; their structure and mechanical and electrical systems; their effect as real property that adds value to the land on which they are built; their environmental impact; and their social, cultural, and symbolic meaning as well as their esthetics.

In practice, such comprehensive criticism of total buildings is very rare. Many critics, even though they may be considered authorities or experts, are not really expert in all of these aspects of architecture. Their job is made even more difficult by the fact that architecture, unlike music, drama, painting, and so on, is a functional art. In architecture, the art and science of buildings must become so intermingled that one cannot be separated from the other without destroying the total concept of the buildings. Many an architect has struck back at many a critic, saying in effect that the critic could not know what the architect had in mind, could not understand the total problem and therefore had written only superficial criticism. The views of critics have been called biased, invalid, narrow-minded, and inconsequential; and the critics, vandals, parasites, and worse. In an extension of the old saying—those who can, do, those who cannot, teach—comes a third part: those who cannot teach become critics. To these charges, critics reply that they are, by their nature, experts who can take a broad overview of architecture and contribute to its understanding, based on valid information, their experiences, and their imaginations.

Objectively approached, it will be found that criticism has had considerable influence on the arts for a very long time. Perhaps this is more the case in certain arts, such as literature, painting, drama, and poetry, but there is also a history of architecture criticism that goes back a long way.

In architecture as well as in the other arts to some extent, critics very seldom make criticism their sole activity. In fact, it is rare for architecture criticism to be the prime activity of most critics. Instead, they are mostly writers, historians, estheticians, teachers, editors, and even cartoonists, who also write criticism. In literary criticism, almost all advanced college literature courses might be considered preparation for critical writing and in most of the other arts, advanced history courses in specialized fields might also be considered in the same manner. In architecture, the situation is quite different. Only a few universities offer courses in architecture criticism and these are electives, and there are no complete curricula for people who would like to make careers of architecture criticism.

Another factor that prevents architecture criticism from becoming more widespread and effective is the fact that only a few magazines and newspapers publish architecture criticism on a regular basis. On the other hand, music, drama, and other critics have a great number of outlets for their work. Because of the paucity of popular media, most people rarely read any architecture criticism; it is hidden away from the average person in professional and scholarly magazines and books.

History Criticism of the arts is generally thought to have been started by the ancient Greek philosphers, Plato (c. 427–347 B.C.), originally named Aristocles, and Aristotle (384–322 B.C.), both of whom wrote criticism of poetry. Since that time, there have been a large number of other noted critics of literature and the other arts. In the 20th century, they have included such American literature critics as William Dean Howells (1837–1920), Van Wyck Brooks (1886–1963), Thomas Stearns Eliot (1888–1959), and John Anthony Ciardi (1916–   ). All did other kinds of writing. In drama criticism, noted Americans included Henry Louis Mencken (1880–1956), an editor and journalist; Joseph Wood Krutch (1893–1970), a naturalist and writer; and Brooks Atkinson (1894–   ), a journalist and foreign correspondent. American music critics include Deems Taylor (1885–1966) and Virgil Garnett Thomson (1896–   ), both of whom were also composers. An interesting American critic of the 20th century was Gilbert Vivian Seldes (1893–1970), who wrote criticism of what he called the seven lively arts: motion pictures, comic strips, vaudeville, musical comedy, radio, popular music, and ballroom dancing.

The first art and achitecture critic is usually thought to have been the Italian architect and painter Giorgio Vasari (1511–74), who wrote *Lives of the Most Eminent Painters, Sculptors and Architects,* published in 1563. Many others followed, including the Englishmen, John Ruskin (1819–1900), Walter Horatio Pater (1839–94), and Roger Eliot Fry (1866–1934), who was also a painter. Two Americans of importance are Bernard Berenson (1865–1959) in art criticism, and Montgomery Schuyler (1843–1914) in architecture criticism.

Influential critics of the 20th century include the Swiss historian Sigfried Giedion (1888–1968), who wrote *Space, Time and Architecture;* the English historian Sir Nikolaus Pevsner (1902–   ); the Italian historian Bruno Benedetto Zevi (1918–   ); and the Australian Robin Boyd (1919–1971); each of whom has written a number of important books. The dean of American critics is Lewis Mumford (1895–   ). Others still writing include George Robert McCue (1910–   ), of the *St. Louis Post-Dispatch;* Grady Edward Clay (1916–   ), of the *Louisville Courier-Journal* and *Landscape Magazine;* Wolf von Eckardt (1918–   ), of the *Washington Post;* and Ada Louise Huxtable (1921–   ), of *The New York Times.* Others include Henry-Russell Hitchcock (1903–   ), Peter Blake (1920–   ), and Walter McQuade (1922–   ). One of the most incisive architecture critics was Alan Dunn (1900–1974), longtime cartoonist of the *New Yorker* and *Architectural Record* magazines.

Related Articles ARCHITECTURE; BOOK, ARCHITECTURAL; DESIGN, ARCHITECTURAL; ESTHETICS; MAGAZINE, ARCHITECTURAL.

Further Reading Attoe, Wayne: *Architecture and Critical Imagination,* John Wiley, Chichester, England, and New York, 1978; Schuyler, Montgomery: *Architecture and Other Writings,* 2 vols., Harvard University Press, Cambridge, Mass., 1961; Whiffen, Marcus, ed.: *The History, Theory and Criticism of Architecture,* MIT Press, Cambridge, Mass., 1965.

DAM A structure placed across a river or other body of water to stop or control its flow. Although most dams would not be considered architecture by many people, and architects are not often involved in their design, there are some notable exceptions. The purposes of dams include storage of water for drinking, irrigation, and other uses; control of water flow to stop erosion and flooding; and production of electric power through water-flow operation of hydraulic turbines. In addition, dams can form lakes for the benefit of wildlife and for recreational purposes.

Construction Materials Dams may be constructed from many materials, including timber, earth, rock, masonry, and combinations of these elements. Timber is used only for relatively small dams and does not last long. The timber is usually weighted down with rock. Embankment dams are raised structures made of earth, rock, or other fill materials. An earth-fill dam is constructed of fine earth in the center, coarser earth or rock on the outside, with a core of concrete or other means of waterproofing. Rock-fill dams are similar but constructed of heavy rock and boulders. The side of the dam facing the water is covered with concrete or some other waterproofing material. Earth and rock are used together in earth-and-rock-fill dams.

Masonry dams are constructed of cut stone or blocks of concrete. These may be gravity dams, which resist water pressure by their own weight; or arch dams, single or multiple, with structures designed to resist pressures. A single-arch dam is usually constructed in a narrow canyon or gorge and gains its strength from the curved conformation of the arch. A multiple-arch dam may be considerably wider and derives its strength from the shape of the arches and from extra supports called buttresses. Important parts of dams are spillways which allow bypassing of water, valves and gates for releasing water, and powerhouses.

History Dams have been constructed from very early times, at first of timber and later of earth and rock. Ruins and other traces of ancient dams have been discovered in the Middle East and in Egypt. The Romans built quite large masonry dams, many of which are still in use, all over their empire.

American Development In colonial America, modest dams were built. The second quarter of the 20th century saw the great era of dam building. Then came great dams such as the Hoover (1936) in Arizona but only 25 mi from Las Vegas, Nev.; Bonneville (1937), about 40 mi east of Portland, Ore.; and Grand Coulee (1942), about 90 mi northwest of Spokane, Wash.

At the same time most of these dams were under construction, the greatest dam project of all time, the Tennessee Valley Authority (TVA), began in 1933. In all, 20 dams were completed in 20 years along the Tennessee River. Also constructed were eight steam plants and a number of bridges, office buildings, visitor centers, and other structures. As great as were the engineering and construction accomplishments of TVA, many observers also consider the dams and other structures of considerable architectural significance. The architectural success of TVA must be attributed, in large part, to the architects who worked on the project, and especially to the head architects, Roland A. Wank (1898–1972), Rudolph Mock, and Harry Bird Tour (1899–   ). A present-day architect

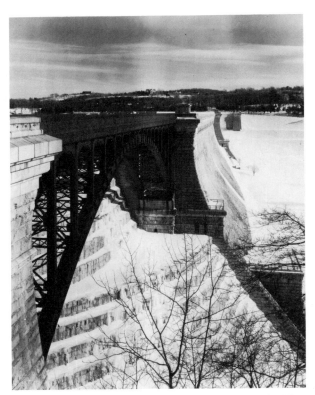

DAM Croton Dam (1906), Croton, N.Y. [*Engineers: City Water Commission. (Joseph W. Molitor)*]

DAM Exterior and Interior, Libby Dam (1973), Libby, Mont. [*Architect: Paul Thiry; Engineers: U.S. Army Corps of Engineers. (Thiry Architects)*]

who consults on the design of dams, including the Libby Dam (1976), Libby, Mont., is Paul Albert Thiry (1904–   ) of Seattle.

Related Articles. ARCH; ENGINEERING; STRUCTURE; VAULT.

Further Reading Kyle, John H.: *The Building of TVA: An Illustrated History*, Louisiana State University Press, Baton Rouge, 1958.

DESIGN, ARCHITECTURAL

The process involved in the development of a mental concept of a building and its parts and expressing the concept in drawings and sometimes in models and written matter. The result of the process, the concept, is also called an architectural design. And one who performs the process is called an architectural designer.

Actually, architectural design is much more difficult to define than any phrase commonly used in architecture. For centuries, architects, philosophers, psychologists, and others have attempted definitions, none universally accepted and certainly not by architects. Architectural design has been called creativity and problem solving; both ideas are implied in the phrase. Design has been called the creation of something new, the changing of man-made things, or the changing of the environment. A long list of other definitions of architectural design, and ideas and beliefs about its nature might be cited. Architects, architectural theoreticans, and critics today discuss the real nature of design whenever they have a chance, and often argue about it too.

Design Phases In any case, architectural design is the creative process used to translate the problems, needs, and aspirations of potential building owners and users into drawings and other documents that depict possible answers to needs and aspirations and eventually translate them into buildings. In architects' offices, architectural design begins after research into the needs, problems, and aspirations of clients, a process called programming; see the article entitled programming. The next part of the process is the schematic design phase. During this phase, along with consultation with the client, studies and analyses of all the most important aspects of the proposed building are made, leading to drawings and information that illustrate a design concept, sometimes with alternate concepts, of the major components of the proposed building, including floor plans, appearance, and other important aspects.

After approval of the schematic design by the client, before which further studies often must be made, the process continues in the design development phase. In this part of the process, the schematic concepts are further studied in greater detail, and drawings and other information produced illustrating more definitively how the floor plans are to be arranged, the appearance of the building, the materials to be used, its structure, and its mechanical, electrical, and other systems. During either or both of the design phases, study renderings or models, or both, and other specific proposals may be made. See articles entitled model making; rendering.

After the design development drawings and other materials have been approved by the client, the process proceeds into the construction document phase; see articles entitled specification; working drawing. Although a major portion of the architectural design work will have been completed previously, the design of many details of buildings and relatively smaller or minor elements and components often continues to the end of the construction document phase, and even afterward.

Along with the architectural design of buildings, other types of design must be performed, including the engineering design of structures, mechanical and electrical systems, and landscape design. While architects sometimes handle such design activities, particularly for relatively small, simple building types, such as single-family houses, structural design is usually the province of structural engineers; mechanical systems design, of mechanical engineers; electrical systems design, of electrical engineers; landscape design, of landscape architects; and so on. In small offices, architectural design is often performed by one or more of the architect-principals. In large firms, design may be performed by one or more of the principals, or under their direction by architects or others employed as architectural designers.

In all but the smallest firms, most architectural designers are specialists. In very small firms, architect-principals and architect-employees alike often perform more than one function. For example, an individual might be involved not only in design but in some or all of the other functions, such as obtaining clients for the firm, management of the office, production of working drawings and specifications, and administration of construction contracts. In most larger firms and many smaller ones, a single individual architectural designer has responsibility for one or more projects, working closely with other architects, production people, engineers, and so on in the design of the buildings.

Design Methods Architectural design today is an incredibly complicated and complex process. So many elements are involved that architectural designers must use every means possible in analyzing the problems of proposed buildings and solving them through design. Traditionally, the major means of architectural design have been study drawings or sketches that begin with simple diagrams of relationships between elements and proceed to more elaborate and definitive drawings. Sometimes study models have also been constructed to allow designers to examine relationships of elements in three dimensions. Such methods remain the primary means of architectural designers today. In addition, many other aids are used, including computers for analysis of data, comparisons of proposed solutions, and other purposes. Computers may be utilized for both written and graphic studies; see the article entitled computer.

Scientific Method A great many systems of problem solving, often computer aided, have been developed. All are based on the scientific method, believed to have been first used by the Italian scientist Galileo Galilei (1564–1642), usually called Galileo. The scientific method has five steps that are intended to lead to orderly problem solving; see the article entitled programming. Based on the steps of the scientific method, many theorists have proposed architectural problem-solving methods. In general, these methods involve (1) definition of the problem, (2) establishment of objectives, (3) collection of data, (4) analysis of the problem, (5) consideration of possible solutions, and (6) solution of the problem. Although the steps may overlap in a given situation and their order of performance may be changed at times, in architecture, steps one through four are generally called programming and steps five and six, design.

Principles and Rules In the past, architectural design could be systematized in a manner that, though not always entirely satisfactory, furnished designers with principles and rules that were useful and generally reliable. Some believe that the same principles may be applied to architectural design today and that when the principles are ignored or the rules broken, excellence in architectural design cannot be achieved. Others argue that principles are subject to change and that rules are made to be broken. In any case, no theory that seems valid for today's architecture has come along to take the place of the set of principles and rules that evolved through centuries of architectural design. And even if principles change and rules are broken, it seems necessary to know and understand the principles before changing them and the rules before breaking them. Without discussing them in detail, some of the principles and rules are enumerated here. In the broadest sense, they include four general areas: (1) needs and desires of people, (2) influences on architecture, (3) major requirements of architecture, and (4) design elements of architecture.

People's Needs The major needs and desires of people are physical, intellectual, esthetic, and emotional. Obviously, all humans need, in their buildings, physical attributes that provide comfort and adequate space in which to live or perform tasks and for other functions. People need to understand the buildings they occupy or use. Although not always apparent to them, people need beauty in their buildings and environments conducive to their emotional well-being. The desires of people often far exceed their actual needs, for example, great spaces, when smaller ones might do, and ornament, when the building would function just as well, physically, without it.

Influences The influences on architecture may be divided into three major types: natural, cultural, and technological. Natural influences on architecture include climate, geography, and geology. Climate affects the proper form, placement on sites, use of windows, insulation, and heating and air conditioning of buildings. Geography affects the design of buildings in their relation to the region or area in which they are to be constructed, to their neighborhoods, and to their actual sites. Geology affects the design of buildings in many ways, including their structures, form, and drainage needs. Cultural influences affect the design of buildings in the large sense of their locations in various countries, states, cities, and so on, and in the smaller sense of their exact sites and neighborhoods. Cultural influences include religion, politics, and others, and also the ideals of the owners and users of buildings and the cultures in which they live. Technological influences are the materials, structures, and systems.

Architectural Requirements The four major requirements of architecture include function, strength, esthetics, and economics. Obviously, a well-designed building should function properly for the uses to which its owners and occupiers will put it. It must be strong enough to withstand the uses and outside influences, such as weather. A well-designed building must satisfy the esthetic standards of the owners and users, and often architects try to exceed the standards of the owners and users. And finally, a building must be designed so that it can be constructed for the stipulated amount of money, or within its budget, and to be an economically sound investment for its owners.

Design Elements The design elements of architecture include plans, form, and composition. Most, though not all, architects believe that the problem-solving process of design begins with the establishment of the elements that compose the plans of a building and the relationships between them. This involves the functions of spaces, their sizes and shapes, their juxtaposition to one another, and, most importantly, circulation, the movement of people and sometimes things within and between the plan elements. Stated simply, a floor plan of a house should be designed so that, for example, the front entrance is properly located, circulation moves smoothly from that point into the house and into living areas that are of the proper sizes and shapes and from there into the private areas of the house, such as bedrooms and bathrooms, also properly sized and shaped. Other relationships in houses must also be studied and designed properly.

In some past eras of architecture, the proper form of buildings was thought to be almost synonymous with their mass or bulk. Today the mass of buildings is still considered important, but their volumes or enclosed spaces are usually considered more important. It is in the volume or space of buildings that people live and function. Mass contributes heavily to the appearance or esthetics of buildings, as does volume. In conjunction with the architectural design of the mass and volume of buildings, other important related considerations include structures, protective elements such as walls and roofs, materials, and ornamental features.

As in the other fine arts, composition is the process in architectural design involved in combining all of

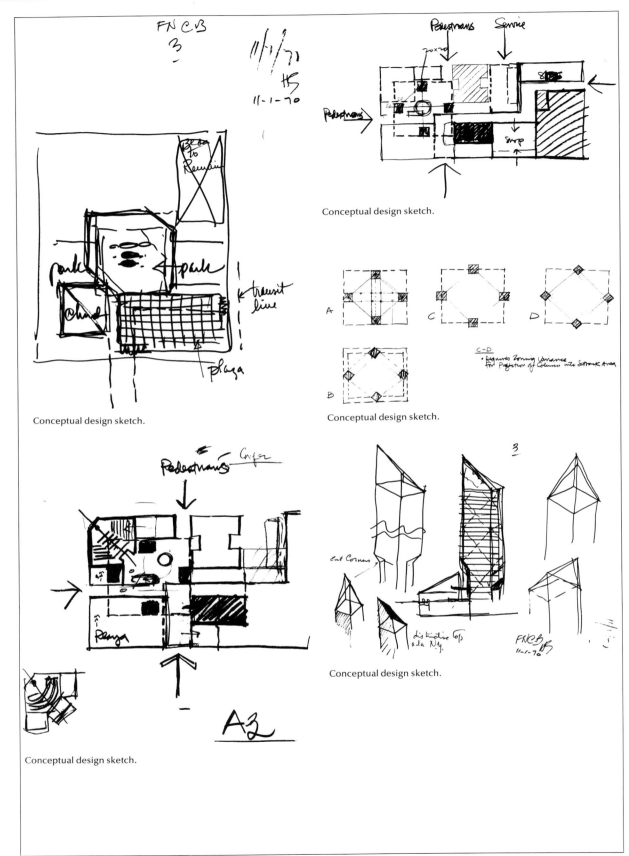

Conceptual design sketch.

Conceptual design sketch.

Conceptual design sketch.

Conceptual design sketch.

Conceptual design sketch.

DESIGN, ARCHITECTURAL   Citicorp Center (1978), New York, N.Y.
[*Architects: Hugh Stubbins, in association with Emory Roth and Sons.*
(Hugh Stubbins and Associates)]

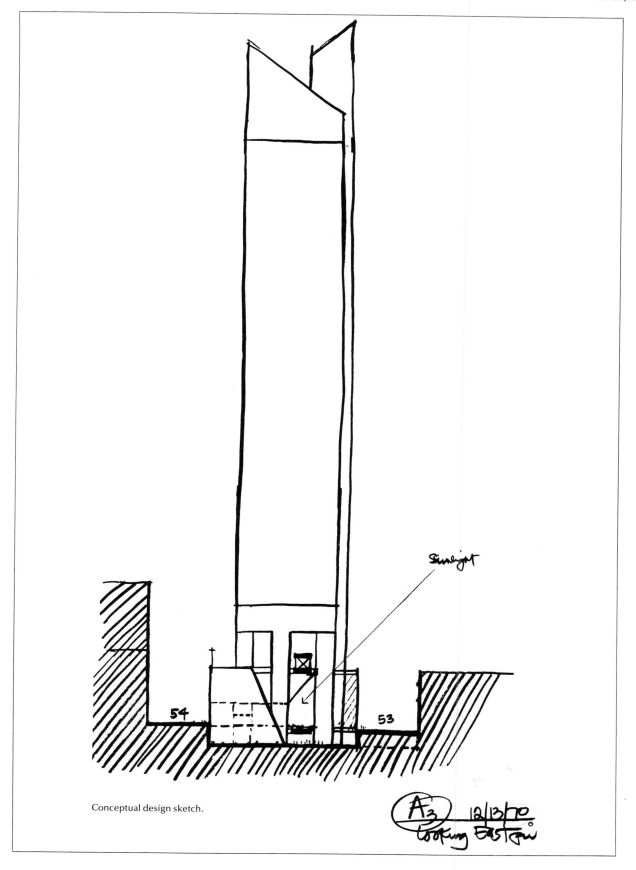

Conceptual design sketch.

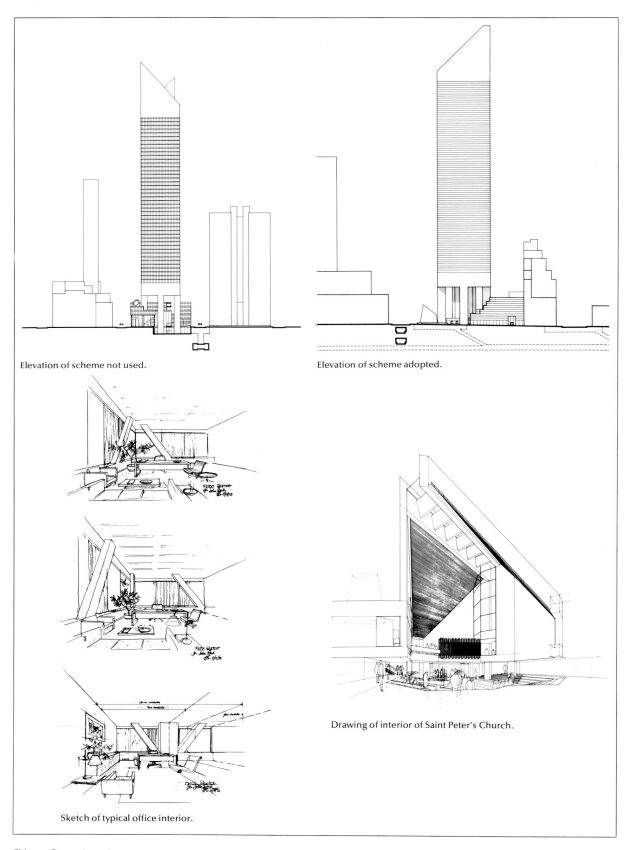

Elevation of scheme not used.

Elevation of scheme adopted.

Drawing of interior of Saint Peter's Church.

Sketch of typical office interior.

Citicorp Center (cont.)

the elements into a coherent whole or design. In the past, the principles of composition in architecture were followed very closely at times, as in the Renaissance, and followed scarcely at all in others, as in the revolt against Renaissance principles, called Mannerism, in the 16th century. The same is true today. There are six major considerations in architectural composition: proportion, scale, contrast, balance, rhythm, and unity. The end result of the combination of such principles of composition establishes the character of a building design.

Proportion is concerned with relationships, or ratios, in size and shape of the various geometric parts of a building to each other and to the building as a whole. Scale refers to the relationships, or ratios, between the sizes and shapes of various parts of a building to the size and shape of the human body in order to produce unity or harmony between them. Contrast refers to the design of various elements of buildings in order for them to have interesting and pleasing differences. Important types of architectural contrast include lines, areas, volumes, masses, sizes, textures, colors, materials, and tones (shades from light to dark).

Balance involves the provision of a state of equilibrium in a building design, not only in actuality but visually. The two types of balance are symmetrical, in which identical parts appear in identical positions on either side of an axis; and asymmetrical, in which the parts on one side of the axis are balanced by ones that are not identical on the other. Rhythm means a regular repetition, according to some system, of elements, such as windows or columns and the spaces between them. Unity means the combination of all the elements into a systematic, identifiable whole.

When all the elements of architecture have been brought into proper relationships with each other and with the whole building or group of buildings, the end result is architectural character. Some believe that there are intrinsic qualities in the character of buildings that cause churches to look like churches or office buildings to proclaim themselves as such. Others do not agree.

To many people, architectural design is exactly what architecture is all about. Some even go so far as to say that architectural design is architecture and all the other functions and pursuits are engineering or something else. In any case, design is the central theme of architecture and is probably the only activity in architecture in which the knowledge and talents of architects are unique. For those with such talents and knowledge, architectural design offers exciting and creative, fulfilling careers. Most architectural designers today have become registered or licensed architects after completion of college professional training, experience requirements in architects' offices, and examinations. Others are architectural graduates who have not yet been registered or licensed to practice on their own. In former times, some architectural designers started out in drafting or other work,

learned on the job and through independent study, and eventually became designers. Today there are few, if any, opportunities to become designers in that manner.

Related Articles ARCHITECTURE; ENGINEERING; ESTHETICS; INTERIOR DESIGN; LANDSCAPE ARCHITECTURE; MODEL MAKING; PRACTICE OF ARCHITECTURE; PROGRAMMING; RENDERING; SITE PLANNING; WORKING DRAWING; Various other articles.

Further Reading Broadbent, Geoffrey: *Design in Architecture—Architecture and the Human Sciences,* John Wiley, London, 1973; Christopher-Jones, J.: *Design Methods—Seeds of Human Futures,* John Wiley, London, 1970; Smith, Harold H.: *Valid Architecture,* Wentworth Books, Sydney, Australia, 1971; Wade, John W.: *Architecture, Problems and Purposes—Architectural Design as a Basic Problem-Solving Process,* John Wiley, New York, 1977.

DOME

DOME A curved roof structure usually, but not always, in the form of a hemisphere or other portion of a sphere. The structural principle on which a dome is based is the same as that of the arch and vault. In fact, a dome might be thought of as a special kind of arch, pivoted along its centerline and spun around to form a partial sphere on a circular base.

Construction Originally of masonry, brick, stone, or tile, domes were constructed with wedge-shaped units of these materials laid in rings, of decreasing diameters, one upon the other from their bases toward their tops. As in an arch or vault, a dome exerts great lateral pressure, or thrust, toward the outside at its base. This thrust must be opposed by heavy, thick

DOME Basketball Arena (1956), Georgia Institute of Technology, Atlanta, Ga. [*Architects: Aeck Associates. (Joseph W. Molitor)*]

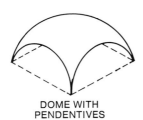

DOME WITH PENDENTIVES

DOME WITH PENDENTIVES SUPPORTING DRUM

DOME Masonry types.

walls or buttresses. A masonry dome is usually supported on a pendentive, a structural element that is a segment of a vault situated in such a way as to provide for the transition from the round base of the dome to a square or polygonal structure supporting it below.

An opening in the middle of the top of a dome is called an eye or oculus. Some domes have lanterns, sometimes called cupolas, small rooms, usually round or polygonal in plan, on their tops. A round or polygonal ring between the base of a dome and the pendentives or other supports is called a drum. Domes may be either smooth-shelled or ribbed and of uniform or varying thicknesses. Also domes can be constructed with one shell or with more. Two shells, one inside the other, were often used to allow different architectural treatment of the interior and the exterior. Sometimes domes are constructed with three shells, with the middle shell supporting the lantern.

Although they may be constructed of masonry and other materials, most domes today are of steel or reinforced concrete, utilizing principles similar to those of masonry, but designed with strong compression rings to resist the outward thrust at the base. A geodesic dome is a special type invented by Buckminster Fuller. Such domes may be constructed from relatively small elements of a variety of materials; see articles botanical building; Fuller, Richard Buckminster.

History The use of domes began in Mesopotamia some 6,000 years ago, soon after the development of the arch and vault. Primitive domes were used in ancient Assyria and Persia, but not in Greece. The Romans carried on the development of the dome to a very high level of sophistication, culminating in the great dome of the Pantheon at Rome (2d century A.D.), still the largest masonry dome (spanning almost 143 feet) in the world. It remained for the Byzantine architects to solve the problem of the pendentive, as in the Hagia Sophia in Istanbul (A.D. 532–537), and the use of the dome spread not only into the rest of Europe but into Turkey, India, Egypt, and North Africa.

The dome was not an important structural element during the Middle Ages, a time which saw great development in the use of vaults, particularly in the Gothic and later churches. Domes again became popular during the Renaissance and later were further developed in such churches as Michelangelo's St. Peter's in Rome, finished in 1590, and Sir Christopher

Wren's St. Paul's in London, finished in 1710, the first with double masonry shells, the second with triple shells.

American Development The introduction of the dome into American architecture came later than the arch and vault, and its use developed more slowly. The early settlers perceived no real need for the great monumental spans of domed roofs and indeed did ⌐ot have the means to construct them. The use of domes became more widespread, especially for churches, state capitols, and other monumental buildings, during the Classic Revival and Eclectic periods of the 19th century and continued into the 20th. Today domes are still widely used, usually of steel or reinforced concrete construction, for such buildings as stadiums in which large areas must be enclosed with a minimum of obstructions, such as columns.

Related Articles ARCH; BRICK; CONCRETE; FULLER, RICHARD BUCKMINSTER; MASONRY STRUCTURE; STEEL; STONE; VAULT.

DOOR An entrance into a building; also called a doorway. The word *door* is also used for the movable portion of a doorway. Doors and doorways have been important elements of architecture since the earliest primitive times.

Classification Doors today are classified in two major ways: by the methods in which they open and close and by the material of which they are made. The major types of door operation are swinging, on hinges or pivots; sliding, on tracks, rollers, or slides; folding, with tracks, rollers, or slides, and also those that fold like an accordion; overhead, ones that swing, roll, or fold up; revolving, like four doors on a central pivot; and bypassing, which open with narrow panels that slide over each other to the side of the doorway.

Types Doors may be placed singly, in pairs, or in multiples. A Dutch door has two leaves, one over the other, making it possible to open half the doorway without opening the other. A French door is made of wood, or other material, with glass inserted from near the top to near the bottom; French doors often come in pairs. A door may have louvers inserted into it for ventilation and would be called a louver door if the louvers extend from near the top to near the bottom. If the louvers are movable, it may be called a shutter door. If the shutters are of glass, it may be called a jalousie door. If a door has insect screening, it is called a screen door. A door with a window over it is said to have a transom. A storm door is an additional door used in conjunction with a regular exterior door to help retard the loss of heat from the interior in winter and to help prevent cold drafts from entering a building. In general, most doors today are either flush, those with plane surfaces, or paneled.

Materials A great number of materials may be used for doors and door frames, the assemblies into which doors fit; the most important are wood, steel, and aluminum. Glass is used extensively in doors and

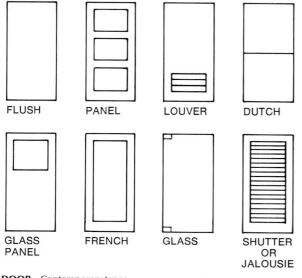

FLUSH   PANEL   LOUVER   DUTCH

GLASS PANEL   FRENCH   GLASS   SHUTTER OR JALOUSIE

DOOR Contemporary types.

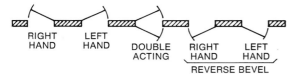

RIGHT HAND   LEFT HAND   DOUBLE ACTING   RIGHT HAND   LEFT HAND
REVERSE BEVEL

DOOR Identification by swings.

some doors, made of tempered glass, may have no frames. Wood doors may be solid or built up with layers of wood and other materials; they come in exterior grades and interior grades that may be hollow core or solid core. Metal doors are generally hollow, sometimes with insulation or other materials inside. Other door materials often used are bronze, stainless steel, and plastics. Many doors are composites, built up of two or several materials, such as a wood flush door with a core of particle board or some other material. Many different types of hardware may be used on doors, ranging from ordinary hinges, locksets, and so on, to door operators that open and close them by means of mechanical or electrical devices. See the article entitled hardware.

Special Types There are a number of special types of doors, including those shielded against the radiation of x-rays, atomic radiation, and so on, and fire-resistant doors. The former ordinarily use lead, steel, or concrete to resist radiation. Fire-resistant doors, which are required in buildings where walls, partitions, and other construction must meet fire-resistance codes, are labeled according to the places where they may be used in buildings, the labeling being based on tests by organizations, such as the Underwriters Laboratories. Another special kind of door is the type often used in entrances to stores and other commercial buildings. These doors are usually metal-framed glass or all glass and are often combined into storefront systems that also include show

windows. They are usually of aluminum or stainless steel, but other materials, such as bronze, may be used. Doors of other types may also be obtained, including insulated ones.

An ordinary swinging door is often spoken of as a left-hand or right-hand door. When such a door is viewed from what is usually considered its outside, a left-hand door has hinges on the left and opens on the right toward the inside; a right-hand door is just the opposite. A left-hand reverse door has hinges on the left and opens toward the outside, while a right-hand reverse door does the opposite. In a door, vertical parts on the edges are called the hinge stile, where the hinges are located, and the lock stile on the other side, where the lock goes; the horizontal edges are the top and bottom rails; a center, or lock, rail is a horizontal member in the door at the height of the lock. These are parts of every door; in paneled types they may be seen, but in flush types they are hidden inside.

Although doors of various types are generally used for specific purposes for which they are designed, for example, overhead doors for garages and storefront doors for commercial buildings, architects today sometimes use them in ways that were not originally intended. For example, almost all types have been adapted to uses in houses, including overhead doors for the protection of vacation houses after the season ends.

Doors can be obtained in many sizes, types, and finishes. Many are stock items, while others are available on special order or may be custom designed to fit a purpose. Many doors, both of wood and metal, are available already mounted in frames, sometimes with all hardware already in place. Frames may be obtained precut but unassembled.

History Although the remains of none of the most primitive doors constructed by ancient people have been found, it is thought that they were rudimentary types of brush or animal skins. In Mesopotamia, doorways were often high with semicircular arches over them. Some doors were made of wood, often with bands of metal, such as bronze; others were thin slabs of stone, paneled to reduce their weight. In Egypt, doorways were rectangular in shape and usually fitted with wooden doors with pivots that acted like hinges. Ancient Greek doors, none of which is known to have survived, are thought to have been of paneled wood and sometimes of metal. Greek doorways were used sparingly and were almost always rectangular, but sometimes were narrowed at the top. Some simple ornament was used on both doors and doorways. An important element of Greek architecture is the colonnade, or peristyle, a row of columns with openings between them but no doors.

The Romans used doorways that were rectangular and others that had semicircular arches at their heads. Doors for important buildings were often of paneled wood covered with bronze that had been hammered into ornamental designs; others were of hollow bronze. In Byzantine architecture, similar doors were used. Notable Roman examples still in existence are on the Pantheon (A.D. 124), Rome; and Byzantine examples on Santa Sophia, or Hagia Sophia (A.D. 537), Istanbul, Turkey. For less important buildings, wood was the door material most often used. A distinguishing feature of Roman architecture is the arcade, a row of arches supported on columns or piers with openings in between but without doors. In Early Christian and Romanesque architecture, doorways were often spanned by semicircular arches, as in Roman times, and doors were of wood or metal and, in some cases, stone such as marble. Some doors were ornamented with carving or other patterns and often doorways were also ornamented.

In Gothic architecture, doorways were ordinarily spanned by pointed arches and were often highly ornamented with moldings or, especially in France, with sculptured likenesses of saints and human figures. Doors were placed where needed, without great regard for symmetry. They were generally made of heavy, vertical wood planks, often ornamented with wrought-iron work, some of it in conjunction with hinges, which were used for the first time in this era. Notable examples include those on the Cathedral of Notre Dame (1163–1250) in Paris. Arcades were used frequently, mostly at first with pointed arches but later with three-centered and four-centered arches, which have several curves of varying radii. The Dutch door is thought to have been developed in northern Europe during the Gothic era for use in houses.

During the Renaissance, door designs were based on those of the classical periods, particularly Rome. Doorways were generally designed with arched heads, and arcades were used extensively. Sometimes arcades were superimposed, one above the other. Arrangements were usually formal and symmetrical, with doorways often ornamented with flanking columns or with architraves, systems of moldings. Along with the fine murals, sculpture, and other art produced by Renaissance architects and artists, doors were an important art form in buildings of the era. Perhaps the most famous doors in the world are those of the Baptistery (6th–16th centuries), Florence, Italy, by Andrea Pisano (c. 1270–1348) and Lorenzo Ghiberti (1378–1455), Pisano's southern door completed in 1336 and Ghiberti's northern in 1424 and eastern in 1447. These doors are of solid bronze, highly sculptured, and became the models for monumental doors of many churches of the Classic Revival and Eclectic eras that followed. Doors for more modest buildings were generally of wood.

After the Renaissance period, doors and doorways were generally derived from those of past eras of architecture, until about the 19th century when the modern movement began. Innovations were made in types of doors, in hardware, and in materials used, but about the only entirely new design was the flush door, a plain type with a flat surface and no ornament. Flush doors, along with a few standardized paneled types, and glass doors of various kinds have become the norm in the architecture of today.

Related Articles ART IN ARCHITECTURE; CLIMATE; GLASS; HARDWARE; INSECT PROTECTION; INSULATION, THERMAL; ORNAMENT; SECURITY SYSTEMS; WALL; WEATHER PROTECTION; Various articles on building materials and systems.

Sources of Additional Information Door and Hardware Inst. 1815 N. Fort Myer Drive, Arlington, Va. 22209.

DRAFTING The process of making drawings. The major uses of drafting in architecture and related fields are in the preparation of conceptual sketches and other drawings for study and design purposes, in the making of drawings or renderings to depict the plans and appearance of buildings to clients and others, and in the preparation of working drawings depicting how buildings are to be constructed. A person who makes a career of drafting is called a draftsman or sometimes today, a drafter. However, architects and others also make such drawings. People who make renderings are usually called renderers, or delineators, instead of draftsmen. People who make design drawings are usually called designers; see articles design, architectural; rendering.

Uses Drafting can be called the true language of architects. They use drawings or sketches to establish relationships between various elements of building designs, to aid in the thought processes of design, to depict buildings in a manner that will be understood, and to prepare working drawings, which are used as guides to the construction of buildings. There are other uses of drafting, but the above demonstrate the importance of drafting in architecture. Drafting is also an important part of the services of other design professionals, such as landscape architects, engineers, and interior designers. And material and equipment suppliers use drafting as an aid in manufacturing and assembly of building products and for the preparation of large-scale shop drawings for the fabrication of other building components and systems.

One of the highest compliments that may be paid to an architectural technician is being called a good draftsman, one who produces excellent working drawings. And one of the highest compliments that can be paid an architectural designer is the same, except that in this case, it means skill in the delineation of sketches and renderings.

Types Architectural drawings may be divided into three major types: conceptual, presentation, and construction. Although the first two types utilize some of the principles of drafting, they are more closely applied to the drawing, painting, and other techniques of the fine arts. Conceptual drawings are usually freehand, sketchy, made with pencil, charcoal, conte crayons, or in other media similar to those used by artists. For further discussion on conceptual drawings, see the article entitled design, architectural. Presentation drawings or renderings primarily depict the designs of buildings for clients and others. This may be accomplished in various ways, as by presentation of the drawings or rendering themselves; by presentation of photographs of the drawings; or by reproduction of the drawings in booklets (brochures), magazines, books, or newspapers; and by slide or filmstrip presentations. For further discussion of various aspects of presentation drawings, see articles entitled graphic design; photography, architectural; practice of architecture; rendering.

The third major use of architectural drawings, the one most people mean when they speak of drafting, is in the preparation of working drawings to be used in the construction of buildings. This kind of drafting is factual, intended to furnish construction information, but not necessarily to depict the appearance of buildings. Therefore it utilizes many techniques, tools, and instruments to produce precise drawings with all the dimensions and other information needed by the contractors, material suppliers, and those who will construct buildings.

Drawing Systems Many systems have been devised for drafting. Only a few are used in architecture, mainly perspective drawing, isometric drawing, and orthographic projection. The first two are included in techniques that are often called pictorial drawing systems because they attempt to depict in two-dimensional drawings, approximations of how three-dimensional objects, such as buildings, appear to the human eye. Orthographic projection attempts to depict the exact shape of objects, such as buildings, together with their sizes or dimensions. Perspective drawing is used mostly for conceptual sketches and drawings and for presentation drawings or renderings. Isometric drawing may also be used for such purposes; and a major application in architecture is in connection with conceptual drawings made with the aid of computers. Orthographic projection is the system used for the preparation of working drawings.

The theory of orthographic projection may be understood by imagining a building enclosed in a clear plastic box. By looking in the front of the box, an observer sees a vertical front view of the building, and by moving around the box, clockwise, the observer may see in turn, the left end view, the back view, and the right end view. These are called the front, side, and back elevations of the building. By looking down on the box, the observer sees a view of the roof, called the roof plan. By taking a horizontal slice through the walls of the building and looking down, the observer may see the floor plan. The observer then imagines that the major points of one of the views, for example, the front elevation, are projected out from the building horizontally and at right angles to the front until these points intersect with the front sheet of plastic. If a draftsman connects the points on the plastic with a pencil, a front elevation drawing of the building will have been made, using the principles of orthographic projection. The other views may be drawn by similar means.

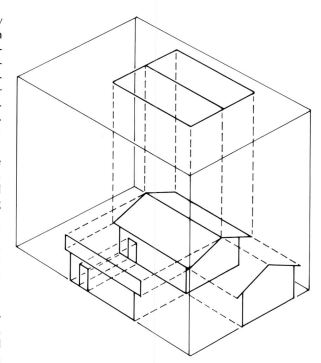

DRAFTING Principles of orthographic projection.

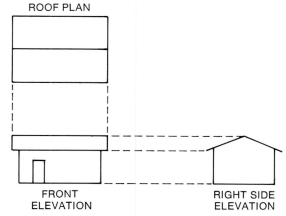

DRAFTING Three orthographic views.

On working drawings, draftsmen show floor plans, roof plans, and elevations, complete with dimensions and other information, along with drawings of other types, including additional plans, such as the site, interior elevations, sections, and details. Sections are made by slicing through the building as in the drawing of floor plans, but the slices may be made horizontally or vertically and may cut through the entire building or any of its parts. Details are drawings, usually in larger scale than those of floor plans or elevations, which contain more information about a building part or component than could be shown otherwise. Working drawings usually contain other information. See the article entitled working drawing.

Instruments and Equipment In making conceptual or presentation drawings, many of the instruments and pieces of equipment used for working drawings may be utilized. In addition, these types of drawings utilize materials, such as paints or pastels, not ordinarily required for working drawings. Many types of drafting instruments and equipment exist. Some of the items are ordinarily not used by architectural draftsmen, but may be used by engineers or others involved in architecture. For example, a drafting machine is like several pieces of drafting equipment, including a T square, scales, triangles, and protractor, combined into one device. Architects very seldom use drafting machines, but engineers frequently do. Many people are familiar with drafting instrument sets, which contain a number of instruments that are commonly a vital part of mechanical drawing courses in secondary and technical schools. Engineers often use sets of instruments such as these, but architects mostly do not, preferring to use only a few instruments selected individually.

The largest piece of equipment is a drafting table, usually made with a drafting surface, or drafting board, that may be raised or lowered and set at various inclines, and ordinarily covered with light-green linoleum, vinyl, or plastic-coated paper to form a surface upon which drawings of good quality may be accomplished easily. A book or storage space should be adjacent, as should a layout table for reference materials. Good overall lighting is a necessity and so are individual flexible lights on drafting tables. Some draftsmen prefer two-tube fluorescent fixtures; others, incandescent lights.

For generations, T squares were used for drawing horizontal lines. Much preferred today are parallel rules, like T squares without heads, which are attached to drafting tabletops with cables. The cables are arranged in such a way that their geometry causes the rules to move up and down drawing boards, always ending in positions parallel to each other. For lines that are vertical or at standard angles, plastic triangles are used, the most common types having one 90° angle with the other two angles either both 45° or 30° and 60°. For angles other than these, adjustable triangles are used. Protractors are used for angular measurements and French curves, together with some special instruments, for drawing irregular, curved lines. For circles, compasses are used, the most popular being bow compasses for most circles and drop compasses for smaller ones. For very large circles, beam compasses are used.

Formerly thumbtacks were used to hold drawings down on drafting boards, but these badly damaged the boards. Today drafting tape is used, a special type much like masking tape but not as sticky. Drafting brushes, sometimes called crumb brushes, are used to keep drawings clean as is drafting powder. Soft pink rubber erasers or other special types that are less likely to damage the drawings are used for correcting mistakes. Erasing shields have slits through which erasing may be accomplished while the area surrounding the slit protects the remainder of the drawing. Electric erasers are also available but must be used with extreme caution, since they cut through drawings very rapidly. Lettering triangles have holes through which pencils may by inserted for making guidelines for lettering on drawings. There are many types of templates, plastic devices with precut slits for drawing circles, plumbing fixtures, kitchen equipment, furniture, and many other items.

Other types of drafting equipment for special purposes include lettering sets. Although architectural working drawings are not ordinarily drawn in ink today, some engineering drawings may be inked, and ink is often used for certain kinds of presentation drawings. The old nib-type drawing pens widely used in the past have now been replaced by much more efficient and easier to use fountain drawing pens.

Of utmost importance to draftsmen are scales of various kinds. Resembling rulers, scales are devices with divisions along their edges indicating the size of drawings in relation to the actual size of buildings. Two major types are used in architecture: a civil engineer's scale and an architect's scale. A civil engineer's scale is divided into tenths, twentieths, and so forth of an inch and is used for large area drawings, maps, and similar purposes. When using one, the scale of a drawing is said to be, in the case of the twentieths scale, 1:20, or 1 in on the scale equals 20 ft on the actual site or area. An architect's scale is divided into ⅛'s, ¼'s, and so on and is used for most architectural working drawings. When using an architect's scale, a drawing is said to be, for example, in the case of the ⅛ portion, in the scale of ⅛ in/1 ft, or ⅛ in on the drawing equals 1 ft on the actual building. Architects learn to think in scale, mentally projecting themselves inside buildings they are drawing as if they could experience them at the drawing sizes and scales.

Undoubtedly, the single most important instrument for a draftsman is the common pencil, though drafting pencils are quite different from the ordinary lead pencil. Today wood-encased drafting pencils have been superseded by mechanical holders in which leads may be replaced. There are several types of holders, including one that has a single lead of a size similar to that in wood pencils and another that stores supplies of very thin leads which need little or no sharpening. For the single-lead holder, electric and manual rotary sharpeners are available. Lead comes in many grades, ranging in hardness from the very hard, 9H, through 18 degrees to the very softest, ExB. For architectural working drawings, only a few grades are generally used, H, 2H, and 3H, and perhaps HB, being sufficient for most tasks. For drafting on plastic film, 6 degrees are available usually marked in a different manner, from softest to hardest, 1 to 6, with letter prefixes that vary among manufacturers. The proper hardness to be used depends on several variables, including type of drawing paper or film, relative humidity in drafting room, and touch of individual draftsmen.

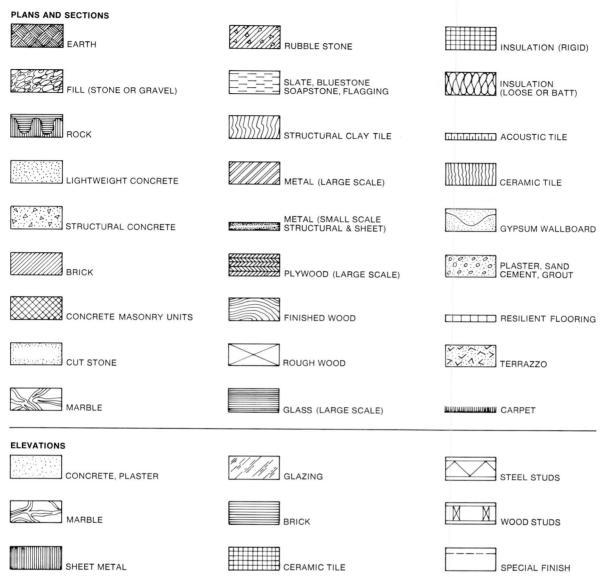

PLANS AND SECTIONS

EARTH

FILL (STONE OR GRAVEL)

ROCK

LIGHTWEIGHT CONCRETE

STRUCTURAL CONCRETE

BRICK

CONCRETE MASONRY UNITS

CUT STONE

MARBLE

RUBBLE STONE

SLATE, BLUESTONE
SOAPSTONE, FLAGGING

STRUCTURAL CLAY TILE

METAL (LARGE SCALE)

METAL (SMALL SCALE
STRUCTURAL & SHEET)

PLYWOOD (LARGE SCALE)

FINISHED WOOD

ROUGH WOOD

GLASS (LARGE SCALE)

INSULATION (RIGID)

INSULATION
(LOOSE OR BATT)

ACOUSTIC TILE

CERAMIC TILE

GYPSUM WALLBOARD

PLASTER, SAND
CEMENT, GROUT

RESILIENT FLOORING

TERRAZZO

CARPET

ELEVATIONS

CONCRETE, PLASTER

MARBLE

SHEET METAL

GLAZING

BRICK

CERAMIC TILE

STEEL STUDS

WOOD STUDS

SPECIAL FINISH

DRAFTING Material indications for architectural drawings.

Drafting Rudiments

Drafting Rudiments It takes a great deal of training, practice, and experience to become an established draftsman. The subject is too large for other than a cursory discussion here. But it should be pointed out that the rudiments consist of the ability to draw lines properly, without which no one can master architectural drafting. At the risk of oversimplification, it must be pointed out that a parallel rule is used for horizontal lines, with the sharpened point of the pencil pulled along it from left to right by right-handed people. As the pencil moves, deliberately and at an even speed, it is held always in a position slanted to the right and is rotated between the fingers to keep the point sharp. Similarly, vertical lines are drawn by right-handed people from the front of the drafting board toward the rear along the left side of a triangle resting firmly against a parallel rule, with the pencil slanted toward the back of the board and rotated. Left-handed people draw horizontal lines from right to left and vertical lines along the right side of a triangle. Draftsmen must also learn to draw lines in a variety of weights, or thicknesses, and of several types, including full and broken, or dash, and other types. Another all-important, rudimentary part of good drafting is proper freehand lettering. Architects usually use roman letters, those with their vertical strokes straight up and down, while many engineers use italic lettering with slanted vertical strokes. Both employ guidelines for lettering.

A great number of new techniques have recently been developed to make drafting more efficient and faster, to take some of the drudgery out of the work, and for other purposes. The first innovation was printing drawing sheets of standard sizes with borders, title blocks, and other standard items. Later developments include paste-up drafting, rub-on techniques, typesetting methods to replace some hand lettering, freehand detailing, half-size techniques, photodrafting, and computer drafting. For a fuller discussion of these techniques, see the article entitled working drawing.

Many architects and other design professionals perform drafting work, particularly in the years just after graduation and when they have recently established their own practices. Some of these professionals continue to do drafting, but the more usual case is for technicians to perform this work. Drafting work requires not only skill in the mechanics and techniques of making working drawings but a considerable knowledge of buildings, including their design and construction. Drafting technicians usually obtain the knowledge and experience they need by attending architectural or other design schools, by training in technical schools, and by on-the-job training in offices of architects or other design professionals. Even with some formal training in architectural drafting, it usually takes some years of broad and diversified exerience before a person can master the craft. For those who would like to participate in important ways in the creation of buildings and related structures wihout becoming professionals in one of the fields, careers as draftsmen can be challenging and rewarding. Many draftsmen go on to become chief draftsmen or other managers in architectural offices, and some eventually become registered architects after gaining sufficient experience and passing architectural registration or licensing examinations.

History Since drawings of buildings have been made by humans from the earliest times, it might be said that there have been architectural draftsmen for a time equally as long. In a sense, this is true. On the other hand, it is not really known when the first drawings were used for construction of buildings. Since the earliest architects were master builders who actually worked in construction, they seem to have had little need for elaborate drawings. In any case, judging by examples of architectural drawings from ancient architects and those of the architects of the Middle Ages, such drawings consisted of very little more than rudimentary floor plans and elevations, most of them drawn by the architects, or master builders.

The major change in drafting in the Renaissance was the introduction of perspective drawings, which helped depict buildings realistically. Although most Renaissance architects and those following in later years did not actually help construct buildings, they were ordinarily available almost constantly to explain to workers what they had in mind.

Not until the late 18th or early 19th century did architects begin to prepare more elaborate sets of drawings. A set of working drawings might consist of floor plans, the most important elevations, and a section, all drawn in a rudimentary way at small scales and often with imprecise dimensions. About the middle of the 19th century, architects began to produce sets of drawings more like those of today.

Young people who aspired to become architects often did the drafting work in offices, a practice that still exists today. And about that time, people began to make careers as draftsmen, as they do today. In the intervening years up to the present time, working drawings have become more and more complex, now consisting of a large number of drawings that can reach a total of 300 sheets or more for a large and complex building. Until the last few decades, drafting techniques lagged behind the changes in working drawings, remaining approximately the same as they had been in the mid-19th century. During later years, methods, instruments, and equipment changed radically.

One thing that has not changed much is drawing lines with a pencil. For years, students in architectural schools have been told that they should learn to think with their pencils, which might be considered extensions of their arms which were in turn extensions of their brains. Architects still think with their pencils, but the day may come when computers or other technologies will finally replace the lowly pencil. Some architects still believe that day will never come.

Related Articles CAREER; COMPUTER; DESIGN, ARCHITECTURAL; ENGINEERING; GRAPHIC DESIGN; INTERIOR DESIGN; LANDSCAPE ARCHITECTURE; PHOTOGRAPHY, ARCHITECTURAL; PLANNING, CITY; PRACTICE OF ARCHITECTURE; RENDERING; WORKING DRAWING.

Further Reading Bellis, H., and W. Schmidt: *Architectural Drafting*, 2d ed., McGraw-Hill, New York, 1971; Hepler, D., and P. Wallach: *Architecture—Drafting and Design*, 2d ed., McGraw-Hill, New York, 1975; Liebing, Ralph W. and Mimi Ford Paul: *Architectural Working Drawings*, John Wiley, New York, 1977; French, Thomas, and Charles J. Vierck: *A Manual of Engineering Drawing for Students and Draftsmen*, 8th ed. rev., McGraw-Hill, New York, 1974.

EARTHQUAKE PROTECTION The provision of structural qualities intended to allow buildings and their elements and systems to resist the effects of earthquakes. Although earthquakes occur somewhat infrequently, they produce forces of high magnitudes that often cause considerable property damage to buildings and other structures and injuries and loss of life among people.

The threat of earthquakes in California has been well known for many years, and that state has long recognized the threat to buildings and their occupants by the establishment of strict earthquake design criteria in building codes and in requirements for knowledge and skill in earthquake-resistant design of engineers and architects registered to practice there. It is not so widely known that many other parts of the United States are also high-risk areas. Legal requirements for earthquake-resistant design have gradually been instituted in states other than California in recent years.

Earthquakes are literally that: quakes, vibrations, or shaking, of the earth's surface or crust, which having been continually stretched or compressed by forces within the earth, reaches a strain too great for its strength. At this point, rocks break or rupture, causing cracks called faults. Faults exist in many places on the earth; some are hidden beneath the surface but others are visible, as the San Andreas fault in California, the largest in the United States, stretching some 600 miles. The San Andreas fault is a part of an earthquake-prone area, called the circum-Pacific belt, that stretches along the edge of the Pacific Ocean, including New Zealand, Japan, the Aleutian Islands, and the coasts of Alaska, Canada, the United States mainland, Mexico, and Central and South America. Another major earthquake zone, the Alpide belt, stretches from Burma to the Alps in Europe.

U.S. Areas In the United States the major earthquake-prone areas, in addition to that along the San Andreas fault, include Alaska; Hawaii; the area around Seattle, Wash.; two large Western areas that include large parts of Montana, Idaho, Nevada, California, and Utah; an area that includes parts of Missouri, Kentucky, Illinois, Tennessee, Alabama, and Arkansas; western New York State; the area around Boston; and the area around Charleston, S.C. About a third of the people in the United States live in these areas. Much larger areas of the United States are believed to be in some danger of earthquakes.

Seismic Waves In an earthquake, almost incalculable forces are released by the sudden movements of rocks along fault lines, up, down, or sideways. Seismic waves are set up by the release of forces, mostly traveling away from the fault. Vibrations occur, for the most part, around the place of rupture, or focus, of the earthquake. Seismic waves are of three types: compressional, which tend to cause rocks to shrink; shear, which tend to change the shape of the rocks; and surface, which move along the earth's surface. All the waves can cause great damage and loss of life. In addition, earthquakes can cause tidal waves that are as dangerous as the quakes and can cause damage that often starts fires, perhaps the greatest danger of all. Damages from an earthquake often occur within a few seconds after the first tremor and consist of breakage not only by the force of the quake but from falling rubble from buildings and other structures, and damage to water lines as well as those for electricity and gas service, which can lead to fires.

Earthquake-Resistant Design To design buildings and other structures properly for earthquake resistance, analyses must be made by competent professionals. It is considered impossible, or improbable, that buildings can be designed and constructed to completely resist the impact of earthquakes. The technological requirements would be overwhelming and the costs so high as to make such a course infeasible. Therefore the usual assumption is that earthquake-resistant design should be confined to reducing the loss of life and property caused by structural failure, by falling debris, and by fire.

The design process for earthquake resistance starts with an analysis of such factors as the seismic activity of the region in which a building is to be constructed,

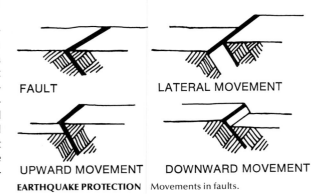

EARTHQUAKE PROTECTION Movements in faults.

149

the geological conditions on the site, the consequences of possible earthquake activity in injuries and loss of lives and damage to the building, the losses while the building cannot be used after an earthquake, and the costs of providing earthquake resistance in the building.

Measurements Seismic activity in a region is studied from data derived from geological evidence, such as faults, history of earthquakes and their locations, and determinations of the quantitative measurements of earthquakes in the area. Measurements for earthquakes have not been made absolutely uniform. However, the major measure is the magnitude or size of an earthquake, usually on the Richter scale, a logarithmic scale that measures the energy of earthquakes, from 1.5, the smallest that can be felt, to 8.5, a very devastating earthquake. This scale was named after American seismologist Charles R. Richter (1900–   ). Another measure is the intensity of earthquakes, referring to the degree of shaking. Intensity is usually measured on the Mercalli scale, which goes from I to XII, with a reading of I, which denotes nothing will be felt, except in rare circumstances, and a reading of XII, which denotes almost total damage. Another measure is seismicity, most often taken to mean the frequency of earthquakes in a region, in number per area of measurement.

Instruments Seismology is the science of earthquakes, and a seismologist is a scientist engaged in studying this activity. A seismograph is an instrument for the detection and recording of the magnitude of earthquakes on the Richter scale. Such instruments, in groups of three, measure vertical movement in earthquakes and movements along north-south and east-west lines. They can also be used to determine locations, called epicenters, of earthquakes.

Other instruments used in the study of earthquakes and which may lead to better earthquake prediction in the future include surveyor's levels, detecting changes in elevation; tiltmeters, indicating tilting of the earth; scintillation counters, indicating changes in water pressure underground; creepmeters and laser instruments, registering horizontal movement; magnetometers, measuring changes in the earth's magnetic field; resistivity gauges, indicating changes in electrical conductivity in rocks; gravimeters, measuring the rise and fall of the ground; and strainometers, measuring expansion and contraction of rock.

Resistance Criteria The actual methods for earthquake-resistant design of buildings and other structures are beyond the scope of this book and must be handled by experts who have both the knowledge and the ability required for proper design. However, some criteria may be cited. Structures that must resist earthquakes should be simple in form, should be as symmetrical as possible, and should tend more toward squares in plan and elevation than toward elongated forms. In addition, structures should be uniform in design, with continuous distribution of strength; tall buildings should not be too slender;

and setbacks in building forms should be avoided.

Structural materials used in buildings affect their earthquake resistance considerably. For high-rise or medium-rise buildings, steel or reinforced concrete frames are considered best. For medium-rise buildings, prestressed concrete may also be used, but many experts think precast concrete and reinforced masonry should not be used. For low-rise buildings, timber structures are considered best, closely followed in order of preference by reinforced concrete and steel.

In the proper structural design of buildings to resist earthquakes, several factors should be considered, including uniform loadings on all load-bearing columns, beams, and other members. All should be continuous in shape without offsets or abrupt changes in section and should be coaxial and as monolithic as possible. Reinforced concrete beams and columns should be approximately of equal width.

After the proper structural forms and materials have been determined, earthquake-resistant design must take into consideration the effects of earthquakes on other elements of buildings. Much damage can be done to improperly detailed elements, such as walls, doors, windows, and ceilings as well as to the structure. Another important consideration is the design for earthquake resistance of service systems and equipment, such as electrical, heating, air conditioning, plumbing, and water supply.

In addition to the requirements for the prevention of as much damage as possible to these systems, they must be designed not to release dangerous substances, such as steam or gas. Emergency equipment, such as that for fire protection or fire fighting, must remain usable after an earthquake. In the 1971 earthquake in southern California, in the hospitals that were destroyed, some of the deaths were attributed not to the earthquake itself but to failure of the life-support systems for patients.

Earthquake-resistant design is a very important part of architecture and, with the great growth of populations in earthquake-prone areas, becomes of even greater importance with time.

History Together with volcanic eruptions, hurricanes, and tidal waves, earthquakes have been one of the most terrifying disasters experienced by human beings from the earliest times. Often the types of violence inflicted by these natural calamities are interrelated. For example, some scientists believe Crete and other Mediterranean communities to have been destroyed about 1450 B.C. by tidal waves, earthquakes, and great quantities of falling ash caused by the explosion of a volcano on the island of Thera, some 70 miles north of Crete. A great number of people were killed and injured, and a highly developed early civilization destroyed.

Many other natural disasters have occurred since, including the eruption of Krakatoa, near Java, in 1883. This disaster took some 36,000 lives, but is believed to have been only about one-fourth of the magnitude of the explosion of Thera. One of the most famous volcanic eruptions was that of Mount Vesuvius in Italy, A.D. 79, which buried the cities of Herculaneum and Pompeii, preserving them until they were excavated, beginning in the 18th century.

Many devastating eathquakes have taken place over the centuries. In 526 about a quarter of a million people were killed by an earthquake in Syria. Since that time, more than 60 major earthquakes have occurred in many parts of the world. More than 35 of them have each taken 10,000 or more lives and some of them have taken many times that number. The worst, in Shensi, China, in 1556, claimed some 830,000 lives.

U.S. Occurrences In the United States, earthquakes have occurred with some frequency. Although the number of deaths in the United States has been small compared to those in other countries, earthquakes present a definite threat to life and property. An earthquake occurred in New England in 1755, to be followed by what may have been the worst earthquakes in the United States, in New Madrid, Mo., in 1811 and 1812. These are believed to have measured 7.2 on the Richter scale. Few people lived there at that time, so a relatively small number of lives were lost. In 1857 an earthquake occurred in southern California and was followed by one in Charleston, S.C., in 1886.

In 1906 the San Francisco earthquake, measuring 8.3 on the Richter scale, destroyed the city and took 500 lives. The Alaska earthquake in 1964, measuring 8.5, claimed 114 lives and was followed by another in the state of Washington the following year. In 1971 another, measuring 6.5, occurred in southern California, killing 65 people. All these earthquakes also took a huge toll in damage to buildings and other structures. Because of the heavy concentration of people in some of these earthquake-prone areas today, much heavier tolls in both property damage and lives might be taken by a major earthquake today.

A considerable amount of research on earthquakes and earthquake-resistant building design has been accomplished over the past few decades. Such research is continuing and may be expected to produce meaningful results in the future, not only in the structural design of buildings but in codes and regulations on earthquake-resistant design and in the infant science of earthquake prediction.

Related Articles FIRE PROTECTION; STRUCTURE; WEATHER PROTECTION.

Further Reading Dowrick, David J.: *Earthquake Resistant Design—A Manual for Engineers and Architects*, John Wiley, London and New York, 1977; Okamoto, Shunzo: *Introduction to Earthquake Engineering*, John Wiley, New York, 1973; Numerous reports of scientific studies have been published by organizations, such as the American Institute of Architects, American Society of Civil Engineers, and the Seismological Society of America; by universities, including the California Institute of Technology, Pasadena, University of California, Berkeley, and Massachusetts Institute of Technology, Cambridge; and by many institutes and conferences, notably in New Zealand and Japan.

Source of Additional Information Seismological Society of America, P.O. Box 826, Berkeley, Calif. 94701.

ECLECTIC ARCHITECTURE A style or movement, in which forms and details are selected from any of the styles or buildings of the past. In more extreme examples, forms or details selected from more than one building or style of the past are recombined into a single building design. The movement began about the middle of the 19th century and has continued into the 20th in the United States and elsewhere.

For many years after the modern movement in architecture had begun, the architects who created Eclectic architecture were denigrated, even reviled. Needless to say, Eclectic architecture was quite different from the functional architecture that followed. Eclectic work has been severely criticized as being irrelevant, derivative, dishonest, unfitted to its purposes, sentimental, even undemocratic. In many cases, some of these accusations may be true, at least partly. But what has become increasingly evident, as the 20th century runs its course, is the very high excellence of some of the buildings of the eclectic era and the proficiency and talent of some of the architects.

Melange of Styles What makes Eclectic architecture so difficult to grasp is the widely varied approaches, the great melange of historical models used, and the strange appearance it brought to many American cities, which often found several styles of office buildings, many of them incompatible with each other, in a single block of a single street. The same thing happened on residential streets. And admittedly, many of the eclectic buildings in which details and forms from several styles were combined often turned out to be unfortunate, at best.

The first few examples of Eclectic architecture were constructed in the United States quite early. And even dedicated architects, who usually designed buildings in other styles, were sometimes eclectic. For example, the dedicated Classic Revival architect Thomas Ustick Walter (1804–87) built Moyamensing Prison (1832), Philadelphia, in a sort of English Gothic style. When he added the Debtor's Wing (1835), he chose a sort of Egyptian style. Equally dedicated classicist John Haviland (1792–1852) used a similar style for Tombs Prison (1840), New York City, later demolished.

Perhaps the earliest real eclecticist was John Notman (1810–65), who designed buildings in Gothic, Romanesque, Renaissance, Baroque, and other styles. Eclectic architecture became more prevalent after the Civil War and, before it faded out in the 20th century, produced a great number of styles. Some of these were the Italianate, Queen Anne, Stick, Victorian, French Second Empire, Romanesque Revival, Shingle, Eclectic Gothic Revival, Eclectic Classic Revival, often called Classic Eclecticism, Renaissance Revival, Colonial Revival, Baroque Revival, Jacobethan, Eastlake, Beaux Arts, and many others.

Many of these styles were short-lived fads. Italian-

ECLECTIC ARCHITECTURE Old Boston City Hall (1865), Boston, Mass. [*Architects: Bryant and Gilman. (Detroit Publishing, Co., Library of Congress)*]

ECLECTIC ARCHITECTURE Dakota Apartment (1884), New York, N.Y. [*Architect: Henry J. Hardenbergh. (Wurts Brothers)*]

ECLECTIC ARCHITECTURE Warner Hudnut Building (1880), formerly B. Altman Store, New York, N.Y. [*Architects: David and John Jardine. (Wurts Brothers)*]

ECLECTIC ARCHITECTURE Plaza Hotel (1907), New York, N.Y. [*Architect: Henry J. Hardenbergh. (Wurts Brothers)*]

ate architecture vaguely resembled that of Italy in the late Middle Ages and early Renaissance, while Queen Anne was thought to be vaguely reminiscent of the architecture of her era. Neither was very important in the evolution of architecture and neither lasted very long. The so-called Stick style was vaguely patterned after medieval half-timbered buildings and did not last long. Victorian architecture was important from about 1860 to 1890. The term is most often used to denote vaguely Gothic houses and other buildings, often with wooden scroll-saw ornamentation, sometimes referred to as gingerbread, and eclectic details. Actually, other eclectic work in Renaissance, French Second Empire, and other revival styles were part of the Victorian movement.

ECLECTIC ARCHITECTURE Public Library (1911), New York, N.Y. [*Architects: Carrère and Hastings. (Detroit Publishing Co., Library of Congress)*]

ECLECTIC ARCHITECTURE Bush Terminal Building (1918), New York, N.Y. [*Architects: Helmle and Corbett. (Wurts Brothers)*]

ECLECTIC ARCHITECTURE Williamsburgh Savings Bank (1929), Brooklyn, New York, N.Y. [*Architects: Halsey, McCormick and Helmer. (Wurts Brothers)*]

ECLECTIC ARCHITECTURE Union Club (1932), New York, N.Y. [*Architects: Delano and Aldrich. (Wayne Andrews)*]

The Second Empire style, derived from the architecture of France during the reign (1852–71) of Emperor Napoléon III (1808–73), was used for a number of major public buildings in many places in the United States. Romanesque Revival became firmly implanted in the United States from about 1875 to the end of the century, mainly because of the masterful designs of Henry Hobson Richardson (1838–86). Richardson also designed buildings in other styles, including the Shingle style, which, in wood shingles for exterior wall coverings, resembles his other work in stone.

Noted Eclectics   Many of the greatest architects of the last part of the 19th and the early part of the 20th century, though eclectics, became noted for their designs in one or other of the more important styles. For example, the Eclectic Gothic churches and other buildings of Ralph Adams Cram (1863–1942) and Bertram Grosvenor Goodhue (1869–1924), who were partners for many years, are still admired today. Other eclectic architects, whose work is still admired, designed in more than one style. Some of the most notable were Richard Morris Hunt (1827–95), George Browne Post (1837–1913), Frank Furness (1839–1912), Charles Follen McKim (1847–1909) and his partner Stanford White (1853–1906), Cass Gilbert (1859–1934), and John Russell Pope (1874–1937). Their major styles were Classic Eclecticism, Renaissance Revival, Eclectic Gothic, and some styles derived from various periods in France. Most were graduates of the École des Beaux Arts in Paris, or had been trained by architects who had attended the school. They developed a type of Eclectic style, derived from various historical sources, that came to be referred to as the Beaux Arts style.

In addition to the styles previously named, a great plethora of others have arisen, most of them briefly,

153

in American architecture, including Spanish Colonial; the Mission style, supposedly derived from the mission churches of California; Italian Villa; Swiss Chalet; along with Japanese, Chinese, Indian, Egyptian, Muslim, and others too numerous to be mentioned. Today, except in certain instances, such as in tract houses, most of these styles have long ago been discarded. (See color section for other illustrations.)

Related Articles BEAUX ARTS, ECOLE DES; CLASSIC REVIVAL ARCHITECTURE; COLONIAL ARCHITECTURE; GOTHIC REVIVAL ARCHITECTURE; HISTORY OF ARCHITECTURE; PRESERVATION; Various articles on eclectic architects.

Further Reading Kidney, Walter C.: *The Architecture of Choice—Eclecticism in America 1880–1930,* Braziller, New York, 1974; See also listing in the article entitled history of architecture.

Sources of Further Information See listing in the article entitled history of architecture.

ECOLOGY

The branch of biology that is concerned with the relationships between living things and their environment. While architecture might be said to have always been concerned with the ecological results of what is built, the concern has deepened in the past few decades. Not only are human beings affected by ecological considerations but the rest of nature is also affected when buildings and other structures are constructed.

Branches The science of ecology may be divided into two major branches—plant and animal—but some think this unnatural because plants and animals ordinarily live together in an environment. Another division sometimes used is that of terrestrial or land ecology; and marine or sea and ocean ecology. All the branches of ecology deal with such subjects as how living things adapt, anatomically, physiologically, and in other ways, to environmental conditions, such as moisture, light, temperature, winds, solar conditions, and interrelations of various plants and animals.

Ecology is also concerned with what are called successions: series of stages of changes that take place in the kinds of animals and plants that live in a specific environment. As an example, in an area that has lost its plant life as the result of some disaster, such as fire or flooding, the succession that follows may vary but would generally include the stages of first flowers, and then grasses, then trees. The final stage of succession is called a climax which produces a climax community. In a climax community, animal and plant life remain relatively stable and unchanging for very long periods of time, thousands of years. In all the stages, the geographical area in which specific animals and plants live is called their range; and the kinds of places in which they prefer to live within the ranges are called their habitats.

Life Zones Environments that exist on land are usually classified as seven types, or life zones, which are different from each other in major ways, and which stretch from the poles to the equator. In the United States, starting from the North Pole, there are six regions: arctic; tundra; taiga, sometimes called bo-

real, or northern, forest; deciduous forest; prairie, sometimes called grassland, steppe, veldt, or pampas; and desert. The seventh, tropical rainforest, is found south of the United States, in Central and South America.

The arctic zone is an area in which few animals or plants live on the land, though abundant life exists in the seas. The tundra is the area south of the arctic, in which there are no trees, but in which animals and some plants live. The taiga is an area of evergreen trees, called conifers, and of other plant and animal life. The deciduous forest zone is the next most northerly area and contains deciduous trees, sometimes called hardwoods, and other plant and animal life. The prairie zone has a heavy growth of grasses and a variety of animal life. The most southerly zone in the United States is the desert, an area in which the climate is hot and dry and in which cacti and a few small trees grow, along with mostly nocturnal or night-moving animals. The tropical rainforest is an area of hot temperature and heavy rainfall, in which many trees, plants, and animals live.

Ecological Concerns Some of the major ecological concerns of architects and other environmental designers are with populations; for example, how many animals, including human beings, or plants can live together without doing harm to each other or to their environment. Ecological population studies are also concerned with the removal or reduction in the numbers of harmful plants and animals, such as rats and mice, insects, and poisonous plants.

Another important ecological consideration of architects and other designers is the study of the interactions between plants and animals, including human beings, and also among animals and among plants. Two or more dissimilar organisms living in a close relationship that benefits each of them is called symbiosis. Many architects and other professionals today believe symbiosis to be one of the most important goals in the design of buildings and other structures.

Finally, architects and other design professionals are greatly concerned today about the conservation of natural things, not only land, air, and water but also the important ones that exist in the multitudinous forms of animal and plant life and the human race.

Related Articles ENVIRONMENTAL PROTECTION; LANDSCAPE ARCHITECTURE; PARKS; PLANNING, CITY.

Further Reading Colinvaux, Paul Alfred: *Introduction to Ecology,* John Wiley, New York, 1973; Knowles, Ralph L.: *Energy and Form—An Ecological Approach to Urban Growth,* MIT Press, Cambridge, Mass., 1974.

EDUCATION

In architecture, primarily the processes involved in teaching the arts, sciences, skills, and disciplines required to practice the profession of architecture. Another important role of education in the building industry is teaching engineers, landscape architects, and others who perform specialized functions in architecture. See articles entitled engineering; interior design; landscape architecture; planning, city. Another important aspect is the education of technicians, such as draftsmen and specification writers. And, of course, continuing education is necessary for maintaining and enhancing the knowledge and skills of those already engaged in architecture.

For a young person who wants to become an architect, the usual method today involves preparation in a secondary school, followed by study at an architectural school, of which there are more than 100 in the United States. For further discussion, see the article entitled career.

Schools Architectural schools are divided into two major types: undergraduate schools, with curricula leading to professional degrees in architecture; and graduate schools, which require undergraduate degrees, though not necessarily in architecture, before students are admitted to graduate programs that lead to professional degrees. While it is difficult to generalize about the secondary school credits required for admission to schools of the first sort because of their great diversity, a typical architectural school might require or prefer approximately the following: four units of English, three to four units of mathematics, two to three units of science, two or more units of social science, and often two or more units of foreign language. Although again difficult to generalize a typical graduate school of architecture might require an acceptable degree or its equivalent from an accredited undergraduate college or university, together with successful completion of specific courses, such as mathematics, sciences, art and architectural history.

In an undergraduate architectural course of five or sometimes six years duration, successful completion earns a professional degree of a bachelor of architecture (B.Arch.), and in a graduate professional school, ordinarily lasting three or more years, a master of architecture (M.Arch.). Students who have earned a B.Arch. may also complete the M.Arch., and a limited number earn a doctor of philosophy (Ph.D.).

In an undergraduate course, students usually take mathematics, sciences, social sciences, and humanities, along with professional courses. In a graduate professional school, such courses will have been completed before students enter. In both types of schools, the professional courses typically include architectural design, usually during all years of attendance; technology, in structures, materials, mechanical and electrical equipment and systems, lighting and acoustics; history of art and architecture; city planning; and architectural practice. Some schools require students to complete a major design project or thesis in the last year, and some require two summers or more of practical experience in architectural offices.

Professional electives available to students in architectural schools are numerous and varied, including such subjects as advanced urban planning, computer technology, advanced structures, visual and graphic communications and design, building law, experimental structures, urban transportation, systems anal-

ysis, social factors in architecture, economics of building construction, real estate, and courses in specific building types, such as schools or hospitals.

Architectural education is in a state of change today. Many different kinds of courses are therefore available, in addition to the ones described above. For example, many schools have what they sometimes call platforms or modules of study that allow students to pursue the regular course and at the same time to attain some degree of specialization in subjects of particular interest to them. Other undergraduate and graduate schools have special curricula that not only allow specialization but often lead to specialized degrees in such areas as urban design, architectural history, architectural technology, health services planning and design, historic preservation, and environmental systems. Some of these courses lead to B.Arch. or M.Arch. degrees; while others offer specific degrees, for example, a master of science in historic preservation or in one of the other specialties.

School Selection Architectural schools are located in both private and public universities. Their entrance requirements, curricula, costs, and facilities vary so much that prospective students should study the bulletins or catalogs thoroughly. If possible, students should choose a university that meets their specific goals and needs and, above all, should choose an architectural school that has been accredited by the National Architectural Accrediting Board. Graduation from an accredited school greatly simplifies the process of becoming registered or licensed architects. As in other fields, architectural education has become increasingly more costly. In general, state schools cost much less than private schools, particularly for residents of the state. A considerable number of grants, scholarships, and loan funds are available to all college and university students, and there are many others specifically for architecture students. Some schools offer cooperative programs, in which students alternate class attendance with periods of work to help pay for their education.

Architectural schools are occasionally part of larger colleges that offer courses in subjects closely related to architecture. Sometimes called colleges of environmental design or architecture and planning or some similar title, these institutions often offer courses in such fields as city planning and landscape architecture, and occasionally in interior design, building construction, and other fields.

In some smaller colleges, courses in prearchitecture offer students a chance to complete the first two years of professional architectural school or to prepare themselves to become architectural technicians in such fields as drafting, specification writing, estimating, construction inspection, and others. Architectural technicians are trained in two other important ways: in vocational and technical schools and in on-the-job training in architects' offices.

American Development In the colonial era, there were no architectural schools in America. The earliest

American architects were trained either by participation in the actual construction of buildings or by study of books and travel. Architectural students were then trained as apprentices in the offices of practicing architects. A large number of important American architects were trained in this manner until late in the 19th century. About the middle of the 19th century, architectural students went to Europe to study, particularly in the École des Beaux Arts in Paris. The first American to enter this school, in 1846, was Richard Morris Hunt (1827–95), who became one of the most noted architects of his time. Many other American architects were trained at the Beaux Arts and in the ateliers of architects who had trained there, well into the 20th century. The first American woman graduate of the Beaux Arts was Julia Morgan (1872–1957).

The first architectural school in the United States was founded in 1868 at Massachusetts Institute of Technology, Cambridge, with nine students, by architect William Robert Ware (1832–1915), follower of Hunt and acknowledged as the father of architectural education in this country. Ware also started a tradition in American architecture in which many practicing architects devote part of their time to teaching; and architectural teachers, to practice. Since that time, there has been a distinguished list of architect-teachers. The first woman to graduate from M.I.T. was Sophia Hayden (c. 1868–1953).

Other architectural schools quickly followed, at the University of Illinois, Urbana, and Cornell University, Ithaca, N.Y., both in 1870; and at Syracuse University, Syracuse, N.Y., in 1873. In 1881 Ware established another architectural program at Columbia University, New York City, in of all places, the School of Mines. All these schools are still in existence; by 1896 there were nine schools in the United States, with a combined total of 273 regular students. Now there are more than 100 architectural schools in many locations in the country, with considerably more than 25,000 full-time students.

During their early years, the first architectural schools in the United States were under the influence of the architects who had been educated at the Beaux Arts. Some of these men founded an organization dedicated to these principles, the Society of Beaux Arts Architects in 1894, in New York City. In 1916 the Beaux Arts Institute of Design was founded in New York City, and this organization dominated the teaching of architectural design in schools all over the United States, through the medium of standard design problems which students solved and which were then graded, according to Beaux Arts principles, by juries chosen from the membership of the Institute.

In the late 1930s Walter Adolf Gropius (1883–1969) brought the more modern philosophy of another famous school, the Staatliches Bauhaus, from Germany to Harvard University. One by one, other schools around the country deserted the Beaux Arts system until soon after World War II, it had become only a memory. The Beaux Arts organization then changed its name to the National Institute for Architectural Education; its major purpose today is providing grants and scholarships for higher architectural education and travel.

Architectural education has been undergoing considerable change in the recent past, reflecting greater concern with the people who use buildings, the new technology, conservation and preservation, and the sociological aspects of architecture.

Related Articles BAUHAUS, STAATLICHES; BEAUX ARTS, ÉCOLE DES; CAREER; CONSTRUCTION, BUILDING; ENGINEERING; GROPIUS, WALTER ADOLF; HUNT, RICHARD MORRIS; INTERIOR DESIGN; LANDSCAPE ARCHITECTURE; PLANNING, CITY.

Further Reading *Barron's Profiles of American Colleges,* vols. 1 and 2, latest editions, Woodbury, N.Y.; *The College Handbook,* latest edition, College Entrance Examination Board, Educational Testing Service, Princeton, N.J.; Hegener, Karen Collier, and David Clarke, eds.: *Architecture Schools in America,* Peterson's Guides, Princeton, N.J., 1976.

Sources of Additional Information The American Institute of Architects, Association of Collegiate Schools of Architecture, National Architectural Accrediting Boards, Inc., all at 1735 New York Ave., N.W., Washington, D.C. 20006; National Institute for Architectural Education, 20 W. 40th St., New York, N.Y. 10018.

Periodicals *ACSA News* and *Journal of Architectural Education,* 1735 New York Ave., N.W., Washington, D.C. 20006.

ELECTRICAL ENGINEERING

A major branch of engineering that deals with distribution, controls, and use of electricity in buildings. An electrical engineer is a person who has been registered or licensed to perform professional services on work of this type.

Working closely with the architects and coordinating the work with that of the other engineers and consultants, an electrical engineer is primarily responsible for the design of the electrical systems in a building; preparation of the construction documents, drawings, and specifications for their construction; making estimates of construction costs; and inspecting the electrical work to ensure that it is properly constructed.

Systems The major systems in the buildings for which electrical engineers are responsible are electrical service and distribution, lighting, electrical heating and cooling, communications, and electrical generation and transmission. Electrical service and distribution includes the wiring, meters, conduits, controls, switches, and other devices required to bring electrical power into a building and distribute it properly and safely. Lighting includes the design or selection of fixtures and other equipment for proper illumination, exterior and interior, and for lighting for ornamental, safety, and other purposes. Lighting is sometimes designed by specialists, who may or may not be electrical engineers. Electrical heating and cooling includes self-contained electrical fixtures and equipment for these purposes, and for snow melting and freeze control. Communications includes systems and equipment for telephones, telegraphs, radio and television, public address and paging, alarms, and the like. Electrical generation and transmission includes motor-powered or turbine-powered generators, overhead or underground transmission lines, and related equipment and systems.

In addition, electrical engineers are responsible for special systems, such as lightning protection and emergency light and power. Elevators and other conveying systems, automated systems, and data-processing systems are often handled by electrical engineers, in many cases by specialists in these fields.

Electrical engineering has increased rapidly in importance since the beginning of the 20th century, as electric power became available all over the country. New inventions and the widespread availability of electrical laborsaving devices and equipment have contributed heavily to its importance in architecture. Today most buildings are full of electrical appliances and equipment; many of them were luxuries just a few years ago but are now considered necessities by most people. Electrical work in buildings consumes an ever-larger portion of construction budgets as time passes. Electrical systems in buildings are also among the most important consumers of energy, and electrical engineers have an important function in the provision of efficient means both to use and to conserve energy.

Work Phases The professional work of electrical engineers is ordinarily divided into phases that are the same as those for architectural and other engineering work: schematic, design development, construction document, and construction administration. Electrical engineers make studies of the site, utilities, building programs, and important problems during the schematic phases, and produce preliminary drawings, specifications, and cost estimates for the electrical work. The problems are further studied during the design development phase and the drawings, specifications, and estimates are refined. During the construction document phase, drawings and specifications, from which the electrical work will be constructed, are prepared, along with further refined cost estimates. In the construction phase, electrical engineers assist the architects in the administration of the work and inspect it to ensure that it conforms to the construction documents and good practices.

In addition to the major functions of their work, electrical engineers are often required to prepare revised drawings and specifications, to make as-built drawings, after a building is complete, and other services. In all their work, electrical engineers work closely with the architects and other engineers and consultants to achieve the purposes of the total building as well as the purposes of the systems for which they are primarily responsible.

The education, registration or licensing, and practice of electrical engineers today parallels that of the other professional engineers; for further discussion, see the article entitled engineering.

Related Articles BUILDING CODES AND STANDARDS; BUILDING INDUSTRY; COMMUNICATION SYSTEM; COST

CONTROL; DRAFTING; ELECTRIC POWER AND WIRING; ENERGY; ENGINEERING; LIGHTING; LIGHTNING PROTECTION; SPECIFICATION; WORKING DRAWING.

Further Reading See the article entitled engineering.
Additional Sources of Information Illuminating Engineering Society, 345 E. 47th St., New York, N.Y. 10017; Institute of Electrical and Electronic Engineers, 345 E. 47th St., New York, N.Y. 10017; see also list in the article entitled engineering.
Periodicals *Actual Specifying Engineer*, 5 S. Wabash Ave., Chicago, Ill. 60603; *Electrical Consultant*, 1760 Peachtree Rd., N.W., Atlanta, Ga. 30309; *IEEE Spectrum*, 245 E. 47th St., New York, N.Y. 10017.

ELECTRIC POWER AND WIRING The systems that provide and distribute an important source of energy, electricity, in buildings. Electrical energy is such an integral part of architecture today, and of the lives of the people who occupy or use buildings, that it seems unbelievable that electricity was completely unavailable for such uses until about 100 years ago. Electricity is the energy that powers almost all of the great number of kitchen appliances in buildings, including ranges, ovens, dishwashers, garbage grinders, trash compactors, knife sharpeners, can openers, hot plates, and mixers. Electricity also powers laundry washers, ironers, dryers, and other appliances. Electric power is used for pumping water and for television sets, radios, electric blankets, vacuum cleaners, and a great array of other items. For extremely important uses of electricity, see articles entitled communication system; fire protection; heating, ventilating, and air conditioning; lighting; security systems; vertical transportation. For a discussion of electric signs, see the article entitled graphic design.

Composition of Matter Although various theories of the characteristics of matter have been held at various times in the past, scientists today generally agree that all matter is composed principally of electrical particles. These particles, called protons (positively charged), electrons (negatively charged), and neutrons (no charge), in various combinations make up the atoms of elements. Hydrogen atoms are the simplest, ordinarily having one electron and a nucleus of one proton. This is the ordinary or neutral (uncharged) state of an atom, when the number of protons in the nucleus and the total number of electrons are equal. Elements, other than hydrogen, have nuclei of more than one proton, along with neutrons and sometimes electrons. These elements also have varying numbers of free electrons. When it loses free electrons, an atom becomes positively charged. When it gains free electrons, it becomes negatively charged. Such charged atoms are called ions, and it is the property of losing or gaining electrons that causes electric currents to flow in materials.

Some elements, such as metals, have greater numbers of free electrons than others, and therefore are better passages, or conductors, for electric currents. In metals, the electrons flow from atom to atom, the positive charges being attracted to the negative and vice versa. In liquids and certain gases, ions flow in a similar manner. Although it is common to consider electricity as flowing from positive to negative in construction and other industries, it is now believed that electrons actually flow from negative to positive.

Electrical Current Electrical energy flows through good conductors very rapidly, at almost the speed of light, 186,282 mi/s (299,792 km/s). This produces an electrical current which powers all the appliances and other electrical equipment. Electrical current is measured by the amounts of electrons that pass a given point in a given period of time. Sometimes referred to as the intensity or rate of flow, the amount of current is measured in amperes (A). The pressure or potential of electricity that causes it to flow, is measured in volts (V). The resistance of the material, through which the current flows, to the flow is measured in ohms (Ω). These three variables were named for physicists who worked with electricity: André Marie Ampère (1775–1836) of France, Count Alessandro Volta (1745–1827) of Italy, and Georg Simon Ohm (1787–1854) of Germany.

Ohm discovered the basic relationship between the three characteristics of electricity and expressed it in what is now called Ohm's law: the current in amperes is equal to the potential in volts divided by the resistance in ohms. The power of electrical current is measured in watts (W) and is equal to volts times amperes. The watt was named for the Scottish mechanical engineer James Watt (1736–1819), who invented many machines utilizing power, particularly steam. Delivered electrical energy is measured in terms of power in a certain unit of time, such as watt-hours (W·h), or more commonly 1,000 watt-hours, or kilowatt-hours (kW·h). In the International System, the SI units are the joule (J) and 1 million (10^6) joules, called a megajoule (MJ). One kW·h equals 3.6 MJ.

Production Electricity may be obtained in several different ways. One is a battery which utilizes the action of chemicals on metals to produce electric current. Thermocouples, consisting of two dissimilar metals attached together, produce electricity when heated. Photoelectric cells, sometimes called electric eyes, produce electricity from rays of light. Solar cells produce electricity by use of the rays of the sun. All these devices have uses in architecture and are discussed elsewhere in this book. The major source of electric current for most of the applications in architecture is huge generators powered by steam, water-power, or other means. See the article entitled energy.

The electric energy produced by generators is transmitted from the places where it is produced to various areas of the country and finally to the sites of buildings. The electric currents produced are either direct current (dc), which flows at a fixed time rate in one direction in a circuit, or alternating current (ac), which has a varied time rate and flows alternately in two directions in a circuit. In ac, one time interval of flow in one direction plus one in the other is called a cycle. One cycle per second is called a hertz (Hz). Or-

dinarily, ac systems today operate at 60 Hz, or 60 cycles per second. The generators for ac are often referred to as alternators, and when dc is changed to ac, the device for this accomplishment is called a rectifier.

Ac and dc electricity are both used in architecture, the ac for most purposes and dc for such purposes as powering elevators, telephone equipment, certain controls and other devices, and for standby or emergency electrical systems. Although electricity usually is generated and transmitted at very high voltages, transformers are used to reduce the voltage for use in buildings, most of which are supplied with 120/208 V or 120/240 V systems. In such cases, the 120-V current is available for purposes such as lighting, and the 208 or 240 V for large motors, cooking ranges, water heaters, and other machinery.

Electric Service The electric current enters buildings through an electric service, which may be overhead, wires strung between poles, or underground, cables or wires, often in pipe or other containers. Because of the unsightly appearance of overhead systems, many architects and other environmental designers often specify underground systems. In some locations, underground systems are required by building or other codes. However, underground systems are much more expensive than overhead ones and much harder to maintain and repair. Ordinarily the utility companies furnish the service facilities up to the meter loops of buildings. However, in some building developments, underground services are constructed with a special system, called underground residential (UR) distribution, which uses direct burial high-voltage cables. Such systems require small transformers that may be installed indoors or outside. Often developers share the costs of such systems with the utility companies.

Where electric services enter buildings, meter loops with utility company meters are installed, usually one in a single-family house or other small building, but more than one in larger, more complex building types. The meters register the amount of electricity that passes through them into the buildings in kW·h. From these measurements, checked periodically by meter readers, the utilities bill for the electricity consumed. Electric utility rates, governed by various laws and regulations, are quite complex. The basic charge is a certain number of cents per kW·h, often with lower rates for commercial, industrial, and other large consumers, and sometimes sliding scale rates for quantities above certain levels. Many variations in these rates may occur, including those based on the relative costs of fuels used to generate the electricity; relative demands for power, such as the increased demand in summer because of air conditioning; and time of use, with higher rates during peak demands during days and lower rates during low-demand hours at night. The only method by which architects and other environmental designers may project the costs of electricity in their building designs is by calculation of amounts of electricity that will be required, or electrical loads, combined with a complete analysis of the various rates of the utilities that will supply the power.

Equipment From meters, electric current passes through various pieces of equipment, called switchboards or panelboards. Each is equipped with a service switch that disconnects all electric service into a building, except that required for emergencies. For small, relatively simple types of buildings, panelboards are ordinarily used. They are small boxes with the service switch and arrangements for the incoming service to be directed into various individual circuits of the building. While fuses have often been used in panelboards in the past, more prevalent today is the use of circuit breakers. These devices, unlike fuses which protect electrical circuits with metal parts that melt under high loads, are tripped by heat or magnetic forces. Since circuit breakers may be reset after tripping, they need no separate switches. Panelboards may be surface-mounted on walls or recessed into walls so that their faces are flush with the planes of the walls. In addition to the main panelboards at the electrical service entrance of buildings, auxiliary panelboards may be located within buildings for such purposes as the protection of groups of motors or other devices.

Switchboards are used for relatively large and complex buildings for purposes similar to those of panelboards. Usually freestanding and often quite large, switchboards contain fuses, switches, circuit breakers, and so on for the control and protection of large electrical systems with numerous circuits. A unit substation, sometimes called a transformer load center, is another relatively large assembly, installed indoors or outside, which not only contains equipment as in a switchboard but also meters, controls, transformers, and other electrical devices required in large and complicated buildings.

From panelboards, switchboards, or unit substations, electric power is directed into distribution systems that carry it to various parts of buildings and ultimately to appliances, lights, motors, and other devices. This is accomplished with electrical conductors, usually made of copper or aluminum. Large conductors (usually rectangular in section and insulated), called busways, are used for heavy power loads. For smaller loads, insulated wire or cable is used. The sizes of the busways and gauges of wire in cables for carrying loads of various amounts are specified in electrical, building, and other codes. Cables that are ordinarily used include a type armored with flexible steel covering, called BX; and NM or NMC cable sheathed with plastic or rubber coverings, called Romex. Neither may be embedded in concrete or similar materials. High-voltage cables are available, as are other special types. Codes also govern their uses.

Raceways Electric cables are often installed in buildings in raceways, devices for the containment and protection of electrical wiring. Raceways of many types and sizes can be obtained, including conduits, which may be rigid or flexible steel types; thin-wall (EMT) steel types, plain or coated with plastic; and aluminum, plastic, asbestos-cement, and fiber types. Larger raceways may be obtained in square or rectangular surface-mounted metal types and floor raceways. The latter include metal types that may be installed in floor structures, with their top surfaces flush with the finished floor surfaces. Also available are cellular metal and precast concrete types that serve not only as raceways but as the structural systems of floors in buildings. Raceways are also provided in integrated floors and ceilings, along with the structure; lighting, heating, and air-conditioning distribution systems; and telephone systems. The other types of raceways may also be used for telephone and other communication and sound installations.

Other Devices In addition to the cables, busways, and raceways required in electrical systems in buildings, a great variety of fittings and other devices are used. There are various kinds of connectors, including types that are clamped, screwed, bolted, or otherwise affixed to connect electrical conductors. Soldering is still used for large cables, and welding is used sometimes. Various types of conduit and raceway connectors are used, including outlet and junction boxes. Many electrical appliances and devices, such as light fixtures, are wired directly but for many others, receptacles of various types are used. The most common is the duplex, which accommodates two caps, or plugs, from the usual types of movable fixtures, such as table or floor lamps. A duplex outlet has two parallel slots for each plug, along with a third hole for the ground. A triplex outlet takes three appliance plugs. Special outlets of various kinds include locking types, waterproof types with covers, safety types, and clock outlets.

In addition, various types of switches and other devices are used. Switches have ampere ratings and sometimes also horsepower ratings. The proper types must be used for given purposes. Many switches close or open circuits by simple metallic contacts. Others use electromagnets, the small ones called relays, to operate the switches; throwing the handle activates the relay by means of low-voltage current, and the relay opens or closes the switch. Such switches may be used in low-voltage wiring systems, which are much more flexible than regular types. For example, with such a system, one light fixture may be turned off and on from a number of locations by means of small-gauge wiring carrying low-voltage, usually 12 or 24 V dc, current to activate the single relay required. If more than two such switches were required for a fixture in the usual system, the wiring would not only carry the regular voltage current but would be extraordinarily complex. To finish outlets and switches, wall plates are generally used. A single-gang plate is used for a single outlet or switch; a double-gang plate, for one with two switches or outlets; and so on. Plates come in metals or plastics and various finishes.

Design Requisites The design of electrical power and wiring systems for buildings can be quite complex. The main principles are to provide complete systems that will be adequate for the needs of building occupants, designed for expansion for future needs and with flexibility for changing needs. Systems must be safe and reliable, yet economically feasible. They must provide for the necessary uses in buildings, such as lighting; heating and air conditioning; vertical transportation; kitchen equipment; communication; plumbing equipment; sound and warning systems; fire, security, and other hazards; motors; and other uses of electricity, some quite special in certain building types. In addition, special provisions must be made in many building types, such as hospitals, and for certain building functions, such as elevators, emergency lighting, and so on, and also in many other types, for standby or emergency power systems. Emergency equipment often consists of standby generators or battery systems.

The various steps in the design of electric power and wiring systems vary somewhat for buildings of different types, complexities, and sizes. However, general steps include determination of an estimate of the expected electrical power loads for lighting, equipment, and so on; power requirements in various locations in the building; requirements of the utility for service and related factors; and determination of the required electrical equipment, including switchboards, panelboards, and other items and their locations in the building. Based on such data, the design of the electrical system may proceed, including lighting circuit layouts; circuits required for other purposes; special layouts for communications, sound, warning, and other systems; electrical appliances and equipment, together with raceways, conduits, fittings, and other devices required.

In addition to spaces for panelboards or switchboards, unit substations, and transformers, space must be provided for special equipment and controls in what are called electric closets, located in convenient positions in the building. All must be protected with proper circuit breakers or other devices. The major circuits up to circuit breakers or other protective devices are called feeder circuits. From that point on, circuits are called branch circuits. Spare circuits must be provided for future uses. And the entire electrical system must be properly grounded. In addition, some systems are so complex that computers are used to control them.

Because of the great importance of electricity in the buildings of today and the relatively high expense of systems installations and operation, which consume a large portion of every building construction and operation dollar, the need for conservation of energy and other reasons, the proper design of electrical systems is all-important. Their design is usually performed by electrical engineers, some of whom specialize in building design rather than in more esoteric fields of electronics. Working closely with architects, engineers, and other environmental designers, electrical engineers can provide efficient, functional, safe systems in the buildings of today.

History The time that humans first learned about electricity has not been established. It is known that the Greek philosopher and scientist Thales (c. 640–546 B.C.) discovered that rubbing a piece of amber with a cloth produced static electricity. Not much progress was made with electricity for more than 2,000 years, until about the 16th century, when the English physician and physicist William Gilbert (1540–1603) experimented with static electricity and magnetism. Many scientists experimented with electricity and made important discoveries after.

The discovery in 1831 of the principle of generation of electricity with magnets and coils of wire was made independently by an English scientist, Michael Faraday (1791–1867), and an American scientist, Joseph Henry (1797–1898). This was the fundamental discovery that eventually led to the widespread use of electricity today. Generators were developed soon afterward and by 1882, a generating station was supplying power to private consumers in London. In the same year, the first generating plant in the United States was built in New York City by American inventor Thomas Alva Edison (1847–1931), who had invented in 1879 a practical incandescent light bulb. For some years previously, electric arc lights had been in use in limited installations, such as in lighthouses and for street lighting.

The early generating plants all produced direct current. In 1886 American inventor and industrialist George Westinghouse (1846–1914) built the first alternating current generating plant. Since that time, thousands of generating plants have been built in the United States, and electricity has become the most important type of energy used in architecture for such purposes as lighting and others. Today some 2,000 generating plants are operating in the United States, utilizing mostly steam, gas, or water turbines, called hydroelectric, sources for electrical production. Since the first atomic plant was established in 1951, others have been built in many places in the United States, but they produce only a small portion of the total output.

Most of the electricity produced in the United States comes from privately owned plants, but the federal government owns and operates a large system, including the Grand Coulee plant in the state of Washington and the sprawling system of the Tennessee Valley Authority (TVA), which was built beginning in the 1930s along the Tennessee River and tributaries in portions of Tennessee, Alabama, Georgia, Kentucky, and Virginia.

Over the years, many developments in the use of electricity in architecture have taken place. Electric lighting got off to a slow start in the late 19th century and little progress was made until the 20th, when a spectacular increase in electric lighting and in the use of electricity for other purposes took place. Today electric lighting is utilized all over the United States, with very few exceptions in extremely remote locations. Great improvements have been made in light bulbs and in lighting fixtures, and newer types such as fluorescent, sodium-vapor, and mercury-vapor lights have been developed.

Electric appliances are widely used in architecture today. Electric elevators are commonly used in buildings of more than a few stories and escalators are used in others. Electric heating has become important and electricity is the main type of energy used for air conditioning. New appliances and other applications of electricity are developed each year and the end seems nowhere in sight, unless curtailed by the shortage of energy being experienced in the latter part of the 20th century.

Related Articles COMMUNICATION SYSTEM; COMPUTER; ELECTRICAL ENGINEERING; ENERGY; FIRE PROTECTION; SECURITY SYSTEMS; VERTICAL TRANSPORTATION.

Sources of Additional Information Institute of Electrical and Electronic Engineers (IEEE), 345 E. 47th St., New York, N.Y. 10017; National Fire Protection Assoc. (NFPA), 80 Batterymarch St., Boston, Mass. 02110.

ENERGY The capacity to perform work. Energy is also closely related to force and power. A force is the action of one body on another, such as in pushing or pulling, which causes the second to move or tend to move. Work is accomplished by the application of a force that causes an object to move a certain distance. Power is the rate of doing work, involving the force applied to a body, the distance it is moved by the force, and the time required for the movement.

Energy is contained in oil, natural gas, coal, and other substances. Electricity is a form of energy derived from such sources and others. Energy has always been important in architecture for heating, lighting, cooling, and many other purposes. Recently, energy has assumed even greater importance because of increasing problems with shortages caused by accelerating depletion of supplies of energy sources, such as oil and natural gas, rising prices, embargoes by foreign countries, and other factors. As the problems have spread and become more acute, their effects on architecture have intensified.

Sources For many years, sources of energy for uses in architecture were, in turn, water, coal, petroleum products, and nuclear reactions. Sources of such forms of energy seemed almost inexhaustible and when problems rose with one form, people simply turned to another. Recently, it has been amply demonstrated that the supplies of energy sources are actually quite limited and that extreme measures must be adopted to ensure that energy will be available in the future. The realization of the energy problems, some of which have developed into crises, has caused a great number of proposals to be made and actions to be taken to alleviate the situation. Many of the proposals and actions affect architecture.

It is believed that about half of the energy consumed in the United States goes into buildings, about 15 percent to construct them and about 35 percent in their operation. Thus architects and other professionals who design buildings are in a position to make great contributions to the conservation and efficient use of energy.

The two major ways by which energy problems in buildings may be met involve improved design for energy efficiency and use of new methods, systems, and sources or rediscovery and modernization of older ones. For a discussion on architectural and engineering methods, including proper orientation of buildings, architectural devices and materials, and mechanical and electrical systems that may be used for increasing energy efficiency in buildings, see articles entitled climate; heating, ventilating, and air conditioning.

Alternative Sources Alternative forms of energy mostly involve natural sources that have always been available, some that were once used but are now virtually ignored, others that have been used only sporadically or on a small scale, and still others that have not been used at all. Such sources include water, air, the earth itself, the remains of living things on earth, and the sun. While all these sources exist in great abundance, the use of many of them has been considered economically unfeasible. However, research and development may well lead to discoveries that might cause some of them to become increasingly usable and affordable.

Waterpower Waterpower was the first source of energy used by human beings other than that of humans and animals. Today the major use of waterpower is in the generation of electricity by the flow of backed-up rivers over and through dams. In France, th energy contained in water waves that flow in and out with tides powers an electric generating plant. Other projects of this sort are under development. Of course, both of these systems are but adaptations and improvements of ancient systems used for other purposes, such as grinding grain. Some people believe that such uses of energy from the flow of water may again help solve part of the energy problem. Another source of energy, in the research stage for almost 100 years, involves extraction of thermal energy from the sea. And some work has been done on extraction of heat from ponds that have been heated by the sun.

Air Another early source of energy was the air, the first applications having been windmills of various sorts and sails for ships. Windmills were used for many purposes, including grinding grains, powering woodworking and other machinery, pumping water, and so on. Today the use of windmills is mostly in an experimental stage, concerned with the generation of electricity instead of direct work applications.

Another source of energy from the air is called an air-to-air heat pump. This is a device that works like a window air conditioner in reverse, extracting heat from the outside air and releasing it into the interiors of buildings. So far such heat pumps have been small, inefficient, and adaptable only to relatively warm climates. A heat pump of this type may also be reversed to perform as an air conditioner. Future development may produce more efficient types. A more efficient heat pump is the water-to-air type which extracts heat from well water or other sources, stores it, and releases it into buildings. The cycle can be reversed, air-to-water, to air-condition buildings by removing heat from their interiors. Heat pumps of this type have been considerably improved in recent years.

Geothermal Energy The earth itself is a source of huge quantities of energy, called geothermal, in the form of heat contained in molten rock, or magma, and in other heated rock. So far, the only way to obtain use of this energy has been by natural escape or tapping water heated by the rocks and released in either liquid or steam form. It is well known that ancient civilizations, in particular the Roman, used such sources for heating buildings and public baths and for other purposes. For many years after the era of the Romans, the major use was in hot baths used for therapeutic purposes.

Sources of geothermal energy, of course, exist under the surface of the entire earth. Sources that are relatively easy to tap exist in many parts of the world, including very large areas of the Western and Gulf states of the United States. Very few of these sources have been utilized so far, including some in Mexico, Iceland, Italy, Turkey, Japan, the Philippines, and New Zealand. Most are used for generation of electricity, but some also furnish heat for buildings and for cooking. The United States, with one of the best geothermal potentials, has only one generating plant, at the Geysers, Calif., where the steam from the earth drives turbines. Geothermal energy is one of the most prevalent forms available, producing not only heat but sulfur fumes and other substances that can create wastelands.

Biofuels The remains of animals and vegetation that once lived upon the earth, often called biofuels, can be used as sources of energy. Oil and coal are examples of such fuels; these come from fossils and are not renewable. Other biofuels are generally renewable and include organic wastes; peat, a form of decomposed vegetation; algae from the oceans; gasoline made from organic materials; and methane gas, which is similar to natural gas but made from organic materials by a chemical process. Such sources of energy hold promise for the future. Of course, the most important of all is wood, used as a source of energy for many centuries, its use partly abandoned later, but now coming back into its own.

To some people, wood seems almost the perfect fuel. It is plentiful, grown without too much difficulty, easily renewable in relatively short periods of time, and quite efficient. Disadvantages are relatively high costs when compared to some other fuels, such as coal, but not when compared to oil and natural gas, the prices of which have risen very rapidly in recent years. Other vegetation can also furnish energy, including sugarcane, which is said to produce almost 6

times more burnable material per acre than pine trees. Most of the plentiful biological sources may be used to produce alcohol, already in use in some countries, and to some extent in the United States, as a fuel for automobiles and other vehicles. Alcohol may be used alone for such purposes or in a mixture with gasoline, sometimes call gasohol.

Solar Energy Many people believe that solar energy holds the most promise for alleviation of energy problems. The energy from the sun seems inexhaustible, readily available everywhere most of the time, clean, and safe. Three forms of energy are available from the sun: thermal; photovoltaic, which produces electricity; and photochemical, which produces chemical changes. Only thermal energy is of importance at the present time, the others being quite complex and difficult to use.

Solar energy is used in architecture in several different ways today. First, there is the simple and relatively inexpensive admission of the sun into buildings, when desired, to warm the interiors. This requires proper orientation of buildings, devices such as sunshades to control the sun, and appropriate architectural measures, such as proper insulation and glazing, to admit and retain the heat. Next, in terms of costs and complexity, are solar collectors that receive heat from the sun and store it, usually in water, which may then be used for bathing, dishwashing, and similar purposes and for heating buildings. More complex and higher costing systems have relatively complicated mechanical and electrical equipment which collect, store, and circulate heated water in cold weather or convert the heat into absorption cooling in hot weather. In many cases, the energy received from the sun must be supplemented by energy from fuel oil or another source to provide an adequate amount of heating and cooling. In other cases, standby equipment using energy sources other than solar must be provided for use in winter and for extended cloudy periods.

A number of buildings have been constructed in recent years with solar energy systems of various types. The more complete ones have been quite expensive to install. And it usually takes many years for their higher total costs of installation to be repaid by lower operating costs. Beginning in the second half of the 20th century, the number of buildings constructed with solar systems, at least partial systems, has been increasing. A considerable amount of research and development work has been going on and continues to the present time. One of the most interesting projects involves work on solar batteries, called solar cells, which convert sunlight directly into electricity. So far, solar cells have been inefficient and very costly; therefore their use has been limited. Other work is going on in the field of photochemistry and other advanced fields.

Many people think that all of the research and development work will lead to efficient, relatively low-cost systems that will eventually supplant conventional systems in many buildings. A few think that the research will also lead to communities in which hot water and electricity derived from solar energy will supply all the needs. Be that as it may, the use of solar energy seems to have become a permanent part of architecture, in limited applications that may be expected to expand in the future. For a discussion on present-day uses of solar energy, see the article entitled heating, ventilating, and air conditioning.

History In prehistoric times, the prime source of energy which was converted into power to perform work was furnished by human beings. At first, these were individuals and groups who contributed their energy for the accomplishment of certain purposes. Later slaves were used in a similar manner to accomplish the purposes of their masters. With the advent of the domestication of animals in the Neolithic period, they became another source of energy. The only other major energy source was wood, used for heating and cooking.

Although the time of its first use has not been determined, the next form of power utilized flowing water to operate rudimentary water mills. These mills probably originated in the Middle East and were later used by the ancient Greeks. The Romans improved the design of water mills, making them faster and more efficient, and later improvements were made in other parts of Europe. Water mills of various types have been used almost continuously ever since.

It is thought that the first real windmills to be used as sources of energy were developed in the Middle East about the 7th century. Again, as in the case of water mills, windmills were further developed and improved and have been used almost continuously until the present time.

There is little evidence that coal was used before the birth of Christ, even though it was found in many places. Some coal may have been used in Europe about the 4th century but no evidence exists of its use in Europe after that until about the 12th century, when it became a major source of energy. Coal had been used in China for a long time previously. Great coal deposits were found in France and England and these were exploited over the years. Some of the greatest deposits were found in the United States, about one-third of the world supply, and these too have been exploited, but at a slower rate than in some other countries.

Coal, water, and wind were the chief sources of energy in the 18th century. In 1698 the first practical steam engine was invented by an Englishman, Thomas Savery (1650–1715). In time, it revolutionized the use of coal as an energy source. The first primitive steam engine had been invented by a Greek scientist, Hero, in Alexandria, Egypt, about the third century A.D., or earlier. Hero's invention led nowhere and Savery's was not very efficient. Improvements were made by another Englishman, the inventor Thomas Newcomen (1663–1729), and by a Scottish engineer, James Watt (1736–1819). Steam engines came into wide usage in

the 19th century and many improvements were made later. Steam engines powered the great railroad trains of the 1800s and early 1900s, but were later replaced by diesel engines. Steam was also used to power many other types of machinery and still does so today, particularly steamships. With the invention of the steam turbine, which utilizes steam to run wheels with blades, the stage had been set for large-scale generation of electric power.

The advent of internal combustion engines again revolutionized the use of power and the energy that supplied it. Internal combustion engines had been developed even earlier than the first practical steam engines. The first is thought to be a rudimentary model invented by a Dutch scientist, Christian Huygens (1629–95). Others followed, but none were capable of continuous operation until 1859, when a Frenchman, Étienne Lenoir (1822–1900), developed a type that utilized an explosive mixture of gas and air. Many other types have since been developed, including those that use oil or gasoline. Such engines have been tremendously improved up to the present time. Two of the most important developments were the diesel engine, named after its inventor, a German engineer, Rudolf Diesel (1858–1913), and the high-speed gasoline engine in the late 1800s by the German Gottlieb Daimler (1834–1900).

Petroleum was known to early humans. It seeped from the ground and later was taken from dug wells to be used for such purposes as paving streets. It is thought that the Chinese used natural gas for fuel as far back as the 10th century B.C. The modern oil industry probably started in Romania in the 19th century, but its real beginning is usually taken to have been with the drilling of the first oil well in the United States in 1857, near Titusville, Pa., by Edwin L. Drake (1821–84). Kerosene, distilled from petroleum or coal, had been in use since 1852. Gasoline occurs naturally, along with oil and natural gas, but in the early days was considered dangerous and a nuisance since it was explosive, unlike oil or kerosene. Gasoline today is produced from natural gas and oil. It can also be extracted from coal, but the process is very expensive. However, some experts think this will be feasible later in the 20th century.

Other products made from petroleum include asphalt, lubricants, fuel oil, jet airplane fuels, chemicals (called petrochemicals), and liquefied petroleum (LP) gas. Today petroleum is an all-important source of energy.

Electricity had been known to humans for many centuries before the birth of Christ. However, for many centuries, it remained a curiosity and a subject for study and invention by a long line of famous scientists. Then an English scientist, Michael Faraday (1791–1867), and an American scientist, Joseph Henry (1797–1878), independently discovered, in 1831, the primary principle of the generation of electricity. This involved the movement of a wire near a magnet that induced an electrical current in the wire. Soon afterward, primitive generators were produced commercially in London. During the 19th century, many improvements were made in generators.

In 1882 the first power-generation station to supply private consumers began operating in London. Others soon followed in that city and elsewhere, including the United States. Many early generators were powered by steam turbines that derived their power from the energy contained in coal. Today more than two-thirds of the power generated in the world and about four-fifths of that in the United States comes from steam turbine generators. Most of the remainder comes from water turbines, or hydroelectric plants, about a third in the world and a sixth in the United States. Other important electric generating systems include gas turbines, atomic energy plants, and diesel engines. Gasoline engines are often used to power small generators. Electricity has become one of the all-important forms of energy used today. It is not a source of power itself but energy produced by other power sources.

Atomic energy was first used for purposes of war. After the first experimental atomic bomb was exploded on July 16, 1945, in the desert near Alamogordo, N.Mex., nothing would ever be the same again in the world. On August 6, 1945, an atomic bomb was dropped on Hiroshima, Japan, and three days later another on Nagasaki. Both cities were destroyed, with 92,000 people dead or missing in Hiroshima and about 40,000 in Nagasaki. Bombs of even greater power have since been developed, including H-bombs, utilizing hydrogen fission instead of the fusion process of the original A-bombs. Atomic energy was later used to power naval vessels and for other military weapons.

Atomic energy was first turned to peaceful uses in 1955, for the generation of electricity in Arco, Idaho. This was followed by the first full-scale nuclear-power generating station in Calder, England, in 1956, and the first in the United States in 1957 in Shippingsport, Pa. Other peaceful uses began, including the powering of merchant ships, the first being the *Savannah*, launched in 1959. By the beginning of the fourth quarter of the 20th century, more than 60 nuclear plants were producing electricity in the United States. They produce more than 8 percent of the total amount of electricity generated and are thought to conserve many billions of barrels of oil or millions of tons of coal. At that time, more than 15 additional nuclear generators were under construction. The construction of nuclear power plants has slowed somewhat in recent years, partly because of public opposition to them based on the dangers of accidents that would release radiation. In addition, the cost of construction of such plants is very high, as is the cost of uranium, and these costs have risen radically in recent years. One proposal has been the construction of nuclear plants that might be less expensive to build and that would consume less energy to produce a given amount of electricity. One of the methods may use a thermonuclear, or fusion, reactor which in-

volves combining atoms rather than splitting them. Another may be the breeder nuclear reactor which produces more energy than it consumes.

Energy Shortages For a very long time, Americans and people in other nations conducted themselves as if fuels for the production of energy were inexhaustible. Architects were no different. In fact, one of the commonly held beliefs about contemporary architecture has been that its designers really did not have to worry too much about the natural climate in which their buildings existed or with natural aids to climate control. All that was necessary to provide comfort within buildings was to utilize the great technology available for heating, lighting, air conditioning, and so on. Good engineers, with the proper techniques and equipment, could provide any artificial climate desired. And that is what they did, giving due regard to the costs of installation and operation, of course, but no consideration to the effect on world fuel supplies.

To be sure, there were a few people who saw what was coming, but not many listened to them. Then from the 1960s, one energy crisis has followed another. Perhaps the beginning may be said to have been the massive power failure that blacked out an area in the Northeast of some 80,000 mi², including New York City, on November 9, 1965. Some 30 million went without electric power for light, heating, or any other purpose that night. Until the blackout, few realized how dependent people are on energy and the devastating effects its loss can have on them.

Nothing much came of it, though, except that the electric utility companies attempted to rectify the problems that had caused the blackout. Very little or nothing was said about the possibility of energy shortages, but in the late 1960s proposals were made for what were called total-energy, or all-fuel, buildings in which electricity from utilities would be replaced by electricity generated at the building site through use of other fuels. Such a course might have prevented a blackout in specific buildings, but the cost in depletion of other fuels, such as oil and natural gas, would have been very high. The electric utilities countered the threat by promoting all-electric buildings, ones in which all of the energy needs would be supplied by the utilities. It seems hard to believe now, but that was the existing situation in the late 1960s and early 1970s.

In 1970 electric power shortages began to develop, particularly in the Northeastern states, prompting pleas to families and industries to curtail power use, particularly at peak-load times. Some selective temporary interruptions of service were also employed. Some shortages of fuel oil and other energy also developed, mainly because of troubles in the Middle East. In 1971 shortages, particularly in natural gas, continued but there really was no crisis. However, at the World Energy Conference in Bucharest, Romania, experts foresaw crises, but thought recent oil and natural gas discoveries, particularly in Alaska and the Arctic, could meet the demand for several decades to come. During 1972 costs of fuels and electricity rose and shortage of natural gas continued. Some had begun to call the situation a crisis.

During the summer of 1973, many gasoline service stations closed because they could not obtain adequate supplies. When gasoline was available, service stations limited the amount sold to each customer. Then on October 6 the fourth Arab-Israeli war in 26 years broke out. Later in the month, the Arab oil-producing countries, which control almost 70 percent of the world's oil production, totally banned oil exports to the United States and other countries. In November, President Richard Nixon (1913–   ) announced that heating oil would be allocated, that a national speed limit of 55 miles per hour for automobiles was to be imposed to save gasoline, and that the nation would return to daylight saving time in January 1974 to save heating fuels. The year 1973 also saw the first of a series of laws requiring manufacturers to produce automobiles that would consume less gasoline. In December 1973, the Arab countries doubled their price for oil, but continued the ban on sales to the United States, the Netherlands, and Denmark. The embargo was lifted in March 1974.

During 1974 shortages of fuels continued and prices continued to rise, even after the lifting of the Arab embargo. In spite of all the troubles, or because of them, U.S. oil companies reported huge profits during the last quarter of 1973, in many cases showing increases of over 50 percent more than in the same period of the preceding year, and in some cases up to 70 percent increases. Late in 1974, President Gerald R. Ford (1913–   ) established an Energy Resources Council to work out national energy policies and converted the Atomic Energy Commission into the Energy Research and Development Administration (ERDA) and the Nuclear Regulatory Commission, to deal with total energy problems.

ERDA announced plans for dealing with fuel shortages, including recovering oil from abandoned wells and shale, production of synthetic oil and gas from coal, increased coal production, further development of atomic energy, and development of solar and other energy sources. Prices for energy sources of all kinds continued to rise during 1975, but in September price controls were placed on domestic oil and in December the U.S. Energy and Policy and Conservation Act took effect, rolling back the price of crude oil. In spite of everything, prices rose during the year and shortages continued during 1976. In December of that year came another blow: the Arab oil-producing countries again raised oil prices.

Severe Weather Problems Then disaster struck. The fall of 1976 was colder than normal and followed a summer of widespread drought in the United States. Early snows, beginning in October, set records, presaging a very cold winter that brought snow to Miami for the first time in recorded history; unusually severe blizzards; record snowfalls in many places; frozen lakes, rivers, and bays into the Deep South; and record low temperatures to much of the nation. Oddly enough, the winter that devastated much of the United States produced record warm weather in Alaska, bringing bears out of hibernation.

The winter of 1976–77 brought a realization of the energy crisis unequaled by anything that had happened before. It is conservatively estimated that some 200,000 people were put out of work by natural gas shortages alone. Other fuels ran out in many localities. People were forced to endure temperatures that often dropped well below zero, without adequate fuel to heat their homes, or in some cases no fuel at all. For those lucky enough to have fuel, prices continued to rise and huge amounts of fuel were consumed.

It has been estimated that the winter cost more than $5 billion in extra fuel bills. The costs in lost crops, joblessness, damage, and other effects of the weather, though astronomical, have never been accurately estimated. In terms of economic growth alone, the U.S. Department of Commerce estimated a loss of some $3 billion. The winter of 1977–78 was equally as bad, with great blizzards and subnormal temperatures that lasted much longer than usual, well into spring. To make matters worse, some experts believe that the long-term trend in the world is toward colder weather in the future. Other experts believe there is a warming trend, but the winter of 1978–79 was again very cold and fuel shortages were again experienced. And the winter of 1979–80 began in many parts of the United States, with the earliest cold weather and snows (in October) in the history of U.S. weather records. Fortunately, the weather later moderated in many parts of the country.

Remedial Actions Some progress has been made in the alleviation of the energy crisis, and progress can be expected to continue and to accelerate. Oil from Alaska is flowing through the pipeline, after various setbacks, as is that from the North Sea. Developments are going ahead in the use of nuclear and solar energy as well as from other sources. Importantly, architects and others involved in the design and construction of buildings now take the situation more seriously and are taking steps to improve the efficiency of the use of energy in their buildings and to provide alternate sources. All such measures will help. In 1977, a new cabinet-level department was established, the Department of Energy (DOE).

If necessary, the federal government may take quite drastic measures to ensure fuel conservation. Some experts believe that the energy crisis in the United States is not really one of shortages, but of the policies and practices that affect the use of energy sources. For example, estimates of U.S. reserves in crude oil range from about 100 to 160 billion bbl, of natural gas from about 500 to 900 trillion ft^3, and coal up to more than 200 billion tons. This information does not suggest that energy from these sources should not be conserved, but it does represent informed projections that enough fuel exists to fulfill

U.S. needs for several centuries. Other experts place the blame for the current fuel shortages and those expected in the future squarely on the seeming inability of U.S. presidents and Congress to develop rational energy policies and enact them into law.

As if to demonstrate how desperate the situation is and the seeming inability of the government to deal with it, severe gasoline shortages occurred in 1979, accompanied by steadily rising prices. During 1979, the cost of fuel oil for heating also rose dramatically, about 60%. In less than ten years, its price had gone up more than 400%.

By early 1980, the nation, and the world, had been suffering from energy crises for more than 10 years. Middle East conditions had resulted in decreasing supplies from that area. Prices of fuels had rapidly spiraled upward, while profits of oil companies had soared, unchecked by governmental, or any other, action. Only a few relatively ineffective actions had been taken, such as standby gasoline rationing, not put into effect, and regulations holding temperatures to 78° F in summer and 65° F in winter in certain types of buildings. During the decade of the 1970s, three U.S. presidents and the U.S. Congress had accomplished little to solve the ever-worsening energy crisis.

Related Articles CLIMATE; DESIGN, ARCHITECTURAL; ELECTRICAL ENGINEERING; ELECTRIC POWER AND WIRING; ENVIRONMENTAL PROTECTION; HEATING, VENTILATING, AND AIR CONDITIONING; INSULATION, THERMAL; LIGHTING; MECHANICAL ENGINEERING; PLUMBING.

Further Reading Beckman, William A., Sanford A. Klein, and John A. Duffie: *Solar Heating Design by the f-Chart Method*, John Wiley, New York, 1977; Considine, Douglas M., ed.: *Energy Technology Handbook*, McGraw-Hill, New York, 1977; Griffin, Charles W.: *Energy Conservation in Buildings—Techniques for Economical Design*, Construction Specifications Institute, Washington, 1974; Halacy, Daniel S., Jr.: *Earth, Water, Wind and Sun—Our Energy Alternatives*, Harper and Row, New York, 1977; Stein, Richard G.: *Architecture and Energy*, Doubleday, Garden City, N.Y., 1977; Szokolay, S. V. *Solar Energy and Building,* John Wiley, New York, 1975.

Sources of Additional Information Association of Energy Engineers, 464 Armour Circle, Atlanta, Ga. 30324; Department of Energy, Forrestal Building, Washington, D.C. 20314; International Solar Energy Society, Inc., 300 State Road 401, Cape Canaveral, Fla. 32920.

ENGINEERING

ENGINEERING The profession that deals with the science involved in the design, construction, and operation of buildings and other structures, machines, systems, and devices used by humans. An engineer is an individual who is licensed or registered to practice the profession of engineering. Since others, such as boiler operators and locomotive drivers, are sometimes called engineers, those licensed or registered to practice professional engineering are usually called professional engineers.

Branches Today the major branches of engineering are civil, chemical, electrical, mechanical, mining, and metallurgical. Civil engineering is concerned with the design, planning, and construction of structures, including buildings, dams, docks, railroads, tunnels, highways, canals, bridges, and water and sewage systems. Civil engineering therefore has a number of specialty fields, including structural, highway, transportation, sanitary, hydraulic, and city planning. Chemical engineering is concerned with the design, construction, and operation of industrial plants in which raw materials are changed into other products by chemical processes. Electrical engineering is concerned with the design, construction, and operation of structures, devices, and systems for the production, transmission, distribution, control, and uses of electricity. Specialty fields within electrical engineering include electronics and illuminating engineering. Mechanical engineering is concerned with the design, construction, and operation of engines and other machines and mechanical systems. Specialties include aeronautical or aerospace, automotive, and heating and air conditioning. Mining and metallurgical engineering are concerned with the discovery, removal from the ground, and processing of minerals. Petroleum engineering is a special branch that deals with oil and natural gas. Other types of engineering include agricultural, nuclear, and textile.

Many of the engineering specialists participate, to some extent, in the design and construction of buildings, including civil engineers who specialize in soils and foundations or in sanitary engineering, the specialty that deals with water and sewage systems. However, the major types of engineering involved in the design and construction of buildings are structural, a branch of civil, electrical, and mechanical engineering. Sometimes these specialties, taken together, are called architectural engineering when applied to building design. Structural engineers design the structures of buildings. Electrical engineers design the electrical, and often the lighting, systems. Mechanical engineers design the heating, ventilating, and air conditioning; plumbing; and other mechanical systems.

Engineers may work in special fields, such as research, development of devices or products based on research, testing, construction of buildings and other structures, sales or service functions, teaching, production functions, or in the operation of machinery, factories, or specialized devices.

Firms The most important function in architecture is the engineering design and planning of buildings and other structures. Design or planning engineers often have their own firms and perform engineering services for buildings for several architects. In such cases, they are often referred to as consulting engineers. Some engineers work for consulting firms. In other cases, engineers are employees of architectural firms and perform services only for those firms. Engineers may also be partners of stockholders in architectural firms. In these cases, the firms may be called simply architects, but are often called architects and engineers, referred to as A-E firms. Sometimes, if engineering comprises a relatively large part of a firm's work as compared to its architecture, the firm is called an E-A firm, or engineers and architects.

In all cases, the engineers work closely with the architects in the design of buildings, each specialist group designing the parts of the building and the systems for which it is primarily responsible and each coordinating this specialized work with that of the architects and other engineers to produce the proper results in the totality of the building.

Engineering offers a great diversity in the kinds of work performed. Some engineers work indoors primarily, others outdoors, or in some combination. Some engineers perform research and studies in a quiet, introspective manner; others spend their time in more active pursuits, such as inspection of the construction of high-rise buildings. Some work in cities, others in rural areas, still others in foreign countries around the globe. Accordingly, the opportunities for careers in engineering are numerous and diverse. For people who are naturally curious, imaginative, industrious, and responsible, engineering careers offer a great deal of satisfaction.

Education   To prepare for careers in engineering, young students should demonstrate aptitudes and interest in mathematics and the sciences. In addition to the usual college-preparatory secondary school courses, students should prepare for engineering school with four years of mathematics and science if possible. In college, engineering students ordinarily take courses in humanities, social sciences, mathematics, sciences, and basic engineering. These are followed by courses concentrated in the areas of choice, such as mechanical, supplemented by fundamental courses in the major fields. Upon successful completion of four or five years, students are awarded bachelor's degrees. Some students earn master's degrees, usually requiring an additional year or more, and a few earn doctor's degrees, requiring two or more years past the master's level.

People interested in an engineering career have a wide choice of educational institutions. There are more than 150 accredited engineering schools offering bachelor's degrees in the United States. In addition, there are many colleges and institutions that offer the first two years of education in preengineering courses. The schools of engineering are located in universities all over the country and preengineering courses are offered in many junior, community, and other types of colleges in many localities.

For people who would like to do engineering work, without becoming professional engineers, there are many technical schools and institutions that offer courses for engineering technicians. Engineering technicians assist professional engineers in their work, often performing such functions as drafting, specification writing, field supervision, and so on.

Registration   In order to call themselves professional engineers and to practice professional engineering, graduates must be licensed or registered, thus establishing their competence to perform engineering that will safeguard the health, safety, and welfare of the public. To accomplish this, they must meet the requirements of the registration or licensing board of one of the states or territories. Upon successful completion of the requirements, they are granted licenses or registrations allowing them to call themselves professional engineers (P.E.'s) and to practice engineering. The general requirements of all the states and territories are good character, U.S. citizenship or a declaration to become a citizen, a minimum age (usually twenty-five), and a high school diploma.

In addition, candidates for registration or licensing as professional engineers must have had a minimum combination of engineering education and experience acceptable to the board. The usual combination is graduation from an accredited engineering school and four years of experience that is acceptable toward the development of professional judgment, capacity, and competence to practice. Various other combinations of education and experience may be accepted by boards, such as eight years of experience with no college. Laws vary between the states and territories. For example, some allow older, experienced candidates to become registered or licensed without written examinations.

The practice of an engineer is often not confined to one state. In general, the states and territories allow engineers registered in other states to practice in their jurisdictions temporarily, for periods of 30 days or more. An engineer may also obtain reciprocal registration or licensing in other states by endorsement, a process that waives another examination, but may require an interview or other action. The National Bureau of Engineering Registration issues Certificates of Qualification to engineers, attesting to their prior registration or licensing and other qualifications. These are usually accepted for reciprocal registration or licensing by states and territories.

The written examinations required for registration or licensing of professional engineers are generally divided into two parts, the first on fundamentals and engineering sciences, lasting eight hours or more; and the second on professional engineering subjects in the candidate's specialty and related specialties. The first-day examination covers such subjects as mathematics, sciences, economics, professional ethics, and contract law. The second-day examination covers all the specific areas of specialty, such as civil engineering for civil candidates, and certain areas of related specialties, such as mechanical and electrical engineering. The examination for mechanical engineers includes, in addition to mechanical subjects, certain areas of civil, electrical, and metallurgical engineering. The electrical examination, in addition to electrical subjects, includes civil and mechanical engineering.

The two parts of the written examination may be taken at different times. The first fundamental part may be taken immediately after graduation, under a program called Engineers in Training, when most people are best prepared for the examination, or it may be taken later. The second part must be taken after completion of the required years of practical experience.

History The history of engineering goes back to prehistoric times when humans first made tools, tents, and other devices. For many centuries, engineering was performed by people who were not specialists in the field. Architecture and engineering were parts of the work of the person who the Mesopotamians called *batu,* the builder, and the Egyptians called the master builder. Many of the great works of these earlier cultures, often referred to as architecture, such as the pyramids, aqueducts, and other structures, were as much engineering as architecture, or more. In ancient Greece the master builder became known as the *architekton,* arch technician or builder. In Rome the master builder was called an *architectus,* an architect who was also an engineer. In ancient Greece, engineering feats were accomplished in such fields as tunnels, water supply systems, harbors, city planning, mining, and buildings, even though they were not called engineering at that time. The Romans were great engineers, excelling in the design and construction of roads, bridges, aqueducts, mines, harbors, buildings, and other structures.

Many ancient Greeks and Romans made inventions and otherwise contributed to what later became engineering, but they were scientists or philosophers and cannot be called engineers. About the third century A.D., a war machine was called an *ingenium,* an invention of genius, and later the word *engin* came into use for such machines. It was not until the Middle Ages that a person who designed, constructed, or operated such machines came to be called an *ingeniator,* an engineer. Thus the first use of the word *engineer* was applied to the work of the military engineer.

Most other work involving engineering, including military engineering, continued to be performed by master builders. By the time of the Renaissance, the role of master builders changed, dividing along the lines of those who constructed buildings, the builders, and those who designed them, the architects. And architects designed not only buildings but other structures, including war machines and fortifications. Many of the architects were also artists.

Engineering and architecture continued to be practiced simultaneously until the 17th century, when some distinction was made between military engineers and architects. Sébastien Le Prestre, Marquis de Vauban (1633–1707), became a great engineer in France, designer and builder of many forts, and dedicated himself to the profession of engineering. He has been called the first engineer. In the 18th century, modern engineering had its beginnings in France. At that time, civil engineering of structures, such as bridges, canals, and water supply systems, was often handled by men who specialized in such work.

By the end of the 18th century, civil engineering had become partly separated from architecture in both France and England, but the real separation was not to be accomplished until near the end of the 19th century. Since then, the two professions have continued to overlap in important ways. In 1750 the great English engineer John Smeaton (1724–92) first used the term *civil engineer* to describe his work. Others began to call themselves civil engineers and later organized an engineering society in England. In 1818 the Institution of Civil Engineers was founded in London and a few years later the Société des Ingénieurs Civils de France was founded in Paris. Soon afterward, lectures in engineering were delivered in French and English universities, and in 1840 a professorship in engineering was established in Glasgow University, Scotland.

U.S. Schools and Societies Civil engineering became established in the United States in the early 19th century. The American Society of Civil Engineers was founded in 1852. At first its title included "and Architects," but that portion was dropped in 1869. The first engineering school in the United States was the U.S. Military Academy, West Point, N.Y., which started teaching engineering when it was founded in 1802 and has continued to do so ever since. Rensselaer Polytechnic Institute, Troy, N.Y., was the second, beginning in 1824, and it granted the first engineering degree in 1835.

Mechanical engineering had its beginnings with the start of the industrial revolution in the 18th century but did not come into its own until the 19th. The American Society of Mechanical Engineers was founded in 1880. Electrical engineering began in the 19th and came into its own in the 20th century. The Institute of Electrical and Electronics Engineers was founded in 1884. Structural engineering, as one of the specialties of civil engineering, started in the 19th century and became solidly established in the 20th.

Related Articles ARCHITECTURE; BUILDING CODES AND STANDARDS; BUILDING INDUSTRY; ELECTRICAL ENGINEERING; MECHANICAL ENGINEERING; PLANNING, CITY; ROAD AND TRAFFIC DESIGN; SURVEYING.

Further Reading Constance, John D.: *How to Become a Professional Engineer,* 3d ed., McGraw-Hill, New York, 1978; Finch, James Kip: *The Story of Engineering,* Doubleday, Garden City, N.Y., 1960; Hicks, Tyler: *Professional Achievement for Engineers and Scientists,* McGraw-Hill, New York, 1963.

Sources of Additional Information American Consulting Engineers Council, 1155 15th St., N.W., Washington, D.C. 20005; Engineers Council for Professional Development, 345 E. 47th St., New York, N.Y. 10017; Engineers Joint Council, 345 E. 47th St., New York, N.Y. 10017; National Council of State Boards of Engineering Examiners, P. O. Drawer 752, Clemson, S.C. 29631; National Society of Professional Engineers, 2029 K St., N.W., Washington, D.C. 20006.

Periodicals *Consulting Engineer,* 217 Wayne St., St. Joseph, Mich., 49085; *Engineering News-Record,* 1221 Avenue of the Americas, New York, N.Y. 10020; *Professional Engineer,* 2029 K St., N.W., Washington, D.C. 20006.

ENVIRONMENTAL PROTECTION
The guarding, preservation, and conservation of nature and natural resources, such as air, water, land, animals, plants, and natural fuels. Architecture, of necessity, changes

the environment in which it is placed. Therefore architects and other environmental designers must make efforts not to destroy or deplete, any more than is absolutely necessary, nature and the natural resources affected by their buildings.

Ecological Effects of Architecture Architecture is so deeply involved with all aspects of nature and life that almost every decision an architect or other environmental designer makes has serious environmental implications. The manner in which a subdivision is planned affects the entire ecology of the area. The planning of a city, or a portion of one, will probably have even greater ecological effects. Such activities greatly affect the potential pollution of the air from heating systems and fireplaces, and by other means. They affect the potential pollution of rivers and other water bodies through increased needs for waste disposal. They may affect erosion by changing drainage patterns, shaping the land with machinery, destruction of trees and ground-cover vegetation, and in other ways. They may destroy the natural habitat of birds, animals, vegetation, and other forms of life. The list could be extended to embrace many other factors, including increased noise levels from automobiles and other sources and from visual or esthetic pollution.

For many individual buildings, the environmental effects may be equally as great and in some cases, for example, factories, even greater. Therefore many architects and other environmental designers today consider environmental protection as one of their major professional responsibilities, whether required by laws or regulations or not. In their architecture, they attempt to solve the functional, esthetic, and other problems, while disturbing the environment as little as possible. Occasionally, they have even improved the environment in some respects, for example, by correcting conditions that cause erosion; by providing parks, open spaces, natural trails, and the like; by blocking noises; by conservation of natural resources, such as fuel oil and gas; and by provision for the cultural, esthetic, and psychological needs of people as well as their functional and physiological ones.

Such architects and other environmental designers have dedicated a major part of their efforts to the protection of the air, water, land, animals, birds, vegetation, natural resources, and other aspects of the environment. Some have even turned away from the more usual types of practice of their professions to become specialists in environmental fields. Other environmental specialists come from varied backgrounds and educational experiences, including science, from such disciplines as forestry, agriculture, horticulture, wildlife management, and geography.

Environmental Laws Architects and other environmental designers, in addition to their own professional environmental concerns, must often follow state and federal environmental laws and regulations in their work. These vary from state to state, and

sometimes between localities within states. The major federal environmental law is the National Environmental Policy Act and the major federal regulatory agency is the Environmental Protection Agency (EPA). For major projects to be constructed with federal funds, EPA requires what are called environmental impact analyses (EIA) and environmental impact statements (EIS). Architects and other environmental designers are often involved in such analyses and statements when their projects may be expected to have major environmental implications.

In general, the procedure involved in the preparation of an EIA is as follows: (1) determine whether or not the project can be expected to have major effects on the environment, by comparison to lists of types of projects; (2) identify activities of the project that may have environmental effects, such as site preparation and excavation, foundations, construction materials and methods, and so on; (3) evaluate the potential impact of each activity on the environment and summarize the impacts; (4) review the alternatives; and (5) analyze the findings. If at this stage a project does not appear to have significant adverse environmental impacts, is not controversial, and is not a major federal budget item, the process stops and the results are used to verify that fact in an EIA report. If a significant adverse environmental impact does seem to exist and the project is controversial or a major budgetary item, an EIS must be filed. If the decision is made not to file an EIS for a project on the published list of those normally requiring one, a negative declaration (ND) must be filed for the public record, stating the reasons why an EIS was not filed.

If an EIS is required for a project, the contents are expected to include detailed information on the (1) project description, (2) land-use relationships, (3) probable impact of the proposed action on the environment, (4) alternatives to the proposed action, (5) probable adverse environmental effects which cannot be avoided, (6) relationship between local short-term uses of the environment and the maintenance and enhancement of long-term productivity, (7) irreversible and irretrievable commitments of resources, and (8) other interests and considerations of federal policy that offset the adverse environmental aspects of the proposed action.

History Until the 18th century, little thought was given to protection of the environment. As a result, timber was cut and not replanted; soil eroded; and birds and animals were killed in great numbers; for example, the passenger pigeon, once estimated to number up to 5 billion, and other birds became extinct, and the American bison or buffalo almost became extinct. Rivers became polluted, partly because water runoff from the land carried with it various harmful substances and partly because raw sewage was customarily dumped into them. The list could be extended almost indefinitely. And the situation in America was even worse than it was in Europe and other places. Some people were concerned and tried to do something about the situation. For example, Thomas Jefferson (1743–1826) and George Washington (1732–99) attempted to control erosion on their farms. But their efforts fell far short of what was needed.

Beginning in the 19th century, some people began to write about environmental subjects and make other efforts to improve conditions, including the naturalist and writer Henry David Thoreau (1817–62) and the landscape architect Frederick Law Olmsted (1822–1903). The first book to excite wide interest in conservation in the United States was *The Earth as Modified by Human Action,* written in 1864 by lawyer and diplomat George Perkins March (1801–82). The first textbook on the subject, not published until 1910, was *The Conservation of the Natural Resources of the United States,* written by geologist and college president Charles Richard Van Hise (1857–1918).

Many others worked for environmental protection and wrote about the subject, including Theodore Roosevelt (1858–1919), naturalist John Muir (1838–1914), planner Benton McKaye (1879–1972), drama critic and naturalist Joseph Wood Krutch (1885–1970), marine biologist Rachel Carson (1907–64), and U.S. Supreme Court Justice William Orville Douglas (1898–1980). The naturalist and journalist Jay Norwood Darling (1876–1962), under the pseudonym of Ding, drew cartoons to promote interest in conservation. Many others have been active in environmental protection and conservation and many are still active today.

Numerous organizations have fought and continue to fight for environmental protection and conservation; for example, the Conservation Foundation, National Wildlife Federation, Sierra Club, Izaak Walton League, National Audubon Society, American Forestry Association, Future Farmers of America, and Conservation Education Association. On the international level, conservation has been the subject of conferences of the United Nations, which also has continuing programs of studies and activities.

U.S. Regulations Partly because of the activities of such conservation-minded organizations and individuals, federal, state, and local governments in the United States have enacted a great number of laws and taken other actions concerned with environmental protection and conservation. Although some previous efforts had been made, the first important federal action is thought to have been the establishment of the U.S. Fish Commission in 1872. In the same year, Yellowstone National Park was established, the first of many public parks. In 1885 the U.S. Bureau of Biological Survey was established in the Department of Agriculture. In 1891 the U.S. Congress enacted a law authorizing the creation of certain forest reserves and in 1897, and later, authorized additional lands to be set aside for such purposes. In 1898 a Division of Forestry was established in the U.S. Department of Agriculture and Gifford Pinchot (1865–1946), considered the first professional forester in the United States, became its first chief.

The conservation movement in the United States greatly accelerated under the leadership of Theodore Roosevelt, while he was president (1901–09). During his tenure in office, and largely because of his deep interest in conservation, a number of progressive steps were made. The Reclamation Act was passed in 1902. The following year, Roosevelt established federal bird reservations. The U.S. Forest Service, with Pinchot as its chief, was established in 1905. Roosevelt added more acres of land to the national forests than any other president and established regulations for grazing in them. In 1908 he held the first conservation conference of state governors, with the result that many states soon afterward created conservation commissions. In the same year, he created the National Conservation Commission, under the leadership of Pinchot.

Since the time of Theodore Roosevelt, many other laws have been enacted and other actions taken by the federal government. Among the most important were the Weeks Law, enacted in 1911, allowing purchase of lands for national forests; the establishment of the National Park Service in 1916; and the first migratory bird treaty with Canada in the same year. Federal conservation efforts lagged somewhat until 1928, when the Forest Research Act was passed by Congress.

President Franklin Roosevelt (1882–1945) gave considerable impetus to conservation during his terms in office (1933–45). From 1933 to 1942, thousands of unemployed young men joined the Civilian Conservation Corps (CCC) to work on conservation projects, including planting some 2 million acres of trees. During Roosevelt's tenure, a number of important conservation laws were sponsored by him and passed by Congress, including those creating the Tennessee Valley Authority (TVA) and the Soil Erosion Service, later called the Soil Conservation Service, in 1933. In 1934 the Taylor Grazing Act was passed; in 1935, the Soil Conservation Act; and in 1936, the Flood Control Act.

Many other laws have subsequently been passed and other actions taken by the federal government, including the Water Pollution Act of 1948, and other later acts on this subject, the Watershed Protection and Flood Prevention Act of 1954, and the Wilderness Act of 1964. Actions have also been taken in the various states for environmental protection and conservation. A leader has been the State of New York, which began conservation programs very early and now has almost 3 million acres in forest preserves in the Adirondack and Catskill Mountains. Other leaders have been the states of Michigan and California.

During the 1960s and 1970s, many people, sometimes called environmentalists, and including a number of college students and other young people, were not at all satisfied with governmental efforts in environmental protection and conservation. Together with environmental organizations, they demanded better environmental policies and controls. In 1970 the National Environmental Policy Act became law and was subsequently amended. In addition to establishing policies and criteria for environmental protection and maintenance of quality in the environment, the act provided for a Council on Environmental Quality in the Executive Office of the President, for the submission by the president of annual environmental quality reports to Congress, and for the preparation of environmental impact analyses and statements for all proposed legislation or other major actions of the federal government or by others when supported with federal funds.

In December 1970, a new Environmental Protection Agency (EPA) was created. To it were assigned the many agencies and administrations concerned with environmental problems then scattered among the Departments of the Interior; Health, Education and Welfare; and others. EPA was thus given the overall responsibility for water quality, air pollution, solid wastes, pesticides, radiation, and other environmental concerns.

Efforts to improve the quality of the environment and to protect it in the future are continuing by individuals, organizations, and federal and state governments. Many believe that the efforts made so far have not been enough and often have come too late. Some disagreements have arisen in later years between people and organizations who generally support the same or similar positions on the importance of environmental protection and conservation. One of the most serious of such disagreements has been between those who are most deeply concerned about environmental quality and those whose deepest concerns are with growing energy shortages. For example, those concerned primarily with energy often support the increased use of coal of which there are greater reserves than those of oil or other fuels. Those primarily concerned with air pollution maintain this would greatly increase that problem. People who advocate the use of nuclear electric generating plants cite their advantages in the conservation of fuels and the relatively low degree of pollution of the air. Those opposed to nuclear plants cite the dangers of accidents, radiation, and pollution by radioactive wastes.

Such questions must be resolved, together with all the other important issues, if the environment is to be protected and preserved for humans and the animals and plants with which they share it. Architects and other environmental designers today are in an exceedingly good position to help bring about meaningful changes for the better.

Related Articles CLIMATE; DESIGN, ARCHITECTURAL; ECOLOGY; ELECTRIC POWER AND WIRING; GARDEN; HEATING, VENTILATING, AND AIR CONDITIONING; INSECT PROTECTION; LANDSCAPE ARCHITECTURE; PARK; PLANNING, CITY; PLUMBING; ROAD AND TRAFFIC DESIGN; SITE PLANNING.

Further Reading Callison, Charles H., ed.: *America's Natural Resources*, rev. ed., Ronald, New York, 1967; Jain, R. K., L. V. Urban, and G. S. Stacey: *Environmental Impact Analysis—A New Dimension in Decision Making.* Van Nostrand Reinhold, New York, 1977; McHenry, Robert, and Charles Van Doren, eds.: *A Documentary History of Conservation in America,* Praeger, New York, 1972.

Sources of Additional Information Association of Conservation Engineers, P. O. Box 180, Jefferson City, Mo. 65101; Conservation Foundation, 1717 Massachusetts Ave., N.W., Washington, D.C. 20036; Environmental Protection Agency, 401 M St., S. W. Washington, D.C. 20460; National Parks and Conservation Assoc., 1701 18th St., N.W., Washington, D.C. 20009; National Wildlife Federation, 1412 16th St., N. W., Washington, D. C. 20036; Sierra Club, 530 Bush St., San Francisco, Calif. 94108.

Periodicals *National Parks and Conservation Magazine,* 1701 18th St., N.W., Washington, D.C. 20009; *National Wildlife,* 1412 16th St., N.W., Washington, D.C. 20036.

ESTHETICS The subject that deals with the nature of beauty or the nature of art, including architecture. Esthetics (also spelled aesthetics) is concerned with experiencing beauty and with that which constitutes beauty. It is concerned with the essential character of beauty and the perception of, response to, and judgment of beauty. Thus esthetics is one of the most important considerations in architecture.

A considerable amount of confusion exists about esthetics, perhaps because of its subjective nature. What is beautiful? Why is it beautiful? How does one know it is beautiful? Questions such as these have no simple answers. Yet esthetics attempts to answer these questions, though it is not easy even for professional estheticians who devote their careers to such studies.

Definitions In this subject so essential to architecture, vast differences of opinion exist. Some define esthetics as a science, along with mathematics, physics, chemistry, and so on. Others define it as a branch of philosophy, which they define, in turn, as the science of the principles and truths of reality, knowledge, and human nature and conduct. There is some difference of opinion about the nature of philosophy itself, some maintaining that it should be subdivided into three major fields: natural, moral, and metaphysical, the study of the nature of reality. Others hold that all philosophy is metaphysical. Still another view is that the division must be four parts: metaphysics; logic, the study of correct reasoning or validity; epistemology, the coordination of knowledge with the natural world; and axiology, the study of values in such concepts as art, morals, and religion. Thus axiology includes both ethics, the study of moral character, principles, quality, and practice, and esthetics.

Further confusing the issue, philosophy is usually classified today, not as a science but as one of the humanities, along with music, literature, religion, and art, including architecture. In this way, esthetics may be thought of as closely allied to the arts, the very subjects into which it attempts to impart meaning. Even in this, there is disagreement, some maintaining that esthetics must be restricted to study of the fine arts, usually, but not always, considered to include painting, drawing, and architecture, to which are often added, music, dance, drama, poetry, and other literature. Others believe even this extended list is too restrictive and should include such activities as industrial design; printmaking, such as engravings, woodcuts, silk-screen prints or serigraphs, etchings, and so on; and motion pictures.

In such a state of affairs, it is not surprising that those who are called upon to design buildings so often find confusion, uncertainty, and controversy surrounding their architecture, the central essence of which is esthetics. No wonder that the principles of esthetic design are so hard to formulate, to teach, and to put into practice by architects, so nearly impossible to explain to clients and others, and so often impossible for architecture critics to deal with.

Yet architects must deal with esthetics if they are to create architecture, no matter how its esthetic qualities be defined or codified. Esthetics crosses many of the lines of other disciplines. The social sciences, such as history, archeology, sociology, anthropology, and so on, help to explain how the arts are related to human beings, and how people live. Psychology helps in the understanding of how human beings think, perceive, feel, learn, and act when creating art, when thinking about it, and when experiencing it. Many other disciplines, including the natural sciences, are helpful in the study of esthetics.

Branches Esthetics is often thought of as divided into five major branches: psychology of art, the study of human behavior when creating, contemplating, or experiencing art; sociology of art, the study of how art affects and is affected by human activities in religion, government, and so on; esthetic morphology, the study of forms and styles in art; esthetic value theory, the study of the functions of art and principles for its judgment; and esthetic semantics, the study of the language used in describing and discussing art.

Philosophies Sometimes esthetics is divided into two major philosophies: the objective, which maintains that beauty is contained, or is inherent in, the art object itself, such as a building or painting; and the subjective, which maintains that beauty is contained not in the object but in the perception the observer has of the object. Needless to say, there are many gradations and variations of belief between the two extreme positions.

Functions In any case, the functions of esthetics involve several types of activity, including the collection, organization, and interpretation of information. Estheticians attempt to discover how artists work, use their imaginations, and make their performances; and how people use and enjoy art and how they feel about it. They also study the principles of beauty, what makes one object beautiful, another not. And they study the moods, beliefs, and attitudes of artists and the people who experience their creations. Other specific subjects for study are perception, the awareness or consciousness in the mind of a person whose senses are stimulated by an object; esthetic value, the property of an object that allows it to be perceived with pleasure or displeasure; and taste, the quality of

being able to express preferences among esthetic values, based on sensitiveness to perceptions caused by stimulation of the senses by objects.

The principles and theories of esthetics require considerable study, and not a little contemplation, if they are to be understood and translated into buildings that are great architecture, if they are to be meaningfully and justly criticized by architecture critics, and if they are to be understood and appreciated by those interested in art, architecture, and their environment.

History From its beginnings, the history of esthetics, irrespective of how it is classified today, as one of the sciences of humanities or in some other way, has been part of the history of philosophy, and therefore the province primarily of philosophers. The great ancient Greek philosophers, Aristotle (384–322 B.C.) and Plato (427–347 B.C.), originally named Aristocles, were both deeply concerned with esthetics as well as with the other aspects of philosophy. Since that time, esthetics has been of concern to a number of philosophers, though it was not actually called by that name until the 18th century.

Beginning late in the 18th century, a number of great philosophers wrote important books on esthetics. Among them are two Germans, Immanuel Kant (1724–1804), who wrote *Critique of Judgment,* published in 1790, a valuable book, though less well known than his earlier work, *Critique of Pure Reason,* 1781, and George Wilhelm Friedrich Hegel (1770–1831), whose *Philosophy of Fine Arts* was published after his death. Englishman Roger Eliot Fry (1866–1934) wrote *Vision and Design,* 1920. The Italian philosopher Benedetto Croce (1866–1952), wrote several books on esthetics, including *Aesthetic,* published in 1921. George Santayana (1863–1952), a Spanish philosopher, educated at Harvard University, Cambridge, and professor of philosophy there from 1889 to 1912, wrote a number of books on esthetics, including *The Sense of Beauty,* 1896, and *Reason in Art,* 1905. Since 1952, when the two giants of esthetics, Croce and Santayana both died, no philosophers of esthetics have reached the heights they occupied.

Related Articles ARCHITECTURE; ART IN ARCHITECTURE; BOOK, ARCHITECTURAL; CRITICISM, ARCHITECTURE; DESIGN, ARCHITECTURAL; SOCIAL SCIENCE.

Further Reading Berlyne, D. E.: *Studies in the New Experimental Aesthetics—Steps Toward an Objective Psychology of Aesthetics: Appreciation,* John Wiley, New York, 1974; Lee, Harold Newton: *Perception and Aesthetic Value,* Prentice-Hall, New York, 1938.

EXPOSITION Educational and usually festive exhibition, often called a fair, especially one of international scope. Most expositions and their buildings are of a temporary nature, but there are exceptions. Some of the buildings left standing, and many others that were demolished, have strongly influenced architecture. And many highly regarded architects have participated in master planning of expositions and in the design of their buildings.

EXPOSITION World's Columbian (1893), Chicago, Ill. [*Chief architect: Daniel Hudson Burnham. (Chicago Historical Society)*]

It is impossible to generalize about the design of expositions, since each is a unique event, with its plan, buildings, and content, subject to the inventiveness of its promoters, exhibitors, and architects. However, there are in almost all expositions structures of four major types: buildings for display of arts, sciences, manufactures, and so on; buildings and other structures for recreation, such as shows, rides, games, and the like; buildings for administration and maintenance; and structures that usually serve no other purpose than the symbolic.

Origins Expositions, as we now know them, started in England in the middle of the 18th century, but the grand era did not begin until the Great Exhibition (1851) in London. Here the famous Crystal Palace, designed by Sir Joseph Paxton (1801–65), was built of glass and iron. Its structure and size, 408 ft wide by 72 ft high by 1,848 ft long, caused a sensation and has influenced both architecture and expositions ever since. The building was moved to Sydenham, England, and was destroyed by fire in 1936. In 1853 another version of the palace was constructed at the New York City Exhibition. In 1855 in the Paris Exposition, the glass and iron Palais de l'Industrie was even larger than its London counterpart, and in 1889 the Galerie des Machines, longer.

A number of other great European expositions followed, including those in London in 1862, 1908, 1924–25, and 1951; Brussels in 1935 and 1958; Montreal in 1967; and Paris in 1855, 1867, 1878, 1889, 1900, 1931, and 1937. All had some influence on architecture and were notable in other ways. Perhaps the most lasting and well-known structure of any of them is the Eiffel Tower (1889), erected for the Paris Exposition of that year. It was designed by engineer Alexandre Gustave Eiffel (1832–1923). An interesting building at Brussels, in 1958, was the U.S. Pavilion by Edward Durell Stone (1902–78).

U.S. Expositions Major 19th-century American expositions include the Philadelphia Centennial (1876) and the World's Columbian Exposition (1893) in Chicago. The latter was a showplace for eclectic architecture, its character determined by New York architects, including Charles Follen McKim (1847–1909) and Richard Morris Hunt (1827–95). Daniel Hudson Burnham (1846–1912) was its chief architect. All these architects designed buildings for the exposition as did Charles B. Atwood (1848–95), whose Palace of Fine Arts later became the still-existing Rosenwald Museum of Science and Industry. Sophia Hayden (c. 1878–1953) designed the Women's Building, the commission for which she had won in a competition. Louis Henri Sullivan (1856–1924) designed the Transportation Building, the only pioneering modern effort, but it was later destroyed.

The Chicago exposition was followed by the Pan-American (1901), Buffalo, N.Y., and the Louisiana Purchase (1904), St. Louis. The latter leaned heavily on

EXPOSITION Century 21, Federal Science Pavilion (1962), Seattle, Wash. [*Architect: Minoru Yamasaki. (Glenn M. Christiansen)*]

EXPOSITION New York State Pavilion, New York World's Fair (1964) New York, N.Y. [*Architect: Philip Cortelyou Johnson. (Joseph W. Molitor)*]

Beaux Arts architecture and produced a building that still exists, the Palace of Fine Arts, now the St. Louis Museum, by Cass Gilbert (1858–1934). The Panama-Pacific Exposition (1915), San Francisco, produced the Palace of Fine Arts of Bernard Maybeck (1862–1957), now reconstructed, and the Panama-California Exposition at San Diego in the same year produced an eclectic Spanish style under the design direction of Bertram Grosvenor Goodhue (1869–1924) of New York. Some of these buildings still exist. The 1933–34 Chicago exposition, A Century of Progress, with Louis Skidmore (1897–1962) as director of design, produced mostly fanciful, futuristic buildings.

The 1939–40 Golden Gate Exposition was held on artificial Treasure Island, made from earth dredged from San Francisco Bay and now the location of a naval base. Also in 1939–40, the New York World's Fair produced little in the way of architectural innovation, except the Swedish, Finnish, and Brazilian pavilions, all of which were taken down after the fair. The 1964–65 fair on the same site as the earlier fair produced several buildings still in existence, the Museum of Science and Technology, by Harrison and Abramovitz, Wallace Kirkman Harrison (1895–   ), and Max Abramovitz (1908–   ); the United States Pavil-

ion by Charles Luckman (1909–   ); and the New York State Pavilion by Philip Cortelyou Johnson (1906–   ).

Many smaller expositions and fairs have been held, and are still being held, all over the world. Some of them have produced innovative, even pioneering, architecture. The German Pavilion of Ludwig Mies van der Rohe (1886–1969) at the Barcelona Exposition (1929) became world famous and deeply affected the development of modern architecture. There are many other notable examples, including the buildings (1962) at the Seattle Century 21 Exposition by Minoru Yamasaki (1912–   ) and the Berlin Congress Hall (1957) at the Berlin Exposition, designed by Hugh Stubbins (1912–   ).

Related Articles BURNHAM AND ROOT; CASS, GILBERT; HARRISON, WALLACE KIRKMAN; HUNT, RICHARD MORRIS; JOHNSON, PHILIP CORTELYOU; MAYBECK, BERNARD; McKIM, MEAD AND WHITE; MIES VAN DER ROHE, LUDWIG; SKIDMORE, OWINGS AND MERRILL; STONE, EDWARD DURELL; SULLIVAN, LOUIS HENRI; YAMASAKI, MINORU.

Further Reading Gardner, James, and Caroline Heller: *Exhibition and Display*, F. W. Dodge, New York, 1960; Luckhurst, Kenneth W.: *The Story of Exhibitions*, Studio Publications, London and New York, 1951.

FACTORY A building, often called an industrial building, or a group of buildings in which products or goods are manufactured or assembled. At one time, the word *factory* was used for any building in which people worked. By the time of the industrial revolution, the word had come to mean a place in which mostly standardized goods were manufactured as contrasted with the shops of craftsmen. Today a factory is apt to be highly organized and automated, with specialized buildings and assembly lines designed specifically for the type of goods to be manufactured. Formerly architects tended to regard factory design as nonarchitectural, but today this has become one of the most important architectural building types.

Classifications Factory buildings are sometimes classified by the type of industries in which they are used: heavy or light. Heavy industries are concerned with relatively large products and processes, such as steel, automobiles, aircraft, and ships. Light industries manufacture or assemble relatively small products, such as machine tools, television and other electronic items, food, and paper. Factories are also sometimes classified by their involvement in processing or assembly. Processing industries are concerned with changing natural materials into some other form, and include such activities as oil refining, papermaking, grain milling, and the like. Assembly industries are involved with combining natural or manufactured items into completely assembled products, and include textile, automobile, and baking plants.

Elements The major elements of factories are the areas used for manufacturing or assembly, warehousing, research and control, administration, and employee facilities. The proper relationships between these elements must be established in a well-planned factory. Of utmost importance is the layout of the spaces for the manufacturing or assembly operations. These operations are generally planned with the aid of flow diagrams, which indicate the sequence of all of the activities required from the receipt of the raw materials to the delivery of the finished products for transportation. Plant layouts are generally used in factories that produce relatively large numbers of only a few product types. Process layouts are used in plants that produce relatively small numbers of many products, all of which require similar processes.

The manufacturing or assembly areas of factories vary considerably between industries and types of products. But all must be designed for ease of operation, efficient flow of materials, flexibility, and good supervision. It is an axiom of factory design that provisions must be made for changes and expansion. Warehousing must provide for efficient storage and movement of both raw materials and finished products. The research and control areas must be designed to allow new product development and testing, and control and testing of current products. The types of laboratories and other facilities required are determined by the type of industry.

Administration areas in factories are similar to those of office buildings, but there may be some specific requirements because of the nature of the operations. Employee facilities include such areas as lounges, lockers and rest rooms, cafeterias, meeting rooms, and first aid stations.

Factories must often be designed to meet special requirements necessitated by the operations, the people who perform them, and the products. For example, in some factories natural lighting is very important and special provisions must be made for windows, skylights, and the like. In other factories artificial light may be used exclusively and no windows are required. Transportation of raw materials into factories and finished products away from them often requires special attention to rail lines and sidings, truck roadways and parking, and loading docks.

In other factories, provisions must be made for storage tanks, incinerators, and water tanks. Provisions may be required for handling dangerous wastes, materials that pollute the air or water; fire hazardous materials and operations; and operations that are noisy or produce unpleasant odors. In many industries, the requirements for heating and cooling, water distribution, electrical and other power may be quite important, complex, and costly. Many are now highly automated and use sophisticated controls and computers. Early factories, usually built in cities, were mostly three or four stories high. Today factories are often built outside cities and are generally single story, but sometimes have two or more stories. And some multistory factories, of eight stories or more, have been built in recent years.

Recently, a trend has developed in the United States toward planned insustrial districts, sometimes called industrial parks. These areas range in size from about eighty to several thousand acres. Individual sites are provided for a great number of factories in a planned area with roadways, parking, and utilities. In

FACTORY Willow Run (1943), Ford Motor Co., Ypsilanti, Mich. [*Architect: Albert Kahn. (Hedrich-Blessing)*]

some industrial parks, restaurants, shops, recreational facilities, and even motels are provided.

Industrial buildings of all kinds, particularly factories, have now become a very important building type. Their design is complex and demanding, but it is also challenging and rewarding. The number of factories built each year fluctuates because of such factors as the state of the economy, but in times of slow building activity, there are usually numerous remodeling projects and changes from one type of process or product to another. In good years, industrial buildings comprise a large and important segment of the construction activity in the United States.

History Although factories of a sort have existed to some extent since the 16th century, it is only since the middle of the 18th that factories, as now known, were built. With the beginning of the use of coal, coke, and waterpower and with the increasing development of water and land transportation for materials and products, factories for the manufacture of iron and textile products were constructed first in England, then in other European countries. Matthew Boulton (1728–1809), an English engineer and manufacturer, built several innovative factories and then teamed up with Scottish inventor James Watt (1736–1819), who had invented improved steam engines, to produce the engines and to design new factories. One was a pioneering seven-story cotton mill (1801) near Salford, England. Although improvements were made in factories and in the use of power in the buildings, the design of factories for the safety and welfare of the workers lagged behind.

American Development In colonial America, there were no real factories. In the years before in-

dependence, most manufacturing processes were handcrafts. The only operations that used power were mills that manufactured lumber, flour, paper, and gunpowder. During the last decade of the 18th century and the first of the 19th, some 200 textile mills, many of them using steam for power, were built in New England and the Middle Atlantic states. During the next decade an industrial town was built in New Hampshire, not only with a factory but housing and other buildings for the workers, a harbinger of later company towns in many parts of the United States.

The advent of wrought, and later cast, iron for building structures changed the design of factories considerably. Now a building could be built with a frame of relatively unobtrusive metal members that did not get in the way of the processes as did the earlier heavy walls. In 1848 James Bogardus (1800–74), inventor and engineer, designed and built a five-story factory in New York City, using iron framing. This was followed by many others, in both wrought and cast iron, all over the United States. Some of the most notable were in New York City and St. Louis. Still most factories were constructed with brick walls and timber floors and roofs. The invention of the skeleton frame and steel changed factory construction drastically. And the widespread use of reinforced concrete starting in the early 20th century brought with it the virtual end of the old types of construction.

Most of the other changes in factory design were brought about by improvements required for the safety and welfare of workers and by increasing mechanization and later automation. Otherwise, factory design did not change much. Architects continued to consider it nonarchitecture and avoided factory design or relegated it to an unimportant place in their practice. Then a few European architects, including Walter Adolf Gropius (1883–1969), began to design handsome, functional factories. And Albert Kahn (1869–1942) revolutionized factory design, first with his significant automobile plants in and around Detroit, and later in other buildings. These factories were not only efficient and functional but comfortable for the workers, and so elegant in appearance that many consider them among the best-designed American buildings. The tradition established by Kahn continues in the design of factories today.

Related Articles BOGARDUS, JAMES; GROPIUS, WALTER ADOLF; KAHN, ALBERT; LABORATORY; STRUCTURE; WAREHOUSE.

Further Reading Munce, James F.: *Industrial Architecture—An Analysis of International Building Practice,* F. W. Dodge, New York, 1960; Peters, Paulhans, ed.: *Design and Planning—Factories,* Van Nostrand Reinhold, New York, 1970.

FARM BUILDING A building, or group of buildings, used for production of agricultural or horticultural products or for housing farm families. While ranchers might not readily admit it, a ranch is a special kind of farm for raising cattle or sheep. Although farm buildings do not form an important building type designed by architects, they were among the first buildings constructed in America. They were then very important in the life and progress of the country and they remain so today.

A great variety of buildings may be found on farms today, some nothing more than sheds for sheltering machinery, some very complex and specialized. First, of course, is the farmhouse, the dwelling for a farm family, and sometimes for employees, farmhands and others who work on the farm. Farmhouses have always been very much like other houses, ranging from very modest dwellings, similar to those found in towns and cities, to great plantation houses, as large and lavish as the great town houses of the same eras.

The design of farmhouses has closely paralleled the design of other houses, except that perhaps in later years it has tended to be more founded in tradition, less progressive than other house design. A family living in a city or suburb might accept a very modern design, or even prefer it, while their counterpart living in the country might choose a design adapted from a historic style from the past. In other respects, farmhouses and town houses are quite similar, except that kitchens, shared much of the time by all members of families for pursuits other than just meal preparation, have been the rule in farmhouses from the beginning. These so-called live-in kitchens, or family rooms, have only started to become popular in suburbia in the recent past.

Building Types The most important building on a farm, other than the house, is the barn. There are many types of barns, but the most prevalent is the general-purpose barn used to house farm animals, shelter machinery and equipment, and store feed and other supplies. There are many specialized barns, including those for dairy cattle, horses, and other animals. Barns are divided into spaces that are specialized by use, such as stalls for horses or dairy cattle, or pens for other animals. Dairy farms often use loose housing or stanchion barn systems. Loose housing systems have several buildings and other elements, including a building for bedding and milking cattle, one for storage, a feeding area with silo, a milkhouse, and a hay storage building. A stanchion barn, more expensive than loose housing but requiring a smaller site, incorporates all the elements into one building, with a silo nearby. Barns may be built of many materials, including wood, masonry, and metal. The most commonly used materials today are wood structures, with sides and roofs of metal or wood. A building closely associated with the barn is the silo, often a tall structure, usually round in plan, for storage of animal feed, usually called silage.

Farms often have many other types of buildings. Storage is most important, not only for animal feed but for canned goods, root vegetables, and other food for the farm family. Root cellars for food storage have long been a fixture on farms, but today farm families often supplement them with freezers. Smokehouses and baking ovens have often been provided for food preparation.

Many specialized buildings are used on farms. Buildings for various kinds of farm animals, such as chicken houses, cattle sheds, hog sheds, and so on, are often required. In addition, many farms raise other animals, which require specialized structures, including rabbits, ducks, geese, pigeons, and turkeys, and on some farms, even catfish and crayfish. Other farms are devoted to horticulture, raising flowers and their seeds or bulbs, trees, or shrubbery. Such farms often require special buildings for handling the products and others, including greenhouses for raising and propagating plants. Some farms have stringent requirements for cold storage of the products. Obviously dairy farms have such requirements, but so do other types, including fruit and nut farms.

As somewhat independent operating units using a great variety of machinery and tools, farms must have good provisions for the storage of these items and for their repair and servicing. Special buildings are often provided for these purposes, with spaces for storing machinery and maintenance and service parts and materials, and a shop.

One of the most important aspects of the design of farms is provision for mechanical and electrical equipment and systems. Farms require large electrical systems, not only for the usual residential services and equipment but lights and machinery in the barns and other buildings; often heat and ventilation in animal shelters, greenhouses, and other places; power for water pumps for farmhouses, animals, and sometimes irrigation of crops. Water piping runs to barns, animal houses, shops, gardens, and other locations. Sewage disposal is dependent on grease traps, septic tanks, and drainage fields. Waste disposal of other kinds must also be provided for, including animal waste, used chemicals, and so on.

All in all, farms are quite complex and would present interesting design problems to architects. For the most part, this does not happen today, for most architects never get the chance to design more than an occasional farmhouse or horse barn.

History Farms have a very old history, dating back to the Neolithic period, beginning about 8000 B.C. or earlier, in Mesopotamia, Egypt, and other countries of that area. During the centuries following, Neolithic people developed cultivation of barley, wheat, and other grains and domestication of cattle, sheep, goats, and pigs. Farms have been an important part of the culture of humans ever since.

American Development The first farms in America were established immediately after the colonists arrived, in the Upper South and East. The first farmhouses were very modest, many of them built with wood frames filled in with wattle and daub, a method using wattles, twigs, or other materials woven together and inserted into the house frame, and then covered on both sides with daub, a mixture of mud and clay with chopped straw or other materials. These were followed by farmhouses made entirely of wood and then of sun-dried brick. In the French settlements of the Deep South, New Orleans and others, wooden buildings were also erected and they were followed by a method called *briquette entre poteaux,* soft brick inserted between timbers.

Later some of the finest houses in America were built on farms, or plantations, of the South. Many were designed by talented amateur architects whose names have been lost; others by some of the best American professional architects. Beginning in the 19th century and continuing into the 20th, the design of farmhouses has often been done by builders and by farmers themselves.

Related Articles BOTANICAL BUILDING; HOUSE.

Further Reading Foss, Edward W.: *Construction and Maintenance for Farm and Home,* John Wiley, New York, 1960; Kauffman, Henry J.: *The American Farmhouse,* Hawthorn Books, New York, 1975; Sloane, Eric: *An Age of Barns,* Ballantine Books, New York, 1967.

FEASIBILITY STUDY
The practicality of a proposed building project, established through research and analysis of its use, financing, construction, and other aspects of importance. A feasibility study is made to determine whether or not the construction of a project is advisable.

Whenever some doubt exists about the advisability of a building construction project, a feasibility study should be prepared. While such studies might seem necessary for all projects in this category, they are absolutely essential for development projects proposed by developers, who must sell the concepts to those who will finance them and to those who will lease or buy them.

Feasibility studies of a somewhat limited sort are of-

ten done by architects for their private clients, and some architectural offices are capable of handling more complicated studies. Upon becoming involved in a development project, an architect often participates in the study of feasibility, together with other people, such as real estate counselors and mortgage bankers. For a project for a private client, the situation is relatively simple. A private owner may decide to do without a feasibility study, relying only on needs and wishes based on experience and judgment. If a feasibility study is prepared for a private owner, the decisions about whether to build or not, what to build, and so on may be made directly by the owner. For development projects and many other profit-making projects, establishment of feasibility is all-important.

Some confusion exists regarding the term *feasibility study.* The term may be used to mean a complete study of all the facets of a proposed building project, including markets for products or services; appraisal of the value of the project; analysis of the project as an investment; economic feasibility; and use of the building. Sometimes the term is applied only to an economic feasibility study, which determines the maximum project budget that will produce the return the owner expects on the investment.

Although the determination of economic feasibility is the most important single element in a complete feasibility study, only analysis of all the elements can produce a reliable basis for making all the proper decisions on real estate projects.

Study Phases A complete feasibility study begins with a market analysis. This analysis is concerned generally with the market, the supply and demand for particular types of real estate projects, such as shopping centers, stores, apartments, or factories. It then proceeds to the study of a proposed project. Answers must be derived to such questions as estimations of future markets, availability of transportation, population trends, rent and occupancy levels, and growth in the area in which the site is located.

An appraisal of the value of the project may then be made, not based solely on the cost of the project but on its value in terms of the net income that it can be expected to generate. An economic feasibility study may then be made, based on the appraised value of the project, together with the mortgage terms, acceptable rate of return on the equity, or ownership, investment in it. From these data, a calculation can be made of the maximum cost of the project, or budget, which can be expected to produce the expected return. The cost of the project or budget in this case includes all costs, such as those for land; professional fees for architects, engineers, and others; interest; taxes; equipment; moving expenses; and so on; in addition to the actual costs of construction. A special type of economic feasibility study, called a highest-and-best-use study, is prepared when several different uses might be made of a site. A study of this sort compares the uses to determine which will produce the maximum return on equity investment.

In any type of economic feasibility study, the final question is whether a project is feasible, that is, whether it will produce the rate of return expected by the investor. At this point, an investment analysis may be made to determine the effects of depreciation on the project, capital gains if the project is to be sold upon completion or later, and other tax considerations. By means of such a study, the leverage of the investor may be determined. Leveraging is a technique used to create the maximum profit to an investor for the least amount of equity or investment. The higher the profit-equity ratio can be made, the better the investment. In some cases, through adroit handling of project financing, very high profits in relation to equities may be produced.

Other Factors Other aspects of feasibility studies should be noted. Successful real estate projects depend on such factors as their locations; control of costs by the architect, owners, and others involved; the ability to obtain good financing terms; the ability to lease or sell the projects or to operate them efficiently; and the ability to complete projects on time, including all phases, from establishment of the concepts, through feasibility studies, architectural and related services, and construction.

Thus the creation of a sound real estate investment depends on doing everything right: selecting the right site for the right kind of enterprise, making the right real estate and financial decisions, providing the right management for the right owners, and providing the right kind of architectural and other design services.

Related Articles BUILDING INDUSTRY; COST CONTROL; FINANCE; PROGRAMMING.

Further Reading Golemon, Harry A., ed.: *Financing Real Estate Development, Aloray* Publishers, Englewood, N.J., 1974; Griffin, C.W.: *Development Building—The Team Approach,* American Institute of Architects (distributed by Halsted Press of John Wiley), Washington, 1972; Hunt, William Dudley, Jr., ed.: *Comprehensive Architectural Services—General Principles and Practice,* American Institute of Architects and McGraw-Hill, New York, 1965.

Sources of Further Information American Society of Real Estate Counselors, 155 E. Superior St., Chicago, Ill. 60611; National Association of Real Estate Boards, 155 E. Superior St., Chicago, Ill. 60611; Society of Industrial Realtors, 1300 Connecticut Ave., N.W., Washington, D.C. 20036.

Periodical *National Real Estate Investor,* 461 Eighth Ave., New York, N.Y. 10001.

FINANCE The provision of capital, and its management, for the development, design, and construction of buildings. In the past, architects had little or nothing to do with the financing of buildings. Ordinarily, clients simply arranged for the financing of the amounts needed, in addition to the funds they already had available from savings, corporate capital, or otherwise, with a lending institution or private investors. Then the clients engaged architects, who proceeded with the regular architectural services.

Today the situation has changed. Some clients need assistance from their architects to obtain financing. In other cases, architectural projects are initiated and developed by people called developers, who may or may not end up as the owners or users of the buildings. In such cases, the architectural services become part of the total development scheme, thus involving the architects. In yet another type of case, the architects participate as principals in development work or initiate such projects and act as developers. To deal with situations of the sort described, and particularly to participate in development projects, architects must have knowledge of and experience in the financing of buildings. This is true of those involved in such work today and may be expected to become the case for other architects in the future. For information on development building, see the article entitled real estate.

Ownership of Buildings Buildings and other real estate are owned in a number of ways. The simplest, of course, is ownership by a single individual in fee simple: absolute ownership with rights to dispose of the property. Almost as simple is ownership by more than one person in joint tenancy, tenancy in common, and tenancy of the entirety. Joint tenancy is the situation that exists when two or more people own property together in such a way that when one of the joint owners dies, that share goes to the others. Tenancy in common is the situation that exists when two or more people own shares, not necessarily equal shares, in property that may be willed to people other than the surviving owners. Tenancy of the entirety, allowed in some states, treats a husband and wife as one entity, each with rights of survivorship.

The other major ways that groups own real estate is through partnerships or corporations. A partnership is a relationship between two or more people who contract together to join in business in which they share profits. The two major types of partnerships are a general partnership, in which any partner can commit the group and each partner is liable for all the obligations of the partnership; and a limited partnership, in which there must be one or more general partners and may be any number of limited partners who are not liable for the obligations of the partnerships. Limited partnerships are often used in the ownership of real estate.

A corporation is a legal entity separate from the people who own it, ordinarily called stockholders, set up to conduct business under the applicable laws of a state. Corporations are used in real estate ownership primarily because of the limited liability of the stockholders, ease of transferring portions of ownership, and the possibility of acquiring capital through sales of stock. The fact that corporations report, for tax purposes, as separate entities may be an advantage in some situations and a disadvantage in others. Another form of real estate ownership is a real estate investment trust (REIT), which allows a number of investors to pool their money to invest in real estate. A REIT is most often used to spread the risk of investment or development over a relatively large number of projects.

Financing Types There are two major types of financing involved in building construction: interim and long term. Interim financing takes the form of an interim loan or loans, producing funds that are used to finance the construction of buildings. Long-term financing involves permanent loans, usually secured by first mortgages, which pledge the property and its improvements as security for debts. A second mortgage is an additional mortgage used to obtain more funds, pledging the property and its improvements as security after first mortgage claims have been satisfied. To secure an interim loan, it is usually necessary to obtain what is called a commitment, or standby commitment, from a long-term lender, agreeing to make the long-term loan. Only part of the long-term funds are usually obtained from lending institutions, the remainder, sometimes called front-end money, comes from cash or its equivalent in services from those participating in the ownership of the project and represents the value of their ownership, or their equity in the project. After a building has been completed and the long-term money received, the interim loan is paid off.

Equity Money The capital, equity money or its equivalent, for real estate acquisition may come from sources other than the owner or developer. Sometimes a joint venture, in which more than one person participates, is used, as are options on land, ground leases, and other types. In leasehold financing, the lessor, one who owns property, leases it to a lessee, one who uses the property. Leasehold financing is generally used when land is unusually high priced or not for sale. The lessor owns the land and the improvements made on it while the lessee has the right to its use. On this basis, long-term financing may be obtained. Equity capital may also be obtained by the process of having a lending institution become a partial owner in a joint venture. Another technique is called a sale leaseback. In this type of venture, a developer sells all, or a portion, of a project to a lending institution or other investor, who in turn leases it back to the developer to use. A sale-buyback arrangement, rarely used, entails the purchase of property by a lending institution or other investor, who then sells it back to the developer on an installment payment contract, payable over a number of years. Sometimes a contingent interest or participation system is used. This is an agreement in which the interest rate on a loan is a combination of a fixed percentage and an additional amount based on the degree of success of a project. Another method is a variable rate mortgage, which allows interest rates to shift up or down, within fixed limits, based on the current cost of capital as determined at various times by an agreed-upon index.

A great number of other types of financing construction may be used and no doubt other types will be developed in the future. Other types used today include joint-pool financing, in which several lenders share in the loan on a project; and balloon loans, in which only partial payments are made on the loan periodically, with a relatively large final payment, called a balloon payment.

Loans Loans backed by mortgages for building construction and other real estate purposes may be obtained from a number of sources, including individuals, businesses, lending institutions, and governments. By far the greatest proportion of loan money comes to borrowers from intermediaries which receive the savings of savers and lend them to borrowers. In real estate, the most important are life insurance companies, saving and loan institutions, commercial banks, savings banks, and mortgage bankers, who specialize in placing mortgage loans with investment institutions of the other types. Other sources of loans for real estate investment include credit unions; Federal Land Bank associations, which lend money on farm and rural property; and the federal government, which makes loans on some types of projects, such as new communities. The federal government also makes grants of various kinds, particularly for low-rent housing for low-income families, but its greatest involvement in real estate financing is through the loan insurance programs of the Federal Housing Administration (FHA) and the loan guarantee programs of the Veterans Administration (VA).

While the figures vary from year to year, some idea of the availability of mortgage loan funds is indicated by the relative loan positions of the major sources of such funds in a recent year, when life insurance companies, savings and loan institutions, commercial banks, and savings banks together had about $1,200 billion in total investments. Of this total, about 56 percent was invested by commercial banks, but only about 13 percent of this was in mortgages, divided into two-thirds residential, one-third nonresidential. Life insurance companies accounted for about 19 percent of the total investment, but 34 percent of their funds were in real estate, of which one-third was residential, the other two-thirds nonresidential. Savings and loan associations accounted for 17 percent of the total investments, but almost 85 percent of their investments were in mortgages, only one-tenth of which was nonresidential. Savings banks, which had only 8 percent of the total investments, had 62 percent of their money in real estate mortgages, of which 86 percent was in residential, the remainder in nonresidential. Savings banks, concentrated mostly in the Northeastern and a few other states, were first among institutions making FHA and VA loans, which represented almost 50 percent of their real estate investments; and they held almost one-fourth of all the mortgages underwritten by the federal government.

In investments in houses for one to four families, savings and loan institutions held about 47 percent of the total amount of the loans, commercial banks about 16 percent, savings banks about 13 percent, life insurance companies about 8 percent, the federal government about 9 percent, and miscellaneous lenders held the remainder.

Long-term Financing Ordinarily the method of obtaining long-term financing for building projects involves preparation of materials describing the project with which to approach potential lenders, the making of applications for loans, and negotiation of the terms of the loans and mortgages. Although the details of these steps vary with different types and sizes of projects, some general principles may be enumerated. For some projects, such as single houses, presentations to lenders may be quite simple; in others, such as large-scale shopping center developments they are quite complex. In the first case, the presentation may consist of only working drawings, specifications, and financial information. In the second kind of presentation, made before working drawings and specifications have been prepared, the materials presented might consist of general information about the proposed projects, schematic drawings, feasibility studies, outlines of materials and methods of construction, legal information, financial and economic information, surveys' lessee information, a description of the organization of the developers, and other information. These materials are submitted to potential lenders in order to determine their interest. When an interested lender has been identified, an application for a loan is made and negotiations begin on interest rates, mortgage terms, and other important matters. Today the work of analysis of a development project and preparation of a presentation to potential lenders, sometimes called the mortgage package, has been much simplified and improved through use of computers.

For architects contemplating becoming involved in financing building projects or acting as developers, knowledge and abilities are required that are not ordinarily dealt with thoroughly in an architect's education or experience. Therefore architects must turn to experts in the field, such as mortgage bankers or real estate counselors, for the knowledge and abilities needed to be successful in pursuits of this kind. For some architects, participation in such pursuits can be exciting and satisfying, architecturally as well as financially. For others, the financing and development of real estate projects might better be avoided.

Related Articles BANK; BUILDING INDUSTRY; COMPUTER; FEASIBILITY STUDY; GOVERNMENT; PRACTICE OF ARCHITECTURE; REAL ESTATE.

Further Reading Golemon, Harry A.: *Financing Real Estate Development,* Aloray Publishers, Englewood, N.J., 1974; Griffin, C. W.: *Development Building—The Team Approach,* American Institute of Architects (distributed by Halsted Press of John Wiley), Washington, 1972; Halperin, Dan A.: *Construction Funding—Where the Money Comes From,* John Wiley, New York, 1974; Portman, John, and Jonathan Barnett; *The Architect as Developer,* McGraw-Hill, New York, 1976; Seldin, Maury, and Richard H. Swesnik: *Real Estate Investment Strategy,* John Wiley, New York, 1970.

Sources of Additional Information American Bankers Assoc., 90 Park Avenue, New York, N.Y. 10016; American Society of Real Estate Counselors, 155 E. Superior St., Chicago,

Ill. 60611; Mortgage Bankers Association of America, 1125 15th St., N.W., Washington, D.C. 20006; National Association of Real Estate Boards, 155 E. Superior St., Chicago, Ill. 60611; Society of Industrial Realtors, 1300 Connecticut Avenue, N.W., Washington, D.C. 20036; United States Savings and Loan League, 221 N. LaSalle St., Chicago, Ill. 60601; Urban Land Inst., 1200 18th St., N.W., Washington, D.C. 20036.

Periodicals *The Mortgage Banker,* 1125 15th St., N.W., Washington, D.C. 20006; *National Real Estate Investor,* 461 Eighth Avenue, New York, N.Y. 10001.

FIREPLACE An incombustible compartment in which a fire may be made, located at the base of a chimney which conducts the smoke and gases of the fire vertically to the outside.

From the earliest times, fire has had a fascination for humans unlike almost any other phenomenon on earth. Ancient cultures are known to have considered fire one of the major elements of the universe, to have believed it had mystical qualities, and to have held it sacred. Although the use of fires as direct sources of light has ended in modern times and its use for cooking and heating curtailed, the mystical qualities are still present for many people. And with the shortage of fuels, other than coal and wood, people have recently turned back to fireplaces not only for their emotional qualities but for heating as well.

Types Fireplaces may be large or small and of several types. They may be very plain, almost like simple openings in walls, or highly ornamented. Fireplaces may be specifically designed for the buildings into which they will go or they may be obtained prefabricated. Those specifically designed for individual buildings are ordinarily constructed of brick or concrete block, but sometimes of concrete or stone. Prefabricated types are usually made of steel or cast iron.

Fireplaces may be attached to walls or freestanding. Those attached to walls may project into rooms or be situated so that their faces are flush with the walls. Projecting types may be open only on their fronts or on the fronts and one or both sides. Freestanding fireplaces may have openings of the same kinds or on all four sides.

Components The usual types of fireplaces have a number of parts in addition to the fire chamber, the space in which the burning of wood or other fuels is accomplished. Above this space is a narrowed opening called the throat, in which a steel or cast-iron device, called a damper, may be placed to control the flow of smoke from the fireplace and to allow the chimney to be closed off when not in use. Above the damper is a larger space, called a smoke chamber or shelf, which helps prevent downdrafts into the fireplace and helps establish updrafts. Above is the chimney, generally of masonry, which is lined with flue liners, usually of clay tile or asbestos-cement but sometimes of double-walled metal, to form a stack up which smoke and gases rise. At the top of the chimney, clay tile chimney pots may project or openings may be made at the sides for smoke and gases to escape, with a hood over the top to help prevent down-

FIREPLACE Choate Road Dormitory (1959), Dartmouth College, Hanover, N.H. [*Architects: Campbell and Aldrich. (Joseph W. Molitor)*]

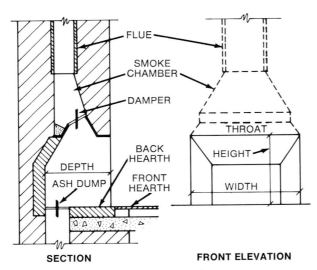

SECTION   **FRONT ELEVATION**

FIREPLACE Section and elevation of typical masonry type.

drafts and precipitation from entering the chimney.

The walls of the fire chamber are finished with materials that resist heat, usually firebrick but sometimes soapstone or other materials. Fireplaces can also be built around prefabricated liners or fireboxes of steel or iron that ensure the proper shapes and dimensions and are equipped with dampers and smoke chambers. Such prefabricated types may also be obtained with grilles that allow cold air near the floor in a room to flow past the firebox, where it is heated and then discharged into the interior of the room from high grilles.

The bottoms inside fireplaces or back hearths are usually covered with heat-resistant materials, such as firebrick, and in front of the fireplaces, other fire-resistant materials, such as clay tile or stone, form front hearths. The face of a fireplace around the opening, the surround, may be finished with any of a number of materials, including ceramic tile, marble or other stone, and wood. If wood is used, it must be held back from the sides and top of the opening for fire safety.

The complete surround of a fireplace is called a mantelpiece, and may include a shelf above the opening, called a mantel shelf or simply mantel. A hole in the back hearth may be provided for an ash dump and covered with a cast-iron, pivoted door to allow ashes to be dropped to a basement or the bottom of the chimney, where they may be removed periodically. Fireplaces usually have devices called andirons placed inside, upon which logs may rest, or grates, into which coal or coke may be placed. For safety from flying sparks, they are often furnished with fire screens, usually of metal mesh that may be pulled to the side like curtains but sometimes of special glass made like doors.

Design For the fireplace to operate or draw properly, it must be designed properly. This means that the fire chamber, smoke chamber, flues, and so on must be in the proper sizes, in relationship to each other and to the whole fireplace, and in the proper shapes. Proper design of a fireplace starts with its opening, for which there are definite ratios of heights to widths. Depths should not be less than half the height of the opening and should not, except in very special cases, exceed 2 ft. For best radiation and for control of fires, smoke, and gases, the side walls should slant inward from front to back; back walls should be vertical to a certain point, then slant toward the front. In very large fireplaces, hoods are often used to decrease the effective openings or hearths may be raised for the same purpose. Both methods may be used purely for design reasons.

Flue sizes are directly related to fire chamber sizes and usually have an area of 10 percent of the fireplace opening. The throat should have an area equal to or larger than that of the flue; if the throat is too small, a fireplace may smoke or if too large, will waste heat. Similarly, certain dimensions and shapes are proper for smoke chambers. To draw properly, chimneys should rise to a point at least 2 ft above the peaks of pitched roofs and 3 ft above flat ones. More than one fireplace may use a single chimney, but building codes require each to have a separate flue. Other code requirements apply to the design and construction of fireplaces and should be consulted. Proper dimensions for various sizes and types of fireplaces and their individual components are available from a number of sources and should be strictly followed.

If the established principles for their proper design and the code requirements are followed, fireplaces of many kinds can be useful, enjoyable, and important features of architecture. In addition to those specifically designed for individual buildings, some of the prefabricated types, available in several shapes and sizes, can be obtained complete with necessary accessories and with flue and chimney hood systems.

While fireplaces can be counted upon today to furnish some amount of heat in buildings, they are not really very efficient. Of all the types, the most efficient are those constructed with prefabricated liners or fireboxes with grilles; and certain prefabricated free-standing types, with openings generally on only one side. Various stoves available today, many of them based on the principles of the Franklin stove, are quite efficient. The less efficient fireplaces are generally those with more than one side open and the least efficient, the type with all sides open.

History The time of the first use of fire by humans is unknown. Evidence of its use has been found in all ancient cultures discovered so far. At first fires were used only out of doors, but later, it is not known when, fires were brought indoors for light, cooking, and warmth. The first fireplaces were very primitive, consisting of a shallow hole scooped out of the ground and lined with stones or clay. There was no chimney; smoke simply rose through a hole in top of the hut or tent. For safety, such hearths were usually located in the centers of huts and tents. Wood was often burned, though coal is known to have been used as a fuel from very early times.

By the time, beginning about 3000 B.C., of the great civilizations around the Mediterranean Sea, braziers of stone and metal, with pierced sides and legs, had been developed. Charcoal was often burned in them. This practice has continued until today in certain parts of the world.

In masonry buildings, hearths were sometimes placed adjacent to walls, though the central type was still used. Instead of holes in roofs, rudimentary exposed flues were used to exhaust the smoke. Andirons were developed, not only for holding logs but for supporting cooking pots; later grates were developed, along with tongs and bellows for starting fires and keeping them burning. Gradually, fireplaces that were partly enclosed, resembling to some extent those of today, were developed along with chimneys and flues.

By the time of the Romans, fireplaces were in general use. However, the Romans, dissatisfied with such a rudimentary heating system, developed the first central heating system, called a hypocaust. During the Middle Ages, in Gothic buildings, the idea of central heating was not pursued. Many buildings, including the great cathedrals, were not heated at all. In other buildings, heating was primitive, consisting of wood-burning, open hearths in the centers of rooms with louvered holes in the roofs to let out smoke. By the 13th century, fireplaces were sometimes placed against walls and furnished with flues, chimneys, and sometimes hoods. Coal was once again used as a fuel. But the older practices persisted in some places until the 16th century. Fireplaces were placed only in the most important rooms. Some Gothic buildings had ornamented fireplaces, often with arches over their openings, and were quite large.

During the early Renaissance, fireplaces, complete with chimneys, developed into the types known today. The custom was to provide a fireplace in every room, including bedrooms, rather than only in the most important rooms as in the past. As they did with other architectural elements, the architects of the Renaissance ornamented the fireplaces and often the chimneys. Some of the designs were quite elaborate. They also put ornamental firebacks of cast iron in fireplaces to protect the masonry from heat. Fireplace openings gradually became smaller than those of the Gothic period and the custom of using mantelpieces, sometimes used in the past, became common practice. Mantelpieces were often of fine wood, marble, or other stone. In the 17th century, the first stoves for heating the interiors of buildings were developed in Northern Europe, particularly in the Scandinavian countries. Stoves thus began to replace fireplaces to some extent.

American Development In early colonial America, rudimentary fireplaces, of the types then in use in Europe, were the first devices for cooking and heating. Later, fireplaces became important architectural elements of American buildings, and gradually became more efficient. About the beginning of the 18th century, stoves for heating appeared and these were also gradually made more efficient. In 1740 the master of all trades, Benjamin Franklin (1706–90), invented a very efficient type that came to be called the Franklin stove. Widely copied and emulated, Franklin's invention was never patented by him. Stoves of this sort, in which coal or wood may be burned, are still available and used today. Other types of stoves and heaters were developed later, including gas and electric types.

Beginning in the 19th century and continuing during the 20th until the present time, central heating systems were developed and continuously improved, originally steam and hot-water, followed by hot-air and other types. By the beginning of the 20th century, the end of fireplaces and stoves as the prime sources of heating for most buildings was in sight. Today major buildings and many others are completely heated, and often air-conditioned, by central systems. Fireplaces have become mainly ornamental and emotional, it might even be said sentimental, vestiges of the past. Regrettably, in terms of architectural honesty and excellence, some fireplaces today hold only fake logs with gas fires issuing from them and some hold no fires at all, only electric lights that glow. With the fuel shortages of the fourth quarter of the 20th century, fireplaces and stoves of improved types, including some newer ones from Scandinavia, have made something of a comeback.

Related Articles DESIGN, ARCHITECTURAL; ENERGY; HEATING, VENTILATING, AND AIR CONDITIONING.

FIRE PROTECTION The use of devices, systems, and materials for the prevention of fires, warnings when fires occur, and saving property and life in fires. The major considerations in building design for fire safety consists of provision of fire-resistant materials and construction, provisions for fire detection and alarms, provisions for escape or refuge from fires, and provisions for bringing fires under control. Fires are sometimes caused by lightning or earthquakes; for further discussion, see articles entitled earthquake protection; lightning protection. Because of dangers to life and property in fires and because of the huge losses of both each year, architects and other environmental designers must give serious consideration to fire protection in buildings. Detailed requirements for fire protection are contained in applicable building, fire, and other codes and regulations.

Ignition Point Various materials ignite at different temperatures; paper, for example, at about 450°F and wood at about 500°F. Fires in buildings move rapidly upward, through convection, carried by the motion of air. Fires spread more slowly horizontally. Fires can also spread by conduction, transfer of heat through solid materials, in particular metals; or by radiation, transfer by waves. Temperatures in fires may reach 1000°F or higher very quickly, igniting combustible materials at considerable distances away. Humans can only withstand temperatures of 250°F for some 15 minutes and 350°F for about 30 seconds. In spite of the inherent danger of such levels of heat, most deaths in fires result from inhalation of toxic gases and smoke.

The rate of burning of fires is controlled by two major factors: the ventilation available and the fuel load, the presence of combustible materials. If ventilation is poor, as in a closed room, and the fuel load is high, the rate of burning will be slow and the fire prolonged. If the opposite is true, as in a room with ample ventilation and a small fuel load, the rate of burning will be fast and the fire of short duration. In any fire, there is danger of flashover, the almost instantaneous ignition of all or most combustible materials in a room when air temperatues near the ceiling reach 800°F or more.

Code Requirements Certain factors must be taken into consideration in the proper design of buildings for fire protection. One is called the fire load, a measure of the amount of combustible materials in various types of buildings. A given fire load is the fuel contribution of the combustibles in a building converted to that of a certain number of pounds of wood per square foot (psf) of floor area. Fire loads are specified in fire, building, and other codes, and range from about 8 psf in an apartment to 36 psf in library bookstacks up to 50 psf in clothes closets and to 86 psf in file rooms.

Codes also require buildings of certain types and in certain locations to have specific levels of fire resistance. The usual classifications of fire resistance in buildings include fire resistive, with three to four hour rating for primary structures, two to three hours for secondary structural members and partitions around stairways and other vertical openings and incombustible materials elsewhere; noncombustible, with fire-resistive bearing walls, floors, and roofs; heavy timber; protected combustible, with incombustible exterior walls; and unprotected combustible, or wood frame. The fire rating requirements vary considerably between building types and between various components of each type, from four hours resistance down to none.

Fire requirements also limit the allowable heights of buildings. No limit, for fire reasons, is placed on fire-resistive construction for any type of building. Typical restrictions on other classifications are noncombustible, three stories for residential buildings, two for other types; protected combustible, four stories for residential and commercial buildings, three for factories, and two for educational buildings; heavy timber, three stories for residential, commercial, and industrial buildings, and two for educational. In some cases, restrictions are also placed on the actual heights of buildings in feet. Restrictions are also made on allowable floor areas of buildings of various types, except for fire-resistive construction upon which there is no limit. Typical limits for other types of construction include 13,200 ft² for noncombustible, 10,000 for protected combustible, and 8,800 for heavy timber residential and educational buildings. Applicable codes contain the exact requirements for various classifications of construction.

Fire, building, and other codes also contain other requirements for fire protection of buildings. For example, fire-resistive construction is the most usual requirement in central city areas, while lesser classifications are generally allowed in less congested areas, in which exposures are not considered as dangerous. Fire walls, with no openings and extending several feet above roofs, are often required between apartment units that may otherwise be of unprotected combustible construction. Tall buildings, in general, must be sealed to fire at every story and have automatic, electric motor-driven fire-resistive covers for escalators. Vertical shafts must be enclosed in fire-resistive construction. Often provisions for smoke shafts or other means for venting smoke and gases to the outside must be provided. Careful attention must be paid to electrical wiring and devices to prevent the possibility of fires originated by overloading or other malfunctions. Automatic dampers are required in heating and air-conditioning ductwork in many cases. Other important considerations are also necessary for the prevention of fires in buildings.

One of the most important considerations requires that structural components must be protected from damage from fire, which might cause them to fail. The most important methods, often used for fire-protection purposes with structural steel, involve covering the steel with prescribed thicknesses of materials, such as gypsum or other types of plaster, mineral wool, gypsum board, concrete, or other fire-resistive materials. Such materials may also be used for protecting walls, partitions, and other building components. Reinforced concrete, properly designed, is highly fire-resistive, as are brick, concrete block, and other masonry materials. Recently, the columns of some buildings have been fire-protected by water which transmits heat to a storage tank, to be vented to the outside as steam.

Detectors The detection of fires in buildings is usually accomplished with heat or smoke detectors. Several types are available for detection of various kinds of fires, including those that smolder or flame up, flash fires, and so on. In order to be effective, the proper types must be selected, must be located properly and in sufficient numbers, and must be properly maintained. Heat and smoke detectors may sound alarms or warnings of fires either directly from the units or through wiring to various locations in buildings. Manual alarms are also widely used in buildings. These require a person who discovers a fire to open an alarm box or break its glass cover and pull a handle. Such alarms may be uncoded, simply sounding warnings, or coded, to indicate where fires are located. Both types should be placed in obvious locations in plain view of building occupants.

Exit Routes Once a fire alarm has sounded, the most important aspect of human safety is the availability of safe escape or egress routes or refuges. Fire, building, and other codes specify requirements for egress and refuge. Such requirements include escape routes that are direct, unimpeded, wide enough, not too far away, and no too long. Maximum limits for travel distances to exits vary according to building types and whether or not buildings have sprinkler systems. For example, buildings with sprinklers may have the following maximum travel distances: hotels, dormitories, apartments, commercial and industrial buildings, 150 ft; most educational and assembly buildings, 200 ft; office buildings, 300 ft. Without sprinklers, these travel distances are reduced by 50 ft, except for office buildings which are reduced by 100 ft.

Exit route minimum widths are often taken to be 3 ft. The number of exits required depends on the number of people per amount of floor area, or occupant density, of various building types. Assumed occupant densities range from 15 ft² per person in assembly rooms with fixed seats, to 20 in classrooms, 30 to 60 in commercial buildings, 100 in office buildings and factories, and 200 in residential buildings. The capacity of an exit is the number of people who can pass through one unit of exit, defined as 22 in wide, in 1 minute. Exit capacities vary in different building types, from 30 people per unit of exit width in sleeping areas of institutions such as hospitals, 60 in residential buildings, to 100 in most other types.

For stairs used as exits, the exit capacities are lower, 22 people per exit unit in sleeping rooms of hospitals and other institutions, 45 in residential buildings, and 60 to 75 in most other types. To determine the required exit widths, the total area of a floor of a building is divided by the density and the exit capacity. For example, a factory with 30,000 ft² on a floor, divided by a density of 100 and by a capacity of 100 for horizontal exits, would require three exit units, totaling 66 in. For stairways, the factory would require 5 units, or 110 in.

In addition to exit width requirements, codes require fire doors of fire-resistive construction, self-closing, equipped with horizontal bars, called panic hardware, which open the doors when people press against them. Minimum stair widths, often 44 in, are required, along with approved types of handrails. Multistory buildings must have certain minimum number of stairs, protected by fire-resistive materials, extending the full heights of the buildings. Such enclosures must also be smokeproof and may be pressurized to accomplish this. Approved types of illuminated exit signs must be provided. In some cases, certain areas of buildings may be designed as safe refuge areas to which people may move until they can escape from the buildings. It is possible to enclose elevators in safe areas and pressurize them for limited use during fires by invalids or other incapacitated people and by fire fighters. A minimum of two exits should be provided on every floor leading to safe exit routes. Corridors should not dead-end, creating traps for smoke and for building occupants.

Control Systems A number of considerations are related to the control and extinguishing of fires in buildings. Sprinkler systems that automatically release water to extinguish fires are required in certain types of buildings and in spaces in other buildings in which high risks of fire exist. Standpipes are often provided in buildings for use by people fighting fires. A dry standpipe system is one which includes piping that usually does not contain water. Fire fighters attach hoses to the systems inside buildings and receive water, pumped by fire trucks, from hydrants on the ground level. Some of these systems are actually dry until used, while others are primed with water that is not under pressure until pumps are attached. Wet standpipe systems contain water under pressure at all times, from storage tanks located on the roof or upper floors of buildings. Water from these is available at all times to building occupants as well as to fire fighters. Sometimes wet and dry systems are used in combination. And often hose cabinets, with hoses ready to be used, are located in the corridors of buildings with wet or combination systems.

In addition, fire extinguishers of various types are often provided in buildings. Fire extinguishers are classified by the types of fires they are designed to extinguish. The A type is for ordinary combustibles, such as wood and paper; the B type for flammable liquids, such as gasoline; the C type for electrical fires; the D type for combustible metals, such as magnesium. Labels on extinguishers indicate their type and care should be taken to use each type properly. For example, an A type used on a gasoline fire will not extinguish it but may cause it to burn or spread more rapidly. On the other hand, an ABC type may be used on gasoline fires as well as ordinary combustible materials and flammable liquids. Fire extinguisher charges last from a few seconds up to about a minute and a half.

In architecture, it is also important for provisions to be made for the professional fire fighters. Adequate space should be provided on building sites for fire trucks and other equipment; an adequate number of hydrants, properly located, should be provided. Windowless buildings present great problems to fire fighters. When more than two stories high or with more than certain prescribed floor areas, windowless buildings must be sprinklered. In addition, access openings for use in fire fighting should be provided on each side of windowless buildings facing streets or other public areas on every floor.

Fire protection of buildings is one of the most important technical considerations in design and construction. While fire, building, and other codes specify certain requirements, architects and other environmental designers often consult experts and organizations that have the experience and knowledge to aid in the design of buildings that will be as fire safe as possible. Such organizations and many of the individual experts are engaged in continuing research and testing to determine improved methods for fire safety. Advantage should be taken of their continuing important work on such matters.

History The threat of fire has always existed in architectural structures. In the earliest primitive huts and tents, the use of fires inside undoubtedly often led to their destruction. Lightning took its toll. The earliest primitive wooden buildings have all been destroyed by fires, weather, insects, and other disasters.

In the buildings of the ancient civilizations in Mesopotamia, Egypt, Crete, and Greece, no particular precautions against fire seem to have been taken, partly because masonry was the major material used. The Romans were much more conscious of the threat of fire to their buildings, which were very close together in towns and cities. During the first century A.D., after several bad fires, regulations restricted the heights of buildings, prohibited party walls between buildings, required use of fire-resistant materials, restricted use of timber, and required flat roofs from which fires could be fought. The Romans also placed roads through cities to act as firebreaks and to provide access to fires, and they established a well-equipped fire-fighting corps. In addition, the Romans had adequate sources of water for fire fighting, available from aqueducts and other systems.

During the Middle Ages and the Renaissance, fires were frequent and were not controlled or extinguished as efficiently as they had been in Roman times. Streets were often narrow and crooked, making access to fires difficult. Roof structures were often of timber, easily ignited by lightning. Water supplies

were inadequate. And fire fighters were less well trained and equipped. During both periods, disastrous fires occurred in many parts of Europe. One of the worst was the Great Fire of London in 1666, which lasted four days and virtually destroyed the city.

As a result of the Great Fire, regulations for buildings were formulated in the London Building Act of 1667, prohibiting timber-framed houses, setting minimum thickness for walls, and requiring nonflammable roof coverings. In 1680 the first fire insurance company was founded and since there were no public fire fighters, the company organized its own. The fire fighters fought only the fires in insured buildings. Later other private fire-fighter companies were formed and this continued to be the practice in early colonial America.

Starting in the 18th century, with the advent of iron-framed buildings, methods for making structures fire resistant, or fireproof, as it was called then, were developed. At first earthenware pots were used but later most utilized bricks, hollow-tile or terra-cotta units to enclose structural members. In some cases, plaster was used, and sometimes brick arches were used to form floors and roofs between the iron girders.

U.S. Fire Disasters Many disastrous fires have occurred in America since the time of the first colonization. Among the worst were the fire in New York City in 1835, which destroyed some 500 buildings; the great Chicago fire of 1871, traditionally started by Mrs. O'Leary's cow, which destroyed the city and took 250 lives; and in the same year, a forest fire near Peshtigo, Wis., which destroyed several small towns and took 1,182 lives. In 1876 fire in a theater in Brooklyn, N.Y., claimed 295 lives; and in 1903 another in the Iroquois Theater, Chicago, 602 lives were lost. In 1904 a large portion of Baltimore burned, but no lives were lost.

U.S. Fire Codes In 1905 the first model fire code was produced by the National Board of Fire Underwriters, now known as the American Insurance Association, and the code was subsequently adopted by many cities and towns. In spite of the requirements of this code and others that followed it, disastrous fires have continued to occur, including that in 1942 in the Coconut Grove Club, Boston, in which 491 people died, only about a week after it had been approved in a fire inspection. In spite of increasingly stringent code and other requirements for building construction, destructive fires continue to occur with regularity, including that of the Beverly Hills Supper Club, Southgate, Ky., which took 164 lives in 1977. In the recent past, some 1 million fires, causing over $3 billion in property losses, have occurred each year.

Gradually over the years, more reliable information on fires, how they start, how they spread, how they are fueled, and so on, has been developed through research and testing. Building, fire, and other codes and standards have been improved. Fire detection devices and fire-fighting equipment and techniques have also been vastly improved. Today rigid requirements for fire resistance in buildings are contained in building, fire, and other codes and standards, as are requirements for fire detection, fire fighting, and evacuation of people from buildings.

Because of the great frequency of fires in buildings and the devastating toll they take in human lives and property damage each year, provision of proper fire protection in buildings is one of the major concerns of architects and other environmental designers.

Related Articles BUILDING CODES AND STANDARDS; COMMUNICATION SYSTEM; EARTHQUAKE PROTECTION; LIGHTNING PROTECTION; Articles on various building components and systems.

Further Reading Egan, M. David: *Concepts in Building Firesafety,* John Wiley, New York, 1978; Prztak, Louis: *Standard Details for Fire Resistive Building Construction,* McGraw-Hill, New York, 1977.

Sources of Additional Imformation American Insurance Assoc., 85 John St., New York, N.Y. 10038; American Society for Testing and Materials, 1916 Race St., Philadelphia, Pa. 19103; National Fire Protection Assoc., 470 Atlantic Ave., Boston, Mass. 02210; Underwriters Laboratories, 333 Pfingsten Rd., Northbrook, Ill. 60062.

FLOOR The bottom surface within a building or room, usually but not always horizontal, on which furniture and other objects may be placed and people may walk. The term *floor* may be applied to the complete system, including its structure and surface material, or to the surface material only. Such surfacing materials are sometimes referred to as flooring. The word *floor* may also be used to denote the separation between stories of a building, as in a building with five floors or stories.

Materials A great variety of flooring materials are available, with many types of characteristics, useful lives, textures, colors, forms, and costs. Major materials include wood, burned-clay types, stone, terrazzo, concrete, carpeting, and resilient flooring. Flooring is usually installed on wood or concrete subfloors. For all kinds of flooring, subfloors must be properly designed and constructed.

Wood flooring comes in strips, up to 25/32 in in thickness, from 1½ to 3½ in wide; and squares, ranging in size up to about 10 by 10 in. The squares may be laminated with veneers like plywood for less costly installations or made with solid strips, often called parquet flooring, fastened together with metal splines or other devices, for more costly work. Parquet flooring in the past was often made with chevron or other patterns.

Wood flooring is available in both softwoods and hardwoods. The former are less expensive but do not wear as well. Softwoods include Douglas fir, pine, hemlock, and larch. Hardwoods include oak, beech, birch, and maple. Wood-strip flooring ordinarily is manufactured with tongues and grooves on the sides, which enable it to be attached to wood subflooring by blind nailing into the tongues, with the grooves hiding the nails. When wood subflooring is used, it is considered good practice to cover it with a felt fabric before the finished floor is laid. When wood-strip flooring is installed over concrete subfloors, small wood strips, called sleepers, to which finish flooring may be nailed are generally used. Parquet and other wood blocks are often laid in mastic or other adhesives.

Burned-clay flooring materials include ceramic tile, quarry and similar tiles, and brick. Stone flooring is mostly of marble or slate. Colors and textures are generally limited in all types except ceramic tile, which comes in many varied colors. All are available in squares or rectangles of various sizes and are laid in cement mortar. Terrazzo is a flooring material, which may be obtained in a number of colors and textures, composed of about two parts marble chips and one part portland cement. Terrazzo may be laid in sand beds, bonded to concrete toppings, or may be used as a thin topping for uncured concrete slabs. Divider strips are used in the sand-bed and bonded types. Terrazzo can also be precast. A type of flooring, much like very thin terrazzo, is sometimes installed with adhesives.

Concrete is often used for flooring, particularly in utilitarian buildings, such as factories. In such cases, the structural concrete of floors is usually finished with a thin topping of special concrete bonded to the structural concrete before it has completely cured. Carpet can be laid, with proper precautions, on almost any kind of floor or subfloor that has been properly prepared.

Among the types most often used today are resilient flooring, made from a variety of materials. Linoleum has been available the longest, from about the third quarter of the 19th century in the United States. It is composed of a thin layer of wearing surface material, made mostly of wood or cork flour in resin binders, adhered to backings of various materials. It comes in many colors and patterns and may be obtained in tiles, rolls, or sheets. With the advent of other types of resilient flooring, linoleum is no longer used to any great extent in new buildings. However, it is a flooring material that is relatively inexpensive and has fair durability; the use of linoleum on concrete slabs on or below grade is not recommended.

Other types of resilient flooring include vinyl, which comes in both sheets and tile; vinyl-asbestos tile; rubber tile; and asphalt tile; generally listed in the order of their probable useful lives, with vinyl tile the best. All can be used, if proper precautions are taken, on subfloors of all kinds, including concrete slabs or on below grade. Another flooring material is cork tile, made of raw cork granules embedded in resins. By its nature, cork tile is not as durable as some other types, but both its durability and the limits of loads to be placed on it can be improved considerably by vinyl coatings. Cork tile should not be used on slabs on or below grade.

In general, resilient tiles indent or will be damaged if loads that are too heavy are placed on them. Rubber and vinyl tile will withstand the greatest loads, followed by vinyl sheet and vinyl-coated cork tile, then by regular cork tile and linoleum, with the least amount of load allowed on asphalt and vinyl-asbestos tile. The two last-named types are generally the least expensive, followed by linoleum, with rubber, cork, and vinyl tiles the most expensive. For quietness, cork tile is the best, followed by rubber and vinyl tiles, then by linoleum and vinyl sheets, then vinyl-asbestos; and the noisiest is asphalt tile.

Other available types of flooring include a number of specialized kinds for specific uses, such as conductive flooring for use in hospital operating rooms and other places where static electricity may build up and cause explosions, and types for heavy-duty uses in places where heavy machinery or vehicles are used.

In addition to their selection for such attributes as the appearance desired, useful lives, degree of maintenance required, and costs, flooring in buildings may be designed as unobstrusive bases or backgrounds for other architectural features or may become such features themselves by the use of patterns, colors, textures, or ornamental designs, including representational as well as abstract or geometrical types. Flooring can also become the base or background for rugs or carpets, ranging from solid unobstrusive colors and weaves to ornamental or pictorial qualities found in fine rugs, such as Orientals or those by modern designers.

History No floor system was used in ancient primitive huts and tents; the ground served as both floor and flooring. Later buildings are thought to have had floors built of wood logs and branches. By about 3000 B.C., in the great civilizations around the Mediterranean Sea, floor systems of stone or brick laid on the ground and wood for upper stories had come into use. For many years, the structure of floors on the ground level was also the flooring. Wood structures of upper stories often supported wood flooring.

Later developments included the use of concrete in Mesopotamia. Made of lime, sand, and broken limestone, it was used on ground levels with waterproofing of bitumen and flooring of stone slabs. In Egypt the roofs of temples were often of cut stone, and served the additional purpose of roof terraces or floors used in ceremonies. In Crete floor structures were often rounded logs, and polished gypsum was used for flooring.

Clay tile was also an important floor material in ancient times and was used in Mesopotamia, Crete, Egypt, Greece, and Rome. However, the most important flooring material used in ancient Greece was stone, particularly marble. In addition to clay tile, the Romans used stone, wood, concrete, and mosaic, usually made by inlaying small pieces of stone into a concrete base. The Romans usually placed ground floors on bases of concrete and floors of upper stories on concrete or wood-framed structures. In Byzantine architecture elaborate mosaic floors were often used, together with flooring composed of several different colors of marble slabs.

In the Romanesque and Gothic periods of architecture, floor systems were generally of stone and wood,

as was flooring. In the Renaissance, the previously available types of floor systems and flooring were used and a new type, terrazzo, was developed.

American Development In early colonial America, floors were tamped earth inside buildings. Later, floor systems and flooring similar to the types in Europe were used. During the revival and eclectic periods in American architecture, floor designs were generally derived from periods of the past. With the beginnings of the modern movement in architecture in the 19th century came the development of skeleton-framed, steel, and reinforced concrete construction. Floor structures were constructed of those materials, using new systems. Wood-framed floor systems were important, particularly in house construction. Floor systems of these types are still used in architecture. A vast array of flooring materials are available today, including all the types used previously.

Related Articles CONCRETE STRUCTURE; FIRE PROTECTION; FOUNDATION; MASONRY STRUCTURE; STEEL STRUCTURE; WOOD-FRAME STRUCTURE; Articles on various materials.

Sources of Additional Information Asphalt and Vinyl Asbestos Tile Inst., 101 Park Ave., New York, N.Y. 10017; Carpet and Rug Inst., 310 Holiday Dr., Dalton, Ga. 30720; Ceramic Tile Inst., 700 Virgil Ave., Los Angeles, Calif, 90029; Maple Flooring Manufacturers Assoc., 424 Washington Ave., Oshkosh, Wis. 54901; National Oak Flooring Manufacturer Assoc., 814 Sterick Bldg., Memphis, Tenn. 38103; National Terrazzo and Mosaic Assoc., 2-A West Loudoun St., Leesburg, Va. 22075; Resilient Floor Covering Inst., 26 Washington St., East Orange, N.J. 07017; Tile Council of America, Princeton, N.J. 08540; Wood and Synthetic Flooring Inst., 1201 Waukegan Rd., Glenview, Ill. 60025.

FOUNDATION The lowest part of a building which supports the loads of the structure above and transmits the loads to the ground. Ordinarily, foundations today are constructed of reinforced concrete, though mass concrete without reinforcing is sometimes used for support of heavy walls, chimneys, or similar heavy loads. The term *foundation* is often taken to mean the entire substructure of a building, and may be partly concrete, brick, or stone masonry, while the lowest portion of reinforced concrete, resting directly on the soil, is called a footing.

Foundations and footings serve the primary purpose of supporting weights of buildings and other loads above them, but they also resist heaving of the earth caused by freezing and thawing. In buildings with basements, foundations also resist the sideways or lateral forces of the earth outside and are expected to protect the interior from water infiltration. See the article entitled waterproofing.

The design of foundations and footings for buildings and other structures must take into consideration several major factors: the loads to be carried, the characteristics of the soil on building sites, climate, and water conditions. The loads to be carried by foundations and footings are determined by the weights of the materials and construction used, the number of stories to be constructed, snow and wind loads, and the loads of people and furnishings. The determination of the loads of foundations and footings, and their design to carry the loads, is a function of a structural engineer. Sometimes simple types, such as those for single-family houses on soil with good load-bearing qualities, are handled by architects and other environmental designers. See articles entitled structural engineering; structure.

Soil Properties The qualities of soils on building sites are determined by the science of soil mechanics or soil engineering. Soils are the thin layer of particles of rock that cover a large portion of the land in the world. Topsoil is the uppermost, richest layer and is usually 6 in or less in thickness today. Subsoil is the next lower strata, about 2 or 3 ft deep ordinarily. Below that may be additional soil until the depth of bedrock is reached. To determine the effects of the soil on foundations and footings for a building, it is necessary to know many facts, including such things as the range of sizes of grains and their shapes, chemical makeup, and others. Of particular importance in architecture are determination of the weight or density of soil, strength of its components, cohesion of the soil, and changes that take place when forces are applied to it. Other considerations include the quantities of organic materials contained in the soil, along with quantities of such materials as limestone.

Identification of soils and their properties and characteristics is usually accomplished by borings. Building and other codes determine the minimum number of borings for a given site; and boring depths and locations must be carefully determined. Although borings were made in other ways in the past, the usual method today utilizes a device called a boring spoon, which is driven into the ground. This produces core samples of soils in layers, and establishes the resistance of the soil to forces and the depths of underground rock and water. The test samples are then analyzed in laboratories for such properties as specific gravity, grain size and shape, ratio of voids to solid matter or void ratios, water content, strength, and others. Based on such information, proper foundations and footing may be designed and constructed.

If necessary, soils may be modified by compaction or densification; by adding portland cement, sand, crushed cinders, or other materials; by rolling with machinery; by reducing the water content; and by other methods. All are intended to improve the bearing qualities of the soil. It must be noted that all soils compact to some extent, and all foundations and footings therefore settle somewhat.

Climatic Effects The climate in which foundations and footings are to be constructed is of great importance, because of the damage that can occur from alternating cycles of freezing and thawing. The bottoms of foundations and footings must therefore be extended approximately 1 ft below the frost line, the lowest level of soil that can be expected to freeze in a given location. If foundations or footings are too shallow, damage may occur to them and to the building

structures they support. In very warm places, such as southern Florida, the soil does not ordinarily freeze. For small buildings, such as single-family houses in warm locations, reinforced concrete slabs with thickened portions under bearing walls are often used. In colder areas, care must be taken to construct foundations and footings to the proper depths, which vary from about 1 in, in the lower part of the Deep South, to several feet in the upper parts of New England.

Types Several types of foundations are commonly used in architecture. The simplest, other than a thickened slab, is a spread footing. This type of footing is ordinarily of reinforced concrete, in a rectangular cross section, laid continuously in locations where bearing walls are to be erected, and usually in square shapes under columns. Spread footings must be considerably wider than the walls or columns they support. Sometimes they are constructed in stepped shapes, with wide portions at the bottoms and narrower portions above. Another relatively simple type of foundation is called a grade beam, usually reinforced concrete of rectangular section, only slightly wider than the walls supported. Basement walls are sometimes made of reinforced concrete in a manner similar to relatively tall grade beams, but for the most part, they are constructed on top of spread footings.

Other types of foundations and footings are sometimes used, including combined and strapped types. Combined footings are much like the spread footings used under columns, except that they support two or more columns, while spread footings support only one. In combined footings, care must be taken to ensure that the centers of gravity of the loads coincide with the actual centers of the footings. A strapped

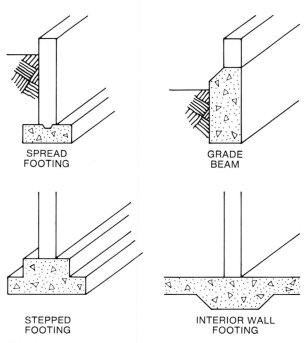

SPREAD FOOTING

GRADE BEAM

STEPPED FOOTING

INTERIOR WALL FOOTING

FOUNDATION Sections of typical types.

footing is similar to a combined type and is used to support two columns. Instead of being poured in one piece as in combined footings, strapped footings are poured under individual columns, with straps of reinforced concrete that act like beams connecting them. Strapped footings may be somewhat less expensive than combined types. Neither type can be used on sites with soils that are soft and wet, which have low load-bearing capacities.

For soft, wet soils, mat or raft foundations are often used. Much like concrete slabs, mat or raft foundations float on the soft, wet soil much like a raft or boat. They may be used for the support of entire buildings. Another method for soft, wet soil, with low load-bearing capacities, utilizes long structural members called piles or piling, driven or otherwise forced into the soil, after which foundations or footings are placed on top of them. Piles support the loads above them by frictional resistance along their lengths and by bearing on the soils near or at their lower ends. Bearing piles are driven down to bedrock or near it. Friction piles support loads by frictional resistance along their lengths and are assumed to have no bearing at their lower ends.

Piles may be made of a number of materials, including most kinds of timber; H piles; precast, plain, or reinforced concrete; and steel shells into which concrete is poured, the shells being either left in place or removed. Timber piles that remain wet at all times deteriorate very little, but alternating dry and wet cycles eventually cause failure. Timber piles that must extend above water levels are pressure-treated with creosote to preserve them.

Piles are usually driven into the ground by machines called pile-driving hammers or pile drivers, which hold the piles in position while the hammer rises and falls or is driven onto their tops. Sometimes piles are placed in the ground by using water jets or by other means. The load-carrying capacities of piles were often determined in the past by the resistance of the piles to the impact or driving forces of the hammers; when a pile had been driven to a depth in which a certain number of blows of the hammer were required to move it a certain additional distance into the ground, tables indicated its bearing capacity. This method is still used today, but actual tests by loading test piles are considered more reliable. Sometimes the bearing capacity is determined by computation.

Other methods sometimes used in foundation work include excavating the ground to various levels and then bracing the sides of the excavation with structural members of steel, wood, or concrete, to construct temporary, essentially watertight walls, called cofferdams. Structural members used for the walls are called sheeting or sheet piles. A caisson is like a cofferdam, but it is a complete structural shell that can sink by its own weight, sometimes aided by excavation. Caissons may also be placed in holes drilled with well-drilling machinery and by other methods.

The design of foundations and footings may be quite complex, and all but the simplest are usually designed by structural engineers and in the most complex situations, by specialists. Foundations and footings must be of adequate strength to carry the loads imposed on them, must provide controlled settlement, must resist displacement by heaving of the ground or other causes, and must not deteriorate or fail. Thus their design and construction is all-important in architecture, for if foundations and footings do not function properly, the other elements of buildings cannot.

History The first buildings made by humans, huts and tents, had no foundations as such. In the masonry buildings of the great civilizations around the Mediterranean Sea, foundations sometimes were used to support the weight of the walls and other construction above. The foundations of ancient Egyptian and Greek buildings were usually of stone, while those of Rome were often of concrete, though they also used stone.

During the Middle Ages, foundations were not always as strong as earlier ones. For example, some cathedrals have foundations of layers of logs, covered with weak concrete. In others, foundations were better, consisting of concrete on compacted clay, with stone above, or of wood piling. During the Renaissance, foundations were constructed along the lines of those of the Roman era, but usually of brick or stone instead of concrete. Although most were quite strong, some of these foundations proved faulty, including those of several leaning towers in Italy.

American Development During the early colonial era in America, foundations were generally of brick and sometimes of stone for more important buildings. Mats of logs were sometimes used. These continued to be the practices for most buildings until the rediscovery of concrete and steel in the 18th century, and the development of reinforced concrete in the 19th.

By the late 19th century, with the advent of the modern movement in architecture, attempts were made to predict the amount of settlements to be expected in buildings and to allow for it in their design. Foundations were often of concrete or grillages of iron rails, and usually each column of tall, skeleton-framed buildings had its own separate foundation. Piling also came into widespread use, mostly of steel or concrete, and later of steel casings into which concrete was poured. Wood piling is still used, often in installations where it will remain continuously under water.

Today, with improved engineering and testing techniques, not only for foundations but in the mechanics of soils, many types of foundations, usually of reinforced concrete or piling of various kinds, are used in architecture.

Related Articles CLIMATE; CONCRETE; CONCRETE STRUCTURE; STRUCTURAL ENGINEERING; STRUCTURE; WATERPROOFING.

Further Reading Johnson, S., and Thomas Kavanagh: *The Design of Foundations for Buildings*, McGraw-Hill, New York, 1968; Tomlinson, M. J.: *Foundation Design and Construction*, John Wiley, New York, 1975.
Source of Additional Information American Society of Civil Engineers (ASCE), 345 E. 47th St., New York, N.Y. 10017.

FOUNTAIN An ornamental feature of the landscaping of buildings, which produces a display with jets of water. The use of water in fountains and in other ways has been an important element of architecture since ancient times and remains so today. Although fountains and other displays of water were often very complex in the past, today they tend to be simpler but no less effective.

Water Elements In addition to fountains, the major ways of using water as an architectural element today include pools or ponds of various kinds, such as reflecting pools, waterfalls, and cascades. Water as an element of architecture is almost always used in conjunction with landscaping and often with sculpture. In some cases, pools or ponds and even fountains are planted with water plants to form water gardens, and often fish or other aquatic animals are part of the overall design.

In any case, water in an architectural setting seems to add something that is impossible to achieve in any other way, an almost universal esthetic experience composed of the delights of the sound and touch of the water itself or of its humidity on the skin, the motion of the water as well as its appearance. Water is essential to life and its inclusion in an architectural setting seems to bring to the human mind and emotions a sense of tranquility, repose, peace, and restfulness.

Fountains and other water elements may be conceived of as freestanding works of art or as integrated elements of buildings. The play and motion of water may be the major esthetic elements or they may be combined with landscaping or sculpture, or both, to achieve the desired effects. Special lighting may be provided to enhance the effects. Plantings in the water may or may not be a major part of the design. Water may be almost completely still, as in a reflecting pool, or may be continuously in motion, changing direction and height, from thin sprays that go high in the air in various patterns to simple cascades that flow slowly down from one rock or bowl to another. The variety that may be achieved is only limited by the imagination of designers and by the spaces and budgets available.

The sizes and complexities of water elements in architecture are extremely varied. A pond or pool, for example, may have only a few square feet of area in the garden of a small house or inside the house, or on a balcony or rooftop of an apartment building. Even in such a very small area, a fountain or cascade may be included. From such small and simple types, the scale increases to pools of great size and fountains of immense size and complexity. Landscaping and sculpture may become a part of both the modest type and the grand, elegant type.

Construction Materials For small ponds, pools, and fountains, prefabricated units, mostly of plastic, may be purchased in various sizes and shapes. Larger ponds and fountains are most often constructed of reinforced concrete, though other materials, such as brick or stone, may be used. When brick, stone, or materials other than concrete are required, they are most often used as surfacing with concrete as the structural base. Concrete is more waterproof than the other materials and need not be painted or otherwise treated. However, if plants or fish are to be introduced into a concrete pool or fountain, the material must be well seasoned to eliminate harmful lime. This is usually accomplished by filling the structure with water and letting it stand for five or more days, repeating the process several times. Then the pool or fountain is completely drained and treated with a solution of 1 part of common vinegar diluted with 10 parts of water, scrubbed with a brush, and the vinegar solution completely washed away.

For all but the simplest and smallest of pools, an overflow pipe, more than one for a large pool, should be provided along with a drainage system. If a pool is to be painted, latex or epoxy masonry paints are recommended. If plants or fish are to be introduced, a pool should be at least 2 ft in depth; if not, any depth may be used that creates the effects desired.

Aquatic Plants Pools may be informal, natural, or formal as determined for the effects desired. Planting, in and around pools, is often restricted to types of vegetation that might naturally grow there and to types hardy enough to survive the climate in which the pool is located. In concrete pools, water plants are usually encased in plastic containers or buckets which are then arranged in the water. The major types of aquatic plants are water lilies, lotus plants, bog plants, and floating plants. Water lilies are of two major types: hardy and tropical. Hardy lilies ordinarily bloom during the day, while tropicals may be either night or day bloomers. Hardy lilies may be left in ponds or pools during winter if their crowns and roots do not freeze. Tropical water lilies are very difficult to protect during cold winters and are therefore usually treated as annuals, with new ones planted each year. Tropical lilies come in a much greater variety of forms, colors, and types than hardy lilies. Lotuses make spectacular displays in water gardens and are hardy if the crowns of the plants are below the freezing depth of the water.

A great variety of bog plants are readily available for ponds and pools. They are easy to grow and for the most part, hardy. Some useful types are cattail, arrowhead, water canna, arum or sweet flag, marsh marigold, water plantain, water iris, and pickerel plants. Among floating plants, which are decorative and also oxygenate pools for fish, are duckweed, water chestnut, salvinia, water poppy, ludwigia, and water violet.

Aquatic Animals Fish and other aquatic animals,

such as salamanders, tadpoles, snails, and so forth, are often introduced into pools. Not only do they add life and color to pools but they also take in oxygen from the water giving off carbon dioxide that is beneficial to plants. Fish and other aquatic animals also fertilize plants to an extent and play a very important role in controlling insect life, particularly that of mosquito larvae in the water. The most common fish used in pools are ordinary goldfish, members of the carp family. They need little care, almost no feeding (none in a balanced pool), and may be left in the water during the winter in most parts of the United States if the ice in the pond does not get too deep. Other fish may also be used in ponds but require more care and are not as hardy as goldfish.

Recirculating Pumps For many centuries, supplying water with adequate pressure to be sprayed out of nozzles or otherwise displayed in fountains was difficult. The pressure was strictly derived from the height of the water above the fountains and could only be achieved by having water that ran down from mountains or other high places or by lifting water to heights with mechanical devices. Today water pressure in fountains is generally supplied by recirculating electrical pumps, which are relatively simple and inexpensive. The advent of the recirculating pump has put fountains within the economic reach of almost anyone who thinks them of importance in architecture.

Jets In general, flowing water descends in waterfalls or in cascades or is ejected from fountains to fall into a pool or other container. All may be powered by recirculating pumps of various sizes.

Jets for fountains may be of several types, producing straight streams of water, ribbons, droplets, or other forms. The simplest is a single jet that ejects water vertically into the air to a certain height from which it falls generally straight down if no wind is blowing. In addition, such jets may be placed so that they slant inward or outward or on diagonals; they may be placed to arch from jet sources toward other areas; or they may produce many other effects.

Multiple jets produce various effects, including tiers of water and funnel shapes, and jets may be timed to produce sprays in different sequences of heights, types, and shapes. Various amounts of turbulence and movement of the water will be produced in the pool or other container below the jets. Some plants, including certain water lilies, do not survive well if subjected to great turbulence or movement of water; many others do very well under such adverse conditions.

Design Fountains and other water elements may be designed by several kinds of professionals, including architects, landscape architects, and sculptors. Such a wide variety of forms, types, landscaping, artworks, and other factors must be considered that it is impossible to generalize about the principles of their design, except that they are similar to designs of other architectural elements. To many architects and other design professionals, the design of fountains, pools, ponds, waterfalls, cascades, and other water elements and the landscaping and the sculpture often incorporated into their design is one of the most gratifying and fulfilling aspects of architecture. And many believe that creative use of lighting, both underwater and around water elements, can produce very satisfying architectural designs.

History Water has been an important element in architecture from the earliest times. Primitive communities were often established near bodies of water; pools or ponds were introduced into the architecture of the early cultures around the Mediterranean Sea. Even in the Middle East and Egypt, with only modest amounts of annual rainfall, pools or ponds were placed in gardens to relieve the effects of the arid, hot climate. The ancient Greeks used water in conjunction with their architecture, in pools and springs over which buildings were constructed.

FOUNTAIN Downtown (1977), Wilkes-Barre, Pa. [Architects: Bohlin, Powell and Brown. (Joseph W. Molitor)]

The time of the first use of a fountain has not been established. However, the ancient Mesopotamians, Egyptians, and other cultures are known to have practiced irrigation, dam building, and piping water. They also built rudimentary machines for lifting water, the basic requirement for establishing the water pressure needed for fountains. The earliest known fountains all utilized the principle that water flowing from a high place built up pressure that would allow it to be directed into the air in sprays, jets, or in other ways to form the ornamental displays of fountains.

One of the greatest accomplishments of the Romans was their extensive water systems. For these systems, the Romans constructed many famous aqueducts but also a number of lesser known elements, such as wells, cisterns, dams, and piping or conduit systems. The most notable Roman accomplishment with water was, no doubt, the provision of adequate, reliable, safe supplies of water for drinking, public baths, irrigation, and other purposes. However, the Roman concerns with water also produced the first great era of fountain design and other architectural uses of water.

The Romans built many fountains in public areas of cities and in the courtyards and gardens of their houses. They built them everywhere, not only in Rome but in the countries they conquered. Most were powered by the pressure of the water coming down from the mountains in aqueducts, but others by lifting machinery and not a few by some natural spring or formation that allowed water to flow or fall. Many of the fountains were combined with sculpture or sculptured spouts from which the water ejected. Some Roman fountains still exist, especially in Rome. The early fountains and the great later examples of the Middle Ages and Renaissance are major elements contributing to the architectural quality of the city of Rome.

During the Middle Ages, though fountains were still important in Rome and other parts of Italy, few were constructed elsewhere in Europe. Fountain design flourished again during the Renaissance, a period when great numbers were built, including some of the most ornate and complex of all time. In Italy, fountains were built in the most insignificant little towns and in the gardens of many houses as well as in almost every public space where there was room for one. Magnificent examples were constructed on the grounds of villas.

A list of the great fountains and other architectural uses of water in Italy would be very long indeed. The greatest collection, from many eras, is to be found in Rome. However, in Tivoli, only a few miles from Rome, spectacular examples of several types are still to be seen. In Tivoli are the remains of several villas and other buildings dating from Roman times and after. The Temple of Vesta (c. 80 B.C.) still exists, as do several other buildings of the Roman era, including the Temple of the Sibyl and portions of the Villa (A.D. 124) of Emperor Hadrian (A.D. 76–138) and the Villa

d'Este (1550), designed by Pirro Ligorio (c. 1520–80).

Equally as interesting as the buildings at Tivoli are the many varied uses of water as an element of architecture. Here may be seen examples of most of the important methods of architectural uses of water, ranging from the natural beauty of a great waterfall, through the several kinds of pools in Hadrian's Villa to the complexities of sprays, cascades, pools, and other water uses at the Villa d'Este. Here may be seen water in all of its moods: the tranquility of reflecting pools, the wild rush of water downward through a rocky landscape, the spectacular displays of hundreds of jets in the several types of fountains at Villa d'Este. In addition, landscaping, sculpture, buildings, and other architectural elements are combined with water in many ways to produce a great range of total effects.

Many other great fountains and other architectural uses of water were constructed during the Renaissance and after. One of the most spectacular is the great displays of water, used in many ways, designed by the landscape gardner André Le Nôtre (1613–1700) at the Palais de Versailles (1661–1756) in France. The original part of the palace was designed by Louis Le Vau (1612–70), who joined with Le Nôtre to create another great integration of architecture, landscaping, and water at the Chateau of Vaux-le-Vicomte (1661), France. At Versailles, a great complex of various fountains, pools, landscaping, and sculpture was created by Le Nôtre. The water was made to flow by raising it to a height of 500 ft with machinery.

A great number of magnificent uses of water, including fountains, exist in many places around the world, not only in many other parts of Europe but in Egypt and the Middle East, India, China, and Japan.

American Development In colonial America, fountains were not important elements of architecture, partly because of the utilitarian nature of the early buildings and partly because of the mechanical difficulties of raising water to heights from which it could descend to jet or cascade in fountains and other elements. By the end of the 18th century or the beginning of the 19th, the construction of great fountains and other water elements in architecture, with only a few exceptions, had come virtually to an end in Europe, with the end of building immense palaces, villas, and public buildings. With the beginning of the modern movement in architecture in the late 19th century, ornaments of all kinds, including fountains and other water elements, were gradually almost completely excluded from building designs.

During the 20th century, interest in ornamental features of architecture has been revived to an extent and with the advent of relatively inexpensive electric recirculating pumps, the technical problems of providing water pressure have been almost eliminated. Fountains and other water elements of architectural design are often relatively simple and modest in scale today, when compared to some of the most spectacular examples of past eras. On the other hand, many contemporary examples are delightful additions to

FOUNTAIN   Pool, IBM Building (1975), Mount Pleasant, N.Y. [*Architect: Edward L. Barnes. (Joseph W. Molitor)*]

FOUNTAIN   Constitution Plaza (1964), Hartford, Conn. [*Architect: Charles DuBose. Landscape architects: Sasaki, Dawson and DeMay. (Joseph W. Molitor)*]

the architecture, not only in great public spaces but in commercial buildings and even in the gardens of modest houses. Many examples today are combined with landscaping and many, with sculptural elements.

A list of notable examples in the United States would be too long for the space available, but a few should be mentioned to give some indication of the various types and locations. These might include the sculptured fountains by the Swedish sculptor Carl Milles (1875–1955) at the Cranbrook schools, Mich., designed in the 1930s by Eliel Saarinen (1873–1950); the Kaufmann House (1937), Bear Run, Pa., designed by Frank Lloyd Wright (1869–1959) and called Falling Water for the waterfall over which it was built; the various pools and fountains at the Lincoln Center for the Performing Arts (1968), some with sculptures by the English sculptor Henry Moore (1898–   ); and Lovejoy Plaza (1966), Portland, Ore., a fountain made for walking in, climbing on, and bathing as well as esthetic enjoyment, designed by landscape architect Lawrence Halprin (1916–   ). Many other excellent examples of fountains and other water elements of architecture are located in many places in the United States.

Related Articles ART IN ARCHITECTURE; DESIGN, ARCHITECTURAL; GARDEN; LANDSCAPE ARCHITECTURE; MONUMENT; ORNAMENT.

Further Reading Bishop, Minor L., ed.: *Fountains in Contemporary Architecture*, the American Federation of Arts, New York, 1965; Jellicoe, Susan, and Geoffrey Jellicoe: *Water—The Use of Water in Landscape Architecture*, St. Martin's Press, New York, 1971; Kramer, Jack: *Water Gardening—Pools, Fountains and Plants*, Charles Scribner's Sons, New York, 1971.

Sources of Additional Information American Federation of Arts, 41 E. 65th St., New York, N.Y. 10021; American Society of Landscape Architects, 1750 Old Meadow Rd., McLean, Va. 22101; National Sculpture Society, 75 Rockefeller Plaza, New York, N.Y. 10019.

FULLER, RICHARD BUCKMINSTER

FULLER, RICHARD BUCKMINSTER American architect, engineer, philosopher, and inventor (1895–   ). Almost impossible to categorize, Richard Buckminster Fuller has had a very full and rewarding career. His inventions have challenged the imagination of people; his philosophies have stirred their minds; his books, articles, and lectures have brought his ideas to a great many, making them question the world in which they live and the way they live in it. Largely self-educated, having never finished college, Fuller has obtained a view of nature, the universe, and the minds of human beings unequaled in its time for its universality and scope.

Superactive all his life, he has been some distance ahead of his contemporaries for a long time. He has managed to influence architecture and the world in which it exists in a way that is unique. Fuller has never been an architect or an architectural designer, in the usual sense. His concerns have always been larger than life. His view encompasses all that is around him: physical, mental, and emotional. His domain is everywhere and he is deeply concerned with everything.

FULLER, RICHARD BUCKMINSTER 4-D House Model (1927; full size house never built). *(Buckminster Fuller Archives)*

FULLER, RICHARD BUCKMINSTER Dymaxion House (1946), Wichita, Kans. *(Buckminster Fuller Archives)*

Out of all this comes an architecture of invention that foresees the future in ways that are sometimes tangible, sometimes not. His designs have deeply affected architecture and architects. And some, such as his geodesic domes, have affected people everywhere.

Inventions The story of Fuller's architecture is in his inventions, primarily, rather than in individual buildings. The first important invention was the Dymaxion House, designed in 1927 in an attempt to adapt house construction to mass production in factories. Supported on a central mast and engineered like an airplane, the house was to be completely prefabricated, even to its bathroom and all its equipment. Fuller experimented with the design of these houses, gradually perfecting his ideas, for many years. The culmination was the construction of a prototype model in the Beech Aircraft Plant at Wichita, Kans., in 1945–46. The houses were to cost about

FULLER, RICHARD BUCKMINSTER U.S. Pavilion (1967), Expo '67, World's Fair, Montreal, Canada. [*Architects: Fuller & Sadao. Architects of exhibition: Cambridge Seven. (Joseph W. Molitor)*]

$3,700 complete, when the plant had gone into full production. Orders for almost 4,000 houses were received, but the financing of the project was never worked out and the houses never produced. Fuller produced other inventions, such as a Dymaxion car (1934), based on the principles of aircraft design, and new world maps with minimal distortion.

Geodesic Domes Starting in 1952, Fuller began to develop what he called geodesic domes. He utilized tetrahedrons, geometrical forms with four triangular faces, combining them into icosahedrons, which have

20 faces, and connecting them together so that they formed domes that closely resembled portions of spheres. He found that light, strong dome structures could be constructed in this way with relatively small pieces of aluminum or other materials. The domes could then be waterproofed with plastic, fiberglass, or other light materials.

One of the first domes was placed on the Rotunda Building (1953) of the Ford Motor Company, Dearborn, Mich. In 1954 others were designed as mobile shelters for the U.S. Marine Corps and were so light they could be transported by helicopters. Some were used to house radar installations, beginning in 1956. Still later, geodesic domes were constructed, often by unskilled workers including college students, all over the country, in every imaginable material, for example, aluminum, steel, wood, folded cardboard, and even bamboo.

Some notable uses of geodesic domes have been the Union Tank Car Plant (1958), Alsen, La., then the largest clear span (384 feet) in the world; the Climatron (1961; see illustrations in article botanical garden) in the Missouri Botanical Gardens, St. Louis, designed by Joseph D. Murphy (1907–) and Eugene J. Mackey (1911–68); and the U.S. Pavilion (1967) at Expo 1967, the World's Fair, Montreal, Canada.

Buckminster Fuller placed his domes on many other buildings in many different locations. They have become a part of the landscape and something of a symbol of an inventive phase of American architecture.

Life Buckminster Fuller was born on July 12, 1895, in Milton, Mass., the son of a merchant. As a boy, he was interested in boats and boatbuilding, but not in formal education. After attending the Milton Academy from 1904 to 1913, he entered Harvard University, stayed two years, and was dismissed in 1915.

Fuller went to Canada where he worked for a while for a machine fitter, then returned to Harvard where he was again dismissed. Except for a short course at the U.S. Naval Academy, Annapolis, Md., while he was in the U.S. Navy, 1917–19, he never again had any formal education. He thoroughly enjoyed his navy experience, learned a lot, made several inventions (harbingers of things to come), and rose to the rank of lieutenant.

In 1917 Fuller married Anne Hewlett and they had two daughters; the oldest died when she was five. Fuller's father-in-law was James Monroe Hewlett (1869–1941), an accomplished architect, mural painter, and stage designer. After several years in various jobs, none of them related to architecture, in 1922 with his father-in-law, Fuller started a firm to develop and manufacture a new fibrous concrete block that Hewlett had invented. In 1927 they lost financial control of the company and Fuller started another company, called 4-D, in Chicago and embarked on his long and varied career.

His first venture was the design of the Dymaxion House in 1927, though this name was not used until 1929, which he later worked on for more than 15 years. After working on mass-produced bathrooms for the Pierce Foundation for a year, he founded the Dymaxion Corporation in 1932. He founded a number of companies, all with exotic names he invented or adapted: Dymaxion Dwelling Machines (1944–46); Synergetics, Inc. (1955–59); Geodesics, Inc.; Plydomes, Inc.; and Tetrahelix Corp.

The inventions poured from him all these years and the companies were founded to develop, manufacture, and market them. Concurrently, Fuller kept a schedule that would have been impossible for a lesser man. He wrote numerous articles and books on many subjects, all related to his Promethean views of the universe, its present state, and what it might become. He lectured whenever there was an audience. When scheduled for an hour, he often took three or five and sometimes ended in the early hours of the morning. Never fond of education as he found it, he nevertheless accepted visiting professorships and lectureships at universities and colleges all over the world, even one at Harvard in poetry. He served as consultant, researcher, board member, or in other capacities for many companies, agencies, and organizations.

In 1959 he moved to Carbondale, Ill., to become professor of generalized design science exploration at Southern Illinois University, a position he held until 1974. Characteristically, he built a house there in 1960 for himself, using a new wood frame and plywood dome he invented and which later was mass produced. Later, he moved to Philadelphia.

Fuller has always been an enigma to the architectural profession and the world at large. Architects have been intrigued by him and his inventions and ideas, but they have been puzzled by the question of whether to accept him as a fellow architect. And in truth, he never has been an architect in the usual sense. He is unique. Misunderstood he might be, but his work and ideas have challenged the minds of people, including architects, for many years. And he always seemed to keep on coming up with new ideas. In spite of his opposition to formal education in his youth, he has been the recipient of a large number of honors, including more than 25 honorary doctor's degrees and election to the American Academy of Arts and Sciences and the National Institute of Arts and Letters.

In accordance with the ambivalent nature of Buckminster Fuller's relationships with the architectural profession, a strange series of events has taken place over the years. In 1959 the American Institute of Architects (AIA) elected him an honorary member, a category reserved for nonarchitects. In 1963 it gave him its Allied Professions Medal, for nonarchitects. In 1970, while he was still an honorary member, the AIA gave him its highest honor, the Gold Medal, reserved only for architects, though Fuller was still not eligible for registration or licensing as an architect or for regular membership in the AIA. Fuller later became eligible, having received his registration, became a member, and in 1975, at age eighty, was elected a fellow of the AIA. In Europe he had been recognized earlier, in 1968, with the Royal Gold Medal of the Royal Institute of British Architects.

Whatever he might be called, Buckminster Fuller is certainly a great man of his time and one who may have seen the future. He deserves to be called architect as well as futurist, engineer, inventor, writer, and philosopher.

Related Articles. CONTEMPORARY ARCHITECTURE; DOME; EDUCATION; MODERN ARCHITECTURE; PREFABRICATION.

Further Reading Fuller, R. Buckminister: *Education Automation*, Southern Illinois Press, Carbondale, 1962; idem: *Ideas and Integrities*, Prentice-Hall, New York, 1963; idem: *Nine Chains to the Moon*, Lippincott, New York, 1938; idem: *No More Second Hand God*, Southern Illinois University Press, 1962; idem: *Operating Manual for Spaceship Earth*, Southern Illinois University Press, 1968; idem: *Utopia or Oblivion*, Overlook Press, New York, 1973; Marks, Robert W.: *The Dymaxion World of Buckminster Fuller*, Reinhold, N.Y., 1960; McHale, John: *R. Buckminster Fuller*, Braziller, New York, 1962.

FURNESS, FRANK American architect (1839–1912). Designer of over 300 buildings, most of them in or around Philadelphia, Frank Furness was the victim of circumstances beyond his control. He established an office in Philadelphia, his home city, that soon became successful. An eclectic designer, he worked most often in the Gothic-derived style of the Victorian era. As times and tastes changed, he was unable to change with them. During his last years, everything went into decline for him, his reputation as an architect and as a person, and the commissions became fewer and fewer until they almost stopped. He died, almost forgotten, and at least half of his buildings have now been demolished.

Furness left his mark on architecture, as a talented and inventive designer, in his important buildings that have survived, and his reputation has been restored beginning in the middle of the 20th century. His first building was a church that has now been demolished, as has almost every other structure he did in his first 10 years of practice. Most of those remaining have been radically altered. Fortunately, one of his best of that time has been preserved, the Pennsylvania Academy of Fine Arts (1876; see color section), Philadelphia. It is Victorian and highly ornamented.

Works Furness designed several types of buildings, but perhaps was most recognized for his churches, banks, and houses. A number of these buildings have survived, including the interesting church he did for his father's old parish, the First Unitarian Church (1886), Philadelphia. In addition, he designed many other types of buildings, including offices, clubs, hotels, institutions, a number of buildings for railroads, and three buildings at the Philadelphia Zoological Gardens, all of them now gone except the gatehouse (1876).

The crowning point in the architect's career was his design of the Library of the University of Pennsylvania (1891), Philadelphia. A Victorian building with great ornamentation of the exterior and interior, the library, now renamed the Furness Building, has been considerably altered. His last known work was an alteration, as were three out of the last five of his commissions. His last complete building, a factory, has been demolished.

Life Frank Furness was born in Philadelphia on November 12, 1839, the last child of a Unitarian minister, who was artistic and intellectual and imbued those traits in his children. Ending his formal schooling early, Furness worked for a while in the office of a Philadelphia architect, John Fraser, and decided he wanted to become an architect. Since there was no professional school of architecture in the United States then, he did the next best thing. He entered the atelier or studio of the foremost architect he could find, Richard Morris Hunt (1827–95), in New York. Here he stayed until the outbreak of the Civil War.

He enlisted in the Union cavalry in 1861. By the time he was discharged in 1864, he had been promoted to captain, a title he liked to use in later life. He had also won his country's highest military award, the Congressional Medal of Honor, though because of a technicality it was not bestowed until 1899.

After the war, he worked for about a year in Hunt's office, but returned to Philadelphia in 1866, thoroughly indoctrinated in the eclectic Beaux Arts inspired architecture of which Hunt was the first acknowledged American master. He had also discovered that he had an innate talent for drawing caricatures of people, which were at once comical and biting. He continued to draw caricatures all his life. Starting his own office in Philadelphia, Furness designed a few buildings by himself, but in 1867 he formed a partnership with his former employer, John Fraser, and another architect, George W. Hewitt (1841–1916). The partnership lasted four years and established Furness as an architect. After Fraser moved to Washington in 1871, Furness and Hewitt continued to practice together until Hewitt left in 1875. During this time, in 1873, a budding young architect, Louis Henri Sullivan, aged sixteen, worked in their office for a time.

After Hewitt left, Furness continued the growing practice. In 1881 a draftsman, Allen Evans (1845–1925), who had been employed in the firm for 10 years, was taken in as a partner and in 1885, the firm was renamed Furness, Evans, and Company to reflect the fact that Furness kept taking in increasing numbers of silent partners. Good commissions continued to come in and the firm prospered. Considered a genuine eccentric, Furness, with a red beard and drooping mustache and dressed in loud plaids, strode around the office and the town in a military manner, swearing and domineering. Among others, Sullivan was impressed by the fact that he could draw and swear at the same time.

In 1879 Furness began work for the Philadelphia and Reading Railroad Company and later worked for other railroads, designing hundreds of buildings and alterations all over the country. His work for the railroads continued until just a few years before he died. The practice prospered until, by 1895, it was no longer possible for Furness to control the designs and details as he had in the past. Thus much of the later work does not measure up to the earlier.

As he grew older, Furness began to dwell more and more on his Civil War record. He liked to be addressed as captain, and he accepted the Congressional Medal of Honor which he had refused, at age twenty five, when he won it in battle. Many people

FURNESS, FRANK Pennsylvania Academy of Fine Arts (1876), Philadelphia, Pa. *(Lawrence S. Williams, Inc.)*

FURNESS, FRANK Furness Building, formerly the Free Library (1891), University of Pennsylvania, Philadelphia, Pa. *(Library of Congress)*

considered him very disagreeable and the incoming commissions slowed almost to a halt. He spent his last years in relative obscurity, in ill health, playing old soldier, and neglecting architecture. When he died, on June 27, 1912, his obituaries in the Philadelphia papers dwelt on his war record and the lives of his father and brother, hardly mentioning his buildings at all.

His architecture and his reputation remained in almost total eclipse for 40 years until the 1950s, when architects and critics began to take a new interest in the importance of his work.

Related Articles ECLECTIC ARCHITECTURE; HUNT, RICHARD MORRIS; SULLIVAN, LOUIS HENRI.

Further Reading O'Gorman, James F.: *The Architecture of Frank Furness*, Philadelphia, Philadelphia Museum of Art, 1973.

FURNITURE Equipment, such as tables, chairs, and cabinets, for use in or around buildings. Furniture may be movable or built-in. Furnishings include furniture and also floor and wall coverings, curtains, and other movable articles.

In many cases, architects become involved in the selection of furniture and other furnishings for the buildings they design. In some cases, architects collaborate with interior designers who perform the interior design work, together with the selection of furniture and furnishings. In other cases, architects handle the interior design and the selection of furniture and other furnishings, or departments in their firms perform these services. A few architects today design furniture and furnishings for production and sale to the general public. And many others design custom items, in particular built-in furniture, for the buildings of their clients.

Properties In order to properly select or design furniture and other furnishings, the major considerations are similar to those common to other elements of architecture: function, strength, appearance, and cost. Although not always the case, most pieces of furniture or other furnishings have relatively simple functions. A chair is for sitting; a bed is for lying down; a carpet is for standing upon. These are primary functions, though each piece may have others. Each furniture or furnishing item must be strong enough to perform its function or functions. In addition, there is a need for stability. A chair may be strong enough, for example, to easily withstand the weight of a person but, at the same time, so unstable that it falls over when a person leans from it. The appearance or visual effect of a piece of furniture or furnishing item depends not only on its form, color, texture, and the like but also upon its fitness to its purpose, structure, and materials. From this it might be gathered that the most successful pieces are those that excel in all the elements mentioned. That this is not always true can be demonstrated by the simple process of sitting in some types of chairs that seem to have all the above excellent attributes, but turn out to be comfortable only if a person sits in a single posi-

tion. On the other hand, so-called overstuffed chairs, though not designed in a modern manner or constructed with the latest types of materials, are often extremely comfortable.

Types A great variety of pieces of furniture and other furnishings are available today, including newly manufactured items, older ones, and antiques. An architect, or interior or other environmental designer, is thus faced with an often bewildering array of types, at widely varied prices. The selection therefore becomes partly a matter of taste of the owners or occupiers of buildings and the building designers. In addition, attention should be paid to other aspects of the furnishings, including function, structure, materials, and safety as well as price. The most expensive items are not necessarily the most appropriate choices.

To make matters more difficult, there exists the problem of compatibility between various items of furnishings. At one time, many believed that modern furniture could not be mixed successfully with furniture from other periods. Many architects and other designers today believe that good, well-designed furniture from many eras and of many styles can be successfully mixed. Perhaps heavy bulky furniture, of highly ornamented wood, from some periods may not be quite right with attenuated types made of metal, plywood, and plastics. However, the best individual pieces, particularly if they are authentic not merely adaptations or copies, are often very much at home together. For example, Thonet bentwood rockers seem quite appropriate when used in otherwise modern interiors. So do Windsor chairs, Shaker furniture, and good pieces of many of the other furniture designers of the past.

When considering the selection of furniture and other furnishings, function is quite important. Each piece should perform its primary function well. In addition, each should be safe and easy to maintain and repair. Furniture or other furnishings should be structurally sound. This means being well made, of good design, construction, and materials. Materials must be proper for the use intended and strong enough to function properly. They should also present a pleasing appearance. The form of a piece of furniture, along with its texture, color, and other factors, join with the materials and structure to produce a visual effect that is satisfying or one that is not. Then there is the question of comfort. The piece should provide the utmost in comfort to the people who use it. Furniture and other furnishings should pass all these tests before being selected for use in well-designed buildings.

The structures of furniture today are often quite complicated, utilizing many of the contemporary construction types and techniques employed in other building elements. As pointed out previously, structures must not only be of adequate strength but must have adequate stability to resist overturning. The structural design of furniture therefore resembles that of buildings. Strength in furniture is derived from the

FURNITURE Reynolds Metals Co. Building (1960), Detroit, Mich. [*Architect: Minoru Yamasaki. (Hedrich-Blessing)*]

strength of the individual parts and, very importantly, from the strength of the joints between the parts. In addition, the frame of a piece of furniture and other working parts must have complete structural integrity when joined together in a system, such as a chair.

Structural Materials The major structural materials used in the construction of furniture today are wood, steel, iron, aluminum, and plastics. Many other materials are often used for finishes and for other purposes, including fabrics for upholstery, other metals for hardware and similar purposes, and stone and glass for tops, doors, and the like.

In general, wood used for furniture today may be either softwood, used mostly for utilitarian purposes such as breakfast tables or for hidden parts of furni-

ture; and hardwoods, used for exposed parts of furniture. Among the most used softwoods are various kinds of native American pine, fir, and redwood. Among the most used hardwoods are such native American woods as oak, birch, maple, and walnut, and woods from other countries, including mahogany, rosewood, ebony, and numerous others, some very ornamental and many quite rare. Although solid hardwoods were often used for furniture in the past and are still used to some extent, the more common practice today utilizes veneers of the desired woods glued to cores of less desirable species or to particle board.

Plywood is also widely used. Both veneers and plywood are currently available in a great variety of woods. Grain, color, and the like are important in wood furniture. And it should be strongly constructed with stable rigid frames, proper joints, and excellent workmanship. For a discussion of various aspects of wood for use in furniture, see articles entitled paint; wood; woodwork.

Two special uses of wood in furniture are bentwood and molded plywood. Bentwood is made by placing shaped pieces of wood in chambers where they are subjected to steam until they become flexible. They are then bent in molds to the desired forms. Molded plywood is made by placing the required number of wood plys and external veneers, with glue between them, in molds. Pressure and heat are applied to help in the process of molding and to cause the glue to set, or high-frequency radio waves can be used.

Until the 20th century, metal was used in furniture sparingly, at first for hardware and other minor purposes and later for wrought-iron or cast-iron outdoor or garden furniture. Such uses continue today. However, some of the finest modern furniture for other purposes is made, at least partly, of steel or aluminum tubing, bars, sheet, or other shapes. These metals are also often used for utilitarian pieces of furniture, such as kitchen chairs. Metal furniture can be constructed with great strength and durability and often may be less expensive than comparable pieces made of fine woods. For a discussion of the various metals used in furniture today, see articles entitled aluminum; construction materials; iron; steel. For a discussion of their finishes, see the article entitled paint.

Although the first plastics had a bad reputation in architecture, perhaps because they copied, and were considered cheap substitutes for, other materials. Today plastics are widely used in architecture for furniture and other purposes. In furniture, their uses include complete glass-fiber reinforced shells of chairs and other pieces; foam for pads, mattresses, and the like; woven and other flexible materials for upholstery; laminated types for tops of tables, counters, and the like; in glues and other adhesives; in finish materials such as paints and others; and for hardware. Plastics are also widely used for other furnishings, such as curtains, carpets and rugs, and other items. For further discussion of plastics, see the article entitled plastics.

Other materials used in furniture include glass, mostly tempered plate but sometimes other types, for tabletops, doors, and other purposes. Glass is also used in mirrors and the form of glass fibers for reinforcing plastics and for curtain fabrics. Stone is sometimes used for tabletops and similar purposes. The most used stone is marble but others, such as granite and slate, are sometimes used. See the article entitled stone. A rather large group of additional materials are often used in furniture. See the article entitled construction materials. They include natural and synthetic rubber in foamed types for such uses as upholstery pads and in other forms for minor purposes. Textiles of many kinds and materials are widely used,

not only for finish upholstery fabrics but as canvas and other materials for hidden construction in chairs, sofas, and beds. Felt, hair, down, and feathers are often used, alone or in combination with plastic or rubber foams, for cushions.

Furniture may be either movable or built-in. Most movable furniture used in architecture is selected from standard stocks of various manufacturers, though special pieces are sometimes designed by architects or other environmental designers. Built-in furniture may be selected from stock, as is usually the case with kitchen cabinets, or designed by architects or others for special applications. For further discussion of both types, see the article entitled woodwork. Movable furniture runs the gamut from the very simplest of pieces to quite complex units. For many young as well as some older people today, the less movable furniture the better seems to be the theme. Often they seem perfectly satisfied with a pad on the floor to sit on and perhaps to sleep on, and very little else.

Systems Most people, however, select furniture that is a bit more formal and considerably more comfortable. In addition to single, freestanding pieces of furniture, such as individual chairs, sofas, tables, and bookcases, systems of furniture are often used today. Sometimes called sectional or modular, these systems are made up of pieces that may be interconnected or placed side by side to form large units or moved apart to be used individually. Perhaps the first of such pieces were sectional sofas and bookcases, individual pieces that may be joined together at will. A number of systems of this sort are available for use in various building types, such as houses, offices, and others. Some of the systems are quite complex. For example, in certain office systems, tables, desks, bookcases, file cases, and other elements may be joined in a great variety of combinations according to the needs of the users and the ingenuity of the designers. Some systems also serve as room dividers, creating open-planned offices or office landscaping.

Specialized furniture, and sometimes systems of furniture, are available for many building types, including hotels, hospitals, schools, libraries, and churches. Special outdoor furniture, often made of such materials as redwood, iron, and glass, may be obtained in many different designs.

Furnishings In addition to furniture, a large number of other types of furnishings are available today. Perhaps the most important are floor coverings and materials for windows. Other than the more permanent flooring materials, the major floor coverings are carpeting and rugs, mostly machine-woven. Carpeting is generally used to cover entire floors of rooms in buildings, cut to size and installed more or less permanently. Rugs, sometimes called area rugs, are usually smaller than the dimensions of rooms and are not permanently left in place. Such a vast variety of fibers, colors, patterns, and textures exist in carpets and rugs that they cannot be adequately described here. In general, both carpeting and rugs are made of wool or any of a variety of synthetic fibers, often in combinations. They may be obtained with plain undersides or backs, or with various backing materials, including rubber sponge or sheet materials.

Carpeting generally is available in widths ranging from about 4 ft 6 in up to 15 ft and in any reasonable length. Special carpeting for stairs comes in smaller widths. Rectangular rugs come in sizes from about 3 by 5 ft up to 12 by 18 ft, and round rugs in diameters from about 4 ft, sometimes less, up to about 12 ft. Underlayment or pads for use under floor coverings are made of hair, fiber, rubber foam or sponge, and combinations of such materials. Plastic carpets for outdoors and indoors are generally available in 3 to 12 ft widths and reasonable lengths. Both outdoor and indoor carpeting usually comes in 12-in squares for fastening to floors with adhesives. Handwoven rugs of many kinds can be obtained in a considerable variety of sizes. Carpeting is usually sold by the square yard or square meter, and rugs by the individual item.

Materials for curtains and drapery for windows are available in a great variety of fibers, textures, patterns, and colors. They may be very sheer or completely opaque, lined or unlined, in a great variety of types. They may be obtained in stock sizes or may be custom-made for individual windows. Perhaps the most important type in architecture today is the draw curtain, which is ordinarily hung from a traverse track. Pulls at the sides allow the curtains to be drawn to the sides for opening or together in the middle for closing. Traverse tracks are available for one-way, two-way, and multiple drawing, in lengths up to 30 ft or more for the one-way and two-way types and up to 60 ft or more for the multiple type. Traverse tracks can be obtained in various degrees of strength, lighter ones being used for such buildings as houses and heavier ones, for public and commercial buildings.

Other systems, often used with windows, include Venetian blinds with horizontal slats of aluminum or sometimes wood or other materials, which can be inclined at various angles to permit or prevent vision and to allow light and breezes to enter or to exclude them. Venetian blinds also may be raised to the top or lowered to the bottom of windows. The blinds come in various stock sizes, ranging up to 16 ft or more in width and 20 ft or more in height, and in several colors. Vertical blinds, like the Venetian type except with the slats vertical instead of horizontal, are often used. Made of aluminum or fabric, they come in sizes up to 16 ft in width and 25 ft in height and in several colors. Other devices sometimes used with windows include louvered blinds and roll-up shades of cloth, wood, bamboo, or other materials.

Furniture designers today come from a variety of disciplines: architecture, interior design, industrial design, and crafts. For many people, the field is exciting and fulfilling. For those who are deeply interested in design, people, and craftsmanship, careers as furniture designers offer a great deal. For architects and other environmental designers the occasional chance to design a custom piece of movable or built-in furniture represents a welcome departure from ordinary practice.

History From the time the first rude huts and tents were constructed by primitive humans, furniture and other furnishings have been important attributes of architecture. None of the earliest examples has survived, and almost none from the ancient civilizations in the Middle East, Crete, Greece, and Rome. The little that is known about furniture and furnishings of those early times has been learned from illustrations on vases or in paintings. The ancient Egyptians believed that various objects needed in life should accompany the dead in their afterlife. The Egyptians therefore buried furniture, furnishings, and other things with the dead. Thus objects that would have been destroyed under ordinary circumstances have been preserved and may be seen in museums today. The furniture and other objects show a high level of design and workmanship and include beds, chairs, storage cases, tables, and other useful and decorative items.

From the fall of the Roman Empire, and the beginning of the Middle Ages, furniture has been closely related to the other aspects of interiors in architecture. For a discussion of the developments from that time to the beginning of the modern movement in architecture in the 19th century, see the article entitled interior design.

Although the beginning of the modern movement in architecture is often taken to have occurred in the late 19th century, it can be foreseen in some buildings and in the design of furniture of earlier eras. Still greatly admired for simple, functional designs and fine workmanship is the furniture of the Shakers, a religious sect that originated in England about the middle of the 18th century and spread to America about two decades later. Another forerunner of the modern movement was the work of the English architect and interior and furniture designer William Morris (1834–96), one of the leaders of the Crafts Movement. Morris and others turned away from the heavy ornament of the Victorian era to simpler furniture designs and better craftsmanship. The work of the members of the Crafts Movement were also antimodern in that they also turned away from factory production to handcrafts.

Another movement, mostly in France and Belgium, called Art Nouveau, also turned away from the past toward nature for inspiration. The Belgian architects Henry van de Velde (1863–1957) and Victor Horta (1861–1947) and the French architect Hector Guimard (1863–1942), the leaders of the movement, not only designed buildings but also furniture and furnishings. The Scottish architect Charles Rennie Mackintosh (1868–1928) also designed furniture that presaged the coming modern movement, as did that of the Spanish architect Antoni Gaudí (1852–1926) and the Austrian architect Josef Hoffman (1870–1956). In the United

States, Henry Hobson Richardson (1838–86) and Louis Henri Sullivan (1856–1924) often designed furniture for use in their buildings.

Perhaps the real beginnings of modern furniture design may be found in the work of the German furniture maker Michael Thonet (1796–1871). With his brothers, Thonet pioneered the design of molded plywood and bentwood furniture, mostly in chairs. He started manufacturing such furniture before the middle of the 19th century. Considered strictly utilitarian at first, the furniture designs were later recognized for their spare, machine-age, modern beauty and are still much admired today. Together with later designs, many are still being manufactured.

In the late 19th century, Frank Lloyd Wright (1867–1959) began to design furniture and continued to do so for certain of his buildings the remainder of his life. Wright's designs were as special and customized as the designs of his houses and other buildings and their interiors. During the same period the German architect Peter Behrens (1868–1940) designed furniture, which had a more universal appeal and which deeply affected later designs. Behrens also affected the work, in architecture and in furniture design, of three architects who worked in his office at various times: Walter Adolf Gropius (1883–1970), Ludwig Mies van der Rohe (1886–1969), and Charles Édouard Jeanneret (1887–1965), known as Le Corbusier. All three designed furniture, Le Corbusier quite a number of individual pieces and a system that was the forerunner of later storage walls. Mies designed several pieces that became famous, including his Tugendhat chair in 1930, and his Barcelona chair, designed in 1929, still being produced and as handsome and admired as ever. Gropius and Mies were associated at the famous German architectural and design school, the Bauhaus, with another architect who also designed excellent furniture, Marcel Lajos Breuer (1902–   ). Breuer designed many pieces of furniture over the years, including some in wood and some in other materials. His most notable designs, however, have been in bent metal tubing, an early and excellent example of which, designed in 1925, is still produced and admired today.

The furniture of the great Finnish architect Alvar Aalto (1898–1976) was first shown in the United States at the New York World's Fair in 1939. Constructed mostly of birch plywood, the furniture was widely praised at the time and today is still considered as some of the greatest modern furniture designs. In 1940 the Museum of Modern Art in New York City sponsored a furniture design competition, entered by a number of noted designers. First prizes for a molded plywood chair and modular storage cases went to two young designers, later to become famous for their work in architecture as well as in furniture design, Eero Saarinen (1910–61) and Charles Eames (1907–1978). Eames later designed many notable pieces of furniture, not only in molded plastics and other materials, many of which are still marketed today. Saarinen also designed excellent furniture, but is best known for his designs of buildings.

Near the end of World War II, a New York city company was established to construct and market modern furniture and other furnishings by Hans G. Knoll (1914–1958). Its first designer was a Dane, Jens Risom (1916–   ), who produced a number of notable furniture designs. Later called Knoll Associates, the company attracted many of the best designers from all over the world and has consistently produced fine pieces to this day. The Herman Miller Company in Grand Rapids, Mich., an old-line producer of solid but scarcely modern pieces, turned to modern furniture after World War II. Architect George Nelson (1907–   ) had designed, with another architect, Henry Wright (1910–   ), a revolutionary system for houses called storage wall and, with the same collaborator, had written an equally revolutionary book, Tomorrow's House, about modern house design. Nelson became director of design for Herman Miller and proceeded not only to completely modernize its line of furniture but its promotion pieces, catalogs, and the whole image of the company. The first postwar furniture made by the company was designed by Nelson and he continued to design other pieces and systems for them for many years. He also attracted other designers to the company, including Charles Eames and Harry Bertoia (1915–1978). The company is still very active today, not only in the design and production of individual furniture pieces but of systems for open-planned offices and other purposes.

Today a large number of companies manufacture modern furniture designed by architects, furniture designers, and others from many nations of the world as well as the United States. Some offer general lines of furniture; others specialize in systems for such buildings as libraries, schools, churches, and offices.

During the 20th century, modern furnishings of such types as rugs and carpets, textiles for upholstery and curtains, and tapestries have been designed, and sometimes made, by many talented designers and artists in other fields. Notable examples of such furnishings are designed and manufactured today in many parts of the world. In the United States, perhaps the greatest textile designers and weavers have been Anni Albers (1899–   ) and Dorothy Liebes (1899–1972). Others, including architect Alexander Hayden Girard (1907–   ), have designed notable textiles. Incidental furnishings, such as ceramics, lamps, wallpaper, tableware, tablecloths, and cooking utensils are available in excellent designs, made both in the United States and other countries.

Related Articles ART IN ARCHITECTURE; GARDEN; INTERIOR DESIGN; ORNAMENT; WOODWORK; Articles on various materials.

Further Reading Caplan, Ralph: The Design of Herman Miller, Whitney, New York, 1976; Dal Fabbro, Mario: How to Build Modern Furniture, F. W. Dodge Corp., New York, 1955; Dal Fabbro, Mario: Upholstered Furniture—Design and Construction, McGraw-Hill, New York, 1969; Pile, John F.: Modern Furniture, John Wiley, New York, 1978.

GARAGE A building, or a room in a building, in which automobiles, trucks, or other motor vehicles are kept or repaired.

Types There are three major types of garage: residential, repair, and parking. Residential garages shelter one or more cars and are attached to or located near houses. A special type is a carport, a covered shelter for the same purpose but not closed in on all sides. Repair garages are commercial buildings in which automobiles and other vehicles are kept temporarily for service, maintenance, and repair. Residential garages and carports are elements of house design, and repair garages are most often design elements of automobile or other vehicular sales and service commercial buildings.

With the growth in automobile traffic, parking garages have become an important building type. Their function is the temporary shelter of vehicles, particularly in densely populated areas where street parking is scarce or impractical. Parking garages may be either separate structures or attached to or integrated with other building types, such as apartments, hotels or motels, and office buildings. In all cases, the principles of design are similar.

Parking garages are usually multistory. When automobiles are parked on one level, the area is usually called a parking lot and no building, except a small one for the attendants and cashier, is required. Multistory parking garages are classified by the types of floors: flat; sloping; and staggered or split-level. They are also classified according to the type of system used for traffic to and from the floors: ramps, used with flat and staggered floors; sloping floor, where the floor itself serves in place of the ramps; and mechanical, using elevators. Ramps may be straight or helical, shaped like a spiral, and may have one-way or two-way traffic. Some parking garages utilize mechanical elevators for moving automobiles into and out of place. In some garages of this type, the automobiles must be driven on and off the elevators by attendants; in others, dollies automatically perform these functions. The elevators are counterweighted so that, in case of power failure, they will rise when empty and descend slowly when loaded with automobiles.

In addition to the parking areas and the ramps or vehicle elevators, the major elements of parking garages are the public areas, which may include waiting rooms, rest rooms, passenger elevators, and a booth for the cashier and attendants. Major considerations in their design include efficient and economical use of space to park the maximum number of vehicles safely and the problems presented by irregular and

GARAGE Parking Garage (1962), New Haven, Conn. [*Architect: Paul Rudolph. (Ezra Stoller)*]

relatively small sites. Because of problems of this sort, many parking garages are designed individually, but for more straightforward sites, prefabricated buildings and systems are often used.

History Some sort of shelter has been used for vehicles ever since they were invented. In Europe the carriage house, and later the coach house, was used to shelter horse-drawn vehicles. Such shelters were ordinarily attached to or near private houses or built in conjunction with inns. The same practice was followed in colonial America and for many years after independence. With the advent of the automobile, the need for parking garages might have been foreseen, but no one seems to have predicted the phenomenal growth in both the number of automobiles and the population of cities. Thus the parking garage has only become an important building type within the last few decades.

Related Articles APARTMENT; HOTEL; HOUSE; HOUSING; OFFICE BUILDING.

Source of Additional Information National Parking Assoc., 1101 17th St., N.W., Washington, D.C. 20036.

GARDEN An area of ground primarily used for growing flowers, shrubbery, and trees; also an area used for growing fruits, nuts, or vegetables. Gardens for use and enjoyment are important parts of the lives of many people. While a garden of vegetables may assume esthetic qualities, most gardens in conjunction with architecture contain ornamental plants. In addition, such gardens often contain other elements, as rocks, lawns, outdoor furniture, paving, garden houses or gazebos, water in fountains or pools, special lighting, and greenhouses.

In any case, gardens have been an important adjunct of architecture since its earliest beginnings and remain so today. Gardens come in a variety of sizes, from the smallest in a window box or planter to that in a yard of a modest house to the great gardens, often many acres in size, in public areas of cities and on large estates.

It has been said that parks should provide opportunities for visual, mental, and physical recreation. Gardens might be said to have the same functions, though not always in the same degree as parks. Activities in gardens are not usually as strenuous as in many parks. And the opportunities for quiet contemplation or reflection and the appreciation of beauty and nature may be even greater in gardens than in most parks.

Types Throughout history, gardens have been of two major types: those in which people are more important (or of equal importance), than plants; and those in which people are subordinated to the plants. The first type might be called a living garden and the second one, a show garden. In addition, in the past, gardens have had varying degrees of formality, ranging from completely informal, naturalistic types to rigidly formal ones. These principles are still applied to garden design today.

The two major types of gardens may be subdivided into a number of variations. One may be a general garden, with plants of many kinds; another may be special, containing only plants of certain varieties, such as a rose garden, or certain kinds of plants, such as alpine, aquatic, rock garden, and so on. They may be even more specialized, as in a cutting garden for production of flowers for display indoors. Gardens may be outdoors or indoors. They may be placed at ground level or elevated, enclosed or not, on roofs, or on level or hilly sites. They may be enclosed in patios or courtyards or on porches. Plants may be set into the ground, or in pots or planters.

Essentials The primary elements of any garden are plants and people. Other essentials are natural features, such as soils, rock, water, topography, and climate, and constructed features such as structures. All these elements must be properly integrated to create a successful garden.

To meet the needs of plants and people, the ideal garden should live in harmony with nature, the soil, the sun, the weather, birds and other animals, and insects. Since ideal conditions never exist, the goal of a designer might be to create gardens in which conditions can be controlled to produce states as near the ideal as possible or practical.

For most gardens, sites that are open to the sun all day are best. Land that slopes gently provides the best drainage. Therefore, for plants that grow well in the sun, eastern and southern exposures are ideal. Trees or large shrubbery planted on the northern and eastern sides protect plants that like sun from winter winds, while those on the southern and eastern sides protect those that prefer shade from the hot summer sun. Walls, windbreaks, and proper placing of shrubbery can also help protect a garden and channel the flow of air through it or around it as desired.

Soil To succeed, a garden must have appropriate soil, properly drained. Rocky soil makes growing plants difficult, as does sandy or clay soil. If the soil remains too wet or too dry, the growing of many plants will be difficult if not impossible. Of course, there are exceptions, for example, many cacti prefer sandy, dry soils. If the soil in a garden site does not have the proper characteristics, they must be provided, using decayed vegetable matter, or humus, to improve sandy or clay soils and working the soil with tools to break it up. In the same way, garden sites that are too dry or too wet must be corrected by improving drainage or by provision for watering.

Another important factor in successful gardens is the acidity of soils, this may be measured with simple kits available from companies that sell plants or seeds or the tests can be made by state agricultural extension services. The measure of acidity of soils is called the pH factor, which is the symbol for the amount of hydrogen ion present. The values of pH range from 0 to 14, with 0 the most acid, 14 the most alkaline, and a value of 7 representing neutrality. Most natural soils in the United States are neutral or slightly acid, except for the Western states where soils tend to be alkaline. For many plants, a neutral or slighlty acid state is ideal. For others, such as azaleas and rhododendrons, acid soils are required. After determination of the plants to be grown in a garden, along with their preferences in pH, acidity in soils may be reduced by the addition of lime and raised by the addition of certain common chemicals.

Water Water is another essential of a successful garden. A sufficient quantity must be applied in the correct manner for plants to grow properly, and excessive quantities must be controlled by proper drainage. Other than in those with desert plants or other types that require only small quantities of water, gardens must receive water regularly, either through rain or other precipitation or by irrigation. While the quantities required vary for plants of different kinds and sizes, a rule of thumb often quoted calls for a minimum of an inch of water per week. A good soaking over a relatively long period is more effective than a great quantity deposited in a short time. Much of the water given too quickly runs off instead of sinking into the soil. On the other hand, an inch of water received over a longer period of time will wet the soil to a depth up to 6 in, a proper level.

Inexpensive rain gauges may be used to measure rainfall and also sprinkler water. Although not truly accurate, these gauges are adequate for garden purposes. Some experts maintain that irrigation by means of such devices as soaker hoses, ones that have a series of holes and are laid on the ground to water plants at their bases, are better for plants than sprinklers. When watering by hose, several hours may be required to apply an inch. The time required will be shorter on light sandy soils, longer on heavy clay soils. Less water will be lost by evaporation if gardens are watered in the late afternoon or early evening, instead of during the hotter times of the day. However, some think that water left on the foliage of plants at night is conducive to diseases.

In dry weather, when gardens must be watered, it is thought that a good soaking once a week is best, rather than more frequent applications of smaller quantities. Gardens may be watered with watering cans, hoses with nozzles, soaker hoses or sprinklers. In some cases, permanent systems, with underground piping, are provided, either with sprinklers attached or with soaker or trickle devices. They must be buried deep enough to prevent freezing in winter or be equipped for draining.

Animals Many people maintain that a garden without animals, in particular birds, is not complete. However, most would agree that animals, like insects, in gardens can be welcome additions or pests. Some harmless animals might include toads and frogs; nonpoisonous garter, king, and other snakes; and fish, tadpoles, snails, and salamanders in ponds to control mosquito larvae and other pests.

Insects Many varieties of insects attack plants. Without controls, they can destroy a garden very quickly. Some people advocate biological controls; others believe that only chemical insecticides or other devices can do the job. Many methods for biological control of insects are used today, including helpful insects, such as the praying mantis and the ladybird beetle, or ladybug, which kill harmful insects; devices that interfere with insect reproduction through sterilization or other means; plants that repel certain insects; symbiotic plant pairings that protect each other; and parasites that destroy the eggs of other insects. Some gardeners also capture harmful insects by picking them off plants or by various kinds of traps.

People who use pesticides maintain that, regardless of preference for biological or other means of insect control, nothing really works properly except chemicals. Several types are available, though some are eventually withdrawn from the market for environmental protection reasons.

Insecticides for control of various insects are available in forms that may be dusted or sprayed on plants. It is also possible to obtain some, in combination with fertilizers, which are absorbed by the roots of plants. In any case, the insecticides must be selected for their specific insect control properties. All of them are poisons and must be handled and applied properly and with extreme caution.

Proper gardening practices can be of great aid in the control of insects. Gardens should be kept clean. Diseased or dead vegetation should be quickly removed. Rotation of plantings may help. Proper cultivation aids in control of insects as well as in plant growth. These measures also help to control plant diseases, which can be as destructive as insects. Plant diseases are also controlled with chemicals, the most important being fungicides. Other chemicals for control of various kinds of garden pests include miticides for mites, herbicides for weeds, nematocides for nematodes (very small eelworms), molluscides for snails and slugs, and rodenticides for mice and rats. All these chemicals are poisonous and should be handled properly and with extreme caution.

Plants An almost endless list of plants of various types may be used in gardens to suit every purpose and whim. The major types of plants include trees, shrubbery, flowers, and vegetables. Trees may be evergreens, those with needlelike leaves that are not usually shed in winter, and deciduous trees, those with other types of leaves that are shed. Many types are available, including dwarf and regular fruit and nut trees. Shrubbery may also be evergreen or deciduous and of various sizes and habits. Some are dwarf types; others are creepers; still others grow very large. Some have flowers, and many have colorful berries that are decorative and provide food for birds.

Flowers exist in an almost endless variety. For example, there are some 9,000 varieties of daffodils alone. The major types of flowers are perennials, which come back every year, and annuals, which die after one season. Biennials are flowers that take two years to mature and then die. Some flowers are grown from seeds; others, such as daffodils and tulips, from bulbs; and still others, such as gladiolus, from bulb or rootlike corms. Bulbs or corms may be hardy, those that usually live through winter in the ground, or tender, those that often do not. Many types of plants and flowers are available for specialized gardens or garden areas, such as rock gardens. Vegetables are also classified as perennials, such as asparagus, and annuals, such as peas. Vegetables are usually grown from seeds, except for bulb plants, such as onions or garlic, which can be grown from bulbs or seeds.

Plants in gardens may be arranged in various ways. When shrubbery or other plants are placed close to buildings, they are often referred to as foundation plantings. Plants may be placed in beds, in borders along walks or fences, or in other places. Larger plants in front of which smaller ones are planted are often referred to as background plantings. For embankments, under trees, and on hillsides, plants are often placed as ground covers. Climbing plants or vines are often grown on fences or walls.

Fertilizers All plants in gardens should be placed and planted with care, at the proper depth in the soil and in proper relationships to each other. Almost all plants require feeding from their roots as well as from the sun. Fertilizers for plant feeding should be chosen with care to ensure that they will perform properly for the specific plants to be grown. Complete fertilizers contain primarily nitrogen, phosphorus, and potash, along with traces of other elements. A set of numbers on a fertilizer bag denotes the percentages of the primary minerals it contains. For example, a common garden, all-purpose fertilizer is called 5-10-5, indicating, in order, 5 percent nitrogen, 10 percent phosphorus, and 5 percent potash. Various plants have specialized requirements for fertilizer which should be determined before application.

As in the controversy between those who espouse biological control of insects and those who use insecticides, there is a division of opinion about fertilizers. Most gardeners today rely on chemical fertilizers; however, a growing number espouse the use of organic fertilizers. Organic fertilizers include well-rotted manure, leaf mold, bone meal, treated sewage sludge, peat moss, and dried animal blood. Also a good source of organic fertilizer is a compost pile, an uncovered box or other container into which kitchen scraps, leaves, and other organic materials are placed, limed to hasten rotting, and, then, when sufficiently rotted, applied to gardens.

Some plant feeding is furnished by decaying organic mulches, materials placed around plants to control weeds, retain moisture, and prevent erosion. Many materials may be used for mulches, including straw, leaves, rotting sawdust, and tree bark.

Planting Devices Although many gardeners start all their plants in the ground where they will remain, others use various devices for starting them, including cold frames, hot beds, and greenhouses. A cold frame is a box laid on the ground outdoors, contain-

GARDEN Peachtree Summit Building (1975), Atlanta, Ga. [*Architects: Toombs, Amisano and Wells. (Hedrich-Blessing)*]

GARDEN Union Carbide Research Building (1966), Eastview, N.Y. [*Landscape architects: Zion and Breen. (Joseph W. Molitor)*]

ing soil in which seeds are planted. A plastic or glass top, hinged at one end, covers the top of the cold frame, letting sun in during the day and retaining some of its heat through the night. The top may be opened for ventilation and to let heat escape on warm days and closed on cold ones and at night. Seeds may be planted in a cold frame much earlier than in the ground and later transplanted into the garden.

A hot bed is like a cold frame, except that fresh manure is placed under the soil. As the manure deteriorates, it produces heat within the hot bed. Today electric coils may be embedded in the soil for heating. A greenhouse is like a large cold frame, a structure of metal or wood with glass or plastic panels or coverings. Greenhouses come in a great variety of sizes, from those that fit outside a standard window to very large commercial types used by horticulturists and nursery operators. Greenhouses may be fitted with equipment to control the climate inside, including fans for ventilation, heaters, and watering systems.

Materials for gardens are of two major types: natural and manufactured. Natural materials are primarily those of the soil, rocks, and water. Manufactured materials may include almost all of those used for other architectural purposes. In gardens, an attempt is often made to express the natural features and to improve upon them for esthetic and functional reasons. In addition to the plants, garden designers may use a variety of structures and devices, including benches and tables, walkways, screens, walls, embankments, lawns, paved areas, changes in levels, ramps, steps, urns, plant containers, ponds and pools, fountains and waterfalls, garden houses or gazebos, and bird feeders and birdbaths.

Design The skillful design of a garden requires the establishment of the proper functional and esthetic relationships among the many elements. Garden design begins with the surroundings, the climate, and the site. In general, the climate or planting zone in which a garden exists, often called macroclimate, cannot be changed and will determine which plants can be grown successfully; smaller climates within gardens, called microclimates, can be created by skillful use of walls, trees, shrubbery, and other elements. The principles to be followed are the same as those in any other kind of landscape architecture or, for that matter, in the architecture of buildings. However, there are a few important additional principles. Unlike some other types of design, that of gardens must be more concerned with the blending of natural and manufactured elements and with the interactions between humans and the rest of nature. Gardens are often self-contained, causing the surroundings to be of lesser importance than might otherwise be the case. Such a condition may also restrict the view from and into the garden, causing it to be more intimate than other architectural forms. Nevertheless, views from the gardens of nearby buildings and from buildings into the gardens are important design considerations.

Special Considerations Plants are growing organisms; some grow quite rapidly. Therefore garden design must take into consideration not only the initial sizes and shapes of plants, and the relationships of these sizes and shapes to other plants and elements of the garden, but must also deal with the sizes to which the plants will eventually grow and the shapes they will take. Other special considerations in garden design include ensuring that the garden itself and nearby structures are protected from damage from such sources as flooding and wind. The maintenance of gardens is also a major consideration. Provisions must be made for receiving plant and other materials and for removal of debris. Storage for gardening tools and equipment must be provided and often space for potting plants and other functions. A watering system is a necessity, and often special lighting is placed in gardens.

Seasonal Nature Perhaps the most important special design consideration is the seasonal nature of gardens. All too often, a garden is designed and constructed as if it is not to exist except in spring and summer. Some experts think that the design of gardens for winters, when flowers usually cannot grow and many trees and much shrubbery have lost their leaves, is a primary consideration. Be that as it may, there are no overriding reasons why a garden cannot be attractive and functional all year. In the winter, evergreens, some with berries, can be very beautiful, especially in snow. Deciduous trees may have a stark beauty. Ground covers often stay partly green in many places, and songbirds may be attracted with feeders. In the spring, if the garden has been properly designed and planted, crocuses and other early plants begin the growing season even when snow is on the ground, to be followed by daffodils and tulips, and then an everchanging panorama of greenery, colors, and forms as successive waves of plants leaf out, bud, grow, and blossom.

In the autumn, many summer flowers are still in bloom and late bloomers, such as chrysanthemums, join them, to be followed by colchicum, the so-called autumn crocus. In a properly designed garden, autumn can also be splendid with great masses of colored leaves of deciduous plants and trees.

For many architects, landscape architects, and others, the design, planting, maintenance, and use of gardens are challenging and gratifying.

History The first gardens are thought to have been planted in the Neolithic period, beginning about the 50th century B.C. in the Middle East. In this period, people were becoming sedentary, instead of nomadic, settling in one place where they developed agriculture and domesticated animals. The first examples of gardens are assumed to have had only edible plants. From that period to the present, gardens have been an important adjunct of architecture.

In all the early civilizations, public and private gardens were designed and planted. The early Egyptians established gardens near their temples and homes, combining usefulness with beauty by planting a variety of edible fruits, vegetables, and herbs; trees; shrubbery; and flowers. The Egyptians developed the first irrigation systems for gardens. In the Middle East, great gardens were established, one of which, the Hanging Gardens of Babylon, constructed by King Nebuchadnezzar II (605–563 B.C.), became known among the wonders of the world.

The ancient Greeks and Romans constructed ornamental gardens, many of which contained herbs that were used for medicinal purposes. The Greeks developed the science of botany. They also planted groves of trees, called arboretums, an art that they had learned from the Persians, who had also introduced the Western world to formal planting of courtyards or patios. The Romans also built roof gardens. In other

GARDEN Ford Foundation Building (1967), New York, N.Y. [*Architects: Kevin Roche and John Dinkeloo. (Ezra Stoller)*]

areas in the Middle East, courtyard gardens were used as well as gardens enclosed with walls to separate them from their surroundings and to insulate them from heat and the dry climate. These were rectangular gardens built along axes, containing plants, water, and paving. Early gardens were also constructed in the Far East, notably in China.

During the Middle Ages, the building of gardens languished, except for those in monasteries and castles, in which were grown fruits, vegetables, and herbs. During the Renaissance, a great wave of gar-

den design and construction began. These were mostly gardens intended to complement the architecture. Plants were of less importance than the architectural element of the gardens: walls, terraces, paving, fountains, pools, waterfalls, and sculpture. These gardens were usually axial and formal, but with sculptural qualities. Flowers, shrubbery, and trees were planted in a very controlled manner and often clipped or shaped to resemble architectural forms rather than left in their natural state.

The design of gardens during the Renaissance began in Italy, where it has remained strong ever since, and spread throughout Europe to France, England, Spain, and other countries. In France, gardens were formal and regular; in Spain, they were mostly planted in patios or courtyards. In England, great formal gardens, ranging in size to more than 30 acres, often had covered walks, the coverings made by training the upper branches of trees to shut out the sky. And English gardens often had terraces, garden houses or gazebos, and shrubbery and trees clipped or shaped to reflect the formal characteristics of the entire garden. Many of the great public gardens of the Renaissance were not public in any real sense, but were intended for the use of the wealthy, the nobility, and sometimes certain other privileged classes.

After the Renaissance, beginning in the 18th century in England, gardens were often designed to create illusions of long ago or faraway places or of an imagined nature that was not natural but contrived to appear the way the garden designers thought it should look. The French called this type of garden *le jardin Anglais* and soon adopted the style; the idea eventually spread all over Europe. These gardens were the antithesis of the formal, axial gardens that had come before. Some gardens of the time were given a romantic, wild appearance, with irregular planting, faked dead trees, and faked building ruins. This type of garden was mostly promulgated by two English architects, William Kent (1684–1748) and Batty Langley (1696–1751), who started the trend, and by an English landscape gardener, Lancelot Brown (1716–83), known as Capability Brown. Having constructed a fake river, Brown is said to have remarked, "Alas, the Thames will never forgive me." Another English landscape gardener, Humphrey Repton (1752–1818), attempted to restore a more rational approach to the design of gardens.

Few changes have taken place in garden design since the 18th century, except for the adoption of ideas from non-European sources, notably from the Chinese, Japanese, and Muslims. A change of another sort has been in the democratization of public gardens, a process that began primarily with the work of the great American landscape architect Frederick Law Olmsted (1822–1903). Olmsted designed parks, including gardens, for private estates, but he also designed the first significant examples intended for use by all the people, not only by the privileged.

American Development In the American colonies, gardens were established very early. They were simple and utilitarian, geometrical in plan, and usually axial. The earliest gardens were strictly utilitarian, containing mostly fruit trees and vegetables; flowers and other ornamental plants were soon added. Later American gardens followed the various styles prevalent in Europe at the time: some formal and axial, others informal and naturalistic, and still others a combination of the two design philosophies.

Today there are gardens everywhere in America, in great public places, in parks, in botanical buildings and arboretums, on the grounds of great estates, and in the yards of more modest dwellings. They are widely varied in design and purpose, as specialized types, roof gardens, inside gardens, pot gardens, patio or courtyard gardens, and water gardens. They are a very valuable and important element of architecture.

A great many fine public gardens of all kinds, and others sometimes open to the public, exist in many places in the United States. Perhaps the greatest concentration can be found in the Southeastern states. Among those of greatest interest and beauty are the following: in Washington—the gardens of the U.S. Capitol; in Virginia—Mount Vernon and Woodlawn Plantation (both in Mount Vernon), Gunston Hall (Lorton), and the gardens of colonial Williamsburg; in North Carolina—Orton Plantation (Wilmington), Tryon Palace (New Bern), Elizabethan Garden (Manteo), and Biltmore (Asheville), designed by Frederick Law Olmsted; in South Carolina—Middleton Place, considered to be the oldest landscaped garden in the United States, and Magnolia (both in Charleston) and Brookgreen Gardens (Murrell's Inlet); in Tennessee—Cheekwood (Nashville) and Botanic Garden (Memphis); in Georgia—the gardens of Savannah and Callaway Gardens (Pine Mountain); in Alabama—Bellingrath Gardens (Theodore); in Mississippi—D'Evereux and Cherokee (both in Natchez); in Louisiana—Afton Villa and Rosedown (both in St. Francisville), Jungle Gardens (Avery Island), and Longue Vue (New Orleans).

GARDEN Old Orchard Shopping Center (1957), Skokie, Ill. [Architects: Loebl, Schlossman, Bennett and Dart. (Hedrich-Blessing)]

Related Articles ART IN ARCHITECTURE; BOTANICAL BUILDING; ECOLOGY; FOUNTAIN; LANDSCAPE ARCHITECTURE; OLMSTED, FREDERICK LAW; PLANNING, CITY; SITE PLANNING.

Further Reading Abraham, George: *The Green Thumb Book of Fruit and Vegetable Gardening*, Prentice-Hall, Englewood Cliffs, N.J., 1970; Church, Thomas D.: *Gardens Are for People*, Reinhold, New York, 1955; Hay, Roy, and Patrick M. Synge: *The Color Dictionary of Flowers and Plants for Home and Garden*, Crown, New York, 1969; Hunter, Margaret K., and Ernest H. Hunter: *The Indoor Garden—Design, Construction and Furnishing*, John Wiley, New York, 1978; Kramer, Jack: *Container Gardening Indoors and Out*, Doubleday, New York, 1971; Kramer, Jack: *Water Gardening—Pools, Fountains and Plants*, Charles Scribner's Sons, New York, 1971.

Sources of Additional Information The American Horticultural Society, Mount Vernon, Va. 22121; American Society of Landscape Architects, 1750 Old Meadow Rd., McLean, Va. 22101; U.S. Department of Agriculture, The Mall, between 12th and 14th Sts., N.W., Washington, D.C. 20250; Various agricultural extension services of states and county agents.

Periodicals *American Horticulturist*, Mount Vernon, Va. 22121; *Horticulture*, 300 Massachusetts Ave., Boston, Mass. 02115; *Landscape Architecture*, 1500 Bardstown Rd., Louisville, Ky. 40205.

GEORGIAN ARCHITECTURE

A movement, or style, in architecture that was developed in England and used forms that were derived, according to strict rules, from classical buildings. Named for the English kings, George I, II, III, and IV, during whose reigns (1714–1830) it flourished in England, the Georgian was an important style in America, before and for a short period after independence. The early American Georgian style has often been called Colonial, a misnomer since Georgian was only one of a number of styles of architecture in the colonies.

Georgian architecture followed the rules of design and proportion formulated by several great English architects, including Inigo Jones (1573–1652), Sir Christopher Wren (1632–1723), James Gibbs (1682–1754), and Sir William Chambers (1726–96), who were trying to create a national architectural style as the Renaissance was coming to an end in England. They based their concepts on those of architects of the Italian Renaissance, particularly Andrea Palladio, (1508–50) who had studied classical Roman architecture and had published his concepts of the proper use of Roman details.

Principles These principles led to architecture which was symmetrical in plan and exterior appearance. The buildings were quiet and serene. Mostly of brick, sometimes of stone or brick with stone details, Georgian buildings are quite elegant, but in a subdued manner.

Typically, Georgian buildings had either simple square or rectangular plans, often with two symmetrical flanking wings, and the form was also generally rectangular. A Georgian house often had a central stair hall with high-ceilinged rooms on either side, and tall windows in the rooms. The number of stories varied, but there were usually two and sometimes more. Entrances were imposing, with large, paneled doors and often with porches or projected hoods, with columns and narrow windows alongside the doors, all finely detailed. Well-proportioned chimneys, often quite large in size, were symmetrically placed. The edges of the roofs, or cornices, were quite ornamental and also finely detailed. Inside, the walls were often of wood divided into paneled areas by ornamental moldings. At the top of the walls where they met the ceilings were rich, ornamental cornices. Fireplaces were included in all major rooms, and often in most other rooms. As elsewhere, they were finely detailed and had ornamental mantels.

Other Georgian buildings followed the design and detailing of the houses, with changes as required by their relative sizes and purposes. For example, Georgian churches often had imposing steeples or towers, designed and detailed to reflect the rules of the style.

Criticism Elegant as they were, restrained but rich, Georgian buildings have often been criticized for sometimes sacrificing function, comfort, and convenience to the demand for symmetry and to the rules of design, proportion, and correctness of form. Another criticism is that the Georgian style produced clichés that were repeated over and over. The most famous is the so-called Palladian motif, introduced by Palladio into the design of an arcade for the Basilica at Vicenza, Italy, in the 17th century. The Palladian motif consists of a round-arched opening supported by columns or pilasters, with smaller rectangular openings at the sides.

American Development The Georgian style was brought to America during the first half of the 18th century, several decades after its beginnings in England, by emigrants who had seen or read about it in England. The first efforts to use the style in the colonies were in houses of wood, attempting to simulate the form and details of the brick and stone buildings in England. Among the early architects was Peter Harrisson (1716–75), who produced a number of buildings following Georgian principles, at first in wood and later in brick. Another was Edmund Woolley (1696–1771), who produced what is considered by many the masterpiece of American Georgian public buildings, Independence Hall (1732–55), Philadelphia.

A house, Westover (c. 1730), Charles City Co., Va., is another masterpiece. Richard Taliaferro (1705–79) was probably the architect, but that is not certain. Westover is a plantation house in a rural setting. As a contrast, the Hammond-Harwood House (1773) Annapolis, Md., is often said to be the finest Georgian town house in America. Its architect was William Buckland (1734–74). Many American Georgian buildings were derived from designs by English architects, among them Sir Christopher Wren and James Gibbs, adapted for use in this country. This was true of Harrison's buildings and those of others. In addition, English architects sometimes prepared designs and plans for buildings to be built in America, even

GEORGIAN ARCHITECTURE Westover (c. 1730), Charles City Co., Va. [*Architect: possibly Richard Taliaferro. (Wayne Andrews)*]

GEORGIAN ARCHITECTURE Christ Church (1732), Lancaster Co., Va. [*Architect: unknown. (Wayne Andrews)*]

GEORGIAN ARCHITECTURE St. Michael's Church (1761), Charleston, S.C. [*Architect: unknown. (Wayne Andrews)*]

GEORGIAN ARCHITECTURE Nassau Hall (1756), Princeton University, Princeton, N.J. [*Architect: Robert Smith. (Detroit Publishing Co., Library of Congress)*]

GEORGIAN ARCHITECTURE Mount Pleasant (1762), Philadelphia, Pa. [*Architect: unknown. (Wayne Andrews)*]

GEORGIAN ARCHITECTURE Miles Brewton House (c. 1769), Charleston, S.C. [Architect: unknown. (Wayne Andrews)]

GEORGIAN ARCHITECTURE Wren Building (1795, rebuilt later), College of William and Mary, Williamsburg, Va. [Architect: possibly Sir Christopher Wren. (Robert Tebles, Library of Congress)]

though they had never been in the colonies. Thus the so-called Wren building, at William and Mary College, Williamsburg, Va., is widely believed to have been designed by Wren. First constructed in 1795, the building was burned and rebuilt several times in altered forms, perhaps also designed by Wren. Other Georgian buildings in America, such as the Capitol (1705), reconstructed in 1934, and the Governor's Palace (1720), reconstructed in 1932, both in Williamsburg, so resemble the other work of Wren that some historians think he may have designed them also.

History The Georgian era is sometimes said to have begun in 1702, thus covering the reign of Queen Anne (1702–14) as well as the four kings George. Some historians think of the architecture of Queen Anne's era as a separate style. Some consider the end of the Georgian style to have coincided with the end of the reign of King George III in 1820. In any case, the Georgian style was developed in England early in the 18th century, and was based primarily on the work of Inigo Jones and Sir Christopher Wren, who were deeply affected by their studies of Palladio's writings even more than by his architecture. The publication of a new edition of his *Antiquities of Rome: The Architecture of Andrea Palladio* in 1742 made his theories, rules, and drawings readily available.

In 1759 Sir William Chambers reformulated the principles of Palladio and other Italian architects of the Renaissance in his *Treatise on the Decorative Part of Civil Architecture,* and this was followed by Robert Adam's *Ruins of the Palace of Diocletian in Dalmatia* in 1764. Such books spread the principles widely and they were readily accepted by many English and American architects. The Georgian style thus became a kind of literary architecture, based more on reading about past architecture than by the buildings themselves. The style also deeply affected other arts, particularly furniture design, as may be seen in the work of the great furniture makers of the time, Chippendale, Hepplewhite, and Sheraton.

In the second half of the 18th century, the Georgian style became firmly entrenched in America for houses as well as more ambitious buildings. American architects then drew most of their inspiration, and often their forms and details, from the books they imported from England. By the end of that century, its popularity had begun to wane in the face of the growing preference for what was to become the Classic Revival style, and by 1830 the real end had come, though some vestiges have persisted ever since, even into the 20th century. The real end was signaled when American architects turned away from Georgian to the Classic Revival for important public and other monumental buildings of the new republic. In fact, Thomas Jefferson (1743–1826), who had built his home, Monticello, near Charlottesville, Va., in the Georgian style in 1775, remodeled and rebuilt part of it in the Classic Revival style, beginning in 1796.

Related Articles BULFINCH, CHARLES; CLASSIC REVIVAL ARCHITECTURE; COLONIAL ARCHITECTURE; FURNITURE; HARRISON, PETER; HISTORY OF ARCHITECTURE; JEFFERSON, THOMAS; LATROBE, BENJAMIN HENRY; PRESERVATION.

Further Reading Architects' Emergency Committee: *Great Georgian Houses of America* 2 Vols., Dover, New York, 1970; See also listings in articles entitled colonial architecture and history of architecture.

Sources of Additional Information See the article entitled history of architecture.

GILBERT, CASS American architect (1859–1934). Although Cass Gilbert had very little architectural training, a year at Massachusetts Institute of Technology, a year traveling in Europe, and two years as an assistant to Stanford White (1853–1906), all of it was under the influence of the principles of design taught at the École des Beaux Arts in Paris. It is therefore only natural that Gilbert should have become an architect in the Beaux Arts tradition, designing eclectic buildings in many styles derived from the past.

GILBERT, CASS Exterior, U.S. Customs House (1907), New York, N.Y. *(Wurts Brothers)*

GILBERT, CASS Interior, U.S. Customs House (1907), New York, N.Y. *(Wurts Brothers)*

GILBERT, CASS Woolworth Building (1913), New York, N.Y. *(Joseph W. Molitor)*

GILBERT, CASS George Washington Bridge (1931), New York, N.Y. [*Engineer: Othmar Hermann Ammann. (The Port Authority of New York and New Jersey)*]

Like his contemporary, John Russell Pope (1874–1937), Gilbert was very good at it. He produced buildings that were scholarly, well designed, and quite popular, but like those of Pope, something of an anachronism in the years just before World War II. He also became a very skilled draftsman, producing fine drawings and renderings to show his clients and others his proposed building designs. And his designs have long been considered among the very best of the late Eclectic period in American architecture. He had little patience with the developing modern movement in American architecture, continuing to produce eclectic buildings to the last, some of which were completed in the late 1930s, after his death.

Gilbert also became one of the most successful architects in the United States, producing a very large number of buildings during his almost 50 years of private practice. Unlike some architects of the time, who tended to design buildings only in and near the cities in which their offices were located, Gilbert built a national practice, designing buildings not only in New York City but in Washington, the Midwest, Arkansas, West Virginia, Missouri, and many other places.

Gilbert also designed a large number of building types, such as office buildings, public buildings, art museums, libraries, and banks. In addition, he planned college campuses for the University of Minnesota, Minneapolis, and the University of Texas, Austin. Gilbert also did architectural designs for bridges, including, in New York City, the Bayonne Bridge between Staten Island and New Jersey and the

great George Washington Bridge between Manhattan and New Jersey, both completed in 1931, and both engineered by the noted Swiss-American engineer, Othmar Hermann Ammann (1879–1965). See article entitled bridge.

Works Some of the most notable of Gilbert's buildings in New York City are the U.S. Customs House (1907); the Woolworth Building (1913), the tallest building in the world when it was built; the New York Life Insurance Building (1928); the New York County Lawyers Building (1930); the North Building (1930), of the National Institute of Arts and Letters and American Academy of Arts and Sciences; and the U.S. Courthouse, completed by his son, Cass Gilbert, Jr., in 1936. His deteriorated Customs House is now being restored, for use as a federal office building.

Notable buildings of Gilbert's in Washington are the U.S. Treasury Annex (1919), the U.S. Chamber of Commerce Building (1925), and U.S. Supreme Court Building (see illustration in article capital, United States), finished by his son in 1935. Important buildings in other locations include the Minnesota State Capitol (1903), St. Paul; the Festival Hall and Art Building (1904), now the St. Louis Art Museum, at the Louisiana Purchase Exposition, St. Louis; the Ives Memorial Library (1905), New Haven, Conn.; the Central Public Library (1912), St. Louis; the Detroit Public Library (1914); the Allen Memorial Art Museum (1917), Oberlin College, Oberlin, Ohio; and the Federal Reserve Bank (1924), Minneapolis.

Life Cass Gilbert was born on November 24, 1859, in Zanesville, Ohio. When he was young, his family moved to St. Paul, Minn., where Gilbert grew up and received his early education. At eighteen, he went to work for an architect in St. Paul for about a year. In 1878 he entered Massachusetts Institute of Technology, Cambridge, where he studied for a year, and in 1879 he went to Europe where he studied and traveled in England, France, and Italy.

Upon his return from Europe in 1880, Gilbert went to work for the New York City architectural firm of McKim, Mead and White, and became an assistant to one of the partners, Stanford White. After two years, Gilbert left the firm in 1882 to form a partnership in St. Paul with James Knox Taylor (1857–1939), which lasted more than 10 years. The firm was moderately successful, but Gilbert did not come into prominence until 1896 when, after dissolving the partnership, he won the competition for the design of the Minnesota State Capitol, St. Paul. In 1898 he won another important competition, that for the U.S. Customs House, New York City. After winning the second competition, Gilbert moved his office to New York City and practiced there the remainder of his life.

In 1887 Gilbert married Julia T. Finch and they had a son, Cass Gilbert, Jr., who became an architect and a partner in his father's firm, and carried on the practice after his father's death. The Minnesota State Capitol brought Gilbert considerable recognition and soon his practice began to grow very rapidly. Eventually, he became one of the most successful architects of his time.

Gilbert was very active in civic and professional affairs, belonging to a number of organizations, including the American Academy of Arts and Letters and the National Academy of Design. He served as president of the American Academy and also, in 1908–09, of the American Institute of Architects. He received honorary degrees from a number of universities. Appointed to the chairmanship of the National Council of Fine Arts by President Theodore Roosevelt (1858–1919), he later served on the National Commission of Fine Arts, 1910–18, under presidents William Howard Taft (1857–1930) and Woodrow Wilson (1856–1924). On May 19, 1934, after nearly a half-decade of practice, Cass Gilbert died while on a trip to England.

Related Articles ECLECTIC ARCHITECTURE; MCKIM, MEAD AND WHITE.

Further Reading Gilbert, Cass: *Reminiscenses and Addresses*, Scribner, New York, 1935; Thompson, Neil B.: *Minnesota State Capitol—The Art and Politics of a Public Building*, Minnesota Historical Society, St. Paul, 1974.

GILL, IRVING JOHN

American architect (1870–1936). In spite of having had no formal training in architecture, Irving Gill nevertheless became one of the most important pioneers of the modern movement in architecture. He developed a unique design style, apparently from study, experimentation, and participation in the construction process. He believed that the interiors and landscaping of buildings were integral parts of the architecture. He was concerned with the sociological aspects of low-cost housing. He was an experimenter, innovator, and inventor, using the newest building materials and methods. Thus his work has deeply affected architecture ever since.

A contemporary of the Greene brothers, Gill was, like them, deeply interested in good craftsmanship. This interest led the Greenes to elaborate, handcrafted details and forms, mostly in wood and other natural materials, combined into a rich and even more elaborate overall design for buildings. Gill's interest led him in the opposite direction to details and forms simplified almost to abstractions, in new materials, particularly reinforced concrete, combined into designs for buildings composed of masses that are angular, cubic solids, with broad surfaces and deep voids. To achieve a high level of craftsmanship, Gill trained his own construction crews, made up mostly of German, English, and Scandinavian immigrants. With the Greenes, everything was richly ornamented and handcrafted. With Gill, there were plain, clean surfaces, with little ornamentation.

Experimental Materials and Devices Gill started his own practice in 1895, and the first 10 years or so gave only a slight indication of his later development. His designs were eclectic, in a variety of styles and materials, but were also beginning to show experimentation with building materials and methods and with form. In 1907, in the Klauber and Laughlin

houses in San Diego, he used concrete and hollow-tile structure. And in the latter, he used concrete floors that curved up at their edges to form smooth surfaces with the walls above. He had done this in kitchens and bathrooms before, but here he used the process throughout the house. He was experimenting with laborsaving devices for housewives which made his houses more sanitary than others. Among these were a disposal that dropped garbage into a basement incinerator, a vacuum cleaner system that carried dust and debris from outlets in all rooms through pipes to the furnace, rooms with no dust-catching moldings, flush doors that had invisible hinges or slid into walls, a refrigerator with a door in the outside kitchen wall for milk deliveries, and a system in the garage that sprayed an entire car for washing.

Works Gill continued using concrete and hollow tile in other buildings. A notable example was the five-story Wilson Acton Hotel (1908) in La Jolla, his tallest building. In 1908 he began to experiment with monolithic concrete structures in Scripps Institution for Oceanography Building (1908), the Holly Sefton Memorial Hospital (1908), Bishop's School (1909), all in La Jolla, and in the Christian Science Church (1909) and Bishop's Day School (1909), both in San Diego. All showed his progress toward near-ultimate simplification of forms.

In 1911 Gill bought, from the U.S. government, equipment for tilt-slab construction, a method of pouring concrete into steel-reinforced hollow-tile forms laid on a large table. With this equipment, a whole wall could be poured with metal door and window frames in place, and after having been cured and finished with a coating of fine cement, could be raised to the vertical by a small engine. In 1912 he used tilt-slab in the Banning House, Los Angeles, and in 1913 in the Women's Club, La Jolla. In 1914 he used tilt-slab walls 60 ft long for the Community House at Scripps Institution. Such was Gill's interest in concrete that he established a laboratory in his office for experiments and tests on concrete. He used concrete for the Walter Luther Dodge House (1916), generally considered his greatest building, but now destroyed, and for the Ellen Scripps House (1916), now the Art Center, in La Jolla. The latter house, now drastically altered, was the epitome of Gill's mature style.

During his whole career, Gill was deeply interested in low-cost housing for laborers, the unemployed, and others who ordinarily could not afford decent housing. He designed a number of projects of this kind, always seeking to provide economical solutions to the problems of good housing. Among his designs of this kind was Lewis Courts (1910), Sierra Madre, which he always said was his favorite design. Following this were a series of low-cost projects, including barracks for Mexican laborers and housing for resettled Indians.

After 1917, commissions became fewer as potential clients turned away from Gill's designs to the new Spanish Colonial style made popular by the Panama

GILL, IRVING Dodge House (1916, demolished 1970), Hollywood, Calif. *(Julius Shulman)*

GILL, IRVING Art Center, formerly the Scripps House (1916), La Jolla, Calif. *(Wayne Andrews)*

Pacific Exposition of 1915. After that, he designed only two additional major works, the Civic Center, Oceanside, and the Christian Science Church, Coronado, both built in 1929. Neither building was experimental. Gill's pioneering of forms and materials had come to an end.

Life Irving John Gill was born in Syracuse, New York, in 1870, the son of a building contractor. He had only a high school education. His early architectural training came from his contact with his father's business and from working for a short time in an architect's office in Syracuse. Becoming aware of the work of Louis Henri Sullivan (1856–1924), Gill went to Chicago in 1890 and was hired by the firm of Adler and Sullivan, joining another young employee, Frank Lloyd Wright (1867–1959), almost three years older than Gill, who had come to this office two years earlier.

Gill worked and studied with Sullivan for two years, participating in the drawings for Sullivan's Transportation Building for the Chicago World's Columbian Exposition of 1893. Tired from overwork and ill, Gill went to Californa in 1892 for a rest. Arriving in San Diego, Gill was impressed by the climate, the surroundings, and the quality of the life. He decided to stay and, except for short periods, lived in California the rest of his life.

Gill's first building, the Normal School (1895), in San Diego, but now demolished, was an undistinguished building with Ionic columns, a form he never used again. During the next few years, he designed other buildings in eclectic styles, including one in Gothic Revival. In 1898 he formed a partnership with W. S. Hebbard, and together they continued designing houses and other buildings in various styles. The partnership was dissolved in 1906, and Gill's buildings began to show evidence of his future directions.

Those who knew Gill thought him sincere and straightforward, with a winning personality. As a result, during the next few years, Gill's office grew and prospered until by 1911, he had six draftsmen, a field supervisor, and a secretary, a mighty accomplishment in a town of 25,000 in which contractors did almost all the design and construction of buildings. Among the draftsmen were his nephew, Louis J. Gill, John Lloyd Wright (1892–1978), the son of his former fellow-draftsman in Sullivan's office, and Hazel Wood Waterman (1865–1948). All later became noted architects.

During this period, Gill had been expected to be named chief architect of the San Diego Panama Pacific Exposition to be held in 1915. Instead, an Eastern architect, Bertram Grosvenor Goodhue (1869–1924) was selected, turning the design of the fair away from Gill's developing modernism to the eclecticism of the Spanish Colonial style. This style made an immediate hit in Southern California and, after 1915, the work of Gill's office radically declined.

The work revived somewhat when Frederick Law Olmsted, Jr. (1870–1957) and his half brother John Charles (1852–1920), son, and stepson of the great landscape architect, received a commission to plan a new industrial town, Torrance, near Los Angeles. The Olmsteds promoted Gill's nomination as chief architect for the building of the town. They had met Gill some years before and in fact the architect had designed a house for John Charles in Newport, R.I. The brothers had also been instrumental in his receiving commissions for two other large houses in Rhode Island. Excited by the prospect of the new town, Gill established an office in Los Angeles to be near the work, leaving his nephew, Louis, in charge of the San Diego office. Again the architect was to be disappointed. He saw only a few small buildings, a railroad station, and a bridge of his built. Of the hundreds of houses that were planned, only 10 were built, but not as Gill had designed them. His designs for simple, economical concrete houses were rejected after having been opposed by labor for having dispensed with traditional details. In their stead were built wood houses in traditional styles.

In 1916 Gill closed the San Diego office and had little to do but remodeling work. By that time, he had designed about 100 houses and 50 other buildings in the San Diego area. After that, he designed only a few buildings, only one or two of them notable examples of his work.

In 1928, at age fifty-eight, Gill married Mrs. Marion Brashear of Palos Verdes, where he went to live, and they moved a year later to a small house in Carlsbad that belonged to his wife. Here, in 1929, he suffered a heart attack. In 1933, after a second attack, he moved to Lakeside to design and supervise the construction of cottages and a chapel for the resettlement of Indians at Rancho Barona. His last design was a small building in Redondo Beach in 1936. His client took the drawings to be blueprinted and Gill never again saw his drawings or his client. Gill died on October 7, 1936, almost forgotten, his contributions to architecture unrecognized.

Some 34 years after his death, the Dodge House, owned many years by the city, was sold and in spite of the fervent efforts of those who wanted to preserve it, was demolished in 1970. His masterpiece is gone, but Gill's reputation as one of the pioneers of modern architecture has now been reestablished.

Related Articles GREENE AND GREENE; SULLIVAN, LOUIS HENRI.

GLASS An important building material, usually transparent or translucent, made from sand (silicon dioxide), soda (sodium oxide), and lime (calcium oxide), and used for windows and many other purposes.

Types There are literally hundreds of thousands of kinds of glass, most of them for specialized purposes. Among the most used in architecture are flat glass, for windows, doors, and similar purposes; blown glass, for such things as light bulbs; corrugated glass; and pressed glass, as in block; and glass fibers, for such purposes as thermal insulation, textiles, and reinforcing for plastics.

The most important type used in architecture is flat glass; there are three major kinds: sheet, plate, and float. All three are used for glazing windows and similar purposes. Sheet glass, drawn molten from furnaces through rollers that flatten it, is most widely used for glazing windows. The only polishing it receives is from the fire in the furnace. Plate glass is made in a similar manner, but is then ground and polished. It is also used for glazing windows and similar purposes, particularly for those, such as show windows of stores, in which exceptional clarity is required. Float glass, made by floating molten glass on top of molten metal, usually tin, has smooth, flat surfaces similar to those of plate glass, without requiring grinding and polishing operations. Float glass is used in applications similar to those of plate.

Flat Glass Many special types of flat glass are widely used in architecture, including patterned, heat-strengthened, structural, laminated, tempered, tinted or heat-absorbing, reflective, and wire glass. Patterned glass is produced by rolling the molten material through rollers that have designs. Available in numerous designs, patterned glass is usually translucent and may be tempered or heat-absorbing. Heat-strengthened and structural glass are used mostly for curtain-wall panels or facings for walls or partitions. Heat-strengthened glass is about twice as strong as plate glass and has ceramic, colored glazes fused to its surface. Structural glass has integral colors produced with metal oxides. It may be heat-strengthened or tempered to improve its strength.

Laminated glass is manufactured in two major types: safety glass and bullet-resisting glass. The types are similar except that safety glass has one layer of plastic to which are laminated two layers of glass, while bullet-resisting has at least three layers of plastic and four of glass. Both types are resistant to damage from impact and, when broken, the plastic holds the pieces of glass, preventing them from flying loose. Safety glass is available with heat-absorbing qualities, tinted, translucent, reflective, or clear. It is used in architecture where there is danger of impact, such as in sports arenas. Bullet-resisting glass is used in architecture for drive-in windows of banks and similar places where dangers of burglaries exists.

Tempered glass is heavy sheet, plate, or float glass that has been given a special heat treatment, consisting of reheating the glass and cooling it very quickly with jets of cold air. Tempered glass is quite resistant to breakage by impact. If broken, which rarely happens, it shatters into small rounded fragments that are not as dangerous as the sharp pieces of broken glass of other types. It is available in clear, tinted, reflective, and patterned forms, and in a special glazed form, used for school chalkboards. Tempered glass is used for all-glass doors in buildings and for glazing where impact damage may be expected to occur. Tempered glass cannot be cut or drilled. Therefore it must be made in accurate sizes, with holes for hardware formed in advance.

Tinted, or heat-absorbing, glass may be heavy sheet, plate, or float glass. Available generally in gray, bronze-colored, or blue-green, heat-absorbing glass is used for glazing that is expected to reduce heat gains in buildings. It may be obtained in tempered, laminated, and patterned forms. Reflective, sometimes called mirror, glass may be used for the same purpose. Coated on one side with thin-metal coatings, reflective glass reduces the amount of heat that enters buildings by reflecting it away in a manner similar to a mirror. In fact, this glass is sometimes called a one-way mirror, because people on its darker side, inside buildings, can see through it while those on the brighter outside cannot. At night, in lighted interiors of buildings, the phenomenon works in reverse. Reflective glass is available in the same colors and forms as heat-absorbing glass.

Wire glass is heavy sheet, plate, or float glass in which hexagonal, square, or other forms of wire mesh are embedded. It resists damage from impact and upon breaking under heavy impact, the wire holds the pieces of glass intact. Wire glass is used in architecture for applications in which breakage from impact may be expected to occur and where the danger of flying glass must be avoided. It is also resistant to fires and may be used, subject to building code requirements, in firedoors and other places where fire resistance must be provided. It is available plain, patterned, and corrugated.

Assembled Glass Insulating glass is used to prevent heat gains in buildings in hot weather, and heat losses in cold. It is fabricated by joining two or three pieces of glass together with air spaces between them, dehydrating the air spaces, and sealing the edges of the glass. Insulating glass is available in sheet, plate, and float types. It can also be obtained as heat-absorbing, patterned, tempered, or laminated glass. The edges of insulating glass may be sealed in two ways: by use of molten glass to form the edges or by use of special metal alloys. Insulating glass can reduce heat losses or gains to less than half of those experienced with single panes of sheet, plate, or float glass.

Glass blocks are building units that are usually a nominal 4 in thick, made by pressing glass into square or rectangular shapes that have bottoms and sides like bowls. Pairs of these shapes are then fused together to form hollow units, in which the air inside has been dehydrated and partly evacuated. Glass blocks are used in interior and exterior walls, particularly in places in which control of light and good insulating qualities are required.

Many other uses of glass are made in architecture, including applications as glass fibers or foamed glass in thermal insulation; see the the article entitled insulation, thermal. Other special types include mirrors, made with thin coatings of metals, and one-way mirrors, with even thinner coatings of metal. Installed on a wall with an opening behind it, a one-way mirror allows observers on the dimly lighted back side to see into a brightly lighted space on the other side, where

GLASS IBM Building (1975), Mount Pleasant, N.Y. [*Architect: Edward L. Barnes. (Joseph W. Molitor)*]

GLASS Continental Oil Co. Building (1972), Stamford, Conn. [*Architect: Victor Bisharat. (Joseph W. Molitor)*]

the glass appears to be a mirror. One-way mirrors are used in places where activities or experiments must be observed unseen by those being observed, such as nursery schools, laboratories, psychiatric hospitals, and so on.

Other types of glass sometimes used in architecture include heat-conducting glass, treated with chemicals to conduct heat; radiation-absorbing glass, available in types that control the transmission of heat, x-rays, and other rays; and radiation-transmitting glass, in types that may allow heat but not light to be transmitted or, unlike regular glass, admit ultraviolet rays while excluding heat rays.

Properties A very large number of types and sizes of glass are available for use in architecture, with widely varied properties and characteristics. While most types of sheet, plate, and float glass transmit 85 to 95 percent of visible light and exclude ultraviolet rays, other types are available with very different transmission properties. Most types of glass may be fabricated by such methods as pressing, blowing, rolling, grinding, polishing, and bending to no less than a 6-in radius. However, some glass, such as the tempered type, cannot be fabricated at all after it is made. While the most generally used glass is clear, many types may be obtained in a variety of colors. The selection of specific glass types to be used for various purposes in individual buildings requires definition of the functions to be served and determination of building and other code requirements concerning glass uses, allowable sizes and conditions, and installation procedures.

Sheet glass comes in two major types: window and heavy sheet. Window glass comes in single strength, used mostly for framing pictures and similar purposes, and double strength, used for window glazing and similar purposes. Grades of double-strength glass, in ⅛ in thickness, from the most perfect to the least, are AA, A, and B, usually designated as DSAA, DSA, and DSB. Heavy sheet glass is available in the same grades, in thicknesses ranging from $3/16$ to $7/16$ in. Both types of glass come in many standard sizes up to 7 by 10 ft. Float glass is available in the same grades, in thicknesses from ⅛ to 1 in, and in sizes up to slightly more than 10 by 25 ft. Plate glass, for window glazing and similar purposes, comes in thicknesses from $5/16$ to $1\frac{1}{4}$ in, and in sizes up to the same maximum as float glass. Special types of glass are available in a variety of sizes and thicknesses. Glass blocks come in nominal sizes of 6, 8, and 12 in² and 4 by 12 in, rectangular.

Information on the properties, characteristics, sizes, and other aspects of glass are available from manufacturers, along with information on proper installation. In general, glazing is usually accomplished with putties or glazing compounds, specifically formulated for use with wood, aluminum, steel, and other frame materials, Another method involves the use of special gaskets made of rubber, neoprene, or plastics.

Architectural design with glass can produce results that are often quite exciting in contemporary buildings. It is very important to select the proper kind of glass, have it installed properly and in acceptable sizes, with proper clearances for expansion, and in accordance with applicable building and other codes.

History Glass is one of the oldest materials used in architecture and one of the best liked. The first knowledge humans had of the material came from natural glass, fused by the heat of lightning or volcanoes. When the first glass was made by humans is not known, but it is believed that the first use was for glazes on ceramic jars or other vessels, about 3000 B.C. Glass rods and beads are also thought to have been made in Mesopotamia and Egypt about that time. The first use of glass for drinking vessels and similar purposes is thought to have occurred about 1,500 B.C. in the same countries. By 750 B.C., glass was widely used in the Mediterranean civilizations. The blowing of glass began before 30 B.C.

The Romans knew how to make both important types of glass: crown and cylinder. Crown glass is made by blowing the molten material into a rough sphere, then spinning it until it is flattened into a fairly flat, round form. Cylinder glass is made by a more complicated process, which also begins with blowing the molten glass into a bulb approximately the shape of a sphere. Then the bulb is swung to give it the shape, approximately, of a cylinder, after which both ends are pierced and opened wide. Again heated, the open-ended cylinder is split with a hot iron, and the glass flattened into a sheet. The Romans were skilled glassmakers and used the material extensively for many purposes, including bowls, vases, and other vessels; jewelry; and other relatively small objects. The Romans also made and used the first window glass, starting about A.D. 50, in small pieces but quite clear. After the Romans, the making and use of glass declined until about 1000, when it was revived in Venice, Italy. Glass was also made in the Middle East.

During the Middle Ages, glassmaking was dominated by the Venetians for some time, after which the art spread throughout Europe. Both crown and cylinder glass were made and used in architecture. By about the 12th century, glass, mostly in small panes, was widely used in churches and by the 14th in important residences, such as palaces and villas. One of the glories of Gothic architecture, particularly in churches and cathedrals, is stained-glass windows. Actually, much of the so-called stained glass was colored with translucent paints. Others were colored with metallic oxides while melted, and still others were regular glass with thin layers of colored glass fused to their surfaces. The latter type was called flashed glass. The usual method for installing glass included shaping the pieces to size, firing those that had been painted in kilns, inserting the pieces in lead channels that were soldered together, and finally installing the assembly of glass and lead into a framework of iron.

Medieval glass had many imperfections, mostly in the form of trapped air bubbles. Although the Romans had made glass that was quite clear, the Gothic artisans were unable to duplicate the feat, their ordinary glass being somewhat colored. The art of making clear glass was rediscovered in Venice in the 15th century and was afterward widely used in buildings from the time of the Renaissance to the present. In the 16th century, Venetian glassblowers brought the art of making clear, crown glass to England, after which crown glass was widely used there until the 19th century. By that time, the use of glass in Europe had spread to modest homes, after its price came down to an affordable level. About the third quarter of the 17th century, the method of casting glass was developed in France and was subsequently widely used. Cast glass had numerous defects, but later it was considerably improved.

American Development Glassmaking began very early in the American colonies, a factory having been established at Jamestown, Va., in 1608, a year after the first colonists arrived. It closed a year later after a famine. In 1621 the Jamestown colonists tried again, but glass manufacturing ceased once again, this time mainly because of the massacre of colonists by Indians in 1622. Other glasshouses, as they were then called, were started in a number of places in the colonies. All failed soon after being founded, until an emigrant from Germany, Caspar Wistar (1696–1752), built one in New Jersey, near Philadelphia, in 1739; it operated until 1780.

Many of the earliest colonial buildings in America utilized oiled paper and other materials in their windows because of the shortage of glass, which continued for some years. When glass was used, it generally was nailed into window frames instead of puttied as was the custom later. During the 17th century, cast glass was first produced in Europe, and methods were later developed for grinding and polishing it. After that, few improvements were made in glass for use in architecture until just before the 20th century began.

In the late 19th century, with the beginning of the modern movement in architecture, glass became one of the most important building materials. The early modern architects began to use glass in large panes, often in continuous, or almost continuous, strips of windows in many of their buildings. Later the amount of glass used in each building increased even further. Such major uses of glass in architecture were made possible by the introduction of new methods of glassmaking. In 1901 the first method for making large sheets of glass, called the Fourcault process, was developed. Named after a Belgian, Émile Fourcault, the process consisted of drawing molten glass directly from a furnace through a slot. By 1917, an American mechanical engineer, Irving W. Colburn (1861–1917), had developed a glass drawing machine for making sheet window glass, a process still in use today. About 1887, a process for making rolled plate glass was developed in England.

Other developments in glass have since followed. In 1926 production of safety glass began, followed by the first manufactured insulating glass, or double glazing, in 1930. Glass block was introduced in 1933. Glass fibers, widely used today for insulation and other purposes, were introduced in 1938 and foamed glass, used for insulation, in 1942. Float glass was introduced in England in 1959. Glass, produced by this process, has very flat surfaces and a brilliant finish as if it had been polished. Beginning in the 1950s, other developments have taken place, including heat-resistant, or absorbing, glass and reflective, or mirror, glass, both often used in building today.

In the 20th century, an important element in architecture has been large areas of glass, often fixed in place in many buildings. Very large windows were used in the Fagus Factory (1911), Alfeld, Germany, designed by Walter Adolf Gropius (1883–1969), foreshadowing curtain walls and window walls, so much a part of architecture since the late 1940s. Such walls would never have become feasible without the development of dependable and economical air-conditioning systems. However, their forerunners go back to such buildings as the glass-enclosed Crystal Palace (1851), designed by Sir Joseph Paxton (1801–65) for the Great Exhibition, London, and the Bibliothèque Nationale (1868), Paris, designed by Henri Labrouste (1801–75).

Today glass of many kinds is widely used in buildings of all types. Perhaps the most important types are sheet window, plate, and float glass, and glass-fiber insulation. Double and triple glazing are also of importance, as are heat-absorbing, tempered, and reflective glass types. Stained glass, which had been such a powerful element in Gothic architecture, was used less frequently afterward and virtually stopped being used by about the 18th century. It came back into demand during the Gothic Revival and Eclectic periods of architecture in the 19th century. Today stained glass is again frequently used in religious and other building types, some designed by great contemporary artists. In recent years, the use of large areas of glass in building has declined somewhat, mainly because of the problems of shortages and sharply rising prices of fuels used to cool and heat buildings.

Related Articles CLIMATE; DOOR; ENERGY; HEATING, VENTILATING, AND AIR CONDITIONING; FARM BUILDING; INSULATION, THERMAL; LIGHTING; OFFICE BUILDING; RELIGIOUS BUILDING; WALL; WINDOW.

Further Reading Hunt, William Dudley, Jr.: *The Contemporary Curtain Wall—Its Design, Fabrication and Erection*, F. W. Dodge, New York, 1958.

Source of Additional Information Stained Glass Association of America, 1125 Wilmington Ave., St. Louis, Mo. 63111.

GOTHIC REVIVAL ARCHITECTURE An architectural movement, or style, in which the forms and details of buildings were derived from the Gothic style

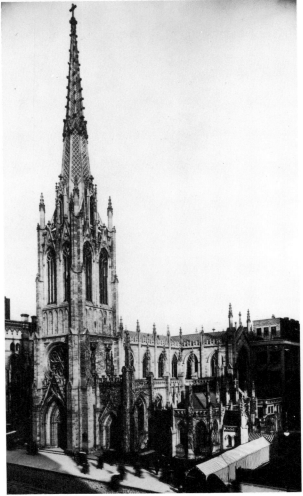

GOTHIC REVIVAL ARCHITECTURE Grace Church (1846), New York, N.Y. [*Architect: James Renwick. (American Studio, Library of Congress)*]

GOTHIC REVIVAL ARCHITECTURE Harral House (1846), Bridgeport, Conn. [*Architect: Alexander Jackson Davis. (Wayne Andrews)*]

GOTHIC REVIVAL ARCHITECTURE Afton Villa (1849, later demolished), St. Francisville, La. [*Architect: unknown. (Wayne Andrews)*]

GOTHIC REVIVAL ARCHITECTURE Exterior, St. Mary's Church (1854), Burlington, N.J. [*Architect: Richard Upjohn. (Wayne Andrews)*]

GOTHIC REVIVAL ARCHITECTURE Interior, St. Mary's Church (1854), Burlington, N.J. [*Architect: Richard Upjohn. (Wayne Andrews)*]

GOTHIC REVIVAL ARCHITECTURE Lyndhurst (1865), Tarrytown, N.Y. [*Architect: Alexander Jackson Davis. (Wayne Andrews)*]

of the Middle Ages. Beginning in Europe in the early 18th century, the movement spread to America where it strongly influenced many architects and their buildings until the end of the 19th century and afterward. Architecture in this style, during the last 60 years of the 19th century, is often called Victorian, after Queen Victoria (1819–1901), during whose reign (1837–1901) it was built. Great impetus was given the movement when the Queen insisted that architects Sir Charles Barry (1795–1860) and Augustus Welby Northmore Pugin (1812–52) use the Gothic Revival style for the English Houses of Parliament, designed in 1836 and completed in 1860.

Characteristics   While Classic Revival architecture, which had begun earlier in America, was based on the cool, rational ideals of classicism, Gothic Revival, from about the beginning of the 18th century, was based on imagination, emotions, the unconventional, mysticism, and the implied true Christianity of medieval forms and ornament. Gothic Revival architecture got off to a rather slow start in the United States. Although a few buildings in the style were designed previously, the first of national importance was Trinity Church (1846), New York City, designed by Richard Upjohn (1802–78). This church received widespread recognition and helped greatly in the establishment of Upjohn as the dominant church architect and Gothicist of his time and one of the most successful architects of all time. It also helped greatly in establishing a tradition of Gothic Revival as the predominant style for churches, a tradition that has lasted in some degree to the present time.

English Influence   Gothic Revival architecture in the United States was greatly inspired and influenced by that in England and by books on the subject by English writers, including architects Pugin and his father, Augustus Charles (1762–1832) and by the critic John Ruskin (1819–1900). Upjohn was influenced by their writings and designed a great number of church buildings, houses, and other buildings in the Gothic Revival style. Another architect who became famous for his designs in the Gothic Revival style, James Renwick, Jr. (1818–95), was also deeply influenced by such books and by Gothic architecture. However, Renwick sometimes designed buildings in other styles, such as the Romanesque. Upjohn and Renwick are usually acknowledged as the greatest Gothic Revival architects.

Another architect who approached their level, and surpassed it in residential work, was Alexander Jackson Davis (1803–92), who started out working in the Classic Revival style, but later turned to the Gothic. With his partner Ithiel Town (1784–1844), Davis designed many fine Gothic Revival houses as well as other buildings in Gothic and other styles. Another important Gothic Revival architect, who also designed buildings in other styles, was Minard Lafever (1797–1854).

By the beginning of the Civil War, the great era of Gothic Revival architecture was beginning in the United States. Its exponents had by then designed and constructed a large number of great churches in many places, together with numerous houses and buildings of other types. Upjohn had published a book of plans that were used to erect modest wood Gothic churches and other buildings in even the smallest towns in out-of-the-way places. Many people admired the mystical, ornamental, and soaring aspects of the style and many still do. The beginning of Eclectic architecture had taken place as early as the 1830s and the movement had gradually achieved some importance in the United States by the time the Civil War began.

Amalgamation After the Civil War, Gothic Revival architecture entered another phase, this time as one important style, alongside all the rest, Romanesque, Renaissance, Colonial, Classical, and so on, that collectively are called eclecticism. From this time, for many years to come, architects would choose what they thought an appropriate style for each new building from all of those available from the past. Eventually they would employ every imaginable style, and combine several styles in single buildings, though the effect would often be disconcerting, even chaotic in some cases. In others, especially when the most talented architects of the time, such as Henry Hobson Richardson (1838–86), Ralph Adams Cram (1863–1942), Stanford White (1853–1906), or Frank Furness (1839–1912), were involved, the results turned out to be architecture of the highest excellence.

Related Articles ECLECTIC ARCHITECTURE; HISTORY OF ARCHITECTURE; PRESERVATION; RENWICK, JAMES, JR.; UPJOHN, RICHARD; Various articles on other Gothic Revival and Eclectic architects.

Further Reading Andrews, Wayne: *American Gothic—Its Origins, Its Trials, It Triumphs,* Random House, New York, 1975; Loth, Calder, and Julius Trousdale Sadler, Jr.: *The Only Proper Style—Gothic Architecture in America,* New York Graphic Society, Boston, 1976; See also listing in the article entitled history of architecture.

Sources of Additional Information See listing in the article entitled history of architecture.

GOVERNMENT The system of social control, under law. Government on every level, from the local to the federal, strongly affects architecture in many ways. Among the most important are controls on architecture by means of codes and standards, statutes, and regulations; licensing of architects, engineers, and others in the building industry; control of financing of buildings by agencies, such as the Federal Housing Administration (FHA) and Veterans Administration (VA); and as the owners, clients of architects, of a great number of buildings and building complexes of every size and almost every type.

The role of government in architecture on every level is so all-pervasive that information on the subject is included in a number of articles in this book. Among the most important are those listed at the end of this article. Governments on all levels are very important clients of architects. There are so many variations between the ways municipalities, counties, and states handle the design and construction of buildings that no meaningful discussion is possible here. However, some information of this sort is contained in articles on various building types in this book.

Federal Programs The federal government has many wide-ranging programs of design and construction. While the subject is too complex to be covered in detail, federal government construction programs are of such importance to architects and other building design professionals that the major considerations should be discussed. While the number and types of buildings, and the amount of money spent on them vary considerably from year to year, the federal government, by any measure, is the biggest client for American architects. And through various programs of federal grants and subsidies for public housing, community development, and other purposes the biggest client, in effect, becomes even bigger.

The General Services Administration (GSA), an independent agency, has the responsibility for the design, construction, operation, and maintenance of more public buildings, some 10,000, than any other federal department or agency. These include buildings of many types, other than military, and make GSA the most important federal agency to architects. GSA operates through regional offices.

Military construction is accomplished by the U.S. Department of Defense (DOD), through the services, Air Force, Army, and Navy, all of which have regional offices. Other executive departments that contract for architectural and related services are Agriculture, through its Agricultural Research Service and U.S. Forest Service, both with regions, and Animal and Plant Health Inspection Service; Health and Human Services (HHS), which has regional offices; Housing and Urban Development (HUD), also with regional offices; Interior, through its bureaus of Indian Affairs and Land Management, and the National Park Service, all with regional or divisional offices; Justice, through the Bureau of Prisons; State, in its Foreign Service and foreign civilian agency programs; Transportation (DOT), through its Federal Aviation Administration, with regions, U.S. Coast Guard, with districts, and Federal Railway Administration; and the Department of Education, established in 1979.

Two other independent agencies, each responsible for its own building design and construction program, are the U.S. Postal Service, which has regional offices, and the Veterans Administration. A few other federal agencies sometimes contract for architectural and related services, mostly for studies and research or development projects.

Regulations Federal contracting for architectural and related services, which in government parlance is called procurement, is subject to a host of statutes and regulations that are not only difficult to understand but which vary between types of construction and between departments and agencies. Some departments and agencies have at least a portion of their buildings designed by architects and engineers, and other design professionals who are their employees. Others contract with independent practitioners exclusively.

In addition to the statutes and regulations that apply to federal construction in general, each department or agency generally has regulations and standards of its own. These vary considerably. In general, an architect, engineer, or other design professional seeking a federal commission must submit an information questionnaire that must be brought up to date periodically. If a proposed project costs more than a certain maximum amount, it is required by law to be announced in the *Commerce Business Daily*, published by the U.S. Department of Commerce. Professionals who have current questionnaires on file are automatically considered for these commissions, if they do not involve large amounts of money in professional fees. Those without questionnaires on file must submit another kind of questionnaire for each specific project. If a proposed project will involve large amounts in professional fees, every architect, engineer, or other design professional must submit a special questionnaire for each job.

Criteria Certain criteria must be met in the selection of an architect, engineer, or other design professional for federal work. These include geographical considerations, requirements that a share of the work go to small businesses and to firms owned by minorities, and others, in addition to the required experience, competency, and capacity of design firms to perform the work properly.

Work Requirements Architects, engineers, and other design professionals who would like to be considered for federal work should obtain information about the general requirements for such work and the specialized requirements of the various departments and agencies. They should also submit questionnaires and should follow announcements in the *Commerce Business Daily* to determine when additional questionnaires are required for specific projects. If they are to perform professional services for federal departments and agencies, firms must be prepared to deal with a vast array of regulatory material and often with considerable red tape.

Related Articles BUILDING CODES AND STANDARDS; BUILDING INDUSTRY; CAPITAL, UNITED STATES; CAREER; ENERGY; FINANCE; MILITARY BUILDING; PLANNING, CITY; PUBLIC BUILDING.

Further Reading *Contracting with the Federal Government—A Primer for Architects and Engineers*, 2d ed., Committee on Federal Procurement of Architectural and Engineering Services, Washington, 1974; *The Federal Marketplace—Are You Prepared?*, American Institute of Architects, Washington, 1976; Publications of various government departments and agencies.

Sources of Additional Information Committee on Federal Procurement of Architectural and Engineering Services, c/o American Institute of Architects, 1735 New York Ave., N.W., Washington, D.C. 20006; General Services Administration, 18th and F Sts., N.W., Washington, D.C. 20405; U.S. Department of Agriculture, 6505 Belcrest Rd., Hyattsville, Md. 20782; U.S. Department of Defense, The Pentagon, Washington, D.C. 20301; U.S. Department of Health and Human Services, 330 Independence Ave., S.W., Washington, D.C., 20201; U.S. Department of Housing and Urban Development, 451 7th St., S.W., Washington, D.C. 20410; U.S. Department of Interior, 18th and C Sts., N.W., Washington, D.C. 20240; U.S. Department of State, 2201 C St., N.W., Washington, D.C. 20520; U.S. Department of Transportation, 400 7th St., N.W. Washington, D.C. 20590; U.S. Postal Service, 475 L'Enfant Plaza, S.W., Washington, D.C. 20260; Veterans Administration, 810 Vermont Ave., N.W., Washington, D.C. 20420.

Periodical *Commerce Business Daily*, Superintendent of Documents, Government Printing Office, Washington, D.C. 20402.

GRAPHIC DESIGN
The art and science of drawing, according to mathematical and artistic principles. Graphic design, or graphics, is important in architecture, not only in plans and other working drawings for the construction of buildings but in drawings and renderings for presentations to clients and for other purposes, in brochures showing the work of architects and other environmental designers, in books and magazine articles, and in signs and other uses in and around buildings.

All such uses of graphic design in architecture, other than for brochures and similar uses and in and around buildings, are discussed in articles listed at the end of this article. For a discussion of graphic design, along with the basic principles of printing processes, see the article entitled book, architectural.

Functions Other than in working drawings and similar work, architectural drawings and renderings serve two important functions: presentation of buildings to clients, potential clients, and others, by showing the actual drawings and renderings or photographic representations in slides; and reproduction of the drawings and renderings in brochures, magazines, and books. In many cases, architects and other environmental designers expect the same drawings and renderings to be used in all these ways. Although it is often impossible to use them for all these purposes, they can be used in most cases if drawings and renderings are prepared properly, with the various end uses in mind. This involves attention to the size and scale of drawings, use of color, gradations of tone, drawing techniques, and other factors.

For example, in preparing a drawing or rendering that will be shown to clients full size and later reproduced in a reduced size in a brochure, magazine, or book, the need for full-size presentation must be balanced with the need for reproduction at reduced size. In general, drawings or renderings to be reproduced should be approximately $1\frac{1}{2}$ to 2 times the reproduction size. If properly drawn, the reduced size of the reproduction will sharpen line and other work when it is printed. Care must be taken not to make the line and other work so detailed or complex that it will not reproduce properly. Any lettering on the rendering or drawing should be simple and large enough to be perfectly legible when it has been reduced.

Drawings or renderings in color are often reproduced in black and white. If the color will not photograph in black and white with considerable variation, or contrast, in tones of grays, the reproduction will not be satisfactory. In making a color drawing or rendering, it must be kept in mind that various colors photograph in black and white in different ways. For example, reds tend to photograph black. In order to check what may happen when a drawing or rendering is reduced for reproduction, reduced photostats may be made while it is in progress, or a reducing glass that works like a magnifying glass in reverse may be used. If the line weights are too heavy or too light, if the lines are so close that they may fill in or so fine that they might break up, or other problems are present, the photostat or reducing glass indicates them.

Reproduction Methods Drawings and renderings are reproduced in brochures, magazines, books, and other places by two major methods: line drawings or halftones. Line drawings reproduce solid lines much as they exist in a drawing. In this method, tones or gradations will not reproduce, but some suggestion of them can be obtained with self-adhering plastic sheets containing cross-hatching, dots, and other graphic devices. Drawings for line reproduction are almost always made with ink.

When the reproduction of tones or gradations is required, as in most pencil drawings with shading, color renderings, and other types, halftones are generally used. Halftones involve a process of photography that breaks up the drawing or rendering into very small dots of various sizes and spacing. The larger the dots, the closer they will be to each other, thus creating relatively dark areas; smaller dots, farther apart, produce lighter areas. For precise work, such as floor plans, details, or diagrams, line drawings are often preferred; for more subtle work, such as perspectives of interiors or exteriors of buildings, the halftone process is usually preferred. For four-color work, halftones are mostly used, separated into four colors, magenta (red), yellow, cyan (blue), and black, and sometimes, for very fine reproductions, into additional colors.

The same principles of reproduction discussed above apply to photographs. In general, large photographs made with large cameras set on tripods reproduce better than small ones made with small hand-held cameras. Photographs with considerable contrast of grays reproduce better than those with less contrast. Color photographs, to be reproduced in black and white, must follow the same principles as color renderings. Finally, only very fine photographs, reproduced properly, show good architecture as it should be shown in brochures, books, and magazines. (See the article entitled photograhy, architectural.)

Not much can be said here about writing for brochures, articles, and books, except to point out that architects and other environmental designers tend to be more graphically minded than verbally minded. In addition, many are not well trained in writing. (For a discussion of some of the principles of preparing and publishing a book, see the article entitled book, architectural. Similar principles apply to the preparation of magazine articles. To be effective, such writing should be well organized; discussions should be straightforward, without too many flourishes; and faith should be put in good editors. And one last point, many architects and other environmental designers are notoriously bad spellers. Good copy editors can help correct this, but care should be taken in spelling, especially in lettering on drawings and renderings to be reproduced.

Typography The typography used in the preparation of brochures and for other purposes is a complex subject. Type faces are so numerous, come in such a wide variety of sizes, and have such a diversity of uses that architects and other environmental designers must usually obtain the services of graphic designers to deal with the typography and layout of brochures and other publications. Magazine and book publishing staffs ordinarily handle these functions for their publications. However, it should be pointed out that type with serifs is generally easier to read than sans serif type. Also important for legibility and ease of reading are the size of types and faces used, the size relative to the length of lines, and the amount of space between lines, or leading, provided.

Brochures and other graphic materials should be prepared to perform their purposes effectively and powerfully. They should be well organized, well designed, written for the audiences they are intended to serve or impress, well illustrated, and direct and complete. Many architectural and other design offices have found that flexible brochures, systematized so that they can be bound together in many ways for various purposes, serve their needs best. With such a system, one type of brochure might be put together for a hospital board considering the construction of a new hospital and a quite different brochure assembled for a school board. Both would contain general information on the firm, including its experience, size, staff, former clients and their buildings, and similar subjects, and specialized information on the building type proposed by a potential client.

Many architects and other environmental design professionals prepare their own brochures and other graphic materials, or have them prepared by people in their offices. Some offices have their own graphic design departments to accomplish this sort of work; a few perform such work for clients and others. For the most part, good brochures and other graphic materials are prepared by free-lance, professional graphic designers, who work as individuals or in design studios.

Brochure Preparation In general, a graphic designer setting out to prepare a brochure or other graphic materials for an architect or environmental firm would start with the purpose to be served, the audience to be reached, and the problems to be solved. A schedule for production of the finished piece might then be established. Materials to be used, such as information and existing drawings and photographs, would then be assembled. The size and shape of the piece would be determined and its format would be designed, including page layouts, title pages and the like, and cover. Type faces and sizes would be selected, including body type and, for the main text, head types and types for other purposes.

The paper, or stock, for printing would be selected, along with the binding material. After the layout has been completed, along with the writing of text and other matter and the illustrations selected or prepared, the project can be readied for printing. The text manuscript must be copy edited for factual and typographical errors, and copy-fitted to the spaces in the layout in which it will appear. Heads and other matter must also go through a similar process. Illustrations must be sized for reproduction, and portions not to be reproduced indicated by marks, or cropped. All items must be marked with instructions for the printer.

In some cases, a graphic designer will prepare, for the printer, camera-ready copy, or mechanicals, sheets on which all the type is placed in proper positions, along with the illustrations or indications of where they will be stripped in by the printer. In other cases, the graphic designer will furnish the printer with detailed layouts, called comprehensives, and the printer does the actual placement of the type and other elements. Sometimes rough sketches are furnished to printers for such purposes, but this practice should be avoided.

After the manuscript and other copy have been typeset by a compositor, galley proofs usually come back to be read for typographical and other errors. The brochure or other publication may then be set into pages and page proofs made, which are read again for errors. Finally, the publication is printed, bound, and ready for use. Many architects and other environmental design professionals consider the work of a graphic designer to be finished when a design for a publication has been submitted and approved. Such a course is not really effective, for some of the most vital services of a graphic designer are in following through on the design with the compositor, printer, binder, and others to ensure that the final product is what was envisioned and expected. In addition, graphic designers should be able to determine and control the costs of publication production and should know where best to have the work accomplished.

Building Signs Signs and other graphic devices in and around buildings are of considerable importance in architecture. Many years ago, the only graphic design in most buildings might consist of Roman lettering, sometimes in Latin, carved into the cornerstones or over the main entrances. Today graphic design is used for those and many other purposes in buildings. In addition, many kinds of signs are used, including types for giving directions, for identification, for warnings, for instruction, for advertising, and simply for ornament. Some considerations that must be taken into account include lettering, colors, pictures,

GRAPHIC DESIGN Steeple Run Elementary School (1977), Naperville, Ill. [*Architects: Orput Assoc. (Hedrich-Blessing)*]

GRAPHIC DESIGN Good Samaritan Hospital (1976), Downers Grove, Ill. [*Architects: Burnham and Hammond. (Hedrich-Blessing)*]

GRAPHIC DESIGN IBM Building (1970), Hawthorne, N.Y. [*Architect: Carl Petrelli. (Joseph W. Molitor)*]

symbols, and lighting. Signs and other graphic devices for buildings are usually designed by specialists, who work in graphic design companies or studios. Large architectural and other environmental design firms may have such specialists on their staffs.

Education Students who think they would like to become graphic designers should have many of the same interests as architects and other environmental designers and artists. For the most part, a general cultural course in secondary school should be pursued, followed by advanced work in an art school, college, or university, Drawing and painting courses in secondary schools vary considerably. If they are not creative, they are thought by many to do more harm than good. In urban centers and sometimes in other places, it is often possible for secondary school students to take certain art and design classes at night or during summer vacations.

Higher education for graphic designers varies considerably. However, a typical course might include, in addition to the usual general and cultural subjects, courses in communication, art and design history, drawing, painting, graphic design, photography, printing processes, layout, makeup, and research. Many graphic designers today have studied such curricula, while others have come from industrial design, architectural, or art schools, and still others have learned through on-the-job training.

In any case, for individuals who like the arts, particularly the visual arts, and want to work in the creation of art that can communicate ideas, graphic design offers meaningful and exciting career opportunities, not only in architecture and the other environmental design fields but in magazine or book publishing, advertising, newspaper work, and other fields.

Architects have always been interested in graphic design, and they are today. Perhaps this can be explained by the fact that while the primary function of architects is the design of buildings and other structures, graphic design, as well as the other arts, is closely and intimately related to architectural design. Another reason is that the creation of architecture is largely accomplished by graphic means, with sketches and drawings of various kinds. The presentation of architectural designs to clients and others is by graphic means, sketches and renderings. Buildings are constructed primarily from working drawings, a graphic means. Architects also often design signs and other graphic devices for buildings and they use graphic design in presentations, brochures, and exhibits.

Thus graphic design naturally pervades many of the thoughts and activities of architects and other environmental designers.

Related Articles ART IN ARCHITECTURE; BOOK, ARCHITECTURAL; COMPUTER; DESIGN, ARCHITECTURAL; DRAFTING; MAGAZINE, ARCHITECTURAL; PHOTOGRAPHY, ARCHITECTURAL; PRACTICE OF ARCHITECTURE; RENDERING; WORKING DRAWING.

Further Reading Abercrombie, Stanley *The Best in Environmental Graphics*, RC Publications, Washington, 1977; Ballinger, Louise Bowen, and Raymond A. Ballinger: *Sign, Symbol and Form*, Van Nostrand Reinhold, New York, 1972; Constantine, Mildred, and Egbert Jacobson: *Sign Language for Buildings and Landscape*, Reinhold, New York, 1961; Gray, Nicolette M.: *Lettering on Buildings*, Reinhold, New York, 1960; Jones, Gerre L.: *How to Prepare Professional Design Brochures*, McGraw-Hill, New York, 1976; Kliment, Stephen A.: *Creative Communications for a Successful Design Practice*, Whitney, New York, 1977; Stevenson, George A.: *Graphic Arts Encyclopedia*, 2d ed., McGraw-Hill, New York, 1979.

GREENE AND GREENE American architectural firm of two brothers, Charles Sumner (1868–1957) and Henry Mather (1870–1954). The Greene brothers had a remarkable life together. Born a short time apart, they went to high school and college together and remained close all their lives. Most importantly, their joint architectural practice, most of the time in Pasadena, Calif., lasted 21 years and had profound effects on modern architecture as well as on the lives of their clients and all who experience their buildings.

Trained in Classical Eclectic architecture, the brothers turned away from this foremost trend of their time to an architecture composed of good planning, fine use of materials, development of ornament, and, perhaps most important of all, excellent craftsmanship, in particular handcraftmanship. They became the foremost of American proponents of what came to be known as the Craft Movement. Begun about the middle of the 19th century in England, primarily by William Morris (1834–96), inventor of the Morris chair, an architect turned painter and promoter of handcrafted articles of wood, metals, textiles, and the like, the movement soon spread to America. The Greenes had attended a high school where they had learned and espoused craftsmanship, and had become deeply engrossed in nature, including the nature of materials. They also became deeply interested in Japanese domestic architecture and the wood houses of Switzerland and other European countries.

Bungalow Style Out of these interests came a steady stream of livable, beautifully detailed and constructed houses, admirably suited to the climate in which they were situated and molded to their sites as if they had grown there. Out of it also came a proliferation of houses, many of them badly copied from the work of the Greenes and crudely constructed. This came to be called the Bungalow style, and when handled by the Greenes, was of the highest excellence; but as the building of such houses spread all over the United States, their quality worsened with time. This situation existed through the first quarter of the 20th century. But the fact that their work was badly copied and eventually became an unfortunate movement in architecture does not detract from the importance of the achievements of the Greenes, or from their part in the early development of modern architecture in this country.

The first decade of the Greene and Greene practice, from the establishment of their office in 1893, found them designing houses in many of the popular styles

GREENE AND GREENE Blacker House (1907), Pasadena, Calif.
(Marvin Rand)

of the past. Later their work took on more of an open, Japanese feeling, and their interest in craftsmanship, particularly in wood, was developed. During their second decade, they produced a proliferation of good houses.

Works Perhaps the greatest houses were those for R.R. Blacker (1907) and David B. Gamble (1908), both in Pasadena; that for William R. Thorsen (1908), Berkeley; and the Pratt House (1909), Ojai. All these houses show the mature Greene style and their detailing is apparent, as is their devotion, especially that of Charles, to close work with the craftsmen and their materials, both in their shops and during the construction of the houses. The most elaborate of these houses is the Blacker, which cost $100,000 in 1907, a very large sum indeed for what is essentially a relatively small house. The Gamble House is the best place to experience the total effect of a Greene and Greene house today. Through the efforts of a group of Pasadena citizens, it has been magnificently preserved, together with its gardens and the Greene brothers' designed furniture, carpets, lighting fixtures, silverware, linens, and the like. Here, as in many of their other houses, the Greenes had designed an entire environment for the occupants.

Though their reputation was founded almost entirely on their wood houses, often redwood, the Greenes also experimented with other materials. For example, in the L. A. Robinson House (1906) in Pasadena, the ground-floor walls are brick, covered with stucco, and the second floor has an exposed wood frame with stucco panels between the timbers. In the Cornelia Culbertson House (1911) in Pasadena, they went even further; the framing is wood, but the wood is covered with sprayed-on concrete, a pioneering use of this material. With its clay-tile roof, this house does not look like other Greene brothers houses; it is in Mission style, derived from the design of California mission churches and other buildings.

If they had been able to foresee it, the Greenes might have considered the Culbertson House an omen of what lay ahead. The brothers drifted apart, not in their personal relationship but in their philosophies, into separate practices. Charles, who had become deeply interested in philosophy and art, moved to Carmel where he designed a few houses, mostly in the Mission style, and wrote, mostly about Oriental philosophy. Henry stayed in Pasadena, where he designed a few houses, mostly unlike the older work of the brothers, in stucco with tile roofs.

The great era of the brothers ended in the second decade of the 20th century. And they, along with their achievements, lapsed into obscurity. After World War II came a revitalized interest in architecture of wood, led by architects in California and the Pacific Northwest. With this resurgence came a strong, new interest in the work of those early pioneers, the Greene brothers. Called out of retirement, they were given accolades and awards from their fellow architects for their accomplishments. In one acceptance speech, Henry Greene made it clear that the brothers had lived in the right time, that for them the 20th-century

GREENE AND GREENE Exterior, Gamble House (1908), Pasadena, Calif. *(Marvin Rand)*

GREENE AND GREENE Interior, Gamble House (1908), Pasadena, Calif. *(Marvin Rand)*

GREENE AND GREENE Detail, Gamble House (1908), Pasadena, Calif. *(Marvin Rand)*

GREENE AND GREENE Detail, Gamble House (1908), Pasadena, Calif. *(Marvin Rand)*

practice of supervising or inspecting the work could never take the place of being completely involved in and participating in the work of construction themselves. An era was indeed over.

Life The brothers Greene were born in Cincinnati, Ohio, just over a year apart, Charles on October 12, 1868, and Henry on January 23, 1870. Their lives and careers were interlocked from then on. Their family having moved to St. Louis, Mo., they attended a high school sponsored by Washington University, in which handwork in wood, metals, and other materials was stressed, along with the more academic subjects. Thus the brothers received an early knowledge of craftsmanship and acquired a love for it that they never lost. Entering the Massachusetts Institute of Technology in 1888, they received the classical tradition, Beaux Arts, education of the architecture schools of the time. Graduating in 1891, the brothers worked for a short time in Boston and then went to Pasadena, Calif., for a visit with their parents who had again moved. They never went back to Boston.

In 1893 the Greenes established their office in Pasadena, their first commission being a small house for a friend of their father's; their second, a tombstone. The next 10 years found the brothers designing houses in most of the fashionable styles of the day, eclectic in a way that reflected their classical tradition education but also giving some promise of what was to become their mature style.

Henry married Emeline Augusta Dart in 1899, and built a house for her four years later. Here their four children were raised. In 1901 Charles married Alice Gordon White, an Englishwoman, and also built a house for his family, which was eventually to include five children. Neither house was particularly notable, but Charles's house was to become so for he almost continually added to it and remodeled it, using it for studies and experiments with architectural forms and materials.

In 1903 the Greenes closed their office in Pasadena and opened one in Los Angeles. The number of their commissions in Pasadena continued to grow, however, and in 1906 they again established an office there, closing the one in Los Angeles a short time later. Their practice grew rapidly and they soon occupied additional space. As long as their partnership lasted, until 1914, they did not move their office again.

The decade ending in 1914 saw their practice flourish. It was a period in which they designed a great number of houses. Although the exact number is uncertain, it is believed that they designed 540 in Pasadena alone. This also was a period that saw their style and craftsmanship flourish in such great architectural accomplishments as the Blacker, Gamble, Thorsen, and Pratt houses. Toward the end of this era, work in the Pasadena area dropped off and the Greenes had fewer commissions. For the first time, the brothers began to practice separately, though their close personal relationship continued. Charles accepted a commission for the D. L. James House (1921), near

Carmel, and captivated by that area, soon moved there. He continued to practice in Carmel, though with few commissions, until he died on June 11, 1957.

Henry continued parcticing in Pasadena, under the old partnership name. After an episode of sickness that lasted four years, he again practiced for a time as an individual, first in the brothers' former Pasadena office, then in a studio at his home. As had been the case with Charles, Henry obtained only a small number of commissions after the end of the partnership. Their work as individuals never had the high degree of style, craftsmanship, and excitement of their best years, the 21 they spent practicing together. After his wife's death in 1935, Henry sold their house and moved in with his eldest son in Altadena, Calif., where he died on October 2, 1954.

The brothers left a legacy that has deeply affected architecture ever since. Quite a few of their houses still exist, and some neighborhoods of Pasadena seem to be almost entirely composed of the architecture of Greene and Greene.

Related Article MODERN ARCHITECTURE.

Further Reading Makinson, Randell: *Greene and Greene: Architecture as a Fine Art,* Peregrine Smith, Inc., Salt Lake City, 1977.

GROPIUS, WALTER ADOLF

German-American architect and educator (1883–1969). As a young man, Walter Adolf Gropius decided to become an architect, and he never swerved from the path he had chosen. It turned out to be a very good choice, for he became one of the great pioneers of modern architecture, an educator who revolutionized architectural education, and an influential social critic who affected not only architecture but life in general.

The Gropius influence was many-sided. He designed influential buildings early in his career and continued to do so all his life. He changed architectural education from the eclecticism of the 19th and early 20th centuries based on the prestige and philosophy of the École des Beaux Arts in Paris to the geometric purity, technical excellence, and functionalism of the philosophy of the Bauhaus in Germany, which he founded and directed for nine years, and in the department of architecture, Harvard University, of which he was chairman for 14 years.

The influence of the Bauhaus had a profound effect on architectural education everywhere, and the Bauhaus principles applied at Harvard marked the end of the Beaux Arts system in America. The architects and other designers Gropius attracted to the faculties of these schools have made great accomplishments on their own and have profoundly affected the design philosophies of their students, many of whom have in turn made their marks on architecture.

The sphere of the Gropius influence was enlarged beyond his own buildings and his teaching through many speeches and articles. He was never satisfied to occupy himself only with the buildings he designed. He had to go beyond that into the social implications of architecture in the society in which it exists.

Architectural Influence It has been said that the influence of Gropius was mostly in his teaching and philosophy rather than in his architecture. As great as his educational accomplishments were, they complement rather than overshadow his other achievements. He was one of the first to express his belief in the technology of the machine, and to act upon it. As early as 1909, he experimented with production-line panels for buildings and with the prefabrication of building parts. This interest continued throughout his career. He was one of the first to express the belief that future architecture must be the result of a group or team working together on building designs, rather than one person who acted as sole designer. He practiced with other architects almost all his life, first with Adolph Meyer (1881–1924), followed by Edwin Maxwell Fry (1899–   ), then Marcel Lajos Breuer (1902–   ), and finally in a group practice with The Architects' Collaborative (TAC).

Works The impact of Gropius on architecture also came from his building designs. Starting with his early German work, the Fagus Factory (1911), Alfeld, on which he was associated with Adolph Meyer, the Werkbund Exhibition (1914), Cologne, and the Bauhaus buildings (1926), Dessau, his designs have had a clarity and consistency not often found in the work of other architects. The early buildings brought him worldwide recognition as a modern architect and influenced architecture everywhere.

During his Bauhaus days, Gropius designed very few buildings. Although some of those he designed were pioneering and inventive, most were never built. Two, however, were built: a prefabricated house (1927) for the Werkbund Exhibition in Stuttgart, a continuation of his interest in production line units, and the Siemensstadt Housing (1929), Berlin, a continuation of his lifelong interest in housing for large numbers of people. During his three years in England, he and Maxwell Fry designed Impington College (1936), near Cambridge.

After coming to America, Gropius and Marcel Breuer, who had been on the Bauhaus faculty and was now on that of Harvard, designed a number of houses around the Boston area, including one for Gropius (1937) in Lincoln; Aluminum City Terrace Housing (1941), New Kensington, near Pittsburgh; and buildings for Black Mountain College, Lake Eden, N.C., that were never built. The first big project of Gropius, after he had formed the group practice, The Architects' Collaborative (TAC), in 1946, was the Harvard Graduate Center (1949), Cambridge, Mass. Like some of his other later buildings, such as the Pan American Building (1963; see illustration in article art in architecture), New York City, for which Gropius and Pietro Belluschi (1899–   ) served as design consultants, the Harvard complex has been criticized as being not up to the early standards set by the architect. The most important later Gropius-TAC buildings were the U.S. Embassy (1961), Athens, Greece; the Boston Back Bay Center (1953); the John F. Kennedy Federal Office

GROPIUS, WALTER Gropius House (1937), Lincoln, Mass. [*Architects: Walter Gropius and Marcel Breuer. (The Architects Collaborative)*]

GROPIUS, WALTER Aluminum City Terrace Housing (1941), New Kensington, Pa. [*Architects: Walter Gropius and Marcel Breuer. (The Architects Collaborative)*]

GROPIUS, WALTER Harvard Graduate Center (1949), Harvard University, Cambridge, Mass. [*Architects: The Architects' Collaborative. (The Architects' Collaborative)*]

GROPIUS, WALTER University of Baghdad (1969), Baghdad, Iraq. [*Architects: The Architects' Collaborative. (Robert D. Harvey)*]

Building (1964), Boston; and the last great design of his career, the University of Baghdad (1969), Iraq.

The Gropius philosophy and principles live on in the work of the many architects he taught and influenced. The Architects' Collaborative continues to practice as an influential and successful firm in Cambridge, which has designed such buildings as the headquarters of the American Institute of Architects (1972) in Washington. In 1979, TAC completed the Bauhaus Archive Building, Berlin, developed from a Gropius design, made some years before he died.

Life Walter Gropius was born on May 18, 1883, the son of an architect who held high governmental positions, into an artistic and successful family. After a

236

boyhood spent among a congenial and intelligent family and circle of friends, he entered the University of Munich in 1903 to study architecture. His education was interrupted by a trip to Spain (1904–05) and by service in the Hussars of the German Imperial Army (1905–06). He completed his education at the University of Berlin in 1907. The next year he went to work in the office of a noted German architect, Peter Behrens (1868–1940), where he stayed three years. Behrens was one of the pioneers of modern architecture, and trained three of the greatest future modernists, Gropius, Ludwig Mies van der Rohe (1886–1969), who later distinguished himself in America, and the great Swiss-French architect Le Corbusier (1887–1965), whose real name was Charles-Èdouard Jeanneret.

In 1910 Gropius set up his own office in Berlin. His first buildings were successful, and set the stage for his designs the rest of his life. During this period, he also did industrial designs for wall hangings, furniture, and a railroad engine and car.

His career was interrupted by World War I, during which he served in the German army from 1914 to 1918. During the war, in 1916, he married Alma Mahler and they had one daughter. After his divorce, he married Ise Frank in 1923, and they also had a daughter. In 1918, Gropius was appointed director of both the Grand Ducal Saxon School of Applied Arts and the Grand Ducal Academy of Arts in Weimar. In 1919 he merged the two schools into the Staatliches Bauhaus (State Building School), an action that was destined to revolutionize architectural education and to have far-reaching effects on the design of buildings, furniture, and industrial products. In 1925, disturbed by hostility in Weimar, Gropius moved the school to Dessau. During the Weimar years, Gropius designed few buildings; he submitted a design in 1922 in the Chicago Tribune competition, which still looks fresh and modern today. The move to Dessau provided him with a great new opportunity: design of the buildings for the new school (see illustration in article Bauhaus, Staatliches).

Under political pressure, he resigned as director of the Bauhaus in 1928, visited the United States, and then resumed private practice in Berlin. In 1929 he was elected vice president of the International Congresses of Modern Architecture (CIAM), an organization started to consolidate and promote the new architecture. He served in this capacity until 1957. CIAM was disbanded in 1959.

In 1934, disillusioned and saddened by the political situation under the Nazis in Germany, Gropius went to England where he formed a partnership in 1935 with the noted English architect Edwin Maxwell Fry. After three years in which most of the designs were for houses, in 1937 Gropius accepted an invitation to take a professorship in the Harvard University Graduate School of Design, offered by the dean, Joseph Hudnut (1886–1963), and the university president, James B. Conant (1893–   ). This was a great challenge to a man as deeply interested in education as Gropius, the chance to apply the principles of the Bauhaus in an outstanding school that, along with the others in America, was still immersed in the Beaux Arts system of architectural education. In 1938 he became chairman of the department of architecture. Again he made educational history and remained in this position at Harvard until 1952.

TAC Practice In 1938 Gropius opened an architectural office in Cambridge, this time in partnership with Marcel Breuer, whom he had first attracted to the Bauhaus faculty and then to that of Harvard. They practiced together until 1943, designing mostly houses. After 1943, each went into his own private practice. In 1946 Gropius, together with several young architects, founded a group practice, The Architects' Collaborative (TAC), in Cambridge which was unique in its organization and methods. TAC was composed of partners who were theoretically equal to each other, each serving as the architect for individual buildings which were subject both to criticism by the other partners and assistance from them. This is quite different from the usual architectural partnership in which each partner specializes, at least to a degree, one in design, one in administration, and another in obtaining commissions for the firm. TAC continued to practice and grow during the lifetime of Gropius, and has continued to do so.

After his retirement from the Harvard faculty, Gropius devoted his time to the architectural practice of TAC. Early in his career, he had begun to make speeches and write articles, many of which were collected into books. He continued to write and speak on all the subjects that so greatly interested him: design and practice of architecture, education, and social issues. It was a fruitful time for a man who had lived a long and productive life, and had achieved the stature of a sage.

Great honors piled up. Over the years, he had been elected to Phi Beta Kappa, awarded honorary doctors' degrees from universities all over the world, including a doctor of arts from Harvard, and elected a fellow of the American Academy of Arts and Sciences. In 1956 he received the Gold Medal of the Royal Institute of British Architects and in 1959, that of the American Institute of Architects. Perhaps the ultimate was the high recognition from his native country which the Nazis had caused him to leave. In 1958 the Federal Republic of Germany awarded him the Grand Cross of Merit with Star and in 1960, the Grand State Prize in Architecture.

Respected, admired, and loved, Walter Adolf Gropius died on July 5, 1969. He had changed architecture and architectural education.

Related Articles Bauhaus, Staatliches; Breuer, Marcel Lajos; Education; Modern Architecture.

Further Reading Fitch, James Marston: *Walter Gropius,* Braziller, New York, 1960; Giedion, Sigfried: *Walter Gropius — Work and Teamwork,* Reinhold, New York, 1954; Gropius, Walter: *Apollo in the Democracy,* McGraw-Hill, New York, 1968; Gropius, Walter: *Scope of Total Architecture — A New Way of Life,* Harper, New York, 1955.

HANDICAPPED, FACILITIES FOR THE Architecture for people with disabilities. Design for the handicapped is an important architectural consideration, not only in buildings specifically for them but in barrier-free architecture in all buildings. It is estimated that about 15 percent of all the people in the world have some kind of disability. In the United States, disabled people constitute about 12 percent of the population. Of these, about 6 out of 10 are capable of leading normal productive lives.

Some handicapped persons who cannot lead normal productive lives are cared for at home by their children, parents, or others. Many are cared for in such institutions as long-term hospitals and special homes. The majority of the disabled lead normal productive lives, live in houses or apartments, work in offices or other buildings, shop in stores and shopping centers, go to restaurants, stay in hotels, and use other buildings in much the same way as nondisabled people. Obviously, specialized buildings for the handicapped must be designed with their disabilities in mind. Until about the end of World War II, it may have been obvious that other buildings should be designed for use by the handicapped, but almost none were so designed.

Today design for the handicapped has become a very important part of architecture, and, in some cases, because of federal and state regulations, has become a legal responsibility of architects and others in the building construction industry. This has brought about barrier-free architecture, not only in specialized buildings for the handicapped but in other building types.

Disabilities Handicapped people generally include those who have become disabled because of birth defects, accidents, or illness. The major disabilities are deafness, blindness, crippling, and mental disability. Deafness is defined as the state that exists when a person cannot hear any sounds. One whose hearing is impaired is called hard of hearing. Mental disabilities are of two types: mental illness, affecting people who were once normal but later developed a mental disability, and mental retardation, a condition of people born with intelligence far below normal.

Barrier-Free Design The primary purpose of barrier-free design is to overcome problems in the physical environment of people with major disabilities. Disabled people are also protected by law against discrimination in employment and in many cases by federal and state laws concerning architectural barriers. Many experts believe the major disabilities to be only part of the architectural-barrier problem, since many other people have handicaps of other kinds, including those inherent in children because of their age; obesity; physical size or stamina; and lack of coordination. People become disabled, temporarily at times, for example, because of pregnancy, fractured bones, convalescence from accidents and illnesses, and other causes. And in the end, everyone who lives long enough becomes handicapped by the infirmities of old age.

In 1974 the American Institute of Architects adopted a position statement that ''. . . it shall be national policy to recognize the inherent right of all citizens, regardless of their physical disability, to the full development of their economic, social and personal potential, through the use of the manmade environment.'' Subsequently, this statement was endorsed by such organizations as the National Easter Seal Society for Crippled Children and Adults, the President's Committee for Employment of the Handicapped, and the Paralyzed Veterans of America. Some think this statement did not go far enough, since it does not mention mental disabilities.

Some also think that the goal of creating a barrier-free environment will greatly benefit, not only those with handicaps but also those without disabilities. For example, ramps are often easier to ascend and descend than stairs by those carrying loads, bicyclists, or mothers with baby carriages. Grab bars in toilet stalls, tubs, and showers make these facilities safer for all people—the nonhandicapped as well as the elderly, the ill, and the handicapped. Barrier-free design does not have to be only a passive response to existing physical or mental disabilities, but may be an active one in the prevention of accidents that cause disabilities. In other words, barrier-free design may lead to better, more comfortable, safer environments for all people.

To help solve the problems of the handicapped, some barrier-free design enthusiasts have let their concerns for the disabled obscure the benefits for all people. It is certainly understandable that a share of the automobile parking spaces near building entrances should be reserved for the disabled; it is quite another, as is the case in some buildings in Washington, D.C., to restrict ramps to the disabled. Which disabled? People in wheelchairs only? Why not a pregnant woman with a baby on one arm and a bag of groceries on the other? The concept of barrier-free architecture should be one that is barrier-free for all.

Barriers Common barriers which barrier-free architecture attempts to deal with are those of building sites, exteriors, interiors, rest rooms and bathrooms, kitchens, and services. Common problems include narrow parking spaces, curbs or other obstructions, narrow doors, unsafe stairs, slippery or varied-level floors, small toilet stalls, fixtures at awkward levels, low hanging elements, service fixtures such as water fountains and telephone booths that are too small or in positions hard to reach, kitchen equipment that impedes use, and many others.

To overcome these problems, the objectives of barrier-free design include proper design of the sizes, shapes, and positions of architectural elements of buildings and their sites, including the larger elements such as rooms, furniture, and equipment and the smaller elements such as doorknobs, water fountains, and kitchen, bath, and rest room appliances and equipment. In addition, limits must be placed on the amounts of effort and energy required to use the various elements of buildings and their sites. Finally, signs and other signals, including alarm or warning systems, should be specifically designed for quick understanding and ease of use.

Barrier-free design has come a long way in a relatively short time, but there are problems still to be solved. Some will require a considerable amount of study and research. Like the problems of the barriers in automobiles, such as steering wheels and columns, some architectural problems will not be solved until designers repudiate the approaches of the past and attack the problems in a free and creative manner. For example, why have steering wheels and columns in automobiles? Why not a completely new system for steering that does not form a physical barrier with which a driver's head may impact in a collision?

Problems Some of the current problems in barrier-free architecture include products that operate in ways that make them difficult to use; specialized safety problems, such as the exit from a burning building of people confined to wheelchairs; making existing buildings barrier-free, and providing ramps for wheelchair-bound people, thus eliminating curbs used for orientation by blind people with their sticks or by their guide dogs. Another problem is the cost of barrier-free architecture. There is much disagreement about this subject; some say the cost is very high, others that it is not. Some analyses have indicated that the cost of providing barrier-free environments in new buildings might be as little as 0.5 percent of the total construction costs, in other words $5,000 for a $1 million building. If these analyses are correct, this seems a small price to pay for the great benefits to be derived from barrier-free architecture.

History In prehistoric times and in the early historical eras, handicapped people were thought to be threats to the societies in which they lived because they did not contribute to the welfare or safety of their communities. Such people were often abandoned or driven out by nomadic people. The ancient Greeks abandoned deformed babies; in Rome, it was legal for parents to drown them. During the Middle Ages, handicapped people were reviled and ridiculed or treated as objects of entertainment. Many were burned to death.

It was not until the 19th century that handicapped people were cared for and became accepted by society. In the 20th century, progress continued and accelerated with World War I. World War II and the Korean War resulted in great numbers of casualties, including a large percent of disabled people, again bringing about progress in the status of the disabled; this progress has steadily grown.

U.S. Standards and Laws Since the early 1960s, much progress has been made in barrier-free architecture. In the United States, this started with the formulation of standards in 1961 by the American National Standards Institute, Inc. (ANSI). The ANSI Standards have since been the basis of federal and state legislation on the subject. The first major federal law was the Vocational Rehabilitation Act of 1965, since amended. This act dealt with employment discrimination against the disabled on federal government work or by those doing business with the government. This was followed by the Architectural Barriers Act of 1968, the creation of the Architectural Barriers Compliance Board in 1973, and the Rehabilitation Act of 1973. A majority of the states have passed building code requirements or other legislation dealing with the subject. In 1979 ANSI issued revised standards for barrier-free architecture.

Related Articles BUILDING CODES AND STANDARDS; DESIGN, ARCHITECTURAL; GOVERNMENT; HOSPITAL; HOUSING; Other articles on building types and systems.

Further Reading Bednar, Michael J., ed.: *Barrier Free Environments*, Dowden, Hutchinson & Ross, Stroudsburg, Pa., 1977; Goldsmith, Selwyn: *Designing for the Disabled*, 3d ed., RIBA Publications, London, 1976; Harkness, Sarah P., and James N. Groom, Jr.: *Building Without Barriers*, Whitney, New York, 1976; Kliment, Stephen A.: *Into the Mainstream — A Syllabus for a Barrier-Free Environment*, American Institute of Architects, Washington, 1974; *Specifications for Making Buildings and Facilities Accessible to and Usable by Physically Handicapped People*, 2d ed., American National Standards Institute, Inc., New York, 1979.

Sources of Additional Information American National Standards Institute, Inc., 1430 Broadway, New York, N.Y. 10018; The Committee on Barrier-free Design, 1111 20th St., N.W., Washington, D. C. 20210; National Center for a Barrier-Free Environment, 7315 Wisconsin Ave., N.W., Washington, D.C. 20014; National Easter Seal Society for Crippled Children and Adults, 2023 W. Ogden Ave., Chicago, Ill. 60612; National Information Center for the Handicapped, P.O. Box 1492, Washington, D.C. 20013; U.S. Department of Health and Human Services (HHS), Washington, D.C. 20225.

HARDWARE Products, or fittings, mostly made of metal, used in conjunction with larger parts of buildings, including such items as nails and screws, or rough hardware, and locks and hinges, or finish hardware. Rough hardware is primarily used for the general construction of buildings, including foundations, walls, structures, and so on, and is generally but not always concealed. Sometimes rough hardware items are called fasteners since so many types are primarily used for fastening two or more materials or parts together. Finish hardware is generally exposed in buildings and includes types for a great variety of purposes, such as those that enable doors or windows to operate or those for security purposes. Thousands of kinds and sizes of hardware items are available as stock items, in many metals, with various finishes and colors. Many can be obtained on special order, and some manufacturers will fabricate certain special types to order.

Rough Hardware The most common types of rough hardware are nails, screws, nuts, and bolts, but also turnbuckles, washers, anchors, ties, inserts, and other fasteners of every conceivable kind for every type of function. The most basic and oldest fastener is the nail, which is known to have been used in ancient building construction. There is a great variety of types of nails, in numerous shapes, materials, and sizes for many purposes. A nail has a head, a shank, and a point. Many kinds of heads are available; the two types most frequently used are the flat head on common nails, in rough carpentry and other ways; and the smaller head on finishing or casing nails, meant to be set, driven below the surface of materials with a nail set and puttied or otherwise finished. Nails are often specified by the pennyweight, as in eight penny, or 8d, which reflects the fact that several hundred years ago one hundred 8d nails sold for 8 pence in England. Common nails come in sizes from 2d, 1 in long of no. 15 gauge wire to 60d, 6 in long of no. 2 gauge wire. Finishing nails are generally available in the same sizes up to 40d.

A variety of other nails are available for various purposes, including fence, roofing, sheet metal, flooring, lath, molding, shingle, and slating. Some nails have heads that are large and flat, double, cupped, offset, oval, or round; and nails may be headless. Special types are made for such materials as concrete or masonry. Very large nails are called spikes and come in several types, in sizes from $\frac{1}{2}$ to $\frac{5}{8}$ in^2, and in lengths from 3 to 12 in or more and with various types of heads. Nails may be driven by hand with hammers or other tools, or by mechanical and power-actuated devices. Most nails are made of iron or steel, plain or coated with zinc or other metals to increase their resistance to rust. Nails are also made of other metals, such as copper and aluminum.

Other rough hardware items that are often used include bolts, screws, nuts, and related types. A bolt is like a rod with a head on one end and external screw threads along its shank. Bolts are used with nuts, devices usually square or hexagonal in shape, with internal threads to mate with those of bolts. A machine bolt has a square or hexagonal head, while a carriage bolt has a rounded head with a square portion below it to keep the bolt from turning when inserted into a square hole. A stove bolt usually has an oval or a round head into which a screwdriver may be inserted. Bolts range in diameter from $\frac{1}{8}$ up to $\frac{1}{2}$ in and in some types to a full inch or more, and in lengths from about $\frac{1}{2}$ to 6 in or more. Nuts come in sizes to fit the bolt sizes. A special type is a lag bolt that has a tapered shank. Washers (metal disks) are often used in conjunction with bolts and nuts, and may be flat or cut, spring locking, with external teeth.

Screws are of two major types: one called a wood screw that is like a bolt but tapered toward its point to allow it to be driven with a screwdriver into various materials; and another that is similar to a bolt and used for similar purposes. The two most used types of screws of the second type are machine screws, which come with round, flat, oval, or other types of slotted heads; and cap screws, which come with slotted, round, flat, hexagonal, or other heads. Slotted head screws may be driven by ordinary screwdrivers; those with two slots, by Phillips screwdrivers. Nuts may be obtained with the types of heads used for bolts and screws and as cap nuts, wing nuts, and in a great number of other forms.

Many other types of rough hardware are available for any imaginable purpose in architecture, including hangers for pipes and other elements, anchors for holding one component securely to another, ties for similar purposes, inserts that go into one material to allow another material or some device to be attached, and fasteners of every shape and kind for every problem and purpose. Among the most useful are staples, roughly U-shaped devices with two pointed ends, for fastening a variety of materials by staple guns or staple hammers; and studs, usually driven partly into materials with power-actuated or mechanically actuated guns, leaving their ends exposed for screwing on, or otherwise attaching, materials or devices. Another special device is a shield, or anchor, usually of lead, fiber, or other material, which is inserted into a material and expands when a screw is driven into it. Another device, for similar purposes, is a toggle bolt which has a flap or flaps that may be aligned with the shank while the device is inserted into a hole, after which the flaps may be caused to spread out to hold the toggle bolt in place.

Finish Hardware This hardware also comes in a great variety of types, sizes, finishes, and materials, and in a somewhat wider range of prices, for many architectural purposes. In some cases, finish hardware usually comes with an assembly, as in most windows today. In other cases, such as in doors, the hardware is often selected separately. So many variations are possible in finish hardware that a complete discussion is not possible here. However, some idea of the scope of the subject may be gained by examining the hardware for doors alone.

Door Hardware This hardware may be obtained in a number of metals, including brass, bronze, aluminum, and steel; steel may be plated with brass, bronze, or chromium or may have a prime coat of paint or other material. In addition, certain finish hardware items, such as doorknobs, may also be obtained in such materials as glass, china, and plastics. Plastics are often used for other parts of door hardware. And the various materials may be obtained in a number of textures, such as bright, semimatte, or matte (sometimes called brushed) finishes.

Many separate items of finish hardware are used with doors. Hinges may be exposed or concealed and special types are available. Doorknobs or levers may be used for opening and closing. Locks may be integral with knobs or separate; and special types, including door bolts, may be used. Thresholds or saddles are located beneath doors when they are closed and, for exterior doors, may be fitted with weatherstripping devices. Weatherstripping around the sides and heads of doors is also recommended. Push plates or bars are often used on doors, particularly in public and commercial buildings. In addition, in buildings of all types, closers which automatically close doors, holders which hold them open when desired, silencers which keep them from making noises when slammed, stops which limit the amount they may open, letter boxes, and other devices are often used. Bars which open doors when people press on them from inside, called panic hardware, are often used in buildings occupied by many people and are required by building codes in some types, such as theaters.

The types of hardware used for windows are equally as varied and numerous. And there are other types of hardware for many different purposes in buildings. Rough hardware, except in special cases, is usually considered part of the construction of the various elements and often is not made a part of the specifications for buildings, except in standards for performance. Finish hardware comes as part of assemblies, such as is usually the case in windows, or is specified in schedules of hardware included in the working drawings or specifications. Sometimes a monetary allowance is made for the total cost of all finish hardware, instead of specifying each item separately.

Since there is such a variety of hardware available today, sometimes architects obtain the services of hardware consultants, who specialize in this field, to aid in selecting and specifying the various items.

History It is believed that the first fasteners used by primitive humans in building construction were vines with which parts were tied together, followed by shaping wooden parts to fit into each other, as in log cabins, and by wooden stakes driven into holes to function much like nails. Metal nails have been used since very early times and were originally forged by hammering pieces of iron. Nails continued to be forged until the 18th century and some were forged in the 19th. In 1786 Ezekiel Reed, an American inventor, patented a machine that made nails out of wire. This method, though improved over the years, is still used for most nails today. Other types of rough hardware

were developed when needs for them arose and have been improved over the years.

Finish hardware was also used in buildings in very early times. From about 3000 B.C. in the great civilizations around the Mediterranean Sea, hardware for various kinds of doors were developed, including pivots that acted like hinges. Later locks and other types of hardware were developed, followed by the first real hinges during the Middle Ages. Some Gothic hinges were highly ornamented features of doors. During the years following, various types of finish hardware were developed, gradually producing the vast array of types available today.

Related Articles DOOR; SECURITY SYSTEMS; WINDOW; Various articles on building materials, components, and systems.

Sources of Further Information American Society of Architectural Hardware Consultants, P. O. Box 549, Mill Valley, Calif. 94941; Door and Hardware Inst., 1815 N. Fort Myer Dr., Arlington, Va. 22209.

HARRISON, PETER English-American architect (1716–75). The buildings of Peter Harrison occupy a very important place in American architecture. He is the first colonist known to have made designs for buildings to be erected by others. He has therefore been called America's first architect. As noteworthy as his accomplishments were, he was not really a professional architect. His vocation was that of merchant and sea captain. Architecture, important as it must have been to him, was an avocation only. He was only slightly involved in the construction of his buildings, if at all. He had no architectural training, except what he learned from books. He also derived all his designs for buildings from books. And it is known that he never received proper professional fees for his work, only token gifts or payments instead.

However, these factors have little or nothing to do with the importance of his work, the largest number of buildings attributed to any architect of his time, at least five major buildings, a number of homes, a fort, a lighthouse, and a map of the town and harbor of Newport, R.I. For his time, he was a first-rate draftsman, something of an engineer, and a self-educated architect, possessed of refinement and taste; in short, a gentleman-amateur architect. He possessed the best architectural library of its time in the colonies, composed mostly of books collected on his trips to England as a ship captain. He was one of the first, and perhaps the most important, of the colonial architects who participated in the development of Georgian architecture in America, adapting it from books about the English style.

Works His first building is thought to be a large house, Shirley Place (1746), in Roxbury, Mass., designed for Gov. William Shirley (1694–1771) of Massachusetts. Two stories high with a basement, this house is Georgian in appearance, but is constructed of wood rather than stone or brick as in English Georgian houses. Since masonry materials were unavailable, the architect used exterior wood, cut in such a

HARRISON, PETER Interior, Christ Church (1761), Cambridge, Mass.
(Wayne Andrews)

HARRISON, PETER Redwood Library (1750), Newport, R.I. *(Wayne Andrews)*

HARRISON, PETER Exterior, Christ Church (1761), Cambridge, Mass.
(Wayne Andrews)

HARRISON, PETER Exterior, Touro Synagogue (1763), Newport, R.I.
(Wayne Andrews)

HARRISON, PETER Interior, Touro Synagogue (1763), Newport, R.I.
(Wayne Andrews)

way as to resemble masonry, and painted, with sand in the paint, to resemble the color and texture of masonry. This was to be the device used in his first public building, the Redwood Library (1750), Newport, R.I., named for its founder, Abraham Redwood.

Harrison's next major building, usually considered his most important work, King's Chapel (1754), in Boston, was designed to be constructed of granite from Quincy, Mass. This was the first church in America to be built of stone, but the columns and the porch or portico were built of wood and were not completed until some 30 years after the main church. The great spire of stone, which Harrison had envisioned, was never built. Although the architect's designs for the exterior were never fully realized, his designs produced the most magnificent interior space in any church in the colonies.

Other important buildings by Harrison are Christ Church (1761), Cambridge, Mass.; and Touro Synagogue (1763) and the Brick Market (1772), both in Newport, R.I. As was the case with King's Chapel, Christ Church was never completed. Built of wood, the exterior was to have been covered with a rough stucco intended to resemble masonry and was to have a tall steeple; neither was accomplished. Touro, the first synagogue in America, like King's Chapel, has a marvelously refined and elegant interior. So much so that the elegance seems out of place in a Jewish house of worship. Knowing nothing of the Hebrew faith, Harrison simply followed his usual procedure of adapting the design from books. The architect's last major building, the Brick Market, is an adaptation from the 17th-century Somerset House in England. It is of brick with an open-air, arcaded market on the ground floor. The two stories above, also of brick, have wooden pilasters attached.

In addition to Shirley Place, Peter Harrison designed many other houses. The number is uncertain, but some of the important ones include Vassall-Longfellow House (1760), Cambridge; Lady Pepperell House (1760), Kittery Point, Maine; and Francis Malbone House (1760), Newport. In addition, he designed a remarkable series of three houses, all different and all designed for members of one family: the first Apthorp House (1760) in Cambridge for the rector of Christ Church, the Rev. East Apthorp; the second for the minister's father (about 1763), in Brighton, Mass.; and the third for his brother in New York City (1767).

All of Harrison's major buildings as well as the houses have designs based on English books studied by the architect. Among the most important were a 1736 translation of the works of Andrea Palladio (1518–80), an Italian Renaissance architect and theorist; *Vitruvius Brittanicus*, by Colen Campbell (c. 1676–1729) and others (published 1715–71); and James Gibbs' books. Harrison has been accused by some purists of being only a literary or bookish architect. However, it must be remembered that none of the colonial architects had been formally trained in archi-

tecture. They were builders or wood-carvers or men of other vocations, who were deeply interested in architecture. And they learned what they knew from books. Harrison, it must be conceded, learned his lessons well and produced notable and important buildings with the help of his books.

Life Peter Harrison came to Newport, R.I., when he was about twenty-two, as a member of the crew of his brother's ship. Soon becoming a ship captain himself, he showed an early interest in drawing and architecture. Captured by the French in 1745, he was imprisoned at Fort Louisbourg on Cape Breton Island, Nova Scotia. After his release, he drew an accurate map of the fortifications which helped the colonial troops to capture the fort. Governor Shirley of Massachusetts, who instigated the attack, was so pleased with Harrison's map that he asked the young ship captain to design a house for him; this was Harrison's first building.

From this beginning, Harrison went on to become an important colonial architect. Originally a Quaker, he became a member of the Church of England soon after reaching America. Though a colonist, he considered himself an Englishman and, as the movement toward independence of the colonies progressed, was known as a Tory in politics. Toward the end of his life, he moved to New Haven, Conn., where he was appointed Customs Collector, a post most harmful to his reputation among those who opposed the English crown. After his death in 1775, on the eve of the Revolution, a mob broke into his house and burned what was one of the great architectural libraries in the colonies and all his drawings.

Related Articles BOOK, ARCHITECTURAL; COLONIAL ARCHITECTURE; GEORGIAN ARCHITECTURE; HISTORY OF ARCHITECTURE.

Further Reading Bridenbaugh, Carl: *Peter Harrison: First American Architect,* University of North Carolina Press, Chapel Hill, 1949.

HARRISON, WALLACE KIRKMAN American architect (1895–   ). Although he had little formal education after age fourteen, and almost none in architecture, Harrison became an architect in the manner that many others had before him, by working in the offices of other architects and also by studying on his own.

In spite of the seeming handicaps of his lack of formal education and his childhood in a relatively small city, Wallace Kirkman Harrison eventually became an urbane and successful architect. Although he worked in offices of other architects most of his early life before becoming a partner, Harrison eventually designed a number of New York City skyscrapers and many other buildings.

Harrison also performed another role that is probably unique in architecture in America and perhaps in any other country. For a very long time, it seemed that whenever some great complex of buildings was to be designed and constructed by a number of architects,

HARRISON, WALLACE K. Exterior, Metropolitan Opera House (1966), Lincoln Center for the Performing Arts, New York, N.Y. (Joseph W. Molitor)

HARRISON, WALLACE K. Interior, Metropolitan Opera House (1966), Lincoln Center for the Performing Arts, New York, N.Y. (Joseph W. Molitor)

Harrison always turned out to be the architect who was called on to direct and administer the project, to keep the peace, and to ensure that the job was done properly. Yet he never relinquished his role as a building designer; rather, he combined the roles of designer and administrator.

Building Complex Harrison's first experience with a great complex came with the design and construction of Rockefeller Center, New York City (see illus-trations in article complex, architectural, and in color section). Although he did not direct this work, he was deeply involved and is considered one of the architects, the others being Harvey Wiley Corbett (1873–1954) and Raymond Hood (1881–1934), who contributed most to the design.

The design of Rockefeller Center began in the 1920s; its construction was started in 1931 and was not completed until 1940. The architectural work was performed by an association of three architectural firms: Reinhard and Hofmeister; Corbett, Harrison and MacMurray; and Hood and Fouilhoux.

The next complex, the United Nations Headquarters, New York City, was begun in 1947, completed in 1950. The UN Headquarters was designed by an international team of 15 architects, headed by Harrison and including Le Corbusier (1887–1965) of France, Oscar Niemeyer (1907–) of Brazil, and Sven Markelius (1889–1972) of Sweden. (For illustration, see article entitled public building.)

Idlewild, now John F. Kennedy, Airport (see illustration in article airport) in Jamaica, near New York City, a great complex of individual terminals and numerous other buildings, was begun in 1942 and virtually completed by 1962, with Harrison as consulting architect. The terminals and other buildings were designed by a number of architectural firms to fit into the master plan. Buildings were designed by Skidmore, Owings and Merrill; Kahn and Jacobs; Tippetts, Abbett, McCarthy and Stratton; Eero Saarinen (1910–61); Edward Durell Stone (1902–78); White and Mariani; William B. Tabler (1914–); Reinhard, Hofmeister and Walquist; I. M. Pei (1917–); George J. Sole; Bloch and Hesse; and Edgar Tafel (1912–).

While Kennedy Airport was under construction, Harrison received a commission to direct the design and construction of another important complex, the Lincoln Center for the Performing Arts, in New York City, begun in 1962 and completed in 1968. In this complex, six buildings were designed by as many architects, including Philip Cortelyou Johnson (1906–); Eero Saarinen; Pietro Belluschi (1889–); Skidmore, Owings and Merrill; the Philharmonic Hall (1962) by Max Abramovitz (1908–), then Harrison's partner; and the Metropolitan Opera House (1966) by Harrison. (See article entitled theater.)

Other Buildings Harrison designed many other buildings, most of them in partnership with Max Abramovitz, including airport buildings, apartments, auditoriums, churches, museums, college buildings, and research buildings. Some of the more notable buildings include the African Building (1941) at the Bronx Zoo, the New York Aquarium (1955), the Loeb Student Center (1959) at New York University, the Museum of Science and Technology (1964), and La-Guardia Airport (1965), all in New York City; the First Presbyterian Church (1959), Stamford, Conn.; and the Assembly Hall (1962), University of Illinois.

Perhaps the most notable buildings designed by Harrison and Abramovitz are office buildings, includ-

HARRISON, WALLACE K. Assembly Hall (1962), University of Illinois, Champaign, Urbana, Ill. [*Architects: Harrison and Abramovitz. Engineers: Ammann and Whitney. (Ezra Stoller)*]

HARRISON, WALLACE K. U.S. Steel Building (1971), Pittsburgh, Pa. [*Architects: Harrison and Abramovitz. (Joseph W. Molitor)*]

ing the Alcoa Building (1952; see illustration in article aluminum) in Pittsburgh; Corning Glass (1959) and Time-Life (1960), both in New York City; and U.S. Steel (1971) in Pittsburgh.

Life Wallace Kirkman Harrison was born in Worcester, Mass., on September 28, 1895. Leaving school early, he went to work in 1909 at age fourteen for a contractor in Worcester but soon left to work in an architectural office there. In 1916 he went to New York where he worked in the office of McKim, Mead and White for a short time before entering the U.S. Navy during World War I.

After the war, Harrison entered the École des Beaux Arts in Paris where he studied for a year and then remained in Europe to travel and study for a year. Returning to the United States, he went to work in the New York City office of Bertram Grosvenor Goodhue (1869–1924) and after Goodhue's death, joined Helmle and Corbett, which eventually became Corbett, Harrison and MacMurray, and participated in the design of Rockefeller Center. In 1926 Harrison married Ellen Milton and they had one daughter. In 1935 Harrison formed a partnership with another architect who had worked on Rockefeller Center, J. Andre Fouilhoux (1879–1945). They were joined in the partnership by Max Abramovitz in 1940. After Fouilhoux was killed in a construction accident during World War II, the firm became Harrison and Abramovitz, which it remained until it was dissolved in 1977.

In his later years, Wallace Harrison was awarded honorary degrees by many universities all over the United States, including Harvard, Oberlin, Dartmouth, and Michigan. In 1957 he was awarded the highest honor for an American architect, the Gold Medal of the American Institute of Architects.

Related Articles COMPLEX, ARCHITECTURAL; CONTEMPORARY ARCHITECTURE; MODERN ARCHITECTURE; OFFICE BUILDING; PUBLIC BUILDING; THEATER. For illustration of interior of Westinghouse Design Center (1971), Pittsburgh, Pa., see LIGHTING. For illustrations of Science Building (1964), New York World's Fair, see

MUSEUM. For illustration of First Presbyterian Church (1960), Stamford, Conn., see RELIGIOUS BUILDING.

HEATING, VENTILATING, AND AIR CONDITIONING
Major systems that provide proper temperatures, ventilation, and humidities for the occupants of buildings. Such systems are often called heating, ventilating, and air conditioning, or HVAC, systems. HVAC systems also help keep buildings and their furniture and furnishings from deteriorating by providing relatively constant levels of temperature and humidity. For a discussion of the requirements for human comfort, heat flow, heat losses and gains, and other principles, see the article entitled insulation, thermal.

Heating of buildings is generally accomplished by convection, the heating of air which then heats the occupants; by radiation, which does not heat the air, but travels from a heat source to the persons being heated by rays or waves as in heat from the sun; or by combinations of the two. Some heating is also received from conduction, the movement of heat within a material, from molecule to molecule.

Heating Methods Four major methods are used for producing heat in the interiors of buildings: steam, hot water, hot air, and electric coils. Steam and hot-water types are called hydronic systems. Any of the systems can be used with unit, or space, heaters which are placed in various locations within buildings and heat only certain areas. Space heaters, such as portable electric types, are often used for temporary heating and for places, such as bathrooms, where additional heat may be required at times. Large space heaters are also often used for heating factories or warehouses. Fireplaces and heating stoves, which are actually types of space heaters, are often used for supplementary heating. See the article entitled fireplace.

Today the general method in most buildings, other than those in very warm climates, is central heating, involving a central source of heat, such as a boiler or furnace, from which air, water, or steam is pumped or blown to various locations in the buildings. Boilers may produce steam or hot water. In the past, the steam or hot water was delivered to devices called radiators, which actually heated partly by radiation and partly by convection. Today steam is usually delivered to devices called convectors, which may also be used with hot water. In addition, hot water can be delivered to baseboard heating units, which are often placed at or near the bases of walls. Baseboard units have one or more pipes surrounded by metal fins, which heat by radiation with some convection. Hot water may also be used in conjunction with radiant panels, composed of coils of piping placed in floors, ceilings, or walls through which the hot water is circulated.

Hot-air systems employ furnaces of various kinds for heating relatively large volumes of air which are then blown through a system of metal ducts to various areas of buildings. The heated air enters rooms through grilles, registers, or diffusers located in floors, walls, or ceilings and returns to the furnaces through return air grilles or registers. In the furnace, this warm air is often combined with some percentage of fresh outside air to improve the ventilation in buildings. Return air grilles are not installed in bathrooms, kitchens, or other places where fumes or odors might enter the system. Ductwork for warm-air heating may be installed in a number of ways, including the perimeter loop system, in which supply ducts are placed around the outside walls of buildings, and the radial system, in which supply ducts radiate to outside walls from the center of buildings.

Electric coils for radiant heating may be embedded in plaster or other ceiling and wall materials or in concrete floors. Separate controls may be installed for each space. Electric baseboard heating may also be obtained but it is practical only in relatively warm climates or in well-insulated spaces. Electric heat sources of other types are also available, including infrared lamp fixtures and panels and electric boilers.

Fuels In addition to electricity, the fuels most used for heating are gas, fuel oil, and coal. As is the case with electricity, gas requires no storage on building sites, except when liquefied, or bottled, gas is used in areas in which gas is not supplied from central municipal systems. Fuel oil requires storage tanks, which are often buried in the ground outside buildings and may be strapped down to concrete slabs to keep them from rising when nearly empty or sinking when full. Coal, formerly the major fuel for heating, is not used as much today. When coal is used, special containers or bins must be provided in sheltered spaces for its storage. Today coal-burning furnaces are usually fed by mechanical stokers which automatically feed proper amounts of coal to the furnaces at regular intervals.

Electricity has advantages because of the simplicity of installing systems, easy control, cleanliness, and easy maintenance; and because it does not produce pollution in buildings. Fuel oil is a very efficient source of heat in modern furnaces and boilers. It has the disadvantages of requiring storage in or near buildings, need for regular maintenance, and the air pollution produced. Gas, both natural and manufactured, is a relatively clean-burning fuel, contributing less to air pollution than fuel oil. It does not require storage, and furnaces and boilers that use it are relatively easy to maintain. Coal produces considerable air pollution, particularly the bituminous or soft type, while anthracite or the hard type produces less. Coal requires storage facilities and machinery to feed it to furnaces and boilers, which may require frequent maintenance to assure their efficiency. Coal also has the disadvantage of undependable availability at times, because of the frequency of strikes in the industry. The costs of equipment to be used with each type of fuel, supplies of the fuels over the years of operation, and maintenance should be considered when selecting the types of systems to be used in buildings.

Steam and hot-water heating systems, with convectors, are often more expensive to install than hot-air systems, but may be more efficient to operate. A problem with both types is that, since warm air rises, uneven temperatures may occur in rooms, with the area near the floors and the floors themselves difficult to heat. Also, unless strictly controlled, the air currents caused by convection may be unpleasant. Radiant heating is found to be more comfortable than other types by many people, since it causes no air waves. And because the air itself is not heated, only people and objects, a quite pleasant atmosphere is created.

Air Conditioning Many people consider air conditioning to be a system that only cools the interiors of buildings in hot weather. Some systems, including central systems and unit or room air conditioners, are in fact used in hot weather to cool and to remove moisture from air in interiors, or dehumidify them. They also clean the air with filters and other devices and may be used to introduce fresh air from outside. Today many systems provide air conditioning all year, performing the above functions in summer and introducing fresh air and cleaning and heating it in winter. They also provide moisture, or humidify the air, to replace the moisture lost during the heating process. Complete year-round air-conditioning systems require heat sources, such as boilers or furnaces, along with equipment for cooling air or chilling water, humidity and air-cleaning devices, and blowers or other devices to introduce heated or cooled air into the interiors of buildings.

In general, air conditioners operate by the compression and liquefaction of refrigerants, such as Freon, causing them to give off heat, and then through evaporation causing them to absorb heat. The major parts of air conditioners and their operations are generally as follows: a compressor compresses the refrigerant, which then is pumped into a condenser, in which fans blow cool air or pumps circulate cool water, which liquefies the refrigerant causing it to release heat that is exhausted to the outside air or to the water; the liquid refrigerant under high pressure then flows through an evaporator, which turns the refrigerant back into a gas, which absorbs heat thereby cooling air blown over it or chilling water pumped over it. The cooled air is then blown into the interior of the building or air is blown over the chilled water coils and into interiors. In some systems, the chilled water itself is pumped to various locations in buildings, where devices, called air-handling units, are equipped with fans that blow air over the chilled water in finned coils and into interior spaces. In the case of year-round air conditioning, heated air is supplied to the interiors in the first type of system, while hot water is supplied to air-handling units in the second type during cold weather.

Many variations of the equipment discussed and the methods of heating and cooling are possible today. In the simplest systems, unit or room air conditioners, all components are contained in packaged units that may be placed in windows or built into walls. Larger, self-contained units of this sort, with greater capacities, usually stand on the floor near outside walls through which they exhaust heat. Other packaged units may be placed on roofs or under floors. Still others have all components installed inside, except for remote condensers that are placed outside. Air-cooling types are often used in conjunction with or combined with warm-air heating systems. Chilled-water types are often used in a similar manner, with steam or hot-water boilers.

While the air-cooling types require no water sources, the chilled-water types must have reliable sources of large quantities of water. Most often, the water is stored in cooling towers, which ordinarily have fans and other machinery to help cool the heated water returned to them. Cooling towers may be located on the roofs of buildings or on the sites outside. Sometimes a pond or lake is used as the source for chilled-water systems.

A special type of year-round air-conditioning system that has come into use in later years is called a heat pump. Heat pumps operate like summer air conditioners in which the processes may be reversed to extract heat from the outside in cold weather to produce heated air inside buildings. In summer, they operate in the same manner as ordinary summer air conditioners. Heat pumps are of two general types. The air-to-air type takes heat from inside air in summer exhausting it to the air outside and performs in the opposite way in winter. The air-water-air type exhausts heat from the air inside buildings in summer and passes it off into water taken from a well, or sometimes a pond; and in winter, the system extracts heat from the water and directs it into the interiors of buildings.

In houses and small buildings of other types, various kinds of packaged air conditioners are installed. In larger buildings much more complicated systems are used. In addition to the compressive refrigeration types previously described, other types, including absorption and thermoelectric, are often used. Absorption types, which have fewer moving parts than the compressive types, are quieter and often require less maintenance. Instead of compressors, absorption types use tanks filled with chemical salts that soak up water from evaporators causing some of the water to evaporate, thereby cooling that remaining. Thermoelectric types are used today only for relatively small installations because of their expense. Such systems generally operate by electricity passed through thermocouples, made by joining two dissimilar metals. When direct current is passed through the thermocouples, they give off heat at one place and absorb heat at another.

Control Devices Controls for heating, air-conditioning, and year-round air-conditioning systems for houses and other small buildings are relatively simple. Some controls are required in connection with the operation of the equipment itself, but the only one readily apparent to building occupants is the thermostat, which controls the starting and stopping of the equipment, when heating or cooling is needed or when a sufficient amount has been supplied. Ordinary thermostats simply react to temperatures inside buildings. More elaborate types may have timers which, for example, automatically lower the amount of heat called for at night and raise it in the morning in winter. Other types have outdoor sensors that can anticipate to an extent future changes in outdoor temperatures. The controls for year-round air-conditioning and other systems in large buildings are usually very complex, and may include many types of controls, timers, gauges, switches, and other devices, not only for the operation of the central system but for sensing and controlling conditions in many parts of buildings. When various rooms or areas of a building have different heating or cooling requirements, the system is zoned to provide flexibility. Thus at a given time, one area might be receiving cooling, another heating. Some control centers or panels today have become so complex that computers are used in conjunction with them.

Design Temperatures In general, the selection of boilers or furnaces for heating and the design of heating systems are based on the hourly rate of heat loss to be expected from buildings and the temperatures to be maintained inside when outdoor temperatures are at certain low levels, called design temperatures. The amount of heat is generally measured in British thermal units (Btu), defined to be the amount of heat required to raise the temperature of 1 pound of water by 1°F. The rate of heat flow, loss or gain, is measured in Btu per hour (Btuh). Winter design temperatures in the United States vary from 55°F in Key West, Fla., to 5°F in New York City, to −30°F in Billings, Mont., and −57°F in Fairbanks, Alaska. Winter design conditions in other parts of the country do not depend on their latitude only, but on other factors as well. For example, Anchorage, Alaska, about 250 miles south of Fairbanks, has a design temperature of −24°F and Kodiak, another 250 miles south, 4°F. Boilers and furnaces are generally selected to replace the hourly heat losses in buildings, with somewhat more in capacities often provided for safety factors.

Heat gains in hot weather are also measured in Btus, and cooling systems are selected and designed to produce selected inside temperatures when certain summer outside design temperatures are reached. In Key West the summer design temperature is 100°F; in New York City, 90°F; and Fairbanks never reaches a level high enough to require cooling. Cooling units are sometimes rated in tons, the amount of heat, 288,000 Btu, required to melt 1 ton of ice in 24 h. A 1-ton cooler can remove this amount of heat in 24 h, or 12,000 Btu. The horsepower ratings of cooling equipment are also often cited. Small window units may be

quite small, a fraction of a horsepower, while the largest may have several thousand. In addition to the heat gains or losses in heating or cooling buildings, other factors must be taken into account when designing these systems, such as air infiltration, the number of air changes per hour required inside rooms, and the effect of the sun.

In addition to the usual parts of heating and air-conditioning systems, other devices may be added, including humidifiers and dehumidifiers; several types of air cleaners which remove smoke, dust, pollen, and even bacteria from the air; and heaters for supplying hot water for various uses in buildings.

Solar Heating For many years, architects and other environmental designers have been interested in solar heating. Many have designed buildings that take advantage of the sun rays in winter, while excluding them in summer by architectural devices such as sunshades and roof overhangs. Some have designed systems which, at least in part, heat the interiors of buildings and provide solar cooling in hot weather. Others have designed solar systems for heating water. In the second half of the 20th century, interest in solar heating has increased considerably because of growing concern about conservation of natural resources and about increasing shortages and rising costs of fuels for heating and cooling.

Solar heating may utilize any of several methods for converting solar radiant energy into forms that may be used in buildings. The rate of delivery per square unit of horizontal surface of solar energy is called insolation. Solar cells, chemical converters that convert the radiation into electricity, and collectors of various kinds in which water, air, or other materials are heated may be utilized for converting solar energy into useful forms. Chemical converters have had no applications in architecture and solar cells, because of their cost, very few applications. However, continuing research may produce solar cells that are economically feasible.

Most solar heating systems in buildings today utilize collectors in which tubing or other channels are provided through which water or some other liquid may flow. These collectors are usually made into panels with glazing on the outside to enable radiation to enter, with a collector or absorber under the glass to trap radiation, and with insulation under the collector. Panels of this sort are placed on the roofs of buildings or in other places and oriented to receive the maximum amount of solar energy.

Water, with a liquid or substance such as ethylene glycol added if there is danger of freezing, is circulated through the collector where it is warmed by the rays of the sun. From there, the liquid is pumped to storage tanks and from them into distribution system piping to be delivered to radiators, convectors, or radiant floor heating systems. The liquid is then returned to storage and back to the collector. Many variations of such a system are possible. In some installations, in which additives such as ethylene glycol are not needed, the systems also produce hot water for bathing, dishwashing, and other purposes. In those in which antifreeze is required, heat exchangers may be installed for supplying a separate hot-water system.

Solar collectors may also be used to heat air. Instead of piping, these systems have ductwork to carry heated air to storage, often in crushed rock or other materials with high capacities for absorbing heat. Air is blown by fans through the storage into ductwork which supplies the interiors of buildings through grilles or registers. Sometimes the heat from such storage places is used to heat water as in the system first described. Solar heating systems, in all but the warmest climates, require auxiliary heating by boilers or furnaces at times. To reduce the use of the auxiliary equipment to a minimum, various chemicals, with high capacities for heat retention, are sometimes introduced into systems, thereby often making it possible for stored solar heat to last through several cloudy winter days.

Complete solar heating systems are often quite expensive to install, when compared to systems of other types. In spite of this, many complete systems of varied types are being designed and constructed today. As the systems become more standardized and more widely used and as the technology of solar heating improves, their use may be expected to increase.

Solar Cooling Solar cooling systems have not been used as widely as the heating types. In general, solar cooling or air conditioning may be produced in two major ways. In the first type, solar panels are heated by the sun as in solar heating systems. Instead of circulating the heated water to heat rooms, it is used to operate an engine that in turn operates equipment, compressors, condensers, evaporators, and so on very much like a conventional air-conditioning system. In the second type, solar heat is used to operate an absorption cooler, which works like a gas refrigerator. Absorption coolers, or air-conditioning systems, may use heat from solar energy or from other sources. Absorption coolers contain refrigerant liquids which when heated vaporize. Directed into a condenser, the vapor condenses losing heat as it does so; the liquid refrigerant is then directed into an evaporator, in which it rapidly evaporates, cools, and absorbs heat from the rooms in buildings. The heated refrigerant is then pumped back to the solar collector or other heat source to repeat the process. Further research and development is being carried on in solar air conditioning and is expected to produce valuable results. Some believe this will produce a nearly perfect system that involves maximum energy uses coupled with the possibility of maximum energy collection. Others are more skeptical.

Design The proper design of heating, air-conditioning, and year-round air-conditioning systems is quite complex and requires a great deal of skill and knowledge. In a time of increasing shortages and prices of fuels, proper design is even more necessary

than before. And the growing initial costs of such systems and the increasing amount they require out of the total budget for buildings make their proper and creative design a necessity today. Mechanical engineers, particularly those who specialize in heating, refrigeration, and air conditioning, usually design all but the simplest, packaged unit systems. They coordinate their work closely with architects, other engineers, and environmental designers to produce the best systems for the functions to be served. In the future, further improvements in heating and air conditioning may be expected.

History Early primitive huts and tents were probably not heated at all, but in time fires were used, the smoke and gases escaping through holes in the roofs. From this rudimentary beginning was developed the fireplace which has been used in architecture ever since. With few exceptions, fireplaces were the major means of heating buildings until heating stoves were manufactured in the 17th century. Such stoves were first used in the American colonies in the following century. For further discussion on fireplaces and heating stoves, see the article entitled fireplace.

No attempt was made to provide central heating in buildings until the time of the Romans, who invented an efficient system called a hypocaust. Used for heating public baths and sometimes other buildings, hypocausts consisted of floors raised on short pillars, creating spaces through which hot air and smoke from furnaces could pass, thus heating the floors. The smoke and gases were then vented to the outside air. This was not only the first central heating system but the forerunner of radiant panel floors and ceilings of the 20th century. After the Roman era, buildings were again heated only by fireplaces, and further development of central systems ceased until the 18th century.

During the 18th and early 19th centuries, rudimentary central heating systems were developed, including a type that utilized waste steam in a factory. Also developed were gravity warm-air systems and hot-water systems with radiators. Gradually these systems were improved and stock boilers and warm-air furnaces were produced along with radiators. Artificial ventilation, using fans and other devices, was also developed. Early in the 20th century, studies began of the conditions of human comfort, eventually leading to criteria and standards for heating and air conditioning buildings. They also led to improved systems.

Natural ice and snow have been used to provide some cooling effects since the time of the Romans. In the early 20th century, manufactured ice, over which air was blown by fans, was used to cool motion picture houses and other buildings. The first building to be air-conditioned in the modern manner was a motion picture house in Los Angeles, completed in 1922, and the first fully air-conditioned office building was the Milam Building (1928), San Antonio, Tex., designed by George Willis. Air conditioning for buildings received its greatest impetus from the installation in Rockefeller Center, New York City, in 1932.

Before World War II, central heating had become the norm for all but the most modest houses and other buildings. After the war, air conditioning also began to have a similar wide usage. Over the years, heating and air-conditioning systems have been greatly improved in operation and efficiency and in their controls. Hot-water and steam systems are now used extensively, as are hot-air systems.

Other systems have been developed, including radiant heating, which utilizes hot water in pipes or electric coils embedded in floors, walls, or ceilings. Another form of radiant heating utilizes baseboards, with piping or electric coils. While coal was the major fuel for heating in the 19th century, more commonly used today are fuel oil, gas, and electricity. A 20th-century heating system, called a heat pump, has had growing acceptance. Another recent development is the use of computers to control and monitor heating and air conditioning in relatively large, complex systems in buildings. Since the mid-1950s when fuel shortages started to occur, there has been considerable interest in solar heating and cooling.

Related Articles CLIMATE; COMPUTER; ELECTRICAL ENGINEERING; ELECTRIC POWER AND WIRING; ENERGY; ENVIRONMENTAL PROTECTION; FIREPLACE; GLASS; INSULATION, THERMAL; LIGHTING; MECHANICAL ENGINEERING; PLUMBING.

Further Reading Beckman, William A., Sanford A. Klein, and John A. Duffie: *Solar Heating Design—by the f-Chart Method*, John Wiley, New York, 1977; McGuinness, William J., and Benjamin Stein: *Mechanical and Electrical Equipment for Buildings*, 5th ed., John Wiley, New York, 1971; Szokolay, S. V.: *Solar Energy and Building*, 2d ed., John Wiley, New York, 1977.

Sources of Additional Information American Society of Heating, Refrigerating and Air Conditioning Engineers (ASHRAE), 345 E. 47th St., New York, N.Y. 10017; American Society of Mechanical Engineers (ASME), 345 E. 47th St., New York, N.Y., 10017; Plumbing, Heating and Cooling Information Bureau, 35 E. Wacker St., Chicago, Ill. 60601.

HISTORY OF ARCHITECTURE

The story or record of the past of mankind, as expressed in architecture, together with the understanding and explanation of the record or story. To understand and explain American architecture, it is necessary to have some understanding of that which preceded it and from which it evolved.

Great architecture has been produced all over the world, including China, Japan, India, and the Islamic countries. Although it has been affected by the architecture of such countries at various times, American architecture evolved most directly and generally from that of the countries around the Mediterranean Sea and in Europe. Therefore the simplified account that follows is devoted to the direct line of evolution.

Architectural Periods Scholars disagree to some extent about the periods of architectural history, but for all useful purposes the major periods, starting from the earliest, may be taken to be Prehistoric, Ancient, Classical, Early Christian, Byzantine, Romanesque, Gothic, Renaissance, Baroque, Classic Revival, Gothic Revival, Eclectic, and Modern. Many of these periods may be subdivided, for example, the Renaissance into the early period, the high period, and the later period, sometimes called Mannerism. Scholars also disagree somewhat on the dates for various periods, partly because the periods do not cover the same span of years in all countries. For example, the Renaissance, which is taken to have originated in Italy about 1400 or earlier, did not spread to France until later in the 15th century and to England until the 16th.

Prehistoric Period Architecture may be taken to have begun in prehistoric times in the New Stone, or Neolithic, Age, starting about the 50th century B.C. or earlier. During that time, humans first left the nomadic life of wanderers and settled down to the sedentary life of villages, to domesticate their first animals and to plant their first crops. The earliest buildings were made of branches of trees, brush, mud, and other readily obtainable simple materials, constructed into rudimentary huts or tents. Remains of these early civilizations have been found in the Middle East and Egypt, but only traces of buildings. Not much is know about the progress of architecture until about the 30th century B.C., by which time advanced civilizations had been established in several places.

Ancient Period The major civilizations of the time were those in Mesopotamia and other areas of the Middle East, Egypt, the islands of the Aegean Sea, in particular Crete, and on the mainland of Greece in Mycenae and Tiryns. Architecture flourished in all of these civilizations, from about 3000 B.C., ending at different times.

In Mesopotamia, architecture may be divided into four major periods: the Babylonian, from the earliest times to about 1250 B.C.; the Assyrian, from about 1250 to 612 B.C.; the Neo-Babylonian, 612–539 B.C.; and the period after the conquest by Persia, 539–331 B.C.. Wood and stone were used in buildings in Mesopotamia, but the major material was brick, sun-dried at first, then later burned in kilns. In the area, the two major structural systems of the time were both used: the trabeated, or post and lintel system; and the arcuated, based on the principles of the arch. Thus Mesopotamian buildings were constructed with vertical and horizontal members and with arches, vaults, and domes.

Some of the important buildings, of which remains exist today, are: the Temple (c. 3000 B.C.), Khafaje, Iran; Ziggurat (2020 B.C.), Ur, Iraq; the city of Babylon, Iraq, first built about 2500 B.C. and rebuilt, along with the famous Hanging Gardens, by King Nebuchadnezzar II (605–563 B.C.); the Ziggurat (c. 1300 B.C.), near Susa, Iran, where was found the Code of King Hammurabi (18th century B.C.), the earliest legal code known, containing laws for building; the Palace (705 B.C.) of King Sargon II (722–705 B.C.), Khorsabad, Iraq; and the Palace (465 B.C.) at Persepolis, Iran.

Egyptian architecture may be taken to have begun

HISTORY OF ARCHITECTURE Egyptian, Rameseum (1301 B.C.), Thebes, Egypt. [*Architect: unknown. (The Bettmann Archive)*]

about 3000 B.C. and to have continued until about the first century A.D. The history of Egyptian architecture is usually divided into three long periods covering the 30 dynasties of Egyptian rulers, or pharaohs: the Ancient Kingdom about 3000–2130 B.C., dynasties I–X; the Middle Kingdom, about 2130–1580 B.C., XI–XVII dynasties; and the New Empire, about 1580–332 B.C., dynasties XVIII–XXX. Later periods are the Ptolemaic (332–30 B.C.), named for Ptolemy (c. 367–268 B.C.), a general of Alexander the Great (356–323 B.C.), who ruled Egypt after Alexander's death; and the Roman period (30 B.C.–A.D. 395), when the country was ruled by Roman emperors.

Materials used in Egyptian architecture include wood, stone, and sun-dried (later kiln-dried) brick. For the most important buildings, stone was usually the major material, while the others were used for lesser structures. The main structural system was the trabeated, post and lintel, but the arcuated system, with rudimentary arches and vaults, was sometimes employed. The Egyptians had strong beliefs in religion and in an afterlife. Their monumental architecture, massive and mysterious, reflects these beliefs, as do the many major buildings still in existence, all of which are tombs or temples.

Among the most important Egyptian buildings still in existence, at least in part, are: the Step Pyramid of Zoser (c. 2800 B.C.) and the rest of the complex of buildings at Saqqara; the Pyramids and Sphinx (c. 2700–2500 B.C.) at Giza, near Cairo; the Rock Tombs (c. 2100–1800 B.C.) at Beni Hasan; the Temple of Hatshepsut (c. 1500 B.C.), Deir- el-Bahari; the Temple of Amon (started c. 1500, completed c. 300 B.C.) and others at Karnak; the Temple of Amon (c. 1300 B.C.) at Luxor, and others; the Great Temple (c. 1300 B.C.) and others at Abu Simbel; the Temple of Horus (c. 300

B.C.) and others at Edfu; and the Temple of Isis (247 B.C.) on the island of Philae.

Aegean architecture existed from about 3000 to about 1100 B.C. and centered in the islands of that sea and on the mainland of Greece. The major materials were brick, stone, and wood and the major structural system, the post and lintel, or trabeated. Also used were rudimentary arches, vaults, and domes. The Aegean people developed a highly sophisticated architecture, often of great size and magnificence and mostly of nonreligious building types. Among the most important buildings still in existence, at least in part, are: on Crete—the Palace of Minos (completed about 1600 B.C.) at Knossos and Palace of Radamanthus (completed about 1300 B.C.) at Phaistos; the so-called Treasury of Atreus (c. 1325 B.C.), acually a tomb, and the Lion gate (c. 1250 B.C.) at Mycenae; and the Palace (c. 1300 B.C.) at Tiryns.

None of these early architectural periods influenced architecture in America to any great extent. However, they did influence the classical architecture of Greece and therefore indirectly that of America. Egyptian architecture had some influence in America, since it was one of the styles sometimes adapted by American architects, mostly in the 19th century, for the design of certain buildings, including many early prisons.

Classical Period The greatest influence on ancient Greek architecture was that of the Aegean, but after the end of the great Aegean period about 1100 B.C., little progress was made in architecture in Greece until about 650 B.C. This date is often taken to mark the beginning of the Golden Age, called the Hellenic period of Greek civilization. This great period is considered to have ended about 323 B.C., and was followed by the Hellenistic period which ended about 30 B.C.

HISTORY OF ARCHITECTURE Greek, The Parthenon (c. 432 B.C.), Athens, Greece. [*Architects: Callicrates and Ictinus. (The Bettmann Archive)*]

The Hellenic period produced some of the greatest architecture the world has ever known, the major examples of which were religious in character. During the Hellenistic period, the quality of architectural design declined, but progress was made in the architecture of public buildings and other types and in city planning. Although the Greeks used wood, brick, and other materials, stone was the major material for important buildings. Most frequently used was the trabeated, post and lintel, structural system, but arches and vaults were used to some extent during the Hellenistic period and later.

Although the Greeks made architectural progress of many kinds, including further development of residential designs, perhaps the greatest progress was in esthetic design refinements of monumental buildings. The Greeks not only produced buildings of excellent form and proportions but invented a system of proportions still much admired today. They also learned how to correct the forms and proportions of their buildings to allow for optical distortions produced by the human eye. The Greeks also developed design systems for the columns, bases, and other elements used in their buildings. These systems, called orders, from the earliest developed and simplest in design to the latest and most ornamental, are the Doric, Ionic, and Corinthian. The orders gave the Greeks a useful system for design, but the actual appearance and proportions of the columns and other elements varied considerably from place to place, between buildings, and at different times. The Romans

adapted these orders to their own uses and they were used later on, in varied forms, in Renaissance and Classic Revival architecture.

A large number of Greek buildings still exist, at least partly, not only in Greece but in many other places, including Italy and Sicily. A list of the great examples would be very long, but some of the most important are: three Temples at Paestum, Italy, the Basilica (c. 530 B.C.), Demeter (c. 510 B.C.), and Poseidon (c. 460 B.C.); the Treasury of the Athenians (c. 485 B.C.), the Theater (c. 510 B.C.), and other buildings at Delphi; the Choragic Monument of Lysicrates (c. 334) and other buildings at Athens; and the Theater (c. 350) at Epidaurus.

The most important architectural remains in Greece are those of the several buildings on the Acropolis in Athens, including the Erechtheion (c. 405 B.C.) and Propylaea (c. 432 B.C.) designed by Mnesicles (5th century B.C.), the Temple of Athena Nike (c. 427 B.C.), probably designed by Callicrates, and the crowning glory of the Acropolis, the Parthenon (c. 432 B.C.), designed by Callicrates and Ictinus (both 5th century B.C.).

Traditionally, Rome has been said to have been founded by the twins Romulus and Remus in 753 B.C. At first Rome was ruled by the Etruscans, who inhabited west-central Italy. The Etruscans had a highly developed architecture that flourished from about 750 to 100 B.C. They were accomplished builders and engineers, using burned bricks, terra-cotta, and stone and are thought to have developed the first true arches.

HISTORY OF ARCHITECTURE Roman, The Pantheon (A.D. 124), Rome, Italy. [*Architect: unknown. (The Bettmann Archive)*]

They developed a new architectural order called the Tuscan. They are also believed to have developed houses with atriums or patios.

By the start of the third century B.C., the Romans were well on the way toward developing their own architecture which continued until about A.D. 365. The Romans were not great designers in the sense that the Greeks were. But they were great engineers and builders and took ideas for their architecture wherever they found them, mainly from the Middle East, the Greeks, and the Etruscans. The Romans used brick, stone, and many other materials but, after a while, their favorite material was concrete, which they often veneered with stone or plastered. They were noted for the great size of their buildings and other structures and for daring engineering feats.

From the Etruscans, the Romans took the arcuated system, based on the principles of the arch, and further developed it to produce great vaults and domes. From the Greeks, they took the trabeated, or post and lintel, system, which they often combined with the arcuated. They also took the Doric, Ionic, Corinthian, and Tuscan orders, adapted them to their own ends, and elaborated upon them. One of their elaborations produced a new order, the Composite, which has some of the attributes of the Corinthian combined with some from the Ionic.

The Romans constructed a great number of buildings and other structures in Italy and in all the coun-

tries they conquered, including France, England, Spain, Lebanon, Syria, and Germany. These included forums, temples, law and commerce buildings or basilicas, public baths, theaters, amphitheaters, palaces, houses, and other types of buildings and structures. A list of the notable examples still in existence would be quite long. Among the most important of those existing today, at least in part, are: the forums of Vespasian, Augustus, Nerva, Trajan, and Caesar, and the Forum Romanum, in Rome; temples such as Bacchus (second century B.C.), Jupiter (A.D.10–249), and others at Baalbek, Lebanon; Portunus (31 B.C.) and Fortuna Virilis (c. 40 B.C.) in Rome; the Maison Carrée (c. 16 B.C.), Nîmes, France; the Pantheon (A.D. 124), Rome; the Basilica of Constantine (A.D. 313), sometimes called that of Maxentius, Rome; baths such as those in Rome, Caracalla (A.D. 217) and Diocletian (A.D. 302), part of which was made into the Church of Santa Maria dei Angeli in 1563 by Michelangelo (1475–1564).

Other great Roman buildings existing, at least in part, are: theaters, Marcellus (13 B.C.) in Rome and that in Orange, France (A.D. 50); amphitheaters such as the Colosseum (A.D. 82) in Rome and that in Verona, Italy, completed in A.D. 290; residences such as the Palace of Diocletian (A.D. 300) in Split, Yugoslavia, Hadrian's Villa (A.D. 124) in Tivoli, Italy, and the House of Livia (c. 55 B.C.) in Rome. The most complete groupings of Roman houses, and of other buildings

HISTORY OF ARCHITECTURE Byzantine, Cathedral of San Marco (1085, with latter additions), Venice, Italy. [*Architect: unknown. (The Bettmann Archive)*]

and structures, exist at Pompeii and Herculaneum, Italy, both of which were covered with lava and volcanic ash by an eruption of Mount Vesuvius in 79 A.D. Both towns have been well preserved and include houses, forums, amphitheaters, and other buildings constructed from about the 5th century B.C. to the first century A.D.

The classic architecture of Greece and Rome have greatly influenced that of succeeding eras, particularly the Roman on the architecture of the Renaissance and both Roman and Greek on the Classic Revival during the 18th and 19th centuries.

Early Christian and Byzantine Periods Early Christian and Byzantine architecture developed side by side at the same time in history, beginning in the early 4th century. Both styles of architecture were mainly used for churches and other religious buildings. The era of Early Christian architecture is usually thought to have begun in 313, when the Roman Emperor Constantine (c. 280–337) declared Christianity to be the Roman state religion. The beginning of Byzantine architecture is taken to have been 330, when Constantine moved the capital of the Roman Empire to Byzantium, later called Constantinople and still later Istanbul, Turkey.

The major development in Early Christian architec-

ture was the basilica church, named after the halls of justice and commerce of the Romans. Basilica churches are typically constructed of stone, with timber roof structures. The main church, or nave, is higher than the side aisles, thus making it possible for the nave section to have rows of windows, called clerestories, above the roofs of the aisle areas. Some basilica churches have post-and-lintel structural systems, some arches, and some combinations of the two types. Many of these churches are relatively simple in design. The amount of ornament varies.

Byzantine architecture took another course in church design, that of the arcuated system, mainly relying on the use of domes, the design of which the Byzantines developed into a high art. Byzantine churches were highly ornamented.

Among the important Early Christian churches are Santa Sabina (425) and Santa Maria Maggiore (432), both in Rome; Sant'Apollinare Nuovo (525) and Sant'Apollinare in Classe (539), both in Ravenna, Italy; and San Demetrius (550) in Salonika, Greece. Masterpieces of the Byzantine style include Santa Sophia (536), often called Hagia Sophia, which was converted into a mosque in 1453 and later into a museum, in Istanbul; San Vitale (547) in Ravenna; and San Marco (1085, with later additions) in Venice.

HISTORY OF ARCHITECTURE Romanesque, Durham Cathedral (1093–1133), Durham, England. [*Architect: unknown. (The Bettmann Archive)*]

Both types of architecture have had an effect on that which came later, establishing traditions in church design some of which have come down to the present day. The end of the Byzantine era in architecture is often taken to be about 1450, or even later. The end of the Early Christian era came much earlier, with the advent of Romanesque architecture in the 9th century.

Romanesque Period Romanesque architecture flourished in Europe, mainly in Italy, France, Spain, Germany, and England, until about the 12th century when it was superseded by the Gothic of which it was the forerunner. Romanesque architecture was developed mainly from that of the Romans, but it was also influenced to some extent by Byzantine and other earlier types. Romanesque architecture was massive and heavy in character, utilizing stone, mostly in religious buildings, particularly in churches and cathedrals. Based on the Roman system of semicircular, or barrel, vaulting, Romanesque architecture gradually developed systems of ribs to replace the heavy groins used by the Romans where vaults crossed each other. This was the beginning of further developments to be made later in Gothic architecture.

Among the most important Romanesque buildings still in existence are: in Italy—the Church of San Miniato al Monte (1090), Florence; the Cathedral (1092), Baptistery (1278), and Campanile (1174), better known as the famous leaning tower, at Pisa; Church of San Ambrogio (1128), Milan; and Monreale Cathedral (1182), Palermo, Sicily; in France—the Church of Sainte Madeleine (1206), Vezelay; and at Caen, Saint Étienne (1086), often called Abbaye-aux-Hommes founded by William the Conquerer (1027–87) and

where he is buried, and La Trinité (1140), called Abbaye-aux-Dames, and founded by William's wife, Matilda.

In Germany, notable examples are the cathedrals of Aix-la-Chapelle (Aachen; 804), established by Emperor Charlemagne (742–814) and where he is buried; Speyer (1030); Mainz (1036); and Worms (1181). In England, notable examples, sometimes called Norman in style rather than Romanesque, are Canterbury (1071–1126), Durham (1093–1133), and Peterborough (1117–93) cathedrals.

Romanesque architecture greatly influenced the Gothic that followed, having established the principles of ribbed vaulting, which were later developed to their ultimate limit in Gothic architecture. Romanesque architecture also influenced some of the architects of the 19th century, in particular Henry Hobson Richardson (1838–86), who established a revival of Romanesque principles and adapted them into designs for buildings.

Gothic Period Gothic architecture is thought to have started in the 12th century and to have flourished until about the 16th. Gothic architecture is arcuated, having evolved slowly from the Romanesque. The major structural change from the older type was the use of pointed arches, derived from those of Mesopotamia, instead of the round or barrel arches as in Romanesque and Roman buildings. Instead of the heavy, massive stone used in Romanesque buildings, Gothic buildings were designed with high, soaring ribbed vaults that exploit the properties of stone to their ultimate. Eventually, this resulted in structures that, unlike the somewhat ponderous earlier Romanesque examples, seem thin, attenuated, almost lace-

HISTORY OF ARCHITECTURE Gothic, Chartres Cathedral (1194–1260), Chartres France, [*Architect: unknown. (The Bettmann Archive)*]

like. In Gothic architecture, the ribs where two vaults crossed are the major structural members supporting roofs. The ribs are supported on tiers of columns.

The central portions, or naves, of churches and cathedrals are higher than the side aisles, allowing high windows to be placed over the roofs of the aisles. These windows and others are often glazed with magnificent stained glass, arranged to make patterns or to depict religious or other subjects. Stone was used with great economy in small pieces, which were accurately cut and set with thin mortar joints to form elegant and craftsmanlike building elements.

Instead of the heavy masonry buttresses used previously to resist the forces, or thrusts, of the vaults, Gothic architecture employed flying buttresses which utilized arches and piers to resist the thrusts, thereby lightening structures and making them more open.

The result is an architecture, quite unlike that of the past, composed of piers, columns, buttresses, and ribbed vaults in a structural system in which each member has been properly designed to receive and

resist the thrust of others. This produced true skeleton structures, not unlike those of steel and reinforced concrete buildings today, in which the walls with their stained-glass windows were used only to enclose space rather than for structural purposes.

The crowning achievements of Gothic architecture are churches, cathedrals, and other religious buildings, of which a great number are still in existence all over Europe. Many of these required a century or more to construct and therefore various stages of the development of Gothic architecture may often be seen in a single building.

A list of significant Gothic religious buildings would be quite long. Among the most notable, still in existence, are: in France—the cathedrals of Notre Dame de Paris (1163–1250), Chartres (1194–1260), Rheims (1211–90), Amiens (1220–88), Strasbourg (1230–1365), and Rouen (1318–1515), and the church of La Sainte Chapelle (1248) in Paris; in England—the cathedrals of Winchester (1079–1235), Lincoln (1192–1320), Salisbury (1220–65), and York (1261–1324); Westminster

Abbey (1055–1269), with the Chapel (1515) of King Henry VII (1407–1509), and the King's College Chapel (1519), Cambridge.

In other European countries, some examples are Saint Gudule (1220–1475), Brussels, Belgium; Antwerp Cathedral (1352–1411), the Netherlands; in Germany—The cathedrals of Cologne (1248–1880) and Ulm (1377–1492); Saint Stephen (c. 1300–1510), Vienna, Austria; Burgos Cathedral (1221–1457), Spain; and in Italy—the cathedrals of Siena (1226–1380), Milan (1385–1485), and Florence (1296–1462), the last-named designed by Arnolfo di Cambio (1232–c. 1300), with a dome added later (1434) by Filippo Brunelleschi (c. 1337–1446).

Nonreligious Gothic buildings include such types as houses, manor houses, hospitals, market halls, guild halls, forts, and castles. A number of examples are still standing, of which the following may be representative: in England—the Guildhall (c. 1529), Lavenham; Hampton Court Palace (c. 1520); and the colleges, constructed from the 12th to the 16th centuries, of Oxford and Cambridge; in France—the House of Jacques Coeur (1453), Bourges; and the Hôtel de Cluny (1498), Paris; in Italy—the Doge's Palace, Venice, started in the 9th century and completed 1550; the Palazzo Pubblico (1289–1302), Siena; and Cloth Hall (1202–1304), Ypres, Belgium.

Representative medieval forts, castles, and fortified towns still in existence include the walled city of Carcassonne (13th century), France; Caernarvon Castle (1323), Wales; the Tower of London (begun in the 11th century); Windsor Castle (begun in the 12th century), London; Castello Nuovo (1283), Naples, Italy; and Castle Krak (1131), Jordan, built by Crusaders.

Gothic architecture deeply affected that of America in many ways. When the colonies were first founded in the New World, the Gothic was the prevailing style in England and on the continent of Europe, and thus deeply influenced the architecture of the English colonies in America. Later, American architects went back to it in the Gothic Revival style and again during the Eclectic period in architecture. The principles of stone, skeleton-framed buildings developed during the Middle Ages also contributed to the development of skeleton structural systems in iron, steel, and reinforced concrete.

Renaissance Period The Renaissance began in Italy in the 15th century at about the time the Middle Ages were coming to an end and spread northward to France later in that century, reaching Germany, the Netherlands, Belgium, and England in the 16th century. Turning away from the style and forms of Gothic architecture, the Renaissance adopted those of classical times, in particular the Roman, including barrel vaults and domes. Renaissance architects used all the Classic Roman orders (Tuscan, Doric, Ionic, Corinthian, and Composite) in their buildings and the first attempts to codify and standardize the orders were made by the Italian architects Andrea Palladio (1508–80) and Giacomo Barozzi da Vignola (1507–73).

Their standards became those of later generations of architects, though they were not usually strictly followed.

The Renaissance was a time of great developments in architectural design, based on the old forms, but using the emerging new scientific methods in the creation of well-designed buildings. It was also a time for a return to older principles of garden and city design and to a new interest in the entire environment in which buildings exist. It was a time of ornament in and on buildings and some of the greatest buildings ever produced by collaboration of architects and artists. It was also a time when architects emerged from their former almost complete anonymity to design buildings that were constructed by others, almost in the manner of today.

The Renaissance produced a prodigious number of significant buildings, of every type imaginable, designed by a great number of talented architects. No list could do justice to the great output and to the architects who produced it. Among the greatest examples in Italy, where the period started, are the churches of San Lorenzo (1460) and San Spirito (1482) and Pazzi Chapel (1446), all by Brunelleschi; Palazzo Medici-Riccardi (1460), by Michelozzo di Bartolommeo (1396–1472); the churches of Santa Maria Novella (1470), all in Florence, and Sant'Andrea (1494), Mantua, and Palazzo Rucellai (1451), Florence, by Leon Battista Alberti (1404–72); Palazzo Strozzi (1539), Florence, by Simone Pollaiuolo (1454–1508), known as Il Cronaca; the Tempietto (1510) by Donato Bramante (1444–1514); Palazzo Farnese (1545), Rome, by Antonio da Sangallo, the younger (1485–1546), with additions by Michelangelo Buonarroti (1475–1564), known as Michelangelo; the Villa Madama (1516), Rome, and Palazzo Pandolfini (1527), Florence, by Raphael Santi (1483–1520), known as Raphael. Many other significant examples still exist in Italy.

Beginning in the second quarter of the 16th century, Italian architects began to develop more personal styles, generally retreated from the conventional principles of design to adopt a somewhat capricious use of forms and theories. This movement has been called Mannerism and has been held by some to be similar to what they consider self-centered, idiosyncratic architecture produced by some architects today.

While there is no real agreement on the subject, Mannerism is thought to have started about 1525, in the late Renaissance, and may be first detected in work of the great painter, sculptor, poet, and architect, Michelangelo, in his Laurentian Library (1542), Florence, later completed by another architect considered to have been Mannerist, Giorgio Vasari (1511–74), and his Medici Chapel (1532), in which are his sculptured tombs of the Medicis. Vasari also designed the Mannerist Uffizi Court (1574) in Florence and other buildings.

Other important Mannerist buildings are Palazzo Farnese (1549), Caprarola, and the churches of San

HISTORY OF ARCHITECTURE Renaissance, Basilica of St. Peter (1506–1667), Rome, Italy. [*Architects: Donato Bramante, Raphael, Michelangelo, and others. (The Bettmann Archive)*]

Andrea (c. 1550) and Il Gesu (1584), both in Rome, by Vignola; and the Basilica (1549) and Villa Capra (1569), also known as Villa Rotonda, both in Vicenza, and the Church of San Giorgio Maggiore (not completed until 1610), by Palladio.

One of the most important of late Italian Renaissance buildings, often thought of as Mannerist, is the Basilica of Saint Peter (1506–1667) in Rome. For this great building which took more than 150 years to construct, the services of some 11 architects were required, including Bramante, Raphael, and Michelangelo.

Some of the important Renaissance buildings in France are the Chateau of Azay-le-Rideau (1527), Chateau de Blois (1524 and later), Palais de Fontainebleau (1540 and later), and the Palais de Louvre, Paris, begun in 1546 by Pierre Lescot (c. 1510–78) and not completed until 1857, after having been worked on by at least 10 architects. Renaissance architecture came late to the other countries in Europe and was never nearly so highly developed as it was in Italy. These countries held on to the Gothic style long after it had been supplanted in Italy. During the Renaissance, styles in England were usually designated by the names of the ruling monarchs at the time: thus the Elizabethan (1558–1603) for Queen Elizabeth I (1533–1603); the Jacobean (1603–25) for James I (1566–1625); the Stuart (1625–1702) for the reigns of Stuart rulers af-

ter James I; and the Georgian (1702–1830) for George I, II, III, and IV.

The Elizabethan and Jacobean styles are usually taken to coincide with the early Renaissance style in other countries and the Stuart and Georgian with late Renaissance. Elizabethan buildings include Hardwick Hall (1597), Derbyshire, by Robert Smithson (c. 1536–1614), and Longleat House (1580), Wiltshire, probably by the same architect. Jacobean buildings include Hatfield House (1611), Hertfordshire, and Charlton House (1612), Kent. The Stuart era was the time of the work of one of England's great architects, Inigo Jones (1573–1652), including his Banqueting Hall (1622), Whitehall Palace, London. The towering figure of the Stuart era was Sir Christopher Wren (1632–1723), who designed more than 60 important buildings in London alone, including his magnificent Saint Paul's Cathedral (1710), London.

Renaissance architecture strongly affected that in America. The English Elizabethan, Jacobean, and Stuart styles were exported to the colonies, but never became well established on a wide scale. On the other hand, the Georgian style was the first to become deeply rooted in the architecture of the American colonies, and has been a part of American life ever since. When American architects began to move away from the Georgian style, they turned to the architecture of classical Greece and Rome to replace it,

HISTORY OF ARCHITECTURE Baroque, Church of St. Louis des Invalides (1691), Paris, France. [*Architects: Libéral Bruant and Jules Hardouin-Mansart. (The Bettmann Archive)*]

often utilizing Renaissance interpretations of those styles instead of the originals. Later in the period of Eclectic architecture, some American architects again turned to the Renaissance for inspiration.

Baroque Period Much of Wren's work is considered to have been in the style called Baroque, which had started in Italy early in the 17th century. Some consider the style to have started even earlier in some of the works of Michelangelo and Vignola. In any case, the Baroque style was one of great sizes, grand spaces, curved forms, complexities, rich materials, and drama.

Among the important Baroque buildings in Italy are Church of Santa Susanna (1603), Rome, by Carlos Maderna (1556–1629); churches of San Carlo alle Quattro Fontane (1641) and San Ivo della Sapienza (1650), both in Rome and by Francesco Borromini (1599–1667); and the Piazza (1667) of the Cathedral of St. Peter and the Church of Sant'Andrea al Quirinale (1670), both in Rome and by Giovanni Lorenzo Bernini (1598–1680).

Important Baroque buildings in other places include: in Paris—the Pantheon (1790), formerly the Church of Saint Geneviève, by Jacques Germain Soufflot (1713–80), where many heroes of France are buried, and the Church of Saint Louis des Invalides (1691), by Libéral Bruant (1635–97) and Jules Hardouin-Mansart (1646–1708), where Emperor Napoleon I (1769–1821) is buried.

The last phase of the Baroque, called Rococo, is not so much a style in architecture as a method of ornamentation often utilizing seashell, rock, and scroll forms. Rococo ornament was profuse, and not always composed into an organic whole. Two important German buildings with Rococo ornament, designed by Balthasar Neumann (1687–1753), are the Kaisersaal (1744), in the Palace, Wurzburg, and the Church of Vierzehnheiligen (1772), near Banz.

During the period of Eclectic architecture in the United States, Baroque was one of the styles revived by American architects. However, it never became as popular as some of the other historical styles.

American Development In the earliest years of the colonies in America, architecture generally followed the styles of the countries in Europe from which the colonists had emigrated. Architecture in America generally lagged behind that in Europe to some extent, and was neither as large in size nor as grand in scale. There were other differences between the architecture in America and in Europe mainly due to the materials, craftsmen, and machinery available; differences in climate and social conditions; and needs for protection.

The history of architecture in America may be taken to have begun in pre-Columbian times before Europeans came to the New World. After that, the history generally parallels that of Europe, sometimes lagging behind, sometimes leading. Separate articles in this book are devoted to the various phases of American architecture. Some differences of opinion exist about American architecture historical periods. However, the subject can be covered, as in the separate articles in this book, approximately in chronological order, as follows: pre-Columbian, Colonial, Georgian, Classic Revival, Gothic Revival, Eclectic, Modern. To round out the history in America, see the article entitled contemporary architecture.

Related Articles ARCH; ART IN ARCHITECTURE; BOOK, ARCHITECTURAL; COLUMN; CONSTRUCTION MATERIALS; DOME; INTERIOR DESIGN; MAGAZINE, ARCHITECTURAL; PLANNING, CITY; STRUCTURE; VAULT; Various articles on American architectural periods and individual architects.

Further Reading Andrews, Wayne: *Architecture in America—A Photographic History from the Colonial Period to the Present*, 2d ed., Atheneum, New York, 1977. Burchard, John, and Albert Bush-Brown: *The Architecture of America*, Little, Brown, Boston, 1961; Cowan, Henry J.: *Master Builders—A History of Structural and Environmental Design from Ancient Egypt to the Nineteenth Century*, John Wiley, New York, 1977; Cowan, Henry J.: *Science and Building—Structural and Environmental Design in the Nineteenth and Twentieth Centuries*, John Wiley, New York, 1978; Fletcher, Sir Banister: *A History of Architecture on the Comparative Method*, 18th ed., Charles Scribner's, New York, 1975; Hammett, Ralph W.: *Architecture in the United States—A Survey of Architectural Styles Since 1776*; John Wiley, New York, 1976; Kidder-Smith, George E.: *A Pictorial History of Architecture in America*, 2 vols., American Heritage, New York, 1976; Norwich, John Julius, ed.: *World Architecture—An Illustrated History*, McGraw-Hill, New York, 1963; Whiffen, Marcus: *American Architecture Since 1790—A Guide to the Styles*, MIT Press, Cambridge, Mass., 1969.

Source of Further Information Society of Architectural Historians, 1700 Walnut St., Philadelphia, Pa. 19103.

HOLABIRD AND ROCHE American architectural firm. In 1883 William Holabird (1854–1923) and Martin Roche (1853–1927), American architects who had worked in the office of Major William Le Baron Jenney (1832–1907), formed a partnership in Chicago that was to last 40 years, until the death of Holabird in 1923. They became deeply involved in the movement toward functional design of tall skeleton-framed buildings, along with other architects, including Jenney, who came to be known as the Chicago school.

Standard Forms In their long years of practice together, they handled a very large number of commissions, consisting mostly of office and other commercial buildings. In the commercial area of Chicago alone, they did 72 major buildings. They developed the most consistent approach to the problems of tall buildings of any of the Chicago school. Attacking the problems of structure, utility, and shape of tall buildings in crowded urban areas, they developed rational methods for their design. They developed standard forms that were repeated in all their buildings with variations only to meet special problems. Thus their buildings have a family resemblance that is not always recognizable in the work of other architects. They have been criticized for both the uniformity and the lack of inventiveness of their work. Instead of allowing these characteristics to become faults, they capitalized on them by letting each succeeding design evolve from those that preceded. In the process, they achieved a consistent excellence in a great number of buildings that has seldom been equaled and never surpassed.

Works After some years of designing buildings that were the forerunners of their mature style, Holabird and Roche designed one that heralded the excellence to come, the Tacoma Building (1889), in Chicago. It was the first or second building to be designed with the skeleton frame supporting almost the entire exterior wall. The other was Jenney's Home Insurance Building (1885). The question of which was first has never been resolved, but the fate of both landmarks was. They were demolished in 1925 and 1927.

This was followed by the Pontiac Building (1891) in Chicago. Starting in 1894, with the construction of the Marquette Building, the firm designed a remarkable series of fine buildings in Chicago. Among the best were the Old Colony Building (1894), Gage buildings (1898; see illustration in article modern architecture), the Williams Building (1898), Crown, formerly McClurg, Building (1900), the Chicago Building (1904), the Champlain, formerly Powers, Building (1903), and the Brooks Building (1910). Their last important building together was a church with offices inside, topped by a great carillon tower and spire.

The great work of the partnership came to an end in 1923, with the death of William Holabird. Hola-

HOLABIRD AND ROCHE Marquette Building (1894), Chicago, Ill. (Hedrich-Blessing)

HOLABIRD AND ROCHE Champlain Building (1903), Chicago, Ill. (Hedrich-Blessing)

HOLABIRD AND ROCHE Chicago Building (1904), Chicago, Ill. *(Hedrich-Blessing)*

HOLABIRD AND ROCHE Mandel Brothers Building (1905), Chicago, Ill. *(Hedrich-Blessing)*

bird's son, John Augur Holabird (1886–1945), came into the partnership and, upon the death of Martin Roche, brought in the son of another great Chicago architect, John Wellborn Root, Jr. (1887–1963), to form a successor partnership, Holabird and Root. It too became large and successful, and it is still in practice today.

Holabird's Life William Holabird was born on September 11, 1854, in American Union, N.Y. During his early years, he had no intention of becoming an architect. Instead he expected to have a military career and entered the U.S. Military Academy at West Point, N.Y. After two years, he resigned because he had been disciplined for aiding a sick friend. In 1875, having decided to become an architect, he went to Chicago to begin work, as a draftsman, in the office of Jenney.

In 1880 he formed a partnership with Ossian C. Simonds (d. 1931) and in 1881 brought Martin Roche, with whom he had worked in Jenney's office, into the firm which now became Holabird, Simonds and Roche. After Simonds left the firm in 1883, the name was changed to Holabird and Roche, which lasted 40 years. William Holabird died on July 19, 1923.

Roche's Life Martin Roche was born in Cleveland, Ohio, on August 1, 1853, and moved with his family to Chicago two years later. After a high school education, he went to work for Jenney in 1872, remaining in that office until he joined forces with Holabird in 1881. In the early years, Roche and Holabird divided the design of buildings between them, sometimes acting as codesigners on certain jobs. Roche designed the interiors for the most part. As the office grew, the partners hired other designers who worked under their direction. Martin survived Holabird by four years; he died on June 6, 1927.

Related Articles JENNEY, WILLIAM LE BARON; MODERN ARCHITECTURE.

HOOD, RAYMOND MATHEWSON American architect (1881–1934). In 1922, when he was forty-one, Raymond Mathewson Hood burst on the architectural scene, after a life of obscurity, by winning, with John Mead Howells (1868–1959), the competition for the office building for the Chicago Tribune (1925). The design was Hood's and the resulting steel-framed skyscraper, clothed in an eclectic stone Gothic Revival exterior complete with flying buttresses, brought him worldwide renown. Though it brought its architects fame and commissions for other buildings, the Tribune Tower did not advance the art of the skyscraper design or the modern movement in architecture, as did many of the buildings of other early modern architects in America and Europe.

In little more than a decade, the architectural career of Raymond Hood started and ended. But it was a decade of almost unparalleled accomplishment, one that saw him develop from a provocative but largely outmoded eclectic into the leader of the New York City designers of modern skyscrapers.

HOOD, RAYMOND Chicago Tribune Tower (1925), Chicago, Ill. [*Architects: Hood, Fouilhoux and Howells. (Hedrich-Blessing)*]

HOOD, RAYMOND Daily News Building (1929), New York, N.Y. [*Architects: Hood, Fouilhoux and Howells. (Joseph W. Molitor)*]

HOOD, RAYMOND American Radiator Building (1924), New York, N.Y. [*Architects: Hood and Fouilhoux. (Wurts Brothers)*]

HOOD, RAYMOND Old McGraw-Hill Building (1930), New York, N.Y. [*Architects: Hood and Fouilhoux.*]

Works Hood continued to design buildings in the eclectic manner for sometime. His first tall building, in New York City, 20 stories in height, the American Radiator Building (1924), is also Gothic Revival but with more subdued forms, and ornament on the top stories is gilded.

Only five years later, again with John Mead Howells, Hood's Daily News Building (1929) became the pacesetter for tall buildings in New York City. Its simple, unadorned limestone walls are arranged in uninterrupted vertical bands from the bottom of the building to the top, expressing both the steel-skeleton structure and the essential verticality of skyscrapers. The old McGraw-Hill Building (1930) in New York City was also a pacesetter, but in this design, Hood, who always tried something new in each building design, used terra-cotta bands that are horizontal and continuous around the building.

During these years Hood played a very important role in the design of Rockefeller Center (see illustrations in article complex, architectural), for which construction began in 1931 and was not completed until 1940, some years after Hood's death. Rockefeller Center has become world famous, not only for the design of its buildings on the midtown New York City site of several blocks but for the excellence of the relationships between buildings and the open spaces between them. (See also color section.)

Rockefeller Center was designed by an association of three architectural firms: Reinhard and Hofmeister; Corbett, Harrison and MacMurray; and Hood and Fouilhoux. The major contributions to the design of the complex were made by Harvey Wiley Corbett (1873–1954), Wallace Kirkman Harrison (1895–   ), and Hood.

In a short time, Raymond Hood had made great progress and had accomplished a great deal. Each new building was a challenge that produced fresh design, evolving from those that preceded. If he had lived longer, Hood might have realized his seeming ability and aspiration for further evolution and accomplishment.

Life Raymond Mathewson Hood was born in Pawtucket, R.I., on March 2, 1881, the son of well-to-do parents. After high school, he entered Brown University in 1898, stayed two years, and then enrolled in the architectural school of Massachusetts Institute of Technology, staying two years. After leaving MIT, Hood worked as an apprentice in the office of Cram, Goodhue and Ferguson in Boston. Here he was influenced by the Gothic styles of both Ralph Adams Cram and Bertram Grosvenor Goodhue, but wanting to further his education, he stayed for only a short time.

He went to Paris, where he enrolled in the École des Beaux Arts in 1905, after having failed to be accepted on his first try in 1904. One year later, Hood was back working for Cram, Goodhue and Ferguson by mid-year 1906, in their New York offices, but was fired after only a few months. He then went to Pittsburgh to work for Henry Hornbostel (1867–1961).

After much indecision, Hood went back to the Beaux Arts in 1908, and for the first time in his life seems to have committed himself to finish something he started, graduating in 1910 at age twenty-nine. After traveling for a time with his brother in Europe, Hood returned in 1911 to the Hornbostel office in Pittsburgh, this time as chief designer. He went back to New York in 1914, and set up an office with another architect, Rayne Adams. For the first years, the commissions were few and insignificant in size, mostly remodeling or alterations. Hood kept the office going by working on competitions for other architects. Hood was now more than forty years old and had not yet designed a building of any importance.

Then in June 1922, the Chicago Tribune announced an international competition for its building. A New York architect, John Mead Howells, familiar with Hood's competition work, asked him to collaborate on a design. Out of 263 designs submitted, that of Howells and Hood won the $50,000 first prize and the commission to do the building. Hood borrowed money to go to Chicago to receive the award. In 1920 Hood had married his secretary, Elsie Schmidt. When Hood returned to New York, his wife showed the check to all their many creditors.

In the years following, Hood became a very successful and influential architect. In the early 1920s, Hood took in a French engineer, Jacques André Fouilhoux (1879–1945), as a partner and in 1924 took in Frederick Augustus Godley (1886–1961). As it turned out, Godley worked mostly on buildings of his own, rather than those of Hood, until he left the firm in 1931 to become a professor at Yale. Howells and Hood also practiced independently of each other, except for the Tribune Tower, the Daily News Building, and an apartment house.

Outside his office work, Raymond Hood pursued other interests that were almost exclusively related to architecture. He was active in the Beaux Arts Institute of Design, an organization founded by graduates of the Paris school to prepare and judge design projects of architectural students. He was also active in the Architectural League of New York, an organization of architects and artists.

Hood designed a number of other buildings, playing a key role in the Century of Progress Exposition in Chicago (1933). During the Depression, there was almost no work in the office. After almost a year of illness, Raymond Hood died on August 15, 1934, at age fifty-three. His major buildings had been done in less than 10 years. But in that short time, he had come a long way, from the Gothic eclecticism of the Tribune Tower to the modernism of the Daily News and McGraw-Hill buildings.

Related Articles BEAUX ARTS, ÉCOLE DES; CRAM, GOODHUE AND FERGUSON; MODERN ARCHITECTURE.

Further Reading Kilham, Walter H.: *Raymond Hood, Architect—Form Through Function in the American Skyscraper*, Architectural Book Publishing Co., New York, 1973.

HOSPITAL A building, group of buildings, or part of a building for the treatment and care of the sick or injured. The first purpose of a hospital is the diagnosis of health problems and the second is to cure them if possible. In addition, hospitals are concerned with the prevention of health problems and with the rehabilitation of those who have been treated. Hospitals are also involved, in varying degrees, with the education of medical students, interns, and nurses, and many are active in research.

In a way, a hospital is like a hotel, providing almost everything required for the general welfare of its patients and, in addition, the health services they need. The great complexity involved in providing good health care has made hospitals one of the most important building types and one of the most challenging for the architects who design them.

Classification Hospitals are classified according to the treatment they offer their patients. A general hospital provides treatment for all kinds of diseases and injuries, sometimes with the exception of such diseases as tuberculosis and mental illness. Patients with these diseases are often treated in special hospitals, specifically designed for such care. Other special hospitals include those for children, contagious diseases, maternity, chronic diseases, and convalescence or rehabilitation. Hospitals are also classified according to the length of time patients stay in them. Short-term hospitals are those in which patients generally stay less than 30 days. For patients whose treatment may be expected to last more than 30 days, such as those with chronic or mental illnesses, long-term hospitals are provided.

The sizes of hospitals are usually expressed by the number of patient beds. Thus a 100-bed hospital can care for 100 bed patients. Hospitals vary in size from only a few beds, the average in the United States is about 22, to a thousand or more. It is usually thought that general hospitals with fewer than 100 beds cannot be designed to operate as efficiently as those that are larger.

Ownership Hospitals are owned and operated in various ways. Some are owned by nonprofit groups organized in communities and are financed by funds donated by concerned citizens, often supplemented by financial help from city, county, state, or federal government. A board of governors or trustees is responsible for the overall operation, and the board employs a hospital administrator to manage the hospital. Other nonprofit hospitals are owned, and sometimes administered, by religious, fraternal, or union groups. Another type is a hospital owned and operated by a university. Often called teaching hospitals, these are generally operated in conjunction and cooperation with medical schools. A proprietary hospital is owned by an individual or organization and operated for profit.

States, counties, and cities operate hospitals, many of which are for long-term patients with mental or chronic illnesses. A number of hospitals are owned

HOSPITAL Meadowbrook (1973), Meadowbrook, N.Y. [*Architect: Max Urbahn. (Joseph W. Molitor)*]

HOSPITAL Exterior, Wilson Health Center (1974), Rochester, N.Y. [*Architects: Wolf, Zimmer, Gunsul and Frasca. (Joseph W. Molitor)*]

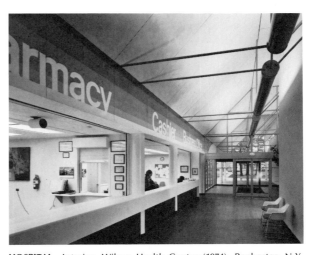

HOSPITAL Interior, Wilson Health Center (1974), Rochester, N.Y. [*Architects: Wolf, Zimmer, Gunsul and Frasca. (Joseph W. Molitor)*]

HOSPITAL Mailman Clinic (1970), Miami, Fla. [*Architects: Ferendino, Grafton, Spillis and Candela. (Joseph W. Molitor)*]

and operated by the federal government. Among these are hospitals for the health care of people in the armed services and those operated by the Veterans Administration for former service people.

Elements The major elements of a hospital are the areas devoted to the primary services performed: diagnostic and treatment, nursing, supply, food, administrative, and maintenance.

The diagnostic and treatment element consists of facilities for outpatients and inpatients. For outpa-

tients, examination and treatment rooms are provided in a close relationship with laboratories and radiological (x-ray) suites. Usually the emergency room is nearby. All have access to other hospital facilities primarily related to diagnosis and treatment of inpatients. These include surgical suites with anesthesia, operating, recovery, and other facilities, and obstetrical suites with similar facilities and nurseries nearby. The radiology suite provides for diagnosis and for treatment by x-ray and other radiological methods.

HOSPITAL St. Mary's (1976), Chicago, Ill. [*Architects: Perkins and Will. (Hedrich-Blessing)*]

Also included in the diagnostic and treatment element are laboratories and facilities for a number of special services.

Nursing elements consist mainly of a group of patient rooms, together with nurses' stations, treatment rooms, storage and utility rooms, and often patients' lounges. The term nursing unit is often used to refer to a group of beds, usually from 8 to 14, that a nurse or team of nurses can handle. The term is also sometimes used to refer to the number of beds a head nurse can supervise. Specialized nursing units include those for intensive care, in which seriously ill patients may be observed continuously, and pediatric units for children.

Patient rooms vary in size greatly and may accommodate single patients in private rooms and two or more patients in semiprivate rooms. A ward is a large room for a large number of patients.

The supply services element of a hospital is quite complex. Not only are such things as linen supplied, as in a hotel, but a host of medical and surgical supplies. A pharmacy is available for the preparation and dispensing of medicine. A central supply room handles the sterilization and dispensing of instruments, gloves, and many other items required for treatment and surgery. A laundry is a necessity. The general stores supply stocks almost everything else needed in the hospital.

The food services element of a hospital performs a variety of functions. Not only must it provide meals each day for the patients, it must also make them available to the hospital staff and often to some extent to visitors. For many patients, meals must be delivered to their rooms. Many of these are special diets, specifically prescribed for individual patients. For ambulatory patients, a cafeteria or similar operation must be maintained. In many cases, vending machine food operations and snack bars are also available.

The administrative element of a hospital ordinarily includes the offices for hospital administrators and staff who handle admitting, purchasing, record-keeping, and other business functions of the hospital. In addition, there are dressing and locker spaces, food services, and employee lounges. In many hospitals, there is a social service department to aid patients and their families to solve problems caused by the patients' hospital stay.

The maintenance element usually includes two major functions: housekeeping and engineering. The housekeeping department is responsible for janitorial services and sometimes for laundry. The engineering department is responsible for the mechanical and electrical systems, including heating and air conditioning, water, gas, electrical system, and oxygen system, and often for repairs and upkeep, including carpentry, plumbing, gardening, and the like.

All of the diverse elements of any hospital must be combined in such a way that the purpose of the hospital, health care, can be efficiently and effectively served. Serious study, planning, and design are re-

HOSPITAL Holy Cross (1962), Silver Spring, Md. [Architects: Faulkner, Kingsbury and Stenhouse. (Joseph W. Molitor)]

quired if this is to be accomplished. In addition, comfortable and pleasant surroundings are an integral part of the recovery process of ill or injured patients and for the well-being of staff and visitors as well. Thus the design of hospitals is both demanding and rewarding.

History Some type of hospital, if it could really be called that, has existed since prehistoric times at least as early as 3000 B.C. These early hospitals were operated by religious groups and were used mostly to care for the poor. Other patients were treated in their homes or in doctors' offices. Gradually, hospitals were developed in which other than poor people were treated. The oldest existing hospital is Hôtel Dieu (c. 600) in Paris and the oldest in the Americas, the 16th-century Jesus Hospital in Mexico City.

American Development One of the earliest hospitals in what became the United States was started in New Amsterdam, now New York City, in 1658. But the earliest that could be called a general hospital was not built until the 18th century. The Pennsylvania Hospital (1756), Philadelphia, was the first chartered hospital in the United States. It was designed by Samuel Rhoads (1711–84). Philadelphia General, called Old Blockley (1732), and Bellevue (1736), New York City, opened as institutions for the poor and were made into hospitals later. The first maternity hospital (1762) in the colonies was that owned by William Shippen (1736–1808) in Philadelphia and the first mental hospital was the Mad House (1769), later called Eastern State Hospital, in Williamsburg, Va. It is still in existence, though the original building, designed by Robert Smith (1722–77), has been destroyed.

In the 19th century, hospitals began to take in paying patients. The use of anesthetics began late in that century, antisepsis or complete cleanliness became accepted, and the use of x-rays began. Hospital nursing schools were established at that time. These developments led to the present-day practice of treatment of serious illnesses and injuries in hospitals rather than at home or in doctors' offices. And they led to the building of large numbers of much improved hospitals all over the country.

Hospital construction speeded up after World War II. An important force was the Hill-Burton Act, which provided federal funds for building new hospitals and improving old ones. The act also provided for establishment of standards of quality, administered by the U.S. Public Health Service. These standards helped considerably in improving the efficiency of hospitals built under this program. The building of hospitals and the improvement of their design has continued to the present time.

Related Article HANDICAPPED, FACILITIES FOR THE.

Further Reading Allen, Rex Whitaker, and Ilona von Karolyi: *Hospital Planning Handbook*, John Wiley, New York, 1976; Redstone, Louis G., ed.: *Hospitals and Health Care Facilities*, 2d ed., McGraw Hill, New York, 1978.

Sources of Further Information American Association for Hospital Planning, 122 S. Michigan Ave., Chicago, Ill. 60603. American Association of Hospital Consultants, 2341 Jefferson Davis Hwy., Arlington, Va. 22202; American Hospital Assoc., 840 N. Lake Shore Dr., Chicago, Ill. 60611.

Periodicals *Hospitals*, 840 N. Lake Shore Dr., Chicago, Ill. 60611; *Modern Hospital*, 230 W. Monroe St., Chicago, Ill. 60606.

HOTEL A building in which travelers and others may obtain food and shelter, and often entertainment and other services. The forerunner of the hotel of today was the inn of colonial times. Inns were simple buildings in which travelers could find a few plainly furnished rooms, along with food and drink.

In the hotels of today, travelers find accommodations that are quite different from those of the earlier era, ranging from comfortable but somewhat utilitarian to the utmost in luxury. Rooms are larger, better furnished, better lighted, heated or cooled according to the season, and most have private bathrooms. Hotels today vary in size as they do in degree of luxury, from only a few rooms to several thousand. There is also considerable variance in the services provided. A small hotel may have a limited number of staff people, providing only the most necessary housekeeping and maintenance work, while a very large hotel may have a staff of thousands performing a great variety of services.

In a small hotel, dining facilities may consist only of a cafeteria or limited restaurant, while a large hotel may have a number of dining facilities, ranging from relatively inexpensive coffee shops to expensive and elegant restaurants, sometimes with entertainment. Some hotels provide newsstands, flower shops, clothing shops, laundry and valet service, barber and beauty shops, and many other services for their guests. Larger hotels often have ballrooms, banquet rooms, and meeting rooms, for use by large groups of people and for conventions. Many have recreational facilities, such as swimming pools and tennis courts. Some have steam baths and saunas, and even golf courses.

Classification Hotels are often classified into four types: transient or commercial, motels, resort hotels, and apartment or residential hotels. A transient or commercial hotel caters to travelers who usually stay only one or a few nights. Many of the guests are business people. Others are individuals or families on a short holiday or stopping over enroute to some other place. Because of the needs of such travelers, these hotels are ordinarily located downtown in cities.

At one time a motel, then called a tourist court, was a modest building or group of cabins adjacent to a well-traveled highway which provided rudimentary lodging for travelers in much the same manner as did the earlier inns. Often poorly maintained and serviced and not very comfortable, these were replaced by better facilities that came to be known as motor courts, motor hotels, or motels. At first, motels were usually one or two stories in height, provided automobile parking near the rooms, and generally had only a few services for guests. Today the distinctions between motels and regular hotels have become blurred. Many motels are a number of stories high, with elevators, are located in cities, and provide many of the services of hotels. Motels, wherever located, continue to provide convenient parking, but now some hotels do also.

Resort hotels are located in the mountains, on the seashore, on lakes, or in other recreational areas for the use of guests on holidays or vacations. Resort hotels provide services similar to those of commercial hotels. In addition, they provide, or have nearby, facilities for golf, tennis, swimming and other water sports, horseback riding, and other activities. Resort hotels often have game rooms, television rooms, and nightclubs. Along with their commercial counterparts, many resort hotels have facilities for conventions.

Apartment or residential hotels provide permanent homes for people who prefer living in apartments but also want many of the conveniences of hotels. In an apartment hotel, residents occupy their own complete apartment units of varying sizes and receive maid and maintenance services from the hotel staff. Linens are also usually available as are public dining and other facilities. Another kind of hotel is a youth hostel. These provide simple lodgings, food services, and recreational facilities for traveling young people, usually for no more than three days at a time.

Hotels are further classified as either European or American plan. The European plan means that there is a set charge for lodging with the cost of meals extra. In the American plan, which was derived from the custom in colonial days, the set charge includes both rooms and meals. Most hotels and motels use the European plan, while some, in particular resort hotels, have the American or offer a choice. Many hotels and motels are owned and operated as chains by established companies, but there has been a trend in recent years toward ownership by real estate investment interests and management by hotel companies.

Elements The major planning elements of a hotel

HOTEL Exterior, Hyatt-Regency (1972), San Francisco, Calif. [*Architect: John C. Portman. (Alexandre Georges)*]

HOTEL Interior, Hyatt-Regency (1972), San Francisco, Calif. [*Architect: John C. Portman. (Alexandre Georges)*]

are the guest areas, sometimes called the front of the house, and the service-administration areas, sometimes called the back of the house. These major areas are kept as separate as possible. Guests experience only the guest area, while the administration-service area caters to their needs but is hidden from the guests.

The guest area of a hotel may be further subdivided into public areas and private areas. Public areas include the lobby; front desk, where guests register, obtain mail and keys, and pay bills; elevators and corridors; restaurants; shops; and other facilities. If convention facilities are included, they too are public areas, but are often separated from public areas used by all guests. The private areas of a hotel are the guest bedrooms and baths, and often suites of two or more rooms.

The administration-service area of a hotel includes space for seven major types of activity: management; laundry services; food and beverage preparation and service; housekeeping services; mechanical and electrical spaces, including heating and air conditioning; maintenance areas, sometimes including carpenter and other shops; and storage for furniture, equipment, and supplies.

At one time, people went to hotels only because they needed a place to stay while traveling. They still go for that reason, but they have come to expect much more, such as comfort, a pleasant staff, a bit of luxury, good meals, and recreation. And hotels are being designed and built to satisfy these requirements.

American Development In the earliest times in America, travelers slept on the ground and cooked their meals over campfires. The more enterprising built crude shelters of tree branches or brought along skins or cloths that could be fashioned into tents. It soon became the custom for travelers to be invited into private houses along the way, for food, drink, shelter, and entertainment. The travelers supplied conversation and news about other places to isolated families, and were in turn furnished hospitality without charge.

Early in the 17th century, public inns were established along well-traveled roads and waterways. Often called taverns or ordinaries, these inns provided meals, drink, and shelter for modest prices. About the middle of the 17th century, stagecoaches came into use, bringing with them an increase in the number of inns along the roads traveled. Toward the end of that century and the beginning of the next, the building of great toll roads, called turnpikes, flourished, creating a vast increase in stagecoach travel and in the building of inns along the roads. The building of canals, starting in the late 18th century, and of railroads, starting in the early 19th century, brought with them the need for additional inns and eventually, hotels.

Starting in the early part of the 19th century, hotels as we now know them were built. Early examples were the Tremont House (1829) in Boston, the Astor

(1836) in New York City, both designed by Isaiah Rogers (1800–69), and the St. Charles (1836) in New Orleans. In the middle of the century, with expansion of the railroads, many other hotels were built all over the country. Some were quite luxurious. During the latter part of the century and the first years of the next, the building of hotels was stimulated by new developments in steel skeleton-framed and fire-resistant structures. Some of the greatest, all now destroyed, were the old Waldorf-Astoria (1897), New York City, designed by Henry J. Hardenbergh (1847–1918); and the Great Northern (1892) by Burnham and Root, the Hyde Park (1891) by Theodore Starrett, and the Metropole (1881) by Clinton J. Warren, all three in Chicago.

Distinguished early hotels still in existence include the Plaza (1907) by Hardenbergh, the St. Regis (1904) by Trowbridge and Livingston, both in New York City; and the Congress (1893), Chicago, by Warren.

In the 1920s and 1930s, there was another wave of hotel building, and after a lull of about 20 years, still another starting in the late 1950s and continuing, generally, until the present time. This has been a time for building numerous hotels and motels for the large chains. It has also produced some of the best hotels, including several Hyatt Regency Hotels, designed by John Calvin Portman, Jr. (1924–   ).

Related Articles HOUSING; RECREATION BUILDING; ROAD AND TRAFFIC DESIGN.

Further Reading Architectural Record: *Hotels, Motels, Restaurants and Bars*, 2d ed., F. W. Dodge, New York, 1960; Davern, Jeanne M., ed.: *Places for People*, McGraw-Hill, New York, 1976; Lawson, Fred: *Hotels, Motels and Condominiums—Design, Planning and Maintenance*, Cahners, Boston, 1976; Smith, Douglas: *Hotel and Restaurant Design*, Van Nostrand Reinhold, New York, 1978.

HOUSE A building in which people live, as an apartment house, row house, or duplex or single-family house. All these types of houses are discussed in other articles in this book except single-family houses, which comprise the type with which most people are familiar, since they live in them, or their neighbors, friends, or relatives do.

Single-Family Houses These houses also comprise the building type of which there is the greatest number in existence and the greatest number are built every year. In addition, single-family houses are likely to be the first building type with which an architect becomes familiar, early in his architectural school days. And more often than not, such houses will be the building type designed first by a young architect starting out in practice. Because of this familiarity with houses, most people are apt to take their design for granted, as if the design of a house should be the simplest thing in the world.

In actuality, the design of houses is not simple. What could be more complicated than a building in which people of varied ages must live, in relatively close quarters, and perform such a great variety of functions as individuals and in small and large groups? What could be more complicated than a

HOUSE Exterior, Dow Residence (1941), Midland, Mich. [Architect: Alden Dow. (Hedrich-Blessing)]

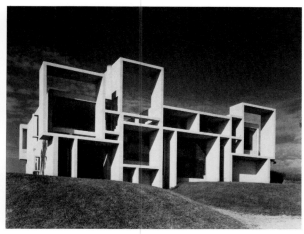

HOUSE Exterior, Milam Residence (1961), Sarasota, Fla. [Architect: Paul Rudolph. (Joseph W. Molitor]

HOUSE Interior, Dow Residence (1941), Midland, Mich. [Architect: Alden Dow. (Joseph W. Molitor)]

HOUSE Interior, Milam Residence (1961), Sarasota, Fla. [Architect: Paul Rudolph. (Joseph W. Molitor)]

building in which most people spend more time than they do anywhere else during their lifetimes? What could be more complicated than a building in which people work, play, study, cook, eat, sleep, argue, fight, procreate, are born, are ill or injured, and die?

In a manner of speaking, a house is a multiuse building, incorporating many of the functions of a number of other building types. The proper design for all those functions is anything but easy. And to further complicate the situation, each family is different from any other and each individual in a family is different. It is no wonder that some of the greatest designers of houses maintain that to design houses properly, a designer should almost live with families, sharing in all their activities.

Social Factors　In addition, other factors deeply affect the design of houses today. In the past, it was common for three generations (grandparents, parents, and children) to live in one house. Today this is very rare. In the past, a husband and wife would usually live in one house all their lives. And then the house would often be passed on to their children,

who would then repeat the process. Today it is very uncommon for a husband and wife to live in one house only. People are more mobile today than in the past. Changing jobs or occupations often calls for moves from one place to another and this might happen several times in a lifetime.

People are also more mobile, socially, today than in the past. Formerly, children tended to follow their father's vocation, often in the same places in which they grew up; today children aspire to increasingly better educations, followed by better jobs and higher incomes than those of their parents. And the parents, as their income increases, aspire to better houses in better locations. As a result, houses, which in the past were more or less permanent residences for their occupants, are today often transient residences for those who will eventually move on. Therefore house design must take into account both resale value and the fact that a house should be designed to fit the requirements of its occupants. Of course, a house can become so special that it is hard to find a buyer for it.

Recently, there has been a tremendous increase in

HOUSE Foster Residence (1968), Wilton, Conn. [*Architect: Richard Foster. (Ezra Stoller)*]

the number of working women, including working wives, and in the number of women who are heads of households. This has deeply affected house design, partly because no one in these families is at home all or most of every day, and housekeeping, once the almost sole province of housewives, is now often a shared responsibility. Servants, once a fixture in the houses of the great middle class, have now become relatively rare. Whereas such households used to have live-in or daily servants, today's householders, excluding the wealthy, do without servants or have someone come in once or maybe twice a week. In some cases, these are maids working as individuals, but often the work is accomplished by cleaning service establishments.

As the hours of work for most people have decreased, a greater amount of time has been released for other activities. At one time, many thought this would produce a situation in which houses would have more use as recreation centers than before. In actuality, what has happened is a boom in recreational opportunities outside the home. Television, of course, tends to keep people home, but except for the occasional group that gathers to watch a game on TV or some other special, the use of television for recreation has been a more or less solitary occupation and has not had a great effect on house design. Perhaps the development of TV sets that can project images on walls or large screens will affect house design in the future.

Convenience Appliances Other factors that affect the design of houses are the great number of comfort, laborsaving, and convenience appliances available. In the past, many of these were optional, but now are considered necessities by many people. Heating and electric lighting have become standard in houses, of course, as have gas or electric stoves and ovens, sinks, and bathroom fixtures. In addition, many people would not live in a house without air conditioning and others would not want to give up automatic clothes washers and dryers, dishwashers, trash compacters, garbage grinders, knife sharpeners, can openers, microwave ovens, grilles, toasters, waffle irons, food warmers, and a great variety of other electric appliances. Others feel they cannot get along without shower massagers, sunken tubs, light dimmers, stereo systems, motion picture and slide projectors, barbecue facilities, and so on. And the TV set, or sometimes several, has become a fixture.

All of this has resulted in another factor affecting the design of houses: the shortages and high prices of energy in the form of gas, electricity, and fuel oil. Now designers must make efforts to reduce the total energy loads of houses they design and to make sure that energy will be employed efficiently. Thus better use of materials, such as insulation, is required, and better design and orientation of houses for taking advantage of natural phenomena, such as solar and wind energy. Other factors and trends will have to be taken into account in the design of houses in the future, and those who design them will have to keep up with new developments.

Elements In a sense, the major elements of a house might be said to be the communal areas, those shared by family members and often guests, such as living rooms, dining rooms, playrooms, and so on, and the private areas, such as bedrooms, bathrooms, and so on. Through such consideration, some direction can be given to house design, since the shared areas have functions that are quite different from those of the more private areas. Kitchens were formerly more or less private areas in which a servant or a housewife worked, but today they have become more communal places where other members of the family work, eat, and entertain.

In another sense, the elements of a house might be said to consist of the following: living areas, in which individuals, families, and guests relax, talk, play games, and the like; sleeping areas, which often also double as areas for study, reading, and other pursuits; dining areas, which can be part of the living space, separate, or part of kitchens, and are used for both family dining and entertaining; bathrooms; work centers, in which meals are prepared, laundry done, and various other functions performed; storage spaces; and space for mechanical-electrical equipment. This is also a useful way to consider the design of a house.

It is, of course, entirely possible to design a house today along the lines of traditional plans, with separate rooms for the various functions, according to the needs, wishes, and financial status of those who will occupy it. Such a house might have only a living room, with a dining wing or alcove, a kitchen, and any number of bedrooms and bathrooms. This concept might be enlarged to include any or all of the following: a study, sometimes called a den; a separate dining room; pantry; breakfast room; breakfast bar in the kitchen; music room; playroom or family room; bar; laundry room; dressing rooms; servants' rooms; and so on. Such a house might have a carport, open on the sides, or a garage, for one or more automobiles. It might have porches, patios, decks, or other outdoor living areas. And it might have a swimming pool, a tennis court, a billiard room, or even a bowling alley.

Deterrents There are two major deterrents to the design of houses with separate rooms as in the past: the economics of house building which have driven costs very high, often beyond the means of many families, particularly young ones; and the trend toward informal living today. Because of these factors and the preferences of some people, the trend in recent times has been toward open planning.

In an open-planned house, the various spaces may no longer be separate rooms, each with four walls separating it from the other spaces, but may be organized in such a way that various spaces are separated only by space dividers, low walls, planters, and other means that allow them to function together, flexibly and in a variety of ways. For example, a house might have a kitchen-work center that opens into the dining area which in turn opens into the living room, then to decks, porches, or patios, thus creating a complex of spaces in which people and their activities may flow from one space to another comfortably, easily, and flexibly. In such a complex of spaces, a person, or several, may cook meals yet continue to be part of a family gathering or social affair. In a plan of this sort, the kitchen-work center might also open into a family room or outdoor living area. In a similar manner, bedrooms may open into play or study areas that are private or shared, living rooms into libraries, and so on. The possibilities are almost endless, only dependent on the requirements of the occupants and the skill of their architects.

House design, then, is involved with understanding the needs and wishes of the occupants and their finances, relating the elements properly to each other, and providing the best possible solution to the problems. The designer must make sure that if and when the time comes for the first occupants to move on that the house will attract potential buyers.

Prefabrication Recently, methods for reducing the costs of houses have included prefabrication, sometimes called precutting or preassembly. Prefabrication of houses involves construction or fabrication of the lumber and other materials that go into houses in factories rather than on the building sites. The prefabricated parts may then be assembled into components, such as whole or partial walls, often with windows and doors in place, which can be shipped to the building sites and erected. Many house components may be prefabricated and preassembled, including tub and shower combinations, and even whole bathrooms and kitchen components. In their most complete form, prefabrication and preassembly can be used to manufacture entire houses which are then trucked to their sites and erected on previously prepared foundations. The most prevalent example of this today is the mobile home. See the article entitled housing.

HOUSE Franzen House (1956), Rye, N.Y. [*Architect: Ulrich Franzen. (Ezra Stoller)*]

HOUSE Canavan Residence (1964), Hanover, N.H. [*Architects: E. H. and M. K. Hunter. (Joseph W. Molitor)*]

Vacation Homes In the past, some families maintained vacation places, sometimes very rudimentary houses, often called camps or cabins. Located in scenic spots, for example, in the mountains or on the seashore, these camps or cabins were places to get away from the everyday life at home and to rough it to an extent. People still have such places, but today the trend is toward much more elaborate vacation homes, with all or most of the comforts of primary residences. Sometimes these second, or vacation, homes are rented to vacationers at certain periods, while the owners use them at other times and during off-seasons. The design of vacation homes is very similar to that of other types, except that the emphasis is often on recreational features and easy maintenance.

History Shelter was of primary concern to primitive humans. Since no remains of the earliest shelters have survived, what they were like is a matter for conjecture. The first shelters were probably natural caves. Humans may then have dug their own caves, and later erected rudimentary tents made of poles and skins or huts of poles and brush, leaves, or thatch. As in houses built later, the primary considerations were the climate in which the people lived, the materials available, and the dangers present. Humans, who

lived in places where mud with proper characteristics existed, covered their huts of twigs or thatch with the mud which then dried to protect the interiors. In places like the Middle East, where trees were scarce but clay was plentiful, people used sun-dried bricks for the walls of houses.

By about 4000 B.C., the lake dwellers of Europe built houses over the water on logs driven into lake bottoms. And by about 3000 B.C., the Egyptians and others built sun-dried brick houses. A few hundred years later, the processes of hardening bricks in fire and glazing to make them more impervious to water were discovered.

The ancient Greeks built elaborate homes, often of stone, and usually with atriums, open courtyards or patios, in the middle. The Romans generally followed the ideas of the Greeks, but in addition to the private town house, or *domus*, developed the country house, or *villa*, and apartment, or *insula*. The Romans also introduced central heating, using hot air or water piped into houses, and were the first to use glass in windows. During the Middle Ages, house building continued and the concepts of fortified castles and walled towns were developed. In the Middle Ages, houses in town were generally built close together and often a number of families lived in one building. Also during this period, the building of half-timbered houses was begun. These buildings utilized heavy timbers with cross braces between them and with the spaces filled in with plaster, made of a mixture of clay and straw, or with brick.

During the Renaissance, an important development was the building of great palaces, most of which were designed by architects. This started a trend toward the design of important houses by architects and the trend has persisted ever since.

American Development The earliest colonists in America built crude shelters very much like those of the American Indians. They dug caves in the sides of hills, dug pits in the ground and erected walls above using poles and brush or thatch, or drove logs in the ground close together and roofed them with branches, covered with thatch or grass. Gradually, the colonists started to build more permanent houses, first with wattle and daub, which utilized wattles, twigs, or other materials woven together, placed in the house frame and covered with daub, a mixture of clay or mud with straw or similar materials. In the French settlements, another method called *briquette entre poteaux*, using soft brick between timbers, was employed.

When the colonists were settled enough to build permanent homes, they turned to local materials, mostly timber and brick in the East, and brick or adobe in the Southwest. The designs of the houses followed those the colonists had known in Europe, and soon developed into styles that became known as New England Colonial, adapted from English buildings; Dutch Colonial in New York and other places settled by the Dutch, adapted from buildings in the homeland; Southern Colonial in the South, adapted to the needs and climate from English buildings; and French and Spanish Colonial, adapted from the buildings in those countries. Thus regional styles were created, derived from those of other places but changed to fit the specific requirements in America.

When the colonists began to migrate toward what later became the Western states, they built houses out of the materials they found at hand. Thus in many places, the pioneers built log cabins by laying timbers on top of each other and attaching them together at their ends for strength. When pioneers reached the great plains of the Midwest, where trees were in short supply, they often built sod houses, made from dirt, or dug caves in which to live.

As time went on, Americans built more and more elaborate houses as well as modest ones. Many of the great plantation houses of the South and the great town houses of the cities were among the best examples of architecture of their time. During the 1800s many improvements were made in houses, including heating, using iron stoves rather than only fireplaces; artificial lighting with kerosene and then with gaslights; and indoor toilets. During the early part of the 19th century, other developments that improved homes were electricity for lighting, heating, and appliances; and central heating, first with coal, then with gas or fuel oil, and finally with electricity. These were followed by air conditioning and a great variety of other types of laborsaving and convenience appliances and equipment.

A boom in house building began after the federal government established the Federal Housing Administration (FHA) in 1934 to help families who had not been eligible for loans for financial or other reasons obtain mortgage loans at reasonable interest and with reasonable monthly payments. The Depression and World War II slowed down house building almost to a halt; but after the war, a building boom swept across the country and very large numbers of houses were built. The rate of house building slowed yet again during subsequent periods, but single-family houses are still one of the most important building types.

One result of the boom in single-family house building has been that an ever-smaller percentage of smaller houses has been designed by architects. Their builders or owners make their own plans, or buy them from what are called plan services, often with unsatisfactory, even disastrous, results. The apocryphal story is that of the architect, who when told by a friend that he had designed his own house, asked if he had also removed his own appendix. Some builders and plan services have their houses designed by architects, who often make several basic designs, with variations, which assure more acceptable results and often very good designs.

Related Articles APARTMENT; PREFABRICATION; Articles on individual architects and firms; Articles on other individual building types.

Further Reading *Architectural Record: Great Houses for View Sites, Beach Sites, Wood Sites, Meadow Sites, Small Sites, Sloping Sites, Steep Sites, Flat Sites*, McGraw-Hill, New York, 1976; *Architectural Record: Houses Architects Design for Themselves*, McGraw-Hill, New York, 1974; *Architectural Record: The Architectural Record Book of Vacation Houses*, 2d ed. McGraw-Hill, New York, 1977; Eckbo, Garrett: *The Art of Home Landscaping*, McGraw-Hill, New York, 1956; Hunter, Margaret K., and Edgar H. Hunter: *The Indoor Garden—Design, Construction and Furnishing*, John Wiley, New York, 1978; Nelson, George, and Henry Wright: *Tomorrow's House—A Complete Guide for the Homebuilder*, Simon and Schuster, New York, 1945; Wagner, Walter: *A Treasury of Contemporary Houses*, McGraw-Hill, New York, 1979.

Source of Additional Information National Association of Home Builders of U.S.A., 15th and M Sts., N.W., Washington, D.C. 20005.

Periodicals *Housing*, 1221 Avenue of the Americas, New York, N.Y. 10020; *NAHB Journal of Homebuilding*, 15th and M Sts., N.W., Washington, D.C. 20005; *Professional Builder*, 5 S. Wabash Avenue, Chicago, Ill. 60603.

HOUSING In general, the buildings, or groups of buildings, which provide shelter and other accommodations for people. Housing includes the usual types of shelter for individuals and families, such as single-family and multifamily houses, apartments, garden apartments, town houses, farmhouses, and so

HOUSING For the elderly, High-Rise (1969), Syracuse, N.Y. [*Architects: Sargent, Webster, Crenshaw and Folley. (Joseph W. Molitor)*]

on. Housing also includes special types, such as shelter provided in hotels and motels, schools, colleges and universities, hospitals, military buildings, and prisons. (See titles listed at end of this article.) However, there are other special types of housing, including public housing, sometimes called low-income or low-rent housing, housing for the elderly, and mobile homes and parks.

Public Housing Housing for low-income families started in the United States in the 1930s, the first two units having been built in Greenbelt, Md., in 1936. These were two-story apartment buildings, built under the Public Works Administration (PWA). In all, 59 projects were built by the PWA in 36 cities before World War II. The federal government had built temporary housing during World War I for war workers, but these were later demolished. Some so-called model tenements had also been built previously in cities, but these were sponsored by charitable institutions.

Starting in 1937, the newly created U.S. Housing Authority took up the task of providing public housing; in 1942 the work was carried on by the National Housing Agency; in 1947, by the Housing and Home Finance Agency; and since 1965, by the Department of Housing and Urban Development (HUD). Today public housing programs are administered by local housing authorities, which may build new housing, buy housing from developers, or lease housing, usually on a short-term basis. The federal government

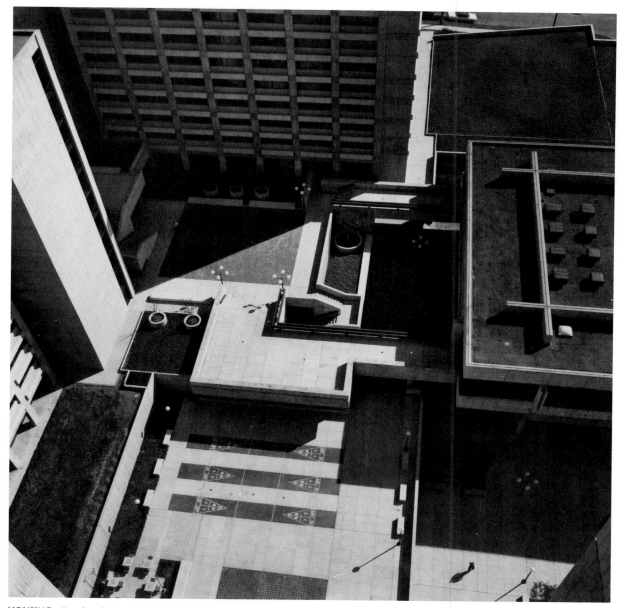

HOUSING For the elderly, High-Rise (1969), Syracuse, N.Y. [Architects: Sargent, Webster, Crenshaw and Folley. (Joseph W. Molitor)]

lends technical and financial assistance, in the form of loans and grants, to the local authorities.

At the start, most public housing was one to a few stories in height. Although not considered the very best of architectural design, it was superior to any other accommodations low-income people could find or afford. In later years, public housing has been mostly confined to high-rise buildings and has been widely criticized, not only for its unimaginative and unesthetic designs but for creating new ghettos, almost slums, in which unsanitary conditions and crime have flourished. This situation has improved considerably in the last few years and some of the latest low-income housing complexes have been well designed. Architect Elizabeth Coit (1892–   ) made significant contributions to public housing design, particularly in New York.

The design of public housing is very similar to that of privately owned apartment buildings, except that architects doing this work must deal, not only with the building codes and other regulations governing private buildings but also with a mass of local, state, and particularly federal regulations governing materials, room sizes, finishes, techniques, and almost every detail of design and construction.

Housing for the Elderly Although elderly people live in all kinds of housing, there has lately been a trend for them to occupy housing specifically designed for them. Not all authorities agree with this, some maintaining that the elderly should not be segregated, as that does not reflect the society they live in. In any case, there are several reasons for specially designed housing for the elderly, including the dramatic increase in life span, the decrease in, almost the end of, three-generation households, and the needs of the elderly for easily maintained quarters, specialized recreational and other facilities, and close proximity to medical and other facilities.

Housing specifically designed for the elderly may be in the form of single-family homes or any of the other usual types, but there is something of a trend today toward apartment buildings for those who can take care of themselves and nursing homes for those who cannot. Apartment buildings for the elderly may be privately owned, government owned, or government-assisted low-income housing. Nursing homes and other long-term care facilities may be owned and operated by private companies, government, or church or charitable groups.

The design of houses and apartment buildings for the elderly is very similar to that for occupants of other ages in some respects. However, buildings for the elderly should be located near medical facilities, recreational facilities such as parks, shopping, churches and synagogues, and public transportation. Since many elderly people are handicapped, and eventually all will become so, housing for them should take this into consideration. Also, since many of them are retired, they need more social, recreational, and enrichment opportunities in their residences than do other people.

The major considerations in the design of housing for the elderly are economical size of apartments and rooms for convenience and ease of housekeeping, construction resistant to fires and other hazards, and pleasant surroundings that are livable, private, and safe. Every effort should be expended in the design of these buildings to anticipate the needs of the elderly by convenient placement of rooms and furniture, safety devices such as nonskid tubs and shower receptors with controlled water-temperature devices and grab bars, no thresholds for doors, stove controls on the front, handrails for walkways, nonskid rugs, slow-closing doors, emergency signals, ramps instead of stairs, and many others. Otherwise, the design considerations are those that would apply to good architecture for housing of any other type.

Nursing Homes These homes are generally long-term care facilities for the elderly who need custodial care or who have moderate physical or mental disabilities. For those who are more seriously disabled mentally or physically, or both, other long-term facilities are required, including chronic and mental hospitals and appropriate wards in hospitals of other types. (See the article entitled hospital.) The major elements of nursing homes are nursing units, with nursing stations and rooms in which patients live; supportive and rehabilitative units such as recreational, dining, and therapy areas; medical and treatment units; and administrative and service units.

Nursing units are similar to those in hospitals with the trend today mostly double rooms, with private or adjoining baths, and a few single rooms for problem patients or isolation. In addition to dining rooms, supportive and rehabilitative areas include dayrooms, exercise rooms, and spaces for physical therapy, oc-

HOUSING Nursing Home, Steuben County (1969), Bath, N.Y. [Architects: Sargent, Webster, Crenshaw and Folley. (Joseph W. Molitor)]

cupational therapy, heat therapy, and hydrotherapy. Medical and treatment areas in nursing homes are much less extensive than those in hospitals, and usually include only limited spaces for examination, relatively minor treatments, and dispensing of medicines and medical devices. Administrative areas include dietary kitchens, offices, storage areas, workrooms, janitorial spaces, and spaces for mechanical and electrical equipment. There are some special storage requirements for such things as stretchers, wheelchairs, and walkers, and for furnishings such as mattresses.

The design of a nursing home involves providing a safe, healthy, and efficient environment for patients in surroundings that are pleasant and as comfortable as possible. Many of the older nursing homes have been forbidding and institutional, in the worst sense of the word. More recent examples have been well designed for their purpose and at the same time with taste and refinement of the architecture, beautifully landscaped grounds, and warm and inviting interiors. The design of nursing homes can be challenging, especially when their architects strive toward making them examples of the best of residential architecture.

Mobile Homes For a long time, mobile homes have been a residential type that held great promise as one solution for housing shortages. Often in the past called trailers, a word now used for vehicles pulled behind cars for traveling and camping, mobile homes today are not really mobile, at least after they have been trucked to their sites. After that, most are never, or seldom ever, moved again. In one way, mobile homes have lived up to their promise, since they are relatively low in cost as compared to other types of housing. As a result, several million people in the United States now live in them. They have also proved to be highly efficient in their use of space. However, few mobile homes are very attractive, architecturally, and none, unless remodeled radically, can compare in their design with that of the best examples of other houses. Many think that their design can be vastly improved, and some have tried to accomplish this, but so far first-rate design is still in the future. Future designs that are better, architecturally, will also have to permit savings in costs by means of production line construction in factories.

The major problem related to mobile homes faced by architects is planning sites for them, sometimes individual and sometimes mobile home parks. Individual sites may be planned in a manner very similar to those for other single-family homes. Mobile home parks in the past have simply been cleared areas with minimal space for individual homes; with electrical, water, and sewage hookups; and sometimes with community buildings for limited shopping and clothes washing and drying facilities; recreational facilities; and so on. Some of these have been very poorly planned and have become eyesores that other people, and sometimes the inhabitants themselves, abhor. Today efforts are being made to improve the design of these areas with well-planned roads and sidewalks, landscaping, adequate-sized sites, and other amenities such as would be provided in any well-planned suburban development for other single-family houses.

Related Articles APARTMENT; COLLEGE AND UNIVERSITY BUILDING; FARM BUILDING; FULLER, RICHARD BUCKMINSTER; GOVERNMENT; HANDICAPPED, FACILITIES FOR THE; HOSPITAL; HOTEL; HOUSE; MILITARY BUILDING; PREFABRICATION; PRISON.

Further Reading Lawton, M. Powell: *Planning and Managing Housing for the Elderly*, John Wiley, New York, 1975; Macsai, John, Eugene P. Holland, Harry S. Nachman, and Julius Y. Yacker: *Housing*, John Wiley, New York, 1976; Weiss, J.: *Better Buildings for the Aged*, McGraw-Hill, New York, 1971.

Sources of Additional Information American Association of Homes for the Aging, 1050 17th St., N.W., Washington, D.C. 20036; Manufactured Housing Inst., 14650 Lee Road, Chantilly, Va. 22021; National Association of Housing and Redevelopment Officials, 2600 Virginia Ave., N.W., Washington, D.C. 20037; National Council of Aging, Inc., 1828 L St., N.W., Washington, D.C. 20036.

Periodicals *Housing*, 1221 Avenue of the Americas, New York, N.Y. 10020; *Journal of Housing*, 2600 Virginia Avenue, N.W., Washington, D.C. 20037; *NAHB Journal of Homebuilding*, 15th and M Sts., N.W., Washington, D.C. 20005.

HUNT, RICHARD MORRIS

HUNT, RICHARD MORRIS American architect (1827–95). During his practice of architecture, lasting more than 40 years, Richard Morris Hunt established himself as the most influential architect of his time in the United States.

He was the first native-born American to be thoroughly trained in architecture. He was the first to establish an atelier, or studio, in which he personally taught young men to become architects. He was the pioneer of the Eclectic style in the United States, based on the principles of the École des Beaux Arts in Paris, where he had studied. He deeply affected the work of other architects, not only through his atelier but in his encouragement of students to go to Europe for training at the Beaux Arts. As a result of his early influences and those of later Beaux Arts graduates, a system of architectural education, based on Beaux Arts principles, was established in the United States during his lifetime and dominated the training of architectural students until well into the 20th century.

Hunt also wielded considerable influence on architecture in the United States through his building designs. He was an eclectic, who designed buildings in many styles for the most powerful and wealthy people in the United States. Hunt's buildings became well known, and the designs of a great many other architects were deeply influenced by them. Although Hunt designed buildings based on those of many historical periods, perhaps his most spectacular buildings were derived from French châteaus.

Hunt's influence also spread through his work for his profession. One of the founders of the American Institute of Architects, he worked very hard for that organization for many years.

Works During his professional career, Hunt designed a large number of buildings of many types, in-

HUNT, RICHARD MORRIS Central section, Metropolitan Museum (1902), New York, N.Y. *(Joseph W. Molitor)*

cluding apartments, libraries, art museums, and office buildings. He also designed monuments, but was perhaps most noted for the great mansions he designed in New York City, Newport, R.I., and other places for wealthy families. Among his first designs was a studio apartment building (1857) in New York City, considered to be one of the first multiple dwellings, if not the first, in the United States. He also designed several other apartment buildings, all since demolished. He designed a number of office buildings in New York City, all of them since demolished, except the Roosevelt Building (1874) and a number of town houses for members of the Astor, Vanderbilt, and other families all gone now including the best one (1881) for William Kissam Vanderbilt (1849–1920).

The only other important buildings by Hunt remaining in New York City where he practiced and made his reputation are the Jackson Square Library (1887) and the Metropolitan Museum of Art, the central portion of which was completed before his death, with the remainder completed in 1902 by his son Richard Howland Hunt (1862–1931). The Metropolitan was the building for which Hunt himself wanted to be remembered. Also still in existence in New York City is Hunt's Vanderbilt Mausoleum (1886) in the Moravian Cemetery. And in that city is his base for the much-loved Statue of Liberty (1886; see illustration in article monument), with the figure of Liberty by the French sculptor Frédéric Auguste Bartholdi (1834–1904) and the structure of the sculpture by the French engineer Alexandre Gustave Eiffel (1832–1923), who designed the Eiffel Tower in Paris and helped design the Pan-

ama Canal. Hunt was one of the New York architects who controlled the eclectic designs of the World's Columbian Exposition (1893), Chicago, and he designed one of its most important structures, the Administration Building.

Two of Hunt's great mansions, both completed in 1895, the year of his death, still exist: The Breakers, Newport, R.I., for Cornelius Vanderbilt II (1843–99), and Biltmore, near Asheville, N.C., for George Washington Vanderbilt (1862–1914). The great landscape architect Frederick Law Olmsted (1822–1903) designed the grounds for the latter house. Biltmore is considered the most impressive of Hunt's house designs and is certainly the most ambitious. Another of his buildings, less prepossessing than the other two, was also finished in 1895, the Fogg Art Museum, Harvard University, Cambridge, Mass. The Museum was later renamed Hunt Hall, for its architect, after the building of new Fogg Art Museum (1927), designed by Coolidge, Shepley, Bulfinch and Abbott.

Richard Morris Hunt took little heed of the changes that were beginning in architecture with the pioneering work of Henry Hobson Richardson (1838–86), who had been the second American at the Beaux Arts in Paris, Louis Henri Sullivan (1856–1924), Major William Le Baron Jenney (1832–1907), and other architects of the Chicago school who were laying the groundwork for what would become the modern movement in American architecture. Hunt continued designing eclectic buildings and so did his followers. Architects have continued to design in eclectic styles ever since, but the later buildings have not closely approached

HUNT, RICHARD MORRIS Biltmore (1895), near Asheville, N.C. (*Wayne Andrews*)

the great size, splendor, perfection, and scholarship of the buildings of Hunt and other early eclectics.

Life   Richard Morris Hunt was born in Brattleboro, Vt., on October 31, 1827, into an artistic family that included his brother, the noted painter, William Morris Hunt (1824–79). As a young boy, he showed considerable artistic talent. He studied at the Boston Latin School, graduating in 1843, and then in Geneva, Switzerland.

In 1846 Hunt entered the École des Beaux Arts in Paris, the first American to go there, to study architecture, painting, and sculpture simultaneously. He chose architecture as his lifework and was the first American to graduate from the Beaux Arts. He then traveled in Europe and the Middle East for two years. In 1854 he was appointed inspector of construction in Paris and worked on additions to the Louvre and the Tuileries, both of which had been under construction since the 16th century, and on other buildings.

On his return to the United States in 1855, Hunt established an architectural office in New York City, where he practiced the rest of his life, except for a few years spent in Europe in the 1860s. In 1857 Hunt established an atelier, or studio, in connection with his office, modeled after those in which the students of the École des Beaux Arts studied. In his atelier, Hunt trained a great number of young men, who were later to make their marks in architecture in the Eclectic style, based on Beaux Arts principles of design that he had learned in Paris. Among the most noted of his students were Frank Furness (1839–1912), George Browne Post (1837–1913), and William Robert Ware (1832–1915), who founded the first American architectural school at Massachusetts Institute of Technology, Cambridge, in 1868.

In 1861 Hunt married Catherine Clinton Howland and in 1862 they had a son, Richard Howland Hunt, who was educated at MIT, the École des Beaux Arts, and in his father's atelier, and who became an architect and his father's partner until the death of the elder Hunt. Another son, Joseph Howland Hunt (1870–1924), also an architect, later joined his brother in a partnership.

Early in his career, Hunt was unable to obtain commissions for important buildings, but after his trip to Europe in the 1860s he began to win numerous commissions, many for mansions for the wealthy, including the Vanderbilts, Astors, and Belmonts, but also for other important buildings. By the end of his career, Hunt was the most influential architect in the United States, successful in his practice and financially, respected by his profession and by the public.

HUNT, RICHARD MORRIS Interior, The Breakers (1895), Newport, R.I. *(Wayne Andrews)*

In 1857 Hunt was one of the founders of the American Institute of Architects (AIA) under the leadership of Richard Upjohn (1802–78). Upjohn became the first president of the organization, serving for 18 years, and Hunt became the first secretary. After serving in

that position for several years and also as vice president, Hunt became the third president of the AIA and served in that office from 1887 to 1890. Later, one of his students, George Browne Post, became president.

Toward the end of his life Richard Morris Hunt received a great many honors for his work in architecture, in his profession, and in education. He did not live to see the almost wholesale demolition of most of his New York buildings and many of those in other places. On the site of one of those demolished, the Lenox Library on Fifth Avenue in New York City, a monument to him was erected after his death on July 31, 1895. A more lasting monument appears on the great bronze doors he added to the masterpiece of Richard Upjohn, Trinity Church (1846), in New York City. The sculptor of the doors, Karl Theodore Francis Bitter (1867–1915), who was Hunt's friend and had executed the sculpture of the entrance of his Metropolitan Museum of Art, placed a sculpture, on the frame of the right-hand door, of the head of Hunt, complete with beret and Van Dyke beard.

Related Articles BEAUX ARTS, ÉCOLE DES; ECLECTIC ARCHITECTURE; EDUCATION; EXPOSITION; FURNESS, FRANK; POST, GEORGE BROWNE; UPJOHN, RICHARD.

Further Reading Ferree, Barr: *Richard Morris Hunt—His Art and Work,* private edition, New York, 1895; Schuyler, Montgomery: *The Works of the Late Richard M. Hunt, Architectural Record,* New York, 1895.

HUNT, RICHARD MORRIS Exterior, The Breakers (1895), Newport, R.I. *(Wayne Andrews)*

INSECT PROTECTION   Devices and methods used in buildings to control insects, protect building occupants from annoyance or injury caused by them, and protect building materials and components from damage or failure caused by them. While many insects, such as butterflies, are considered beneficial, many others are harmful to humans and their architecture. Houseflies, mosquitoes, and other insect pests are annoying; some bite or sting humans and animals; some carry diseases; and some damage or destroy materials. Termites and wood borers damage or destroy wood. The larvae of moths destroy certain fabrics, such as wool; silverfish damage paper, books, and other articles. Pests, other than insects, such as fungi, also harm buildings. Certain actions may be taken in the design and construction of buildings to prevent or minimize the dangers and damage caused by these pests.

Insects are small, six-legged animals, of which almost a million kinds have been classified by entomologists, zoologists who study them. Some entomologists estimate that there may be millions of insects that have not yet been identified. In any case, the kinds of insects outnumber other kinds of animals by at least 4 to 1. Of the insects identified so far, several thousand types are considered harmful, while the remaining million or so are not, and many types are beneficial. In architecture only a few types of harmful insects are of great importance, including those that bite or sting humans and animals; those that may carry disease; those that destroy furnishings, fabrics, and other interior elements; those that destroy wood structural members; and those that are just considered nuisances. In addition, harmful insects destroy plants, shrubbery, trees, and flowers. (See the article entitled garden.)

Harmful Pests   Mosquitoes, houseflies, and other insects may carry disease, including such dangerous types as malaria, encephalitis, plague, typhoid fever, and cholera. Some insects, such as lice, fleas, bees, and wasps, inflict bites or stings, which are not only painful but in some cases cause sickness or even death. Although not insects, ticks also bite and may carry Rocky Mountain spotted fever. Some insects, including roaches and flies, spoil food. Moths and beetles eat clothing, carpets, upholstery, and other fabrics. Silverfish and some beetles destroy books and other paper items. Sometimes ants also cause problems in buildings.

Wood Damage   A number of insects damage or destroy wood structural members and other components used in buildings. Certain types of beetles and wood wasps bore holes in unseasoned wood but not in seasoned wood. Powder-post beetles attack and destroy all wood. Carpenter ants chew holes in wood in which to make nests. Wood in contact with salt or brackish water is subject to destructive attack by various marine borers. By far the most destructive insect is the subterranean termite, which contrary to popular belief, is known to have caused great damage in wood buildings in every state of the mainland United States. Nonsubterranean termites are also very destructive in many states, including California, Arizona, New Mexico, Texas, Louisiana, Mississippi, Alabama, Florida, Georgia, and North and South Carolina.

Pest Control   Only a few architectural methods are available for control of the more common insect pests, such as mosquitoes and houseflies. Provisions for tightly closed storage of food, clothing, and other materials eaten by insects helps considerably. Provisions for good housekeeping, minimizing dirt, spilled food, and other debris also help, as does good housekeeping practiced by the occupants of buildings. Elimination of standing water anywhere on or near building components, without cracks, crevices, or other openings through which insects may enter, is very important. This will also prevent other pests, such as mice and rats, from entering buildings. Certain electronic and other types of devices are available to trap or kill insects. In addition, building occupants often apply insecticides, or subscribe to extermination services, to control insects.

The only other important architectural device for control of common pests is woven wire cloth, usually called screening or sometimes fly screening, over all openings in buildings, including not only windows and doors but foundations and attic vents. Woven wire cloth or screening is usually made of 22-gauge wire woven to produce 12 openings per inch in each direction. The most commonly used types are made of steel or aluminum wire, but other types are available in bronze, copper, stainless steel, and other metals, and in plastics. Generally available in rolls, up to 6 ft in width and 100 ft in length, screening is ordinarily installed into metal or wood frames, often called screens or screen doors, with tacks, staples, or plastic or neoprene strips which hold the screening into slots in the frames. The least expensive types are steel, aluminum, and plastic; the most expensive are copper, bronze, and stainless steel. The cheaper types do not last as long or maintain their shape under impact as well as the expensive group.

Many beetles, borers, and wasps that attack unseasoned wood may be avoided by using only wood that has been properly seasoned. Other insects that attack dry wood may be controlled with insecticides, including types that may be used with oil on the wood. Treating lumber with perservatives can also help to control such insects. The major types of preservatives are creosote, creosote combined with coal tar, water-soluble metallic salts, and carbolic acid, generally called phenol, compounds Although such materials may be brushed on the surfaces of wood, or the wood may be dipped in them, the most effective method is impregnating the wood with the substances under pressure, called pressure treating. While many of these materials are effective against most insects, the only effective method for marine borers requires pressure treatment with creosote or creosote–coal tar solutions. It also helps to prevent damage from insects if wood is kept completely dry or completely submerged in water.

Termites   These insects are much more destructive and much harder to control than the other nonmarine insects. Subterranean termites live in the ground where they can obtain the moisture they need for survival. Emerging from undergound colonies, they make their way to wood which they eat until it fails or crumbles. Nonsubterranean, sometimes called drywood, termites, found only in a narrow strip across the southern United States, do not require contact with the soil to live. They are almost as destructive as the other type but do not destroy wood as rapidly.

Control of termites requires a number of actions. Wood treatments, as outlined above, are helpful. So are well-ventilated areas around wood and screening of openings through which the insects may enter buildings. Wood must not come into contact with the ground or with moisture. Solid masonry walls, with portland cement joints, or concrete walls will bar their entry as will concrete slab floors. Poisoning of the soil under buildings and around foundations is thought to provide protection for up to 20 years. In some cases, roll roofing or plastic, properly sealed, is used on the ground in crawl spaces under buildings to prevent entry. All litter, particularly pieces of wood, should be removed from such spaces. And precautions should be taken to ensure that no paths are left open for the insects to reach wood members from the ground.

In the case of subterranean termites, sheet metal guards, called termite shields, are often placed under the lowest portion, the sill, of the wood structures of buildings. Termite shields have turned-down edges to prevent the insects from reaching the wood. Termite shields are not necessarily effective against the non-subterranean types. Treatment at regular intervals with insecticides is also recommended. If in spite of all precautions, termites enter the wood members of buildings. They must be promptly exterminated and the damaged wood replaced. Extermination can often be accomplished by fumigation with special poisons of the areas affected.

Fungi   Although not insects, but plants, fungi can also damage and destroy various components of architecture. Whereas some fungi are beneficial, including mushrooms and the rare truffles, some, such as mold, mildew, and other decay-producing fungi, must be controlled in architecture. Fungi do not produce food for themselves by photosynthesis like most other plants, but live as parasites on living things or as saprophytes on dead organic matter. In order to damage or destroy components or objects in buildings, they need organic food sources: air, relatively warm temperatures, and adequate moisture. While some of the damage of fungi, such as the mildewing of articles placed on damp concrete floors on grade, may only be annoying, the great damage, even destruction, is of wood structures and other components of buildings.

Fungi cause wood to decay, reducing its strength and fire resistance, and eventually may cause it to fail. In order for such damage and destruction to take place, fungi must have all the conditions cited above. Wood continuously under water will not be attacked by fungi because of the lack of air. Wood that is continuously dry will not be attacked because of the absence of moisture. Even dry rot, a great destroyer of wood components in buildings, cannot occur unless the fungi that cause it have access to moisture.

Dry rot and other damage to wood from fungi can be prevented by taking proper precautions. In the first place, heartwood is more susceptible to attack than sapwood. And certain species of wood are more susceptible than others. For example, many cedars, cypress, redwood, and black walnut are quite resistant to decay caused by fungi. Almost as durable are such woods as Douglas fir, Southern yellow pine, and white oak. More susceptible are such woods as beech, birch, hemlock, hickory, maple, red oak, and spruce.

Other precautions to take against dry rot and other fungus infections of wood include pressure treatment as previously described for insect protection, adequate ventilation around wood members, and separation of wood from sources of moisture, including condensation. Proper maintenance, including periodic washing of wood or other architectural components with mildew-reducing solutions, proper painting, and so on, will also aid in preventing decay caused by fungi. If wood is attacked, the damaged portions should be replaced and the new wood properly protected to prevent recurrence.

Crawl spaces under buildings without basements should provide a minimum of 18 inches clearance under wood joists or other members. Openings in masonry or concrete walls for the ends of joists and other members should be large enough to allow adequate air space around their sides and ends. Crawl spaces should also be provided with an adequate number and sizes of screened vents for cross ventilation.

As in the protection of buildings and their occupants from other hazards, protection from insects and other pests is very important. Fungi, termites, and other pests cause great amounts of damage to buildings every year. And much of it could be avoided by proper design and construction.

Related Articles DOOR; FOUNDATION; GARDEN; WINDOW; WOOD; WOOD-FRAME STRUCTURE.

Source of Additional Information American Institute of Timber Construction, 333 W. Hampden Ave., Englewood, Colo. 80110.

INSULATION, THERMAL
Often simply called insulation, materials used in buildings to decrease loss of heat in winter and gain of heat in summer. In architecture, the term *insulation* is also used for sound control or acoustical materials and for electrical insulation. (See articles entitled electric power and wiring; sound control.) All building materials resist the flow of heat to some extent. For example, masonry materials, such as brick, stone, and concrete, resist the flow of heat, mainly because they can absorb relatively high amounts of heat when the sun shines on them and the air is warm, store it in a heat sink, and then release it at night and when the air is cooler. When thermal insulation is spoken of today, the term usually means nonstructural materials that have the property of impeding the flow of heat, rather than storing it as in masonry.

Kinetic Energy Heat is a form of energy, called kinetic, that results from the motion of molecules within various substances. The amount of kinetic energy or heat in a substance at a given time is dependent on how fast the molecules move; the faster, the more heat. Temperature, in degrees Fahrenheit (F) or Celsius (C), is dependent on how fast the molecules are moving, and is a measure of the average kinetic energy of the molecules. Heat, in British thermal units (Btus), joules (J), or kilojoules (kJ), is dependent on both the speed and the number of molecules in a substance, and is a measure of the total kinetic energy in the substance. Heat flows from a warm substance to a cool one in three ways: conduction, convection, and radiation. Conduction involves the movement of heat from molecule to molecule, as in heat that travels from a heated end of an object to the other end. Convection involves the movement of heat from one substance to a cooler one, usually in air, causing currents that rise as the air is heated. Radiation involves the movement of heat by means of waves that do not heat the intervening air, as in heat received from the sun. Heat transfer in buildings occurs in all three ways. The purpose of thermal insulation is to minimize the effects of the heat transfer.

Heat is measured in Btus, generally taken to be the amount of heat required to raise the temperature of 1 pound of water 1°F, or in joules. Heat flow, or thermal conductivity (K), is a measure of the amount of heat in Btus that will flow through a material 1 ft², 1 in thick with a temperature differential of 1°F between its sides, in 1 hr, or in joules per second, called watts (W). Today insulating materials are often taken to be those that have thermal conductivities of less than 0.5 Btu, or 0.5275 kJ.

Thermal conductance (C) is a similar measure applied to the thickness of an actual material, such as a brick or concrete block. The overall conductance (U) is a similar measure applied to a complete building component, such as a wall, a roof, or a floor. Resistance (R) is the reciprocal of conductivity or conductance (K, C, or U); for example, in a material with a C factor of 0.5, the R factor would be 1/0.5, or 2. R factors are very useful in the calculations of heat transfer, because, unlike the other values, R factors of the various materials that make up a building component, a wall, for example, can be added together to determine the resistance of the entire component.

In buildings, heat losses in winter and heat gains in summer occur mainly through walls, ceilings, roofs, and floors. Glass in windows or doors is a very large source of heat loss or gain. Heat losses and gains through walls and roofs may be minimized by the provision of dead air spaces within them and by proper insulation in sufficient amounts. Heat losses and gains through glass can be minimized by reducing the number and sizes of such openings and by the use of double or multiple glazing, storm windows and doors, or heat-absorbing glass.

Resistances Some differences of opinion exist about the proper resistances that buildings should have today. Since the beginning of the fuel shortages in the second half of this century, many have maintained that very high resistances should be provided to minimize the use of fuels. However, many others believe that a given building should provide an interior climate that is healthy and comfortable at the minimum cost, including annual operating and fuel costs for heating and air conditioning and the original costs of the mechanical systems, the insulation, and other materials and elements used to produce thermal comfort, prorated over 10 years or more.

Resistances, sometimes referred to as desirable to produce comfortable interiors, range from 10 when the outside temperature is 30°F, to 17 when it is 0°F, to 25 when it is 30°F below zero. These resistances are necessary to produce interior wall temperatures of 68°F, which most people find comfortable in winter when air temperatures inside are about 70 to 75°F. In general, resistances of 24 for ceilings, 13 for walls, and 19 for floors over vented crawl spaces have often been considered acceptable. Some might maintain today that these R's are too low in a time of fuel shortages.

Resistances for materials ordinarily used today vary greatly, from about 0.0031 for 1-in-thick steel, which has little resistance to heat flow, to about 0.40 for whole face brick, to about 0.89 for window glass, to as much as 16 for some types of insulating materials. R-factor tables for materials, and tables of overall resistances for various types of walls, floors, roofs, and so on are widely available.

Overall resistances may also be calculated by adding the resistances of individual materials used in a wall or other building component to the resistances of air spaces within the component and the resistances of the film of air on the outside of the component and that on the inside. In a relatively common situation, such as in the walls of a wood-frame house with nominal 2 by 4 in studs, the materials might include ¾-in wood siding ($R = 1.05$), building paper ($R = 0.06$), ⅜-in plywood sheathing ($R = 0.59$), 3½-in glass-fiber insulation ($R = 15.75$, at 30°F), and ½-in gypsum board ($R = 0.45$).

In addition, for the outside surface air film in a 15 miles per hour wind, $R = 0.17$; for the inside surface air film, in still air, $R = 0.68$; and for the air space in the wall, $R = 0.84$. The overall total resistance of this will be the sum of all the R's of its components and will equal 19.59, over 80 percent of which is attributable to the insulation. With the same materials, except for nominal 2 by 6 in studs and 5½ in of glass-fiber insulation, the total R would be 28.59. Both of these R factors are well above the recommended figure of 13 for walls, mentioned previously. However, if the insulation were left out of this wall, the resulting R would be only 4.84, well below that recommended. It should be remembered that additional insulation beyond a certain point produces diminishing returns in resisting heat flow. In the wall example above, an approximate 57 percent increase in insulation produced an approximate 46 percent increase in resistance. Further increases in insulation would produce further diminished results.

Savings in heat transmission can be accomplished by the use of insulating glass. While ordinary window glass has an R of only 0.89, double glazing with a single air space has an R or about 1.50, and triple glazing with two air spaces, about 2.20. Storm windows have R factors of about 1.80; in addition, they help prevent wind infiltration, as does weather stripping.

Insulation Forms Thermal insulation for buildings comes in a number of forms: batts or blankets, usually enclosed on one or both sides with waterproof paper or other materials, in pieces or rolls; loose materials; rigid boards or sheets; reflective types; and plastic foams that may be made into boards or foamed into place in buildings.

Batts and blankets are made of mineral wool (sometimes called rock wool), glass fibers, and sometimes wood or other fibers. Loose materials include mineral wool, glass fibers, cork granules, and such materials as vermiculite and perlite which can be expanded by heating to produce trapped air pockets. Boards and sheets are made of cork, glass and other fibers, and cellular glass, sometimes called foamed glass. Reflective insulations are usually of aluminum foil, often fabricated to produce air pockets between sheets. Foamed insulations are generally of polystyrene or polyurethane plastics; the latter produces poisonous gas in fires. Thermal insulating materials may be laid, nailed, blown, or foamed into place in buildings.

With the use of insulation in buildings, the problem of condensation of water vapor in the air is intensified. Water vapor acts in a manner similar to any gas and therefore very much like air. The flow is generally from warm places toward colder ones, from the interiors of buildings toward the exteriors in winter, and in the opposite direction in summer. In the winter, as warm air, laden with water vapor, moves from the interior toward the exterior, it may reach its dew point, at which it deposits condensation in the cooler insulation or exterior building components.

To counteract such conditions, vapor barriers are used in conjunction with insulation, always applied on the warm side. This means that vapor barriers should be on the inside of insulation in the winter and on the outside in summer. However, temperature differentials in winter can vary 60°F or more between outside and inside, while in summer they seldom vary more than about 15°F. Thus vapor problems, in most instances, will be more serious in winter than in summer.

Vapor barriers are usually made from impervious materials, such as aluminum foil, bituminous-treated building papers, and plastics. If vapor barriers are used on the outside of insulation, they must have the capability of letting trapped vapor escape to the outside. Also walls, roofs, including spaces in attics, and other building components are often vented to the outside for the same purpose.

The use of insulation in buildings today has become a necessity in most areas of the United States, not only to provide comfort for the occupants but for reducing the initial costs of heating and air-conditioning systems and for lower operating costs and conservation of fuels. Efficient insulating materials are available as well as information on design and installation.

History Thermal insulation of the types used today did not exist during earlier periods of architecture. The masonry buildings of the past, with thick walls, resisted the inflow of heat in the summer and its loss in the winter. Windows and other openings were relatively small and contributed little to heat flow. To keep warm in winter in colder climates, people huddled around fires and stoves and wore heavy clothing indoors. In warmer climates, during the heat of the day in summer, people stopped work or other activities, for siestas. Also, since heating was relatively primitive, there was little need for efficient insulation.

Beginning in the 19th century came the development of better heating systems and of skeleton-framed walls that did not depend on thick masonry for structural strength. Thermal insulation was needed to allow the thin walls to resist heat flow as had the masonry walls of the past, but nothing much was done about the problem until after 1920. Then people began to wear lighter clothing indoors and to expect, at the same time, an increased degree of comfort. The advent of air conditioning increased the requirements for insulation and thin curtain walls further increased them, as have the fuel shortages of the 20th century.

In the 20th century, many new types of thermal insulation materials have been developed, including glass fibers, first produced in 1908 but not commercially until 1938, expanded minerals such as vermiculite and perlite, aluminum foil, and foamed plastics.

Related Articles CLIMATE; ELECTRIC POWER AND WIRING; ENERGY; HEATING, VENTILATING, AND AIR CONDITIONING; SOUND CONTROL; WATERPROOFING; WEATHER PROTECTION.

Further Reading Rogers, Tyler Stewart: *Thermal Design of Buildings,* John Wiley, New York, 1964.

Source of Additional Information Acoustical and Insulating Materials Assoc., 205 West Touhy Ave., Park Ridge, Ill. 60068.

INTERIOR DESIGN
The process of developing concepts of the finishes, furniture, and furnishings to go into the interiors of buildings and individual rooms. People who program, plan, design, and execute interiors of buildings are called interior designers, a title that only came into wide usage after World War II. Formerly, interior designers were called interior decorators, as some still are today, a title that had been in use since the 19th century.

Before the latter half of the 19th century, interiors were usually designed by architects, cabinetmakers, or furniture designers, though some evidence exists of designs by others, including amateurs. Interior design, though it was not called that at the time, was the first design field in which women became prominent, dating back at least to the time, in France, of Jeanne Antoinette Poisson (1721–64), better known as Madame de Pompadour, mistress of Louis XV (1710–74), and of Marie Antoinette (1775–93), wife of Louis XVI (1754–93), who wielded considerable influence over the interior design of buildings for the nobility and royalty. The influence of women on interiors has remained strong since that time.

Classification Interior designers today may be classified into two major categories. First, there are the professionals who design interiors for fees, as architects usually design buildings, and who, though they may select and purchase furniture and furnishings for their clients, do so on a professional fee basis. Second are the commercial interior designers, often called decorators even today, who work for or own commercial firms, in which profits on the sale of furniture and furnishings are often paramount, with those for design services either nominal or absorbed by the firms in order to make sales. Interior-design operations of the first type are usually carried on by interior design departments of architectural firms, by independent professionals, and in some cases by subsidiaries or departments of commercial furniture or other firms. Independent interior designers often work with architects, but in other cases compete with them for work. Interior design operations of the second type are often found in department stores, furniture stores, home furnishings stores, and in smaller retail operations owned and operated by designers.

Services Most interior design operations offer a variety of services, including design and planning of interior layouts; design of walls, ceilings, and other interior elements; color coordination; design or selection of built-in elements such as bookcases, cabinetwork, and the like; selection of movable furniture, carpets, curtains, and other items for interior use; selection of wall coverings, flooring, lighting, and the like; purchase of items for clients; and administration of the construction work, including inspection to ensure that it is performed properly. Interior designers usually handle the design of interiors for buildings of all types, including houses, offices, banks, theaters, and schools. A few specialize in one type, such as offices, or a few types.

Space Planning A special type of interior work, closely related to interior design, is called space planning. By this is meant the activities involved, in an office building, for example, in the analysis of operational needs, flow of people from one department or office to others, flow of paperwork between various offices and departments, space requirements, and so on. This process goes much deeper into the organizations and operations of offices than do the usual procedures of interior design. However, the programs and schedules prepared by space planning may then be translated into interior designs.

Open Planning A relatively new type of interior design, often used in office buildings but adaptable to other types, is open planning, or in office work, office landscaping. Open planning was first espoused by early modern architects, such as Frank Lloyd Wright (1867–1959), in their house designs. Instead of placing four walls around every room, thus effectively cutting each off from the others, they designed spaces that had no walls on some sides, spaces that flowed into each other so that people could move easily from living areas to dining to cooking and to outside spaces.

In the newer concept of office landscaping, there are no interior walls, or almost none, thus creating an open space in which divisions between activities are accomplished by placement of special furniture: space dividers, planting, and other partial barriers which do not rise to the ceilings. For some functions, such as those that are similar or closely related, the concept seems to work very well. For others, for example, those in which one occupation that is noisy and outgoing is placed next to one that is quiet and introspective, the concept works very poorly. Whole systems of furniture, space dividers, and other elements for open office planning are available.

Although the processes involved in interior design may vary considerably, they are somewhat similar to those in architectural services. Generally, the phases include programming; space planning; design; preparation of procurement documents, working drawings, and specifications; and construction, including

INTERIOR DESIGN Hempstead Bank (1971), Hempstead, N.Y. [*Architects: Bentel and Bentel. (Joseph W. Molitor)*]

INTERIOR DESIGN Bohlin summer house (1975), Conn. [*Architects: Bohlin and Powell. (Joseph W. Molitor)*]

INTERIOR DESIGN Johnson House (1965), Old Lyme, Conn. [*Architect: King Lui Wu. (Joseph W. Molitor)*]

INTERIOR DESIGN Douglas House (1964), Mich. [*Architect: Richard Meier. (Ezra Stoller)*]

INTERIOR DESIGN Douglas House (1964), Mich. [*Architect: Richard Meier. (Ezra Stoller)*]

administration, inspection, and actual procurement of items of furniture and furnishings.

For people who are motivated toward creative work that is also functional, work that requires taste and professionalism and which also results in tangible results that are actually constructed, a career in the field of interior design can be very gratifying. Interior designers are motivated by much the same things that motivate architects. Yet their work is usually on a smaller scale, and often more concerned with the fine details of arts and crafts than that of architects. In other ways, interior design is very much like architecture. As is necessary for architects, interior designers must work with people, manage offices, study and analyze problems, prepare programs for their solutions, design interiors, make construction documents such as working drawings and specifications, and administer the construction process.

Education Preparation for higher education in interior design begins with a broad preparatory course in secondary school, including sciences, mathematics, social sciences, and humanities. Drawing and other art courses, if they are highly creative, may be helpful, but otherwise should be avoided. In a college or university or one of the specialized schools of interior design, the course consists of four years, sometimes less, of general college courses, together with others in design, history of art and architecture, interior design, sketching and rendering, drafting, lighting design, construction materials, furniture, furnishings, color, and so on.

Today three to four years of practical experience in the office of a professional interior designer is recommended after graduation, before an interior designer starts an independent practice. Another avenue for those who want to become professional interior designers is a two-year, general college course, followed by three years in a specialized school of interior design and three to four years of experience. After completion of such requirements, a person should have become fully qualified as an interior designer, and to become a member of the professional association, the American Society of Interior Designers (ASID), must then subscribe to the ethics of the organization. ASID was founded in 1931, but only in 1961 did it drop the name Decorators from its title and add Interior Designers.

History Interior design, though it was not called that until the 20th century, was practiced from the earliest times when humans first furnished their caves and decorated them with painted and sculptured walls. The ancient Egyptians, Greeks, and other Middle Eastern and Mediterranean people decorated the interiors of their houses and other buildings, often in elaborate styles. This practice was continued by the Romans.

During the early Middle Ages, interiors of buildings were mostly simple, utilizing hangings and furniture that was usually made of heavy oak, unadorned or decorated with paint. Very few early Gothic pieces of furniture or other interior furnishings have been preserved. Later, furniture and furnishings were given more attention and resulted in better designs, including those for tapestries, hangings woven with yarns of different colors to form pictures or designs. Tapestry weaving was highly developed in the Middle Ages, particularly in France, and a number of fine examples are still in existence, including *The Lady and the Unicorn* in the Cluny Museum, Paris; the *Burgundian Sacraments,* in the Metropolitan Museum of Art; and *The Hunt of the Unicorn,* in the Cloisters, a branch of the Metropolitan, both in New York City.

During the Renaissance, the art of tapestry making was further developed in Brussels, Belgium, and in Paris by the Gobelin family after 1663. The arts of furniture and interior design were also highly developed during the Renaissance period and the years immediately following. Italian designs were mostly derived from classical Greece and Rome, and designs in France and England, from the Italians. At this time, walnut came into use for furniture, partly replacing oak which had been widely used previously. Very few examples of Renaissance furniture and furnishings, other than tapestries and a few minor pieces, have survived and these are hard to authenticate.

By about the end of the Renaissance period, interior design was profoundly affected by a succession of styles, some of which lasted only a short time, and most of which were different in various countries. Some of these interior styles took their names from the architectural styles of the day, others from furniture styles, still others from various influences. Italian leadership in interior and furniture design began to wane, and was replaced by that of other countries, including France and England.

French Styles In France, at first the styles were named for the kings in whose reigns they occurred. Thus there was the Louis Quatorze style (1643–1715), named for Louis XIV (1638–1715); the Louis Quinze style (1715–74), named for Louis XV (1710–74); and the Louis Seize style (1774–94), named for Louis XVI (1754–93). During the Louis XIV period, interiors and furniture and furnishings were based on classical designs and were very formal. During the Louis XV period, designs were still classical but were lighter, more delicate, more ornamented, and were done with more gaiety. During the Louis XVI period, designs were much more simple and subdued than before.

The succeeding styles in furniture and interiors included the Directoire, named for the Directory, the five men who ruled France (1795–99) after the overthrow of Louis XVI in 1792. This style was even more simplified and subdued than the one it superseded. The next great style was the Empire, named for the reign (1804–14) of Emperor Napoleon I, the title assumed by Napoléon Bonaparte (1769–1821), who had been First Consul in the Consulate, which took over the rule of France (1799–1804). The Empire style returned to grand forms in interiors and furniture, based on those of Imperial Rome, and lasted until about 1840. Later, a Second Empire style (1852–70) was developed, but it was very heavy and often incongruous, unlike the style it tried to emulate.

English Styles In England, beginning with the Renaissance, furniture and interior styles took their names from the architecture of the periods. And the architectural styles were named for the reigning monarchs. The earliest was the Elizabethan style (1558–1603), named for Elizabeth I (1533–1603). This was a transition style between that of the Gothic in the Middle Ages and that of the Renaissance. Next came the Jacobean style (1603–25), named for James I (1566–1625), Jacob being an ancient form of the name James. This style was more in the spirit of the Renaissance and used forms derived from that period.

Next came the Stuart style (1625–1702), named for the Stuart rulers of England, not including James I. The Stuart style was predominant in England during the time of Charles I (1600–49), who was beheaded, through the Commonwealth (1649–60), when the country was ruled by Oliver Cromwell (1599–1658), and through the reigns of Charles II (1630–85) and James II (1633–1701); it ended in 1702, with the death of William III (1650–1702), who had reigned jointly with Mary II (1662–94). Architecture and interior design during the William and Mary era is sometimes called by that name. The Stuart style saw the development of great English Renaissance interiors and furniture as well as architecture.

The next style was the Georgian (1702–1830), named for the Hanoverian kings of England, George I (1660–1727), George II (1683–1760), George III (1738–1820), and George IV (1762–1830). Sometimes other names are used for styles in certain portions of this period; Queen Anne in the period (1702–14), when Anne (1665–1714) reigned, and Regency for the period 1811–20, when the Prince of Wales, later George IV, ruled as regent while George III was mentally and physically unable to reign. The Georgian style was based on concepts of design from the Renaissance, particularly in Italy. The style was predicated on rules of design, many of which were developed by English architects and other designers from the books of an Italian Renaissance architect, Andrea Palladio (1518–80).

Later styles in England are sometimes called by the names of the architects or cabinetmakers who predominated in interior and furniture design at the time. Thus the graceful, ornate style of cabinetmaker Thomas Chippendale (c.1718–79) and of his son Thomas (d. 1822) is often called the Chippendale style, while the delicate style of cabinetmaker George Hepplewhite (d. 1786) is often called the Hepplewhite style. These men were the greatest furniture designers and makers of their time and examples of their work are very much admired today.

Perhaps even more influential, certainly in interior design if not in furniture design, were the brothers Adam, who were architects, interior designers, and furniture designers. Of the four brothers, Robert (1728–92) and James (1730–94) were the most talented. They deeply influenced architectural and interior design, not only in England but in America as well, with their light, decorative designs. Another Englishman was Thomas Sheraton (1751–1806), who was strictly a furniture designer and who published widely admired books of his designs.

American Development In the earliest days in colonial America, interior design was almost nonexistent, the settlers using what little furniture and furnishings they had brought from home and later supplementing these with crude items made from native woods, pewter, and homespun fabrics. Early American homes were smaller than many of those in Europe, and the furniture the colonists made was usually smaller than the European prototypes. Since colonial architecture, for some time, usually reflected that of the buildings the colonists had known in Europe, so did interiors.

In New England the architecture, including interiors, was adapted from that in England and became known as New England Colonial. In the English Southern colonies, the source of inspiration was the same, but buildings and interiors were modified to meet the special requirements of the climate and for other purposes. In New York and other places settled by the Dutch, Dutch Colonial became the style, as did French Colonial and Spanish Colonial in places settled by people from France and Spain. Interiors in New England houses in the early days often had white or off-white walls, with colorfully patterned carpets and curtains. Furniture was simple and only a few pieces were used in rooms. On the other hand, in the South, much of which was settled by more affluent people, houses were larger and more splendid and were often furnished, at least partly, with furniture and furnishings imported from England.

The earliest furniture made in the English colonies in America was based on the Jacobean style, prevalent in the home country at the time of the earliest colonization. In America the style came later than in England, about 1650, and lasted until about 1670. Subsequent furniture and interior designs generally followed those popular in England, but they also ordinarily came to America later. Certain phases of the Stuart era were popular in America, such as the William and Mary style in the 18th century, and of the Georgian era such as the Queen Anne style, which became popular in America after the death of the queen and remained so at least until the middle of the 18th century.

The Chippendale style reached America about the middle of the 18th century. Fine furniture derived from it was made by American craftsmen, particularly in Philadelphia, in what came to be called American Chippendale. After this, the style of the brothers Adam became widely accepted in American architecture, including interiors, mainly because of the books they wrote about it; the Adam style never caught on in furniture in America because the brothers Adam did not publish their furniture designs. As had happened with Chippendale, the Hepplewhite style came to America in the late 1700s, after the Revolution, and was closely followed by the Sheraton style. Hepplewhite furniture was forceful and original, while the Sheraton was delicate and eclectic, based on the work of other men, including not only Hepplewhite but Chippendale and the brothers Adam. Many other styles were imported to America in the 19th century, including the French Directoire and Empire styles.

However, the greatest influences on American interiors in the late colonial period, and afterward, came from architects, many of whom were cabinetmakers and craftsmen, the others having studied the architecture of interiors in books. Also of great importance were the American cabinetmakers who designed furniture. Often using mahogany or walnut, such craftsmen were to be found in every colony. Some of the best were John Goddard (1724–85) of Dartmouth, Mass.; William Savery (1721–87) of Philadelphia; and the man usually considered the greatest craftsman Scottish-American Duncan Phyfe (1768–1854) of New York City. Phyfe produced furniture based on the ideas of Sheraton, but sometimes his work is referred to as the Phyfe style, rather than American Sheraton.

During the latter part of the 19th century and continuing to some extent in houses to the present, architects designed buildings in a variety of eclectic styles based on those of the past. Interior design has generally followed the lead of architecture in these buildings, but in some cases has been eclectic even when the architecture was not. Thus there have been Classic Revival, Gothic Revival, Renaissance Revival, and almost every other imaginable revival in both architectural and interior design.

There have also been many fads, inspired by one thing or another. These have included a vast potpourri of styles, some more long lived than others, such as the Victorian style, named for Queen Victoria (1819–1901) of England; the Eastlake style, named for Sir Charles Lock Eastlake (1793–1865), an English painter and critic; the General Grant style, named for Ulysses Simpson Grant (1822–85), Civil War general and later president of the United States; and the Arts and Crafts Movement, espoused by interior and furniture designer William Morris (1834–96), who designed the Morris chair. All were interesting but derivative, and none contributed much to the future development of architectural or interior design. One of the most interesting fads was the Steamboat Gothic style, utilizing the elaborate ornament of river steamboats in buildings, some of which were thousands of miles from a river.

Also part of American architectural design, including interiors, of the late 19th and 20th centuries, was a vast outpouring of styles based on very exotic places and times that were far away and long ago. Thus buildings and their interiors were designed in styles based on the Romanesque, Gothic, Classic, and other eras in Greece, Rome, Egypt, France, Italy, Spain, England, Germany, and almost everywhere else, including Japan, China, India, and other countries.

Beginning in the latter half of the 19th century, American architects and those of other countries began to develop a type of architecture, including interior design, which has come to be called modern architecture. Led by Major William Le Baron Jenney (1832–1907) and other architects of what is often called the Chicago school of design, they turned away from designs based on those from the past toward architecture that was expressive of the time in which it was created. Although some of the earliest modern architects were not deeply involved in interior design, those who came a bit later, including Louis Henri Sullivan (1856–1924) and Frank Lloyd Wright, began to consider the design of interiors as integral parts of their buildings.

Wright, together with other young architects in the early 20th century, often designed the complete interiors of their buildings, including in some cases furniture and other furnishings. This practice has been continued to some extent today. For discussion of late-20th-century interiors, see the article entitled furniture.

Many present-day architects continue to perform the interior design of their buildings, or have interior design departments in their firms which handle this function. Other interiors are designed by independent designers. Not a small amount of interior design today, more often than not still called interior decoration and mostly for houses, is handled by amateurs or people who work part-time. Many of the professional designers work only in modern idioms. Others still attempt interiors intended to be period pieces, particularly in such building types as houses and restaurants. A specialized form of period work, requiring great scholarship and skill, is restoration and reconstruction of historical interiors.

Related Articles ART IN ARCHITECTURE; DESIGN, ARCHITECTURAL; ESTHETICS; FURNITURE; HISTORY OF ARCHITECTURE; PROGRAMMING.

Further Reading *Architectural Record: Interior Spaces Designed by Architects*, McGraw-Hill, New York, 1974; Friedmann, Arnold, John F. Pile, and Forrest Wilson: *Interior Design—An Introduction to Architectural Interiors*, 2d ed., American Elsevier, New York, 1976; Halse, Albert O.: *The Use of Color in Interiors*, 2d ed. McGraw-Hill, New York, 1978; Pile, John F.: *Interiors Third Book of Offices*, Whitney, New York, 1976; Pile, John F.: *Interiors Second Book of Offices*, Whitney, New York, 1969; Saphier, Michael: *Office Planning and Design*, McGraw-Hill, New York, 1968; Siegel, Harry: *This Business of Interior Design*, Whitney, New York, 1976.

Source of Additional Information American Society of Interior Designers, 730 Fifth Ave., New York, N.Y. 10019.
Periodicals *Contract Interiors*, 1515 Broadway, New York, N.Y., 10036; *Interior Design*, 150 E. 58th St., New York, N.Y. 10022.

IRON A metallic element, mined from the earth, that has wide usage in architecture for everything from nails to structures. Iron, produced today in a blast furnace, is used in buildings mainly in cast and wrought forms. After having been refined into steel, the material has a great number of additional uses in architecture.

The second most abundant metal, surpassed only by aluminum, iron is found in most countries in the world. The Soviet Union leads in mining iron ore, with the United States second. Although every state in the United States contains iron ore, the richest deposits are in Minnesota and Michigan, near Lake Superior, where 75 percent of the U.S. iron is mined.

Types Two forms of iron are used in architecture: wrought iron, which has less than 0.1 percent carbon, usually much less; and cast iron, which usually has from 1.7 to 4 percent carbon. The most important use is in steel, which has up to 2 percent carbon. Wrought iron is relatively soft, malleable or easy to work by forging, bending, or other processes, and can be welded. Available in a variety of shapes, including pipe, plate, sheets, and bars, wrought iron is used in architecture mostly for pipe, furniture, fences, hardware, and sometimes ornamental ironwork. Cast iron is a hard, brittle metal that can be easily cast in many forms in molds, but generally cannot be worked by forging, bending, or other usual methods. Malleable cast iron, sometimes called malleable iron, is produced by heating cast iron and holding it at an elevated temperature long enough to relieve the internal stresses. This process, called annealing, produces a metal that can be machined and worked by other methods. Cast iron may be alloyed with other substances, including nickel, chromium, molydenum, and silicon, to produce types with added strength and corrosion or chemical resistance. Cast iron is available in pipe, sheet, plate, bars, and other shapes, and is used in architecture for many purposes, including pipe, plumbing fixtures, fireplace dampers, gratings, stairs, and ornamental ironwork.

Production The usual method for making iron from ore utilizes a blast furnace, a tall, round furnace made of steel lined with refractory brick. Usually operated continuously, 24 h a day, a blast furnace is charged with iron ore, crushed limestone, and coke. Wood is set on fire to start the coke burning, after which additional iron ore, limestone, and coke are added continuously, at the top, to keep the furnace operating. Burning is intensified by a steady blast of air, heated by gas in stoves, from nozzles near the bottom of the furnace. This blast of air gives the furnace its name. The hot air together with the burning of the coke produces carbon monoxide which rises through the iron ore and other materials melting them and causing some of the carbon to combine with the molten iron.

The molten iron falls to the bottom of the furnace to a crucible or hearth, and every few hours is drawn off, or tapped. Impurities, called slag, float on top of the molten iron, now called pig iron, with 95 percent iron, up to 4 percent carbon or slightly more, and traces of impurities. The slag is also drawn off. The pig iron is tapped into special vehicles called ladle or bottle cars. The ladle cars transport the molten pig iron to casting houses, where it is cast into bars called pigs, or directly to an open-hearth or other type of furnace to be made into steel. Blast furnaces are of different sizes; the largest can produce as much as 2,400 tons of pig iron a day. A furnace that large would also produce about half that much slag, useful in architecture for such purposes as the manufacture of portland cement, aggregates for concrete, building streets, and others. Another by-product is gas drawn off from the top of the furnace, treated to remove useful substances, and then employed as fuel in steel making or other operations.

In addition to the above uses in architecture, iron has such other uses as inclusion as an alloying metal to increase the strength of aluminum, brass, bronze, copper, and other metals; as a color pigment in glazes for clay tile and porcelain enamel products; and as a preservative.

Corrosion Protection Although wrought and cast iron have some resistance to corrosion, they are almost always protected with coatings. Several types of paint or other organic coatings may be used. Proper types should be carefully selected for the material to be painted and for the function of the product. Different paints or coatings are available for interiors, exteriors, and areas with chemical fumes, saltwater, air pollution, and so on. Iron may also be protected with asphalt coatings where extreme conditions exist.

Iron may also be protected from corrosion by treating it with phosphates to produce rust-resistant surfaces, by plating with other metals, and by galvanizing, a process that covers the iron with a thin coat of zinc. Galvanized iron is often painted. Properly selected or designed, installed, and protected, products of wrought or cast iron are very useful and reliable. Both can be used for ornamental objects. Wrought iron, in particular, was widely used for such purposes in the past. Still highly admired, it is not used so frequently for ornament today, to the regret of some people. Although the intricate and often delicate forms possible in wrought iron cannot be duplicated in cast iron, the latter material has had a place in architectural ornament in the past and might well be used more often today. And it is hard to imagine how the great variety of iron functional architectural components (stairs and grilles) could be effectively replaced by ones made from another material.

History Eventually, iron became the most useful metal in architecture, particularly after methods of making steel were developed. However, this took a long time to get started. While copper was beginning to be used by about 5000 B.C. or even earlier, iron, in the form of meteorites, was not known to humans until about 1,000 years later. Another 1,000 years passed before experimental iron smelting was tried and almost another 2,000, before the beginning of the Iron Age, about 1200 B.C..

IRON Stewart-Wannamaker store (1862, demolished 1956), New York, N.Y. [*Architect; John Kellum. (Wurts Brothers)*]

Before that time, iron had been used in Mesopotamia and Egypt, mostly for jewelry and other ornament, and sometimes for weapons. The earliest of these were of meteoric iron fashioned into primitive forms. Later, globules of iron were obtained by heating ores in primitive smelters. The globules were then reheated and hammered into wrought iron. The making of steel was discovered soon after the earliest production of iron. The ancient Egyptians and other people around the Mediterranean Sea developed improved smelters and discovered the method of hardening iron by quenching the hot metal in cold water. The ancient Greeks made wrought iron and steel and also cast iron, which was used only rarely.

When the first use of iron in architecture occurred is unknown, but the earliest uses are thought to have been for relatively small components. The Greeks used it for clamps and other fasteners to hold various components of stone and wood together or to fasten them to buildings. For example, iron dowels were sometimes used to join sections of stone columns. Iron was also used at times for structural members. The iron in Greek buildings rusted away long ago, but traces of it may be found on stone elements that have survived.

The Romans made iron, using simple hearth furnaces very much like earlier ones. Although they also made steel, the best kinds were imported from the early steel-making centers in India, Persia, and Damascus, Syria. In architecture, the Romans used iron for clamps and other fasteners in conjunction with masonry, which sometimes acted somewhat like the reinforcing of concrete or masonry today. The Romans also used iron for other parts of buildings, including hardware, nails, and structural elements, such as beams and girders.

During the Romanesque period of architecture, iron was widely used for such purposes as hardware and grilles and for strengthening doors with iron plates, nails, and heavy, strong locks and bolts. Little structural use of the material was made. During the Middle Ages, new types of more efficient forges were introduced in several places in Europe; they used forced drafts induced by bellows, instead of the natural drafts of chimneys. Except for modest amounts of steel, all these forges produced wrought iron. By about 1350, forges had been further developed into the first blast furnaces, producing cast iron, and thus establishing the basis for iron and steel production from that time on. The major uses of iron in architecture during the Middle Ages were in grilles, placed in windows, to strengthen the masonry and glass and to prevent burglars from breaking in; for fastening together stone components; for hardware, including nails; and for relatively minor structural purposes. Iron was sometimes used, especially in Germany, for ornament.

During the Renaissance, iron continued to be used for purposes much like those of the past, but its use in structures increased spectacularly. In addition to its use for fastening stone components and similar purposes, iron was also used in chains placed around the great domes of the period to resist the outward forces, or thrusts, of the masonry. Some of these chains were plated with tin or enclosed in lead to prevent rusting. Iron bolts and other fasteners were used to construct timber trusses.

The early American colonists established blast furnaces for making iron during the first half of the 17th century. The first blast furnace was located at Falling Creek, Va., in 1621, and the second in Braintree, now West Quincy, Mass., in 1644. Furnaces were soon built at other places in Massachusetts, New Jersey, and Connecticut, and later in other colonies. The early blast furnaces produced only modest amounts of iron for local usage, mostly nonarchitectural, except for nails which were always in short supply in the colonies.

The art of making steel, which had been lost or ignored after ancient times, was rediscovered in 1740. In 1856 the English engineer Sir Henry Bessemer (1813–98) invented the Bessemer converter, an improved method for making steel, still in use today. In 1864 the open-hearth furnace, another improved method and still in use, was first used in England by Sir William Siemens (1823–83), who in 1878 developed the first successful electric furnace for making steel. An open-hearth furnace had been independently developed in 1864 by a French engineer, Pierre Émile Martin (1824–1915). These inventions were followed by other improved methods for handling iron ore, iron, and steel.

During the late 18th and early 19th centuries, new developments occurred in the use of iron as a structural material. For example, one of the first real applications of wrought iron as a reinforcing agent for masonry was in the Classic Revival Church of Ste Geneviève (completed 1790), later renamed the Panthéon, in Paris and designed by Jacques Germain Soufflot (1713–80). The English architect Thomas Rickman (1776–1841) built four Gothic Revival churches in Liverpool, England, including Saint George's (1814), in which almost every component was of cast iron, including door and window frames, structure, pulpit, and ornament. Iron was first used in a bridge for a span over the Severn River, at Coalbrook Dale, England, in 1781. It was designed by an architect, Thomas Farnolls Pritchard, constructed by Abraham Darby III, and is still in existence. Other iron bridges soon followed.

American Usage Both cast and wrought iron were important building materials in 19th-century America, their use perhaps first popularized by the success of the Crystal Palace (1851), at the Great Exhibition in London, designed by Sir Joseph Paxton (1801–65), with a structure entirely of iron. In other buildings, iron was used for such purposes as grilles, fences, ornament, columns, and complete structures. Buildings with iron structures, and sometimes with other important iron components, were erected in many places in the United States during the 19th century, including notable examples in New York City and St. Louis. At first, these were structures of moderate height, usually only a few stories. A remarkable group of cast-iron buildings were constructed in New York City during the 1850s and 1860s, and somewhat later, designed by prominent architects and manufacturers, including James Bogardus (1800–74) and J. P. Gaynor. Many have long since been demolished, but a few examples remain, including Gaynor's Haughwout Building (1857).

In the late 19th and early 20th centuries, an even more remarkable series of iron buildings was constructed in Chicago by architects of the so-called Chicago school of design. Although iron had been used previously in Chicago for relatively tall buildings, the first skeleton frame of the material was used in the 10-story Home Insurance Building (1855), designed by William Le Baron Jenney (1832–1907), and later demolished. This was also the first use of Bessemer steel for beams in a building. Although masonry bearing walls continued to be used after that time, the end of their use in buildings was clearly in sight. Other iron-framed tall buildings soon followed. In 1874 the first use in the United States of Bessemer steel for any type of structure was in the Eads Bridge, St. Louis, designed by engineer James Buchanan Eads (1820–76), for whom the bridge was named. The Reliance Building (1895), designed by Burnham and Root, was the first tall building in which steel columns as well as other structural members were used. The steel in these early buildings was riveted to form the frames. Riveting became the most used American fastening system for steel structures for many years. Later welded steel structures were often used.

Today steel remains one of the most important architectural materials for structural purposes, including concrete reinforcing, and for a host of other uses. Stainless steels are also used for many purposes. Cast iron is extensively used for pipe, hardware, ornamental work, and many other purposes. Wrought iron is used mostly for corrosion-resistant pipe, railings, fences, and grilles.

Related Articles BOGARDUS, JAMES; BRIDGE; BURNHAM AND ROOT; CONCRETE STRUCTURE; JENNEY, WILLIAM LE BARON; PREFABRICATION; STEEL; STEEL STRUCTURE; Articles on various building components and systems.
Source of Additional Information American Iron and Steel Inst., 1000 16th St., N.W., Washington, D.C. 20036.

J

JEFFERSON, THOMAS American statesman, farmer, writer, and architect (1743–1826). The many achievements of Thomas Jefferson have been so well documented and praised that the excellence of his architecture has often been overshadowed. Yet in spite of the years spent in service to his country and in a host of other pursuits, in all of which he excelled, he designed some of the greatest buildings in American history. His architectural training, as did that of other amateur gentlemen-architects of his time, came almost entirely from books.

Unlike many other American architects of his time, Jefferson was able to augment the book learning by close study of the Georgian buildings of Williamsburg and later of French and Roman buildings during the five years he was U.S. Minister to France. In addition, he was a scholar of classical literature, having learned both Greek and Latin as a boy.

Many-sided Scholar His deep interest in classical culture led him away from the Georgian style so prevalent at the time to an architecture derived from the Roman buildings he had seen and studied in books. An early proponent of Classic Revival architecture, Jefferson used both his own buildings and his official positions to influence the designs of buildings, particularly those of the new American republic. His own taste was classical, based on the strict principles of proportion and decoration of ancient Rome. As time went by, he became more and more anti-British in his architecture as well as in his politics and philosophy. Thus he played an important role in the evolution of American architecture as he had in its government.

For Jefferson, architecture was not merely a way to occupy himself pleasantly; he was most serious about it. He worked at perfecting his drawing skills until he became a very accomplished draftsman. He was one of the first American architects to use drawings as a means of studying designs. He prepared plans for his buildings and wrote specifications for them. He ordered materials, hired workers, supervised construction, and kept strict financial records.

Jefferson designed both buildings and town plans, among them a checkerboard scheme that envisioned squares of buildings alternating with open space squares, a revolutionary idea at that time. Among his town plans were one for Richmond, Va., and another for portions of Washington. He designed master plans and groups of buildings, including those for the University of Virginia at Charlottesville. He helped foster good planning through his support of the L'Enfant plan for Washington, and good architecture through his appointment, while president, of Benjamin Henry Latrobe (1764–1820) as surveyor of public buildings for the federal government.

Jefferson was an architectural scholar who collected the greatest library of books on the subject of that era. He was an architectural educator, helping to train young architects; his most notable student was Robert Mills (1781–1855), who spent two years studying and working with Jefferson. He was an innovator and inventor in the use of materials and systems, working out methods for manufacturing brick and other elements of buildings, and inventing systems of double glazing of windows to minimize heat losses, hot-air heating systems, and double doors that opened simultaneously.

Works It is in his own buildings, though, that Jefferson's genius as an architect is most apparent. His first work was his own house, Monticello, originally built (1769–75) in Georgian style, then remodeled and altered many times and drastically remodeled (1808) in Roman Revival style. In fact, Jefferson designed and redesigned, built, tore down, and rebuilt Monticello continually from 1769 almost until the time of his death, except for periods when he was absent on governmental affairs. (See also color section.)

Monticello is a magnificent building, some think Jefferson's masterpiece, in a beautiful setting on top of a hill near Charlottesville, Va. With a domed central element and porticoes on two sides, the two-story house was constructed of brick with wood trim, fabricated at the site under Jefferson's supervision. Underground passages led from either side to long wings that housed servants, and contained the kitchen, stables, an office, and other rooms. Sold after Jefferson's death to help settle his debts, the house deteriorated badly over the years, until it was bought by the Thomas Jefferson Memorial Foundation, which has had the house and grounds restored and many of the original furnishings reinstated.

Jefferson designed a number of other Virginia houses. Among the finest of those still standing are Belle Grove (1796) in Middleton and Poplar Forest (1820) in Forest. After the state capital of Virginia was moved from Williamsburg to Richmond, Jefferson designed a Capitol Building in 1784, adapted from the

JEFFERSON, THOMAS Monticello (1769–75, remodeled 1796–1808),
Charlottesville, Va. *(Detroit Publishing Co., Library of Congress)*

JEFFERSON, THOMAS State Capitol (1791), Richmond, Va. *(Detroit
Publishing Co., Library of Congress)*

JEFFERSON, THOMAS University of Virginia Rotunda (1825), Charlottesville, Va. *(Library of Congress)*

Roman Maison Carrée (c. 16, B.C.) in Nîmes, France. After arriving in Paris as U.S. Minister, he did additional work on the design and had a model of the building made by a French architect, C. L. A. Clerissau. The drawings and models were sent to Richmond in 1786. The work on the building had begun in 1785 and was finished in 1791. Jefferson also designed a governor's house for Richmond, based on the Villa Rotunda (c. 1657) at Vicenza, Italy, but it was never built. The Virginia Capitol was the first building in the United States with a design adapted from a pure temple form and was some 20 years ahead of the first in France, the Church of the Madeleine, begun in 1806.

Jefferson's last great work, which, though he loved Monticello, he considered his finest, was the campus and buildings of the University of Virginia (1825) in Charlottesville. Here Jefferson designed what he described as an academic village. For his village, Jefferson produced a master plan with five major elements: two long ranges of buildings each consisting of five two-story pavilions in which professors lived and taught, interconnected with single-story dormitory rooms for students; at one end of the range is the focal point of the plan, the library, now called the Rotunda; behind each of the ranges, and separated from them by landscaped grounds, are two additional long buildings, each with three dining rooms separated by additional dormitories. The University of Virginia is still considered one of the greatest master plans in all American architecture. (See also color section.)

For each pavilion, Jefferson chose the style of an actual great classical building or a design from the books of the 16th-century Italian architect Andrea Palladio (1518–80). For the Rotunda, the model was the Pantheon (A.D. 124) in Rome but half the size of that building. In 1851 Robert Mill, who much earlier had studied architecture with Jefferson, designed a large annex behind the Rotunda. In 1895 the annex caught fire and burned, the fire spread and the Rotunda was seriously damaged. Stanford White (1853–1906), of McKim, Mead and White, renovated the Rotunda in 1912, but in the process changed Jefferson's design considerably. The building has now been restored almost to its original design. And Jefferson's famous serpentine garden walls have been rebuilt to the design of the originals.

For the University of Virginia, Jefferson designed the campus and its buildings, supervised the construction, kept the construction accounts, and trained and directed the workmen. He went on to design the curriculum, select the books for its library, and to choose the faculty members. In the end, he came to call himself the father of the university, which he undoubtedly was in a sense. He might also be called the father of the Roman Revival movement as well as one of the two or three founders of the Classic Revival style in America.

Life Thomas Jefferson was born at the family home, Shadwell, in Albemarle (then Goochland) County, Va., on April 13, 1743. He was the son of Peter Jefferson, surveyor, colonel of militia, and landholder, and Jane Randolph, a member of one of the oldest and best families in Virginia. Jefferson's early education consisted of studying with his father and in local schools.

After his father's death, when young Jefferson was only fourteen, he continued his education at the school of the Rev. James Maury in Charlottesville. At

JEFFERSON, THOMAS University of Virginia Wall (1825), Charlottes-ville, Va. *(Library of Congress)*

JEFFERSON, THOMAS University of Virginia Ranges (1825), Char-lottesville, Va. *(Detroit Publishing Co., Library of Congress)*

age sixteen, he entered the College of William and Mary in Williamsburg, Va. By this time, he had already learned a considerable amount of French, Greek, and Latin and to play the violin. These were to become lifelong interests. In Williamsburg, Jefferson got his first introduction to architecture in the buildings of the colonial capital. This was another interest that would last all his life.

After graduation in 1762, Jefferson remained in Williamsburg to study law with George Wythe (1726–1806), a learned lawyer and judge. In 1767 he was admitted to the bar. He had by that time grown tall, 6'2", was freckled and red-haired. He had studied deeply in the arts and sciences and in music and literature. Formally trained as a lawyer, and having delayed as long as possible, he now entered the practice of law. By his own admission and the observations of others, it is certain that he never really enjoyed the law very much. But it was a stepping stone to the great career as a politician and statesman that lay ahead. And though he never really liked it, his career as a lawyer was most successful.

Dividing his time between Williamsburg and the family home, Shadwell, Jefferson began to pursue another of his enthusiasms, architecture. He had studied the architecture of Williamsburg, most of which he did not like, and he had studied classical architecture in the library that had been assembled by William Byrd (1674–1744), at Westover. The finest of its day, it included 26 architectural books, particularly those of Andrea Palladio. Jefferson began to collect architectural books for his own library. Soon after his admission to the bar, he began the design of a house for himself, on the top of the 500-ft-high hill he called Monticello (little mountain), near Shadwell. The top of the hill was leveled and construction began in 1769 on the first phase, a one-room house, finished late that same year. This was the beginning of an architectural career as brilliant as that of any American of his time.

In 1770 Shadwell burned, destroying all of Jefferson's papers and library. Because of the loss of the papers, little documentation of his earlier years exists. Of the later years, the information is voluminous in his own journals, in the thousands of his letters that have been preserved, and from other sources. In addition, over 500 of his architectural drawings have survived. He immediately began to assemble a second library that eventually had some 6,000 volumes. This second collection was sold to the United States, at about half its value, to form the basis of the Library of Congress, replacing the books that had been burned by the British in the War of 1812. Jefferson moved to Monticello and continued work on his house.

During his lifetime, Jefferson designed a number of other houses, a church, two courthouses, all of them notable, and in addition to Monticello, two other masterpieces, the State Capitol at Richmond and the University of Virginia.

In 1772 Jefferson married a widow, Margaret Wayles Skelton. It was a happy marriage, producing a son and five daughters, but only Martha and Mary lived to maturity. Jefferson's wife died 10 years later and he never remarried.

Political Career Jefferson's brilliant career as a politician and statesman started with his election to the Virginia House of Burgesses, where he served from 1769 to 1775, and ended with his two terms as president of the United States (1801–09). During the interim, he had been a delegate to the Continental Congress (1775–76) in Philadelphia, for which he wrote the Declaration of Independence, and again a delegate (1783–85); had been governor of Virginia (1779–81); and had written the Virginia Statute of Religious Freedom. He served as U.S. Minister to France (1785–89), during which he enlarged his architectural knowledge; as U.S. secretary of state (1790–93), during the presidency of George Washington (1732–99); and as vice president (1797–1801), during the presidency of John Adams (1735–1826).

During all this time, Jefferson continued his architectural work. He had turned official Washington architecture away from the Georgian toward Classical Revival, in particular Roman Revival which he thought a fitting style for the new republic. He had, in fact, come close to becoming the designer of the White House, then called the President's House, placing second in a competition he had entered anonymously, which was won by James Hoban (c. 1762–1831). Later, as president (1801–09), he made designs for additions, including the garden front portico to the house.

In 1809, when his second term as president ended, Jefferson returned to Monticello to stay. Years before he had said, "All my wishes end, where I hope my days will end, at Monticello." He had turned away from politics, which he had served so well, as he had earlier turned away from law. He could now spend his days in the place he loved and in the way he wished to live, in study and contemplation, in invention and design and building, both on his own house and buildings for others. And the grand finale of his architectural work began.

Model University For many years, Jefferson had been thinking about the design of a model university. By 1805, while he was still president, he had come up with a scheme that envisioned a university as a small village in which professors and students lived and worked, with a great library as its focal point. He asked Benjamin Henry Latrobe and William Thornton (1759–1828), who had designed the U.S. Capitol, to think about the design and advise him. With some help from their ideas, Jefferson chose a building with a dome for the library, the central feature of the plan. The design of this building, however, was Jefferson's.

The construction of the university began in 1817 and was completed in 1825. Though somewhat aged, Jefferson supervised the work until its completion, in person, and with the aid of a telescope mounted on the terrace at Monticello.

During his last years, his happiness in being at Monticello and with his studies and work was marred by financial troubles with which he was never able to deal with properly, and later with ill health.

In 1824 he entertained the Marquis de Lafayette (1757–1834), an old friend, at Monticello and at a formal dinner in the still-unfinished Rotunda. By 1825, when Lafayette returned from his trip to the Western United States to say his farewells, Jefferson was so weak that he had to receive him while lying on a couch. His condition worsened during the next few months, and on July 4, 1826, the fiftieth anniversary of the signing of the Declaration of Independence, Jefferson died.

He had lived a life full of accomplishment, unequaled by that of any other American before or since. And he had written his own epitaph, which now appears on his gravestone at Monticello: "Here was buried THOMAS JEFFERSON Author of the Declaration of American Independence of the Statute of Virginia for Religious Freedom and Father of the University of Virginia."

Related Articles CLASSIC REVIVAL ARCHITECTURE; GEORGIAN ARCHITECTURE; LATROBE, BENJAMIN HENRY; MILLS, ROBERT.
Further Reading Guinness, Desmond, and Julius Trousdale Sadler, Jr.: *Mr. Jefferson: Architect*, Viking, New York, 1973; Kimball, Fiske: *Thomas Jefferson: Architect*, Riverside Press, Boston, 1916.

JENNEY, WILLIAM LE BARON

American engineer and architect (1832–1907). Although trained as an engineer rather than as an architect, and though his talents were mostly in engineering rather than in architecture, William Le Baron Jenney became one of the most influential architects of his time. Probably because of his interest in and knowledge of structural engineering, Jenney was the first proponent of the early style for tall buildings of the group of architects who came to be known as the Chicago school. Never a school, in the real sense of the word, these architects, led by Jenney, began to design buildings late in the 19th century, utilizing iron and later steel skeleton structures. As time went on, they designed the exteriors of their buildings to express the structure underneath, instead of attempting to adapt older traditional styles to the new tall buildings. These then were some of the earliest antecedents of what was to become modern architecture.

Jenney led the way, both in his own buildings and in his influence on younger architects of the Chicago school. In fact, of the five most influential younger men, four, Louis Henri Sullivan (1856–1924), Martin Roche (1855–1927), William Holabird (1854–1923), and Daniel Hudson Burnham (1846–1912), had worked in Jenney's office. Only John Wellborn Root (1850–91) had not worked for Jenney, but he was influenced by his partner, Burnham. All were to become fine architects in their own right and all were to contribute to the progress of the Chicago school and the movement toward modern architecture. Much earlier than in any other American city, they were to establish solid principles for the design of modern skyscrapers.

Works What Jenney and the others were beginning to develop became apparent in his First Leiter Store (1879) and was further developed in the Second Leiter Store (1891), now a Sears Roebuck store, both in Chicago. The latter had a boldness and vitality not seen before. Jenney continued the development in other Chicago buildings, the Manhattan Building (1890), the Fair Store (1891), now a Montgomery Ward store, and the Ludington Building (1891). In 1885 Jenney's masterpiece, the 10-story Home Insurance Company Building, was completed. This was a real breakthrough. Some call it the first skyscraper. The structure utilized cast-iron and wrought-iron columns, and wrought-iron and steel beams, the first use of Bessemer steel in a building, though it had been used previously in bridges. This was also the first building in which both floors and exterior masonry walls were supported by the metal skeleton. Consid-

JENNEY, WILLIAM LE BARON Manhattan Building (1890), Chicago, III. *(Hedrich-Blessing)*

JENNEY, WILLIAM LE BARON Sears Roebuck Store, formerly the Second Leiter Store (1891), Chicago, III. *(Hedrich-Blessing)*

ered the most important building of its era, and one of the most important in American history, the building was demolished in 1931.

The Isabella Building (1893) and the Association, or Central YMCA, Building (1893), both in Chicago, were the last of Jenney's buildings to maintain the high standards of design he had reached. It seemed that he had pioneered as far as he could, and the later buildings were anticlimax. Jenney had already proved himself an original structural designer, not overly concerned with the esthetic qualities of his buildings, but a creative architect who was unafraid to break with precedent. He had set an example for innovative work to be done by later architects.

Life William Le Baron Jenney was born in Fairhaven, Mass., on September 25, 1832. The son of a wealthy whaling fleet owner, Jenney had a first-rate education in engineering, studying for two years at the Lawrence Scientific School at Harvard University. In 1853 he went to the École Centrale des Arts et Manufactures in Paris and was graduated in 1856.

He was a daring man, a trait he was to demonstrate in his buildings. Before going to Paris, he had participated in the gold rush of 1849, and later in the construction of a railroad in Panama. In 1861 he entered the Union Army as an engineer and served during the Civil War until 1866. His army career was exemplary. He rose rapidly in rank to major, a title he was to use the rest of his life, and served on the staffs of generals Ulysses S. Grant (1822–85) and William Tecumseh Sherman (1820–91).

Jenney went to Chicago in 1867, and opened his office the following year. He practiced in Chicago the rest of his life. His first buildings were not impressive, but he rapidly developed the style of architecture that was to become the hallmark of the Chicago school.

Jenney was considered by those who knew him to be an easygoing, impressive gentleman and gourmet. He enjoyed being a guest but enjoyed even more being a host. He was a cultured man, learned in science and history as well as in his chosen profession. He gave interesting lectures, among them a series at the Chicago University in 1883 that was published in *Inland Architect and Builder* in 1883–84.

In both the number and the consistent excellence of his buildings, 1891 was the high point in Jenney's career. In that year, he took in William B. Mundie (1863–1939) as a partner, an arrangement that was to last until Jenney's death. In 1905 he took in another partner, Elmer C. Jensen (1870–1955), who had worked for him since 1885. The firm then became Jenney, Mundie and Jensen, but only two years later, on June 15, 1907, Jenney died. Though mainly an engineer, he had not failed to make a lasting mark on architecture of his time and the future. He left a legacy in his buildings and in those he had helped train to carry on.

Related Articles BURNHAM AND ROOT; HOLABIRD AND ROCHE; MODERN ARCHITECTURE; SULLIVAN, LOUIS HENRI.

JOHNSON, PHILIP CORTELYOU American architect (1906–). Having become an architect relatively late, after graduating in architecture from Harvard in 1943, when he was thirty-seven years old, Johnson nevertheless has had a great influence on the architecture of his time. As a writer, critic, and lecturer on architecture, and as director of the department of architecture of the Museum of Modern Art, New York City, Johnson and his ideas made a considerable impact on architecture and architects.

International Style With critic and historian Henry-Russell Hitchcock (1903–), Johnson invented the term International style to denote what they considered to be important developments in modern architecture that were leading toward building designs that were simple, unadorned, and expressed their structure with modern materials. In their view, these trends, adopted by architects all over the world would lead to a modern architecture devoid of local or regional characteristics.

Johnson and Hitchcock collaborated on a book espousing this position, *The International Style —Architecture Since 1922,* published in 1932. And that same year, Johnson organized the first International Exhibition of Modern Architecture at the Musuem of Modern Art. Johnson believed that the architecture of Ludwig Mies van der Rohe (1886–1969), who had emigrated to the United States from Germany and had become director of the architecture school at the Illinois Institute of Technology, Chicago, was the epitome of the International style. Mies decried the phrase and even the word *style* in his work, but the book and exhibition were very influential. Many architects and critics espoused the cause, but later many were to declare that while some of the principles may have been valid, there never really was an International style.

Works After becoming an architect, Johnson designed mostly houses for a while. He continued to write and lecture and he continued his interest in and espousal of the work of Mies. Johnson incorporated his principles in a house he built for himself (1949) in New Canaan, Conn. Three years were spent in its design and the resulting glass-enclosed house brought its architect much recognition and is still considered one of his best buildings. (See also color section.)

Johnson continued to design other buildings, mostly houses, which demonstrated the principles of the International style. Some of his best houses of that period were the Hodgson (1951), Ball (1953), and Wiley (1953), all in New Canaan; Leonhardt (1956), Lloyd's Neck, Long Island, N.Y.; and the Boissonnas (1956) in New Canaan. Beginning with his houses, Johnson's influence began to spread by means of his designs as it had previously through his writing, lectures, and other work.

JOHNSON, PHILIP Johnson house (1949), New Canaan, Conn.
(Ezra Stoller)

JOHNSON, PHILIP Asia House (1959), New York, N.Y. *(Joseph W. Molitor)*

JOHNSON, PHILIP Kline Science Tower (1964), Yale University, New Haven, Conn. *(Joseph W. Molitor)*

Johnson designed a new wing (1950) for the Museum of Modern Art, designed its sculpture garden (1953), and added another wing (1964). He also designed a number of nonresidential buildings, including the Kneses Tifereth Israel Synagogue (1956), Port Chester, N.Y.; University of St. Thomas auditorium and classrooms (1957), Houston, Tex.; the Roofless Church (1960), New Harmony, Ind.; and two art museums, the Munson-Proctor-Williams (1960), Utica, N.Y., and the Amon Carter Museum of Western Art (1961), Ft. Worth, Tex. He designed buildings of other types, including the Nuclear Reactor (1961), Rehovot, Israel; the New York State Theater (1964) at the Lincoln Center for the Performing Arts, New York City; and the Kline Science Tower (1964), Yale University, New Haven, Conn. He also was associated with Mies van der Rohe on the great Seagram Building (1958; see illustration in the color section), New York City, a commission which he helped Mies to obtain, and he designed an elegant restaurant, the Four Seasons (see illustration in article restaurant), which is located in the building.

Philip Johnson has not designed a large number of buildings during his career, but those he designed have continued to have considerable influence on architecture. His early theories of an International style have been largely superseded. But few architects of Johnson's era have been able to approach the crisp elegance, the sophistication of his best designs. And Johnson is still producing such designs. One of his latest, designed with John Henry Burgee (1933–   ), the twin towers of Pennzoil Place (1976), Houston, Tex., has been widely acclaimed.

Life Philip Cortelyou Johnson was born in Cleveland, Ohio, on July 8, 1906. He attended Harvard University at various times beginning in 1923 and graduated with an A.B. in 1930. He was interested in the arts, particularly in architecture, though he had no intention of becoming an architect. After the Museum of Modern Art was chartered in 1929, Johnson became its first director of architecture in 1930. In this position, he became familiar with the modern buildings of the time and with the architects who were designing them. He also became familiar with many of the architecture critics of the day, and he started to write critical articles and books.

In 1932 Johnson and Henry-Russell Hitchcock published their book on the International style and it had great influence on the modern movement in architecture. Johnson continued to write critical articles on

JOHNSON, PHILIP Exterior, Johnson Museum (1966), New Canaan, Conn. *(Ezra Stoller)*

JOHNSON, PHILIP Interior, Johnson Museum (1966), New Canaan, Conn. *(Ezra Stoller)*

architecture. In 1936 he left his position at the Museum of Modern Art and traveled in Europe studying the new architecture firsthand. Returning to the United States, he entered the Graduate School of Design at Harvard University and received his architectural degree in 1943. At age thirty-seven, he had finally embarked on his career as an architect. Before graduation though, he had designed his first houses and continued designing others after leaving Harvard.

In 1946 Johnson returned to the Museum of Modern Art as director of the department of architecture and design, and remained there until 1954. He continued designing houses during this time, including his own famous glass house. By this time, he had become deeply interested in and impressed by the architecture of Mies van der Rohe and wrote the first important American book on his work, published in 1947 and revised in 1953.

Johnson continued to write and to design houses, but after 1956 began to devote a major portion of his energies and talents to other building types. Since that time, he has designed buildings of many types in a number of locations in the United States and abroad. Many of these have been significant examples of contemporary architecture. Some have felt that there was a period in Johnson's career during the late 1960s and early 1970s when his work was less interesting than it had been before. That may be, but his later work, designed in partnership with John Burgee, has brought worldwide recognition. For the excellence of his architecture, Philip Cortelyou Johnson received the highest award of the American Institute of Architects, the Gold Medal, in 1978.

Related Articles CONTEMPORARY ARCHITECTURE; EXPOSITION [for illustration of New York State Pavilion, New York World's Fair (1964–65)]; MIES VAN DER ROHE, LUDWIG; MODERN ARCHITECTURE.

Further Reading Hitchcock, Henry-Russell, Jr., and Philip Johnson: *The International Style—Architecture Since 1922*, Norton, New York, 1932; Jacobus, John M., Jr.: *Philip Johnson*, Braziller, New York, 1962; Johnson, Philip C.: *Mies van der Rohe*, 2d rev. ed., Museum of Modern Art, New York, 1953.

KAHN, ALBERT German-American architect (1869–1942). Emigrating with his family from Germany when he was eleven, Albert Kahn received his professional training from apprenticeship in an architect's office and from a year's study in Europe on a scholarship. Starting out as an eclecticist, Kahn continued to design in various styles all his life, except on industrial buildings or factories, in which he became one of the greatest pioneers of modern architecture. In the practice of architecture he was also a pioneer, developing one of the largest and most successful offices ever. His office became a complete entity, handling all phases of the architectural and engineering work for his buildings.

Innovative Factory Design Beginning in 1903, Kahn started a long series of innovative factories of reinforced concrete and steel. He introduced factories that were all under one roof and later factories that were all on one floor, revolutionary techniques at that time. At the time, factory design in most offices was relegated to junior draftsmen. Kahn introduced rigorous planning into his factories, designed by himself and by the best designers in his office, including Ernest Wilby, a good designer who worked with him from 1903 to 1908.

Kahn was the first architect to use industrial steel sash, which had to be imported from Europe, with a concrete frame. He helped develop buildings to house continuously moving assembly lines. Kahn originated the practice, later almost standard in factories, of maximum natural lighting and ventilation through the use of continuous bands of windows, skylights, and roof monitors. Over the years, Kahn introduced many structural innovations in both concrete and steel, including the use of long, flat-span trusses to provide interior spaces unobstructed by columns.

Works Among the milestone industrial buildings of Albert Kahn, the earliest was the Packard Motor Car Company Plant (1903), Detroit, in which he used steel sash in a concrete-framed building. This was followed by another first, a building for Ford Motor Company (1909) in Highland Park, Mich., in which the Ford production line was housed under one roof. Kahn added several other buildings at this plant, culminating in a building (1918) with cantilevered balconies inside to facilitate handling of materials and parts. In 1926 Walter Adolf Gropius (1883–1969), one of the European

architects who had become interested in the work of Kahn, used similar balconies in his Bauhaus at Dessau, Germany. Other important buildings of this era were the plants for Burroughs Adding Machine Company (1919), Detroit, and Fisher Body Company (1921), Cleveland, Ohio.

Starting in 1917, Kahn produced a number of buildings for the large Ford River Rouge Plant, Detroit. The first of these, called Building B, was revolutionary. A half-mile long, the building sheltered the entire assembly line for automobiles in a steel frame enclosed entirely with windows. In the De Soto Division Press Shop of Chrysler Corporation (1936), Detroit, Kahn produced an elegant design utilizing large trusses beneath which glass curtain walls enclosed the interior. In 1938 he produced similar elegance in the Half-Ton Truck Plant of the Dodge Division of Chrysler. This time, the effect came from long-span trusses, butterfly monitors on the roof, and curtain walls. The Ohio Steel Foundry Company Building (1938), Lima, Ohio, is similar in design.

Then came the great World War II war plants. Among these were the large bomber plant for Glenn L. Martin Company (1937), Baltimore, and the even larger, in fact the largest in the world, Willow Run Bomber Plant for Ford (1943; see illustration in article factory), later converted to automobile manufacture and assembly. In the latter, because of wartime blackout regulations, Kahn turned away from glass-curtain walls to a windowless, artifically lighted factory. Other important wartime buildings were American Steel Foundries Cast Iron Plant (1941), East Chicago, Ind., and American Locomotive Company Machine Shop (1942), Auburn, N.Y.

Albert Kahn, in a career that lasted 57 years, worked right up to the time of his death in 1942. He had accomplished a great deal. He had made factory buildings into architecture, his own best architecture. His other nonindustrial buildings, which seemed to him to be of a higher order, never actually approached the excellence of his factories. In the factories, he influenced the growth of modern architecture at home and abroad.

Life Albert Kahn was born in Rhaunen, Germany, on March 2, 1869, the oldest of six children of a rabbi and teacher. Kahn's family emigrated to the United States, settling in Detroit in 1880. As a youth, he wanted first to become a musician, then an artist. By

KAHN, ALBERT Chrysler Corp. Plant (1936), Detroit, Mich. *(Hedrich-Blessing)*

KAHN, ALBERT Chrysler Corp. Plant (1938), Warren, Mich. *(Hedrich-Blessing)*

the time he was sixteen, however, the family had eight children and to help out, Kahn took a job in 1885 as office boy in the architect's office of Mason and Rice in Detroit. He soon became a draftsman. In 1891 Kahn won a scholarship for a year of travel and study in Europe. In Florence, he met Henry Bacon (1866–1924), later to become a noted architect himself, and also on a scholarship. The two young men traveled together through Italy, France, Belgium, and Germany, sketching and studying.

Back from his travels, Kahn was to practice in Detroit the rest of his life. He returned to the office of

Mason and Rice, where he remained until 1896. In that year, he married Ernestine Krolik and formed a partnership with George W. Nettleton and Alexander B. Trowbridge, who left in 1897 to become dean of the Cornell University College of Architecture. The two remaining partners continued on until the death of Nettleton in 1900. For a short time, he then had a partnership with his old employer, George D. Mason (1856–1948), but it was dissolved in 1902. During these years, the work of Kahn and the others was eclectic and Kahn continued designing most of his buildings in this manner the remainder of his life. His industrial buildings were something else again. From a rather inauspicious beginning with a building for a machine company in 1901, Kahn was to design numerous industrial buildings for many of the great American companies, including Ford, General Motors, and Chrysler. Most were innovative and experimental, many of them daring and creative.

In 1929 a Russian commission visiting Detroit was so impressed with Kahn's work, they asked him to design a tractor plant (1930) in Stalingrad. This building was so successful that the Soviet government hired Kahn to help industrialize Russia. For this purpose, he sent over a group of architects and engineers from his office, under the direction of his brother, Moritz Kahn. In two years, they built 521 factories all over the Soviet Union and trained over 1,000 Russian engineers and technicians to handle the work.

For many years, Kahn was commissioner of the Detroit Institute of Fine Arts. In this capacity, he was able to have Paul Philippe Cret (1876–1945) of Philadelphia chosen as architect for the Institute Building (1927).

Kahn's office rapidly expanded, including about 400 people by 1938. The office was then handling about one-fifth of all the architect-designed industrial work being done in the United States. The office handled all the architectural, structural, and other engineering work. Improved techniques shortened the necessary time for making working drawings. When World War II began, the office expanded to about 600 people and was plunged into the design of a large number of factories for war production. In addition, the office did naval bases in Alaska, Hawaii, Puerto Rico, Midway Island, and Jacksonville, Fla.

Active all his life, the heavy burden and long hours of the war work proved too much. Under strain and overtired, he contracted a bronchial ailment and died on December 8, 1942. The organization he had built so well survived to continue the work he started and, as Albert Kahn Associates, is still in practice today.

Related Articles BACON, HENRY; CRET, PAUL PHILIPPE; FACTORY; MODERN ARCHITECTURE.

Further Reading *Legacy of Albert Kahn,* the Detroit Institute of Fine Arts, 1970.

KAHN, LOUIS ISADORE

KAHN, LOUIS ISADORE Estonian-American architect (1901–74). Although he only designed slightly more than 100 buildings, many of which were never built, Louis Isadore Kahn was one of the most notable and influential 20th-century architects. Much of his time was spent in study, contemplation, and introspection. He wrote little, but he did manage to impart to his students and to others a philosophy, which some have called more poetry than philosophy, of an architecture that would serve people and at the same time be a high form of art.

Philosophy Louis Kahn's designs illustrate his philosophy. They are bold forms, composed of masses and voids, with the materials, the structure, and even the mechanical and other engineering aspects strongly expressed. He said he depended mostly on inspiration, not on knowledge. He favored no style, no methods, no technology. Instead, he sought to find out what the building wants to be; or what a brick wants to be. He was something of a mystic, even a guru, who led his students and other followers toward order in architecture, the sense of the relationships and bonds between all things. And a very creative and personal kind of architecture it produced. He worked closely, for the last two decades of his life, with the noted engineer August E. Komendant.

Kahn believed that in the complete set of laws of nature, which of course no one understands, there exists a force than can produce order in architecture as well as in everything else. During his career, he made a great number of speeches, or rather they might be called lectures, to students, fellow professionals, and others. His message was cryptic and had to be sensed more than understood. Those who received the message properly believe it is expressed in his designs. Although the believers are many, there are some who have doubts about his philosophy, if not about his buildings.

Works After he began his own practice in 1935, Kahn designed a small number of buildings during the next decade other than government housing projects. His first important commission was the Art Gallery (1953), Yale University, New Haven, Conn. This brought him to the attention of architects but brought only a few new commissions. Then came a wave of publicity about a new and controversial design on which he was working, the Alfred Newton Richards Medical Research Building (1961; see illustration in color section), at the University of Pennsylvania. Controversial the building may have been and still is to some extent, but many have come to consider it Kahn's best design and one of the best of its era.

Other commissions started to come in. Kahn designed about 20 houses, about half of which were built. During the next few years, he designed a number of notable buildings, including the Tribune-Review Newspaper Plant (1961), Greensburg, Pa., and the Indian Institute of Management (1963), Ahmedabad, India. Then he designed what has been called his masterpiece, the Salk Institute for Biological Studies (1965), La Jolla, Calif., for the world-famed inventor of the polio vaccine, Dr. Jonas Edward Salk (1914–   ).

During the next decade, Kahn designed other notable buildings, including Temple Beth El (1966), Chappaqua, N.Y.; the First Unitarian Church (1967), Rochester, N.Y.; the Olivetti-Underwood Factory (1970), Harrisburg, Pa.; the Kimbell Art Museum (1972), Fort Worth, Tex.; the Library and Dining Hall (1972) at Phillips Exeter Academy, Exeter, N.H.; and a great master plan and buildings for the capital at Dacca, East Pakistan, now Bangladesh, part of which was still under construction when he died. His last building was the British Art Center (1976), Yale University, New Haven, Conn.

Life Louis Isadore Kahn was born on February 20, 1901, on the island of Saaremaa (Oesel), Estonia. Al-

KAHN, LOUIS   Salk Institute (1965), La Jolla, Calif. *(Ezra Stoller)*

KAHN, LOUIS   First Unitarian Church (1967), Rochester, N.Y. *(Wayne Andrews)*

KAHN, LOUIS Kimbell Art Museum (1972), Fort Worth, Tex. *(Ezra Stoller)*

though Estonia was later incorporated into the Soviet Union, Kahn always insisted he was an Estonian, not a Russian. In 1905 the family emigrated to the United States and settled in Philadelphia. In 1915 Kahn became a naturalized U.S. citizen. Having graduated from the Industrial Art School of Philadelphia in 1917, he spent the next three years studying at the Pennsylvania Academy of Fine Arts, receiving a number of prizes for drawing and painting. He then enrolled in the architectural school of the University of Pennsylvania in 1920, was a student of Paul Philippe Cret (1876–1945), and graduated in 1924.

After working in an architectural office for a short time, he became the chief designer for the Sesquicentennial Exposition (1925–26) in Philadelphia. During the next few years he traveled and studied in Europe, returning to Philadelphia in 1929, during the Depression. In 1930 and later, he worked in the office of Paul Philippe Cret, who had been his teacher. In that same year, he married Esther Virginia Israeli and they had one daughter. In 1931 he organized a number of unemployed architects and engineers into the Architectural Research Group, which studied planning, housing, and other problems.

In 1935 Kahn started his own practice and later was associated in practice with George Howe (1886–1955) from 1941 to 1943 and with Oskar Stonorov (1905–70) in 1942–43. Kahn served in various civic positions most of his professional life, starting with his appointment as consultant architect for the Philadelphia Housing Authority in 1937, and then for the U.S. Housing Authority in 1939. Never a man to let one area of activity satisfy him, Kahn continued his practice over the next years and still found time to serve as consultant architect to the Philadelphia Planning Commission, a position he held six years starting in 1946 and then again in 1961. He became professor of architecture at Yale University, New Haven, Conn., in 1947, remaining there until 1952, with time out for a year as resident architect of the American Academy in

Rome, Italy (1950–51). He was a professor at Massachusetts Institute of Technology, Cambridge, in 1956. In 1957 he was appointed professor of architecture at his alma mater, the University of Pennsylvania, a position he held until 1971.

Although Kahn was considered something of a mystic, private and reserved in manner and introverted, his philosophy and his architecture made him world famous. His buildings that were constructed, and even some of those that were not, had an impact on architects and architecture completely out of proportion to their number. His later life was filled with almost every honor that might come to an architect: seven honorary doctor's degrees; exhibits of his work; and election to the National Institute of Arts and Letters, to the Royal Swedish Academy of Fine Arts, and to fellowship in the American Academy of Arts and Sciences and the Royal Society of Arts of England. In 1971 the architects of his adopted country gave him their highest honor, the Gold Medal of the American Institute of Architects. The following year, the architects of Great Britain gave him theirs, the Royal Gold Medal of the Royal Institute of British Architects.

In 1974 Louis Isadore Kahn was at the pinnacle of his career. He had several interesting projects under way, including a redevelopment project in Iran and the buildings at Dacca, Bangladesh. Returning from a trip to Bangladesh and India, Kahn reached New York's Pennsylvania Station to take a train back to Philadelphia, collapsed with a heart attack, and died on March 17, 1974.

Related Articles CRET, PAUL PHILIPPE; EDUCATION; MODERN ARCHITECTURE.

Further Reading Giurgola, Romaldo, and Jaimini Mehta: *Louis I. Kahn,* Westview Press, Boulder, Col., 1975; Komendant, August E.: *18 Years with Architect Louis Kahn,* Aloray Publishers, Englewood, N.J., 1975; Scully, Vincent, Jr.: *Louis I. Kahn,* Braziller, N.Y., 1962; Wurman, Richard Saul, and Eugene Feldman, eds.: *The Notebooks and Drawings of Louis I. Kahn,* 2d ed., MIT Press, Cambridge, Mass., 1974.

LABORATORY A building, group of buildings, or room, used for scientific experiments or other research and testing. Laboratories, or research buildings, have become an important building type only in the last 50 years or so. Research had previously been carried on mostly in buildings not specifically designed as laboratories.

Types Research is often divided into basic or fundamental, sometimes called pure, research and applied research. Basic research is concerned with the discovery of basic laws of nature, while applied research is concerned with the application of basic knowledge to practical problems or needs. Regardless of the type of research, laboratories must be designed to allow the activities to be carried out efficiently and effectively. Laboratories are used by many organizations that sponsor and perform research, including governments, associations, universities, businesses, and foundations. Laboratories are used in every discipline or field of human knowledge and endeavor, including the biological and chemical sciences, mathematics, agriculture, education, physical sciences, medicine, engineering, social sciences, business, and industry.

Elements The design of a laboratory begins with the classification of the research to be performed: (1) the principal science, as in chemistry or agriculture; (2) the activity, as either basic or applied research; and (3) the field of investigation, as in fuels or fertilizers. The major elements of a laboratory are the research areas, the administrative areas, the support areas, and the service facilities.

The research areas contain rooms, called laboratories, with necessary benches and other equipment for the type of work to be done. In many cases, laboratories require an environment in which temperatures, humidity, air purity, and other factors can be controlled. Frequently there are requirements for special

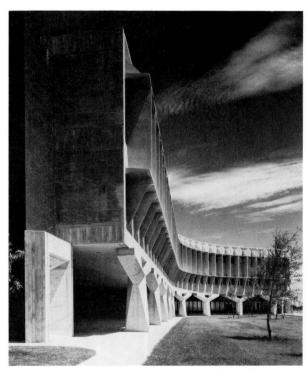

LABORATORY IBM (1974), Boca Raton, Fla. [*Architects: Marcel Breuer and Robert Gatje. (Joseph W. Molitor)*]

LABORATORY Multicategorical Research (1974), Cornell University, Ithaca, N.Y. [*Architect: Ulrich Franzen. (Norman McGrath)*]

LABORATORY Environmental Laboratory, National Oceanic and Atmospheric Administration (1973), Miami, Fla. [*Architects: Ferendino, Grafton, Spillis and Candela. (Joseph W. Molitor)*]

services, such as steam, distilled water, compressed air, vacuum, and other systems. Offices or desk space and meeting rooms are needed.

Administrative areas contain offices and other related rooms. Support areas may include an auditorium, lecture rooms, library, computer room, cafeteria, and so on. Service areas include provisions for electrical and mechanical equipment, shops, and other rooms for service and maintenance. In addition, laboratories require special facilities for washing or cleaning equipment; disposal of harmful wastes; and receiving, storage, and shipping. Some need special provisions for animal quarters, radiology, nuclear work, photography, and other operations.

The design of a laboratory is involved with the provision of all the many diverse requirements in a building, where the researchers and other staff may perform their experiments under controlled conditions, safely, effectively, and comfortably. Designs must allow for flexibility, not only of the laboratory building but individual spaces within the building. The complex and demanding requirements of laboratory design are challenging and rewarding to architects.

History Research has always been carried on by members of the human race. Until the 16th century, true research, which involves experimentation, did not exist on a wide scale. During the 16th century and afterward, researchers worked as individuals in small rooms, which might be called the first laboratories, of their own or provided by their patrons. One of these men, the English philosopher Sir Francis Bacon (1561–1626), was the first to cite the need for organized research. His idea did not come to fruition until the latter part of the 19th century.

American Development In the American colonies, as in Europe and elsewhere at the time, there was no real research and no laboratories. The first laboratories were founded by individual American researchers, mostly inventors, starting in the late 1800s. They were followed by research activities in universities. One of the first real research laboratories was built by the Bell Telephone Company at about this time. A tremendous boost to organized research was given by the establishment of the U.S. National Research Council in 1916. Subsequently, a number of laboratories were built, but with the advent of World War II, laboratory construction boomed and today has become a major building type.

Further Reading *Architectural Record: Buildings for Research,* F. W. Dodge, New York, 1958; Ferguson, W. R.: *Practical Laboratory Planning,* John Wiley, New York, 1973.

LANDSCAPE ARCHITECTURE The art and science of the design, planning, and construction of outdoor spaces around buildings, including gardens, plazas, and outdoor furniture and fixtures.

A person who has been educated to practice landscape architecture is called a landscape architect, or sometimes a land planner or site planner. A landscape architect is primarily responsible for the design and construction of the outdoor spaces around and between buildings and in other places, such as parks and playgrounds. The work of a landscape architect on one project may entail only the land planning and landscaping for a single building; on another it may include similar work for a large residential development or other complex. Landscape architects design small city squares and great national parks. Some work on even larger projects, such as in city or regional planning.

Functions For buildings, a landscape architect's major responsibilities include establishment of proper relationships between buildings and between buildings and features of their sites, shapes and grades of the land, planning of various areas of sites, and design of walkways, driveways, walls, fences, steps, fountains, pools, and planting arrangements. In all of these functions, the landscape architect works closely with the architects, and sometimes with civil engineers.

Landscape architects perform another important function, the study and evaluation of land to determine its usefulness for buildings or other purposes. In this work, they consider the effects of the composition of the subsurface soil; the surface soil, or topsoil; surface characteristics of the topography, or form, of the land; vegetation; climate; views; landmarks; and water-supply proximity to other buildings.

Work Phases Landscape architects work for governmental agencies, as consultants, or in architectural firms. Some, including practitioners, teach. As consultants, they often are engaged by architects to handle the landscape work. When performing this function, landscape architects generally follow the same phases as the architects, that is, schematic, in which studies, preliminary drawings, specifications, and cost estimates are prepared; design development, in which refinements are made; and construction document, in which final drawings and specifications are prepared, from which the actual construction may be performed; and a more refined estimate is made. Finally comes the construction phase, in which landscape architects inspect the site and landscaping work to ensure that it is properly constructed. A landscape architect may be called upon for other services when required on specific projects.

For people who are naturally imaginative and creative, yet practical and of sound judgment, landscape architecture can offer a fulfilling and exciting career. Not only does it offer ample opportunity for creative design, it also is a functional art in which the creative aspects can be put to practical purposes.

Education In addition to the usual college preparatory secondary school courses, students should take courses in biology and botany if possible. In college, they take general courses in humanities, social sciences, mathematics, and sciences. They also take courses in design, history of art and architecture, site planning, construction materials, and specialized courses in landscape architecture. There are only a few landscape architecture schools in the United States, and most of these operate as part of architectural schools.

History The exact time of the beginning of landscape architecture, or landscape gardening as it was called for a long time, is hidden in ancient history. However, from hieroglyphs, tomb paintings, and other sources, it seems apparent that humans may

have begun cultivating gardens for their pleasure as early as the Neolithic period, beginning about the 50th century B.C. in the Middle East. Egyptian nobles placed pools, trees, and other plants around their houses no later than the 26th century B.C. And the hanging gardens of Nebuchadnezzar II (d. 562 B.C.), king (605–562 B.C.) of Babylon, are famous.

Little is known about ancient Greek gardens except that they existed and that they contained trees, vineyards, and flowers. The Romans created numerous parks and gardens as well as private gardens, not only in Rome but in conquered areas, such as Constantinople, now Istanbul. Other early gardens of importance were established in such places as Persia, now Iran, and in Japan, beginning about the third century A.D.

Little is known of the gardens of the Middle Ages, except that they were usually enclosed with walls, as were monasteries, castles, and towns, and were mostly simple in design and contained a small number of types of plants and flowers. During the Renaissance, landscape gardening flourished and the term landscape gardener came into use to denote a person who designed and constructed gardens. Great gardens, plazas, and parks, intended mostly for use of the nobility and the wealthy, were designed and constructed in cities and for town houses and country villas. In France and Italy, landscape gardening produced a great number of magnificent gardens; and in England, examples that were great but not as spectacular as those on the European continent.

During the 18th century, landscape gardeners in England designed gardens to produce an illusion of foreign, exotic, or old places, such as a Chinese or ancient Greek garden. This type of garden, which the French called *le jardin Anglais*, was soon built in France and elsewhere in Europe. These too were gardens for the wealthy and the nobility. And they soon became more picturesque than formal, designed to be beautiful, not functional.

American Development The early colonists started gardens soon after reaching America. Most were simple in concept and were built near private houses. New England gardens featured a device called a forthright, which was a path leading from the house lengthwise through the garden. After a few years, the colonists also began to build civic gardens, most of which were based on the formal models of earlier gardens in Europe.

One of the first American landscape architects, though he did not call himself that, Andrew Jackson Downing (1815–52), turned away from formalism toward more natural or picturesque landscape design. As the editor of *The Horticulturist* (1846–52), as the author of several books, and as the landscape architect for the U.S. Capitol, the Smithsonian Institution, and the White House, all in 1849 and all located in Washington, Downing exerted considerable influence on landscape architecture in the United States. Before his untimely death at age thirty-seven in a steamboat accident on the Hudson River, he also practiced architecture for a time in partnership with Calvert Vaux (1824–95), who later became the partner of the dominant figure in landscape architecture of the time, Frederick Law Olmsted (1822–1903). Olmsted was the first person to sign his drawings as a landscape architect and he designed a great many parks, including, with Vaux, Central Park, New York City. Olmsted rejected the idea that landscape design was only for the wealthy and powerful and established the first parks in the United States that were intended for the people.

Olmsted continued to practice until the latter part of the 19th century and more than anyone else was responsible for the establishment of landscape architecture as a profession. He also deeply influenced landscape design. His son, Frederick Law Olmsted, Jr. (1870–1957), and his stepson, John Charles Olmsted (1852–1920), became famous landscape architects, as did his partner Charles Eliot (1860–97). His two sons, together with nine others, established the professional organization, the American Society of Landscape Architects, in 1899. And in 1900 the first professional school of landscape architecture was founded at Harvard University, Cambridge, Mass., and named for his former partner, Charles Eliot.

The profession of landscape architecture has since become well established and has made great progress, not only in the landscaping of individual buildings and groups of buildings but in land planning and city and regional planning. Some of the noted landscape architects of the 20th century are Garrett Eckbo (1910–), Daniel Urban Kiley (1912–), John Ormsbee Simonds (1913–), Lawrence Halprin (1916–), Hideo Sasaki (1919–), and Ian McHarg (1920–).

Related Articles ECOLOGY; FOUNTAIN; GARDEN; OLMSTED, FREDERICK LAW; PARK; PLANNING, CITY; SITE PLANNING.

Further Reading Clifford, Derek: *A History of Garden Design*, Praeger, New York, 1963; Eckbo, Garrett: *Home Landscape—The Art of Home Landscaping*, rev., McGraw-Hill, 1978; Tobey, George B., Jr.: *A History of Landscape Architecture—The Relationship of People to Environment*, American Elsevier, New York, 1973.

Source of Additional Information American Society of Landscape Architects, 1750 Old Meadow Road, McLean, Va. 22101.

Periodical *Landscape Architecture*, 1500 Bardstown Rd., Louisville, Ky. 40205.

LATROBE, BENJAMIN HENRY English-American architect and engineer (1764–1820). Often considered the first professional architect in America, Latrobe exerted considerable influence on the architecture of his own time and that which came later. He was one of the founders and leaders of the Classic Revival movement in American architecture. A designer and an innovator, he was also a voluminous writer, particularly of searching and thoughtful letters, and a talented artist. He was responsible for the architectural training of two men, who also became great archi-

tects, Robert Mills (1781–1855) and William Strickland (1788–1854). Most of all, he was a great architect. The buildings he did were well thought-out, pioneering in some respects, and excellent examples of the architecture of his time.

Latrobe was also a talented and inventive engineer, designing waterworks, canals, and docks as part of his practice. The experimental design of his buildings and other structures and his work with industrial machines, steam engines, water looms, water systems, and steamboats were ahead of their time. Many of the experiments that led him to disastrous financial losses later brought fame and fortune to others.

Works Emigrating to America from England in 1796, Latrobe began his practice with the Pennock House (1796), Norfolk, Va., and the Harvie-Gamble House (1799), Richmond, Va. In 1797 Latrobe won a competition for the new State Penitentiary (1800) in Richmond. This was a milestone, his first important big building; perhaps of even greater importance, it allowed him to meet Thomas Jefferson (1743–1826), an event that was to affect the lives of both men. Jefferson's interest in advanced prison design had been one of the reasons for the competition. Jefferson was interested in the prison and its architecture, and Latrobe was influenced by Jefferson's theories that design could lead to reform and hope rather than to punishment and despair. In 1798, Latrobe moved to Philadelphia.

In Philadelphia, Latrobe soon had a number of buildings to do, the most notable being the Bank of Pennsylvania (1801), the first real Classic Revival building in America; it was later demolished. In all of his early work, Latrobe worked in this style, with forms derived from those of ancient Greece and Rome, adapted to the needs, materials, and methods of the day. This was to continue in other important houses: Sen. John Pope House (1811), Lexington, Ky., and the Robert Carter Burwell House (1812), Clarke Co., Va.

As always, Latrobe had surprises in store; a notable example is his Gothic Revival Sedgeley House (1799), Philadalphia, considered the first building in that style in America.

For perhaps his most important building, the Cathedral of the Assumption (1818), Baltimore, Md., Latrobe's ideas went through many phases. He later said he designed it seven times before it was completed, including one scheme utilizing the Gothic Revival style. In the end, the cathedral was in the Classic Revival style. Many consider this the best use of the style in any American building. He also designed another important building in Baltimore, The Exchange (1820).

Other notable churches are Christ Church (1805) and St. John's Church (1816), often called the church of the presidents, both in Washington, D.C. He also designed a number of important houses, notably the Taft House (1820), Cincinnati, Ohio, and Decatur House (1818), Washington, D.C., until recently the headquarters of the National Trust for Historic Preservation. Some also attribute another great Classic

LATROBE, BENJAMIN HENRY Homewood (1801), now owned by Johns Hopkins University, Baltimore, Md. [*Architect: probably Latrobe. (M.E. Warren)*]

LATROBE, BENJAMIN HENRY The Cathedral of the Assumption (1818), Baltimore, Md. *(M. E. Warren)*

Revival house to him, Homewood (1801), now part of Johns Hopkins University, Baltimore, Md., partly because of its resemblance to the Taft House.

Another significant aspect of Latrobe's professional life was his work for the U.S. government. In 1803 Thomas Jefferson (1743–1826) appointed Latrobe surveyor of the public buildings of the United States, to superintend the construction of the Capitol Building (illustrated in capital, United States, and color section); that occupied a large part of his time until 1812,

and also from 1815 to 1817. Latrobe made important contributions to the construction of the building and to its design, particularly in the south wing, in repairs and alterations of the north wing, and in many details. The interior of the central portion is primarily from his design. Latrobe also worked on the White House (see illustration in article capital, United States), or President's House, as it was then called. He redesigned the interiors and added terrace pavilions. Later, porticoes he had designed were added. And he designed the buildings of the Navy Yard (1804) in Washington.

Latrobe went to New Orleans in 1818. While there, he designed the Louisiana State Bank (1821), still in existence, and a tower (1820) for the Cathedral of St. Louis. The tower was demolished when the cathedral was rebuilt in 1850.

Life Benjamin Henry Boneval Latrobe was born on May 1, 1764, in Fulneck, Yorkshire, England. His father, an Irish-born Moravian minister whose antecedents were French, had moved to England before young Latrobe was born. His mother, also a Moravian, was born in Pennsylvania; she was descended from German nobility. Originally named Boneval de La Trobe, the Latrobe family was descended from French nobility. In later life, Latrobe again took up the use of Boneval as a third given name.

Benjamin Henry Latrobe attended the Moravian school at Fulneck until 1776, when he was twelve years of age. He had a good mind, did well in his studies, and showed considerable talent in drawing, particularly landscapes and buildings. From 1776 to 1784, Latrobe attended Moravian schools in Germany. After traveling in Europe, Latrobe returned to London in 1784, apparently determined to become an architect.

After a period of searching, during which he studied and wrote, he went to work in 1787 for a London architect, Samuel Pepys Cockerell (1754–1827). Little is known about his architectural experiences there. In 1791 he opened his own architectural office in London and work, mostly alterations and remodeling, came in almost immediately. Two of his houses still stand in England: Hammerwood Lodge (1792), Sussex, and Ashdown House (1793), Berkshire. The lodge was his first independent design. Both houses were forerunners of the Greek Revival buildings he designed in America. He also made designs for a canal that was never built.

On February 27, 1790, Latrobe married Lydia Sellon. They had a son and a daughter, but his wife died in childbirth with the third child in 1793. Latrobe suffered a serious nervous breakdown and his practice came almost to a standstill.

In addition to his depression which adversely affected his architectural practice, France and England went to war in 1793 and building construction came to a halt. Adding to his problems were his sympathies for the new American republic and for the French revolutionaries. In late 1795, he made up his mind to go to America. Sending his books and instruments ahead, he left England on November 25, 1795, and landed in

Norfolk, Va., about the middle of March 1796. He had good letters of introduction and started practice immediately, designing the Pennock House within weeks of his arrival. A year later, after designing a few houses, he won the competition for the Virginia State Penitentiary.

After moving to Philadelphia in 1798, Latrobe received commissions for other buildings, including an important bank. On May 2, 1800, he married Mary Elizabeth Hazelhurst. Eventually they had three daughters and two sons, one of whom, John Hazelhurst Boneval Latrobe (1803–91), became an architect and lawyer. Another son, Henry Sellon Latrobe (1792–1817), by his first wife, became an architect and builder and worked as superintendent of construction for his father.

Latrobe soon was very busy. In addition to his architectural work, he was appointed engineer of the Philadelphia waterworks. That he was busy did not mean that he had an easy time starting his practice. He believed in complete architectural services, from the idea to the completed building, much as architects of today practice. But his practice was opposed by the powerful Carpenters' Company, whose members thought only they should design and construct the buildings of Philadelphia. In spite of their opposition, Latrobe received commissions for several houses and the Philadelphia waterworks during this period. He also spent a lot of time on buildings never built, competitions not won, and prospects for commissions never received.

Starting in 1798, Latrobe worked on several federal government projects, including a 165-ft-wide by 800-ft-long covered drydock, suggested by President Thomas Jefferson, in 1802. The drawings were finished in just a few weeks but despite the architect's and Jefferson's satisfaction with them, the drydock was never constructed. Impressed by Latrobe's abilities, Jefferson appointed him surveyor of public buildings of the United States in 1803. The title implies more than it means. Actually, Latrobe's job was to take over the direction of the U.S. Capitol construction. Two talented architects, Stephen Hallet (1755–1825) and James Hoban (c. 1762–1831), had already tried to construct the building. Both had found working with its architect, Dr. William Thornton (1759–1828), impossible and had resigned. Latrobe soon found himself in the same position, but he persisted longer than the others, staying with the work until 1812.

In 1807 Latrobe moved his family to Washington. He not only worked on the Capitol but also designed a lighthouse, buildings for the navy, and other projects for both the government and private clients. He also did work on the White House. By 1812, Latrobe's reputation had suffered, mostly because of the troubles with Thornton. Never able to handle his personal finances properly, he had also suffered losses in money and prestige in various schemes that failed.

Disillusioned and disheartened, he left Washington in 1813, moving his family to Pittsburgh, where he had become involved in a steamboat building venture with Robert Fulton (1765–1815), who had designed and built the first successful steamboat. The Pittsburgh venture was not fruitful. Latrobe managed to build up an architectural practice while there but all his income from it and his capital disappeared in the ill-fated project. With Fulton's death in 1815, the venture failed. Financially ruined and deeply in debt, Latrobe had another nervous breakdown.

Early in 1815, Latrobe was recalled to Washington by President James Madison (1751–1836) to rebuild the Capitol, burned by the British in the War of 1812. Again he found himself embroiled in controversy and late in 1817, resigned his position. Soon afterward, he was declared bankrupt, and in 1818 moved to Baltimore where he had buildings under construction. After less than a year, Latrobe moved to New Orleans.

During much of his career, Latrobe acted as engineer and architect for waterworks, including those in Philadelphia. Starting in 1810, with time out during the War of 1812, his waterworks in New Orleans had been under construction. He not only designed the waterworks but arranged for their financing and constructed the project. Latrobe's son, Henry, who had assisted him in the work on the Capitol and other buildings, was the construction superintendent and also designed and constructed buildings on his own. On September 3, 1817, Henry died, at age twenty-four, of yellow fever. The grief-stricken father went to New Orleans to take over the work on the waterworks, replacing his son.

His spirits revived by the new environment, Latrobe started designing buildings in New Orleans. At fifty-six, he had survived financial losses, controversy, the premature death of his first wife in childbirth and three other children, and the loss of his reputation. Then yellow fever struck him and he died on September 3, 1820, three years to the day after his son. He died worn out by overwork, despondent, and almost penniless. But all of his troubles and his tragic death could not obscure the greatness of his architecture.

Related Articles. CAPITAL, UNITED STATES; CARPENTERS' COMPANY; CLASSIC REVIVAL ARCHITECTURE; JEFFERSON, THOMAS; MILLS, ROBERT; STRICKLAND, WILLIAM.

Further Reading Hamlin, Talbot: *Benjamin Henry Latrobe*, Oxford University Press, New York, 1955.

LIBRARY A building or a room in which a collection of books, and sometimes other materials, is kept for reading and reference. Of all the building types, none is more important to the culture and civilization of the human race than the library. The books and other materials contained in libraries are essential to the understanding of history and progress and to the education of those who will provide the progress of the future. And a library is one of the most challenging and rewarding buildings to design.

A library may be a small room with a modest collection of books in a private residence or it may be a

LIBRARY Exterior, Brydges (1968), Niagara Falls, N.Y. [*Architect: Paul Rudolph. (Joseph W. Molitor)*]

LIBRARY Interior, Brydges (1968), Niagara Falls, N.Y. [*Architect: Paul Rudolph. (Joseph W. Molitor)*]

LIBRARY Exterior, University of Maine (1976), Orono, Maine [*Architect: Alonzo Harriman. (Joseph W. Molitor)*]

LIBRARY Interior, University of Maine (1976), Orono, Maine. [*Architect: Alonzo Harriman. (Joseph W. Molitor)*]

great public institution with books and other materials in the millions. Libraries may constitute limited collections made by individuals for their own pleasure and needs or they may be highly specialized and virtually complete collections of materials on limited subjects, used only by scholars.

Types There are many types of libraries owned by government on all levels, from national to local, by schools from kindergartens through universities, by businesses, and by religious groups. In fact, there is no field of human endeavor in which there are no libraries.

Public libraries are owned by and located in cities and towns for the use of people living there. These range in size from a few thousand volumes in the smallest localities to millions in the largest cities. Libraries in schools, colleges, and universities also vary considerably in size according to needs and to financial resources available. It has been said that an educational institution can be judged, in large part, by the quality of its library. In some schools, libraries are called by such names as instructional materials, instructional resource, learning resource, or information resource centers, apparently in an attempt to describe the expansion of such libraries to include media other than books, such as periodicals, cassettes, records, tapes, closed-circuit TV, moving pictures, slides, microfilm, and the like. Materials of this sort are now available in other types of libraries.

In addition to the libraries of colleges and universities, which are often research libraries, there are others for research supported by private organizations, foundations, associations, and government. Some of these are highly specialized. Other special libraries are maintained by businesses and other organizations for their own specific purposes. For example, newspapers, manufacturers, and professional associations often have libraries dedicated strictly to their own endeavors and needs. All states have libraries and the U.S. government has a great number in all of its de-

partments and three national libraries, all in or near Washington, D.C., the Library of Congress, the National Library of Medicine, and the National Library of Agriculture.

There are architectural libraries in architectural schools all over the country. Perhaps the greatest is the Avery Library, Columbia University, New York City. Another important architectural library is that of the American Institute of Architects in Washington, D.C.

Many public libraries, in addition to their main buildings, maintain branch libraries located in convenient places in neighborhoods of cities. An extension of branch units is the bookmobile, a van or truck that can be driven to various points in cities or elsewhere bringing books to those who find it inconvenient to visit the library building.

In addition to their primary functions of storing and lending books and other materials, libraries perform a number of other services. They often serve as archives for important papers, original manuscripts, biographical information, government records, and so on. Many provide Braille books and talking books, articles and books on records or tape, for those who are blind. Many sponsor performances, discussion groups, and other educational and entertaining programs for children and adults. Others stage exhibits of various kinds.

Elements The major elements in libraries are the spaces for books and other materials, readers, meetings, administration, and equipment and maintenance. Books, other than those in reading rooms or on display, are ordinarily stored in bookstacks, tiers of shelves specifically designed for library use. In some libraries, the bookstacks or stacks are open, making them accessible to readers; in others, stacks are closed and attendants must bring books to readers. In the stacks, as elsewhere in libraries, books are filed according to a system, ordinarily the Dewey decimal or that of the Library of Congress. Sometimes,

LIBRARY Selby (1975), Sarasota, Fla. [*Architects: Skidmore, Owings and Merrill. (Hedrich-Blessing)*]

LIBRARY Interior, Selby (1975), Sarasota, Fla. [*Architects: Skidmore, Owings and Merrill. (Hedrich-Blessing)*]

especially in research libraries, cubicles, called carrels, are provided in which scholars may work.

Readers are accommodated in reading rooms. Some are general reading rooms, but others may be classified according to the types of materials available or by the people who use them. Thus there may be periodical reading rooms for newspapers and magazines, microfilm rooms, reference rooms, and children's and young adults' rooms. Books and materials used in a given type of reading room may be stored in stacks nearby, or in central stacks. Important parts of a library, located in the reading room or nearby, are the card files in which titles may be located, and checkout desks where materials may be signed out and returned. Meeting rooms and rest rooms must be provided in convenient locations. Some libraries have small kitchens adjacent to meeting rooms and some have auditoriums for large groups.

Administrative areas are generally of three types: offices for librarians and other employees; workrooms where books and other materials may be processed, cataloged, and repaired; and employee areas, such as lounges, rest rooms, and dining facilities. Equipment and maintenance areas must be provided for mechanical and electrical equipment and for the upkeep and repair of the building.

All the elements of libraries must be planned together in a manner that will make their use pleasant, comfortable, and rewarding for readers. At the same time, libraries must be efficient and easy to operate and must have provisions for protecting books and other materials. The planning and design of libraries that meet these criteria have been continuing concerns of architects for many centuries.

History For at least 5,000 years before the birth of Christ, pictorial and written records were made on clay tablets in Mesopotamia. It is believed that libraries of these tablets were assembled at about the same time. A library from the 21st century B.C. has been discovered as have later ones. Papyrus scrolls are known to have existed as far back as 2500 B.C. and papyrus continued to be used well into the Christian era, not only by the Egyptians but by other people living around the Mediterranean Sea, including the Greeks and Romans. Many of these scrolls were assembled into libraries but almost all have disappeared because of the rapid decay of papyrus. Leather was used instead of papyrus in some cases, and by the end of the 5th century A.D., parchment, the untanned skin of animals, had supplanted papyrus. Vellum is a very fine grade of parchment.

Some of the most famous ancient libraries were those of Ramses III, Egyptian pharaoh in the 13th century B.C.; Assyrian King Sennacherib in the 7th century B.C. in Nineveh; and the library of Alexandria, Egypt, founded by Alexander the Great and developed by pharaohs Ptolemy I and II in the 4th century B.C. The Greeks established the first public library in Athens, about 500 B.C., and Aristotle founded another great library. The Romans, starting with Julius Caesar, built at least 25 public libraries in Rome by the 5th century and also built libraries in the countries they conquered.

During the Middle Ages, the important libraries were in monasteries and churches. Although paper had been invented by the Chinese in the second century A.D.., it did not reach Europe until about the 12th. By the 15th century, paper had mostly replaced parchment, and printing with movable type was invented by Johann Gutenberg about 1450. Thus began the age of libraries of books rather than handwritten manuscripts. One of the world's great libraries, that of the Vatican, in Rome, was founded about the same time. Other great European libraries were founded, including the Bibliothèque Nationale in Paris in the 14th century, and the Bodleian, at Oxford University, England, and the Laurentian, in Florence, Italy, both in the 16th century. Many other great libraries, all over the world, have been founded since.

American Development In the American colonies, the first libraries were private collections made by individuals for their own use and pleasure. The library at Harvard University, Cambridge, Mass., was founded in 1638 when John Harvard (1607–38) left his private library and money from his estate to help start both the university and its library. The first public library was founded in 1653 in Boston; many libraries were built in the years succeeding. The Library Company of Philadelphia was founded in 1731 by Benjamin Franklin (1706–90). It was the first of many subscription libraries which bought books with members' dues and loaned the books to them free.

In 1800 the Library of Congress was established, but the British burned its books during the War of 1812. The private library of Thomas Jefferson (1743–1826) was purchased to form the nucleus of what has become the largest library in the United States. The first tax-supported public library was opened in Peterborough, N.H., in 1833. The industrialist and humanitarian Andrew Carnegie (1835–1919), a Scottish-American who made a fortune in steel, gave millions of dollars toward the construction of more than 2,500 libraries in the United States. The building of libraries has continued in the United States ever since. Many libraries are notable examples of good architecture designed by talented architects.

Related Articles. BOOK, ARCHITECTURAL; COLLEGE AND UNIVERSITY BUILDING; MAGAZINE, ARCHITECTURAL; SCHOOL; Articles on architects.

Further Reading Langmead, Stephen, and Margaret Beckman: *New Library Design—Guidelines to Planning Aca-* *demic Library* Buildings, John Wiley, New York, 1971; Thompson, Godfrey: *Planning and Design of Library Buildings*, 2d ed., Nichols Publishing Co., New York, 1977.

Source of Additional Information American Library Assoc., 50 E. Huron St., Chicago, Ill. 60611.

LIGHTING The system that provides illumination in buildings and their surroundings. Lighting can be natural, as that received from the sun through windows, or artificial, as in electric lighting. For further discussion of natural lighting, see articles entitled climate; window. Beginning in the fourth quarter of the 19th century, electric lighting has steadily increased in importance in architecture. Today it is difficult to imagine what life was like before that time. And reliable electric lighting, at relatively low cost, deeply affects the design of buildings.

Electromagnetic Energy Light is a form of radiant energy that permits vision. Light is also considered to be one type of electromagnetic energy, similar to cosmic rays, gamma rays, x-rays, ultraviolet, infrared or heat, radio, and electrical waves. Each type of wave travels at certain ranges of velocity and each operates in a range of frequencies, or cycles per second, measured in hertz (Hz). The shortest waves, with the greatest frequencies, are cosmic rays, measured in a miniscule fraction of an inch and with frequencies of about 10^{22} Hz. At the other end of the spectrum are radio waves which may be miles in length and up to about 10^4 Hz. Light waves fall somewhere in the middle between the two extremes, about 10^{15} Hz, and from slightly less than 400 to more than 800 nanometers (nm), or about $400–800 \times 10^{-9}$ meters (m). Light is believed to travel at a speed of 186,282 miles per second (299,792 km/s).

Color The color of visible light is dependent on the wavelengths and frequencies. Light with the longest wavelengths and lowest frequencies, near the infrared or heat range, is red; as wavelengths decrease and frequencies increase, the color changes, in turn, to various shades of orange, yellow, green, blue, and violet until the visible light approaches the ultraviolet range. White light is produced when a source emits approximately equal quantities of light from all portions of the visible spectrum.

Color Temperatures Light is sometimes described by its color temperatures. This measure, named for English physicist William Thompson, Lord Kelvin (1824–1907), is based on the fact that when light-absorbing bodies are heated, they at first glow deep red, then brighter red, then shades of yellow until at the highest temperatures, they glow white, or at white-hot.

Color temperatures are measured in International System (SI) units, on the kelvin temperature scale in kelvins (K). (The degree Celsius has been adopted as a special name for the kelvin for use in expressing Celsius temperatures or intervals in the SI system.) The kelvin, sometimes called the absolute, scale, used mostly for scientific work, is related to the Celsius scale, ordinarily employed for most purposes in

LIGHTING Westinghouse Design Center (1968), Pittsburgh, Pa. [*Architects: Harrison and Abramovitz. Interior design: Knoll Planning Unit. (Joseph W. Molitor)*]

the metric system. In SI units, 0°C represents the freezing point of water; 100°C represents its boiling point. On the kelvin scale, 0 K is called absolute zero and occurs at −273°C or −456°F. Thus 273 K is equal to 0°C, and 373 K is equal to 100°C. Some typical color temperatures include candle flames at about 1700 K; incandescent lamps from 2500 to 4000 K; and fluorescent lamps from 3500 to 6500 K. Blue sky overhead has a color temperature of more than 10,000 K as contrasted to the first rays of a sunrise at about 2000 K.

Light Measures Several measurements are used in lighting design. The most basic is luminous intensity, the light-emitting power of a source, measured in candelas (cd). Luminous flux is the measure of the flow of light, in lumens (lm). Luminance is the light emitted by a unit area of surface of a source, measured in candelas per square meter (cd/m²). Illuminance, sometimes called illumination, is the light falling on a unit area of surface, measured in lux (lx), a quantity equal to lumens per meter squared. The quantity of light is measured in lumen-seconds (lm·s); light exposure in lux-seconds (lx·s); and lu-

minous efficacy, formerly called efficiency, in lumens per watt (lm/W).

Characteristics of Light Lighting affects the eye and without those effects would have no purpose in architecture. Four basic characteristics of light primarily affect the eye: luminance, which is almost synonymous with brightness; size; contrast; and time. Visual tasks are dependent on these four factors and also on the perception of detail, low contrast levels, and levels of brightness. When lighting is being designed for various tasks or purposes, these characteristics must be taken into consideration. Various tasks require various combinations of characteristics. In terms of luminance or brightness, fine work requires greater brightness than that which is less fine. Reading type on a page generally requires less brightness than reading handwriting. In sewing by hand, some 10 times as much luminance is required as for reading type, if the work is with white thread on white cloth; black thread on white cloth may require as much as 30 times the luminance for reading type.

The size of objects is important in lighting and

seeing. Larger objects are easier to see than smaller ones, but smaller ones can be made easier by moving them nearer the eye. Contrast required for various tasks varies considerably. For example, in reading type on a page, black type contrasted with white paper aids in the reading. On the other hand, black type on a gray page is harder to read. However, high contrasts between the work being performed and the background are considered detrimental. It is therefore often considered best to have the brightness of the work no greater than 3 times that of the background. The time of viewing an object is important in seeing and lighting. An object will be seen better if viewed over a relatively long period of time than if viewed only briefly. An object viewed only briefly will require more brightness than one of the same size viewed over a longer period of time. Minimum levels of luminance have been established for various tasks, and tables of these quantities are widely available.

Qualitative Characteristics Another important consideration in lighting is the quality of the light. One of the characteristics of quality is glare, light received by the eye directly from light sources, causing discomfort and interference with good vision. The amount of glare is rated by brightness, size, and position of the glare-producing light source. Glare is generally controlled by reducing the brightness of the source or its size or changing its position. Reflected glare, from mirrors or other polished surfaces, must also be controlled.

Another qualitative characteristic of lighting is diffusion, the direction or directions from which light emanates. If light were perfectly diffused, it would come from all directions with equal intensities. At the other extreme would be the least diffused, a light emanating from a single direction. In architectural lighting for general purposes, such as the overall lighting of offices, classrooms, and the like, diffused lighting is most often used. For specific tasks, such as fine detailing in a drafting room, directional lighting is used to supplement the general lighting. Diffused lighting produces relatively uniform levels of light in rooms, tending to eliminate shadows and contrast, and therefore tending to make things look flat. Directional lighting produces shadows and contrasts. For many purposes, some combination of the two types will be found useful and comfortable. For example, in an art museum, sculpture might have diffused lighting for general vision, with directional lighting to illuminate the three dimensions with shadows and highlights.

Another important qualitative characteristic of lighting is color. When light strikes surfaces, portions of it are absorbed and portions reflected. White light striking a black or white surface is partly absorbed and partly reflected in the entire spectrum of colors of which the light is composed. White light striking surfaces of other colors is selectively absorbed and reflected. For example, a white light striking a blue wall has various components of its spectrum absorbed, except the blue which is reflected and is seen to be blue. The attribute that is usually called a color is actually a hue: red, yellow, green, or others. Black, white, and gray, composed only of black with white, are colorless or neutral, and therefore have no hues. The brilliance or brightness of a color is called its value. In general, white is the most brilliant and black the least, with the various hues in positions in between the extremes. The saturation of a color is an indication of its vividness. For example, starting with a gray that has no hue and a relatively low brilliance or value, the addition of another color, such as red, changes the saturation or vividness of the gray, but does not change its brilliance. Saturation is sometimes referred to as chromaticity.

Colors strongly affect lighting; for example, the greater the value of a color, the greater its reflectance of white light, with white surfaces the most reflective, black the least, and the hues in between. Colors are also considered to have strong psychological effects. Colored light and objects may be used to alter the appearance of things. For example, bluish or greenish lights or walls make the interiors of buildings, their contents, and people look quite different from reddish lights. Many other psychological effects are created by colors, including the feeling that warm colors, like red, make rooms look smaller, and cool ones like blue, make them look larger. In addition, warm colors are thought to produce tensions in people, while cool colors have calming effects.

Proper Lighting This is of extreme importance in architecture today. Good lighting for various tasks and purposes helps prevent tension, tiredness, eyestrain, discomfort, and even illness in occupants. Proper lighting promotes efficiency in the work of the occupants, helps prevent accidents and reduce errors, and aids in good visual health by helping to prevent eye defects or to keep them from becoming worse. Improper lighting can produce any of the opposite effects or all of them, in combination. In addition, proper lighting can produce a great many kinds of exciting, ornamental, and esthetic effects in architecture, outdoors as well as in interiors.

Sources The most universal source of light is the sun which provides daylight. (See articles entitled climate; window.) Another important source, from the earliest times, is fire, still used in some parts of the world for certain kinds of lighting. Today the all-important sources of artificial lighting in buildings are various electrical devices. Such devices include various types of lamps, in the form of bulbs, tubes, and panels. The major types are incandescent, gaseous discharge, and electroluminescent lamps. Incandescent lamps generally operate on the principle of wire filaments, enclosed in glass bulbs, heated by electric currents. Gaseous lamps operate generally on the principle of gases, which conduct electricity through glass tubes. Electroluminescent lighting is based on the principle of direct excitement of phosphors in thin sheets or panels by electric currents.

For many years, incandescent lamps were the most

LIGHTING Westinghouse Design Center (1968), Pittsburgh, Pa.
[*Architects: Harrison and Abramovitz. Interior design: Knoll Planning Unit. (Joseph W. Molitor)*]

important source of electric lighting in architecture. In general, they are sealed glass bulbs, in which tungsten filaments are located. The filaments are heated by electric currents, producing light and heat. Such lamps are not very efficient sources of light, dissipating some 90 percent of the electric power in heat. Most incandescent lamps are either frosted or coated inside with silica for diffusion of the light. Incandescent lamps are available in a number of shapes, with several types of bases, and in numerous capacities for uses in architecture. Very small lamps, similar to flashlight bulbs, are sometimes used for warning and control lights for mechanical and electrical equipment. From these very-low-wattage types, lamp capacities range up to 300 W and higher. For lighting in buildings, lamps have various types of bases, including the smallest for use with standard 120 V current, called the candelabra base, and the next larger, intermediate, both used for ornamental purposes. The most commonly used is the medium base, and the mogul base is used for very large capacity lamps.

Incandescent lamps are available in various specialized types, including ones with reflector surfaces inside; colored glass types; single lamps with two filaments, providing three different levels of lighting; safety lamps; and low-voltage lamps. Extended service lamps have longer useful lives than regular lamps, up to 2,500 hours or more, but are not as efficient. Other types are also available for special purposes. One is the tungsten-halogen type, which is an incandescent lamp, with a tungsten filament enclosed in a quartz tube, filled with one of the halogens: iodine, chlorine, bromine, or fluorine. These lamps have useful lives twice as long as those of ordinary incandescent types, because the halogens prevent evaporation of the tungsten filaments.

While incandescent lamps are still widely used in architecture, particularly in residential buildings and for ornamental, stadium lighting, and other purposes; fluorescent lighting has come to be used very widely for many purposes in many building types. Fluorescent lamps are generally tubular types filled with inert gases, such as low-pressure argon, and mercury vapor. Passing electricity through the mercury vapor causes it to arc, producing ultraviolet light that excites the interior coatings of fluorescent phosphors in the tubes. The phosphors then emit visible light.

Fluorescent lamps require devices called ballasts to produce the very high voltages necessary to start arcs in the mercury vapor and to limit the current after the arcs have started. Fluorescent lamps are usually rapid-start, requiring about 1 s for starting, or instant-start. Fluorescent tubes generally come in lengths ranging from 24 to 96 in, representing wattages from 25 to over 200. They are available with regular or mogul bipin, single-pin, or double-contact bases. Fluorescent lamps also require starters, including a type in which a button must be held in momentarily, and others that start almost instantaneously. Most fluorescent lamps are straight tubes, but special types are also available in U shapes, circles, and panels. The efficiency of fluorescent tubes depends on many vari-

LIGHTING Architect's office (1960), Raleigh, N.C. [*Architect: G. Milton Small. (Joseph W. Molitor)*]

ables, such as frequency of starting, hours of burning, and temperatures. In general, they are more efficient than incandescent types.

A number of other gaseous discharge lamps are available for uses in architecture. Neon lighting, in which neon gas conducts the electricity to produce light, is used mostly for signs. High-intensity discharge lamps are used for special purposes. They operate on the principle of the production of light in high-pressure gases or vapors. Three types are currently available, in capacities up to 1500 W: mercury vapor, metal halide, and high-pressure sodium. All require ballasts and are used for street lighting and other purposes.

Electroluminescent light sources are generally available in sheet form for use with 120 V current. The sheets are made of phosphor materials, with aluminum foil and electrical leads enclosed in plastics. Emitting light from their entire surfaces, these light sources are used mostly for ornamental purposes and are available in several colors in addition to white.

A number of other types of light sources are sometimes used in architecture for lighting and other purposes, including ultraviolet, or black light, used for ornamental and other purposes; carbon arc lights, used in searchlights and motion picture projectors; and cold-cathode lamps, used for purposes similar to neon types. Other specialized types include infrared lamps for heating, laser lamps for security purposes,

light-emitting diodes (LED) for indicators and controls, and ozone and germicidal lamps for sterilization of the air in buildings, such as hospitals.

Luminaires Literally thousands of types of lighting fixtures, sometimes called luminaires, are available today. They range from simple, utilitarian types to ones that are very ornamental. They may be fixed, as in ceiling fixtures, or movable, as in floor types. They may be acquired with lamps of any of the kinds previously discussed. There are indoor and outdoor types. Ceiling fixtures may be surface-mounted, recessed, or hung permanently or on tracks. There are types for installation on walls, poles, and in other locations. Lighting fixtures may distribute light in many kinds of patterns, asymmetrical as well as symmetrical. They may also emit light directly, indirectly, or in combinations. They may emit diffused direct light or combinations. Such fixtures may be square, round, rectangular, or other shapes. They may have reflectors, louvers, lenses, filters, or any of a number of other accessories. Light fixtures may also be mounted above a hung plastic luminous ceiling that emits light from a large area rather than a single point or line.

Luminaires generally illuminate in one of five ways: direct, in which most of the light in downward; indirect, in which 90 percent or more of the light is upward; semidirect, in which 60 to 90 percent is downward, the remainder upward; semi-indirect, with 60 to 90 percent of the light upward, the remainder downward; and general diffuse, which directs approximately equal amounts of light upward and downward. Among the thousands of luminaires available, there are types for every imaginable architectural purpose. The best source of information on luminaire types is included in catalogs issued by manufacturers. Also available are many kinds of special switches, dimmers, timers, and other devices often used in conjunction with lighting systems.

Lighting Design The design of lighting for general and special uses within and outside buildings is quite complex and varies considerably between building types. In general, the purposes of such design are to provide functional, efficient, and economical lighting for all the general and special needs in buildings, together with pleasing ornamental architectural effects. Proper lighting levels, of the proper quality, should be provided for the various tasks and activities to be performed in buildings. Lighting design begins with analysis of the functions and problems in a proposed building, proceeds to selection of proper light sources including fixtures, then to calculation of the loads and to establishment of fixture patterns for the overall or general lighting. Supplemental lighting for special purposes or effects may then be calculated and sources and fixtures selected. Finally, the entire design must be reviewed, and altered if necessary.

The design of lighting, in all but the simplest applications, is ordinarily handled by lighting designers, many of whom are electrical engineers. Others were trained in architecture or other disciplines. Lighting designers must coordinate their work closely with that of other environmental designers, particularly with that of architects and electrical engineers who design electric power and wiring systems in buildings. Lighting design offers great opportunities for the achievement of ornamental and dramatic effects in architecture, in addition to the purely functional requirements.

History The first lighting in architecture was the natural light from the sun that came through openings in primitive huts and tents. Natural lighting has remained an important element of architecture to this day.

The first artificial lighting used by humans came from campfires and from burning branches removed from the fires. Later, fires inside huts and tents gave off light; for portable lights, torches of resinous woods, such as cedar, were used. Early humans had little use for such lighting, since they usually went to bed when the sun went down and arose with the sunrise. This continued to be the most usual practice for many centuries. In the early civilizations around the Mediterranean Sea, Egypt, the Middle East, and the mainland of Greece as well as in islands such as Crete, candles of wax or tallow were used as far back as 3000 B.C. People also used simple lamps, usually no more than a hollowed stone in which a wick and oil were placed. Later, improved lamps were made of pottery, seashells, and metals. The ancient Greeks and Ro-

mans used candles, lamps, and torches for lighting. Fuels were various oils, such as olive, castor, linseed, and others. The first use of petroleum is thought to have occurred in Mesopotamia.

The use of candles and lamps for lighting was quite widespread in Roman times, but during the Middle Ages less artificial lighting was used than previously. Oil for lamps and candles was scarce and expensive and therefore used mostly in churches, cathedrals, and castles. Some light was, of course, supplied by the great fireplaces used to heat Gothic castles, but the churches and cathedrals were unheated. During the Renaissance, artificial lighting was almost as little used as in the Middle Ages. Fireplaces gave some light, and lamps and candles were scarce and expensive, affordable only by wealthy people.

American Development In early colonial America, candles and oil for lamps were scarce and expensive. For the most part, people arose at sunrise and went to bed at sundown. Some light came from fires in fireplaces. In the 18th century, artificial lighting began to improve, mostly because of the increasing availability of oil from the sperm whales, pursued and captured by New England whalers. Candles also became more plentiful, but were still expensive. Most households had their own candle molds, in which they made their own, until candle-making machines were developed much later. Modest homes and other buildings were then lighted with candles in holders, while more important buildings and larger homes were often lighted with candelabra and chandeliers which often held a great number of candles.

In 1792 an English engineer, William Murdock (1754–1839), revolutionized artificial lighting when he first installed coal-gas lights, fueled with a by-product of the coking process. In 1802 he used this kind of lighting for the exterior of a factory and in 1806, in the interior of another. In the latter year, coal gas was first used for lighting in the United States. By 1824, natural gas was used, in a limited way, for lighting. By the middle of the 19th century, gas lighting was used in buildings all over the United States. The quality of the light from gas was greatly improved by the invention of the Bunsen burner, which premixed air and gas, and the Welsbach mantle, a cloth hood treated with chemicals. Bunsen burners produced hot, blue, smokeless flames, and are still used in laboratories today. Welsbach mantles produced very hot, white, incandescent flames, and are still in use today in gas and gasoline lanterns, such as those used by campers. By the end of the 19th century, manufactured and natural gas were firmly established as fuels for lighting.

Rudimentary incandescent light bulbs had been made during the first half of the 19th century, but Thomas Alva Edison (1847–1931) produced the first practical type in 1879. Arc lights had been used on a limited scale for illumination previously. By the end of the century, electric generating plants had been built in many places in the United States, and electric lighting was beginning to replace gas lighting. The changeover proceeded rapidly, but the use of gas for lighting lingered on for some time into the early part of the 20th century. In 1881 a mile of Broadway, in New York City, had been lighted with carbon arc lights; other cities soon followed suit.

With the spread of electric lighting for buildings and cities came new kinds of lives for people, who now could use the night hours for purposes previously only possible in the daytime. And the new development changed architecture radically. No longer would buildings be constructed almost entirely for daytime activities. No longer would their occupants be dependent on daylight or the relatively inefficient light produced by burning gas. Eventually, the easy availability and efficiency of electric lighting led to what many think are excesses in architecture. In some buildings, there was little or no provision for natural lighting. In others, artificial lighting was provided in amounts considerably greater than needed for activities. Such buildings have been criticized for their often unnatural, even inhuman, interior qualities and in later years, for their waste of energy.

From the beginning of its use, electric lighting has been almost continually improved. More efficient incandescent light bulbs have deen developed and the quality of the light improved. Other types of electric light sources have been developed, including the fluorescent tube, which produces high levels of light with less energy than do incandescent types. Fluorescent lighting in architecture has increased rapidly since World War II and has become the standard general lighting for many building types, including office buildings and stores. Along with the improvements and new developments in light sources, there have been corresponding improvements in lighting fixtures.

Today many types of light sources are available for architectural uses, including high-intensity lamps, electroluminescent lamps, and germicidal lamps. Neon and cold-cathode lamps, first invented in 1911, are widely used in signs on buildings and elsewhere to the delight of some observers and with the opposite effect on others.

Related Articles CLIMATE; ELECTRICAL ENGINEERING; ELECTRIC POWER AND WIRING; ENERGY; INTERIOR DESIGN; WINDOW.

Further Reading Nuckolls, James L.: *Interior Lighting—For Environmental Designers*, John Wiley, New York, 1976.

Source of Additional Information Illuminating Engineering Society of North America (IES), 345 E. 47th St., New York, N.Y. 10017.

LIGHTNING PROTECTION
System used to protect buildings from damage and their occupants from injury or death by lightning strokes. Compared to many other hazards, lightning causes relatively little damage to buildings and relatively few injuries and deaths. In the United States, about 350 people are killed and 1,500 injured each year by lightning. Of the fires in buildings each year, slightly over 1 percent are caused by lightning. However, lightning protection is a very important architectural consideration in certain kinds of buildings and other structures, including those that are isolated or relatively tall or with tall portions, such as church steeples.

Lightning Stroke A lightning stroke is an electrical current or spark of very high magnitude, as much as 15 million V and 8 mi long, between a cloud and the earth and can travel that distance in approximately 0.0004 s. Lightning occurs when clouds, or the waterdrops within them, become sufficiently charged with electricity. It is believed that as waterdrops fall through rising columns of air, they break up into larger particles with positive charges and smaller ones with negative charges. When enough electric potential has been built up, a stroke of lightning flashes from a positively charged portion of the cloud toward a negatively charged area, a different part of the same cloud, another cloud, or some object or area or a water body on the earth. When lightning strikes the earth, it may cause considerable damage to buildings, other structures, and trees, may start fires, and may kill or injure people.

Need for Protection Current practice in architecture does not require lightning protection for every building or structure. The need for lightning protection may be determined by a careful analysis of a building or other structure of such factors as exposure; height; monetary value; historical value; potential dangers to building occupants; and the frequency, duration, and intensity of thunderstorms in the area of the site. Buildings of relatively great height, such as tall offices or other types, and tall structures, such as water towers, chimneys, or steeples, usually require lightning protection. So do those in exposed locations, as in rural areas with no other buildings nearby. Valuable tall trees also need protection, particularly if standing alone.

Air Terminals The only known system of lightning protection involves the provision of air terminals, or lightning rods, at the highest points of buildings, other structures, or trees, to attract lightning strokes away from the other parts, connected to metallic downconductors, usually of copper or other alloys, which carry the electricity to the ground. Ordinarily, a number of air terminals are required. In addition, anything of metal on roofs should be connected by conductors to the downconductors. The downconductors are connected to adequate grounds in the earth. The grounds may be pipes (ground rods), ground plates, or loop (counterpoise) conductors of wire with an adequate number of electrodes. Radio and television antennas should always be grounded in a similar manner and provided with devices called lightning arresters.

In steel-frame buildings, the frames may be used as conductors; and in concrete-framed buildings, the reinforcing bars in the concrete should be welded together to provide continuous conductors. In all types of construction, conductors should prevent electricity from passing through nonconducting portions, in which heat could start fires or where the great force could cause damage.

The design of proper lightning protection is specialized. Various standards and codes govern the subject, including the materials and equipment to be used, notably those of the National Fire Protection Association and the Underwriters Laboratories. Improperly designed or partial systems may increase the likelihood of lightning damage, rather than preventing it. Accordingly, most lightning protection systems today are designed by specialists in the field.

History Although humans have always held lightning in awe, its essential nature as electricity was not understood until Benjamin Franklin (1706–90) flew a kite in a thunderstorm in 1752. In that same year, Franklin also invented the first lightning rod and erected it on his house.

Related Articles BUILDING CODES AND STANDARDS; COMMUNICATION SYSTEM; CONCRETE STRUCTURE; COPPER ALLOY; FIRE PROTECTION; STEEL STRUCTURE; WEATHER PROTECTION.

Further Reading Marshall, J. Lawrence: *Lightning Protection*, John Wiley, New York, 1973.

Source of Additional Information Lightning Protection Inst., 2 N. Riverside Plaza, Chicago, Ill. 60606.

MAGAZINE, ARCHITECTURAL Periodical containing articles about architects, architecture, and related subjects. For many years, architectural magazines have been important to architects and other environmental designers and they continue to be so today.

Definition A magazine is a periodical, published on a regular basis, usually weekly or monthly; each issue contains a collection of articles or stories, usually on diverse subjects, with illustrations. A magazine is distinguished from another type of periodical, a newspaper, by the fact that it usually does not attempt to cover daily news, is printed on better paper, and is bound. Magazines published every week are called weeklies, those published every month, monthlies, those published every two months, bimonthlies, and those appearing every three months, quarterlies. Magazines may be published at other intervals, such as twice a month for semimonthlies or every two weeks for fortnightlies.

Types Sometimes magazines with broad audiences composed of members of the general public are called mass magazines, while those with limited audiences which have certain special interests are called class magazines. Magazines published for specific audiences of various professional, trade, or business groups are often called trade magazines or journals. In other instances, such publications may be called business or professional magazines. Architectural magazines today fall into the professional group. Many thousands of magazines of a great many types are published in the United States, and many millions are distributed every day through the mails or sold on newsstands.

In the past, a number of architectural magazines were published in the United States; today there are only three national magazines that can be called architectural in the strict sense: *AIA Journal, Architectural Record,* and *Progressive Architecture.* All are monthlies; the first two also publish special extra issues; and all are distributed through the mails to specific audiences. In addition, a number of regional architectural magazines are published in the United States. These have audiences limited to certain geographical areas. Many other magazines, of interest to architects and other environmental designers, are published in such fields as construction, engineering, interior design, landscape architecture, and city planning. Many are listed in various articles in this book.

Qualified Audience Although magazine publishing, including architectural magazines, is quite complex, the general principles may be stated rather simply. All the architectural magazines serve the interests of certain specific audiences, sometimes called their qualified circulation. These audiences vary somewhat between the individual magazines, but are generally composed of architects, together with engineers and other environmental design professionals who perform services for buildings, and others in the building industry.

Editorial Content To these audiences, the magazines furnish editorial services of interest to them, along with advertising pertinent to architecture. The editorial content of magazines is the key to success. If they are able to attract subscribers, in sufficient numbers, who wish to obtain the editorial content, if the subscribers actually read the content and are in a position to select and specify the products advertised, the magazines can then sell advertising to product manufacturers who wish to bring their promotional messages to the magazine audiences. A portion of the income of the magazines is obtained from subscriptions, but the major portion comes from the sale of advertising.

Good editorial content thus generates circulation among people of importance to both editors and advertisers and creates good readership. The audience or circulation may then be translated into advertising that produces product sales for manufacturers and others and income for the magazine. With increasing income, the editorial content can be further improved in quality as well as in quantity.

Architectural magazines are thus able to serve the interests of both readers and advertisers. To readers, the magazines present each month, or more frequently, a colorful package of information in text and pictures, generally covering their professional needs, as the management and, in particular, the editorial staffs of the magazines view those interests. In each magazine there exists a ratio between the pages of editorial content and the pages of advertising, called the editorial-advertising ratio. If this ratio falls too low on the editorial content side, readership may suffer; if too high on the editorial side, the profitability of the magazine may suffer. In national architectural magazines today, editorial-advertising ratios range from about 35:65 to 50:50.

In addition, each architectural magazine has what is

called an editorial mix, a balance between types of editorial content, news, feature articles, and so on. Each magazine strives to make its own mix the unique one preferred by its audience. A striking feature of architectural magazines is the high ratio of pictures to text, reflecting the fact that architecture is a visual art and that architects usually react more strongly to graphic content than to reading matter. Recently, there has been a strong tendency toward publishing an increasing number of color pictures.

Organization Although it varies somewhat between individual publications, the general organization of architectural magazines includes a management group, an editorial staff, and a business group. The management is directed by a publisher, who usually though not always has overall responsibility for the entire magazine. The editorial staff has responsibility for the editorial content and is usually headed by an editor or editor in chief. Next in authority is the managing editor, who usually handles the day-by-day management of editorial matters. The business group handles advertising, circulation, and other business matters.

Editors on architectural magazine staffs perform many kinds of tasks. One is to keep up with architecture, including design, practice, and other important matters. Architectural editors initiate articles, find authors for them, and aid in their writing; write articles themselves; obtain illustrations, including photographs and drawings; edit articles; and perform other related functions. Today most photographs in architectural magazines are made by free-lance architectural photographers, who usually license their photographs for onetime use in magazines. Other photographs are sometimes obtained from archives, and in some instances editors take their own. Drawings for use as illustrations are usually obtained directly from architects or other environmental design professionals. Many are redrawn for reproduction, often by free-lance illustrators.

Architectural magazines today have editorial staffs ranging in size from about 8 to 15 people, plus secretaries and assistants. In addition to the editor and managing editor, each has several classifications of editorial positions, starting with the highest, senior editors, followed by associate editors, then assistant editors. All have varying degrees of responsibility, according to their ranks, and all perform editorial functions that are generally similar. In addition, each magazine staff has an art director and assistants who are responsible for the design and layout of the magazine. Each also has a production editor or manager, who handles the details of actually producing the magazine, working with typesetters, printers, and so on as well as with the editors. In addition, some architectural magazines have part-time advisers, mostly environmental design professionals, called correspondents, contributing editors, or editorial consultants. Sometimes the magazines utilize various news services.

Sections All architectural magazines are large in size, 9 by 12 inches, and all are bound with a glue system that is fairly permanent and strong, but not so strong as the sewn bindings of hardbound books. In each issue of the magazine, there are three major sections, often called front, center, and back of the magazine, bound into a cover. The front of the magazine contains the contents page, or pages, with a masthead listing the staff, together with various combinations of editorials, news, and continuing features, called departments, interspersed with advertising pages. The center of the magazine is devoted exclusively to editorial content, including articles, picture features, and other matter. The back of the magazine generally resembles the front and contains departments, news, and advertising.

There is some resemblance between the national architectural magazines, but the resemblance is somewhat superficial. Each has its own editorial mix, editorial philosophy, and special departments. The magazines have in common departments for publishing news, calendars of events, letters to the editor, notices of various kinds, book reviews, and others. Two publish product reports, product literature, and law columns, and have engineering or technical departments. One has regular departments devoted to building costs, construction statistics, and office management. All have advertisers' indexes and reader inquiry cards. All publish articles about new buildings, but the number of buildings published each issue and the pages devoted to them varies considerably. Two are mostly staff written, with only occasional articles by others, while the third is primarily composed of articles written by people other than staff members.

Processes In general, magazine processes include planning issues, editorial preparation of articles (writing, illustrations, editing, and production), plant operations (typesetting, printing, and binding), and mailing operations. The planning process for an issue of a monthly magazine starts months in advance of the issue date and includes such considerations as estimated pages of editorial content and mix of articles and other content. Editors receive assignments and start to acquire or prepare articles. Other editors work on the content of the various departments assigned to them. Drawings are prepared or acquired, along with photographs. Some weeks before the issue date, layouts of articles are prepared, last minute changes are made in articles, and the content is copy edited to correct errors and to ensure that articles properly fit their assigned pages, and other adjustments are made. After the text and other manuscript for various departments and articles have been completed, they are marked with instructions for typesetting and sent to typesetters, who set them in type and pull long proofs, called galley proofs or galleys. These are carefully proofread for errors and proper page fit, and then cut up and pasted on sheets of paper the size of magazine pages, along with copies of photographs and other artwork, headlines, credits, and so on, in what is called a dummy. Where they occur together, editorial and advertising pages are combined in the dummy.

When certain portions of the magazine have been dummied and everything else is in readiness, they are sent to the printer to be made into pages. Ordinarily, these portions are sent out in multiples of 8 to 64 pages, which eventually will be printed at one time, or in one form, on offset presses. After the content has been made into pages, page proofs are pulled and read for errors. Then various forms may be approved for the actual printing. The printed press sheets are then folded into signatures. If necessary for special reasons, an editor or production person may examine actual press sheets as they come from the printing press to assure quality. When all the signatures have been printed and folded, they are gathered together, bound into their covers, trimmed, wrapped in paper covers (sleeves), and mailed.

The business group of an architectural magazine usually consists of four major functions: circulation management, advertising sales, advertising production, and general management. The circulation department, usually headed by a circulation director or manager, solicits subscriptions, manages subscription lists, and attends to processes, called fulfillment, involved in delivery of magazines to subscribers. The advertising sales department, usually headed by a sales manager, solicits contracts for the publication of advertising in the magazine from building product manufacturers and other companies interested in the architectural market. Each national architectural magazine has from 5 to 12 salespeople who make direct calls and otherwise attempt to persuade advertisers of the importance of their magazine's coverage of the significant selectors and specifiers of architectural products and other items, of the completeness of their coverage of such people or the market, of the readership of the magazine, and of other reasons why the advertisers should place their faith in a particular magazine. The advertising salespeople, often called space salespeople, attempt to persuade both manufacturers and their advertising agencies. Space salespeople may be members of the staffs of architectural magazines or independent contractors, often called magazine representatives, who sell advertising in more than one magazine.

Most advertising pages in architectural magazines are designed and prepared by advertising agencies. The advertising production department of the magazines prepare the few that are not and also oversee the production processes of the advertising received from agencies. The magazines also have staffs who aid in the preparation and placement of the magazines' own promotional efforts, mostly in the form of direct mail campaigns and promotional pieces for sales purposes. Promotion departments are ordinarily headed by research or promotion managers. The business management department administers the general business affairs of a magazine.

Editorial Services Architectural magazines perform many editorial services for their readers, including furnishing news of the environmental design professions, the building industry, and related topics; and information on new building types, practice, legal matters, design, engineering, and many other subjects. All the magazines try to provide inspiration in addition to information. Advertising in the magazines, together with product reports and literature, keeps professionals up to date on building products, materials, and systems. In addition, the magazines sponsor award programs, round-table discussions, educational meetings, and other events of interest to architects and others.

Because of their wide-ranging interests, attendance at meetings and seminars, interviews, reading, and other activities, many architectural editors are good sources of many types of information. And many editors answer specific questions from members of design professions and others. Architectural magazines are also of great importance to architects and others as media for the publication of their building designs and completed buildings. Such publication carries a certain amount of recognition, even prestige, and also offers an opportunity to obtain tear sheets or reprints of the articles in the business development and public relations programs of architects.

Many architects, particularly young ones, often ask what they should do to get their buildings published. There is no easy answer, but the most obvious one is to design good buildings. It also helps to know architectural editors, though it is possible, if a building is of sufficient excellence and out-of-the ordinary interest, to have it published by simply mailing a description, along with drawings and photographs, to an architectural magazine. In any case, the availability of good photographs and good reproducible drawings can be very helpful in getting a building published. See articles entitled graphic design; photography, architectural.

Another way to be published in architectural magazines is to write well-illustrated articles. Generally, the procedure might start with an attempt to interest an editor in an outline, together with suggested illustrations. For a discussion on some writing details of this sort, see the article entitled book, architectural. Many architects gain recognition and sometimes prestige, along with publicity, by writing articles for nonarchitectural magazines, in particular those that reach audiences of potential clients, in such fields as hospitals, schools, office buildings, hotels, and other building types. In many cases, editors of such magazines welcome well-written, timely articles directed to their audiences.

For many architects and other design professionals as well as people educated as journalists or in other disciplines, work on the editorial staffs of architectural magazines offers a chance to contribute heavily to their professions, to architecture, and to society in ways that are quite different from the work of most professional practitioners. For those with interests in language, graphic design, printing, people, and communication as well as in architecture and other types of environmental design, architectural magazines offer interesting and rewarding careers, unlike any others in architecture.

Some knowing editor, a long time ago, described an editor as a person who is able to think and plan, organize, and execute. The editor must know writing and reporting, people, and production, and must be able to establish and keep deadlines, write, and inspire good copy, bright headlines, and exciting article leads. The editor must believe that all articles can be better when shorter, and must be willing to work toward that goal. It should be added that an architectural editor must also know and believe in good architecture.

History Although there is some disagreement about which was the first magazine, the most likely candidate is *Journal des savants*, first published in Paris in 1665. The first English magazine is considered to be *Gentleman's Magazine*, which began publication in 1731. The first periodicals in America, appearing in 1741, were *American Magazine* and *The General Magazine* of Benjamin Franklin (1706–90). Since that time, a great number of magazines are started every year, covering every possible subject, and a great number are discontinued each year.

American Development It is not easy to establish the time when the first American architectural magazine appeared. In colonial times, various building publications somewhat like magazines were published, some periodically. Unlike later magazines, these did not devote themselves to articles on diverse subjects. Most contained collections of drawings or patterns, often called plates, from which various elements of architecture could be derived and constructed. The first real architectural magazine, if its title can be believed, may have been *The Architectural Magazine*, published for about five years beginning in 1834.

Next came the *Architectural Review and American Builder Journal*, which lasted only a short while after its debut in 1869. In 1876 *American Architect and Building News* was published by the James K. Osgood Co. of Boston. This magazine was later bought by the Hearst newspaper and magazine chain and renamed *The American Architect*. In 1938 it was bought by and merged into *Architectural Record*. In 1879 the *Inland Architect and Builder* was published in Chicago. By 1885, these three magazines had been joined by a number of others, including: *Building; Carpentry and Building; Builder and Woodworker; Decorator and Furnisher; Building Review;* and *The Builder*.

In 1891 *Architectural Record*, the first of the architectural magazines still published today, was founded as a general magazine for lay people interested in architecture as well as for architects. A quarterly in those days, the magazine had a broad range of editorial content, including essays, critical and historical articles, poetry, and even a serialized novel by the first editor of the magazine, Harry W. Desmond.

In 1896 another magazine of importance was established; this was *Architectural Review*, not to be confused with the English publication of the same name. Later, its editor was an architect who had a distinguished career in architectural journalism, Henry H. Saylor (1880–1967). Saylor was editor of *Architecture* in the 1920s and 1930s and became the first editor of the *Journal of the American Institute of Architects (AIA)* in 1944, serving in that capacity until 1957. The AIA had previously published a magazine of the same title, from 1912 to 1928, under the editorship of Charles Harris Whitaker, and before that, from 1900 to 1912, the *American Institute of Architects Quarterly Bulletin*. In 1892 *The Brickbuilder* was started.

All the early magazines were not really professional magazines, but rather for members of the general public who wanted to be informed about architecture, or for the building trades, such as brick masons, plumbers, carpenters, and so on. In 1914, under the leadership of its editor-publisher, Dr. Michael W. Mikkelson, *Architectural Record* was converted from a magazine for the lay public to one for professional architects. Thus began a trend that has continued, with some exceptions, ever since. In 1917 *The Brickbuilder* became *Architectural Forum*, an important professional magazine for many years. And in 1920 *Architectural Review* spawned a new magazine, *Pencil Points*, slanted mostly to draftsmen, designers, and specification writers rather than to professional architects. The magazine had only three editors, Eugene Clute, Russell Whitehead, and Kenneth Reid (1893–1960), before becoming a more complete professional magazine and being renamed *Progressive Architecture*, the title it still bears today. Architect Thomas Hawk Creighton (1904–) became its editor at that time, in 1946, and remained in the post until 1963.

By the late 1920s, the leading architectural magazines were *American Architect*, published by Hearst; *Architectural Record*, then edited by Mikkelson; *Architectural Forum*; *Architecture*, then published by Scribner's and edited by Saylor; and *Pencil Points*. In 1932 *Architectural Forum*, under the direction of editor-publisher Howard Myers (1894–1948), was purchased by Time, Inc. From a professional circulation of some 5,000 in 1932, the magazine grew to more than 70,000 by the time of Myers' death in 1948. Perry Prentice then became editor-publisher and continued the course toward becoming a large circulation, generalized architectural magazine. In 1950 the name was changed to *The Magazine of Building*, though the *Architectural Forum* title was also retained.

In 1952 this magazine was split into two, *Architectural Forum* once again and *House and Home*, for professionals and house builders. In 1954 Douglas Haskell (1899–1979), who had previously been an editor of *Architectural Record* for 20 years and of *Architectural Forum* for 5, became the magazine's editor.

As it turned out, he was the last in the Time, Inc., era, as the magazine was suspended in 1964. The other, *House and Home*, was sold to McGraw-Hill, Inc., and is published today under the title, *Housing*. *Architectural Forum* again began publication in 1965, having been given, by Time, Inc., to a nonprofit organization, Urban America, Inc., which published it, with Peter Jost Blake (1920–   ) as editor. In 1970 the magazine was sold to Whitney Publications, and again published under the editorship of Blake until 1973, when it ceased publication.

Progressive Architecture suffered similar vicissitudes, but has survived. Sold to a conglomerate, Litton Industries, resold and then resold again, it continues to be published today. After Creighton, its editors have been Jan Christopher Rowan (1924–   ), Forrest Wilson (1918–   ), and the present editor, John Morris Dixon (1933–   ).

The *Journal of the American Institute of Architects* was often called the *AIA Journal*, from 1957 when Joseph Watterson (1900–72) became editor. From 1964, when William Dudley Hunt, Jr. (1922–   ), formerly senior editor of *Architectural Record*, became its first publisher, serving until 1972, the official name has been the *AIA Journal*. In 1965 Robert Earl Koehler (1924–   ) became editor, and he was succeeded by Donald James Canty (1929–   ) in 1973.

After becoming a strictly professional magazine in 1914, *Architectural Record* continued to grow, though not without periods of trial, until it became the largest and most successful architectural magazine in the world. In 1938 it absorbed *American Architect* and *Architecture*. Having become a monthly in 1902, the magazine added a new fillip in 1956, a thirteenth regular issue, published ever since and now called *Record Houses*. In 1961 the magazine, together with its parent company, F. W. Dodge Corporation, was sold to McGraw-Hill, Inc., and has been published by that company ever since. In a few years, *Architectural Record* will be 100 years old, the oldest continuously published architectural magazine in the United States. Since World War II, its editors have been Kenneth Stowell (1894–1969), Harold Dana Hauf (1905–   ), John Knox Shear (1917–58), and Emerson Goble (1901–69). The present editor is Walter Frederick Wagner, Jr. (1926–   ).

A number of other architectural, or architecturally related, magazines were started after World War II, only to cease publication a few years later. Among them were: *Building Products; Architectural and Engineering News;* and *Architecture Plus*. One of the most influential, *Arts and Architecture*, was published from 1940 to 1960. Originally called *California Arts and Architecture* and edited by John Dymock Entenza (1905–   ), it later expanded to a national circulation. Among the accomplishments of the magazine and its editor was the sponsorship of pioneering house designs, which were actually built and featured in the magazine, designed by many noted architects of the era.

The only primarily architectural magazines being published in the United States today are the *AIA Journal, Architectural Record*, and *Progressive Architecture*. In addition to their chief editors, many of whom have been named previously, all three magazines have had many distinguished staff editors and famous authors. Some idea of the importance of the people who have written for architectural magazines might be gained from a sampling of the lengthy list of authors: critic Montgomery Schuyler (1843–1914), critic and historian Lewis Mumford (1895–   ), and historian Henry-Russell Hitchcock (1903–   ) for *Architectural Record*. Mumford and Hitchcock also wrote for *Architectural Forum*, whose writers and editors included Jane Jacobs (1916–   ) and Walter McQuade (1922–   ). While the other magazines have been mostly staff written, the *AIA Journal* for most of its existence has usually published articles by outside authors, a list of whom would include most of the well-known American architects, other environmental designers, critics, and historians of the 20th century.

A number of provocative and important books have been made out of articles in architectural magazines. Some idea of their importance may be gained from the mention of only a few: first published in the *AIA Journal*, the *Autobiography of an Idea* by Louis Henri Sullivan (1856–1924), and in *Architectural Record, In the Cause of Architecture* by Frank Lloyd Wright (1867–1959).

A large number of important continuing series have appeared in architectural magazines over the years, including the critical series published by *Progressive Architecture* and *Architectural Forum*, beginning in the 1940s, the series on architectural philosophy in the 1950s, and the *Image of the Architect* series in the 1950s and 1960s in *Architectural Record*, together with its *Building Types* series, which has been running continuously since 1937. Important series in the *AIA Journal* have included the *Urban Design* series written by Paul Spreiregen (1931–   ) of the 1960s, which had great impact on the architecture and planning of cities, and the *Comprehensive Architectural Services* series of the same era, which pioneered concepts of broad areas of architectural practice which have been adopted today. Both series eventually were made into books. Another important series was the *Office Practice series*, which was spawned from the *Image of the Architect series* in *Architectural Record*, beginning in the 1960s. Edited by senior editor William B. Foxhall (1913–75), this series was also later made into an important book. For a number of years, the *AIA Journal* has published the finest architectural book review department in the United States, under the editorship of Mary E. Osman (1913–   ).

In addition to their editorial content, the architectural magazines serve their audiences in other ways. Over the years, they have sponsored numerous round tables, discussion meetings, and other important events. Notable among these have been the round tables of *Architectural Forum*, beginning in the

1940s, and of *Architectural Record* recently. The magazines have given aid to out-of-work or needy architects in bad times, for example, by engaging them to write articles, as in the case of Louis Henri Sullivan for the *AIA Journal* and Frank Lloyd Wright for *Architectural Record.* Wright edited special issues of his work for *Architectural Forum,* which also helped architects in another way during the era of Howard Myers, by staging competitions for building designs, with money prizes for the winning architects. A more recent example of this kind of service to architecture, architects, and the public is the international competition, called Human Settlements, sponsored by *Architectural Record,* under the general editorship of senior editor Mildred Floyd Schmertz. Judged in 1976, the competition involved the design of complete urban environments for underdeveloped countries. An example of a continuing service to architects and architecture is the annual design award program of *Progressive Architecture,* published every year since the mid-1940s.

Related Articles BOOK, ARCHITECTURAL; CRITICISM, ARCHITECTURE; GRAPHIC DESIGN; LIBRARY.

Sources of Additional Information Architectural Index; Art Index; Avery Index to Architectural Periodicals; Engineering Index; Reader's Guide to Periodical Literature.

Periodicals *AIA Journal,* 1735 New York Ave., N.W., Washington, D.C. 20006; *Architectural Record,* 1221 Avenue of the Americas, New York, N.Y. 10020; *Progressive Architecture,* 600 Summer St., Stamford, Conn. 06904; Engineering, landscape architecture, interior design, and other related magazines are listed in various articles in this book.

MASONRY STRUCTURE A system in which masonry units (bricks, concrete block, and stone) are used to form the structure of buildings, as opposed to masonry veneer in which the units only function as a covering or finish for walls or other building parts. Although the word *masonry* originally referred only to stonework, the term is used today to denote work with any materials that are held together with mortar, including brick, structural clay tile, other types of tile, concrete block, cement brick, gypsum block, glass block, and stone.

Uses Although masonry materials were often used in the past for the construction of roof structures, particularly domes and vaults, today the major structural uses are for bearing walls, which support their own weights, those of other building elements above them, and the live loads imposed by snow, wind on roofs, furniture and furnishings, and people. In such walls, masonry arches are sometimes used over openings, but steel or concrete lintels are more commonly used today. Brick walls may also be used in skeleton-frame buildings to resist lateral forces of wind on the structures. Masonry is often used in the foundations of buildings which may have wood-frame, masonry, or other types of wall structures, and is sometimes used, with reinforcing, in columns and beams. Masonry materials are often used for nonstructural, non-load-bearing walls, and for such purposes as curtain walls on the exteriors of buildings and partitions in their interiors.

Types The major types of masonry used for structural purposes in buildings today include brick, structural clay tile and facing tile, concrete block, and stone. These may also be utilized for nonstructural purposes. Other nonstructural masonry types include other kinds of clay tile, such as ceramic mosaics and other tiles intended for floor and wall coverings, gypsum block, and glass block.

Major considerations in the structural design of walls with masonry units include the strength and other properties of the types of units to be used; laying and bonding of the units, so that they act together as an integral system; types and placement of mortar; height and thickness of walls; bracing or support for loads from the sides, called lateral support; support provided by foundations or footings; and reinforcement if used.

Code Requirements Requirements for masonry structures are contained in building codes and other codes and standards. In general, requirements begin with the allowable compressive stresses, those that result when masonry is pushed upon by weights, or loads, from above, the major stresses that masonry withstands. Such stresses are dependent on the type of masonry unit and the type of mortar used. They cover a wide range and apply to the gross cross section of complete walls or other structural elements of buildings. Structural clay-tile masonry allowable compressive strengths are low, ranging from about 70 to 100 pounds per square inch (psi), according to the type of unit and the mortar used. Concrete block masonry has similar allowable strengths. Solid brick masonry has allowable compressive strengths ranging from about 75 to 500 psi, according to the type of brick and mortar. Stone masonry has allowable compressive strengths ranging from about 80 psi for rubble work, with certain mortars, to 800 psi or more for ashlar granite work, with the strongest mortars.

The allowable compressive strengths for various types of mortars are determined by the portland or masonry cement used in them and the proportions of cement to hydrated lime or lime putty. The strongest mortar, designated M, is usually made with 1 part by volume of portland cement, 1 part masonry cement, and 4½ to 6 parts aggregate. Sometimes type M mortar is made with ¼ part hydrated lime or lime putty, 1 part portland cement, and 2½ to 3¾ parts aggregate. Type M mortar has an allowable compressive stress of 2,500 psi. Type S mortar has an allowable compressive strength of 1,800 psi, type N 750 psi, and type O 350 psi. In addition, there are high-strength mortars with high tensile as well as compressive strengths. Allowable loads for specific building locations must be determined from the applicable building and other codes and standards. Upon this basis and that of the actual loads to be supported, proper masonry systems may be designed.

The laying and bonding of masonry units to conform with codes and for proper practice generally requires the proper amount of mortar to be used, its proper placement, and the proper bonding of masonry units by laying them in positions that produce bonding or by the use of corrosion-resistant metal ties. Practices vary between masonry types. (See articles entitled brick; stone; tile.)

The thickness and height of masonry walls are also included in codes. In general, masonry bearing walls are required to be a minimum of 12 in in thickness, except that residential buildings not more than 3 stories tall or 35 ft high may have walls 8 in thick. Nonresidential buildings, taller than 35 ft, must have the lower portions of their walls thickened an additional 4 in for each 35 ft, or fraction, of additional height. Thus a 105-ft-high building would have 20-in walls for the lowest 35 ft of height, 16-in walls for the next 35 ft, and 12-in walls for the uppermost portion. Exceptions to these rules exist; for example, rubble stone walls must usually be 4 in thicker than the walls previously mentioned. Other exceptions also exist. Nonbearing masonry walls may generally be 4 in less in thickness than bearing walls, but not usually less than 8 in.

Another requirement for masonry bearing walls is that certain ratios between heights to thicknesses and lengths to thicknesses must not be exceeded. In general, the ratios are 20:1 for solid walls and 18:1 for walls with hollow units or cavity walls. Thus a 12-in solid wall should not be higher or longer than 20 times 12 in, or 20 ft. If the height or length exceeds 20 ft, the wall must be supported laterally, generally by the use of cross walls, buttresses, piers, floors, roofs, or other means. All must be solidly anchored or bonded to the supported wall. The unsupported height of piers should not exceed 10 times their smallest dimensions. In calculating the ratios for masonry work, the thicknesses of veneers are not included, unless they are bonded in such a way as to become integral portions of the structural walls. Nonbearing walls may have higher ratios.

Masonry walls may be reinforced by various means, including integrating them with reinforced concrete, and use of special joint reinforcement devices. Masonry is also used for retaining walls that resist the forces of earth on one side. The structural design of reinforced and retaining walls is ordinarily accomplished by structural engineers to suit the needs of individual buildings. Masonry walls may also be used for garden walls and similar purposes. For all masonry structures, proper design of foundations is required to prevent settling, cracking of walls, or other deterioration or failure. (See the article entitled foundation.) Other methods for preventing cracking are limitation of moisture penetration and movement in walls, use of control or expansion joints, and use of reinforcement.

In general, expansion joints are provided in long walls, where offsets occur, at junctions of walls, and other places where movement may be expected. Steel reinforcement may be placed in walls to limit move-

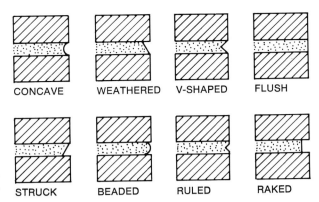

CONCAVE WEATHERED V-SHAPED FLUSH

STRUCK BEADED RULED RAKED

MASONRY STRUCTURE Sections of typical joints.

ment resulting from temperature changes and other causes. Moisture penetration into walls may not only cause movement, but is undesirable because of its effects on strength and appearance and the need to prevent moisture from reaching the interiors of buildings.

Moisture Resistance Certain masonry products have better moisture resistance than others, and this factor should be taken into consideration in their selection. It is also important to use the recommended mortars, particularly in such cases as in masonry below grade. Mortar should solidly fill the spaces between masonry units. Several types of mortar joints are employed in masonry work, including concave or rodded, weather, and V-shaped, all considered good protection against water infiltration; flush joints, considered fair protection; and beaded, raked, and struck joints, considered poor protection. In brick of more porous types, concrete block, and sometimes other masonry structures, painting with special paints or coating with bituminous products, silicones, or other kinds of coatings or finishes are required to prevent moisture infiltration. In cavity walls, weep holes are required to allow moisture to escape from the cavities. For all types of masonry, proper flashing is required. (See the article entitled waterproofing.)

The above discussion about masonry structures must be considered as general, providing only guidelines for design and construction. In practice, governing codes and standards must be followed as well as principles of good design and construction to ensure that masonry structures will be adequate in strength, will resist cracking and moisture penetration, will properly perform the required functions, and will present the appearance desired for specific buildings.

History Masonry structures have been used in architecture since early primitive times. Their uses in the early civilizations around the Mediterranean Sea and in Europe are discussed under the titles listed at the end of this article.

The pre-Columbian American Indians living in Southwestern lands that later became part of the United States never developed the high level of stone architecture constructed in Mexico, Central America, and Peru. However, they did construct brick and sometimes stone walls in front of their cliff dwellings and well-designed pueblos of adobe. Some of these are still in existence, at least in part, mostly in Colorado, Arizona, and New Mexico. Stonework was usually laid without mortar and adobe was constructed much as it is today. Pre-Columbian use of these materials was for walls only; their builders did not know the principle of the arch.

American Development   American colonists used stone and brick for construction early in the 17th century in the English colonies and even earlier in the Spanish. Used at first for relatively minor architectural elements, such as building foundations and chimneys, brick and stone were later used for columns; bearing wall structures; and arches, vaults, and domes. Brick and stone masonry was used for the structures of many buildings in the United States, particularly the more important ones, until nearly the end of the 19th century. Although supplanted to some extent by structural steel and reinforced concrete, they are still extensively used, but not usually in tall structures. During the 19th century, several innovations occurred in masonry work. Included in these innovations were hollow clay blocks, similar in purpose to the structural clay tile of today; reinforced masonry, making stronger structures possible; and both solid and hollow cement and sand-lime bricks, often marketed as artificial stone. Concrete block came into widespread use in the 20th century. All these materials are important masonry materials today. Walls of masonry with the exterior courses separated from those of the interior, called cavity walls, also were developed in the 19th century. They were then considered to be superior to solid walls in the prevention of moisture infiltration and in insulating qualities. For some years, cavity walls were used extensively, but are used less frequently today.

More commonly used today are solid masonry walls of brick, structural clay tile and facing tile, concrete block, or stone; and used even more extensively are walls of building, sometimes called common, brick, structural clay tile, or concrete block, with exterior facings of stucco, face brick, stone, ceramic veneer (formerly known as terra-cotta), or structural facing tile, and the interiors covered with plaster or other materials.

Related Articles   ARCH; BRICK; COLUMN; CONCRETE; DOME; FOUNDATION; GLASS; ROOF; TILE; VAULT; WALL.

Sources of Additional Information   Brick Institute of America, 1750 Old Meadow Rd., McLean, Va. 22101; Building Stone Inst., 420 Lexington Ave., New York, N.Y. 10017; Facing Tile Inst., 1750 Old Meadow Rd., McLean, Va. 22101; International Masonry Inst., 823 15th St., N.W., Washington, D.C. 20005.

MAYBECK, BERNARD

MAYBECK, BERNARD   American architect (1862–1957). Somewhat of an enigma as an architect, Bernard Maybeck has been called eclectic, mystic, romantic, bohemian, actor. He played all these roles; in short, he was a character. He selected the forms and themes of his architecture from wherever he found them. In one of his most famous buildings, the First Church of Christ, Scientist (1910), in Berkeley, Calif., elements of Byzantine, Romanesque, Gothic, Renaissance, Japanese, and perhaps even Chinese architecture may be found, along with that of Swiss and American wood buildings. He was a faddist, espousing vegetarianism and other prevalent movements. When he designed the terra-cotta cornice for an early building he worked on, he contrived a fanciful monogram of the initials of his future wife, which was repeated all around the top of the building. He also designed his own clothes, including high-waisted trousers to serve as vests.

Despite his apparent eccentricities, Maybeck was a gifted designer. His plans were ingenious and functional. The forms he used for his buildings were inventive in ornament and appearance, but no less inventive was his use of materials, structural systems, and other engineering aspects of his buildings. Through all the eclectic elements of his buildings, there is a glimmer of the modern movement in architecture.

Works   In many of Maybeck's early buildings may be seen a preoccupation with the Craft Movement, begun in the 19th century by William Morris in England. As time went by, he never deserted the precepts of fine craftsmanship, but he did gradually abandon the simplicities of wood architecture that occupied his contemporaries, the Greene brothers, most of their lives. Instead, he employed a much more complex and eclectic use of diverse forms and materials. In his first major building, Hearst Hall (1899), University of California, Berkeley, he pioneered the use of laminated arches, built up of glued layers of wood, which eliminated the need for columns in the entire central portion of the building. This was a structural milestone. Destroyed by fire in 1922, the building had an exterior of redwood shakes with the form of the great arches exposed on the front. He used laminated arches for many later buildings. Other buildings of about the same time still exist on the Berkeley campus: the Faculty Club (1902), now much enlarged, and the Hearst Memorial Gymnasium for Women (1925), designed in association with Julia Morgan (1872–1957), the architect of part of William Randolph Hearst's estate, San Simeon.

Maybeck continued his structural innovation in his Town and Gown Clubhouse (1899), Berkeley, where he utilized wood king-post trusses; in the Outdoor Art Clubhouse (1905), Mill Valley, with its posts and beams projecting outside and ornamented; and in the Hopps House (1906), Moss Valley, which had paired rafters with posts between them. At the time, he was designing other buildings, mostly houses, including a house for Mrs. Hearst, now destroyed, which cost $100,000, a very large sum for those days, especially when compared to the $4,000 to $5,000 houses he had been designing. In 1907 he turned his attention to a monolithic reinforced concrete structure in the Lawson House, Berkeley.

Then came Maybeck's greatest opportunity, one that many think produced his best building, the commission for the design of the First Church of Christ, Scientist (1910) in Berkeley. In this design, his creative powers, now fully developed, were employed to their fullest. This is the church previously mentioned as combining parts of so many styles and cultures. In this building, Maybeck produced a rich and ornamental effect throughout the interior and exterior. His experiments with materials and structure continued: great carved wood trusses, exposed inside the building, intersect in the middle to form a Greek cross that reflects the floor plan. New materials, such as asbestos panels, metal factory windows, and reinforced concrete, are skillfully combined with redwood in a building of the present, but with its roots in the past. After this, his commissions declined. He did the charming wood-shingle Chick House (1913) in Berkeley and the Bingham House (1917) in Montecito.

Then he produced the splendid Palace of Fine Arts (1915) for the San Francisco Panama-Pacific International Exposition. The structure of the palace was formed with daring three-hinged steel arches that had been used in buildings only a few times before, but its exterior was as eclectic as any Maybeck had done previously. The palace made an immediate hit with San Franciscans. Unlike the other fair buildings, it was allowed to remain standing after the fair had closed. But though its structure was sound, the materials covering it were not and soon began to deteriorate. Gradually, it turned into a ruin, which may well have been what Maybeck had intended. In 1967, with the aid of $2 million given by a San Francisco citizen, Walter Johnson, and matched by the State of California, the palace was rebuilt in more permanent building materials by architects Welton Becket and Associates, following the original Maybeck plans housed in the library of the University of California.

Maybeck had reached his peak. He did town plans for two small towns, but nothing came of the first one and only two buildings from the second. In 1923 he designed the Glen Alpine Cabins, Lake Tahoe, simple buildings of granite, with factory windows and corrugated iron roofs, integrated into the rugged landscape. In 1927 he did the Hearst Gymnasium, and found a new client who kept him going for awhile. For this client, Earle C. Anthony, (1880–1967), Maybeck designed an elaborate house (1927) in Los Angeles that had 21 levels and was constructed of stone from Caen, France, and roof tile from Barcelona, Spain. The cost was $500,000. He also designed two showrooms for Packard automobiles in Berkeley and San Francisco, built in 1928, for the same client. Though he continued to go to his office until 1942, when he was eighty, his last important commission was for the master plan and buildings of Principia College, Elsah, Ill. The eight buildings were not completed until 1938. Maybeck did not supervise their construction, and though the college shows traces of his better work, the vigor and creativity were gone.

MAYBECK, BERNARD Exterior, First Church of Christ, Scientist (1910), Berkeley, Calif. *(Julius Shulman)*

MAYBECK, BERNARD Interior, First Church of Christ, Scientist (1910), Berkeley, Calif. *(Julius Shulman)*

MAYBECK, BERNARD Palace of Fine Arts (1915; rebuilt 1965), Panama-Pacific International Exposition, San Francisco, Calif. [*Architects: Welton Becket Assoc. and Hans Gerson. (Morley Baer)*]

MAYBECK, BERNARD   Exterior, Chick House (1913), Berkeley, Calif.
(Morley Baer)

MAYBECK, BERNARD   Interior, Chick House (1913), Berkeley, Calif.
(Morley Baer)

Maybeck lived to see his work highly regarded and himself praised as one of the great pioneers of modern architecture. He felt that he could make things of the past come alive again, in harmony with the present in a world of his own creation. Many think that he succeeded.

Life Bernard Maybeck was born in New York City on February 7, 1862, the son of German immigrant parents. His father, a wood-carver, wanted his son to follow him into that trade, but his mother, who died when he was three, had wanted him to be an artist. Maybeck always remembered a childhood spent drawing instead of playing ball like other boys. He also took extra courses in French, German, and philosophy. Young Maybeck turned out to be an indifferent student and left school at seventeen, to be apprenticed to a wood-carver as his father had wished. This lasted only a short time and he soon found himself working for his father who directed a large New York wood-carving shop.

At eighteen, Maybeck was sent to Paris as an apprentice in furniture design. The shop in which he worked was across the street from the famous École des Beaux Arts. Becoming interested in architecture and architects, Maybeck, with his father's permission, entered that school of classical academic tradition. This seemed to suit him just fine, for he had become captivated with Classic Greece and the Romanesque and early Gothic eras, and their architecture. This romantic and eclectic approach to architecture stayed with him all his life, as did his pronounced flair for invention.

After passing his final examination at the École in 1886, Maybeck returned to the United States to his first architectural job with Carrère and Hastings, a New York firm, recently established by his roommate at the École, Thomas Hastings (1860–1929). This firm, later to become a leading eclectic office, was engaged in the design of the now-demolished Ponce de Leon Hotel (1888) in St. Augustine, Fla. Hastings and Maybeck produced a design that was a mixture of Spanish and Mexican forms which foretold the future of eclecticism of both men.

After the hotel was finished, Maybeck formed a short-lived partnership with James Russell in Kansas City, Mo., where he met Mark White and his sister, Annie, who was to become the architect's wife in 1900. Mark White worked with Maybeck for many years as superintendent of construction. Moving on to Berkeley, Calif., with the Whites in 1889, Maybeck worked a while for an architect, then as a furniture designer and carver, and then as a draftsman with another architect, A. Page Brown (1859–96). In this office, he worked on the Church of the New Jerusalem (Swedenborgian), built in 1894 in San Francisco.

In 1894 Maybeck took a position teaching descriptive geometry in the department of drawing at the University of California, Berkeley, and later taught architecture. These were the rudimentary beginnings of the College of Architecture at that university. While teaching at the university, Maybeck initiated and administered an international competition for a campus master plan, sponsored and paid for by Mrs. Phoebe Apperson Hearst, activities that took him to New York City and Europe and brought him considerable recognition and publicity. However, the competition cost Maybeck his job, for architect John Galen Howard (1864–1931), brought from New York in 1901 to supervise the work, took over as professor of architecture. While administering the competition, Maybeck had received several commissions, including one from Mrs. Hearst for Hearst Hall, later destroyed by fire.

Before his career ended, Maybeck designed at least 250 buildings. An innocent in money matters, Maybeck started offices in San Francisco on three separate occasions, commuting from Berkeley, but none was profitable. His wife, soon after their marriage, had taken over their financial affairs, both private and professional, and she managed to keep things fairly solvent, until about 1910. During the next few years to keep going, he sold, one by one, some lots he had bought some years before. Maybeck was then forced by his circumstances to take a job as a draftsman with another architect, Willis Polk (1867–1924), one of his former students. Polk had received a commission to design the Palace of Fine Arts in San Francisco. Too busy to do the work, Polk asked his draftsmen to try their hands at its design. Maybeck produced a design that so impressed a member of the architectural commission, Henry Bacon, architect of the Lincoln Memorial, that Bacon insisted it be constructed. Polk gave Maybeck full charge of the work and also the credit. Although he grumbled about doing this work for draftsman's wages, Maybeck went on to produce what many think is a masterpiece.

Maybeck maintained and visited his office until 1942. His name remained in the lobby directory and on an office door because the old man had told his young associate, William Gladstone Merchant, he never wanted to retire. During World War II, his fame obscured, Maybeck lived in a cabin he had designed, busying himself with various ideas and projects. After the war, he returned to the old Maybeck house in Berkeley. The late 1940s saw a resurgence of interest in his work, as it had in that of the Greene brothers. Yet his carpenter, Ivan Melvin, called him a real common man. As an architect, his peers thought otherwise. In 1951 they awarded him the Gold Medal of the American Institute of Architects, their highest honor.

At age 95, on October 3, 1957, Bernard Maybeck died. He left a legacy of highly original and creative buildings that have influenced architecture ever since.

Related Articles BEAUX ARTS, ÉCOLE DES; ECLECTIC ARCHITECTURE; GREENE AND GREENE; MODERN ARCHITECTURE.

Further Reading Cardwell, Kenneth H.: *Bernard Maybeck—Artisan, Architect, Artist*, Peregrine Smith, Santa Barbara, Calif., 1976.

McINTIRE, SAMUEL American architect and wood-carver (1757–1811). Samuel McIntire became one of the greatest architect-builders of colonial times and the early years of the American republic. Although self-taught in architecture, he had great skill in working with wood that complemented his innate sense of the right way to develop the inherent qualities of wood into sensitive and beautiful elements of buildings. This was particularly apparent in his interiors, which are still considered as some of the most finely detailed and executed in America.

Works McIntire's buildings, most of which were houses for the wealthy of Salem, Mass., are usually considered to be Georgian in style, though certainly a rather late Georgian that is sometimes called Adam or Early Federal style. Perhaps his masterpiece was the Gardner-Pingree House (1805) in Salem. The exterior is a rather austere, restrained squarish building of three stories, beautifully proportioned and detailed. Inside, the art of McIntire comes into full play in the masterfully designed and executed fireplaces and mantels, doorways, and windows.

Another fine McIntire house is the Pierce-Nichols (1785), Salem, also noted for its fine proportions and details. Among others in Salem are the Elias Hasket Derby House (1780) and a remarkable series of houses on the west side of Washington Square. Two of McIntire's nonresidential buildings still exist in Salem: Assembly House (1783), remodeled about 1796, and Hamilton Hall (1807).

Life Samuel McIntire was born in Salem, Mass., in January 1757, where he subsequently designed and built his buildings. In fact, he never traveled very far from his birthplace. Trained as a wood-carver by his father, he became an architect and builder through the study of books and from experience. His work for the wealthy of Salem, most of them shipowners or otherwise involved in commerce of the sea, developed into a long and successful career. Starting out on his own, he later employed his son, two brothers,

McINTIRE, SAMUEL Gardner-Pingree House (1805), Salem, Mass. (Wayne Andrews)

and a nephew, all craftsmen, in his work. In 1792 he took part in the competition for the design of the U.S. Capitol, a prize that went to an amateur gentleman-architect, Dr. William Thornton (1759–1828). McIntire died in Salem on February 8, 1811.

Related Articles CAPITAL, UNITED STATES; COLONIAL ARCHITECTURE; GEORGIAN ARCHITECTURE.

Further Reading Cousins, Frank, and Phil M. Riley: *The Woodcarver of Salem—Samuel McIntire, His Life and Work,* AMS Press, New York, 1970; Kimball, Sidney F.: *Mr. Samuel McIntire, Carver—The Architect of Salem,* Essex Institute, Salem, Mass., 1940.

McKIM, MEAD AND WHITE American architectural firm. Charles Follen McKim (1847–1909), William Rutherford Mead (1846–1928), and Stanford White (1853–1906) formed the firm of McKim, Mead and White in New York City in 1879. It became one of the largest and most successful architectural firms in the world. The three partners practiced together more than 25 years, and produced more than 500 buildings. The firm continued until the 1960s, long after all three original partners were dead. Starting out as eclectic architects working in a number of styles, the firm gradually turned almost exclusively to buildings in a style developed from the architecture of the Renaissance and adhering quite strictly to the tenets of the École des Beaux Arts in Paris, where McKim had been educated. Their buildings were noted for classical good taste, constrained and discriminating rather than inventive.

Firm's Works Important houses were those for H. Victor Newton (1881), Elberon, N.J., W. G. Low (1887), Newport, R.I., both with shingle exteriors; that for H. A. C. Taylor (1885), Newport, in Colonial Revival style; and the Villard residences (1884), New York City, originally six separate houses in Italian Renaissance style. The firm designed a great number of clubs, among the finest being the Century Association (1891); the Harvard Club and the Metropolitan Club, both in 1894; and the University Club (1900); all in New York City. Among the libraries designed were the Boston Public Library (1895), often considered the firm's best building; and the Low Library (1897) at Columbia University, and what has been called the jewel of Renaissance Revival style, the Morgan Library (1906), both in New York City. The firm designed many other notable buildings, including several others at Columbia University, the First Methodist Church (1882), Baltimore, Md., in Romanesque Revival style, and Pennsylvania Station (1910; see illustration in article railway station), New York City, now demolished. The firm was also deeply involved in the design of the World's Columbian Exposition in Chicago in 1893, and designed the Agricultural Palace for that fair.

McKim's Life Charles Follen McKim was born at Isabella Furnace, Chester County, Pa., on August 24, 1847, the son of a Presbyterian minister father and a Quaker mother. McKim originally planned to become a mining engineer and entered Harvard University,

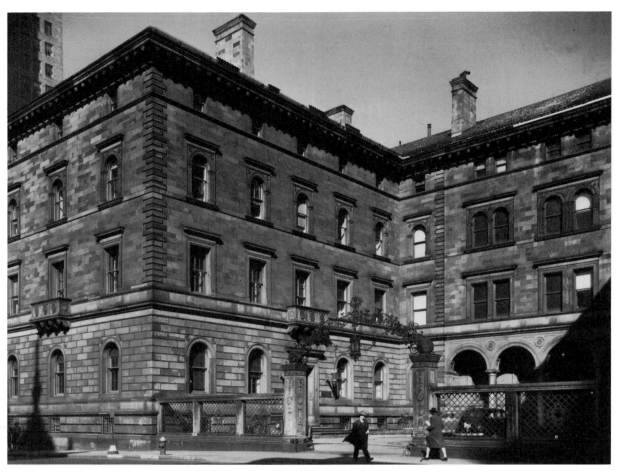

McKIM, MEAD AND WHITE Villard residences (1884), New York,
N.Y. *(Wayne Andrews)*

McKIM, MEAD AND WHITE Boston Public Library (1895), Boston,
Mass. *(Library of Congress)*

McKIM, MEAD AND WHITE Century Association (1891), New York, N.Y. *(Wayne Andrews)*

McKIM, MEAD AND WHITE University Club (1900), New York, N.Y. *(Wurts Brothers)*

Cambridge, Mass. While spending a few months working in the office of an architect, Russell Sturgis (1836–1909), he decided that he would rather be an architect. In 1867 he entered the École des Beaux Arts in Paris and after three years of schooling and travel in France and England returned to America in 1870, to enter the office of architect Henry Hobson Richardson (1838–86), then practicing in New York City. He stayed there until 1872, working on, among other buildings, Richardson's Trinity Church (1877) for Boston, across from which McKim's firm would place its own Boston Public Library some 25 years later.

In 1872 McKim formed a partnership with William Rutherford Mead and William B. Bigelow, which lasted until 1878, when Bigelow retired. In 1879 Stanford White, who had been working in Richardson's office, joined the other two in partnership, with McKim as senior partner. McKim distinguished himself not only in architecture, but in his encouragement of patronage of the other arts by his wealthy clients and in his service to architectural education and to his profession.

Just as McKim, Mead and White built a reputation for buildings derived from those of the Renaissance, McKim acquired a reputation as a sort of Renaissance man. He felt that art and architecture were the prime civilizing influences on society. And he spent much of his time in fine clubs, often designed by his firm, in luxurious parlor cars, and in European travel, enjoying cultural activities and conversation while he persuaded potential clients to entrust their buildings to his firm and to allow him to commission sculpture, murals, and other art to go into the buildings. A tall, redheaded man, he was genial, dignified, urbane, and discriminating.

All his energies went into his professional and public life. He never really had much of a private life. Married in 1874, at age twenty-five, to Annie Bigelow, the

sister of his partner, they had one daughter, Margaret. The marriage ended in divorce in 1878. He then married Julia Amory Appleton in 1885, but she died two years later. He did not see his only daughter for 20 years, until 1899, but later she became his companion. Busy all his life designing great houses for his friends and other clients, McKim never had time to design one for himself. All his time went into his practice, his profession, and his other interests.

In the architectural profession, he was one of the giants. Of his many services to his profession perhaps the most important was serving as president of the American Institute of Architects for two years, 1901 to 1903. During his tenure, the notable house designed by Dr. William Thornton (1759–1828) for Col. John Tayloe, now called The Octagon (1800), was purchased to become the AIA headquarters with funds personally underwritten by McKim. It was also a time in which he served on the Park Commission of the District of Columbia, working to complete the planning of Washington that began with the plans Pierre Charles L'Enfant (1754–1825) had designed in 1791.

McKim worked all his life for the cause of architectural education, establishing scholarships and fellowships for students. With other architects, especially Daniel Hudson Burnham (1846–1912), who had also designed buildings for the World's Columbian Exposition in Chicago in 1893, McKim originated the idea for a postgraduate school for architecture and other arts in Italy. In 1895 this idea became a reality with the opening of the American Academy in Rome, called at first the American School of Architecture. McKim became its first president and continued in that position for 15 years.

In his later life, McKim received many honors for his work, honorary doctor's degrees from Columbia University and the University of Pennsylvania, honorary membership in the Royal Institute of British Archi-

McKIM, MEAD AND WHITE Morgan Library (1906), New York, N.Y.
(Detroit Publishing Co., Library of Congress)

tects, and its highest honor in 1903, the Royal Gold Medal.

On January 1, 1908, suffering from ill health, McKim left the office of McKim, Mead and White for an extended vacation. But he was never able to return to work, and on September 4, 1909, he died. On December 15, 1909, the Gold Medal of the American Institute of Architects, voted to him a year before, was received by the last surviving original partner of McKim, Mead and White, William Mead, and presented by him to the architect's daughter, Margaret McKim. To a large and distinguished audience, the major address was made by the President of the United States, William Howard Taft (1857–1930).

Mead's Life William Rutherford Mead was born in Brattleboro, Vt., on August 20, 1846. After graduating from Amherst University, Amherst, Mass., in 1867, Mead worked for a while in the office of an engineer and in 1868 for an architect, Russell Sturgis (1836–1909). During 1871 and 1872, he studied architecture at the Accademia de Belle Arte in Florence, Italy.

After returning to the United States, Mead formed an architectural partnership, McKim, Mead and Bigelow, with Charles Follen McKim and William B. Bigelow. In 1878 Bigelow left the firm and was replaced the following year by Stanford White; the name of the firm was then changed to McKim, Mead and White. Unlike the other two partners, both of whom were noted for their design abilities, Mead was more talented in the management of the firm than in design. He was considered a very good critic of the design work of the others and helped them to improve their work. He occasionally made conceptual designs of buildings.

In 1884 he married a Hungarian, Olga Kilenyi. After the death of McKim in 1909, Mead took over the presidency of the American Academy in Rome, and remained in that position until he died. Mead withdrew from the firm in 1919, but continued as a consultant for the rest of his life. Having survived his partner, White, by 22 years, and McKim by 19, William Rutherford Mead died on June 20, 1928.

White's Life Stanford White was born in New York City on November 9, 1853, the son of Richard Grant White (1821–85), a noted writer, editor, and music critic. White showed considerable talent in drawing and the arts as a young child. After having attended private schools in New York City, he entered New York University, but stayed only a short time. At nineteen, White worked in the office of Henry Hobson Richardson, where he met his future partner, McKim, who was working there on Richardson's magnificent Trinity Church, to be located in Boston.

When McKim left the office in 1872 to start his own practice, White took over some of the work on the plans and details of the church. Most of McKim's ideas were eventually supplanted. In 1878 White left Richardson's office to travel and study in Europe, returning in 1879, to become a partner in McKim, Mead and White. He also returned to his studies and graduated from New York University in 1881.

White married Bessie Springs in 1884, and a year later they had a child who died the same year. They had a son, Lawrence Grant White (1887–1956), who later graduated from Harvard, became an architect, joined McKim, Mead and White in 1914, and became a partner in the firm in 1920.

Stanford White was a talented draftsman and designer, not only of buildings but of interiors, picture frames, magazine covers for Scribner's and The Century, book bindings, and jewelry. A tall, well-built, redheaded man, White was a bon vivant, exuberant and flamboyant in his professional work and in his behavior. Considered Bohemian in his habits, he hobnobbed with a rather racy set, many of whom were connected with the theater, including the great actor John Barrymore (1882–1942). White and his wife lived apart after the first few years of their marriage, White staying in various apartments and studios in New York City.

White was considered a connoisseur of beauty in architecture, other arts, antiques, decoration, and women. Much of his work in the firm was devoted to ornamental or decorative details of buildings, and to their interiors, including furniture and furnishings. A collector all his life, he amassed a huge personal collection of art, antiques, and other art objects. He also selected and purchased such articles for clients of the firm.

In addition to his work on most of the buildings designed by the firm, White made designs on his own. One of his best was the Farragut Monument (1881), in Madison Square, New York City, for which White designed the base, and the famous sculptor Augustus Saint-Gaudens (1848–1907) did the sculpture, the first such collaboration between sculptor and architect in the United States. Another was also a monument, Washington Arch (1892), in Washington Square, New York City.

White was associated most closely with the design of certain buildings, houses, and clubs, mostly in New York City. The few that are still standing include the club for the Century Association (1891), the Metropolitan Club (1894), and the Hall of Fame (1900) at New York University.

White lived a full life, one that was full of triumphs and ended with scandal and tragedy. In 1890 his masterpiece, Madison Square Garden, was completed. This was a great complex that included a theater, a restaurant, a concert hall, a tower with studios, and a roof garden. White occupied one of the studios, while his wife lived in their country home in Long Island. White had a reputation for staging wild and voluptuous parties, and associating with theatrical people, including chorus girls. In 1901 he met a sixteen-year-old artist's model and chorus girl, Evelyn Nesbit with whom he became involved, she claimed intimately. Later Evelyn Nesbit married Harry Kendall Thaw, the profligate son of a wealthy Pittsburgh railway tycoon. Thaw, irresponsible, wild, and reckless, and some said a drug addict, was also madly jealous.

In 1905 disaster struck White; his great collection of art was totally destroyed in a New York City warehouse in which it had been stored. Then on June 25, 1906, while seated in the Madison Square Roof Garden, Stanford White was shot to death with a revolver held close to his head by Harry Kendall Thaw, who was obsessed with the idea that White had grievously wronged his wife and himself.

What followed was also tragic. At Thaw's trial for murder, which began in January 1907, his wife's testimony about intimate details of her relationship with White created a sensation. Printing the lurid details, newspapers called White a beast and worse. None of White's old cronies stepped forward to defend his reputation. Noted reporters covering the trial, included Irvin S. Cobb (1876–1944) and Elizabeth Meriwether Gilmer (1870–1951), who wrote under the name Dorothy Dix and later became famous for her advice column in newspapers all over the country. Only the upright Richard Harding Davis (1864–1916), a friend of White's but never a member of his inner circle, whose activities were being questioned, upheld the reputation of his friend and defended him in print.

The trial ended in April 1907, with a hung jury. Five voted not guilty by reason of insanity; seven guilty, as charged, of first-degree murder. In January 1908, Thaw's second trial began and on February 1, the verdict was not guilty on grounds of insanity. He was committed to the Asylum for the Criminal Insane, Matteawan, N.Y. In 1913 he escaped, went to Canada, was extradited, and tried again in 1915, again bringing out most of the lurid testimony of the other two trials. Judged sane, he was freed only to be judged insane again in 1917 for the kidnapping and whipping of a nineteen-year-old man. Committed to the Pennsylvania State Hospital, he was again released in 1924. Divorced in 1915, Thaw and Evelyn Nesbit reconciled for a while in 1925–26. He continued to get into trouble of various kinds until he died in 1947. Evelyn dropped from sight, but reportedly moved to California.

The two had caused not only the murder of Stanford White but the loss of his personal reputation. Neither Evelyn Nesbit nor Harry Thaw could be called stable people and, on many occasions, were proved to have been unreliable witnesses. The truth about White's actions cannot be known; he was a victim of his behavior and times. Although his name will always be linked with scandal, his reputation as a great architect has been enhanced with time.

In the years following, three of White's finest buildings, Madison Square Garden (1890), the Herald

Building (1893), and the Madison Square Presbyterian Church (1906), were demolished.

Related Articles ASSOCIATION, BUILDING INDUSTRY; BUILDING INDUSTRY; ECLECTIC ARCHITECTURE; EDUCATION; RICHARDSON, HENRY HOBSON.

Further Reading Baldwin, Charles C.: *Stanford White,* Dodd, Mead, New York, 1931; Granger, Alfred Hoyt: *Charles Follen McKim—A Study of His Life and Work,* Houghton Mifflin, Boston, 1913; Langford, Gerald: *The Murder of Stanford White,* Bobs Merrill, Indianapolis, 1962; Moore, Charles: *The Life and Times of Charles Follen McKim,* Houghton Mifflin, New York, 1929.

MEASUREMENT The extent, degree, capacity, dimensions, or amounts of anything, determined by measuring it; also the act of measuring or a system of measures. In architecture, a number of measurements are employed, including not only the dimensions of buildings, sites, and components but also time, temperature, forces, and heat flow.

In the United States, two major systems of measurement are used in architecture. One is the English, now often called the customary system, since England has adopted the metric system. Of growing importance in the United States is the metric system, now often called the Système International d'Unités (SI), or International System of Units. As the last major nation to adopt this system, the United States is embarked on a voluntary conversion to the International System and its SI units. In other parts of the world, actions are being taken to convert the metric units of all countries to the International System of Units (SI).

Major types of SI units utilized in architecture are those of length, area, and volume. For engineering and other purposes in architecture, important SI units are utilized to measure quantities in mechanics, the branch of physics that deals with forces on bodies; in heat and related phenomena; and in electricity, lighting, and acoustics. For further discussion on forces and related measurements of bodies not in motion, see the article entitled structure; on heat measurements, articles entitled heating, ventilating, and air conditioning; insulation, thermal; on acoustical measurements, the article entitled sound control; on lighting measurements, the article entitled lighting.

Customary versus SI Units Architects and other environmental designers in the United States measure buildings and their components in feet, inches, and fractions of inches in the English, or customary, system. In SI units, buildings and their components are usually measured in millimeters (mm), very much simplifying the preparation of working and other types of drawings, since no fractions are required. Also, when millimeters are used exclusively on drawings, the use of the abbreviation mm is not required. In the customary system, a dimension might appear on a drawing as 2'-7½". The equivalent SI unit measurement, in millimeters rounded off, would appear as 800. In drawings of larger elements of architecture, such as a site plan for a subdivision, the meter (m) may be used. And for even larger distances, the kilo-

meter (km), or 1,000 m is the proper SI unit rather than the mile as in the customary system. For land areas, as on building sites, the SI unit employed is the square kilometer (km²), and for smaller areas, the square meter (m²), while the acre and the square foot are ordinarily used in the customary system. The basic preferred module for the design and construction of buildings is 4 inches (in) in the customary system and 100 mm, slightly less than 4 in, in SI units.

There are major differences between customary and SI units. SI units have rational relationships based on powers of 10, or decimals, with each other, while most customary units are based on arbitrary measurements, many of them derived from assumed dimensions of the human body. SI units comprise an organized system, in which only seven base units and two supplementary units may be used to derive all the many kinds of measurements needed in the world of today and in its architecture. Multiples of the base and derived units all use the same prefixes to denote the same powers of 10 by which the base and derived units are multiplied. For example, milli means 1/1000, or 10^{-3}. Thus a millimeter is 1/1000 of a meter or 0.001 m, and a milligram (mg) is 0.001 gram (g).

Engineering and scientific calculations are greatly simplified by the use of SI units, not only because of decimalization but because of the greater coherence and versatility of the system. For example, 24 customary units for pressure and stress can all be expressed by one SI unit, the joule (J). In some cases, because of their usefulness and widespread acceptance, certain non-SI units are retained. They include the time units of minute, hour, and day; the angular measurements of second, minute, and degree; and the nautical mile.

History It is believed that crude measurements were used by humans in prehistoric times. The earliest were based on measurements of the human body and on weights of plant seeds. Since the dimensions of the human body are anything but standard, different measurements were adopted in different places at different times. Even after the adoption of standard measurements, different countries and even cities and localities within countries continued to use their own standards. The result was a confused, even chaotic, situation, which exists to the present time.

Units of length are thought to have been the first measurements developed, mainly because they would have been needed in building huts and tents and for other purposes. The primary unit of length was the cubit, considered to be the length of the human forearm from the elbow to the tip of the middle finger. Other measures were the palm, the width usually taken across the palm at the base of the fingers; the digit, the width of a finger; and the foot, the length of that extremity. Although these measurements varied between localities, their relationships were somewhat as follows: 4 digits equal 1 palm; 4 palms, or 16 digits, equal 1 foot; 1 foot equals ⅔ of a cubit; 6 palms equal 1 cubit; 4 cubits equal 1 fathom. All these are still used today in some places.

The earliest weights were used for the measurement of gold. They were based on the weights of plant seeds, and the term *grain* is still used in weighing gold and some other materials. Later such weight measurements were made equal to other quantities, such as the shekel, which varied in size from 120 to 218 grains (gr) in the ancient civilizations. Measures of volume were also developed very early and varied considerably between localities. By about 3000 B.C., attempts were made in the ancient lands to standardize the measures, at least within their own territories, by preserving specimen weights and measures in temples, by order of the rulers.

However, the variations between countries and localities persisted. For example, the Egyptian royal cubit, 20.63 in (524 mm), measured 7 palms or 28 digits, while the short cubit, 17.68 in (449 mm), was 6 palms or 24 digits long. The ancient Greek Olympic cubit, 18.23 in (463 mm), equaled 25 digits. An Olympic foot measured ⅔ of an Olympic cubit, 12.15 in (309 mm), while the ordinary cubit, 12.45 in (approximately 316 mm), more often used, equaled 16 digits.

The Romans attempted to standardize measurements in their empire. In spite of this effort, their measurements continued to vary somewhat in different places and at different times. One set of Roman measurements included the digit *(digitus)*, 0.73 in (slightly more than 18 mm); 4 *digiti* equal 1 palm *(palma)*, 2.9 in (approximately 74 mm); 4 *palmae*, 11.6 in (almost 1 foot or 296 mm), equaled 1 Roman foot *(pes)*; 1½ *pedes*, 17.5 in (approximately 443 mm), equaled 1 cubit *(cubitus)*.

After the time of the Romans, little or no attempt was made to standardize measurements, each nation, and often localities within nations, continuing to develop their own. By the 18th century, it is believed that there were almost 300 variations of the foot being used in Europe. A high degree of standardization was achieved in England in what came to be called the English system of measurement, and this system spread throughout the British Empire.

The first colonists who emigrated from England to America brought the English system, which was later somewhat modified and became the standard in America. Colonists from Spain, France, the Netherlands, and other places brought the systems of their own countries, and some of their measurements were absorbed into the American system.

The metric system was developed in France in the late 18th century; laws were passed in 1795 and 1799 making it the official system. Not until 1837 was the system made compulsory in France. And even today, some of the older terms for measurement, such as pound, are still used. Subsequently, the metric system was adopted in many of the nations of Europe and after World War II, in China, India, and other Eastern countries. The major group of nations still using the older system in the second half of the 20th century included England, the British Commonwealth, and the United States. Although the metric system seemed, on the face of it, to be standardized; in actuality it was not. Practices and standards varied from nation to nation, even though all used the same or similar units of measurement.

In 1875 an International Bureau of Weights and Measures (BIPM) was founded for the purpose of imposing standards. In 1885 the United Kingdom joined the bureau. In the United States in 1866, Congress passed a law making the metric system legal, but optional. For many years, the system was used only for a few applications, such as optometry. However, after 1866, the United States began to base its standard measurements on the metric system and that is the practice today. Over the years, those standards have changed, the present one for the meter, for example, having been established only in 1960. In the same year, the General Conference on Weights and Measures (CGPM), the governing body of the international bureau, adopted an international system of units, called Système International d'Unités, or SI units. Not only are SI units standardized so that they represent the same measurements wherever they are used, but an attempt has been made to make relationships between units as simple as possible.

England began conversion to the metric system, using SI units, in the 1960s, leading to complete conversion of all measurements in the 1980s. Australia and Canada followed the English lead during the 1970s, as did other nations of the Commonwealth, leaving the United States as the only major holdout. For many years, efforts were made to have the United States convert to the metric system. All failed. In 1975 the U.S. Congress enacted a law calling for voluntary conversion, without any deadline for completion. Congress also created a U.S. Metric Board, with members to be appointed by the president. In 1978 the members were appointed. Over the years, the metric system has been taught to some extent in American schools, colleges, and universities and has been used in certain disciplines, such as chemistry. During the 1970s, the process of teaching the metric system accelerated on most educational levels, including engineering and scientific schools. And SI unit sizes are gradually being adopted by various industries. When the U.S. conversion to the metric system will be completed is still a matter of conjecture.

Since 1972, the American National Metric Council has actively promoted conversion to the metric system. Participating in this effort are other private and governmental groups, such as the American National Standards Institute and the National Bureau of Standards of the U.S. Department of Commerce.

Further Reading Barry, Brother B. Austin: *Construction Measurements,* John Wiley, New York, 1973; Braybrooke, Susan, ed.: *AIA Metric Building and Construction Guide,* John Wiley, New York, 1980; Fairweather, Leslie, and Jan A. Sliwa: *VNR Metric Handbook,* Van Nostrand Reinhold, New York, 1969; Lytle, R. J.: *American Metric Construction Handbook,* Structures Publishing Co., Farmington, Mich., 1976.

Source of Additional Information American National Metric Council, 1625 Massachusetts Ave., N.W., Washington, D.C. 20036.

SI BASE UNITS

Physical Quantity	Unit	Symbol
length	meter	m
mass	kilogram	kg
time	second	s
electric current	ampere	A
thermodynamic temperature	kelvin	K
luminous intensity	candela	cd
amount of substance	mole	mol

DERIVED UNITS WITH COMPOUND NAMES

Physical Quantity	Unit	Symbol
area	square meter	m^2
volume	cubic meter	m^3
density	kilogram per cubic meter	kg/m^3
velocity	meter per second	m/s
angular velocity	radian per second	rad/s
acceleration	meter per second squared	m/s^2
angular acceleration	radian per second squared	rad/s^2
volume rate of flow	cubic meter per second	m^3/s
moment of inertia	kilogram meter squared	$kg \cdot m^2$
moment of force	newton meter	$N \cdot m$
intensity of heat flow	watt per square meter	W/m^2
thermal conductivity	watt per meter kelvin	$W/(m \cdot K)$
luminance	candela per square meter	cd/m^2

DERIVED UNITS WITH SPECIAL NAMES

Physical Quantity	Unit	Symbol	Derivation
frequency	hertz	Hz	s^{-1}
force	newton	N	$kg \cdot m/s^2$
pressure, stress	pascal	Pa	N/m^2
work, energy, heat	joule	J	$N \cdot m$
power	watt	W	J/s
electric charge	coulomb	C	$A \cdot s$
electric potential	volt	V	W/A
electric capacitance	farad	F	C/V
electric resistance	ohm	Ω	V/A
electric conductance	siemens	S	Ω^{-1}
magnetic flux	weber	Wb	$V \cdot s$
magnetic flux density	tesla	T	Wb/m^2
inductance	henry	H	Wb/A
luminous flux	lumen	lm	$cd \cdot sr$
illumination	lux	lx	lm/v^2
activity	becquerel	Bq	s^{-1}
absorbed dose	gray	Gy	J/kg
temperature	degree Celsius	°C	K

PREFERRED MULTIPLES AND SUBMULTIPLES

Prefix	Symbol	Factor	Magnitude
exa	E	10^{18}	1 000 000 000 000 000 000
peta	P	10^{15}	1 000 000 000 000 000
tera	T	10^{12}	1 000 000 000 000
giga	G	10^{9}	1 000 000 000
mega	M	10^{6}	1 000 000
kilo	k	10^{3}	1 000
milli	m	10^{-3}	0.001
micro	μ	10^{-6}	0.000 001
nano	n	10^{-9}	0.000 000 001
pico	p	10^{-12}	0.000 000 000 001
femto	f	10^{-15}	0.000 000 000 000 001
atto	a	0^{-18}	0.000 000 000 000 000 001

CONVERSION FACTORS FOR THE MOST COMMON UNITS USED IN ARCHITECTURE

Metric to Customary   *Customary to Metric*

Length

1 km	= 0.621 371	mile	1 mile (int)	= <u>1.609 344</u>	km	
	= 49.7097	chain	1 chain	= 210.1168	m	
1 m	= 1.093 61	yd	1 yd	= <u>0.9144</u>	m	
	= 3.280 84	ft	1 ft	= <u>0.3048</u>	m	
1 mm	= 0.039 370 1	in		= <u>304.8</u>	mm	
			1 in.	= <u>25.4</u>	mm	

Area

1 km²	= 0.386 102	mile²	1 mile²	= 2.59000	km²
1 ha	= 2.471 04	acre	1 acre	= 0.404 687	ha
1 m²	= 1.195 99	yd²		= 4046.87	m²
	= 10.7639	ft²	1 yd²	= 0.836 127	m²
1 mm²	= 0.001 550	in²	1 ft²	= 0.092 903	m²
			1 in²	= <u>645.16</u>	mm²

Volume, modulus of section

1 m³	= 0.810 709 × 10⁻³	acre ft	1 acre ft	= 1233.49	m³
	= 1.307 95	yd³	1 yd³	= 0.764 555	m³
	= 35.3147	ft³	100 board ft	= 0.235 973	m³
	= 423.776	board feet	1 ft³	= 0.028 316 8	m³
1 mm³	= 61.0237 × 10⁻⁶	in³		= 28.3168	L
			1 in³	= 16 387.1	mm³
				= 16.3871	mL

Capacity

1 L	= 0.035 314 7	ft³			
	= 0.264 172	gal (US)			
	= 1.056 69	qt (US)	1 gal (US)	= 3.785 41	L
1 mL	= 0.061 023 7	in³	1 qt (US)	= 946.353	mL
	= 0.033 814	fl oz (US)	1 fl oz (US)	= 29.5735	mL

Second moment of area

1 mm⁴	= 2.402 51 × 10⁻⁶	in⁴	1 in⁴	= 416 231	mm⁴
				= 0.416 231 × 10⁻⁶	m⁴

Plane angle

1 rad	= 57° 17′ 45″	degree	1 degree	= 0.017 453 3	rad
	= 57.2958	degree	1 minute	= 290.888	μad
	= 3437.75′	minute	1 second	= 4.848 14	μrad
	= 206 265″	second			

Velocity, speed

1 m/s	= 3.280 84	ft/s	1 ft/s	= <u>0.3048</u>	m/s
	= 2.236 94	mile/h	1 mile/h	= <u>1.609 344</u>	km/h
1 km/h	= 0.621 371	mile/h		= <u>0.447 04</u>	m/s

Acceleration

1 m/s²	= 3.280 84	ft/s²	1 ft/s²	= <u>0.3048</u>	m/s²

Volume rate of flow

1 m³/s	= 35.3147	ft³/s	1 ft³/s	= 0.028 316 8	m³/s
	= 22.8245	million gal/d	1 ft³/min	= 0.471 947	L/s
	= 0.810 709 × 10⁻³	acre ft/s	1 gal/min	= 0.063 090 2	L/s
1 L/s	= 2.118 88	ft³/min	1 gal/h	= 1.051 50	mL/s
	= 15.850 3	gal/min	1 million gal/d	= 43.8126	L/s
	= 951.022	gal/h	1 acre ft/s	= 1233.49	m³/s

Equivalent temperature value (^{t}°C = ^{t}K − 273.15)

^{t}C	5/9 (^{t}F−32)		^{t}F	= 9/5 ^{t}C + 32

Temperature interval

1 °C	= <u>1 K = 1.8 °F</u>		1 °F	= 0.555 556 °C or K
				= 5/9 °C = 5/9 K

Mass

1 t (metric ton)	= 1.102 31	ton (2000 lb)	1 ton	= 0.907 185	t (metric ton)
1 kg	= 2.204 62	lb		= 907.185	kg
	= 35.2740	oz	1 lb	= 0.453 592	kg
1 g	= 0.035 274	oz	1 oz	= 28.3495	g
	= 0.643 105	pennyweight	1 pennyweight	= 1.555 17	g

NOTE: Underlined values are exact conversions.

CONVERSION FACTORS FOR THE MOST COMMON UNITS USED IN ARCHITECTURE *(Cont.)*

Metric to Customary			Customary to Metric		

Mass/unit length

| 1 kg/m | = 0.671 969 | lb/ft | 1 lb/ft | = 1.488 16 | kg/m |
| 1 g/m | = 3.547 99 | lb/mile | 1 lb/mile | = 0.281 849 | g/m |

Mass/unit area

1 kg/m²	= 0.204 816	lb/ft²	1 lb/ft²	= 4.882 43	kg/m²
1 g/m²	= 0.029 494	oz/yd²	1 oz/yd²	= 33.9057	g/m²
	= 0.003 277 06	oz/ft²	1 oz/ft²	= 305.152	g/m²

Density
(Mass/unit volume)

1 kg/m³	= 0.062 428	lb/ft³	1 lb/ft³	= 16.0185	kg/m³
	= 1.685 56	lb/yd³	1 lb/yd³	= 0.593 278	kg/m³
1 t/m³	= 0.842 778	ton/yd³	1 ton/yd³	= 1.186 55	t/m³

Moment of inertia

| 1 kg·m² | = 23.7304 | lb·ft² | 1 lb·ft² | = 0.042 140 1 | kg·m² |
| | = 3417.17 | lb·in² | 1 lb·in² | = 292.640 | kg·mm² |

Mass/unit time

| 1 kg/s | = 2.204 62 | lb/s | 1 lb/s | = 0.453 592 | kg/s |
| 1 t/h | = 0.984 207 | ton/h | 1 ton/h | = 1.016 05 | t/h |

Force

1 MN	= 112.404	tonf (ton-force)	1 tonf	= 8.896 44	kN
1 kN	= 0.112 404	tonf	1 kip	= 4.448 22	kN
	= 224.809	lbf	1 lbf	= 4.448 22	N
1 N	= 0.224 809	lbf (pound-force)			

Moment of force, torque

1 N·m	= 0.737 562	lbf·ft	1 lbf·ft	= 1.355 82	N·m
	= 8.850 75	lbf·in	1 lbf·in.	= 0.112 985	N·m
1 kN·m	= 0.368 781	tonf·ft	1 tonf·ft	= 2.711 64	kN·m
	= 0.737 562	kip·ft	1 kip·ft	= 1.355 82	kN·m

Force/unit length

| 1 N/m | = 0.068 521 8 | 1bf/ft | 1 lbf/ft | = 14.5939 | N/m |
| 1 Kn/m | = 0.034 260 9 | tonf/ft | 1 tonf/ft | = 29·187 8 | kN/m |

Pressure, stress, modulus of elasticity (1 Pa = 1N/m²)

1 MPa	= 0.072 518 8	tonf/in²	1 tonf/in²	= 13.7895	MPa
	= 10.442 7	tonf/ft²	1 tonf/ft²	= 95.7605	kPa
	= 145.038	lbf/in²	1 kip/in²	= 6.894 76	MPa
1 kPa	= 20.8854	lbf/ft²	1 lbf/in²	= 6.894 76	kPa
			1 lbf/ft²	= 47.8803	Pa

Work, energy, heat (1 J = 1 W·s)

1 MJ	= 0.277 778	kWh	1 kWh	= 3.6	MJ
1 kJ	= 0.947 817	Btu	1 Btu	= 1.055 06	kJ
1 J	= 0.737 562	ft·lbf		= 1055.06	J
			1 ft·lbf	= 1.355 82	J

Power, heat flow rate

1 kW	= 1.341 02	hp	1 hp	= 0.745 700	kW
1 W	3.412 14	Btu/h		= 0.745 700	W
	= 0.737 562	ft·lbf/s	1 Btu/h	= 0.293 071	W
			1 ft·lbf/s	= 1.355 82	W

Heat flux density

| 1 W/m² | = 0.316 998 | Btu/(ft²·h) | 1 Btu/(ft²·h) | = 3.154 59 | W/m² |

Thermal conductance (heat transfer coefficient)

| 1 W/m²·k) | = 0.176 110 | Btu/ft²·h·°F) | 1 Btu/(ft²·h·°F) | = 5.678 26 | W/(m²·K) |

Thermal conductivity

| 1 W/(m·K) | = 0.577 789 | Btu/(ft·h·°F) | 1 Btu/(ft·h·°F) | = 1.730 73 | W/ (m·K)· |

NOTE: Underlined values are exact conversions.

OTHER MULTIPLES AND SUBMULTIPLES

Prefix	Symbol	Factor	Magnitude
hecto	h	10²	100
deka	da	10¹	10
deci	d	10⁻¹	0.1
centi	c	10⁻²	0.01

MULTIPLES OF SI UNITS

Physical Quantity	Name	Symbol	Magnitude
volume	liter	L	10^{-3} m³ = 0.001 m³
mass	metric ton	t	10^{3} kg = 1000 kg
area	hectare	ha	10^{4} m² = 10 000 m²
pressure	millibar	mbar	10^{2} Pa = 100 Pa

SI SUPPLEMENTARY UNITS

Physical Quantity	Unit	Symbol
plane angle	radian	rad
solid angle	steradian	sr

NON-SI UNITS USED WITH SI

minute	min
hour	h
day	d
nautical mile	n mile
knot	kn
kilometer per hour	km/h
revolution per minute	r/min
degree (angle)	°
minute (angle)	′
second (angle)	″
kilowatt hour	kW·h

METRIC UNITS NOT RECOMMENDED FOR USE

Names of Unit	Symbol	Physical Quantity	Value
are	a	area	100 m²
atmosphere	atm	pressure	$1.013\ 25 \times 10^{5}$ Pa
bar	b or bar	pressure	10^{5} Pa
calorie	cal	energy, work	4.186 8 J
dyne	dyn	force	10^{-5}N
erg	erg	energy, work	10^{-7} J
kilogram-force	kgf	force	9.806 65 N
kilopond	kp	force	9.806 65 N
maxwell	Mx	magnetic flux	10^{-8} Wb
micron	μ	length	10^{-6} m
millimicron	mμ	length	10^{-9} m
oersted	Oe	magnetization	$7.957\ 747 \times 10^{1}$ A·m⁻¹
quintal	q	mass	100 kg
stere	st	volume	1 m³
stilb	sb	luminance	10^{4} cd·m⁻²
torr	torr	pressure	$1.333\ 224 \times 10^{2}$ Pa

CONVERSION FACTORS FOR THE MOST COMMON UNITS USED IN ARCHITECTURE *(Cont.)*

Metric to Customary			Customary to Metric		
Calorific value (mass and volume basis)					
1 kJ/kg	= 0.429 923	Btu/lb	1 Btu/lb	= 2.326	kJ/kg
1J/g				= 2.326	(J/g)
1 kJ/m³	= 0.026 839 2	Btu/ft³	1 Btu/ft³	= 37.2589	kJ/m³
Thermal capacity (mass and volume basis)					
1 kJ/(kg·k)	= 0.238 846	Btu/(lb·°F)	l Btu (lb·°F)	= 4.1868	kJ/(kg·K)
1 kJ/(m³·K)	= 0.014 910 7	Btu/ft³·°F)	1 Btu/(ft³·°F)	= 67.0661	KJ/(m³·K)
Illuminance					
1 lx	= 0.092 903	lm/ft² (footcandle)	1 lm/ft²	= 10.7639	lx
Luminance					
1 cd/m²	= 0.092 903	cd/ft²	l cd/ft²	= 10.7639	cd/m²
	= 0.291 864	foot lambert	1 footlambert	= 3.426 26	cd/m²
1 kcd/m²	= 0.314 159	lambert	1 lambert	= 3.183 01	kcd/m²

NOTE: Underlined values are exact conversions.

MECHANICAL ENGINEERING

A major branch of engineering concerned with the production, use, and distribution of mechanical power, including water, heat and air conditioning, and waste disposal in buildings. A mechanical engineer has been licensed or registered to perform professional services for work of this kind.

Working closely with the architect and coordinating the work with other engineers and consultants, a mechanical engineer is primarily responsible for designing the mechanical systems in a building; preparing the mechanical construction documents (working drawings and specifications); making estimates of the construction cost of the mechanical work; and inspecting the work while the building is under construction to ensure that the mechanical work is free of defects and is properly constructed.

Mechanical Systems The two major systems in buildings for which mechanical engineers are responsible are plumbing; and heating, ventilating, and air conditioning, sometimes referred to as HVAC. Plumbing includes all the piping, fittings and other devices, and fixtures required for supplying bathrooms, kitchens, laundry rooms, drinking fountains and water coolers, janitors' sinks, and the like, and also the piping and other devices for disposal of wastes. Heating, ventilating, and air conditioning includes all the ductwork or piping, devices, equipment, and controls for these purposes. In addition, mechanical engineers are often responsible in some buildings for refrigeration equipment and systems, fire protection systems, and other types of mechanical work.

In times past, mechanical engineering was not nearly so important as it is today. Systems were simpler then and the needs and wishes of the people who used buildings were relatively simple. Today elaborate heating and air-conditioning systems are thought of as necessities, along with a variety of kitchen, laundry, and other appliances, and many other increasingly elaborate systems. Other factors have heightened the importance of mechanical engineering today. Mechanical engineers are responsible for much of the equipment which requires energy in the form of electricity and fossil fuels. Thus mechanical engineers carry a considerable part of the burden for efficient use of energy in buildings and conservation of energy supplies.

Mechanical engineering has become more important, architecturally, in still another way in recent years. In the past, the norm in building design was to hide pipes, ducts, and equipment; yet for some time there has been a move to express the structure of buildings. Ducts and other items, in some buildings today, are openly exposed to become elements of the exterior, and sometimes interior, appearance of buildings. Thus the mechanical work previously carefully hidden or disguised can become a major esthetic design element. Mechanical work in buildings increases in both complexity and costs, with time, taking an ever large portion of total building construction budgets.

Work Phases The professional work of mechanical engineers in buildings is usually divided into phases that are the same as those of the other architectural and engineering work: schematic, design development, construction document, and construction administration. Mechanical engineers work closely with the architects and other engineers during all phases. During the schematic phase, mechanical engineers make studies of the building site, program, and problems, and prepare preliminary drawings, specifications, and estimates of construction costs of the mechanical systems. During the design development phase, they study the problems further and refine the drawings, specifications, and estimates. During the construction document phase, they prepare final drawings and specifications which will be used in the actual construction of the building and prepare further refined estimates of costs. During the construction administration phase, they assist the architects in the administration of the work and inspect the actual construction of the mechanical systems to ensure that they are properly constructed.

In addition to the major functions of the mechanical engineers, other services may be required, such as revisions in drawings, specifications, or estimates or preparation of as-built drawings after construction has been completed. In all their work on buildings, mechanical engineers strive, not only to achieve the purpose of the systems for which they are primarily responsible but to cooperate with the architects and other engineers and consultants in the creation of buildings which, in their totality, achieve their purposes.

The education, registration or licensing, and practice of mechanical engineers today are similar to those of other professional engineers. (See the article entitled engineering.)

Related Articles BUILDING CODES AND STANDARDS; BUILDING INDUSTRY; COST CONTROL; DRAFTING; ENERGY; ENGINEERING; FIRE PROTECTION; HEATING, VENTILATING, AND AIR CONDITIONING; PLUMBING; SPECIFICATION; WORKING DRAWING.

Additional Sources of Information American Society of Heating, Refrigerating and Air Conditioning Engineers, Inc., 345 E. 47th St., New York, N.Y. 10017; American Society of Mechanical Engineers, 345 E. 47th St., New York, N.Y. 10017; See also list at end of the article entitled engineering.

Periodicals *Actual Specifying Engineer,* 5 S. Wabash Ave., Chicago, Ill., 60603; *ASHRAE Journal,* 345 E. 47th St., New York, N.Y. 10017; *Mechanical Engineering,* 345 E. 47th St., New York, N.Y. 10017.

MIES VAN DER ROHE, LUDWIG

German-American architect (1886–1969). Although he was destined to become one of the world's most influential architects, Ludwig Mies van der Rohe had no formal education in architecture. A member of a quartet of architects that included Frank Lloyd Wright (1867–1959), Le Corbusier (1887–1965), and Walter Adolf Gropius (1883–1969) which brought modern architecture to fruition, Mies saw only a small number of his designs built. He wrote very little and what he did write was terse and to the point.

Yet in spite of his relatively small output, Mies profoundly affected the architecture of his time and of the future. He was fond of aphorisms and some of them were widely repeated: "Architecture is the will of an epoch translated into space; living, changing, new," and "Form is not the aim of our work, but only the result." Later he was to refer to his buildings as "skin and bones," to his design philosophy as "less is more," and to say "God is in the details." But his great influence came from his architecture, not his aphorisms.

The buildings of Mies are predominantly rectangular. They have a clear, clean logic in their plans and appearance that makes their designs seem as rational as pure science. All the elements of a Mies design seem abstract, the lines and planes of the walls, roofs, and floors forming a functional composition that seems quite formal. It is as if he were seeking to reduce the building and all its details to the absolute irreducible minimum. Though almost all his American buildings reveal their structure on the exterior, they all have a dignified subtlety and elegance that comes from considerably more than just their structure. His austere formalism had a powerful effect on the designs of architects, not only those who studied at the Illinois Institute of Technology, where he taught, but on architects everywhere.

Works The designs of Mies started having a degree of influence on architecture early in his career, mostly because of visionary projects that were widely published, but never built. Then in 1929 he burst on the world scene with one of the most published buildings of all time. This was the German Pavilion for the International Exposition, Barcelona, Spain. An abstract design of simple planes, the pavilion was not designed to house exhibits but to serve as an exhibit itself. It was considered a masterpiece of modern architecture and brought quick recognition to Mies. For the pavilion, he also produced another masterpiece, a chair (called the Barcelona chair), made of curved steel bands cantilevered to support cushions. This chair is considered by many to be the finest single piece of modern furniture and it is still being produced. A year later, he produced the Tugendhat House, Brno, Czechoslovakia, also considered one of his best buildings, and for which he designed another fine chair.

His first commission, after he came to America, was for the design of the campus and buildings at Armour Institute, which was later renamed the Illinois Institute of Technology (IIT; see illustration in color section), Chicago. Beginning in 1939, this project occupied him for some 20 years, and produced a unified group of buildings. Before he retired from IIT in 1958, he designed several other notable buildings. First came the Promontory Apartments (1949), Chicago, originally designed in steel but built of concrete, followed by the Farnsworth House (1950), Plano, Ill., a simple, elegant cube with glass walls. His 860 Lake Shore Drive Apartments (1951), two towers in Chicago, was another landmark design, followed by Commonwealth Promenade Apartments (1953), a complex of four towers, also in Chicago. The only building by Mies in New York, the Seagram Building (1958; see illustration in color section) designed with Philip Cortelyou Johnson (1906–   ), is one of the most notable skyscrapers of later years, in its plan, appearance, use of the site, and interiors. It contains an elegant restaurant, The Four Seasons (see illustration in article restaurant), completely designed by Johnson right down to the tableware. Mies's last building completed before his death was the National Gallery (1968) in West Berlin. Several other buildings were in the process of design at that time. The major legacy of Mies is to be found in his buildings and his students and in the influence they have had on architecture.

Life Ludwig Mies van der Rohe was born on March 27, 1886, in Aachen, Germany, the son of a stonecutter and mason. Later he added his mother's name, van

MIES VAN DER ROHE, LUDWIG Farnsworth House (1950), Plano, Ill.
(Hedrich-Blessing)

der Rohe, to his father's. As a boy, Mies learned stone masonry by working with his father. He attended the Cathedral School in Aachen and at thirteen entered the trade school there. At fifteen, his formal schooling ended when he left the trade school, but his education in the practical side of architecture continued. From age fifteen to nineteen, he worked as a designer and draftsman of ornamental details in stucco for Classic style buildings. In 1905 he went to work for an interior and furniture designer in Berlin. In 1907 he left to embark on his architectural career and that same year designed a house in classical style. In 1908 he went to work in the office of Peter Behrens (1868–1940), a pioneering German architect. While there, another future great architect, Walter Adolf Gropius, joined the firm and later the great Swiss-French architect Le Corbusier, real name Charles Édouard Jeanneret, worked in the office.

Mies left the Behrens office in 1911, and went to The Hague, Netherlands, in 1912 to work on the design of a house for Mme H. E. L. J. Kroller. Although he stayed for a year, finished the design, and had a full-size model of wood and canvas erected on the site, the house was never built. Here again, the style was traditional classical. Returning to Berlin, Mies opened his own office, designed several buildings, all traditional, only one of which was built. In 1914 he was called into the German army in World War I, and served until the Armistice in 1918.

Returning to Berlin, he opened a practice in 1919. Lacking commissions for actual buildings, he spent his time designing exhibitions and writing. He also designed a remarkable series of five building projects,

none ever built, but all different and all very much ahead of the times. These were schemes for a glass office building (1919), another for a glass skyscraper (1921), one for a concrete office building (1922), and two for country houses, one in brick (1923), the other in concrete (1924). These projects were widely published and established Mies as a pioneering visionary architect, though not a very practical one. He still designed projects, but most were never built.

In 1926 Mies was appointed first vice president of the German Werkbund, an organization of architects and industrialists attempting to improve the quality of industrial design in Germany. In this position, he directed the Second Werkbund Exposition (1927) in Stuttgart. To design the buildings, he brought in many of the best European architects, including Peter Behrens, Walter Gropius, Le Corbusier, and the fine Dutch architect Jacobus Johannes Pieter (J.J.P.) Oud (1890–1963). Mies designed one building. He served in this position until 1932.

In 1929 he designed a masterpiece, the Barcelona Pavilion, which brought him worldwide recognition and the following year he designed his great Tugendhat House. Also in 1930, Mies was appointed director of the Bauhaus, the famous design and arts school, in Dessau. Political pressures caused the school to move to Berlin in 1932 and the following year it was closed by the Nazis.

Mies continued designing projects, including an innovative series of houses with courtyards, but again none was actually built. In 1937 he came to America, a very influential and famous architect, who by age fifty had designed many buildings, but only about 19

MIES VAN DER ROHE, LUDWIG 860 Lake Shore Drive Apartments (1951), Chicago, Ill. [*Architects: Ludwig Mies van der Rohe, in association with Pace Associates and Holsman, Holsman, Klekemp and Taylor. (Hedrich-Blessing)*]

MIES VAN DER ROHE, LUDWIG Exterior, Museum of Fine Arts (1958 and 1973), Houston, Texas. [*Architects: Ludwig Mies van der Rohe, in association with Steub, Rather and Howze. (Hedrich-Blessing)*]

MIES VAN DER ROHE, LUDWIG Interior, Museum of Fine Arts (1958 and 1973), Houston, Texas. [*Architects: Ludwig Mies van der Rohe, in association with Steub, Rather and Howze. (Hedrich-Blessing)*]

MIES VAN DER ROHE, LUDWIG Colonnades (apartments, 1960), Newark, N.J. *(Joseph W. Molitor)*

had been built. These include 11 houses, 2 apartments, and 6 exhibits destroyed at the end of the expositions in which they appeared. In addition, he had designed a monument that was built, but was later torn down by the Nazis.

After a short time in America, in 1938 Mies was named director of architecture at Armour Institute, later renamed Illinois Institute of Technology. Soon afterward, he was commissioned to design a whole new campus and the buildings for the school. Starting in 1939, he designed the master plan for the school and eventually the buildings for the campus. He was occupied with the buildings at IIT and with the Architecture School for the next 20 years until he retired, in 1958, to practice full time in Chicago. He designed a number of other important buildings and continued to do so for the remainder of his life.

The profession that he embraced gave him numerous awards, including the Gold Medal of the Royal Institute of British Architects (1959). He had become an American citizen in 1944, and the architects of his adopted country, the American Institute of Architects, awarded him the Gold Medal in 1960. His last important building, the National Gallery (1968), was built in West Berlin. On August 19, 1969, Ludwig Mies van der Rohe died, the last of the great quartet that had made modern architecture flower. He had outlived Wright by 10 years, Le Corbusier by 4, and Gropius by a little over a month.

Related Articles ART IN ARCHITECTURE [for illustration of Federal Center (1964), Chicago]; BAUHAUS, STAATLICHES; EDUCATION; GROPIUS, WALTER ADOLF; MODERN ARCHITECTURE.

Further Reading Blaser, Werner: *Mies van der Rohe: The Art of Structure*, Thomas and Hudson, London, 1965; Drexler, Arthur: *Ludwig Mies van der Rohe*, Braziller, New York, 1960; Johnson, Philip C.: *Mies van der Rohe*, Museum of Modern Art, New York, 1947.

MILITARY BUILDING A building for use in military defense, training, or waging war. Military buildings may be classified into two major types: those that have specialized uses in defense or in waging war, such as ancient forts or modern missile silos; and those usually employed for ordinary purposes that have been adapted to military functions.

Throughout history, architects have been deeply involved in the design and construction of military buildings. And it is only necessary to go back a few hundred years to find architects also deeply involved in the weapons of war and defense. Today architects are still engaged in the design and construction of military buildings and other structures, but not ordinarily with weapons. In the recent past, military construction formed a large and important part of the practice of quite a few architects and, for some, it continues to be important.

For various reasons, including their very specialized, often classified, nature, discussion of the specialized kinds of military buildings is beyond the scope of this article. Architects who become involved in such work are often required to obtain security clearance and have to work closely with the military services to determine how to program and design such buildings. In general, these architects find that work of this kind entails meeting many kinds of criteria, requirements, regulations, and specifications not ordinarily found in work for nonmilitary clients.

Architectural services for buildings of the second type more closely resemble those for nonmilitary clients. However, here again architects find a great number of special regulations and requirements. On the other hand, the design of such buildings has much in common with that of the same types used for nonmilitary purposes.

Building Types Military bases today are much like cities or towns and have requirements for many of the same types of buildings and other structures. Among the major building types usually found on military bases are apartments, banks, hospitals, houses and other types of housing, libraries, office buildings, parks, prisons, recreation buildings, religious buildings, restaurants, schools, shopping centers and stores, theaters, and warehouses. Other types of buildings often found on military bases include airport facilities, barracks that are similar to college dormitories in some respects, hotels, laboratories, museums, and railway stations. In addition, many military bases have buildings and structures so specialized that specific research must be accomplished by architects before they can be designed properly. Also certain structures, such as docks and bridges, are found on military bases, but are not ordinarily designed by architects today.

The military services also use buildings that are not located on the usual type of military base, including the college buildings of the service academies and office buildings, such as the Pentagon, in Washington, D.C. Architects who wish to design military buildings should establish contact with the various services to determine their requirements.

History Since prehistoric times, human beings have made war on each other, seeking such goals as territory, wealth, power, and security. Therefore military buildings and other structures have been part of human life ever since. No one knows exactly what form military structures took at first. It is believed that they were simply rocks or boulders piled up for protection, probably followed by palisades or stockades made of tree trunks. In the Middle East, after people began to create towns, protective walls of mud or sun-dried brick were erected. In Mesopotamia and other nearby areas, town walls might be 20 ft or more in thickness and were made of sun-dried brick, sometimes framed with timbers and erected on stone bases. Many of them had towers at intervals. Some had double walls and at strategic places within the walls, forts or citadels, with additional walls to protect the most important buildings. In other cases, the circumferential walls were augmented by cross-walls within.

The city of Babylon, rebuilt by King Nebuchadnezzar II (c. 605–563 B.C.), was heavily fortified with an inner wall protecting the principal buildings and outer walls surrounding the entire city. In the Middle East, forts were also built at important places away from cities, such as river fords.

The ancient Greeks also placed walls around their towns. In fact, it is thought that by the 4th century B.C., every sizable Greek city was protected by walls. These were constructed of mud brick, later of stone, irregular shapes at first, followed by squared stones. These thick walls usually had towers and also ditches outside.

The Romans built walls around their towns and those they conquered. These walls were usually of masonry and were erected in pairs about 20 ft or so apart with as many as three ditches outside. Some towns even had three walls. In between the walls, parapet walks were constructed of rammed rock and earth. The outer wall was quite high and had alternating solid and open sections, called crenelation, at the top. Such a wall is often called a battlement. The inner walls were lower, allowing easy access from inside the towns. Gates had elaborate baffles to delay or prevent entry by enemies. Galleries at different levels, elaborate stairways, chambers and towers served a similar purpose.

During the Middle Ages, early forts and fortified castles were constructed with wooden stockades placed on mounds and had wooden towers called keeps. Later stone was used for fortifications, at first in simple walls without towers, then in elaborate ones, with towers and galleries of wood, later replaced by stone, or hoardings, which projected from the tops to the outside. From the hoardings, objects could be dropped on invaders below.

By the 13th century, design and construction of castles and other fortifications had become much more complex. Walls were strengthened, elaborate towers of various sizes were placed in important locations, and certain areas of forts or castles were designed to be held by the defenders even if other parts fell to the invaders. About the 13th century, the French began construction of fortified towns, called *bastides*. The introduction of gunpowder into Europe in the 14th century, long after its first use in China, revolutionized warfare and fortifications. Walls were made wider to accommodate defensive artillery and lower to reduce the effects of the artillery of the attackers.

During the Renaissance, after the advent of artillery, forts and fortified towns were not usually constructed with high walls which would present excellent targets to enemy gunners. In their stead, the main walls were made stronger, of masonry, but just high enough to prevent scaling and were sloped. Massive earthworks and ditches were placed outside the walls, making it difficult for artillery to score direct hits on the walls. Rocks, trees, and other objects behind which enemies might be protected were removed for great distances beyond the mounds and ditches. And various obstacles were erected to impede the progress of the invaders, including stockades or palisades of poles, called *fraises*, cut down trees with branches trimmed to points, or *abatis*, and wooden stocks with pointed ends placed radially, called *chevaux-de-frise*. Other types of fortifications were developed, including polygonal structures that were thought to be more easily defended than some other types.

In the late 16th and early 17th centuries, many systems of fortification were developed, though no radical changes were made like those necessitated by the introduction of artillery. The science of fortification was systematized during this period, in which an important role was played by the French engineer Sébastien Le Prestre Vauban (1632–1707). Vauban worked out a system of fortification unequaled by any that preceded it. His principles included provisions that fortifications must be strong enough to withstand cannon fire, that all parts must be positioned so no hiding places were available to enemies, and that every part must be within reach of defensive musket fire from other parts. Acting upon these principles, Vauban took part in the erection of more than 30 new French forts and the improvement of about 300 others, with the result that his nation developed the best fortification system in Europe. Vauban also directed some 50 sieges during the almost unending series of wars fought by France during his lifetime. The work of Vauban had considerable influence on fortifications and upon military tactics and strategy in colonial America as well as in Europe.

American Construction   In early colonial America, forts were among the first structures to be built. American forts generally were modeled after those of the European nations, mainly France, Spain, and England, which had established colonies in the New World. Over the years, forts and other military buildings and structures have continued to be built, each succeeding example reflecting the needs at the time and the prevailing theories of defense. Many of these forts and other military buildings and structures are still in existence, though some are in ruins. A number have been reconstructed.

Although anything approaching a history of military construction in America is far beyond the scope of this book, some understanding may be gained through examination of a place that might represent that history, in microcosm, the city and surrounding area of Pensacola, Fla.

Pensacola   The site of Pensacola is thought to have been discovered in 1540, by the crew of a ship of the Spanish explorer Hernando De Soto (c. 1500–42). Tristan de Luna established a colony, called by its Indian name Ochuse, in 1559, but it was abandoned two years later, thus bringing to a temporary end a city that was six years older than the oldest existent in the United States, St. Augustine, Fla. Almost 140 years passed before another Spanish settlement was made in Pensacola in 1696. Although the original colony may have had fortifications, the first known structure of this kind in Pensacola was Fort San Carlos de Austria, completed in 1699, and constructed of two rows of pine logs with sand between them. Other forts of wood had earlier been built near what is now Jacksonville, Fla., and St. Augustine. About 1719, the Spanish built another fort on Santa Rosa Island, across Pensacola Bay from the present city. In 1719, when war broke out with the Spanish, the French attacked Pensacola, burned the town, and destroyed the fort.

In 1723, three years after the war ended, the French restored Pensacola to Spanish rule. The town was rebuilt but was again destroyed in 1754, by a hurricane. In 1763, as a result of the Treaty of Paris, Spain ceded Florida to Great Britain and Pensacola became a British colony. The entire Spanish population of the city, except for one man, deserted Pensacola. The city then became the British headquarters for West Florida and soon several forts were built, including Fort George and Fort Redoubt, about 1770. In 1781 a French and Spanish force headed by the governor of Spanish Louisiana, Bernardo de Galvez (c. 1746–86), attacked the British at Pensacola and erected Fort Bernardo a short distance from Fort George. From Fort Bernardo, the Spanish successfully bombarded the British fort and it surrendered. Galvez renamed it Fort San Miguel and Pensacola went back under Spanish rule.

About 1787, a more permanent Fort San Carlos was built by the Spanish. The earlier forts have long been demolished, but portions of this fort still remain. In 1813, during the War of 1812, the British invaded Pensacola and seized the forts. Within a few months, the British were defeated by General Andrew Jackson (1767–1845), returning the town to the Spanish. In 1818, during the so-called Seminole War, Jackson again entered the city, capturing the forts. In 1821 he returned to the city to receive West Florida from Spain and to become its first U.S. provisional governor.

MILITARY BUILDING Fort Pickens (1834), Santa Rosa Island, near Pensacola, Fla. [*Engineer: Col. William H. Chase. (National Park Service)*]

MILITARY BUILDING Fort Barrancas (1844), Pensacola, Fla. [*Engineer: Col. William H. Chase. (National Park Service)*]

MILITARY BUILDING Advanced Redoubt (c. 1859), Pensacola, Fla. [*Engineer: Col. William H. Chase. (National Park Service)*]

After the War of 1812, the United States embarked upon a major construction program of permanent forts. At Pensacola, Fort Pickens was constructed in 1834, on Santa Rosa Island at the site of the earlier Spanish fort; in 1839 Fort McRee, across Big Lagoon was completed. Fort Barrancas was built in 1844, adjacent to the site of old Fort San Carlos, and Advanced Redoubt (c. 1859) nearby was begun a short time later. The engineer for all was Col. William H. Chase, U.S. Army. None of these forts ever fired a shot at a foreign enemy or were fired upon by one. However, they did figure in the American Civil War. Forts Barrancas and McRee were occupied by Confederate troops, as was the Navy Yard, which had been established in 1826, but Fort Pickens became one of the few forts in the South to be occupied by Federal troops throughout the war. The others were Fort Taylor (1845), Key West, Fla.; Fort Jefferson (1845), Garden Key, Fla.; and Fort Monroe (1827), Hampton, Va. Occasional artillery duels between the guns at Fort Pickens and those of the Confederates occured early in the war. In 1862 the Confederates abandoned the city to the Federal troops who occupied it for the remainder of the war.

In 1898 improvements were made at Fort Pickens and, later, disappearing guns of the U.S. Army Coast Artillery were placed there. The fort protected the port of Pensacola during the Spanish-American War and World Wars I and II, but was later abandoned, to become a Florida State Park in 1949. From 1886 to 1888, the famed Apache Indian Chief Geronimo (1829–1909) was imprisoned in Fort Pickens.

All the forts built in Pensacola after the War of 1812 are still in existence, except Fort McRee of which only a few ruins remain underwater. Fort Monroe is still in use. The forts in the Florida Keys are also still in existence. Fort Jefferson was made into a prison after the Civil War; its most famous inmate was Dr. Samuel A. Mudd (1833–83), convicted of conspiracy in the assassination of President Abraham Lincoln (1809–65), because he set the broken leg of the murderer, John Wilkes Booth (1838–65). Mudd was later pardoned because of his services in a yellow fever epidemic. None of the forts was considered effective against rifled cannon, invented about the time of the Civil War.

The long military history of Pensacola continues today. In 1914 the old Navy Yard was converted into the Pensacola Naval Air Station and since that time has had a major role in the flight training of naval pilots and other flying personnel. In addition to the main base, there are three other naval flying fields in the area.

U.S. Forts Many old American forts are still in existence, at least partly, from all eras of colonial and U.S. history, or have been reconstructed. Among the old Spanish forts are the Castillo de San Marcos, St. Augustine, Fla., begun in 1672 and not completed until 1756, and Fort Matanzas (1742), near that city. The earliest English fort, a very small one made of earth and logs, believed to have been built about 1584, has

MILITARY BUILDING Battery Langdon (1917) for disappearing Coast artillery guns, Fort Pickens, Santa Rosa Island, near Pensacola, Fla. (National Park Service)

MILITARY BUILDING Navy pier (1916), Chicago, Ill. [Architect: Charles S. Frost. Restored 1976; Architect: Jerome R. Butler, Jr. (Hedrich-Blessing)]

been reconstructed at Manteo, N.C., on Roanoke Island. This is the site of the lost colony, the first English colony in America, established under the sponsorship of Sir Walter Raleigh (c. 1552–1618), who never saw it. Here Virginia Dare was born in 1587, the first English child to be born in America, but Virginia and other colonists vanished and were never found.

The remains of Frederica, an early and unusual English fortified town built in 1736, are located on Saint Simons Island, near Brunswick, Ga. In 1754 an early British fort was built by Colonel George Washington (1732–99). Called Fort Necessity and located near Farmington, Pa., the fort has been reconstructed. Two early French examples are Fort Ticonderoga (1755), Ticonderoga, N.Y., and Fort Pitt (c. 1750), Pittsburgh, Pa.

British fortifications as well as those of the Americans and their French allies, built in 1781, exist at Yorktown, Va. Here the British General, Lord Charles Cornwallis (1738–1805) surrendered to General Washington on October 17, 1781, ending the Revolutionary War. Fort McHenry, Baltimore, Md., built soon after the war, in 1790, was made famous during the War of 1812, when Francis Scott Key (1779–1843), held prisoner on a British ship, wrote the words to *The Defense of Fort McHenry,* later known as *The Star Spangled Banner,* in the early morning of September 14, 1814. A later fort, begun in 1827 but never finished, Fort Sumter, on an island in the harbor of Charleston, S.C., became famous as the scene of the first shots fired in the Civil War, on April 12, 1861.

Two forts which figured in the westward expansion of the United States are Fort Davis (1854), Tex., a base in the U.S. actions against the Apache and Comanche Indians, and Fort Laramie (c. 1834), Wyo., which protected the Oregon Trail and was the scene, in 1868, of a treaty ceding lands to the Indians. Many other historical and interesting forts and other military buildings and structures exist in other parts of the United States.

Related Articles APARTMENT; BANK; HOSPITAL; HOUS-ING; LIBRARY; OFFICE BUILDING; PARK; PRISON; RECREATION BUILDING; RELIGIOUS BUILDING; SCHOOL; STORE; WAREHOUSE.

Further Reading *Historic American Buildings Survey— Catalog of the Measured Drawings and Photographs of the Survey in the Library of Congress, March 1, 1941,* U.S. Government Printing Office, Washington, D.C., 1941, catalog supplement, 1959, catalogs by states; Robinson, Willard B.: *American Forts—Architectural Form and Function,* Amon Carter Museum of Western Art and the University of Illinois Press, Urbana, Ill., 1977

MILLS, ROBERT

American architect and engineer (1781–1855). After graduating from Charleston College, Robert Mills obtained his architectural education while working for James Hoban (1762–1831), the architect of the White House; Thomas Jefferson (1743–1826); and Benjamin Henry Latrobe (1764–1820). Thus Mills became one of a growing number of men who early in the 19th century were trained for the professional practice of architecture in all of its aspects: design, engineering, and construction.

Mills became one of the most important architects of his time. A believer like his mentors, Jefferson and Latrobe, in Classic Revival architecture, in particular the Greek Revival style, Mills designed a great number of buildings during his career: houses, churches, courthouses, and other public buildings.

It was for his large public buildings and monuments that he became best known, imparting to them meticulously fine proportions, simple unadorned great masses that produced monumental effects unlike most buildings built before that time. His buildings were simple, yet bold, with excellent engineering.

Works Although it is unclear when Mills left the office of Latrobe, it is known that in 1808 he received his first important independent commission for the Sansom Street Baptist Church (1809), followed by the Octagon Unitarian Church (1813), both in Philadelphia. Neither building has survived. But the most important development at this stage of his career was his winning of a competition to design a church intended

MILLS, ROBERT Bethesda Presbyterian Church (1820), Camden, S.C. *(Wayne Andrews)*

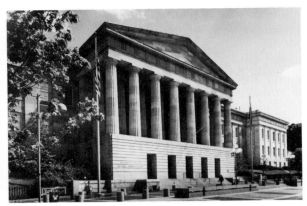

MILLS, ROBERT National Portrait Gallery, formerly U.S. Patent Office (1840), Washington, D.C. *(Joseph W. Molitor)*

MILLS, ROBERT Fireproof Building (1827), Charleston, S.C. *(Wayne Andrews)*

MILLS, ROBERT U.S. Treasury Building (1842), Washington, D.C. *(Joseph W. Molitor)*

to memorialize 71 people who had died in a fire. This commission produced what many think is one of the architect's best buildings, the Monumental Church (1812), Richmond, Va., which fortunately is still in existence. The church is simple and straightforward in concept, inside and out, with refined, restrained details. The building has a dual purpose: a memorial to the dead and an active church. The porch and the main building seem therefore almost to exist independently of each other. The main church building is octagonal in plan, of brick and stucco, with a low dome of wood construction, plastered inside. The porch, of stone, is square in plan, much like a Greek Doric temple, a building type from which it is derived. In the center of the porch, a rather large funerary urn symbolizes the receptacle of the ashes of those who died in the fire. The building became a milestone in the development of Classic Revival architecture in America.

Another milestone, though for a different reason, was the Record Office (1827), Charleston, S.C. This building, one of the most innovative of its time, came to be known as the Fireproof Building, for that is what Mills set out to accomplish. Here again Mills expressed his talent for simple, dignified classic forms,

but it is in the function of the building and its engineering that his greatest accomplishments were made. Two stories high with a basement, the Fireproof Building contains eight rooms on each floor, all opening on halls and all with outside exposures. All the walls and partitions are brick covered with stucco, and the ceilings of the basements and first floor are brick vaults, covered with stucco. Thus no wood was used except for the roof structure, from which the second floor ceiling of suspended plaster was hung. The roof was covered with copper and all the windows and shutters were of iron. In the center of the building, a central stairwell extends from the basement to the second floor and is covered with a skylight in the roof. Here too the materials were incombustible, the stairs and landings of stone, the railings of iron. In this building then Mills established himself as a complete architect, dedicated to his profession and skilled in design, engineering, and construction.

Most of the important later work of Mills was accomplished in Washington, where he spent the remainder of his professional life after 1830. Appointed architect of public buildings, a post in which he served from 1836 to 1851, Mills designed a number of U.S. government buildings and monuments, among

MILLS, ROBERT Washington Monument (1884), Washington, D.C.
(*Joseph W. Molitor*)

them the Patent Office (1840), now the National Portrait Gallery; the Treasury Building (1842); the Old General Post Office (1869), now the Tariff Commission Building; and the Washington Monument, a project not finished until 1884, long after the death of the architect.

Of the government work of Mills, the Treasury Building is considered his masterpiece. Here again, Mills demonstrated the simple, straightforward design that had become his style, but in a building of monumental size, three stories and basement, 190 ft deep and 336 ft long. The plan is simple, sort of like a letter E laid on its side with great courtyards in the spaces between the strokes. The long side of the E, the major elevation, has 30 gigantic Greek Ionic columns, each three stories high imposed on the basement. Behind this great colonnade are strictly utilitarian office spaces, designed for the functional purposes to which they are put, much as in the earlier Fireproof Building. As in that building, the architect paid considerable attention to engineering and fire safety, using incombustible materials, in this case mostly Acquia stone, and vaulted ceilings. And as in that earlier building, Mills again provided a magnificent curved stair extending up through the building.

At one point, in 1838, it looked as if this magnificent building would never be completed. Mills had been the subject of mounting criticism in Congress, led by Levi Lincoln, a Massachusetts congressman. It was much the same position in which Latrobe had found himself when his work for the government had been attacked, and seemed to have stemmed from the same reason, politics and jealousy. The congressman had a young Philadelphia architect, Thomas U. Walter (1804–87), appointed to make a report on the Treasury Building. This report led to a bill in Congress to demolish the Treasury Building, before completion. After much debate and maneuvering, the bill was narrowly defeated, 94 to 91, and the building went on to completion in 1842.

Life Robert Mills was born in Charleston, S.C., on August 12, 1781, of a Scottish father and an American mother. He seems to have decided upon a career as a professional architect when quite young. After graduating in liberal arts from Charleston College at 20, he began his architectural education in the office of Hoban who practiced for a while in Charleston, went with him to Washington in 1800, then to Monticello where he worked and studied with Jefferson for about two years. In 1804 he continued his education by visiting a number of architects, including Charles Bulfinch, in the Eastern United States, and studying their buildings firsthand. He entered the office of Latrobe and spent about five years there, working and learning. About 1808, he began his own practice, doing work in Philadelphia, Washington, Richmond, and Baltimore.

In 1820 Mills received an appointment as engineer and architect of the State of South Carolina, and moved his family back to Charleston. Returning to Washington in 1830, Mills was appointed architect of public buildings by President Andrew Jackson (1767–1845), in 1836. He held this post until 1851, a period that saw him design his three notable government buildings in Washington. Mills died on March 3, 1855.

Related Articles CLASSIC REVIVAL ARCHITECTURE; JEFFERSON, THOMAS; LATROBE, BENJAMIN HENRY.

Further Reading Gallagher, Helen M. P.: *Robert Mills: Architect of the Washington Monument, 1781–1855*, Columbia University Press, New York, 1935.

MODEL MAKING

MODEL MAKING The construction of three-dimensional, usually small-scale, representations of buildings, groups of buildings, or other architectural projects for study purposes or for presentation of design concepts to clients and others.

Types In the last few decades, making models of buildings has become increasingly important in architecture. Models have come to be accepted as the best means of accomplishing many purposes. In architecture, models are of four major types: study models, finished models, working models, and mock-ups. Study models are usually made of simple, common materials assembled in a somewhat unfinished manner and without undue expenditure of time, to help designers visualize various aspects of their designs, such as relationships to sites, orientation, relationships between buildings in groups, form of buildings, materials, circulation of people around and within the buildings, and such details as room sizes, entrances, and so on.

Finished models are made from a variety of materials to simulate as closely as possible what a completed building will be like. They are constructed with care, usually require many hours of work, and are often quite costly to build. Though finished models may also be of help in the study of building designs, their major purpose is for presentation of clients and others of completed designs, in a way that drawings or renderings, which often supplement models in presentations, cannot duplicate. The major function of finished models is to sell the building design to potential buyers. Photographs of a model are often used, and some of these may be made by superimposing photographs of the model on photographs of its site and surroundings.

Working models, more rarely used than the types described above, are made when some movement of parts of a building, such as a stadium dome which may be opened or closed, must be studied or demonstrated. Mock-ups, either full-size or scaled down, are used for purposes similar to those of working models and also for testing building elements or components, such as testing water infiltration through a new type of wall.

In addition to the four major types, other types of models are used in architecture, including structural models, showing structures or parts of them; landscaping models, showing grading of sites, planting, and other aspects; planning models, showing cities or

MODEL MAKING Study model, scheme 1. Citicorp Center (1978), New York, N.Y. [*Architects: Hugh Stubbins, in association with Emery Roth and Sons.*]

MODEL MAKING Finished model, adopted scheme. Citicorp Center.

portions of them; and interior models showing space planning of interior spaces, colors, materials, furniture, and furnishings.

Architectural students, and often those in related fields, learn how to make models as part of their curricula in professional schools. Therefore all architects have had some experience in model making. Other model makers learned their craft through experience or as a hobby. In practice, some architects make their own models, particularly study models, but also finished or presentation models and other types. However, finished or presentation models are more often made by specialists, who may have their own businesses or work for others. Some model makers are employees of architectural firms, but only the largest firms can usually afford staff members who perform solely this function.

Tools The tools of model makers are many and varied. There are numerous kinds of hand tools, such as knives, rasps, drills, tweezers, planes, strippers, scissors, and clamps on the market, many of them designed specifically for model makers. There are also many types of power tools available, some of which are regular shop tools but others specifically intended

for model making, including hand-held electric tools that use as bits an array of grinders, cutting wheels, polishers, cutters, routers, and so on. There are special tools for plastics, wood, and metals, and there are several types of sprayers for paints.

Materials The materials used by model makers comprise a bewildering array. A skilled and inventive model maker may use almost any material available on the market for any purpose to help depict in miniature the actual materials and form of buildings. Such materials include most woods, metals, plastics, paper products, glass, and others. Also of importance are the great number of materials and other items produced to scale specifically for use in models, including materials that simulate structural steel shapes, brick, stone, wood siding and the like, roofing, windows, doors, landscaping, and many other elements of buildings and their sites. In addition, various glues, cements, and adhesives are used for the assembly of models, and paints and other coatings are used for finishes. First-class architectural models are the result of careful selection of the materials and other items and careful workmanship by skilled and creative model makers.

Construction The actual construction of models varies widely, not only because of the different purposes for which they may be used but because of the varied skills and techniques of architects and model makers. In general, though, the first step in making a model should be careful study of its purpose, followed by study of the proper size and scale of the model. Residential models are often built at a scale of ¼ in equals 1 ft, while larger buildings may be at a scale of ⅛ in to 1 ft. For even larger projects, such as a college campus or a portion of a city, smaller scales such as 1 in equals 50 ft, 1 in equals 200 ft, or even smaller must be used. In general, the smaller the scale of the model, the less detail is shown. Another important early consideration in model making is the choice of a proper base on which to construct it and a plastic cover for the model if it is to be displayed publicly or for a long period of time.

The actual construction of the model may proceed after the preliminary decisions have been made and the required materials have been collected. The first step, if required by the model to be constructed, is the preparation of the site of the building on the model base. This may require the building up of the form of the site into contours that represent the slope of the land. Then follows the gradual building up of the remainder of the model, starting with the large forms and proceeding to ever smaller details, until the whole model building has been completed, together with its landscaping and with figures of people, automobiles, and other things to indicate its scale.

History Model making is one of the oldest crafts practiced by humans, small-scale, three-dimensional representations of boats and other articles having been made at least as far back as the 40th century B.C. Some of these models still exist. Whether the earliest architects made models or not is uncertain. It is known that early Egyptian architects and others made drawings of buildings, and this practice has continued to the present time. These drawings have served several purposes. They have been a means of studying the designs of buildings and their parts; they have been used as a means of explaining or demonstrating the designs to clients; they have been used as guides to the actual construction of buildings; and they have served as a record of what has been built. In later times, they have also served for obtaining publicity for architects' work.

Architectural model making was practiced in ancient Greece and Rome, and the practice was continued to an extent in later periods of history. However, the use of drawings, for the most part, to serve the purposes cited above continued until the late 19th century. In the late 19th and in the 20th centuries, the use of study models made of clay and later claylike plastic substances came into wide usage. These models were valuable for study of form, of little or no use in study of volumes or space, and virtually useless in presentation of a building design to clients or others.

During the 20th century, many new model-making techniques have been developed, along with new materials. As a result, making architectural models has become quite widespread, not only for study and presentation purposes, but also in full-size models, or mock-ups, for testing and other purposes. A recent development has been building models for wind tunnel testing to determine building performance in hurricanes and other storms.

Related Articles DESIGN, ARCHITECTURAL; RENDERING.

Further Reading Burden, Ernest: *Architectural Delineation—A Photographic Approach to Presentation*, McGraw-Hill, New York, 1971; Taylor, John R.: *Model Building for Architects and Engineers*, McGraw-Hill, New York, 1971.

MODERN ARCHITECTURE.

Usually taken to mean the architectural movement that began in the late 19th century in opposition to the eclectic architecture then prevalent. In the strictest sense, the word *modern* may be defined as characteristic of the present or of the most recent era. Thus the phrase *modern architecture* is a somewhat unfortunate choice to describe this movement, since what was modern in the 19th century is now historical. Some have suggested that the phrase *contemporary architecture* replace modern architecture. Since the word *contemporary*, strictly defined, means living, occurring, or existing at the same time, its choice is also unfortunate.

For purposes of discussion here, the well-established phrase, modern architecture, though somewhat inappropriate, is employed, because of its widespread usage to denote the architecture that turned away from past historical styles toward designs of buildings expressive of their own time. This article discusses modern architecture from its beginnings in the 19th century through the end of the most significant work of the great modern architect-theorists, Walter Adolf Gropius (1883–1969), Le Corbusier (1887–1965), Ludwig Mies van der Rohe (1886–1969), and Frank Lloyd Wright (1867–1959), after the middle of the 20th century. For a discussion of architecture after World War II, see the article entitled contemporary architecture. Inevitably, there is some overlap between the two eras and the two articles.

Forerunners of Modern Movement There is no general agreement about the beginning of the modern movement. Some have placed it in the early and middle parts of the 19th century, with the advent of such buildings as the Crystal Palace (1851) in London, designed by Sir Joseph Paxton (1803–65); the Bibliothèque Ste Geneviève (1850) and Bibliothèque Nationale (1868), both in Paris and designed by Henri Labrouste (1801–75); and Les Halles Centrale (1858, demolished in 1970), Paris, designed by Victor Baltard (1805–74). Such buildings utilized materials and techniques developed during the industrial revolution, such as iron framing and large amounts of glass, and were considerably more functional than many buildings of the time. However, all used eclectic forms, in iron rather than stone or other materials of the past. Yet some prediction of things to come later can cer-

MODERN ARCHITECTURE, EARLY Monadnock Building (1891), Chicago, Ill. [*Architects: Burnham and Root. (Hedrich-Blessing)*]

MODERN ARCHITECTURE, EARLY Reliance Building (1895), Chicago, Ill. [*Architects: Burnham and Root. (Hedrich-Blessing)*]

tainly be detected in them today, if not at the time when the buildings were constructed. Even before, some hints of the coming modern movement were present in various factories and other industrial buildings constructed in Europe and elsewhere.

In the United States, the first glimmerings of the modern movement may be seen in the work of James Bogardus (1800–74) and many others who designed and constructed cast-iron buildings in New York City and other places all over the country. In these buildings as well as those in Europe, the materials and techniques tended to be expressions of the industrial revolution and their purposes were functional, but the forms were eclectic.

Beginning of Modern Movement Therefore all these early buildings might be considered forerunners of the modern movement, and its real beginning placed in the late 19th century, with the work of the architects who, reacting against eclecticism, began to develop new kinds of architecture. Their reactions to eclecticism took a number of different forms, but the two most important came to be known as the Art Nouveau style and the Chicago school of architecture. Other reactions, of lesser importance, included what came to be called the Craft Movement.

Art Nouveau This style started out, about 1890, as a revolt of architects, artists, and artisans against the work of the past. It flourished in Europe for about 10 years and held on for about another 10 after that. Before it had run its course, Art Nouveau had affected not only architecture and interiors but furniture, jewelry, typography design, sculpture, painting, and other fine and applied arts. Its main characteristics were undulating, fluid forms and lines, sometimes extremely contorted into strange and exotic shapes resembling living organisms.

The earliest proponents of Art Nouveau were two Belgian architects, Victor Horta (1861–1947) and Henry Van de Velde (1863–1957). Other architects affected by the style include a Scot, Charles Rennie Mackintosh (1868–1928); a Spaniard, Antoni Gaudi (1852–1926); and a Frenchman, Hector Guimard (1867–1942). In painting, the style is perhaps best exemplified in the work of Henri Marie Raymond de Toulouse-Lautrec (1864–1901). Art Nouveau had very little effect on American architecture, but did influence other arts, including the stained-glass designs of Louis Comfort Tiffany (1848–1933).

Art Nouveau affected the work of architects in other parts of Europe, including the Austrian pioneer, Otto Wagner (1841–1918), who started out as an eclectic architect and later became the inspiration of the movement known as the Austrian Secession. Wagner also influenced two younger architects who became the leaders of the Austrian Secession, Joseph Marie Ohlbrich (1869–1908) and Joseph Hoffmann (1870–1956). Another Austrian pioneer of modern architecture, Adolf Loos (1870–1933), rebelled against the secession as well as against eclecticism. Other European pioneers of modern architecture were Hendrik Petrus Berlage (1856–1934) of the Netherlands, Peter Behrens (1868–1940) of Germany, and Auguste Perret (1874–1954) and Tony Garnier (1869–1948) of France.

MODERN ARCHITECTURE, EARLY Gage buildings (1898), Chicago, Ill. [Architects: two on left, Holabird and Roche; one on right, Louis Henri Sullivan. (Hedrich-Blessing)]

Although the Art Nouveau architects had little effect on American architecture, other pioneer architects had great influence: their ideas of architecture for its own time, functionalism, use of modern materials and techniques, and discard of eclecticism reflecting and influencing the ideas of the American pioneers of the modern movement.

The Craft Movement had a considerable effect on the work of a few American architects, but very little on most architects. Originated by an English architect, William Morris (1834–96), the movement turned away from industrial machines to handcrafted elements of architecture, furniture, and other arts and crafts. Among the important American architects deeply affected by the movement were the Greene brothers, Charles Sumner (1868–1957), Henry Mather (1870–1954), and Bernard Maybeck (1862–1957), architects of creative buildings, all highly ornamented with handcrafted details and furnishings.

Chicago School The most important accomplishments in the establishment of the modern movement in the United States were those of the architects of the so-called Chicago school. Sometimes their work is called the Commercial style, since most of it was devoted to office buildings, warehouses, department stores, and other commercial building types.

The prime mover of the Chicago school was Major William Le Baron Jenney (1832–1907), an engineer turned architect who began late in the 19th century to turn away from the eclectic architecture of the time. The prime impetus to the Chicago school was the great fire of 1871, which virtually destroyed the downtown area of Chicago. After the fire, the architects who came to be known as the Chicago school started to rebuild in a distinctly different manner. Iron had been used quite often for structures in Chicago before the great fire, but afterward for some years, architects turned back almost exclusively to brick and stone. Gradually, the use of iron, at least for the interior columns of some buildings, was resumed. Then several events came at once: some technological innovations and one purely architectural change.

The major technological changes included the invention of a safe elevator; the first was installed by its inventor, Elisha Graves Otis (1811–61), in the five-story Haughwout Building (1857), New York City, designed by J. P. Gaynor. The second technological change was the growing use of central heating. Together, the elevator and central heating helped establish the beginning of tall buildings, or skyscrapers. And central heating, along with new insulating methods, allowed the use of large areas of glass in walls. The important architectural change was the growing disenchantment with eclecticism that eventually led to the functional architecture later called modern. Another factor that affected the architecture of the time was the development of methods for making iron, and later steel, structural members fire resistant, or fireproof, as it was called then, by enclosing them with masonry.

MODERN ARCHITECTURE   Chrysler Building (1930), New York, N.Y. [*Architect: William Van Alen. (Wurts Brothers)*]

MODERN ARCHITECTURE   Empire State Building (1931), New York, N.Y. [*Architects: Shreve, Lamb and Harmon. (Wurts Brothers)*]

MODERN ARCHITECTURE Rockefeller Center (1940), New York, N.Y. [*Architects: Reinhard and Hofmeister; Corbett, Harrison and Mac-Murray; Hood and Fouilhoux. (Bo Parker)*]

MODERN ARCHITECTURE Equitable Building (1948), Portland, Ore.
[*Architect: Pietro Belluschi. (Morley Baer)*]

Led by Jenney in whose office most of them worked at one time or another, the Chicago school architects created a new kind of architecture in the late 19th century: functional with ornament used sparingly, of iron (later steel) skeleton framed tall buildings with large areas of glass in exterior walls. In New York City and other places, architects had also begun designing tall buildings, many of them exceeding in height those in Chicago. But the Eastern buildings were eclectic, while those in Chicago were designed in forms more appropriate to the time and its technology and needs.

MODERN ARCHITECTURE Lever House (1952), New York, N.Y.
[*Architects: Skidmore, Owings and Merrill. (Ezra Stoller)*]

In the First Leiter Building (1879), Chicago, Jenney used brick columns for the exterior and iron columns for the interior. Six years later, his Home Insurance Co. Building (1885, since demolished) was built with a complete skeleton frame, mostly of iron but with some steel beams. His former employees followed his lead. Daniel Hudson Burnham (1846–1912) joined in partnership with John Wellborn Root (1850–91), who had not worked for Jenney, to design some of the great Chicago buildings of the era. Two former Jenney employees, William Holabird (1854–1923) and Martin Roche (1855–1927), formed another firm that did masterful work. And the greatest of all of the former Jenney employees, Louis Henri Sullivan (1856–1924), outperformed them all in a series of fine buildings designed and built in the late 19th and early 20th centuries. (See articles entitled Burnham and Root; Holabird and Roche; Jenney, William Le Baron; Sullivan, Louis Henri.)

By the early 20th century, the Chicago school architects had developed a new kind of architecture, now called modern, that was almost purely American, demonstrating few if any influences from the modern movements taking place in Europe at that time. From the commercial buildings of Chicago and other places, the new architectural design spread to other building types. And the work of the Chicago school architects began to affect that of younger architects, including one destined to become a towering master, Frank Lloyd Wright. From the time of his employment in the office of Louis Henri Sullivan, Wright deeply affected architecture.

First acclaimed in Europe for his work, Wright eventually became the best-known and greatest architect of his time, some think of all time. In California, the Greene brothers and Bernard Maybeck, affected by the Craft Movement in Europe, created masterfully detailed and crafted buildings, some of them, particularly in the case of Maybeck, very romantic, even mystical. Another California architect, Irving John Gill (1870–1936), believed to have been influenced by the emerging modern architecture in Europe, particularly that in Germany, Austria, and the Netherlands, created a personal kind of architecture of excellent quality. Gill turned his back on handcrafts but not on craftsmanship. His architecture was strictly of its time, finely detailed, using modern technology and methods. (See articles entitled Gill, Irving John; Greene and Greene; Maybeck, Bernard; Wright, Frank Lloyd.)

Modern Movement Established In the 1920s and 1930s, the modern movement became firmly established not only in the United States but in Europe and elsewhere. Eclecticism still held on strongly and has persisted, to some extent, ever since. Frank Lloyd Wright continued to be the towering figure in the United States, always dedicated to what he called organic architecture and increasingly influential with younger architects all over the world. In Europe, the towering figure was a Swiss, who practiced in France, Charles Èdouard Jeanneret, almost always called Le Corbusier. Others deeply affected modern architecture, including a German, Eric Mendelsohn (1887–1953), who later became a British subject and still later practiced for a time in Israel and the United States; a Swede, Sven Markelius (1889–1972), and two Dutchmen, Jacobus Johannes Pieter (J.J.P.) Oud (1890–1963) and Marinus Dudok (1884–1974).

U.S. Architect-Émigrés To the United States emigrated a number of remarkable people who were already, or were destined to become, accomplished architects. The first to arrive was a German, Albert Kahn (1869–1942), at age eleven; Kahn became a great pioneer of modern factory design. A Finn, Eliel Saarinen (1873–1950), already famous in Europe, arrived in the 1920s and deeply affected architecture in the United States. Another architect who had an important part in the development of modern architecture, an Austrian, Richard Joseph Neutra (1892–1970), arrived about the same time, to become famous later, particularly for his houses and schools. Just before World War II, two German architects, already established and famous, arrived in the United States, Walter Adolf Gropius and Ludwig Mies van der Rohe, the former to revolutionize modern architectural education as he had already done in Germany and the latter, also an educator, to establish a spare, beautifully detailed architecture of planes and modern technology that had deep effects on the architecture of the time and afterward. (See articles entitled Gropius, Walter Adolf; Kahn, Albert; Mies van der Rohe, Ludwig; Neutra, Richard Joseph; Saarinen, Eliel.) Others also came to the United States, one of the most notable being an Austrian, Rudolph Schindler (1887–1953).

The architecture of Frank Lloyd Wright and some other American architects of the time was warm, often utilizing exotic forms and natural materials, with modern technological methods. The work of Mies, Neutra, Schindler, and often that of Gropius and others was composed mostly of simple, rectangular forms, using almost entirely modern materials, such as glass and steel. The work of Wright and others of his persuasion affected the architecture of other architects.

The International Style However, the work of Mies and the others, and some architects in Europe, had an even wider influence at the time. So widespread did their ideas become that some thought that a new style was being created that would eventually become established around the world. Called the International style in the 1932 book of the same title, written by the historian and critic Henry-Russell Hitchcock (1903–) and Philip Cortelyou Johnson (1906–), not as yet an architect, the phrase caught on with architects and others. Although the phrase was later denigrated by most of those who were supposed to have developed the style, including Mies and Gropius, there was a great deal of truth in the idea at the time, and some truth even today.

A Decade of Notable Architects During slightly more than a decade starting in 1895, a number of peo-

MODERN ARCHITECTURE   Citicorp Center (1978), New York, N.Y.
[*Architects: Hugh Stubbins, in association with Emery Roth and Sons.
Engineer: William Le Messurier. Landscape architects: Sasaki Associates.
(Nick Wheeler)*]

ple destined later to become notable architects were born. In Europe, they included the Finn Alvar Aalto (1898–1976), Spaniards José Luis Sert (1902–) and Eduardo Torroja (1899–1961), the Englishman Edwin Maxwell Fry (1899–), the Italian Gio Ponti (1897–1979), and the great Italian engineer Pier Luigi Nervi (1891–1979). Modern architecture was making inroads in other places too, including Brazil in the work of Lucio Costa (1902–) and Oscar Neimeyer (1907–).

Born in approximately the same decade were Americans who later became notable architects, including William Wilson Wurster (1895–1973), Buckminster Fuller (1895–), Wallace Kirkman Harrison (1895–), Bruce Goff (1904–), Philip Cortelyou Johnson, and three architects who established one of the world's most successful firms, Skidmore, Owings and Merrill, Louis Skidmore (1897–1962), Nathaniel Alexander Owings (1903–) and John Ogden Merrill (1896–1975). (See articles entitled Fuller, Richard Buckminster; Harrison, Wallace Kirkman; Johnson, Philip Cortelyou; Skidmore, Owings and Merrill; Wurster, William Wilson.)

The same era produced a number of architects, who emigrated to the United States and practiced there, including Pietro Belluschi (1899–) from Italy, Louis Isadore Kahn (1902–74) from Estonia, Marcel Lajos Breuer (1902–) from Hungary, and Eero Saarinen (1910–61) from Finland, brought by his family to the United States when he was young. Others of importance are William Lescaze (1896–1969) from Switzerland and Serge Chermayeff (1900–) from the Soviet Union. (See articles entitled Belluschi, Pietro; Breuer, Marcel Lajos; Kahn, Louis Isadore; Saarinen, Eero.)

By the 1940s and 1950s, two trends, that of the organic architecture of Wright or something resembling it, and that of the International style, whatever it might be called, had been firmly established in the United States. Architects like Goff and Alden B. Dow (1904–) and others followed the Wrightian philosophies, while architects like Johnson, Skidmore, Owings, Merrill, Harrison, Breuer, and others followed the philosophies of Gropius and Mies. Other architects, such as John Ekin Dinwiddie (1902–59), Harwell Hamilton Harris (1903–), and Belluschi, seemed intent on establishing regional styles on the West Coast, styles somewhat more akin to the ideas of Wright than of Gropius and Mies.

By this time, Wright's concepts had evolved into the use of free-form, sculptural shapes in his architectural designs. And other architects, including Belluschi and Breuer, some of whom had been going in other directions, sometimes used such forms. The trend was toward an architecture that was not only thought of as sculptural but was also sometimes called sensual or emotional. And ornament also began to come back into building designs. Some of the younger architects became involved in work of this kind, including Minoru Yamasaki (1912–) and Paul Rudolph (1918–). Although he started out designing buildings much like those of Mies, Eero Saarinen turned to sculptural, emotional forms for many of his later buildings. Louis Isadore Kahn designed great sculptural buildings that have deeply affected architecture since that time. (See the article entitled Yamasaki, Minoru.)

During this era, Le Corbusier and others went even further, developing a phase of the sculptural style that came to be called the Brutal style, not to be critical of it, but in recognition of its use of heavy sculptural forms, often in quite large sizes.

The era of great pioneers of the modern movement in the United States—Jenney, Burnham, Root, Roche, Holabird, and Sullivan—came to an end when the last of them, Martin Roche, died in 1927. Before that, their influence had given way to that of the great masters of the movement: Wright, Mies, Gropius, and Le Corbusier. Wright died in 1959, Le Corbusier in 1965, and both Mies and Gropius in 1969. This was the end of another great era. By that time a group of younger architects, many of them in their thirties, forties, or early fifties, were making names for themselves. For a discussion of their accomplishments, see the article entitled contemporary architecture.

Illustrations The illustrations in this article indicate the history of the growth of modern, high-rise buildings, or skyscrapers, from the late 19th century to today. The 16-story Monadnock Building (1891), Chicago, Ill., designed by Burnham and Root, was the last tall building with masonry bearing walls, which were 6 ft thick for the first story. The 14-story Reliance Building, completed in 1895 in Chicago, by Burnham and Root, has a steel skeleton frame, fire-protected by masonry. The Gage buildings (1899), Chicago, two by Holabird and Roche and one by Louis Henri Sullivan, illustrate the further development of the style of the Chicago school and of the three-part Chicago window. By 1930, when the Chrysler Building, New York City, designed by William Van Alen, was completed, the record height for a building had gone from less than 20 stories to 75.

The height record of the Chrysler Building lasted only a year, until the 102-story Empire State Building (1931), New York City, by Shreve, Lamb and Harmon, was completed. This record lasted until 1973, when the 110-story World Trade Center, New York City, designed by Minoru Yamasaki, in association with Emery Roth and Sons, was completed. Its height was equaled a year later by Sears Tower (1974), Chicago, Ill., by Skidmore, Owings and Merrill. Rockefeller Center (1940), New York City, by Reinhard and Hofmeister; Corbett, Harrison and McMurray; and Hood and Fouilhoux, was the first great group, or urban complex, of tall buildings to be completed in the United States.

While the Chrysler Building, Empire State Building, and Rockefeller Center are all eclectic in design, the Equitable Building (1947), Portland, Ore., by Pietro Belluschi, returned to the direct line of evolution of modern architecture and has one of the earliest thin metal and glass curtain walls. Lever House (1952),

New York City, by Skidmore, Owings and Merrill, continued the evolution also in a curtain-wall building, placed on its site to allow a great plaza on the ground level and another elevated above it.

Citicorp Center (1978), New York City, designed by Hugh Stubbins in association with Emery Roth and Sons, continued the evolution. Structurally engineered to take advantage of the most advanced technologies, with heating and air-conditioning systems designed for energy conservation and with a very advanced curtain wall, the Center was designed to provide great open spaces, not only outside the building but within as well, with shops, restaurants, sitting areas, and other spaces for people that are occupied both during the daytime and until late at night.

See additional illustrations in color section.

Related Articles CONTEMPORARY ARCHITECTURE; ECLECTIC ARCHITECTURE; GROPIUS, WALTER ADOLF; HISTORY OF ARCHITECTURE; MIES VAN DER ROHE, LUDWIG; SULLIVAN, LOUIS HENRI; WRIGHT, FRANK LLOYD; Various articles on other modern architects.

Further Reading Benevolo, Leonardo: *History of Modern Architecture*, 2 vols., MIT Press, Cambridge, 1971; Condit, Carl W.: *The Chicago School of Architecture*, University of Chicago Press, Chicago, 1964; Giedion, Sigfried: *Space, Time and Architecture—The Growth of a New Tradition*, 4th ed., Harvard University Press, Cambridge, 1962; Hitchcock, Henry-Russell: *Architecture in the Nineteenth and Twentieth Centuries*, Penguin Books, Baltimore, 1958; Hitchcock, Henry-Russell, and Philip C. Johnson: *The International Style—Architecture Since 1922*, Norton, New York, 1932; Jordy, William H.: *American Buildings and Their Architects*, vol. 3, *Progressive and Academic Ideals at the Turn of the Century* and vol. 4, *The Impact of European Modernism in the Mid-Twentieth Century*, Doubleday, Garden City, N.Y., 1972; McCoy, Esther: *Five California Architects*, Reinhold, New York, 1960; See also listing in the article entitled history of architecture.

MOLDING Part of a building usually in the form of a relatively narrow strip primarily used as ornament around doors and windows, at the intersections of exterior walls with roofs and interior walls with ceilings, and in many other places. Moldings (sometimes spelled mouldings) are ordinarily rectilinear or curved or some combination of these forms.

In many of the past periods of architecture, moldings were one of the major ornamental elements of building interiors and exteriors. With the advent of the modern movement in architecture, their importance declined to the point that today moldings are considerably smaller, simpler, and sparingly used. Most are made in stock sizes and shapes and their most frequent use is in covering joints between surfaces or materials in buildings.

Materials In the past, moldings were made of such materials as wood or plaster, but the highest development came in stone, which was often carved or otherwise ornamented. In some periods, certain types and systems of moldings were developed of which vestiges still exist today. In contemporary architecture, moldings, when used at all, are apt to be of wood or metal, in simple, standardized or stock

shapes, in relatively small sizes and unornamented. Many of the available moldings are named for their purposes, such as crown, corner, picture, base, rail, stop, and so on; others are named for their shapes, as round, half round, and quarter round.

History At the time of the great ancient civilizations around the Mediterranean Sea, moldings were not important ornamental elements in architecture. The scale of Egyptian, Middle Eastern, And Aegean architecture was so great that moldings would have seemed insignificant. They were used on columns, however, and in a few cases moldings of relatively large size were used on Egyptian buildings.

As they did in other architectural elements, the ancient Greeks developed moldings to a high degree of perfection. Refined and delicate, Greek moldings were usually carved into stone. So important were moldings to the Greeks that they developed a whole system, which has been followed to an extent in the moldings of subsequent architectural periods. The most important moldings of the Greeks were the fillet, a flat band; and seven curved types: astragal; torus, now called half round; ovolo, called quarter round, even though the Greek ovolo was more egg-shaped than like a quarter segment of a circle; cavetto, called cove; scotia; cyma recta, called crown; and cyma reversa, called ogee. Some moldings used on Greek buildings were plain; others had skillfully carved ornament on their surfaces.

The Romans used moldings that were largely derived from those of the Greeks. The major Greek types were all used, often with abundant carved ornament, and less skillfully executed than that of the Greeks. Roman moldings also differed somewhat in shape from those of the Greeks.

Both the Greeks and Romans often placed moldings of various kinds adjacent to each other to form highly ornamental major building elements. The classic molding types have had a very important place in American architecture in almost every period, except the present one, but most particularly during the Classic Revival and Eclectic eras.

Moldings in Early Christian architecture were usually rich but crude, often using acanthus leaf motifs. In Byzantine architecture, moldings were seldom used because mosaics, wall paintings, and other ornament almost completely covered every important architectural element. Romanesque moldings were mostly rather heavy and coarse, elaborately carved in stone, in designs adapted from those of the Romans. The moldings of none of these eras have had any appreciable effect on American architecture.

During the Gothic period of architecture, moldings at first were used sparingly and were simple in design, but later became very complex and vigorous, with quite extreme variations between different centuries and different countries. In Italy, moldngs remained similar to those of Roman times; in Spain, they were usually somewhat crude, often in designs adapted from those in France; in Germany, they were intricate

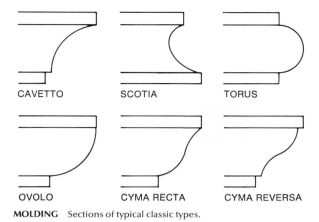

| CAVETTO | SCOTIA | TORUS |
| OVOLO | CYMA RECTA | CYMA REVERSA |

MOLDING Sections of typical classic types.

and highly detailed; and in France, they were large and bold, but not so ornate as in some other countries. Moldings were, perhaps, most highly developed in England, where rich, bold applications were made to a great number of architectural elements, including columns, arches, and openings. Often elaborately carved, English Gothic moldings utilized a number of motifs, including chevrons, cables, dogteeth, cones, flowers, and scrolls. These moldings were often deeply undercut and different types were frequently used together, sometimes passing behind and in front of one another. Gothic molding types, especially those of the English, were used in later architecture in Europe and America, particularly during the Gothic Revival and Eclectic periods.

During the Renaissance, moldings were mostly derived from those of the Classic periods, particularly the Roman era. Using combinations of the classic Roman molding types, or variations of them, Renaissance architects created complex moldings, often with alternating flat and curved bands, for many architectural elements, including cornices, the highest part of the elements supported by columns, and other parts of the buildings. Cornices often were designed to project out a considerable distance and were ornamented in such a way as to make them of considerable importance in building designs. Such combinations of classic moldings varied considerably between Renaissance buildings. Another ornamental feature, developed during this period, is a railing system, or balustrade, often used above the cornices of buildings.

American Development In early colonial America, moldings were used sparingly and were mostly of wood, in designs derived from those in Europe. In later architecture, moldings were adapted from those of historical periods of European architecture as shown in books, most of which were published in England, or as established through scholarly research of the older examples from which they were derived. By the end of the 19th century, the use of ornamental moldings was declining and in the 20th, came virtually to an end. Today vestiges of the ornamental uses of moldings are sometimes found in the design of hand-

rails for stairways and other building elements. The main use of moldings today is not actually ornamental but to cover joints that might otherwise be objectionable, between building materials or elements.

Related articles ARCH; ART IN ARCHITECTURE; BOOK, ARCHITECTURAL; COLUMN; DESIGN, ARCHITECTURAL; HISTORY OF ARCHITECTURE; ORNAMENT; Various articles on American architectural history.

MONUMENT A building or other structure erected to commemorate a person or event, and sometimes to denote a natural geographical feature or historical site. Monuments range in size from simple grave markers to the gigantic carvings at Mount Rushmore in the Black Hills, near Rapid City, S.D. Some monuments have functional purposes; others are purely symbolic.

Types There are many kinds of monuments. A grave marker in a cemetery is used to commemorate a person who has died. Memorial markers, called cenotaphs, are used in places other than where the person memorialized is buried. A mausoleum is a building in which the dead are entombed and which also acts as a memorial. Monuments may also be buildings, streets, highways, parks, sculpture, or pillars. And canyons, mountains, water bodies, and land areas are sometimes named as monuments.

History From the earliest times a great number of these types of monuments have been constructed. In prehistoric times, monuments were usually made of large stones and were called megaliths, or from a single stone called a stele. Early people in the Middle East and in Egypt erected pyramids, obelisks, pillars, and other monuments. The Romans built numerous monuments, including columns, mausoleums, and triumphal arches. Many of these early monuments are still standing.

Monuments have been built ever since all over the world. They vary a great deal, from the magnificent Taj Mahal (1653), in Agra, India, a mausoleum built by Shah Jahan (1628–58), to the awe-inspiring pyramids built in the 28th to 26th centuries B.C. at Gizeh, Egypt, near Cairo, to the Arc de Triomphe de l'Étoile (1836), Paris, designed by Jean François Chalgrin (1739–1811).

American Development In colonial America, few monuments were built other than grave markers or simple types. After the Revolution, Americans erected monuments for every conceivable historical event and person. Many of the monuments were designed by architects, whose names read like a Who's Who of American architecture. Among them were Louis Henri Sullivan (1856–1924) who designed a number of mausoleums and Paul Phillippe Cret (1876–1947) who designed monuments of many kinds.

Although monuments are to be found all over the United States, the biggest collection is in Washington, D.C. A selection of these will demonstrate the range of types. In and near the U.S. National Cemetery, Ar-

MONUMENT Statue of Liberty (1886), New York, N.Y. [*Architect of base: Richard Morris Hunt. Engineer: Gustave Eiffel. Sculptor: Frederick Auguste Bartholdi. (Library of Congress)*]

MONUMENT Memorial, Amphitheatre (1920), U.S. National Cemetery, Arlington, Va. [*Architects: Carrère and Hastings. (Theodore Horydczak, Library of Congress)*]

MONUMENT Tomb of the Unknowns, formerly Tomb of the Unknown Solder (1931), U.S. National Cemetery, Arlington, Va. [*Architect: Lorimer Rich. (Library of Congress)*]

lington, Va., in addition to the thousands of single grave markers, there are the Memorial Amphitheater (1920) designed by Carrère and Hastings, the Tomb of the Unknown Soldier (1931; renamed Tomb of the Unknowns in 1958 when two more unknowns, one from World War II and one from the Korean conflict were buried there) by Lorimer Rich (1891–1978), the Memorial Gate and Memorial Bridge, both designed by McKim, Mead and White, and built in 1932, and the John F. Kennedy grave (1966), designed by John Carl Warnecke (1919–   ) Across the river in Washington are the three most famous monuments in the area: the Washington Monument (1885), designed by Robert Mills (1781–1855), the Lincoln Memorial (1922), by Henry Bacon (1866–1924), and the Jefferson Memorial (1943), by John Russell Pope (1874–1937).

Related Articles BACON, HENRY; CAPITAL, UNITED STATES; CRET, PAUL PHILIPPE; McKIM, MEAD AND WHITE; MILLS, ROBERT; POPE, JOHN RUSSELL; SULLIVAN, LOUIS HENRI.

MUSEUM A building, or group of buildings, or a room in a building, in which are housed collections of rare and educational objects or works of art. Many museums also have gardens or other outdoor areas for display of certain objects.

Types Sometimes an art museum may be referred to as an art gallery, a term also applied to stores in which works of art are displayed for sale. Other kinds of museums include those that specialize in archeology, history, natural history, applied science, or other fields of knowledge. A general museum houses collections in a number of these fields. Some museums are specifically for children. Others limit themselves to some relatively small subject, such as the site of a battle or other event, a home of a famous person, or a single art style or period. In some cases, whole areas

that preserve or re-create the environment in which people lived in the past operate as museums. Two of the most famous are the colonial area of Williamsburg, Va., and old Sturbridge Village, Mass.

Functions Museums may be located almost anywhere, but for the most part they are in cities, on college and university campuses, and on historical sites. In addition to their functions in the preservation of objects and display to the public, most museums are cultural centers, in which experts engage in research; monographs, books, and other publications are published; theatrical and musical performances are staged; and many other activities are pursued.

Museums acquire their collections by outright purchase, trading with other museums, gifts, and searching for them in archeological and other expeditions. Museums are financed primarily by governments on various levels, from the local to the federal, and by donations of money by individuals and other institutions.

Elements Although a somewhat small number of museums is built in any given period, museum design is interesting and challenging to architects. And since museums always seem to be constantly acquiring new objects, making changes in exhibits, and expanding their facilities, a goodly number of architects may be involved in their design. Although every museum presents different problems to its architect because of its location, size, type of collections, and other factors, all museums have several common elements, public and private. Public spaces include display areas or exhibition rooms which are the primary museum spaces, shops where souvenirs and other items are sold, and rest rooms. Often lecture rooms, auditoriums, and libraries, and restaurants, cafeterias, or snack bars are provided. Important private areas of a museum are administrative offices; spaces for preparation of exhibits and storage of objects not on display; shops for repairs and maintenance; rooms for scholars; and rest rooms, lounges, and other rooms for the staff.

Of primary importance in the design of a museum are provisions for flexibility in mounting and arranging exhibits, for expansion, and for lighting the displays, either with natural or artificial light or a combination of the two.

History of Museums The history of museums dates back at least to the 5th century B.C. Some of the earliest were in Egypt and nearby countries. Museums of the kind known today began during the Middle Ages, but really became important during the Renaissance. Most of these museums came from collections of art or other objects made by private collectors and donated to institutions, such as universities. Probably the first of these museums was the Ashmolean (1683) at Oxford University, England. The establishment of museums speeded up in the 18th century and included the British Museum (1753), London, and the Louvre (1783), Paris. The fastest growth in the number of museums took place in the 19th century, when

MUSEUM Exterior, Oakland (1969), Oakland, Calif. [*Architects: Kevin Roche and John Dinkeloo. Landscape architect: Daniel U. Kiley. (Morley Baer)*]

MUSEUM Interior, Oakland (1969), Oakland Calif. [*Architects: Kevin Roche and John Dinkeloo. Landscape architect: Daniel U. Kiley. (Morley Baer)*]

MUSEUM Exterior, Science Building (1964), New York World's Fair, New York, N.Y. [*Architects: Harrison and Abramovitz. (Joseph W. Molitor)*]

MUSEUM Interior, Science Building (1964), New York World's Fair, New York, N.Y. [*Architects: Harrison and Abramovitz. (Joseph W. Molitor)*]

such museums as the Prado (1819) in Madrid, Spain, the Berlin museums (1830), the Victoria and Albert (1857) in London, and the Hermitage (1852) in Leningrad, which was then St. Petersburg, Russia, were founded.

American Development The first museum in America was founded in 1759 in Charleston, S.C., but the great era of American museum building was also in the late 19th century. At that time, important museums such as the Smithsonian Institution (first building, 1849) in Washington, the Metropolitan Museum of Art (1870) in New York City, the Boston Museum of Fine Arts (1870), the Philadelphia Museum (1876), and the Art Institute of Chicago (1879) were built.

Related Articles ART IN ARCHITECTURE; CAPITAL, UNITED STATES; COLLEGE AND UNIVERSITY BUILDING; LIBRARY.

Further Reading *Architectural Record: Buildings for the Arts*, McGraw-Hill, New York, 1978.

Source of Additional Information American Association of Museums, 2233 Massachusetts Ave, N.W. Washington, D.C. 20007.

NEUTRA, RICHARD JOSEPH Austrian-American architect (1892–1970). Although his work has often been considered to parallel that of other great 20th-century architects—Le Corbusier, Mies, Gropius, and Wright—Richard Joseph Neutra started much later than they did. Neutra began his architectural practice in 1926, some 15 years after the first three architects above and 30 years after Wright. Although his career ran concurrently with theirs for more than 30 years, his work always seemed to be somewhat overshadowed by their work. Through his lifetime, Neutra's work was a source of some controversy. There were those who thought it derivative from that of the other architects and those who thought it creative and original in itself.

Time has seemed to have justified those who supported the latter view. Neutra's buildings have a grace and lyrical style all their own, related to the work of other architects but not derivative. Neutra was deeply concerned with the environment in which his buildings would exist. Experienced as a landscape gardener in his youth, he respected building sites and developed them as creatively as any architect of his time. He was concerned with technological progress. He respected industrial products, but did not worship them as some did. He was keenly interested in the biological sciences and his designs reflected that interest. Most of all, Neutra was interested in people, especially the people who would inhabit and use his buildings. And he was interested in large-scale planning and devoted a measure of his talents to master plans, city plans, and development projects. As a result, he designed some notable buildings of his era and strongly influenced the architecture of his time and of the future.

Works Opening his office in 1926, Neutra made a rather slow start, but Lovell House (1929; see color section), Los Angeles, drew the attention of the world's architects. Often called the Health House because of the interest of Neutra and its owner in natural living and health; the Lovell House, with a steel skeleton, thin concrete walls, and glass, was hailed as a technological breakthrough and a masterpiece. Over the next few years, he designed several notable houses, including one for himself (1933) and the Von Sternberg House (1936), both in Los Angeles. He also designed a military academy and a school, his first of many, and several other buildings. The school, Corona Avenue (1935), was the first with one-room-deep classrooms, with glass on both sides, and a wall that could be opened with sliding doors to the outside. He also worked on ideas for prefabricated houses, but none was ever built. His great design for the Kahn House (1940) in San Francisco included furniture that he also designed. This was followed by other California houses, including the Nesbitt House (1942), West Los Angeles; another masterpiece, the Kaufmann House (1946), Palm Springs; the Tremaine House (1948), Santa Barbara; the Moore House (1952), Ojai; and the Singleton House (1959), Los Angeles. During this period, he had designed a number of other California buildings, the most notable of which are Holiday House (1948), a seaside motel at Malibu, and Eagle Rock Club House (1953), Los Angeles. He also designed a pioneering housing development, Channel Heights (1942), San Pedro, Calif., and its furniture.

After the formation of Neutra's partnership with Robert Evans Alexander (1907–   ) in 1949, the firm produced a number of buildings of other types, including the Child Guidance Clinic (1954) in Los Angeles, Miramar Chapel (1959) in La Jolla, Alamitos Elementary School (1957) in Garden Grove, all in California; the Lincoln Memorial Museum (1959), Gettysburg, Pa.; and the U.S. Embassy (1961), Karachi, Pakistan.

While in partnership with Alexander, Neutra continued to handle certain designs by himself. Two important ones were the Gemological Institute (1956),

NEUTRA, RICHARD Corona Avenue School (1935), Los Angeles, Calif. *(Julius Shulman)*

NEUTRA, RICHARD   Lovell House (1929), Los Angeles, Calif. *(Julius Shulman)*

NEUTRA, RICHARD   Kaufmann House (1946), Palm Springs, Calif. *(Julius Shulman)*

West Los Angeles, and an open-air classroom school, based on what he called the ring plan, first projected in 1928 and finally built in Lemoore, Calif., in 1960. It is named the Richard J. Neutra School.

Neutra had a lasting effect on modern architecture, through his own designs and through the large number of books and articles he wrote.

Life Richard Joseph Neutra was born on April 9, 1892, in Vienna, Austria, the son of the owner of a small factory that made brass and bronze castings. As a boy, he became interested in architecture and enrolled at the Vienna Technical High School, the equivalent of a college in the United States. When he was sixteen, he left school to join the Austrian army artillery and served as an officer, in the Balkans, during World War I. Returning to Vienna in 1917, he went back to school to receive his degree. While still a student, he met the pioneering modern architect and critic Adolf Loos (1870–1933), and worked in his office for a time. The architectural design philosophy of Loos made a deep and lasting impression on him. Loos also interested him in the United States, particularly its industrial design. He was greatly impressed by the designs of Frank Lloyd Wright (1867–1959), which were published in Europe at that time.

Since Austria was in the middle of a revolution when he graduated from school, Neutra went to Switzerland in 1919, where he worked for a landscape architect and gardener. Then he worked for the municipal government of Brandenburg, Germany, helping to resettle workers from the city to the country. While there, he designed a chapel and gatehouse for a cemetery. In 1921, interested in Eric Mendelsohn (1887–1953), he went to Berlin to visit and stayed to work in his office as a draftsman. Neutra later collaborated with Mendelsohn on the design of buildings, including four exhibition houses in Berlin (1922), and in 1923, on a competition for a business center in Haifa, Israel, then Palestine, which they won. The building was never built.

Neutra married Dione Niedermann, a cellist, in 1922. The next year, alarmed by the inflation and turbulent conditions in Germany, they went to the United States. For a few months, Neutra detailed Gothic ornament for buildings in New York and in November 1923, moved to Chicago, where he went to work for the office of Holabird and Roche, the large firm that had designed many of the tall (Chicago school) buildings. Soon after arriving in Chicago, Neutra visited Louis Henri Sullivan (1856–1924), who was then sixty-seven, ill, with less than a year to live. At Sullivan's funeral, in April 1924, Neutra met Frank Lloyd Wright, whose work had so impressed him in his youth. During the year Neutra visited Wright at Taliesin in Spring Green, Wis. several times and in 1925 stayed there to work with Wright for several months.

In 1926 Neutra went to Los Angeles to open his own practice, sharing office space with R. M. Schindler (1857–1953), a pioneering modern architect, fellow Austrian, and former draftsman for Wright. The two architects collaborated on a few designs that were not built. That same year, a son, Dion (1926–   ), was born to Richard and Dione Neutra. Neutra's first design, on his own, was for the Jardinette Apartments (1927), Los Angeles, but it showed little promise of his later style. In 1928-29, Neutra taught architecture at the Academy of Modern Art, Los Angeles. The Depression slowed his progress as it did that of all architects. But he had begun to receive recognition for his work and commissions came in more rapidly. In 1930 Neutra became an American citizen. During the early postdepression years, he continued to design houses and other building types, including schools and apartments. From 1939 to 1941, he was a member and served as chairman of the California State Planning Board.

During World War II, commissions slowed and Neutra turned to nonessential materials (redwood, common brick, and glass) in his house designs. In 1942 Neutra's son, Dion, aged sixteen, came to work in his father's office and continued to do so with time out for his architectural education until 1960. After the war, in addition to houses, schools, and apartments, Neutra received commissions for other building types, including those for offices, clubs, churches, and clinics.

In 1949 Neutra formed a partnership with Robert Evans Alexander, architect and city planner, which was to continue for nine years until 1958, when Alexander left to organize his own firm.

In 1951 Neutra and Alexander were appointed planning consultants and architects to the government of Guam, a role that Neutra had played in Puerto Rico during the war years. The 10-year master plan for Guam was one of a number of planning projects handled by Neutra with Alexander.

In 1965 Neutra's son again joined the firm, which was renamed Richard and Dion Neutra, and they practiced together until the elder Neutra's death. The firm continued with Dion.

On April 16, 1970, at age seventy-eight, Richard Neutra died in Wuppertal, West Germany, while on a lecture tour. He had helped pioneer the development of modern architecture, in a very American way, though he had been born and educated in Austria. He was deeply concerned with the environment and sites of his buildings and with the people who occupied and used them. In 1977, seven years after his death, he was awarded the highest architectural honor of his adopted country, the Gold Medal of the American Institute of Architects.

Related Articles MODERN ARCHITECTURE; SULLIVAN, LOUIS HENRI; WRIGHT, FRANK LLOYD.

Further Reading Boesiger, W., ed.: *Richard Neutra, 1950–60: Buildings and Projects,* Praeger, New York, 1959; Boesiger, W., ed.: *Richard Neutra, 1961–66: Buildings and Projects,* Praeger, New York, 1966; McCoy, Esther: *Richard Neutra,* Braziller, New York, 1960; Neutra, Richard: *Survival Through Design,* Oxford, New York, 1954.

OFFICE BUILDING A building in which business is transacted or professional services performed. A room, for the same purposes, in such a building is called an office. Office buildings are one of the most important building types and almost all architects design them.

Office buildings can be any size, from one room to thousands, from 1 story to over 100, from about 10 ft in height to more than 1,300, from less than 100 ft² of floor area to millions. Most office buildings in the past were approximately square or rectangular in plan, but today they may be any shape their architects can devise for construction.

Types of Organizations Business and professional groups are organized as proprietorships, owned by a single person; partnerships, owned by two or more people; or corporations, owned by stockholders who own shares of stock in them. Another type of ownership is a joint venture, in which two or more individuals or companies share the ownership of a venture for some specific purpose. Business trusts are formed to allow one group, the trustees, to manage property owned by others; and a syndicate is a special type of joint venture formed for joint selling of the goods or services of several companies. A syndicate may go further, forming a cartel, sometimes called a pool or a trust, a group of companies banded together not only for joint selling but to limit production, divide markets, fix quotas, and divide profits.

The most usual organization, for all but companies of relatively small size, is the corporation. Until recently, organizations of professionals, such as doctors, lawyers, engineers, or architects, were always single proprietorships or partnerships. Now professionals may form corporations, but are often subject to special legal or ethical requirements that limit some of their corporate activities.

Most corporations are organized generally along the following lines. The stockholders, who are the owners, elect members of the board of directors who are responsible for overall policy, for the election of the chairman, and the appointment of top management executive officers, including the president, who is usually the officer charged with carrying out the policies. Vice presidents, responsible to the president, manage the various functions of the company.

Functions of Organizations Companies and professional groups operate in many different ways, according to their size and objectives. For example,

small architectural offices operate quite differently from the offices of large manufacturing companies. However, in every office, certain functions take place, including management, production, finance, and general services. In almost every organization, there is a sales or marketing function and in many a technical services or research function. The major problems

OFFICE BUILDING Gulf Life Tower (1967), Jacksonville, Fla. [*Architects: Welton Becket, in association with Kemp, Bunch and Jackson. (Joseph W. Molitor)*]

OFFICE BUILDING CBS (1965), New York, N.Y. [*Architect: Eero Saarinen. (Joseph W. Molitor)*]

OFFICE BUILDING Equitable (1960), New York, N.Y. [*Architects: Skidmore, Owings and Merrill. (Joseph W. Molitor)*]

in designing an office building come from the provisions for the needs of all these functions and allowing for the proper interrelationships between them.

Group Needs The management group, including the top executives, the middle management group, and those at the lowest level require offices designed for efficiency and comfort in doing their work. Space for clerical workers, conference rooms for meetings and other gatherings, and other facilities are usually needed. The financial group has similar requirements for office space and an even greater need for clerical space. In addition, the financial group requires facilities for a great variety of office machines and computer, or data-processing, functions. Often related to this group are purchasing and personnel departments.

Facilities for the production group vary considerably among business and professional organizations. In a manufacturing company, for example, the production group may have offices in or near the plant in

which the manufacturing operations take place. In a doctor's office, "production" is the work of the doctor himself and his professional staff. In an architectural office, production is the process of making drawings, specifications, and other documents for the construction of buildings. In some companies, production may be far away from the home office in another building in another location.

Sales or marketing groups vary considerably. In a doctor's office, there is no sales group. In an architect's office, a sales group might be small and consist of members of the firm or employees who also perform other functions. In the offices of a manufacturer, the sales group might well be one of the largest in the organization. The sales group has requirements for offices and related spaces, along with spaces for meeting with customers, display of products, training, conferences, demonstrations, and storage for samples, catalogs, and other sales literature.

The general services group provides services for all

the others, among which may be mail handling, duplication and printing, stenographic pool, central files, library, and general communications. It requires office and other spaces adapted to the specialized needs of each service.

The technical services or research group also varies considerably from firm to firm. A product manufacturer might have a very large department that designs and improves products, investigates new materials and methods, and performs other services. In a small office, such as an insurance agency, there might be no research group or one of limited size. The space required by the research group varies widely according to industry, process, or type of business. Some require extensive and very specialized laboratories and related facilities, others only office and clerical space very much like that used by other groups.

All the groups in office buildings have requirements for rest rooms and other management and employee facilities, often including lounges, cafeterias or snack bars, libraries, first aid rooms, and other spaces. Many offices have special requirements for storage including vaults, teletype and other communications equipment, stockrooms, and other purposes. All offices need space for janitorial work and some require other facilities for upkeep and maintenance.

OFFICE BUILDING   Xerox Square (1968), Rochester, N.Y. [*Architects: Welton Becket and Assoc. (Joseph W. Molitor)*]

OFFICE BUILDING Blue Cross (1973), Chapel Hill, N.C. [*Architect: Arthur Gould Odell. (Joseph W. Molitor)*]

Office Areas Within an office building, and also within each department or group, there are three major areas: the reception area, the office space, and storage. In the past, offices were designed in one of three ways: completely enclosed spaces, or private offices; open spaces, often called bull pens, in which workers were not separated from each other by walls; and semiprivate spaces, in which workers were separated from each other by partial partitions, often with glass above a certain level. In a given office building, any or all of the types might be used. For example, executives might have private offices, clerical workers might use open spaces, and salespeople might have semiprivate offices. All three types are still in use.

Another method that has come into use is open planning, sometimes called office landscaping. In this method, first espoused by German architects and interior designers, the basic office space is open, but it is subdivided by special furniture, storage units, planters, and low partitions. The method has advantages over traditional office layouts, including greater flexibility, better interaction between workers, and the possibility of providing an environment that is more expansive and satisfying than a group of enclosed offices can be.

In practice, many open office plans have been less than satisfactory. The failures seem to have come, at least partly, from trying to place diverse kinds of work in a single office landscape. This does not work well when employees whose occupations require quiet contemplation, writing, research, or similar activities are given space adjacent to employees who have a stream of visitors, use noisy machines, or cause disturbances. For those whose work is similar, it often seems to function well, for example, in an office occupied by copy editors, all quietly working on similar tasks. Even then, good acoustics are all-important.

In any office building, great attention should be given in the design to the flow patterns of the work, including paperwork, people, and communications. In the best designs, work, including paperwork, moves from one worker to another with the least amount of fuss and the smallest loss of time. Visitors should be able to move from the entrance to reception to an office in a similar manner. Workers should be able to move from the entrance to their desks or other work stations, then from their work stations to those of others in a similar efficient manner. In addition, all the spaces and their interrelationships should be planned for the degree of security and privacy required by the functions of the organization occupying the office building and the individual offices or work stations within it.

Specialized Types There are many specialized types of office buildings, all with out-of-the-ordinary requirements. For example, architectural and engineering offices need large drafting rooms with excellent lighting. These may be the bull-pen, semiprivate, or office-landscaped type. Insurance companies, banks, and other organizations require larger than usual facilities for data processing. Medical offices must have examining and treatment rooms often with special equipment, radiological or x-ray rooms, laboratories, and so on. Each presents special design problems unlike those of other office buildings. Dental offices require operating rooms, and law offices require unusually large libraries and vaults. Each special office building must be designed to meet the special needs of those who will occupy and use it.

History It is impossible to say when the first room or office, was set aside for the use of a person in conducting a business or profession. Certainly this occurred very early and almost certainly the first office was in a dwelling home. Office buildings were unknown before the Middle Ages, when the guilds constructed guild halls that were partly used as offices. Beginning during and accelerating toward the end of the 19th century, in Europe and America, commercial buildings, including offices, became important building types. Some of the best and most innovative architecture of the late 1800s were the tall buildings in Chicago, many of which were office buildings. And office buildings, large and small, have been a major part of architecture ever since. Many architects have designed them and many designs have produced great architecture.

Related Articles FACTORY; INTERIOR DESIGN; LABORATORY; STRUCTURAL ENGINEERING.

Further Reading Saphier, Michael: *Office Planning and Design*, McGraw-Hill, 2d ed., New York, 1978; Schwartz, M.: *Office Building Design* McGraw-Hill, New York, 1975.

OLMSTED, FREDERICK LAW
American landscape architect (1822–1903). Usually considered the first professional landscape architect in the United States, Olmsted is thought to be the first person to have placed the words, *landscape architect*, on a set of plans. These plans were for his masterpiece, Central Park, the designs for which were begun in 1857 by Olmsted and his partner, Calvert Vaux (1824–95).

Professional Innovations Olmsted was not the first person to design landscaping, a practice which goes back to ancient times. But he was the first to practice landscape architecture, called landscape gardening earlier, as a profession. One of his most important innovations was charging fees for his work, in a manner similar to the practice today in landscape architecture, rather than working for wages, as landscaping employees would, or taking profits on the cost of the work, as landscaping contractors would. In this and other ways, Olmsted pioneered the character of landscape architecture and the professional role of landscape architects, as they are known today.

Olmsted was a pioneer of landscape architecture in other ways. Landscaping had been largely the province of landscape gardeners, who worked mainly for the nobility and other wealthy patrons. Most of their work was for gardens and other landscaping of palaces, large country estates, and great city gardens and plazas, which were designed to be beautiful but not functional. Thus landscape gardening was mostly for the wealthy and powerful. Olmsted also designed landscaping for the estates of the wealthy and for gardens and plazas, but his main interest was design of great public parks, intended for public use. He also designed suburban developments intended for low-income and middle-income families.

Having started out as a farmer, Olmsted never lost his admiration for nature. And he brought this quality into his designs. English gardeners before him, in the early 19th century, had tried to impart natural qualities into their designs for country estates, but often what they achieved was only designed naturalness, contrived through their talents to look like what they thought nature should look like. Olmsted also tried to keep nature in his designs, but he had had experience with nature as it really exists, and had a great respect for it. In his designs, natural scenery was left alone as often as possible and then enhanced by the additon of designed landscaping elements. In this way, he was often able to create a sort of rural atmosphere that was beautiful and functional.

Thus Olmsted was ahead of his time in many ways. He was an intellectual and a socially conscious person who believed in simplicity, not pomp and circumstance. His abilities and philosophy transcended those of the new profession of landscape architecture, which he had pioneered.

Works Olmsted applied the principles of professional landscape architecture to the design of a great many projects, including estates, plazas, suburban housing developments, an exposition, and parks. His greatest works are undoubtedly parks. And the greatest of these is his masterpiece, Central Park. He and Vaux won the competition for its design in 1857, and Olmsted worked another 20 years continuing to design and build its elements. The result was a park that has brought pleasure to millions of people and stands today as one of the world's great monuments to creative design.

Olmsted designed many other parks all over the United States. Some of the most notable parks are Prospect (opened 1867), Brooklyn, New York City; in Boston, Franklin (1875) and the Fenway, together with its parkway system, the first in an American city, starting in 1879; and others in Buffalo, N.Y., Chicago, and elsewhere. Among his most important designs of other types are the grounds of the U.S. Capitol, including the west terrace (1875), and the site plan for Stanford University, Stanford, Calif., beginning in 1886, with the first buildings by Shepley, Rutan and Coolidge, the successor to that of Olmsted's friend and associate, Henry Hobson Richardson (1838–86). Another important project was landscaping the immense estate, Biltmore, of George Washington Vanderbilt (1862–1914), near Asheville, N.C. The building (1895) was designed by Richard Morris Hunt (1827–95) and the grounds, beginning in 1888, by Olmsted. His last great project was the design for landscaping the grounds for the World's Columbian Exposition (1893) in Chicago.

Life Frederick Law Olmsted was born in Hartford, Conn., on April 26, 1822, the son of a merchant and a descendant of one of the founders of that city. His

OLMSTED, FREDERICK LAW Central Park (1857–77, and later), as it appeared in 1931, New York, N.Y. [*Landscape architects: Olmsted and Vaux. (Wurts Brothers)*]

OLMSTED, FREDERICK LAW Central Park (1857–77, and later), as it appeared about 1941, New York, N.Y. [*Landscape architects: Olmsted and Vaux. (Wurts Brothers)*]

mother died when he was three years old and his father married again when the child was five. His early education was in dame's schools, named for the ladies who conducted them, and then in a series of other schools to which he was sent by ministers with whom he lived. By 1842, when he was twenty, Olmsted had been instructed by some 12 schools and tutors. Not much had come out of it but he had developed three interests that he would retain the rest of his life: nature, reading, and travel.

Olmsted joined the crew of a sailing ship, the bark *Ronaldson*, in April 1843 and sailed from New York around the Cape of Good Hope to China. He arrived back in New York a year later, very tired and ill. For about a year and a half, he lived on farms and studied farming while recovering, then attended lectures at Yale for about three months and returned to rural life. In 1847 he moved to a farm which his father had bought for him near Guilford, Conn. Still restless, he left there in 1848 to move to another farm bought by his father in Staten Island, N.Y., and farmed there until the early part of 1850. Olmsted then spent the next six months traveling in Europe. Back from his travels, Olmsted brought awakening enthusiasms for public parks, stirred by those he had seen in England, and for social issues, particularly the plight of the poor, sailors, and slaves.

Social Issues Now determined to become a writer, Olmsted published his first article, on the subject of cruelty to sailors in 1851, and his first book, *Walks and Talks of an American Farmer in England,* in 1852. The book was concerned more with social problems than with the practice of farming. He continued to travel and to write about his travels the rest of his life. In 1852–53 and again in 1854, he traveled in the South and wrote a series of articles on the effects of slavery in those states for the *New York Daily Times.* In 1856 his book on the same subject, *Journey in the Seaboard Slave States,* was published.

Central Park Most of his efforts went into writing until 1857, when he met an English architect, Calvert Vaux, who had moved to New York City to practice. The meeting changed Olmsted's life. Having determined sometime before to build a great public park in New York City, Central Park, the Board of Park Commissioners appointed Olmsted its superintendent. That same year, work on the site began and a competition was held for the design of the park. Vaux talked Olmsted into collaborating on an entry, which they called Greensward, in the competition, and in 1858, they were awarded the commission for the park design.

Olmsted and Vaux worked on the design and construction of the park until 1863, resigned, and then were reappointed in 1865. By 1876, they had essentially finished the main features of the park and in that year, Olmsted was dismissed, Vaux staying on until 1883. Vaux did some further work on the park later and Olmsted continued to make recommendations for important design improvements for many years.

Family In 1857 Olmsted's younger brother, John Hull, died at age thirty-two. The brothers had always been very close and Olmsted was grief stricken. In 1851 John had married May Cleveland Bryant Perkins and they had three children. In 1859 Frederick Olmsted married his brother's widow. They had a son a year later, but the baby died before its first birthday. A daughter followed in 1861. A second son was born in 1866, but died on the day he was born. In 1870 a third son was born and christened Henry Perkins. The elder Olmsted was determined that this son should become a landscape architect and carry on the tradition that had been started. Accordingly, he renamed him Frederick Law Olmsted, Jr. (1870–1957), when the child was four years old. The boy did become an important landscape architect, city planner, and college professor.

Later Life During the Civil War, Olmsted served as secretary of the Sanitary Commission, a group formed to investigate and improve health conditions in the Union camps and hospitals. In 1863 he resigned as secretary of the commission and went to California, where he had taken a position as superintendent of the development of the Mariposa, a 70-square-mile estate, near the future Yosemite Park, which contained great mines and a number of villages. His work on the development of the estate was not too successful, but he gave considerable aid to the proposals for reserving Yosemite and the Mariposa Big Tree Grove, with its ancient sequoias, for future designation as United States parks.

When Olmsted had first started working with Vaux, the two men had formed a firm called Olmsted, Vaux and Company, which continued until 1872. Over the years, they designed the landscaping for a great many estates, suburban developments, and parks. Olmsted was later associated with other landscape architects and architects, including Henry Hobson Richardson. Beginning in 1878, he moved part of his practice to Cambridge, Mass.; in 1881 he left New York City and moved to Cambridge permanently. His nephew and stepson, John Charles (1852–1920), began working in his office in 1875, and in 1884 became a partner, with the firm renamed F. L. and J. C. Olmsted. In 1893 another noted landscape architect, Charles Eliot (1860–97), joined the firm and it was renamed Olmsted, Olmsted and Eliot.

By 1895, Olmsted was having serious mental problems and John Charles became senior partner. Olmsted's memory began to fail and he began to show signs of increasing senility. In that year his son, Frederick Law, Jr., joined the firm. The elder Olmsted's condition continued to worsen until September 1898, when he was committed to McLean Hospital, Waverley, Mass. Frederick, Jr., had been appointed his father's legal guardian and often stayed with him in his cottage at the hospital. With Frederick, Jr., at his bedside, Frederick Law Olmsted died on August 28, 1903. He had accomplished much: his great design for parks, especially Central Park; his devotion to the solution of social problems; and his tremendous influence on the establishment of the profession of landscape of architecture. He had received numerous honors, including honorary doctor's degrees from both Harvard and Yale. But perhaps the greatest honor was the founding by his two sons, along with nine other landscape architects, of the American Society of Landscape Architects on January 4, 1899, a little more than three months after he had been committed to the mental hospital and 3½ years before he died. A year later, the first professional curriculum in landscape architecture was started at Harvard University and named for his former partner, Charles Eliot.

Related Articles LANDSCAPE ARCHITECTURE; PARK; PLANNING, CITY.

Further Reading McLaughlin, Charles Capen, ed.: *The Papers of Frederick Law Olmsted, Vol. I. The Formative Years, 1822 to 1852,* Johns Hopkins University Press, Baltimore, 1977; Olmsted, Frederick Law, Jr., and Theodora Kimball, eds.: *Forty Years of Landscape Architecture—Central Park,* MIT Press, Cambridge, 1973; Roper, Laura Wood: *FLO—A Biography of Frederick Law Olmsted,* Johns Hopkins University Press, Baltimore, 1973.

ORNAMENT   An element of a building primarily intended as embellishment or decoration. While the line of demarcation may be blurred between ornament and art in architecture, ornament is usually taken to mean elements that are integrated into buildings, while artworks generally are complete, or almost complete, within themselves independently of the buildings in which they are placed.

However, the distinction is not quite that clear. A carved molding may certainly be called ornament and freestanding sculpture art, but sculpture attached, or engaged, partly integrated into a column or wall might be classified either way. For a discussion on artworks not integrated in architectural elements, see the article entitled art in architecture. See also the article entitled molding.

Ornament of many kinds has been a very important element in architecture from very early times. Various civilizations developed a great array of styles and forms of ornament, each often derived to some extent from those preceding but each with specific attributes peculiar to its own era.

History   In the earliest times, little ornament was used on buildings, but by the time of the great ancient civilizations around the Mediterranean Sea, beginning about 3000 B.C., ornament had come to be of considerable importance.

The Egyptians used ornament extensively in their buildings, around openings, on walls, on floors, and in other places. Most of the ornament consisted of stylized or conventionalized symbolic depictions of natural objects, including the sacred beetle (scarab), feathers, palm leaves, lotus blossoms, papyrus, the sun, and people. Such ornament was ordinarily carved into building elements and often painted with primary colors. In Mesopotamia, ornament generally followed the precedents of the Egyptians, using stylized, natural forms in pavings, on walls, and around openings. In Crete, both stylized and naturalistic forms of ornament were used, mostly painted on walls and other architectural elements.

These earliest forms of ornament have affected the architecture of America very little, except for an occasional use of Egyptian types mainly during the Eclectic era.

The Greeks greatly admired architectural ornament and used it extensively in their buildings. Beautifully executed, Greek ornament was derived mainly from natural and geometric forms and was often highly stylized. Among the preferred forms were acanthus leaves; anthemia, derived from palms or honeysuckle; egg and dart, or egg and tongue; bead and reel; fluting; scrolls; birds' beaks; and dentils, bands of small, separated blocks. It is believed that much of the ornament as well as the buildings were originally painted in bright colors.

The Romans also used ornament extensively, much of it derived from the Greeks and some executed by Greek artists. While ornament in Greece was ordinarily delicate, refined, well executed, and located with esthetic discretion, that of the Romans was often somewhat coarse, not always well executed, and placed almost everywhere imaginable.

Greek and Roman ornament have had an important effect on the architecture which came later, including that of America, in most periods up to the modern movement.

In both Early Christian and Byzantine architecture, ornament was often very elaborate and decorative, in some cases overpoweringly so. Using many kinds of subjects, including geometric, natural, and religious, as depictions of saints and symbols, such as doves, anchors, peacocks, and olive branches, Early Christian and Byzantine ornament has had considerable effect on the architecture in some countries, for example, the Soviet Union, but very little in America

Romanesque ornament was often heavy and crude, utilizing mostly forms derived from vegetation and sometimes from animals. It has not had a great effect on American architecture. On the other hand, Gothic ornament has had important effects on the architecture, not only of America but of other countries, on church architecture especially, during the Gothic Revival and Eclectic periods. Gothic ornament was mystical and religious in nature and was developed to a high level of excellence, using plant, animal, and human forms somewhat realistically or conventionally. Many Gothic churches and cathedrals were almost literally covered with a profusion of ornament, much of it sculpture attached, or engaged, to walls and other building elements. Figures of animals, monsters, and people, often grotesque in appearance, called gargoyles, are interesting works of Gothic art. Used as ornamental waterspouts for roofs, they were usually carved in stone for major buildings and made of lead for minor ones. Perhaps the highest form of Gothic ornament is the stone figures of many of the cathedrals, particularly those in France.

During the Renaissance, there was a great outpouring of building ornament of every kind imaginable, not only based on religious subjects and symbolism but on subjects that had preceded Christianity: pagan gods, classical mythology, and other aspects of Greek and particularly Roman life and beliefs. Ornament was produced in a vast variety of materials, including stone and metals. Many elements of architecture were ornamented during the Renaissance, including door and other openings, doors, walls, and columns. However, the overwhelming accomplishments in ornament in the Renaissance are to be found in the work of the large number of great artists of the period, many of whom were also architects. Using every conceivable material and medium, these artists produced a profusion of murals, sculpture, and other works of art, never equaled in volume and scarcely in excellence, in any period before or since. Renaissance ornament is closely related to the art in architecture of the period. (See the article entitled art in architecture.)

American Development Early American architects in the colonies used ornament derived from that which was current in their homelands. During the various periods of architectural revivals, ornament was derived from the Classic, Gothic, Renaissance, and other earlier periods. Toward the end of the 19th century, with the beginning of the modern movement, ornament came to be used with less frequency, until it virtually disappeared from American buildings in the 20th century. Some American architects of the modern movement attempted to develop systems of ornament suitable to the new style. Important buildings using ornament were designed by such architects as Louis Henri Sullivan (1856–1924), Bernard Maybeck (1862–1957), the Greene brothers, Charles Sumner (1868–1957), Henry Mather (1870–1954), and Frank Lloyd Wright (1867–1959). Their efforts had some considerable effect, but not enough to prevent most modern buildings from being designed with little or no ornament.

Related Articles ARCH; ART IN ARCHITECTURE; COLUMN; DESIGN, ARCHITECTURAL; HISTORY OF ARCHITECTURE; MOLDING; Various articles on American architectural history.

P

PAINT A liquid, which upon being applied to a surface in a building, dries to form a protective and decorative coating. Paints and other coatings today often contain pigments, which impart color, opacity, and other properties, suspended in a liquid vehicle of oil, plastic, or other material. Paints and other coatings often have additional ingredients. In addition to its protective qualities, paint is mostly used for the effect of the colors obtained. For a discussion on other kinds of finishes that may be used to impart textures, patterns, and colors to architectural elements and surfaces, see articles entitled construction materials; plastics.

Composition A great variety of paints and other coatings for use in architecture exists today. Paint and other coatings are made up of liquids in which various materials have been dissolved. The liquid or vehicle, in which the other materials may be contained, allows paint to spread on surfaces where it will harden into a protective coating when it dries. Vehicles usually contain solvents or thinners, binders, plasticizers, and driers that control the spreading, drying time, and other characteristics of the paint. Suspended in the vehicle are pigments, such as titanium dioxide, that give paints their hiding power. Other pigments impart color, and inert substances make paints last longer and give them other desirable characteristics.

The major types of vehicles are natural such as rosin, opal, or shellac, or synthetic resins, such as alkyd plastics. Solvents or thinners in paints are either water (water-based paints), or organic liquids (oil-based paints).

Properties In general, paints and other coatings used in architecture should have certain basic properties, including proper workability, flow and spreading characteristics, fast drying, good adherence and hiding power qualities, stability, flexibility, durability, hardness, fade-resistant colors, and stability under exposure. Exterior paints and coatings, in particular, should have good resistance to abrasion and to the effects of weather and the sun. In addition, certain paints and coatings for special purposes should have such properties as heat resistance, fire retardation, rust inhibition, and resistance to chemicals, mold, and fungus.

Types Selection of the proper paint or coating for use in architecture must be made from a vast and bewildering array of types and formulations. In addition to oil-based and water-based paints, other types of coatings include varnish, enamel, lacquer, shellac, stains, bituminous, cement-mortar, sealers, primers, and waxes. Varnish is a transparent coating, usually made of drying oil and natural or synthetic resins. Enamel is a coating with a varnish vehicle and pigments. Enamels may be applied in the field or in a factory, where they are baked on and are called baked enamels. Lacquer is a quick-drying coating with nitrocellulose as its basic ingredient. Shellac is a fast-drying, transparent coating made with resins, obtained from lac insects, dissolved in denatured alcohol.

Stains utilize various vehicles, such as water, alcohols, or oils, together with small amounts of pigment that color but do not obscure the grains of woods. Bituminous coatings have bases of either coal-tar pitch or asphalt. Cement-mortar coatings generally consist of water as a vehicle, with portland cement, pigments, and other ingredients. Sealers are special coatings for use on wood, knots in wood, or other purposes, in preparation for other coatings. Primers are used for similar preparation of surfaces, such as plaster, for application of further coatings. Waxes are natural coatings, obtained from bees or plants, used mainly to protect other coatings. In addition, many other types of materials are often used in conjunction with paints and coatings: putties and wood fillers, to repair minor defects in materials; glazing compounds, for installation of glass in windows; caulking compounds, for sealing against moisture penetration in buildings; and a variety of thinners, driers, and paint and coating removers.

When selecting paints or other coatings for specific purposes in architecture, first consideration must be given to the functions, qualities, and appearances required; to the materials to which they will be applied; and to the circumstances of the applications, such as interior or exterior uses. Also to be considered is the question of whether the paint or coating will be applied on the job at the building site or in a mill or factory. Painting of materials at building sites is usually done with brushes, rollers, or spray guns. Mill or factory painting may be accomplished by any of these methods or by one of several others, including dipping, coating between rollers, and silk screening. Mill or factory paint may also be baked on. Finish painting may be handled in a mill or factory or materials may be only primed there, to be finish-painted at the building site.

Special coatings For painting masonry, brick, concrete block, and concrete, several types of paints and coatings, with widely varying characteristics, are available, including bituminous; cement mortar; oil-based; water-based; varnish-based; various types made with plastics, such as epoxies, alkyds, urethane, vinyls, and acrylics; and paints with synthetic rubbers. A special kind contains silicone for water-infiltration resistance. Many of these paints and coatings are also suitable for plaster and for asbestos-cement products. There are also special paints for concrete floors.

Several types of paints and coatings for iron and steel include those with coal-tar pitch or oil bases; and those that utilize various plastics, such as alkyds, phenolics, epoxies, polystyrenes, urethanes, vinyls, and synthetic rubbers. Primers used for painting these metals usually contain red lead or other ingredients for inhibiting rust. For such metals as aluminum, copper alloys, and galvanized iron, special paints and coatings are available.

There are many types of paints and coatings for use on wood. For exteriors to be painted white or in colors, types formulated with alkyds, epoxies, latex, or oil bases are generally used. Alkyd, latex, oil-based, water-based, and vinyl paints are also used for painting interior wood. Stains may be used for exterior or interior work, as may varnishes, when transparent coatings are required. Urethane coatings are sometimes used for the same purpose indoors. Lacquers, either clear or colored, are used indoors, where high-gloss, hard finishes are desired. There are special varnishes for interior wood floors and for exterior floors. Many paints and coatings may be obtained in various degrees of gloss, from flat, sometimes called matte, to semigloss to high gloss. Many are available in a wide variety of ready-mixed standard colors, and other colors may be mixed for special purposes.

Special paints and coatings may be obtained for other materials or conditions. For example, fire-resistant paints and coatings are incombustible and therefore do not contribute to the spread of flames. Heat-resistant paints and other coatings are used for the finishing of boilers, in which high temperatures are encountered. Fire-resistant paints are used to protect building elements by swelling up when flames touch them. Other special paints and coatings are also available, formulated for resistance to mold, fungi, marine borers, and other pests. Some ordinary paints may also be obtained with ingredients for such purposes.

Many factors must be considered when selecting paints for various architectural uses. Hiding power for opaque paints, measured by what is called the index of refraction, is of utmost importance. White lead, the most used material for obtaining hiding power in the past, has now been supplanted by titanium dioxide, which has a greater degree of hiding power, from 6 to 8 times that of white lead, which is harmful to human health. Other requirements for paints and coatings are contained not only in federal regulations but in various building and health codes.

Paints and other coatings vary in appearance and color under different types of lighting. A paint in natural light does not have the same hue under artificial light. And paint under fluorescent lighting looks quite different under incandescent.

After the proper paint or coating has been selected for the material on which it is to be used, it must be properly applied. Thickness and number of coats, drying times, effects of temperature and humidity during the time of application and drying, proper preparation of surfaces to ensure that they are dry, clean, free of grease, and so on, and proper priming are all of utmost importance to ensure good workmanship and long-lasting painted or coated surfaces.

To ensure that the proper paints and other coatings are selected and that they are applied properly, specifications of manufacturers, associations, government sources, and others should be consulted. For special problems, manufacturers can often help.

History Paints existed before humans constructed their first buildings. Although the time of the first use of paint is unknown, wall paintings in a number of caves in Europe date back at least to about 15,000 B.C. in the late Paleolithic, or Old Stone, Age. Primitive humans also painted designs on such things as clay pots, and on their bodies for religious or ceremonial purposes.

By the time of the great civilizations around the Mediterranean Sea, beginning about 3000 B.C., paints were used extensively. The ancient Egyptians are thought to have been the first people to develop a wide range of colors, which they made from minerals and other materials mixed with such substances as bitumen, eggs, and waxes to make them adhere. By about 1500 B.C., paints were also used in ancient Greece and Crete. Generally, these early people used paint for ornamental purposes rather than for protection of the building materials. Paint making, as well as its use, was considered an art and was a jealously guarded secret. The Romans used paint, mostly for ornamental purposes, and some think they were the first to use white lead in paints.

By about the fifth century A.D., the art of making paints had largely disappeared, not to be rediscovered until about the 15th century when the Middle Ages were coming to an end. Paints at that time were used on public buildings to some extent. Artists had not only continued to use them all along for paintings but mixed their own paints, using secret ingredients.

In the 18th century in the United States and in Europe, manufacturing paints for utilitarian purposes, including protection of buildings, began. The first of these paints were made with hand-ground pigments and various natural materials as vehicles. Most could be thinned with water. About the end of that century, paint materials were first made with machinery. The materials were then mixed by painters. In 1867 the first complete, ready-mixed paints were offered on the market.

Many new paints and other coatings have since

been developed, including sundry kinds of synthetic pigments and vehicles. Today many types for general and even specialized purposes are available.

Related Articles ART IN ARCHITECTURE; ORNAMENT; PLASTICS; WATERPROOFING; Articles on various materials, systems, and components of architecture.

Source of Additional Information National Paint and Coatings Assoc., 1500 Rhode Island Ave., N.W., Washington, D.C. 20005.

PARK A tract of land set aside for the enjoyment and recreation of the public, in or near a city or town, or in a natural or wilderness area. A park may be a small open area with a few trees and plants in a city where people may stop for a while to relax; a much larger landscaped area in which facilities are provided for many types of sports, cultural activities, and other pursuits; or a vast national park with provisions for hiking, camping, and enjoyment of nature in the wilderness. In any case, parks have become what many people view as necessities in the world of today. A playground is a special area set aside for games and play by children and others. Playgrounds may be located in parks, school yards, or other places.

Types Parks today are of many kinds. Some are specialized, such as those located at historic sites, or those established as nature trails for nature study. Other parks are general-purpose types, and may include not only natural areas but facilities for several different activities, such as recreational sports, games, athletics, educational pursuits, contests, concerts and other performances, and so on. Some parks have restaurants; others have overnight facilities in lodges or cabins or for camping.

Parks are an important part of architecture. They are designed by landscape architects or city planners, and architects and engineers are usually involved in the design of their buildings and other structures. However, parks are of so many types, purposes, and sizes that it is almost impossible to generalize about the elements of their design.

Purposes Perhaps the best way to start examining the design of parks is to determine their purposes. The primary purpose of any park is recreation, or enjoyment by people. Recreation is an elusive concept. For one person, it may consist of quietly sitting in the sun or shade, contemplating nature. For another person, it may mean participation in a game, such as chess, with one opponent, or in a card game with several participants. For still another person, recreation may mean active participation in sports, individually or as a member of a team or in dramatic performances or concerts. And recreation may mean a vast number of other pursuits. In addition, to further complicate the subject, one person may find recreation in quiet contemplation on one occasion and in very active games or sports on another. The attempt is made in many parks to provide for a whole spectrum of recreational pursuits.

It might be said that parks provide, in general, opportunities for visual, mental, and physical recreation.

And that in doing so, parks cater to the emotional needs of people. To accomplish these goals, a park must have a purpose and everything in the park must also have purpose. The park must be designed to function properly for these purposes and each part must be in the proper relationship with the others. For example, bicycle riders should not interfere with those who are resting or reading. Finally, a park should provide experiences to its users, including esthetic experiences.

Elements In beginning the design of a park, consideration must be given to existing factors, including such natural elements as soils, topography, presence of water bodies, subsurface characteristics, vegetation and wildlife, climate, seasonal temperatures, and precipitation. Consideration must also be given to man-made factors, such as boundaries, streets and roads, utilities, and so on. Consideration must also be given to esthetic factors, such as views and surroundings.

In general, a park might be divided into major elements for such purposes as nature study, group sports and games, picnics, camping or sleeping, circulation of automobiles and pedestrians, parking, service and maintenance, and areas left in the wild state. Not every park contains all these elements, and they vary in importance in parks of different types. Some parks may have other elements, such as provisions for boating and other water sports.

Design Goals After studying the purposes and the existing conditions of a park, a program outlining the goals of the design and criteria and methods for meeting the goals may be prepared. Based on the program, the design of a master plan for the park can proceed.

Locations for the various activities may be established, taking into consideration the sizes of areas needed, orientation to views and to prevailing winds and the sun, operating needs, supervisory requirements, circulation, safety, budgets, and other factors. Playing fields and other important spaces may be located, as may buildings, parking lots, and other structures. Areas to be left in the natural state may be selected. Site changes and landscaping of the park may be determined.

Then the elements may be properly related to each other, to the site, and to the overall concept of the park. If all these factors have been properly handled in the design and construction of the park, it will then have become a place where people can find recreation and a place where people and the other elements of nature can coexist and commingle, in harmony.

Playgrounds Although often reserved for children, playgrounds may also be used by young adults and older people. Ordinarily, a playground for very young children contains only play spaces, with simple devices such as swings, slides, seesaws, sand piles, and perhaps carousels operated by pushing. For older children and young adults, playgrounds often have facilities for sports and athletics, such as basketball, football, and softball or baseball. For adults, facilities for tennis, horseshoes, and other games may be provided and many of these may also be used by younger people. In some cases, playgrounds have swimming pools and facilities for track and other activities.

Playground facilities are often divided into elements that are somewhat separated from each other on the basis of the age groups that use them and by the nature of the uses. Playgrounds must be designed to be functional and safe. The major problem in their design is the provision of the proper facilities in the proper relationships to each other and to the overall plan. Playgrounds are usually located in parks or in school yards, but some are separate entities.

American landscape architects, city planners, and architects have designed many notable parks, most of them during the late 19th and the 20th centuries. Others will be designed and built in the future, and the design professionals who create them will find in their design very satisfying and fulfilling experiences.

History Since ancient times, certain areas have been set aside for recreational purposes. In Egypt and the Middle East, these were areas such as hunting preserves, whose use was restricted to the rulers and the nobility. The first public areas for recreational purposes are thought to have been established by the ancient Greeks; most of these were for athletic purposes, and had groves of trees for people to walk through. The Romans built small parks; although a few were open to the public, most constituted hunting preserves, which were restricted to the ruling classes and the wealthy. This practice was continued for many centuries. During the Renaissance, parks were mostly promenades or formal gardens, and few were open to the public.

During the 18th century in England and Scotland, the practice of establishing great hunting preserves for the nobility continued, often at the expense of farmers and shepherds who were displaced from their homes to make way for the preserves. City parks of the time, in London and other cities, were not public, being restricted to certain classes of people or requiring admission fees for entry. During the 19th century, many of these became public parks and many hunting preserves and other parks of the nobility were converted to public use.

American Development The first city park in colonial America is thought to have been the Boston Common, established in 1634. Commons were located in other New England cities, and later other types of public parks were built. These parks were generally formal in concept, suitable for walking or sitting, but not very much else. Such was the situation when Frederick Law Olmsted (1822–1903) won, with his partner, Calvert Vaux (1824–95), the competition for the design of Central Park in New York City.

Olmsted, the first person to call himself a landscape architect, and Vaux set out, in 1857, to create the first park in the United States that was planned from the beginning. They created a masterpiece that was planned not only in a natural, almost rural, manner

PARK Armonk Recreation Center (1967), Armonk, N.Y. [*Architects: Norton and Hume. (Joseph W. Molitor)*]

PARK Harper's Ferry Center (1969), Harper's Ferry, W.Va. [*Architect: Ulrich Franzen & Associates. (George Cserna)*]

but provided the public with a park in which all who wished to do so could find recreation. Olmsted designed many other parks in such cities as Buffalo, N.Y., Washington, Philadelphia, and Boston. He also helped establish the national park system, by his recommendations for the Yosemite Valley in California, which ultimately became Yosemite National Park in 1890. The first national park, Yellowstone National Park, Wyo., had been founded in 1872.

Olmsted was devoted to the establishment of city parks as natural, rural retreats for those who could not go to the country. At that time, others involved in park establishment and planning followed his philosophy, which came to be known as one of passive recreation. Beginning in the early 20th century, some planners believed that parks should provide active recreation, playgrounds, areas for sports and athletics, nature study, arts and crafts work, and other activities. These opposing viewpoints resulted in two types of facilities: parks that were natural and passive, and recreation areas for the more active pursuits. Parks were planned properly, recreation areas planned almost not at all. This situation persisted until the end of World War II. Then the two opposing camps tended to merge their interests, also merging passive and active recreation in park design.

In the United States today, there are parks of many kinds: small and large, owned by cities and towns, counties, states, and the federal government. In addition to the above purposes, they serve as places for educational pursuits; musical, dance, and dramatic performances; contests; and other activities. Or as some park planners put it, they provide refreshment for mind and body.

There are literally tens of thousands of parks in the United States, occupying millions of acres. The 100 largest cities alone have more than 7,000 parks and the states more than 2,000, occupying more than 5 million acres. The national park system has about 40 national parks, about 20 national historic parks, and a great number of national battlefield parks, military parks, national memorials and monuments, and historic sites.

Some of the most notable city parks in the United States, in addition to those already mentioned, are Prospect, Brooklyn, New York City; Lincoln and Jackson, Chicago; Rock Creek, Washington; Golden Gate, San Francisco; Fairmount, Philadelphia; Druid Hill, Baltimore; and Belle Isle, Detroit.

Related Articles GARDEN; LANDSCAPE ARCHITECTURE; OLMSTED, FREDERICK LAW; PLANNING, CITY; RECREATION BUILDING.

Further Reading American Institute of Architects: *Architectural Graphic Standards*, 7th ed., John Wiley, New York, 1980; Davern, Jeanne, ed.: *Places for People*, McGraw-Hill, New York, 1976; De Chiara, Joseph, and John Hancock Callender: *Time-Saver Standards for Building Types*, McGraw-Hill, New York, 1973; Rutledge, Albert J.: *Anatomy of a Park—The Essentials of Recreation Area Planning and Design*, McGraw-Hill, New York, 1971.

Sources of Additional Information National Parks and Conservation Assoc., 1701 18th St., N.W., Washington, D.C. 20009; National Recreation and Park Assoc., 1601 Kent St., Arlington, Va. 22209.

PHOTOGRAPHY, ARCHITECTURAL

The art and science of making pictures of architecture with a camera. In the past 40 years or so, architectural photography has become increasingly important to architects, until today it would be difficult to imagine how they could do without it. Photography is the major medium for two very important functions in an architectural office: gaining recognition for completed buildings, and attracting clients to commission the architect to design new buildings. In former times, architects used renderings and other drawings for these purposes, almost exclusively. Today they mostly use photographs.

Photographs are often made by architects, who seem to be fascinated with photography. Some are made by commercial photographers who make many kinds of pictures. But the most important photographs are made by a relatively small number of professional photographers, perhaps no more than 30 in the United States, who specialize in architectural work and call themselves architectural photographers. These architectural photographers make the majority of the fine photographs that are so important in architecture.

Uses Architects use photographs in several ways, all related to recognition for past work and obtaining new commissions. Architectural photographs, both black and white and color, are used for illustrations of buildings in magazines, books, and newspapers. They are used in the preparation of office brochures, which architects use to explain their services and illustrate their accomplishments to potential clients. For the same purposes, they are assembled into albums or framed for hanging on the walls of architectural offices. Photographic slides, almost exclusively in color, are organized into complete slide shows for making presentations to potential clients and others. And the architect's collection of prints and slides forms a record of his work, documenting his accomplishments in a unique way.

Requirements Fine photography requires considerable knowledge of cameras, films, accessories; it requires knowledge of the principles of light, color, composition, form, texture, and the like, similar to those that must be mastered by an artist. And fine photography requires talented photographers. Fine architectural photography also requires a deep understanding of the design and meaning of architecture. In addition, architectural photographers say it requires patience; one must wait for the right light, endure days of inclement weather, and discover exactly the proper angles for photographs. It also requires good equipment. Therefore most architectural photographers work only with precision, high-priced, tripod-supported view cameras with which they make 8×10 or 4×5 inch negatives and with the best 35-mm hand-held cameras for slides. And most take along a staggering amount or other equipment: floodlights, flash equipment, lenses, filters, film, and several cameras.

History Photographing buildings began in the early 19th century. In fact, the first known photograph of any kind was of buildings in a rural landscape. In spite of these early beginnings, architectural photography developed very slowly until the late 19th century, when several talented photographers began to record on film many of the notable buildings of the time.

U.S. Progress The real progress of architectural photography in the United States may be said to have started with the work of the Wurtz brothers of New York, beginning in 1894 and continuing to the mid-20th century. Another famous early architectural photographer was Raymond Trowbridge of Chicago, who photographed many of the buildings of early modern architects, including Louis Henri Sullivan (1856–1924) and Frank Lloyd Wright (1867–1959). Another was Samuel Gottscho, whose work continued until after the mid-20th century. In 1930 Ken Hedrich, a young photographer in Chicago, challenged the documentary way of photographing architecture. His photographs had new and dramatic viewpoints and he was a pioneer in the use of the wide angle lens as it is known today.

Overall view.

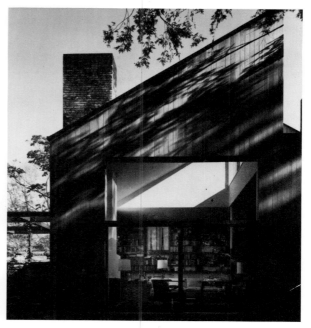

Exterior and interior.

Main Entrance.

Interior.

Another view of entrance.

PHOTOGRAPHY Selection of photographs of a country house. [*Architect: Edward L. Barnes. (Joseph W. Molitor)*]

Other talented architectural photographers have carried on the work started by these pioneers and have developed it to high pinnacles of excellence and invention. Many of their names are in the credit lines with their photographs in this book. Also to be seen are the tangible results of their talent, knowledge, and patience.

Related Articles PRACTICE OF ARCHITECTURE; RENDERING.

Further Reading Molitor, Joseph W.: *Architectural Photography*, John Wiley, New York, 1976; Shulman, Julius: *The Photography of Architecture and Design—Photographing Buildings, Interiors and the Visual Arts*, Whitney, New York, 1977; Woolley, A.: *Photography—A Practical and Creative Introduction*, McGraw-Hill, New York, 1974.

PLANNING, CITY

PLANNING, CITY The art and science of the design, planning, and construction of cities and parts of cities; also called town or urban planning. City planning principles can also be extended to include areas larger than cities, as in regional planning. Persons who practice city planning are often called city planners or urban or town planners, though some prefer to be called simply planners.

Modern Planning City planning is an ancient calling, but as practiced today, it is a product of the 20th century. Early in the century, planners were mostly privately sponsored, but this changed rapidly to sponsorship by local, municipal, or county governments. Early in the century, planners were mostly concerned with the major visual elements of cities, parks, boulevards, civic centers, and parkways. Today planners are concerned with the total fabric of cities, not only the physical aspects, now seen in three dimensions rather than two as before, but the economic, social, legal, and human aspects. Previously, planners devoted much attention to streets and squares, public buildings, docks and harbors, and railroads, Today they are still concerned with these factors but also with transportation of all kinds; buildings of all kinds, including housing; utility distribution; and all other aspects of urban life.

Practitioners In the past, most planning was performed by architects, engineers, and landscape architects. Today many planners come from those professions, but there are also planners trained as economists, sociologists, geographers, and so on, reflecting the attention given to factors other than the physical planning of urban areas.

Planning Commissions Planning was given a big boost with the creation of planning commissions in urban areas during the first part of the 20th century. Two of the first were those of Hartford, Conn., started in 1907, and Chicago, founded in 1909. The idea. spread to other communities all over the United States. The commissions were not very effective, because the laws affecting planning were loosely constructed or nonexistent. Starting in 1916, when New York City adopted the first zoning law in the United States, regulations for land use and building heights, bulking, and uses gave planners the tools with which to enforce their plans.

Work Areas The work of planners may be divided into five major areas: preparing master plans, ordinances and regulations, and improvement programs for urban areas; preparing regional master plans for larger areas; planning of portions of urban areas, such as shopping centers, neighborhoods, and so on; planning for urban renewal, slum clearance and redeveloping older areas; and planning new towns.

To accomplish this work, planners generally follow a process that includes development of long-range goals and objectives; study and analysis of existing conditions, physical, economic, and social; study and analysis of the problems; preparation of master plans covering aspects such as land use, transportation, buildings, and other facilities; and putting the master plans into effect, with the aid of zoning and subdivision regulations, codes, ordinances, and other means.

Most planners today work for planning commissions that are government agencies, mostly at the municipal level. Others practice as consultants who perform services for municipalities which do not have their own planning staffs or wish to have special studies made. Planners make studies of many kinds, including projections of future employment patterns; population growth; movement of people, industries, and businesses into and out of areas; needs for transportation and utilities; and so on. They then translate these studies into reports and master plans that define the future needs and character of cities and demonstrate how the needs can be met and the character fulfilled in the best manner. They also make studies of portions of cities or specific problems and translate these into reports and plans to meet the needs or problems. Planners also are concerned with zoning and building codes, and with development and redevelopment that take place in cities. Regional planners are concerned with the same subjects as city planners, but perform their work for whole regions rather than single cities.

Planning offers careers to many types of people, since it involves social and economic planning, and the physical planning of cities, in a manner similar to the work of architects, landscape architects, and engineers. A great variety of functions are performed by planners, some by people who are essentially creative, others by those who are primarily studious, and still others by those who are active by nature. All must be interested in urban life and in the process of improving urban life and its setting, the cities.

Education Preparation for planning may be acquired in a number of ways. Many architects, landscape architects, and engineers, in particular civil engineers, ultimately find their true careers in planning. All these professionals take some related courses in college. More than 30 universities offer degrees in planning in the United States. Some are attached to architectural schools; others are not. Many are graduate schools, which require an undergraduate degree in some related field before a student may be accepted. A few schools allow architectural students to specialize in planning, after their first few years of general architectural training.

History Humans founded urban settlements during prehistoric times. Although the first of such settlements have not been accurately dated, it is known that by the beginning of the Neolithic period, about the 80th century B.C., some humans left the nomadic life and had begun to settle in villages in Mesopotamia, Egypt, and other Middle East areas. Some of the villages grew into cities. These early villages and cities were located on easily defended sites.

During the Neolithic period, large cities were developed, not only in the Middle East but in India and

China. Two of the greatest, Nineveh and Babylon, are believed to have been founded in early Neolithic times, to have flourished about the 20th century B.C., and to have been destroyed sometime during the 7th century B.C.

Most early cities were not planned, in the meaning of today. They were founded in locations where natural resources, such as minerals, existed, near trade routes or water bodies, or near populated rural areas, which were food sources. Then these cities developed without planning around temples and forts. Some early cities were planned, mostly with public areas at their centers and with two main streets, one running north and south and the other east and west. Other streets divided the cities into what has come to be called a gridiron or grid plan, in which the blocks of the city form squares or rectangles bounded by streets on all four sides. The gridiron plan was used for many thousands of years and can still be seen in most American cities. An early gridiron-plan city, still in existence, is Alexandria, Egypt, founded about 332 B.C. by Alexander the Great (356–323 B.C.).

The Romans founded cities in many conquered places. Some cities, not including Rome which just developed naturally and haphazardly, had grid plans. Typical examples are Gloucester and Lincoln, England; Florence and Turin, Italy; Cologne, Germany; and Barcelona, Spain.

During the Middle Ages, cities declined somewhat and their place was taken to some extent by monasteries and castles. The cities that existed grew in an unplanned manner, mostly with narrow, crooked streets, behind protective walls. Starting about the 11th century in Italy and spreading to the rest of Europe later, a resurgence took place in cities. Many new ones were built. Most had plans based on the grid, unlike such older cities as Paris and London. Some of the new ones were *bastide*, or fortress, towns. They were laid out with a regular pattern of streets and blocks, gridiron fashion. Such towns were built in many places in Europe. Monpazier, France, founded in the 13th century, typifies their planning: a walled and fortified town with blocks approximately 125 ft wide by 150, 250, and 300 ft long, separated by major streets 24 ft and minor ones 16 ft wide. Through the blocks ran alleys about 6 ft wide. Near the center was a market square surrounded by arcades, with the nearby church the major architectural feature.

During the Renaissance, planning of towns and cities followed the principles of the *bastides* for a time. But the Renaissance was also a time of great theorizing about city planning as well as architecture. Some important books dealing with the subject were written by the Italian architects Leon Battista Alberti (1404–72) and Andrea Palladio (1518–80), and the philosophers, Italian Tommaso Campanella (1568–1639) and the Englishmen, Sir Francis Bacon (1561–1626) and Sir Thomas More (1478–1535).

Many projects for new towns and for replanning of older ones were developed during the Renaissance.

Most of these projects were never executed, but some notable examples that were built include partly replanned open-space areas, such as the great plazas in Italy at San Marco, Venice; the Campidoglio by Michelangelo Buonarroti (1475–1564), and San Pietro by Giovanni Lorenzo Bernini (1598–1680), both in Rome. Pope Sixtus V (1521–90), with the help of architect Domenico Fontana (1543–1607), replanned a portion of Rome.

Later great plans for European cities include that of Sir Christopher Wren (1632–1723) for rebuilding London after the Great Fire of 1666. This plan, with radial major streets, was never adopted nor were those prepared by two nonarchitects, John Evelyn (1620–1706), a minor government official and writer, and Robert Hooke (1635–1703), philosopher and scientist. Other important city plans of the era were those for Bath, England, by architects John Wood, Sr. (1704–54) and his son John Wood (1728–81), and the replanning of portions of Paris by Baron Georges Eugéne Haussmann (1809–91).

Others who deeply affected city planning were the Englishmen, Sir Patrick Geddes (1854–1932), planner and sociologist, who worked for slum clearance through planning, and Sir Ebenezer Howard (1850–1928), who originated the concept of the modern garden city, an urban area surrounded by a rural one. The first garden city, Letchworth, England, was begun in 1903. Laws enabling cities to carry out planning were passed in Europe in the second half of the 19th century, in Italy in 1865, and in England in 1875.

American Development Planning in colonial America began with the founding of St. Augustine, Fla., in 1565 by the Spanish. This city was given a plan, more or less on the grid pattern, but quite irregular. Later Spanish towns followed the gridiron plan more strictly, as the plan for San Antonio, Tex., founded about 1730 as the villa of San Fernando de Bexar; Pensacola, Fla., first settled in 1559, destroyed and rebuilt several times since; and Santa Fe, N.Mex., founded in 1609. French settlements in what eventually became the United States started much later, Detroit, Mich., in 1701; New Orleans, La., in 1721; Mobile, Ala., in 1702; and St. Louis, Mo., in 1764, all with grid plans.

The earliest English colonies in America had plans that were somewhat similar to the *bastides*, fortified cities of the Middle Ages in Europe, but much more primitive. Jamestown, Va., founded in 1607, is thought to have originally had a stockade of logs around a triangular plan, within which the buildings were located. The first permanent New England settlement, at Plymouth, Mass., founded in 1620, is thought to have originally had two rows of houses with a street separating them, all surrounded by a stockade. St. Mary's, Md., founded in 1633, is thought to have had meandering streets that followed Indian trails. A good early plan was that of New Haven, Conn., in 1638, a square plan with nine large squares, the central one being referred to as the town common.

Both Virginia and Maryland passed new town acts in the 17th century, and these resulted in policies for planned towns in these states. Many new towns were planned as a result of these acts and a number were established, mostly utilizing grid plans. Most of the new towns were planned by administrators, who were amateur planners, rather than by architects or others who practiced planning. Some of the most important were Norfolk (1682) and Richmond (1737), Va., and Baltimore (1729), Md., all with grid plans; and Annapolis (1694), Md., planned by Sir Francis Nicholson (1655–1728), with major streets radiating from the center rather than on a grid plan. Later, Nicholson also planned Williamsburg (1699), Va., reverting to the grid plan. Nicholson had an interesting career, as the governor at various times of Virginia, Maryland, South Carolina, and Nova Scotia, and lieutenant governor of New England.

In New England, most early towns had grid plans that were modified to fit the topography and other natural features and to accommodate farms nearby. New England town plans often had central open spaces, called greens or commons, where townspeople could congregate and around which meeting houses and other public buildings were often built. Before 1635, at least 20 towns had been established in what is now Massachusetts, including Salem, founded in 1626, and Boston, in 1630. Many others soon followed in Massachusetts and in the other New England states. Towns were built in the other colonies, beginning in the 17th and continuing into the 18th century. New Amsterdam, which became New York City, was founded in 1624. Philadelphia, founded in 1682, was planned by William Penn (1644–1718), with the aid of a surveyor, on a grid system with five great squares reserved for parks. Another grid town plan was that for Savannah, Ga., founded in 1733 by James Edward Oglethorpe (1696–1785).

None of these early significant plans were designed by architects, engineers, or planners, who had formal training in the subject or practiced any of the design professions. They were able administrators who had the knowledge, ability, and foresight to envision what cities of the time should be like and the power to see their plans realized. This was a situation that lasted for a long time in the United States, as settlers spread westward and built new towns in the territories that eventually became states.

The most striking attempt to plan a new town of the time was that for what eventually became the city of Washington, D.C., the nation's capital. President George Washington (1732–99) chose a French engineer, who had served as an engineering officer in the Continental Army, Pierre Charles L'Enfant (1754–1825), to design the plan in 1791. L'Enfant made the plans for the city, the results of which are so apparent today. In 1792 L'Enfant was dismissed after a series of disputes about the work. He had designed a magnificent plan, with locations for the most important government buildings, from which radiated broad avenues. Great open spaces and vistas were envisioned, the greatest of them being the mall which stretched from the Capitol building, or Federal House as it was then called, to a great monument at the other end behind the White House, or President's House as it was called. L'Enfant's original map was mislaid and the surveyor of the capital city, Andrew Ellicott (1754–1820), redrew it from memory, not exactly as L'Enfant had laid it out, but close.

Thus the city was actually laid out according to the map of Ellicott and the work continued later according to a revised plan of 1797. For the next 100 years, development continued in the city in a haphazard manner, with few planning and no zoning controls. By 1900, L'Enfant's envisioned mall had turned into a shambles of disorganized planting, railroad tracks, and a railroad station. In 1900 a new plan was devised under the leadership of architects Daniel Hudson Burnham (1846–1912) and Charles Follen McKim (1847–1909), landscape architect Frederick Law Olmsted (1822–1903), and sculptor Augustus Saint-Gaudens (1848–1907). From that time, the city of Washington has been developed following this plan and the later work of a great many other talented architects and planners on various commissions.

In the years following the planning of Washington, many new towns were planned and new plans made for older cities. Much of this work was by architects and engineers, who had an interest in planning. Most of the plans were of the gridiron type.

Thomas Jefferson (1743–1826) had long been interested in city planning, and had proposed plans for both Washington and Richmond, Va., that were never used. Early in the 19th century, Jefferson proposed a radically new type of plan, which came to be called the checkerboard plan. It consisted of a gridiron pattern with blocks for buildings alternating with open squares in both directions. This was a fresh concept and it was put into practice in the town of Jeffersonville, Ind., in 1802, but within 15 years a decision was

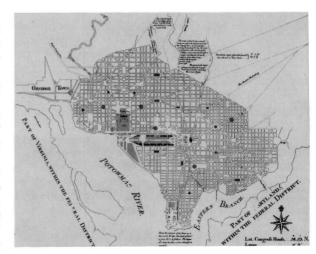

PLANNING, CITY Original plan of Washington, D.C. (1791). [*Planner: Maj. Pierre Charles L'Enfant.*]

made to sell lots in the open squares and the original concept of the plan was destroyed. The same thing happened in Jackson, Miss., after its founding in 1822, and the checkerboard plan was never used again, in spite of its seeming merits.

During much of the 19th century, cities became overcrowded, land speculation reached new heights, and little was done in the way of planning. An exception was the significant work of Frederick Law Olmsted and his partner Calvert Vaux (1824–95) in the planning of suburbs and towns, which followed the natural contours and other features of the land on which they were built. Late in the century, attention once again turned to good planning, and its leading exponent was the architect Daniel Hudson Burnham.

Starting with the classic, Beaux Arts, eclecticism of the World's Columbian Exposition in Chicago in 1893, Burnham, who had been chief consulting architect of the fair, proposed for Chicago and other cities new designs based on those of the fair. Burnham's proposals and those like them later came to be known as the City Beautiful Movement. As an attempt to revamp modern city plans to something approximating those of older, great European cities with their wide boulevards and impressive public buildings, the movement made a great stir for some years and then disappeared under the onslaught of more progressive city planning principles.

Burnham designed inventive plans for many cities, including the one for Chicago. His theories have been superseded, not because of any inherent flaw in the ideas but because of the increasing desire and need to make cities more efficient, a state often, but not always, achieved by making them less beautiful. More importantly, Burnham had established city planning as an essential part of American life, a place it has occupied ever since.

Speaking at the first international meeting of planners held in 1910 by the Royal Institute of British Architects, Burnham made it plain that planning was here to stay. The first national conference on planning in America had been held in Washington the year before. In 1917, five years after Burnham's death, the American City Planning Institute, composed mainly of architects, engineers, and landscape architects, was organized and it eventually became the present-day American Institute of Planners. A few years later, the first specialized college courses were established at Harvard University, Cambridge, Mass. Since then, the profession of planning has grown rapidly to the point where there is scarcely a government body in the United States on any level that does not have a planning commission, and many have professional planners on staff.

The work of planning goes on. Some of the most significant work of the 20th century was that of Clarence S. Stein (1882–1975) and Henry Wright (1878–1936), both planners and architects. Drawing on the garden city theories of Ebenezer Howard and his predecessors, Stein and Wright planned important

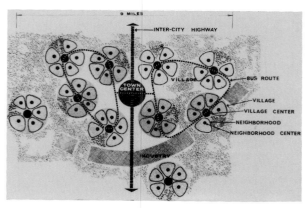

PLANNING, CITY Diagram of new town, Columbia, Md. (begun 1964). [*Planners: Community Research and Development, Inc., James W. Rouse; William E. Finley; Wallace Hamilton; Morton Hoppenfeld.*]

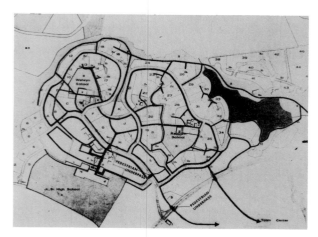

PLANNING, CITY Plan of new town, Columbia, Md. (begun 1964). [*Planners: Community Research and Development, Inc., James W. Rouse; William E. Finley; Wallace Hamilton; Morton Hoppenfeld.*]

new towns such as Radburn, N.J., and Chatham Village, Pittsburgh, both built in the 1930s. Stein went on to plan other projects that came to be called greenbelt cities, taking the garden city ideas to a new level of achievement. During the second half of the 20th century, a number of new towns have been built, including Columbia, Md., and Reston, Va.

Other noted planners of the 20th century include Albert Mayer (1897–   ), Edmund Norton Bacon (1910–   ), Christopher Tunnard (1910–   ), Kevin Lynch (1918–   ), and Ian McHarg (1920–   ). Of great influence on the planning of cities has been the writing and philosophy of Lewis Mumford (1895–   ).

Related Articles BUILDING, CODES AND STANDARDS; BURNHAM AND ROOT: CAPITAL, UNITED STATES; ENGINEERING; HOUSING; JEFFERSON, THOMAS; LANDSCAPE ARCHITECTURE; OLMSTED, FREDERICK LAW; PARK; ROAD AND TRAFFIC DESIGN; STEIN, CLARENCE S.; SURVEYING.

Further Reading Golany, Gideon: *New-Town Planning— Principles and Practice*, John Wiley, 1976; Hecksher, August:

Open Spaces—The Life of American Cities, Harper and Row, New York, 1977; Reps, John W.: *The Making of Urban America—A History of City Planning in the United States,* Princeton University Press, Princeton, N.J., 1965; Reps, John W.: *Tidewater Towns—City Planning in Colonial Virginia and Maryland,* the Colonial Williamsburg Foundation (distributed by University of Virginia Press), Williamsburg, Va., 1972; Spreiregen, Paul D.: *Urban Design—The Architecture of Towns and Cities,* McGraw-Hill, New York, 1965; Whittick, A.: *Encyclopedia of Urban Planning,* McGraw-Hill, New York, 1974.

Sources of Additional Information American Institute of Planners, 917 15th St., N.W., Washington, D.C. 20004; American Society of Planning Officials, 1313 E. 60th St., Chicago, Ill. 60637.

Periodicals *American City,* Pittsfield, Mass. 01201; *Nation's Cities,* 1612 K St., N.W., Washington, D.C. 20006.

PLASTICS Synthetic materials made from chemicals derived from such raw materials as coal or petroleum and used extensively in buildings. First developed in the 19th century, plastics have been vastly improved and newer types formulated in the 20th. Today they have many uses in architecture. Hundreds of types of plastics exist and new ones appear with some regularity. The various types have widely varied properties and characteristics. Some are hard or rigid; others are soft and pliable. Some are colored; some are clear. Some are opaque, others translucent, and still others transparent. Some withstand heat very well; others do not. Some may be spun into fibers; others cannot. Some burn, others melt, and still others are non-flammable or even highly heat resistant.

Characteristics The properties and characteristics of plastics depend primarily on the chemicals and other materials used to make them and how they are made. About the only property they all have in common is that they can be molded, which is where the word *plastics* originated. The major classifications of plastics are thermoplastic types, those that become soft when heated and harden again when cooled; and thermosetting types, those that cannot be softened by heat after they have been formed. Thermoplastics may be softened and hardened many times. Heating thermosetting plastics, after they have been formed, may cause damage.

Production Methods Plastic products may be made by several methods, including molding, casting, extrusion, calendering, and laminating. Molding is accomplished by melting plastic resins, forcing the liquid into molds under pressure, and curing the plastics, by cooling for thermoplastic types and by heat and pressure for thermosetting types. Casting is like molding except no pressure is applied. Extrusion is accomplished by forcing melted plastic through dies. Calendering, used for coating paper, cloth, or other materials with plastics, involves feeding the material to be coated, along with melted plastic, between rollers. Calendering may also be used to produce thin sheets of plastic. Laminating involves joining plastics to materials, such a metal or others, by heat and pressure exerted in a press or with contact adhesives, as used for laminated plastic countertops and other products.

In selecting plastics for various uses in architecture, an examination must be made of the properties that will properly fulfill the purposes. Among the most important properties are hardness, transparency, color, resistance, weight, insulating qualities (electrical or thermal), strength, and resistance to corrosion or other deterioration. Plastics are available today with a great variety of combinations of such properties.

Uses A list of the uses of plastics in architecture would be very long. Some of the more important uses include resilient flooring; roofing and siding materials; paints and coatings; light fixtures; skylights; synthetic fabrics and other materials for curtains, upholstery, carpeting, and the like; electrical and thermal insulation; glazing materials; countertops; surfacing for football and other athletic fields; piping; vapor barriers; and adhesives.

Other important uses of plastics in architecture include acrylics, such as Lucite and Plexiglas, for glazing windows, doors, and skylights, for light fixtures, and for other purposes; several types used for making adhesives, including caseins and epoxies; melamines for plastic laminated countertops; polybutene for caulking and sealing compounds; polyvinyls for outdoor carpeting and athletic field surfaces; and urea formaldehydes and alkyds for baked enamels. Plastics are often used in composite materials, called reinforced plastics, which are strengthened by the addition of glass fibers or other materials. Polyester plastic sheets and others reinforced with glass fiber, usually in corrugated form, are often used for exterior siding and roofing, particularly in botanical buildings, greenhouses, and other building types into which light and sunshine must be admitted. Polystyrene plastics and others are made into boards, tiles, and sheets for interior wall finishes. Plastics are also used for making hardware, electrical appliances, and plumbing fixtures.

Plastics are used today for more exotic purposes, such as nuclear shielding and detection of radiation; artificial parts for the human body; protection against acids and other chemicals; nose cones and other uses in rockets; in tent, air, and cable structures; and in clothing of almost every type.

Appearance Qualities In the past, plastics often had a bad reputation among architects and other environmental designers, partly because they were considered synthetic substitutes for superior materials. This came about because the early plastics manufacturers thought of their products as substitutes and, starting with fake wood grain in Bakelite, have tried to simulate wood, marble, and various other quality materials. Today the true characteristics of plastics can be exploited. Architects and other environmental designers can find plastic products that express only their function, as thermal insulation or vapor barrier materials. Other products to be exposed in buildings are quite beautiful in their own right. For example, no

PLASTICS Screens, curtains, and furniture made of plastics. Apartment (1970), New York, N.Y. [Architect: Paul Rudolph. (Joseph W. Molitor)]

PLASTICS Screens, curtains, and furniture made of plastics. Apartment (1970), New York, N.Y. [Architect: Paul Rudolph. (Joseph W. Molitor)]

material, natural or otherwise, duplicates the feel, sheen, colors, and optical effects of acrylics.

When their inherent qualities are exploited, plastics are probably the most versatile of materials. Easily and inexpensively formed and worked, plastics have a bright future in architecture, only waiting to be discovered by thoughtful and creative designers.

History Although plastics are often thought of as a 20th-century material, their beginning was in the early 19th century, when the first experimental forerunners of present-day plastics were made. In 1869 American inventor John Wesley Hyatt (1837–1920) invented the first commercially successful plastic, Celluloid. Hyatt won a prize for making composition billiard balls, which replaced natural ivory, the main source of which had been elephant tusks. Celluloid later was widely used, not only for billiard balls but for other small articles, such as combs, men's collars and cuffs, and early photographic film.

Many other types of plastic were developed during the latter half of the 19th century, including rayon, the

first synthetic fiber, used in making cloth. In 1909 Bakelite was developed by a German-American chemist, Leo Hendrik Baekeland (1863–1944). After 1920, development of new plastics accelerated. Cellulose acetate was used during World War I for making lacquers and, beginning in 1929, for molded plastics articles. Acrylics were developed about 1930, polystyrenes in 1937. Since the beginning of World War II, many new types have been developed, including polyethylenes, silicones, and epoxies. Today plastics of many kinds are used for a great variety of purposes in architecture.

Related Articles BOTANICAL BUILDING; ELECTRIC POWER AND WIRING; FLOOR; FURNITURE; INSULATION, THERMAL; LIGHTING; PAINT; PLUMBING; ROOFING; WATERPROOFING; WINDOW; Various articles on other building components and systems.

Sources of Additional Information Manufacturing Chemists Assoc., 1826 Connecticut Ave., N.W., Washington, D.C. 20009; Society of Plastics Engineers, 656 W. Putnam Ave., Greenwich, Conn. 06830.

PLUMBING A system in a building consisting of piping, fixtures, appliances, and other parts through which natural and manufactured gas and hot and cold water are supplied, and through which the wastes of these systems are removed. Until the 19th century, plumbing systems were either very simple or nonexistent in buildings. Today such systems are considered necessities and may be quite complex. Plumbing systems are now major elements of architecture and among the most expensive systems in buildings.

Plumbing, generally taken to mean systems in and closely related to buildings, primarily consists of the piping and other devices required to supply gas and water, the appliances and fixtures in which these substances are used, and the waste disposal system. Supply systems conduct water to kitchens for cooking, drinking, and dishwashing; to laundry rooms for clothes washing; to bathrooms for bathing, washing, and use in toilets, or water closets; to drinking fountains; to hose outlets for outdoor use; and to many other kinds of outlets, fixtures, or appliances. A very important supply problem is water for fire fighting and for fire-sprinkler systems. (See the article entitled fire protection.)

Central Water Systems Water is generally supplied to buildings in cities and towns from central water systems usually operated by municipalities. The runoff from precipitation drains into streams, rivers, and lakes or soaks into the ground. Water is drawn directly from rivers and lakes or from reservoirs that are like artificial lakes constructed for water storage. Most large cities obtain their water supply from such sources. Many smaller cities and towns, and some of the larger ones, obtain their supplies from wells drilled to tap underground water sources. Water obtained from any of the sources is often stored in water tanks, or towers, as well as in reservoirs.

While some water obtained from these sources is pure enough for human use, most of it must be treated in settling tanks, with filters and chemicals. After treatment, the water is pumped into the main system that supplies buildings and other users. At building sites, water ordinarily flows through meters which measure quantities for which building owners and users then pay. In rural areas, central water systems are not ordinarily available. Buildings in such areas usually rely on private water systems, consisting of wells equipped with pumps and storage tanks. Shallow wells, less than 25 ft deep, may be used where the level of water in the ground, or water table, is high. Where greater depths are needed, deep wells are required. Shallow wells are often dug, while deep wells are usually drilled. For impure water obtained from wells, private systems for chlorination, or chlorinators, are available. Systems are also available for changing hard water to soft (water softeners), and for reducing the acidity of water.

Sewage Systems Waste disposal or sewage systems outside buildings in cities and towns are usually municipally operated. From the buildings, sewage and waste flows into collecting systems which carry them to plants removing and treating solids to form sludge, which may be further treated and dried for use in fertilizers. The liquid materials are filtered and treated with chemicals to form a liquid, called effluent, which is safe and can be discharged. In rural areas, private sewage disposal systems are required. Today there are two main types: grease-trap and drain-field systems, and septic tanks and drain-field systems. Grease-trap systems are used mostly for wastes that contain grease, such as that from kitchen sinks and dishwashers. In the trap, grease remains while the effluent flows into the field system of clay tile or other types of piping to be discharged into the ground. In a septic tank, bacteria act upon sewage changing it into harmless solids that remain in the tank, gases which escape, and effluent that flows into the ground through drain fields. In both grease traps and septic tanks, solids must be periodically removed.

In order for a private sewage disposal system to be installed, health and other codes require that the ground be capable of absorbing the effluent that will be discharged into it. This is often determined by a percolation, or perc, test, in which a hole of a specified diameter and depth is made in the ground, water poured into it, and the distance it drops in 30 min recorded. If the water drops enough within the allowable time, a septic system will be allowed; if not, its use will not be permitted. Much of the rural land in the United States cannot pass percolation tests because of its clay composition, high water tables, and other reasons. Therefore buildings cannot be constructed in many rural areas unless patented private sewage disposers are employed. Several types are available, but have not been widely accepted under various health and other codes. In some localities soil survey maps and test borings are used, sometimes in conjunction with perc tests, for the determination of soil suitability for septic systems.

Rural water and sewage systems, as well as other types, must be kept separate at all times. Until the 19th century, the fact that the relationship of water supply to sewage contributed to the spread of disease was unknown. For rural systems, certain code and good practice requirements specify the distance that must be maintained between wells and septic systems. In other installations, care should be taken to eliminate the possibility of contamination of water supplies by sewage.

Gas Services Gas supplies in buildings furnish either natural or manufactured gas for heating, cooking, clothes drying, and other purposes. In cities and towns, gas services are usually supplied by the municipalities through mains and meters into buildings. In rural areas, gas is ordinarily supplied to buildings in containers of manufactured, liquefied gas, sometimes called bottled gas. When the contents of one have been exhausted, another is obtained or the first refilled.

Piping System For water supplies entering buildings, complex systems of piping and fittings are required to direct the water to the places where it will be used. Piping is often of steel, wrought iron, or copper, with the latter considered the best. Today plastic piping is also used for many purposes. In some buildings, such as wood-frame houses, piping is often concealed in floors, walls, and other elements, but in other buildings, particularly large ones, special spaces, called pipe chases, are provided. The piping is joined with a variety of fittings, such as elbows, couplings, and tees, for connecting pipe lengths and making turns. In small buildings, the pressure of the water flowing from the mains is sufficient to distribute it to the places where it will be used. In larger buildings, especially tall ones, pumps are used to raise the water to upper floors, where it is stored in tanks and from which gravity causes it to flow downward.

In the supply system, cold water flows to all the fixtures in buildings, including bathtubs, wash basins, water closets, bathrooms, kitchen sinks and dishwashers, laundry tubs and clothes washers, drinking fountains, hot-water or steam heating systems, and hose outlets. In certain buildings, fire, building, and other codes require water reserves to be held for firefighting purposes. Sprinkler systems in such buildings must also be supplied. Cold-water supply lines are connected with hot-water heaters (gas or electric), which are of three major types: storage tank heaters, with heating coils inside of them; tankless heaters, which operate when a demand for hot water is made on them; and hot-water tankless heaters that are installed in or in connection with boilers used for heating the interiors of buildings. (See the article entitled heating, ventilating, and air conditioning.) Often hot-water pipes are covered with special insulation to avoid heat losses during transmission, and insulation is often used for cold-water pipes to keep condensation from them and to avoid freezing in exposed locations. Shutoff valves are installed at various points in the water supply systems to allow stopping the flow of water to certain portions of the system for specific fixtures, repairs, or other purposes. Sewage, or sanitary drainage, systems, are completely separate from water supply systems. Fixtures in buildings are equipped with traps, curved sections of pipe that hold water which prevents sewer gases from entering the interiors of buildings. From the traps, fixture branch piping, of cast iron, copper, plastic, or steel, takes the waste from fixtures and allows it to flow, by force of gravity, to pipes called waste stacks and then down to the main drains, all made of the same materials. In order to let air enter the system so that waste will flow freely and discharge gases from it, vertical pipes of the same materials, called vents, are provided. These rise above the roofs to discharge gases. In the sewage lines, cleanouts, with removable threaded plugs, are provided to allow cleaning of the system if clogs occur. The main drain passes through a main trap to the outside sewer on the site, made of clay tile, cast iron, or plastic pipe, to the public sewer lines or to the lines of private septic tank and grease-trap systems.

Fixtures A great variety and number of fixtures are available, including various kinds of sinks of procelain enamel and baked enamel steels, stainless steel, and others; tubs and showers of many types and sizes; and other fixtures. These come in many colors and finishes. There is a wide variety of appliances: hot-water heaters of various types and capacities; dishwashers; gas-fired and electric stoves; separate ovens and stove tops; clothes washers and driers, both gas-fired and electric; water softeners; built-in grilles; and microwave ovens. These appliances are available in a range of colors and finishes, for both domestic and commercial use.

Plumbing systems in buildings are designed by mechanical engineers. Building, health, and other code requirements are very strict today for both design and construction, specifying how many fixtures may be attached to drain lines, types of traps to be used, types of piping and sizes required, vents required, and many other things related to such systems.

History In the most ancient primitive buildings, there was no plumbing. Water for drinking and other purposes was supplied by springs or other water bodies, used at its source, and later carried and stored in clay and other vessels. By the time of the great ancient civilizations around the Mediterranean Sea, methods had been developed for obtaining water from wells, springs, cisterns, and other sources; transporting it through aqueducts and conduits made of brick, hollow timbers, or stone; and lifting it with primitive machines, using ropes, buckets, and levers. The water was used, not only for all human needs but for animal needs and for irrigating farmlands. Later pottery pipes were used for conducting water and still later, lead and bronze pipes. Similar pipes were also used to drain away waste water and sewage. Remains of such systems have been found in many places, including Mesopotamia, Crete, Mycenae, on the Greek mainland, and in Egypt. These early people also had primitive latrines or toilets, showers, and bathtubs.

The ancient Greeks built water and drainage systems, using mostly terra-cotta pipes, but sometimes lead or bronze ones. The Romans built remarkable water supply and drainage systems that were never equaled until modern times. They also built plumbing systems, with many things in common with those of today. To supply water, the Romans built a vast system of aqueducts, wells, cisterns, reservoirs, and conduits, resulting in the most plentiful and reliable water system up to that time. From the sources, the water was conducted to settling tanks, in which sediment was allowed to settle out, then to water mains of wood, strengthened with iron, terra-cotta, bronze, or lead, from which fountains, baths, and buildings were supplied. Since the Romans had no reliable method of purifying water, they kept the supplies from various sources separate, using the purest for drinking and the others for sundry purposes.

The Romans had sewage disposal systems and the overflow from baths, fountains, and other places was often disposed of by the systems. The water supply, plumbing, and sewage disposal system of Rome was complete and highly developed. In other parts of the Roman Empire, such systems were constructed, but usually on a smaller scale and not so elaborate as that in Rome. In other places, the supplies of water were not always adequate to the needs, and sometimes water had to be rationed.

The public baths, or *thermae*, constructed by the Romans are well known. Often quite complex, they contained not only hot and cold baths but often rooms for exercise, recreation, and other pursuits. They also had central heating with hypocausts, through which hot air and smoke circulated under floors. Not so well known are the Roman toilets, or *foricae*, which had groups of seats located over water flowing in channels. *Foricae* were located in various places in Rome, including apartment buildings. The sewage flowed, untreated, into the Tiber River, through a great sewer, the construction of which had begun in the 6th century B.C. Private bathtubs, very much like those of today, were used in the residences of wealthy people. And the Romans had provisions for water to be used in fire fighting.

After the time of the Romans, the systems for water supply, plumbing, and sewage disposal declined in number and quality. In some cases, the aqueducts and other parts of Roman systems were maintained, but in others they were not. Water from the roofs of buildings poured into open gutters, which also carried sewage. Wells and other water sources were often polluted with sewage or other refuse. Cleanliness became less important to people than it had been in Roman times and standards of hygiene worsened. All these negative factors contributed to the spread of the plague and other epidemics through Europe during the Middle Ages.

Beginning about the 13th century, conditions began to improve. Water supplies became more reliable, and sewage was discharged through pipes or directly into rivers and other water bodies. Since there were shortages of metals, pipes were often made of wood. Public baths were again instituted and toilets were used to some extent, but often their contents were thrown on the street or emptied into moats, rather than disposed of properly.

During the Renaissance, conditions improved somewhat and better concepts of hygiene were adopted. Roman aqueducts were repaired and new ones constructed. In palaces and other residences of the nobility and wealthy, bathrooms were constructed, often with elaborate tubs filled and emptied with buckets. Pots were used for toilets or people went to outside privies. Sewage was not handled properly for the most part, and epidemics of diseases carried in sewage were frequent. Often the sewage was discharged into streams, which were also used for water supplies, thus compounding the disease problems. Major sewage systems were not constructed until the 17th century in Paris and the 19th century in London.

American Development In early colonial America, water supply, plumbing, and sewage systems did not exist. Water came from natural sources, such as springs, and then from wells and cisterns. Outdoor privies were constructed or pots were used inside and emptied out-of-doors. Baths were taken in washtubs. Such conditions existed well into the 19th century. During that century, public sources of water, including reservoirs, were established in many places. Pumps and piping were installed to conduct the water to buildings. The quality of water did not improve much but the quantity available did. There were no sewers, but later elaborate systems were built, discharging directly into rivers and other water bodies. For places without sewers, cesspools and later septic tank systems were developed. Primitive types of toilets, or water closets, were introduced early in the 19th century.

During the same century, water filtration plants, using sand, came into use and were followed by chemical treatment plants. The relationship between water and sewage, in the spread of disease, was recognized and sewage treatment plants were constructed. Water closets became more efficient and gradually the inside toilet replaced the outdoor privy. By the late 19th century, inside bathtubs with water connections and drainage were installed, along with wash basins or lavatories, which were ofen placed in bedrooms. About the same time, sinks, with running water and drains, were installed in kitchens. The goal became a bathroom and kitchen with plumbing in every house.

In later years, one bathroom per house became the exception, with many houses containing several, including private ones connected to individual bedrooms. Equipment for kitchens and bathrooms has become increasingly more prevalent and elaborate during the 20th century, with the addition of built-in tubs and shower enclosures in bathrooms, and dishwashers, food disposers, and other appliances in kitchens. People today find other uses for plumbing, for example, in heating and air-conditioning systems; for ponds, fountains, and other purposes; and for swimming pools near or in houses. There has been a similar increased use of plumbing and appliances in buildings of most other types.

Related Articles DAM; ENERGY; ENVIRONMENTAL PROTECTION; FIRE PROTECTION; FOUNTAIN; GARDEN; HEATING, VENTILATING, AND AIR CONDITIONING; MECHANICAL ENGINEERING.

Further Reading McGuinness, William J., and Benjamin Stein: *Mechanical and Electrical Equipment for Buildings,* 6th ed., John Wiley, New York, 1979.

Sources of Additional Information American Society of Mechanical Engineers, 345 E. 49th St., New York, N.Y. 10017; Cast Iron Soil Pipe Inst., 2020 K St., N.W., Washington, D.C., 20006; Plumbing, Heating and Cooling Information Bureau, 35 E. Wacker Dr., Chicago, Ill. 60601.

POPE, JOHN RUSSELL American architect (1874–1937). A good student and an inspired man, John Russell Pope became one of the foremost architects in the United States. Some count it a misfortune that he lived in an era when architecture was changing radically from the eclectic styles that had dominated it for so many years to the modern movement.

Pope started his career under the tutelage of an architect, William Robert Ware (1832–1915), who had been influenced by the principles of the Ecole des Beaux Arts in Paris. Then he won a scholarship given by another Beaux Arts architect, Charles Follen McKim (1847–1909), to the American Academy in Rome, a school McKim had helped found and of which he was president. Pope then attended and graduated from Ecole des Beaux Arts. Coming back to the United States, he met McKim and, highly impressed, fell almost completely under the spell of the Beaux Arts philosophy and the man.

Thus Pope had very little choice, except to become an architect who based his work on Beaux Arts principles and produced buildings in the Eclectic style. Whether he had a choice or not, Pope designed buildings in this manner throughout his lifetime. And Pope was very good at it. The only others of his time about whom this may be said were Cass Gilbert (1859–1934) and Paul Philippe Cret (1876–1945). Although many of the buildings of these three architects were notable, some are anachronisms since they were built in the 1930s and 1940s.

Pope started out as a talented and scholarly architect, who designed striking and popular buildings in a variety of styles. He ended by becoming one of the most successful architects in the United States, practiced almost 40 years, and designed a great number of buildings of many types, including public buildings, colleges, churches, houses, and museums. He also designed a large number of monuments.

Works Although Pope practiced in New York City,

POPE, JOHN RUSSELL Temple of the Scottish Rite (1910), Washington, D.C. *(Library of Congress)*

POPE, JOHN RUSSELL National Archives Building (1935), Washington, D.C. *(Library of Congress)*

POPE, JOHN RUSSELL Constitution Hall (1930), Washington, D.C. *(Detroit Publishing Co., Library of Congress)*

POPE, JOHN RUSSELL National Gallery of Art (1941), Washington, D.C. *(Hirst Milhollen, Library of Congress)*

his most important buildings were constructed in other places. Of his work in New York City still in existence, the two most important commissions involved remodeling and additions to existing buildings. Pope remodeled the home of Henry Clay Frick (1849–1919), steel industrialist, originally completed in 1914 by Carrère and Hastings, into an art gallery (1935) to house the Frick Collection and added a library. The building is now known as the Frick Museum. He also added, to the complex of the American Museum of Natural History, a building called the Roosevelt Memorial Building (1936), named for President Theodore Roosevelt (1858–1919). The original portions of the complex (1877) were by Vaux and Mould. The only other important Pope buildings in New York City are the Spence School (1929) and the house of William Kissam Vanderbilt II (1878–1944), now the headquarters of the Rumanian delegation to the United Nations.

Pope designed plans for a number of campuses, including those of Yale University, New Haven, Conn.; Johns Hopkins University, Baltimore, Md.; Syracuse University, Syracuse, N.Y.; and Dartmouth College,

Hanover, N.H. He designed buildings and monuments in many locations, including Syracuse and Plattsburgh, N.Y., and Baltimore. One of his most important monuments was the American Battle Monument (1937), Montfaucon, France.

The greatest collection of Pope's works is in Washington, where he designed the Temple of the Scottish Rite (1910), Washington International Center, or Meridian House (1915), Constitution Hall (1930), and the National Archives Building (1935). Three of his most important commissions were not completed until after he died: the National City Christian Church (1939); the National Gallery of Art (1941), given to the city by the industrialist and financier Andrew Mellon (1855–1937); and the Jefferson Memorial (1943). The last-named two were the last great eclectic buildings in Washington.

Life John Russell Pope was born in New York City on April 2, 1874, the son of an artist. After studying at the College of the City of New York, now City University of New York, Pope enrolled in 1891 in the architectural program, established in 1881 at Columbia University, New York City, by a former student of

Richard Morris Hunt (1827–95), William Robert Ware. In 1894 Pope graduated with a bachelor of philosophy degree, which seems unlikely enough, from the architectural program in the Columbia University School of Mines, which seems even more unlikely.

In 1895 Pope won the McKim scholarship, allowing study at the American Academy in Rome. Winning another scholarship the following year, Pope was able to stay two years in Rome, studying architecture. He then entered the École des Beaux Arts in Paris, where both Hunt and McKim had studied. Completing the architectural course in two years, Pope graduated in 1900. Returning to New York, Pope worked for a while in the architectural office of Bruce Price (1845–1903), the father of Emily Price (1873–1960) who later became famous on her own, using her married name Emily Post, as the foremost authority on etiquette in the United States.

Pope then established his own office in New York and soon had a successful practice that brought him commissions, not only in many parts of the United States but in England and France. He practiced almost 40 years and became one of the most respected architects in the United States. He was active in many organizations and served on several national commissions, including the National Council of Fine Arts, to which he was appointed by President Woodrow Wilson (1856–1924), and the National Board of Consulting Architects, appointed by President Herbert Clark Hoover (1874–1964). He received many honors, including election to membership in the National Institute of Arts and Letters and the National Academy of Design. Pope served as president of the American Academy in Rome from 1933 until August 27, 1937, when he died.

Related Articles BEAUX ARTS, ÉCOLE DES; ECLECTIC ARCHITECTURE; EDUCATION; HUNT, RICHARD MORRIS; McKIM, MEAD AND WHITE.

Further Reading Cortissoz, Royal: *The Architecture of John Russell Pope*, 3 vols., Halburn, New York, 1924–30.

POST, GEORGE BROWNE

American architect (1837–1913). George Browne Post was an eclectic architect who designed buildings of many styles derived from the past. He learned his architecture from the pioneer of the Beaux Arts principles of design in the United States, Richard Morris Hunt (1827–95). Perhaps because of his earlier training as a civil engineer and because of his inquisitive nature, Post made a greater number of contributions to architecture than many other Beaux Arts architects, who were preoccupied with scholarship, past styles, and ornament.

In spite of the eclectic nature of his building designs, George Post was an architectural innovator. He was one of the first New York City architects to design tall office buildings, later known as skyscrapers, including the 25-story St. Paul Building (1900) in New York City. He was one of the first architects to use elevators. He pioneered in the design of modern hotels, many of them for the Statler chain in cities around the United States, and was a good planner. He also took a deep interest in good materials, sound construction, and meeting the needs of his clients.

Works During the more than 40 years he practiced, Post produced a great number of buildings of many types, including office buildings, banks, hotels, apartments, college buildings, and houses. He also designed a remarkable series of New York City buildings for national marketing groups: the Produce Building (1884), considered one of his best designs, and the Cotton Exchange (1885), both since demolished; and the New York Stock Exchange (1904), still in use.

Post designed a number of houses, the best of which was that for Cornelius Vanderbilt II (1843–99), built in New York City in 1880, enlarged in 1894, and since demolished. Other important New York City buildings by Post include the Williamsburgh Savings Bank and the Western Union Building, both completed in 1875; the Long Island Historical Society Building (1878); the old Times Building (1889), now part of Pace College; the Old Borough Building (1897), Brooklyn; and the Vincent (Astor) Building (1890), Fordham University. In 1900, he designed a master plan for the College of the City of New York, now the City University of New York, and later designed buildings for the campus (1907). These buildings are still in existence, except for the Western Union Building, which was demolished.

Post designed buildings in other parts of the country, including Newark, N.J., Pittsburgh, Detroit, and Cleveland. He also designed the Manufacturers' and Liberal Arts buildings for the World's Columbian Exposition in 1893 in Chicago. His last important building, completed in 1917, four years after his death, was the State Capitol of Wisconsin, Madison.

Life George Browne Post was born in New York City, on December 15, 1837. He attended Churchill's School, a military institution, in Ossining, N.Y. After graduation, he entered New York University, graduating in 1858 with a degree in civil engineering. He then entered the architectural atelier, or studio, of Richard Morris Hunt, who was the acknowledged master of the Eclectic style based on the principles of the École des Beaux Arts in Paris, where Hunt had studies. In 1960 Post left the atelier to form an architectural practice in New York City, in partnership with Charles D. Gambrill (1832–80), who later was the partner of Henry Hobson Richardson (1838–86).

In 1861 the office was closed when Post went on active duty as a captain in the U.S. Army, during the Civil War. He served until 1865, participating in battles, and was eventually promoted to colonel. After the war, Post returned to New York City and opened a new office, this time without a partner. Soon commissions began to come in and before long Post was one of the busiest architects in the city. He became one of the most successful of his time, always practicing in New York City and designing most of his buildings to be constructed there.

In 1863 Post married Alice Matilde Stone. They had

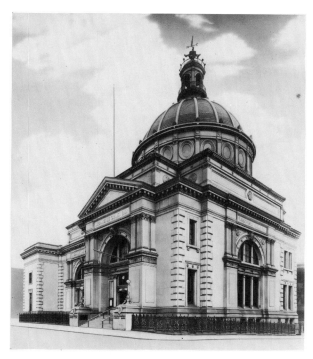

POST, GEORGE BROWNE Williamsburgh Savings Bank (1875), Brooklyn, New York, N.Y. *(Williamsburgh Savings Bank)*

POST, GEORGE BROWNE New York Stock Exchange (1904), New York, N.Y. *(Library of Congress)*

two sons, William Stone Post (1866–1940) and J. Otis Post (1874–1951), who became architects. In 1904 both sons were taken as partners by the elder Post and the firm was renamed George B. Post and Sons, which it remained until the death of the father. The

brothers continued the firm for many years afterward, designing buildings of many types. They also continued the hotel work for the Statler chain, begun by their father, and designed the Statler-Hilton (1924), New York City. This hotel, originally called the Pennsylvania, was immortalized for big band fans by a song using its telephone number, "Pennsylvania Six-Five Thousand," written by band leader Glenn Miller (1904–1944)

George Browne Post was much admired and he received many honors. He was very active in architectural, arts, and other types of organizations. He was elected president of the American Institute of Architects in 1896 and served in that position until 1898. He was a member of the National Institute of Arts and Letters, the American Academy of Arts and Letters, and several other organizations. In 1911 Post received the highest honor the AIA can bestow on an architect, the Gold Medal. After a life that was active right to the end, George Browne Post died on November 28, 1913.

Related Articles ECLECTIC ARCHITECTURE; HUNT, RICHARD MORRIS.

Further Reading *Recent and Current Work of George B. Post and Sons,* Harwell-Evans & Co., New York, 1909; Sturgis, Russell: *The Work of George B. Post, Architectural Record,* New York, 1898.

PRACTICE OF ARCHITECTURE
The functions, actions, and processes performed by architects and other environmental design professionals and technicians in the design, planning, and construction of buildings.

In a sense, every article in this book is concerned with architectural practice. However, practice may be divided into major areas, including basic architectural services, related services, and special services. Another major consideration in practice is the management of firms and architectural projects.

The basic architectural services include the phases of schematic design: design development, construction documents, bidding or negotiation, and construction contract administration. The major related services include interior design; landscape architecture; structural, mechanical, and electrical engineering; site planning; surveying; city planning; and road and traffic design. Such services are sometimes performed by independent professionals in various fields. For further discussion of these various phases and services, see the titles listed at the end of this article.

Special services include programming, feasibility studies, remodeling, preservation and restoration, graphic design, acoustics, lighting, building construction, and others. Some architectural firms offer such services; in other cases, they are performed by other professionals. While some architectural firms offer only basic services to their clients, the trend today is toward comprehensive services, which include not only the basic but a combination of related and special services needed by their specific clientele.

Architectural Firms It has been estimated that

there are more than 10,000 architectural firms in the United States, employing more than 100,000 people. Firms range in size from one-person offices to those with several hundred. The one-person offices, about 20 percent of the total, are usually those of young architects just starting out for themselves, or other architects, such as college professors, who practice part-time. In such offices, the architect-owners, or principals, perform all the architectural services, except those for which outside consultants, such as engineers, are retained, and occasional part-time help in drafting and other functions. In larger offices, the principals and employees tend to specialize in one or more aspects of practice.

Some firms practice on a very limited geographical scale, in some cases within a single state or even within the environs of a single city. Most firms practice in broader geographical areas, regionally or nationally. Quite a few firms have international practices that extend to Europe, the Middle East, and other areas. In some cases, such work is handled in the U.S. offices of the firms; in others, branch offices are maintained in foreign countries or temporary offices are set up as needed.

The average office in the United States has about nine people, including principals and employees. Some 25 percent of the offices are about that size, while only about 1 percent have more than 75 people. One-person offices, of course, have single owners, or proprietors. For offices of larger size, the owners may be single proprietors but in the more usual case, two or more partners. In the past, architects were not allowed, under state laws, to incorporate, but today most states allow corporate practice. Some allow general corporations, in which anyone may own stock; others allow only so-called professional corporations, in which stockholders must be registered or licensed architects or other environmental designers.

Architectural firms that perform only architectural services, acquiring the services of engineers and other professionals from consultants, are usually called simply by the names of the single proprietor, partners, or major professional stockholders, followed sometimes by AIA or FAIA to denote membership or fellowship in the American Institute of Architects, and by the title architect or architects. Firms that perform both architectural and engineering services may also call themselves simply architects. In other cases, they are called architects and engineers, and are sometimes referred to as A-E firms. A few firms, in which engineering services form a larger portion of the work than do architectural, are called engineers and architects, or E-A firms. Any of these firms may offer additional related or special services, such as construction management, interior design, or landscape architecture. In some cases, such services are offered by the firms themselves; in others, firms own subsidiaries that perform such services. Some larger firms also operate branch offices in various parts of the country. Some architectural firms own other architectural firms which they operate as subsidiaries.

Commissions The most usual situation today is for a single architectural firm to obtain a commission from a client, performing all the required services either with its own personnel or with the aid of consultants for portions of the work. For very large or complex projects, those far away from a firm's office location or in other special cases, a firm obtaining a commission may choose, or be required by the building owners, to associate with another firm to perform the services. In such cases, the firms divide the work between them, the primary firm, for example, managing the project and performing design and production services, and the associated firm administering the construction contract during the actual construction of the building. In other cases, two or more firms may form a joint venture in order to obtain certain commissions and to handle them properly. A joint venture is like a temporary partnership between firms for specific purposes. In a joint venture, the work is usually divided in a manner similar to that of an association. In either case, many variations are possible.

Fees Architects receive fees from their clients, usually the owners of the buildings for which the services are performed. The most usual type of fee arrangement is a percentage of the cost of the construction. Often thought to be 6 percent, such fees actually range both higher and lower than 6 percent, according to the types of buildings, their size and complexity, the repetition of certain building elements, and for other reasons. Two other types of fee arrangements are often used: the multiple of direct personnel expense type, and the fee plus expenses type. Percentage fees generally cover only basic architectural and engineering services, with other services incurring additional fees.

Multiple of direct personnel expense fees cover all services performed, regardless of type. In this fee system, records are maintained of the payrolls of people working on a project, along with their fringe benefits, such as insurance, social security, retirement plans, and the like. The fee charged is some multiple of the total of these costs, usually 2.5 times the costs or more. The multiple thus covers the direct costs of services plus overhead and profit for the firm. In the fee plus expenses system, an architectural firm receives a fixed amount for its fee, in addition to reimbursement of all costs of the project, including personnel and fringe benefits, other expenses, and overhead.

Some architects have experimented with other fee systems, including lump sum fees that cover everything, and combination fees that entail multiples of expenses during the early stages of services through the design development phase when the costs of the services are difficult to estimate in advance and a lump sum fee for the remainder of the services. For some years, architectural associations and other groups published suggested schedules of minimum fees for services. This practice is now illegal.

Organization Architectural firms are organized in

various ways. Of course, in a one-person office, the entire organization is the single practitioner. As a one-person office grows through the addition of secretarial, drafting, and other personnel, some sort of organization must be established. Organizational forms vary considerably, but there are two major types sometimes called the horizontal or staff organization and the vertical organization. In general terms, a horizontal organization is composed of specialized departments, such as administration, business development, design, working drawings, specifications, construction administration, and so on. The administration department performs the overall management functions. The business development department is engaged in sales of the firm's services to potential clients. The other departments perform the basic, and sometimes other, services, each building project progressing through each department in turn, each performing its own special functions. The design department performs the design services for all projects, the working drawings department makes the construction drawings for all, and so on.

A vertical organization has similar functions but instead of a project proceeding through departments, people with various kinds of knowledge and talents are assigned to the project and, working as a team, perform all the services required. In horizontal organizations, other than a small one, rarely does a single individual perform functions other than in a single specialty. In a vertical organization, individual members of a team often perform more than one function; indeed, in some cases most or all of the functions. Many variations of these two types of organization are possible and are used in architectural offices today. One of the most common is a combination of the two types, certain functions being performed only by specialists while others are performed by people who, though specialists in a sense, are also generalists.

While smaller offices usually have only a few departments, or none at all, when a firm reaches a size of about 10 or more people, departmentalization is often found to be a necessity. In a medium-sized firm, the only departments required might be administration, including business development, design, production, and construction contract. In larger firms, a separate business development department is usually provided, often with a public relations office attached to it. Larger firms may have many other types of departments, including project management, scheduling, cost control, financial, personnel, rendering, model making, contract management, computer services, libraries, printing shops, and contract departments. In addition, many firms have structural, mechanical, and electrical engineering departments. And those that offer comprehensive services may have any of a number of others, including graphic design, landscape architecture, construction management, feasibility, programming, city planning, and interior design. In some firms, such services are offered by subsidiaries.

Office Functions Many kinds of people perform many kinds of functions in architectural offices. In each firm, there is a person who acts as the executive head of the entire operation. In a single proprietorship, this person is an architect who owns the firm, generally called the principal or simply the architect. In a partnership, with two or more principals, one is usually chosen to be the executive officer and may also head one or more major departments, while the others head one or more. In such firms there may also be a management board or committee that deals mainly with overall policies. Most architectural corporations have boards of directors to deal with policy and an executive officer, usually with the title president, who provides overall top management. In all but the smallest firms, departments are headed by department heads or principals; in corporations, these people are often given the title vice president.

Staff In the past, almost all the top management people in architectural firms and all the principals were either architects or engineers. Today some firms have taken in, as partners or stockholders, others, such as business managers, other environmental design professionals, or experienced people from related fields. However, in some states, this is not legal. The employees of a small architectural firm are generally secretaries, draftsmen (or drafters), specification writers, and field people who administer construction contracts and inspect construction work. In larger firms, a great variety of specialists may be employed, in addition to the above. They might include sales and public relations specialists in the business development department, engineers and engineering production people, cost control experts, computer programmers and operators, renderers, model makers, librarians and other information specialists, and programmers. In firms offering comprehensive services, others on the staff might include landscape architects; interior designers; space, site, or city planners; accountants; and contract experts. Most of these people will have had considerable education, often requiring college degrees in their fields, and many will be quite experienced.

Student Employees Some architectural firms make it a practice to encourage young people, including, in some cases, secondary school students as well as college students, by offering employment during summer vacations. A few also offer part-time employment to young people during the school year. In this way, young people may benefit and learn from actual practical experience in architectural offices, and at the same time earn experience credits toward those needed for registration or licensing. The firms that hire students perform a service for their professions as well as for the students, and may very well find that they are developing continuing relationships with people who may become their future employees, trained in the firm's business methods. For further information on education and careers in architecture, see articles entitled career; education.

Additional information on the major areas of practice is included in various other articles in this book, resulting in some fragmentation of the subject. In an attempt to remedy this situation, a simplified description of a single project, Citicorp Center (1978), New York City, is included on the following pages.

Citicorp Center is a significant example of the kind of excellent architecture that can be achieved when enlightened clients, cooperative governments, and talented architects and other environmental designers join together in a building project. Citicorp Center is a mixed-use, or multiple-use, complex composed of the following major elements: a 65-story, 914-ft high office tower, integrated with a church, a 7-story low-rise building containing shops, restaurants, and other retail establishments surrounding a glassed-in atrium and a landscaped plaza.

This combination of uses together with creative design and good construction have produced a complex that functions efficiently and is at the same time exciting and satisfying. Most importantly, it has produced an urban oasis that is filled with people from early morning until late at night. People going to and from work, by foot and by subway. People shopping, eating, or drinking. People listening to music played by groups who appear in the atrium regularly. People reading, sitting, playing games, or just looking at other people. Thus in this building complex, the amenities and excitement that once were considered to be normal in the central cores of cities and towns have been reborn.

In the 1960s, the First National City Bank, now called Citibank, completed the acquisition of the site, a process that took five years. In an unusual agreement, Citibank purchased the property of Saint Peter's Lutheran Church on the site, forming a condominium that would allow the congregation to build another church on the site, one that would be freestanding but closely related to the life of the rest of the Center. From the first, the owners wanted a mixed-use complex, partly out of the conviction that this would help restore city life to the area and partly because the inclusion of public spaces would make the Center more feasible, economically, since under New York City laws, additional rentable floor space would be allowed. The architects enthusiastically supported this course of action from the beginning. In such a nearly ideal situation, everyone wins: the architects and other environmental designers in the creation of a fine design, the owners in terms of both satisfaction and economics, and, most of all, the people who populate the plaza, atrium, shops, and restaurants of the comfortable, exciting, and useful spaces of the Center.

The plans and other illustrations on these pages convey some of the aspects of Citicorp Center, though it is impossible to portray in a book the hustle and bustle of the activities carried on there at times or the quiet restfulness of the church and certain areas of the plaza and atrium.

In other articles in this book, an attempt has been made to demonstrate some of the aspects of architectural and other design services for a large complex such as Citicorp Center. In the article entitled design, a number of conceptual sketches illustrate some of the processes involved in architectural design, including one of the six design schemes prepared before reaching the one actually used. Also a few schematic drawings are shown. In the article entitled working drawing, three partial working drawings are shown. These were part of a set of 372 sheets, each of which was 36 by 42 inches in size. In the article entitled specification, four pages of specifications, part of a set of 1309 pages, are shown. In addition, there were 69 sheets of drawings and 454 pages of specifications for the church.

In the article entitled rendering, a number of examples of various types of renderings are shown, including ones of an unadopted scheme, interiors, and a final rendering of the accepted design scheme. In the article entitled model making, a study model of an unadopted scheme is shown, along with the final model of the accepted design scheme. In the article entitled structure, a section of the building shows the trussed-frame structure and a sketch shows the tuned mass damper that reduces building sway in the wind. Many features could not be shown, including the energy efficiency of the double-glass and aluminum walls and the computer-controlled heating and air-conditioning system, and the fact that the slanted roof is oriented for possible later addition of solar collectors, though the building was originally designed that way for the inclusion of balconied apartments on top. The owners and their architects were unsuccessful in obtaining a zoning variance to permit the apartments, and they were subsequently eliminated from the design.

Related Articles BUILDING CODES AND STANDARDS; CAREER; COMPUTER; CONSTRUCTION CONTRACT ADMINISTRATION; COST CONTROL; DESIGN, ARCHITECTURAL; EDUCATION; ENGINEERING; FEASIBILITY STUDY; GRAPHIC DESIGN; INTERIOR DESIGN; LANDSCAPE ARCHITECTURE; MODEL MAKING; PLANNING, CITY; PRESERVATION; PROGRAMMING; REMODELING; RENDERING; SITE PLANNING; SPECIFICATION; WORKING DRAWING.

General References American Institute of Architects (AIA): *Architect's Handbook of Professional Practice, vols. 1 and 2*, latest edition, AIA, Washington; AIA and Charles G. Ramsey and Harold R. Sleeper, Robert T. Packard, ed.: *Architectural Graphic Standards*, 7th ed., John Wiley, New York, 1980; Callender, John J.: *Time Saver Standards for Architectural Design Data*, 5th ed., McGraw-Hill, New York, 1974; Caudill, William W.: *Architecture by Team —A New Concept for Practice of Architecture*, Van Nostrand Reinhold, New York, 1971; Class, Robert Allan, and Robert E. Koehler, eds.: *Current Techniques in Architectural Practice*, AIA and Architectural Record Books, Washington and New York, 1976; Foxhall, William B.: *Techniques of Successful Practice for Architects and Engineers*, McGraw-Hill, New York, 1975; Hunt, William Dudley, Jr.: *Total Design —Architecture of Welton Becket and Associates*, McGraw-Hill, New York, 1972; Hunt, William Dudley, Jr., ed.: *Comprehensive Architectural Services —General Principles and Practice*, McGraw-Hill, New

PRACTICE OF ARCHITECTURE Citicorp Center (1978), New York, N.Y. [*Architects: Hugh Stubbins and Associates; Associated Architects: Emery Roth and Sons; Structural engineers: LeMessurier Associates/SCI and the Office of James Ruderman; Mechanical and electrical engineers: Joseph R. Loring Assoc.; Landscape architects: Sasaki Assoc.; Graphic and church furniture designers: Vignelli Assoc.; Construction managers: HRH Construction Corp.; Owners: Citibank/Citicorp. (Norman McGrath)*]

Interior.

Interior.

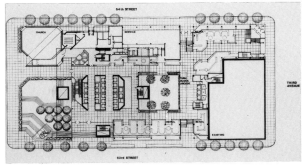

Street Floor Plan

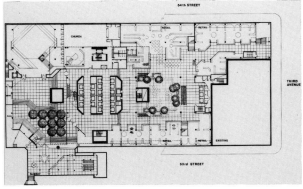

Concourse Floor Plan

PRACTICE OF ARCHITECTURE Citicorp Center (1978), New York, N.Y. [Architects: Hugh Stubbins and Associates; Associated Architects: Emery Roth and Sons; Structural engineers: LeMessurier Associates/SCI and the Office of James Ruderman; Mechanical and electrical engineers; Joseph R. Loring Assoc.; Landscape architects: Sasaki Assoc.; Graphic and church furniture designers: Vignelli Assoc.; Construction managers: HRH Construction Corp.; Owners: Citibank/Citicorp. (Norman McGrath)]

York, 1965; Kemper, Alfred M.: *Architectural Handbook — Environmental Analysis, Architectural Programming, Design and Technology, and Construction,* John Wiley, New York, 1979; Merritt, Frederick S., ed.: *Building Construction Handbook,* 3d ed., McGraw-Hill, New York, 1975; Wills, Royal Barry; *This Business of Architecture,* Reinhold, New York, 1941.

Business Practices Architectural Secretaries Association (ASA): *Architectural Secretaries Handbook,* ASA, Washington, 1975; Bockrath, Joseph T.: *Environmental Law for Engineers, Scientists and Managers,* McGraw-Hill, New York, 1977; Case and Company: *Methods of Compensation for Architectural Services,* AIA, Washington, 1969; Case and Company: *Profit Planning in Architectural Practice,* AIA, Washington, 1968; Dibner, David R.: *Joint Ventures for Architects and Engineers,* McGraw-Hill, New York, 1972; Guttmann, Hans P.: *The International Consultant,* McGraw-Hill, New York, 1976; Hauf, Harold D.: *Building Contracts for Design and Construction,* 2d ed., John Wiley, New York, 1976; Koehler, Robert E., ed.: *The American Institute of Architects Personnel Manual,* AIA, Washington, 1978; Walker, Nathan, Edward N. Walker, and Theodor K. Rohdenburg: *Legal Pitfalls in Architecture, Engineering and Building Construction,* 2d ed., McGraw-Hill, New York, 1979.

Business Development Cooper, David: *Architectural and Engineering Salesmanship,* John Wiley, New York, 1979; Coxe, Weld: *Marketing Architectural and Engineering Services,* Van Nostrand Reinhold, New York, 1971; Jones, Gerre L.: *How to Market Professional Design Services,* McGraw-Hill, New York, 1978.

Source of Additional Information The American Institute of Architects, 1735 New York Ave., N.W., Washington, D.C. 20006.

PRE-COLUMBIAN ARCHITECTURE

The buildings and other structures by the American Indians and their ancestors before Christopher Columbus landed in America in 1492. The ancestors of the American Indians are believed to have come to America across a strip of land connecting what are now Alaska and the Soviet Union. The land connection has disappeared and Bering Strait is located there. Although the exact time these people reached America has not been established, and it is not known what they called themselves, it is believed that the migrations started at least 20,000 years ago and continued for quite a long time.

Traces of these early people have been found in North America, including caves they occupied in the west and tools they used as far back as 15,000 B.C. in what is called the Folsom culture. No remains of these early humans have been found. Their architecture, if they had any other than caves, also remains a mystery. However, it is believed that they began to construct crude huts from limbs of trees and brush and tents from limbs and animal skins sometime before 5000 B.C. The remains of none have been found.

Medicine Wheels The earliest constructions of the Indians still in existence in the United States are medicine wheels, though their real purpose has not been firmly established. Found in many places in the Western United States and in Canada, they are geometric arrangements of stones, roughly in the shape of wheels with spokes. Thought to have had astronomical and religious purposes, some of these wheels are 200 ft or more in diameter and are thought to have been built about the time of the pyramids in Egypt, about the 27th century B.C., or earlier. It is believed

that there may be literally millions of these located in the area stretching roughly from Texas into southern Canada.

Mounds Other early structures made by Indians are mounds of various kinds. Some are thought to have been constructed as early as 300 B.C., while others have been dated as late as A.D. 1200. Thousands of these mounds have been found in many places in the United States, the greatest number in the states of Ohio and Illinois, with lesser numbers in Indiana, Wisconsin, Arkansas, Kentucky, Tennessee, Iowa, Louisiana, and Georgia. The mounds are of three major types: burial; temple, earthen pyramids on top of which temples were built; and effigy, shaped like crude representations of animals, birds, or snakes. The effigy mounds probably had religious significance, but their exact use is not known.

Some of the most notable mounds still in existence are Effigy Mound, near Lake Koshkonong, Wis.; Azlatan, near Madison, Wis.; Etowah, near Cartersville, Ga.; and Cahokia Mounds, near East St. Louis, Ill. Among the many important mounds in Ohio are Great Serpent, Hillsboro; Mound City; Newark Earthworks, Newark; Fort Ancient, Lebanon. Hopewell mounds, for which the culture of the Mound Builders has been named, are to be found in many locations, in the eastern half of the United States.

Early Buildings The earliest buildings of most of the Indians in America, other than that of the Pueblos, have not survived because of the perishable materials used in their construction. However, their construction has been documented quite well because the types continued to be built by Indians long after the colonization of America by Europeans. The architecture of the Indians was regional in character, and varied considerably from place to place, in order to fit the climatic conditions and the way of life of the users.

Later Buildings Later Indian architecture may be divided into five major groups: Eastern Forest, Great Plains, Pacific Northwest, California, and Southwest. Eastern Forest Indians lived by farming or by combining farming with hunting. The farmers in the Southeast generally built houses of wood, with thatched roofs and walls plastered with mud. In Florida, the Indians built chickees: open-sided, thatched huts. The farmer-hunters of the Northeast built two main types of buildings: dome-shaped wigwams, huts made of limbs or small trees, covered with bark; and longhouses, made in a similar manner, but large enough for several families to live together.

The Indians of the Great Plains were hunters or farmers, and sometimes combined both pursuits. The nomadic tribes lived in tepees, or tipis, cone-shaped, often highly ornamented tents, constructed of poles and covered with animal, often buffalo, skins. A single tepee required some 15 to 30 poles and an equal number of buffalo hides. More sedentary Indians built earth lodges, often partly underground and covered with logs, brush, and dirt. In the Pacific North-

PRE-COLUMBIAN ARCHITECTURE Pueblo Bonito (c. 1100), Chaco Canyon National Park, N.Mex. [*Architect: unknown. (David Muench)*]

west, where the Indians were generally sedentary fishermen, wood dwellings of split planks were constructed and were highly ornamented.

California Indians, sedentary for the most part, gathered seeds, roots, and nuts for food. Some tribes lived almost entirely on acorns. Their major type of dwelling was the wickiup, a framework of poles in a sort of beehive shape, covered with brush and sometimes with dirt. Many of the Indian tribes also built communal buildings, or meeting houses, of various types. In the Southwest, some of the earliest Indians, who were seminomadic, lived in slab houses, or pit dwellings, made of logs and mud, partly underground, and sometimes lined with stone slabs. Others lived in hogans, houses made like log cabins, with earthen roofs.

Basket Makers The crowning architectural achievements of the early Indians are the magnificent structures of the Southwest. The origins of the people who constructed these buildings have not been firmly established. It is known that they descended from a culture called the Basket Makers that has been traced to approximately the time of the birth of Christ. The Basket Makers were pit dwellers and are the earliest definitely known ancestors of the people who later became known as the Cliff Dwellers and still later as the Pueblo Indians. Perhaps more to the point is the name by which the Navaho called them, Anasazi, the ancient ones.

Beginning about A.D. 500, the culture of the Basket Makers advanced considerably until, by about 700, they had learned to construct remarkable buildings of adobe brick, and sometimes stone; these were not only single residences but apartments with a great number of units, and structures of other types, including ceremonial chambers, called kivas. The buildings of the Basket Makers came to be known as pueblos, the name by which they are still called. Although the Basket Makers built pueblos on level sites, some of the most spectacular were located on the sides of cliffs and in canyons. In these pueblos, they were relatively safe from enemies. They farmed areas near their cities and hunted elsewhere.

By 1100, these Indians had a very highly developed culture, making pottery and many other kinds of vessels, implements, tools, and weapons; and clothing of skins and woven from cotton and other fibers. But in their architecture, they reached their highest level of accomplishment. Sometime before 1300, these Indians began to leave their cliff and other pueblo homes. No one has determined exactly why they left or where they went. Two theories have been advanced for their departure: increasing attacks by enemies and a severe drought that is known to have occurred during the last quarter of the 13th century. In any case, by 1300, all had departed, probably to be absorbed into other related tribes in the area, now known as the Pueblo Indian tribes.

PRE-COLUMBIAN ARCHITECTURE Spruce Tree House (*c.* 1100), Mesa Verde National Park, Colo. [*Architect: unknown. (David Muench)*]

PRE-COLUMBIAN ARCHITECTURE Cliff Palace (*c.* 1100), Mesa Verde National Park, Colo. [*Architect: unknown. (David Muench)*]

PRE-COLUMBIAN ARCHITECTURE Taos Pueblo (begun *c.* 1300), Taos, N.Mex. [*Architect: unknown. (David Muench)*]

They left a magnificent and spectacular architectural heritage. Some of the greatest of the cliff and other dwellings existing today, at least in part, include: Chaco Canyon, N. Mex. (see also color section), and the Mesa Verde, Colo., perhaps the most magnificent of all; also in New Mexico, Gila Cliff, and Aztec, a misnomer since the Aztecs had nothing to do with this pueblo; and in Arizona, Canyon de Chelly, Kayenta, Montezuma Castle (which the Aztec chieftain never saw), Sunset Crater, Tonto, Walnut Creek Canyon, and Wuptaki.

When the Spanish explorers arrived in the Southwest during the 16th century, they found many descendants of the Anasazi, or their relatives, living in pueblos located on mostly level sites rather than in canyons and on the sides of cliffs. An exception was Acoma, N. Mex., constructed on top of a massive butte and still in existence. Another famous pueblo, still in existence and still inhabited, is located in Taos, N. Mex. Some 30 other pueblos, including those at Laguna and Zuni, N. Mex., are still in existence in Arizona and New Mexico, mostly along the Rio Grande Valley.

Although the architecture of the American Indians has generally influenced that of succeeding eras very little in the United States, the great pueblos of the Southwest did have considerable influence on the early Spanish architecture of that region. And adobe is still widely used in the region for buildings that continue to reflect the early Spanish culture and that of the Anasazi, who preceded them.

Related Articles COLONIAL ARCHITECTURE; HISTORY OF ARCHITECTURE.

Further Reading Bunting, Bainbridge: *Early Architecture in New Mexico,* University of New Mexico Press, Albuquerque, 1976; Current, William, and Vincent Scully: *Pueblo Architecture of the Southwest,* Amon Carter Museum of Western Art, University of Texas, Austin, 1971; Morgan, Lewis H.: *Houses and House Life of American Aborigines,* University of Chicago Press, Chicago, 1965; Muench, David, and Donald G. Pike: *Anasazi—Ancient People of the Rock,* American West Publishing Co., Palo Alto, Calif., 1974.

Sources of Additional Information See listing in the article entitled history of architecture.

PREFABRICATION A system of construction in which standardized components or elements of buildings are manufactured and assembled in factories instead of on building sites. Prefabrication has always been of some importance in architecture. Recently, because of rising costs of construction at building sites, scarcity of skilled craftspersons, the greater precision and efficiency of factories, and the possibility of lower costs, prefabrication construction has become increasingly more important.

Prefabrication is sometimes called industrialized construction, since components are manufactured in factories. Prefabrication is also sometimes called systems building and the use of prefabricated units, systems design or the systems approach to design. The integration of prefabrication systems into the total construction of buildings is often called an industrialized building system.

Types Three major types of prefabrication are important in architecture: components; systems composed of components; and complete, or nearly complete, buildings. A component is usually a relatively small unit, made to be used with other units of the same kind and others in the construction of buildings. A system is a number of such components, joined together in a manner allowing the whole to perform some function or functions. However, it should be remembered that small components, like bricks, may be joined together in a system, such as a wall, that in turn may be considered a component of the structural system of a building. The structure then becomes a component of the entire building system, which is in turn a component of the environment in which it exists.

Thus prefabrication can be seen to be concerned with a large array of products and materials, ranging in size from the smallest manufactured item, such as a nail or other fastener, through a whole spectrum of sizes and complexities, to complete buildings. It is not too difficult, at least in theory, to imagine an even greater extension to groups of buildings and even entire communities.

In practice, prefabrication is of importance in architecture on a somewhat smaller scale. Increasingly, architects and other design professionals must design buildings with manufactured or prefabricated products, over which they exercise no design prerogatives except selection, the products having previously been designed by others beyond the control of architects. Architects may also design with products that are precut to size, such as wood studs or steel beams. In such cases, architects exercise some control over the products to be used. At the next level of complexity, products or components are combined in a process sometimes called preassembly into systems, some of them relatively small and simple, such as windows, some large and complex, such as entire curtain walls for tall buildings. Some of these systems, including most windows today, were designed by others, with architects only making selections from stock types. In other cases, such as curtain walls, architects may either select or design systems, the choice often being determined by function, esthetics, and economics.

Design Practicing architects may design complete prefabricated buildings, but most are designed by the staffs of the companies that produce them. These companies occasionally commission practicing architects to make designs for prefabricated buildings. Because of this situation, many architects are convinced that prefabricated buildings are not good architecture, and that these buildings are in competition with their own. The prefabricated building companies reply that they can provide buildings that are perfectly adequate for many purposes and are acceptable to certain clients at lower cost than those designed by architects; they are more speedily erected, saving the time, energy, and money expended in having buildings designed by architects and constructed by contractors or others. Architects reply that no stock building can be as good as one designed by a competent architect.

Short of selecting complete prefabricated buildings from catalogs, architects and other design professionals find that they must be up to date on the latest components and systems. And many also find that methods may be discovered for combining prefabricated components in new and imaginative ways. As the cost of on-site fabrication and assembly of buildings and their parts continues to rise because of continuing inflation, the use of prefabricated components and systems may be expected to increase. And architects will have to deal with that fact in their designs. Some think this will necessitate a systems approach to design. Others hope that architects will be called upon more frequently to design the components and systems, as they have occasionally in the past. Admittedly, such architects will have to learn the principles of design for industrial production in order to accomplish good designs in this field. A few have done so in the past and some people believe that a greater number of future architects may specialize in design for fabrication of entire buildings as well as components and systems.

History Although prefabricated building construction is often thought of as quite modern, actually such practices began soon after humans constructed their first huts. When the first builder cut poles that were properly sized and transported them to a building site to be erected, the practice of prefabricated construction had its rudimentary beginnings. This was followed by making sun-dried brick in standard sizes so that they could be combined together to make walls and other systems.

Other prefabrication methods were developed over the years, using mostly craft labor and rudimentary machines for the production. Not until after the beginning of the industrial revolution in England, about the middle of the 18th century, did prefabrication, or industrialized building, as practiced today actually start. However, some prefabricated wood houses had been produced in England and shipped to the American colonies and other places early in the 17th century and, by the end of the first quarter of the 18th, such houses were produced in the colonies.

By the middle of the 19th century, buildings were prefabricated not only of wood but also of cast and wrought iron in England, New York, and other places and shipped to countries as far away as Australia. In 1851, with the construction of the Crystal Palace, at the Great Exhibition in London, designed by Sir Joseph Paxton (1801–65), the practice of prefabrication was given a great impetus. For this building, English engineer Sir Charles Fox (1810–74) devised a structural system, with standardized sizes of iron columns and other structural members, including only three sizes of trusses, and with 300,000 panes of window

glass all of the same size. All fit into a planning unit or module of 8 by 8 feet. All the parts of the Crystal Palace were prefabricated, transported to the site, and erected with the aid of machinery. For this very large building, of some 754,000 ft² of ground floor area, the whole process of fabrication and erection was accomplished in nine months, a feat made possible by its modular design, standardized parts, and prefabrication.

The design, prefabrication, and erection of the Crystal Palace was so well done that it was later dismantled and erected again at Sydenham, England, only to be destroyed by fire in 1936. Although the Crystal Palace was not really appreciated as a work of architecture until some 50 years after it was built, it nevertheless had an almost immediate effect on the use of iron and glass in buildings and on standardization and prefabrication of buildings and their parts. Others soon followed, including major ones at the Paris expositions of 1855 and 1889.

By the end of the 19th century, iron and timber prefabricated buildings were relatively common. Some systems even lent themselves to the construction of any of a number of types of buildings, including churches, houses, and stores. Some not only included prefabricated structures, but fronts or facades as well. Prefabrication of iron structures and facades for office and similar buildings was further developed by several people and companies in New York City in the latter half of the 19th century. The best known and most successful was an American inventor, James Bogardus (1800–74), who designed and fabricated a number of such buildings in New York City and in other American cities. Beginning in 1905, another important system of prefabrication, precast concrete, has been used in buildings.

U.S. Prefabrication During the early part of the 20th century, in the United States considerable progress was made in the standardization of building components, such as windows and doors. Some prefabricated buildings were constructed for war workers during World War I, but they were mostly crude and of a temporary nature. After the war, various attempts were made to develop new prefabrication systems for complete buildings. One of the most interesting was a design for an aluminum building, called the Dymaxion House, made in 1927 by Richard Buckminster Fuller (1895–). Designed to be constructed on assembly lines in aircraft plants, idled after World War II, the first prototype was manufactured in 1946. The revolutionary building went into production.

Earlier, the production of trailers, begun in the 1930s, led to the development of mobile homes, fabricated in factories and transported mostly by truck to their sites. Never truly mobile, since most of them are never moved again, mobile homes have become the most successful housing prefabrication system in the United States. Several million people live in them and relatively large numbers are sold each year.

A large number of other prefabricated systems for

PREFABRICATION New Haven Housing (1971), New Haven, Conn. [*Architect: Paul Rudolph. (Joseph W. Molitor)*]

PREFABRICATION Bubble Houses (1954), Hobe Sound, Fla. [*Architect: Eliot Noyes. (Eliot Noyes)*]

houses have been developed in recent years. Although many of these systems, like those of mobile homes, leave much to be desired in terms of esthetic design, many of the systems have been successfully marketed in the United states and elsewhere. And like mobile homes, other prefabricated house systems, because of their lower costs as compared to conventional construction, have made it possible for millions of Americans to own their homes. Some of the most interesting and well-designed prefabricated houses were those designed by Carl Koch (1912–), including his Acorn and Techbuilt houses, introduced in the 1950s.

In prefabricated systems for buildings other than houses, considerable progress has been made in the 20th century, particularly after World War II. Industrial and other types of buildings of precast concrete, timber, and metals have been developed and are widely available. Components such as curtain walls of metals and other materials have come into widespread use and have been considerably improved over the years. Completely fabricated in factories and often delivered to building sites in large assemblies, such curtain walls are not only improvements over older types of walls but may often be more inexpensively manufactured and can be erected quickly. Just how quickly, if need be, was demonstrated by the erection, perhaps mostly as a publicity stunt, of an entire aluminum curtain wall on a tall building in New York City in a single day in 1954.

Precast concrete units have been widely used in buildings in recent years. These include both very large wall and other structural panels, and complete rooms, prefabricated in their entirety and lifted into place in buildings like blocks. Similar systems have been developed in other materials.

One of the most important recent developments in prefabrication has been the gradual increase of open system components and other building elements. As opposed to a closed system, in which components and elements may be interchanged only with those in the same system, open system components and elements are designed and manufactured to fit together properly in a great variety of ways and systems.

Great impetus was given to open system prefabrication in the 1930s and 1940s by the development of a dimensional coordination system for buildings and their components and other elements. Called modular coordination, the system was started by an American manufacturer, Albert Farwell Bemis (1870–1936), in the 1920s and later continued by the Modular Building Standards and the American Standards associations. Their work resulted in standards for building components and building dimensions, based on a module of 4 in. The system was later adopted in other countries. In countries using the metric system, a module of 100 mm (millimeters), slightly less than 4 in, was adopted. Modular standards have gradually made it possible for building components to fit together properly in generally open systems. And the standards have also made design, detailing, and drafting for buildings more efficient.

Many interesting and important improvements in design for prefabrication have recently taken place in many parts of the world, including England, the Soviet Union, and the United States. One of the most interesting and important was a program called School Construction Systems Development (SCSD), during the 1960s. Under the direction of Ezra D. Ehrenkrantz (1932–), the SCSD program produced, with cooperation of manufacturers of various components and systems and with funds provided by Educational Facilities Laboratories, a series of 13 schools in California, designed specifically as demonstrations of a systems approach to building prefabrication. These schools were notable not only for their rather complete use of prefabrication but for the integration of lighting, heating, and other comfort systems within the overall systems of structure and other elements.

Today in the United States, as elsewhere, prefabrication of all kinds is growing rapidly. Hundreds of thousands of mobile homes are produced each year, and it is estimated that about one-fourth of all American families now live in prefabricated houses of some kind. What are sometimes called pre-engineered buildings, for many purposes, are widely available. And the number of prefabricated components and systems increases as time passes. Many architects believe that the advent of widespread prefabrication is not an unmixed blessing. Admitting that factory production of building components has many desirable aspects, they are less than happy as they envision the possibilities for a faceless, dehumanized, standardized environment.

Related Articles BOGARDUS, JAMES; BUILDING INDUSTRY; FULLER, RICHARD BUCKMINSTER; HOUSE; Articles on various building components and systems.

Further Reading Cutler, Laurence Stephan, and Sherrie Stephens Cutler: *Handbook of Housing Systems for Designers and Developers,* Van Nostrand Reinhold, New York, 1974; Dietz, Albert G. H., and Laurence Stephan Cutler: *Industrialized Building Systems for Housing,* MIT Press, Cambridge, 1971; Lewicki, Bohdan: *Building with Large Prefabricates,* American Elsevier, New York, 1966.

Sources of Further Information Educational Facilities Laboratory, 850 Third Ave., New York, N. Y. 10022; Manufactured Housing Inst., 14650 Lee Road, Chantilly, Va. 22021; Metal Building Manufacturers Assoc., 1230 Keith Bldg., Cleveland, Ohio 44115.

PRESERVATION Taking appropriate actions to prevent further changes or deterioration in a site, building, group of buildings, or other structure. Thus preservation accepts sites, buildings, or other structures generally as they exist and does not attempt to make changes for historic or similar reasons. An architect who does preservation work on buildings is often called a preservationist, as are other people interested in the subject.

Definitions Some confusion exists about the precise meanings of some of the processes related to preservation work. Repairs are work performed on a building in order to correct problems that may further injure it. Restoration is the rehabilitation of a building in a manner that will closely approximate its state when it was first constructed or at some other time in its history. Reconstruction means the construction of a new building that resembles an old building as closely as possible, on the basis of studies of historic, archeological, and other types of evidence. Remodeling means rehabilitation of, or making changes in, a building without any particular regard to its history or original form. A recent type of rehabilitation, sometimes called adaptive use or recycling, involves changing a building that was originally designed for certain functions into one to be used for different functions, for example, a barn into a house or a warehouse into an apartment building.

In preservation work, it is often said that the best and most honest procedure is that of preservation, if at all possible, followed in descending order of desirability by repairs, restoration, and reconstruction. A wide range of opinion exists on the subject of specific buildings that should be preserved, restored, or reconstructed. At one extreme end of the range are those who have no interest in their historic or architectural heritage and do not care if anything is saved. At the other extreme are those who think everything from the past is worth preserving.

Yet even among those who are dedicated, there is considerable difference of opinion. Some believe that the buildings worth saving are those considered to be excellent architecture. Others believe that buildings of historic interest should be saved. The most widely held and accepted view is that buildings, groups of buildings, other structures, and sites that make cultural contributions to society should be preserved, that those of historic or architectural significance, or both, should be saved. This philosophy still leaves room for debate, some maintaining that sites of single events, such as the Wright brothers' first flight at Kitty Hawk, N. C., the birthplace of a president, or some other place, should be preserved, restored, or reconstructed, while others may disagree. The debate will no doubt continue.

Many architects are involved in some kind of preservation work. To do effective work in this field, they must be scholars as well as architects. For such work to have authenticity, architects must understand the background of the building upon which they will work, not only the architectural background but the historic, together with the lives, manners, goals, and other characteristics of the people who first constructed the building and those who occupied it. Such pursuits are of great interest to some architects, but not to others. Those of no particular historic bent, who are not willing to spend time in study and research, and who are not willing to sublimate their own creative talents to those of the architect or other designer of the original building, should leave preservation work to persons who do have the requisites.

Research The process of preservation, restoration, or reconstruction begins with research. The amount and depth of the research required varies considerably. For example, if only repairs and modest rehabilitation are to be undertaken, the research might be minimal. On the other hand, if a reconstruction is to be attempted, research might begin with the remains, if any, of the foundation of the former building and extend to searches of old records, documents, books, and many other sources limited only by the abilities and imagination of the researcher

Research is of three major types: historic, archeological, and architectural. Historic research involves investigation of every source that might yield information on the building, its builders, and those who lived in it or used it and their times. Archeological research involves investigation of the site of the building for artifacts and other remains that may then be identified, preserved, restored, cataloged, and studied. Architectural research is involved with the character and dates of the building, its details, and site.

Such research is usually initiated at the beginning of a project and often proceeds during the entire process until the construction work has been completed. Based on the initial research, a program may be prepared for the work, outlining the goals to be achieved and methods for reaching them. First, the importance of the building must be established, along with the facts of its plan, structure, size, location, and so on. Next, the use to which the building will be put must be determined. Although many of these buildings are used as museums, the trend today is often toward other and more vital uses, such as offices, homes, information centers, and so on. Care must be taken not to destroy the architecture of these buildings in order to provide such uses.

Once the use has been determined, the next important decision is the date or era to which the building will be returned. In some cases, this may be the time in which it was originally constructed; in others, it might be some time of historic importance. In still others, a decision might be made to retain some elements of each of the various eras in a building's history. The selection should be made with extreme care and should be based on thorough and painstaking research. After the purpose has been determined, the use to which the building will be put must be examined in detail. If it is to become a museum, what are the requirements for large groups, offices, storage, or spaces of other types?

Preparatory Phases Other than the requirements for scholarly research and the translation of the research into period construction that will appear authentic, architectural services in preservation, restoration, and reconstruction are generally similar to those for other buildings. There is one great difference and that is the necessity for keeping scrupulous records, written and graphic, of everything discovered about the buildings through research and during the construction.

After the completion of a program for a building, the next steps are preparing a schematic design, along with preliminary specifications; developing them more fully, during the design development phase; and preparing contract documents, working drawings and specifications from which the work can be constructed. Cost estimates are also prepared.

Contracts for the construction are then bid or negotiated and the actual construction may begin. All these phases are similar to those for other buildings, except that in this work, there are unusual requirements for old materials and objects to be found or reproduced and for a very high level of craftsmanship. During the construction phase, the architect ordinarily spends more time than he would on that of a new building of relatively the same size and complexity. As construction work proceeds, parts of the building are revealed, often furnishing bits of information that will be useful in later work or problems that could not have been foreseen. Old parts must be carefully removed, numbered, cataloged, and stored. A major

problem, of course, is in finding contractors interested in this sort of work and skilled craftsmen to execute the work.

After a building has been completed, there remain a few other services the architect may perform, including sometimes the interior design and furnishing of the building. Another important service is the provision for display of features of the building, such as characteristic details, various types of construction, unique features, and the like. Information on good operating and maintenance practices should be furnished to the owner. An architectural record should also be prepared, completely illustrating and documenting the work that has been performed, including what was done, and why and how. Copies of such reports should be filed in the Historic Buildings Survey section of the U.S. Library of Congress, Washington.

Historic Sites Literally thousands of buildings and other structures of historic or architectural importance have been preserved, restored, or reconstructed in the United States, including whole towns, or parts of them, as in the Vieux Carré, New Orleans, La.; Williamsburg, Va.; and Sturbridge Village, Mass. Many thousands of others have been destroyed for economic reasons, as the old Pennsylvania Station (1910), New York City, designed by McKim, Mead and White; or allowed to collapse into ruins, as the great houses of Rosewell Hall (1740) in Gloucester, Va., by an unknown architect, and Belle Grove (1857), Iberville Parish, La., designed by James Gallier, Jr. (1827–68), two of the many truly great houses that have been lost through neglect. Many other buildings are still in need of preservation or restoration, and their chances of survival are probably better today than at any other time in the history of the United States, mainly because of laws passed in recent years by the states and the national government and efforts of dedicated preservationists. In spite of these efforts, many significant buildings continue to be demolished all over the country.

Laws Preservation began early in the United States, though at first it was almost completely confined to sites and buildings of importance in the early history of the country. About the middle of the 19th century, preservation work accelerated as a result of the efforts of governments and individuals. By the early 20th century, various laws had been passed attempting to encourage preservation, among them the National Antiquities Act of 1909. Also organizations dedicated to preservation were founded about that time or somewhat earlier, including the Society for the Preservation of New England Antiquities and the Association for the Preservation of Virginia Antiquities.

Starting in 1933, the work of preservation has been helped enormously by the Historic American Buildings Survey (HABS). Beginning in that year, HABS has systematically collected data, photographs, and drawings of buildings and other structures all over the United States and its territories. Administered by the

PRESERVATION Exterior, Colonial Capitol (1705, burned, rebuilt, burned again, reconstructed 1934), Williamsburg, Va. [*Architect: uncertain, but may have been Sir Christopher Wren.* [*Architects of reconstruction: Perry, Shaw and Hepburn. (Colonial Williamsburg Photograph)*]

PRESERVATION Interior, Colonial Capitol, General Court room. [*Architect: unknown. Architects of reconstruction: Perry, Shaw and Hepburn. (Colonial Williamsburg Photograph)*]

PRESERVATION Exterior, Raleigh Tavern (1735, burned 1859, reconstructed 1932), Williamsburg, Va. [*Architect: unknown. Architects of reconstruction: Perry, Shaw and Hepburn. (Colonial Williamsburg Photograph)*]

PRESERVATION Interior, Raleigh Tavern, Apollo Room. [*Architect: unknown. Architects of reconstruction: Perry, Shaw and Hepburn. (Colonial Williamsburg Photograph)*]

PRESERVATION George Reid, formerly Captain Orr, House (c. 1782), Williamsburg, Va. [*Architect: unknown. (Colonial Williamsburg Photograph)*]

PRESERVATION Smokehouse at Reid House. [*Architect: unknown. (Colonial Williamsburg Photograph)*]

National Park Service of the U.S. Department of the Interior, under an agreement with the American Institute of Architects and with the Library of Congress, where the records are deposited, HABS has collected information on more than 16,000 buildings. In 1935 the National Historic Sites Act was passed, establishing a list of a number of sites to be protected and preserved.

In 1949 the National Trust for Historic Preservation was chartered by the U.S. Congress for such purposes as the collection and provision of information, consulting services, publishing of materials, grants, and preservation and maintenance of a number of historic buildings. With over 100,000 members, the National Trust does much to encourage and promote preservation. In addition, there are many other groups, on local, state, and national levels, involved in such work. Several hundred government programs are involved in preservation in some way and most states have preservation commissions.

In 1966 the National Historic Preservation Act gave a giant boost to preservation. It expanded the list of historic sites into a National Register of Historic Places that now includes some 15,000 properties considered significant. In general, these properties must be more than 50 years old, but significant later ones may be exempted from this requirement. The act also established an Advisory Committee on Historic Preservation, composed of people in government and in private life, to advise the president and Congress. Most importantly, the act established funds for grants to the National Trust and to the states for preservation work, millions of dollars of which have been spent since the first grants in 1968. Many other federal and state programs that encourage preservation and aid in its funding have since been established. A very important one is the Tax Reform Act of 1976, which establishes tax incentives for those who rehabilitate historic structures and tax penalties for those who demolish such structures.

For people who have a deep interest in history as well as architecture, preservation work can be very rewarding. Some people, including a number of architects, specialize in this work. In order to prepare themselves to handle the many requirements, specialized training is required, especially in general history, archeology, and the other social sciences as well as architectural history. Many architectural schools offer electives of value in preservation work and a few offer specialization in the field and specialized degrees.

Related Articles ARCH; COLUMN; DOME; SOCIAL SCIENCE; VAULT; Various articles on history and architects.

Further Reading Bullock, Orin M., Jr.: *The Restoration Manual—An Illustrated Guide to the Preservation and Restoration of Old Buildings,* Silvermine Publishers, Norwalk, Conn., 1966, *Historic American Buildings Survey—Catalog of the Measured Drawings and Photographs of the Survey in the Library of Congress, March 1, 1941,* U.S. Government Printing Office, Washington, D.C., 1941, catalog supplement, 1959, catalogs by states, National Trust for Historic

Preservation, Tony P. Wrenn and Elizabeth D. Mulloy: *America's Forgotten Architecture,* Pantheon Books, a division of Random House, New York, 1976; Noel-Hume, Ivor: *Historical Archaeology—A Comprehensive Guide for both Amateurs and Professionals to the Techniques and Methods of Excavating Historical Sites,* Alfred A. Knopf, New York, 1969.

Sources of Additional Information The Historic American Buildings Survey, National Park Service, Department of the Interior, Washington, D.C. 20240; Library of Congress, Division of Prints and Photographs, Washington, D.C. 20450; National Trust for Historic Preservation, 1785 Massachusetts Ave., N.W., Washington, D.C. 20036.

Periodicals *American Preservation,* 620 E. Sixth St., Little Rock, Ark. 72203; *Historic Preservation* and *Preservation News,* both at 1785 Massachusetts Ave., N.W., Washington, D.C. 20036.

PRISON A building, or group of buildings, in which people convicted or accused of breaking the law may be confined. Prisons, including jails and other types, have been designed by architects since about the 16th century. Although they never comprised a building type of great numbers, prisons have been an important fact of life since that time and a number of architects have contributed to improvements in their design.

Types Prisons may be classified into three major types: lockups, jails, and correctional institutions. Lockups are usually part of police stations operated by municipalities and are used for holding people, temporarily, for investigation, hearings, or trials. Jails are usually operated by cities or counties and are used both for temporary detention, as in lockups, and for people serving sentences of less than one year. Correctional institutions, sometimes called prisons or penitentiaries, are usually operated by a state or federal government and are used for those serving sentences longer than one year, and in the case of federal institutions, for those convicted of federal crimes. There are several specialized types of correctional institutions, including maximum-security and minimum-security prisons and special detention facilities for children, formerly called reform schools or reformatories, now usually called juvenile halls or homes. There are also special institutions for convicts who are physically or mentally ill.

Controversial Principles Prisons are as controversial as are the concepts of law and order, punishment, and rehabilitation. Authorities have debated these principles for a very long time. On the one hand, there are those who espouse retribution and punishment, including prison terms, for those convicted of breaking laws. Some argue that such punishment acts as a deterrent to crime. On the other side are those who believe that the risk of punishment does not deter crime and that prison sentences may help make hardened criminals out of wrongdoers, who happened to commit crimes but who have not actually embarked on lives of criminality. The social costs of imprisonment are very high indeed, but are immeasurable. The economic costs are more easily understood. It costs more for a person to spend four years in San Quentin, a California state prison, than four years at Harvard University. Because of the controversies surrounding the whole subject of law and order and of justice, design philosophy for prisons has also become quite controversial.

Elements The design of prisons may be as simple as the provision of a few cells in a small police station lockup to the major problems of large maximum-security prisons, which in addition to housing prisoners in cells must have most of the elements of a complete city. The major elements of all but the smallest prisons are housing, dining services, recreation, reception and discharge, visiting, and administration.

Housing for inmates may be of several types, dependent on the type of institution and its security requirements. Housing units include interior cells usually back to back in the center of cell blocks and exterior cells on outside walls. Cells are usually barred and are equipped with toilet fixtures. Other types of housing include individual rooms, and dormitories, shared by up to 30 inmates. Near the inmate housing, other facilities are often provided, including dayrooms for recreation.

Dining services must be provided not only for the inmates, but for the prison staff. Such facilities may include central dining halls, localized dining halls near the various cell-block units, and dining in the cells. The latter is considered the least desirable.

Correctional services include facilities for counseling, clinical testing and treatment, academic and vocational education, and inmate work areas. Inmate services include libraries, commissaries, barber and beauty shops, and chapels. Medical services include facilities for medical, psychiatric, and dental care of both bed and ambulatory patients. Recreational facilities include provisions indoors for sports, physical education, games, moving pictures, and other activities, and provisions outdoors for exercise, sports, and games.

The reception and discharge element has provisions for booking in and out prisoners, storage of prisoners' clothing and other property, medical examinations, issue of prison clothing, and fingerprinting and photographing. Visiting facilities may be closed, with inmates and visitors completely separated physically, but able to see each other through tempered glass and to talk using telephones; and open, either indoors or outdoors, allowing normal contact. Administration includes offices and other facilities for the warden, guards, and other officials of the prison.

The proper design of a prison involves provision of all the elements required and establishment of proper relationships between them. In addition, the design must provide adequate security against escape by inmates, for inmates from each other, prison property, and the administrative personnel. The degree of security required varies considerably between institutions of different types. For example, a maximum-security prison is completely surrounded by a strong wall or fence, with guards patrolling it and others manning towers that overlook the entire facility. In-

mates are housed in individual cells blocks each with its own toilet facilities. On the other hand, a minimum-security prison might have no walls, fences, or towers and the inmates might be housed in open dormitories or individual rooms. Sometimes a single institution houses inmates of varying security risks, and various areas of the complex have provisions for security at maximum, medium, and minimum levels.

In any prison, there must be provisions for proper communications, often including closed-circuit television and paging and public address systems as well as telephone and alarm systems. In addition, provision of secure locking systems and control of their keys is a necessity.

History In the earliest times, there were no prisons. Punishment of criminals took other forms. Beginning about the 12th century, prisons were established for certain kinds of offenders. Some of the great castles incorporated dungeons or keeps. The Tower of London, completed in the late 12th century and added on to later, is one of the best-known fortress-castles incorporating a keep in which, for centuries, illustrious prisoners were jailed. Prisoners in the Tower include two wives of Henry VIII (1491–1547), Anne Boleyn (born 1507, beheaded 1536) and Catherine Howard (born about 1520, beheaded

PRISON Metropolitan Correction Center and Federal Courthouse Annex (1975), Chicago, Ill. [*Architect: Harry Weese. (Hedrich-Blessing)*]

PRISON Cook County Correction Center (1976), Chicago, Ill. [*Architects: A. Epstein and Sons. (Hedrich-Blessing)*]

PRISON Marion Prison (1964), Marion, Ill. [*Architects: Hellmuth, Obata and Kassabaum. (Hedrich-Blessing)*]

1542). Other famous inmates were the great English statesman and writer Sir Thomas More (born 1478, beheaded 1535), Lady Jane Grey (born 1537, proclaimed queen in 1553, imprisoned in the Tower 10 days later, and beheaded in 1554), and Sir Walter Raleigh (would-be colonizer of North Carolina and Virginia, born about 1552, beheaded 1618).

Another famous early prison was the Bastille (built in the 14th century) in Paris. It too jailed many famous prisoners, including a French government official, Nicolas Fouquet (1615–80), thought to be the model for *The Man in the Iron Mask*, written by Alexandre Dumas (1802–70), and the great writer Voltaire (1694–1778), the assumed name of François Marie Arouet. The prison was destroyed by a mob on July 14, 1789, the date marking the beginning of the French Revolution, and later celebrated as the French national holiday, Bastille Day.

Other prisons were built later, but in the 16th and 17th centuries a new method was widely employed:

the prison ship or galley rowed by prisoners. Houses of correction were used, starting in the 16th century, mostly for people awaiting trials. Another innovation was the debtor prison for confining those who owed money. In most of the early prisons, sanitation was almost nonexistent and overcrowding was the rule. Treatment of prisoners was inhumane and corporal punishment was widely practiced. Prison reforms later changed these conditions, starting about the end of the 18th century, by which time imprisonment had been adopted as the most generally used method of punishment.

American Development The early colonists in America built jails, houses of correction, and debtor's prisons, and conditions in them were no better than they were in Europe, until prison reforms started in the 1800s. A number of famous American architects designed prisons, including the Walnut Street Prison (1776), Philadelphia, by Robert Smith (1722–77), since demolished; the Virginia State Prison (1800), Richmond, by Benjamin Henry Latrobe (1764–1820); Moy-amensing Prison (1835), Philadelphia, by Thomas Ustick Walter (1804–87); the Tombs (1838), New York City, designed by John Haviland (1792–1852), and later destroyed; and the Allegheny County Jail (1888), Pittsburgh, by Henry Hobson Richardson (1838–86). Many of the early prisons were Egyptian in appearance, which their architects seemed to think was proper to their purpose, but Richardson changed to Romanesque. Early American architects also designed jails, as have their later counterparts. Then, and today, jails were often associated with courthouses and almost every early American country seat had a building of each type.

Related Articles Latrobe, Benjamin Henry; Richardson, Henry Hobson; Walter, Thomas Ustick.

PROGRAMMING The process involved in developing a statement of the requirements, conditions, and goals, and of methods for satisfying these aims, in a proposed building. An architectural program is a report containing information of this type. Before a problem of any kind, including an architectural design problem, can be solved, it is necessary to know what the problem is. Then steps may be taken to solve it. Thus in architecture, the process of design is the solving of architectural problems, and the process of programming is the determination of the problems to be solved. This is also the case in other types of design involved in architecture. For example, interior designers, landscape architects, and city planners prepare both programs and designs.

Scientific Method Although not always recognized as such, even by architects, architectural problem solving utilizes what is known as the scientific method, a system for problem solving thought to have been first used by the Italian astronomer and scientist Galileo Galilei (1564–1642), called simply Galileo. The scientific method involves five major steps for orderly problem solving: statement of the problem; formulation of a hypothesis, or tentative theory; collection of data through observation and experimentation; testing and interpretation of the data; and drawing conclusions.

In architecture, the process is often broken down somewhat differently into six steps: definition of the problem; establishment of objectives; collection of data; analysis of the problem; consideration of possible solutions; and solution of the problem. The first four steps of the problem-solving process are included in architectural programming. The last two steps, which are involved in the solution of the problem, are included in architectural design. In other words, the steps in architectural programming might be said to include establishment of goals to be achieved and needs to be met, collection and analysis of data, development of concepts expected to lead to the solution of problems, and a statement of the problems.

The process in programming is collection and analysis of data, or the separation of the problem and the information gathered into their constituent parts or elements so that they may be studied. The process in design, is composition, or synthesis: putting together the component parts or elements to form a whole, in other words, a building. In the complex world of architecture today, good building design depends on good programming, even for smaller building types such as houses.

In practice, architectural programming occurs in three major ways: by building owners, if they have competent staffs and construct numerous buildings; by architects, based on data furnished by their clients; and by architects, who handle the entire process. Although some buildings are still designed today without adequate programs, many architects believe so strongly in programming that they will not undertake commissions that do not include it; and many prefer to handle the processes themselves to ensure they are performed properly and thoroughly. In all these cases, it is necessary for architects to work closely and smoothly with clients' representatives.

Data Classifications The goals and needs of owners of proposed buildings must be clearly understood by architects performing programming functions. These are determined through conferences, study, and analysis. Many types of data are ordinarily required in programming; the amounts and types required depend on the type of building, its size and complexity, and other factors. The kinds of data required may be generally classified into six major groups: area or regional characteristics of the surroundings of the building site; the site itself; user needs and goals; budgets and other financial information; concepts for problem solving, or design; and schedules. Each of these categories may include many types of information. For example, site and related information ordinarily includes property boundaries, easements, and locations of natural features (rocks and trees), walkways, streets, curbs, pits, ditches, electrical and telephone posts and services, elevations and contour lines, subsoil conditions, views, prevailing winds, and so on. The programmer must determine which items of information will be required in each category and then gather the data.

After going through all the steps of programming, the program itself may be prepared. A program may be used for several purposes. First, it is used to demonstrate to the client what is involved in the project, and the program itself is subject to approval by the client. Second, the program may be used to explain the project to those expected to finance it, those who will use it, and others. Finally, the program serves as a guide for design by the architects and other design professionals involved in the work.

A program may take one of several forms, according to the preferences of those who prepare it and those who will use it, and the requirements of the project. However, as a guide, a program might be organized in a manner similar to the following outline.

Outline of Program

I. Introduction
   A. Programming work performed and how
   B. Work performed by whom
   C. Outline of report
II. Goals and Objectives
   A. Architectural
   B. Operational
III. Data
   A. Use
   B. Site
   C. Climate
   D. Regulations
   E. Legal
IV. Concepts
   A. Organization
   B. Space requirements
   C. Functions
   D. Operations
   E. Land requirements
   F. Equipment
V. Economics
   A. Budgets
   B. Schedules
   C. Project phases
VI. Problems
   A. Architectural
   B. Operational

Programs for specific buildings may vary considerably from the outline, but most will generally follow its concepts. As may be seen in the outline, the final category of information in a program constitutes a set of premises upon which the design of a building may be based. Thus a program is not an end in itself, but a tool used in the process of designing and constructing buildings. Also a program should not be thought of as a self-contained product or a procedure that takes place before design, and that design is another self-contained procedure that follows programming. In fact, the two are closely related and intertwined.

Some architects view programming procedures as part of the design process and believe that both should be performed by the same people, while other architects believe that programming (mostly analysis) and design (mostly synthesis) require different kinds of talents. In the first instance, programming and design might be performed by an architectural designer. In the second, a programmer would do the programming, a designer the design. The most important thing, however, is the preparation of informative and well-studied programs upon which creative designs may be based, regardless of who performs the various functions and how they are accomplished. Programming is also widely used in architectural schools for design problems to be solved by students. Sometimes a design professor furnishes a program to students; in other cases, students prepare the programs.

Programming has become such an important, even essential, part of architecture today that it is hard to imagine how architects functioned without it. Yet it is believed that no architectural programs were prepared for buildings until about the middle of the 19th century. And it is only in the past few decades that programming of the sort described above has come into widespread use. Today no important building, and very few minor ones, would be started without first preparing a program. And the process of programming has been greatly eased and expanded by use of computers for storage and retrieval of large amounts of data.

Related Articles COMPUTER; DESIGN, ARCHITECTURAL; FEASIBILITY STUDY; PRACTICE OF ARCHITECTURE.

Further Reading Paterson, John: *Information Methods for Design and Construction,* John Wiley, London and New York, 1977; Pena, William, William Caudill, and John Focke: *Problem Seeking—An Architectural Programming Primer,* Cahners, Boston, 1977; Sanoff, Henry: *Methods of Architectural Programming,* Dowden, Hutchinson & Ross, Stroudsburg, Pa., 1977; Wade, John W.: *Architecture, Problems & Purposes—Architectural Design as a Basic Problem-Solving Process,* John Wiley, New York, 1977.

PUBLIC BUILDING A type of building, or group of buildings, owned and operated by a governing body, and often occupied by a governmental agency. Government buildings exist on every level, from the borough or town to the city, county, state, and federal.

Some government buildings are similar to those in use by private organizations. Other government buildings are uniquely related to functions that are purely governmental. Some of the major types are city and town halls, courthouses, fire and police stations, state capitols and related buildings, embassies, and the Capitol and other buildings of the national capital, Washington, D.C.

The U.S. Capital The capital of the United States is unique. It contains a great many public buildings of all sorts, many of them magnificent buildings by talented architects, others not up to that level. The greatest is undoubtedly the U.S. Capitol, upon which construction work and design and redesign have been going on since the competition for its design was won by an amateur architect, Dr. William Thornton (1759–1828), in 1792. For further discussion on the many interesting and important government buildings in Washington, see the article entitled, capital, United States.

State Capitols State capitol buildings are not an important building type today since none is being built. The latest was the State Capitol of Hawaii (1969), designed by John Carl Warnecke (1919–) in association with Belt, Lemmon and Lo. Many of the capitols were designed by eminent architects, starting in colonial times, and some are distinguished architecture. One of the most notable of the early buildings is the Colonial Capitol (1705), Williamsburg, Va., burned in 1749, and reconstructed in 1931. It may have been designed by the noted English architect Sir Christopher Wren (1632–1723). Others are Independence Hall (1755), Philadelphia, formerly the State House of Pennsylvania, designed by Edmund Woolley (1696–

1771); the Maryland State House (1772), Annapolis, by Joseph Horatio Anderson (d. 1781); the Massachusetts State House (1798), Boston, designed by Charles Bulfinch (1763–1844); and the Capitol of Virginia (1791), designed by Thomas Jefferson (1743–1826). Notable later capitols include those of Tennessee (1859), by William Strickland (1788–1854); Rhode Island (1901), by McKim, Mead and White; Minnesota (1905), by Cass Gilbert (1859–1934); Wisconsin (1917), by George Browne Post (1837–1913); and Nebraska (1928), by Bertram Grosvenor Goodhue (1869–1924).

Governors' Residences State governments build many other types of buildings, including office buildings and colleges. Some notable residences for governors include the Governor's Palace (1614), Santa Fe, N.Mex.; the Governor's Palace (1749), San Antonio, Tex., reconstructed in 1931; the Governor's Palace (1720), Williamsburg, Va., reconstructed in 1933, all by unknown architects; and the Governor's Palace (1767), New Bern, N.C., by John Hawks (1731–90), burned in 1798, and reconstructed in 1959.

Town and City Halls These halls are still being built today, though not in great numbers. Their major elements are departments requiring considerable contact with the public, those requiring contact on occasion, those requiring contact for special purposes, city council chambers, offices for officials including mayors and city managers, storage, rest rooms, locker rooms and related facilities, and mechanical and electrical equipment spaces. Often a city or town hall also has courtroom facilities.

Such departments as those of tax collectors require frequent contact; departments such as building permits or city planning require contact on occasion; police and fire departments require contact for special purposes. In the design of city and town halls, emphasis must be put upon providing the special kinds of facilities needed by different departments, placing them in the proper relationships to each other, and locating them according to needs for contact with the public. In localities where town meetings, gatherings of voters, are held, special provision for this purpose must be made in town halls.

City and town halls were constructed in Europe in very early times and this tradition was later followed in America, when towns and cities started to grow. A great number of architects have designed such buildings and continue to do so today. In colonial America, there were no town halls in most of the country, other than New England, since the earliest local seats of government were usually counties.

A number of early town halls are still in existence, including that in Marblehead, Mass. (1727); Fairfield, Conn. (1794), later restored; Wilmington, Del. (1798), designed by Peter Baudry; and the Cabildo (1799), New Orleans, La. Later city and town halls of note include that in New York City (1812) by Joseph François Mangin (d. 1818) and John McComb, Jr. (1761–1853); the old City Hall (1850), New Orleans, La., by James Gallier, Sr. (1798–1868), now called the Gallier Build-

ing; the Old Boston City Hall (1865), by G. J. F. Bryant (1816–99) and Arthur Delevan Gilman (1821–82); Baltimore (1875), by George A. Frederick (1842–1924); Philadelphia (1890), by John McArthur Jr. (1823–90); and San Francisco (1915), by Bakewell and Brown.

A striking and innovative new city hall (1969) for Boston was designed by Gerhard M. Kallmann (1915–   ), Noel M. McKinnell, and Edward F. Knowles (1929–   ) in association with Campbell, Aldrich and McNulty.

Customs Houses Customs houses are much like other office buildings and the principles of their design are similar. This is a venerable building type and American architects have designed notable examples since colonial days. An early Customs House (1715) by an unknown architect still exists at Yorktown, Va. Other interesting examples that survive include the Customs House (1770) at Williamsburg, Va., by Robert Smith (1722–77); the Exchange and Customs House (1771), Charleston, S.C., by Samuel Cardy (d. 1774) and William Rigby Naylor (d. 1773); and the Customs House (1841), New York City, by Ithiel Town (1784–1844) and Alexander Jackson Davis (1803–92), later used as a subtreasury building and now called the Federal Hall National Memorial. Over the years, a number of mints have been built in various locations, including Charlotte, N.C., Denver, Colo., New Orleans, and San Francisco.

Courthouses These constitute an important building type. The highest court in the country is the U.S. Supreme Court, in Washington, which occupies a building, completed in 1935, designed by Cass Gilbert (1859–1934). Other federal courts include district courts, which hold trials for federal cases, and courts of appeals, which hear appeals from district courts. Special federal courts include the Court of Claims and the Customs Court. On the state level, the highest courts are the state supreme courts, and some states have appeal courts on the next lower level. Trial courts include county and municipal courts and, on the lowest level, the courts of justices of the peace, police courts, and special courts, such as those for probate proceedings.

The design of courthouses, on all levels, includes all or most of the following elements: one or more courtrooms; one or more judge's suites; court officers' offices; jury rooms; and witnesses' rooms. In addition there may be libraries, press rooms, assembly rooms, conference rooms, and other spaces. Criminal courts also require holding cells for the accused and related facilities for the use of marshals and other law officers. The design of courthouses is quite complex. There are a number of diverse functions to be performed in them. There are times when the performers must come together, as in the courtroom during trial appearances, and times when they must be strictly separated from each other, as when juries or prisoners are not in court.

Courts have existed from ancient times. At first the courts were held by rulers or religious officials in their

PUBLIC BUILDING Orange County Government Center (1970),
Goshen, N.Y. [*Architect: Paul Rudolph. (Joseph W. Molitor)*]

PUBLIC BUILDING United Nations Headquarters (1950), New York,
N.Y. [*Architects: Wallace K. Harrison, Le Corbusier, Oscar Niemeyer,
Sven Markelius, and others. (Joseph W. Molitor)*]

palaces, in churches, or in other locations. By the Middle Ages, it had become the custom in England for officials to travel around the country holding court in various local buildings. By the time of the English settlements in America, special courthouse buildings were constructed and this practice was followed in the colonies. In many cases, the judges still traveled to the localities to hold court and this practice still exists, to some degree, today. For the most part, courthouses and the judges and other officials hold court in fixed locations at the municipal, county, state, and federal levels.

In colonial America, a courthouse was built in almost every county. Some still exist, including a remarkable series in Virginia, thought to have been designed by Richard Taliaferro, pronounced Toliver (1705–79). If he were in fact the architect, he was prolific indeed. In addition to many other buildings, he designed at least eight courthouses, including four that still exist in the counties of Charles City (1730), King William (1746), Hanover (1750), and Isle of Wight (1750). Many interesting courthouses have been designed since by architects all over the country.

Fire Stations Firehouses are an interesting building type. There are two major types: those operated by paid fire department employees, and those operated by volunteers. The design of both types is essentially the same, the major difference being in the facilities required for the personnel. The main elements of a fire station are the apparatus room, where the fire vehicles are housed, and the personnel areas. In an apparatus room, space is provided for one or more vehicles. Since hook-and-ladder aerial trucks might be 70 ft long, they require considerable space. Also in the apparatus rooms are the watch station, or room, rack or tower for drying hoses, facilities for storing and drying fire-fighting clothing, rest rooms, mechanical and electrical equipment areas, and sliding poles. Facilities for the personnel include sleeping quarters, cooking and dining areas, lockers, rest rooms and showers, study rooms, libraries, and recreational facilities.

In a fire station manned by volunteers, frequently a hall for meetings and social events is provided, and space for rescue vehicles is often required. In these stations, sleeping facilities are not usually required, unless the fire company employs paid drivers.

The history of fire fighting is as old as the history of the use of fire by humans. Pumping machines of various sorts were used in ancient Egypt in the second century B.C., and the Romans later invented improved machines. Hand-held squirt guns were used in 17th-century England, until mechanical pumps operated by levers and treadles were introduced about the middle of that century. Soon afterward, machines of this sort were brought to colonial America. Horse-drawn, steam-operated fire vehicles came into use in both Europe and the United States about mid-19th century, but were gradually replaced by engine-powered vehicles in the 20th century.

Police Stations These stations may be in separate buildings or incorporated into city or town halls. They usually have lockups or jails and police courts incorporated into them. Police stations may be quite small, in small towns, or quite large, in large cities. In either case, the major elements are administrative operations, divisional operations, prisoner facilities, public facilities, rest rooms and other personnel facilities, courts, storage, and mechanical and equipment spaces.

Administrative operations include offices and other facilities for the chief and other officials, and spaces for training, photographing and fingerprinting, communications, and record keeping. Divisional operations require spaces for the various law-keeping divisions, including detectives, juveniles, public safety, and others. Prisoner facilities include receiving, processing, and booking areas; cell blocks; cooking and dining facilities; and other spaces. Public facilities are those used by people who come to the station on business, and include waiting rooms, information centers, traffic violation bureaus, and complaints sections. Personnel facilities include such spaces as lounges, locker rooms, rest rooms, gymnasiums, lunchrooms, and snack bars. Police court requirements are similar to those of other courts but simpler, and in addition to the courtroom may include judges' chambers, offices, prisoners' rooms, and other spaces. Major aspects of the design of police stations involve the proper relationships between the various elements and proper precautions to prevent prisoner escapes and to protect police officials and the public as well as the prisoners.

There has been some sort of police authority since ancient times. In England, in the 9th to 11th centuries, the kings appointed people, called reeves, to represent them in the counties, called shires. From the combination of these words into shire reeve comes the present-day word *sheriff*. For police protection, all men over sixteen had to stand what was called watch and ward duty under the direction of the sheriffs. By the early 19th century, cities had watchmen, and by the second quarter of the century, paid police had been organized, thus creating the need for the first police stations.

The American colonists followed the English system of watch and ward for many years. In 1838 Boston hired a paid police force of six men, and New York followed with a larger one in 1844. Since that time, the construction of police stations has followed and their development has closely paralleled that of courthouses.

Recent Public Buildings Many other kinds of public buildings have been constructed in the past and are being constructed today. Interesting, varied, and important public buildings constructed in the recent past, include the United Nations Headquarters (1950, library 1963), New York City, designed by an international team of 15 architects, headed by Wallace Kirkman Harrison (1895–   ) of the United States, and

PUBLIC BUILDING Daley Center (1965), Chicago, Ill. [*Architects: C. F. Murphy Assoc.; Loebl, Schlossman and Bennett; Skidmore, Owings and Merrill. (Hedrich-Blessing)*]

including Le Corbusier (1887–1965) of France, Oscar Niemeyer (1907–) of Brazil, and Sven Markelius (1889–1972) of Sweden. Another joint effort is the Chicago Civic Center (1967) by an association of firms: C. F. Murphy; Skidmore, Owings and Merrill; and Loebl, Schlossman, Bennett and Dart. Other important buildings are the Marin County Civic Center (1972), San Rafael, Calif., completed many years after the death of its architect, Frank Lloyd Wright (1869–1959); the twin-towered World Trade Center (1973), New York City, by Minoru Yamasaki (1912–) and Emery Roth and Sons; and the Post Office and Federal Building (1976), Saginaw, Mich., by Smith, Hinchman and Grylls.

Embassies One of the most interesting kinds of public buildings constructed in the second half of the 20th century has been a series of U.S. embassies. A truly remarkable demonstration of good American architectural design was disseminated all over the world in these new embassies built in many countries. Although they vary in their degree of excellence, the embassies make an impressive list: The Hague, Netherlands (1956), by Marcel Breuer (1902–); Athens, Greece (1961), by Walter Adolf Gropius (1883–1969) and The Architects Collaborative; Havana, Cuba (1953) and Rio de Janeiro, Brazil (1954), by Harrison and Abramovitz; Rabat, Morocco (1961), by Morris Ketchum, Jr., (1904–), Francis X. Gina (1910–), and Stanley Sharp (1914–); Seoul, Korea (1957), by Ernest Kump (1911–); Karachi, Pakistan, (1961), by Neutra and Alexander; Stockholm, Sweden, and Copenhagen, Denmark, both 1954, by Ralph Rapson (1914–); Djarkarta, Indonesia (1958), by Antonin Raymond (1888–1976) and Ladislav Rado (1909–); Amman, Jordan (1957), by Paul Rudolph (1918–); London, England (1956), and Oslo, Norway (1959), by Eero Saarinen (1910–61); Baghdad, Iraq (1956), by José Luis Sert (1902–); New Delhi, India (1954), by Edward Durell Stone (1902–78); Bangkok, Thailand (1959), by John Carl Warnecke (1919–); and Accra, Ghana (1958), by Harry Weese (1915–).

Related Articles CAPITAL, UNITED STATES; Individual architects and firms; Various building types.

Further Reading Hitchcock, Henry-Russell, and William Seale: *Temples of Democracy—The State Capitols of the USA,* Harcourt Brace Jovanovich, New York, 1976; Institute of Continuing Legal Education: *The American Courthouse,* University of Michigan Press, Ann Arbor, 1973.

RAILWAY STATION A building for the arrival, loading, handling, and departure of railroad trains and their passengers, crews, and freight. There are two major kinds of stations: passenger and freight. Each station is usually operated by one railroad company but some stations are used by more than one railroad company and are often called union stations.

Today railway station design is almost completely a thing of the past, except for remodeling and construction of a few small stations. Railway stations, particularly those in large cities, in the golden era of railroading, were almost like complete cities with facilities for almost every need of passengers and visitors. Today a few of these great stations are still in existence, but no new ones are being designed. Perhaps this will change in the future if the Amtrak system becomes more successful.

Elements In the small railway stations of today, the major elements are few: a waiting room, a ticket office, a baggage room, rest rooms, mechanical and electrical equipment spaces, and canopy-covered platforms.

Sometimes there is a newsstand or a snack bar. The design of these stations is straightforward, mainly consisting of placing the various elements in an efficient relationship with each other. This is a far cry from the complications and complexities of the great terminals of the past.

History The history of railroading began in England with the invention of the first steam locomotive in 1804, with the first locomotive to pull cars in 1814, and with the first regularly operated railroad in 1825. Since that time, many railway stations, large and grand or small and modest, have been built all over the world.

U.S. Development The first railroad locomotive in the United States started operating in 1825 and the first scheduled railroad in 1830. The railroads started building stations soon afterward. None of the earliest stations has survived. And many of the buildings constructed in the era of railroad expansion during the second half of the 19th century has been demolished.

The grand era of railroad station design came in the

RAILWAY STATION Pennsylvania Station (1910, demolished 1966), New York, N.Y. [*Architects: McKim, Mead and White. (Wayne Andrews)*]

RAILWAY STATION Cincinnati Union Terminal (1933, later partially demolished), Cincinnati, Ohio. [*Architects: Fellheimer and Wagner. (George Stille)*]

late 19th century and the first quarter of the 20th. A large number of stations were designed by many of the best American architects. Many of the buildings were small and some architects, including Frank Furness (1839–1912), made a specialty of their design. Others were very large and some quite opulent. A number of these are still in operation, including Union Station (1908), Washington, by Daniel Hudson Burnham (1846–1912), later remodeled; Grand Central Station (1913), New York City, by Reed and Stem in association with Warren and Wetmore, often threatened but still standing; Union Station (1926), Chicago, by the successors to Daniel Hudson Burnham, Graham, Anderson, Probst and White; and Union Station (1926), Richmond, Va., by John Russell Pope (1834–1937).

Related to the regular railways are rapid transit systems, including subways and elevated railroads. The first elevated railroad in the United States was built in Chicago in 1892, the first subway in Boston in 1897, followed by New York in 1904. A subway system was built in Chicago, starting in the 1930s. Until recently, these were the only American cities with such rapid transit systems.

In the past few years, other cities have studied the possibilities of more efficient public transportation and two have constructed systems: San Francisco, the first part opened 1972, and Washington, the first part opened 1975. Harry Weese (1915–) designed the stations for the Washington system, called Metro.

More than 14 architects and 8 landscape architects participated in the design of the San Francisco system, Bay Area Rapid Transit, or BART. From the beginning of BART, in 1960, to 1966, Donn Emmons (1910–) served as consulting architect, and from that time to 1970, the position was held by Tallie B. Maule (1917–74). An effort has been made over the past few years to improve the grim and dreary appearance of the subway stations of the old New York City system.

Other cities, including Atlanta, are planning rapid transit systems, but there is consderable doubt that they can be constructed and operated economically.

Related Articles AIRPORT; HOTEL; RESTAURANT; Articles on individual architects and firms.

Further Reading Grow, Lawrence: *Waiting for the 5:05 — Terminal, Station and Depot in America*, Main Street/ Universe, New York, 1977.

REAL ESTATE Land and all things, such as buildings, trees, and minerals, more or less permanently attached to it. The concept of property has been a part of human affairs since prehistoric times. Although hard to define precisely because of the different interpretations given to the concept in various societies and in various periods in history, property, in general, means things of value that are owned or which people have rights to use, enjoy, and dispose of. Property is generally divided into two major types: personal property, or personalty, and real estate, or realty. In the United States, real and personal property may be owned by individuals, groups of people, partnerships, corporations, governments, associations, religious groups, and others. Most types of personal property may be bought, sold, or given away freely without the necessity of contracts. Real estate in the United States may be sold or given away only by written contracts.

Functions of Agents   Real estate is a very important part of the building industry and has a considerable effect on architecture. Real estate agents, of various kinds, acting for owners and sometimes for themselves, actively engage in buying and selling land and buildings, in real property leasing, in development of projects, and in management of real property. In the performance of these functions, real estate agents are frequently involved with architects. They often represent owners, or themselves, in the assembly and development of land. By placing evaluations on land and other real property, they affect the financing of building projects. They advise owners on building projects and they often procure the financing for them. Sometimes they engage in the construction of buildings.

The basic function of real estate agents is selling real property for owners. A person who performs this function is often called a real estate broker. A broker may have real estate salespeople who are responsible to and work under the direction of the broker. Some people in the field specialize in real estate appraisal, evaluation of land and other real property; in real estate counseling, advising owners and others on purchases, sales, and similar matters; or in real estate management, administration of leasing, maintenance, and business matters for real properties.

Developers   Often called entrepreneurs or promoters, developers actively promote the creation of building projects, including the assembly of land on which they are to be built and their financing, design, construction, and leasing or sale. Developers are often engaged in real estate work of other kinds, or come into development by way of such work, but this is not always the case. Anyone with the knowledge and business acumen necessary for putting together projects that are often large in size and quite costly can become a developer. And this includes some architects, who act as developers or who join with others to create developments.

A developer may promote a development, which is ultimately sold to others, in the expectation of profits; but perhaps the more usual case is that in which the developer retains total or part ownership in the completed development. Sometimes developers sell all or a portion of a development to others and then lease it back from them; this is called a sale-lease back transaction. When a developer sells a project and contracts to buy it back on a long-term basis, the transaction is called a sale-buy back or installment-sale contract. Architects also may participate in these processes.

In a typical development by a group, the major interests may be an investor, who supplies the equity capital, sometimes called the front money, to get the project started; a real estate agent, who assembles the land; a mortgage banker, who obtains the long-term financing, secured by a mortgage, a lien on the property; an architect, who performs the architectural services; and a contractor, who constructs the building. Also sometimes involved in such a group are an attorney to handle the legal aspects, an economist to ensure the feasibility of the project, and engineers and other consultants. Often the users of a development may also be involved, for example, in the case of the major tenants of a shopping center.

In a development by an individual developer or a development company, all the risks are taken by the developers, and the ownership or potential for profits is all theirs. For the other functions, architects, contractors, and others are engaged to perform their own functions as they would in any building project. When the development is handled by a group, or team, such as previously described, each participant performs specific functions for which each receives a fee, salary, or other payment; all share in the risk and divide the profits or ownership.

A development organization may be a single proprietorship, a partnership, a corporation, or a real estate investment trust (REIT). A joint venture, which may also be used, is like a partnership for one specific project or a series of projects. An REIT is an institution organized, usually by large developers or mortgage lenders, to spread the risk of development over a relatively large number of projects.

Development Stages   Developments ordinarily go through a number of important stages: establishment of the concept; determination of users' requirements; determination of approximate building size and costs and land requirements; feasibility and economic analysis of the venture; securing of land options; determination of financing sources; development of programs, schematic designs, and refined cost estimates and economic analyses; proposal to users; project design and preparation of construction documents, working drawings, and specifications; construction; and delivery of completed project to the users. Many developments have much more complicated steps than those outlined. In all cases, each step must be performed properly, efficiently, and with knowledge and foresight if a development is to be successful.

Regulations   In the past, real estate transactions were not well regulated and real estate agents were neither well regulated nor well trained. Today there is a body of laws and regulations governing the actions of real estate agents and the functions they perform. Local real estate boards, located in every sizable municipality and the state associations of the National Association of Real Estate Boards (NAREB) govern the actions of their members in matters of ethics and other conduct. Real estate brokers must be licensed and must pass examinations to obtain their licenses. And for a person to use the title realtor, it is necessary to be licensed and a member of NAREB, who subscribes to its code of ethics. Real estate salespeople must also be licensed. In the United States, more than a half million people are licensed real estate brokers and salespeople. An increasing number of brokers and salespeople have taken courses in real estate in the more than 250 U.S. colleges and universities offering such study. And an increasing number have graduated from one of the more than 50 colleges and universities offering degrees in real estate.

Related Articles BUILDING INDUSTRY; FEASIBILITY STUDY; FINANCE; PROGRAMMING

Further Reading Golemon, Harry A., ed.: *Financing Real Estate Development,* Aloray Publishers, Englewood, N.J., 1974; Griffin, C. W.: *Development Building—The Team Approach,* the American Institute of Architects (distributed by Halsted Press of John Wiley), Washington, 1972.

Sources of Additional Information American Society of Real Estate Counselors, 155 E. Superior St., Chicago, Ill. 60611; National Association of Real Estate Boards, 155 E. Superior St., Chicago, Ill. 60611; Society of Industrial Realtors, 1300 Connecticut Ave., N.W., Washington, D.C. 20036.

Periodical *National Real Estate Investor,* 461 Eighth Ave., New York, N.Y. 10001.

RECREATION BUILDING

RECREATION BUILDING Any of a wide variety of building types, where people may congregate to enjoy cultural pursuits, participate in athletics, watch sports, or engage in other activities. Recreation buildings are closely related to outdoor facilities used for similar purposes.

Recreation is a very personal thing. To some, it is represented by a quiet chess or card game. To others, it is flying an airplane, racing automobiles, or surfing. Recreation for many consists of spectator sports, either by attending games and other events or watching them on television. For others recreation is found in travel, gardening, studying, or collecting stamps, coins, or any of an almost boundless list of articles. Many pursuits provide recreation to some people, but are actually the vocations of others, who seek recreation in different activities. Because of the great variety and number of recreational pursuits possible, a discussion of recreation buildings must necessarily be quite general, touching only on buildings and related outdoor areas that are primarily and specifically recreational in nature.

Classifications The major recreational facilities may be classified as follows: those for participant sports and athletics; those for spectator sports; clubs; camps; community recreation centers; and a miscellaneous category that would include amusement parks, fairgrounds, gambling casinos, dance halls, and other types. For further discussion of specific cultural recreation building types and open recreation areas, see titles listed at the end of this article.

There is no hard and fast line of division between recreation facilities of the various types, two or more often being combined in one facility. For example, a golf club usually provides facilities for recreational golfing, a participant sport, and for tournaments, a spectator sport. And a country club may provide for both these functions and also have facilities for other sports, dining, dancing, card playing, other games, and so on.

Ownership Recreation facilities are owned and operated in several ways: by governments on all levels, federal, state, county, and municipal; by church groups; by associations or other organizations; by corporations or other businesses; and by individuals. Recreation facilities may be open to the public at large or to segments of the public, such as the inhabitants of a neighborhood or city; or to members and their guests as in most clubs; or they may be intended only for the private enjoyment of a family or an individual and guests.

Participant Sports There is a long list of participant sports, for which indoor or outdoor facilities are often provided. Some of them are bicycle riding; boating, in marinas, boat ramps, and other facilities; bowling; fishing, boats, docks, camps, and other facilities; golf; hunting camps and other facilities; rifle and pistol ranges; skating, ice and roller; softball; skeet and trap shooting; swimming; and tennis. Of course there are a number of others and new ones are being invented all the time. Some of the later additions include the use of vehicles of various kinds, such as dune buggies, four-wheel-drive recreational vehicles, go-carts, hang gliders, motorbikes, motorcycles, skateboards, and snowmobiles. Many think these latter pursuits are nourished by thrill-seeking and intoxication with speed and noise, and as these fads become unfashionable, they will be replaced by new ones. Some of these pursuits have become problems since many of their devotees have been known to destroy public and private property and natural resources and to create public nuisances.

Spectator Sports The major spectator sports are football, baseball, and basketball; but boxing, soccer, tennis, horseracing, and ice hockey are also popular. Facilities for these sports may be buildings, often called arenas, in which the contests take place indoors, and other structures, often called stadiums or parks, in which the games are played out-of-doors. A recent development has been stadiums that are completely or partly roofed, and in a few cases stadiums in which the roofs may be opened or closed as occasion demands.

Clubs Clubs, for recreational and other purposes, include youth clubs, adult clubs, golf clubs, tennis clubs, country clubs, and other types. Among the most important clubs for youths are the Young Men's Christian Association (YMCA), Young Women's Christian Association (YWCA), and the Young Men's Hebrew Association (YMHA), the last named often combined into a club for both men and women (YM&YWHA).

Camps In addition to sports camps, such as those for fishing or hunting, many other camps exist for those traveling with trailers or campers and for those who like to vacation in more or less natural surroundings, in cabins, tents, tent campers, travel trailers, or

RECREATION BUILDING Exterior, State Fair Pavilion (1954), Raleigh, N.C. [*Architects: Matthew Nowicki and William H. Dietrick. Structural engineer: Fred Severud. (Joseph W. Molitor)*]

RECREATION BUILDING Interior, State Fair Pavilion (1954), Raleigh, N.C. [*Architects: Matthew Nowicki and William H. Dietrick. Structural engineer: Fred Severud. (Joseph W. Molitor)*]

on the ground. Such camps range from those that have small parking spaces for camping or travel vehicles, with hookups for electricity, water, and plumbing, and other facilities such as shower rooms, coin-operated laundries, and stores, to primitive camping sites accessible only to hikers or sometimes four-wheel-drive vehicles.

Community Centers Community recreation centers provide facilities in which people of all ages can engage in numerous activities, including sports, games, dances, craft and artwork, meetings, and so on.

Amusement Parks Among the miscellaneous recreational types, a popular one today is the amusement park. In the past, such parks were relatively simple, providing a few rides, such as a ferris wheel, carousel, and roller coaster; a midway where games could be played; a few concessions selling hot dogs, soft drinks, and cotton candy; and perhaps a fun or ghost house, and a few sideshows featuring jugglers, snake charmers, and the like.

Now amusement parks have become much more complicated and contrived. An attempt has been made in many parks to fabricate an illusion of some exotic place far away or in some olden time, or both. These are often called theme parks. In some, for example, Disney Land, Anaheim, Calif., and Disney World, near Orlando, Fla., the result has been a sort of fantasy environment, based on the creative motion

RECREATION BUILDING Exterior, Civic Auditorium (1961), Pittsburgh, Pa. [*Architects: Mitchell and Ritchey. (Joseph W. Molitor)*]

RECREATION BUILDING Interior, Civic Auditorium (1961), Pittsburgh, Pa. [*Architects: Mitchell and Ritchey. (Joseph W. Molitor)*]

pictures of the Disney artists and technicians. In other theme parks, the result has often been only a vast potpourri of contrived fake buildings, shops, games, overpriced food and drink, shows of little or no artistic merit, and rides that must be made ever more elaborate and scary to hold their appeal.

Amusement parks can be more creative than such theme parks, with better architecture too. This is demonstrated by some examples around the world, perhaps the most famous of which is Tivoli Gardens, founded in 1843, in Copenhagen, Denmark. Here, in an imaginatively conceived park, light, landscaping, buildings, fountains, pools, rides, displays, top-quality ballet, drama, pantomime, concert and circus performances, and other interesting and provocative things have been combined in such a way as to bring mirth, laughter, even a degree of happiness to those who visit the park. Perhaps, if given a chance, architects of today might design amusement parks of such delightful fantasy and fun through flights of creative imagination, rather than only parks contrived to be something of which they can only be pale and unconvincing copies.

Design Problems The major problems in the design of recreation buildings and related facilities of any kind are proper provision for the functions to take place in them and for the age groups that will use them, in comfortable, attractive, and safe surroundings. There are so many types of recreation facilities

RECREATION BUILDING Armonk Recreation Building (1967), Armonk N.Y. [Architects: Norton and Hume. (Joseph W. Molitor)]

that the designer must become familiar with the rules and requirements for the type to be designed. For example, there are standards for football fields to which the designer must adhere and there are specific requirements for the needs of players, officials, coaches, concessions, and spectators. In a bowling alley, there are different specific requirements.

Requirements vary considerably between clubs of various types. And the same holds true for the great number of other types of recreation facilities. In attempting to satisfy the specific requirements, the designer must also remember that recreation facilities are intended for the enjoyment and entertainment of people in their leisure time. In their design, recreation buildings should reflect those sometimes elusive pursuits.

History One of the basic needs of human beings is for recreation, activities engaged in for pleasure, relaxation, and excitement by choice, but no one knows when such activities started. It can be presumed that primitive humans engaged in recreational activities, but no records have been found indicating what they were. From the earliest historic times, it is known that many recreational activities were pursued, including dancing, music, games, festivals, and contests between animals and between animals and humans.

The ancient Minoans practiced a form of bull fighting as far back as 3000 B.C. and the custom was carried on by both the Greeks and Romans. The ancient Egyptians had a number of recreational pursuits, such as games of various kinds and athletics, including wrestling, and by about 1500 B.C. had developed races by horse-drawn chariots. The ancient Greeks and Romans continued all these activities. In addition, the

Greeks developed drama and music, as these arts are understood today. They also enjoyed athletic contests that were highly developed in Olympic Games, which began in 776 B.C. The greatest athletic event in ancient Greece, the games were abolished at the end of the 4th century B.C. In 1896 the Olympics were revived and the first modern games were held in Athens.

The Romans loved recreational activities and were very inventive in the establishment of some of the more barbarous types, including battles between gladiators and between gladiators and wild animals, and throwing criminals and Christians to wild animals. The Romans also played games, attended theaters, and visited the public baths, where entertainment was furnished by acrobats, magicians, and other performers. Both the Greeks and the Romans built theaters. And the Romans built very large amphitheaters for certain spectacles, and what they called circuses, arenas in which chariot races were held.

During the Middle Ages, recreation of any but the simplest sort was not available to the peasants or serfs. The lords amused themselves in many ways, including such games as dice, chess, and checkers; plays and festivals; and jousting, in which two knights fought, and tournaments in which two groups of knights did combat. After the Middle Ages, recreational pursuits of all kinds began to flourish and new ones were started. For example, the kind of circus of today was started in the 1700s in England.

Many other kinds of recreational pursuits have since been invented and many have required new kinds of buildings and other structures. Some have been interesting and important works of architecture; others simply reflected the evanescent fashions and fads of the day, or lacked any distinguished features.

In the 20th century, with the trend toward continuing reduction of the hours people must work to make their living, there has been a plethora of recreational pursuits, and requisite buildings or structures have been built in ever-increasing numbers. Some pursuits have many redeeming features; but many people believe that others cater to mere escapism that comes from too much idle time and a failure to engage in more meaningful activities.

Related Articles BOTANICAL BUILDING; HOTEL; LIBRARY; MUSEUM; PARK; THEATER; ZOOLOGICAL BUILDING.

Further Reading AIA and Ramsey and Sleeper, Robert T. Packard, ed.: *Architectural Graphic Standards*, 7th ed., John Wiley, New York, 1980; Davern, Jeanne M., ed.: *Places for People*, McGraw-Hill, New York, 1976; DeChiara, Joseph, and John Hancock Callender: *Time-Saver Standards for Building Types*, McGraw-Hill, New York, 1973.

Sources of Additional Information American Society of Golf Course Architects, 221 N. LaSalle St., Chicago, Ill. 60601; National Recreation and Park Assoc., 1601 N. Kent St., Arlington, Va. 22209; National Swimming Pool Inst., 2000 K St., N.W., Washington, D.C. 20006.

RELIGIOUS BUILDING

A building, or group of buildings, such as a church, a synagogue, sometimes called a temple, or a mosque, in which people worship, or other buildings used for religious or secular purposes by the worshipers, or for housing religious orders.

World Religions In order of their number of members, from the largest to the smallest, the major religions of the world are Christianity (Protestant, Roman Catholic, and Eastern Orthodox), Islam, Hinduism, Confucianism, Buddhism, Shinto, Taoism, and Judaism. While some of the other religions are established in the United States in a relatively small way, the major religious bodies in this country are Protestant, with some 70 million members, Roman Catholic, with some 50 million, Judaism, with about 4 million, and Eastern Orthodox, with about 4 million.

U.S. Religious Bodies The major U.S. religious bodies operate more than a quarter-million churches and synagogues and a large number of schools, hospitals, colleges and universities, seminaries, monasteries, and other institutions. There are some 300 Protestant denominations in the United States and about 15 Eastern Orthodox denominations, usually divided along national lines, including Greek, Russian, Syrian, and so on. Some of the Eastern Orthodox churches include the word *Catholic* in their titles. Judaism, in the United States, is divided into three groups: Orthodox, Conservative, and Reformed. Thus for these major U.S. religions, religious buildings constitute a major building type. The other religious groups in the United States construct very few buildings.

Common Elements Buildings of the major religious groups in America all have some things in common. The churches or synagogues are all designed for the worship of God. Most have provisions of some sort for other purposes, including religious instruction, social activities, and the like. All have ritualistic requirements of some kind. But their requirements are quite different in many ways. Therefore the only way to understand the design of buildings for the various religions or denominations is to examine each individually. For a discussion on buildings constructed for purposes other than worship and related activities, see articles entitled college and university building; school.

Synagogues The places of worship of the Jews, the followers of Judaism, are synagogues. Practices vary in other religions, but almost every synagogue has three major elements: a sanctuary, for worship and other ritual events; an educational center; and a social center. The sanctuary, or synagogue proper, is not considered a place of mystery, and should be bright and well lighted. The service consists of prayers, readings from sacred texts, songs, responsive readings, and sermons.

In practice, the three groups of Judaism (Orthodox, Conservative, and Reformed) have certain practices that are the same and others that are different. The focal point of the sanctuary for all three is the sacred Torah, the scrolls containing the first five books of the Old Testament of the Bible. The Torah is kept in the ark, a niche or chest, usually located on the eastern wall. A paroche or curtain covers the ark. An eternal light hangs near the ark and on one or both sides are placed seven-branched candelabra, called menorahs. The Tablets of the Law usually hang above the ark. A raised platform (bema, bimah, or almemar) is provided and on it are located a table or desk on which the Torah is placed to be read. In Orthodox services, the reader faces the ark; in the Reform, the congregation; and in the Conservative, may face either way. Sometimes the table or desk is used also as a pulpit by the rabbi and the cantor, who chants the liturgical music. In other cases, one or two pulpits may be provided. The Orthodox place the bema in the center of the sanctuary, the other groups at the end in front of the ark. Choirs, and sometimes pianos or organs, are often involved in Conservative services, always in the Reform, but never in the Orthodox. Choirs may be visible or concealed. Seating is provided for the congregation in the sanctuary and the usual practice today is to provide a center aisle for weddings and other ceremonies. In addition, there is a vestibule or foyer and cloakroom. In some synagogues, chapels are provided for smaller groups.

Other elements of a synagogue are the educational center, which has classrooms for religious instruction, and the social center, which not only serves for plays, meetings, dances, and so on, but also is used in Jewish rituals which require festive meals during Passover and on other holidays. Social centers have banquet rooms, kitchens, and stages. In addition, synagogues have offices, libraries, and other facilities. Synagogues are often decorated with stained-glass windows, sculpture, tapestries, and other works of

RELIGIOUS BUILDING Exterior, Church of the Redeemer (1959), Baltimore, Md. [*Architects: Pietro Belluschi; in association with Rogers, Taliaffero and Lamb. Artist: Gyorgy Kepes. (Joseph W. Molitor)*]

RELIGIOUS BUILDING Interior, Church of the Redeemer (1959), Baltimore, Md. [*Architects: Pietro Belluschi; in association with Rogers, Taliaferro and Lamb. Artist: Gyorgy Kepes. (Joseph W. Molitor)*]

art. Until recently, these were expected to be purely symbolic, but today some representational art is allowed in Reform synagogues.

Roman Catholic Churches Whereas Roman Catholic churches often have such elements as classrooms, parish halls for gatherings, rectories in which priests live, and others, the only major element is the church itself. The church is considered a sacred place, set apart from other things, in which there is a Divine Presence, the Holy Eucharist. Therefore the design of a Roman Catholic church involves mainly the provision of a building in which the liturgy can be performed properly. The major element is the church proper, divided into the sanctuary, in which the priests perform their functions, the choir, and the body of the church or nave in which the congregation gathers. The choir may be placed in any of a number of places, in the sanctuary, at the back of the church, and others. The body of the church contains chairs or pews for seating the congregation, though in the early church the congregation often stood during services.

The sanctuary is usually elevated higher than the floor of the nave and is divided from it by the communion rail, at which communicants kneel or stand to receive the Holy Eucharist or Communion. The central and most important element of the sanctuary is the altar, which may be placed against a wall or may be freestanding. The altar cross, which must have the figure of the crucified Christ, may be placed on the altar, suspended above it, or mounted on a staff behind the altar. Although not required, a canopy is often placed over the altar. On the altar is permanently fixed the tabernacle, a strong vault or box, in which is kept the Holy Eucharist or Sacrament. It is covered with a tentlike veil. A sanctuary light, sometimes more than one, burns continuously near the tabernacle, but not over the altar. At one side is located the credence table which holds articles used in the masses and other services. Sermons may be delivered from the predella, a space in front of the altar used also in celebration of Mass, from a lectern, or from a special place, a pulpit, provided specifically for sermons. Two other important furnishings of the sanctuary are priedieux, kneeling benches with shelves in front, for use by priests, and sedilia, benches on which priests and others may sit at times during Mass.

Other important elements of Roman Catholic churches are a vestibule, called the narthex; baptistery, where baptisms are held; confessionals, small rooms in which priests hear confessions; and sacristy, in which various church articles are stored and in which priests don their robes or vestments. Often an atrium or courtyard is located in front of the church, providing a division between the church and the outside world. A church may have one or more chapels, additional altars and shrines, and other elements. Churches usually have depictions of religious history and beliefs on their walls, windows, and elsewhere. These may include sculpture, paintings, stained glass, carvings, mosaics, and other art forms. Although some are relatively plain, many are highly ornamental. Additional elements of Roman Catholic churches, such as church schools, parish houses, and the like, are similar to those of other denominations or those used for lay purposes.

Eastern Orthodox Churches There is some resemblance between Eastern Orthodox churches and Roman Catholic churches. Some of the latter churches are small, simple, and restrained, but Eastern Orthodox churches are always richly ornamented, with spacious interiors and high curved ceilings, in keeping with the doctrine that they are the dwelling places on

RELIGIOUS BUILDING Priory of St. Gregory the Great (1961), Portsmouth, R.I. [*Architects: Pietro Belluschi; in association with Anderson, Beckwith and Haible. Sculptor: Richard Lippold. (Joseph W. Molitor)*]

RELIGIOUS BUILDING Temple (1965), West Hartford, Conn. [Architect: Philip DiCorsia. (Joseph W. Molitor)]

earth of God, the Eternal King of Heaven, and therefore should have royal splendor.

Orthodox churches are always built on east-west lines, with the sanctuaries on the eastern ends. They often have domes and belfries, each of which is always topped with a cross. Some churches have vestibules at the western ends, above which are located choir lofts. Inside, the nave is divided into a rear section for the congregation and a front section, the chancel, for the priest and cantors, or chanters of liturgical music. The chancel is always elevated higher than the rest of the nave. Behind the chancel is the sanctuary, separated from the rest of the church by a screen, called an iconostasis, with tiers of icons or pictures of Jesus Christ, Mary, Mother of God, and saints. The sanctuary represents the dwelling of God, the Most High, Holy of Holies. In it are located the altar or holy table, representing the table on which Jesus and the Apostles had the Last Supper, the cross on which Jesus was crucified, the sepulchre in which he was buried, and the throne on which he sits at the right hand of God, his Father.

Protestant Churches Architecturally, Protestant churches are more difficult to describe than those of the other denominations. There are some 300 denominations, each with beliefs that vary from the others, and each with liturgical requirements that also vary considerably. Therefore it is only possible to describe the major requirements of Protestant churches and to furnish some particulars of the churches of some of the predominant denominations in the United States. As in buildings of other religious groups, Protestant churches may have such facilities as social, educational, and other types. Their design is similar to that for the other groups and those for lay purposes.

In general, Protestants can be divided into Episcopal, Presbyterian, and Reformed groups. These three groups vary in their doctrines and in the way they are administered or governed. They also vary in the degree of ritual, from the most elaborate, the Episcopal, to the least, the Reformed, which includes the church denominations usually called Congregational. Architecturally, the churches designed for the three groups vary from the often more elaborate and ornamented churches of the Episcopal to the quite simple for the Reformed churches, which are often called simply meetinghouses.

The main body of the church, for all Protestant denominations, is divided into two elements: the nave where the congregation is seated and the chancel, sometimes called the sanctuary, where the ministers or priests and other officiants perform their functions. In most churches, the central focal point of the chancel is an altar, sometimes called the Lord's Table. Often a cross is placed on, over, or near the altar. Also located in the chancel are a pulpit and sometimes a lectern, which often holds the Bible. In some denominations, such as the Church of Christ, Scientist, and some of the reformed groups, the central focal point is the pulpit instead of an altar. Also the baptismal font is placed in the chancel where it can be seen by the entire congregation in meetinghouses for reformed groups and churches for other denominations, such as the Lutherans, instead of in some other location.

A Protestant church often has a vestibule or narthex. In churches in which the priests or ministers wear special garments or vestments, there are sacristies or vesting rooms. Where choirs also wear vestments or robes, there is a choir robing room. In Protestant churches, choirs may be located in a number of places, such as behind the altar, in the nave in front of the altar, in the rear of the church, in a loft above the main level of the nave, or in an alcove, at the side of the chancel. The organ console, if there is one, is usually located within or near the choir, in a position that is unobtrusive but allows the organist to see the entire chancel and also give cues to the choir.

In some churches, communion rails, at which communicants kneel to receive Communion or the Lord's Supper, are provided. Most Protestant denominations practice baptism, usually of infants or small children by sprinkling or pouring water taken from a container (a font) on the head. In some denominations, fonts may be located in or near the narthex or in a separate room, called a baptistery. Baptist denominations practice baptism only of older persons and by total immersion, submerging people completely in water.

Many Protestant denominations use ornament in their churches, including stained glass, sculpture, mosaics, paintings, and so on. Other denominations use little or no ornament. In addition to the main body of the church, many denominations provide other kinds of facilities, such as chapels, parish halls, banquet halls, and others for use by members for both religious and lay activities.

In the past, churches of most denominations were ordinarily rectangular or cruciform, in the shape of a cross, in plan. Today many denominations allow the plans of their churches to be almost any form that can

RELIGIOUS BUILDING First Presbyterian Church (1960), Stamford, Conn. [*Architects: Harrison and Abramovitz; Sherwood, Mills and Smith. (Joseph W. Molitor)*]

be made to function properly for the rites and services to be held. One development, which has often been used in recent years, is the concept of a central plan, in which the altar is located in the middle of the church with the congregation seated around it. Such plans may be circular, hexagonal, or other shapes.

Churches and synagogues form an important building type and many architects design them. Buildings of this sort can be challenging and gratifying to design. To design a church or synagogue properly, an architect must understand the tradition and rituals of the particular religious group. Since these vary so widely, adequate time must be spent in research to determine the specific requirements. Once these have been determined, many denominations today allow considerable freedom to their architects.

History Although no real facts have been established, it is believed that primitive humans practiced some type of religion. There is reason to believe that the first religious activities involved worship of natural objects, or naturism, and that this was followed by animism, the belief that all natural objects have souls. The next step may have been spiritism, which includes the belief that the spirit or soul lives on after death and may have contact with the living. The important early religions are believed to have been based on such principles. They also included fetishism, the belief in the magical powers of objects of nature, or the possession of people and objects by spirits other than their own. Polytheism was the worship of a number of deities, each responsible for certain natural phenomena, and in the simplest form these

RELIGIOUS BUILDING Priory of St. Mary and St. Louis (1962), St. Louis, Mo. [*Architects: Hellmuth, Obata and Kassabaum. Landscape architect: Hideo Sasaki. (Hutchinson Photographers)*]

deities resembled people. Henotheism was the belief in one deity, but did not preclude belief in others. Monotheism is the belief in one God, to the exclusion of others.

The ancient Egyptians practiced polytheism in some localities, worshiping gods each of whom rules over certain natural phenomena, such as air, moisture, earth, and sky. In other localities, the people worshiped one god. Some of the earliest religious buildings, temples, were built in Egypt, starting about 2700 B.C., and many later ones are still in existence. The earliest religious building ruins are located in the Middle East, in what was Mesopotamia. The ancient Greeks practiced polytheism, as did the early Romans in a somewhat different form. Both cultures produced great religious architecture, some of which is still in existence. Although Christianity was introduced into Rome and Greece in the first century A.D., it was not established as the state religion in Rome until the 4th century, and polytheism did not die out in Greece until the 6th century.

Of the major religions of the world today, Hinduism and Shinto are thought to be the oldest, beginning about 2500 B.C. Hinduism is polytheistic, having three

gods, as is Shinto, with many gods. Three major religions were founded about the 6th century B.C.: Buddhism, Confucianism, and Taoism. Islam was founded in the 6th century A.D.

Judaism, the oldest monotheistic religion, is believed to have been founded by Abraham, to have been given form by Moses about the 13th century B.C., and to have been developed into a form closely resembling that of today by the 5th century B.C. In the United States, Judaism is divided into three groups: the Orthodox, who believe in strict interpretation of the Torah, the first five books of the Old Testament, and Jewish traditions and laws; the Conservative, who believe in Jewish law and tradition, but allow interpretations of some religious doctrines; and the Reform, who believe that people of each generation have the right to accept or reject traditions.

Christianity was founded by Jesus Christ and is therefore almost 2,000 years old. For almost 1,000 years, there was essentially one Christian religious body. Beginning in the 9th century, differences began to develop between the Western church in Rome and the Eastern in Istanbul, then called Constantinople. In the 11th century the two bodies separated, forming in the West, the Roman Catholic church, and in the East, the Greek Orthodox, which later spread to other countries and became known as the Eastern Orthodox Church. Beginning in the 16th century, during the Protestant Reformation, large numbers of people left the Roman Catholic church to form Protestant churches, and later these divided to become the approximately 300 denominations in existence today.

Throughout their history, the Jewish, Roman Catholic, Protestant, and Eastern Orthodox groups have built churches and synagogues. Early Christian churches were built in Rome and other places. Christian churches in what came to be know as the Byzantine style were built in the domain of the Eastern Orthodox. These were followed by the great churches in the Romanesque style and then by the magnificent Gothic style cathedrals of the Middle Ages. Many of these early churches and cathedrals are still standing. The products of unknown master builders, these buildings are among the world's finest architecture. During the Renaissance, the building of churches and cathedrals continued, and their architects were the greatest of the time, including Filippo Brunelleschi (c. 1377–1446), Leon Battista Alberti (1404–72), Donato d'Agnolo, called Bramante (1444–1514), and Michelangelo Buonarroti, called simply Michelangelo (1475–1564). From that time on great churches and synagogues have been designed by many, including some famous, architects, and their designs have produced some of the best architecture.

U.S. Religious Buildings In the United States, the early colonists built churches and synagogues soon after they arrived. The first church in America is believed to have been built at Jamestown, Va., in the early 1700s but was later destroyed and another built on its foundation, only to be partly destroyed. Other old churches still in existence include St. Luke's, sometimes called Old Brick (c. 1682), Smithfield, Va.; Christ Church (1732), Lancaster Co., Va.; and the Old Ship Meeting House (1681), Hingham, Mass. The first synagogue in America, Touro, was built at Newport, R.I., in 1763, and was designed by Peter Harrison (1716–75). The first Spanish colonial churches in what is now the United States were probably built in the Southwest near the end of the 16th century in what later became New Mexico. Since that time, numerous churches and synagogues have been built all over America. Many architects have designed them and the building continues. Some of these buildings in every era are considered among the finest examples of American architecture.

Related Articles ART IN ARCHITECTURE; COLLEGE AND UNIVERSITY BUILDING; HOSPITAL; HOUSING; RECREATION BUILDING; SCHOOL.

Further Reading *Architectural Record: Religious Buildings,* McGraw-Hill, 1979; Christ-Janer, Albert, and Mary Mix Foley: *Modern Church Architecture,* McGraw-Hill, New York, 1962; Thiry, Paul, Richard M. Bennett, and Henry Kamphoefner: *Churches and Temples,* Reinhold, New York, 1953.

Sources of Additional Information Guild for Religious Architecture, 1777 Church St., N.W. Washington, D.C. 20036; Stained Glass Association of America, 1125 Wilmington Ave., St. Louis, Mo. 63111.

Periodical *Faith & Form,* 1777 Church St., N.W., Washington, D.C. 20036.

REMODELING Rehabilitation, renovation, repairs, or alterations performed on an existing building. Often considered part of remodeling but actually new construction, an addition is an expansion that adds height or floor area to an existing building. Remodeling work is very similar to what is called restoration work. However, in restoration, an attempt is made to rehabilitate a building to a state resembling that when it was first constructed or that of some other period in its history, while remodeling involves rehabilitation without regard to the history of buildings.

Types of Work Remodeling may involve rehabilitation of only portions or all of a building. It may involve only rehabilitation of the building so it will perform its current function better, or it may be concerned with what has come to be called adaptive use, or recycling, of a building to change it to new uses, for example, from a hotel to an apartment building. Some remodeling projects are very small, involving only relatively small amounts of work and relatively low budgets; others may be quite extensive and involve millions of dollars in expenditures.

Practitioners Traditionally, remodeling work and additions to existing buildings have been the kinds of commissions, other than modest houses, which architects starting out in practice were most likely to receive. This is still the case, but it should not be inferred that only young, beginning architects do this kind of work. In fact, most architectural firms perform remodeling and addition work to some extent, if only for their established clients. And it is estimated that more than 75 percent of the architectural firms in the United States do some of this work on a regular basis. Some do remodeling work only as a service to their regular clients and do not expect to make appreciable profits on it. Other firms take on any remodeling and addition work which they can obtain and make profits that compare favorably with those for new buildings.

Building Types In any case, remodeling and addition work seem to be plentiful, and commissions for this type of work often seem easier to obtain than those for new buildings. Although the situation varies at different times, remodeling and addition work are usually available for most building types. However, such commissions are ordinarily most plentiful in certain types, such as offices, schools, houses, religious buildings, and stores. Not so plentiful, but still numerous enough to be attractive to architectural firms, are such types as apartments, hospitals, banks, factories, and public buildings. It might be assumed that most of these commissions would be for buildings of some considerable age, as is usually the case in preservation work, but actually that is not always the case. Surveys have shown that of the buildings remodeled

Exterior of building before remodeling. *(Henri Czechorowski)*

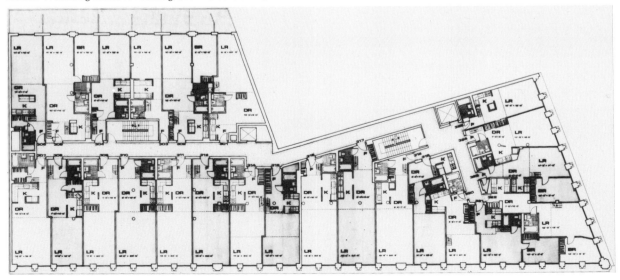

Typical floor plan.

Exterior of building after remodeling. *(Stephen B. Jacobs)*

Interior of typical apartment. *(James Brett)*

Isometric of typical apartment.

REMODELING Cast Iron Building, formerly McCreery's Dry Goods Store (1868), New York, N.Y. [*Architect: John Fellum. Remodeled into apartments (1978). Architect: Stephen B. Jacobs.*] Original five-story building converted into seven-story building by adding additional floors in ground and top stories. Apartments are two-level, with living areas on lower levels and bedrooms on second level.

at any given time, about one-half were less than 25 years old and about one-third were less than 15. It has also been shown that over one-third of these projects involved major additions of floor area.

It may therefore be seen that remodeling and addition work comprise a quite important part of architecture today. This kind of work is prevalent for several reasons. One of the most important is economic; building costs have gone up so radically in recent years that it is often possible to remodel an existing building much less expensively than it would be to construct a new one. In many cases, the structures and exteriors of older buildings are satisfactory, needing only minor work, and could not be duplicated by new construction for anything approaching the cost of remodeling. In such cases, the major work is usually renovation of the interiors and provision of up-to-date systems, such as heating, air conditioning, electrical, lighting, and elevators. Many other reasons exist for remodeling and addition work, including needs for changes in function, improvements for comfort and efficiency, increasing profitability, and needs for meeting code requirements set after a building had been constructed.

Remodeling Requirements Remodeling or addition work is usually handled by architects in a manner similar to that in which they handle new work. However, remodeling or addition work may often be considerably more complicated, and there may be problems not found in work on new buildings. These include factors related to the existing condition of buildings, some aspects of which may be hidden; the need sometimes for demolition; requirements for nonstandard materials to match or blend with existing ones; needs for changing certain elements of building, such as plumbing or electrical systems or structures and materials, to conform to building and other code requirements from which the buildings were formerly exempt; requirements for cutting, patching, and refinishing work and for removal of old materials and equipment from the building and the site.

Remodeling and addition work differs from that on new construction in other important ways. There will often be more concern with the economic and technical advisability, or feasibility, of a remodeling or addition project than a new one. Budgets for remodeling or addition work are often more difficult to prepare than for other jobs, because of the unknowns that are always present regarding the condition of existing buildings.

In spite of all of the problems, many architects find remodeling and addition work challenging, satisfying, and profitable. Because of its complications, such work usually brings higher fees to architects, sometimes up to twice as much as for new work with the same budget. For these reasons, many architects actively seek commissions for work of this type. Others are able to find clients, such as chain stores or chain hotel organizations which seem to be continually expanding their operations, making acquisitions of existing businesses and their buildings or seeking new markets. For many of these clients, remodeling and addition work also seem to go on continuously. Such continuing clients do much to make an architectural practice function more smoothly, efficiently, profitably, and most importantly, with continuity.

Architectural Services Very few, if any, architects have specialized departments to handle remodeling and addition work. Instead, services for these commissions are performed by the same people who handle such services for new buildings. And the services performed are generally the same as those for new buildings: programming; schematic design, along with preliminary specifications; design development; preparation of contract documents, working drawings, specifications, and others; and construction contract administration, including inspection of the work to ensure conformance with the contract documents. In addition, construction budgets are prepared early and gradually improved as more information becomes available during the architectural processes.

Some differences do exist in the manner in which services are performed for remodeling and addition work as compared to those for new buildings. In the first place, it is almost always necessary to make measured drawings of existing buildings. These are done by making actual measurements which are noted on sketches of floor plans and elevations. From this information architectural drawings may be drafted. Often much of the information that would ordinarily be in the specification may be placed instead on the working drawings. Specifications often vary more from job to job in remodeling and addition work than in new. There is usually an increased need for special conditions, such as patching, cutting, refinishing, demolition, and removal, not required for new work.

Another important difference is that remodeling and addition work often require more time and effort in the programming, schematic design, and design development phases than does new work. Remodeling and addition work also often require architects to spend more time on the construction site than they would for a new building of comparable size. And remodeling and addition work require, for proper execution, contractors, subcontractors, and craftspersons who are both experienced in and enjoy such work.

Sometimes a contractor may be selected very early, at the time of the schematic design phase or earlier, to allow the architect to obtain advice and counsel on materials, systems, and construction methods while the project is being designed. As in preservation work, as-built drawings, showing the work as actually constructed, are often required in remodeling and addition work.

Other design professionals, such as engineers and interior designers, often become involved in remodeling and addition work. In fact, the largest expenditures on some jobs of this type are for new or improved mechanical and electrical systems. And some jobs consist almost entirely of interior renovation and improvements.

Related Articles Construction Contract Administration; Cost Control; Design, Architectural; Feasibility Study; Practice of Architecture; Preservation; Programming; Specification; Working Drawing.

Further Reading Daizell, J.: *Repairing and Remodeling Guide for Home Interiors —Planning, Materials, Methods,* 2d ed., McGraw-Hill, New York, 1973; Scharf, R.: *The Complete Book of Home Remodeling,* McGraw-Hill, New York, 1975.

RENDERING

A drawing that illustrates floor plans, exteriors, interiors, or details of a building or a group of buildings. The word *rendering* is also used to denote the process of making such a drawing. Renderings have two main purposes. They are a means by which an architect or other designer visualizes and studies the design of a building, and they portray the appearance of a building to the owner of the building and to others. Renderings of the latter type are often called presentation drawings.

Terms Defined Delineation is often used as a synonym for a rendering, but more properly means any drawing, or the act of making a drawing. Other terms are important in rendering. Entourage is the landscaping and other features around a building in a rendering, and sometimes applied to the same elements around an actual building. An esquisse is a sketch or rendering, made in a relatively short time, to show the most important and general features of a building or a portion of it. A rendu is another name for rendering, and sometimes used for the color of a rendering. A wash is a method of applying watercolors in a rendering, usually in relatively large areas, as in a sky, by wetting the paper and letting the color flow from the brush onto the wet paper. A graded wash, in which the color is graded from dark to light, as often actually seen in the sky, is made by putting a small amount of color in the water on the paper and gradually adding more color as the wash proceeds across an area, or by starting with a dark color and gradually diluting it with water. A stretch is the preparation of watercolor paper for a rendering by soaking it in water, stretching it by hand onto a drawing board, then fixing it with vegetable glue. After drying, the stretch prevents buckling and rippling when watercolors are applied to the paper.

Characteristics Renderings may be quite small or very large. They may be in full color or in a single color. They may depict a complete building or group of buildings or only a small detail, such as a doorway. They may be made with quick, sketchy drawing techniques or controlled, painstaking techniques that take many hours. They may show only an impression of a building or a complete and realistic picture. They may have two dimensions as in a rendering of a floor plan or they may utilize perspective, a method that simulates depth, or three dimensions, in a rendering that has only two dimensions.

Renderers All architects learn to make renderings as a part of their education. And many continue to make sketches at least as part of their study of the design of their buildings. Some architects also make presentation renderings as part of their professional work, and in some architectural offices, one or more people may specialize in making these drawings. A person who makes renderings is called a renderer or delineator. Some renderers have their own specialized, free-lance offices and make renderings for architects, owners, or others. Some renderers, in architectural offices or in free-lance work, are not architects but learned their craft in architectural or art schools.

Much of the knowledge and many of the abilities required by artists in other fields are the same as those for renderers. All must have basic art knowledge and skills of drawing, perspective, shades and shadows, color, textures, form, and composition. In addition, a renderer must acquire a deep knowledge and understanding of architecture, in school, through experience, or from other studies.

Tools Renderers use all the basic equipment and tools employed by architectural and other draftsmen:

drafting tables, T squares, triangles, scales, pencils, and so on. In addition, they use a wide variety of other equipment and tools similar to those used by other artists, working with watercolors, inks, charcoal, special papers, and the like.

Pen and India ink, pencil, and watercolor, or combinations of these, all on paper, are the traditional rendering media. Renderers often use other media for all or a portion of their renderings: pastels; charcoals; Chinese ink, like India ink except that it comes in a stick which the renderer grinds and mixes with water; tempera, watercolors that are opaque rather than transparent like regular watercolors; and others. Sometimes a renderer will use a photograph as part of the rendering, for example, in a rendering of a building superimposed on a suitable photograph of its actual site. Montages, in which various pieces of other materials or other appropriate elements are arranged, are sometimes used; for example, in an interior rendering where it is considered important to show actual colors, materials, and textures of furniture, carpets, and curtains.

Other tools used by the renderer are brushes, watercolor, and others; a wide variety of pencils, black and a variety of colors; special papers; and a host of other items, some of which are artists' tools; some are everyday items like sponges, blotters, and cheesecloth; and others that are limited only by the ingenuity and needs of the renderer. In the past, when watercolor was the usual medium for a color rendering, special papers were used that when wet could be stretched onto a drawing board. These papers tighten as they dry, preventing curling or buckling when watercolors are applied. Today such renderings are often done on illustration, or poster, board made of a fine quality paper bonded to a cardboard backing.

Preparation of a Rendering The actual processes used in making renderings are as varied as the media in which they are done, the buildings they portray, and the knowledge, skill, and ingenuity of the renderers. Some idea of these processes may be gained through a generalized example of the preparation of a rendering. First, the renderer must determine the purpose of the rendering, what should be shown and how this is to be accomplished. The renderer then thinks the problem through, usually with the help of study sketches. Next, a medium, or combination of media, a size for the rendering, and a point of view for the people who will see the rendering might be selected. A perspective of the building would then be drawn, together with major landscaping or other required features and, when satisfactory, transferred to the final rendering paper. At this point, the techniques begin to vary widely. Some renderers start by lightly painting in the sky and lawn, continuing on to the general form of the building, then to details and to the final touches in the landscape, gradually developing each element of the rendering to its finished appearance. Others work directly on the whole rendering, in the manner of many painters. Some do

Rendering of scheme not used. *(Hugh Stubbins and Associates)*

Rendering of scheme not used. *(Hugh Stubbins and Associates)*

Rendering of adopted scheme. *(Hugh Stubbins and Associates)*

Rendering of atrium interior. *(Hugh Stubbins and Associates)*

Rendering of interior of Saint Peter's Lutheran Church. *(Hugh Stubbins and Associates)*

Rendering of exterior of Saint Peter's Lutheran Church. *(Hugh Stubbins and Associates)*

RENDERING Citicorp Center (1978), New York, N.Y. [*Architects: Hugh Stubbins in association with Emery Roth and Sons.*]

much of the detail work with pen and ink or with pencil. Some execute sharp, crisp lines for building corners and the like; others use a looser style. The variations are endless.

History Rendering has a very long tradition stretching back to prehistoric times. The Egyptians developed architectural symbol hieroglyphs and drew floor plans and elevations of buildings on papyrus, stone, or wood. The development continued in ancient Greece and Rome, though few examples of the drawings exist today, and through the work of monks and master masons (architects) on the Gothic churches and other buildings of the Middle Ages. These renderings represented little more than did the floor plans and elevations of the earliest times, though of course the later ones were more complex and complete.

Rendering took a giant step during the Renaissance, influenced by three major events. Paper became widely available. The invention of the printing press allowed architectural renderings and other materials to be widely disseminated, thus affecting architecture everywhere. And the first rules were formulated for the proper use of perspective to simulate the three-dimensional character of buildings. Renaissance architects used these new techniques extensively, making possible the construction of a building from drawings by an architect, who might appear on the site only occasionally rather than remaining there almost constantly as in the Middle Ages. Renaissance architects were deeply interested in rendering, and studied and practiced it with great skill. This interest has remained with architects, the subject studied and the skill actively sought, to the present day.

American Development The earliest drawings in America that would now be called renderings were done by amateur architects, who were self-taught from European books in their libraries. Later architects were knowledgeable and skillful in rendering, which they had learned in Europe before emigrating to the colonies. Shortly before the middle of the 19th century, American-born architects obtained their education, including rendering, in Europe. Many continued to do so even after American architectural schools had been established. One of the notable European schools, the Ècole des Beaux Arts in Paris, trained many American students. This school strongly emphasized rendering in its curriculum. This emphasis continued in U.S. schools of architecture until about the middle of the 20th century by means of architectural projects prepared and judged by members of the Beaux Arts Institute of Design in New York. Today the trend in rendering is toward newer techniques, including photography to complement or supplement the older methods, and others such as acrylic plastic paints, computer-assisted drawings.

Related Articles DESIGN, ARCHITECTURAL; DRAFTING; EDUCATION; ESTHETICS.

Further Reading Atkin, William Wilson: *Architectural Presentation Techniques*, Van Nostrand Reinhold, New York, 1976; Burden, Ernest: *Architectural Delineation—A Photo-graphic Approach to Presentation*, McGraw-Hill, New York, 1971; Capelle, Friedrich W.: *Professional Perspective Drawing for Architects and Engineers*, McGraw-Hill, New York, 1969; Halse, Albert O.: *Architectural Rendering—The Techniques of Contemporary Presentation*, 2d ed., McGraw-Hill, New York, 1972; Kemper, Alfred M.: *Drawings by American Architects*, John Wiley, New York, 1973; Kemper, Alfred M.: *Presentation Drawings by American Architects*, John Wiley, New York, 1977.

RENWICK, JAMES, JR. American architect (1818–95). Although he had been educated as an engineer, thus following the profession of his father, James Renwick, Jr. wanted to become an architect from an early age. Completely self-taught, he learned architecture from books, notably those of the French-English architect-theorists August Charles Pugin (1762–1832) and his son Augustus Welby Northmore Pugin (1812–52), both of whom wrote about the glories of Gothic architecture. To the knowledge he gleaned from books, Renwick added practical experience working in construction.

From a socially prominent New York City family, Renwick started out in architecture in 1843, by winning the commission for the design of Grace Church (1846; see illustration in article Gothic Revival architecture), the home parish of many of the wealthiest and most fashionable families in the city. For this church, he produced a fine design in Gothic Revival style, based on his studies of the books by the Pugins and others. He soon received other commissions and he eventually became one of the most successful American architects of his time. He was also one of the most consistent in design philosophy, never deserting the Gothic Revival style in any important way.

Works Although Renwick designed buildings of many types, including hospitals, schools, houses, and museums, he is remembered for his churches. Among the best of these churches still in existence in New York City are Grace Calvary (1846), St. Stephen's (1854), Riverdale Presbyterian (1863), St. Ann's (1869), and All Saints (1894). He did churches in other cities, including a little gem in Washington, Oak Hill Chapel (1850), but his masterpiece is St. Patrick's Cathedral, New York City, for which he received the commission in 1853. Delayed by the Civil War, St. Patrick's was essentially completed by 1879. Renwick added a rectory in 1884.

Other Renwick buildings still in existence in New York City include the Cleveland E. Dodge House (1863), known as Greystone and now a conference center for Teachers College, Columbia University; Cathedral High School (1869); and the Graymore Friars' Residence (1869), formerly St. Joseph's Church School. In Washington, the finest Renwick works are the first building of the Smithsonian Institution (1849); and St. Mary's Episcopal Church (1887).

James Renwick, Jr., practiced architecture for more than 50 years and designed many buildings, some of which are heralded as among the best examples of Gothic Revival architecture of all time in the United States. During his long career, Renwick had another

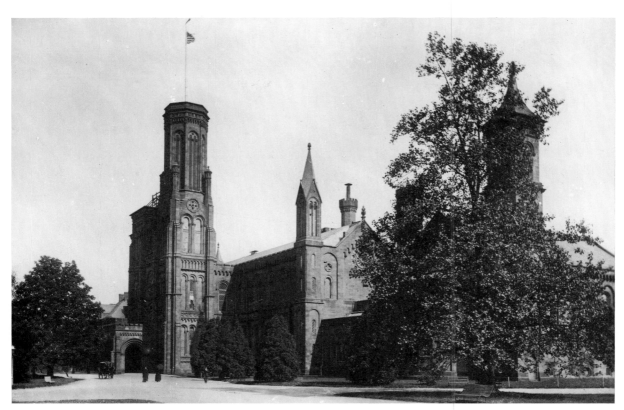

RENWICK, JAMES, JR. Smithsonian Institution (1849), Washington,
D.C. *(Detroit Publishing Co., Library of Congress)*

RENWICK, JAMES, JR. Renwick Gallery, formerly Corcoran Gallery
and Court of Claims (1859), Washington, D.C. *(Library of Congress)*

RENWICK, JAMES, JR.   Exterior, St. Patrick's Cathedral (1879), New
York, N.Y. *(Irving Underhill, Library of Congress)*

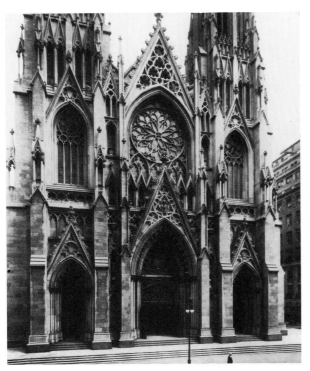

RENWICK, JAMES, JR. Exterior, St. Patrick's Cathedral (1879), New York, N.Y. *(Wurts brothers)*

important accomplishment: he trained a large number of young men who worked in his office. Some of these trainees became important architects, including Bertram Grosvenor Goodhue (1869–1924) who worked with Renwick from 1884 to 1891 and became thoroughly indoctrinated in Gothic Revival design. Having become disenchanted with the style late in life, Goodhue designed a notable building with modern overtones, the Nebraska State Capitol, Lincoln, completed in 1928 after his death. Another esteemed architect who trained in Renwick's office was John Wellborn Root (1850–91) who worked there in 1869 and 1870, after graduating in civil engineering. Root became more deeply involved in the modern movement than did Goodhue, and much earlier. With his partner, Daniel Hudson Burnham (1846–1912), Root designed some of the pioneering tall, skeleton frame buildings in Chicago that presaged the architecture of today. Goodhue's influence on modern architecture was minimal because he started too late; Root's influence was never fully realized because he died at age forty-one.

Life James Renwick, Jr., was born in New York City on November 1, 1818, and named for his father, an engineer, professor at Columbia University and amateur watercolorist. When he was young, Renwick exhibited artistic talent and expressed a desire to become an architect. Entering Columbia University, he graduated in 1836 and took an engineering position with the Erie Railroad. In 1839 he took a job as superintendent of the construction of the Croton Reservoir, completed in 1843 on a prominent site in mid-

town Manhattan, but demolished in 1900 to be replaced by the New York Public Library (1909) by Carrère and Hastings. On this job, Renwick gained his first experience in architecture and building construction.

In 1843, the year the reservoir was completed, Renwick entered and won a competition for Grace Church, which started him on an architectural career that became one of the most successful of the time. By the early 1870s, Renwick had become one of the most famous architects in the United States, and received more commissions than he could handle. To help with the buildings, Renwick took in a partner, Joseph Sands (d. 1880), and the firm became Renwick and Sands. After the death of Sands, James L. Aspinwall (1854–1936) became a partner and a short time later, Renwick's nephew, William W. Renwick (1864–1933), who had been trained in architecture in his uncle's office, became a partner. Still later, after William H. Russell (1854–1907) had become a partner, the firm became Renwick, Aspinwall and Russell. Regardless of what name it operated under, the firm did a large amount of work, most of it in and around New York City.

Other than in New York City, the most important Renwick buildings are in Washington. One of them, the Old Corcoran Gallery (1859), later used by the Court of Claims, was restored in 1972 by architects John Carl Warnecke (1919–), exteriors, and Hugh Newell Jacobsen (1929–), interiors. The building was then renamed the Renwick Gallery in honor of its original architect who, during his lifetime, had been an avid oriental art collector. A house on Fifth Avenue, New York City, was the last building by James Renwick, Jr., completed shortly before he died on June 23, 1895.

Related Articles BURNHAM AND ROOT; CAPITAL, UNITED STATES; CRAM, GOODHUE AND FERGUSON; GOTHIC REVIVAL ARCHITECTURE.

RESTAURANT A building, or rooms in a building, in which food and drink are prepared and served. Restaurants are an important building type, and almost all architects design them as individual buildings or as groups of rooms in buildings of other types. Restaurants may be very small to very large, serve low-cost, simple meals or snacks to very costly, sumptuous dinners. Their buildings or rooms and their interiors, furniture and furnishings, may be quite simple, even severe and relatively inexpensive, to very ornate and expensive. Restaurants may be located almost anywhere, by roadsides, in hotels, in office buildings, and so on. Restaurants serve fixed-price meals, with one price covering everything, or a la carte, with separate prices for each item; some offer both.

Types There are many kinds of restaurants, including hotel and motel dining rooms and coffee shops, fountain lunch counters often found in drugstores, sandwich shops, and complete restaurants. A

RESTAURANT Arnie's (1974), Chicago, Ill. [*Interior designer: Richard Himmel. (Hedrich-Blessing)*]

cafeteria is a special type with food displayed on counters by which patrons pass with their trays to be served or to serve themselves. An Automat is another special type of self-serve restaurant in which coins are inserted to open glass doors to obtain food and drink items. A vending machine restaurant operates in a similar manner, but offers only a limited choice of food and drink items, rather than the large selection often found in an Automat. Another type that has recently become popular is the fast-food restaurant. These restaurants, many of which are franchised or operated by large chains, sprawl across the country. Most of them serve simple foods, such as fried chicken, fish and chips, hamburgers, hot dogs, or sandwiches. Fast-food restaurants sometimes have seating for patrons, sometimes only food service with patrons eating in their automobiles or elsewhere.

Merchandising The success of any type of restaurant depends on good merchandising. The location must be right. The exterior must be inviting to the prospective clientele. The interior must satisfy the expectations of the clientele, as must the meals and beverages served. Patrons must be served in the manner they expect. The cost of dining must be appropriate to the level of quality of meals and service. Even when all these requirements are satisfied properly, there is no guarantee of success for a restaurant. There are too many intangibles, too many fads, too many fickle aspects of human nature. A badly designed restaurant, in a good location, serving popular meals at reasonable prices may well be a huge success, while one that is well designed, but lacking in some of the other aspects, may fail. Thus the construction of restaurants may be something of a gamble. To decrease the risk, architects and restaurant owners and operators must be very scrupulous in their study of the various factors and in the planning of everything from the building, its interiors and furnishings, to the menus to be served, the service to be provided, and the ambience.

Common Elements There are considerable differences in the design of various kinds of restaurants. A fast-food operation is different from a fancy French restaurant in important ways. However, all restaurants have some elements in common, including the dining areas, the serving areas, and the production areas. These elements and their relationships with each other must be properly designed. Important factors are the type of restaurant, type of menu to be served, type of service, volume of service, equipment to be used, traffic patterns, and storage.

RESTAURANT The Four Seasons (1958), New York, N.Y. [*Architect: Philip Johnson. (Joseph W. Molitor)*]

In a regular restaurant, regardless of location, serving full meals, the dining areas ordinarily have provisions for separate tables for one or two people, four people, and larger groups. In a simple restaurant, as little as 10 to 12 ft² of floor space per diner might be allowed; in a fancier one, as much as 20 ft². In some restaurants, banquette seating, which resembles sofas placed along walls, is used. This type of seating can only replace a portion of the movable chairs. Other seating arrangements include booths, often used in simpler establishments or coffee shops, and counter seating, used mostly in lunchrooms, sandwich shops, and coffee shops. Cafeterias, Automats, and vending machine restaurants may have any or all of these types of seating, as may fast-food operations, some of which provide no seating at all.

The serving areas of restaurants vary considerably. The menus to be served, the expected volume, and, most importantly, the type of service, all affect the design of serving areas. In a regular restaurant, in which waiters or waitresses serve tables, service stations are located in various parts of the dining areas. In the service stations, provisions are made for the preparatory work of waiters or waitresses, and for easy access to tableware, napkins and tablecloths, condiments, but-

ter, and so on. In a cafeteria, the serving area is a counter on which food and beverages are displayed in containers that may be heated or cooled as required, located between the dining and production areas. Fast-food serving areas are similar, but with fewer requirements for heating and cooling. Where food is served at counters, the counters are the serving areas.

The production areas also vary considerably because of the differences between types of restaurants. All types must provide for certain necessary functions, including receiving, storage, preparation, cooking, serving facilities, and sanitation. The spaces required for each of these functions depend on the size, menu served, and volume of the individual restaurant.

All restaurants must have facilities for receiving and for dry, low-temperature, freezer, and other types of storage. Preparation areas of restaurants may be quite simple, as in a fast-food operation where only a few simple foods are served. In a large, full-service restaurant, these facilities might be quite extensive and include specialized areas for preparation of meat, vegetables, salads, and sandwiches. Cooking facilities required also vary considerably between restaurants.

RESTAURANT McDonald's standard design. [*Architect: McDonald Corp. Staff. (Joseph W. Molitor)*]

In a fountain lunch, for example, a limited number of cooking appliances are located on the work area, or back bar, separated by an aisle from the counters. In a full-scale restaurant, the appliances required are determined by the menu served. One restaurant might limit the types of cooking, while another might do all types, including roasting, broiling, baking, grilling, frying, baking bread and pastries, and so on. Facilities must be provided for all these types and also for steam tables to keep meals warm and for plate warmers.

The serving facilities required in the production areas of restaurants also vary considerably from what amounts to almost none at all at a lunch counter to full facilities, including pickup points in the cooking area, pantries, cold food service areas, and checkout areas.

Sanitation requirements of all restaurants are similar, though they vary in size and complexity. Typical facilities include dishwashing, pot and pan washing, and waste disposal. In addition to the major elements, restaurants have requirements for cashiers; guest rest rooms; and locker, lounge, rest rooms, and dining facilities for employees. And some restaurants have provisions for entertainment; some have dance floors. Such establishments are often called nightclubs and may offer full food service or only drinks and snacks.

Except in the restaurants of chain operations, which tend toward standardized designs, each restaurant presents a unique set of problems to its designer. If it can be made to satisfy the wishes of the clientele it expects to attract, the design problems will have been properly solved. If it fails, at least a part of the problem will undoubtedly have been in its design.

A bar or cocktail lounge is an establishment in which alcoholic and other drinks are served, and sometimes light meals or snacks. A bar or cocktail lounge may be part of a restaurant or it may exist in-dependently. In either case, the required elements are similar to those of restaurants, as are the design considerations. In an establishment of this sort, the bar is a counter similar to that of a lunch counter, though often more ornate. Bars also have work areas, or back bars, as in lunch counters. The cocktail lounge portions provide seating at tables, in booths, and so on as in restaurants. Sometimes entertainment is provided, such as music by a piano player or a small group. And sometimes the piano may have a counter around it to form a piano bar. Nightclubs often operate in a manner similar to that of cocktail lounges, but ordinarily provide more elaborate entertainment.

History The first restaurants, called taverns or ordinaries, were located in the inns of 16th-century England. At first only travelers staying in the inns were served, but later others were allowed to come in, usually for one meal a day at a fixed time and price. A tavern or ordinary was later called a coffee house in England and in France, a *café*, the French word for coffee. In the 18th century, in France a *café* came to be called a *restaurant*, the French word for a restorative.

American Development The first restaurants in America were taverns or ordinaries similar to those in England at the time. They were located in inns along well-traveled roads and waterways, and later in towns and cities. Some of the early taverns are still in existence in various parts of the country, including the Fraunces Tavern (c. 1750), New York City, and Gadsby's (1752), Alexandria, Va. As the building of turnpikes, canals, and, later, railroads progressed, so did the building of inns and taverns.

The first restaurant of the sort known today was established in New York City, about 1834, by Lorenzo Delmonico (1813–81). Although no longer in its original building or location, Delmonico's Restaurant is still in existence. Soon after its founding, other restaurants were established in New York City and elsewhere. And many great restaurants have been designed during the years following. The first cafeteria, called the Exchange Buffet, was opened in New York City in 1885. Fast-food restaurants were first established early in the 20th century, multiplied after World War II, and in the past decade or so have mushroomed everywhere.

Related Articles HOTEL; RECREATION BUILDING.

Further Reading *Architectural Record: Hotels, Motels, Restaurants and Bars,* 2d ed., F. W. Dodge, New York, 1960; Davern, Jeanne M., ed.: *Places for People,* McGraw-Hill, New York, 1976; Smith, Douglas: *Hotel and Restaurant Design,* Van Nostrand Reinhold, New York, 1978.

RICHARDSON, HENRY HOBSON.

American architect (1838–86). Known as a romantic because of his espousal of the Romanesque Revival style, Richardson was nevertheless a creative architect who adapted the Romanesque into his own personal and logical style. His was the first of the styles of the eclectic era in architecture which was developed by an American architect and not adapted from the European revivals.

Although he lived less than 50 years, practiced only about 20, and designed less than 100 buildings, he became the most influential, some think the greatest, architect of his time. He is now acclaimed one of the greatest American architects of all time. Richardson has often been called the first modern architect, but he never really was that. He was a traditionalist, taking his inspiration from the architecture of the past and recasting it into buildings that were peculiarly and personally his own. He was not an innovator who invented new forms or used new materials or techniques.

Appraisal Richardson's buildings were designed to utilize the techniques and materials of the past, in particular masonry, mostly stone masonry, and wood, in a controlled and masterful manner. He was deeply concerned with the spaces within his buildings and the forms of the masses that composed them. Many of his buildings have a sculptural quality that was almost nonexistent in other buildings of his day, a quality that sometimes seems a prediction of the sculptural architecture of many other later architects. Richardson's buildings are bold in form and in details, also qualities of much of today's architecture. They are consumately three dimensional, as opposed to much of the architecture of his time that seemed as if it had leaped from the two dimensions of the drawing board to two dimensions in the buildings. Richardson spent a lot of time with the craftsmen working on his buildings, altering his designs as the actual job conditions warranted until he had everything the way he wanted it.

Richardson's architecture was accepted very well in his own day, by clients and by the public. Even the architects of the day were impressed. In 1885, a year before his death, they voted his Trinity Church the best building in America; it received 84 percent of the votes. And four of his other buildings were named among the 175 best buildings.

After his death, Richardson's architecture had little influence on the work of most architects, who now espoused an academic eclecticism. There were some notable exceptions. John Wellborn Root (1850–91), one of the Chicago pioneers of modern tall-building design, was influenced by Richardson's work. And Louis Henri Sullivan (1856–1924), the greatest of the early Chicago modern architects, admired and was deeply affected by the Richardson designs. Frank Lloyd Wright (1867–1959) was also impressed with and learned from Richardson's buildings.

During his career, Richardson designed a number of significant buildings. This is not to say that all his buildings were great. Many were below the standards of his best work. And the best examples intermingle with the others from the beginning to the end of his professional life.

Works The first important designs by Richardson were for the Church of the Unity, Springfield, Mass., and Grace Church, West Medford, Mass., both completed in 1869, both in a Victorian Gothic style. Richardson designed a great number of churches afterward, though he never considered himself a very religious person.

After designing houses, offices, a school, a bank, and so on in other styles, it is appropriate that his first building in the Romanesque style should be a church, this time the Brattle Square Church (1872), Boston. It is also considered one of his more significant buildings. He then designed a number of other buildings, including a school, a hospital, a courthouse, and houses. Next came the building many think his masterpiece, Trinity Church (1877; see color section for additional illustration), Boston, the first full expression of his Romanesque style.

Over the next few years, he designed a number of buildings, including three important Massachusetts libraries: the Winn Memorial (1878), Woburn; the Ames Memorial (1879), North Easton; and the Crane Memorial (1883), Quincy. He also designed the City Hall (1882), Albany, N.Y., and two important buildings at Harvard University in Cambridge, Mass.: Sever Hall (1880) and Austin Hall (1883), which house the law school.

Over the years Richardson designed a number of houses. Among the best are the Sherman House (1875), Newport, R.I.; the Stoughton House (1883), Cambridge, Mass.; the Brown House (1882), Marion, Mass.; and the Sard House (1883), Albany, N.Y.

During the last few years of his life, Richardson designed a great number of buildings, 30 of them in the last three years. He was an extremely popular architect, who took on a greater number of commissions than he could handle properly. These last buildings, 20 of which were incomplete at the time of his death, include some of the best of his work and some of the worst. Certainly three of the best, completed after his death in 1886, are the Marshall Field Wholesale Store and Warehouse (1887), Chicago, since demolished; the Allegheny County Courthouse and Jail (1888),

RICHARDSON, HENRY HOBSON Sherman House (1875), Newport, R.I. *(Wayne Andrews)*

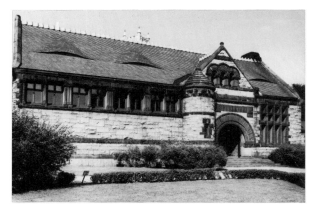

RICHARDSON, HENRY HOBSON Crane Memorial Library (1883), Quincy, Mass. *(Wayne Andrews)*

RICHARDSON, HENRY HOBSON Allegheny County Courthouse and Jail (1888), Pittsburgh, Pa. *(Joseph W. Molitor)*

Pittsburgh; and the Glessner House (1887), Chicago. Many think these three measure up to his Trinity Church and were the forerunners of what would have been a whole new creative era in his life, had he not died at age forty-seven.

Life Henry Hobson Richardson was born on September 29, 1838, at Priestley Plantation, St. James Parish, La., which is located about halfway up the Mississippi River from New Orleans to Baton Rouge. His father, a prominent businessman, died when the boy was sixteen. Richardson then spent the summers on the plantation and the winters in New Orleans, where he attended a private school. After a year at the University of Louisiana, now Tulane University, Richardson went to Cambridge, Mass., to be tutored for entry into Harvard University. After a rather undistinguished undergraduate career, he graduated from Harvard in 1859, with a degree in civil engineering, now determined to become an architect. In June of that year, he went to Paris. In the fall, he took the examinations for the École des Beaux Arts in Paris and failed everything except mathematics.

Richardson stayed on in Paris for a year, studying. In November 1860, he tried again and was admitted, becoming the second American to study there. Entering an atelier or study group, he began his architectural education, but after two years the Civil War in America disrupted his financial support. Going back to Boston, he could not find work, perhaps because as a Southerner, he would not take a loyalty oath to the Northern States. Returning to Paris, he worked as a draftsman in the office of Theodore Labrouste and possibly in others until 1865, when he returned to the United States. Urged by his family to come to New Orleans and by his friends to Boston, he did neither. He went to New York City, thus establishing once and for all that his career would be in the North instead of in Louisiana, to which he never returned.

The next few years were uneventful. Richardson worked for a while for a builder, then designed gas light fixtures for Tiffany's, and did other odd jobs. He was in extremely bad financial straits and was forced to sell his library, except for his architectural books. His first real break came in 1866 when he won a competition for the design of the Church of the Unity. In January 1867, Richardson married Julia Hayden, who had been his fiancée since his Harvard days. In October of that year, he formed a partnership with Charles Gambrill (c. 1832–80) that lasted with ever-decreasing effectiveness until 1878. In 1867 Richardson won the competition for Grace Church. The newly married couple settled in Staten Island, an unlikely choice of a home for an architect who never had any real commissions in the New York City area.

Commissions in Massachusetts began to come into the office in increasing numbers and even a few from places such as Buffalo, N.Y. One, a little building, the Agawam National Bank (1870), Springfield, Mass., since destroyed, gave the first hint of a later predilection for the Romanesque Revival style.

RICHARDSON, HENRY HOBSON Trinity Church (1877), Boston, Mass. *(Joseph W. Molitor)*

In 1870, his philosophy of architectural design still tentative and unformed, Richardson acquired his first assistant, Charles Rutan (1851–1915), who was associated with him the rest of his life. Another, Charles Follen McKim (1847–1909), just back from the École des Beaux Arts and destined to become a famous architect himself, joined the firm and stayed until 1872. Commissions continued to come in and Richardson won competitions for others, the most important of which were the Brattle Square Church in Boston and the Lunatic Asylum, now known as the State Hospital, in Buffalo, N.Y., which was not finished until 1878.

The eventful year in Richardson's life was 1872. In that year he received the commission for Trinity Church. In that year, McKim left to start his own practice and another young architect, who later made his own name, Stanford White (1853–1906), joined Richardson to stay until 1878. White afterward became a partner, with McKim, in the firm of McKim, Mead and White. Also in 1872 Richardson moved part of his practice to Boston, and in the spring of 1874, moved the rest of his firm and his family to Brookline, Mass. For the next 15 years, the firm produced some of the finest American buildings and Richardson became a famous architect.

By 1882, Richardson was tired, overweight, and ill. That summer, he returned to Paris for his only visit since he had worked there. He also went to London, consulted doctors about his health, and journeyed on to Italy and Spain. Everywhere he went, he collected photographs of Romanesque architecture. Returning to the United States, he received more commissions than he had ever had at one time in the past. As his health deteriorated, his designs became increasingly erratic.

In 1884 two young architects joined his firm, George Foster Shepley (1860–1903) and Charles Allerton Coolidge (1858–1936). On April 27, 1886, after a long illness, Richardson died at age forty-seven. A successor firm, Shepley, Rutan and Coolidge, was formed to finish the work on hand. The firm, now known as Shepley, Bulfinch, Richardson and Abbott, is still in existence. Thus this firm has had one of the longest-lasting practices in America. In 1973, in recognition of its work, it received the Architectural Firm Award of the American Institute of Architects.

Related Articles BEAUX ARTS, ÉCOLE DES; ECLECTIC ARCHITECTURE; MCKIM, MEAD AND WHITE; MODERN ARCHITECTURE; PUBLIC BUILDING; RELIGIOUS BUILDING.
Further Reading Hitchcock, Henry-Russell: *The Architecture of H. H. Richardson and His Times,* MIT Press, Cambridge, rev. ed., 1975.

ROAD AND TRAFFIC DESIGN The process of developing designs for facilities for vehicular traffic. Road and traffic design, or engineering, affects architecture in many ways. Since automobiles and other vehicles have become such an important part of life today, the design of facilities for them is of major concern in regional and city planning, which produce the total background or setting in which architecture exists. Streets and other vehicular facilities, such as parking adjacent to sites, also strongly affect the design of buildings placed on the sites. Provisions for vehicular facilities on building sites are of great importance and, in the case of architectural complexes, such as housing developments or shopping centers, can become dominant features of the designs.

Roads are strips of land on which vehicles travel. Roads within cities and towns are usually called streets, while major roads between urban areas are usually called highways, a name they acquired when roads were first constructed with their surfaces higher than the level of the ground.

U.S. Roads Several types of roads and highways are used in the United States. Local roads are used in smaller areas; secondary roads are used to connect smaller communities and for access to the primary highways that connect larger communities. The term *freeway* is used for a major highway, which theoretically allows free flow of traffic and which has controlled access at specific locations, called interchanges. Freeways are sometimes called superhighways or expressways and may require toll payments. When freeways pass through urban or congested areas, they are often elevated above or depressed below city streets. These are called grade separations.

Freeways that charge tolls were originally called turnpikes and some are still called that today. A parkway is like a freeway except that it is located in a landscaped, parklike setting and often only automobiles are allowed to use it. An interstate highway is a freeway, without tolls, connecting major urban areas of the United States. Freeways almost always have median strips, open land between the set of traffic lanes going in one direction and those going in the other, often with fencing or other devices to control accidents. Bypass highways are located so that traffic may go around or past towns and other urban areas. Circumferential highways, sometimes called beltways, go around large cities, allowing access to various neighborhoods or local areas directly, without passing through other areas of the cities.

Streets are very much like other roads, but are located in urban areas. Arterial streets handle major portions of the traffic; they are often larger than other streets and may have medians. Sometimes arterial streets are called avenues or boulevards.

Pertinent Factors Road, highway, and traffic design, planning, engineering, and construction are quite complex, because of the great number of important factors that must be taken into consideration. Long-range studies must be made of subjects, such as where people live or goods are produced, where they will go, how they will get there, and so on. The future of urban, suburban, regional, and larger areas must be studied. Traffic counts must be made and projected to indicate needs for the future. Utility requirements, lighting, landscaping, drainage, safety, grading, and other factors must be studied. Decisions must be made on the preparation of the land, surfacing, intersections, bypasses, grade separations, and other questions.

Government Finance Road, street, and highway construction is financed by governments, towns and cities on the urban level, and mostly states but sometimes counties on the rural level. The funds come from several sources: taxes, bond issues, tolls, and federal monies. The interstate system has been paid for, 10 percent by the states and 90 percent by the federal government, from a highway trust that receives money from taxes on items related to highway usage, such as vehicle fuels, tires, and tubes, and by trucks and buses.

Design Professionals Several design professionals are involved in the design, planning, and engineering of roads, highways, and streets: city and regional planners, highway and traffic engineers who have civil engineering degrees, landscape architects, and architects. The major functions in the analysis of their design and in their programming are often performed by city planners and traffic engineers; the major functions in their engineering, by highway engineers. Landscape architects often design the landscaping and architects become involved in relation to the buildings and building complexes they design.

History The history of roads goes back to prehistoric times, the first examples being trails and paths thought to have been made originally by animals and used by humans to track the animals. Later humans made their own trails while seeking water, food, and fuel.

During the Neolithic period, starting about the 40th century B.C., rudimentary roads were built and used for pack transport, first by women who carried the loads, while the men, presumably, protected the women. Following their domestication, some animals were trained to carry packs. The first is thought to have been the ass, beginning very early in the Neolithic period. the first vehicles for transport were sledges which slid on runners when they were pulled by humans and, later, by oxen or other animals.

After the invention of the wheel about 3500 B.C., road building began in earnest. Some of the first surfaced roads utilized what is called the corduroy system, logs or brushwood laid on the ground parallel to each other, to cross soft ground. These were followed by rut roads, made with grooves cut into the ground in which the wheels of vehicles could run. Roads were paved with stone no later than the 25th century B.C. Although travel by water continued to be used extensively, roads were built by the ancient Egyptians and by other people in the Middle East, and streets were paved in both Mesopotamia and Egypt with flagstones, some of which were set on brick bases with a mortar made of bitumen. Roads were also built in many other places, including China.

The ancient Greeks were not noted as road builders; most of the roads they built were rudimentary types, such as rut roads. The Romans were great road builders, not only in the extent of the network of roads they constructed all over Italy and their conquered territories but in the technical excellence of their work. The Roman roads were of two main types: paved; and sanded or graveled. Both were well designed and constructed. In one type of paved Roman road, for example, the surface of the ground was excavated to a proper level, then sand was laid down with cement mortar on top of it; on top of this were laid successive layers of stone slabs or blocks in mortar, concrete and a surfacing of stone set in mortar or concrete. The roads were sloped from the centers to the sides for water drainage and ditches were dug alongside to take away the water.

The Romans are thought to have built more than 50,000 miles of roads, some in Africa and Persia and some as far away as England. The first of their roads and perhaps the most famous was the Appian Way, begun in 312 B.C. This road runs 162 miles from Rome south to Terracina. Many Roman roads are still in use today.

During the Middle Ages and the Renaissance, road building came almost to a stop, even though many architects of the Renaissance period were interested in road design. Most of the roads that were built were unpaved, primitive tracks, often passable only by pedestrians, horseback riders, and pack animals. Starting in the reign of Louis XIV (1638–1715) of France and continuing through the era of the Emperor Napoleon (1769–1821), good roads were built in France for military purposes. In the rest of Europe, roads were not improved very much until the 17th century and later.

In the late 18th and early 19th centuries, two Scottish engineers revolutionized road building. First, Thomas Telford (1757–1834), also noted for his bridge designs, designed and built a network of good roads in Scotland, constructed of layers of stone with gravel. Then another engineer, John Loudon McAdam (1756–1836), developed even better and less costly methods of road building. For the more costly hand-laid stone foundations used previously, McAdam substituted thin packed layers of crushed stone by a method that was named for him, macadam, and which is still used today. Concurrent with the improved roads came the establishment of stagecoach travel, and in England, the building of the first toll roads, or turnpikes as they came to be called.

American Development In colonial America, the first roads were primitive trails. Until the end of the 18th century, most roads were unpaved and followed trails made by Indians. Travel was almost entirely by foot or horseback, later by stagecoach. The first hard-surfaced road, of crushed stone and gravel, in the United States was the Lancaster Turnpike, 62 miles long, constructed in Pennsylvania in 1795. Early streets were unsurfaced, but cobblestones and wooden blocks were used later and still later stone was used. In 1873 the first brick street was constructed in Charleston, W.Va. Bituminous paving was also used about that time. The first concrete street was built in 1893, and the first concrete road in 1908, in Detroit.

With the advent of automobiles, road and street building accelerated in the early part of the 20th century. In the 1920s a great deal of this sort of construction was carried on; then the activity slowed down during the Depression and World War II and accelerated again after the war. Since the 1950s, the Federal Interstate Highway System has added many thousands of miles of roads all over the United States. In all, there is a total of some 4 million miles of roads and streets in the country today.

Related Articles ENGINEERING; HOTEL; PLANNING, CITY.

Further Reading Halprin, Lawrence: *Freeways*, Reinhold, New York, 1966; Ritter, Paul: *Planning for Man and Motor*, Macmillan, New York, 1964; Robinson, John: *Highways and Our Environment*, McGraw-Hill, New York, 1971; Rose, Albert C.: *Historic American Roads—From Frontier Trails to Superhighways*, Crown, New York, 1976.

Source of Additional Information Institute of Transportation Engineers, 1815 N. Ft. Myer Dr., Arlington, Va. 22209.

Periodical *Traffic Engineering*, 1815 N. Ft. Myer Dr., Arlington, Va. 22209.

ROOF The weatherproofed topside of a building, including its structure and covering, or roofing. One of the major structural systems that protect buildings, their contents, and occupants from the effects of weather, roofs have always been important elements of architecture.

Forms Roofs come in many different forms, a traditional response to climatic conditions. In relatively arid areas of the world, roofs have tended to be flat. In other areas, with relatively large amounts of snowfall or rainfall, roofs have usually been sloped to drain off the precipitation. Today these principles still apply in architecture; however, improved materials and structural methods have made it possible for architects to use just about any form of roof they wish in almost any climate.

Sloped Roofs These roofs are often covered with shingles or tiles, which come in small units and depend on their overlaps and the slope of the roofs to prevent leaking. The slope of a roof is usually referred to as its pitch, meaning the ratio between the vertical

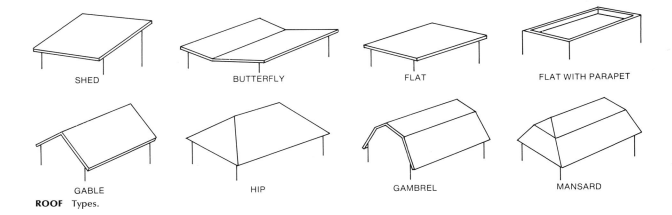

SHED   BUTTERFLY   FLAT   FLAT WITH PARAPET

GABLE   HIP   GAMBREL   MANSARD

ROOF Types.

rise of the roof and its horizontal span. For example, if a roof spans 10 ft and rises 5 ft, it is said to have a half-pitch, one in the ratio 5:10. For convenience, roof pitches are usually expressed in rise per foot of span; therefore a one-half pitch would be expressed as 6:12, denoting a 6-in rise in a 12-in span. Pitches may also be expressed in ordinary fractions, in which case the 6:12 example would be a ½ pitch. Some other commonly used pitches for roofs include: 0 for a roof that is flat or nearly flat; 3:12, or a ¼ pitch; 4:12, or a ⅓ pitch; and 5:12. Sometimes roof pitches may be even greater than the above.

Types The simplest roof is a flat one, though it usually has some slight slope or pitch. If it has a steeper slope, in only one direction, a roof is often called a lean-to or shed type. A roof that slopes in two directions from the top or peak toward the outsides is called a gable type and its form makes triangles at the ends, which the ancient Greeks termed pediments. A butterfly roof also slopes in two directions, but from the outsides down to its center. A hip roof has slopes on all four sides, the shorter ones usually being called the hips. A gambrel roof slopes up from only two sides, but has two different pitches on each side, the lower portions of the roof having steeper pitches than the upper portions. A gambrel roof is sometimes called a mansard roof, but often the latter term is applied to a roof sloping from all sides, like a hip type, but with two different pitches on each of the four sides. Other types are the sawtooth roof, often used in factories or other large area, low-rise buildings to permit the entry of more light, and sometimes air, than would otherwise be possible; and the monitor roof, which has raised sections with windows on their sides for the same purpose.

For the usual types of sloped roofs, the line along which two slopes meet at their highest level is called the ridge, the line along the lowest level is called the eave and, if it projects beyond the wall, is often called an overhang. The trough where two roof planes intersect is called a valley. The top of a wall that projects above the eave of a roof is called a parapet. A wall that projects through a roof surface, for fire-resistance purposes, is called a fire wall.

Other Forms Today there are a great variety of other roof shapes, made possible by advanced structural methods, particularly in reinforced concrete, steel, and aluminum. These include various kinds of vaults and domes in several geometric shapes, such as segments of spheres and cylinders, conoids, hyperbolic paraboloids, and hyperboloids. Many other roof forms are possible through the use of relatively new structural systems, such as lamella, laminated-wood arch, thin concrete shell, stressed-skin, suspension, and space frame.

Elements The major elements of a complete roof system are the roof structure and the deck or other surface upon which is placed roofing, the material used to weatherproof the roof deck. Two other elements are often used: a vapor barrier, laid on the deck to prevent moisture from the heated interior of a building from reaching the roofing; and thermal insulation, placed over the vapor barrier to retard the flow of heat into the building interior in hot weather and out of it in cold. A fifth element, almost always necessary to complete the weatherproofing of a roof, is flashing, a device usually made of metal, but sometimes of other materials, used to prevent water infiltration where roof planes meet and where roofing meets the edges of roofs, chimneys, or other building elements. Associated with flashing are devices to direct the flow of water from roofs, including gutters and downspouts and other types. For further discussion on vapor barriers, see articles entitled insulation, thermal; waterproofing. The latter article also covers flashing, gutters, downspouts, and so on. For further discussion on roof structures of various materials, see articles entitled concrete structure; steel structure; wood-frame structure. See also the article entitled roofing.

Roof systems are one of the most important determinants of architectural design, primarily because their forms have a great deal to do with the overall appearance of buildings; and because of their textures, colors, and patterns. Architects today design roofs in a variety of forms and may choose roofing from a great variety of types. The architectural treatment of roofs, their slopes and how they intersect, also strongly affects the appearance of buildings. A great deal of attention is therefore paid to the esthetic design of roofs.

In addition, a great deal of attention must be paid to proper structural design, detailing, and workmanship. Roof structures, including roof decks, must be strong enough to withstand the loads to which they will be subjected. They must be stiff enough so that undue deflection will not weaken their structures, lessen their weatherproofing qualities, or cause other problems. They must be designed and constructed in accordance with the fire-resistance qualities required in building codes. In many roofs, expansion joints must be provided to prevent damage to the materials when they expand and contract with changes in temperature.

In addition, roofs are often the location for building elements of many kinds, including penthouses for elevator or other types of machinery, water tanks, ventilators, skylights, scuttles for roof access, and dormer windows. All such elements must be properly designed, structurally as well as esthetically, and must be properly flashed or otherwise protected from water infiltration. Flat roofs are often used for terraces or other areas for various types of activities. If they are to be used in this manner, special provisions must be made so that their structures will withstand such loads, and they must be surfaced so that the roofing will be protected from damage.

History Ancient primitive buildings had roofs constructed of poles set in a conical shape. In Mesopotamia, roofs were flat and constructed of wood, or had vaults or domes constructed of brick, at first sundried and later kiln-dried. In Crete, wood was also used for roof structures, which were generally flat, and sometimes had slabs of gypsum over the timbers. Roofs in Egypt were generally constructed of stone slabs and were flat, making it possible to use them for various activities.

In ancient Greece, roof structures were generally framed in timber, in low-pitched, gable shapes. The Romans used a variety of roof forms (gables, vaults, and domes) constructed of a variety of materials, including wood, stone, and concrete. Early Christian buildings generally had gable roofs, made with wood members. Byzantine architecture utilized mostly domed roof structures of brick, stone, and concrete. In Romanesque architecture, barrel-vaulted roofs of stone were used along with timber roofs; sometimes both types were used for various portions of a single building.

During the Gothic period in architecture, roofs were constructed mostly with timber trusses, which were sometimes exposed on the interiors and some-

times placed over stone vaults. When exposed, the trusses were usually ornamented with carvings, especially in England. Gothic roofs were generally in gable shapes, with low pitches in Italy, medium pitches in England, and high pitches in France.

During the Renaissance, roof structures of several types were used, including gable roofs, with trusses of timber, and domes and barrel vaults of brick, stone, and sometimes concrete. In Italy, except for domes, roofs were generally low-pitched and were often concealed from view by railings or balustrades, or other ornamental architectural features. In the countries north of Italy, domes were often used as were gable, high-pitched roofs. Hip roofs, used only rarely before, were also sometimes used, as were flat roofs and the type of roof with two pitches, called a gambrel or a mansard roof, after the French architect Francois Mansart (1598–1666), who used it often and who even developed a type with three pitches. Renaissance roofs, particularly in France, often had many dormers and ornamental chimneys.

After the Renaissance, roofs used on buildings varied widely and included all the types previously used. As time went on, stone and brick were gradually abandoned as roof structural materials in America as well as in Europe and other places, to be replaced today by three major materials: steel, reinforced concrete, and wood. During the various revival and eclectic periods of architecture, roof styles were derived from those of the past.

After the beginning of the modern movement in architecture in the 19th century, flat roofs were used quite widely and the trend has continued to the present time. A type not ordinarily used in the past is the lean-to or shed roof, previously used only on the most ordinary buildings. Today many types of roofs are used, including all of those in the past. In addition, various curved and other shapes may be used in concrete, steel, and other materials. Also roof structures today may be space frames, made up from relatively small members of various materials in a variety of shapes; laminated timbers; and other types.

Related Articles ARCH; CONCRETE STRUCTURE; DOME; INSULATION, THERMAL; MASONRY STRUCTURE; ROOFING; STEEL STRUCTURE; VAULT; WATERPROOFING; WOOD-FRAME STRUCTURE.

Further Reading Griffin, C. W., Jr.: *Manual of Built-Up Roof Systems*, 2d ed., McGraw-Hill, New York, 1980; Krishna, Prem: *Cable-suspended Roofs*, McGraw-Hill, New York, 1978; Parker, Harry: *Simplified Design of Roof Trusses for Architects and Engineers*, John Wiley, New York, 1953.

Sources of Additional Information Asphalt Roofing Manufacturers Assoc., 757 Third Ave., New York, N.Y. 10017; National Roofing Contractors Assoc., 1515 N. Harlem Ave., Oak Park, Ill., 60302; Red Cedar and Handsplit Shake Bureau, 515 116th Ave., N.E., Bellevue, Wash. 98004.

ROOFING The materials used to make the top of buildings weatherproof. Roofing is the outer element of a roof system that also includes a structure of some sort with a deck over it, upon which the roofing may be placed. The system often includes a vapor barrier placed over the deck to prevent moisture from coming up from heated areas below and insulation over the vapor barrier to decrease the amount of heat entering a building interior in summer or escaping in winter. For further discussion on these other elements of complete systems, along with roof flashing, see articles entitled insulation, thermal; roof; waterproofing. Roofing is usually measured in squares, the amount that will weatherproof 100 ft² of roof structure.

Types The major types of roofing are classified by the forms they take and include large units called sheets; small units called shingles; and tiles, rolls, liquids, and composite systems, usually called built-up roofing. Each type of roof may also be classified according to the materials used. The sheet forms may be obtained in metals, such as aluminum and galvanized iron, and in asbestos-cement and plastics. Other metals, used less frequently because of higher costs, include stainless steel; copper; lead; zinc; terneplate, which is sheet steel coated with terne, an alloy of lead and tin; and Monel, a nickel-copper alloy. Many sheet roofing materials may be obtained in flat, corrugated, or crimped forms. Small-unit roofing may be obtained as wood shingles, or shakes, the latter like shingles but handsplit; asbestos-cement; asphalt and metal shingles; clay and concrete tiles; and slates.

Roll roofing is made of asphalt coated with mineral granules, and of plastics. Liquid roofing materials are types of plastics that are brushed, rolled, or sprayed on. Built-up roofing, sometimes called bituminous roofing, is made up of several layers of asphalt or tarred felt, which comes in rolls, alternated with layers of either liquid ashpalt, a by-product of petroleum, or liquid coal-tar pitch, a by-product of the manufacture of coke from coal.

For so-called flat roofs, those with very slight slopes or pitches, built-up systems are generally used, though liquid plastics or flat-seam metal roofs of copper, lead, or terneplate, or of stainless steel with welded joints may be used. Flat-seam and welded types are quite costly. All these types of roofing may be used on buildings of any types.

For most pitched roofs, shingles, tiles, or slates are used for roofing. Any of these materials may be used for any building type, but the most general use is for houses. For pitched roofs, any of the other types of roofing may also be used, including flat-seam metal roofing if required. However, if there is an adequate pitch, a simpler, easier to install and less costly type is a standing-seam metal roof, which is suitable for all types of buildings. Roll roofing and flat, corrugated, or crimped galvanized iron or aluminum roofing are mostly used for industrial, farm, or other utilitarian buildings. Corrugated plastic or plastic with glass fibers is often used in installations in which light must be admitted through the roofs, as in greenhouses. Liquid plastic roofing is used mostly for unusual shapes, such as domes and hyperbolic paraboloids.

Roofs of buildings are subject to great forces that tend to damage or destroy them, such as sun, rain, snow, and wind; and alternate freezing and thawing, wetting and drying. The first requirement for good roofing is proper design and construction of the roof structure and deck. These must be designed not to deflect unduly under loads placed on them and must be smooth, clean, and dry before application of the roofing.

For most roofing materials, a layer of roofing felt is first nailed, or otherwise adhered with asphalt or coal-tar pitch, to the roof deck. In a built-up roofing system, successive layers of felt are then adhered until a total of three, four, or five piles have been laid. The top of the last layer of felt is then covered with asphalt or coal-tar pitch and usually finished with gravel or slag. Hot asphalt or coal-tar pitch is usually applied to built-up roofs, but sometimes cold applications are made, though they are not often recommended except for making repairs. Single-ply roofing, sheets of bitumen or asphalt with plastics, or of plastics alone, are also used for such purposes and, increasingly, for simpler roof structures.

Some types of shingles and tiles come in a variety of shapes which create different patterns when they are placed on roofs. Some shingle types, such as asphalt, are made in large sizes, each cut and shaped to resemble several shingles. Ordinarily, shingles and tile are nailed to roofs over asphalt roofing felt or rosin paper.

Characteristics The selection of roofing for an individual building presents an architect with an almost endless variety of types, forms, appearances, textures, colors, life expectancies, fire resistances, and costs. Built-up roofs are restricted to the colors available in the gravel or other materials with which they are covered, unless they are surfaced with tile or some other material for use as roof terraces or for some other purpose. Natural materials, such as slate or wood, generally cedar but also available in redwood or cypress, have color, texture, and weathering characteristics peculiarly their own. Each of the metals has its own color and other characteristics. Galvanized iron should be painted and thus has unlimited color possibilities. Most other roofing materials have limited color and texture ranges, except for asphalt shingles.

Life expectancies for roofing range from about 15 years for wood shingles, somewhat more for asphalt shingles, up to about 20 years for some built-up types, and somewhat more for such materials as asbestos-cement shingles, slate, clay tile, copper, stainless steel, terneplate, and a few other metals. Fire resistances of roofing materials range from the lowest for wood shingles which are combustible and asphalt shingles which have little resistance, through the metals which are incombustible, to asbestos-cement clay and concrete tile and slate which are quite fire resistant. The fire resistance of built-up roofs varies considerably with differences in structures, decks, types of application, and surfacing materials. Building codes determine which roofing materials meet fire-resistance requirements.

The cost of roofing materials varies widely from the lowest, roll roofing, through intermediate levels, including asphalt shingles, usually considered to be the lowest-priced acceptable material for houses, to very high-priced types such as flat-seam roofs of several metals.

History In the primitive cultures of early history, roofing is thought to have been of animal skins or brush, thatch, or other vegetation. In Mesopotamia, roofing was usually of clay and reeds or bitumen on masonry. In Egypt, roofing was not employed on top of roof structures, but the stone of the structures had channels cut in it to take away rain.

Roofing in ancient Greece was of marble or terra-cotta tiles. In Rome, roofing was of terra-cotta tiles, but sometimes marble tiles or bronze were used. In Byzantine architecture, no roofing at all was used for many buildings; in others, metals, such as lead, were sometimes used.

During the Middle Ages, in the Romanesque and Gothic periods, slate and lead were the major roofing materials. During the Renaissance, both materials were used, as were tile and slabs of other kinds of stone. By the end of the Renaissance, many of the various kinds of roofing materials used today had been developed. Notable exceptions are galvanized iron, which dates from about the middle of the 19th century; asphalt and aluminum, from about the end of that century; and plastic, a 20th-century roofing material.

Related Articles ROOF; Various articles on individual building materials.

Further Reading Griffin, C. W., Jr.: *Manual of Built-Up Roof Systems,* 2d ed., McGraw-Hill, New York, 1980.

Sources of Additional Information See listing in the article entitled roof.

SAARINEN, EERO Finnish-American architect (1910–61). Son of a famous architect-father and a talented artist-mother, Eero Saarinen was almost preordained to become an architect. Instead, he decided to become a sculptor but later changed his mind, and became one of the most sculptural architects. He was also one of the most inventive, particularly in the forms of his buildings.

After graduating from Yale University School of Architecture in 1934, he joined his father in 1937 in a partnership, Saarinen and Saarinen, located in Bloomfield Hills, Mich., and the two worked together until the death of the father in 1950.

In 1948 Eero Saarinen won the competition for the design of the Jefferson National Expansion Memorial in St. Louis, with a giant stainless-steel-covered arch that came to be known as the Gateway Arch. The favorable publicity his design received brought in commissions independently of his father. After the death of his father, he started his own firm, called Eero Saarinen and Associates. In the little more than a decade he had left to live, Saarinen designed a number of buildings, many of which received sensational receptions in the press and among architects. Most of the buildings were sculptural in form and each seemed to have been designed with little or no reference to those that preceded it.

Works Among the first were the Kresge Auditorium and the Chapel (both 1955) at the Massachusetts Institute of Technology, Cambridge. These were followed by the U.S. embassies in London (1956) and Oslo, Norway (1959); two 1956 buildings for International Business Machines at Rochester, Minn., and Yorktown Heights, N.Y. (see illustration in article stone); the John Deere Administration Center (1957), Moline, Ill.; two buildings at Concordia College (1958), Fort Wayne, Ind.; the Ingalls Hockey Rink (1959) at Yale University, New Haven, Conn.; the University of Chicago Law School (1960), Chicago; and the TWA Terminal (1960) at John F. Kennedy, then Idlewild, International Airport, New York City. Several of his most interesting buildings were completed after his death, including the Samuel F. B. Morse and Ezra Stiles colleges (1962) at Yale University; the CBS Building (1965; see illustration in article office building), New York City; the Vivian Beaumont Theater (1965), Lincoln Center for the Performing Arts, New York City; and the Gateway Arch (1965). His great and pioneering design for Dulles Airport (see illustration in color section), Chantilly, Va., was not finished until 1963. Many people think it his masterpiece.

Appraisal Eero Saarinen was something of an enigma to the public as well as to his fellow architects. He never quite seemed to fit into any mold or pattern. Each building design seemed to present him with a specific challenge which he then answered in an original way. He always seemed to be searching for something newer or better, or both. And he never seemed to find it, at least not for long. He never seemed to have been interested in developing a style in his work, unless it was the style of treating each new problem as if there were no precedents for its solu-

SAARINEN, EERO Kresge Auditorium (1955), Massachusetts Institute of Technology, Cambridge, Mass. *(Joseph W. Molitor)*

SAARINEN, EERO Chapel (1955), Massachusetts Institute of Technology, Cambridge, Mass. *(Joseph W. Molitor)*

tion. His accomplishments startled and surprised many people. He was always fresh and intriguing. Many people called him a genius, but others are still not completely convinced.

Life Eero Saarinen was born on August 2, 1910, in Kurkkonummi, Finland. His father, Eliel Saarinen (1873–1950), was already a famous architect in Europe. Something of a prodigy, who could sketch with either hand, young Saarinen had little formal training in his early years. But he designed, drew, painted, and modeled. In 1922, when he was twelve, he won a contest for a design with matchsticks. In that same year, his father placed second in the competition for the design of the Chicago Tribune Tower, and received great acclaim for the design which many critics thought superior to that of the winner.

As a result of the prominence that came from the Tribune Tower competition, Eliel Saarinen moved to the United States and Eero and the rest of the family joined him in 1923. In 1925 the family moved to Bloomfield Hills, Mich., where Eliel became director

of the Academy of Art. Eliel designed the Kingswood School for Girls (1929) there, for which Eero designed sculptural wood furniture. Having decided to become a sculptor, he then enrolled in 1929 in the Grande Chaumière in Paris. After a year, he changed his mind and transferred to the architectural school at Yale University. Graduating with honors in 1934, he won a two-year traveling scholarship and went to Europe.

After returning from Europe, Saarinen went back to Cranbrook in 1936, to serve as a design instructor and in 1937, to join his father's architectural firm, which was renamed Saarinen and Saarinen. Some of the notable buildings they did together are the Kleinhaus Music Hall (1938; see illustration in article Saarinen, Eliel), Buffalo, N.Y.; the Crow Island School (1939; see illustration in article school), Winnetka, Ill., in association with a Chicago firm destined for success, Perkins, Wheeler and Will; and the Tabernacle Church of Christ (1940; see illustration in Saarinen, Eliel), Columbus, Ind. In 1939 he married Lily Swann, a student of ceramics at Cranbrook. In 1940 he and

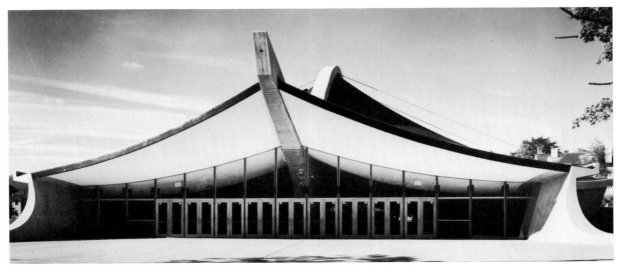

SAARINEN, EERO Ingalls Hockey Rink (1959), Yale University, New Haven, Conn. *(Joseph W. Molitor)*

SAARINEN, EERO TWA Terminal (1960), John F. Kennedy International Airport, New York, N.Y. *(Ezra Stoller)*

SAARINEN, EERO Gateway Arch (1965), St. Louis, Mo. *(Hutchinson Photographers)*

SAARINEN, EERO John Deere Administration Center (1957), Moline, Ill. *(Ezra Stoller)*

Charles Eames (1907–1978) won two first prizes for furniture design in a competition of the Museum of Modern Art in New York City. During World War II, Saarinen served with the Office of Strategic Services from 1942 to 1945. Even during his wartime service, he found time to work with his father on building designs.

After the war, the Saarinens received commissions for important buildings and other projects, among them campuses for several colleges. The largest and most comprehensive project was the General Motors Technical Center, Warren, Mich. The design of this more than $20 million complex, with associated architects Smith, Hinchman and Grylls, began soon after the war but was not completed until 1957, seven years after the elder Saarinen died. In 1948 Eero Saarinen won the competition that established him as an individual architect, the Gateway Arch, which was not finished until 1965, after his death.

In 1953, having been divorced, Saarinen married Aline B. Louchheim (1914–72), an art critic and later a television commentator. After winning the Gateway Arch competition, he received a great number of commissions for buildings of all types. For each one, he seemed to be able to come up with a design unlike that of any of the others. The large number of projects required a large staff, which eventually reached about 100 people. Among them were some talented younger men, including the Irish-American architect Eamonn Kevin Roche (1922–   ) and John Gerard Dinkeloo (1918–   ) who later formed a successor firm to that of Saarinen and have themselves since designed many notable buildings.

At age fifty, Eero Saarinen seemed to have everything. His architectural design was inventive and virile. Commissions were pouring in. His personal life was happy. Honors were coming in, including election as fellow of the American Academy of Arts and Letters. Then tragedy struck him down at age fifty-one

at the peak of his powers. On September 1, 1961, he died after brain surgery. The following year, he was awarded, as had been his father, the highest honor of the American Institute of Architects, the Gold Medal. The posthumous award was accepted in his name by his widow, Aline Saarinen.

Related Articles CONTEMPORARY ARCHITECTURE; MODERN ARCHITECTURE; SAARINEN, ELIEL.

Further Reading Saarinen, Eero, and Aline B. Saarinen, eds.: *Eero Saarinen on His Work—A Selection of Buildings Dating from 1947–1964*, Yale University Press, New Haven, Conn., 1968; Temko, Allen: *Eero Saarinen*, Braziller, New York, 1962.

SAARINEN, ELIEL Finnish-American arthictect and planner (1873–1950). Originally having expected to become a painter, Eliel Saarinen changed his mind and instead became one of the foremost architects, planners, and educators of his era. His buildings and city plans left their mark on the development of modern architecture. His philosophy, as expressed in his books, and especially as expressed in the school he built, Cranbrook Academy of Art, Bloomfield Hills, Mich., had an even greater effect on modern architecture.

Only about six years after Walter Adolf Gropius (1883–1969) started the Bauhaus, the influential German school of modern design, Saarinen instituted a similar program in the United States, at Cranbrook. There were differences in philosophy between the two schools, of course. The Bauhaus, for example, was perhaps more dedicated to design for machine-made products. Cranbrook was more dedicated to humanism. In both schools, the emphasis was on the integration of all the design arts, not just architecture alone. And both schools attracted talented faculty members and students, who went on to great accomplishments in their chosen fields.

Saarinen had a considerable reputation in Europe before he arrived in the United States in 1922. The only thing known about him in America was his masterful design for the Chicago Tribune Tower, which won second place in the competition but engendered a great deal of publicity. In Finland, he had designed a number of notable buildings and city plans. And he continued to do so in the United States.

Works He designed almost the entire educational complex at Cranbrook, including the Kingswood School for Girls (1929), the Cranbrook School for Boys (1930), and the Cranbrook Academy of Art (1941). His son, Eero Saarinen (1910–61), joined him in a partnership, Saarinen and Saarinen, in 1937, and together they designed a whole series of interesting buildings, including the Kleinhaus Music Hall (1938), Buffalo, N.Y.; the pioneering Crow Island School (1939; see illustration in article school), Winnetka, Ill., in association with Perkins, Wheeler and Will; the Tabernacle Church of Christ (1940), Columbus, Ind.; the Tanglewood Opera House (1944), Lenox, Mass.; Christ Lutheran Church (1949), Minneapolis, in association with Hills, Gilbertson and Hays; and the more than

SAARINEN, ELIEL Kleinhaus Music Hall (1938), Buffalo, N.Y. [*Architects: Saarinen and Saarinen. (Wayne Andrews)*]

SAARINEN, ELIEL Tabernacle Church of Christ (1940), Columbus, Ind. [*Architects: Saarinen and Saarinen. (Hedrich-Blessing)*]

$20 million General Motors Technical Center, Warren, Mich., in association with Smith, Hinchman and Grylls, completed in 1957, seven years after Eliel Saarinen died.

Eliel Saarinen left a legacy for future architects and all those who enjoy architecture, in his buildings, in his books, and especially in the students whose careers he helped to mold.

Life Gottlieb Eliel Saarinen was born in Rantasalmi, Finland, in 1873, the son of a Lutheran minister. The family moved to Ingermanlandia, Russia, about 30 miles south of Leningrad, then called St. Petersburg, when young Saarinen was two years old. Here he spent his childhood in a rural atmosphere, while his father ministered to the Finnish-speaking peasants of the area, recently released from serfdom. From an early age, he drew and painted and thought he would like to become an artist.

Saarinen went back to Finland to attend high school in Wiipuri. Passing through St. Petersburg on his trips to and from school, he spent many hours in the Hermitage, one of the world's greatest art museums. These visits strengthened his desire to become a painter but he also had reason to believe that architecture might prove to be more practical. In 1893 he enrolled simultaneously in the Polytechnic Institute in Helsinki as an architecture student and in the University Art School as a painting student. Before graduating in 1897, Saarinen had made up his mind to practice architecture. But he never lost his deep interest in painting and the other arts.

Even before he left school, Saarinen started an architectural firm in 1896, in partnership with Herman Gesellius and Armas Lindgren. His Finnish Pavilion for the Paris Exposition of 1900 brought him recognition

SAARINEN, ELIEL Cranbrook Academy of Art (1941), Bloomfield Hills, Mich. [Architects: Saarinen and Saarinen. (Hedrich-Blessing)

in Europe as a talented architect and his National Museum (1902) and Central Railroad Station (1904), both in Helsinki, firmly established his reputation.

In 1902 Saarinen and his partners designed and built a studio house with 38 rooms, Hvittrask, on a bluff overlooking a lake 18 miles from Helsinki. In 1904 he married Loja Gesellius, a sister of his partner, and in 1905 their first child, Eva-Lisa, always called Pipsan (1905–79) was born.

Loja was a talented artist, who did sculpture, weaving, and photography. Pipsan later became a noted designer. In 1910 a son, Eero, Finnish for Eric, was born and he, like his father, became a famous architect. The house-studio was the early training school in the arts for both children. Surrounded by such activities, they too soon began to design, paint, draw, and model. And all these pursuits became a family affair, a situation that continued during the later part of their lives. The house-studio was also a center of cultural pursuits, attracting a number of the great men of the time who came not only for the good conversation but for recreation. Among the regular visitors were Eliel Saarinen's good friends, Jean Sibelius (1865–1957), the Finnish composer, and Carl Milles (1875–1955), the Swedish sculptor, who later joined Saarinen at Cranbrook. And they were often joined by others, including the Russian writer Maxim Gorki (1868–1936), the Austrian composer Gustav Mahler (1860–1911), and another close friend of Saarinen's, Julius Meier-Graefe (1867–1935), the German art critic and writer.

In 1907 Saarinen left the partnership but continued to practice architecture; and having become involved in city planning, he designed plans for Reval and Helsinki, Finland. In 1922 he won second prize in the Chi-

cago Tribune Tower competition, with a design that many people preferred to the winner. Having come to America to receive his prize, he decided to stay, and later brought his family to New York and then to Michigan a short time later. Named director of the Cranbrook Academy of Art (see illustration in article art in architecture) in 1925, a position he held the rest of his life, Saarinen transformed the school into an institution where all the design arts were integrated and taught together.

Saarinen started another architectural practice in Bloomfield Hills, and soon the work again became a family affair. On one early project, the Kingswood School for Girls, Saarinen designed the building; his wife, Loja, did the rugs, draperies, and furniture coverings; his daughter, Pipsan, designed the auditorium and dining hall interiors; and his son, Eero, designed the furniture. In time, Saarinen designed the campus and buildings for the entire Cranbrook complex.

The reputation of Cranbrook spread and soon the school began to attract students who would later become noted designers themselves. Some of them were Charles Eames (1907–78), designer; Harry Bertoia (1915–78), sculptor; Harry Weese (1915–), architect; and Ralph Rapson (1914–), architect and architectural educator.

His partnership with his son, Eero, produced a number of notable buildings and lasted until Eliel Saarinen died on July 1, 1950. He had accomplished a great deal in architecture, in planning, and in education. By that time, he had gained worldwide recognition for his work in all three fields. In 1947 the architects of his adopted country awarded him their highest honor, the Gold Medal of the American Institute of Architects.

Related Articles BAUHAUS, STAATLICHES; EDUCATION; HOOD, RAYMOND MATHEWSON; MODERN ARCHITECTURE; SAARINEN, EERO.

Further Reading Christ-Janer, Albert: *Eliel Saarinen,* University of Chicago Press, Chicago, 1948; Saarinen, Eliel: *The City—Its Growth, Its Decay, Its Future,* Reinhold, New York, 1943; Saarinen, Eliel: *Search for Form—A Fundamental Approach to Art,* Reinhold, New York, 1948.

SCHOOL A building, or buildings, in which students are given organized instruction at levels below that of a college or university. The main purposes of schools are to impart knowledge and skills to young people, and to teach them how to live productive, useful, and satisfying lives as members of society.

School Systems For many years in the United States, school education was divided into the 8–4 system: elementary, the first eight grades, followed by secondary, the last four grades. Elementary education was the minimum that was considered acceptable and secondary education, in high schools, was considered highly desirable. A secondary education is now considered the minimum. And those who only achieve this minimum are expected to learn at least the rudiments of trades or skills, with which they can work after graduation, in addition to the academic and physical education they receive. For students expected to enter college, the emphasis has been on academic preparation for further education.

During the first half of the 20th century, the trend was toward further subdividing school systems, in order to help meet some of the stresses students face in adolescence and in the process of maturing. Thus the so-called 6–3–3 plan was introduced, with elementary schools providing grades 1 through 6; junior high schools the last two elementary grades, 7 and 8, and one of the secondary, 9; and senior high schools providing grades 10 through 12. There has been a trend toward the addition of another grade to precede the first, kindergarten, intended to prepare young children, usually five-year-olds, for elementary school, thus making K–6–3–3 school systems. Kindergartens have existed for a long time in the United States, but only recently have come to be considered a mandatory part of education in some communities. Often kindergartens are located in elementary schools. This system spread all over the United States, though not all school systems adopted the exact system in its entirety. For example, some systems combined the two higher schools into junior-senior high schools, the K–6–6 system. Recently, there has been a tendency to separate grades even further. In many systems, other types of schools have been added, and the types are elementary, K–4; middle, 5–8; and high, 9–12; the K–4–4–4 system. And some systems have gone even further, to elementary, K–4; middle, 5–6; intermediate, 7–8; and high, 9–12; the K–4–2–2–4 system.

Most secondary schools offer both practical and academic training to students, thus preparing them for either vocations or for further education. In some school systems, particularly in large cities, some high schools specialize in vocational training, along with academic courses. Such institutions include trade schools, technical schools, business schools, and agricultural schools.

Other Types Other kinds of schools include community, neighborhood, regional (central or consolidated), and special schools for students who are retarded, handicapped, or unusually intelligent. In community schools, facilities are provided for regular use during nonschool hours for athletic, social, educational, and other activities by children and adults, including the elderly. Other schools may be used occasionally for such purposes. Neighborhood schools serve small community areas where students can ordinarily walk to and from school. Regional (central or consolidated) schools serve larger areas, such as counties, where students usually ride buses to and from school. Regional (central or consolidated) schools serve larger areas, such as counties, where students usually ride buses to and from school. Special schools for the retarded, handicapped, or unusually intelligent are sometimes provided in communities, but the trend today seems to be incorporation of these students in the general school system.

In addition to the above schools, there are over 4,000 nursery schools in the United States. These are mostly private schools, for children aged three and four, which teach basic skills. They also provide for small children of working parents, as do day care centers.

Ownership and Operation School systems are owned and operated by governmental bodies, usually towns, cities, or counties, called public schools; private schools, by private organizations that are usually nonprofit; or parochial schools, by church organizations. Some private and parochial schools are called preparatory schools, reflecting the fact that their primary function is to educate students to enter colleges and universities. Private and parochial schools are administered by individuals, often called principals or headmasters, appointed by the governing boards which set policies. Public schools are usually administered by principals, appointed by superintendents of education, the top administrative officers of these systems, often called districts. Superintendents are elected by the voters or appointed by boards of education, the top policymaking bodies in the public school districts. Members of boards of education, often called school boards and sometimes boards of trustees or school trustees, may be elected by the voters, or appointed by city councils, county commissioners, or other community officials.

New Schools In the United States, there are some 100,000 elementary schools with an enrollment of more than 30 million students, and over 30,000 junior, senior, and junior-senior high schools with more than 14 million students. The need for new schools varies considerably over the years, due mainly to fluctuations in the birthrate at various times. Therefore,

SCHOOL Exterior, Crow Island (1939), Winnetka, Ill. [*Architects: Saarinen and Saarinen and Perkins, Wheeler and Will. (Hedrich-Blessing)*]

SCHOOL Interior, Crow Island (1939), Winnetka, Ill. [*Architects: Saarinen and Saarinen and Perkins, Wheeler and Will. (Hedrich-Blessing)*]

though schools are a very important building type, the number being designed and built at various times fluctuates considerably. Education is now compulsory in all the United States, but the length of time students must attend or the ages that they must attain before leaving school varies between the states. These factors also affect the number of schools built in a given period in various localities. In spite of the variations, schools constitute a building type designed by a great number of architects, and in many cases constitute an important part of their practice.

Facilities The design of any school begins with the establishment of an educational program, stating the educational concept, its goals and purposes, the activities to be carried on, and the detailed area, space, and equipment requirements. Based on the educational program, study can then be made of the major facilities of schools: instructional, academic and vocational; athletic, physical education and recreational; service; administrative; and maintenance and mechanical-electrical equipment.

Academic and vocational instructional facilities include classrooms, laboratories, workshops, libraries, auditoriums, band and choral rehearsal rooms, and sometimes art studios, theaters, and lecture halls. Athletic, physical education and recreational, facilities include such indoor spaces as gymnasiums and swimming pools and such outdoor areas as playing fields and stadiums. Closely related to the instructional ele-

SCHOOL Sarasota High (1960), Sarasota, Fla. [*Architect: Paul Rudolph. (Joseph W. Molitor)*]

ments are the service facilities, such as cafeterias, restrooms, student lockers, student lounges, and parking lots. Administrative facilities include offices for principals, teachers and counselors, faculty lounges, and sometimes dining rooms, first aid or health rooms, and conference rooms. Maintenance and mechanical-electrical facilities include spaces for janitorial services and heating, air-conditioning, and other mechanical and electrical systems.

Educational Improvement In some schools, several functions may be performed in one area of the building, often called an all-purpose or multipurpose room. Here any two, or all three, functions of an auditorium a cafeteria, and a gymnasium may be provided. Another method for converting spaces to multipurpose uses is provision of movable partitions, folding or accordion doors, or other means for subdividing large rooms for use by either small or large groups.

Another method to improve the learning processes in schools is the conversion of libraries into learning resource centers (LRC), instructional materials centers (IMC), or information resource centers (IRC). In this concept, libraries take on responsibilities for materials and activities, in addition to the more traditional ones, for example, audiovisual materials, including tapes, records, cassettes, closed-circuit TV, films, and other media. In such centers, provisions are often made for listening rooms, audio laboratories, video laboratories, and other activity areas.

Another trend intended to improve the education of students involves the provision for different kinds of learning experiences. Some experiences seem to be more meaningful if performed by an individual alone, such as reading a book, while others, such as laboratory experiments, are better when participated in by two or more students, as in discussions or lectures.

Educators and educational psychologists are continually studying and researching new methods for the improvement of education. One result has been the concept of team teaching, which involves the education of students, not by a single teacher in a single subject but by a team of several teachers who can bring to students various aspects of larger areas of learning.

Another method, first tried in the 1920s but mostly developed since the middle of the 20th century, involves what is often called programmed learning, frequently using teaching machines. Programmed learning uses devices that enable students to receive pieces of information in some kind of order and then to make responses, repeating the process over and over, with increasing amounts of information and degrees of difficulty. The simplest form is a book, or other printed material, arranged in such a way as to elicit a response from a student, who is then directed to another section or chapter to learn whether or not the response was correct and whether to proceed or go back for another try. There are many variations of this system. Other systems, in ascending order of sophistication, are student-operated machines that display information and receive responses; audiovisual systems that present visual programs on film, filmstrips, or slides with sound on records or tapes, to which students respond using microphones; and computer systems.

Elements Architectural requirements for schools vary widely according to the type, the number of students, the grade levels, and many other factors. Generally, the elements required are fairly simple for a nursery school and range through various levels to the most complex in high schools.

Nursery schools ordinarily have only a few facilities, often all contained in one or a few rooms, and a playground. Inside the schools are areas for group activities, reading and listening, art activities, play, storage, restrooms, and sometimes cubicles for individual tutoring. Often included are observation areas where teachers and others may observe children while remaining unseen by them.

In elementary schools, the most important educational elements are classrooms, one or more libraries or resource centers, gymnasiums and cafeterias or

SCHOOL Patrick Henry High (1962), Roanoke, Va. [*Architects: Caudill, Rowlett and Scott. (Joseph W. Molitor)*]

multipurpose rooms, and playgrounds. In higher elementary and lower secondary schools, provisions must also be made for laboratories, shops, music rooms, auditoriums, and athletic facilities outdoors. In high schools facilities are similar to those of the other schools, with the addition of more elaborate athletic facilities and sometimes theaters, art studios, observatories, and automobile education driving ranges. In boarding schools, where students live while school is in session, provisions must also be made for dormitories, dining rooms, and housing for administrators and teachers.

History Education has been a very important human activity since prehistoric times. At first, teaching the young was handled within families and by tribe elders. By about 3000 B.C., with the invention of writing, schools began to appear, but they were mostly for boys. In ancient Greece, schools became highly developed but in early Rome, most teaching was done at home until about the second century B.C. The Romans then established schools, with emphasis on what they called the liberal arts: arithmetic, astronomy, geometry, grammar, logic, music, and rhetoric. The phrase liberal arts is still in use today, but now generally means all the natural and social sciences and the humanities. From about the second century A.D., the Romans established public schools which eventually replaced most of the private schools. During the Middle Ages, church schools were established. All types of schools (church, public, and private) flourished during and after the Renaissance.

American Development The earliest schools in colonial America were set up soon after the colonists arrived. They were mostly one-room schools, in which up to 40 students of varying ages were taught. The one-room school was the most predominant type until well into the 19th century and thousands of them still exist today. Gradually, the colonists set up other types of schools, including trade schools. Beginning about the end of the first quarter of the 19th century, various states established public school systems to augment those operated by churches and other or-

ganizations. These school systems were supported by taxes and children could attend without charge. The first elementary schools were started in the early 1800s; the first public high school was opened in Boston in 1821. During the remainder of the 19th century, public school buildings continued to grow and by 1900, students in public high schools outnumbered those in private and parochial schools, and this has been the case ever since.

Gradually, during the 19th century, many one-room schools were expanded to make room for additional students. Some of the expansion was done without much planning and resulted in buildings that were often unsatisfactory for their purposes, unhealthy, and unsafe. Early in the 20th century, educators and architects developed principles that led to better schools designed for their functions, with safe and healthy environments for students. A great many architects have designed schools, and some have produced innovative improvements. One of these is the so-called open plan which, instead of having self-contained classrooms, provides larger spaces that can be readily subdivided into modular areas for different activities by groups of varying sizes. Other ideas have been one-room-deep classrooms with windows on both ends, allowing better control of sunlight and ventilation. Another is the cluster plan which consists of pavilions for instruction connected together with open or closed corridors. As progress continues in both educational psychology and architecture, better schools will be possible in the future. To their architects, they will present challenging design problems.

Related Articles HOUSING; LABORATORY; LIBRARY; RECREATION BUILDING; RESTAURANT; THEATER.

Further Reading Leggett, Stanton, C. William Brubaker, Aaron Cohodes, and Arthur C. Shapiro: *Planning Flexible Learning Spaces*, McGraw-Hill, New York, 1977.

Sources of Additional Information American Association of School Administrators, 1801 N. Moore St., Arlington, Va. 22209; Council of Education Facility Planners, 29 W. Woodruff Ave., Chicago, Ill. 43210; Educational Facilities Laboratories, 850 Third Ave., New York, N.Y. 10022.

Periodical *Nation's Schools*, 230 W. Monroe St., Chicago, Ill. 60606.

SECURITY SYSTEMS Systems or devices used in buildings to prevent burglaries, vandalism, or other criminal acts. Security systems used in buildings today are of four major types: those intended to prevent intrusion into buildings, those that detect and give warnings when intrusions occur, those that safeguard valuables after intrusions occur, and those that make records of intrusions. The types used and the extent of their use depend, to a large extent, on the degree of risk of human life or property involved and the value of property to be protected. In high-risk areas, such as certain central areas of cities, more safeguards must be taken than in certain low-risk rural or other areas. Certain types of safeguards may be effective in cities, while suburban or rural areas may require other types. More safeguards are ordinarily required for buildings in which money and high-value, easily marketed items, such as television sets or jewelry, are stored than in those in which only low-value or difficult-to-market items, such as supplies in a barber shop or paperwork in a real estate office, are located.

Security Measures Guarding the interior of a building against intrusions generally involves strong doors, windows, and other openings; strong and reliable hardware; and similar architectural elements. Watchmen and other guards are also employed for security purposes. Intercom systems, with units at building entrances, allow voice identification of visitors before allowing them to enter; and peephole devices in doors or closed-circuit television systems allow visual identification before allowing entry. In a well-lighted, low-crime area, with reliable police protection, elements of this sort may provide adequate security for most buildings in normal times. In times of riots and other disorders, such as those that occurred in Washington in April 1968 and in New York City during the blackout in July 1977, architectural measures cannot provide total security for buildings and their occupants.

Warning Devices Criminals have been known to brag that no amount of security of the types suggested can prevent them from burglarizing buildings. Certain types of systems and devices are therefore often used in buildings to give warning when intrusions occur. Guards or watchmen may also perform this function, and sometimes watchdogs are used. The usual method of protection by guards or watchmen involves making rounds within, and sometimes around the outsides of, buildings. The simplest method uses a series of boxes with time clocks inside, which a watchman opens, inserts a key, and records the time. More sophisticated systems employ similar boxes connected electrically to a central location, in which lights on a board show the progress and locations of watchmen. Some watchmen carry portable telephones which may be plugged into jacks along the inspection route, or carry portable radios or walkie-talkies.

Other systems used for detecting and warning of intrusions include types that operate by contact, photoelectric cells, proximity, or radar. Contact systems use wires, pads, metallic tape, magnetic switches, and other devices that set off alarms or give other warnings when they are touched. A photoelectric cell performs similar functions when a light beamed on a receiver is interrupted. Proximity devices are generally used to safeguard single items, such as files or safes. They trip alarms or give other warnings when a person comes near. Radar systems emit signals which give alarms when motion occurs in their paths. Other similar types of security systems employ ultrasonic signals or magnetic fields which, when interrupted, give warnings. Closed-circuit television is also often used for detection and warning of intrusions.

Any of the intrusion types of security systems can be used to sound alarms and transmit information to central places in buildings. They may also be connected with police stations or private security organizations, activating alarms or signals that show an intrusion has taken place and where it has occurred.

Safes and Vaults The major types of devices used for safeguarding valuables are safes and vaults of various kinds and sizes. Such devices may be very small and simple in construction for use in houses, stores, and so on, or very large and complicated, as those used in banks and other places where large quantities of money and other valuables are stored. Safes may be freestanding or built into floors, walls, and other building elements. Attempts are often made to conceal their existence. Vaults are ordinarily constructed of heavy, fire-resistant materials with complicated doors that are very difficult or impossible for intruders to open. Often safes and usually vaults are interconnected with sophisticated electronic and other security systems. Many vaults are also electronically timed, so that they cannot be opened except at regular intervals and under specific conditions set by the users.

Devices for recording intrusions and other criminal acts include closed-circuit television systems, which can be used to monitor such activities as well as to record them on video tape, and automatic cameras. Either may be hidden or exposed according to the needs of the buildings in which they are used.

Security systems may have sizable effects on the operating costs of buildings, since insurance rates vary considerably in individual cases. Security systems for buildings are quite specialized and are usually designed by specialists in consultation with architects and building owners. In many cases, they involve secrets, which architects must protect, unlike the architects of ancient Egypt who were often put to death after designing royal tombs and pyramids.

History Security, the provision of protection of people and their property from invaders, burglars, and other risks, has always been a factor in architecture. The earliest settlements that later became towns and cities were usually founded on easily defended sites. Later walls and other fortifications were provided to protect towns and cities. The practice of building walls around towns and cities continued until about the 15th century. The practice of protecting towns and cities with forts continued even longer, until after the American Civil War.

Other types of security measures began early, including devices to bar doors against intruders, followed by locks of various kinds. Windows were barred or shuttered for the same purpose. The need for security against burglars and other intruders has varied considerably during different periods of history. For example, the Romans were able to police their cities quite well. This fact was reflected in more open plans and larger windows during the era of Roman supremacy. In contrast, after Rome began to decline a period of lawlessness existed in Europe. Walls were built for protection against enemies; windows were small and protected by bars and other devices; doors were strengthened with iron bands and heavy hardware. During the Renaissance, when there was less lawlessness, windows were made larger and had fewer security devices. The building of walled cities began to decline, not so much because there was less danger from enemies but because gunpowder rendered them ineffective.

Since the Renaissance, the situation has fluctuated between periods of war and peace, and greater or reduced incidence of lawbreaking. Today the provision of security for the occupants of buildings and their property is of considerable concern in architecture.

Related Articles DOOR; ELECTRICAL ENGINEERING; HARDWARE; MILITARY BUILDING; PLANNING, CITY; WINDOW.

Further Reading Hopf, P. S.: *Handbook of Building Security Planning and Design*, McGraw-Hill, New York, 1979; Keogh, James, and John Koster: *Burglarproof, A Complete Guide to Home Security* McGraw-Hill, New York, 1977; Robinson, Robert L.: *How to Burglarproof Your Home*, Nelson-Hall, Chicago, 1978.

SHOPPING CENTER
A building, or group of buildings, in which a number of stores and service establishments are located, with provisions for automobile parking nearby, often in a suburban location but may be in a city or town.

Big Stores Shopping centers are just big stores which contain a collection of smaller stores. They therefore resemble the downtown shopping areas cities and towns have had for many years and which shopping centers have tried hard to replace. Shopping centers are different from their downtown counterparts in some ways. First, there probably never would have been any shopping centers if there had not been a mass movement of people out of cities and towns to suburbia. And there might not have been any real suburbia if it had not been for the proliferation of automobiles. In a sense then, shopping centers had their genesis in the widespread use of automobiles and have been automobile-oriented ever since. In fact, the earliest centers had large parking areas which almost dominiated the stores that faced them. Later centers have turned inward, the stores

facing spaces for people and turning their backs on automobiles.

Merchandising Principles Since shopping centers are essentially stores, they must be designed to sell goods effectively if they are to be successful. Like any store, a shopping center must arouse the interest of potential customers, and lure them inside. Then customers must be attracted into the individual stores whose interests are served by selling products. Merchandising principles apply to both stores and shopping centers, but the latter must draw potential customers who arrive in automobiles as a rule rather than on foot as is often the case in downtown stores. (See the article entitled store.)

A shopping center is also different in that it contains individual stores, any of which may offer any combination of staples or demand goods, convenience products, and impulse or luxury items. In addition, the whole shopping center functions much like a large department store, with the individual stores acting like departments. Thus the merchandising of the entire shopping center is important, but once inside the individual stores must also be merchandised. Customers must be able to flow easily through the entire shopping center, must be attracted into various individual stores and then be lured through their interiors.

Types The two major types of shopping centers are the neighborhood or community center and the regional center. Neighborhood or community centers often contain only a few stores, usually including a su-

SHOPPING CENTER Michigan Square Building (1930), Chicago, Ill. [*Architects: Holabird and Root. (Hedrich-Blessing)*]

SHOPPING CENTER   Galleria (1970), Houston, Tex. [*Architects: Hellmuth, Obata and Kassabaum. (Hedrich-Blessing)*]

SHOPPING CENTER Regency Square (1962), Jacksonville, Fla. [Architects: Toombs, Amisano and Wells. (Joseph W. Molitor)]

permarket and a drugstore, and sometimes one or more small branches of department stores. These centers serve limited marketing areas in cities, towns, or suburbia. Regional centers serve large marketing areas, sometimes drawing customers from many miles away. The keystones of these centers are department stores, of which there may be one to four or more in a single center. There may be as few as 50 other stores in a regional shopping center, though some have up to 100 or more. Regional centers may contain stores of almost every possible kind, from small specialty shops, such as florists, candy stores, or bakeries, to service establishments, such as barber and beauty shops, banks, or diaper services, to large complete department stores and supermarkets. In addition, regional centers may also have entertainment facilities, such as motion picture houses or bowling alleys. Many have drinking and dining facilities, such as restaurants, cafeterias, or cocktail lounges. Some have professional offices for doctors, dentists, and others; post offices; gasoline service stations; and almost every type of commercial operation imaginable.

Master Plans The major types of master plans for shopping centers include row or strip developments, in which stores are lined up along sidewalks with automobile parking often facing a street or highway, and cluster developments, in which the various elements containing stores are arranged around a pedestrian area in the middle, with parking around the perimeter of the cluster. Cluster developments, usually called shopping malls, have open spaces or enclosed malls in the middle between the stores. Shopping centers may be one-story or two-story affairs, the most usual today, and some have more than two stories.

One of the most important principles in the design of a shopping center with a mall is the design of the mall itself. It must be made into an attractive pedestrian area, with appealing shops on the sides with their fronts facing inward toward the mall. Many malls have comfortable seating areas, shrubbery, flowers and trees, sculpture, fountains, even aviaries.

Another important aspect of shopping center design is provision for efficient automobile parking facilities and easy access into the center. Parking may be provided at ground level outside, on the roof, or in parking garages. For shopping centers, a great deal of space is required for parking, ranging from about 2.5 car spaces per 1,000 ft² of leasable store area in a downtown center to 6, or more, car spaces per 1,000 ft² in suburban centers.

Because of the many types of stores and other establishments that may be included, the complexities of providing for buildings, for automobile traffic and parking, and for pedestrian traffic, shopping centers have become a sort of universal building type. They test the design abilities of architects who must somehow put all the pieces of the puzzle together so that the whole functions properly as well as all the various parts.

History No one knows when the first shopping center of ancient times was built, but the ancient Greek merchants brought their wares to the *stoa*, a long *portico*, through which passersby could be sheltered and shop too. A *stoa* was built around an *agora*, or public meeting square, and connected important buildings. The *agora* was the center of public life and therefore there was always quite a lot of traffic, the first consideration in the location of any commercial building. Later the Romans built shopping centers, perhaps the first being the one erected adjacent to the Roman Forum about A.D. 110. Other shopping centers, of various kinds, were later built in European cities.

U.S. Centers The first shopping centers, resembling those of today, were built in the United States in the last few decades before World War II. After the war, the rate of movement of people from cities and towns to suburbs increased rapidly. And suburban shopping centers were not far behind. At first, these were neighborhood or community centers, but starting about the middle of the 20th century, big regional centers were constructed. The trend has continued ever since. Soon after the construction of regional centers began in earnest, great redevelopment projects, intended to slow the movement from cities to the suburbs, helped revitalize the centers of cities. And urban shopping centers quickly followed. This trend too has continued. Thus shopping centers of all types remain a very important building type today.

Related Articles GARAGE; GRAPHIC DESIGN; ROAD AND TRAFFIC DESIGN; STORE; WAREHOUSE; Other individual building types.

Further Reading Gruen, Victor, and Larry Smith: *Shopping Towns—U.S.A.*, Reinhold, New York, 1960; Hornbeck, James S.: *Stores and Shopping Centers*, McGraw-Hill, New York, 1962; Lion, Edgar: *Shopping Centers—Planning, Development, and Administration*, John Wiley, New York, 1976; Redstone, Louis G.: *New Dimensions in Shopping Centers and Stores*, McGraw-Hill, New York, 1973.

Source of Additional Information International Council of Shopping Centers, 445 Park Ave., New York, N.Y. 10022.

SITE PLANNING The process of developing a concept or design for the land on which a building or other structure is to be constructed, or for other purposes, such as parks or playgrounds. Site planning is concerned with many factors, including building location, grading, planting, location, and design of other features of sites, and with the circulation of pedestrians and automobiles and other vehicles. Site planning is ordinarily one of the first processes in the design of architecture and is performed by architects, city and regional planners, engineers, and landscape architects. These professionals also engage in site selection, making investigations and analyses of sites to determine their suitability or feasibility for use as building or other project sites, and to make selections between alternative sites.

Preparatory Phases The first steps in both site selection and site planning are collection of data and their analyses. These procedures develop important information upon which a selection of a site may be made, if required, and which will become part of a program for a building or other project.

Based on the analysis and the program, a land-use plan may then be prepared. A land-use plan shows only the general aspects of a site, such as areas for various functions or activities; the densities, or number of people or families to be accommodated per acre; the circulation of people, goods, and so on; and other important relationships or linkages between the activity areas. All these phases of site planning begin with the concept of the larger area or total environment, in which a site exists and then proceed to the specific environment of the site itself.

The major factors studied in both cases may be classified as natural, man-made, and esthetic. Natural features include soils and other geological conditions, topography, water bodies, vegetation, wildlife, climate, and others. Man-made features include boundaries, streets and roads, sidewalks, existing buildings or other structures, utilities, and so on. Esthetic features include views, surroundings, and others. Many questions must be studied and answered concerning all these features and their interrelationships.

Topographic Maps One of the important tools for site planning is a topographic map, showing natural and man-made features of the site. Maps of this sort may be obtained from the U.S. Geological Survey, or they may be prepared at larger scales and showing more details from information derived by surveying the site. Topographic maps contain such information as property lines; easements; rights of way; storm and sewage systems; woods; water bodies; rock outcroppings; elevations and contours of the land and other objects; locations; and information on first-floor elevations of existing buildings, walls, driveways, parking lots, and other structures.

Contour lines are used on topographic maps and other drawings to indicate levels or elevations of the land, slopes, and similar information. A contour line represents a constant elevation above some selected reference level, or plane, called a datum. A vertical distance, called a contour interval, is selected between contour lines for each map or other drawing.

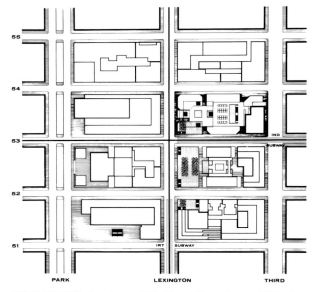

SITE PLANNING Location and Site Plan, Citicorp Center (1978), New York, N.Y. [*Architects: Hugh Stubbins, in association with Emery Roth and Sons. (Hugh Stubbins and Associates)*]

For example, a contour interval might be 2 ft. Thus adjacent contour lines will be 2 ft apart from each other vertically. Contour lines that are close together indicate relatively steep slopes, while those that are farther apart indicate more gentle slopes. In a map with contour lines at 2 ft vertical intervals, if two consecutive lines are 4 ft apart horizontally on the map, the indication is of a slope that rises 2 ft, vertically, in a horizontal distance of 4 ft. The slope, the ratio of the horizontal distance to the vertical, would then be 4:2 or, as it would usually be expressed, its equivalent of 2:1, a very steep slope. Another related term is grade, expressed as the percentage the height, called the rise or fall, is of the horizontal distance. Thus the 2:1 slope is equivalent to the 50 percent grade.

Creative Elements After a program and a land-use plan have been prepared, the process of planning a site can proceed further. Major considerations are locations of buildings or other structures and provisions for vehicular and pedestrian circulation into and on the site and into the buildings. Parking is another important consideration. All these elements must be handled efficiently and economically, with proper consideration given to safety and comfort, to protection of the site and the environment, and to visual design factors. As in all architectural design, the visual considerations include creative use of shapes, volumes, textures, colors, and other factors to produce design elements that are properly balanced, in proportion, and in the proper scale to each other and to the whole design. Natural visual elements include the land itself, along with rocks, plants, water, and others. Man-made visual elements may include paving, walls, outdoor stairs, fountains, pools, sculpture, lighting, and benches and other outdoor furniture. In addition, there may be requirements for playing fields and other facilities.

Visual elements of the above sort are part of every site plan; all must be combined in a manner that will create a harmonious and esthetic overall design. In addition, the site planner must design the elements for proper construction and for efficient maintenance. The planner must also properly handle the technological aspects of the site plan, including grading of the site, water protection and drainage, utility services, roads, streets, parking, and other construction items.

It would be difficult to overstate the importance of proper and creative site planning, for buildings of all types and sizes and particularly for building complexes. Site planning not only affects the individual buildings and complexes, but also the areas that surround them and the entire environment. The changes made in sites affect the ecology of the area as well as the human and esthetic qualities. Therefore site planning is a subject to be taken very seriously and should be performed only by those with adequate knowledge, experience, and creative ability to accomplish worthwhile results that can lead to overall designs of high excellence.

Related Articles DESIGN, ARCHITECTURAL; ECOLOGY; ENGINEERING; FOUNTAIN; GARDEN; LANDSCAPE ARCHITECTURE; PARK; PLANNING, CITY; PRACTICE OF ARCHITECTURE; PROGRAMMING; SPECIFICATION; SURVEYING; WORKING DRAWING.

Further Reading De Chiara, Joseph, and Lee E. Koppelman: *Site Planning Standards,* 2d ed., McGraw-Hill, New York, 1978; Parker, Harry: *Simplified Site Engineering for Architects and Engineers,* John Wiley, New York, 1954; Rubenstein, Harvey M.: *A Guide to Site and Environmental Planning,* 2d ed., John Wiley, New York, 1980.

SKIDMORE, OWINGS AND MERRILL

SKIDMORE, OWINGS AND MERRILL American architectural firm, founded by Louis Skidmore (1897–1962), Nathaniel Alexander Owings (1903–   ), and John Ogden Merrill (1896–1975). Founded in 1936 by Skidmore and Owings, the firm became Skidmore, Owings and Merrill (or SOM) in 1939. From this beginning, the firm grew to become one of the largest and most influential in the world, with offices in New York City, Chicago, San Francisco, Washington, and Portland, Ore.

Most noted for large office buildings, the firm has designed many other building types and continues to do so. Their work is characterized by sophisticated and artful handling of big buildings for big businesses and other institutions, by clear, careful handling of plans and exteriors and interiors down to the smallest details, and by use of glass and metal-curtain walls, prefabricated and sometimes preassembled in factories.

While the work of the firm has sometimes been criticized for a degree of sameness of their buildings, actually there is considerable variety but it is subtle. In a way, the work of SOM, in theory is much like that of Holabird and Roche in the late 1800s and early 1900s in Chicago. Both firms attempted to perfect their designs, with each succeeding design growing or evoloving from those that preceded. By such evolutionary architecture, SOM, like Holabird and Roche, has produced a body of work that is of consistently high quality. The firm has also proved that a large office can produce good work, an idea that many architects have not accepted very readily.

SOM Works During the early years of the SOM practice, commissions were often for small buildings or remodeling jobs. For a firm later to be recognized as a world design leader, there was little to indicate the future. Then the firm was given the commission for the important New York City Building for the 1939 World's Fair in that city. Other commissions came in, and then World War II began. By that time, the firm had become well known enough to be asked in 1942 to design a huge new complex for a secret government project in Tennessee. As it turned out, the firm designed a whole town for 75,000 people who would work on and support the Manhattan Project, which produced the atomic bomb. The town was Oak Ridge, Tenn., and SOM worked on the buildings for several years, finishing after the end of the war. Commissions then flowed in at an ever-increasing rate for some of

SKIDMORE, OWINGS AND MERRILL Manufacturers-Hanover Trust Bank (1954), New York, N.Y. *(Ezra Stoller)*

the most important buildings in the United States. And the commissions have flowed in ever since.

After the war, SOM designed buildings of various types and was recognized as a competent architectural firm. Then in the early 1950s, they produced a building that brought them worldwide acclaim, one that is still acknowledged as one of their best ever, if not the best. This was Lever House (1952; see illustration in color section), New York City. SOM had the vision to design this great building, but they would never have been allowed to design it in the way they did except for the vision of another architect, turned soap company executive, the president of Lever Brothers, Charles Luckman (1909–   ). Later Luckman returned to architecture and built a large and successful practice of his own.

After Lever House, there were steady commissions, some for elegant small buildings like the Manufacturers-Hanover Trust Bank (1954), New York City; others for large elegant buildings, some in the suburbs like the Connecticut General Life Insurance Co. offices (1957), Bloomfield, Conn., and some in the city like the Inland Steel Building (1958), Chicago. Then followed the Crown-Zellerbach Building (1958), San

Francisco, and the Reynolds Metal Co. Building (1958), Richmond, Va. Then came a commission that many architects had sought, but SOM got, the design of an entire campus and buildings for the new U.S. Air Force Academy (1962), Colorado Springs, Col. The Academy, and particularly its Chapel, received wide recognition. Soon SOM was involved in the design of another complete campus and its buildings, the University of Illinois Chicago Circle Campus (first phase completed in 1965), in Chicago.

In succeeding years, SOM has designed a number of other notable buildings. Among them are the Union Carbide Building (1960) and the Chase-Manhattan Bank (1961), both in New York City; the John Hancock Center (1969), Chicago; the Library (1971) at Northwestern University, Evanston, Ill.; the Weyerhaueser Headquarters (1971), Tacoma, Wash.; and the Sears Roebuck Tower (1974), Chicago. The last-named is either the world's tallest or second tallest building, according to whether you ask its proponents or those of the World Trade Center (1973) in New York City. In either case, the Sears Roebuck Tower is considered by many to be SOM's best building effort so far.

SKIDMORE, OWINGS AND MERRILL Inland Steel Building (1958), Chicago, Ill. *(Hedrich-Blessing)*

SKIDMORE, OWINGS AND MERRILL Pepsi Cola Building (1960), New York, N.Y. *(Ezra Stoller)*

Skidmore's Life Louis Skidmore was born in Lawrenceburg, Ind., on April 8, 1897. He served in England during World War I as a private in a construction group. After the war, Skidmore entered the architectural school at Massachusetts Institute of Technology and graduated in 1924. In 1926 he won the coveted Rotch Traveling Fellowship on his second try. This is one of the oldest and most respected awards in architecture, having been awarded almost every year since 1884.

Skidmore used the fellowship for travel in England, France and other European countries, and the Near East, remaining away from the United States almost three years. During his travels, he met Eloise Owings, the sister of his future partner, in Paris where she was studying fashion design. In 1929 she and Skidmore were married. He and Owings then did some architectural work together but nothing much came of it once the Depression started.

In the early 1930s, when word circulated that there would soon be a great fair in Chicago, Skidmore sought out the leaders of the architectural commission, Raymond Mathewson Hood (1881–1934) and Paul Philippe Cret (1876–1945). Skidmore was appointed chief of design for the fair, and took his brother-in-law to Chicago with him to help. The next three years were spent working on the Century of Progress, as the Chicago World's Fair of 1933 came to be known.

After the fair closed, Skidmore and Owings opened an office together in Chicago in early 1936. This was the beginning of what later became one of the largest and most influential firms of the 20th century. Some months later, they opened another office in New York and Skidmore took charge of it. Plagued with ulcers most of his life, he still managed a very busy schedule in New York, but once in a while had to retreat completely away from it all to recuperate. In spite of his physical problems, he managed to establish the office solidly.

In 1956, after the firm had been existence for 20 years and both it and the partners had become hugely successful, Skidmore retired to a house with an orange grove beside a lake in Winter Haven, Fla. In 1957 he was awarded the highest honor his profession can give, the Gold Medal of the American Institute of Architects. He spent his last five years mostly staying at home with his wife, enjoying the lake and the orange grove. On September 27, 1962, Louis Skidmore died.

Merrill's Life John Ogden Merrill was born in St. Paul, Minn., on August 10, 1896. He attended the University of Wisconsin for two years (1915–17). He served as an officer in the U.S. Army during World War I from 1917 to 1919, then transferred to the architectural school at Massachusetts Institute of Technology, from which he graduated in 1921. In 1918 he had married Ross MacKenzie and they had three children, one of whom, John Ogden, Jr. (1923–   ), became an architect and later a partner in Skidmore, Owings and Merrill.

SKIDMORE, OWINGS AND MERRILL Equitable Building (1965), Chicago, Ill. *(Hedrich-Blessing)*

SKIDMORE, OWINGS AND MERRILL Sears Roebuck Tower (1974), Chicago, Ill. *(Hedrich-Blessing)*

Merrill worked in various offices and a short time for the Federal Housing Administration. In 1939 he joined Skidmore and Owings in their partnership and its name was changed to its present form. In 1942 he moved to Tennessee to take charge of the highly secret buildings at Oak Ridge, remaining there until 1945, and directing the work after that from the Chicago office of the firm.

Having been divorced from his wife, Merrill married Viola Berg in 1946. During 1947–49, after having become expert in the technology of buildings and building codes, he directed a major revision of the Building Code of the City of Chicago. In 1948 he retired from practice and went to live in Colorado Springs, Col. On June 7, 1975, John Merrill died.

Owing's Life Nathaniel Alexander Owings was born in Indianapolis, Ind., on February 6, 1903. Impressed by the cathedrals of France on a trip he had won as a boy scout in 1920, he decided to become an architect. First, he entered the architectural school at the University of Illinois, Urbana, and stayed a year.

After passing the entrance examinations to the U.S. Military Academy at West Point, he became very ill and had to give up the appointment. Recovering, he went to Oklahoma to work for a pipe company.

Failing in his new ambition to enter the architectural school at Cornell University, Ithaca, N.Y., he was admitted to its College of Agriculture, later transferred to architecture and graduated in 1927. After graduation, Owings went to New York City where he worked for a while in the office of York and Sawyer. When Louis Skidmore, his brother-in-law and partner-to-be, was named chief designer for the Chicago World's Fair of 1933, Owings went along to work with him.

In 1931 Owings married Emily Hunting Otis and they had four children. After the close of the Chicago Fair, Owings and his wife traveled in Japan and China and then went to Paris where Owings and Skidmore planned the future architectural firm that would bear their names. Early in 1936, they opened their first office in Chicago.

Divorced from his wife in 1953, Owings married Margaret Wentworth Millard on the last day of the year. Having gone to San Francisco to direct the SOM office there, Owings built a house (1957) in Big Sur, on the coast of California, and moved there to live. Much of his time in the past two decades has been spent in important civic work, including the President's Council on Design of Pennsylvania Avenue; beginning in 1963, the California Highway Scenic Roads Commission (1964–67); and U.S. Interior Department Advisory Board on National Parks, Historic Sites, Buildings and Monuments (1966–72), serving as chairman (1970–72). Now retired, Owings lives in Big Sur.

A great number of noted architects have worked for or have been partners in Skidmore, Owings and Merrill over the many years of its existence. Though far from a complete list, some of them are Gordon Bunshaft (1909–   ), Robert Ward Cutler (1905–   ), Bruce John Graham (1925–   ), William Edward Hartmann (1916–   ), John Ogden Merrill, Jr. (1923–   ), Walter Andrew Netsch, Jr. (1920–   ), David Arthur Pugh (1926–   ), Ambrose Madison Richardson (1917–   ), John Walter Severinghaus (1905–   ), and Louis Skidmore, Jr. (1937–   ).

Related Articles AIRPORT [for illustration of International Arrivals Building (1957), John F. Kennedy Airport]; ART IN ARCHITECTURE [for illustration of Daley Center (1965), Chicago]; CONTEMPORARY ARCHITECTURE; EXPOSITION; LIBRARY [for illustrations of Selby (1975), Sarasota, Fla.]; MODERN ARCHITECTURE; OFFICE BUILDING [for illustration of Equitable (1960), New York, N.Y.]; PUBLIC BUILDING [for illustration of Daley Center (1965), Chicago]; STONE [for illustration of Brunswick Building (1963), Chicago]; WOODWORK [for illustrations of Texaco World Headquarters (1976), Harrison, N.Y.]; WURSTER, WILLIAM WILSON [for illustration of Bank of America Building (1971), San Francisco].

Further Reading Owings, Nathaniel Alexander: *The Spaces in Between—An Architect's Journey,* Houghton Mifflin, Boston, 1973; SOM: *Architecture of Skidmore, Owings and Merrill, 1950–62,* Praeger, New York, 1963; SOM: *Architecture of Skidmore, Owings and Merrill, 1963–73,* Architectural Book Publishing Co., distributed by Hastings House Publishers, Inc., New York, 1974.

SOCIAL SCIENCE

The broad area of knowledge, sometimes called behavioral science, which is concerned with human society and the relationships of humans with each other in groups, including families, races, and others. Social science is thus one of the three major divisions usually made of human knowledge, the others being natural science and mathematics, which are concerned with the nature of the physical world, and humanities, concerned with the meaning of human life and with human culture. The natural sciences include such fields as physics, chemistry, and biology. The humanities include such fields as languages, art, music, literature, religion, and philosophy.

Although there is no universal agreement about the subject, the social sciences are often thought to consist primarily of anthropology, criminology, economics, history, political science, psychology, sociology, and law. To this list, others would add education and ethics. To further confuse the issue, portions of other fields deal with human beings in groups, and may be thought of as at least partly social sciences. Thus ecology, geography, linguistics, and other fields are sometimes thought of as social sciences, in part. And psychology seems to be a natural as well as a social science.

Architects and other environmental designers today have become deeply concerned with the effect of social factors on buildings and other structures. This was not always the case, but in the complex world of today the social sciences deeply affect architecture. Although all the social sciences affect architecture to a degree, a few are considered more important than the others today. These are anthropology, economics, psychology, and sociology. This is not to say that an architect designing a prison should not be concerned with criminology, that one designing a school would not consider education, or one designing a public building should not know something about political science. All the social sciences will help at times and in specific cases. But architects designing buildings of any kind should be concerned with the four social sciences cited above.

Definitions Anthropology, actually part social and part biological science, is the study of the place of human beings in the universe and their essential physical characters, origins, and development, and the relations between races. It is of great importance in the design of the spaces in buildings in which human beings live, work, and engage in other activities. Economics is concerned with how humans produce and distribute goods and services. Since much of the work of architects is involved with such processes, economics is also important in architecture. Psychology deals with the behavior of animals, including human beings. Architects have become increasingly aware of the welfare of the users of their buildings, an area in which psychology can be of great benefit. Sociology deals with relationships between people, the manner in which they live, work, and play together. As such, it is essential to the design of good architecture.

Anthropology Because it is concerned with the whole way of life of human beings, how they live, eat, work, play, worship, and so on, anthropology is important in architecture. The other social sciences specialize, more or less, on portions of the lives of people; psychology on how they learn, think, and feel, for example. Anthropology is a more generalized field that crosses over into others, dealing generally with questions that are also dealt with specifically in such fields as history, psychology, economics, sociology, and biology. Anthropology is divided into two major areas, physical and cultural, sometimes called social anthropology. Physical anthropology is subdivided into paleontology, the study of fossil humans; somatology, the study of the development, functions, and structure of the human body; and the study of living humans. In this work, an important tool is anthropometry: measurements of the human body. Cultural anthropology is subdivided into archeology, the study of prehistoric and extinct cultures; ethnology, the study of existing cultures; and linguistics, the study of languages.

Economics This social science is very important to architecture, since it deals with the production and distribution of goods and services, subjects with which architects also have to deal in much of their work. The four basic problems of economics are the goods and services that are to be produced; the methods of producing them; the people who will receive the goods and services; and the rate of growth of the economy. Architects must be concerned with the first three problems in their practices, since they may be said to produce and distribute services, and in the design of buildings and other structures, since every building type they design is involved in production or distribution, or both, of goods or services. The fourth problem, economic growth rate, is also of concern to architects because it is an indicator of the need and demand for building construction and because it affects architecture as a business.

The four major elements in the growth of the economy are natural resources, capital, labor, and technology. Architects are involved with all these. They are also involved in markets, for their services, and with markets, prices and competition in the commercial buildings they design. Obviously, architects are concerned with profits, not only in their practice but in the functioning of their buildings. And they must be concerned with the economic principles of supply and demand.

Psychology This social science is very important in architecture because it deals, among other things, with human behavior. It deals with the kinds of environments that should be designed for human beings to live in and also with the effects the environments have on the thoughts, emotions, and motivations of the people who live in them. Together with anthropological study, psychology can be of great benefit to architects concerned with problems of this sort.

Psychology is a very broad field that has a great number of specialized subdivisions, including abnormal, clinical, comparative, developmental, educational, environmental, industrial, learning, motivation, perception, personality, physiological, social, testing, and thought. All these specialized fields are of importance in architecture at various times. For example, educational and learning psychology are extremely important in the design of schools, colleges and universities, and other building types, as are some of the other psychology specialties.

The major methods used in psychology are experiments, observations, case histories, and surveys. The four major philosophies of psychology today are be-

haviorism, gestalt, psychoanalysis, and structuralism.

Behaviorism is based on the theory that animal and human behavior results from response to stimulus and may be studied by observation. Psychologists who base their work on behaviorism are sometimes called stimulus-response psychologists. Gestalt psychology is based on the theory that animals and humans perceive organized patterns, not individual parts that are then added together, and that meaning comes from the relationship of the parts of stimuli perceived as a whole or pattern. Psychologists who base their work on gestalt psychology are often called cognitive theorists.

Psychoanalysis is based on the theory that needs and desires that are unacceptable to a person or society are repressed and thereafter the subconscious mind influences conscious behavior. Psychoanalysis is founded on the work of Sigmund Freud (1856–1939) in Vienna, Austria. Structuralism is based on the theory that psychology is concerned with conscious experience, including sensations and feelings, often studied by introspection, in which people describe experiences when stimulated. Structuralism was founded by Wilhelm Wundt (1832–1920) in Germany and he also founded the first psychological laboratory in 1879, thus establishing psychology as a science.

Sociology This social science is concerned with how people live together. Obviously, sociology is of great importance in architecture, since it deals with the way people work, play, engage in group activities, join organizations, and generally relate to each other. The major subdivisions of sociology are general, social psychology, demography, community, social organization, and social change. As may be inferred from this list, sociology overlaps the other social sciences in important ways. General sociology is concerned with the culture of society, with the relationships of people in groups of all sizes and in group activities. Social psychology is concerned with the effects made by society on the behavior of people. Demography deals with populations: distribution, movements, and other changes. The community is involved with the study of human beings in relation to their environment and is further subdivided into urban and rural sociology. Social organization is concerned with institutions of humans, such as religion, families, governments, and so on. Social change involves the study of basic forces, such as inventions, fashions, wars, and other conflicts that cause changes. Such forces may either cause changes for the better or may result in social problems, such as crime, unemployment, prejudice, alcoholism, or drug abuse.

The basic processes used by sociologists are surveying, the collection and evaluation of information, and making conclusions from the data collected. Today there are three major philosophies of sociology: one that emphasizes the collection of data and makes intensive use of statistics; one that puts the emphasis on how people interpret the data; and one that emphasizes the belief that different parts of society work together to maintain the stability of the whole society.

It should be apparent that the various fields of social sciences and their specialties hold great promise for the creation of architecture that will better serve the needs and desires of people. The domain of the social sciences is so vast and the fields overlap so much with each other and with the natural sciences and humanities that it is difficult for an architect to obtain and interpret the ideas and information needed to design better buildings. It is probably easier and more fruitful for an architect to consider the whole subject as one of human behavior, ignoring to a degree the nuances and differences between the various specialties. By thinking of the subject in this manner, an architect becomes free to seek information from all sources without formalities. An architect may also establish a principle that the best social science consultants to help with architectural problems are those with broad enough points of view to attack the total problem of human behavior in buildings and other structures, without regard to rigid lines of disciplines or authorities.

Related Articles DESIGN, ARCHITECTURAL; PRACTICE OF ARCHITECTURE; PROGRAMMING.

Further Reading AIA: *Architectural Design and the Social Sciences*, 1975, and *Social Science and Design—A Process Model for Architect and Social Scientists Collaboration*, 1974, the American Institute of Architects, Washington; Canter, David: *Psychology for Architects*, Halsted Press of John Wiley, New York, 1974; Hall, Edward Twitchell: *The Hidden Dimension*, Doubleday, Garden City, N.Y., 1969; Heimsath, Clovis: *Behavioral Architecture*, McGraw-Hill, New York, 1977; Lang, John, Charles Burnette, Walter Moleski, and David Vachon, eds.: *Designing for Human Behavior—Architecture and the Behavioral Sciences*, Dowden, Hutchinson and Ross, Stroudsburg, Pa. 1974.

SOUND CONTROL The materials and other physical characteristics in buildings, or rooms, that determine the loudness or volume, intensity, and quality of sound. Sound consists of the waves, or oscillations, that occur when an object vibrates. These sound waves travel through air or some other material causing vibrations in the eardrum or tympanum, stimulating the auditory nerves and the brain. Acoustics, the science of sound, always involves a source, a transmission, a path, and a receiver of sound. When the science is applied to buildings, it is called architectural acoustics and when applied to rooms in buildings, room acoustics. Architectural acoustics is concerned with two major considerations: the design of buildings for wanted sounds to be heard properly, and for unwanted sounds, or noise, to be controlled or excluded. A third consideration, often of importance, is reduction of the level of reverberations of sounds.

Sound Characteristics When objects vibrate, sound waves are generated. The major properties or characteristics of sound are frequency, wavelength, magnitude, intensity, and velocity. Frequency is the times an object vibrates or a sound wave oscillates in a given period of time. One cycle per second is called

a hertz (Hz), and human hearing encompasses an approximate range of 20 to 20,000 Hz. Wavelengths are measurements of the distance between similar points on two successive sound waves, or the distance sound travels in one cycle, or hertz. Humans can hear sounds of approximately 0.5 in. on the high-frequency side. The magnitude of sound is its power, or energy, measured in watts (W). The intensity of sound refers to its power per unit of area, often expressed in watts per square meter (W/m²).

A decibel (dB) is an abstract number often used to express a certain level of sound value. For every 10 points rise in the decibel scale, the intensity increases tenfold. Thus, 50 dB has 100,000 times the intensity of 0 dB. The loudness of a sound is the apparent power of the sound perceived by the eardrum and transmitted to the auditory nerves and brain. A sound with a certain intensity may seem louder to one person than to another. The velocity of sound is the rate at which it moves through a material. Velocity of sound varies considerably between materials, from about 1,100 feet per second (ft/s) in air at 32°F and normal atmospheric pressure, to some 4,700 ft/s in water and 16,400 ft/s in steel. For comparison, light which may travel in a vacuum, which sound cannot do, has a speed of 186,281 miles per second (mi/s).

Other characteristics of sound are important in architecture. The threshold of hearing or audibility, below which the normal ear cannot hear sounds, is considered to be at an intensity level of 0 dB, and the threshold of feeling, at which sound affects feeling in the ear, and of pain, at which sounds can actually hurt is considered to be at an intensity level of 130 dB. A person who cannot hear sounds below the threshold of pain is considered to be totally deaf. Other approximate intensity levels include an average office at 50 dB, speech from 3 ft away at 70 dB, a shout from 5 ft at 90 dB, rock band at 120 dB or more, and near a jet engine at 140 dB. The Occupational Safety and Health Administration (OSHA) allows a 90-dB maximum level for industrial workers who work eight-hour days. Continued exposure to sound intensities of more than 85 dB will damage the hearing of many people

Sound attenuation is a reduction in the intensity caused by distance from the source or absorption or blocking of the sound by materials or objects between the person hearing the sound, or the receiver, and the source. For sound sources at distances, the intensity of sound is reduced by one-quarter each time the distance between the source and receiver doubles. In sound absorption and blocking or barrier, materials, and objects, various degrees of attenuation occur.

Two or more sounds may combine as in an orchestra. Sound may be reflected as well as absorbed or blocked. Background noise levels affect sounds heard and perceived. Another important consideration in architecture is the reverberation time of sound, its persistence after the sound has stopped issuing from a source. The quality of sound is also important, particularly in concert halls, theaters, and similar building types. The quality of sound is largely determined by the tones that issue from the source of the sound. For example, the tones from a violin are quite different from those of a trumpet. Each instrument produces certain fundamental tones at various frequencies, along with overtones at different frequencies. Overtones are often spoken of as harmonics, the second harmonic vibrating at twice the frequency of the fundamental tone, the third at three times the frequency, and so on. Other factors affect the quality of sound, including resonance, the production of large vibrations by small forces, such as in a piano or cello.

Architectural Acoustics In general, architectural acoustics deals with the provision of good conditions for sound in buildings. This involves the design of buildings for good speech conditions, privacy, and freedom from distracting noises. In such buildings as theaters, concert halls, opera houses, and similar types, architectural acoustics also must provide good conditions for listening to drama and music.

For the provision of good conditions in most buildings, acoustical design involves controlling the amount of sound through absorption or sound insulation, through blocking of sound, and through control of background noises. Good acoustical conditions may also be achieved, at least partly, through design of machines, such as furnaces and boilers, refrigerators, air-conditioning systems, and the like, for quiet operation.

Sound Absorption Sound is absorbed most readily by materials that are fibrous or porous, such as heavy curtains, upholstered furniture, carpets, and the like. Human bodies also absorb sound readily, each person absorbing more sound than a yard of thick carpet. Many sound-absorbing materials are available for use in ceilings of buildings, including tiles made of fiberboard, glass fibers, and others, and acoustical plaster. Standard systems are available for installation of such materials in ceilings or for their use in suspended ceilings. Measures of their effectiveness are sound absorption coefficients, in these materials from about 0.38 for low frequencies in the range of 125 Hz to more than 0.95 for higher frequencies of about 4,000 Hz. As a contrast, concrete ranges from about 0.01 to 0.0 Hz. Sound-absorbing qualities of materials are often referred to by noise reduction coefficient (NRC) numbers, which are averages and range from the lowest, 0.0, upward. Good sound-absorbing, acoustical materials may have NRC numbers from about 0.65 to 0.95, while concrete has 0.0. Heavy carpet on concrete has an NRC number of 0.30, while the same material with a foam rubber backing or pad has an NRC number of 0.55. Medium-weight curtains have an NRC of about 0.55 and heavy-weight, 0.60.

Sound Isolation Sound blocking, or isolation, is accomplished by the use of relatively dense, heavy materials which reflect sound away from the spaces to be protected. While sound isolation is very important in all building types, it is especially needed in such buildings and spaces as airports, offices in conjunction with factories, and the like. Concrete, with an NRC number of 0.0, provides excellent sound blocking. Other good sound-isolating materials are brick, concrete block, and heavy plate glass, with 0.05, and plaster, gypsum board, stone, and tile, with 0.0.

Standards Standards have been established for sound absorption and sound isolation in various building types. The standards for sound absorption involve recommended reverberation times for various types of buildings. For example, the optimum reverberation time, in seconds, at frequencies between 500 and 1,000 Hz include approximately the following: elementary classrooms 0.6–0.8; moving picture houses 0.8–1.2; auditoriums 1.5–1.8; concert halls 1.4–2.1; and so on.

Noise criteria (NC) curves are used for the determination of acceptable noise levels in various kinds of buildings. Some NC values, with their approximate decibel ratings, include concert halls, NC 15–20, 25–35 dB; sleeping rooms, NC 20–30, 30–40 dB; private offices, NC 30–35, 40–45 dB; stores, restaurants, and the like, NC 35–40, 45–50 dB.

The NC curves measure acceptable levels of background noise in various kinds of rooms. Too much background noise may make it impossible to hear and understand conversation and other wanted sounds or to enjoy properly dramatic, musical, and other performances. Too little background noise is also undesirable, for such reasons as privacy of conversations. The aim in controlling background noises then is to achieve the proper balance for the functions to be performed in architectural spaces.

Other Noise Sources Much of the noise to be dealt with in buildings comes from outside sources, such as automobile traffic, or sources in adjoining rooms. Such noises are usually controlled by the methods previously discussed. Other annoying noises to be controlled in buildings are those from various kinds of mechanical equipment, such as pumps, elevators, and air-conditioning components. Such noises can be controlled, at least partly, with sound-blocking materials. However, it is considered better practice to control as much of this noise as possible at the source. Mechanical equipment, such as pumps, fans, air-conditioner components, and others, are often mounted on springs or on concrete or other supports mounted on springs. Neoprene or other resilient pads are also often used. These do not prevent the vibrations of the machinery that produce noise, but help prevent the noise from being transmitted through the building frame. Noise transmitted through ductwork can be minimized by proper design of the airflow through them, by glass-fiber duct linings, and by mufflers. Other methods are sometimes used for controlling noises from mechanical equipment, including special floor systems.

Special Acoustical Problems Auditoriums, including lecture halls, concert halls, opera houses, theaters, and the like, present special acoustical problems. The programs to be presented in such buildings or the range of types of performances must be determined. Sizes of audiences are important, as are the relative levels of sophistication of the performances and the audiences. In general, large auditoriums are more difficult to design, acoustically, than are smaller ones. And auditoriums in which professional opera, drama, or music is to be presented to audiences with extremely high expectations for perfection have quite different acoustical requirements than elementary or high school auditoriums.

The acoustical design of auditoriums involves room acoustics and noise control. Many factors affect room acoustics, including size or volume of the room; shapes of floors, walls, and ceilings; sound absorption; reverberation characteristics; sound reflection; sound scattering or diffusion; and sound flow around objects or diffraction. The acoustical design of auditoriums is quite complex and is usually handled by acoustical specialists. In addition, the design must assure that noises are strictly controlled. Acoustical design for auditoriums often involves the provision of electronic sound systems, consisting of microphones, amplifiers, loudspeakers, and other equipment. (See the article entitled communication system.)

Building types, other than auditoriums, often present specific acoustical design problems. For example, schools house a number of widely varied activities. Provisions must be made for such activities as lectures, quiet studies as in libraries, outdoor and indoor athletics, physical education, and others. Each type of activity presents acoustical problems that must be solved not only for that activity but for other different activities located nearby. Churches, offices (particularly open-planned types), houses and apartments, and many other building types also present varied acoustical problems that must be solved.

Sound control and acoustics in buildings today is a highly complex subject, only discussed in a very general manner in this article. Because of the complexities, acoustical design is generally handled by specialists, acoustical consultants, who are usually engineers or physicists. Architects and other environmental designers also contribute importantly to good acoustical design, since the shapes of rooms, the materials used, the design and placement of mechanical equipment, and other architectural and engineering considerations have great effects on the acoustics of buildings.

History There is little evidence that attention was paid to acoustics and sound control in the buildings of the early civilizations around the Mediterranean Sea or before that time. In early huts and tents, little could be accomplished, and if it could have been, would probably have been considered unnecessary. In the buildings of ancient Mesopotamia, Crete, and Egypt, sound blocking was a natural result of the massive masonry used in construction, but no attention seems to have been paid to other acoustical factors.

In ancient Greek theaters and those of the Romans that followed, excellent acoustics were achieved,

some experts think by accident. In achieving good sight lines from the audiences to the stages, such theaters were usually designed in semicircular or similar forms and had seating that inclined upward away from the stage or orchestra, as it was called. Behind the orchestra, there ordinarily was a wall, sometimes with a canopy, called a *skene*. The combination of the shape of the theater, the inclination of the seating, and the sound-reflecting qualities of the *skene* as well as the absence of distracting noises near the theater produced very good acoustics.

After the time of the Romans, little or no attention was paid to acoustics for several centuries. Theater construction stopped during the Middle Ages and when it was revived, during the Renaissance, theaters were mostly small and had good sight lines, which incidentally produced good acoustics.

The first printed references to acoustics were published in 1486, even though written by a first-century A.D. Roman architect, Marcus Vitruvius Pollio, usually called Vitruvius. His book *De architectura,* now often called *Ten Books on Architecture,* discussed many elements of architecture, including the acoustics of Greek theaters. It had some effect on the architecture of the time when it was published, but has had considerable importance since that time.

The beginnings of the modern science of acoustics may be taken to be the 17th century, when the French mathematician Marin Mersenne (1588–1648) first measured the velocity of sound in 1640, or when the German mathematician Athanasius Kircker (1601–80) published books on sound, music, and acoustics. Other developments in the science of sound and in acoustics also took place in the 17th century, but they had little or no effect on the acoustics of buildings of the Renaissance and Baroque periods and those that followed, until the 19th century.

In the late 19th century, a number of influential books on acoustics were published, including the two volumes, in 1877 and 1878, of *The Theory of Sound* by the English physicist Lord Rayleigh, (John William Strutt; 1842–1919). The science of architectural acoustics began with the work of American physicist Wallace Clement Ware Sabine (1868–1919), who was a professor at Harvard University, Cambridge, Mass. Sabine not only developed important principles of acoustics but applied the principles to the first building in America to be specifically designed acoustically for the performance of music, the Boston Music Hall, now known as Symphony Hall (1900), designed by McKim, Mead and White.

Since the time of Professor Sabine's work in acoustics, the science has advanced very rapidly. Many new techniques have been developed for providing proper acoustics, not only in theaters, opera houses, symphony halls, and other buildings requiring excellent sound but also in other types, such as office buildings. Progress has also been made in sound control of other sorts, including sound blocking and noise control. Today acoustics and sound control are routinely part of architectural design. In the case of structures, such as theaters, acoustical specialists ordinarily handle acoustical design and testing and often they are consulted on other types of acoustical problems.

Related Articles AIRPORT; HEATING, VENTILATING, AND AIR CONDITIONING; RECREATION BUILDING; RELIGIOUS BUILDING; THEATER.

Further Reading Beranek, Leo L.: *Music, Acoustics and Architecture,* John Wiley, New York, 1962; Beranek, Leo L., ed.: *Noise and Vibration Control,* McGraw-Hill, New York, 1971; Egan, M. David: *Concepts in Architectural Acoustics,* McGraw-Hill, New York, 1972; Knudsen, Vern O., and Cyril M. Harris: *Acoustical Designing in Architecture,* John Wiley, New York, 1950; Northwood, Thomas D., ed.: *Architectural Acoustics,* Dowden, Hutchinson and Ross, Stroudsburg, Pa., 1977.

Sources of Additional Information Acoustical and Insulating Materials Assoc., 205 W. Touhy Ave., Park Ridge, Ill. 60068; Acoustical Society of America, 335 E. 45th St., New York, N.Y. 10017; National Council of Acoustical Consultants, 484 E. Main St., East Aurora, N.Y. 14052.

Periodical *Journal of the Acoustical Society of America,* 335 E. 45th St., New York, N.Y. 10017.

SPECIFICATION

SPECIFICATION The process involved in preparing a written document (the specifications), which describes the materials, workmanship, and final results expected in building construction, along with legal considerations, insurance requirements, inspection and testing procedures, and other requirements. Specifications are sometimes referred to as specs.

The written descriptions of the specifications amplify and augment the graphic descriptions of the working drawings, sometimes called the plans. Together, the working drawings and specifications and other required items are often called the contract documents, since they are part of the contracts between owners and contractors for the construction of buildings.

Contract Documents For the construction of buildings, contract documents consist of the agreement (or contract) between an owner and a contractor, the working drawings, the specifications, the general conditions of the contract, any supplementary conditions or addenda issued before the contract is signed, and later modifications signed by the parties to the contract.

An agreement, general conditions, specifications, and working drawings are the basic parts of a set of contract documents. The others are used as required. Sometimes, contract documents, with the exception of working drawings, are collected into what is called a project manual, which also includes several other items, a copy of the invitation or advertisement for bids, instructions to bidders, and sample forms for insurance and bonds. Formerly, general conditions were considered part of the specifications, but the practice today is to consider these as two separate documents, though they are bound together into project manuals. This is because the content of the general conditions today is confined to questions, such as the responsibilities of and relationships between owners, contractors, subcontractors, architects, and others involved in the construction, and with other business and legal requirements. The content of the specifications may then be confined to the technical requirements for the construction of buildings.

The general conditions of the contract for construction has 14 parts: (1) contract document requirements; (2) the functions, responsibilities, and rights of the architect, (3) the owner, (4) the contractor, (5) the subcontractors; (6) rights to award separate contracts for portions of the work and related requirements; (7) miscellaneous requirements, including laws, damages, bonds, royalties, patents, tests, and so on; (8) time, scheduling, progress, and related requirements; (9) payments to the contractor and completion of the job; (10) safety requirements for people and property; (11) insurance requirements; (12) changes in the work; (13) correction of defective or incorrent work; and (14) termination of the contract.

Formats Today specifications are usually based on a format originally developed by the Construction Specification Institute (CSI), and often called the CSI format. Generally such specifications are said to be in the Uniform Construction Index (UCI) format, since that is the title of a guide to such usage, prepared by CSI, along with the American Institute of Architects (AIA), Associated General Contractors (AGC), of America, Consulting Engineers Council (CEC), of the United States, Council of Mechanical Specialty Contracting Industries (CMSCI), National Society of Professional Engineers (NSPE), Producers' Council (PC), and the Specification Writers Association of Canada. Thus the UCI format for specifications has the backing of many of the major building industry associations.

The 16 divisions of the UCI format cover generic types of construction work. The divisions are subdivided into sections, each of which is devoted to a specific unit of construction work. The 16 divisions are (1) general requirements; (2) site work, (3) concrete, (4) masonry, (5) metals, (6) wood and plastics, (7) thermal and moisture protection, (8) doors and windows, (9) finishes, (10) specialties, (11) equipment, (12) furnishings, (13) special construction, (14) conveying systems, (15) mechanical systems, and (16) electrical systems.

In each of the 16 divisions, sections vary in number, according to needs, from 6 to more than 20. For example, in division (12) furnishings, the eight sections are artwork, cabinets and storage, window treatment, fabrics, furniture, rugs and mats, seating, and furnishing accessories. All these sections, as those in other divisions, are broad in scope; other sections may be added as required. Each section is further subdivided into subjects of narrower scope. For example, in division (12), artwork section, are ceramics, paintings, sculpture, and stained glass; but here too other subjects, such as frescoes, photomurals, and so on, may be added if required.

In a set of specifications, reference is often made to the general and other conditions in the various divisions and in the sections. In addition, each specification section is often divided into three parts: general provisions, materials, and execution of the work. In some specifications, the sections contain slightly different parts: general provisions; materials; fabrication, installation, and testing; closeout and continuing requirements; and submissions of samples, test results, shop drawings, and the like.

Philosophies There are two major philosophies of specification writing: the procedure, sometimes called the prescriptive, specification system; and the performance specification system. In the procedure system, materials to be used and methods of construction are specified. In the performance system, the results expected in the construction are specified, but not the materials or means to be used to arrive at the results. Although some specification writers prefer one system over the other, both are generally used to some extent in most specifications, since certain construction requirements can be better expressed in one way, while some are better expressed in the other.

Materials or Products One of the most important aspects of specifications is the information they contain on materials or products. There are two major methods for the handling of products or materials: closed or open specifications. In a closed specification, certain materials or products are specified by name, with no substitutions allowed. This method is used where it is thought that only these products will be acceptable.

In an open specification, certain options are available in the products or materials used. Open specifications may contain provisions of several kinds: a list of all acceptable products or materials, giving the contractor options; a list of products or materials, with the provisions that a contractor may apply to the architect for approval of substitutes, or equals, before or at the time of bidding or during the construction; and a descriptive specification, which lists the qualities, functions, sizes, performance, and so on of products or materials, any of which will be approved if the requirements are met. All these types of material or product specifications are used by architects at various times.

Specification Writing Ordinarily, specification writing begins early during architectural services. When the design of a building has been developed to a point at which its major elements may be determined, preliminary or outline specifications are usually prepared. In a small office, an architect might prepare these; in larger offices, specification writers are usually specialists in this work. Other design professionals, such as engineers, ordinarily prepare specifications for the types of work they handle, and these are then delivered to the architect for approval and to be found with the other divisions.

After approval of the designs and outline specifications by an owner, the preparation of working draw-
ings and final specifications may begin. Working with the outline specifications and the working drawings as they progress, a specification writer develops checklists and other information to be included in the final specifications. In smaller offices, and to some extent in larger ones, specifications previously prepared for similar projects may be used as guides in the preparation of new specifications. In larger offices, a master specification is often maintained for guidance. As the actual writing of the specification proceeds, the writer will need to confer with the project architect, or other person, in charge of the project and with those actually preparing the working drawings. It may be necessary to seek information from other sources, including manufacturers' catalogs, standard specifications prepared by governmental and building industry technical groups, books, magazines, building codes and ordinances, and other sources.

Reproduction Systems When the specifications have been prepared, they must be checked for accuracy and completeness, carefully proofread, and then reproduced and bound. For relatively small and simple projects, specifications are often reproduced by fluid duplicators or similar methods. For larger and more complex projects, specifications are often printed, sometimes by letterpress but more often by offset process. Binding of specifications usually entails only stapling the pages, along with the other parts of the project manual, into covers. Many larger offices today have their own reproduction systems, while smaller ones often obtain such services from commercial sources. Some offices also use automated systems involving typewriters with attachments for recording the specifications on punched paper or electronic tapes, which allow recall, editing, and automatic typing of the specification contents.

Recently, even more sophisticated methods for specification preparation, using computers, have been developed. Some computer methods were developed in architects' offices. Others are national in scope and are available on a subscription or fee basis. One system that has become widely used was developed by Production Systems for Architects and Engineers Inc. (PSAE), a subsidiary of the American Institute of Architects.

In this system, current specification information is collected and stored in a computer system. Architects or others using the system select from a catalog the divisions and sections they require for specific projects. They then receive computer printouts of the materials, edit them to fit their own requirements, and send the edited copy back to PSAE. In return, they receive corrected printouts from which pages of the specifications may be reproduced directly without further typing.

Specification Specialists Specifications are generally prepared by architects, especially in smaller offices, by specialists in specification writing, either in architects' offices or those of other design professionals, or by specialists who have their own consulting

SPECIFICATION Portion of specifications for stairs, Citicorp Center (1978), New York, N.Y. [Architects: Hugh Stubbins, in association with Emery Roth and Sons. (Hugh Stubbins and Associates)]

SECTION 5B - MISCELLANEOUS IRON AND STEEL

5B.5.   STEEL STAIRS

5B.5.1.   Interior stairs, steel pan construction.

5B.5.1.1.   General - Stairs shall be arranged for cement tread and platform finish, shall be fabricated with bent steel plate treads and risers, plain wall and outside steings plain steel bar balustrading on open side with plain steel tube newels, pressed steel molded cap and drop, and black steel pipe railings (wall mounted and with openside balustrading), one (1) or both sides as shown on the drawings or specified. All steel stair members and structural shapes required for the complete installation of the stairs shall be furnished in place, including those members which may be required but which are not shown or specified. Where soffits of stairs and platforms are indicated to be fireproofed with concrete, tread and platform pans shall be omitted. In such case suitable steel angle members shall be furnished and installed to support the concrete fireproofing.

5B.5.1.2.   Quality - Stairs (and platforms) shall be constructed in accordance with the best practice recommendations of the National Association of Architectural Metal Manufacturers, for this class of work.

5B.5.1.3.   Codes and regulations - All stairs shall be fabricated and erected in accordance with the requirements and regulations of the local Building Code, and all local and state agencies having jurisdiction.

5B.5.1.4.   Loading - Stair and platform construction shall be such as to sustain a superimposed (live) load of not less than one-hundred (100) pounds per square foot (in addition to the dead load).

5B.5.1.5.   Construction sequence - All stairs shall be erected as the structural steel framing of the building progresses and at no time shall be more than three (3) stories below the highest steel erectors derrick floor, unless more stringent requirements are set forth by local authorities having jurisdiction, or by local building code regulations. During the erection operations stairs and platforms shall be accurately fitted to all other adjacent construction

SECTION 5B - MISCELLANEOUS IRON AND STEEL

5B.5.1.6.   Risers, treads and platforms for cement filled steel pan stair construction shall be not lighter than .109 inch thick (No. 12 gauge) sheet steel for stairs up to five (5) feet in width, and not lighter than .140 inch thick (No. 10 gauge) sheet steel for stairs over five (5) feet in width. Platforms shall be reinforced with pressed, integral "v" type ribs, two (2) inches deep for platform up to 3' 1½" wide, and three (3) inches deep for platforms four (4) feet wide and over. Ribs shall be spaced approximately two (2) feet on center (three (3) ribs for an eight (8) foot long platform). Riser heights shall not exceed 7 3/4 inches. Tread widths shall be approximately ten (10) inches including nosing.

a. Risers, Treads and Platforms shall be bent to form nosing and pans to receive cement finish by others. Treads shall be formed to receive 1½" inch deep cement finish, and platforms to receive two (2) inch deep cement finish, except that where platforms are greater in width than 3'-1½", cement finish shall be 2½" deep.

5B.5.1.7.   Stair Stringers shall be fabricated from structural steel channels weighing a minimum of 6.5 pounds per lineal foot. Stringers shall be complete with minimum 1¼ by 1/8 inch steel angle carriers riveted or bolted in place. Carrier angles shall be located so as to properly receive risers and treads, and shall be continuous around perimeter of platforms. Bolts and/or rivets shall be not less than 1/4 inch in diameter. Where stair construction requires, because of greater span between supports, heavier stringers shall be furnished 8.4 or 10.6 pound channels as the specific condition may required. Stringers shall be carried continuously around platforms of stairs (concrete fireproofed and steel pan construction) forming a base which shall be trimmed at landings to height and profile shown. Open ends of all stair stringers shall be closed at terminations.

a. Where stairs are fireproofed with concrete, steel angles of sizes shown shall be furnished, in place welded to stringers. Steel angles shall extend continuously for full extent of the concrete fireproofing, and such angles shall receive 1/4 inch round holes punched or drilled on twelve (12) inch

SECTION 5B - MISCELLANEOUS IRON AND STEEL

centers to receive wire mesh reinforcing for concrete.

b. Shelf angles of suitable size and weight (not less then 3/8 inch thick) shall be furnished in place where stair construction is required to carry walls and partitions on top of stringers. Shelf angles shall be continuous for full length of the partitions and walls being supported, and shall be welded in place in an approved manner.

c. Plates of suitable size and weight (not less than 3/8 inch thick) shall be furnished in place where stair construction is required to carry walls and partitions on bottom of stringers. Plates shall be continuous for full length of the partitions and walls being supported, and shall be welded in place in an approved manner. Plates shall be furnished and installed complete with 1/4 inch thick gusset plates located on not more than two (2) foot centers.

5B.5.1.8. Closure plates, fabricated from .109 inch thick sheet steel shall be applied to top flanges of stair stringers where stairs are located up to fifteen (15) inches away from walls and partitions. Closure plates of .109 inch thickness shall be applied to bottom flanges of stair stringers (over tops of walls and partitions) where walls and partitions are offset from, or are only partially in contact with bottom stringer flanges.

5B.5.1.9. Stair hangers shall be furnished in place as required for the proper support of stairs and platforms. Hangers shall be fabricated from round steel bars of not less than 3/4 inch diameter having threaded ends to receive nuts. Hangers shall be installed so that they may be concealed in walls and partitions. In all locations where hangers are suspended through concrete beams, steel pipe sleeves shall be furnished in place. Sleeves shall have a wall thickness of not less than 3/16 inch and an inside diameter not more than 1/4 inch greater in overall size than the diameter of the hanger. Hangers shall be complete with all washers, nuts, and retaining plates, and shall be of required single lengths.

SECTION 5B - MISCELLANEOUS IRON AND STEEL

5B.5.1.10. Newels shall be fabricated from square steel tubes of 3/16 inch wall thickness, and 3½ or 4 inch size as indicated. Newel tubes shall have rounded corners, plain sides and plain pressed steel caps and bottom closure plates welded in place.

5B.5.1.11. Stair Railings

a. Stair and guard railings on open side of steel stair construction shall be furnished and installed complete with all fittings, accessories rails and fastenings. Railings shall consist of 1/2 by 1/2 inch upright steel bars spaced five (5) inches on center and riveted to a continuous 1 by 1/2 by 1/8 inch steel channel at top and bottom, the bottom channel being top screwed to the upper stringer flange and the top channel being surmounted by a 1½ inch nominal size standard black steel pipe handrail. Handrail shall be fastened to sides of newels, and not to fronts, using offset lugs (square newell fittings). Screws attaching to and bottom channel members to stringers and railing members shall be located on not more than twelve (12) inch centers. Where railings terminate against walls, wall bracket shall be furnished in place as specified hereinafter for wall mounted handrail. Railing terminations which are exposed shall be closed by means of plugs welded in place and neatly rounded off.

b. Wall mounted hand railings for steel pan stairs shall be fabricated from 1½ inch nominal size standard black steel pipe, supported on malleable, or cast, iron wall railing brackets, one (1) located at midpoint of run, and one (1) located at each end. Ends of railings shall be bent (90 degrees) to return to wall or partition and shall terminate in a round escutcheon plate of same diameter as bracket supports. All directional changes of railing members shall be bent to true radii.

c. Wall mounted hand railings shall be secured in place as follows:

1. Where mounting brackets are secured to solid masonry units or concrete, furnish not less than three (3) expansion bolts for fastening; where secured to hollow masonry units furnish not less than (3) toggle bolts.

firms. Effective writing of specifications requires considerable knowledge of the building industry, not only of products, materials, systems, and workmanship but of construction procedures, design and working drawing preparation, construction contracts, law, and construction contract administration.

While courses in specification writing as well as in related subjects are available in professional schools, none are detailed and complete enough to suffice for the proper writing of specifications. Therefore specification writing is often performed by professionals and other construction industry people with an interest in and a deep knowledge of the subject gained through experience working with seasoned specification writers. Many of these are architects, engineers, technicians, or construction people, who chose to become specification writers.

History It is believed that the use of specifications began in the 18th century. Until well into the 19th century, such specifications were quite simple and often were organized according to the crafts which performed the work. A textbook by T. L. Donaldson, *Handbook of Specifications,* published in London in 1860, divided the work into two major headings: carcase (or carcass) of a building, and its finishing. The subdivisions under carcase were excavator, bricklayer, mason, slater, founder and smith, and carpenter. Under finishing were joiner, plasterer, painter, glazier, paperhanger, ironmonger, smith and bellhanger, and gasfitter.

At the end of the 19th century, specifications were often divided into three sections: masonry, carpentry, and mechanical work. In 1915 the AIA published the first edition of its general conditions and this document has subsequently gone through a number of revisions. In 1963 the Construction Specification Institute published its CSI format for construction specifications and in 1966, the Uniform Construction Index, based on the CSI format, was published. In 1969 Production Systems for Architects and Engineers, Inc., was founded for the primary purpose of developing the master (computerized) specification it now makes available to the building industry.

Related Articles COMPUTER; ELECTRICAL ENGINEERING; INTERIOR DESIGN; LANDSCAPE ARCHITECTURE; MECHANICAL ENGINEERING; PRACTICE OF ARCHITECTURE; STRUCTURAL ENGINEERING.

Further Reading Ayers, C.: *Specifications—An Introduction for Architects and Engineers,* McGraw-Hill, New York, 1975; Meier, Hans W.: *Construction Specifications Handbook,* Prentice-Hall, Englewood Cliffs, N.J., 1975; Rosen, Harold J.: *Construction Specifications Writing—Principles and Procedures,* John Wiley, New York, 1974; *Uniform Construction Index—A System of Formats for Specifications, Data Filing, Cost Analysis and Project Filing,* 2d ed., American Institute of Architects and seven other building industry associations, Washington, D.C., 1972.

Further Information Construction Specifications Inst., 1150 17th St,, N.W., Washington, D.C. 20036; Production Systems for Architects and Engineers, Inc., 1735 New York Ave., N.W., Washington, D.C. 20006.

Periodical *The Construction Specifier,* 1150 17th St., N.W., Washington, D.C. 20036.

STAIR A part of a building that allows people to walk from one floor level to another. Stairs are usually constructed on an angle, with a series of steps consisting of treads, horizontal members to walk on, and vertical members, one to each tread, called risers. A stair is also sometimes called a staircase or a stairway and the portion of a stair connecting two floor levels, a flight of stairs. The horizontal distance covered by a flight of stairs is often called a run, and the same term is sometimes used for a single tread. The vertical height of a flight of stairs is called the rise, but the same term is also applied to the height from one tread to another.

Types The simplest form of stair is a ladder, still used sometimes today. Almost as simple is a straight-run, unbroken flight type that rises in a certain direction from one floor level to another. Many other stair forms are possible and are often used for reasons of design, appearance, or space limitations. The next simplest form is one that rises a certain distance, usually to the halfway point between floors, where it meets a platform, called a landing, from which it then rises the remainder of the distance in another direction, usually at right angles to or in the opposite direction from the first.

Many other geometrical forms may be used for stairs, including circular, elliptical, and other curves, and helical, sometimes called helicoidal, or spiral, stairs that wind around poles or are constructed with reinforced concrete or other structures that are self-supporting. Treads of curved stairs are called winders.

Construction Methods Stairs may be built to fit into spaces or shafts, called stairwells, or without stairwells. A special kind with no well, called a dog-legged stair, rises to a landing in one direction then resumes its rise in the opposite direction.

The usual construction for stairs involves inclined structural members, called stringers, which span the distance from floor to floor or between floor and landings. Such stairs may be closed underneath or open. If they are open, the underside is called a soffit. Risers may also be closed or open. In open-rise stairs, the vertical spaces between treads are left open rather than being filled in with various materials as in a closed-rise type. Other construction methods may be used, including cantilevers, in which treads project out from a supporting structure. Stairs are usually provided with handrail systems, often called balustrades, which consist of rails of various materials supported by posts at the ends and at landings, called newels, and smaller posts in between, called balusters or banisters.

Construction Materials The most usual materials for the structure of stairs are wood, reinforced concrete, steel, and sometimes aluminum. One special system consists of preformed steel tread and riser assemblies, called stair pans, which are usually supported by steel stringers. Concrete or another material is poured into the pans to form treads. Many materials may be used for treads and risers, including

STAIR Headquarters of the American Institute of Architects (1972), Washington, D.C. [*Architects: The Architects Collaborative. (Ezra Stoller)*]

wood, usually oak or pine but sometimes others, steel grids, marble or other stone, terrazzo, ceramic and quarry tile, and carpeting. Sometimes metal devices, called nosings, are placed on the front edges of treads to protect them from wear and for safety reasons. Specially formed treads, incorporating abrasives or made of rubber or other materials (nonskid treads), are often used for safety.

Many special types of stairs are available for specific purposes, including ships' ladders of steel, cast iron, and aluminum; prefabricated steel stairs for utilitarian purposes; disappearing stairs of wood, aluminum, or other materials for access to such places as attics and available with mechanical or electrical operators; and fire escapes.

Code Requirements The design of stairs is governed by building code requirements and other standards for construction, inclines, widths, ratios of rise to run, handrails, number required in various building types, sizes, and other particulars. Such codes and standards also govern the requirements for spaces at stair ends and doors necessary for the exit of people from stairs during fires or other emergencies.

In addition, certain concepts of good practice in stair design have been developed over the years. Of utmost importance are the proper inclines. In general, outdoor stairs are not made as steep as those indoors, since those on the exteriors of buildings must be used in bad weather. For interior stairs, certain rules of thumb are sometimes cited, such as that the dimension of a riser plus that of a tread should equal 17 or 17½ in or that the dimension of a riser multiplied by that of its tread should equal 70 or 75. There is also a definite relationship between the relative height of risers to the width of treads. Risers of 7½ in with 10-in treads and risers of 7 in with 10½- or 11-in treads are found to be satisfactory by many people. For other proper ratios, a stair designer should consult various stair tables and diagrams that are widely available. A special riser-tread ratio is sometimes used for monumental buildings, in which the intent is to slow walkers to gain certain effects as they approach. In such buildings, risers are often made very low and treads are made very wide. Many people find such stairs uncomfortable unless the treads are made wide enough so that a walker makes several strides before reaching the next riser. Similarly, many people find that the steeper stairs become, above the angle of a 7½-in riser, 10-in tread, the harder they are to climb.

History Although none are known to exist, it is thought that the first structures of more than one story constructed by humans were provided with vines for climbing from one level to another. Later rudimentary ropes were probably used for this purpose and in time primitive ladders made from limbs of trees. The time when the first real stair was constructed is unknown. However, by about 3000 B.C. when the great early civilizations around the Mediter-

STAIR IBM Laboratory (1974), Boca Raton, Fla. [*Architects: Marcel Breuer and Robert Gatje. (Joseph W. Molitor)*]

ranean Sea were well established, stairs were in common use.

Most of the earliest stairs still in existence are monumental exterior types leading to great temples and other important buildings. Stairs of this type are still in existence in such places as the Palace of Persepolis (486 B.C.), Iran, and many places in Greece. An early interior stair is in the Palace (c. 1600 B.C.) of King Minos, Crete, a place where buildings were as many as four stories high, all levels being served by stairs. The Romans constructed buildings of considerable height, up to about 160 ft, with all levels served by stairs; a number of Roman examples have survived at least in part.

Gothic exterior stairs were usually of stone, while interior ones might be of stone or wood. Stairs of this period were usually not emphasized as architectural features and were often in spiral forms that wound around central columns. During the Renaissance, stairs became important elements of architecture and many fine examples were constructed in many places in Europe. A small sampling of the most notable are double stairs of the Palais de Chambord (1547), France; Palazzo Farnese (1549), Caprarola, Italy, designed by Giacomo Barozzi Vignola (1507–73); and Ashburnum House (1662), Westminister, England, thought to have been designed by John Webb (1611–72). An interesting situation exists at the Chateau de Blois (1524, with later additions), France, where a late Gothic stair was built about 1504 and an early Renaissance example in a tower about 1524.

Many notable stairs were constructed in the years following the Renaissance, including the Baroque example in the Opera House (1874), Paris, designed by Jean Louis Charles Garnier (1825–98), and the Art Nouveau stair in the Tassel House (1893), Brussels, Belgium, by Victor Horta (1861–1947).

American Development In early colonial America, stairs were strictly utilitarian. Later notable curved stairs and other types were constructed in many houses and other buildings during the Colonial period and during the years after the Revolution. Many of these stairs were well designed and graceful, but much simpler than the ornate types often constructed in Europe at the time. In the Classic Revival and Eclectic periods of American architecture, the design of stairs, along with that of other architectural elements, was generally derived from past periods. Some monumental stairs were used for important buildings and this practice continues to an extent today.

Most stairs today, though often well-designed architectural elements, tend to be consistently simple and utilitarian rather than important architectural features. In buildings taller than two stories, except for stairs required by building codes for fire and disaster exists, elevators and sometimes escalators have virtually replaced all stairs. An exception is sometimes made in the lobbies of certain buildings and outside the entrances of others.

Related Articles FIRE PROTECTION; HANDICAPPED FACILITIES FOR THE; VERTICAL TRANSPORTATION.

STEEL An alloy of iron with varying quantities of carbon and often with one or more other substances, used in numerous forms and for many purposes in buildings. The three most common forms of ferrous metals in architecture are wrought iron, cast iron, and steel. The main difference between them is in the amount of carbon they contain. Wrought iron contains the least, less than 0.1 percent carbon but usually much less; cast iron the most, usually from 1.7 to 4 percent carbon; and steel falls in between the two types, with up to 2 percent carbon usually.

Production Methods Steel is made from the product of blast furnaces, called pig iron, which contains approximately 95 percent iron, up to 4 percent carbon, or slightly more, and traces of other substances. Molten pig iron, often with scrap steel and iron added, is processed in a Bessemer converter or an open-hearth, electric, or oxygen furnace, thus removing impurities which are taken off as slag, leaving steel with the amount of carbon required. Metals may be added to the molten steel to produce alloys of various kinds.

About 90 percent of the steel made in the United States comes from open-hearth furnaces. In general, a batch of steel, called a heat, is made by charging the furnace with limestone and scrap steel. The mixture is melted by fires fueled with oil, gas, or other fuels. After the mixture has been melted, molten pig iron is added. After a few hours, if test samples indicate that too much carbon is present, iron ore is added and a small quantity of spiegeleisen or spiegel, pig iron with 20 percent manganese and 5 percent carbon, is added to help remove oxygen from the steel and make it stronger. When samples of the mixture indicate that the heat is ready, the molten steel is tapped into ladles, into which manganese is added. Impurities, in the form of slag, float on the top and flow off into a smaller ladle. The molten steel is then poured into molds to form ingots, and small amounts of aluminum are added to remove oxygen. The entire heat will have taken some 8 to 10 hours and have produced some 50 to 500 tons of steel.

Steel is also made by other methods, including Bessemer converters, today largely supplanted by oxygen furnaces that produce considerably less air pollution. Another method utilizes an electric furnace, in which electric currents cause electrodes inserted into the furnace to arc to the scrap steel and alloying metals and back to the electrodes. Electric furnaces are used mostly for making stainless and other special-alloy steels.

At the end of a steel making process, the molten steel is poured into molds to form ingots. The ingots are again heated to an even temperature in a soaking pit, from which they go to a semifinishing mill where they are rolled, while hot, through rollers to form rough shapes called blooms, billets, or slabs, depending on their shapes and sizes. These shapes go to finishing mills where they are rolled again to produce structural shapes, bars, sheets, strips, plates, or other shapes. These shapes may be used as they come from the finishing mills, as is usually the case with structural shapes, or may be further processed into final products.

Classifications Steels for use in architecture are generally classified as carbon or alloy steels. Carbon steels have at least 95 percent iron, up to 2 percent carbon, and unspecified amounts of other substances. Alloy steels have quantities of other substances in amounts large enough to impart such properties as strength or rust resistance, different from those of carbon steel. Some of the major alloying substances, in addition to carbon, include silicon, manganese, aluminum, boron, chromium, nickel, molybdenum, and vanadium. Many different alloys are available with widely differing characteristics, making alloy steel a versatile architectural material. Stainless steels are special alloys that contain more than 10 percent chromium to impart resistance to corrosion or rusting.

Carbon Steels In general, carbon steels may be worked in several ways (rolled, cast, wrought, and forged) and they can be welded. They are used in architecture for such purposes as structural members, concrete reinforcing rods, mesh and cable, rough hardware, windows, doors, and many others. Since they rust readily, they are painted with rust-inhibiting primers and usually finish coats. Carbon steels are generally available in a number of sizes and forms,

STEEL Mercantile Bank (1975), Kansas City, Mo. [*Architect: Harry Weese. (Hedrich-Blessing)*]

WIDE FLANGE   I-BEAM   CHANNEL   ANGLE   TEE   ZEE

STEEL Typical rolled shapes.

such as sheet, strip, plate, bar, pipe, tubing, and structural shapes, including I beams, wide-flange beams, and H beams, angles, channels, pipe columns, and bar joists. Carbon steel sheet is often formed into light-gauge structural shapes, such as studs and joists.

Alloy Steels Alloy steels vary in their workability, based on the amounts and types of alloying substances. Alloy steels are used where high strength and corrosion resistance are required, for such purposes as elevator cables, high-strength bolts and other fasteners, and sometimes special structures.

Stainless steel comes in several types, classified according to the alloying substances used and their amounts. Stainless steel may be worked by casting, forging, bending, rolling, drawing, and extrusion, and may be welded or soldered. Stainless steel is used in many applications in architecture where high quality, strength, and corrosion resistance are considered important, including curtain walls; windows; doors; countertops; grilles; and kitchen, laboratory, and other appliances. Stainless steel generally comes in sheets, bars, structural shapes, strips, and plate. Sheet is available in several finishes, ranging from an as-fabricated finish through matte satinlike finishes to polished mirrorlike finishes. The first major use of stainless steel in architecture was in the Empire State Building (1931), New York City, designed by Shreve, Lamb and Harmon.

Recently, another type of high-strength, low-alloy steel, called weathering steel, has been used quite often in architecture. Alloyed with 0.20 to 0.55 percent copper, 0.30 to 1.25 percent chromium, and small quantities of niobium, formerly called columbium, these steels need no painting; their surfaces gradually oxidize to brownish colors and after a time cease to oxidize further. Many architects believe this to be one of the most important technical developments in the 20th century, a material that can be exposed like redwood, cypress, stone, or bronze to gradually achieve a natural coloring that is unique. Care must be taken, in using this material, to prevent contact with other metals, such as aluminum, which will be corroded by galvanic action, or with copper, which will cause the steel to corrode. Water, in the form of runoff from one material to another, will also cause corrosion for the same reason. Runoff from weathering steel may stain or discolor some materials, such as stone. For the most part, all other types of steel used in architecture must be painted or otherwise protected by such measures as galvanizing, aluminizing, porcelain enameling, plating, or other surface treatments.

Architects and other environmental designers often design buildings, other structures, and their components of steel. Many steel products come in complete forms, from which the ones to be used may be selected. Others, such as sheet metal for flashing, must be designed and detailed for each application. For structural uses, tables of properties, allowable loads, and so on are widely available thereby helping to simplify the structural design of most relatively uncomplicated building structures. For others, structural engineers perform the structural design.

History The making of primitive steel is thought to have started in the civilizations around the Mediterranean Sea sometime after 3000 B.C. Steel was used only to a small extent, while wrought iron and later cast iron were used much more extensively in early architecture. Fine steels were made in various places, but they were used mostly for swords and other weapons and ornament. The secret of steelmaking was lost, not to be rediscovered until the 18th century. Since that time, steel has become increasingly important in architecture, for structural and many other purposes. For further discussion on the history of steel, see the article entitled iron.

Related Articles BURNHAM AND ROOT; CONCRETE STRUCTURE; IRON; JENNEY, WILLIAM LE BARON; PREFABRICATION; STEEL STRUCTURE; Articles on various building components and systems.

Source of Additional Information American Iron and Steel Inst., 1000 16th St., N.W., Washington, D.C. 20036.

STEEL STRUCTURE Building construction system using steel in the form of columns, beams, and other members for the structure of a building. Structural steel construction refers to the use of hot-rolled members, of not less than $1/8$ in thickness, such as I beams, wide-flange beams, columns, angles, channels, tees, zees, and others. Such structural steel shapes are classified into heavy structural shapes, those that have at least one dimension of 3 in or more, and light structural shapes or bars. Light-gauge steel, for structural systems, includes such members as beams, joists, and studs made of sheet steel which has been bent, cold, or otherwise fabricated, for use in relatively small buildings.

Uses Steel members may be used in building structures in many ways, ranging from a single pipe column to take the load of a floor or roof in a wood-frame house to the complete framing of tall buildings. A method often used for relatively small, low-rise buildings consists of bearing walls of masonry or other materials, with floors and roofs framed with steel members. For buildings in which large open, columnless spaces are required, steel may be used for long spans, utilizing trusses of various kinds, large girders, arches, space frames, rigid frames, or long-span joists. For relatively small buildings, often only one story, light-gauge members may be used for walls, floors, and roofs. In some cases, such members are fabricated to produce a slot into which nails may be driven to fasten finishing and other materials.

It can be seen that steel is a versatile structural material that can be employed in buildings in a great variety of ways. One of the most important today is in the construction of skeleton-framed buildings.In such buildings, mostly heavy structural shapes are used to form complete structures of walls, floors, and roofs. Often steel decking is used in roofs that are finished

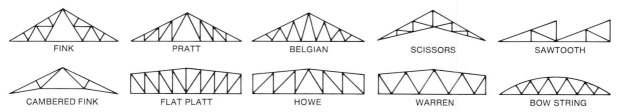

STEEL STRUCTURE Typical trusses.

with fire-resistant materials, such as concrete or plaster. Skeleton-framed steel buildings generally have columns, beams, and girders attached together to form strong frames. Usually, the connections between members are made by riveting or welding, but sometimes in smaller buildings or for relatively minor connections, by bolting. Forces from the sides of skeleton-framed buildings, lateral loads, such as those from wind or earthquakes, are usually resisted by either diagonal steel bracing or by masonry or concrete transverse walls, called shear walls. In many cases, masonry or concrete serves the additional purpose of providing fire resistance for the steel framing members.

While regular steel heavy structural shapes may be used for the construction of floors and roofs in buildings with walls of masonry or other materials, a more usual method employs open-web steel joists. These are prefabricated, flat trusses made of small steel sections, such as angles, tees, and bars. They are available in various depths, lengths, and strengths. Open-web joists, used for relatively short spans, are often called bar joists, and those for longer spans, up to 144 ft, are usually called long-span joists. They are used in relatively close spacing, in a manner similar to that of wood joists in a house, and are usually covered with corrugated steel or other types of materials upon which concrete is poured. The undersides may be left exposed in such building types as factories or warehouses and plastered or otherwise surfaced in shopping centers or other building types in which finished appearances are important.

Light-gauge steel members are available in such sections as channels, zees, angles, and others, and in I sections, made by welding two channels together or two angles to a single channel. Such members come in various sizes and gauges, and special types may also be designed and fabricated. The design of buildings using stock light-gauge steel is somewhat similar to the design of buildings with stock wood-framing members. For special types, a considerable amount of calculation is required, and the procedures are quite different from those involved in design with structural steel sections.

Other important steel structural materials, widely available, are light-gauge roof and floor decking. Such components come in several types, among the most important being the ribbed and cellular types. Ribbed types, in several gauges and in a variety of widths and lengths, are generally used for roof decks and are of-

ten covered with insulation and built-up roofing. Cellular types are made in such a way that spaces are provided in which electrical wiring or other systems may be installed and easily modified. The cellular types come in various sizes and strengths and are used for both floors and roofs, usually with concrete placed on top of them. Their bottom sides may be finished with plaster or other materials. There are also special types with perforated metal undersides above which acoustical materials may be installed.

Many other applications of steel in structures may be made. For example, steel pipe, available in many sizes and strengths, is often used for columns. Sometimes pipe columns are filled with concrete for added strength. Steel, in the form of reinforcing bars, welded wire fabric, and wire rope or cable, is widely used for reinforcing concrete. (See the article entitled concrete structure.)

Assembly Systems An interesting and important use of steel in building construction is assembly of relatively small steel members into systems that can span great distances. A type that has been used for centuries in architecture is the truss, an assembly of relatively small members into a system, composed of triangles, the most rigid geometrical shape possible, for long spans. In steel, five types of trusses are generally used: the Pratt, Fink, Warren, scissors, and bow string. The five vary in shape and in the way the members are arranged. The scissors and bow-string trusses were named for their shapes, the others for their designers, American engineer Thomas Willis Pratt (1812–75), German-American engineer Albert Fink (1827–97), and English engineer James Warren (d.c. 1848). A later type of truss, the Vierendeel, does not depend on triangles for its rigidity but on strong, welded joints between its members.

Other assemblies of relatively small members, used to span great distances, are steel arches of which there are three major types: three-hinged, two-hinged, and hingeless. All are constructed with triangles, like trusses. Three-hinged arches have hinge pins at the base while the crown is rigidly connected. Three-hinged arches are simpler than the two-hinged to design and easier to erect. Two-hinged arches are usually heavier than the three-hinged type. Hingeless arches have no pins, but are rigidly connected. They may be economical for structures built on ground with good bearing strength and where the arches will carry relatively light loads. Another type of steel structural member for long spans is the rigid frame, which may be two-hinged or hingeless for single spans. Rigid frames are assembled from steel structural shapes.

Space Frames   Many other types of steel structures are used today, including space structures or space frames. Strictly speaking, a space frame is any structure in three dimensions and thus includes rigid skeleton frames of buildings and other types. Today the term usually denotes various types of structures, including folded plates, domes, arches, grids, and others, in which the entire structure of a roof, for example, is made up of relatively small members designed and connected in a manner allowing the entire structure to act as an assembly to carry loads. These loads are then transferred directly to columns, foundations, or other structural elements. In other types of structures, for example, trusses, the loads on the roof are ordinarily carried by the roof deck, then transferred to purlins or other structural members, then to the trusses, and finally to the columns. Space frames are capable of spanning long distances in two directions, utilize relatively small steel sections, and are simple to fabricate as compared to many other systems. Space frames also make possible structural forms of buildings that would not ordinarily be possible when other systems are used.

Other Developments   Many other types of structures utilizing steel are possible today, including suspension systems, in which roofs of buildings are hung from cables, as in suspension bridges. Steel is a very versatile structural material and new and modified uses of it continue to be developed. Tables of data and other information are widely available. Computers have simplified calculations and have made additional data available to structural engineers for use in calculations. Many of the procedures used today were very difficult, or impossible, to handle before the advent of computers.

Among the most recent developments is weathering steel, which can be exposed without painting or other treatment. This steel weathers to brownish colors that protect it from further oxidation or rusting. Other important developments have been the use of huge trusses in buildings to resist the lateral forces of wind and earthquakes, and the design of tall buildings based on the structural principle of a tube or group of tubes.

For all but the simplest uses of steel in structures, calculations in structural design may be quite complex. Therefore the discussion here has only covered general guidelines and principles of design and construction. In practice, the applicable building and other codes must be followed, as must good principles of design and construction. Experienced and highly competent structural engineers usually design all but the simplest steel structures. And architects using steel in their buildings must have a keen understanding of its properties, characteristics, and uses in order to exploit the material to the ultimate.

History   Steel making was discovered very early in history, perhaps by 3000 B.C. The early civilizations rarely used steel, preferring wrought iron for architectural and other purposes, most of which were relatively small at first. Probably because steel did not come into widespread use, the methods for making steel were later lost or ignored. In 1740 steelmaking began again. However, steel did not become a structural material for buildings until the late 19th century, with its use for some beams in the Home Insurance Building (1885), in Chicago, designed by William Le Baron Jenney (1832–1907), and later destroyed. In 1895 steel columns were first used in the Reliance Building, Chicago, designed by Burnham and Root. From that time, steel has been a very important structural material, not only for tall buildings but for most other types.

The Reliance Building had 4 floors when it was first built, and was later expanded to 14. Only a few years later, in 1907, the steel-framed Singer Building, New York City, designed by Ernest Flagg (1857–1947), with 47 stories and 612 ft high, was completed. This was the record height for a building until about 1909, when the 700-ft-high Metropolitan Life Insurance Building, New York City, designed by Nicholas Le Brun and Sons, was completed. The record did not last long. In 1913 the Woolworth Building, New York City, designed by Cass Gilbert (1859–1934), was completed, with 55 stories and 760 ft high. Its record lasted the longest, until 1930, when the Chrysler Building, New York City, designed by William Van Alen (1907–   ), was completed with 75 stories, 1,049 ft high, including its spire. A year later, this record was broken by the Empire State Building (1931), designed by Shreve, Lamb and Harmon, 102 stories and a height of 1,250 ft to the top of its never used dirigible mast. Later a tall television antenna was added on top. A the present time, the height record is a tie between the World Trade Center (1973), New York City, designed by Minoru Yamasaki (1912–   ), in association with Emergy Roth and Sons, and the Sears Tower (1974), Chicago, designed by Skidmore, Owings and Merrill. Both buildings have 110 stories and are 1,454 ft tall. How long their record will stand is a matter for speculation. In any case, it is important to know that all the above buildings were framed in steel. Some think that the era of the design of buildings so tall, or taller, is over. Others disagree. One who disagreed was Frank Lloyd Wright (1867–1959) who, in 1958, proposed a mile-high skyscraper, with 528 floors. It was never built, but Wright always insisted it was feasible. Not all architects or engineers were convinced.

While American architects were building ever-higher steel-framed skyscrapers, other important developments were also taking place in structural steel usage. In fact, some of these developments were necessary before tall buildings could be designed and constructed. The connection of steel structural members with rivets was derived from the method of making boilers. The steel-skeleton frame was derived from earlier wrought-iron and cast-iron frames. At first, steel buildings used masonry walls to resist the forces of wind, or lateral forces, and sometimes these forces were even ignored, a practice definitely not followed today.

Before the beginning of the 20th century, another method for providing lateral bracing had been developed: riveting all structural members to form a rigid frame. In a rigid frame, all the beams, girders, columns, and other structural members are rigidly connected together to form a complete system which resists loads. This became a standard method in architecture. Another technique was later developed for this purpose, the provision of diagonal bracing, which has also become a standard method. Steel trusses have been used in a number of buildings to provide diagonal wind bracing.

Of course, tall steel-framed buildings would not have been feasible if Elisha Graves Otis (1811–61) had not invented a safe elevator, first used in an office building in 1857. The development of central heating and later air conditioning were also necessary for tall buildings to function properly.

In the years after the early steel-framed buildings, many new developments were made. Most of them would not have been possible without improved mathematical methods for calculations of structural members and complete structures. In addition, stronger and better steels have been developed. Improvements have also been made in testing structures by means of mock-ups and models. Until the advent of computers in the second half of the 20th century, it was still very difficult or impossible to perform some of the calculations required for complicated structural designs. Computers have now made possible many advanced and sophisticated structures.

Beginning in the 1960s, a new concept of the structure of tall buildings was developed. Instead of considering the frame as a rigid structure assembled of columns, beams, and so on, it is thought of as a tube perforated by windows. Considerable savings of steel can be achieved in structures of this type. In fact, the concept is a tube within a tube, the inner one the elevator and systems core, usually of reinforced concrete, surrounded by an outer tube of structural steel. Used in the John Hancock Center (1970), Chicago, designed by Skidmore, Owings and Merrill, the tubes are braced with diagonal steel members on the exterior of the building.

In the Sears Tower, mentioned above, the concept was a perforated bundle of nine tubes, with diagonal bracing. In this building, the tubes are in sets of two or three, each set terminating at a different height, the lowest at the 50th floor, the highest at the 110th. The tube concept has also been used in other buildings. The structures of both of these buildings were designed by Pakistani-American engineer Fazlur Rahman Khan (1929–   ), of the staff of the architects of the buildings.

Although electric arc welding had been invented in 1881, it was not used in a steel building structure until 1920. Beginning in the 1930s, welding became an important method in steel construction. It allows savings in the amount of steel used, simplifies difficult connections, and, theoretically at least, makes possible connections as strong as the members themselves. Welding is widely used today in making connections in steel-framing buildings. Welding is particularly well adapted to connections required in many types of curved or oddly shaped structures. Such structures include space frames of various types, arches, vaults, domes, and others. High-strength bolts are also used for similar purposes.

Other types of steel structures used in architecture today include two-hinged and three-hinged arches; rigid arches; latticework structures, called lamella; and geodesic domes, invented by Buckminster Fuller (1895–   ); cable-suspended structures. When the ingenuity of architects and engineers are combined with the versatility of structural steel and with the great information retrieval and calculation capabilities of computers, it can be expected that new types of structures will be developed in the future.

Related Articles BRIDGE; COMPUTER; IRON; OFFICE BUILDING; STEEL; STRUCTURAL ENGINEERING; STRUCTURE; VERTICAL TRANSPORTATION; Various articles on individual 19th and 20th century architects, and on building components and systems.

Further Reading Cowan, Henry J.: *Science and Building—Structural and Environmental Design in the Nineteenth and Twentieth Centuries,* John Wiley, New York, 1978; *Manual of Steel Construction,* latest edition, American Institute of Steel Construction, New York; Merritt, Frederick S.: *Structural Steel Designers' Handbook,* McGraw-Hill, New York, 1972; Parker, Harry, and Harold D. Hauf: *Simplified Design of Structural Steel,* 4th ed., John Wiley, New York, 1974; Schueller, Wolfgang: *High Rise Building Structures,* John Wiley, New York, 1977.

Sources of Additional Information American Iron and Steel Inst., 1000 16th St., N.W., Washington, D.C. 20036; American Institute of Steel Construction, 1221 Avenue of the Americas, New York, N.Y. 10020.

STEIN, CLARENCE S.

STEIN, CLARENCE S. American architect and planner (1882–1975). Although he started out as an architectural designer, working mostly in eclectic styles, Clarence Stein soon found that his major interests and talents were in planning. He chose to devote his career to planning some of the most progressive communities in the United States. And he became a leader of the cause for good community and regional planning.

Community Planning With his partner, architect and planner Henry Wright (1878–1936), Stein pioneered many ideas that were in opposition to the meaningless, ugly inconvenient, and uncomfortable sprawl of cities and their suburbs. Stein and Wright were a long way ahead of their time. They advocated and designed master plans for communities in which houses could be located properly on their sites and in proper relationships to each other, to vehicular and pedestrian travel, to open space areas, and to landscaping. In their designs, varying functions, such as automobile and pedestrian traffic, were separated for

STEIN, CLARENCE Area plan (1930), Radburn, N.J. [*Planners: Clarence S. Stein and Henry Wright. (Stein & Wright)*]

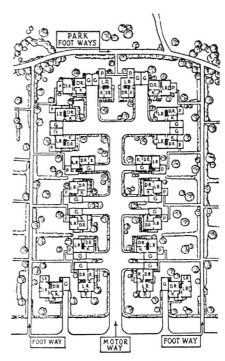

STEIN, CLARENCE Block plan (1930), Radburn, N.J. [*Planners: Clarence S. Stein and Henry Wright. (Stein & Wright)*]

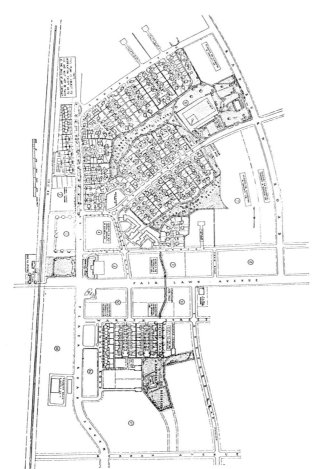

STEIN, CLARENCE Plan (1930), Radburn, N.J. [*Planners: Clarence S. Stein and Henry Wright. (Stein & Wright)*]

convenience and safety. Communities were set in what came to be called greenbelts, areas of trees and other natural elements that protected them. Schools, shopping areas, and so on were located in specific areas so that their activities could function without infringement on others. Groups of houses were arranged into neighborhood units, in which families could achieve a sense of freedom and identification. The houses faced open areas and trees, shrubbery, and grass.

The result of these theories and practices were communities that were far superior to those being built elsewhere in the United States then. And far superior to most of those being built today. Stein and Wright had a vision of something better and they made it work. This is not always the case in the developments of today.

Works The first important development by Stein and Wright was Sunnyside Gardens (1924), Queens, New York City. This was followed by Phipps Garden Apartments (1931), also in Queens, and Hillside Homes (1935), in the Bronx, New York City. Then followed two new communities for which Stein and Wright acted as master planners. The first was Radburn, N.J., for which they started planning in 1928 and which was built in the early 1930s according to their plans but with buildings designed by others. The second was Chatham Village, Pittsburgh, also built in the early 1930s and with buildings by others.

After the death of Henry Wright in 1936, Stein continued to act as planner and architectural consultant for other new communities. He did not design build-

STEIN, CLARENCE Baldwin Hills Village (1940), Los Angeles, Calif. [*Planner: Clarence S. Stein. Architect: Robert E. Alexander. (Julius Shulman)*]

ings for these, but had considerably more success in affecting the quality of their architecture than he had exercised in the earlier projects. He planned a series of three communities, based on his earlier greenbelt ideas, for the Farm Security Administration of the U.S. government: Greenbelt, Md.; Greendale, Wis.; and Greenhills, Ohio. All were notable for their plans but not for financial success. In the early 1940s he planned Baldwin Hills Village, its buildings designed by Robert Evans Alexander (1907–), Los Angeles, and in the early 1950s was associated with British planner Gordon Stephenson on the planning of Stevenage, England. In the latter community, he was able to establish, for the first time, a town center free of vehicular traffic. In 1951 Stein acted as planning director for his last great project, the new industrial town of Kitimat, British Columbia, Canada.

Life Clarence S. Stein was born in Rochester, N.Y., on June 19, 1882, the son of a successful businessman. Frail and often ill as a child, Stein moved with his family to New York City when he was a boy. After graduating from high school, he entered the architectural school at Columbia University, New York City, in 1908, stayed a short while, and transferred to the École des Beaux Arts in Paris, studying there until 1911.

Upon his return from Paris, Stein went to work in the office of Bertram Grosvenor Goodhue (1869–1924) in New York City in 1911, and worked there until 1918. While with Goodhue, he participated in the design of numerous buildings and designed the

master plan for a mining village in Tyrone, N.Mex. In 1918, during World War I, he served in the U.S. Army Corps of Engineers as a first lieutenant.

Having become deeply concerned with housing, particularly for low-income families, Stein started his own architectural practice in 1919 and became involved in the work of New York state committees on housing and planning. At first, he designed buildings as would any other practicing architect but later devoted more and more time to planning, particularly new towns and other developments. In this work, he was one of the earliest pioneers in the United States.

In 1924 his first important housing, Sunnyside Gardens, Queens, New York City, was completed; others followed over the years. From 1918 to 1921, he served as associate editor of the *AIA Journal,* using the magazine as a medium to espouse the cause of good planning and conservation, including the proposal for the Appalachian Trail made in 1921 by the noted and far-sighted forester and planner Benton MacKaye (1879–1976). Thus began Stein's lifelong dedication to the cause of planning, not only his own but that of others, including MacKaye; the famous historian, writer, and critic Lewis Mumford (1895–); Catherine Bauer (1905–64), who later taught at the University of California and was married to William Wilson Wurster (1895–1973); and Henry Wright, who was his partner in planning most of the great communities. Stein arranged for Wright to work out the Regional Plan of New York State in 1923, a classic example of creative planning, still much admired.

In 1928 Stein was married to Aline MacMahon, an actress. He later helped organize a group to promote planning on all levels, the Regional Planning Association of America. Many of the foremost planners of the day were active in this organization. Stein did everything he could for the cause. He wrote articles, lectured, made movies on planning, sent reports and memos to government officials, and edited *Town Planning Review* from 1951 to 1959. He had also embarked on a busy professional career that gradually found him making master plans for communities that are still models of good design. Gradually, he also stopped designing buildings; in his greatest communities, he did not design a single building.

Plagued by illness much of his life, Stein nevertheless accomplished a great deal. Many honors came to him, including the Gold Medal, the highest honor of the American Institute of Architects, in 1956. When he died on February 6, 1975, at age ninety-two, he had come to be considered not only a pioneer of planning but a sage as well.

Related Articles BEAUX ARTS, ÉCOLE DES; CRAM, GOODHUE AND FERGUSON; HOUSING; MODERN ARCHITECTURE; PLANNING, CITY.

Further Reading Stein, Clarence S.: *Toward New Towns for America*, MIT Press, Cambridge, 1967.

STONE, EDWARD DURELL American architect (1902–78). Edward Durell Stone is a controversial architect about whose work architects and other people seem to have widely divergent views. Nevertheless, Stone put his mark on the architecture of his time, in the many important buildings he designed, in his espousal of refined ornament in his later years, and in his establishment of sunscreens, usually grilles, as a major element of his buildings. He also became well known for his dedication to the cultural aspects of his buildings and their proper harmonization with their surroundings.

Works Starting with his first commission, for the Mandel House (1933), in Mt. Kisco, N.Y., Stone designed numerous fine houses all over the country. It took a rather long time for him to become established in the design of other building types, but beginning in the early 1950s, he produced a steady stream of notable buildings. Some of them are the El Panama Hotel (1946), Panama City, Panama; U.S. Embassy (1954), New Delhi, India, which many consider his best building; Stanford University Medical Center (1955), Palo Alto, Calif.; Stuart Company offices (1956), Pasadena, Calif.; U.S. Pavilion (1957) at the World's Fair, Brussels, Belgium; the National Geographic Society Building (1961), Washington; and the John F. Kennedy Center for the Performing Arts (1969), Washington.

Life Edward Durell Stone was born on March 9, 1902, in Fayetteville, Ark. As a boy, he was a good student and was interested in building things like boats, furniture, and birdhouses. His older brother, Hicks (1888–1928), was an architect who practiced in Boston. In 1920 Stone went to the University of Arkansas, but dropped out in 1923 to join his brother in Boston. He then worked in architectural offices, including that of Coolidge, Shepley, Bulfinch and Abbott, and studied architecture nights at the Boston Architectural Club, since 1944, the Boston Architectural Center.

In 1926 Stone won a competition for a scholarship to Harvard University and stayed there a short time and then transferred to Massachusetts Institute of Technology, and stayed until 1927. Having won the Rotch Traveling Scholarship, Stone went to Europe in 1927, and remained there until 1929. Returning to America, Stone went to New York, where he worked for several firms until 1933, when he opened his own office.

In 1931 Stone married Orlean Vandiver and they had two children. These were Depression times and architectural commissions were very few. After Stone first opened his office, he designed a few houses that brought him considerable attention, including one for Henry R. Luce (1898–1967), the noted publisher of *Time*, and later *Life*, magazines. Luce commissioned Stone to design a plantation house and several other buildings (1936) in Moncks Corner, S.C. He was then chosen to design, with Philip L. Goodwin (1885–1957), the new Museum of Modern Art (1939), New York City, to which wings were added in 1951 and 1964 by Philip Cortelyou Johnson (1906–   ). After that commissions started to come into his office in increasing numbers.

STONE, EDWARD DURELL Museum of Modern Art (1939), New York, N.Y. [*Architects: Edward Durell Stone and Philip L. Goodwin. (Wurts brothers)*]

STONE, EDWARD DURELL U.S. Embassy (1954), New Delhi, India. *(Edward Durell Stone)*

STONE, EDWARD DURELL Graf House (1956), Dallas, Tex. *(Edward Durell Stone)*

When World War II started, Stone entered the U.S. Army Air Force in 1942, and was released as a major in 1945. Returning to New York, he reestablished his practice, this time in Great Neck, Long Island, and again started designing houses. Soon commissions for other types of buildings started to come in and his career, other than as a house architect, began.

In 1951 Stone was divorced from his wife, and in 1954 he married Maria Elena Torchio, the American-born daughter of an Italian father and Spanish mother. They had two children, but were subsequently divorced. He then married again, this time to Fiona Campbell and they had one child.

Stone eventually built one of the most successful architectural practices of his time, and designed a great number of important buildings all over the world. His life was not always easy, with two divorces and a long struggle with the problems of alcohol. But he always kept the good humor he was noted for and weathered all his troubles to keep on producing architecture. He also received many honors, including doctor's degrees and membership in the American Academy of Sciences and the National Institute of Arts and Letters. On August 6, 1978, Stone died.

Related Articles CONTEMPORARY ARCHITECTURE; MODERN ARCHITECTURE.

Further Reading Stone, Edward Durell: *The Evolution of an Architect,* Horizon Press, New York, 1962; Stone, Edward Durell: *Architecture—Recent and Future,* Horizon Press, New York, 1967.

STONE Rock used in the construction of buildings for walls, floors, and other purposes. Rock is the hard, solid mass, composed of minerals, that makes up the earth's crust. Soil is composed of rock particles, often mixed with organic matter. Rock used for construction purposes is often called building stone after it has been cut, sized, or otherwise processed for use in architecture. Stone has been a very important building material from the earliest time and until the 19th century was the primary structural and ornamental material for monumental and other notable buildings. Today stone is still widely used for various purposes in buildings, but not often for complete structures.

Types Rock occurs naturally all over the world and stone suitable for architectural uses exists in many places. Rock may be classified into three types: igneous, sedimentary, and metamorphic. Igneous rock was formed by the cooling of molten rock or magma, from within the earth. Sedimentary rock consists of various rock materials that were deposited in layers, or strata, by the action of water, held together by cementitious materials. Metamorphic rock is another type that has had its appearance and sometimes its composition changed by the action of pressure, heat, or chemical action.

Building Stone Stone used for buildings comes from all three types of rock, including granite from igneous, limestone and sandstone from sedimentary, and marble and slate from metamorphic. Many vari-

eties of these stones are found in the United States, with widely varying characteristics and properties of strength, maximum and minimum usable sizes, colors, textures, and the like. Some types are occasionally imported from other countries, including a few from quarries that were first worked by the Greeks and Romans. Thus architects and other designers have a wide choice of available building stones.

Among the most important are limestone, granite, sandstone, slate, and marble. Limestone is a hard, durable type that is relatively easy to work and comes in various shades of buff and gray. Granite is a very hard, very strong type that is relatively hard to work. It comes in a range of gray tones, usually with visible specks of mica, quartz, and other minerals, giving it a mottled appearance, and it can be highly polished. Sandstone is moderately hard, easy to work, and comes in a variety of colors. Some sandstones do not weather well, but others are very weather resistant. Slate may be split into thin forms for use in shingles and flooring; it comes in a limited range of grays, blue-grays, greens, and almost black. Marble is a strong, very durable stone that comes in a variety of colors, often with streaks of other colors. For many centuries marble has been considered the finest building stone, and even today many people would agree. The world *marble* is sometimes loosely applied to limestones, particularly dolomitic types, which can be highly polished.

Quarrying Stone is quarried in very much the

STONE IBM, Watson Research Laboratory (1960), Yorktown Heights, N.Y. [*Architect: Eero Saarinen. (Joseph W. Molitor)*]

same manner as it was in ancient times, except for the use today of power, machinery, and explosives. Rough stone is blasted from quarries with explosives, broken into usable sizes, and used in its rough form or finished. Cut stone is quarried by drilling and cutting channels or sawing and using wedges to break huge blocks, weighing up to 50 tons, from the bedrock. These blocks are then sawed into smaller ones. Smaller blocks are cut into the desired shapes and sizes and finished by polishing or other methods to enhance the texture and color. The final operations may be completed at the quarries or by stone fabricators, located elsewhere.

Other Building Stones Rough stone, called fieldstone, just as it comes from the ground and with no cutting or finishing may be used in walls and other building elements. However, the major types used for such purposes are rubble and dimension stone. Rubble, rough and irregular in shape but sometimes roughly squared, is used for walls and other purposes usually, but not always, uncoursed. Dimension stone comes in specific sizes, square and finished to be used in walls, for wall facings or veneers, and other purposes. In larger sizes, dimension stone is often called cut stone and in smaller ones, ashlar, which may be laid in walls in courses and in patterns of large and small pieces. Laid without continuous joints, such stonework is called random ashlar.

Another type of stone, frequently used in architecture, is flagstone, relatively thin, flat pieces, from about 1 to 2 inches thick, that may be either irregular or squared. Flagstone is used, inside and outside of buildings, for flooring, walkways, terraces, stair treads, countertops, and other purposes. Crushed or broken stone is used for a variety of purposes, including aggregates in concrete and terrazzo, and for walks, roads, and surfacing built-up roofs and asphalt building products. Powdered stone is used in paints, resilient flooring, and other products. Relatively massive stone, either rough or finished, used for such purpses as monuments or sculpture, is often called monumental stone.

Characteristics Stone comes in a great variety of colors, including red, green, blue, yellow, gray, and various color combinations. Some stones, such as granite, have specks of various minerals that sparkle in the sunlight. Other stones, such as marble, often have streaks of various colors in a monotone background. Cut stone may be obtained from any of several surface textures, including relatively rough finishes imparted by the type of saws used. These include shot-sawed, gang-sawed, and chat-sawed types. Other types of textures may be imparted to stone by bushhammering, peen hammering, and other methods. Stone may also be tooled, by hand or machine, imparting grooves or striations in the face; this very expensive method is rarely used today.

Polished stone may be obtained in various degrees of smoothness. From the least smooth to smoothest, the methods include machined, stone directly from a

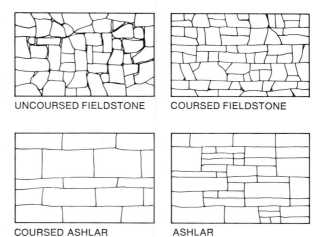

UNCOURSED FIELDSTONE COURSED FIELDSTONE

COURSED ASHLAR ASHLAR

STONE Typical coursing.

planer; Carborundum finished, produced by using a Carborundum machine instead of a planner; wet rubbed, treated with abrasives; rubbed and honed; and honed and polished.

Bonding Methods Stone is erected in buildings in several different ways, by laying it in mortar, by attaching it with anchors, and sometimes by the use of adhesives. Stone used for structural purposes, as in bearing walls, is laid in mortar either in solid walls or as veneers bonded to back-up materials, such as brick or structural clay tile. Bonding may be accomplished by either laying the stone, and other materials when used, in mortar to interlock with each other, forming a strong integral wall, or by use of metal wall ties. When stone is used as a veneer for other wood-framed structures, it is laid in mortar and tied to the structures with metal ties. Mortar for use with stone, other than fieldstone, must be made with nonstaining cement and white sand to avoid discoloration. When used in curtain walls, stone is usually connected to building frames with metal anchors. High-strength adhesives are sometimes employed to attach thin-stone panels. Stone for flooring, walkways, and the like are ordinarily set in cement seating beds; flagstone is sometimes set in sand beds.

Stone is one of the most important architectural materials. Its long life, beauty, and strength have appealed to architects from almost the beginning of building construction. Many architects today believe that no other material can satisfy specific kinds of requirements in certain elements of buildings as well as stone. However, stonework is relatively expensive, compared to other materials, and must be used with care. It is subject to discoloration and deterioration by waterborne or airborne pollution. Some stones are easily stained by such materials as bronze and other copper alloys, steel, and even some types of wood.

To use stone properly, architects and other environmental designers should familiarize themselves with the properties and characteristics of the various types and follow the recommended practices for their uses. Careful selection must also be made of the

STONE Brunswick Building (1963), Chicago, Ill. [*Architects: Skidmore, Owings and Merrill. (Hedrich-Blessing)*]

proper colors, textures, finishes, and variations in the stone. Samples of stone to be used are always required as are accurate shop drawings for its fabrication. Delivery problems and shipping costs should be determined as well as the availability of skilled labor near the locality of building sites.

History Although the time of its first use has not been firmly established, stone is believed to have been used, in crude form, as early as 4000 B.C. In the ancient civilizations around the Mediterranean Sea, stone was used for almost all important buildings in areas where it was to be found. Thus in Mesopotamia, where there was little stone, brick and other clay products, such as terra-cotta, became the primary building materials. In Egypt, where it was plentiful, stone was used. The first important use of stone in construction was for the stepped Pyramid of Zoser (2778 B.C.) in Akkara, Egypt, constructed from relatively small blocks of limestone. Later the Egyptians used very large blocks, in what is called Cyclopean stonework, laid without mortar, named after the mythological one-eyed giant, Cyclops.

The largest stone buildings ever built are the pyramids (c. 2723–2563 B.C.) at Gizeh, Egypt. The largest of the three, the Great Pyramid of Cheops, was orig-

inally 480 ft high and 756 ft on the sides at its base. These pyramids were originally encased in fine limestone, but much of their covering has deteriorated or been taken away. As was customary in Egyptian construction, no mortar was used for setting the stone, but a thin lime mortar was used as a lubricant to help in the placement of the blocks. Although many theories have been advanced, no one really knows how the Egyptians, with only simple machinery, were able to construct these pyramids made with pieces of stone that averaged 2½ tons in weight. For columns, obelisks, sculpture, and other important architectural elements of the sort, the Egyptians mostly used single or monolithic stones. Many kinds and qualities of stone were available in Egypt, but the main kinds used were limestone, granite, and sandstone. In ancient Crete and early ancient Greece, stone was used along with wood, brick, and other materials.

As it had been in Egypt, stone was the major building material used for important buildings in ancient Greece. And the Greeks brought the design of stone buildings and their elements to a level of perfection never equaled except, perhaps, in the Gothic cathedrals of the Middle Ages. Stone was plentiful in Greece, a good deal of it being marble, including the famous Pentelic marble, often used in fine buildings, and the equally famous Parian marble, often used in sculpture. The Greeks designed marble building elements to perfection, cut them to perfection, and erected them to very small tolerances for error, usually without mortar.

Instead of the monolithic elements of Egyptian architecture, the Greeks generally built up columns and other architectural elements in pieces. Columns were made with pieces of stone, called drums, which were placed one above the other without mortar, but with very precise joints. The drums were joined to each other with wooden dowels at first and later with iron ones. Sometimes the Greeks covered the buildings with stucco made of fine marble dust, and highly polished. Stone sculptures and carved ornaments of the finest quality were placed by the Greeks on all their most important buildings. As had been that of the Egyptians, Greek architecture was trabeated, or post and lintel.

The Romans also used stone extensively in their architecture. Although they had sources of fine travertine limestone at Tivoli, Luna marble at Carrara, and marble from Siena, most of the other stones were of lesser quality, at least in appearance. Therefore, for stone that was exposed on buildings, the Romans often imported marble and other stone from all over their empire, including the famous quarries in Greece. Stone was used in walls and other architectural elements in a manner similar to that of the Greeks, except that the Romans generally laid it in walls in mortar and often used monolithic stone for columns and similar elements.

The Romans also used rubble stone set in thin beds of mortar. A more widespread use of stone by the Romans was in facings or veneers for buildings constructed of other materials, mainly concrete. Unlike the Egyptians and Greeks, the Romans used the trabeated, or post and lintel, structural system sparingly, preferring the arcuated structural system, employing arches, vaults, and domes. For such structures, the Romans used stone as well as concrete and brick. They also used stone for sculpture and architectural ornament, often utilizing Greek artists for its creation.

In Early Christian architecture, stone was generally used in a manner similar to that of the Romans, including the use of vaults. Often Roman buildings were stripped of columns and other elements that were then reerected in Early Christian churches. In Byzantine architecture, brick was the material used for most buildings, since almost all stone had to be imported. Unlike Early Christian architecture, which utilized mainly vaults, Byzantine architecture used mainly the brick dome as a structural system. Imported monolithic stone columns were sometimes used, but the major use of stone was in ornamenting almost every available surface, including floors, with patterns made with marbles and other stones of various colors, sizes, and shapes.

During the Romanesque period of architecture, if stone were available, it was used much in the manner of the Romans. In other places, brick was often used. During the Middle Ages, architectural design in stone again became, in Gothic architecture, the dominant material for buildings, using the arcuated structural system, mainly with arches and vaults. However, some buildings were constructed of brick in places where stone was scarce. Stone for use in Gothic architecture was generally cut into smaller pieces than had been done in the past. Most of the stone came from local quarries near the buildings to be constructed, or was transported by ship from quarries located near a waterway to buildings which were also near a waterbody.

In Gothic atchitecture, stone was generally finely cut and fitted, particularly exposed stone. In some cases, especially in large elements such as buttresses, stone rubble laid with lime mortar was used for the structure, with facings of fine cut stone. When using hard stones, such as granite or sandstone, ornament and sculpture were usually more simple and restrained than when using more easily carved stones, such as marble. In Italy, where marbles of various colors were available, some buildings were ornamented with two or more colors of stone, sometimes in strips, or other patterns, producing very rich effects.

During the Renaissance, stone was used extensively, no longer in the rubble method of the Middle Ages but in ashlar, with large pieces of stone, accurately cut and placed in horizontal courses. In Italy, all the fine stones that had been quarried and used by the Romans were employed and new quarries were developed. Local stones were quarried in many other places in Europe. Although stone walls and other elements were sometimes used, a more usual method utilized stone facings on building structures of brick or other materials. Another method used brick walls with stone quoins at corners and adjacent to window and door openings.

American Development In colonial America, wood and then brick were the major building materials. However, rough stone was often used for foundations of early buildings and for fireplaces and chimneys. Good building stone can be found in many locations in the United States today. A number of these locations were soon discovered, and quarrying sandstone and granite began early in the 17th century in what is now the State of Connecticut. Quarrying coquina, a soft limestone with shells embedded in it, began in Florida a short time later.

By the end of the 18th century, sandstone was quarried in Virginia, North Carolina, Ohio, Pennsylvania, Maryland, and New Jersey. Granite was quarried in New Hampshire and Massachusetts; limestone in Pennsylvania, New Jersey, and Ohio; and marble in Pennsylvania, Vermont Massachusetts, and Connecticut. By the middle of the 19th century, stone of various kinds was quarried in New York, Michigan, Nevada, Kentucky, Maine, Utah, Tennessee, and Georgia. Stone is still quarried today in most of these places and in others, such as Missouri, California, Colorado, and Arizona.

As time went on, cut stone was used increasingly in the American colonies, mostly for elements of buildings, such as fireplace facings and mantelpieces, stairs, door and window sills, and quoins in conjunction with brick, but sometimes for complete walls of important buildings. Rubble stonework continued to be used to some extent. Cut stone became an important building material during the 19th century, with the development of transportation by railways and canals. Limestone, granite, marble, and sandstone, in particular the variety called brownstone, were all used as structural materials for many of the most important buildings during the Georgian, Classic Revival, Gothic Revival, and Eclectic periods of architecture in the 19th century.

With the beginning of the modern movement in the 19th century, stone was used less frequently for structures. However, it continued to be widely used as facings for buildings constructed of other materials and for elements, such as stairs. Today stone is used on infrequent occasions for bearing walls and other structural elements. The major uses are in thin slabs for curtain walls and veneers; for sculpture, slate roofs, flooring, stairs, garden walls, and monuments; and in such relatively small building elements as chalkboards, countertops, sills, toilet partitions, and so on. Crushed or broken stone is often used as aggregates in concrete and terrazzo, for driveways and walks, as a finish for built-up roofing, and for other purposes.

Related Articles ARCH; BRICK; COLUMN; DOME; FIREPLACE; FLOOR; MASONRY STRUCTURE; MONUMENT; ROOF; VAULT; WALL.

Further Reading McKee, Harley J.: *Introduction to Early American Masonry—Stone, Brick, Mortar and Plaster*, National Trust for Historic Preservation and Columbia University, Washington, 1973.

Source of Additional Information Building Stone Inst., 420 Lexington Ave., New York, N.Y. 10017.

STORE A building, sometimes called a shop, or a room in a building, in which merchandise is sold. Stores constitute one of the most important building types. They may have one, two, or many floors. They may be very small or very large, simple and utilitarian or complex and ornate, but all stores have one thing in common: they must be designed to sell goods or they do not succeed.

A look around any city, town, or shopping center reveals a myriad of stores, offering every conceivable product: shoe stores, women's shops, men's shops, drugstores, bakeries, gift shops, jewelry stores, and so on. In many instances, such stores are incorporated into a larger one offering many types of goods. And larger stores are often combined with smaller ones to form shopping centers. Whatever the types, whatever the size or combination, the sole purpose of all these establishments is to sell goods in order to make money. Thus the architectural design problem

begins with the question of how to provide spaces in which the products may be merchandised successfully.

Classifications Stores are classified as wholesale, those that sell to retail stores and others, who then sell to consumers; and retail, those that sell to consumers. Wholesale stores vary somewhat between industries, but all tend to be quite similar, in that they must have showrooms appropriate to the goods offered and to the needs of the business people who are the buyers, adequate warehousing, and often libraries of catalogs.

There are many types of retail stores, which vary considerably. The simplest is the specialty shop which offers only goods of a certain type, such as jewelry, groceries, baked goods, women's wear, and so on. At the other extreme are the large generalized stores that offer many types of goods. One of these is the department store which has specific areas or departments, much like many specialty shops gathered into one store. Some department stores are operated as discount houses, which theoretically sell to consumers at lower prices than are available elsewhere. Another large store is the supermarket, a grocery store in which many types of food and drink are offered in departments, as in a department store.

Special Types A special type of store is a mail-order house. These stores may be organized somewhat like large department stores, with a wide range of products, or like single-goods specialty shops. If their business is only by mail order, their merchandising will be entirely by means of advertising mail promotions and catalogs. In other cases, a mail-order business is an adjunct to a regular store and customers have a choice of buying either way.

Another special type is the chain store, one of a group of stores owned and operated by one company or other companies under franchises from the chain. Chain stores exist in the bakery, grocery, drug, clothing, shoe, department, and other industries. Most stores, including chains, are owned by corporations or individuals and operated for profit. A cooperative store is owned by a group of people, its members, and operated for their convenience and benefit, without the store itself making profits. In the past, most generally found in rural communities, cooperatives are now often also located in urban areas. The three major types of cooperatives are marketing, for the selling of goods produced by the members; service, for example, for the purpose of providing loans to its members, operation of cooperative apartments, and the like; and the consumer cooperative, the only type that is actually a store. In the latter type, products are purchased, wholesale, for resale to members and sometimes to the general public.

Merchandising Principles The first principles of merchandising goods in stores are that the interest of the potential customer must be aroused and that the store must then satisfy the interest. These principles also apply to the architectural design of stores for

STORE Patterson Drug Store (1952), Jackson, Miss. [*Architect: N.W. Overstreet. (Joseph W. Molitor)*]

merchandising. Their actual application in stores varies somewhat according to the types of goods offered. Such goods might be divided into staples, or demand goods, those that consumers regularly need and buy; convenience goods, those bought at irregular intervals or for special needs; and impulse goods, often luxury items, that consumers might not really need, but to which they are attracted sufficiently to purchase.

At the one extreme in merchandising are the staples, which in a sense are simply collections of needed products conveniently located for easy pickup by shoppers. At the other extreme are the luxury or impulse items that must be sold by the personality, glamour, or other means of the products themselves and the manner in which they are merchandised. Some stores fall at one of the extremes; for example, some supermarkets handle staples only and some specialty shops, only luxury items. Most stores fall in between. Although they may offer products at one extreme, such as staples, they also offer some convenience and impulse or luxury items.

The major considerations in the design of a store of any kind are location, the site, type of merchandise, exterior and interior character, and proper planning of the spaces. Merchandising experts say that the location of a store is all-important. Without a proper location, nothing else can work. However, it is also important that the building be designed properly for its site and for the merchandise offered, a factor intimately related to the type of clientele to be attracted. All these factors must be properly handled in the establishment of the character of the store and in its plan in order to ensure its success.

Elements The major elements of a store are the selling areas and the work areas. Both must be planned to operate efficiently and effectively not only as individual units but together. The selling areas begin with the storefront, which establishes the image the store presents to potential customers. The shop

windows, if any, should be attractive and contain interesting displays. The entrance should be inviting. The graphic design of signs should help draw customers inside. Inside the store, displays should be arranged for the convenience of both the customers and the salespeople. In addition, they must allow easy and unobtrusive restocking of shelves from the storage areas. As customers are drawn through the store, in some cases primarily by the demand for staple products, they must be motivated to pass convenience items and impulse or luxury goods, inventively placed and displayed. On the other hand, impulse items, such as jewelry, often have the most visual appeal for customers. Next most important are high-impression items, such as women's and men's clothing, and last are the more mundane articles, such as stationery. In any store, the proper placement and display of these types of merchandise must be accomplished. The spaces must also be planned for easy flow of customers, who are drawn from one department, or type of article, to another.

The exterior of the store having established its character and having drawn customers in, the interior must maintain the character and also provide proper fixtures for display of products and proper lighting to show them to their best advantage. Interiors and displays may range from the simple and straightforward through the entire range to the very dramatic. The important thing is to achieve the proper character for the store, the clientele, and the merchandise. The psychology of sales is a study on which much talent, time, and money are continually being spent. To design effective stores, architects must also study this psychology and apply its principles in their designs.

Other important adjuncts of selling areas of stores are cash registers and wrapping stations. These should be conveniently, but safely, located. In a supermarket, there are usually a number of such stations, called checkout counters, located near the exits. In department stores, stations are located in various places convenient to the selling departments. In a small specialty shop, the counter might be out of the way, almost concealed from the customers. Other important spaces related to the selling area are fitting rooms, near clothing sales areas, customer rest rooms and sometimes lounges, cafeterias or other food operations, credit offices, tables for writing cards, and so on. The type of store will determine which of these should be included.

The work areas of stores vary considerably in size but all contain offices and stockrooms. Some stores need large and elaborate storage areas, others only minimal facilities. In addition, certain stores have special requirements, such as alteration rooms for clothing stores, preparation rooms for florists, and special gift-wrapping areas for gift and jewelry shops. All stores require space for electrical and mechanical equipment, janitorial spaces, and the like.

In the past, many stores utilized some forms of automated equipment, such as dumbwaiters for trans-

STORE Mobil Service Station (1966), New Haven, Conn. [*Architect: Eliot Noyes. (Joseph W. Molitor)*]

porting goods from stockrooms to selling areas and pneumatic tube systems for sending sales slips and other paperwork back and forth between sales areas and business offices. Today the trend is toward more use of automation, with certain stores now operating with computer-controlled stocking of shelves and others experimenting with such ideas. Another new idea is the use of electronic scanners that read price codes on products, feed the prices into computers, add up the totals, and furnish the salesperson and customer with a tape indicating the transactions. In less sophisticated but more widespread systems, the salesperson punches the transaction into a computer terminal and receives the completed sales slip back. Such systems can be expected to become better and more widespread in the future.

History Merchandising, at first by barter or trade, has been practiced from the time of the earliest primitive humans. In the beginning, there were no buildings specifically devoted to merchandising. But stores are still one of the oldest building types, having become well established by the 4th century B.C. Stores in some instances specialty shops, were common in ancient Greece and Rome. Though barter was again prevalent after the time of the Romans, retail stores later became the major means of merchandising. And retail stores of all kinds have proliferated ever since.

American Development The early colonists established stores soon after arriving in America. One of the interesting early types was the general store, which came into existence in America in the early 19th century, stocked a little bit of everything, and was a place for people to gather as well. Such stores are still found in rural areas, operated in almost the same manner as in the past. Almost every form of store existed in the early days of merchandising, though it is impossible to date their beginnings accurately. In later times, some of the older practices were again adopted and improved upon. Cooperatives were first founded in the United States in the early 19th century, though the greatest growth of consumer cooperative stores did not occur until after World War I. Some of the chain stores of today were founded in the mid-19th century, but have had their greatest growth in the 20th. Present-day department stores and mail-order stores both started in the late 19th century. Supermarkets, of the type known today, started in the 20th century in America and later spread to other countries around the world. Shopping centers of current types began in the first half of the 20th century and since midcentury have been built all over the United States.

Since the beginning of architecture in the American colonies, many architects have designed stores. Many of these have been well designed and successful in their time, some for quite a long time. In a few instances, store design has produced significant buildings, but for the most part the requirements of the fashions of the time and the changing tastes of people have made specific store designs short-lived, to be soon replaced by other merchandising ideas.

Related Articles GRAPHIC DESIGN; SHOPPING CENTER; WAREHOUSE.

Further Reading Hornbeck, James S., ed.: *Stores and Shopping Centers*, McGraw-Hill, New York, 1962; Redstone, Louis G.: *New Dimensions in Shopping Centers and Stores*, McGraw-Hill, New York, 1973.

STRICKLAND, WILLIAM American architect and engineer (1788–1854). The son of a successful master carpenter, William Strickland spent his early life in and around buildings under construction. Along with another young man destined to become a noted architect, Robert Mills (1781–1855), Strickland served his apprenticeship with Benjamin Henry Latrobe (1764–1820). Before he was twenty-one, he established himself in an architectural practice that became one of the most successful of the time.

Works Strickland's first major building, the Second Bank of the United States (1824), Philadelphia, established him as an important architect. An early Classic Revival building, it also established him as one of the leaders of that movement in architecture. During the next few decades, he designed a number of important buildings in Philadelphia, among them churches, houses, theaters, and other types. Two of his most notable buildings in that city were the Naval Asylum (1833), later called the Naval Home, and the U.S. Mint (1833), both demolished. An even more important building, the Merchants' Exchange (1834), has survived. In 1828 he restored Independence Hall and added the present steeple.

During his career, Strickland handled the engineering for a number of nonbuilding projects. Among these were the survey of a route for the Chesapeake and Delaware Canal (1823), consulting engineer for the Delaware and Raritan Canal (1825), design of the Brandywine Shoal Lighthouse (1827), and the engineering of Delaware Breakwater (1840), Lewes, Del.

Important buildings designed by Strickland for locations other than Philadelphia, include the U.S. mints at Charlotte, N.C. (1835) and New Orleans (1836); the Athenaeum (1838), Providence, R.I.; and the Tennessee State Capitol (1859), Nashville. He designed numerous buildings and consulted on the U.S. Capitol and other buildings in Washington.

Strickland was one of the most successful American architects. There were good reasons for this. His building designs were accepted and admired. He was

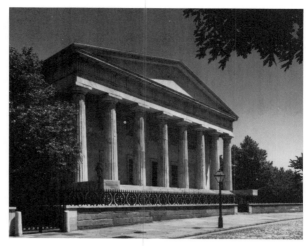

STRICKLAND, WILLIAM Second Bank of the United States (1824), Philadelphia, Pa. *(Lawrence S. Williams)*

STRICKLAND, WILLIAM Merchants Exchange (1834), Philadelphia, Pa. *(Wayne Andrews)*

STRICKLAND, WILLIAM State Capitol (1859), Nashville, Tenn. *(Wayne Andrews)*

a good engineer who insisted on sound practices, good materials, and first-rate workmanship. He was admired for his ability to estimate building costs accurately and to construct buildings within their budgets and within their time schedules. More could scarcely be expected from him as an architect. And his performance might well serve as a model for all those who are or wish to become architects.

Life William Strickland was born in Navesink, N.J., in November 1788, the son of a carpenter. Moving the family to Philadelphia in 1790, the father later became the carpenter for the Bank of Pennsylvania (1801), designed by Benjamin Henry Latrobe. This building is considered to be the first in the Greek Revival style in the United States. The young Strickland played around it during the four years it was under construction, and in 1803, at age fourteen, was apprenticed to its architect. Latrobe thought his apprentice to be intelligent and talented but also undependable. After two years Strickland proved him right by leaving the office without notice and going to New York to sketch. In 1808 he returned to Philadelphia and designed his first building, Masonic Hall (1811), in that city.

A talented artist as well as architect, Strickland supported himself during this time mostly by doing engravings for books and magazines, designing theatrical scenery, and surveying. On November 3, 1812, he married Rachel McCollough Trenschard and they had six children. During the War of 1812, he helped survey the defensive positions for Philadelphia and helped supervise the building of redoubts around the city. Attempting to get his architectural practice started after the war, he entered several competitions and finally won that for the Second Bank of the United States. Strickland's former employer, Benjamin Henry Latrobe, won the second prize and promptly claimed that Strickland had stolen his design. The controversy is still debated by architectural historians to this day. In any case, this building established Strickland's reputation as an architect and led to a successful professional career.

Strickland, a convivial man, attracted people and formed lasting friendshps, which helped him to acquire architectural commissions and honors. He joined many social and intellectual societies, including the American Philosophical Society and the Pennsylvania Academy of Arts, and served as a director of the latter organization for 28 years. He continued painting and sketching all his life. He liked to travel and made several trips to Europe. He was well thought of as an engineer and served in a number of official engineering capacities. As a result, he was elected a member of the Royal Institution of Engineers in London. He composed songs. He wrote essays not only on architecture but on other subjects, including art criticism. He was one of the founders in 1836, and first president, of the American Institution of Architects, the first national architects' organization, which later failed.

In spite of his many other activities and pursuits, Strickland produced a number of notable buildings. He played an important part in the development of Classic Revival architecture in the United States. In 1845 Strickland moved, with his family, to Nashville, Tenn., where he had been selected to design the Tennessee Capitol, his last major building, finished in 1859, five years after his death. During the years in Nashville, he also designed two churches, one of which is in an Egyptian style, and three monuments. He is believed to have designed a number of houses in and around Nashville. His son, Francis Strickland (1818–95), became an architect and joined his father in the work on the Tennessee Capitol and other buildings. In 1851 Strickland became ill and Francis carried on the work. On April 6, 1854, William Strickland died and, by resolution of the state legislature, was buried in a vault in the Tennessee Capitol building he had designed.

Related Articles CLASSIC REVIVAL ARCHITECTURE; LATROBE, BENJAMIN HENRY; MILLS, ROBERT; PUBLIC BUILDING.

Further Reading Gilchrist, Agnes Addison: *William Strickland—Architect and Engineer, 1788–1854*, rev. ed., DaCapo Press, New York, 1969.

STRUCTURAL ENGINEERING

STRUCTURAL ENGINEERING Within civil engineering, one of the major engineering branches, a specialty field that deals with the engineering design and construction of buildings and other structures to withstand the weight, winds, rain and snow, and other forces to which they are subjected. Although people who practice structural engineering are actually civil engineers, who have been licensed or registered to perform professional services for work of this kind, they are often called structural engineers. And what they design is the structure of buildings, the framework of walls, columns, beams, floors, roofs, and so on that will withstand the forces to which buildings are subjected.

For the smallest and simplest buildings, such as houses, architects often design the structures along with their other work. For larger and more complex buildings, structural engineers design the structures.

Structural engineers and architects work closely in the design of buildings, perhaps even a bit more closely than do architects with mechanical or electrical engineers. Structure so often strongly influences the form of buildings and is so interwoven with the other aspects of architecture that it is difficult, if not impossible, to produce a good design without their close cooperation.

Service Phases Working with the architect, a structural engineer performs services in phases that are like those of the architect, but which are confined to the structure from the foundation to the roof. In the schematic phase, a structural engineer starts by studying the site, the building program, and problems; analyzing the work of the architect; and seeking possible structural solutions. Based on the architectural design studies of the architect, the structural engineer prepares structural design studies that lead to schematic or preliminary drawings showing the proposed structure, preliminary estimates of costs for the construction work, and preliminary specifications that outline elements of the construction of the structure. Still working closely with the architect and with the other engineers and consultants as required, in the design development phase the structural engineer refines the drawings, estimates, and specifications. Upon approval of this work, the structural engineer then prepares, in the construction document phase, the structural contract documents, drawings, and specifications that will be used to construct the structure, and a further refined estimate of costs. After the actual construction has begun, during the construction administration phase, the structural engineer assists the architect in administration and inspects the structural work of the building to guard against defects or mistakes and to ensure that the structure is properly constructed.

During construction, the structural engineer may also have to make supplemental drawings and specifications and perform other services to ensure that the construction moves forward efficiently, on schedule, and within the budget for the building. Upon completion of the building, the structural engineer then makes a final inspection of the work and sometimes prepares as-built drawings, which show the building as it was actually constructed.

Education for structural engineering, together with experience, registration or licensing requirements, and methods of practice, are similar to those for other engineering specialties. (See the article entitled engineering.)

Excellence in architecture today is as much a result of excellence in structural engineering as of almost any other factor. To achieve a high level in architecture, structural engineers and architects must work closely and in harmony. Each must understand a great deal about the work of the other and both must work toward the end of buildings designed in their totality, not just in their parts or details. In addition, the structure is often expressed in the appearance of buildings today.

History Until the late 19th century, much of the structural engineering for buildings was done by architects, some of whom were also very talented engineers, who designed bridges, waterworks, and other structures as well. Since that time, many professional structural engineers have made considerable contributions to architecture. Some of them are Othmar Hermann Ammann (1879–1965), Charles S. Whitney (1892–1959), Frederick Severud (1899–   ), Paul Weidlinger(1914–   ), Mario Salvadori (1907–   ), Tung Yen Lin (1911–   ), Lev Zetlin (1918–   ), John Skilling, William J. Le Messurier, and Fazlur Rahman Khan (1929–   ).

Related Articles Building Codes and Standards; Building Industry; Concrete Structure; Construc-

tion Contract Administration; Cost Control; Drafting; Engineering; Masonry Structure; Specification; Steel Structure; Structure; Wood-Frame Structure; Working Drawing.

Further Reading Gaylord, Edwin Henry, and Charles N. Gaylord: *Structural Engineering Handbook*, 2d ed., McGraw-Hill, New York, 1979. See also listing in the article entitled engineering.

Source of Additional Information American Society of Civil Engineers, 345 E. 47th St., New York, N.Y. 10017.

Periodical *Civil Engineering*, 345 E. 47th St., New York, N.Y. 10017.

STRUCTURE The parts of a building that in the proper combination withstand the weight, wind, rain, and snow, and other forces to which a building is subjected. Structure may also mean a building or something else that has been constructed.

Structure, in the sense of the combination of parts in a building which resists forces, is obviously of great importance in architecture. Without a properly designed and constructed structure, a building may fail in some way or even collapse. If the structure has been properly designed and constructed, it will be strong enough to withstand all the forces to which it may be subjected. Some architects and engineers believe that the structure should be just that strong and no stronger. In addition to the function of providing strength in buildings, many architects believe that structure is one of the primary determinants of architectural design.

Forces From an engineering point of view, the primary purpose of structures is resistance to forces, which are the actions of one body upon another, mainly by compression (pushing) or tension (pulling) which cause or tend to cause the body to move. The major forces on the structures of buildings include those imposed by the weights of the buildings themselves, by the people and objects that occupy them, by snow or rain, and by wind. Earthquakes also produce great forces on building structures.

Structures for some buildings may be designed by architects, but for most, including all the more complicated ones, structural engineers perform the structural design functions. In either case, structures are designed by using the principles of a branch of physics often called structural mechanics, which is divided into statics, which deals with equilibrium in bodies produced by balanced forces, and strength of materials, which deals with the behavior of bodies which acted upon by such forces.

In order to work with forces, it is necessary to determine their magnitudes, lines of action, points of application, and directions. When a force, or system of forces, acts upon a building structure, it produces a load in the structure. In this way, a column in a building, for example, may support a certain load placed upon it by the weights above it and other forces, must resist the load without failure, and must transfer it to a foundation and eventually to the ground. In the column the load produces stresses,

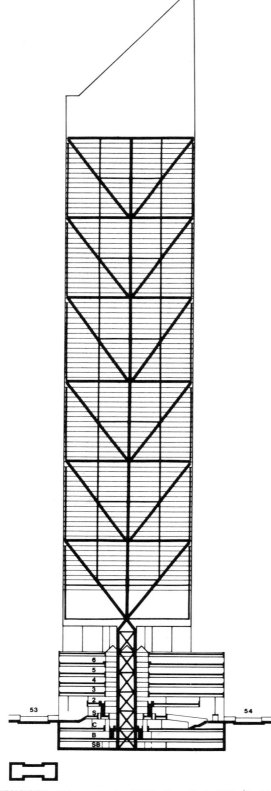

STRUCTURE Citicorp Center (1978), New York, N.Y. [*Architects: Hugh Stubbins, in association with Emery Roth and Sons. (Hugh Stubbins and Associates)*] Trussed frame structure carries wind loads and half of the weight loads.

which are the internal forces within the column that must be resisted.

Stress   There are four main kinds of stress: tension, compression, shear, and torsion. A tensile stress is produced by pulling on an object and tends to stretch the object. A compression stress comes from pushing on an object and tends to crush it. A shearing stress causes parts of an object to tend to slide past each other or split away from each other. These are the most important stresses dealt with in building structures. The fourth, torsion, is of lesser importance and is caused by twisting forces.

Loads   There are several kinds of loads on building structures. Dead loads are permanent loads imposed by the weights of the buildings themselves. Live loads are the less permanent loads caused by people, furniture, and so on. Dead loads on a structure may be calculated by adding their weights together. Live loads are determined statistically and experimentally and are specified in building codes. Snow loads are live loads, but are often added to the dead loads since they act only vertically on structures. In some cases, the live loads of heavy rains must also be dealt with. Another kind of load is that imposed by wind. Wind loads are usually considered to act horizontally, though this is not strictly the case. In calculation, wind is customarily considered to act at right angles to roof structures.

Since maximum snow loads and maximum wind loads cannot occur at the same time, the usual assumption for maximum loading on a building structure may be the dead load plus maximum snow load, dead load plus maximum windload and minimum snow load, or dead load plus maximum snow load and minimum wind load. To these must be added live loads, including those of people and objects within the building. In addition, many other loads must be dealt with in certain structures, including those of earthquakes; those caused by pressure of the earth or of water against foundations and basement walls and the like; unusual loads imposed by heavy machinery or other equipment; loads imposed by motion, including that of vehicles or people; and so on. The actual loads to be dealt with in the deaign of any building structure will be those specified in the appropriate building code for the locality in which the building will be constructed and which conform to good practice in structural engineering.

Structural Failures   Thus a person who designs the structure of a building must make sure that it conforms to a building code and to good practice. In a sense, this means primarily that neither the structure itself nor any of its parts will fail to perform properly. Failure in a building structure may bring to mind a roof that collapsed or some other dramatic destruction of a building or any of its major parts. In actuality, a structure may fail in any of a number of ways, ordinarily considered to include failures in stability, strength, or stiffness, or because of changes in the materials of the structure.

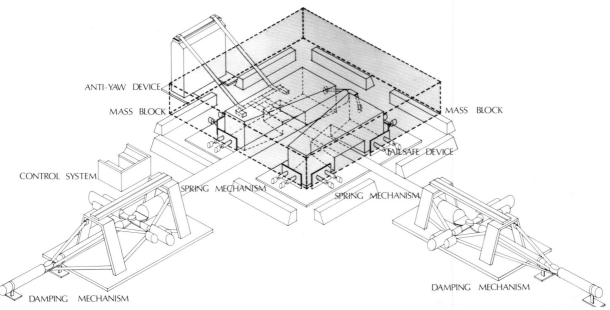

STRUCTURE Citicorp Center (1978), New York, N.Y. [*Architects: Hugh Stubbins, in association with Emery Roth and Sons. (Hugh Stubbins and Associates)*] Tuned mass damper (TMD) reduces building sway caused by winds. TMD utilizes 400-ton concrete mass which moves in opposite direction from building to reduce building sway by some 40 percent.

Stability in a structure means that it has been designed not to tip over, fall down, or move about unduly. It must be noted that buildings do move and this factor must be dealt with in their design. In general, the taller a building is the more it will move. Strength in a building structure is concerned with its ability and that of all its parts to resist, without breaking, the loads placed on them. Stiffness means that a structure and all its parts can resist failure by deformation, any change in the shape or size of the structure or its parts. In some members of structures, such as beams, a deformation of this sort is called deflection and causes them to sag. Excess deflection may cause problems, such as the cracking of plastered ceilings, but can also be extremely dangerous in a structure. Deformation of columns or other members, or buckling, may be equally dangerous. Stiffness in building structures is so important that it often determines the design of certain members.

Changes that may take place in the materials used in building structures are of two major types: those caused by the nature of the materials used, and those caused by deterioration of the materials. In the first instance, a structural designer must thoroughly understand the materials used. Concrete and masonry shrink; wood sags. All materials change sizes, expanding and contracting as temperature rises and falls. And different materials expand and contract at different rates. Each material has its own unique characteristics that must be understood and dealt with.

Deterioration modifies, usually lowering, the loads that structures and structural members can take. Deterioration in building structures may result from many causes, including water infiltration, dry rot, insect activities, fire, chemical changes, abrasion, corrosion, and bacterial action. These threats must be understood and allowed for in structural designs or their occurrence must be prevented.

Structural Systems In the past, structural systems used in architecture were mostly limited to the trabeated, or post and lintel, system using walls, columns, and beams; and the arcuated system, based on the principles of the arch. Today these systems are still widely used, but a vast array of new systems and extensions of old ones are available. The same is true of materials for structures. In addition to wood, brick, and other traditional materials, structures may now be constructed of many types of steel; precast, prestressed, and other forms of concrete; laminated timbers; aluminum; and other materials.

Structural designers today may also utilize new types of domes and vaults, concrete slabs, space frames, lamella systems, laminated wood arches, thin shells, folded plates, stressed-skin systems, suspension systems, rigid frames, a variety of trusses, and other systems. Many of these types of structures were difficult or impossible to design properly in the past. Today new methods of calculation and testing have been developed. The advent of the widespread availability of computers has made complicated calculations feasible which in the past were too time-consuming to were virtually impossible.

In practice, not every structure or part of a structure need be calculated. Load tables and other data are available for every structural material and many structural systems. For relatively simple structural problems, such as the sizes of steel beams or wood floor joists to carry given loads under ordinary conditions, a designer of a structure may select proper sizes from tables. In somewhat more complicated problems, it may be necessary for the designer to make a series of calculations. And in the most complex problems, a design may require complicated calculations whose solution may only be practical with computers.

Structural Expression Many architects today maintain that structure is one of the primary determinants of architecture, that it should be expressed in buildings, or even exposed in them. Others disagree. This is a difference of opinion that has occurred throughout history. It is only necessary to note the expression of structure in Gothic cathedrals as opposed to the hiding of the structure in many Renaissance buildings to understand the wide divergence of approach. This is not to deny that the structure of a building will, to some extent, determine its total form and effect, but to question the relative importance of the structure in that determination. Many people, including architects, are often confused by discussions on such subjects involving principles of structural honesty, expression, fitness to purpose, and similar subjects, frequently engaged in by architects, architecture critics, and others.

Many people find great beauty in objects that are almost pure structural expressions, in fine bridges, for example. Many would agree that great beauty may be found in buildings that express, in more subtle ways, their well-designed, carefully crafted structures. And many architects today attempt to create beauty in their buildings in just such a manner. Other architects exploit the structures of their buildings by exaggeration of the structures to produce sculptural effects or by details that seem to have been designed to look right rather than for the ultimate in structural efficiency. Other architects design buildings in which the essential facts of structure are denied in their appearance.

It would thus appear that many approaches to the structural design of buildings may be taken. It is essential that the approach to structure produce a strong, safe building. The overall influence of structure on the sum total of the architecture of that building is determined by design preference, by the era in which the building is constructed, and by many other social, historic, and cultural factors.

History The first building structures made by humans are thought to have been caves. These were followed by simple structures of limbs or poles taken from trees and covered with animal skins or with brush, leaves, or thatch; and mud houses. Since that time, structures for buildings have changed radically over the years into the sophisticated types that are used today.

The earliest wood building structures had pyramidal forms in which the end of limbs or poles were placed around a circle on the ground with their opposite ends learning inward to form a peak in the middle at the top. In some cases, the limbs or poles were bent into curves, as they rose upward, to increase the headroom inside.

Structural Developments After this primitive beginning, the next big development in building structures was the post and lintel, or trabeated, system, still being used today. The most familiar post and lintel buildings today are wood-frame houses, but many steel-framed and concrete buildings also utilize this system.

In the Middle East, another type of structure was developed in about the 25th century B.C. This is the arcuated system, based on the use of arches instead of posts and lintels to support the weights imposed on buildings. Such structures also utilized vaults and domes, which are based on arch principles. In Egypt, though the arcuated system was used occasionally, the trabeated system was most generally used. In Mesopotamia, where stone was almost nonexistent and wood scarce, the arcuated system was often used, but mostly for relatively minor purposes at first.

The ancient Greeks used the trabeated system for the most part. Stone was plentiful and could be quarried in relatively large pieces, and timber was also available. The Greeks, who were so creative in many disciplines including architectural design, were seemingly content to use a structural system from the past and to add to it very little in the way of innovation.

Roman Engineering Feats The Romans had a quite different attitude toward building structures. Although not considered as creative in architectural design as the Greeks, the Romans were talented engineers and builders. While the Romans did not usually invent new methods, they were masters of the refinement of older techniques and of their extension to perform daring structural feats not thought possible before. The Romans borrowed the principles of arcuated structures, including arches, vaults, and domes, from the ancient Etruscans, who inhabited west-central Italy. From the ancient Greeks, they borrowed the principles of trabeated, or post and lintel, structures. They then combined the two systems to produce buildings and other structures of great size and complexity. The Romans used all types of available materials, mainly brick, wood, stone, and concrete, utilizing each alone or in combination with others as the occasion demanded.

One of the most striking characteristics of Roman architecture is the great spans they achieved using concrete to form barrel, or semicircular, vaults. Many Roman buildings had vaults spanning as much as 90 ft. The dome of the Pantheon (second century A.D.) spans almost 143 ft and is still the largest masonry dome in the world. The Romans also built very tall buildings and other structures. The Flavian Amphitheater, usually called the Colosseum (A.D. 82), is almost 158 ft high. The great aqueduct near Nîmes, France, the Pont du Gard (about A.D. 14.), is 155 ft high, and other Roman buildings and structures approach these heights.

The Romans also surpassed, in sheer size, the buildings constructed previously. The Circus Maximus (first century A.D.), used mainly for chariot races, measured 650 ft wide by 2,000 ft long, and seated 255,000 spectators, more than twice the number of the largest stadiums in the United States. The Temple of Jupiter (second century A.D.) in Baalbek, Lebanon, amply demonstrates the Roman penchant for size. Although the temple is of modest height, 126 ft, the substructure or platform on which it rests is almost 40 ft. high and some of the stones in it measure about 64 by 11 by 14 ft, and each weighs about 725 tons.

Although the Romans used domes extensively and for long spans, they almost always placed them over circular or polygonal substructures because of the problems in building them over square structures. Pendentives, a method of using curved wall surfaces, to make the transition from a square structure below to a round dome above, were used by the Romans but only on relatively small and minor buildings.

Domes In Byzantium, later renamed Constantinople and still later Istanbul, now part of Turkey, the art of building with domes became highly developed beginning about the 4th century. The Byzantines often used pendentives to allow their domes to cover square spaces below. They also developed a system of smaller domes and partial domes which would resist the forces of the main dome. They developed drums, circular structures placed beneath domes to raise them higher and to permit windows below the bases of the domes. The greatest expression by Byzantine architecture is thought to be the Church of the Holy Wisdom (537), Istanbul, formerly called Santa Sophia but now more generally called the Hagia Sophia.

Skeleton System During the period immediately preceding the Middle Ages, no great structural innovations were made. However, the beginnings could be detected of what was to become a revolutionary change during the Middle Ages. The structural systems of the Romans and others who came before them were based mainly on the principle that great masses of stone or other materials could be made to resist the forces of each other by placing them in opposing positions in sufficient quantities. Now a structure system was developed that discarded the principles of great opposing masses and replaced it with one in which each structural member was designed to perform its exact purpose without excess bulk or weight.

Thus, beginning about the 9th century, master buildings began to develop the system which would result in the great soaring, relatively light, skeleton structures of the Gothic style. This was an arcuated system, using the principles of the arch to produce great vaults, at first round and later pointed. These vaults were constructed at right angles to each other

so that each of a pair of intersecting vaults resisted the forces of the other. Eventually, the system became so sophisticated that the major functions of the intersecting vaults could be performed by ribs at the intersections, while the spaces between the ribs could be filled with light materials having only minor structural purposes. As time went by, all the structural members were gradually reduced to the minimum sizes that would serve their purposes, making possible the high, light structures of the great Gothic cathedrals in many places all over Europe.

During the Middle Ages, progress was also made in the use of wood for structures. For example, in earlier buildings, wood-framed roofs ordinarily utilized timbers that were placed as rafters or joists, each acting almost independently in carrying the loads placed on the roofs. During the Middle Ages, various types of timber trusses were developed, thus strengthening and lightening roof structures and allowing longer spans than before. These trusses were designed so that a number of pieces of timber could be fastened together in a manner that allowed the entire structure to work as a unit in resisting the loads placed upon it.

Scientific Calculation The Renaissance was marked by a reawakening of interest in classic Greece and Rome and a turning away from the Middle Ages. It has been said that Renaissance architecture was mostly based on esthetics and therefore the major contributions to architecture were in ornament and esthetic design. The architects of the time deserted the Gothic structural forms, for the most part, including ribbed vaults and pointed arches, to return to semicircular arches and especially domes.

Perhaps the most important development in structures, during the Renaissance, was the introduction of scientific methods of calculation. Renaissance architects utilized these methods to design the structures of the great vaults and domes. Among the most dramatic results were the development of revolutionary methods for designing domes, including the use of chains to resist forces in them and the construction of domes with double, later triple, shells. They also developed the first timber trusses with diagonal members to withstand forces, a method which is still used today. The science of mechanics and strength of materials became established during the Renaissance, paving the way for the future development of structural engineering. The testing of materials, now standard procedure, also began at that time.

Iron Structures After the Renaissance period, scientific and engineering study of structures and related subjects accelerated and considerable progress was made. New developments in structures were not far behind. In 1781 the first major structural use of cast iron was made in a bridge at Coalbrook Dale, England, still in use. Many others soon followed. The first important structural uses of iron, both cast and wrought, in buildings occurred in France in the late 18th century, as framing for roofs. Soon afterward, iron began to be used in buildings in England and in

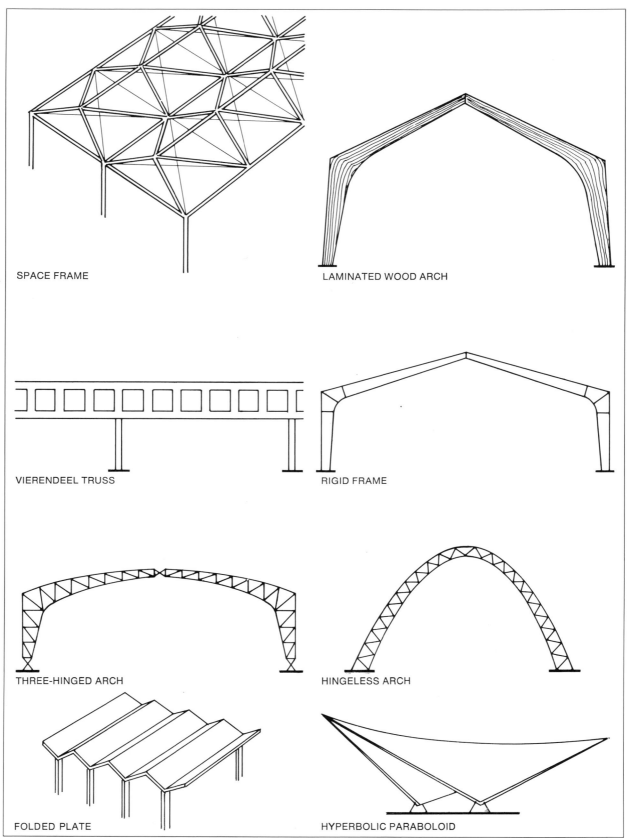

SPACE FRAME

LAMINATED WOOD ARCH

VIERENDEEL TRUSS

RIGID FRAME

THREE-HINGED ARCH

HINGELESS ARCH

FOLDED PLATE

HYPERBOLIC PARABOLOID

STRUCTURE Contemporary types.

1803, William Strutt built what was probably the first building, a mill, with a complete iron frame. From this beginning, the use of iron for building frames spread all over Europe and to the United States. The construction of the great Crystal Palace (1851), London, designed by Sir Joseph Paxton (1801–65), with an iron frame combined with glass, had a considerable effect on architecture all over the world.

After the time of the Romans, concrete as a structural material fell into disrepute. In the early 19th century, methods were developed for making what came to be called portland cement, a product still very much in use today. As time went by, concrete again began to be used in building structures, but only in a limited way. Concrete was not to equal the importance it had in Roman times until the 20th century.

During the latter half of the 19th century, the use of cast-iron structural frames for buildings increased. New methods for making wrought iron were introduced, as were methods for rolling beams of this material, leading to its increased use in buildings. Another development was the construction of iron trusses.

Reinforced Concrete In the early 19th century, iron was experimentally embedded in concrete, thus creating a composite material in which the concrete could withstand compressive forces and iron, tensile forces. In this way, a new type of structural material, eventually to be called reinforced concrete, was developed, possessing the best qualities of both concrete and iron. By the second half of the 19th century, reinforced concrete was used for the structures of both bridges and buildings. Later new and improved methods of calculation made it possible for reinforced concrete to achieve its current prominence as a 20th-century structural material. Beginning in 1905, precast concrete has also been widely used in buildings. Although steel had been developed many years before, the Eiffel Tower (1889), in Paris, designed by Alexandre Gustave Eiffel (1832–1923), was designed with a wrought-iron structure.

New Structural Frames Beginning in the 1800s and continuing in the present century, structural innovations have occurred regularly and rapidly. About 1830, the invention of the balloon-frame system revolutionized wood structures. This system utilized relatively small, light-wood members which could be erected, by semiskilled labor quickly and efficiently. Instead of relying only on the strength of individual posts or columns, beams, and so on, a balloon-frame building has walls, floors, and roof constructed in such a way that all act together to resist forces. For well over 100 years, the balloon frame was the preferred structural method for houses in the United States and in other places. It has now largely been replaced by a similar but even newer and simpler method called western, or platform, framing.

Another great and important innovation was the invention of the metal skeleton frame. Until the late 1800s, buildings generally had heavy masonry bearing walls which supported the weights of the floors and other elements above them. The Home Insurance Building (1885), in Chicago, since demolished, designed by William Le Baron Jenney (1832–1907), became the first building in which the entire structure was of skeleton construction, utilizing both cast and wrought iron and the first Bessemer steel used in any building. This was the beginning of the era of tall, skeleton-framed buildings that still continues today.

Structural Theory Other important developments have take place since the beginning of the 20th century. New structural theory has been developed that allows the design and construction of evermore innovative structures. New testing methods have been developed. And the widespread use of computers in structural design, beginning about the middle of the century, has made possible calculations that were virtually impossible before. Structural theory has now become so complex that only computers can make the most complicated calculations possible or practicable.

New types of structures have been developed in the past few decades. Among the most important are curved structures of various kinds, including domes and shells of concrete and other materials in such shapes as segments of spheres or cylinders, hyperbolic paraboloids, hyperboloids, conoids, and others. Another type of relatively new structure is the space frame, an assembly of relatively small structural members into a three-dimensional framework that for its own weight can resist relatively large forces. Among the best-known space frames are the geodesic domes designed by Buckminster Fuller (1895–   ).

Other types of structures developed during the last few decades include prestressed concrete, pneumatic structures inflated by air pressure, long-span systems, and many others. Also having an impact on structures is the advent of prefabricated and industrialized systems and those in which structural systems are integrated with lighting, heating, air-conditioning, and other service systems.

The use of structures in America parallels their use elsewhere. In the earliest colonial times, the first buildings had wood structures, followed by ones of brick and stone. As wrought and cast iron began to be used in Europe, these materials were also employed in structures in the United States. The same is true of concrete structures and those of other types.

Related Articles ARCH; BUILDING CODES AND STANDARDS; CONCRETE STRUCTURE; CONSTRUCTION MATERIALS; DESIGN, ARCHITECTURAL; DOME; EARTHQUAKE PROTECTION; FIRE PROTECTION; MASONRY STRUCTURE; STEEL STRUCTURE; STRUCTURAL ENGINEERING; WEATHER PROTECTION; WOOD-FRAME STRUCTURE; Various articles on building systems, components, and materials.

Further Reading Cowan, Henry J.: *The Masterbuilders— A History of Structural and Environmental Design from Ancient Egypt to the Nineteenth Century*, John Wiley, New York, 1977; Cowan, Henry, J.: *Science and Building—Structural and Environmental Design in the Nineteenth and Twentieth Centuries*, John Wiley, New York, 1978; Fischer, Robert

E., ed.: *Architectural Engineering—New Structures*, McGraw-Hill, New York, 1964; Gero, John S., and Henry J. Cowan: *Design of Building Frames*, John Wiley, New York, 1976; Howard, H. Seymour, Jr.: *Structure—An Architect's Approach*, McGraw-Hill, New York, 1966; Michaels, Leonard: *Contemporary Structure in Architecture*, Reinhold, New York, 1950; Schueller, Wolfgang: *High-Rise Building Structures*, John Wiley, New York, 1977.

SULLIVAN, LOUIS HENRI American architect (1856–1924). Although not recognized as such during his own lifetime, Louis Henri Sullivan has now come to be regarded as the first great modern American architect.

Appraisal Sullivan struggled to free architecture from adherence to styles of the past, from decoration for its own sake, from suppression of the functions of buildings to their appearance. Instead, he formulated principles that called for architecture which fulfilled the needs of people in their own time, which expressed such social needs in buildings that reflected the technology of their own times. His oft-quoted dictum, that form follows function, was probably first used by sculptor and writer Horatio Greenough (1805–52). In any case, it became a major principle in the philosophy of later modern architects, including Frank Lloyd Wright (1867–1959) who worked and studied with Sullivan. In this, as in his buildings and in his famous writings, *Kindergarten Chats* (1901–02) and *Autobiography of an Idea* (1924), Sullivan was something of an enigma.

He did not always adhere to his own dictum in his buildings, and his writings contain much that is ambiguous. He struggled mightily to become an architect, achieved a high level of important work for a relatively brief period of about 12 years (1888–1900), and sank into almost anonymous, debt-ridden obscurity, made worse by alcohol. He was rescued, at least partly and temporarily, by the publication of the *Autobiography* in the *AIA Journal*, during 1922–23, shortly before his death. Later his reputation was restored and enhanced by the many talented architects, in Europe as well as the United States, who acknowledged him to be the progenitor of modern architecture. In this vein, it is interesting that the American Institute of Architects, which had partly supported him with payments for his *Autobiography*, finally gave him its highest award, the Gold Medal, in 1946, 22 years after his death.

The enigma of his life, his buildings, and his writings, and the late-coming recognition do not detract from his importance. His buildings are important, not only for their overall designs but for his dedication to function and use of ornament. His philosophies are important. Their threads can be found running through architecture to this day. The miracle is that he was able to accomplish what he did, under adverse circumstances, in a short period of time, in only some 30 buildings and two major books.

Works In 1879 Sullivan went to work for Dankmar Adler (1844–1900) and afterward formed a partnership with him. The first important building that felt the imprint of what was to become Sullivan's style and philosophy was the Borden Block (1880), Chicago. In this building, now demolished, could be seen the beginnings of the architect's experimentation with newer types of structure and with what was to become his manner of handling the form and ornamentation of tall buildings. This was followed by another early example, the Chicago Joint Board Building (formerly Troescher) built in 1884 in Chicago, in which these themes were further developed and refined. The Auditorium (1890), also in Chicago, went still further, especially in the use of ornament in the interior.

During the years following the Auditorium, Sullivan as an individual, and Adler and Sullivan as a firm, continued to innovate and mature. This period produced a number of notable Chicago buildings, including the Garrick Theater in the Schiller Building (1892) and the Transportation Building (1893) at the World's Columbian Exposition (1893), both demolished later, and the Stock Exchange Building (1894). Sullivan also found time to develop further his use of ornament on some tombs, such as those for the Ryersons (1889) and the Gettys (1890) in Chicago, and for the Wainwrights (1892) in St. Louis. The Ryersons' tomb was designed for the family which had commissioned Adler and Sullivan to design the Ryerson Building (1884) in Chicago, now demolished. The Wainwright family had commissioned a building by the architects, the Wainwright Building (1891), St. Louis, still in existence and considered one of their masterpieces. The Wainwright is considered to be the first tall building to be designed so that its steel skeleton frame is expressed in the exterior appearance. Soon to follow was the Prudential Building (formerly Guaranty), built in 1895 in Buffalo. This was the last building of Adler and Sullivan. Their partnership dissolved, and Sullivan continued on his own.

It has been said that the career of Louis Sullivan was marked for decline by the dissolution of his partnership with Dankmar Adler. It is true that within five years or so, his private practice had almost disappeared and after that he produced only a few small buildings. But within the five years, he produced what is now considered one of his best buildings, and perhaps the most modern, the most noteworthy example of his philosophy and style. This is the Carson, Pirie, Scott Department (formerly Schlesinger and Mayer) Store (1904; see also color section), Chicago, highly praised for the restrained (almost spare) purity of its exterior appearance, but has also been criticized for its lack of architectural character in the interiors. Other important Sullivan buildings, produced on his own, are the Condict (formerly Bayard) Building (1898), his only New York City building, and the Gage buildings (1899; see illustration in article modern architecture), Chicago.

During his later years, Sullivan produced a series of small, Midwestern banks, some of which are admired for their architectural form, and all, in varying de-

SULLIVAN, LOUIS HENRI   Chicago Joint Board, formerly Troescher,
Building (1884), Chicago, Ill. [*Architects: Adler and Sullivan. (Hedrich-
Blessing)*]

SULLIVAN, LOUIS HENRI Auditorium (1890), Chicago, Ill. [*Architects: Adler and Sullivan. Restored in 1968 by architect Harry Weese. (Hedrich-Blessing)*]

SULLIVAN, LOUIS HENRI Wainwright Building (1891), St. Louis, Mo. [*Architects: Adler and Sullivan. (Hedrich-Blessing)*]

grees, for their use of ornament. The best is the earliest, Security (formerly National Farmers') Bank, built in 1908, in Owatonna, Minn. Others are Peoples' Saving Bank (1911), Cedar Rapids, Iowa; Poweskiek Co. (formerly Merchant's National) Bank (1914), Grinnell, Iowa; People's Savings and Loan Association Bank (1918), Sidney, Ohio; and Farmer's and Merchant's Union Bank (1919), Columbus, Wis.

Functional Architecture During his lifetime Sullivan was an outspoken advocate, in both his buildings and his writings, of what came to be called modern architecture. He turned away from the styles of the past, and the mixing of such styles, eclecticism, to what he thought of as functional architecture that expressed in its appearance the uses to which it was to be put, the materials of which it was made, and the new skeleton structures that supported it. He also became one of the leading proponents of the Chicago school of architects, a group composed of Jenney and the younger architects who had worked for him, the most noted, Sullivan, Holabird, Roche, and Burnham and others influenced by him, including Adler and Root. With some help from a few others, these men invented and developed the architecture of the

SULLIVAN, LOUIS HENRI Exterior, Charnley House (1892), Chicago, Ill. [*Architects: Adler and Sullivan. Designer: Frank Lloyd Wright. (Hedrich-Blessing)*]

SULLIVAN, LOUIS HENRI Interior, Charnley House (1892), Chicago, Ill. [*Architects: Adler and Sullivan. Designer: Frank Lloyd Wright. (Hedrich-Blessing)*]

SULLIVAN, LOUIS HENRI Stock Exchange (1894), Chicago, Ill. Later demolished, but main exchange room shown was dismantled and re-erected in the Chicago Art Institute. [*Architects: Adler and Sullivan. (Hedrich-Blessing)*]

early modern Chicago tall buildings, or skyscrapers. They strongly influenced the architecture of the future. In this, Sullivan played a leading role, one not really appreciated in his lifetime but more apparent in the years after his death.

Life Louis Henri Sullivan was born in Boston, on September 3, 1856. As a youth, he spent most of his summers on the farm of his maternal grandparents near Boston and lived with them other times. Here he acquired an interest in and curiosity about nature and craftsmanship, interests that continued the rest of his life and that were reflected in his architecture. Having

decided early that he wanted to be an architect, he entered Massachusetts Institute of Technology in 1872, at age sixteen. He stayed about a year, thus beginning what was to be a sketchy education at best.

He went to New York where he visited Richard Morris Hunt (1827–95) and then to Philadelphia, where he was hired as a draftsman by the firm of Furness and Hewitt. Lack of work caused him to leave this firm shortly after he was hired. He then went to Chicago where his parents were living and to work for William Le Baron Jenney (1832–1907) for a short time, leaving in 1874 to continue his education at the Ecole

SULLIVAN, LOUIS HENRI Prudential, formerly Guaranty, Building (1895), Buffalo, N.Y. [*Architects: Adler and Sullivan. (Wayne Andrews)*]

SULLIVAN, LOUIS HENRI Condict, formerly Bayard, Building (1898), New York, N.Y. *(Wurts brothers)*

SULLIVAN, LOUIS HENRI Carson, Pirie, Scott, formerly Schlesinger and Mayer, Department Store (1904), Chicago, Ill. *(Hedrich-Blessing)*

des Beaux Arts in Paris. This attempt lasted only about six months and, much disillusioned, he was back in Chicago by early 1875.

After having worked as a draftsman in several Chicago offices, he joined the firm of Dankmar Adler, a moderately successful Chicago architect, in 1879. The talents of the practical-minded, engineering-oriented Adler were perfectly complemented by those of the romantic, design-oriented younger man. In 1881 Sullivan was made a full partner in the firm, renamed Adler and Sullivan, a partnership that was to last almost 15 years and produce some of the masterpieces of that era.

Frank Lloyd Wright joined the firm in 1887 and remained until 1893. This association between Sullivan and Wright profoundly affected the lives and the architecture of both men. Wright always acknowledged his debt to Sullivan, whom he called his master. And Sullivan's own philosophy and work derived much of value from Wright.

During the panic and subsequent depression of 1893, building construction came to a virtual standstill. The firm of Adler and Sullivan held on until 1895, when it was dissolved. During the next five years, Sullivan did not exactly prosper. But these were the years that saw the flowering of his talents.

Sullivan's career then went downhill. His designs had never become acceptable enough to bring him an adequate number of clients. He sank into despon-

SULLIVAN, LOUIS HENRI Security, formerly National Farmers', Bank (1908), Owatonna, Minn. *(Wayne Andrews)*

dency brought on by the slipping of his practice and by drink. At the time of the climax of his career, in 1899, he married Margaret Hattabough, but she left him in 1906 and the marriage ended in divorce in 1917. From 1900 until his death, Sullivan produced only a few buildings, interesting in their designs but modest in size, a few stores and offices, a few small banks, a church in Cedar Rapids, Iowa, and two houses. He died in Chicago, in April 1924, in obscurity, his philosophy and buildings admired by only a few, his accomplishments not yet fully appreciated.

Related Articles FURNESS, FRANK; HUNT, RICHARD MORRIS; JENNEY, WILLIAM LE BARON; MODERN ARCHITECTURE; RICHARDSON, HENRY HOBSON; WRIGHT, FRANK LLOYD.

Further Reading Bush-Brown, Albert: *Louis Sullivan*, Braziller, New York, 1960; Kaufman, Mervyn D.: *Father of Skyscrapers: A Biography of Louis Sullivan*, Little, Brown, Boston, 1969; Sullivan, Louis: *Kindergarten Chats on Architecture, Education and Democracy*, George Wittenborn, Inc., New York, 1901–02; Sullivan, Louis: *The Autobiography of an Idea*, Dover, New York, reprinted, 1956.

SURVEYING A branch of civil engineering concerned with measuring land, determining points on the land and their relationships, areas, and relative heights or elevations. Another kind of surveying is the detailed analysis of materials and equipment with which to construct buildings. This type of surveying is called quantity surveying in Great Britain. For further

discussion on quantity surveying, see the article entitled cost control.

Types There are many types of surveying, including hydrographic surveying, which is concerned with shore lines and bottom contours of water bodies; land surveying (including geodetic), which takes into account the curvature of the earth and is used for large areas; and plane surveying, in which the earth is considered flat, and is used for smaller areas. Other types are named according to their purposes: topographic surveying, for establishing heights or depths, called elevations, of earth features and for producing data for contour maps that have lines of constant elevation; route surveying, for highways and railroads; mine surveying; underground surveying, for locating underground features, such as pipes or tunnels; and construction or engineering surveying, for constructing buildings and other structures. Types of surveying are also classified by the major instruments employed, such as plane table, transit, and photogrammetric surveying.

Instruments A plane table is a drawing board on a tripod with an alidade, a combination ruler and telescope; it is used for rapid work not requiring a great degree of accuracy. A transit is an optical instrument with a telescope that can be elevated or depressed and turned horizontally, mounted on a tripod and with a plumb bob for accurate positioning. A transit is fitted with accurate scales with verniers, devices for reading small fractions of degrees, and spirit levels, and can be used to measure vertical and horizontal angles accurately. A transit can also be used for measuring distances and elevations by sighting at a surveyor's rod held by an assistant at distant points. Photogrammetry involves the use of photography in surveying. A theodolite is similar to a transit, but much more accurate.

Other important tools of surveyors are measuring devices, including Gunter's, or surveyor's, chain; the engineer's chain; and the steel tape. A Gunter's chain is 66 ft long and is divided into 100 links; the engineer's chain is 100 ft long and is divided into 100 links. Gunter's chain came into widespread use because it was useful in laying out land. An acre, 43,560 ft², is exactly 10 square chains; or a piece of land 1 chain wide by 100 chains long contains 1 acre. More prevalently used today is the steel tape, which comes in lengths of 50, 100, and 200 feet. For very precise work, tapes made of invar, an alloy of nickel with steel, are used because they are less affected by temperature changes than regular steel tapes. Surveyor's rods of this material are also used for the same reason.

Another instrument used in surveying is the level, a device much like a transit except that it can be used only for measuring elevations, not for distances or angles. Land and construction surveying are the types most used in architecture, for several purposes, including the layout of housing and other developments, such as roads and streets, and in the establishment of property lines in subdividing land. A most important use of surveying in architecture is in connection with the actual design and construction of buildings. Before proceeding with the design of a building, an architect needs accurate information on the boundary lines and topography of the site; location of streets, curbs, pavements, and utilities; location of buildings or other structures on or adjacent to the site; and location of trees and other major landscaping features. At the beginning of construction, a building must be accurately laid out, as to its position, shape, size, and height. As the construction proceeds, surveying is used to check progress, to correct errors, and to make adjustments, until the building has been completed and its grounds have been landscaped.

Career For a person who likes to work out-of-doors with precision instruments, often on a great variety of projects, such as buildings, dams, bridges, and highways, surveying offers attractive career opportunities. Since surveying theory and practice are based on mathematics, in particular geometry and trigonometry, a person considering this field should have aptitudes and education in those subjects. Professional engineers, in particular civil engineers,

study surveying and many continue to do surveying after graduation. Another way to learn surveying is in technical schools and through experience in the field.

In most of the states, surveyors must become registered or licensed to practice surveying. Typically, the requirements for licensing or registration include six years of acceptable experience, for two years of which acceptable work in an accredited engineering school may be substituted. Candidates for licensing or registration must also pass written examinations lasting one or two days in basic sciences and mathematics; in the principles, theory, and practice of surveying; and in law and ethics. Land surveying boards of the states are often part of the same bodies that regulate architectural and engineering registration or licensing, but in some cases are separate organizations.

History Surveying is an occupation of humans that dates back to ancient times and which had been developed to a high degree of sophistication by the ancient Egyptians. Surveying has held an important place in the history of architecture ever since.

American Development In early colonial America, surveyors laid out township lines and divided the townships into lots. As people pushed west to settle, the early pioneer surveyors were often the first to arrive, braving the dangers of wild animals, weather, and unfriendly Indians. Surveying has always been considered an honorable profession, and many early Americans who were to make their marks later in other fields started as surveyors. Some of the most famous were George Washington (1732–99), Thomas Jefferson (1743–1826), and Daniel Boone (1734–1820).

By the time Washington did his first surveying in the Shenandoah Valley of Virginia in 1748, almost all the major present-day instruments, except the steel tape, were available, though mostly in elementary forms. Since that time, more accurate instruments have become available and old methods have been improved, and new ones developed, such as photogrammetry, which utilizes photographs, especially aerial photographs, for making surveys.

Related Articles CONSTRUCTION, BUILDING; COST CONTROL; REAL ESTATE; STRUCTURAL ENGINEERING.

Further Reading Barry, B. A.: *Construction Measurements*, John Wiley, New York, 1973; Breed, Charles B., and George L. Hosmer: *Principles and Practice of Surveying—Elementary Surveying*, 10th ed., John Wiley, New York, 1966; Davis, R., F. Foote, and J. Kelly: *Surveying—Theory and Practice*, 5th ed., McGraw-Hill, New York, 1966.

Sources of Additional Information American Congress of Surveying and Mapping, Woodward Building, Washington, D.C. 20005; American Society of Civil Engineers, 345 E. 47th St., New York, N.Y. 10017.

Periodical *Surveying and Mapping*, Woodward Building, Washington, D.C. 20005.

THEATER A building or outdoor structure in which audiences watch actors, musicians, and dancers perform. Theaters are sometimes called playhouses.

Types An opera house is a kind of theater in which operas, or musical dramas are presented, while a concert hall is a theaterlike building for the performance of music alone by orchestras, bands, instrumental soloists, or singers. Some theaters have specialized purposes, as a ballet theater, primarily intended for dance performances. Sometimes buildings in which motion pictures are shown are called motion picture theaters. Also buildings in which radio and television shows are enacted are sometimes called theaters, though the more proper term is studio.

Some theaters are used for only one type of performance, such as operas or plays, but others may be used for several or all types. An amphitheater is an outdoor theater often semicircular or elliptical in plan. An arena theater is one in which the seating for the audience surrounds the stage in the middle. Sometimes a theater in which plays are performed is called a legitimate theater.

An auditorium is a room in a building, such as a school, college, or university, used for theatrical and musical performances, meetings, instruction, or other similar gatherings of relatively large groups of people. The word *auditorium* is also used for the part of a theater occupied by the audience. The auditorium is often divided in sections, including the main area or orchestra, on the main floor; the balcony, a gallery projecting over part of the orchestra, or sometimes more than one; the loge, the front part of the lowest balcony; and private seating areas, sometimes called boxes.

Elements All the above types of buildings are essentially theaters and their design, though it varies in details, is similar. The two major parts of a theater are the public areas, sometimes called the front, and the production areas, called backstage. The major element in the front of a theater is the auditorium which the audience occupies; the major element backstage is the stage, on which the performance takes place. These two elements may be combined in theaters in three major ways: in a proscenium theater; a thrust-stage, or open-stage, theater; and an arena theater.

In a proscenium theater, there is a wall between the stage and auditorium, with an opening framing the stage on which the performance is held. The audience sits in rows of seats on one side of the wall; the stage is on the other. A curtain covers the opening and is lifted or drawn aside when a performance begins, and closed when an act or a performance ends. Behind the wall, on either side of the opening, are spaces on the stage called wings. Above the stage is a space called the flies, or fly loft, used for scenery and other equipment which may be raised or lowered by ropes and other rigging.

In a thrust-stage, or open-stage, theater, the stage projects into the auditorium, allowing the audience to be seated around the stage on three sides. One advantage of the open stage is the possibility of action that is more three dimensional than that on the more traditional proscenium stage.

An arena stage takes the principles of the open stage full circle, by placing the stage in the middle of the auditorium, completely surrounded by the audience. This is often called theater-in-the-round. Some theaters have been designed so that they can be converted from one type to another as occasion demands.

Other elements of the backstage areas are dressing rooms for the actors; property rooms for storage of props; storage rooms, called docks, for scenery; rehearsal rooms; green rooms, in which performers may relax or receive visitors; shops for making and repairing costumes, props, and scenery; and offices. In addition, theaters have prompters' boxes at the front of stages and sunken spaces in front of the stages, called orchestra pits.

In addition to the auditorium, the front of a theater must have a lobby or foyer, or both, for circulation of the audience into and out of the theater and, nearby, rest rooms, ticket office, and checkroom. Some theaters also have lounges, restaurants, bars, and cocktail lounges.

In a proscenium theater, the performers enter and leave the stage via the wings. In an arena theater, this is accomplished by openings between groups of seats, called vomitories, at various points in the auditorium. In an open-stage theater, performers may make entrances and exits through the back of the stage and through vomitory tunnels under the auditorium.

Design In the design of any theater, the major considerations are circulation of the audience, seating and sight lines of the audience, good acoustics,

THEATER Radio City Music Hall (1940), Rockefeller Center, New York, N.Y. [*Architects: Corbett, Harrison and MacMurray; Hood and Fouilhoux. (Wurts brothers)*]

safety, lighting, and proper relationships between the various front and backstage elements. The audience should be able to enter the theater with ease, have adequate space in the foyer or lobby, with rest rooms and other conveniences nearby, and easy access to their seats through adequate aisles and spaces between rows of seats. The stage should be in the proper relationship with the auditorium to allow good sight lines from any seat in the house. For the same purpose, seating in theaters is placed on inclined floors, rising away from the stage, and often the rows of seats are curved. Ratios have been established between the depth of auditoriums and their widths for optimum viewing for different kinds of theaters.

Good acoustics are all-important in theaters. The acoustics of theaters are affected by many factors, such as the shape of the stage and the auditorium, the materials, the placement and size of the audience, and so on. The design of theater acoustical systems is therefore very complex and is usually performed by specialists.

Many disastrous theater fires have occurred in the past, some with the loss of a considerable number of lives. Today there are stringent codes and regulations governing design for safety in theaters. The number and position of exits, the widths of aisles, the number of seats next to each aisle, and the locations of storage rooms are all fixed by law. Panic bars, which open doors when pushed from inside the building, are required. Scenery, curtains, and other materials must be made nonflammable and fire resistant. High-risk areas must be protected by automatic sprinkler systems. Exit lights must be provided.

Lighting in theaters is of two major types: the lighting of the public areas and the lighting of the stage. In the public areas, lighting is similar to that in other building types used by the public, except that in the auditorium, provisions must be made for dimming the lights, bringing the house lights down at the beginning of performances and up at intermissions and at the end of performances.

Stage lighting is a complex art. Many types of lights are used in a great variety of positions, colors, and conformations, designed and timed to fit the action taking place on the stage. The lights are controlled by electricians, trained for this work, who operate complicated switchboards, called control boards or consoles. The design of stage lighting for theaters is complex and is performed by specialists in this field.

The major relationships between the front and

THEATER Edens (1970), Chicago, Ill. [*Architects: Perkins and Will. (Hedrich-Blessing)*]

THEATER Performing Arts Center (1966), Saratoga, N.Y. [*Architects: Vollmer Associates. (Joseph W. Molitor)*]

backstage elements of theaters are those between the lobby or foyer and auditorium, between the auditorium and stage, and between the stage and other backstage areas. These must be designed to work effectively and efficiently for the audience, the performers, and the stagehands and other workers backstage. For example, a very important aspect of theater design is the provision for easy changing or moving of sets, scenery, and props.

Special Needs Theaters of various types have some special requirements. For example, a motion picture house must have an adequate projection booth from which the projectors can project films. Today almost every type of theater has a projection booth. In drive-in motion picture theaters, automo-

bile parking, with individual sound speakers, must be provided for the audience, along with a projection house that is sometimes combined with a snack bar or other refreshment facility; in some, seating areas are provided for those who walk in.

In some theaters, special stages are provided. Some roll into and out of place, and some revolve, allowing several sets to be installed in advance and brought onstage when needed. Amphitheaters present special problems to designers, since it is more difficult to provide proper acoustics, lighting, and so on, outdoors. Auditoriums, particularly those in schools, colleges, and universities, often have requirements for band, choral group, and other practice rooms and are also used for purposes other than performances.

THEATER   Red Rock Amphitheater (1941), Morrison, Colo. [*Architect: Burnham Hoyt. (Hedrich-Blessing)*]

Each theater must be designed to function properly for its purpose or purposes and to accommodate performances, the audience, the performers, and other workers. Thus theaters are one of the most intriguing of building types to the architects and others who design them, as well as to those in the entertainment industry and those who comprise the audiences.

History   Drama is one of the oldest art forms, having had its beginnings in ancient times, probably originating in religious rites. In every historic era and in every part of the world, some sort of drama was performed. Theaters too go back to ancient times, though in Egypt and the Near East, performances took place in palaces or other buildings rather than in structures specifically designed as theaters. The ancient Greeks built theaters, or amphitheaters, usually in natural, bowl-shaped depressions on the sides of hills where thousands, sometimes tens of thousands, of spectators sat on the ground or on crude seating to watch performances on the stage below. At first, the performances consisted of dancing and singing by groups of people. Sometime in the 6th century B.C., the Greek poet Thespis, who is thought to have invented tragedy, is believed to have stepped forward from such a group and recited a monologue. Soon after that, Thespis or perhaps the Greek playwright Aes-

chylus (525–456 B.C.) added another actor, creating a dialogue on the stage. This was the beginning of the plays of today and ever since then, actors have often been called thespians. The Greeks built many great theaters, quite a few of which are still in existence. And some of the world's greatest playwrights were early Greeks, including the tragic writer Sophocles (c. 496–406 B.C.), Euripides (5th century B.C.), and the writer of comedies, Aristophanes (c. 448–380 B.C.).

Although there were theaters in ancient Rome, the Romans preferred other pleasures and the theater declined. In other parts of the world, it flourished, particularly in India and China. During the Middle Ages, the theater was revived, for the most part in performances connected with religion. During the Renaissance, other types of theater were revived in Europe. The first theater in England, called simply The Theater (1576), London, was built by the English actor James Burbage (d. 1597). In this building were probably performed the first plays of William Shakespeare (1564–1616). Shakespeare was connected with other theaters, including the famous Globe (1598) in London.

Later many other theaters were built all over the world. Opera, as it is known today, was invented in Italy in the 17th century and the construction of opera houses as well as of concert halls began. Few of the early theaters still exist, for many reasons, but mostly because theaters were very apt to be destroyed by fire or other violent events. For example, the Globe Theater was built in 1598, destroyed by fire in 1613, rebuilt in 1614, and demolished by the Puritans in 1644. Another famous London theater, Covent Garden, was built in 1732, later disintegrated, was reconstructed in 1792, destroyed by fire and rebuilt in 1810, destroyed by fire again and rebuilt in 1858.

American Development In colonial America, theater was popular, but the first permanent building was not built until 1766, in Philadelphia. It was followed by the Chestnut Street Theater (1794) and the Walnut Street Theater (1809), the oldest still existing in the United States, both in Philadelphia. Theaters were then built all over the United States, in every city and in many towns. Although the building of theaters has slowed down at various times, they have continued to comprise an important building type to the present time. A great number of architects have designed theaters and some of them have been significant architecturally.

Efforts were made by many in the late 19th century to discover ways to photograph motion and project motion pictures. No one knowns which person was first successful, but the first showing in the United States was made in 1896 by Thomas Alva Edison (1847–1931). Shortly before that time, showings had been held in France. This was the beginning of the motion picture industry, though the early showings were all in theaters designed for other purposes.

The first theater designed specifically for motion pictures, The Electric Theater, was opened in Los Angeles in 1902. Cinema houses have since been constructed all over the United States. With the advent of sound in 1927, the process speeded up until every hamlet in America had its own movie house, and sometimes more than one. Many architects designed these buildings, some quite ornate, in almost every conceivable exotic style. The construction of motion picture theaters slowed down starting in the 1950s, mostly due to the inroads made by television in the entertainment industry. By the 1970s interest in motion pictures began to revive and so did the building of motion picture theaters.

Beginning late in the 19th century, there was considerable dissatisfaction with commercial theaters. As a result, all over Europe and in the United States, little theaters were started. These new theaters were free of some of the restrictions of commercial theaters since they received financial support from individuals and organizations without the necessity for making profits, so essential to the commercial theaters. The first little theaters in the United States were established in Provincetown, R.I., and New York City in 1915. Later, little theaters were built all over the United States, many of them with financial help from the Federal Theater Project from 1935 to 1939.

Today there are many thousands of theaters of all types across the United States in cities, towns, suburbs, and rural areas. They exist in separate buildings and within other structures, including office buildings, shopping centers, and airports. Many are located in schools, colleges, and universities. Some are part of large theater complexes that contain several buildings, as in the Lincoln Center for the Performing Arts (1968), New York City, and some are in buildings that contain several theaters under one roof, as in the John F. Kennedy Center for the Performing Arts (1969), Washington, designed by Edward Durell Stone (1902–78).

The buildings of Lincoln Center, designed under the general direction of Wallace Kirkman Harrison (1895–) are New York State Theater (1964), by Philip Cortelyou Johnson (1906–); Philharmonic Hall (1962), by Max Abramovitz (1908–); Vivian Beaumont Theater (1965), by Eero Saarinen (1910–61); Julliard School of Music (1968), by Pietro Belluschi (1899–); Library-Museum of the Performing Arts (1965), by Skidmore, Owings and Merrill; and the Metropolitan Opera House (1966) by Harrison.

There seems to be no end to the interest, even obsession, of the American people with the cultural and entertainment values derived from theater attendance.

Related Articles FIRE PROTECTION; LIGHTING; SOUND CONTROL; Articles on individual architects, and on other building types.

Further Reading Beranek, Leo L.: *Music, Acoustics and Architecture*, John Wiley, New York, 1964; Izenour, George C.: *Theater Design*, McGraw-Hill, New York, 1977; Jewell, Don: *Public Assembly Facilities — Planning and Management*, John Wiley, New York, 1978.

THORNTON, WILLIAM English-American architect (1759–1826). Although William Thornton was a medical doctor, he did not practice professionally. He was a dilettante, an amateur artist, philosopher, linguist, scientist, and sportsman. He is remembered today for another of his amateur pursuits: architecture. And in architecture, he is remembered almost entirely for one building, the original designs for the United States Capitol in Washington.

Works To base Thornton's reputation as an architect, amateur or otherwise, on the Capitol alone, even though it is one of the greatest American buildings, does him an injustice. After coming to the United States, Thornton settled in Philadelphia, where he designed his first building for the Library Company (1789; since demolished) of that city. He eventually moved to Washington where he produced designs for a number of notable buildings, mostly houses. Some of his important houses, all still in existence, are Octagon House (1800), designed for Col. John Tayloe III (1771–1828), now preserved by its owners, the American Institute of Architects; Tudor Place (1815), a Classic Revival house considered by many to be Thornton's best building, both in Washington; and Woodlawn Plantation (1805), near Mount Vernon, Va. Thornton also designed St. John's Church (1804) in Georgetown, Washington, now much modified. This

THORNTON, WILLIAM Woodlawn Plantation (1805), near Mount Vernon, Va. A property of the National Trust for Historic Preservation. *(Joseph W. Molitor)*

THORTON, WILLIAM Octagon House (1800), Washington, D.C. *(Wayne Andrews)*

church should not be confused with that of the same name across from Lafayette Square, near the White House, built in 1816 from designs by Benjamin Henry Latrobe (1764–1820).

In spite of all his other accomplishments, Thornton's name is mostly associated with the design of the U.S. Capitol (see illustration in color section), the commission for which he won in a competition in 1792. The construction of the Capitol began the next year, but it soon became apparent that Thornton did not have the knowledge to direct the work. The runner-up in the competition, a French architect, Stephen Hallet (1755–1825), was appointed to direct the

construction. Thornton, having been appointed a city commissioner in 1794, remained involved in the construction until 1802. After that, a number of architects worked on the building, changing and making additions to many of the elements of Thornton's original design, but retaining the major element of a central dome with porticoes front and back and wings on either side.

Life William Thornton was born on May 20, 1759, on the island Tortola, now in the British Virgin Islands, but then considered part of the British West Indies. When he was fifteen, he went to England to attend school and in 1781 entered the University of Edinburgh, Scotland, and studied there until 1784. In that year, he transferred to the University of Aberdeen, Scotland, and received a medical degree in 1784. He came to the United States in 1787, settled in Philadelphia, and became a U.S. citizen in 1788.

He was married in 1790, and while on his honeymoon in Tortola, learned of the competition for the U.S. Capitol. In 1792, though he had no training in architecture, he won the competition. Two years later he moved to Washington and lived there the remainder of his life. In 1794 he was appointed a city commissioner and in 1802, commissioner of patents of the federal government, a position in which he served until his death.

All his life, Thornton pursued a great variety of interests. He made inventions, among them boilers and firearms; he painted; he attempted to found a national university in Washington. One of his major interests from the time he was in his thirty's was in the abolition of slavery. In the 1790s, he proposed that colonies should be set up in Africa, to which ex-slaves could be repatriated. He was one of the first members, and a very active one, in the American Colonization Society, organized in 1817 for just such a purpose. In 1822 the Society managed to establish a small colony for this purpose at Monrovia, West Africa, which eventually grew into the present-day Republic of Liberia.

Thornton had a reputation among some of his contemporaries as a cantankerous and unreasonable man. The architects, including Hallett, James Hoban (c. 1762–1831), and Benjamin Henry Latrobe (1764–1820) who had tried to work with him on the construction of the Capitol, all had trouble with him. To his friends, Thornton seemed just the opposite, a scholar and gentleman, talented but eccentric, full of humor, generosity, and humanity. On March 28, 1826, Thornton died in Washington, his adopted city, and was buried in the Congressional Cemetery.

Related Articles CAPITAL, UNITED STATES; CLASSIC REVIVAL ARCHITECTURE; LATROBE, BENJAMIN HENRY.

TILE A baked clay unit used in building construction for flooring, wall coverings, roofing, structural systems, and other purposes, often laid with mortar in a manner similar to that for brick. The word *tile* is frequently used to denote other materials that are made in relatively small units, such as vinyl tile flooring. However, tile is most closely related to various products made of baked clay.

Types Clay tile used for flooring and wall coverings may be obtained either unglazed, with integral color throughout, or glazed, with ceramic materials in various colors fused to the surfaces. Other types include quarry tile, which is an unglazed tile in earth colors, generally used for flooring. Roof tiles are available in glazed and unglazed finishes, in various shapes, often named for the countries from which they were derived, including Greek, English, Spanish, and French. Structural clay tiles, in the past often called hollow tiles because of their conformation, are used for various building components, including the structures of walls, and are often finished with stucco, plaster, brick, or stone. Structural facing tiles have colored, glazed surfaces that may be left exposed. Clay tile pipes are used for drainage and other plumbing and sewage purposes. Terra-cotta is a baked clay product used for finishes on buildings and may be flat or molded. Because of the relative ease of molding, terra-cotta has often been used for ornamental purposes in architecture. However, it is seldom used today, except in thin tiles, usually called ceramic veneer, which may be obtained with graphic or ornamental designs. Clay flue linings are often used in chimneys.

Floor and Wall Tiles Clay floor and wall tiles are used today for those purposes and sometimes for facing fireplaces and countertops. Tiles of this type are made of clay, usually ball clays (in the industry sometimes called plastics), fillers, often flint or silica, which impart strength and resist shrinkage during firing, and solvents, usually feldspar, callled fluxes. The exact proportions of these materials vary among the various types of tiles.

Floor and wall tiles are made by either the dust-press or the plastic process. Each process requires a number of operations. In general, the dust-press process involves shaping the mixture of clay and other materials in steel dies under great pressure, after which the shaped tiles are fired. The plastic process involves shaping the mixture by extrusion through dies or by hand molding, after which they are fired. The dust-press method produces more precise shapes and sizes than the plastic method, which produces tiles that look somewhat handmade. The surfaces of floor and wall tiles may be unglazed or glazed. In unglazed types the color is integral throughout the body of the tiles and their appearance comes from the materials used. Glazed tiles have ceramic materials fused to their faces in an additional firing. Glazed tile may be almost any color and may have surface textures, such as mottled or stippled. Glazes may be polished or bright, or matte. Floor and wall tiles are also classified by their degree of fusing of the materials, or vitrification, which largely determines their degree of water absorption. From the least impervious to water to the greatest, tile may be nonvitreous, semivitreous, and vitreous or impervious.

The major types of floor and wall tiles, often called ceramic tiles, include glazed wall tiles, ceramic mosaic tiles, and floor tiles. Glazed wall tiles are usually made by the dust-press method. Nominal sizes usually available are $5/16$ in thick, $4\frac{1}{4}$ and 6 in square, and

TILE Wall, Temple Beth Sholom (1965), Framingham, Mass. [*Architects: Henneberg and Hennegerg. (Joseph W. Molitor)*]

4¼ by 6 in. They also come in other sizes and in octagonal shapes. A special type is the weatherproof glazed wall tile, made by either method, and used in locations where freezing occurs. These tiles, in matte finishes, may also be used for flooring in areas with moderate traffic.

Ceramic mosaic tiles, usually unglazed, may be used for interior or exterior floors and walls. They come in two types: porcelain, made by the dust-press method, and vitreous or impervious; and the natural clay type, made by either method. Ceramic mosaic tiles are generally small in size, of nominally ¼ in thickness, and 1 or 2 in² or 1 by 2 in. Because of their small size, they are often furnished with paper attached to their faces to hold them in place while they are being set. Porcelain types come in a wide range of colors, while the colors of the natural tile are generally determined by the types of clay used.

Other than those previously mentioned, floor types include quarry tiles and pavers. Both are available in squares and rectangles, in nominal sizes ranging from 3 to 9 in, and in thickness from ⅜ to ¾ in. Both types are unglazed. Quarry tiles are made by the plastic method and pavers by either method. Both types may be used for interior or exterior installations and both are resistant to wear from heavy traffic. Quarry tiles are generally restricted in color to those produced by the clays from which they are made. Pavers are similar to ceramic mosaics and may be obtained in a variety of colors. In all types of floor and wall tiles, special shapes may be obtained for use in corners, for bases at the bottom of walls, caps at the tops, and so on. Also special fixtures, such as soap dishes, are available for use with tile.

Many other types of tile are available for special purposes, including faience, majolica, and delft. Faience tiles are named after the town of Faenza, Italy, where they were first made during the Middle Ages. They are highly ornamental, resembling Persian tile, usually with striking opaque glazes. Majolica, named for the island of Majorca where it was first made in the Middle Ages, is a special kind of faience, with brilliant, enameled ornament fired on its face. Delft tile, named for the town of Delft, the Netherlands, where it was first made in the 16th century, is a faience, often in blue and white and with ornament derived from oriental sources.

Floor and wall tiles are available in various grades, which are different for the particular types of tile. When tiles are being selected or specified for use in buildings, a determination of the proper grades should be made. Floor and wall tiles may be installed by either of two methods; one using mortar and the other, adhesives. Joints between individual tiles are grouted with special groutings or caulking materials or with portland cement mixed with sand or other materials.

Roof Tiles   Clay roof tiles are available unglazed, in mostly earthly colors, or glazed in a variety of colors, in rounded and other shapes, and as shingles. Sizes

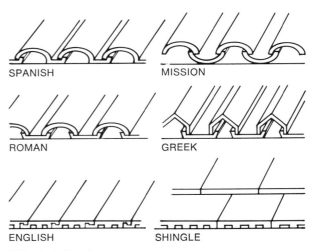

TILE   Typical roofing types.

of the various shapes of roof tiles range from about 8 to 12 in wide and from about 11 to 18 in long. Shingles are generally 12 or 15 in long and 6, 7, or 9 in wide. The minimum pitch of roofs using shaped tiles is 4½ in rise to 12 in of length, or run; for shingles, the minimum is 6 in rise to 12 in run. Clay roof tiles and shingles are generally installed with noncorrosive nails and some types have interlocking features. Special shapes are available for use on roof ridges and similar purposes.

Structural Tiles   Structural clay tiles may be obtained with unfinished faces to be used as backup for exteriors of brick or other materials, which combine to support loads, or as structural facing tile, in which the tile itself supports the entire load and is finished with stucco or other materials. Structural facing tiles may be also obtained with unglazed or glazed finished faces, and with smooth, scored, combed, and other textures. Unglazed types are generally in earth colors derived from the types of clay used, and glazed tile may have any of a number of colors, in solid, mottled, or other finishes that are either shiny or matte. Structural tiles may be obtained as loadbearing for use in masonry structures or nonload bearing for other uses. There are also special types, such as fireproof tile, used to protect steel structural members.

Structural tiles are generally available in nominal sizes of 4 in thick by 12 in long and various heights and 8 in thick and high by 16 in long. Other sizes may also be obtained. Many special shapes are available in structural facing tiles for corners, jambs of doors and windows, bases at the bottom of walls, caps at tops, and so on. Some of the types of structural tile come in several grades for various uses. Structural clay tiles are usually installed in mortar, composed of portland cement, lime, aggregate, and water. The proportions of these materials, the time of their mixing, and the placement of the mortar must be strictly controlled.

Terra-cotta, or ceramic veneer, ordinarily comes in nominal sizes of ⅜ to about 4 in in thickness and in pieces up to about 3 by 4 ft. It may be obtained unglazed, in various earth colors determined by the clays used in its manufacture, and in various textures and finishes. If glazed, many colors are possible. Ceramic veneer is usually installed with mortar and special setting clips. Clay flue tiles for use in the lining of chimneys generally come in round, rectangular, and square forms, in various sizes, from which the proper size may be selected based on the size of the fireplace to be served. Clay pipe comes in unglazed form, usually called drain tile, for use in drains and underground sewage disposal systems, in sizes, based on the inside diameter from 3 to 24 in. A perforated type is also available. Vitrified clay pipe, used for storm sewers, sewers, and other purposes, comes glazed or unglazed and in sizes from 4 to 42 in. Both types have bell and spigot ends for fitting together. Various fittings such as Y's, tees, and so on are available for both types.

Clay products constitute such a variety of types and have such a wide usage in architecture that it is virtually impossible to generalize about their selection. In types for structural purposes, attention must be paid to load bearing characteristics. The degree of water infiltration allowable in specific installations must be determined and tile with sufficient vitrification selected. For exposed installations, colors, textures, finishes, and shapes are important. Since many types of tile come in various grades, selection must be made of the ones that fit the purposes intended.

Proper mortars or adhesives must be selected and the tile installed under the proper conditions and in the correct manner on walls or other bases that have been correctly prepared. If proper selections and safeguards are followed, all clay tile products will give many years of almost maintenance-free service.

History Clay or ceramic materials, such as terra-cotta and tile, have been used in architecture from early primitive times, about 5000 b.c., or even earlier. When the first of such materials was used has not been established, but early types have been found in the oldest remains of civilizations around the Mediterranean Sea, including those in Mesopotamia, Crete, Egypt, and Greece. At first tile and terra-cotta were sun-dried, but later they were kiln-burned.

The ancient Egyptians used both tile and terra-cotta, but not as extensively as in Mesopotamia and other areas of the Middle East. Nor did the Egyptians reach the high level of excellence in the use of color, carvings, and molding achieved in the Middle East where clay was abundant, but other materials were not. The Mesopotamians developed terra-cotta and tile into a high art, ornamenting many of their walls and other building elements with elaborate depictions of animals and people made of these materials. The ancient Greeks used terra-cotta and other clay materials, not so much for ornamental as for functional purposes, such as roofs, sewers, and water conduits. As ornament, the Greeks used terra-cotta for cornices and similar purposes.

The Romans used tile and terra-cotta extensively, not only for ornament and roofs, as had their predecessors, the Etruscans, but also for piping, flooring, in hollow forms for conducting hot air and smoke to heat buildings, and in the form of hollow boxes for construction of vaults and domes. Roman terra-cotta and tile were often unglazed and uncolored, but that was not always the case. Along with brick, tile and terra-cotta were used only infrequently during the Middle Ages. Exceptions occurred in Italy and Germany and, particularly, in Spain and the Muslim countries, where ornamental tile work has been of high excellence since very early times.

During the Renaissance, tile and terra-cotta were widely used, not only for ornamental features of buildings but, in the case of terra-cotta, as a sculptural medium by many of the leading artists of the time. The art of making fine tile spread from Spain to Italy, England, and other countries, in particular to the Netherlands. Terra-cotta was used in England for a time, but by the end of the 16th century, its use had been virtually discontinued there. It continued to flourish in Italy and elsewhere for a time, but by the end of the Renaissance, was no longer widely used in Europe.

American Development In the American colonies, neither tile nor terra-cotta was used. Later tile was imported, particularly delft from the Netherlands, and used mostly for ornamentation and fireplace facings. Tile was later manufactured in America and its use for other purposes grew. The use of terra-cotta was revived in the late 19th century, first for use in Victorian and other buildings and then for ornamental uses in cornices and other elements of early tall buildings. With the modern movement in architecture, the use of terra-cotta for ornamental purposes came to an end, except in latter-day Eclectic buildings. Today structural clay tile, tile pipe, and other types are used for functional purposes. Clay roofing tile is mostly used for buildings designed to reflect a Spanish influence or that of some other country. Ceramic tiles are widely used in bathrooms and kitchens and for other purposes. Ceramic veneer continues to be used to some extent.

Related Articles Brick; Floor; Masonry Structure; Plumbing; Roof; Wall.

Sources of Additional Information Ceramic Tile Inst., 700 Virgil Ave., Los Angeles, Calif., 90029; Facing Tile Inst., 1750 Old Meadow Rd., McLean, Va. 22101; National Ceramic Manufacturers Assoc., 59 E. Main St., Moorestown, N.J. 08057; National Clay Pipe Inst., 350 W. Terra Cotta Av., Crystal Lake, Ill. 60014.

UPJOHN, RICHARD English-American architect (1802–78). Starting out as a cabinetmaker and carpenter, Richard Upjohn studied architecture and drawing. In an earlier era, he might have gone on to become a craftsman-architect as had many before him. But by the time he began practicing architecture in 1833, it had become possible for a career to be made in architecture alone. Thus Upjohn became one of the earliest professional architects in America.

Architectural Influence Although he designed a relatively large number of buildings of many types, it is as a church designer that he made his reputation. He designed more than 100 churches, located in many parts of the United States, remodeled and renovated many more, and influenced the design of many others, mainly through his book on church design, *Upjohn's Rural Architecture,* containing drawings of a prototype church and other buildings, originally published in 1852.

While his commercial and residential work were often exceptions, his designs were almost always in the Gothic Revival style, using forms and details derived from the churches and cathedrals of the Middle Ages. Upjohn's use of this style influenced the architecture of his time, and the architects then as well as those who later turned to Gothic themes in the era of Victorian architecture. He also had a lasting influence on architecture and its practice through his many years of work for the benefit of the profession.

Works It has been said that the reputation of Upjohn rests on his design of one building, Trinity Church (1846), New York City. Although there is some truth in this assessment and Trinity certainly is his masterpiece, Upjohn designed a number of other notable buildings. Among them are the Church of the Ascension (1841), New York City; Christ Church (1842), Brooklyn; Grace Church (1848), Brooklyn; St. James' Church (1850), New London, Conn.; St. Mary's Church (1854; see illustrations in article Gothic revival architecture), Burlington, N.J.; St. Paul's Church, Buffalo, N.Y.; and the Chapel at Bowdoin College (1853) in Brunswick, Maine.

Life Richard Upjohn was born in Dorsetshire, England, on January 22, 1802, the son of a surveyor. His mother died the same year. His father moved the family to Newfoundland in 1808, but soon returned to England. After showing an aptitude for drawing, Richard was apprenticed to a cabinetmaker at seventeen.

UPJOHN, RICHARD Kingscote (1838), Newport, R.I. *(Wayne Andrews)*

UPJOHN, RICHARD   Exterior, Trinity Church (1846), New York, N.Y. *(Wurts brothers)*

UPJOHN, RICHARD   Interior, Trinity Church (1846), New York, N.Y. *(Joseph Byron, Library of Congress)*

While serving his apprenticeship, he began to study architecture, a pursuit he continued after he started his own cabinetmaking business. On November 14, 1826, he married Elizabeth Parry; their son, Richard Michell (1827–1903) became an architect.

In 1828 Upjohn brought his wife and son to the United States, first settling in Manlius, N.Y., and then moving to New Bedford, Mass., where he worked as a draftsman. In 1833 he began his career as an architect with the design of a house in Bangor, Maine. During the next few years, he designed several other houses, and in 1834, moved to Boston. Soon afterward, he designed his first church, St. John's (1839), Bangor, Maine. This was the beginning of a great career in church design. Largely because of the success of the Bangor church, and through his friendship with the newly appointed rector of Trinity Church, N.Y., Dr. Jonathan Wainwright, Upjohn was called to New York to design a new building for the congregation. This church, Trinity (1846), firmly established Upjohn as one of the most important American architects and one of the finest church architects of all time. Over the succeeding years, he designed churches all over the United States and also did a number of other buildings, including houses and university and commercial buildings.

Upjohn formed a partnership with his son, Richard Michell, called Upjohn and Co., in 1853; the firm name was changed several times, to Richard Upjohn, in 1858; and finally R. and R. M. Upjohn, in 1864, reflecting the growing importance of the younger man in the firm.

During the later years of his life, Upjohn began to devote more and more of his time to his profession and less to his own practice. He then took a step which ensured his deeper involvement with his profession. On February 23, 1857, group of architects met in the Upjohn office to discuss the foundation of an architectural organization that would have a great effect on architecture. Out of this meeting came the professional organization, the American Insitute of Architects. Upjohn was elected its first president, a post in which he served for 18 years.

In 1872 Upjohn dissolved his partnership with his son, who carried on his own practice afterward. Retiring to an old house he had bought in Garrison, N.Y., Upjohn spent his last years mostly relaxing with his grandchildren and painting in oils the scenery around the house and the Hudson River. On August 17, 1878, Richard Upjohn died, honored and respected by his profession. Much of his great architecture survived him, as did his architect-son, Richard Michell, and architect-grandson, Hobard B. (1876–1949). A great-grandson, Everard Miller (1903–   ), studied architecture but instead became a professor of fine arts at Columbia University.

Related Articles   Association, Building Industry; Building Industry; Gothic Revival Architecture; Religious Building.

Further Reading   Upjohn, Everard Miller: *Richard Upjohn—Architect and Churchman,* DaCapo Press, New York, 1968; Upjohn, Richard: *Upjohn's Rural Architecture—Designs, Working Drawings and Specifications for a Wooden Church and Other Structures,* repr., DaCapo Press, New York, 1975.

VAULT A structural element of a building using the principles of the arch extended to form a curved roof over an interior space.

As the arch, the vault was originally constructed of masonry, stone, brick, or tile units, shaped so that when assembled they formed a strong structural system that transferred weight down through the vault units to walls or columns. As in the arch, this weight produces forces that thrust outward at the base of the vault as well as downward. To prevent the vault from collapsing, the outward, or lateral, thrusts must be resisted by thick walls or by special structural elements called buttresses. In some cases, vaults are placed side by side so that the lateral thrusts of adjacent vaults resist each other. A flying buttress is a special type, much used in the Gothic architecture of the Middle Ages, consisting of sloping structural elements supported on an arch that tranfers the lateral thrust of the vault to a pier.

Elements Other terms are important in vaults. A crown is the top of a vault. A haunch is the middle part of a vault between the crown and the spring line. A spring line is the lowest part of a vault, where it begins to rise. The rise of a vault is the height from the spring line to the bottom of the crown. Its span is the the width between the interior sides of a vault.

VAULT, CONTEMPORARY Wood Frame, Bar Harbor Junior School (1953), Bar Harbor, Maine [*Architect: Alonzo Harriman. (Joseph W. Molitor)*]

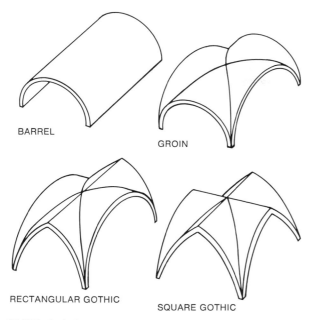

BARREL

GROIN

RECTANGULAR GOTHIC

SQUARE GOTHIC

VAULT Typical masonry types.

Types Masonry vaults are of three main kinds: barrel, groined, and ribbed. The simplest, the barrel vault, sometimes called tunnel vault, is semicircular and spans the space between two walls like a continuous arch. A groined vault is formed when two vaults intersect, the groin being the ridge or rib formed at the intersection. In a ribbed vault, ribs only are constructed where the groins would otherwise be thus creating a skeletonlike structure much lighter in appearance and actuality than a groin vault. The spaces between the ribs may then be filled with relatively light materials, including glass.

Vaults have also been constructed of homogeneous materials, such as concrete, from the time of the Romans. Today such vaults would be built of reinforced concrete. Vaults of reinforced concrete perform in much the same way as those of masonry, except that the side thrusts may be eliminated, thus also eliminating the need for heavy piers and buttresses.

History The use of vaults as structural elements began at about the same time as arches, in Mesopotamia about 6,000 years ago. This tradition was continued by other cultures, including the Egyptian, but not the Greek, and was further developed by the Romans, particularly masonry and concrete barrel and groined vaults. The development of the masonry ribbed vault reached its apex in the Gothic architecture of the Middle Ages, notably in the great cathedrals. In the Renaissance period, vaults were used extensively, though most were the barrel form.

American Development Vaults of masonry have been used in American architecture since colonial times, especially in churches and other buildings in which a monumental effect was desired. Later reinforced concrete vaults came into widespread usage,

for the achievement of similar monumental effects and where relatively long distances were spanned by the roofs.

During the height of the Classic Revival movement in America, vaults of masonry, designed to strict engineering standards, were used by many architects in a daring and innovative manner. Their use continued during the Gothic Revival and Eclectic periods in American architecture and into the 20th century.

Related Articles ARCH; CONCRETE STRUCTURE; DOME; MASONRY STRUCTURE; STEEL STRUCTURE; WOOD-FRAME STRUCTURE.

VERTICAL TRANSPORTATION A system for transferring people or objects between floors in buildings. A stair is the most common and rudimentary of such devices used in buildings today. When vertical transportation is mentioned today, the reference is usually to electrical or hydraulic devices, such as elevators or escalators. Many other devices are used for such purposes. (See the article entitled stair.)

Vertical Transportation Devices An elevator is a conveyance that lifts and lowers people and objects in a building by means of a car, cage, or platform in a vertical shaft. In England and some other places, an elevator is called a lift. The word *elevator* is used in England to denote a platform that can be raised or lowered vertically for such uses as construction of buildings. In the United States, such a device is generally called a scaffold and may or may not be motorized. A special kind of scaffold is sometimes attached to buildings for use in window washing and maintenance.

Temporary elevators for lifting workers and materials during building construction are sometimes called hoists. The word *hoist* may also be applied to lifting machinery, such as that employed in factories or warehouses and in other ways. An escalator is an inclined device for vertical transportation of people on moving stairs. A similar device is a moving ramp. The principle of escalators and moving ramps have also been applied to the movement of people and objects horizontally on moving sidewalks.

A stairlift is a device, used mostly in houses or other residential buildings, for transporting handicapped, ill, or elderly people up and down stairways. A stairlift is like a motorized chair that rides on the railing of a stairway. A dumbwaiter is like a small elevator and is used for raising or lowering objects in buildings. Other vertical transportation devices include pneumatic tube systems for conveying paperwork between various building locations, and many kinds of conveyors for materials and other objects. Information on various kinds of dumbwaiters, conveyors, hoists, and so on are included in articles in this book pertaining to building types and systems in which they are used.

Elevators may be used in all buildings two stories high or more. In buildings higher than two stories, they are considered necessities. Escalators are generally used in buildings where large numbers of people move in a single direction or where it is considered desirable to direct their movement in one direction. Ordinarily escalators are one story high, though some are higher, and groups of them are generally used for only a few stories. At first escalators were mostly used in transportation buildings, such as railway stations, airports, subways, and the like. Stores soon found them useful for directing shoppers through various floors and departments. Today escalators are often used in many other types of building, including hospitals, schools, hotels, and sports arenas and amphitheaters. Elevators, of course, have uses in almost every building type.

Elevator Mechanisms Although elevators may be used for transporting both people and materials, a distinction is often made between passenger and freight elevators. There are two major types of elevator mechanism: hydraulic, for buildings from two to about six stories; and electric, for buildings from two to any number of stories. Electric elevators are of two major types: geared traction and gearless traction. Geared traction elevators are often used in buildings of medium height and in which the elevator speeds do not exceed 350 feet per minute (ft/min). In taller buildings, elevators with speeds up to 1,000 ft/min or more, gearless traction elevators are usually used. Hydraulic elevator installations are limited by the fact that the hydraulic cylinders that furnish the lifting power must extend into the ground a distance equal to or greater than the height to which the elevator rises. Also their speeds are limited to a maximum of about 150 ft/min.

The major components of an electric elevator system are the hoistways, the vertical spaces in buildings in which elevators operate; the penthouse, a room on the roof of a building or above the top floor the elevator serves, in which various machinery is located, including electric motors that power the elevators, motor generators, and control panels; and the elevator cars. Inside the hoistways are guide rails which cause cars to move vertically without moving sideways or twisting. Elevators are hung from their tops on metal cables, called roping, which are raised or lowered by the electric motors above, with the aid of counterweights that help balance the cars and reduce the effective weight to which the motors are subjected.

A number of limit switches, safety devices, car leveling devices, buffers, and other components ensure safe, smooth, efficient operation of the cars. The whole operation is activated when a passenger pushes a button, and is usually controlled by computers or other automated devices, instead of elevator operators as in the past. Hydraulic elevators are similar to the electric, except that the operating mechanisms are hydraulic rather than electric; there is a need for pits underneath and shafts for the hydraulic plungers, but no penthouses are needed.

Passenger Elevator Design The proper design of elevator systems for buildings is quite complex and

VERTICAL TRANSPORTATION Elevator, Hyatt House (1970), Chicago. Ill. [*Architect: John C. Portman. (Hedrich-Blessing)*]

highly specialized. Some electrical engineers design such systems, while others are handled by elevator specialists. Proper elevator design begins with consideration of the characteristics of a building, such as the number of floors, heights of stories, critical periods of elevator travel, number of people using the building or the building population, and so on.

After determinations of this sort, consideration is given to such time factors as interval, the average time a passenger must wait for an elevator, often taken to be a maximum of 30 to 40 seconds (s), but sometimes longer; and average round-trip time. The average round-trip time includes loading time in the lobby, door closing times at each stop, transfer times at each stop, the times taken for unloading and loading, until the highest stop is reached, and similar times for the return trip to the lobby and the opening of the door at that level.

After the time factors and the number of people to be served have been determined, the number of elevators and their capacities may be calculated. A number of other design decisions remain to be made, including location of the hoistways in the building; lobby arrangements and access, control, and operation of the elevators; and specific floors to be served. In some buildings, particularly relatively tall ones, elevators are zoned, that is, certain cars serve certain levels of the building exclusively. For example, some cars might serve only the second through seventh floors, others the eight through fourteenth, and so on. Another method, sometimes used, is called the skip-floor system. In this system, cars stop at alternate floors, For example, in a medium-rise to high-rise building with two-story individual apartment units, elevators might stop on the living levels but not on the bedroom levels. A recent variation of this system utilizes double-decker elevator cars, each two stories tall.

Groupings of elevators usually range from two cars, side by side, up to eight elevators in two groups of four, across from each other. Though not generally recommended, larger groupings are sometimes used. Other important considerations in elevator design for buildings are locations in floor plans, provision for incoming and outgoing traffic, and traffic peak times. Also special considerations must be made in certain building types, such as commercial, apartment, institutional, multiuse, parking garage, and others.

Escalator Design   The design of escalators starts with basic considerations similar to those for elevator design, including building population, number of floors, heights of stories, times of travel and use, and so on. In addition, it is considered desirable to locate escalators so that they are readily seen by potential passengers. Since escalators are essentially devices that run continuously in one direction, they are usually built in pairs, one going up, the other down. Their directions can be reversed if, for example, traffic flows upward in the morning and down in the evening. When escalators are the primary form of vertical transportation, they must be supplemented by elevators for handicapped people, mothers with baby carriages, and people with other problems.

Escalators are rated by their width at the approximate hip level of people and by their speed, which generally ranges from 90 to 120 ft/min. From these factors, their carrying capacity can be determined. Escalators generally occupy relatively large amounts of space. Therefore they are usually grouped, either side by side or crisscrossing each other. Escalators are usually thought to be superior to moving ramps, which take more space because of their relatively low inclines, and because escalators are considered safer.

Freight Elevator Design   Freight and materials handling elevators, including dumbwaiters, are usually designed in a manner similar to that of passenger elevators, except that the basis is the size and weight of loads to be carried rather than the requirements of people. Also passenger elevator cars are better fin-

VERTICAL TRANSPORTATION Escalator, Valley National Bank (1975), Phoenix, Ariz. [*Architect: Welton Becket Assoc. (Hedrich-Blessing)*]

ished than those used for materials. Materials handling elevators may range in size from cars of about 1 ft² of floor area to about 81 ft² for dumbwaiters and, for freight elevators, up to almost any size and to carrying capacities of more than 50 tons. For freight elevators, attention must be paid to needs for loading and unloading. As is the case with other elevators, specialists are usually required for the design of freight and other materials handling elevators.

History Devices for raising people and objects from one level to another have been used by humans from early ancient times. The earliest and most rudimentary were vines, ropes, and ladders, which were developed into stairways. Later, devices powered by humans or by animals were used. The earliest types of elevators usually employed systems of ropes, winches, pulleys, and windlasses, which lifted and lowered platforms carrying people or objects. These early elevators were very limited in the amount of weight that could be handled and the heights to which people and objects could be lifted. They were also quite dangerous for the ropes often broke and the elevator crashed down. The earliest passenger elevator is thought to have been invented about 253 B.C. by the Greek mathematician and scientist Archimedes (c. 287–212 B.C.), who also invented the pulleys with which the elevator operated.

Very little progress was made in elevator design for almost 2,000 years after Archimedes' invention. During that period, crude devices were used for lifting people and objects, but they had no safety devices to stop a fall when ropes broke. Most were powered by animals, usually horses by the late 18th and early 19th centuries. In the early 19th century, steam replaced horses as the source of power and later in that century hydraulic power was used. The real beginning of the elevators of today was in the second half of the 19th century. It is a matter of conjecture whether the desire to construct buildings of more than four or five stories in height led to the modern elevator or whether the development of safe elevators led to the design of tall buildings.

The first elevator with a safety device to keep it from falling if the ropes broke was demonstrated by its inventor Elisha Graves Otis (1811–61) in The Crystal Palace of the New York Exposition of 1853. Until the Otis invention, elevators were mostly used in factories and warehouses. In 1857 Otis installed the first of his new, safe elevators in the five-story Haughwout Building (1857), still in existence in New York City, designed by J. P. Gaynor. After that, elevators began to be widely used in stores and hotels at first, and later in other building types. For some years, both hydraulic and steam-powered elevators were used, but the hydraulic type was faster and could lift to greater heights. In 1889 the first electric elevator was installed in a New York City building by the company of Otis' sons, which later became the Otis Elevator Company of today. In 1894 the same company installed the first automatic push button elevator. In 1900 the Otis Company installed the first escalator in a building of the Paris Exposition. It was later removed and installed in a Philadelphia department store, where it operated until 1939.

As the heights of office buildings increased in the early 1900s, hydraulic elevators, which could not reach the heights accomplished by electric types, were superseded, except for their use in relatively low-rise buildings. This situation still exists today. Other improvements in electric elevators followed: automated and computerized systems, increased safety factors, smoother operation, and considerably higher speeds. Improvements in escalators have also been made and their principles adapted to moving sidewalks for horizontal movement of people and objects. Such improvements continue to be made even today.

Elevators may be very plain in design, very elegant, or anything in between. Many materials may be used and many unusual applications are possible. One has been the provision, in some very tall buildings, of intermediate lobbies to which express elevators take passengers, who then board locals to reach the next group of floors above the lobbies. Elevators can run up the outside of buildings or up the walls of interior open spaces. Such elevators are often, at least partly, glass enclosed. Elevators need not run straight up, but may be placed on inclines. Other innovations may be expected in the future.

Related Articles AIRPORT; APARTMENT; COMMUNICATION SYSTEM; ELECTRICAL ENGINEERING; OFFICE BUILDING; STAIR.

Further Reading Annett, F.: *Elevators*, 3d ed., McGraw-Hill, New York, 1960; Strakosch, George R.: *Vertical Transportation—Elevators and Escalators*, John Wiley, New York, 1967.

WALL A part of a building, usually vertical or nearly so, that encloses it or subdivides it into rooms. A wall that helps to support the weight of the building is called a bearing wall, while an exterior wall that does not is called a curtain wall. An interior wall, bearing or curtain, is often called a partition. Many of the important aspects of walls are discussed in other articles. For example, for further discussion on the structures of bearing walls, see articles entitled concrete structure; masonry structure; steel structure; wood-frame structure. For openings in walls, see articles entitled door; window. See also the article entitled weather protection.

Types In addition to the walls of buildings, others are used in architecture, including garden walls or similar types for enclosing outdoor areas, and retaining walls for preventing earth from sliding down into areas. A cavity wall is made of masonry with a separation between the masonry units on the exterior side and those on the interior side. A party wall is shared between two buildings or units of a building. A fire wall has a certain degree of fire resistance, often measured in terms of the hours, from one to four, it can be expected to withstand flames, before failing. A parapet wall extends above the roof of a building. Fire walls usually have parapets extending about 3 ft above roofs. A window wall is a curtain wall made entirely of glass with metal frames. A spandrel wall in a multistory building occupies the spaces between strips of windows.

Functions Although they may seem quite simple elements of buildings, walls are actually among the most complex because of the great variety of functions they serve. Exterior walls are expected to protect buildings and their occupants from a great many inconveniences, discomforts, and dangers, including intruders, insects, dirt, odors, animals, rain and other precipitation, winds, hot and cold temperatures, lightning, fires, condensation, floods, noise, sunlight, and earthquakes. In addition, exterior walls are expected to provide privacy inside buildings. On the other hand, exterior walls are also expected to allow access to the interior for occupants, visitors, and other people; light; solar heat; breezes; warm or cool temperatures; and pets. At the same time, exterior walls are required, in many cases, to permit views from the interiors of buildings to the outside. Exterior walls are also expected to allow passage from the interior to the outside for occupants, visitors, and other people; pets; air; heat; odors; light; and sometimes to permit views from the outside in. As if all these diverse, sometimes conflicting, functions were not enough, exterior walls are also very important determinants of the appearance of architecture.

Not only are exterior walls expected to have the flexibility to perform all or most of the above functions but they are also expected to be easy to maintain and repair and to be economically feasible. If bearing walls, they must also support the construction above them in buildings. Interior walls may have all the above functions, in some cases, but in most will not be quite so complex. Interior walls are expected to provide the desired architectural effects.

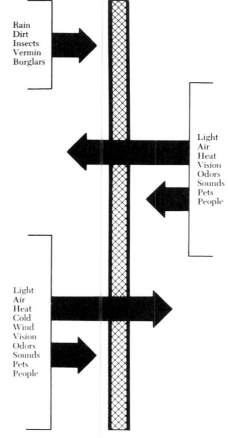

WALL The wall as a filter.

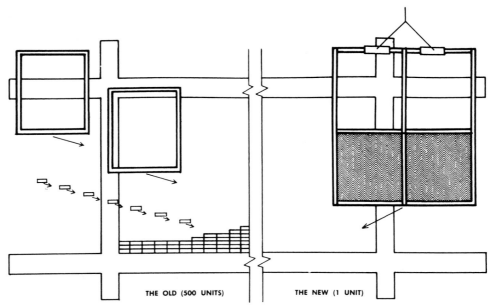

THE OLD (500 UNITS)   THE NEW (1 UNIT)

WALL Former construction method contrasted with a contemporary curtain-wall method.

Exterior Wall Finishes Building exterior walls may be enclosed with any of a great many materials, including most of those used in architecture. Bearing walls of masonry, concrete block or brick, clay brick, structural clay tile, stone, and others may be used. Many of these materials, such as brick or stone, may also be used as veneers for walls of other materials, such as concrete block or structural clay tile. Reinforced concrete may also be used for walls. Masonry walls of certain materials, such as structural tile and concrete block, may be finished with stucco. Others, including those of building brick, are often painted.

Masonry materials, such as stone or brick, may also be used as veneers for light wood-frame walls. Also used for such purposes are many wood materials, such as shingles or shakes; siding of various types; board and batten, consisting of relatively wide boards placed vertically with small strips or battens, sheets of plywood; asbestos-cement shingles or boards; aluminum shingles or sheet; plastic shingles; corrugated or sheet plastic materials; stucco; galvanized iron; and many other materials. Glass is an important material in such walls, for fixed as well as operating windows, and sometimes for doors, and also in the form of glass block.

Exterior Curtain Walls These walls, usually with metal frames, may be obtained with panels of aluminum, porcelain enamel, stainless steel, copper alloys, stone, thin-veneer brick, architectural terra-cotta, now usually called ceramic veneer, clay tiles of various types, glass, plastics, concrete, steel, and other materials. Often prefabricated in relatively large units, such curtain walls may have insulation, windows, exterior and interior finish materials, and other components completely assembled. Delivered to the sites of

buildings, the complete assemblies are erected into walls, with only the installation of weatherproofing and fire-resistant backup walls if required to be added on the job.

If properly designed, such curtain walls have a number of advantages over past types. They efficiently protect from weather and are light, preassembled, and have long useful lives, strength, and flexibility. They also eliminate much handwork on building sites and may be easily erected from inside buildings.

Interior Bearing Walls There walls or partitions may be constructed of and finished with any of the materials used for exterior bearing walls: brick, stone, wood, frame, concrete, and so on. Nonbearing walls may also be constructed of such materials, but may also utilize others, attached to wood or metal studs, including gypsum board, plaster on plaster lath, hardboard, fiberboard, particle board, plywood or solid-wood paneling, and ceramic tile. Some of these materials have integral ceramic, laminated plastic, baked enamel, or other finishes. For materials that do not have integral finishes, paint or other coatings, wallpaper or cloth, various types of fiber cloth, plastics, fabrics, cork, and other finishes may be applied.

Nonbearing Partitions Solid gypsum boards and solid plaster on metal or gypsum lath are also used for nonbearing partitions. Another type of nonbearing partition, called a movable partition, is often used in buildings, such as offices, where frequent floor layout changes may occur. Such partitions are available from manufacturers as complete systems with framing members, wall finish materials, door and frames, and sometimes with integral electric fixtures and conduits for electrical and telephone service lines. Although most types might not be movable in the strictest sense, they do permit considerable flexibility in the arrangement of interior spaces. And many of the components are salvageable for further use after changes have been made.

A special type of nonbearing partition often used in architecture is a folding partition, actually a large folding door that may be closed or opened to convert a large space into smaller ones and vice versa. Another special type, used in open-planned offices, sometimes called office landscaping, is a space divider that acts as a low partition and at the same time as bookshelves, storage, or other office furniture. Partial partitions of other types are also often used, including ones constructed in a manner similar to that of full-height types. Partial partitions of this sort may be any desired height; they may be solid or have glass or plastic from about waist level to the tops.

Hollow types of bearing and nonbearing exterior and interior walls often serve still another purpose, the concealment of piping, ductwork, conduits, vents, and chases or other spaces required for plumbing, heating, air-conditioning, electrical, telephone, and other systems.

Design Both exterior and interior walls come in a wide variety of types, finishes, acoustical ratings, and fire resistances, and with an equally wide choice of accessories, such as windows, doors and other openings, solar shades, provisions for mechanical and electrical systems, and other characteristics. This often bewildering array presents architects and other environmental designers with some of their most intriguing and baffling problems. At the same time, the proper design of walls for both function and appearance is one of the most challenging and gratifying of design experiences. Some authorities have suggested that architects and other designers should consider walls as filters. In this sense, walls may act, flexibly, as barriers, limits, or passages for people, precipitation, temperature, light, views, sounds, odors, and other factors. A perfect wall would function as a barrier, limit, and passage, in various combinations at various times, subject to the will and needs of the occupants.

In addition, walls must be designed with adequate strength to function properly and, in some cases, to provide protection from fires, hurricanes, earthquakes, and other dangers. And all the many functions must be properly performed, while the walls also serve as one of the most important determinants of the appearance or esthetics of buildings. To architects, who customarily design walls except in unusual cases, the challenge is a great one.

History During the most ancient times, humans are thought to have provided their crude shelters with walls of thatch, leaves or brush, or animal skins. By the time of the great ancient cultures around the Mediterranean Sea, beginning about 3000 B.C., quite functional walls had been developed. Walls in Mesopotamia were usually of sun-dried then kiln-dried brick; they were thick and massive to shield the inte-

riors of buildings from the hot sun. In Crete and other places, in and around the Aegean Sea, the lower portions of walls were usually of stone with timber framing above and sun-dried brick between the timbers. Walls were often covered with stucco outside and painted inside.

In Egypt, walls were usually of massive, thick limestone or sandstone or of sun-dried then kiln-dried brick. Walls were usually carved in low relief and often had thin coats of painted stucco. In ancient Greece, walls for the most important buildings were of carefully and skillfully cut and placed stone, with the units usually connected together with cramps and dowels of lead or iron, and set without mortar. In some instances, coarse-grained stone was used and covered with stucco made with marble dust. For houses, stone was often used for the lower parts of wall with stucco-covered brick above.

The Romans used stone and sometimes brick in their walls, but their favorite material was concrete. Often the Romans would cover concrete walls or those of other materials with thin veneers of stone or with plaster or stucco. Roman walls were usually massive, thick bearing walls. Early Christian architecture made use of the Roman methods, employing brick or stone that was often covered with stucco or plaster. Byzantine walls were usually of brick, and highly ornamented with marble or glass mosaics. During the Romanesque period, walls were generally along the lines of those of the Romans, but usually of somewhat heavy, rough construction.

During the Gothic period, walls were generally of cut stone set in lime mortar for cathedrals and other important buildings. For less important buildings timber was used in a system called half-timbered. In the half-timbered system, heavy posts and diagonal members make up the structure of walls. To fill in the spaces between the timbers, bricks or more often wattle and daub, a sort of plaster made of a mixture of clay with straw or sticks, were used. In some Gothic buildings, walls were load bearing, but in others, such as many of those in the cathedrals, the main loads were carried by columns or pilasters with vaults overhead. The walls acted as curtain walls supporting only their own weights. In many cases, particularly in cathedrals and other religious and public buildings, walls were ornamented with carvings or sculpture. Brick walls were rarely used during the Gothic period.

During the Renaissance, walls for important buildings were usually of brick or carefully and accurately cut and placed stone. Those of brick were often covered with facings of stone, but sometimes brick and stone were combined and left exposed. Brick was sometimes used for main walls, with stone quoins at the corners of buildings and around windows and doors. Stucco or plaster was frequently used to cover walls constructed of other materials and was often ornamented. Some of the greatest artists of the Renaissance painted frescoes or other types of murals on the interior walls, mostly of religious buildings.

After the Renaissance, the design of walls of buildings in America as well as elsewhere generally followed the precedents of the past historic styles from which they were derived. Most were bearing walls constructed from the materials that had been used in the past, such as stone, brick, wood, stucco, and so on. In the 19th century, with the beginning of the modern movement in architecture and the use of metal skeleton frames, bearing walls were gradually superseded in many building types by curtain walls of various kinds. The Monadnock Building (1891) in Chicago, designed by Burnham and Root, pushed the use of bearing walls to the limit, 16 stories, requiring 6-ft-thick walls for the first story. This was the last tall brick bearing-wall building. After that, bearing walls were largely outmoded, except for smaller buildings, such as houses.

Although curtain walls had always been used in architecture, the tall skeleton-framed buildings ushered in many new developments in this type of wall. At first, brick and stone were used for curtain walls in much the same way they had been used previously in bearing-wall buildings. Later thin walls, sheathed with various materials, such as copper, bronze, thin-stone slabs, stainless steel, aluminum, or glass, were developed. For walls of this type, building codes required a backup of masonry or other fire-resistant materials, thus effectively reducing the value of the prefabricated, production-line nature of the new walls. Later some of these requirements were relaxed, making it possible to produce curtain walls in relatively large units, complete with windows, insulation, and sometimes interior finishes, deliver them to building sites in large assemblies, and erect them quickly and efficiently on building structural frames.

Today walls for buildings may be constructed of a great variety of materials, in various sizes and shapes, plain or ornamented. Many of the types are available as stock items from manufacturers, while others are designed individually by architects.

Related Articles CLIMATE; DOOR; FIRE PROTECTION; INSULATION, THERMAL; PREFABRICATION; SOUND CONTROL; STRUCTURE; WATERPROOFING; WEATHER PROTECTION; WINDOW; Articles on various materials, components, and systems.

Further Reading Hunt, William Dudley, Jr.: *The Contemporary Curtain Wall—Its Design, Fabrication and Erection,* F. W. Dodge, New York, 1958; Schaal, Rolf: *Curtain Walls—Design Manual,* Reinhold, New York, 1959.

Sources of Additional Information Various industry associations and manufacturers.

WALTER, THOMAS USTICK

WALTER, THOMAS USTICK American architect (1804–87). Thomas Ustick Walter received his architectural training from William Strickland (1787–1854), a great Classic Revival architect, who had in turn received his training from the noted architect Benjamin Henry Latrobe (1764–1820), who had been one of the founders and early leaders of the Classic Revival movement in America. It was only natural then that when Walter became an architect, he would design

buildings in the Classic Revival style, derived mostly from ancient Greece.

Private Practitioner Walter had an unusual career as an architect, divided into three major stages: the first as a private practitioner, the second as a government architect, the third in semiretirement. At twenty-eight, he won a competition for a very important building, Founders Hall, Girard College for Orphans, Philadelphia, winning the commission over some of the greatest architects of the time, all older than he. In this building, completed in 1847, Walter achieved what many think is the climax of the Greek phase of the Classic Revival style. Soon Walter was recognized as a leading American architect and began to receive important commissions for churches, public buildings, office buildings, banks, and houses.

Before the Girard College competition, Walter had received only one important commission, the Moyamensing Prison (1832), Philadelphia, a building that he designed, oddly enough, in Gothic Revival style. Later when he added a Debtors' Wing (1835) to the prison, he utilized an Egyptian style, thought by architects of the time to be appropriate for places where people would be incarcerated. Among Walter's designs for houses, the most notable was that for the Greek Revival Andalusia (1836), near Philadelphia, the home of the banker Nicholas Biddle (1786–1844). Another important Greek Revival building, still in existence, is Hibernian Hall (1835), Charleston, S.C.

Government Architect In 1850 Walter's professional life entered the second stage. In that year he won the competition for a new dome to replace that of the U.S. Capitol (see illustration in color section), in Washington, D.C. Appointed architect of the Capitol the following year, Walter took over the construction of the dome, which is now a dominant feature of the Washington scene. Of cast-iron construction, the dome established Walter as a leader among architects of the time and as a talented engineer as well. During his tenure as architect of the Capitol, Walter confined his architectural practice to work on the Capitol and on other Washington government buildings. In addition to the great dome, completed in 1863, Walter also extended the wings, completing that of the House of Representatives in 1857 and the Senate, in 1859.

While in Washington, Walter did alterations, extensions, and remodeling of a number of other buildings, including the Treasury Building; the Old Patent Office, now the National Portrait Gallery; and the Old Post Office, now a multiuse building with stores and shops.

Semiretirement In 1865 Walter's career entered the third and last stage. Having resigned from his government office because of ill health, Walter practiced architecture only sporadically for the more than 20 years before his death. He spent the last 10 of those years as president of the American Institute of Architects, of which he had been a cofounder in 1857.

Life Thomas Ustick Walter was born in Philadelphia on September 4, 1804, the son of a brick mason

WALTER, THOMAS U. Andalusia (1836), near Philadelphia, Pa. *(Wayne Andrews)*

WALTER, THOMAS U. Founders Hall (1847), Girard College, Philadelphia, Pa. *(Wayne Andrews)*

and builder. Having had little formal schooling, he entered the office of William Strickland in 1819, when he was fifteen, but left after a short time to study mathematics, science, and construction on his own. In 1822 he went back into Strickland's office as an apprentice and remained there for several years.

In 1830 Walter started his own practice and the following year obtained his first important commission, Moyamensing Prison. In 1832 Walter won a competition for an even more important building, Founders Hall at Girard College. The other architects competing were a distinguished group: Strickland, his former employer, who placed second; Isaiah Rogers (1780–1869) of Boston, who placed third; Ithiel Town (1784–1844) and Alexander Jackson Davis (1803–92) of New York City; and John Haviland (1792–1852) of Philadelphia. This was quite a conquest for a young, beginning architect and brought Walter considerable recognition.

After winning the competition, Walter received commissions for other buildings in Philadelphia and elsewhere. In 1836 he was one of the founders of the American Institution of Architects, in New York City, and later, after this organization had failed, helped found the American Institute of Architects, also in that city, in 1857, along with Davis who had been an original member of the earlier group, Richard Upjohn (1802–78), and 11 other architects. Upjohn became the first president of the AIA, serving 18 years until 1877, when Walter became the second president and served until his death 10 years later.

In 1850 Walter won the competition for the design of a new dome for the U.S. Capitol, Washington, to replace that originally designed by William Thornton (1759–1826) and completed by Charles Bulfinch (1763–1844).

In 1851 he was appointed architect of the Capitol by President Millard Fillmore (1800–74) and retained that position for 15 years until 1865. He replaced Robert Mills (1781–1855), who had served in the position since 1836. It is ironical that in 1838, when Walter was thirty-four, he had written a report recommending that the unfinished U.S. Treasury Building (1842) of Mills be demolished. This did not happen but in a further irony, Walter designed additions to the Treasury Building that were completed in 1869. During the 15 years, he worked not only on the Capitol but on a number of other government buildings. After resigning his Washington position because of ill health, Walter returned to Philadelphia. Although he was associated for a time with John McArthur, Jr. (1823–90), the designer of the Philadelphia City Hall (1890), Walter never returned to full-time practice.

Walter married Mary Anne Hancocks and they had 11 children, including a son, Thomas Ustick Walter, Jr., who became an architect. He in turn had a son, Thomas Ustick Walter III (1864–1931), who also became an architect. Walter's wife died in the birth of her eleventh child and, later, he married Amanda Gardiner, by whom he had two children.

Walter was honored in his later years for his work,

receiving several honorary degrees, including a Ph.D. from Harvard University in 1867. When he died on October 30, 1887, at age eighty-three, he had been out of his position as architect of the Capitol for some 22 years, yet the government still owed him $25,000 for his work. The profession he had served so well, respresented by the AIA, petitioned Congress, 10 years later, to pay his heirs the money he was owed. Congress granted the heirs not the full amount but $14,000.

Related Articles CAPITAL, UNITED STATES; CLASSIC REVIVAL ARCHITECTURE; MILLS, ROBERT; STRICKLAND, WILLIAM.

WAREHOUSE A building, or a room in a building, in which objects are stored. In addition, warehouses must have provisions for receiving and shipping. Warehouses are important elements of factories for handling both raw materials and finished products. They are also important in many other kinds of businesses, such as retailing and wholesaling products. A bonded warehouse is one in which goods may be stored without paying taxes or duty until the goods are withdrawn. Similarly, a warehouse in a free zone or free port is one in which goods may be stored without payment of customs duty until shipped.

Design Warehouses are utilitarian and thus are not often highly regarded as an architectural building type. However, these buildings require a considerable amount of design skill to make them economical and efficient. Some of the major considerations are open floors as free of columns and other obstructions as possible; proper heights, widths, and lengths for efficient storage and handling; strong structures to withstand heavy loads on floors; and flexibility of layout to facilitate changes and special storage problems.

Mechanical Handling Devices Perhaps the most important consideration in the design of warehouses today is the provision of mechanical handling devices appropriate to the products to be handled. Most warehouse handling is performed with the aid of such devices, which include forklift trucks, tractor trailers, conveyors, and overhead systems. Forklift trucks have prongs that may be inserted under pallets, portable platforms on which products are stored, lifting, and stacking, and removing the pallets as required. Forklifts may also place pallets on tractor trailers for long horizontal movements. Conveyors of many kinds are used, including belts, chains, chutes, and elevators. Overhead systems include monorails and various kinds of cranes. Recently, there has been a trend toward automation in warehouses, with mechanical handling devices activated by computers or other electronic devices.

Warehouses may be single story or multistory. The decision about which type to construct is based mainly on the articles to be stored, the size of the site available, and which type will be most economical.

History Since prehistoric times, some storage has

been used, at first in caves and later in simple structures. With the expansion of trading activities during the Middle Ages, warehousing, as now known, started. Early warehouses were built along waterways which were the major means of transportation. Later they were built along roads and railroads and then near airports.

American Development   The earliest warehouses in colonial America were built beside the docks in Atlantic seaboard towns to handle the storage of goods arriving from Europe and goods to be shipped there. Gradually, as river transportation developed and roads and canals were built, warehouses also appeared along these trade routes. And the growth of cities, with their increasing mercantile activities, brought warehouses into urban areas, a trend that has been somewhat reversed in later years.

Related Article   FACTORY.

WATERPROOFING   A material or device used to prevent water from entering walls or other surfaces of buildings or to direct water off, away from, or out of buildings. Water infiltration into buildings or other components and dampness are major causes of deterioration.

The term *waterproofing* is often used to designate only those membranes, compounds, or coatings used to keep water from entering building walls or other elements. However, materials of this sort answer only some problems. A great variety of other materials and devices are used in architecture to prevent water infiltration, condensation, and dampness or to control water when it enters, including flashing, weatherstripping, vapor barriers, and drains. And, of course, roofs, walls, windows, doors, and other components have major functions in the exclusion of water from buildings. Vapor barriers, intended to prevent the passage of water existing as vapor in air, are closely related to insulation. See titles listed at the end of this article.

One of the best ways to prevent water infiltration into buildings is proper design, detailing, and construction of various building elements. For example, dense brick of the proper type, laid in the proper manner, with water-shedding joints and correct mortars properly applied, will be quite resistant to water infiltration. On the other hand, less dense brick, if laid improperly and subject to cracking, can be expected to develop leaks.

Water Infiltration   Water may be forced into buildings by the force of gravity as rain falling on a roof or rainwater running or dripping from a building; by pressure differentials between the outside and inside, caused by winds or atmospheric pressure; by pressure of water underground, called its hydrostatic head; by condensation that may occur when the relative humidity is high; and by other conditions. Major problems with water infiltration, other than condensation, often occur in foundation walls of buildings, in basements or other places below the surface of the

ground, or below grade. They also occur at places where surfaces, elements, or materials intersect, such as door or window openings, or where chimneys or other elements go through roofs. Water-infiltration problems often occur in materials that have high permeability, such as many types of masonry materials. Hurricanes and severe storms intensify water-infiltration problems.

Foundation Walls   For foundations of buildings and basement or other walls below grade, either bituminous membranes or bituminous coatings are applied, hot or cold. Usually applied on the exterior, they must have no breaks and must be properly bonded to or overlapped with similar waterproofing materials under concrete slabs on or below grade. Backfill of gravel should be placed against the waterproofed wall or foundation, and foundation drains, usually of clay tile or concrete pipe, with open joints or perforations, are often used to drain groundwater away from the building. Sometimes such waterproofing is applied inside walls below grade, but the practice is not recommended.

Permeable Materials   The soil at finish levels outside should be sloped away from buildings. In addition to the waterproofing methods mentioned, the exteriors of masonry walls are sometimes treated with coatings of portland cement mortar. For waterproofing interior walls, portland-cement-based paints and other coatings are often used. A number of colorless coatings for the exterior of masonry walls above grade are available, including silicone resins and others. Stucco may also be used, as may various kinds of paints and other coatings, some organic in nature, some made with portland cement. To prevent moisture from entering buildings through mortar joints, the joints may be repointed by cutting out and replacing mortar to a depth of about ⅝ inch.

Buildings with concrete structures are generally waterproofed by methods similar to those used for masonry structures. Wood-frame buildings are waterproofed by treating the exterior materials properly with paint, stains, and so on and often by installation of membrane, building paper, or felt over the sheathing, inside the exterior facing. Steel-framed buildings ordinarily have curtain walls made of materials that are impervious to water infiltration, but joints must be carefully detailed and constructed.

Roofing   Roofing for buildings, of course, is mainly a waterproof material. Water infiltration is effectively prevented by well-designed and constructed roofs, with proper slopes or pitches, for the various types. In addition, proper flashing must be used at places where roof planes intersect and where chimneys, vent pipes, dormers, or other elements penetrate the roofs, at roof edges, and where walls penetrate or extend above roofs as in parapet walls.

Flashing   In general, flashing includes devices, made of metals or other materials, that are impervious to water, shaped and placed in such a way as to direct water away from the building elements they protect.

Flashing may be made from many materials, but the most commonly used include copper and aluminum, membranes, and flashing made of combinations of metal and membrane. Galvanized iron, stainless steel, Monel metal, lead, and other metals are sometimes used for flashing. The materials to be used in a given case depend on the function of the flashing, the life span expected, and the possibility that the flashing may cause staining of other materials.

Metal Problems Staining may also occur when copper is adjacent to white stone or other materials, or deterioration may occur when water from one metal passes over another causing the second to deteriorate through a process called electrolysis or galvanic action. In general, flashing should cover the object to be protected or project into it as in the side of a masonry chimney, and should turn down in such a way as to direct the water in the proper direction. In cases where two pieces of flashing are used together, the topmost one is turned down over that below it.

For flat roofs, flashing at the edges or eaves is used in conjunction with metal devices called gravel stops, made in several shapes, often of aluminum. Many other conditions that must be corrected with flashing exist in buildings. For example, flashing is often required at various places in walls, such as their bases and over and underneath doors and windows. Many other conditions require flashing in buildings today.

Weatherstripping Weatherstripping is used around doors and windows to prevent infiltration of water and wind and to help prevent heat losses in winter and heat gains in summer. Weatherstripping is often included with preassembled windows and doors, but may also be applied during the construction of buildings. Weatherstripping is often made of metals, such as bronze, stainless steel, or aluminum, or of plastics, rubber, or neoprene. Two principles are used for various types of weatherstripping: pairs of interlocking units, for example, a type in which one part is attached to a door and interlocks with another part when the door is closed; and types that seal by compression, as in spring metal, plastic, rubber, or neoprene devices that are attached either to a door or its frame and compressed when the door is shut. Special weatherstripping items may be obtained for all types of doors, including sliding units, and for all types of windows. Special sills or thresholds, complete with weatherstripping, are also available.

Other Devices Other methods and devices are often used for controlling water infiltration, including weep holes at the bases of masonry hollow unit walls, cavity walls, and masonry veneers. Good ventilation of certain building spaces and elements can also help control water infiltration. Various types of drains are used on roofs, in basements, and in other places to collect water and drain it away. Roof drains may be built into the surface of flat roofs. The type most generally used for roof drainage consists of gutters placed at the eaves or inserted into the roofs near the eaves. Wood gutters (redwood or fir) may be used, but more accepted are metal gutters made of copper, aluminum, or other metal.

Gutters Gutters come in standard stock sizes and in semicircular, rectangular, and other shapes. Gutters are installed almost horizontally, with a slight pitch toward the downspouts or leaders that conduct the water downward to the ground or to a drainage system. Screens of metal mesh are sometimes placed over gutters to prevent clogging from leaves and other debris; in other cases, perforated metal devices or wire baskets are placed over the top of leaders for this purpose. If the leaders discharge water onto the ground instead of into drainage systems, splash blocks, usually made of concrete with dish-shaped depressions, are placed beneath the bottoms of the leaders to prevent water from splashing on buildings.

Complete waterproofing of buildings requires attention both to many problems and solutions and to proper design, detailing, and construction.

Related Articles BRICK; CONCRETE; CONCRETE STRUCTURE; DOOR; FLOOR; FOUNDATION; INSULATION, THERMAL; MASONRY STRUCTURE; PAINT; ROOF; ROOFING; STONE; WALL; WINDOW.

Further Reading Gratwick, R. T.: *Dampness in Buildings*, 2d ed., John Wiley, New York, 1974.

WEATHER PROTECTION

The provisions employed protect buildings and the occupants from discomfort, damage, injury, or death from the effects of weather, the natural atmospheric phenomena of temperature, wind, sun, humidity, and precipitation in the form of rain, sleet, snow, and hail. Weather, or meteorology, is the science concerned with such phenomena over relatively short periods of time, while climatology is the science concerned with the same phenomena over periods of many years.

Both climate and weather are important considerations in architecture. One set of concerns deals with the usual or relatively normal effects of climate and weather, including protection of buildings and their occupants from heat, cold, precipitation, and humidity, and controlling the admission or exclusion of the sun into buildings. Much of the work of architects and other design professionals is devoted to such considerations and to ways in which weather phenomena may be excluded, controlled, or modified to provide general protection for buildings and protection and comfort for the occupants. For further discussion on considerations of this sort, see titles listed at the end of this article.

Catastrophes Another important concern of architecture is the disastrous effects that weather may have on buildings and the occupants. Along with earthquakes and fires, weather causes the most damaging catastrophes for both buildings and their occupants. Catastrophic weather events include lightning strikes and heavy snow on buildings. (See articles earthquake protection; fire protection; roof; structure.)

Other than the above weather events, the most dangerous are high winds and flooding; flooding may be caused by winds, heavy precipitation, earthquakes, and volcanic eruptions. Catastrophic events are often interrelated in other ways. For example, earthquakes frequently cause fires when gas lines are broken. Similar things may happen during or after other catastrophes. Heavy snows or rains may cause flooding and mud slides which engulf or severely damage buildings.

Winds The major damage to buildings and injuries or deaths of people caused by strong winds result from the tremendous forces of the winds themselves and wind-driven water. It is generally considered impractical or economically infeasible to protect all buildings against all possible catastrophes. However, buildings and their occupants can be protected in high-risk areas by proper measures against the hazards of high winds and flooding.

High winds occur in storms, disturbances of the atmosphere in which differences primarily in temperature and atmospheric pressure cause masses of air to move rapidly in a counterclockwise direction in the Northern Hemisphere, clockwise in the Southern Hemisphere. This circular motion of air is usually called cyclonic and the effects it produces, cyclones. All cyclonic winds revolve around centers of relatively low pressure and the winds blow inward toward the low. Anticyclonic winds blow outward from centers of high pressure. For the most part, such conditions produce only ordinary weather, not storms. When a storm develops, its winds gain in velocity and pick up moisture that eventually may be deposited in the form of precipitation. The high winds of storms over oceans or other sizable bodies of water build tremendous waves and drive them to create unusually large tides, especially when a storm occurs at the same time as normal high tides.

Winds are usually measured on the Beaufort scale, which has been in use since 1805. Numbers on the Beaufort scale range from 0, when air is completely calm, to 17, the strongest possible wind. Another method, employed particularly in boating and other marine activities, classifies dangerous winds and their accompanying sea conditions as warnings, including small-craft warnings when winds are near but do not exceed about 31 miles per hour (mph), gale warnings 32 to 54 mph, whole gale warnings 55 to 73 mph, and hurricane warnings above 73 mph (12–17 on the Beaufort scale). Gale winds may cause damage to buildings and injury to people, and whole gale winds even more extensive damage to buildings and trees and injury or death to people. The major damage to buildings and injuries and loss of life to people are caused by winds of hurricane force. Such winds are found in three major types of storm: hurricanes, cyclones, and tornadoes.

Hurricanes A hurricane may be defined as a large, violent storm, with winds of 74 mph or more, sometimes with gusts to more than 200 mph, which revolves counterclockwise in the Northern Hemisphere. Hurricanes, which are intense tropical cyclones, are formed over the ocean in tropical regions and generally move northward, at first somewhat toward the northwest, then in a northerly direction, and later somewhat toward the northeast. Hurricanes usually begin as tropical disturbances and progress to tropical storms, with winds exceeding 40 mph.

In the center of a hurricane is a region of almost complete calm, some 20 miles (mi) in diameter, around which the high winds spread out as far as several hundred miles. Hurricanes usually move relatively slowly, some 10 to 30 mph, but they are erratic and hard to predict both in velocity and direction of movement. Occurring mainly between June and November, they are most frequent in September. When hurricanes travel over water, they often intensify and accelerate. Over land, friction slows them down and dissipates their energy, raising the pressure and slowing the winds. However, heavy rains may continue for some time. It was formerly believed that only buildings and people on the coasts of the Gulf of Mexico and the Southern Atlantic states were dangerously exposed to hurricanes, but many hurricanes have taken their greatest toll in the Eastern and Middle Atlantic states.

Cyclones Another type of cyclone, called extratropical, revolves counterclockwise around a center in the Northern Hemisphere and may develop winds that can reach hurricane force. Such cyclones in the United States usually originate over the Western states, from which they move generally from the Southwest toward the Northeast. A cyclone of this type may be less than 100 mi in diameter or it may be large enough to cover the entire United States. Large cyclones usually move only 100 or so mi per day, but smaller ones may move more rapidly. While cyclones may cause damage, injury, and death in the same manner as hurricanes, most pass over the country without causing problems of this kind.

Tornadoes An extremely intense storm, like a small cyclone, usually only a few hundred yards to a few miles across, is called a tornado or sometimes a twister. Tornadoes characteristically have tall, narrow, funnel-shaped clouds, move relatively fast, from 25 to 40 mph, and have very short lives, of only about half an hour or so. During their short life span, they are, for their size, the most destructive of all storms, with winds up to several hundred miles per hour.

Tornadoes occur in all parts of the world. In the United States, they occur most frequently in the Midwestern states, but there have been numerous occurrences in many other places, including the states of the Deep South. Although properly designed and constructed buildings may withstand the effects of tornadoes, light-framed houses and other less sturdy types may not. In any case, in areas where tornadoes occur regularly and frequently, concrete storm cellars or other refuges are often provided for protection of people.

Tornadoes at sea are called waterspouts. A typhoon

is what a hurricane is called if it originates over the Pacific Ocean. Typhoons usually occur from July to October, form in the North Pacific Ocean, and travel northwest and then northeast, bringing death and destruction mainly to the islands of the Pacific and Eastern countries, such as China, Japan, and India.

Blizzards A blizzard is an intense winter storm with heavy snowfalls, high winds, and usually quite low temperatures. Blizzards ordinarily occur when very cold Arctic air meets warmer air from the South, forming low-pressure areas called cold fronts along the line where the masses of air meet. In the United States, blizzards are most common in the Midwestern states but may occur in states to the south and east of that area. The snow and low temperatures, made worse by the wind-chill factor, cause blizzards to be extremely dangerous and disruptive to human activities. The greatest dangers to buildings and their occupants, other than failure of heating systems, is from the heavy snow loads that may be deposited on roofs and from high winds. For a discussion of snow loads, see the article entitled structure.

Protection for People People may be protected from severe storms by evacuation before a storm strikes, in shelters, by locations of buildings on less hazardous sites, and by proper building design to resist the effects of wind, water, and other hazards. Another method is the modification or prevention of storms, an activity that, though still in its infancy, has been the subject of considerable research and some practical applications. Recently, the National Weather Service, in cooperation with weather services of other nations, has greatly improved its prediction of storms. Through its hurricane watches and warnings, tornado watches and warnings, and marine advisories and warnings, the Weather Service has made it possible for people to anticipate violent storm activities and to evacuate or take shelter. A watch alerts people to the possibilities of storm activities and a warning indicates that people should evacuate or take shelter. Through the use of radar, airplane surveillance, weather satellites, and other techniques, the loss of lives has been dramatically reduced

Building Protection Protection of buildings from severe storms is mainly a matter of proper location away from hazardous areas and proper structural and architectural design. Very little can be done about the predilection of people to build in high-risk hurricane areas, such as along the beaches of the Gulf of Mexico and Atlantic coasts, the tornado areas of the Midwest, and high-risk areas elsewhere. However, proper structural design of buildings and their location above storm tide levels may prevent major damage during intense storms. In some cases, as in the disastrous mud slides in southern California caused by torrential rains, some experts believe that nothing can prevent major damage short of location of buildings in safer areas.

Wind Damage The structural and architectural design of buildings to resist intense activities of wind and water are governed by requirements in various building and other codes. However, some experts think that these requirements do not go far enough. The criteria to be used in the design of any building in a hazardous area should be based on the records from that area, from which probabilities of similar occurrences can be derived. In any wind storm, the least consequential dangers are the loss of TV antennas, roofing, and the like, followed in gravity by loss of glass and windows or walls, proceeding to structural damage, and finally to building collapse. The winds tend to make buildings overturn, slide from their foundations, or for whole buildings or part of them to be lifted upward. Also winds may hurl debris against buildings, damaging them. In addition, in some cases, particularly in tornadoes, relatively high air pressures within buildings as compared to extremely low pressures outside can cause buildings literally to explode.

Wind Resistance In general, the major factors affecting the design of buildings for wind resistance are the forces of winds that may be encountered, including those in high-velocity gusts, and building shapes, dimensions, and height-width ratios. All these must be carefully considered. For example, a tall narrow building must withstand greater forces than a short wide one. In order to overcome the effects of strong winds, a building structure must be properly designed, particularly in matters that might cause it to be deformed or deflect, in proper anchoring of the building and its elements to prevent uplift or overturning, and in the proper design of enclosure elements, such as roofs, walls, and windows, particularly the glass in windows, to withstand the great forces to which they will be subjected.

Storm Damage The effect of water in severe storms, sometimes called storm surge, can cause coastal areas to be inundated with tides as much as 24 ft or more above normal. When the storm-driven tides coincide with normal high tides, they can reach even greater heights. Storm surges tend to cause buildings to overturn or slide and can also cause erosion or scouring under foundations. Other damage, injury, and loss of life can occur in the inundation by the flood waters or can be caused by the extremely strong forces or currents and wave action and by debris hurled against buildings by the force of the water.

Storm Resistance Proper use of codes and standards will aid in the design of storm-resistant structures. Also the use of proper materials and structures is important. For example, reinforced concrete structures, if properly designed, are thought to be able to resist even the most destructive of storms: hurricanes and tornadoes. Specialized design for storm resistance, by experts, is certainly appropriate in many cases. Adequate insurance against the perils of storms to buildings should be carried. Policies today as well as in the past usually insure against most hazards, except the effects of flooding. Until somewhat recently, flood insurance was not available and those who incurred damage by water found themselves, often to their dismay, not covered for risks of this sort. In other cases, flood insurance, though available, was not carried because of its extremely high cost. Today in some areas of the country, flood insurance, at reasonable rates made possible by federal government sponsorship, is available.

History The hazards of violent weather have always been a factor in human life. Almost every year, a number of people are injured or killed and vast amounts of property damage occur. The first recorded hurricane spawned in America occurred on February 12, 1493, and was noted by Christopher Columbus (1451–1506) on the return trip of his first voyage to America. Since that time, almost 1,000 have occurred, taking a vast toll in human life and injury and in property damage. Since the beginning of the 20th century, more than 100 hurricanes have struck the Gulf and Atlantic coasts from Texas to North Carolina and others have hit the Middle Atlantic and Northeastern states. The worst in U.S. history, in terms of lives lost (6,000), occurred in Galveston, Tex., on September 8, 1900. Loss of lives has recently gone down, primarily due to earlier warnings, but loss of property has been in the billions of dollars.

A great number of tornadoes are reported in the United States each year and they too take a heavy toll in lives, injuries, and property damage. During the second and third quarters of the 20th century, the number of tornadoes reported each year in the United States has varied from less than 50 to a high of more than 1,000, in 1973, and deaths each year, from about 25 to more than 900. The average number of tornadoes per year for the period is about 400 and the average number of deaths, about 175.

Other storms, including blizzards, have also caused many injuries, taken many lives, and damaged a great deal of property. Such extreme hazards require the utmost attention of architects and other design professionals.

Related Articles BUILDING CODES AND STANARDS; CLIMATE; CONSTRUCTION MATERIALS; DESIGN, ARCHITECTURAL; FIRE PROTECTION; HEATING, VENTILATING, AND AIR CONDITIONING; INSULATION, THERMAL; LIGHTNING PROTECTION; STRUCTURE; WATERPROOFING.

Further Reading Flora, Snowden Dwight: *Tornadoes of the United States,* University of Oklahoma Press, Norman, 1953; Houghton, Edward Lewis: *Wind Forces on Buildings and Structures—An Introduction,* John Wiley, New York, 1976; Macdonald, Angus J.: *Wind Loading on Buildings,* John Wiley, New York, 1975; Tannehill, Ivan Ray: *Hurricanes, Their Nature and History, Particularly Those of the West Indies and the Southern Coasts of the United States,* 9th ed., Princeton University Press, Princeton, 1956.

Source of Additional Information National Weather Service, National Oceanic and Atmospheric Administration, U.S. Department of Commerce, 6010 Executive Blvd., Rockville, Md. 20852.

WINDOW An assembly, usually including a frame, glass, and hardware set into an opening in an exterior wall of a building for control of the entry of light, air, and solar heat into the interior. Windows have been used in architecture since its beginning, but in the earliest times were not considered important features; later they became important for both functional and ornamental reasons. Today windows are very important functionally and in many cases are major determinants of the architectural design of buildings, both in their exteriors and interiors.

Types Windows may be classified by the ways in which they operate, by the materials used, and in other ways. The major types used today include projected; fixed; double-hung, which have two operating units, called sash, which slide vertically inside or outside each other; casements, with hinges at the sides, and often used in pairs, swinging horizontally out and sometimes in; horizontal sliding; and pivoted, either at the center top and bottom, called vertical pivoted, or at the center of the sides, called horizontal pivoted. There are also single-hung windows, in which only one sash moves.

Projected windows come in various types. Most swing out from the tops, though some are hinged at the bottom and others may swing in. They range from a single sash hinged at the bottom, called a hopper window, or at the top, through awning windows which have several sash that swing out from the top, and jalousie windows which are like the awning type but in which the sash are smaller and are glass without complete frames. Fixed windows may be used in conjunction with other types or individually; when they are relatively large, they are often called view or picture windows. Some windows combine, in single assemblies, two or more of the above types. For example, an intermediate window may have a fixed glass portion at the top, an outward projecting section in the middle, and an inward projecting hopper at the bottom. Two or more individual window units of various kinds may also be combined, for example, a view window with operating windows at either side.

Window Unit A window unit is a complete assembly in a frame, together with weatherstripping and hardware, and often with insect screens and storm sash, which may be closed to lessen the effects of bad

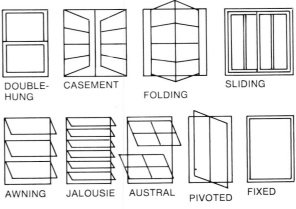

DOUBLE-HUNG   CASEMENT   FOLDING   SLIDING

AWNING   JALOUSIE   AUSTRAL   PIVOTED   FIXED

WINDOW Typical contemporary types.

weather. Storm sash and insect screens may also be applied separately. A sash is a single window assembly, fixed or operating, that ordinarily fits into a window frame, consisting of jambs at the sides and head, and usually a sill at the bottom with a stool on the interior side, and often with casings for trim around the frame. Trim on the interior side at the bottom beneath the stool is called an apron. The vertical side pieces of a sash are called stiles and the horizontal top and bottom ones, rails. Narrow horizontal or vertical bars, called muntins, subdivide sash into what are often called lights. A mullion is a vertical element separating two window assemblies.

Construction Materials The major materials used for window construction are wood, including pine, fir, cypress, cedar, and redwood; aluminum; steel; stainless steel; and bronze. Wood, aluminum, and steel windows are used mostly in houses, while steel is used for factores and other utilitarian buildings. Windows of any available material may be used in buildings of other types, but stainless steel or bronze is often used for the most important ones.

Classification Windows are sometimes classified by such terms as basement or utility, residential, commercial, or monumental. Basement or utility windows are simple, economical types, usually projected from the top or hoppers, often used in garages, service stations, or other utilitarian buildings. Residential windows may be any type described above, but are usually of somewhat lighter weight and sometimes less rugged construction than commercial or monumental types. Commercial, sometimes called industrial, windows are often used in commercial and industrial applications where strong, economical types are most appropriate. Monumental windows are usually heavy, of rugged construction, and often of stainless steel or bronze, for use in monumental, important buildings. A clerestory window is placed high in a wall system, often in a wall that rises above an adjacent roof.

Special-Purpose Types Many types of windows are available for special purposes, including security, detention, and psychiatric. Security windows are heavy, strong, usually of steel, and built to make unlawful entry difficult. These windows usually have inward projecting sash and continuous muntins, horizontally and vertically, welded together for strength and extending over the entire window unit, including the operating sash. Detention windows are heavy and strong, available for various degrees of restraint needed to prevent escape of prisoners from jails. Psychiatric windows are like detention types, but designed to restrain mental patients but without the forbidding heavy appearance of regular detention windows.

Many other special types of windows are available, including sound isolation types and complete storefront systems with both windows and doors, for use in stores and other commercial establishments. Another type of special system is a curtain wall, an assembly of various wall materials complete with windows, wall finishes, insulation, and in some cases interior finishes. Many curtain walls have strips of windows with other materials over and under them, called spandrel covers. In other cases, windows are used to form an entire wall, which is often called a window wall. Windows in both types of walls may be fixed or operable, or in various combinations.

Glazing Glazing for windows is usually accomplished with window glass for small panes and polished plate glass in larger ones. Sometimes double glazing is used for retarding heat losses from buildings in winter and heat gains in summer. Double glazing may be accomplished by the proper setting of two panes of glass in a sash, but the preferred method is the use of factory-produced double-glazing units. Another method of accomplishing such purposes is the use of storm sash which can be obtained with many types of window units, or installed separately, and which can be raised or lowered at will or taken off and stored when not needed. Insect screens are obtainable in similar ways.

Sometimes tempered glass, made by a heating and cooling process to give it strength, or laminated glass, with two or more layers separated by and adhered to plastic materials, are used where greater safety against breakage is required. Glazing of all kinds is usually set into window sash with glazing mastics or compounds or with special plastic or neoprene gaskets. In wood windows, panes are often held in by small metal devices, called glazier's, or push, points over which the glazing compound is placed. In metal windows, glass is often held in by metal clips or beads and waterproofed with glazing compound or gaskets.

Standard Units Window units are available in a great variety of standard sizes and others may be fabricated if required. Many come complete with glazing and weatherstripping in place and standard operating devices, though some are available unglazed or weatherstripped. It is also possible to obtain special operators, including both mechanical and electrical types. Many sizes of panes are available for windows but, to the dismay of many architects, wood sash today often have plastic fake muntins that snap in over large panes to simulate real muntins in windows with small panes.

Finishes The finishes available in windows vary between materials. Although wood windows may have natural finishes, thay are most often painted, and today some types have the wood parts covered with plastic and do not need further finishing. Regular wood windows are obtainable, finished or unfinished. Steel windows are usually galvanized or otherwise treated at the factory and then painted. Aluminum windows have no special finish other than a clear coating of plastic or other material applied at the factory to protect them during shipping and erection. Stainless steel windows need no special applied finishes, but it is possible to obtain them with various surface textures. Bronze windows need no finishes; in fact, one of the qualities most admired in this material, other than its long life, is the patina it acquires as it weathers.

Functions The size, number, and placement of windows in buildings have a considerable effect on the appearance of buildings, when viewed from the inside as well as from the outside. The proper use of windows also has a great deal to do with the comfort and well-being of building occupants, with the benefits to be derived from solar energy and winds, and with conservation of other types of energy. Therefore windows are a very important part of architecture today and must be carefully designed, detailed, and constructed, not only as individual units but as major elements of entire walls. In addition, the design of related elements, such as solar screens, sunshades, and others, must be carefully integrated with the windows and walls. Finally, proper provisions must be made for cleaning, maintenance, and repairs, operations often provided in many buildings today by mechanized scaffolds which may be lowered from the roofs.

History The earliest primitive people who constructed buildings are thought to have covered windows with crude flaps of animal skins or brush. By the time of the Mesopotamians and Egyptians, windows had become highly developed, but were rarely used because doorways usually admitted sufficient light. Windows were usually rectangular and had lintels of stone or wood over them. For protection, stone or carved wood grilles were often placed over the openings. Later crude shutters or lattices were used. The Greeks used windows sparingly, almost not at all in temples. Windows were rectangular and simply designed, but were sometimes narrowed at the tops. Some ornamentation was used around openings.

Most Roman windows had semicurcular arches at their heads, though some were completely rectangular in shape. The Romans often used mullions in window openings to separate windows. In many of the ancient civilizations, attempts were made to develop window coverings that would keep out heat, cold, intruders, and so on, yet admit light. Such materials include thin sheets of stone, shell, horn, mica, oiled paper, pierced stone, and cloth. Although glass had been invented about 2500 B.C., it was not used in windows until the time of the Romans, who used it occasionally and in small panes.

In Early Christian architecture, windows were usually small and had either flat or semicircular heads; their openings were often filled in with ornamented and pierced sheets of stone or plaster. High windows, or clerestories, were also used at this time. Byzantine windows usually had arches at their heads and often were filled in with thin sheets of stone or in some cases glass. Romanesque windows usually had semicircular arched heads and were surrounded by series of ornamental moldings. Circular types called wheel windows and later, when stained glass came into use, rose windows, were also used. Glass had come to be widely used, particularly in important buildings, by the time of Romanesque architecture.

In Gothic architecture, windows were developed to a high degree of excellence. Gothic windows generally had pointed arches at their heads and their surrounds were often ornamented. Wheel and rose windows were widely used, particularly in France, and other types were developed, including lunettes, crescent or other shapes, usually placed over doorways; and lancet windows, tall narrow types, with pointed arches above, most often found in English Gothic buildings. Glass had come into common use in cathedrals and other religious buildings by the beginning of Gothic architecture and in other important buildings by the 14th century.

The crowning glory of Gothic windows is stained glass, combined with tracery, ornamental stone, or wood shapes made to support the glass in devices of lead called cames. Although the glass used in Gothic architecture had imperfections, such as air bubbles, and was only available in relatively small panes, craftsmen used it to create scenes and designs, particularly in Gothic cathedrals, that are now considered masterpieces. Many examples are still in existence. In the Gothic era, pictures were painted on windows. Bay windows of varied shapes that project outside of walls were also used. Special kinds include bow windows, in which the projecting shapes are segments of circles in plan, and oriel windows, which project from upper stories. Casements and dormers were also used.

During the Renaissance, the design of windows, like that of other architectural elements, turned away from the Gothic era to classical architecture, particularly Roman. With greater law enforcement than had prevailed in Gothic times, windows could be made larger. In northern Europe, they were actually made larger to admit additional light, but in the relatively hot southern countries, such as Italy, they were kept small. Windows of the era ordinarily had semicircular, arched heads and, unlike those of the Gothic era, were placed symmetrically in building walls, often in groups that were superimposed one over another. Window designs were usually formal, with surrounds that were often ornamented with flanking columns or architraves, a series of ornamental moldings. By the 16th century, window glass was commonly used in buildings of all types, including houses. Panes were larger than those in previous times, but often smaller ones were used by choice.

Renaissance architects used windows of many types derived from classical examples and developed others of their own. Although used to some extent previously, round windows, called by various names, *oeils-de-boeuf*, bull's-eyes, oxeyes, or oculis, became popular for use in attic walls. During the Renaissance, important types of windows still in use today were developed, including double-hung windows, developed in England, and French windows, sometimes called French doors, that usually come in pairs, open and close like casements, and start at the floor. Another important development was the Palladian window, or Palladian motif, used for windows, doors, and other architectural purposes. First used by the Italian architect Andrea Palladio (1508–80), the motif consists of a three-part opening, the center part of which is arched and supported on freestanding round columns, each of the outer two with a horizontal head, supported by one of the columns on one side and on the other by a rectangular pilaster or column. This motif was used extensively by architects in the Classic Revival and Eclectic periods.

After the Renaissance, in America as well as in Europe, windows were derived from those of past eras. Newer materials came into use, including wrought and cast iron, but window design remained much the same as in previous periods.

During the 19th century, considerably more emphasis was put on the interior environments of buildings than had been placed on such aspects in most periods of the past. Glass had become widely available and architects designed buildings with greater numbers of windows, particularly in such utilitarian buildings as mills and factories. During the latter part of the 19th century, with the beginning of the modern movement, windows became one of the most dominant elements in architecture. The early modern architects were frankly fond of glass as a material and most later architects have agreed with them.

Long ribbons of windows appeared on buildings. One of the most effective designs was used in many of the buildings of the so-called Chicago school of architects in the late 19th century. It consisted of a three-part window system, with a fixed pane of glass in the center, now often called a view or picture window, flanked by operating windows. This idea was later repeatedly used for every type of building, including speculative houses, and though somewhat outmoded is still used to some extent. Other later developments were curtain walls and the all-glass wall, often called a window wall, both of which have also been used extensively.

Today windows are mostly free of ornament, are available in many materials, and may be glazed with window, plate, sealed multiple panes, or heat-absorbent or mirror glass that reflects heat and images. Windows may be obtained in systems, such as window or curtain walls, or individually. They can be fixed or movable in any number or combination, and may have such special attachments as built-in blinds or sun controls of various types.

Related Articles ART IN ARCHITECTURE; CLIMATE; DOOR; GLASS; HARDWARE; HEATING, VENTILATING, AND AIR CONDITIONING; INSECT PROTECTION; INSULATION, THERMAL; LIGHTING; ORNAMENT; PLASTICS; SECURITY SYSTEMS; WALL; WEATHER PROTECTION; Various articles on building materials and systems.

Further Reading Hunt, William Dudley, Jr.: *The Contemporary Curtain Wall—Its Design, Fabrication and Erection*, F. W. Dodge, New York, 1958.

Sources of Additional Information Architectural Aluminum Manufacturers Assoc., 35 E. Wacker Dr., Chicago, Ill. 60601; Stained Glass Association of America, 3600 University Dr., Fairfax, Va. 22030.

WOOD The material in the interior of trees under the bark which is cut into lumber and other forms and used for many purposes. One of the most important uses of wood is in buildings, a practice which began in prehistoric times and continues today. Wood is used in buildings for structures as in wood-framed houses; for finish materials as in floors, wall paneling, and exterior siding; for elements of buildings as doors and windows; and for furniture.

Classification Types of wood are classified into what are called softwoods and hardwoods, in spite of the fact that some softwoods are harder than some hardwoods and vice versa. For example, Douglas fir, classified as softwood, is harder than poplar, a hardwood. The term *hardwood* is applied to wood taken from deciduous trees, those with broad leaves that are shed in the fall. Softwoods are taken from coniferous trees, usually having needlelike leaves, which are evergreen. Among the important hardwoods used in building construction for flooring, wall paneling, woodwork, and furniture are walnut, birch, oak, and maple. Among the most important softwoods, sometimes used for similar purposes but more prevalently used for building structures and related purposes, are fir, pine, spruce, and hemlock.

Uses Wood is a very versatile material. It is used in many forms in buildings as lumber, 2 × 4's, and so on; as heavy timber, 5 × 5's or larger, for structural purposes; as boards, either plain or machined into patterns, for flooring, exterior siding, wall paneling, and the like. Layers of wood can be glued together or laminated, to form relatively large, strong structural elements, such as beams or arches. Wood can also be laminated into large panels, plywood; and as thin sheets, wood veneers, may be laminated to backup wood for use in furniture. Wood chips or shavings can be chemically or mechanically broken down and recombined with filler adhesives to form boards, panels, or other products, or used as an ingredient of plastics.

Wood is more easily worked than most other building materials. It can be sanded, planed, sawed, or drilled with relative ease. It may be fastened to itself and to other materials, with nails, screws, bolts, or adhesives. Wood comes in an almost endless variety of colors and patterns, and with a wide variation of properties of hardness, strength, and durability. It can be given a great range of surface textures and can be finished with paints, stains, plastic or other coatings, and in some cases, as redwood, left unfinished to weather naturally.

Types Wood for building construction comes in three primary types, classified according to the amount of work done on it before it comes to the market. Rough lumber has been sawed, in a sawmill, into shapes with straight sides and rough edges. Rough lumber is not used to any great extent in building construction today. Dressed lumber has been processed, in a planing mill, to make the sides and edges smooth. Worked lumber, sometimes called

WOOD Private house (1974), Evanston, Ill. [*Architects: Keck and Keck. (Hedrich-Blessing)*]

factory or shop lumber, has been dressed and further machined to give it a pattern of decorative or other purposes or to provide for joining pieces together. The last two types are widely used in building construction.

Grading by Usage Lumber for building construction is graded according to its uses. Yard lumber is intended for general building purposes, such as house construction. Structural lumber is most often used in heavier structures, and comes in larger sizes, generally 2 inches (in) or more in both thickness and width. Factory or shop lumber is that intended mainly for further machining into worked lumber which will have patterns in it.

Quality Grading Lumber is also graded by its quality, that is, by its relative freedom from defects, such as knots. Yard lumber is graded select, with a minimum of defects and suitable for exposed, finished parts of buildings; and common, with defects that detract from its appearance but which do not prevent its use for structural and other parts that are not exposed. Select lumber is further graded (1) suitable for natural finishes and (2) suitable for paint finishes, with two further subgrades in each category. Common lumber is further graded (1) for standard construction and (2) for less exacting purposes, with three further subgrades in the (1) category and two in (2). Structural lumber is graded according to its strength, the weights it can hold up or resist safely and efficiently. Hardwood lumber is graded from the best, most free from defects to the least, in the following grades: first; seconds; selects; No. 1 common; No. 2 common; sound wormy; No. 3A common; No. 3B common.

Hardwood Dimension Lumber This is hardwood

lumber that has been sawed into small pieces, free of defects. Plain blocks of such wood are called rough hardwood dimension; if further trimmed, sanded, or otherwise worked, they are surfaced hardwood dimension; and if machined into parts, as in legs or arms of chairs, they are called completely fabricated hardwood dimension.

Sizes of Lumber The sizes of lumber are given in inches for the thickness and width and in feet for the length. These sizes are not the actual sizes, but are called the nominal sizes, those of the lumber before it was dried or seasoned and before it went through the planing mill. The actual sizes are less. For example, a 4-in board actually measures 3½ in today, and for many years in the past measured 3⅝ in. Lumber is sold by the board foot which is a nominal dimension of 1 in thick by 1 ft wide by 1 ft long.

Processing Lumber Trees are brought from the forest to a sawmill, where the logs are moved first to debarkers, which remove the bark, then to a series of saws that cut the log into various sizes of lumber, and finally to a machine called a trimmer which squares up the ends. Lumber may be plain sawed, quarter sawed, or rift sawed. In plain sawing, all boards are sawed from the log in the same direction, parallel to each other. In quarter sawing, one quarter of the log is sawed at a time, with the saws working parallel to each other and generally toward the center of the log. Rift sawing is similar, except the saw cuts are at slight angles to each other. The first method produces strong lumber that costs less because there is less waste. The others produce lumber with edge grain that is pronounced and ornamental.

Seasoning Newly sawed lumber, called green

further worked in milling and other machines to produce patterns for various purposes. If used in buildings where it may be damaged by insects, such as termites, or decay, caused by fungi attacking the damp wood, lumber is often treated with preservatives for protection. The two most widely used types are oil-type preservatives, such as creosote, and chemicals in water.

Veneer Wood One other method for preparing wood for use in buildings, making veneer wood, has increasingly become more important. In this case, instead of being sawed, the log, called a peeler log, is held against a long blade of a machine and rotated in such a way as to peel a thin veneer from it. The veneer thus produced is then laminated, under pressure, with adhesives to other sheets of wood to form plywood and similar products.

History Wood has been used in architecture from earliest prehistoric times. The earliest primitive structures are believed to have been similar to those of the American Indians. The development of wood uses and forms has continued ever since through all the great styles or movements in architecture. Even in an era like the Middle Ages, in which stone was the major material, great roof structures of wood, handled in a skillful and craftsmanlike manner, were used for cathedrals and many other important buildings. And of course, wood never ceased to be used widely for humbler structures.

American Development Wood has played a large part in the architecture of America from the earliest times to today. The Pre-Columbian Indians used wood in the form of branches and logs for wigwams, longhouses, and other structures, and continued to do so well after the establishment of the colonies. The colonists found great forests, which provided ample lumber, the most easily usable material for their earliest buildings. Sawmills, using waterpower, were established in Virginia and New England in the early 17th century; waterpower was replaced with steam by the middle of the 19th. Most of the early colonial buildings were of wood used in a simple manner, but later in a much more sophisticated way, often in forms adapted from buildings of stone and brick in Europe. Wood has continued to be one of the most important building materials in the United States, and notable architecture in wood has been produced in every era and is still being produced today.

Related Articles BUILDING TRADE; CEILING; CONSTRUCTION, BUILDING; CONSTRUCTION MATERIALS; DOOR; FLOOR; FURNITURE; HOUSE; MOLDING; PREFABRICATION; ROOF; ROOFING; STRUCTURAL ENGINEERING; STRUCTURE; WALL; WINDOW; WOOD-FRAME STRUCTURE; WOODWORK.

Sources of Additional Information American Forestry Assoc., 1319 18th St., N.W., Washington, D.C. 20036; American Plywood Assoc., 1119 A St., Tacoma, Wash. 98401.

WOOD Camp Louise (1972), Berwick, Pa. [*Architects: Bohlin and Powell. (Joseph W. Molitor)*]

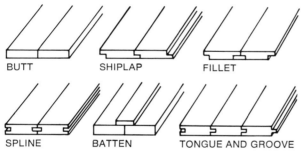

BUTT   SHIPLAP   FILLET

SPLINE   BATTEN   TONGUE AND GROOVE

WOOD Typical joints for siding and other components.

lumber, has a high moisture content. It must be dried or seasoned to reduce the moisture. During this process, the lumber shrinks. If green lumber were used in a building, there would be warping or other distortion. To prevent this from happening, lumber is seasoned either by air drying, stacking it outdoors to be dried by the sun and wind, or by kiln drying, in which the lumber is subjected to controlled heating to drive out the proper amount of moisture. The recommended average moisture content in the United States varies from 6 percent in dry areas to 11 percent in humid areas.

Planing After having been seasoned, all lumber other than that to be used as rough lumber, is further processed in planing mills. Here the lumber is moved through machinery with knife blades that shave and smooth the rough lumber. Factory or shop lumber is

WOOD-FRAME STRUCTURE Building construction system using wood in the form of studs, beams, girders, joists, rafters, and other members for the structure of a building. Wood is one of the most ancient and versatile structural materials used in architecture. The major structural methods used today are light wood framing, utilizing small thicknesses, nominally 2 inches (in), of lumber to form the structures of relatively small buildings, such as houses; heavy timber, sometimes called mill or warehouse, construction, in which much larger structural members are used for relatively large buildings; plank and beam framing, which utilizes relatively large beams and sometimes posts, with roof and floor decking of nominal 2-in planks. Other methods are also used, including wood piling. For further discussion on wood piling, see the article entitled foundation.

Advantages and Disadvantages Wood, in the form of lumber and timber, has marked advantages as a structural material in buildings. It is plentiful in most places and is renewable by replanting trees. Many species of trees furnish structural lumber and timber. Thus a wide variety of characteristics, including strengths, may be obtained. Wood is the most easily worked of all building materials, easy to saw, plane, drill, shape, and fasten, with almost all tools and machines. It is also easy to finish. Wood is one of the most inexpensive structural materials, is strong and durable if handled properly in design and construction, and has insulating qualities. Wood is also one of the favorite materials of many people, including architects and other environmental designers, for its warm appearance and other esthetic qualities. A major disadvantage of wood is that it is subject to damage when attached by certain insects, such as termites, and to deterioration and damage from water and from attacks by various fungi that cause it to decay and eventually fail. All these negative qualities can be avoided through proper design, construction, and maintenance. Perhaps the greatest disadvantage is that wood is combustible; therefore it cannot be used for buildings of certain types, occupancies, and sizes.

Wood Species The major woods used for structural members, both softwoods, are Douglas fir and southern pine (the Georgia pine). In addition, many other softwoods may be used, including various hemlocks, cedars, spruces, redwood, and larch. Each of these types of wood has specific characteristics and properties that must be taken into consideration in the design of structures of various kinds. For basic characteristics and properties, along with sizes, grading, and other information, see the article entitled wood. Engineering data, including allowable stresses in types of wood, load tables for such structural members as joists, rafters and decking, and so on, are widely available.

Light Wood Framing This framing system is often used for construction of houses and other relatively small buildings, one to three stories in height. Ordinarily, light wood-frame structural members are a nominal 2 in in thickness by various depths and lengths. The vertical structural members used for walls, called studs, are usually 2 × 4's erected on 16-

in centers, or for one-story buildings sometimes on 24-in centers. In walls with 2 × 6 studs, 24-in centers are often used. Other primary light wood-frame structural members, such as floor and roof joists and rafters, are usually 2 in in thickness, range up to 14 in in depth and up to 24 ft or more in length. Such members may also be of 3 or 4 in thickness.

Balloon Frame There are two major methods for light wood framing: the balloon frame and the western, or platform, frame. The balloon frame, long the standard method in the United States, utilizes studs that are two stories high in two-story buildings. In this method, usually two 2 × 6's or other sizes of lumber, called the sill, are bolted to the foundation. The studs are nailed to the sill. The horizontal structural members, floor and roof joists, are nailed to the sides of the studs. A plate, two wood members the same thickness and depth as the studs, is nailed along the top of the stud wall. Rafters if used are nailed to the sides of the roof joists. Diagonal wood or plywood sheathing is nailed to the outside of the studs. Wood subfloors are nailed on top of the floor joists and wood roof decking nailed to the top of the rafters in pitched roofs or the roof joists in flat roofs. Wood or metal bracing is used between joists. Wood firestops, the same thickness and depth of the studs, are nailed in place at each floor level and at the mid-heights of the studs. Similar fire-stops are nailed between joists at the outer ends.

Western Frame Today western, or platform, framing has supplanted the balloon method to some extent. Western framing utilizes studs that are only one story high. A sill, usually only one wood member, is bolted to the foundation as in the other type. The first-floor joists are then nailed directly to the sill and the subflooring nailed to the joits. On top of the subfloor, a sole plate, sometimes called a shoe, is nailed and the studs are nailed to it. On top of the studs, a double plate is nailed as in the balloon method. The same process is repeated for the second floor and if required, the third. Cross-bridging is used between joists as before, along with a roof deck. One of the major advantages of this method of framing, as compared to the balloon, is that the framing of walls may be completely assembled and then tilted into place.

Although both methods of light wood framing utilize mostly lumber in small sizes, usually of nominal 2 in thickness, in certain cases heavier timbers are used for girders, columns or posts, and similar members carrying heavy loads. Sometimes steel structural members are used instead. Light wood framing is also often used in conjunction with masonry exterior walls, and in this case is usually called ordinary construction.

Heavy Timber Construction This system utilizes structural members larger than the nominal 2-in thickness of light wood framing. Heavy timber construction has considerable fire resistance since the heavy wood members retain much of their strength for long

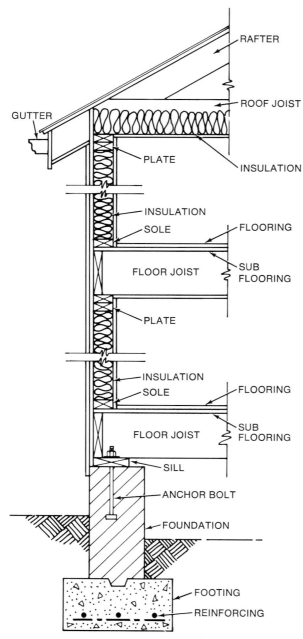

WOOD-FRAME STRUCTURE Section of western, or platform, frame.

periods of time in fires because of the slow rate of surface charring. In order to qualify for a fire-resistance rating, heavy timber construction must be accomplished with structural members of certain minimum sizes or greater, with approved connectors and details, with no concealed spaces under floors and roofs, and with fire-resistance-rated wall, floor, and roof construction. Typical of the nominal sizes for heavy timber structural members are the following: 8 in for columns supporting floors and 6 in for those supporting roofs; 6 in wide and 10 in deep for beams and girders; and other minimums for other members.

In heavy timber construction, either solid or glued laminated timber may be used. Bearing walls in heavy timber construction must have fire-resistance ratings of two or three hours and nonbearing walls must be incombustible, and have fire-resistance ratings of from one to three hours if separated from other construction by less than 30 ft. Buildings of many types, in quite large sizes, may be built with heavy timber construction. Although the most common use of the system is for utilitarian buildings, such as factories and warehouses, it may also be used for many other types, in which open, columnless spaces and long roof spans are needed.

Plank and Beam Framing This framing system is often used for houses and other buildings of relatively small sizes. In this system, the vertical supports may be walls constructed in a manner similar to western framing or wood posts. Instead of joists, beams of relatively large size of solid wood, built-up with smaller members attached to each other or of laminated wood, are used on centers usually of 6 to 8 ft. Nominal 2-in-thick tongue-and-groove planks are attached to the top of the beams to form floors and roofs. Many architects and other people prefer the architectural effects achieved with the exposed beams and planks and the additional ceiling heights that can be obtained at little or no extra expense. On the other hand, concealment of piping, electrical wiring, and ductwork is more difficult than in the more conventional light wood framing systems.

Another structural system, sometimes used for the more utilitarian types of buildings, such as factories or frame buildings, utilizes round timber poles for columns. Often a reinforced concrete floor slab, supported by the ground, is used. Simple connections are possible and simple wood trusses may be used for roofs. This system is one of the most economical of structures available for buildings today.

Special Structural Elements Many types of special structural elements are used in conjunction with the above systems, including trusses, trussed rafters, arches, stressed-skin panels, structural diaphragms, and shell structures. Most of these were developed in the 20th century, except for trusses which go back to ancient times.

A truss is a special kind of structural element used to span long distances. Trusses are made up of relatively small members into rigid shapes, usually composed of triangles; several kinds of trusses are used today, including the Pratt, flat Pratt, bowstring, Belgian, Fink, Warren, Howe, scissors, and sawtooth. The shapes of most of these are illustrated in the article entitled steel structure. Wood trusses may be constructed in two major ways, with wood members only, bolted or fastened together with special connectors; or with compression members of wood combined with steel rod tension members. Large trusses, spaced 8 to 20 ft apart, are used in buildings, such as factories, in which great columnless spaces are required for spans up to 80 ft or more. For smaller buildings, lighter trusses, often called trussed rafters, are used. Trussed rafters are made of small lumber, are placed at 2-ft to 4-ft intervals, and usually span up to 32 ft, though they can be made to span greater distances. Trussed rafters are often prefabricated, trucked to building sites, and erected.

Wood arches may also be used for long roof spans. Often of glued laminated timber, though sometimes built up in other ways, the arches are generally available in several shapes, including A frame, like a gable end; Gothic, curved and pointed; radial, like a segment of a circle; parabolic; three-centered; and Tudor. Such arches may be used for spans up to 100 ft or more. Often left exposed beneath roof decks, laminated arches are used for several building types, including churches and assembly buildings. Many architects and other environmental designers often prefer laminated arches for their building designs, not only for their long spans but for their appearance.

Other structural members made of glued laminated wood are also available, including roof beams, which may be straight, curved, or pitched in one or two directions. Roof beams of this type may span up to 60 ft or more. Columns and other members may also be made of glued laminated wood. Plywood is the most commonly used glued laminated material, for a great many purposes in architecture. As a structural material, plywood is mostly used for wall sheathing, subfloors, roof decking, and the like. In addition to carrying the normal weights or loads in such structures, plywood also may be designed to act as a diaphragm to resist loads from the sides, or lateral loads. Plywood is also sometimes used to construct stressed-skin panels, made by gluing plywood to the tops, and usually the bottoms, of wood frames. Used for strong walls, floors, and roofs, and also for box beams, stressed-skin panels are very strong for their weight and the amount of materials of which they are composed.

Shell construction with wood generally utilizes hyperbolic paraboloids: strong, thin, double-curved shapes used for roofs of buildings. Such structures in wood are usually constructed with laminated or solid wood structural members on the perimeters. Sheathing may be solid wood or plywood attached to the top or bottom, or sandwiched between the perimeter members. Roofs with other types of curves may be constructed of wood, but the hyperbolic paraboloid is one of the easiest to design. It is also relatively easy to fabricate and construct because, though it may seem unlikely, the double-curved surface is actually composed of straight lines that slope but do not curve.

Fasteners Fasteners or connectors for wood structures are extremely important. For light wood frame buildings, the most generally used fastener is the common nail. Standards of good practice have been established for the types, sizes, and number to be used for various purposes, and the driving methods. Many timber structural elements, such as trusses and

others, are connected with bolts and nuts, usually in combination with washers. Today trusses and similar components are frequently connected with special connectors or plates which are often used in conjunction with bolts and nuts, or with nails. These special fasteners not only speed up fabrication but produce stronger joints than bolts and nuts alone. Many kinds of special items of steel or iron are used in conjunction with wood construction. Various kinds of steel or iron plates are used for such purposes as splicing wood members; anchoring wood members to masonry or concrete, bearing plates under beams, and other members; and hangers for beams, joists, and other members. Most types are available from stock, but others must be fabricated for the exact purpose intended. A great number of other fasteners, including wood and lag screws, spikes, and rods, are often required.

For many architects and other environmental designers, the use of wood in building structures is both interesting and satisfying. And some believe that some of the methods, such as laminated wood exposed inside buildings, produce very fine architecture. The information in this article provides only general guidelines for design in wood. Engineering tables are widely available for use in determining various wood structures. However, for all but the simplest structures, such as light wood frame houses, structural design in wood must be accomplished by informed and experienced architects or structural engineers.

History Wood was one of the earliest structural materials used by primitive humans to construct huts and tents. And wood has continued to be an important construction material to the present time. While all the earliest wood structures have long since disappeared as have many that came later, it is thought that the early buildings were simply sticks or branches set in the ground in a circle at the bottom and tied together at the top in the form of a tepee. Over the crude frame were placed branches or leaves or skins of animals. Later, primitive people constructed more elaborate buildings with vertical and horizontal structural members of wood, and sometimes gable roofs, in the system that is known as the post and lintel, or trabeated.

In the ancient civilizations in and around the Mediterranean Sea, Mesopotamia, Egypt, Crete, and the mainland of Greece, wood structures were also used, though stone and burned-clay units were the major building materials. Wood was used structurally in all these places for posts, lintels, and rafters in earliest times and later, mostly for small buildings and for relatively minor uses in important ones. Because of the ravages of time, insects, and weather, none of these early wood structures has survived.

The Romans also used wood extensively. Although none of their wood buildings has survived, there is evidence of them in the works of writers of the time and from archeological excavations. The Romans used structural wood for columns, beams, trusses, joists, roof and floor structures, and complete buildings. They also sometimes constructed wood bridges. Roman wood buildings used the trabeated system, developed elsewhere, with few innovations.

During the Middle Ages, wood structures were used quite extensively for the roof structures of cathedrals and other important buildings and for complete structures of less important types. Some buildings were constructed with split logs, but many were of roughly dressed timbers. Some were highly ornamented with carvings.

One of the major uses of wood in Gothic structures was for the framing of roofs of timber buildings and over the stone vaults of others. Often made of oak, these roof structures were usually joined together with mortise and tenon joints and with wooden pegs. Rafters were usually connected to each other with tie beams to increase their strength and stability and sometimes diagonal bracing was also used for the same purpose, thus creating an assembly that resembled a truss. Some of the roof structures were quite elaborate, particularly in England, where curved ribs were sometimes used in assemblies. The English also used a very ornamental system, called a hammer-beam roof, which had short hammer beams at the side from which rafters and arched ribs rose. Also of importance in Gothic architecture were half-timber buildings, in which wood posts and diagonal members formed the structure with the spaces in between filled with plaster, brick, or other materials.

During the Renaissance, wood was not as important a structural material as were brick and stone. Wood continued to be used, much in the manner of the Middle Ages, in half-timber structures, in roofs, and for other purposes. Renaissance architects sometimes used trusses, somewhat like those of the Romans. Wood trusses were often used for domes which were then roofed outside and plastered inside.

American Development In early colonial America, wood was the most used structural material, particularly in the English and other colonies of the Middle Atlantic and New England areas. The methods of construction were those the colonists had known in the countries from which they emigrated. Later a method called the braced frame was developed. This system utilized large heavy posts and horizontal members called girts, with diagonal bracing. Wood structures have continued to be used in the United States since that time. However, brick and stone and later reinforced concrete and fire-protected steel have become the structural materials used in centers of cities where fire risks are so great.

Wood has continued to be the major structural material used in houses to the present time. Early in the 19th century, a system for wood framing of relatively small buildings, called the balloon frame, was introduced in the United States and was later used elsewhere. The balloon frame is believed to have been invented by a contractor, G. W. Snow (1797–1890). The balloon frame made it possible for a house to be constructed with small pieces of lumber instead of heavy timbers, nailed into place instead of fastened with mortise and tenon joints. The system was fast and inexpensive and could be erected by relatively unskilled carpenters. Soon the balloon frame became the major method for constructing houses. It continued to be widely used in the 20th century. Today western, or platform, framing, a similar and even simpler method, has replaced balloon framing to some extent.

Heavy timber, often called warehouse or mill, construction has been used mostly for factories and other utilitarian buildings for a long time in the United States and continues to be used. Plank and beam structures are often used in houses today. Laminated wood structural members, such as columns, beams, and arches, are often used not only in houses but in other types of buildings. Wood is often used for the structures of prefabricated houses and other building types.

Related Articles BUILDING CODES AND STANDARDS; FACTORY; FOUNDATION; HOUSE; INSECT PROTECTION; PREFABRICATION; STRUCTURAL ENGINEERING; STRUCTURE; WOOD.

Further Reading American Institute of Timber Construction, *Timber Construction Manual*, 2d ed., John Wiley, New York, 1974.

Sources of Additional Information American Institute of Timber Construction, 333 W. Hampden Ave., Englewood, Colo. 80110; American Plywood Assoc., 1119 A St., Tacoma, Wash. 98401.

WOODWORK A part of a building made of wood by carpenters or cabinetmakers, in particular a finished part, rather than the rough work in wood framing in walls. Work in wood on buildings is generally accomplished by two trades: carpentry and cabinetmaking. Carpentry is often classified as either rough, concerned mainly with the wood framing of buildings; or finish, concerned with such work as sheathing, exterior, and interior finish, setting windows, hanging doors, and installation of stairs, flooring, moldings, and the like. Cabinetmaking is concerned with the construction of special items of wood, such as built-in furniture, cabinets, wall paneling, and so on. Although there is some overlap between these trades, woodwork is usually the responsibility of cabinetmakers, and in some cases, finish carpenters. Millwork consists of elements of wood, such as windows, doors, and moldings produced in a woodworking plant.

Woodwork in buildings today consists mainly of furniture and storage, stairs, moldings and other trim, and wall paneling. In the past, wood windows and doors and their frames were often made by cabinetmakers or carpenters. Today most of them are made on assembly lines in factories and put into place in buildings by carpenters, who usually also install the trim around them. For further discussion on doors, moldings and other trim, stairs, and windows, see articles listed at the end of this article.

WOODWORK Texaco World Headquarters (1976), Harrison, N.Y.
[*Architects: Skidmore, Owings and Merrill. (Joseph W. Molitor)*]

WOODWORK Texaco World Headquarters (1976), Harrison, N.Y.
[*Architects: Skidmore, Owings and Merrill. (Joseph W. Molitor)*]

In the past, such items as built-in dressers, chests of drawers, bookcases, special closets, kitchen cabinets, and so on were often built on the job, in place, in buildings. Later many of such items were specially constructed in woodworking shops for specific buildings. Both methods are still employed to some extent today, but a far more prevalent practice is the selection of such items from standard lines of stock types mass-produced in factories. This is particularly true of kitchen cabinets. Also many itmes of this sort, again particularly kitchen cabinets, are produced in metals today rather than in wood.

Prefabricated Cabinets Prefabricated kitchen cabinets, of wood or metal, are available in a variety of sizes, types, qualities, and finishes. Stock kitchen cabinets are of two major types: base cabinets with countertops, placed on the floor, to form storage spaces and work areas; and wall cabinets. Base cabinets are generally 36 in high, 24 to 25 in deep, and 12 to 42 in or more wide. Wall cabinets are generally 13 in deep, 15 to 30 in high, and in widths similar to those of floor cabinets. Special types of cabinets are available for sinks, built-in ovens and stovetops, tray storage, laundry hampers, and other special uses. Metal cabinets come in various colors and with countertops of laminated plastic, stainless steel, and other materials. For most installations, other than the simplest, the countertops are made to order with backsplashes. Wood cabinets may be obtained prepainted, primed for painting, unfinished, stained, or otherwise finished, in woods of various kinds, including birch and maple.

Prefabricated Units Prefabricated dressers, chests of drawers, closets, bookcases, and other items are also available in many combinations and in several woods. Storage and other units for offices, libraries, and other building types, made of steel or wood, come in a variety of types and sizes.

When cabinets, storage units, and the like are to be used in buildings, care must be taken to ensure accurate dimensioning, use of proper finishes, and, above all, proper construction and craftsmanship. In the case of prefabricated units, such considerations may be a matter of observation and understanding of manufacturers' specifications and their actual products. When such work is to be specially designed and constructed for specific uses in individual buildings, extreme care must be taken in the preparation of working drawings and specifications covering the work and in checking large-scale shop drawings from which the items will actually be fabricated.

Cabinetwork A major consideration in cabinetwork is selection of the proper woods. Softwoods, such as pine and fir, are often used for cabinets or other items to be painted, and sometimes redwood, cypress, or cedar for those to be stained or given natural finishes. Aromatic cedar is often used for lining clothes closets. For other pieces to be stained or given natural finishes, hardwoods are generally used, including birch, walnut, maple, oak, and mahogany.

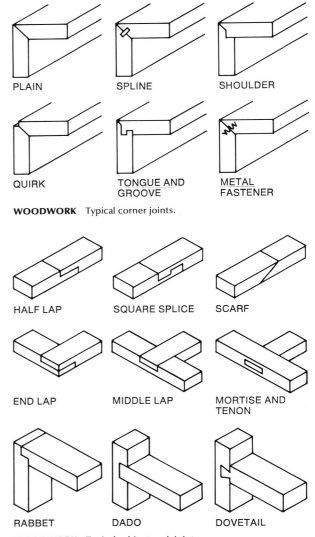

WOODWORK Typical corner joints.

WOODWORK Typical cabinetwork joints.

Although in the past solid woods or solid cores with thin veneers were usually used for cabinetwork, today plywood is generally used. For cabinetmaking and similar purposes, wood should be clear and free of blemishes. (See the article entitled wood.)

Another important consideration in cabinetwork is proper construction. Dimensions should be accurate, corners square, and parts properly fitted. Joints between various wood members are important. In rough carpentry, butt joints, in which one member with a flat end is simply nailed or otherwise fastened to another, are commonly used. In cabinetwork, special joints that are stronger and better finished are used, including tongue and groove, mortise and tenon, rabbet and dado, and dovetail types, all often fastened together with glues or other adhesives.

Hardware Many types of hardware are available for use in cabinetwork and other woodwork, including hinges, locks, slides, and so on, in such metals as brass, bronze, and stainless steel. Special devices may be obtained for almost every conceivable purpose, including shoe, tie, hat, and belt racks; umbrella holders; extension hangers; and pants, blouse, and skirt hangers. Special extension drawer slides are also available, as are adjustable shelf standards.

Paneling As in other woodwork, paneling in the past was mainly made of solid woods, often softwoods for surfaces to be painted and hardwoods for those to be stained or given natural finishes. In other cases, special veneers were used. Today some solid or specially veneered wood paneling is still used in buildings. Many exotic woods from all over the world are available for this purpose, in addition to the more generally used American woods, such as birch, walnut, oak, and maple. For the most part today, paneling in buildings is made of plywood, in which a great number of widely varied woods are available. In many cases, plywood paneling is installed in big sheets with very simple butt joints, often with V grooves or with specially made divider strips. Joints may be recessed or have strips called battens over them. Solid or specially veneered wood paneling may also be installed in large pieces, with various kinds of joints. Such paneling may also be installed in smaller pieces, in square or other shapes, with framing and molding around them.

In the past, many types of ornament were used in conjunction with wall paneling and other woodwork, including wood carving and marquetry, the inlaying of pieces of wood, and sometimes other materials, glued to a background. Such techniques are rarely used today.

History Because of the discovery of various early woodworking tools, it is believed that humans worked in wood almost from the time of the lower Old Stone, or Paleolithic, Age, perhaps as far back as 500,000 B.C. By the time of the New Stone, or Neolithic, Age, people were making excellently designed and crafted objects of wood and had even invented a kind of primitive mortise and tenon joint.

By about 3000 B.C., in Egypt, Crete, the Middle East, and Greece, fine woodworking had become a widely practiced craft. So accepted were various wood forms of the time that these ancient people often copied them later in stone and other materials. From that time, woodworking has been an important part of architecture. It was practiced in Roman times, highly developed, particularly in carving, during the Gothic period, and further developed during the Renaissance.

Except for the magnificent era of Gothic wood carvings, the great age of woodworking was in the 18th century, when some of the finest furniture and other wood objects were produced in England, France, and other places, including America. The traditions that started then were continued to some extent in the 19th century, but by the end of that period, machines had replaced handwork in wood and the end of the great era had virtually come. The early architects of the modern movement turned away from ornament in wood, as they had in other materials, to plain unadorned surfaces, usually in natural finishes. Some of the early modern architects resisted this trend and produced ornamental woodwork still thought to be of the highest excellence. Among those who designed such work are the Greene brothers, Charles Sumner (1868–1957), Henry Mather (1870–1954), and Bernard Maybeck (1862–1957). Other modern architects have designed excellent built-in furniture and other objects of wood, using simple forms, for the most part plain and unadorned. This trend continues today.

Related Articles CEILING; DOOR; FURNITURE; GREENE AND GREENE; INTERIOR DESIGN; MOLDING; ORNAMENT; PAINT; PREFABRICATION; STAIR; WALL; WINDOW; WOOD; WOOD-FRAME STRUCTURE.

Source of Additional Information Architectural Woodwork Inst., 5055 S. Chesterfield Rd., Arlington, Va. 22206.

WORKING DRAWING Plans, elevations, details, and other data that show how a building or other structure is to be constructed. Such information is presented graphically in the working drawings and supplemented by verbal information in the specifications. Working drawings and specifications, together with related items, are called the construction contract documents. They are not only guides for construction work but form part of construction contracts between owners and contractors. Because of their importance and legal status, working drawings as well as other contract documents must be prepared with skill, thoroughness, and care.

Generally, working drawings for the engineering portions of buildings, mainly structural, mechanical, and electrical, are prepared by engineers and their assistants, in close coordination with each other and with the architect. Various other portions may be prepared by other design professionals, such as landscape architects, interior designers, and so on. All the rest of the working drawings are prepared by architects and their assistants.

Production The preparation of working drawings and specifications is usually called production in architectural and other design offices. In the smallest offices, production might be handled by an architect if a sole proprietor, or by one or more partners. In somewhat larger offices, there may be a production department, with a few draftsmen and a specification writer. In still larger offices, the organization of production varies somewhat. In general, there is a production department under the direction of a principal or an upper-level employee of the firm, with a title such as director of production and overall responsibility for the entire production system. Under this individual might be a chief specification writer who directs the work of that department and a chief draftsman who directes the preparation of working drawings. Often there is also a separate cost control department. And sometimes construction contract administration is included in the production department.

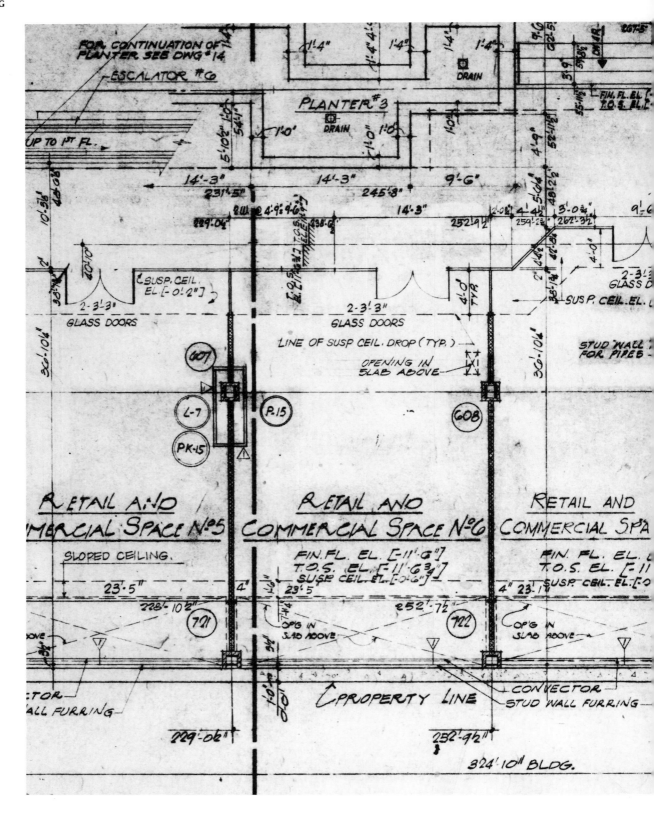

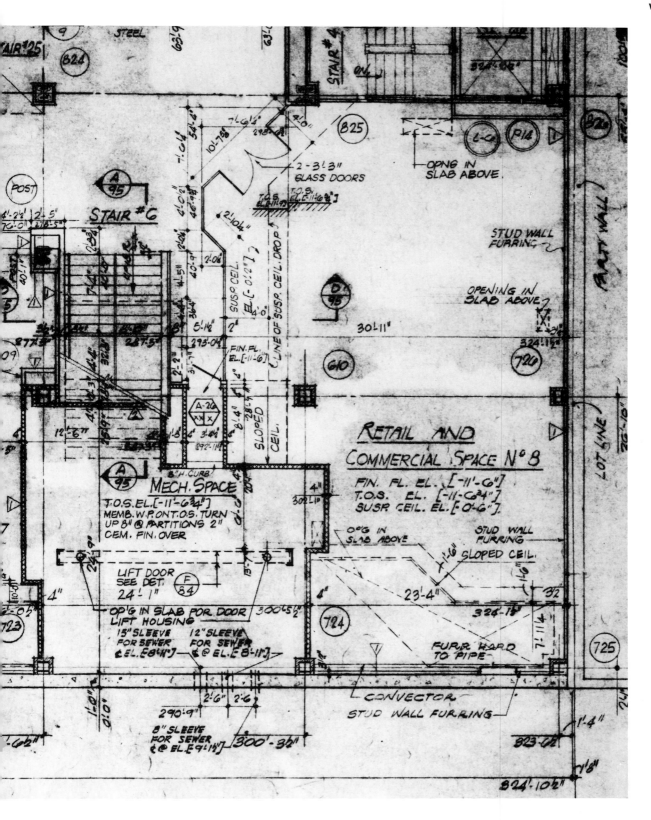

WORKING DRAWING Partial Concourse Plan, Citicorp Center (1978), New York, N.Y. [*Architects: Hugh Stubbins, in association with Emery Roth and Sons. (Hugh Stubbins and Associates)*]

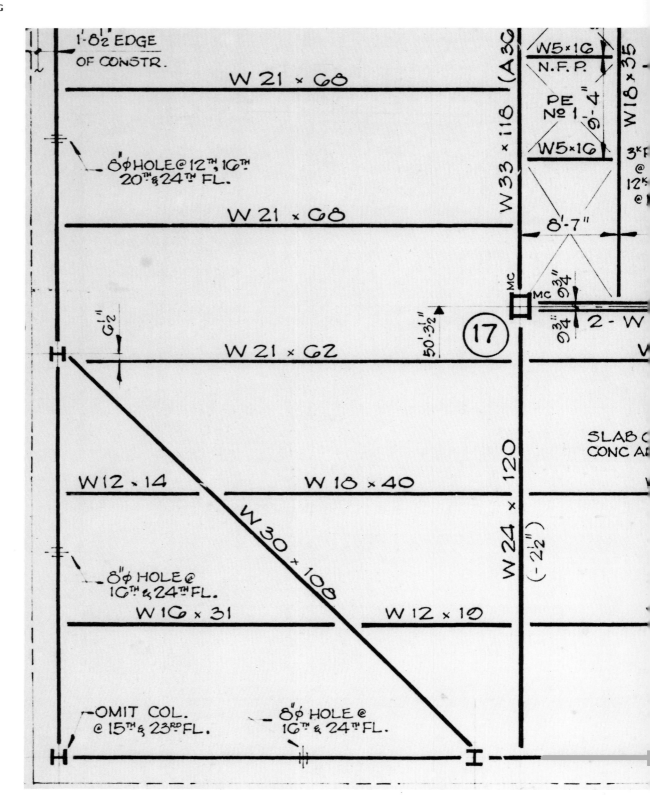

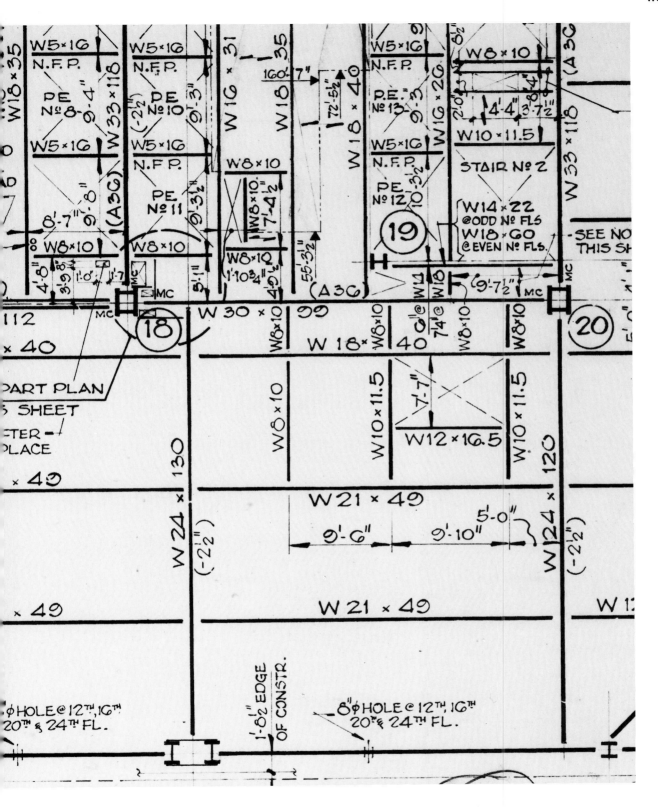

WORKING DRAWING Partial Structural Framing Plan, Citicorp Center (1978), New York, N.Y. [*Architects: Hugh Stubbins, in association with Emery Roth and Sons. (Hugh Stubbins and Associates)*]

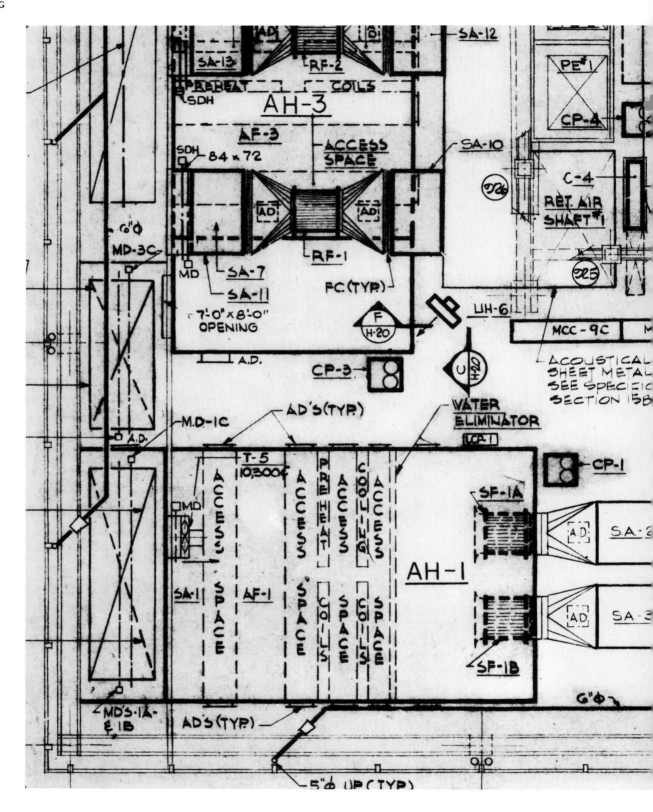

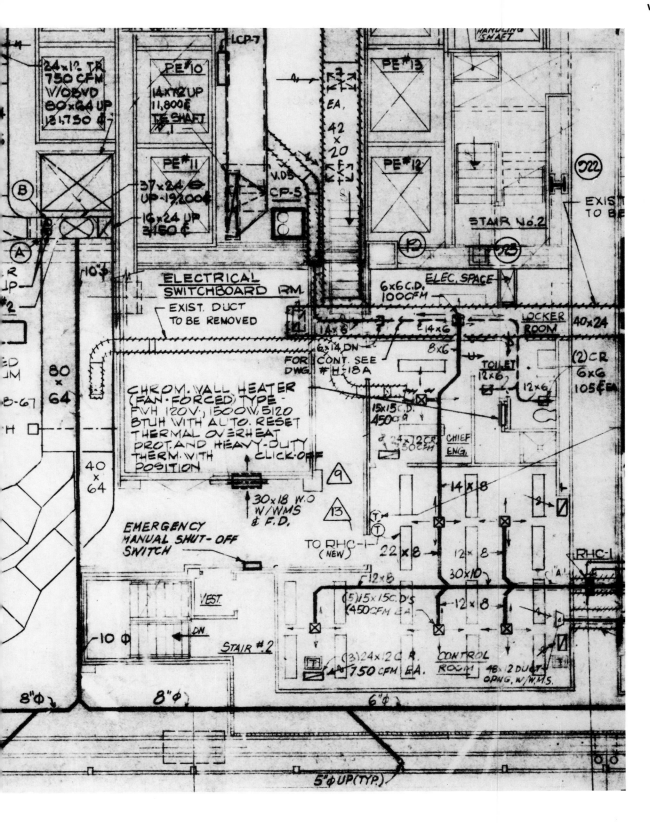

WORKING DRAWING Partial Ductwork Plan, Citicorp Center (1978), New York, N.Y. [*Architects: Hugh Stubbins, in association with Emery Roth and Sons. (Hugh Stubbins and Associates)*]

Methods Of the several methods for the actual production of working drawings, two systems are the most important. One system selects a job captain to direct each individual project, along with draftsmen. These people handle the production of working drawings for the job until they have been completed. The other system also employs a job captain to direct the work, but it is actually performed by draftsmen-specialists, each preparing only certain specific types of drawings for all or a number of the jobs in the office. Many variations of these systems are possible.

In most architectural offices, the individual responsible for an entire project, including all the processes, such as production, administration, design, and so on, is an architect, who is called by some title such as project architect or partner-in-charge. Thus those who actually prepare working drawings are under the direction of a director of production, a chief draftsman, and job captains, but the drafting they perform is directed toward the end result of producing contract documents for projects that are the responsibility of the project architects.

In architectural offices with engineering, landscape architecture, or interior design departments, production of such drawings is usually separate from architectural production, but closely related. When independent consulting engineers and others perform such work, their organizations are approximately similar to those of architects. In either case, each profession produces its own portion of the drawings, coordinating them with the others.

Elements For a very small building, such as a modest house, a set of working drawings may consist of only a few sheets. From this size, sets may range up to more than 300 sheets for a very large and complex building. Regardless of the size or complexity of buildings, all working drawings contain several elements; plans, elevations, sections, details, schedules, and notes.

Plans are drawings that show horizontal views of a project. The most important plan, and usually the first one to be drawn, is the main floor plan. From it, many elements of a building may be developed. Other plans shown on working drawings include those of other floors, site or plot, roofs, foundations, and other elements. A special type is a reflected ceiling plan which shows a ceiling as if it were reflected in a mirror laid on a floor.

Elevations are drawings that show vertical views of buildings, mainly depicting the exteriors or facades and the interior walls. Sections are drawings that are made by theoretically slicing through a wall or other building element, either horizontally or vertically, to show its construction and other features. A wall section is a vertical section through a wall; a building section is a vertical section through a building. Building sections may be either full or part. A section elevation is a building section that shows an elevation. A detail is a drawing, usually at relatively large scale, showing some feature of interest, and may be a section or another type. A schedule is a list or table that gives types and other information about such items as windows or hardware. Notes are used to amplify and explain what may not be clear in the graphic work on working drawings.

Subcategories Ordinarily, working drawings sets are divided into subcategories, including architectural, structural, mechanical, electrical, and sometimes landscaping and others. Some production departments number the sheets of working drawings to indicate this division: A for architectural, S for structural, and so on. In sets of this type, architectural drawings would have numbers such as A-1, A-2, and so on, and structural drawings and the others would be numbered similarly.

A typical set of working drawings would include such individual drawings as plans—site, floor, for all floors including basement levels, roof, and possibly reflected ceilings; elevations—all exterior and important interior walls; sections and details—included as required to explain the building properly; and schedules —for such items as doors, windows, hardware, and room finishes, along with notes as required.

In the structural section would be included individual drawings of the structure, similar to those listed above, along with roof and floor framing plans and other specialized drawings and schedules of lintels, footings, piling, columns, beams, and so on. The mechanical and electrical sections would include drawings similar to those in the architectural section, but usually with outline of walls and so on drawn more lightly and the various systems shown diagramatically and by symbols. Schedules in these sections would include fixtures, equipment, appliances, and the like.

Sheet Composition All the sheets of the working drawings are cross-referenced to each other and various individual drawings, for example, sections and details are cross-referenced to the plans or elevations to which they refer. The first sheet of a working drawing set is called the title sheet; it contains, in addition to the title of the project, important general information, such as the names, addresses, and telephone numbers of the owner, architects, engineers, and others; a vicinity plan; a table of symbols; and other items. On each sheet in the set is a title block, giving the name and location of the project, the professionals involved and their addresses and titles, and the number of the individual sheet, and the seals and signatures of the architect and other professionals who certify the working drawings as having been drawn by them or under their direction. Also space should be provided for information concerning reissues or revisions of each sheet.

Standards and Procedures The preparation of working drawings requires great skill in drafting and considerable knowledge of the building industry, architecture, and construction. Accordingly, it takes some years of experience for a draftsman to become competent in this work. Even skilled draftsmen may not always produce drawings that are of consistently high standards, without proper guidance. In addition to that given by directors of production, chief draftsmen, and others, many architects supply their draftsmen with office manuals that specify standards and procedures. Included in such a manual is information on symbols and abbreviations to be used, line types and weights, lettering sizes, types and quality, dimensioning practices, layout of drawings, coordination of the work, building industry regulations and standards to be followed, and so on. All these and others are factors in the systematic production of high-quality working drawings.

Additional Drawings In addition to the above types of drawings, production departments often prepare others, including preliminary working drawings which serve as the basis for the final documents, revisions of drawings, measured drawings of existing buildings, and supplemental drawings needed during construction, and as-built drawings showing how buildings were actually constructed.

History At the beginning of the 20th century, almost every working drawing was done in ink on tracing cloth. While some are still done with pen and ink, most working drawings today are done with pencil on tracing paper or sometimes cloth. Until a few years ago, this still meant that every line on every drawing had to be done by hand and every letter hand lettered. This was a laborious, sometimes boring, process that was painstakingly repeated for every new job in production.

Tools and Techniques In the past few decades, many improvements have been made in drafting instruments and equipment, including new types of pencils, fountain drafting pens, and tracing papers. There have also been changes in techniques, many of which not only reduce the tedium of drafting but speed the process and facilitate the production of better drawings.

One technique involves the development of standard details that can be used more or less intact on succeeding jobs. Some firms have experimented with systems of detail drawings from which relevant examples may be selected for specific jobs, reproduced over and over, and bound into relatively small books which supplement the larger and more general drawings. Another method, in more widespread use, involves reproduction of details or other drawings, without redrawing, on clear materials that may be affixed to sheets of working drawings with clear tape or by other means. Typed or printed notes, tables, and other text may be affixed in a similar manner.

A quite extensive array of pressure-sensitive products are also available today, including alphabets and numbers, symbols, screens, patterns and tones, and lines. Generally, these are rubbed onto a drawing, covered with clear plastic, and burnished to ensure adhesion. Other types are available with adhesives that are not pressure-sensitive. Some of these materials also take typing or printing, which may then be affixed to drawings. Some offices utilize machines that reproduce details and other data, ready to be adhered to drawings. And many offices make drawings on sheets of plastic, rather than making them on tracing paper.

Other methods for improving the production of working drawings are in use today and others will no doubt be developed in the future. Some present-day methods include freehand detailing, in which details are drawn without drafting instruments on small pieces of drafting paper laid over grid sheets. Much faster than conventional detailing, the freehand method produces individual details that are then affixed to sheets of the working drawings. These working-drawing sheets may be reduced to half size or less, photographically. The smaller sheets are easier to use and often less expensive to reproduce. Other photographic methods are also being used to reduce both the time required and the bulk of the sets of working drawings. The most revolutionary new drafting method involves the use of computers with working-drawing programs used as input, the output being complete or partly complete construction contract drawings.

Reproduction Techniques From the latter half of the 19th century, blueprinting was the method used for reproducing working drawings. Its use was so common until a few years ago, that many people still speak of the working drawings as the blueprints, even though they are not reproduced that way any more. And for some reason, the curious phrase that architects draw blueprints has persisted among certain laypersons, even though architects never did draw them.

Today the most common method for reproduction of working drawings is an ozalid system which is similar to blueprinting, but instead of producing white lines on a blue background, produces blue or black lines on essentially white backgrounds. These prints are sometimes called ozalids, but more often they are referred to as blue-line or black-line prints.

Blue-line and black-line prints are produced by processes in which the drawings, on tracing paper, are used as negatives to make prints on sensitized paper by exposure to ultraviolet light. The image on the print is then fixed by passing it through alkaline ammonia vapor. Additional negatives called vandykes, or sepias because of their color, may also be made by this process. Photographic processes are sometimes used for large complex jobs, in which 100 or more sets each numbering hundreds of sheets of large size must be reproduced. Generally, these processes involve reducing the size of the drawings, photographically, to half size, preparing printing plates, and printing on offset presses. Other new methods, including chronflex, have also been developed in recent years.

Legal Status The legal status of working drawings and other construction contract documents is often misunderstood. Although there are variations, their legal status according to most agreements or contract between owners and architects, is that of instruments of service from which owners' buildings or other structures may be constructed. The ownership of working drawings remains with the architects, whether the building is constructed or not.

Related Articles DRAFTING; ENGINEERING; INTERIOR DESIGN; LANDSCAPE ARCHITECTURE; PRACTICE OF ARCHITECTURE; SPECIFICATION.

Further Reading Liebing, Ralph W., and Mimi Ford Paul: *Architectural Working Drawings*, John Wiley, New York, 1977; Thomas, Marrin L.: *Architectural Working Drawings —A Professional Technique*, McGraw-Hill, New York, 1978; Wakita, Osamu A., and Richard M. Linde: *The Professional Practice of Architectural Detailing*, John Wiley, New York, 1977.

WRIGHT, FRANK LLOYD American architect (1867–1959). One of America's, and the world's, most famous architects, Frank Lloyd Wright had a profound and lasting effect on architecture. His professional career spanned 70 years, starting with an architecture of revivals of past styles and continuing through the era that saw the beginnings of what is now called modern architecture, a movement in which Wright played a major role. It did not end before he had made a solid contribution to the establishment of the modern movement that evolved into the architecture of today.

Assessment Wright lived so long and had such a profound effect on architecture that a considerable mythology about him has been created. His architecture was daring and controversial and so was his life. To separate the man and his architecture from the myths is not easy. It must be admitted that he was one of the most inventive and creative architects of his time, or any time. His was a most unusual life and philosophy: the poetic dreamer-artist, the pragmatic engineer, the freethinking individualist, the reformer, the evangelist. Through all his leanings was a strong reverence for life and nature. These attitudes and convictions recur again and again in this architecture. Above all though, he was an artist whose preferred medium was architecture.

Wright's architecture was always far ahead of its time and the work of most other architects. Just when others started to approach his position, he was off on another creative burst that again widened the gap.

Wright was a structural innovator, experimenting with great steel and concrete cantilevers and with types of poured concrete in many of his buildings. He was one of the first architects to take concrete block seriously, designing buildings of custom-cast blocks with patterns. He introduced open planning in buildings, letting spaces flow into each other instead of rigidly enclosing them with separating walls. He was interested in machines, and utilized factory-manufactured products in his buildings.

In all his work can be seen certain recurring forms; some he had learned in his childhood: circles, cubes, cantilevers, penetrated building elements, and walls with balconies enclosing space. There is also masterful use of ornament, most often machine-made but handcrafted whenever it seemed more appropriate to do so.

In everything, he was always the pioneering architect very much in the forefront of modern architecture. His influence spread around the world and is still being felt. His designs and philosophy remain a subject of debate to this day. But there is no disagreement about his stature in world architecture. He was a giant.

Wright lived and practiced architecture for so long that historians have had a difficult time putting him and his work into perspective. Therefore his architectural career has sometimes been divided into periods, as was done with the Spanish painter Pablo Picasso (1881–1974). In Wright's case, the periods may be called the early (1893–1910), the mature (1910–45), and the late (1945–59).

Early Period After working for Louis Henri Sullivan (1856–1924) for six years, Wright started his own practice, designing houses that gave only slight promise of how his architecture would later develop. Among other buildings he designed during his early period, two masterpieces stand out. They are the Larkin Building (1904), Buffalo, since destroyed, and the Unity Church (1907), Oak Park, Ill. Harbingers of future development, both utilize cubistic forms. The Larkin Building had great balconies in a central hall rising the full height of the building and glassed-over on top. Unity Church was an early reinforced concrete building.

Another of Wright's masterpieces was his Robie House (1909; see illustration in color section), Chicago, one of the last of a long series of houses Wright designed in the Midwest, which he called Prairie houses. All these houses are low and horizontal in profile, and have widely projecting roof eaves and rows of windows. Other notable Prairie style houses are those for Ward W. Willits (1902), Highland Park, Ill.; Arthur Heurtley (1902), Chicago; Darwin Martin (1904), Buffalo; and Avery Coonley (1909), River Forest, Ill. a portion of which burned in 1978. All these finely designed houses illustrate the development and maturing of Wright's architectural philosophy. He had made the first steps toward what he called "organic architecture," an architecture that grew like living organisms by adaptation to specific environments, sites, uses, and materials, one that must change or evolve with changing conditions. By the end of Wright's early period, he was a success, artistically and professionally.

Mature Period The second or mature period of Wright's career began with his desertion of his family. This heralded a turbulent time filled with tragedy and triumph. Between 1910 and the end of World War II, the productive periods in his work were interspersed with periods of almost complete idleness. In 1911 he built his home and studio, Taliesin, in Spring Green, Wis. It burned twice and was rebuilt each time, in 1915 and 1925. Like Jefferson at Monticello, Wright built, rebuilt, altered, and added to Taliesin the rest of his life.

Two notable designs of the mature phase of

WRIGHT, FRANK LLOYD Millard House (1923), Pasadena, Calif.
(Julius Shulman)

Wright's career were for buildings that are quite different. The first was for Midway Gardens (1914), Chicago, a great indoor and outdoor amusement center where large numbers of people could dance, attend concerts and other performances, drink and dine. The other was for the Imperial Hotel, Tokyo, which occupied most of Wright's time from 1916 until its completion in 1922. Hailed as an engineering triumph that survived the great earthquake of 1923, the Imperial Hotel foundation later settled unevenly and was demolished in 1968. Midway Gardens, after a period of success, could not survive Prohibition and was demolished in 1923. Wright also designed some houses during this period, the most notable of which is the Millard House (1923) in Pasadena, Calif. In the 1930s commissions were scarce and most of those that

WRIGHT, FRANK LLOYD Exterior, Taliesin East (1911, rebuilt in 1915 and again in 1925), Spring Green, Wis. *(Hedrich-Blessing)*

WRIGHT, FRANK LLOYD Interior, Taliesin East (1911, rebuilt in 1915 and again in 1925) Spring Green, Wis. *(Hedrich-Blessing)*

WRIGHT, FRANK LLOYD Closeup, Taliesin East (1911), rebuilt in 1915 and again in 1925), Spring Green, Wis. *(Hedrich-Blessing)*

WRIGHT, FRANK LLOYD Kaufmann House, Falling Water (1937), Bear Run, Pa. *(Hedrich-Blessing)*

WRIGHT, FRANK LLOYD Exterior, Taliesin West (1938–59), Maricopa County, near Phoenix, Ariz. *(Julius Shulman)*

WRIGHT, FRANK LLOYD Interior, Taliesin West (1938–59), Maricopa County, near Phoenix, Ariz. *(Hedrich-Blessing)*

WRIGHT, FRANK LLOYD Guggenheim Museum (1959), New York, N.Y. *(Ezra Stoller)*

came in were not built. Later in that decade things started to pick up again. As he had with his Prairie houses, he started a whole new series of houses which he now called Usonian, a term for the United States, used by Samuel Butler in his 1872 novel, *Erewhon*. Many of these were in Califiornia, but some were built in other places. In most, he experimented with custom-designed concrete block, a pioneering effort at the time.

Then came a flurry of creative activity toward the end of that decade. He designed a residential master-piece, the Kaufmann House (1937; see also color section), called Falling Water, because it was built over a stream and waterfall at Bear Run, Pa. Falling Water was followed by a striking design for the Johnson Wax Company Administration Building (1939), Racine, Wis.; the campus and buildings for Florida Southern University, Lakeland, Fla., started in 1940 and completed in 1952; and his own winter house and studio, Taliesin West (see also color section), Scottsdale, Ariz., started in 1938 and worked on until he died.

Late Period The World War II years saw little building activity. After the war, entering his late period, Wright found all the commissions he could handle. He designed houses again, among them the notable one for his son, David, in 1952 near Phoenix, Ariz. Another great building of the era is the Johnson Wax Company Factory and Laboratory Tower (1949; see illustration in color section), adjoining the Administration Building which Wright had previously designed. In religious work, the Unitarian Church (1947), Madison, Wis., was followed by the Beth Sholom Synagogue (1959), Elkins Park, Pa. Along the way, he proposed a mile-high sckyscraper, The Illinois, in 1958, which he claimed to be structurally possible and economically sound. It was never built. A little gem of a building is the V. V. Morris Gift Shop (1950) in San Francisco.

In 1953 the H. C. Price Tower, a 16-story building interspersing professional office spaces with duplex apartments, was built in Bartlesville, Okla. In 1943 he started designing a revolutionary art museum, the Guggenheim, for a site in New York City. A model of the building was first exhibited in 1945, but over 10 years passed before construction was started. The building, which features a continuous ramp around an interior court, was completed in 1959, the year Wright died. He left a number of unfinished projects; some were completed by his students at the Taliesin Foundation. Included was his last important building, the Marin County Civic Center (1972), San Rafael, Calif.

A giant figure, Wright had deeply affected architecture. He was a man of his own time who had visions of the future and set out to find it in his architecture.

Life Frank Lloyd Wright was born in Richland Center, Wis., on June 8, 1867. His father deserted the family when Wright was sixteen; his mother was a strong-willed woman who had decided that her son was to become an architect.

In 1876 Mrs. Wright learned about a new kindergarten teaching method orginated by Frederick Froebel. The student, using a basic set of blocks, folded paper and other simple materials, thought about the object to be built, named the object, drew plans for it, and finally constructed rudimentary buildings, furniture, and other objects. Although young Wright was past kindergarten age, he started to study in this manner when he was seven, under his mother's tutelage, and continued to do so for some years. Wright always maintained that the work with the Froebel system constituted his only early training and that it deeply affected his architecture. When Wright was sixteen, he enrolled in civil engineering at the University of Wisconsin, at Madison, but dropped out after less than two years.

At eighteen, Wright worked for a short time in the office of James Lyman Silsbee (1845–1913) and then went to Chicago to work in the office of the man he would always call master, Louis Henri Sullivan. As a designer and draftsman in the office of Adler and Sullivan, Wright worked on some of their best buildings, including the Wainwright Building (1891) in St. Louis. He also absorbed much of the philosophy and design principles of the master, and the engineering knowledge and talent of the partner Dankmar Adler. It seems evident in the later work of Sullivan that in return the student influenced the master. While working with Sullivan, Wright designed a shingled house (1889) for himself in Oak Park, Ill. It showed little indication of his future directions in design. Here he later set up his practice. The chief of his drafting room was Marion Mahoney Griffin (1871–1961), later a respected architect.

However, the Charnley House (1891), Chicago, designed for Adler and Sullivan, and his first commission after setting up his own practice in 1893, the Winslow House (1893), River Forest, Ill., do hint at his future development. These houses marked the beginning of a long and productive life and an architectural practice that lasted 66 years. It was a life marked by periods of scandal and tragedy, and others of great happiness and satisfaction; a career marked by periods of frustration and failure, but predominantly by accomplishment and success.

During his early career, Wright worked mostly in a studio attached to his home in Oak Park and later in downtown Chicago. This was a very productive period for him. He designed a number of excellent houses, gradually developing what he named his Prairie style, and several other of his greatest buildings, including the Larkin Building and the Unity Church. In 1889 he married Catherine Lee Tobin and by 1909 the family had six children. That year, Wright, as had his father, abandoned his family. He then went to Europe for a year with Mamah Borthwich Cheney, the wife of one of his clients.

After returning to America, Wright stayed for a short time in Oak Park, then went to Spring Green, Wis., where he had inherited his family's farm on which he had grown up. Here, in 1897, he had designed a fanciful windmill, which he had named Romeo and Juliet. Here Mrs. Cheney, now divorced, joined him. His wife, Catherine, did not divorce him until 1921. Wright designed a home and studio on a hill, and called it Taliesin, the Welsh word for shining brow and the name of a 6th-century Welsh bard. This was the beginning a new life for Wright and his entry into the second period of his architecture, the mature years.

Then on August 14, 1914, tragedy struck, while he was in Chicago working on the Midway Gardens. Mamah Borthwick Cheney, her two children, and four workmen were murdered by a crazed servant, who then set fire to Taliesin, destroying it.

In 1915 Wright rebuilt his Spring Green home, naming it Taliesin II. Important commissions came in, including that for the Imperial Hotel in Tokyo. While designing the hotel, Wright made a number of trips to Japan and lived there from 1918 to 1922, while it was being constructed. Accompanying him was a divorcée, Miriam Noel, whom he married in 1923, In 1923 Wright's mother, with whom he had always been very close, died at age eighty-one. He then returned to Taliesin II, in 1924, this time to remain.

The marriage to Miriam Noel lasted only a few months but they were not divorced until 1927. Miriam later accused him of desertion, bigamy, and other charges. In 1925, another tragedy struck. Taliesin II caught fire in a storm.

After his divorce, Wright, in 1928, married Olgivanna Milanoff, who had been a member of the Russian Ballet Company. They then started to build Taliesin III, on which he worked the rest of his life. His former wife, Miriam, continued to press him, through publicity in the newspapers and legal actions, and even had Olgivanna, their daughter, and Wright jailed for several days. In the end, Wright was cleared of all charges, but by then he had been ruined financially and professionally.

In 1928 he was declared bankrupt and all his possessions at Taliesin sold, under the terms of the mortgage on the property. Wright fought back. He paid off the mortgage and he was working on several designs for important buildings, including a glass skyscraper, a retirement town in the Arizona desert, and a New York City apartment. None was ever built. The stock market crash in 1929 and the ensuing Depression stopped all building. During these years, Wright supported his family by giving lectures and writing for the most part, while his architectural practice went into almost total decline.

Things started to get better in the mid-1930s. He did another remarkable series of houses, as he had in his early days, and other important buildings. He also designed Taliesin West, which he started to build in 1938 and continued to work on until he died. In 1932 Wright established the Taliesin Fellowship at Spring Green. This was a combination school and apprenticeship program in which architectural students could study and work. It was also a sociological experiment in communal living, in which the participants worked the Taliesin farm and performed maintenance and other chores. After building Taliesin West, the Fellowship was in residence there in the winter and in Spring Green in the summer. The Fellowship has continued the programs Wright started to the present time.

By the late 1930s, both Wright and his buildings had admirers all over the world. He received recognition and honors from everywhere—Europe, Asia, and South America—except his own country. In the United States, Wright's students and other admirers were dedicated and outspoken, but not so the architectural profession. He had received honors from architectural professions all over the world, but the Gold Medal of the American Institute of Architects was late in coming. It was presented to Wright, who never joined the AIA, in 1949, when he was eighty years old. The opening sentence of his acceptance speech was, "Well, it's about time!"

Work was scarce during World War II, but in 1945 Wright embarked on the final phase of his long career. This was a period of considerable activity and he produced a number of great buildings. He had always been ahead of his profession in creative and innovative designs during the first 50 years of his practice and he continued to hold his lead during the last years. Daring and imaginative all his life, he could not stop now and he worked until just a few weeks before he died, on April 9, 1959. He had practiced 66 years, produced several hundred buildings, some think as many as 600, all innovative, many masterpieces. The exact number of his buildings is hard to determine. Many designs were never built and he disavowed some of his own buildings. He had created a band of dedicated disciples who would carry on the philosophy of his design. Considered arrogant and overbearing by some, he was loved and respected by his disciples. He had led the way for architecture, his way, all his life. He had become one of the world's greatest (some think the greatest) architects.

Related Articles MODERN ARCHITECTURE; SULLIVAN, LOUIS HENRI.

Further Reading Hitchcock, Henry-Russell: *In the Nature of Materials—The Buildings of Frank Lloyd Wright, 1887–1941,* Duell, Sloan and Pierce, New York, 1942; Kaufmann, Edgar, Jr., and Ben Raeburn, eds.: *Writings and Buildings,* Horizon Press, New York, 1960; Scully, Vincent: *Frank Lloyd Wright,* Brazilier, New York, 1960; Sergeant, John: *Frank Lloyd Wright's Usonian Houses,* Whitney, New York, 1976; Tafel, Edgar: *Apprentice to Genius—Years with Frank Lloyd Wright,* McGraw-Hill, New York, 1978; Twombly, Robert: *Frank Lloyd Wright—His Life and His Architecture,* John Wiley, New York, 1978; Wright, Frank Lloyd: *An Autobiography,* Horizon Press, New York, 1977; Wright, Frank Lloyd: *A Testament,* Horizon, New York, 1957.

WURSTER, WILLIAM WILSON

American architect and educator (1895–1973). Although he has been most widely admired for his achievements in the education of architectural, planning, and other environmental design students, William Wilson Wurster was also an accomplished architect.

Beginning in the 1920s, Wurster started designing simple, livable houses in a manner that later was called the ranch style. For the rest of his life, he was preoccupied with house design, in particular warm, human-scaled, modest dwellings. He was deeply concerned with house sites, the surrounding landscapes, construction materials, and the institutions and culture of their locale. These principles deeply affected architects and architecture in an era when many buildings were designed to be different, daring, or provocative.

Works The principles of Wurster's house designs also deeply affected his design of other buildings. In every building, there is a sense of rightness that very few architects have managed to achieve. Wurster achieved it from the first, in the Gregory House (1927), near San Francisco. And many of his other houses, scattered all over northern California, still exist to testify to his principles. Other than the houses,

WURSTER, WILLIAM WILSON Exterior, Ritter House (1957), Atherton, Calif. [*Architects: Wurster, Bernardi and Emmons. (Morley Baer)*]

WURSTER, WILLIAM WILSON Interior, Ritter House (1957), Atherton, Calif. [*Architects: Wurster, Bernardi and Emmons. (Morley Baer)*]

WURSTER, WILLIAM WILSON Ghirardelli Square (1969), San Francisco, Calif. [*Architects: Wurster, Bernardi and Emmons, in association with DeMars and Reay. (Morley Baer)*]

WURSTER, WILLIAM WILSON Ghirardelli Square (1969), San Francisco, Calif. [*Architects: Wurster, Bernardi and Emmons, in association with DeMars and Reay. (Morley Baer)*]

his most notable buildings, all done by the partnership of Wurster, Bernardi and Emmons, are the Center for Advanced Study in Behavioral Science (1955) Palo Alto, Calif.; U.S. Consulate (1959), Hong Kong; Golden Gateway Redevelopment (1967), San Francisco; the redevelopment and restoration of Ghirardelli Square, (1969), San Francisco, in association with DeMars and Reay; and his last important building, the Bank of America headquarters (1971), San Francisco, in association with Skidmore, Owings and Merrill and Pietro Belluschi (1899–   ).

Architectural Education Wurster achieved many accomplishments in education. As dean of the architectural school of the University of California, Berkeley, for many years, he established it as a leader in architectural education. He founded the College of Environmental design at the university in an attempt to integrate and interrelate the teaching of architecture with the other environmental design professions. He deeply influenced the design philosophies of several architects, including John Ekin Dinwiddie (1902–59) and Gardner Dailey (1895–   ). In recognition of his services and those of his wife, Catherine Bauer Wurster (1905–64), to the University of California, the College of Environmental design was renamed Wurster Hall.

Life William Wilson Wurster was born in Stockton, Calif., on October 20, 1895. Deciding early that he wanted to become an architect, Wurster enrolled in the architectural school of the University of California at Berkeley and graduated with honors in 1919. His architectural career had started even earlier when he went to work, at fifteen, as an office boy for a Stockton firm.

After graduating from college, Wurster worked for architects in San Francisco and Sacramento, spent a year traveling in Europe, and then worked in New York City for Delano and Aldrich in 1923 and 1924. In 1926 he started his own firm in San Francisco and practiced as an individual until 1943. In 1940 he married Catherine Bauer, a noted planner and writer. They had one daughter.

In 1943 Wurster formed a partnership with Theodore C. Bernardi (1903–   ), in San Francisco, and a year later Donn Emmons (1910–   ) joined the firm which was renamed Wurster, Bernardi and Emmons. In 1944 he was named dean of the School of Architecture and Planning, Massachusetts Institute of Technology, Cambridge, a position he held until 1950. From 1950 to 1959, Wurster was dean of the College of Architecture, University of California, Berkeley, and then founded the College of Environmental Design in 1959, at that university and became its first dean, remaining in that position until 1963.

Tragedy struck Wurster when his wife, Catherine, who had worked closely with him for many years and was a professor of city planning at the University of California, was lost while on a hiking trip in the mountains near San Francisco and died on November 22, 1964.

After retiring from the faculty at Berkeley in 1963 as dean emeritus, Wurster devoted most of his time to his architectural practice. He received many honors in the United States and in other countries, including an honorary doctor's degree from the University of California and fellowships in the American Academy of Arts and Sciences and the Royal Academy of Fine Arts of Denmark. In 1969 he received the highest honor, the Gold Medal, from the American Institute of Architects. On September 20, 1973, William Wurster died.

Related Articles EDUCATION; MODERN ARCHITECTURE.

WURSTER, WILLIAM WILSON Bank of America Building (1971), San Francisco, Calif. [*Architects: Wurster, Bernardi and Emmons, in association with Skidmore, Owings and Merrill and Pietro Belluschi. (Julius Shulman)*]

Y

YAMASAKI, MINORU American architect (1912–). A controversial architect, Minoru Yamasaki seems to have dedicated supporters and equally dedicated detractors. On the one side, some people are convinced that his buildings are works of art, sensitive to form, materials, and human needs. On the other side, many think that he has been too playful, even capricious, and that his buildings are merely ornamental, decorative forms for their own sake. Yamasaki said that the social function of an architect is to create a work of art. This, his detractors say, proves their point. His supporters, perhaps defining works of art differently, claim that his ornamental forms express the function and structure of his buildings as well as the delight which should be an integral part of great architecture.

Appraisal In spite of the controversy, Yamasaki has exerted a considerable influence on the architecture of today. In a time when many modern buildings were designed as plain, even sterile-looking, products of the industrial age, Yamasaki steadfastly designed buildings with ornament, with sculptural forms particularly in the details, and with gaiety or serenity as the occasion demanded. It may be true, as some claim, that he has not developed a group of followers or disciples. And Yamasaki, unlike many of his contemporaries, has stuck closely to the practice of architecture, rather than combining it with teaching, writing, or lecturing. Yet, many people find his buildings, of which he has produced a rather large number, delightful and exciting. And the work of some architects today reveals their interest in relieving the monotony of design of machine production with sculptural form and ornament. Some architects believe this would happen more often if the costs of construction had not soared to the point where ornament is often not feasible.

Works After working in the offices of other architects for more than 15 years, Yamasaki joined a partnership, in 1949, Hellmuth, Yamasaki and Leinweber. The firm soon had some important commissions, including one for the Lambert–St. Louis Airport (1956; see illustration in article airport), which won several

YAMASAKI, MINORU Exterior, McGregor Memorial Community Conference Center (1958), Wayne State University, Detroit, Mich. (Hedrich-Blessing)

588

YAMASAKI, MINORU Interior, McGregor Memorial Community
Conference Center (1958), Wayne State University, Detroit, Mich.
(Hedrich-Blessing)

YAMASAKI, MINORU Reynolds Metals Co. Building (1960), Detroit, Mich. *(Hedrich-Blessing)*

awards and established Yamasaki's reputation as a designer.

He has since designed more than 85 important buildings of many types. Among the most important are several buildings at Wayne State University, Detroit, including the McGregor Memorial Community Conference Center (1958); Reynolds Metals Company Building (1960), Detroit; Air Terminal (1961), Dhahran, Saudi Arabia; Federal Science Pavilion (1962; see illustration in article exposition), at the World's Fair, Century 21, Seattle; Michigan Consolidated Gas Company Office Building (1963), Detroit, in association with Smith, Hinchman and Grylls; International Business Machines Co. Building (1964), Seattle, in association with Naramore, Bain, Brady and Johanson; Woodrow Wilson School of Public and International Affairs (1965), Princeton University, Princeton, N.J.; the Century Plaza Hotel (1966), Los Angeles; Congregation Beth-El Temple (1974), Bloomfield, Mich.; and Federal Reserve Bank (1973), Richmond, Va. Yamasaki's latest important buildings are the twin towers of the World Trade Center (1973; see illustrations in article column and in color section), New York City, in association with Emery Roth and Sons.

Life Minoru Yamasaki was born in Seattle, Washington, on December 1, 1912, the son of an immigrant Japanese farmer. A top student, he graduated from Garfield High School in 1929. While in high school, he became fascinated with architecture through watching the work of his uncle who was an architect. Determined to rise above the tenement surroundings in which he had been born and to become an architect, Yamasaki worked summers in fish canneries in Alaska, saved his money, and entered the architectural school of the University of Washington.

After graduating in 1934, Yamasaki went to New York City where he worked for eight years in several offices, including Shreve, Lamb and Harmon, Harrison and Fouilhoux, and the noted industrial designer Raymond Loewy (1893–   ). In 1941 he married Teruko Hirashiki and they had three children. He also taught architectural design at Columbia University from 1943 to 1945. He was able to escape internment as a Japanese-American during World War II with the help of the architects for whom he worked. And by bringing his parents to New York to live with him, he also saved them from internment. In 1945 he went to Detroit to work for the large and successful firm of

YAMASAKI, MINORU   Woodrow Wilson School of Public and International Affairs (1965), Princeton University, Princeton, N.J. *(Joseph W. Molitor)*

Smith, Hinchman and Grylls, remaining until 1949.

In 1949 Yamasaki went into practice in Detroit, in partnership with Joseph William Leinweber (1895–   ) and George F. Hellmuth (1907–   ). The partnership lasted until 1955, when Hellmuth withdrew to form another partnership in St. Louis. Yamasaki and Leinweber continued their partnership until 1959. Yamasaki then formed a successor firm, Minoru Yamasaki and Associates, which is still in practice in Troy, Mich., near Detroit.

Soon after the Hellmuth, Yamasaki and Leinweber partnership was formed, the firm received a significant commission for a new airport in St. Louis. Its design brought quick recognition to the firm, resulting in many commissions. In 1953 Yamasaki became dangerously ill with ulcers which necessitated surgery. He recovered and built a good-sized and successful practice. In 1961 he was divorced from his wife.

Minoru Yamasaki has received many honors, including a number of honorary doctor's degrees, awards for several buildings, and fellowship in the American Academy of Arts and Sciences.

Related Articles CONTEMPORARY ARCHITECTURE; MODERN ARCHITECTURE.

Z

ZOOLOGICAL BUILDING A building, or group of buildings, housing a collection of wild, and sometimes domestic, animals for study, display, and enjoyment. Such buildings are ordinarily located in zoological gardens, familiarly called zoos, areas set aside for keeping animals. In the past, most buildings for zoo animals were cages with bars or wire to keep the animals from escaping and to protect animals and visitors. Some cages were glassed-in, for example, those for snakes, which can escape through bars, and for monkeys, which are susceptible to human diseases. Nonswimming animals were sometimes placed behind moats or ditches, filled with water. Fish were kept in tanks; aquatic mammals, such as seals, and water birds were provided with pools. All were severely restricted to relatively small areas of activity. A later trend has been toward keeping the animals in large enclosures, which resemble the natural habitat of the animals as closely as possible.

Thematic Classification Zoo displays are often classified according to themes. The most important themes are systematic, zoogeographic, ecological, behavioral, and general. In the systematic zoo, the earliest type, cats are kept together, hoofed animals together, and so on. The zoogeographic type places animals together according to their place of origin, North American, African, South American, and so on, or by even smaller geographic locations, such as a sin-

ZOOLOGICAL BUILDING Lila Acheson Wallace World of Birds (1972), Bronx Zoo, New York, N.Y. [Architect: Morris Ketchum. (Louis Checkman)]

gle state or region. The ecological exhibit groups animals together according to habitat, such as desert, prairie, forest, and the like. In such exhibits, predators are often separated from their prey by barriers that are invisible to visitors. A behavioral exhibit displays animals that share certain habits, such as flying, burrowing, or swimming. The general zoo simply brings together the most popular animals, without regard to any classification. Many zoos utilize more than one theme in order to bring variety into their exhibits. And some arrange special exhibits, for example, exhibits where children may intermingle with and pet animals. Some of the most successful zoos are combined with botanical gardens to form more logical, complete, and natural exhibits.

Elements Zoos contain three major elements, for animals, visitors, and management and maintenance. The first precedence is given to the animals, which require special considerations according to their individual needs. Some of the specialized buildings include mammal houses, aviaries or bird houses, and aquariums for fish and other aquatic animals. In addition to walks among displays, visitor facilities include parking lots, rest rooms, and concession stands. Administrative and maintenance facilities include offices, food preparation areas, animal hospital, reserve animal areas for those not being exhibited, and employee quarters.

Zoos comprise a limited building type since relatively few exist in the United States, and almost none have been built in the recent past. In existing zoos, some new buildings are being built and others remodeled. They are interesting and rewarding problems for the architects who design them.

History It is believed that the dog was the first wild animal to be captured and kept by human beings, during the Paleolithic, or Old Stone, Age, 10,000 to 20,000 years ago. The first known zoo, or it might have been called a menagerie, was started by Egyptian Queen Hatshepsut about 1500 B.C. Menageries and aviaries were kept by other members of the ruling families of Egypt in ancient times, and in ancient China and Rome. During the Middle Ages and later, menageries were kept for exhibit of animals, often in unsanitary and crowded cages that were repugnant to many visitors. The first modern zoo, and botanical garden, was the Jardin des Plantes (1626) in Paris; it is still in existence. The first zoo in the United States was established in Philadelphia in 1859. Other notable examples are the Bronx Zoo in New York City, and the zoos of San Diego, Chicago, and Cincinnati. The National Zoological Park in Washington, D.C., was founded in 1890.

Related Article BOTANICAL BUILDING.

Index

Article titles are set in all capital letters, with the page numbers in boldface. Illustrations are indicated by italic page numbers. References to the color section (following page 52) are preceded by the word *color*.

A

Aalto, Alvar, 204, 371
Abramovitz, Max, Philharmonic Hall, New York, 244, 535
(*See also* Harrison and Abramovitz)
Accra, Ghana, U.S. Embassy, Weese, 431
Ackerman House, Hackensack, N.J., 89
Acoma Pueblo, N. Mex., 416
San Estévan, *90, 91*
Acoustical tile, 77
Acoustics, 490–492
theaters, 490–491
Acropolis, Athens, 17, 252
Adam, James, 40, 291–292
Adam, Robert, 40, 214, 291–292
Adam Thoroughgood House, Norfolk, Va., 89
Adler, Dankmar, 524, 528, 583
(*See also* Adler and Sullivan)
Adler and Sullivan, 524, 528
Auditorium, Chicago, 524, *526*
Borden Block, Chicago, 524
Charnley House, Chicago, designed by Wright, *527,* 583
Chicago Joint Board Building (formerly Trosecher Building), Chicago, 524, *525*
Garrick Theater in Schiller Building, Chicago, 524
Prudential Building (formerly Guaranty Building), Buffalo, N.Y., 524, *528*
Ryerson Building, Chicago, 524
Stock Exchange Building, Chicago, 524, *527*
Wainwright Building, St. Louis, 524, *526*
Aeck Associates, Georgia Institute of Technology, Atlanta, Basketball Arena, *141*
Aegean architecture, 251
Afton Villa, St. Francisville, La., 211, *224*
Agawam National Bank, Springfield, Mass., Richardson, 460
Air and Space Museum, Washington, Hellmuth, Obata and Kassabaum, *72, 73*
Air conditioning, 247–250
AIRPORT, **1–4**
Alamitos Elementary School, Garden Grove, Calif., Neutra and Alexander, 378
Alamo, San Antonio, Tex., 91
Albany, N.Y., City Hall, Richardson, 459
Albers, Anni, 204
Albers, Josef, Harvard University Graduate Center, 20
Alberti, Leon Battista, 39, 257, 397, 445
Alcoa Building, Pittsburgh, Pa., Harrison and Abramovitz, *6,* 245

Alexander, Robert Evans:
Baldwin Hills Village, Los Angeles, 505, *505*
with Neutra, 378, 380
(*See also* Neutra and Alexander)
Allegheny County Courthouse and Jail, Pittsburgh, Pa., Richardson, 425, 459, *460*
All Saints Church, Brookline, Mass., Cram, Goodhue and Ferguson, 127
All Saints Church, New York, Renwick, 452
All Souls Church, Ashmont, Mass., Cram, Goodhue and Ferguson, 127
ALUMINUM, **4–6**
alloys, 5
architectural products, 5
furniture, 202
Aluminum City Terrace Housing, New Kensington, Pa., Gropius and Breuer, 43, 234, *235*
American Academy, Rome, 66, 341, 404, 406
American Battle Monument, Montfaucon, France, Pope, 405
American colonies, town planning, 397–398
American Indians:
Basket Makers, 414
pre-Columbian architecture, 413–416
pueblo cultures, 414, 416
American Institute of Architects (AIA), 20–22, 279, 282, 541, 550, 552
on handicapped persons, 238
headquarters, Washington, *21,* 70, 341, 535, *536*
library, 318
stairway in headquarters, Washington, *497*
American Institute of Planners, 399
American Locomotive Company Machine Shop, Auburn, N.Y., A. Kahn, 306
American Museum of Natural History, New York, Pope, 405
American National Standards Institute, Inc., 239
American Radiator Building, New York, Hood, *262, 263*
American Society of Civil Engineers, 168
American Society of Landscape Architects, 314, 388
American Society of Mechanical Engineers, 168
American Steel Foundries Cast Iron Plant, East Chicago, Ind., A. Kahn, 306
Ames Memorial Library, North Easton, Mass., Richardson, 459
Amman, Jordan, U.S. Embassy, Rudolph, 431
Ammann, Othmar Hermann, 53, 105, 517
Bayonne Bridge, Staten Island, N.Y., 216
George Washington Bridge, New York, 53, 216, *216*

Ammann, Othmar Hermann (*Cont.*):
Verrazzano-Narrows Bridge, New York, *52*
Amon Carter Museum of Western Art, Fort Worth, Tex., Johnson, 303
Amphitheater, 531, 533, 534
Amusement parks, 436
Andalusia, near Philadelphia, Walter, 550, *551*
Anderson, Joseph Horatio, Maryland State House, Annapolis, 427
Anderson, Beckwith and Haible, Priory of St. Gregory the Great, Portsmouth, R.I., *441*
Annapolis, Md., town plan, 398
Anthony, Earle C., House, Los Angeles, Maybeck, 336
Anthropology, 487–488
APARTMENT, **7–9**
condominium, 7–8
cooperative, 7–8
garden, 7
high-rise, 7, *7*
low-rise, 7, *8, 9*
tenements, 8–9
townhouse, 7
Apthorp Houses (three), P. Harrison, 243
Arc de Triomphe de l'Étoile, Paris, Chalgrin, 373
ARCH, **9–10,** 252–253
contemporary types, *522*
triumphal, Roman, 17
wood-frame structure, 565
Architects, 10–11
associations, 20–22
career, 73–75
commissions, 408
in construction contracts, 108–111
education, 74–75, 154–156
fees, 408
firms, 115, 117, 407–410
license, 75
master builders, 168
Architects Collaborative, The (TAC), 117
American Institute of Architects Headquarters, *21, 497*
Back Bay Center, Boston, proposed, 99, 234
Gropius with, 234–237, 431
Architectural League of New York, 263
ARCHITECTURE, **10–11**
Armonk, N.Y., Recreational Center, Norton and Hume, *393, 438*
Arnie's Restaurant, Chicago, Himmel, *456*
Arp, Jean, Harvard University Graduate Center, wood sculpture, 20
ART IN ARCHITECTURE, **12–20**

N

T